ECONOMICS

FIFTH EDITION

AQA

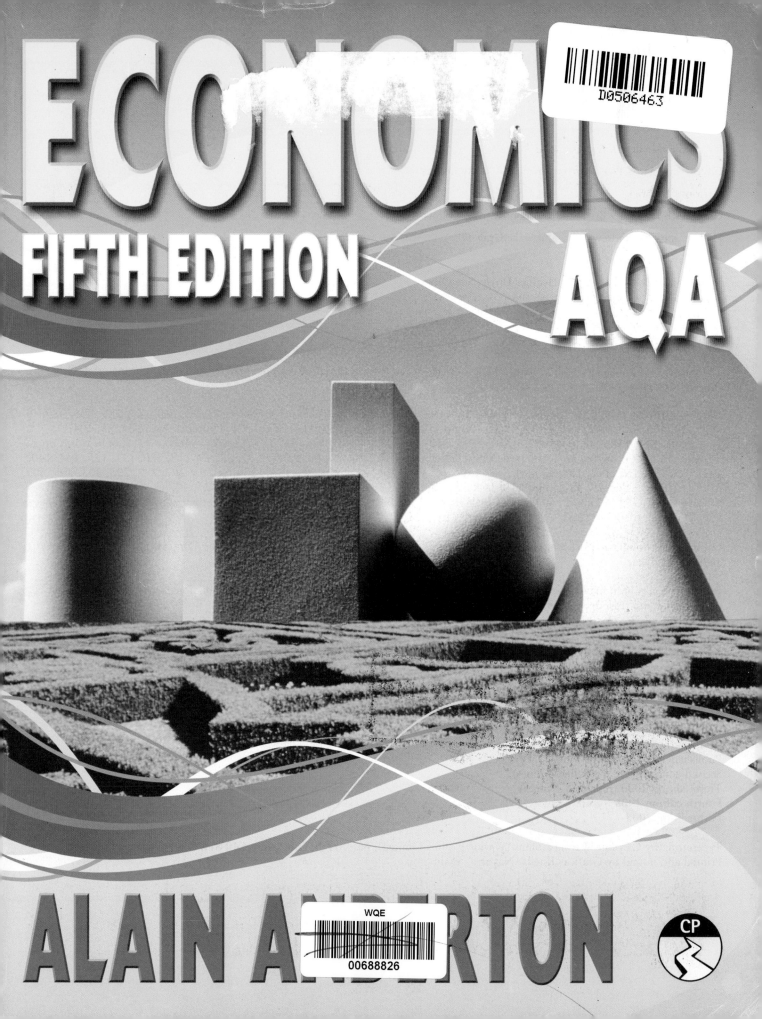

ALAIN ANDERTON

Credits

Original cover design by Susan and Andrew Allen, fifth edition by Tim Button

Cover drawing by Pete Turner, provided by Getty images

Cartoons by Brick

Graphics by Kevin O'Brien and Caroline Waring-Collins

Photography by Andrew Allen and Dave Gray

Edited by Dave Gray

Proofreading by Mike Kidson, Heather Doyle, Sue Oliver

Acknowledgements

The author and publishers wish to thank the following for permission to reproduce photographs and copyright material. Other copyright material is acknowledged at source.

Corel pp 3(t), 21, 339, 392, Digital Stock p 293(c), Digital Vision pp 2, 3(b), 7, 16(b), 67(t), 87, 93, 260, 265, 289, 305, 389, 402, 403, 405, 415, 418(c), 422, 548, Image100 pp 178, 405, 418(b), 435, Photobiz p 338, Photodisc pp 9, 29, 65, 104, 106(bc,br), 124, 138, 246, 264, 292(b), 303, 335, 383, 385, 387, 418(t), 425, 429(b), 512, 527, 546(t), 611, Rex Features pp 90, 101, 130, 173, 284(t), 427, 453, 456, Shutterstock pp 14, 15, 25(t,b), 89, 95 (l,r), 97, 98, 99, 119, 120, 121, 125, 134, 140, 144, 145, 146, 150, 163, 179, 180(l.r), 182, 190, 197, 205, 206, 222, 273, 275, 279, 284(b), 295, 297, 298, 295, 303, 305, 309, 311, 313, 316, 317, 327, 332, 333, 345, 348, 358, 360, 369, 395, 396, 397, 398, 424, 426, 427, 427(t), 481, 482, 484, 595, 543, 544, 567, 595, 600, 602, 603, 618, 624, 638, 641, Stockbyte pp 91(r), 197, 429(t), 452, Stockdisc pp 165, 329(t), 469, 550, Topfoto pp 106(bl), 200.

Office for National Statistics material is Crown Copyright, reproduced with the permission of the Controller of Her Majesty's Stationery Office.

Every effort has been made to locate the copyright owners of material used in this book. Any omissions brought to the notice of the publisher are regretted and will be credited in subsequent printings.

British Library Cataloguing in Publication Data.

A catalogue record for this book is available from the British Library.

ISBN 978 1 4058 9238 4

Pearson Education, Edinburgh Gate, Harlow, Essex, CM20 2JE
Contribution © Alain Anderton
Published 1991 (reprinted 3 times)
Second edition 1995 (reprinted 4 times)
Third edition 2000 (reprinted 4 times)
Fourth edition 2006 (reprinted twice)
Fifth edition 2008

Typesetting by Caroline Waring-Collins (Waring Collins Limited), Burscough, Lancashire L40 8JW www.waringcollins.com
Printed and bound by Graficas Estella, Navarra, Spain.

Contents

A2 Unit 3: Business economics and the distribution of income

Business economics

Welfare economics

Labour markets

A2 Unit 4: The national and international economy

Macroeconomics and government policy

The international economy

Preface

Teachers and students of economics are critical groups of people. Constantly dissatisfied with the materials that they use, they face the problems of limited resources, a wide variety of needs and a constantly changing world. This book is intended to go some way to resolving this example of the basic economic problem.

The book has a number of distinctive features.

Comprehensive The book contains comprehensive materials to satisfy the demands of students taking AQA AS/A Level Economics.

Flexible unit structure The material is organised not into chapters but into shorter units. This reflects the organisation of a number of GCSE textbooks, and therefore students should be familiar with this style of presentation. The unit structure also allows the teacher greater freedom to devise a course. Economics teachers have a long tradition of using their main textbooks in a different order to that in which they are presented. So whilst there is a logical order to the book, it has been written on the assumption that teachers and students will piece the units together to suit their own teaching and learning needs. Cross referencing has been used on occasions. This approach also means that it is relatively easy to use the book for a growing number of courses which encompass part of an AS/A Level specification, such as professional courses with an economics input.

Accessibility The book has been written in a clear and logical style which should make it accessible to all readers. Each unit is divided into short, easily manageable sections. Diagrams contain concise explanations which summarise or support the text.

A workbook The text is interspersed with a large number of questions. These are relatively short for the most part, and, whilst some could be used for extended writing work, most require relatively simple answers. They have been included to help teachers and students assess whether learning and understanding has taken place by providing immediate application of content and skills to given situations. I hope that many will be used as a basis for class discussion as well as being answered in written form. **AQA Economics Teachers' Guide (Fifth Edition)** provides suggested answers to questions that appear in the book.

Applied economics as well as economic theory Many economics courses require teachers and students to have a book covering economic theory and an applied economic text. In this book, a systematic approach to applied economics has been included alongside economic theory. Each unit has an applied economics section and some units deal only with applied economics. It should be noted that many of the questions also contain applied economics material, and where sufficiently significant, this has been referred to in the index.

Use of data Modern technology has allowed much of the book to proceed from manuscript to book in a very short period. This has meant that we have been able to use statistics which were available in 2007. Many statistical series therefore go up to 2006/2007, although some were only available for earlier years. At the same time, experience has shown that too many current stories quickly date a book. Materials have therefore been chosen, particularly for the macroeconomic section of the book, from throughout the post-war era, with particular emphasis on the turbulent times of the 1970s and 1980s, as well as the 1990s and 2000s. This approach will help candidates to answer questions which require knowledge of what has happened 'in recent years' or 'over the past decade'.

Study skills and assessment The last two units of this book provide guidance on effective study and the methods of assessment used in economics..

Key terms Many units contain a key terms section. Each section defines new concepts, which appear in capitals in the text of the unit. Taken together, they provide a comprehensive dictionary of economics.

Presentation Great care has been taken with how this book is presented. It is hoped that the layout of the book, the use of colour and the use of diagrams will make learning economics a rewarding experience.

Specification references Specification section reference numbers can be found on the top right of the first page of each unit. This shows teachers and students precisely how each unit relates to the AQA specification.

Online support MyEconSpace.co.uk is an online support resource for teachers and students using AQA Economics (Fifth Edition). It includes an online student book, an accurate graphing tool, questions from the student book that can be answered and marked online, links to key websites providing access to latest economic data and a regular updated news section

Thanks
I have many thanks to make. Brian Ellis has provided invaluable comments on the fifth edition. Susan Gardner managed the project expertly and provided essential support. Mike Kidson, Sue Oliver and Heather Doyle carried out the unenviable task of proof reading the fifth edition and Waring Collins Limited designed the book with their usual flair and skill. Dave Gray has been a superb editor and, as always, has been an enormous pleasure to work with. Not least, I would like to thank my wife who has performed a variety of tasks, in particular putting up with the stresses and strains of the production of such a large volume. All mistakes in the book, however, remain my own responsibility.

Finally, I would like to thank all those who read this book. It is an enormous privilege to be able to explore the world of economics with you. Your comments are always welcome, whether critical or otherwise. I hope you find the subject as exciting, stimulating and rewarding as I have always found it.

Alain Anderton

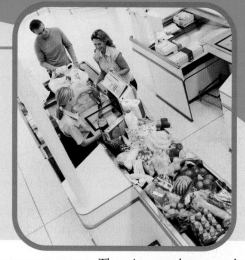

Summary

1. *Nearly all resources are scarce.*
2. *Human wants are infinite.*
3. *Scarce resources and infinite wants give rise to the basic economic problem - resources have to be allocated between competing uses.*
4. *Allocation involves choice and each choice has an opportunity cost.*
5. *The production possibility frontier (PPF) shows the maximum potential output of an economy.*
6. *Production at a point inside the PPF indicates an inefficient use of resources.*
7. *Growth in the economy will shift the PPF outwards.*

Scarcity

It is often said that we live in a global village. The world's resources are finite; there are only limited amounts of land, water, oil, food and other resources on this planet. Economists therefore say that resources are SCARCE.

Scarcity means that economic agents, such as individuals, firms, governments and international agencies, can only obtain a limited amount of resources at any moment in time. For instance, a family has to live on a fixed budget; it cannot have everything it wants. A firm might want to build a new factory but not have the resources to be able to do so. A government might wish to build new hospitals or devote more resources to its foreign aid programme but not have the finance to make this possible. Resources which are scarce are called ECONOMIC GOODS.

Question 1

Time was when people used to take their car out for a Sunday afternoon 'spin'. The novelty of owning a car and the freedom of the road made driving a pleasant leisure pursuit. Today, with 34 million cars registered in the UK, a Sunday afternoon tour could easily turn into a nightmare traffic jam.

Of course, many journeys are trouble free. Traffic is so light that cars do not slow each other down. But most rush hour journeys today occur along congested roads where each extra car on the road adds to the journey time of every other car. When London introduced a £5 a day 'congestion charge', a fee for cars to use roads in central London, the amount of traffic dropped by 17 per cent. This was enough to reduce journey times considerably.

Traffic congestion also greatly increases the amount of pollution created by cars. Our ecosystem can cope with low levels of emissions, but, as cities like Paris and Athens have discovered, high levels of traffic combined with the right weather conditions can lead to sharp increases in pollution levels. The car pollutes the environment anyway because cars emit greenhouse gases. One quarter of CO_2 emissions in the UK come from road transport.

Source: adapted from *Transport Statistics for Great Britain 2007*, Department for Transport; Office for National Statistics.

Explain whether roads are, in any sense, a 'free good' from an economic viewpoint.

Not all resources are scarce. There is more than enough air on this planet for everyone to be able to breathe as much as they want. Resources which are not scarce are called FREE GOODS. In the past many goods such as food, water and shelter have been free, but as the population of the planet has expanded and as production has increased, so the number of free goods has diminished. Recently, for instance, clean beaches in many parts of the UK have ceased to be a free good to society. Pollution has forced water companies and seaside local authorities to spend resources cleaning up their local environment. With the destruction of the world's rain forests and increasing atmospheric pollution, the air we breathe may no longer remain a free good. Factories may have to purify the air they take from the atmosphere, for instance. This air would then become an economic good.

Infinite wants

People have a limited number of NEEDS which must be satisfied if they are to survive as human beings. Some are material needs, such as food, liquid, heat, shelter and clothing. Others are psychological and emotional needs such as self-esteem and being loved. People's needs are finite. However, no one would choose to live at the level of basic human needs if they could enjoy a higher standard of living.

This is because human WANTS are unlimited. It doesn't matter whether the person is a farmer in Africa, a mystic in India, a manager in the UK or the richest individual in the world, there is always something which he or she wants more of. This can include more food, a bigger house, a longer holiday, a cleaner environment, more love, more friendship, better relationships, more self-esteem, greater fairness or justice, peace, or more time to listen to music, meditate or cultivate the arts.

The basic economic problem

Resources are scarce but wants are infinite. It is this which gives rise to the BASIC ECONOMIC PROBLEM and which forces economic agents to make choices. They have to allocate their scarce resources between competing uses.

Economics is the study of this allocation of resources - the choices that are made by economic agents. Every CHOICE involves a range of alternatives. For instance, should the·

Question 2

Draw up a list of minimum human needs for a teenager living in the UK today. How might this list differ from the needs of a teenager living in Bangladesh or sub-Saharan Africa?

Question 3

Over the past 10 years, university students have come under increasing financial pressure. For the previous 40 years, the government paid for all student tuition fees. It also gave a grant to students to cover their living expenses, although this grant was means tested according to the income of parents. In the 1990s, the government froze student grants and introduced a system of subsidised student loans to allow students to make up for the falling real value of the grants. In 1998, students for the first time were charged for part of their tuition fees. The amount they had to pay each year was set at £1 000. In 1999, maintenance grants were replaced completely by loans. In 2006, students began to pay £3 000 a year toward tuition fees. The cost of going to university had risen to average over £7 000 a year to the student.

What might be the opportunity cost of the £7 000 in fees and maintenance:
(a) to parents if they pay them on behalf of their sons or daughters;
(b) to students if they have to borrow the money to pay them?

government spend £10 billion in tax revenues on nuclear weapons, better schools or greater care for the elderly? Will you choose to become an accountant, an engineer or a vicar?

These choices can be graded in terms of the benefits to be gained from each alternative. One choice will be the 'best' one and a rational economic agent will take that alternative. But all the other choices will then have to be given up. The benefit lost from the next best alternative is called the OPPORTUNITY COST of the choice. For instance, economics may have been your third choice at 'A' level. Your fourth choice, one which you didn't take up, might have been history. Then the opportunity cost of studying economics at 'A' level is studying history at 'A' level. Alternatively, you might have enough money to buy just one of your two favourite magazines - *totalDVD* or *DVD Monthly*. If you choose to buy *totalDVD*, then its opportunity cost is the benefit which would have been gained from consuming *DVD Monthly*.

Free goods have no opportunity cost. No resources need be sacrificed when someone, say, breathes air or swims in the sea.

Production possibility frontiers

Over a period of time, resources are scarce and therefore only a finite amount can be produced. For example, an economy might have enough resources at its disposal to be able to produce 30 units of manufactured goods and 30 units of non-manufactured. If it were now to produce more manufactured goods, it would have to give up some of its production of non-manufactured items. This is because the production of a manufactured item has an opportunity cost - in this case the production of non-manufactured. The more manufactured that are produced, the less non-manufactured can be produced.

This can be shown in Figure 1. The curved line is called the PRODUCTION POSSIBILITY FRONTIER (PPF) - other names for it include PRODUCTION POSSIBILITY CURVE or BOUNDARY, and TRANSFORMATION CURVE. The PPF shows the different combinations of economic goods which an economy is able to produce if all resources in the economy are fully and efficiently employed. The economy therefore could be:
- at the point C on its PPF, producing 30 units of manufactured goods and 30 units of non-manufactured;
- at the point D, producing 35 units of manufactured goods and 20 units of non-manufactured;
- at the point A, devoting all of its resources to the production of non-manufactured goods;
- at the points B or E or anywhere else along the line.

The production possibility frontier illustrates clearly the principle of opportunity cost. Assume that the economy is producing at the point C in Figure 1 and it is desired to move to the point D. This means that the output

Figure 1 The production possibility frontier

ABCDE is a production possibility frontier. It shows the different combinations of goods which can be produced if all resources are fully and efficiently utilised. For instance, the economy can produce no manufactured goods and 50 units of non-manufactured, 30 units of manufactured goods and 30 units of non-manufactured, or 40 units of manufactured goods but no non-manufactured.

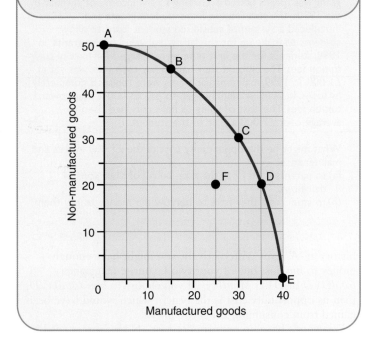

change. At the point C in Figure 1, the economy could produce more manufactured goods, but at the cost of giving up non-manufactured goods. For example, the marginal cost of 5 more units of manufactured goods would be 10 fewer units of non-manufactured goods. This is shown by the movement from C to D along the boundary.

The production possibility frontier for an economy is drawn on the assumption that all resources in the economy are fully and efficiently employed. If there are unemployed workers or idle factories, or if production is inefficiently organised, then the economy cannot be producing on its PPF. It will produce within the boundary. In Figure 1 the economy could produce anywhere along the line AE. However, because there is unemployment in the economy, production is at point F.

The economy cannot be at any point outside its existing PPF because the PPF, by definition, shows the maximum production level of the economy. However, it might be able to move to the right of its PPF in the future if there is **economic growth**. An increase in the productive potential of an economy is shown by a shift outwards of the PPF. In Figure 2 economic growth pushes the PPF from PP to QQ, allowing the economy to increase its maximum level of production, say, from A to B. Growth in the economy can happen if:

- the quantity of resources available for production increases; for instance there might be an increase in the number of workers in the economy, or new factories and offices might be built;
- there is an increase in the quality of resources; education will make workers more productive whilst technical progress will allow machines and production processes to produce more with the same amount of resources.

Production possibility frontiers can shift inwards as well as outwards. The productive potential of an economy can fall. For example, war can destroy economic infrastructure. A rapid fall in the number of workers in a population can reduce potential output. Some environmentalists predict that global warming will devastate world agriculture and this will have a knock-on effect on all production. Global warming could therefore lead to a shift inwards of the world's PPF.

The production possibility frontiers in Figures 1 and 2 have been drawn concave to the origin (bowing outwards) rather than as straight lines or as convex lines. This is because it has been assumed that not all resources in the economy are as productive in one use compared to another.

Take, for instance, the production of wheat in the UK. Comparatively little wheat is grown in Wales because the soil and the climate are less suited to wheat production than in an area like East Anglia. Let us start from a position where no wheat is grown at all in the UK. Some farmers then decide to grow wheat. If production in the economy is to be maximised it should be grown on the land which is most suited to wheat production (i.e. where its opportunity cost is lowest). This will be in an area of the country like East Anglia. As wheat production expands, land has to be used which is less productive because land is a finite resource. More and more marginal land, such as that found in Wales, is used and output per acre falls. The land could have been used for another form of production, for instance sheep rearing. The more wheat is grown, the less is the output per acre and therefore the greater the cost in terms of sheep production.

In Figure 3 only sheep and wheat are produced in the economy. If no wheat is produced the economy could produce 0C of sheep. If there is one unit of wheat production only 0B

of manufactured goods will increase from 30 to 35 units. However, the opportunity cost of that (i.e. what has to be given up because of that choice) is the lost output of non-manufactured, falling from 30 to 20 units. The opportunity cost at C of increasing manufacturing production by 5 units is 10 units of non-manufactured.

Another way of expressing this is to use the concept of the MARGIN. In economics, the margin is a point of possible

Figure 2 Economic growth

Economic growth in the quantity or quality of the inputs to the production process means that an economy has increased its productive potential. This is shown by a shift to the right of the production possibility frontier from PP to QQ. It would enable the economy to move production, for instance, from point A to point B.

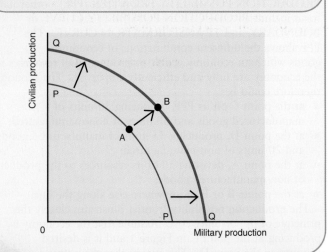

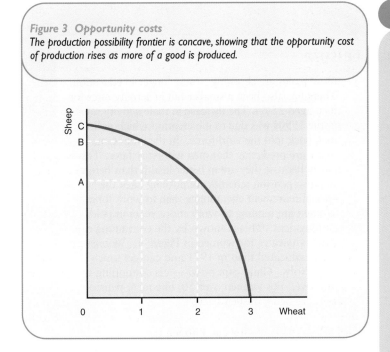

Figure 3 Opportunity costs
The production possibility frontier is concave, showing that the opportunity cost of production rises as more of a good is produced.

of sheep can be produced. Therefore the opportunity cost of the first unit of wheat is BC of sheep. The second unit of wheat has a much higher opportunity cost - AB. But if the economy produces wheat only, then the opportunity cost of the third unit of wheat rises to 0A of sheep.

The PPF by itself gives no indication of which combination of goods will be produced in an economy. All it shows is the combination of goods which an economy could produce if output were maximised from a given fixed amount of resources. It shows a range of possibilities and much of economics is

concerned with explaining why an economy, ranging from a household economy to the international economy, chooses to produce at one point either on or within its PPF rather than another.

Question 4

Draw a production possibility frontier. The vertical axis shows the production of public sector goods and the horizontal axis shows production of private sector goods. The economy is currently producing at point A on the frontier where 50% of all production is devoted to public sector goods and 50% to private sector goods.

(a) Mark the following points on your drawing.
 (i) Point A.
 (ii) Point B which shows production following the election of a government which increases government spending on both education and the National Health Service.
 (iii) Point C where unemployment is present in the economy.
 (iv) Point D where the government takes over production of all goods and services in the economy.
(b) Draw another diagram putting on it the original production possibility frontier you drew for (a), labelling it AA.
 (i) Draw a new production possibility frontier on the diagram, labelling it PP, which shows the position after a devastating war has hit the economy.
 (ii) Draw another PPF labelling it QQ which shows an increase in productivity in the economy such that output from the same amount of resources increases by 50 per cent in the public sector but twice that amount in the private sector.

Key terms

Basic economic problem - resources have to be allocated between competing uses because wants are infinite whilst resources are scarce.
Choice - economic choices involve the alternative uses of scarce resources.
Economic goods - goods which are scarce because their use has an opportunity cost.
Free goods - goods which are unlimited in supply and which therefore have no opportunity cost.
Margin - a point of possible change.
Needs - the minimum which is necessary for a person to survive as a human being.

Opportunity cost - the benefits foregone of the next best alternative.
Production possibility frontier (also known as the production possibility curve or the production possibility boundary or the transformation curve) - a curve which shows the maximum potential level of output of one good given a level of output for all other goods in the economy.
Scarce resources - resources which are limited in supply so that choices have to be made about their use.
Wants - desires for the consumption of goods and services.

Applied economics

Work and Leisure

Paid work

Time is a scarce resource. There are only 24 hours in a day and 365 days in a year. Average life expectancy for a UK male born in 2006 was 76.8 and 81.2 for a female. So people have to make choices about how to allocate their time.

One fundamental choice is how to divide time between work and leisure. Work can be narrowly defined as paid work. Statistics suggest that men are in paid employment for less time over their whole life than before. The position for women is more complicated.

- Table 1 shows that there has been a small reduction in the average number of paid hours worked per week over the past 20 years.
- Holiday entitlements have shortened the working year. All full time workers are now entitled to 4 weeks paid holiday each year which includes bank holidays. In 1970, the average was only 2 weeks.
- Men are working fewer years over their lifetime. Figure 4 shows how economic activity rates have changed since 1971. The economic activity rate in Figure 4 is the percentage of the population (men aged 16-64 and women aged 16-59) in work or seeking work (i.e. officially unemployed). Over time,

more males are choosing to stay longer in education. There has also been a smaller fall in activity rates for men aged 25-64. The increase in male activity rates in the 1990s was due to job creation which pulled men back into the workforce. In the long term, many are predicting that men will retire later. This is partly because they are in better health than before. But also pension schemes are pushing back the official retirement age, forcing men to work longer.
- Women are tending to work more years in paid employment. This is shown by the continuing rise in activity rates for women in Figure 4. Women are better educated than in 1971 and can get much better jobs. Child care provision is continuing to improve. For women over 50, like men, pension ages are being pushed back.

The motivators for paid work

People work for a variety of motives, including the satisfaction of doing a job and enjoying being part of a team. However, the primary motivator is pay. When workers retire, they might choose to undertake voluntary work, or do jobs about the house which previously they would have paid someone else to do, but rarely will they will put the time or the energy into these activities that they put into their previous paid job. Over time, the opportunity cost of not working has been rising because wages have been rising. Since 1945, earnings have roughly been doubling every 30 years in real terms (i.e. after inflation has been taken into account). Workers today can buy far more goods and services than their parents or grandparents at a similar age. If a 40 year old doesn't work today, he or she will have to forego the purchase of far more goods and services than, say, 30 years ago. This is arguably the most important reason why more and more women are choosing to stay in work rather than give up work to stay at home to bring up their families.

For those taking early retirement, the opportunity cost of leisure time is typically far less than for other workers. When they retire, they receive a pension. Hence, the money foregone is only the difference between what they would have earned and their pension. Tax, national insurance contributions and work related payments like pension contributions or costs of commuting to work all help to reduce the monetary value of a wage. Hence, many workers taking early retirement find that their new retirement income is not that much below their old take home pay. The benefits of the extra leisure time they can gain by retiring far outweigh the losses in terms of the goods and services they could buy had they stayed in work.

Table 1 Average weekly hours of full-time employees

	1986	2006
Males	41.8	38.9
Females	37.3	34.0

Source: adapted from *Annual Abstract of Statistics*, Office for National Statistics.

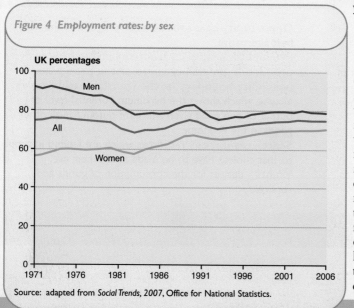

Figure 4 Employment rates: by sex

UK percentages

Men
All
Women

Source: adapted from *Social Trends, 2007*, Office for National Statistics.

Early retirement, however, is likely to become less common in the future. With rising life expectancies, employers are finding it more expensive to provide pensions for workers. The public sector is reacting by trying to force up retirement ages and make it more difficult for workers to retire early. Private sector employers are tending to close down their existing pension schemes and replace them with far less generous schemes where workers have to save more to get the same pension. The result is that the opportunity cost of retiring early is likely to rise substantially. Workers will react by staying on in work longer.

Non-paid work

Paid work is not the only type of work undertaken by individuals. People also have to work at home, cooking, cleaning, maintaining equipment and property and looking after others, particularly children, the sick and the elderly. Table 2 shows that women tend to spend nearly twice as much time on housework and childcare as men. They also spend less time on leisure activities than men. However, men tend to spend more time on employment and study. The traditional stereotype of the man coming home from work and expecting the house to be clean, the children fetched from school and the meal on the table is to some extent still true, even though more and more women are going out to work.

Leisure

Individuals spend their leisure time in a variety of ways. Table 3 shows participation rates in the main home-based leisure activities and how they have changed over time. The most popular leisure activity is watching television. Nearly everybody had watched some television in the four weeks prior to being interviewed for the survey. Equally, seeing friends or relatives is a highly popular activity. Table 3 shows that there are gender differences between leisure activities. Men are far more likely to do DIY and gardening, whilst women are more likely to do dressmaking, needlework and knitting. This time series shows that participation rates in most leisure activities have been rising over time. A greater proportion of the population, for example, read books, did DIY or did some gardening at the end of the twentieth century than they did in the 1970s. This greater variety of leisure activities has probably come about for a variety of reasons: increased incomes, allowing people to afford to engage in particular activities such as listening to CDs; better education, giving people access to activities such as reading; and

Seeing friends is a highly popular pastime.

Table 2 Adults aged 16+, time spent on main activities by sex, 2005

	Hours and minutes per day	
	Males	Females
Sleep	8.04	8.18
Resting	0.43	0.48
Personal care	0.40	0.48
Eating and drinking	1.25	1.19
Leisure		
Watching TV/DVD and listening to radio/music	2.50	2.25
Social life and entertainment/culture	1.22	1.32
Hobbies and games	0.37	0.23
Sport	0.13	0.07
Reading	0.23	0.26
All leisure	5.25	4.53
Employment and study	3.45	2.26
Housework	1.41	3.00
Childcare	0.15	0.32
Voluntary work and meetings	0.15	0.20
Travel	1.32	1.22
Other	0.13	0.15

Source: adapted from www.statistics.gov.uk

Table 3 Participation in home-based leisure activities: by sex

Great Britain			Percentages	
	1977	1986	1996	2002
Males				
Watching TV	97	98	99	99
Visiting/entertaining				
friends or relations	89	92	95	-
Listening to recorded music	64	69	79	83
Reading books	52	52	58	58
DIY	51	54	58	-
Gardening	49	47	52	-
Dressmaking/needlework/knitting	2	3	3	-
Females				
Watching TV	97	98	99	99
Visiting/entertaining				
friends or relations	93	95	97	-
Listening to recorded music	60	65	77	83
Reading books	57	64	71	72
DIY	22	27	30	-
Gardening	35	39	45	-
Dressmaking/needlework/knitting	51	48	37	-

Source: adapted from *Social Trends*, *General Household Survey*, Office for National Statistics.

less time spent at work giving more time for DIY or gardening.

Individuals have to allocate their scarce resources of time and money between different leisure pursuits. Children tend to be time rich but financially poor. 45 year olds tend to be the reverse: time poor but financially better off. Old age pensioners are time rich but less financially well off than when they were working. Their health may also preclude them from activities such as taking part in sport. These constraints could be represented on a production

possibility frontier. For instance, a diagram could be drawn showing the trade off between home based leisure pursuits and leisure activities away from the home. The more time spent in the pub means that less time is available to watch television at home or do gardening. Equally, a production possibility diagram could be used to illustrate the trade-off between work and leisure. The more time spent at work, the less leisure time is available. Ultimately, choices have to be made between work and leisure and individuals have to assume responsibility for the choices they make.

DataQuestion — Production possibility frontiers

The break up of Eastern Europe

When communism in Eastern Europe and the former Soviet Union was replaced by more democratic systems of government at the end of the 1980s, there was a move away from state control of the economy towards a market-led economy. Before, the state had often decided which factories were to produce what products, and would issue instructions about who was to buy the resulting output. In the new market-led system, factories had to find buyers for their products. The result was that many factories closed down. Consumers began buying foreign made goods, or found their incomes drastically slashed as they were made redundant from closing enterprises. Factories making goods for the defence industry were particularly badly affected as governments cut their spending on defence. Some attempted to transfer their skills to making civilian goods, but it often proved impossible to make the jump from the manufacture of fighter jets to the manufacture of washing machines. The total incomes and output of countries such as Russia and Georgia were actually lower in 2006 than they were in 1990. These countries have faced enormous problems in making the transition. Others, such as Hungary, have been more successful and have seen a rise in their total incomes and output.

Table 4 National income, selected countries in Eastern Europe and the former Soviet Union, 2006 as a % of 1990

	%
Albania	64.6
Belarus	39.6
Bulgaria	9.8
Croatia	11.0
Georgia	- 41.9
Hungary	38.7
Romania	19.2
Russian Federation	- 3.4
Serbia	- 28.2

Source: adapted from United Nations, unstats.un.org.

Former Yugoslavia

The collapse of communism in Eastern Europe was a mixed blessing for some. In Yugoslavia, it led to the break-up of the federation of states which formed the country. Serbia, which considered itself the most important part of the federation, strongly resisted the process. In 1992, it fought a war with Croatia and over-ran parts of that country which had majority Serb populations. Serbia then helped fuel a civil war in Bosnia-Herzegovina. In 1999, Serbian forces were accused of attempting to ethnically cleanse the majority Albanian population from its province of Kosovo. This resulted in intervention by US and European troops. Serbia saw its economy shrink as infrastructure, such as houses and factories, was destroyed in fighting. Embargoes by the USA and the EU on trade with Serbia disrupted exports and imports. It was only from 2000 when peace was restored in the region that Serbia's economy began to grow again. Even then, as Table 5 shows, Serbia paid a heavy price for its aggression towards its neighbours. Croatia, which also engaged in war, was less badly affected because it had stopped fighting by the mid-1990s, allowing its economy to begin growing again.

Table 5 Croatia and Serbia, national income, 2006 as a % of 1990

	%
Croatia	+ 11.0
Serbia	- 28.2

Source: adapted from United Nations, *Economic Survey of Europe.*

Source: adapted from www.state.gov; www.washingtonpost.com.

China

Since the mid-1970s, China has been growing dramatically. Currently, it is growing by nearly 10 per cent per annum. This means that output is doubling roughly every seven years. It is not difficult to understand why the Chinese economy has been so successful. By the mid-1970s, it already had a relatively well educated workforce. compared to other poor developing countries. However, its economy was otherwise inefficient and backward. From the mid-1970s, there was a gradual easing of Communist control of the economy which allowed ordinary Chinese people to set up their own businesses in a more free market style economy. Exports began to be encouraged. This linked China to the global economy. Finally, there was a considerable flow of investment money and technological know-how into China. Foreign investors were keen to take advantage of cheap labour and found the lure of what is likely to become the world's largest economy irresistible.

Table 6 China, average annual growth in real national income, 1971-2006

				Percentage
	1971-1980	1981-1990	1991-2000	2001-2006
National income	6.3	9.4	10.5	9.7

Source: adapted from unstats.un.org.

Of all the world's regions, Africa has had the most disappointing economic performance over the past few decades. Sub-Saharan Africa in particular has performed poorly. As Table 7 shows, average annual growth in national income was only 1.8 per cent in the 1980s and 2.4 per cent in the 1990s. This was below other regions of the world. It was also not enough to prevent average incomes falling. This is because population growth was higher than growth in national income.

A number of factors account for these statistics. Economic management was often poor and governments were corrupt. Disastrous borrowing in the late 1970s and 1980s left many countries with foreign debts they couldn't afford to repay. There was a failure to invest in everything from education to health care to roads. Too few businesses were set up. The aids epidemic has also hit incomes because it has hit at people in the prime of their lives when they could be most productive.

Since the start of the new millennium, growth figures have improved. However, Africa needs much higher growth rates to raise its peoples out of poverty. At the moment, with India growing at around 6 per cent per annum and China at 10 per cent, the gulf between Sub-Saharan Africa and the rest of the world is increasing.

Table 7 Sub-Saharan Africa: average annual real growth in national income and national income per head

			Percentage
	1980-89	1990-99	2000-04
National income	1.8	2.4	4.0
National income per head	-1.1	-0.2	1.6

Source: adapted from World Bank, *African Development Indicators 2006*

1. What is a production possibility frontier for an economy?
2. Explain why a production possibility frontier might shift inwards or outwards. Illustrate your answer with examples from the data.
3. A peace group has put forward a proposal that the UK should halve its spending on defence, including giving up its nuclear capability. Using production possibility frontiers, evaluate the possible economic implications of this proposal.

Summary

1. An economy is a social organisation through which decisions about what, how and for whom to produce are made.
2. The factors of production - land, labour, capital an entrepreneurship - are combined together to create goods and services for consumption.
3. The economy is divided into three sectors, primary, secondary and tertiary.
4. Markets exist where buyers and sellers exchange goods.
5. The main actors in the economy, consumers, firms and government, have different objectives. Consumers, for instance, wish to maximise their welfare whilst firms might wish to maximise profit.

What is an economy?

Economic resources are scarce whilst human wants are infinite. An economy is a system which attempts to solve this basic economic problem. There are many different levels and types of economy. There is the household economy, the local economy, the national economy and the international economy. There are free market economies which attempt to solve the economic problem with the minimum intervention of government and command economies where the state makes most resource allocation decisions. Although these economies are different, they all face the same problem.

Economists distinguish three parts to the economic problem.

- **What** is to be produced? An economy can choose the mix of goods to produce. For instance, what proportion of total output should be spent on defence? What proportion should be spent on protecting the environment? What proportion should be invested for the future? What proportion should be manufactured goods and what proportion services?
- **How** is production to be organised? For instance, are DVD players to be made in the UK, Japan or Taiwan? Should car bodies be made out of steel or fibreglass? Would it better to automate a production line or carry on using unskilled workers?
- **For whom** is production to take place? What proportion of output should go to workers? How much should pensioners get? What should be the balance between incomes in the UK and those in Bangladesh?

An economic system needs to provide answers to all these questions.

Economic resources

Economists commonly distinguish three types of resources available for use in the production process. They call these resources the FACTORS OF PRODUCTION.

LAND is not only land itself but all natural resources below the earth, on the earth, in the atmosphere and in the sea. Everything from gold deposits to rainwater and natural forests are examples of land.

NON-RENEWABLE RESOURCES, such as coal, oil, gold and copper, are land resources which once used

Question 1

Consider your household economy.
(a) What is produced by your household (e.g. cooking services, cleaning services, accommodation, products outside the home)?
(b) How is production organised (e.g. who does the cooking, what equipment is used, when is the cooking done)?
(c) For whom does production take place (e.g. for mother, for father)?
(d) Do you think your household economy should be organised in a different way? Justify your answer.

will never be replaced. If we use them today, they are not available for use by our children or our children's children. RENEWABLE RESOURCES, on the other hand, can be used and replaced. Examples are fish stocks, forests, or water.

SUSTAINABLE RESOURCES are a particular type of renewable resource. Sustainable resources are ones which can be exploited economically and which will not diminish or run out. A forest is a renewable resource. However, it is only a sustainable resource if it survives over time despite economic activities such as commercial logging or farming. It ceases to be a sustainable resource if it is cleared to make way for a motorway. NON-SUSTAINABLE RESOURCES are resources which are diminishing over time due to economic exploitation. Oil is a non-sustainable resource because it cannot be replaced.

LABOUR is the workforce of an economy - everybody from housepersons to doctors, vicars and cabinet ministers. Not all workers are the same. Each worker has a unique set of inherent characteristics including intelligence, manual dexterity and emotional stability. But workers are also the products of education and training. The value of a worker is called his or her HUMAN CAPITAL. Education and training will increase the value of that human capital, enabling the worker to be more productive.

CAPITAL is the manufactured stock of tools, machines, factories, offices, roads and other resources which is used in the production of goods and services. Capital is of two types. WORKING or CIRCULATING CAPITAL is stocks of raw materials, semi-manufactured and finished goods which are waiting to be sold. These stocks circulate through the production process till they are finally sold to a consumer. FIXED CAPITAL is the stock of factories, offices, plant and machinery. Fixed capital is fixed in the sense that it will not be transformed into a final product as working capital will. It is used to transform working capital into finished products.

Sometimes a fourth factor of production is distinguished. This is ENTREPRENEURSHIP. Entrepreneurs are individuals who:
- organise production - organise land, labour and capital in the production of goods and services;
- take risks - with their own money and the financial capital of others, they buy factors of production to produce goods and services in the hope that they will be able to make a profit but in the knowledge that at worst they could lose all their money and go bankrupt.

Entrepreneurs are typically the owners of small and medium sized businesses who run those businesses on a day to day basis. However, **managers** in companies can also be entrepreneurial if they both organise resources and take risks on behalf of their company.

Sectors of the economy

Economies are structured into three main sectors. In the PRIMARY SECTOR of the economy, raw materials are extracted and food is grown. Examples of primary sector industries are agriculture, forestry, fishing, oil extraction and mining. In the SECONDARY or MANUFACTURING SECTOR, raw materials are transformed into goods. Examples of secondary sector industries are motor manufacturing, food processing, furniture making and steel production. The TERTIARY or SERVICE SECTOR produces services such as transport, sport and leisure, distribution, financial services, education and health.

Most firms tend to operate in just one of these sectors,

specialising in producing raw materials, manufactured goods or services. Some very large firms, such as BP, operate across all three sectors, from the extraction of oil to its refining and sale to the public through petrol stations.

Markets

Markets play a fundamental role in almost all economies today. Markets are where buyers and sellers meet. For economists, markets are not just street markets. Buying and selling can take place in newspapers and magazines, through mail order or over the telephone in financial deals in the City of London, or on industrial estates as well as in high street shopping centres. A MARKET is any convenient set of arrangements by which buyers and sellers communicate to exchange goods and services.

Economists group buyers and sellers together. For instance, there is an international market for oil where large companies and governments buy and sell oil. There are also national markets for oil. Not every company or government involved in the buying and selling of oil in the UK, say, will be involved in the US or the Malaysian oil markets. There are also regional and local markets for oil. In your area there will be a small number of petrol filling stations (sellers of petrol) where you (the buyers) are able to buy petrol. All these markets are inter-linked but they are also separate. A worldwide increase in the price of oil may or may not filter down to an increase in the price of petrol at the pumps in your local area. Equally, petrol prices in your area may increase when prices at a national and international level remain constant.

How buyers and sellers are grouped together and therefore how markets are defined depends upon what is being studied. We could study the tyre industry or we could consider the market for cars and car components which includes part but not all of the tyre industry. Alternatively, we might want to analyse the market for rubber, which would necessitate a study of rubber purchased by tyre producers.

Many Western economists argue that specialisation, exchange and the market lie at the heart of today's economic prosperity in the industrial world. Whilst it is likely that the market system is a powerful engine of prosperity, we shall see that it does not always lead to the most efficient allocation of resources.

The objectives of economic actors

There are four main types of economic actors in a market economy - consumers, workers, firms and governments. It is important to understand what are the economic objectives of each of these sets of actors.

Consumers In economics, consumers are assumed to want to maximise their own ECONOMIC WELFARE, sometimes referred to as UTILITY or **satisfaction**. They are faced with the problem of scarcity. They don't have enough income to be able to purchase all the goods or services that they would like. So they have to allocate their resources to achieve their objective. To do this, they consider the utility to be gained from consuming an extra unit of a product with its opportunity cost. If there is 30p to be spent, would it best be spent on a Mars Bar, a newspaper or a gift to a charity? If you could afford it, would you prefer to move to a larger but more expensive house, or spend the money on going out more to restaurants, or take more holidays abroad? Decisions are made at the **margin**. This means that consumers don't look at their overall spending every time they want to spend an extra 30p. They just consider the alternatives of that decision to spend 30p and what will give them the highest utility with that 30p.

Sometimes it is argued that economics portrays consumers as being purely selfish. This isn't true. Consumers do spend money on giving to charity. Parents spend money on their children when the money could be spent on themselves. Seventeen year old students buy presents for other people. What this shows, according to economists, is that the utility gained from giving money away or spending it on others can be higher than from spending it on oneself. However, individuals are more likely to spend money on those in their immediate family than others. This shows that the utility to be gained from paying for a holiday for your child is usually higher than paying for a holiday for a disabled person you do not know.

Workers Workers are assumed in economics to want to maximise their own welfare at work. Evidence suggests that the most important factor in determining welfare is the level of pay. So workers are assumed to want to maximise their earnings in a job. However, other factors are also important. Payment can come in the form of fringe benefits, like company cars. Satisfaction at work is also very important. Many workers could earn more elsewhere but choose to stay in their present employment because they enjoy the job and the workplace.

Firms The objectives of firms are often mixed. However, in the UK and the USA, the usual assumption is that firms are in business to maximise their PROFITS. This is because firms are owned by private individuals who want to maximise their return on ownership. This is usually achieved if the firm is making the highest level of profit possible. In Japan and continental Europe, there is much more of a tradition that the owners of firms are just one of the STAKEHOLDERS in a business. Workers, consumers and the local community should also have some say in how a business is run. Making profit would then only be one objective amongst many for firms.

Governments Governments have traditionally been assumed to want to maximise the welfare of the citizens of their country or locality. They act in the best interests of all. This can be very difficult because it is often not immediately obvious what are the costs and benefits of a decision. Nor is there often a consensus about what value to put on the gains and losses of different groups. For instance, in the 1990s the UK government brought

the motorway building programme to a virtual halt following the growing feeling that motorways were destroying the environment and were therefore an economic 'bad' rather than a 'good'. However, many, particularly in industry, would argue that the environmental costs of new motorway building are vastly exaggerated and that the benefits of faster journey times more than outweigh any environmental costs.

Governments which act in the best interests of their citizens face a difficult task. However, it can also be argued that governments don't act to maximise the welfare of society. Governments are run by individuals and it could be that they act in their own interest. Certain Third World countries have immense economic problems because their governments are not impartial, but are run for the monetary benefit of the few that can extort bribes from citizens. There is equally a long tradition of 'pork barrel politics'. This is where politicians try to stay in power by giving benefits to those groups who are important at election times. In the UK, it is expected that MPs (Members of Parliament) will fight for the interests of their constituents even if this clearly does not lead to an overall increase in welfare for the country as a whole.

So governments may have a variety of motives when making decisions. In an ideal world, governments should act impartially to maximise the welfare of society. In practice they may fall short of this.

Question 2

Table 2 Shops selling grocery items in Burscough

	Number
Small independent grocers	2
Convenience store grocers	1
Supermarket grocers	1

Burscough is a town in Lancashire which has shops selling grocery items such as fresh vegetables, dairy products or tinned food.

(a) Who might be the buyers and sellers in the local Burscough market for grocery products?
(b) What is the relationship between this market and the market for (i) meat and (ii) petrol?

Question 3

In April 2005, just weeks before a General Election, MG Rover, the last remaining UK owned mass car manufacturer, announced that it was going into receivership. The Labour government immediately announced a £150 million aid package. This included up to £50 million for training workers made redundant at MG Rover and its suppliers, over £40 million to cover redundancy payments and protective awards for Longbridge workers, £24 million to establish a loan fund to help otherwise viable businesses affected by MG Rover's collapse and £41.6 million for MG Rover suppliers who were left being owed large sums of money for products delivered but not paid for.

It could be argued that the aid package smacked of favouritism and 'election year politics'. MG Rover's main plant at Longbridge in Birmingham, where most of the company's 5 000 workers were employed, was in an area with several marginal constituencies. A swing to the Conservatives of just a few per cent of the voters would have turned those constituencies from being Labour held to Conservative held.

Many commentators pointed out that very few of the hundreds of thousands of workers made redundant each year across the UK received such generous help.

On the other hand, trade unions representing workers at Longbridge argued that the package was too small. There were calls for the government to provide a generous aid package to any buyer for MG Rover which would guarantee the safeguarding of its 5 000 jobs. It was pointed out that it was not just the MG Rover jobs which were at stake. It was also all the jobs at suppliers which would disappear if production ceased at Longbridge.

Source: adapted from www.manifest.co.uk.

(a) Suggest what might have been the motives of the UK government in offering a £150 million aid package for MG Rover.
(b) What might have motivated trade unions to call for government aid to help keep the Longbridge plant open?

Key terms

Capital productivity - output per unit of capital employed.
Factors of production - the inputs to the production process: land, which is all natural resources; labour, which is the workforce; capital, which is the stock of manufactured resources used in the production of goods and services; entrepreneurs, individuals who seek out profitable opportunities for production and take risks in attempting to exploit these.
Fixed capital - economic resources such as factories and hospitals which are used to transform working capital into goods and services.
Human capital - the value of the productive potential of an individual or group of workers. It is made up of the skills, talents, education and training of an individual or group and represents the value of future earnings and production.
Market - any convenient set of arrangements by which buyers and sellers communicate to exchange goods and services.
Non-renewable resources - resources, such as coal or oil, which once exploited cannot be replaced.
Non-sustainable resource - resource which is being economically exploited in such a way that it is being reduced over time.

Primary sector - extractive and agricultural industries.
Productivity - output per unit of input employed.
Profits - the reward to the owners of a business. It is the difference between a firm's revenues and its costs.
Renewable resources - resources, such as fish stocks or forests, which can be exploited over and over again because they have the potential to renew themselves.
Secondary sector - production of goods, mainly manufactured.
Stakeholders - groups of people which have an interest in a firm, such as shareholders, customers, suppliers, workers, the local community in which it operates and government.
Sustainable resource - renewable resource which is being economically exploited in such a way that it will not diminish or run out.
Tertiary sector - production of services.
Utility - the satisfaction derived from consuming a good.
Welfare - the well being of an economic agent or group of economic agents.
Working or circulating capital - resources which are in the production system waiting to be transformed into goods or other materials before being finally sold to the consumer.

Applied economics

Sport and Leisure

Different markets

The sport and leisure market is made up of many different markets. For instance, there is a market for travel and tourism, a market for football, a television entertainment market and a restaurant market. Some of these markets overlap. A Japanese visitor to the UK might eat in a restaurant in London and so the tourism and the 'eating out' markets overlap. Some markets are closely linked. Pubs near a football stadium are likely to benefit from increased trade on the day of matches.

Figure 1 gives data for one segment of this market, the market for visitor attractions, such as historic houses, theme parks and museums. The figures given are for attractions like museums such as the National Gallery, Historic properties such as the Tower of London and steam railways such as the Severn Valley Railway. The data show that the most popular type of visitor attraction in 2006 was museums and art galleries. This was closely followed by historic properties. These two types of visitor attraction accounted for approximately 50 per cent of the market by visitor numbers.

Economic resources

Each market uses land, labour and capital to produce services. For instance, a visit to a National Trust property utilises land as a factor. There is likely to be a house built on land and the gardens too use land as their basic resource. Labour is needed for the upkeep of the property and to provide services to the visitor, including volunteers on the door and in the tea shop. Buildings on the property represent capital.

There are many examples of entrepreneurs in the market. Andrew Lloyd Webber, for instance, is an entrepreneur putting on musical shows for the mass market. Rich owners of football clubs are entrepreneurs too.

Objectives of participants in the market

In a market there are buyers and sellers. The objectives of consumers are to maximise their welfare or utility when buying sport and leisure services. They consider whether they will get more satisfaction per pound spent from going to a pub or going to a nightclub, for instance.

They have to choose between spending on sport and leisure services and all other goods and services, like clothes or consumer durables. They also have to choose between different sport and leisure services.

There is a number of different types of suppliers to the market. First there are firms whose aim is to maximise profit. For example, Table 2 shows that 29 per cent of tourist attractions in the UK were either privately owned by an individual or group of

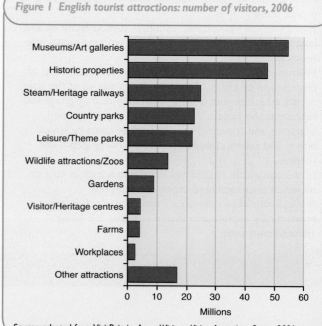

Figure 1 *English tourist attractions: number of visitors, 2006*

- Museums/Art galleries
- Historic properties
- Steam/Heritage railways
- Country parks
- Leisure/Theme parks
- Wildlife attractions/Zoos
- Gardens
- Visitor/Heritage centres
- Farms
- Workplaces
- Other attractions

Millions: 0 10 20 30 40 50 60

Source: adapted from VisitBritain, *Annual Visits to Visitor Attractions Survey 2006*.

individuals, or by a company with shareholders. Their aim is likely to be to make a profit from that attraction. Alton Towers, Blackpool Pleasure Beach, Chessington World of Adventures or Legoland at Windsor are not charities, but run for profit for the benefit of their owners.

Second, however, as Table 2 shows, there are many examples of charities and trusts in the market, making up 31 per cent of visitor attractions. The largest is the National Trust. Charities and trusts do not necessarily have the same objectives, but few are likely to have profit maximisation as their principal objective. The National Trust has as its primary aim to 'preserve places of historic interest and natural beauty permanently for the nation to enjoy'. Financially, it must break even over time to survive. However, it is unlikely to see maximising profits or revenues as its priority. For instance, there are restrictions on the number of visitors to some properties that it owns because more visitors would lead to unacceptable levels of wear and tear.

Third, government is a major provider of services. If English Heritage, Historic Scotland and Cadw are included as part of government, Table 2 shows that 34 per cent of visitor attractions in the UK are owned by different government bodies. They include the British Museum, the Tower of London and London Zoo. The management of these tourist attractions want to maximise resources available to them, particularly by securing larger grants from government. However, government itself is often interested in minimising spending on such bodies because of conflicting objectives. Government may prefer to spend more money on the National Health Service than on museums. The arts and sport have tended to be subsidised by government. Concerning the arts, there is a belief that 'culture' is important to the health of the nation. Hence, the Royal Opera House is heavily subsidised, whilst an Andrew Lloyd Webber production like The Phantom of the Opera receives no subsidy. Some would argue that there is no difference between a Mozart opera like The Marriage of Figaro and The Phantom of the Opera. Indeed, The Phantom of the Opera might be a better case for subsidy because more foreign tourists are likely to see it than a Royal Opera

Table 2 UK distribution of attractions by ownership type, 2002

Ownership	Attraction	Visits
Sample	3,295	284.8m
	%	%
Government	5	17
English Heritage/Historic Scotland/Cadw	7	4
Local Authority	22	23
Privately owned	27	26
Public company/plc	2	3
The National Trust/National Trust for Scotland	10	6
Other trust/charity	21	14
Educational institution	2	1
Religious body	3	5
Other	2	1
UK	100	100

Source: adapted from UK Research Liaison Group, www.staruk.org.uk.

House production. Tourism brings money into the country and creates prosperity.

The same arguments apply to sport. There is an argument that everyone should have access to sporting facilities. Traditionally, local authorities have subsidised swimming pools, leisure centres and sports facilities. Sometimes government is swayed by lobbying from a particular part of the country for spending on the arts or leisure. Local MPs fight for grants for new theatres or recreational facilities. So government is likely to be motivated by a variety of factors when deciding on spending on sport and leisure.

DataQuestion

The oil industry

Figure 2 Brent crude oil price 1966-2006

Source: adapted from UK Offshore Operators Association, *Activity Survey 2006*.

Figure 3 *Capital investment in oil and gas, UK continental shelf; £ billion at 2006 prices*

Source: adapted from UK Offshore Operators Association, *Activity Survey 2006*.

Chancellor announces rise in the tax levied on North Sea oil producers following record crude prices.

Motorists switch to smaller, more fuel efficient cars as petrol prices stay high.

Workers on oil rigs pressing for large pay increases.

North Sea oil producers cut back their spending on investment in exploration and new equipment because of higher costs and taxes

1. Explain the following economic concepts in the context of the UK oil industry:
   (a) economic resources and (b) markets.
2. The world price of oil changed significantly between 2002 and 2006. What might have been the objectives of the following groups when faced with these changes:
   (a) oil companies with North Sea oil installations;
   (b) the UK government; (c) UK motorists;
   (d) workers on North Sea oil rigs?

Summary

1. *Economic data are collected not only to verify or refute economic models but to provide a basis for economic decision making.*
2. *Data may be expressed at nominal (or current) prices or at real (or constant) prices. Data expressed in real terms take into account the effects of inflation.*
3. *Indices are used to simplify statistics and to express averages.*
4. *Data can be presented in a variety of forms such as tables or graphs.*
5. *All data should be interpreted with care given that data can be selected and presented in a wide variety of ways.*

The collection and reliability of data

Economists collect data for two main reasons.

- The scientific method requires that theories be tested. Data may be used to refute or support a theory. For instance, an economist might gather data to support or refute the hypothesis that 'Cuts in the marginal rate of income will increase the incentive to work', or that 'An increase in the real value of unemployment benefit will lead to an increase in the number of people unemployed'.
- Economists are often required to provide support for particular policies. Without economic data it is often difficult, if not impossible, to make policy recommendations. For instance, in his Budget each year the Chancellor of the Exchequer has to make a statement to the House of Commons outlining the state of the economy and the economic outlook for the next 12 months. Without a clear knowledge of where the economy is at the moment it is impossible to forecast how it might change in the future and to recommend policy changes to steer the economy in a more desirable direction.

Collecting economic data is usually very difficult and sometimes impossible. Some macro-economic data - such as the balance of payments figures or the value of national income - are collected from a wide variety of sources. The figures for the balance of payments on current account are compiled from returns made by every exporter and importer on every item exported and imported. Not surprisingly the information is inaccurate. Some exporters and importers will conceal transactions to avoid tax. Others will not want to be bothered with the paper work.

Other macroeconomic data such as the Consumer Price Index (used to measure inflation) or the Labour Force Survey (used to measure employment and unemployment) are based on surveys. Surveys are only reliable if there is accurate sampling and measuring and are rarely as accurate as a complete count.

Some macro-economic data are very reliable statistically but do not necessarily provide a good measure of the relevant economic variable. In the UK, the Claimant Count is calculated each month at benefit offices throughout the country. It is extremely accurate but no economist would argue that the figure produced is an accurate measure of unemployment. There is general agreement that some people who claim benefit for being unemployed are not unemployed and conversely there are many unemployed people who are not claiming benefit.

In micro-economics use is again made of survey data, with the limitations that this implies. Economists also make use of more

Question 1

In November 1998, the Office for National Statistics (ONS) suspended publication of one of the most important economic series it compiles. The average earnings index was found to be giving inaccurate information. The average earnings index is a measure of how much earnings in the whole of the UK are rising. It is calculated monthly by taking data from thousands of returns from businesses. They report on whether or not they have given any pay rises during the previous month and if so, by how much.

Problems arose because of different ways of calculating the average. In October 1998, the ONS launched a new series for average earnings which used a different way of calculating the average than before. But as Figure 1 shows, this revised series gave very different figures from the original series used before. It also didn't fit in very well with what other economic indicators were showing at the time.

A government enquiry found that the revised series was based on inadequate statistical methods which gave too much importance to large changes in earnings by small businesses. In March 1999, a new series was published which followed more closely the old series.

(a) The three lines in Figure 1 should show the same data: the percentage change in average earnings. Give ONE time period when the original series showed an upward movement in earnings when the revised series showed a downward movement.
(b) Why do the three sets of statistics differ in their estimate of changes in average earnings?
(c) Explain TWO reasons why it is important for economic statistics, like growth in average earnings, to be measured accurately.

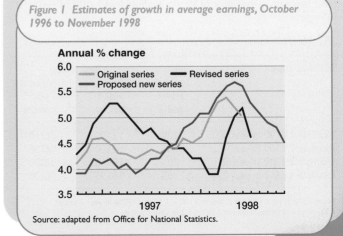

Figure 1 Estimates of growth in average earnings, October 1996 to November 1998

Source: adapted from Office for National Statistics.

experimental data, gathering evidence for case studies. For instance, an economist might want to look at the impact of different pricing policies on entry to sports centres. He or she might study a small number of sports centres in a local area. The evidence gathered would be unlikely decisively to refute or support a general hypothesis such as 'Cheap entry increases sports centre use'. But it would be possible to conclude that the evidence **tended** to support or refute the hypothesis.

In economics it is difficult to gather accurate data and, for that reason, academic economists mostly qualify their conclusions.

Real and nominal values

There are many different **measures** in use today such as tonnes, litres, kilograms and kilometres. Often, we want to be able to compare these different measures. For instance, an industrialist might wish to compare oil measured in litres, and coal measured in kilograms. One way of doing this is to convert oil and coal into therms using gross calorific values. In economics, by far the most important measure used is the value of an item measured in **monetary terms**, such as pounds sterling, US dollars or euros. One problem in using money as a measure is that inflation (the general change in prices in an economy) erodes the purchasing power of money.

For instance, in 1948 the value of output of the UK economy (measured by gross domestic product at market prices) was £12.0 billion. 58 years later, in 2006, it was £1 299.6 billion. It would seem that output had increased about 108 times - an enormous increase. In fact, output increased by only a fraction of that amount. This is because most of the measured increase was an increase not in output but in prices. Prices over the period rose about 25 times. Stripping the inflation element out of the increase leaves us with an increase in output of 4.2 times.

Values unadjusted for inflation are called NOMINAL VALUES. These values are expressed AT CURRENT PRICES (i.e. at the level of prices existing during the time period being measured).

If data are adjusted for inflation, then they are said to be at REAL VALUES or at CONSTANT PRICES. To do this in practice involves taking one period of time as the BASE PERIOD. Data are then adjusted assuming that prices were the same throughout as in the base period.

For instance, a basket of goods costs £100 in year 1 and £200 in year 10. Prices have therefore doubled. If you had £1 000 to spend in year 10, then that would have been equivalent to £500 at year 1 prices because both amounts would have bought 5 baskets of goods. On the other hand, if you had £1 000 to spend in year 1, that would be equivalent to £2 000 in year 10

prices because both would have bought you 10 baskets of goods.

Taking another example, the real value of UK output in 1948 at 1948 prices was the same as its nominal value (i.e. £12 billion). The real value of output in 2006 at 1948 prices was £50.9 billion. It is much lower than the nominal 2006 value because prices were much higher in 2006.

On the other hand, at 2006 prices, the real value of output in 1948 was £306.2 billion, much higher than the nominal value because prices in 2006 were much higher than in 1948. Further examples are given in Table 1.

UK government statistics expressed in real terms are adjusted to prices three or four years previously. In 2007, figures were expressed at 2003 or 2004 prices.

Question 2

Table 2 Components of final demand at current prices

2003=100		£ billion		
	Index of prices	Households' expenditure	Government expenditure	Fixed investment
2003	100.0	697	233	187
2004	102.4	733	251	202
2005	105.5	761	269	212
2006	108.4	795	287	235

Source: adapted from *Monthly Digest of Statistics*, Office for National Statistics.

Using a calculator or a spreadsheet, work out for the period 2003-2006 (a) at constant 2003 prices and (b) at constant 2006 prices the values of:
(i) households' expenditure;
(ii) government expenditure;
(iii) fixed investment.
Present your calculation in the form of two tables, one for 2003 prices and the other for 2006 prices.

Indices

It is often more important in economics to compare values than to know absolute values. For instance, we might want to compare the real value of output in the economy in 1996 and 2006. Knowing that the real value of output (GDP at market prices at 2003 prices) in 2004 was £913.8 billion and in 2006 was £1 209.3 billion is helpful, but the very large numbers make it difficult to see at a glance what, for instance, was the approximate percentage increase. Equally, many series of statistics are averages. The Retail Price Index (the measure of the cost of living) is calculated by working out what it would cost to buy a typical cross-section or 'basket' of goods. Comparing say £458.92 in one month with £475.13 the next is not easy.

So, many series are converted into INDEX NUMBER form. One time period is chosen as the base period and the rest of the statistics in the series are compared to the value in that base period. The value in the base period is usually 100. The figure 100 is chosen because it is easy to work with mathematically.

Table 1 Nominal and real values

Nominal value	Inflation between year 1 and 2	Real values	
		Value at year 1 prices	Value at year 2 prices
Example 1 £100 in year 1	10%	£100	£110
Example 2 £500 in year 1	50%	£500	£750
Example 3 £200 in year 2	20%	£166.66	£200
Example 4 £400 in year 2	5%	£380.95	£400

Note: £100 at year 1 prices is worth £100 x 1.1 (i.e. 1+10%) in year 2 prices.
£200 at year 2 prices is worth £200 ÷ 1.2 in year 1 prices.

Table 3 *Converting a series into index number form*

Year	£ millions	Index number if base year is:		
		year 1	year 2	year 3
1	500	100.0	83.3	62.5
2	600	120.0	100.0	75.0
3	800	160.0	133.3	100.0

Note: The index number for consumption in year 2, if year 1 is the base year, is (600 ÷ 500) x 100.

Taking the example of output again, if 1948 were taken as the base year, then the value of real output in 1948 would be 100, and the value of real output in 2006 would be 423.4. Alternatively if 2006 were taken as the base year, the value of output would be 100 in 2006 and 23.6 in 1948. Or with 2003 as the base year, the value of output in 1948 would be 25.5 whilst in 2006 it would be 108.1. Further examples are given in Table 3.

The interpretation of data

Data can be presented in many forms and be used both to inform and mislead the reader. To illustrate these points, consider inflation figures for the UK economy. Inflation is the general rise in prices in an economy. If there has been 2 per cent inflation over the past year, it means that prices on average have increased by 2 per cent. One way in which inflation figures can be presented is in **tabular form** as in Table 5.

The data could also be presented in **graphical form** as in Figure 2 (a). Graphs must be interpreted with some care. Figure 2 (b) gives a far more pessimistic view of inflation between 2004 and 2006 than Figure 2 (a) at first glance.

Question 3

Table 4 *Consumers' expenditure*

	Food and drink	Transport	£ billion Restaurants and hotels
2003	63.2	104.6	78.9
2004	65.5	109.2	83.6
2005	67.5	112.9	88.9
2006	70.9	116.4	92.0

Source: adapted from *Monthly Digest of Statistics*, Office for National Statistics.

Using a calculator or a spreadsheet, convert each category of expenditure into index number form using as the base year:
(a) 2003 and (b) 2006.
Present your calculations in the form of two tables, one for each base year.

Table 5 *UK inflation (CPI)*

Year	Inflation %
1990	7.0
1991	7.5
1992	4.2
1993	2.5
1994	2.0
1995	2.6
1996	2.5
1997	1.8
1998	1.6
1999	1.3
2000	0.8
2001	1.2
2002	1.3
2003	1.4
2004	1.3
2005	2.1
2006	2.3

Source: adapted from www.statistics.gov.uk.

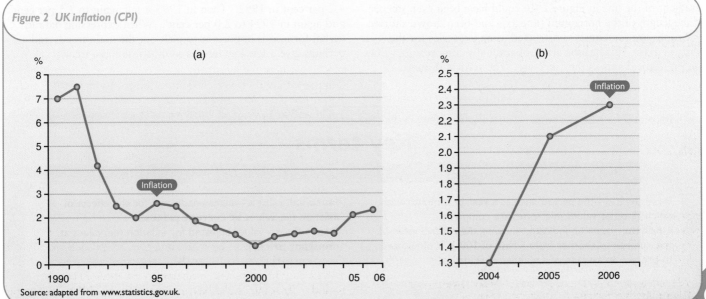

Figure 2 UK inflation (CPI)

Source: adapted from www.statistics.gov.uk.

Question 4

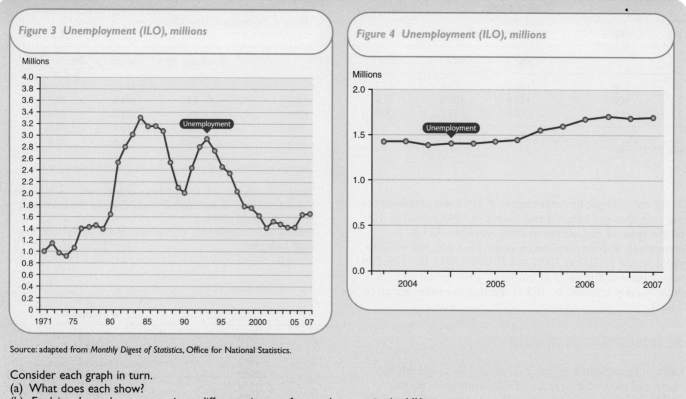

Figure 3 *Unemployment (ILO), millions*

Figure 4 *Unemployment (ILO), millions*

Source: adapted from *Monthly Digest of Statistics*, Office for National Statistics.

Consider each graph in turn.
(a) What does each show?
(b) Explain why each seems to give a different picture of unemployment in the UK.

One reason is that Figure 2 (b) is taken out of the context of its surrounding years. Figure 2 (a) would suggest that inflation between 2004 and 2006 was relatively low for the whole period shown. Figure 2 (b) suggests the opposite, a dramatic increase in inflation. Another reason why Figure 2 (b) suggests a dramatic increase in inflation is because the line is drawn very steeply. This has been achieved through the scales used on the axes. The vertical axis in Figure 2 (b) only covers 1.3 to 2.5 per cent. In Figure 2 (a), in contrast, the vertical axis starts at zero and rises to 8 per cent over the same drawn height. The gradient of the line in Figure 2 (b) could have been even steeper if the length of the horizontal time axis had been drawn shorter.

Graphs are sometimes constructed using log scales for the vertical axis. This has the effect of gradually compressing values on the vertical axis as they increase. The vertical distance

between 0 and 1, for instance, is larger per unit than between 999 and 1 000.

Data can also be expressed in **verbal form**. Figure 2 shows that inflation rose between 1990 and 1991, and then broadly fell to a low of 0.8 per cent in 2000 before fluctuating in the 1.2 to 1.4 per cent range between 2001 and 2004. Inflation then rose to 2.3 per cent by 2006. When expressing data in verbal form, it can become very tedious to describe each individual change. For instance, it would be inappropriate to say 'Inflation in 1990 was 7 per cent. Then it rose to 7.5 per cent in 1991 before falling to 4.2 per cent in 1992. Then in 1993 it fell again to 2.5 per cent and again in 1994 to 2.0 per cent'. When expressing data in verbal form, it is important to pick out the main trends and perhaps give a few key figures to illustrate these trends.

Key terms

Base period - the period, such as a year or a month, with which all other values in a series are compared.
Index number - an indicator showing the relative value of one number to another from a base of 100. It is often used to present an average of a number of statistics.

Nominal values - values unadjusted for the effects of inflation (i.e. values **at current prices**).
Real values - values adjusted for inflation (i.e. values at **constant prices**).

Applied economics

Tourism

Spending on tourism

Tourism is a major industry in the UK. Is it growing in size? There is a number of ways in which growth can be measured. Table 6 shows how total spending on tourism has grown between 1989 and 2005. It divides tourists into three categories - UK tourists who take a holiday within the country, foreign tourists who come to the UK and UK tourists who take holidays abroad. The figures in Table 6 are expressed at current prices. This means that inflation is not taken into account. If there had been very high inflation over the period 1989-2005, the volume of tourism could have declined given the data in Table 6. In fact, consumer prices over the 16 year period rose 67 per cent. So real growth in spending is anything which is above that 67 per cent rise.

Table 6 Spending on tourism at current prices, £ million

| | £ millions at current prices | | |
	Spending on holidays by UK citizens in the UK	Spending in the UK by foreign visitors	Spending on foreign holidays by UK residents
1989	17 071[1]	6 945	9 357
1995	20 072	11 763	15 386
2005	22 667	14 248	32 154

1. Estimated

Source: adapted from *Annual Abstract of Statistics*, Office for National Statistics.

Table 7 shows the figures in Table 6 expressed at constant 2001 prices, i.e. after the inflation element has been stripped out and adjusted to the level of prices in 2001. Taking 2001 as the reference year for prices means that the 1989 and 1995 data at current prices increase as numbers when they become data at constant prices, whilst the 2005 numbers fall.

Table 8 shows the figures in Table 7 in index number form. This has the advantage that it is much easier to

Table 7 Spending on tourism at constant 2001 prices, £ million

| | £ millions at constant 2001 prices | | |
	Spending on holidays by UK citizens in the UK	Spending in the UK by foreign visitors	Spending on foreign holidays by UK residents
1989	25 677	10 446	14 047
1995	23 332	13 674	17 885
2005	25 118	15 789	35 632

Source: adapted from *Annual Abstract of Statistics*, Office for National Statistics.

see which of the three areas of tourism has grown more quickly. At a glance, it can be seen that spending on holidays by UK citizens in the UK fell by 2.1 per cent in real terms over the period 1989 to 2005. In contrast, spending on foreign holidays by UK citizens grew by 153.7 per cent. Foreign visitors to the UK spent 51.1 per cent more. Because these are index numbers, it is not possible to say how important is the 51.1 per cent rise in spending by foreign visitors to the total domestic tourist industry. For instance, if foreign tourists accounted for just 1 per cent of total spending, a 51.1 per cent rise would have almost no impact on tourism. This illustrates one of the disadvantages of using index numbers. To assess the relative impact of the increase in foreign tourists, we have to look back to Table 7. Total spending on tourism in the UK by UK citizens and by foreigners at constant 2001 prices rose from £36.1 billion to £40.9 billion, a 13.2 per cent increase, over the period 1989 to 2005. A 13.2 per cent change over 16 years is not particularly large. The data show that spending by UK citizens has broadly been unchanged over the period. The increase comes entirely from increased spending by overseas visitors.

Employment in tourism

Tables 8 and 9 show that employment in tourist industries grew by 6.6 per cent between 2000 and 2004. Tourism is a major employer in the UK

Table 8 Spending on tourism at constant 2001 prices, 1989 = 100

| | 1989 = 100 | | |
	Spending on holidays by UK citizens in the UK	Spending in the UK by foreign visitors	Spending on foreign holidays by UK residents
1989	100.0	100.0	100.0
1995	90.7	130.9	127.3
2005	97.9	151.1	253.7

Source: adapted from *Annual Abstract of Statistics*, Office for National Statistics.

accounting for 5 per cent of all employment. In some regions of the UK such as the South West of England, it is an even more important provider of jobs.

Table 9 shows that the largest tourism employer is restaurants, bars and canteens, accounting for 43.5 per cent of employment in tourist industries. When Table 9 is converted into index number form in Table 10, this cannot be seen from the data. The largest number in Table 10 for 2004, which is 113.0 for Recreation services, shows the largest increase in employment from 2000.

Trips and prices

Data for UK domestic tourism, trips made by British citizens within Great Britain, reveal some very interesting aspects of tourism. Table 11 shows that the number of trips made increased by 29.1 million between 1989 and 2005. Each trip, though, was shorter. In 1989, the average number of nights spent was 4.0 but in 2005 had fallen to 3.2. Spending per trip at constant prices fell by 1.1 per cent. This compares to the 50.9 per cent increase in real household consumption expenditure over the same period.

Table 11 therefore shows that between 1989 and 2005, people went on more holidays in Britain, but they were shorter and spending on holidays per trip failed to keep up with increases in household spending on all other goods and services. Part of the reason for these trends is that 'short breaks' have now become far more popular. More people are now taking a weekend holiday, for instance. These will be less expensive than longer holidays. The fall in spending per trip could also be an indication that the price of holidays has fallen relative to all other prices in the economy. Since 1989, there has been considerable expansion of chains of budget hotels such as Travel Inn or Travel Lodge. These have exercised downward pressure on the cost of hotel and other accommodation.

Table 9 Employment in tourism, UK

							Thousands
	Hotels and other tourist accommodation	Restaurants, bars and canteens	Transport	Travel agents, tour operators	Recreation services	Rest of the economy	Total employment
2000	230.0	556.1	132.2	135.2	73.2	205.2	1 331.9
2002	222.0	586.8	133.4	138.8	78.4	208.2	1 367.4
2004	229.6	618.2	131.5	146.8	82.7	211.1	1 419.9

Source: adapted from *Annual Abstract of Statistics*, Office for National Statistics.

Table 10 Employment in tourism, UK, 2000=100

							2000=100
	Hotels and other tourist accommodation	Restaurants, bars and canteens	Transport	Travel agents, tour operators	Recreation services	Rest of the economy	Total employment
2000	100.0	100.0	100.0	100.0	100.0	100.0	100.0
2002	96.5	105.5	100.9	102.7	107.1	101.5	102.7
2004	99.8	111.2	99.5	108.6	113.0	102.9	106.6

Source: adapted from *Annual Abstract of Statistics*, Office for National Statistics.

Table 11 UK domestic tourism

	Number of trips, millions	Number of nights spent, millions	Average nights spent	Average expenditure per trip at current prices (£)	Average expenditure per trip trip at constant 2001 prices (£)
1989	109.6	443.2	4.0	99.1	149.1
1995	121.0	526.0	3.6	135.8	157.9
2005	138.7	442.3	3.2	163.4	147.5

Source: adapted from *Annual Abstract of Statistics*, Office for National Statistics.

DataQuestion

Cinema data

Table 12 *Cinema exhibitor statistics, UK[1]*

	Number of sites	Number of screens	Number of admissions, millions	at current prices			at constant 2001 prices		
				Gross box office takings, £ millions	Revenue per admission, £	Revenue per screen, £ 000	Gross box office takings, £ millions	Revenue per admission, £	Revenue per screen, £ 000
1987	492	1 035	66.8	123.8	1.85	118.7	210.6	3.15	201.9
1995	728	2 003	114.6	354.2	3.09	176.8	411.7	3.59	205.5
2006	783	3 569	156.6	762.1	4.87	213.5	677.8	4.34	189.9

Source: adapted from *Annual Abstract of Statistics*, Office for National Statistics.

Table 13 *Cinema exhibitor statistics, UK[1]*

1987=100

	Number of sites	Number of screens	Number of admissions	at current prices			at constant 2001 prices		
				Gross box office takings	Revenue per admission	Revenue per screen	Gross box office takings	Revenue per admission	Revenue per screen
1987	100.0	100.0	100.0	100.0	100.0	100.0	100.0	100.0	100.0
1995	148.0	193.5	171.6	286.1	167.0	148.9	195.5	114.0	101.8
2006	159.1	344.8	234.4	615.6	263.2	179.9	321.8	137.8	94.1

Source: adapted from *Annual Abstract of Statistics*, Office for National Statistics.
1. 1987 data are Great Britain. 1995 and 2006 data are UK.

1. Describe the main trends in cinema admissions shown in the data.
2. Explain the advantages and disadvantages of using index numbers to present data. Illustrate your answer from the data.
3. 'Revenues per admission and the number of screens cannot carry on rising.'
   (a) To what extent does this data support this statement for the period 1987-2006? (b) Discuss whether it is likely to be true in the future.

Summary

1. Positive economics deals with statements of 'fact' which can either be refuted or supported. Normative economics deals with value judgments, often in the context of policy recommendations.
2. Economics is generally classified as a social science.
3. It uses the scientific method as the basis of its investigation.
4. Economics is the study of how groups of individuals make decisions about the allocation of scarce resources.
5. Economists build models and theories to explain economic interactions.
6. Models and theories are simplifications of reality.
7. Models can be distinguished according to whether they are static or dynamic, equilibrium or disequilibrium, or partial or general.

Positive and normative economics

Economics is concerned with two types of investigation. POSITIVE ECONOMICS is the scientific or objective study of the subject. It is concerned with finding out how economies and markets actually work. POSITIVE STATEMENTS are statements about economics which can be proven to be true or false. They can be supported or refuted by evidence. For example, the statement 'The UK economy is currently operating on its production possibility boundary' is a positive statement. Economists can search for evidence as to whether there are unemployed resources or not. If there are large numbers of unemployed workers, then the statement is refuted. If unemployment is very low, and we know that all market economies need some unemployment for the efficient workings of labour markets as people move between jobs, then the statement would be supported. Statements about the future can be positive statements too. For example, 'The service sector will grow by 30 per cent in size over the next five years' is a positive statement. Economists will have to wait five years for the proof to support or refute the statement to be available. However, it is still a statement which is capable of being proved or disproved.

NORMATIVE ECONOMICS is concerned with value judgements. It deals with the study of and presentation of policy prescriptions about economics. NORMATIVE STATEMENTS are statements which cannot be supported or refuted. Ultimately, they are opinions about how economies and markets should work. For example, 'The government should increase the state pension', or 'Manufacturing companies should invest more' are normative statements.

Economists tend to be interested in both positive and normative economics. They want to find out how economies work. But they also want to influence policy debates. Normative economics also typically contains positive economics within it. Take the normative statement 'The government should increase the state pension'. Economists putting forward this value judgement are likely to back up their opinion with positive evidence. They might state that 'The average pensioner has a disposable income of 40 per cent of the average worker'; and 'The average pensioner only goes on holiday once every four years'. These are positive statements because they are capable of proof or disproof. They are used to build up an argument which supports the final opinion that state pensions should be raised.

Normative statements tend to contain words like 'should' and 'ought'. However, sometimes positive statements also contain these words. 'Inflation should be brought down' is a normative statement because it is not capable of refutation. 'Inflation should reach 5 per cent by the end of the year' is a positive statement. At the end of the year, if inflation has reached 5 per cent, then the statement will have been proven to be correct.

The scientific method

There are many sciences covering a wide field of knowledge. What links them all is a particular method of work or enquiry called the SCIENTIFIC METHOD. The scientific method at its most basic is relatively easy to understand. A scientist:

- postulates a THEORY - the scientist puts forward a hypothesis which is capable of refutation (e.g. the earth travels round the sun, the earth is flat, a light body will fall at the same speed as a heavy body);
- gathers evidence to either support the theory or refute it - astronomical observation gives evidence to support the theory that the earth travels round the sun; on the other hand, data refutes the idea that the earth is flat; gathering evidence may be done through **controlled experiments**;
- accepts, modifies or refutes the theory - the earth does travel round the sun; a light body will fall at the same speed as a heavy body although it will only do so under certain conditions; the earth is not flat.

Theories which gain universal acceptance are often called LAWS. Hence we have the law of gravity, Boyle's law, and in economics the laws of demand and supply.

Economics - the science

Some sciences, such as physics or chemistry, are sometimes called 'hard sciences'. This term doesn't refer to the fact that physics is more difficult than a science such as biology! It refers to the fact that it is relatively easy to apply the scientific method to the study of these subjects. In physics much of the work can take place in laboratories. Observations can be made with some degree of certainty. Control groups can be established. It then becomes relatively easy to accept or refute a particular hypothesis.

This is all much more difficult in social sciences such as economics, sociology, politics and anthropology. In economics,

Question 1

London's business leaders are hoping that one of Gordon Brown's first acts as prime minister will be to fund the Crossrail scheme, a new railway linking Heathrow, the City and Canary Wharf. Estimated to cost £16 billion, Crossrail is not cheap. Why does the City think Crossrail is so important? Mostly, because it will link Heathrow airport to the City of London. Currently, rail travellers to the City from Heathrow have to get off at London Paddington and catch a slow tube train. In comparison with other major cities, such as Paris or Amsterdam, the service is poor and slow. It places the City at a major competitive disadvantage with other financial centres.

The City of London is vital to the success of the UK economy. The UK government should give this support to an industry which is a major contributor to the wealth of the country.

Source: adapted from the *Financial Times*, 22.6.2007.

Explain which are the positive statements and which are the normative statements in this passage.

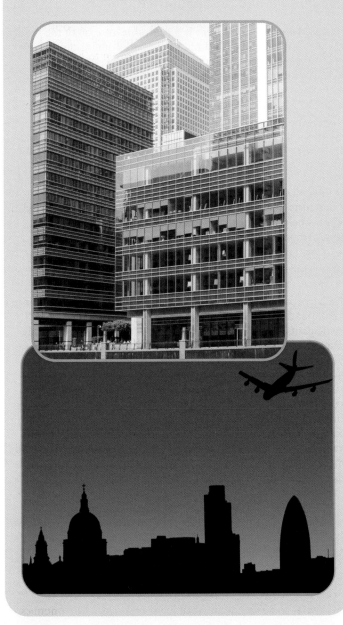

it is often not possible to set up experiments to test hypotheses. It is often not possible to establish control groups or to conduct experiments in environments which enable one factor to be varied whilst other factors are kept constant. The economist has to gather data in the ordinary everyday world where many variables are changing over any given time period. It then becomes difficult to decide whether the evidence supports or refutes particular hypotheses.

Economists sometimes come to very different conclusions when considering a particular set of data as their interpretations may vary. For example, an unemployment rate of 6 per cent in Scotland compared to a national average of 3 per cent may indicate a failure of government policy to help this area. Others may conclude that policy had been a success as unemployment may have been far greater without the use of policy.

It is sometimes argued that economics cannot be a science because it studies human behaviour and human behaviour cannot be reduced to scientific laws. There is an element of truth in this. It is very difficult to understand and predict the behaviour of individuals. However, nearly all economics is based on the study of the behaviour of groups of individuals. The behaviour of groups is often far more predictable than that of individuals. Moreover, we tend to judge a science on its ability to establish laws which are certain and unequivocal. But even in a hard science such as physics, it has become established that some laws can only be stated in terms of probabilities. In economics, much analysis is couched in terms of 'it is likely that' or 'this may possibly happen'. Economists use this type of language because they know they have insufficient data to make firm predictions. In part it is because other variables may change at the same time, altering the course of events. However, it is also used because economists know that human behaviour, whilst broadly predictable, is not predictable to the last £1 spent or to the nearest 1 penny of income.

Theories and models

The terms 'theory' and MODEL are often used interchangeably. There is no exact distinction to be made between the two. However, an economic theory is generally expressed in looser terms than a model. For instance, 'consumption is dependent upon income' might be an economic theory.
'$C_t = 567 + 0.852Y_t$' where 567 is a constant, C_t is current consumption and Y_t current income would be an economic model. Theories can often be expressed in words. But economic models, because they require greater precision in their specification, are often expressed in mathematical terms.

The purpose of modelling

Why are theories and models so useful in a science? The universe is a complex place. There is an infinite number of interactions happening at any moment in time. Somehow we all have to make sense of what is going on. For instance, we assume that if we put our hand into a flame, we will get burnt. If we see a large hole in the ground in front of us we assume that we will fall into it if we carry on going in that direction.
One of the reasons why we construct theories or models is because we want to know why something is as it is. Some people are fascinated by questions such as 'Why do we fall downwards and not upwards?' or 'Why can birds fly?'.
More importantly we use theories and models all the

time in deciding how to act. We keep away from fires to prevent getting burnt. We avoid holes in the ground because we don't want to take a tumble.

Simplification

One criticism made of economics is that economic theories and models are 'unrealistic'. This is true, but it is equally true of Newton's law of gravity, Einstein's Theory of Relativity or any theory or model. This is because any theory or model has to be a simplification of reality if it is to be useful. Imagine, for instance, using a map which described an area perfectly. To do this it would need to be a full scale reproduction of the entire area which would give no practical advantage. Alternatively, drop a feather and a cannon ball from the top of the leaning tower of Pisa. You will find that both don't descend at the same speed, as one law in physics would predict, because that law assumes that factors such as air resistance and friction don't exist.

If a model is to be useful it has to be simple. The extent of simplification depends upon its use. If you wanted to go from London to Tokyo by air, it wouldn't be very helpful to have maps which were on the scale of your local A to Z. On the other hand, if you wanted to visit a friend in a nearby town it wouldn't be very helpful to have a map of the world with you. The local A to Z is very much more detailed (i.e. closer to reality) than a world map but this does not necessarily make it more useful or make it a 'better' model.

Simplification implies that some factors have been included in the model and some have been omitted. It could even be the case that some factors have been distorted to emphasise particular points in a model. For instance, on a road map of the UK, the cartographer will almost certainly not have attempted to name every small hamlet or to show the geological formation of the area. On the other hand, he or she will have marked in roads and motorways which will appear several miles wide according to the scale of the map.

Types of model

Equilibrium and disequilibrium models Equilibrium is a central feature of all the models studied in this book. In economics, EQUILIBRIUM can be described as a point when expectations are being realised and where no plans are being frustrated. For instance, in the model of demand and supply, equilibrium price is achieved when the planned quantity that buyers wish to purchase is equal to the planned quantity that sellers wish to sell. Equilibrium models are models where it is predicted that the market or economy will return to an equilibrium point. Disequilibrium models are ones where there is no tendency to return to the equilibrium point. Disequilibrium models are more complex than equilibrium models and tend to be expressed using complex mathematical language.

Static and dynamic models A DYNAMIC model is one which

contains time as one of its variables. A STATIC model is one which contains no time element within the model. Nearly all the models explained in this book are static models. They tend to be simpler and easier to use. Dynamic models tend to be complex. They are more suited, for example, to computer modelling.

General and partial models A GENERAL MODEL is one which contains a larger number of variables. For instance, a model which includes all markets in the economy would be a general model. A PARTIAL MODEL is one which contains relatively few variables. A model of the oil market or of the demand for labour would be a partial model. A partial model will be one in which most variables are assumed to be in the category of CETERIS PARIBUS. Ceteris paribus is Latin for 'all other things being equal' or 'all other things remaining the same'. It is a very powerful simplifying devise which enables economists to explain clearly how an economy or market market works. For instance, in neo-classical price theory, we assume that income and tastes remain the same when drawing a demand curve.

Equilibrium and disequilibrium models

As stated above, equilibrium is a central feature of all the models studied in this book. All static models are equilibrium models because they deal with equilibrium positions.

An equilibrium position may be stable. If there is a movement away from equilibrium for some reason, there will be an in-built tendency for equilibrium to be restored. If the equilibrium point is unstable, there will be no tendency to move towards an equilibrium point once disequilibrium has been established.

It is easy to make the incorrect assumption that the market (or whatever is being studied) will always return to an equilibrium position; or that the equilibrium point is somehow the optimal or most desirable position. Neither is necessarily true even if economists tend to believe that knowing where is the equilibrium point is helpful in explaining economic events and in making policy recommendations.

Macroeconomics and microeconomics

A macroeconomic model is one which models the economy as a whole. It deals with economic relationships at the level of all participants in the economy. A micro-economic model, on the other hand, deals with the economic behaviour of individuals or groups within society. For instance, the study of the spending decisions of individual consumers or consumers within a particular market such as the market for cars (demand theory) would be micro-economics. The study of consumption patterns for the whole economy (the consumption function) would be an example of macro-economics. The study of the determination of wage rates (wage theory) would be micro-economics. The study of the overall level of wages in the economy (part of national income accounting) would be macro-economics.

Key terms

Ceteris paribus - the assumption that all other variables within the model remain constant whilst one change is being considered.

Equilibrium - the point where what is expected or planned is equal to what is realised or actually happens.

Law - a theory or model which has been verified by empirical evidence.

Normative economics - the study and presentation of policy prescriptions involving value judgements about the way in which scarce resources are allocated.

Normative statement - a statement which cannot be supported or refuted because it is a value judgment.

Partial and general models - a partial model is one with few variables whilst a general model has many.

Positive economics - the scientific or objective study of the allocation of resources.

Positive statement - a statement which can be supported or refuted by evidence.

Static and dynamic models - a static model is one where time is not a variable. In a dynamic model, time is a variable explicit in the model.

The scientific method - a method which subjects theories or hypotheses to falsification by empirical evidence.

Theory or model - a hypothesis which is capable of refutation by empirical evidence.

Applied economics

Positive and normative economics

The *Financial Times*, in a editorial dated 10.9.2007, wrote about 'How government can sustain UK manufacturing success'. The editorial covered why manufacturing industry was currently successful and how best the government can support manufacturing industry in the future.

It starts off with a normative statement, an opinion: 'Rumours of the death of UK manufacturing have been greatly exaggerated.' It then supports this opinion with a number of positive statements, or facts, about UK manufacturing such as 'surveys report bulging order books' and 'productivity growth has outstripped the rest of the economy'.

The article goes on with a number of positive statements about how manufacturing has remained competitive. For example, it states that 'what remains in Britain is often the high-value-added production that cannot easily be shipped overseas; and they 'make complex and innovative products that are hard to copy'.'

The article then turns to the role of government. It argues that government can support manufacturing industry. It makes two value judgements about government buying policies of equipment such as aircraft, and about innovation: 'while government procurement contracts should not favour British manufacturers merely because of their nationality, they could do more to favour innovation.' It then makes another normative statement: 'The biggest contribution the government could make would be to sort out the lamentable state of UK state secondary education and skills training.' It supports this value judgement with a number of positive statements such as 'skills shortages have been filled recently by engineers from eastern Europe.'

The editorial concludes by making the positive statements that 'The manufacturers that have survived the shakeout have devised successful strategies for remaining competitive in the global economy. But they also know that continuing success depends on raising the pace of innovation and further developing the skills of the workforce.'

DataQuestion — The Common Agricultural Policy (CAP)

CAP

In 2005, there were difficult negotiations about the EU budget between member countries. The British Prime Minister, Tony Blair, wanted to reopen a deal made in 2002 about the Common Agricultural Policy which set CAP budgets to 2014. He, in turn, came under intense pressure to give up the 'British Rebate', an annual refund to the UK first negotiated in the 1980s to compensate the UK for its low level of subsidies from the CAP budget. The ten, mainly Eastern European, countries which joined in the EU in 2004 wanted a larger slice of EU spending than proposed. France and Ireland, both major beneficiaries of CAP subsidies, strongly defended the deal made in 2002.

Two contributions to this debate follow, one from Bertie Ahern, the Irish Prime Minister who was against further CAP reform, the other from Tony Blair's Press Spokesperson, who argued for CAP reform.

We must stand by the Common Agricultural Policy

In an article written for the *Financial Times*, Bertie Ahern, the Irish Prime Minister, argued for maintaining the CAP deal made in 2002. His comments included the following.

The defeat of the European Union's proposed constitution in the French and Dutch referendums has led to a renewed debate on the way forward for Europe. As part of this debate, the Common Agricultural Policy has in recent months been the subject of much criticism, with repeated calls for further reform.

2003 saw a radical reform of CAP, decoupling 'subsidies' from production. This reform is in its first year of implementation. It would be both unfair and unwise to ask farmers to accept another radical reform now. Farmers, like other business people, need a reasonable degree of stability in the policy environment in which they operate. However, there is more at stake. To try to overturn an agreement reached unanimously by the European Council as recently as October 2002 would be to send the wrong signal to Europe's people. The public needs to see a Europe that stands by its agreements.

There are other issues too. Reform would mean that European agricultural production would fall rapidly. The food supply gap would be filled by imports from, for example, South America and Australia, which can produce at prices below European levels. Europe's food supplies could, once again, become vulnerable. Reform would also result in serious damage to the social and economic fabric of rural areas across Europe. As for the scale of subsidies, the Organisation for Economic Co-operation and Development (OECD) has estimated that transfers to agriculture from both consumers and taxpayers amount to $103bn (£58bn) in the EU and $92bn (£52bn) in the USA, or 1.32 per cent of GDP for the EU and 0.92 per cent for the US. There is therefore broad comparability of support.

Calls for radical CAP reform are misplaced and outdated; they are based on a misunderstanding of the role of the CAP in European society and the world economy. They are also based on a false premise about the relative cost of the CAP.

Source: adapted from the *Financial Times*, 26.9.2005.

Briefing from the Prime Minister's Official Spokesperson on the Common Agricultural Policy

Our policy all along has been to get rid of subsidies for crops because we believe that this was a distorted way in which to support the rural economy. Therefore what we have always argued for was a managed process of change in which you maintained sustainable livelihoods in the countryside but didn't do so at the expense of distorting world trade. That was why we always argued for fundamental reform of CAP and we recognised that there had been some progress in that direction but we are arguing for more.

We are still in a situation where some 80 per cent of the existing budget is directed towards the original 15 member states, and that does not allow the spending to be prioritised towards providing the infrastructure support that accession countries need. Therefore we still have a distorted system.

There should be a policy of managed change which would include more efficient farming and viable, sustainable rural communities. You cannot have a situation where we go into another decade with 40 per cent of the EU budget being spent on 5 per cent of the population.

Source: adapted from The Office of the Prime Minister, www.number-10.gov.uk/output/page7762.asp.

1. Explain the difference between positive and normative statements. Give at least six examples from the views of Bertie Ahern and Tony Blair.
2. Evaluate the case for and against reform of the CAP using the arguments put forward in the data.

Summary

1. Demand for a good is the quantity of goods or services that will be bought over a period of time at any given price.
2. Demand for a good will rise or fall if there are changes in factors such as incomes, the price of other goods, tastes, and the size of the population.
3. A change in price is shown by a movement along the demand curve.
4. A change in any other variable affecting demand, such as income, is shown by a shift in the demand curve.
5. The market demand curve can be derived by horizontally summing all the individual demand curves in the market.

Demand

A market exists wherever there are buyers and sellers of a particular good. Buyers **demand** goods from the market whilst sellers **supply** goods to the market.

DEMAND has a particular meaning in economics. Demand is the quantity of goods or services that will be bought at any given price over a period of time. For instance, approximately 2 million new cars are bought each year in the UK today at an average price of, say, £8 000. Economists would say that the annual demand for cars at £8 000 would be 2 million units.

Demand and price

If everything else were to remain the same (this is known as the **ceteris paribus** condition), what would happen to the quantity demanded of a product as its price changed? If the average price of a car were to fall from £8 000 to £4 000, then it is not difficult to guess that the quantity demanded of cars would rise. On the other hand, if the average price were £35 000 very few cars would be sold.

This is shown in Table 1. As the price of cars rises then, ceteris paribus, the quantity of cars demanded will fall. Another way of expressing this is shown in Figure 1. Price is on the vertical axis and quantity demanded over time is on the horizontal axis. The curve is downward sloping showing that as price falls, quantity demanded rises. This DEMAND CURVE shows the quantity that is demanded at any given price. When price changes there is said to be a **movement along** the curve. For instance, there is a movement along the curve from the point A to the point B, a fall of 1 million cars a year, when the price of cars rises from £8 000 to £16 000.

It is important to remember that the demand curve shows

Table I The demand schedule for cars

Price (£)	Demand (million per year)
4 000	4.0
8 000	2.0
16 000	1.0
40 000	0.4

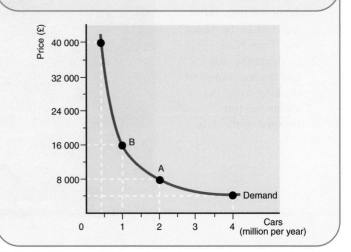

Figure I The demand curve
The demand curve is downward sloping, showing that the lower the price, the higher will be the quantity demanded of a good. In this example, only 0.4 million cars per year are demanded at a price of £40 000 each, but a reduction in price to £4 000 increases quantity demanded to 4 million units per year.

EFFECTIVE DEMAND. It shows how much would be bought (i.e. how much consumers can afford to buy and would buy) at any given price and not how much buyers would like to buy if they had unlimited resources.

Economists have found that the inverse relationship between price and quantity demanded - that as price rises, the quantity demanded falls - is true of nearly all goods. In the unit 'Normal, inferior and Giffin goods', we shall consider the few examples of goods which might have upward sloping demand curves.

Demand and income

Price is not the only factor which determines the level of demand for a good. Another important factor is income. Demand for a normal good rises when income rises. For instance, a rise in income leads consumers to buy more cars. A few goods, known as inferior goods, fall in demand when incomes rise.

The effect of a rise in income on demand is shown in Figure 2. Buyers are purchasing 0A of clothes at a price of 0E. Incomes rise and buyers react by purchasing more clothes at the same

Question 1

Stagecoach operates both bus and train services. It charges different prices to different passengers for the same journeys depending, for instance, on when they travel, their age, whether they are making a single or return journey or whether they have a season ticket. Using a demand curve diagram, explain what happens when:

(a) children are charged half price for a bus journey instead of being charged full price;
(b) senior citizens are given a free bus pass paid for by the local authority rather than having to pay the full fare;
(c) Stagecoach increases its prices on a route by 5 per cent;
(d) passengers can get a 60 per cent reduction by buying a day return if they travel after 9.30 compared to having to pay the full fare.

Figure 2 A change in income

An increase in income will raise demand for a normal good. At a price of 0E, for instance, demand will rise from 0A to 0B. Similarly, at all other prices, an increase in income will result in a level of demand to the right of the existing demand curve. So the demand curve will shift from D_1 to D_2. A fall in income will result in less being demanded at any given price. Hence the demand curve will shift to the left, from D_1 to D_3.

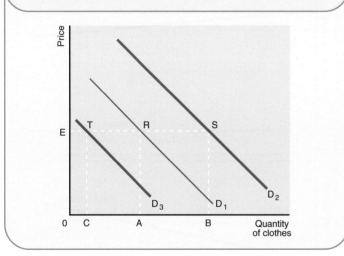

price. At the higher level of income they buy, say, 0B of clothes. A new demand curve now exists passing through the point S. It will be to the right of the original demand curve because at any given price more will be demanded at the new higher level of income.

Economists say that a rise in income will lead to an **increase in demand** for a normal good such as clothes. An increase in demand is shown by a SHIFT IN THE DEMAND CURVE. (Note that an **increase in quantity demanded** would refer to a change in quantity demanded resulting from a change in price and would be shown by a movement along the curve.) In Figure 2, the original demand curve D_1 shifts to the right to its new position D_2. Similarly, a fall in income will lead to a **fall in demand** for a normal good. This is shown by a **shift** to the left of the demand curve from D_1 to D_3. For instance, at a price of 0E, demand will fall from 0A to 0C.

Two points need to be made. First, the demand curves in Figure 2 have been drawn as straight lines. These demand curves drawn show a hypothetical (or imaginary) position. They are drawn straight purely for convenience and do not imply that actual demand curves for real products are straight. Second, the

shifts in the demand curves are drawn as parallel shifts. Again this is done for convenience and neatness but it is most unlikely that a rise or fall in income for an actual product would produce a precisely parallel shift in its demand curve.

Question 2

Table 2

Quantity demanded (million tyres)	Price(£)
10	20
20	16
30	12
40	8
50	4

Table 2 shows the demand curve facing a tyre manufacturer.

(a) Draw a demand curve for tyres from the above data.
(b) An increase in income results in an increase in quantity demanded of tyres of: (i) 5 million; (ii) 10 million; (iii) 15 million; (iv) 25 million. For each of these, draw a new demand curve on your diagram.
(c) Draw a demand curve for tyres which would show the effect of a fall in incomes on the original demand for tyres.
(d) Draw a demand curve for tyres which would show that no products were demanded when their price was £8.

The price of other goods

Another important factor which influences the demand for a good is the price of other goods. For instance, in the great drought of 1976 in the UK, the price of potatoes soared. Consumers reacted by buying fewer potatoes and replacing them in their diet by eating more bread, pasta and rice.

This can be shown on a demand diagram. The demand curve for pasta in Figure 3 is D_1. A rise in the price of potatoes leads

Figure 3 A rise in the price of other goods

A rise in the price of potatoes will lead to a rise in the demand for substitute goods. So the demand for pasta will increase, shown by a shift to the right in the demand curve for pasta from D_1 to D_2.

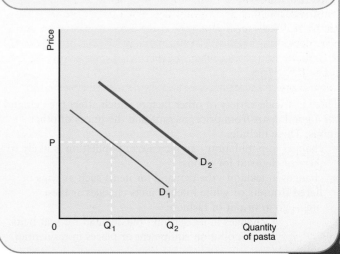

to a rise in the demand for pasta. This means that at any given price a greater quantity of pasta will be demanded. The new demand curve D_2 will therefore be to the right of the original demand curve.

Not all changes in prices will affect the demand for a particular good. A rise in the price of tennis balls is unlikely to have much impact on the demand for carrots, for instance. Changes in the price of other goods as well may have either a positive or negative impact on demand for a good. A rise in the price of tennis rackets is likely to reduce the demand for tennis balls as some buyers decide that tennis is too expensive a sport. On the other hand, the demand for cinema places, alcoholic drink or whatever other form of entertainment consumers choose to buy instead of tennis equipment, will increase.

Question 3

Figure 4 *Brent crude oil price, $ per barrel, 2005-2007*

Between 2005 and 2007, the price of Brent crude oil rose from $38 a barrel and peaked at $79 a barrel. The price of oil was predicted to remain high for the foreseeable future because of growing demand for oil from emerging countries such as China. Explain, using diagrams, what effect you would expect this to have on the demand in the UK for:
(a) oil-fired central heating systems;
(b) luxury cars with high-mileage petrol consumption;
(c) rail travel;
(d) ice-cream;
(e) air travel.

Other factors

There is a wide variety of other factors which affect the demand for a good apart from price, income and the prices of other goods. These include:
● changes in population - an increase in population is likely to increase demand for goods;
● changes in fashion - the demand for items such as wigs or flared trousers or white kitchen units changes as these items go in or out of fashion;
● changes in legislation - the demand for seat belts, anti-pollution equipment or places in residential homes has been affected in the past by changes in government legislation;
● advertising - a very powerful influence on consumer demand which seeks to influence consumer choice.

Question 4

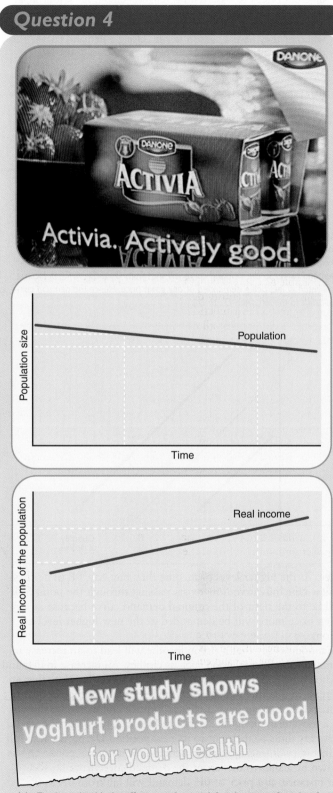

(a) Explain the likely effect on demand for Activia of each of the four factors shown in the data. Use a separate demand diagram for each factor to illustrate your answer.

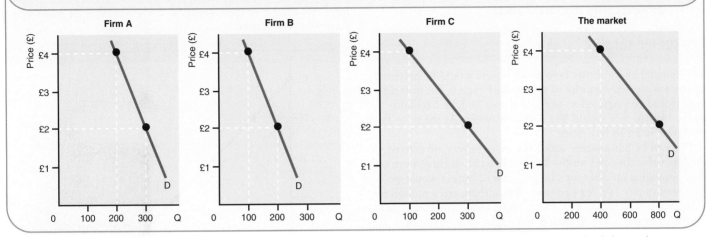

Figure 5 *Individual and market demand curves*
The market demand curve can be derived from the individual demand curves by adding up individual demand at each single price. In this example, for instance, the market demand at a price of £2 is calculated by adding the demand of firms A, B and C at this price.

A summary

It is possible to express demand in the form of a **functional** relationship. The quantity demanded of good N (Q_n) varies according to (i.e. is a function of) the price of good N (P_n), income (Y), the price of all other goods ($P_1, ... P_{n-1}$) and all other factors (T). Mathematically, this is:

$$Q_n = f [P_n, Y, (P_1, ... P_{n-1}), T]$$

At this stage, this mathematical form of expressing the determinants of demand is a convenient shorthand but little else. The major tools for dealing with demand at this level are either the written word or graphs. At a far more advanced level, the algebraic formula for demand is often the most powerful and useful tool in analysing demand.

Individual and market demand curves

So far, it has been assumed that demand refers to demand for a product in a whole market (i.e. MARKET DEMAND).

Question 5

$$Q = 20 - \frac{1}{2} P$$

where Q is the monthly quantity demanded of compact discs (CDs) in millions and P is their price.
(a) Draw the demand curve given by this equation between CD prices of £1 and £20.
(b) A new format results in a fall in demand of CDs of 5 million per month at any given price. (i) What is the new formula for quantity demanded of CDs?
(ii) Plot the new demand curve on your diagram.
(c) A rise in consumer incomes results in consumers being less price sensitive than before when buying CDs. As a result, instead of monthly demand falling by half a million when price is increased by £1, monthly demand now falls only by 400 000. Assume that the original equation for demand is as in part (a) of this question. (i) What is the new formula for quantity demanded of CDs? (ii) Plot the new demand curve on your diagram.

However, it is possible to construct individual demand curves and derive market demand curves from them. An INDIVIDUAL DEMAND CURVE is the demand curve of an individual buyer. This could be a consumer, a firm or a government.

The determinants of demand for an individual are no different from those of the market as a whole. When price rises, there is a fall in the quantity demanded of the product; when income rises, assuming that the product is a normal good, demand will increase, etc.

Figure 5 shows a situation where there are three and only three buyers in a market, firms A, B and C. At a price of £2, firm A will buy 300 units, firm B 200 units and firm C 300 units. So the total market demand at a price of £2 is 300 + 200 + 300 or 800 units. At a price of £4, total market demand will be 200 + 100 + 100 or 400 units. Similarly, all the other points

Question 6

Table 3

Price (£)	Quantity demanded of good Y (000 units)		
	Firm A	Firm B	Firm C
100	500	250	750
200	400	230	700
300	300	210	650
400	200	190	600
500	100	170	550

There are only three buyers of good Y, firms A, B and C.
(a) Draw the individual demand curves for each firm.
(b) Draw the market demand curve for good Y.
(c) A fourth business, firm D, enters the market. It will buy 500 at any price between £100 and £500. Show the effect of this by drawing a new market demand curve for good Y.
(d) Firm B goes out of business. Draw the new market demand curve with firms A, C and D buying in the market.

on the market demand curve can be derived by summing the individual demand curves. This is known as **horizontal summing** because the figures on the horizontal axis of the individual demand curves are added up to put on the market demand curve. But the figures on the vertical axis of both individual and market demand curves remain the same.

Consumer surplus

The demand curve shows how much buyers would be prepared to pay for a given quantity of goods. In Figure 6, for instance, they would be prepared to pay 10p if they bought 1 million items. At 8p, they would buy 2 million items. As the price falls, so buyers want to buy more.

This can be put another way. The more buyers are offered, the less value they put on the last one bought. If there were only 1 million units on offer for sale in Figure 6, buyers would be prepared to pay 10p for each one. But if there are 3 million for sale, they will only pay 6p. The demand curve, therefore, shows the value to the buyer of each item bought. The first unit bought is worth almost 12p to a buyer. The one millionth unit is worth 10p. The four millionth unit would be worth 4p.

The difference between the value to buyers and what they actually pay is called CONSUMER SURPLUS. Assume in Figure 6 that the price paid is 6p. The buyers who would have paid 10p for the millionth unit have gained a consumer surplus of 4p (10p - 6p). Those who would have paid 8p for the 2 millionth unit would gain 2p. So the total consumer surplus at a price of 6p is the shaded triangular area in Figure 6.

Adam Smith, writing in the 18th century, was puzzled why consumers paid high prices for goods such as diamonds which were unnecessary to human existence, whilst the price of necessities such as water was very low. Figure 6 explains this **paradox of valu**e. If there are few goods available to buy, as with diamonds, then consumers are prepared to pay a high price for them. If goods are plentiful, then consumers are only prepared to pay a low price. This doesn't mean to say that they don't place a high value on necessities when they are in short supply. In famine times, diamonds can be traded for small amounts of food. If diamonds were as common as water, buyers would not be prepared to pay much for the last diamond bought. Consumers enjoy large amounts of consumer surplus

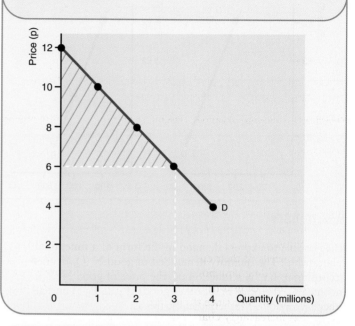

Figure 6 Consumer surplus
The demand curve shows the price that the buyer would be prepared to pay for each unit. Except on the last unit purchased, the price that the buyer is prepared to pay is above the market price that is paid. The difference between these two values is the consumer surplus. It is represented by the shaded area under the demand curve.

Question 7

Demand for a good is zero at £200. It then rises to 50 million units at £100 and 75 million at £50.
(a) Draw the demand curve for prices between 0 and £200.
(b) Shade the area of consumer surplus at a price of £60.
(c) Is consumer surplus larger or smaller at a price of £40 compared to £60? Explain your answer.

on water because the price is low and large amounts are bought. Far less consumer surplus is enjoyed by consumers on diamonds because far fewer diamonds are bought.

Key terms

Consumer surplus - the difference between how much buyers are prepared to pay for a good and what they actually pay.
Demand curve - the line on a price-quantity diagram which shows the level of effective demand at any given price.
Demand or effective demand - the quantity purchased of a good at any given price, given that other determinants of demand remain unchanged.

Individual demand curve - the demand curve for an individual consumer, firm or other economic unit.
Market demand curve - the sum of all individual demand curves.
Shift in the demand curve - a movement of the whole demand curve to the right or left of the original caused by a change in any variable affecting demand except price.

Applied economics

The demand for housing

Housing tenure

The housing market is not a single market because there are different forms of tenure in the market.

Owner-occupied housing Figure 7 shows that most homes today are owner-occupied. This means that they are owned by at least one of the people who live in the house.

Rented from local authorities The single largest group of landlords in the UK are local councils. Since the 1980s, their importance has declined as local authority housing has been sold off.

Rented from housing associations Housing associations are organisations set up to provide housing for rent. They have no shareholders and are not in business to make a profit. Their aim is to serve the needs of their customers. Much of their funding for building new houses comes from the government in the form of grants. Housing associations have grown in importance since the 1980s because the government has increasingly channelled grants for house building in the rented sector away from local authorities and towards housing associations.

Rented from private landlords Private landlords are in business to make a profit from renting property. The 1988 Housing Act (amended in 1996) revitalised the private renting sector. It allowed for new 'assured tenancies' where landlords could charge whatever rent they wished. For the first time in decades, landlords could charge the rent that the market would bear instead of having it capped, typically at a rent far below the market price. Landlords could also end tenancy agreements with an individual. This meant they could reclaim their property if they wanted to get rid of a difficult tenant, move back into the property or sell it without have a sitting tenant in place. The result has been an increase in the number of private properties for rent and a considerable improvement in the quality of housing for rent. In a competitive market where landlords are charging market rents, tenants can shop around not just for the cheapest rent but also for the best quality property at the price. Figure 7 shows that there was a slow rise in privately rented accommodation in the 1990s. However, this rise accelerated and between 2002 and 2006 approximately 100 000 '**buy-to-let**' properties were added to the rented sector each year. Individuals were buying properties with the intention of renting them out to earn a profit and to make capital gains when selling properties. Buy-to-let between 2002 and 2006 accounted for on average half of the increase in all dwellings in the UK.

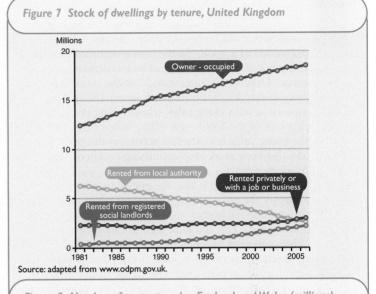

Figure 7 Stock of dwellings by tenure, United Kingdom

Source: adapted from www.odpm.gov.uk.

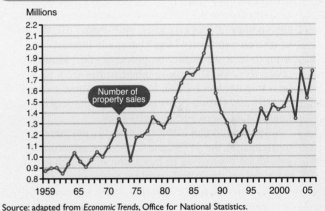

Figure 8 Number of property sales: England and Wales (millions)

Source: adapted from *Economic Trends*, Office for National Statistics.

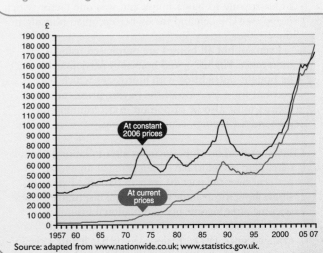

Figure 9 Average UK house prices, £ at constant 2006 prices

Source: adapted from www.nationwide.co.uk; www.statistics.gov.uk.

Factors affecting the demand for housing

There are many factors which determine the demand or quantity demanded of housing.

The price of owner-occupied housing Economic theory suggests that the higher the price, the less will be demanded of a good. In the owner-occupied market, rising house prices should lead to less demand and vice versa. However, Figures 8 and 9 show no evidence of this. In fact, rising house prices in the 1980s were associated with rising sales, whilst falling prices in the first half of the 1990s saw falling house sales. Equally, the house price boom which started in the mid-1990s has also been associated with rising numbers of property sales.

One explanation is that the price of a house is arguably the wrong price to consider when looking at the demand for homes. Most houses are bought with a **mortgage**. This is a loan used to buy property. When potential buyers look at the price of the transaction, they tend to look at the value of the monthly repayments on the mortgage rather than the actual house price. In the short term, the value of monthly repayments is more influenced by interest rates than house prices. If interest rates rise, mortgage repayments rise and vice versa. Comparing Figure 7, the number of property sales, with Figure 10, the level of interest rates, very large changes in interest rates do seem to have an impact on property sales. However, relatively small changes in interest rates seem to have little impact. Since 2000, for example, there seems to be little correlation between the small changes in interest rates seen and property sales.

Subsidies too can affect the monthly payments on a mortgage. In the 1970s and 1980s, the government subsidised borrowing to buy a house through giving tax relief on the interest paid on mortgages. This effectively reduced the monthly repayment cost of the mortgage. Starting in 1987, the value of mortgage tax relief was progressively reduced by the government and was finally abolished in 1999. This increased the cost of borrowing to buy a house and was one factor which dampened the demand for owner-occupied housing in the 1990s.

Even so, not all houses are purchased using a mortgage. Higher priced houses in particular tend to be bought outright or with mortgages which only account for a fraction of the buying price. So other factors must also be important in determining the demand for owner-occupied housing.

Incomes Real incomes (incomes after inflation has been taken into account) have been rising at an average of 2.5 per cent over the past 40 years in the UK. Figure 11 shows how the average real personal disposable income (income after income tax and National Insurance contributions have been deducted) of households has changed since 1971. Rising income has led to a rising

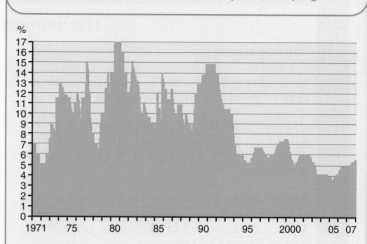

Figure 10 *Interest rates: the base rate set by the Bank of England*

Source: adapted from Bank of England website.

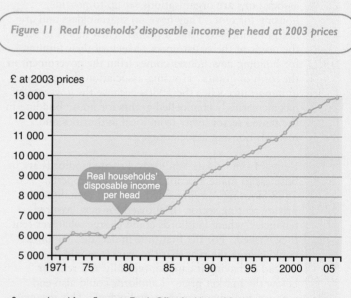

Figure 11 *Real households' disposable income per head at 2003 prices*

Source: adapted from *Economics Trends*, Office for National Statistics.

Table 4 *Population and number of households: UK*

		Millions
	Population	Number of households
1961	52.8	16.3
1971	55.9	18.6
1981	56.4	20.2
1991	57.8	22.4
2001	59.1	23.8
2006	60.5	24.2

Source: adapted from *Social Trends*, Office for National Statistics; *Monthly Digest of Statistics*, Office for National Statistics.

demand for housing. When growth in income slowed or fell, as in the early 1980s and early 1990s, this was associated with slowdowns or falls in housing prices. In the early 2000s, moderate growth in average household income undoubtedly contributed to the housing boom.

The increase in owner-occupation compared to renting is also probably due to rising income. Households in the UK prefer to own their own homes rather than renting them. Rising incomes makes home ownership more affordable to more people. Equally, though, the growth in buy-to-let from the 1990s onwards has also increased demand for housing and contributed to rising house prices.

Population trends Population trends have also been important in increasing the demand for housing. As Table 4 shows, the population of the UK is growing over time. However, the number of households is growing at a much faster rate. A household is defined as a group of people living together in a dwelling. Households have been getting smaller over time. More people are living longer and pensioners tend to live on their own. Divorce rates have increased whilst there are more one parent families than before. Fewer young people want to live at home with their parents once they have left school. So the number of dwellings needed to accommodate households has been rising and is predicted to carry on rising to 2050.

Other factors Other factors may affect the demand for housing apart from prices, income and population trends. One factor which influenced house buying in the 1970s and 1980s, and from the late 1990s onwards, was speculation. Because house prices rose consistently during the 1950s and 1960s, many saw housing more as an investment rather than as a place to live. In the property booms of the early 1970s and late 1980s, higher house prices were encouraging people to buy houses in the hope that their value would go up even further. The 1990s saw far less speculative activity because house price increases remained relatively subdued, but speculation again took off from the late 1990s as house prices soared.

The end of the housing boom in the late 1980s saw a reverse effect to this. Millions of households in the early 1990s were caught in a **negative equity** trap. They bought houses at the top of the property boom in 1988

and 1989, borrowing almost all the money needed for the purchase. House prices fell in the early 1990s. This meant that many owed more money on their mortgage than their house was worth. Hence they had 'negative equity'. This discouraged people from buying houses because it was feared that house prices might fall even further, leading to equity losses. Moreover, due to very high interest rates and high unemployment, many fell behind with their mortgage payments and eventually saw their houses repossessed by their lenders. This experience discouraged households from overborrowing throughout much of the rest of the 1990s.

In the rented housing market, important legal changes led to changes in demand. In 1980, the government gave tenants of council houses the right to buy their homes at very low prices. Over the next two decades, more than one and half million council houses were sold to their tenants. So this legal change led to a rise in demand for owner-occupied housing.

Another important legal change was the passing of the 1988 Housing Act. This gave landlords the right to set their own rents. Previously, rents had been controlled by law and in practice were very low. In theory, higher rents should have led to a fall in demand for rented accommodation. However, two other factors more than outweighed this effect. First, property rented under the 1988 Housing Act arrangements tended to be much better quality than under rent controls. Second, rising prices for houses forced some people into the rented sector because they couldn't afford to buy.

The relative importance of different factors

In the long term, rising incomes and an increasing number of households are pushing up the demand for

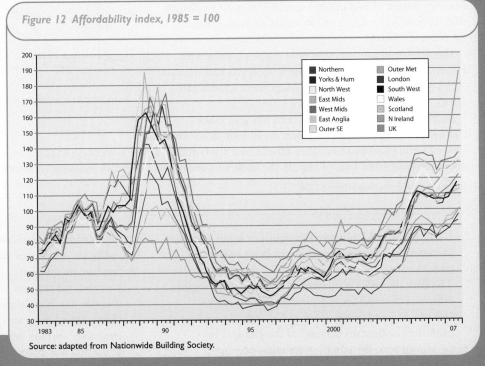

Figure 12 Affordability index, 1985 = 100

Source: adapted from Nationwide Building Society.

both owner-occupied and rented housing in the UK. In the short term, other factors have had a significant impact on the demand for housing, including property speculation, changes in the law, the ending of mortgage tax relief and changes in interest rates.

One measure which attempts to combine a variety of factors is the First time Buyer Nationwide Affordability Index shown in Figure 12. The Nationwide Building Society calculates the index based on first time home buyers. Average mortgage payments depend on the size of the mortgage, and therefore for new house purchases the price of housing, and the rate of interest paid on the mortgage. If house prices fall, interest rates fall, or take home pay rises, then houses become more affordable and the index goes down. If house prices rise, interest

rates rise, or take home pay falls, then houses become less affordable and the index rises.

Figure 12 shows that houses were least affordable at the end of the 1980s due to a combination of relatively high prices and high interest rates. Figure 12 also shows that affordability deteriorated sharply from 2002. Despite low interest rates and rising incomes, the size of mortgages increased rapidly because house prices were rising sharply. What the index cannot indicate, however, is at what level houses would become unaffordable to first time buyers. In the late 1980s, a high affordability index was associated with a housing slump. The same would happen today if the affordability index reached too high a level.

DataQuestion

Independent Schools

The number of school age children might be falling, but the numbers going to private schools are rising. Figures from the Independent Schools Council show an increase of 0.7 per cent in 2006. This is despite rising school fees. Average school fees were up 5.9 per cent this year. The average termly fee for a private day school is £ 2 930, a 6.4 per cent rise, and £6 990 for boarders, an increase of 5.6 per cent.

The increase in student numbers comes after private schools sharply raised spending on advertising and a more professional marketing effort. A survey to be published later this summer will show the average school's marketing budget has risen from £33 966 in 2001 to £59 330 in 2006. Within that, advertising spending has increased on average from £9 500 to £19 600.

The number of affluent, time-poor parents is rising too. Hilary Moriarty, from the Boarding Schools Association, says: 'Time-poor parents value all that independent schools can offer.'

Many private schools have also been trying to make themselves more affordable to poorer families by increasing the amount of financial assistance they offer. About £300 million a year is spent on financial assistance, with almost a third of pupils receiving some kind of help. In the latest year, the number of pupils receiving such help rose by 3.4 per cent to 158 807.

Source: adapted from the *Financial Times*, 4.5.2007.

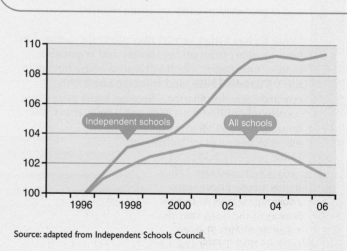

Figure 13 Change in pupil numbers at independent schools, Number of pupils (index, 1996=100)

Source: adapted from Independent Schools Council.

1. Using Figure 13, compare the trends in pupil numbers in independent schools with those in all schools in recent years.
2. The data describes a number of factors which might influence demand for independent school places. Using a demand curve diagram for each example, explain the effect on demand of the changes in (a) school fees; (b) school population numbers; (c) marketing and advertising; (d) numbers of 'affluent, time-poor parents'; (e) financial assistance.
3. Average incomes are rising by around 4.0 per cent per year, but for the top 10 per cent of income earners, this rise has been higher. School fees too have been rising. Using diagrams, discuss whether the amount of consumer surplus derived by parents from independent education has been rising over the past ten years.

6 The supply curve

1. A rise in price leads to a rise in quantity supplied, shown by a movement along the supply curve.
2. A change in supply can be caused by factors such as a change in costs of production, technology and the price of other goods. This results in a shift in the supply curve.
3. The market supply curve in a perfectly competitive market is the sum of each firm's individual supply curves.

Supply

In any market there are buyers and sellers. Buyers **demand** goods whilst sellers **supply** goods. SUPPLY in economics is defined as the quantity of goods that sellers are prepared to sell at any given price over a period of time. For instance, in 2006 UK farmers sold 5.1 million tonnes of potatoes at an average price of £129 per tonne, so economists would say that the supply of potatoes at £129 per tonne over the 12 month period was 5.1 million tonnes.

Supply and price

If the price of a good increases, how will producers react? Assuming that no other factors have changed, they are likely to expand production to take advantage of the higher prices and the higher profits that they can now make. In general, quantity supplied will rise if the price of the good also rises, all other things being equal.

This can be shown on a diagram using a **supply curve**. A supply curve shows the quantity that will be supplied over a period of time at any given price. Consider Figure 1 which shows the supply curve for wheat. Wheat is priced at £110 per tonne. At this price only the most efficient farmers grow wheat. They supply 110 million tonnes per year. However, if the price of wheat rose to £140 per tonne, farmers already growing wheat might increase their acreage of wheat, whilst other non-wheat growing farmers might start to grow wheat. Farmers would do this because at a price of £140 per tonne it is possible to make a profit on production even if costs are higher than at a production level of 110 million units.

A fall in price will lead to a **fall in quantity supplied**, shown by a **movement along** the supply curve. At a lower price, some firms will cut back on relatively unprofitable production whilst others will stop producing altogether. Some of the latter firms may even go bankrupt, unable to cover their costs of production from the price received.

An upward sloping supply curve assumes that:
- firms are motivated to produce by profit - so this model does not apply, for instance, to much of what is produced by government;
- the cost of producing a unit increases as output increases (a situation known as rising marginal cost) - this is not always

Figure 1 The supply curve

The supply curve is upward sloping, showing that firms increase production of a good as its price increases. This is because a higher price enables firms to make profit on the increased output whereas at the lower price they would have made a loss on it. Here, an increase in the price of wheat from £110 to £140 per tonne increases quantity supplied from 110 million tonnes to 150 million tonnes per year.

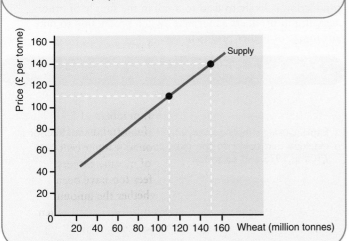

Question 1

Table 1

Price (£)	Quantity supplied (million units per year)
5	5
10	8
15	11
20	14
25	17

(a) Draw a supply curve from the above data.
(b) Draw new supply curves assuming that quantity supplied at any given price:
(i) increased by 10 units; (ii) increased by 50 per cent;
(iii) fell by 5 units; (iv) halved.

true but it is likely that the prices of factors of production to the firm will increase as firms bid for more land, labour and capital to increase their output, thus pushing up costs.

Costs of production

The supply curve is drawn on the assumption that the general costs of production in the economy remain constant (part of the **ceteris paribus** condition). If other things change, then the supply curve will shift. If the costs of production increase at any given level of output, firms will attempt to pass on these increases in the form of higher prices. If they cannot charge higher prices then profits will fall and firms will produce less of the good or might even stop producing it altogether. A rise in the costs of production will therefore lead to a decrease in supply.

This can be seen in Figure 3. The original supply curve is S_1. A rise in the costs of production means that at any given level of output firms will charge higher prices. At an output level of 0A, firms will increase their prices from 0B to 0C. This increase in prices will be true for all points on the supply curve. So the supply curve will **shift** upwards and to the left to S_2 in Figure 3. There will have been a **fall in supply**. (Note that a fall in **quantity supplied** refers to a change in quantity supplied due to a change in price and would be shown by a movement along the supply curve.) Conversely a fall in the costs of production will lead to an increase in supply of a good. This is shown by a shift to the right in the supply curve.

Technology

Another factor which affects supply of a particular good is the state of technology. The supply curve is drawn on the

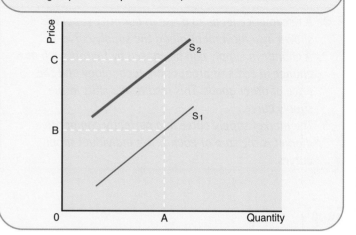

Figure 3 A rise in the costs of production
A rise in the costs of production for a firm will push its supply curve upwards and to the left, from S_1 to S_2. For any given quantity supplied, firms will now want a higher price to compensate them for the increase in their costs.

assumption that the state of technology remains unchanged. If new technology is introduced to the production process it should lead to a fall in the costs of production. This greater **productive efficiency** will encourage firms to produce more at the same price or produce the same amount at a lower price or some combination of the two. The supply curve will shift downwards and to the right. It would be unusual for firms to replace more efficient technology with less efficient technology. However, this can occur at times of war or natural disasters. If new technical equipment is destroyed, firms may have to fall back on less efficient means of production, reducing supply at any given price, resulting in a shift in the supply curve to the left.

The prices of other goods

Changes in the prices of some goods can affect the supply of a particular good. For instance, if the price of beef increases substantially there will be an increase in the quantity of beef supplied. More cows will be reared and slaughtered. As a result there will be an increase in the supply of hides for leather. At the same price, the quantity of leather supplied to the market will increase. An increase in the price of beef therefore leads to an increase in the supply of leather. On the other hand, an increase in cattle rearing is likely to be at the expense of production of wheat or sheep farming. So an increase in beef production is likely to lead to a fall in the supply of other agricultural products as farmers switch production to take advantage of higher profits in beef.

Question 2

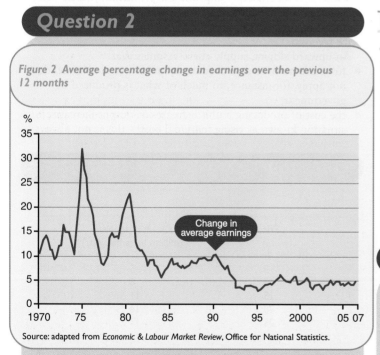

Figure 2 Average percentage change in earnings over the previous 12 months

Change in average earnings

Source: adapted from *Economic & Labour Market Review*, Office for National Statistics.

(a) Explain how a change in earnings can shift the supply curve of a product to the left.
(b) Discuss in which years the supply curves for goods made in the UK are likely to have shifted (i) furthest and (ii) least far to the left according to the data.

Question 3

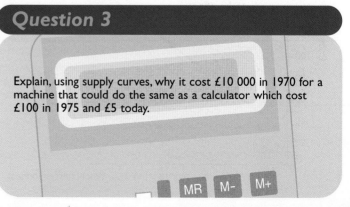

Explain, using supply curves, why it cost £10 000 in 1970 for a machine that could do the same as a calculator which cost £100 in 1975 and £5 today.

MR M- M+

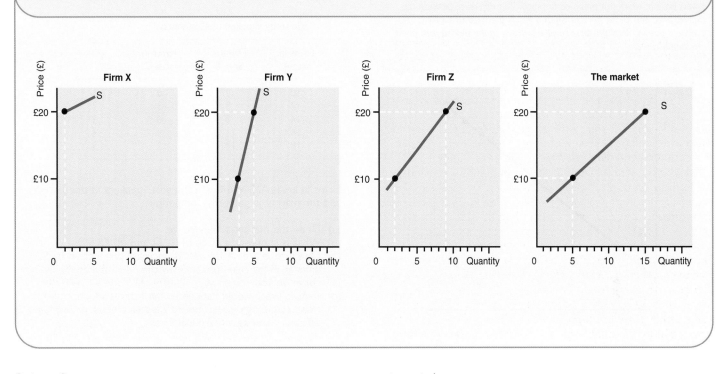

Figure 4 Individual and market supply curves
The market supply curve is calculated by summing the individual supply curves of producers in the market. Here the market supply at £20, for instance, is calculated by adding the supply of each individual firm at a price of £20.

Other factors

A number of other factors affect supply. These include:
- the goals of sellers - if for some reason there is a change in the profit levels which a seller expects to receive as a reward for production, then there will be a change in supply; for instance, if an industry such as the book retailing industry went from one made up of many small sellers more interested in selling books than making a profit to one where the industry was dominated by a few large profit-seeking companies, then supply would fall;
- government legislation - anti-pollution controls which raise the costs of production, the abolition of legal barriers to setting up business in an industry, or tax changes, are some examples of how government can change the level of supply in an industry;
- expectations of future events - if firms expect future prices to be much higher, they may restrict supplies and stockpile goods; if they expect disruptions to their future production because of a strike they may stockpile raw materials, paying for them with borrowed money, thus increasing their costs and reducing supply;
- the weather - in agricultural markets, the weather plays a crucial role in determining supply, bad weather reducing supply, good weather producing bumper yields;
- producer cartels - in some markets, producing firms or producing countries band together, usually to restrict supply; this allows them to raise prices and increase their profits or revenues; the best known cartel today is OPEC which restricts the supply of oil onto world markets.

Question 4

Explain, using diagrams, how you would expect supply of the following goods to be affected by the events stated, all other things being equal.

(a) Wheat. A drought in Romania reduced its wheat harvest by 46 per cent in 2007.
(b) Beef. Embrapa, a Brazilian agricultural research body, developed new strains of grass that allowed Brazilian cattle ranches to feed more cattle per hectare of grazing land.
(c) Houses. The government published a white paper in 2007 which wants to see an easing of planning permission restrictions on land in the South East of England.

Individual and market supply curves

The MARKET SUPPLY CURVE can be derived from the INDIVIDUAL SUPPLY CURVES of sellers in the market (this assumes that supply is not affected by changes in the demand curve as would happen under monopoly or oligopoly). Consider Figure 4. For the sake of simplicity we will assume that there are only three sellers in the market. At a price of £10 per unit, Firm X is unwilling to supply any goods. Firm Y supplies 3 units whilst Firm Z supplies 2 units. So the market supply at a price of £10 is 5 units. At a price of £20, Firm X will supply 1 unit, Firm Y 5 units and Firm Z 9 units. So the market supply at a price of £20 is 15 units. The rest of the market supply curve can be derived by **horizontally summing** the level of output at all other price levels.

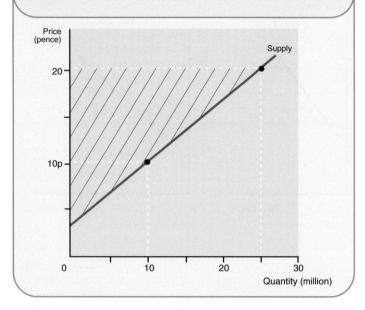

Figure 5 *Producer surplus*
The supply curve shows how much will be supplied at any given price. Except on the last unit supplied, the supplier receives more for the good than the lowest price at which it is prepared to supply. This difference between the market price and lowest price at which a firm is prepared to supply is producer surplus. Total producer surplus is shown by the shaded area above the supply curve.

Question 5

Table 2

Quantity supplied (million units)			Price (£)
Firms in area A	Firms in area B	Firms in area C	
10	2	0	1
12	5	3	2
14	8	6	3
16	11	9	4
18	14	12	5

Firms in areas A, B and C are the sole suppliers in the market and the market is perfectly competitive.

(a) Draw the market supply curve.
(b) What is supply at a price of (i) £1 and (ii) £3.50?
(c) One firm in area A decides to increase production by 5 units at every given price. Draw the new market supply curve on your diagram.
(d) Explain what would happen to the market supply curve if new technology in the industry led to greater productive efficiency amongst individual firms.

Producer surplus

The supply curve shows how much will be supplied at any given price. In Figure 5, firms will supply 10 million units at 10p whereas they will supply 25 million units at 20p. Assume that the price that firms receive is actually 20p. Some firms will then receive more than the lowest price at which they are prepared to supply. For instance, one firm was prepared to supply the 10 millionth unit at 10p. The firm receives 20p, which is 10p more. This 10p is PRODUCER SURPLUS. It is the difference between the market price which the firm receives and the price at which it is prepared to supply. The total amount of producer surplus earned by firms is shown by the area between the supply curve and horizontal line at the market price. It is the sum of the producer surplus earned at each level of output.

Key terms

Individual supply curve - the supply curve of an individual producer.
Market supply curve - the supply curve of all producers within the market. In a perfectly competitive market it can be calculated by summing the supply curves of individual producers.

Producer surplus - the difference between the market price which firms receive and the price at which they are prepared to supply.
Supply - the quantity of goods that suppliers are willing to sell at any given price over a period of time.

The supply of new housing

New housing

There is a number of different markets within the housing market, each of which has its own supply. One way of subdividing the housing market is into the market for new dwellings and the market for second hand dwellings. Approximately 90 per cent of house sales are of existing dwellings. The remaining 10 per cent is of new dwellings.

Figure 6 shows that new dwellings are of two types. Most new dwellings are sold privately, either to owner-occupier buyers or as buy-to-let properties. In 2005/06, 210 000 new properties were sold in this way. The other source of new dwellings is 'Social Landlords'. In practice, this means housing associations. They mainly rent out properties to those for whom owner occupation might be unsuitable. This includes those on below average incomes or the elderly. Social landlords receive most of their funding for new houses from the government. So the supply of new social housing is dependent on the political priorities of governments rather than market forces. Note that local authorities which supply council housing effectively no longer build new houses. Although they own and rent out a large stock of houses, they play no part in the new housing market.

Factors affecting the supply of new private housing

Economic theory would suggest that the supply of new private housing would be affected by a variety of factors including price, costs and government legislation.

Price A rise in the price of new housing should lead to a rise in quantity supplied. Figure 7 shows that the rapid rise in prices since 2000 has lead to a significant rise in private housing. However, the response has been relatively weak. In the 1990s, there was little correlation between the two variables. Over the period 2000-2006,

the 74 per cent price rise led to a 26 per cent rise in supply of new dwellings. This would suggest that other factors are important in determining the supply of new housing.

Costs Costs of new housing have risen over time. Figure 9 shows that the price of land for building has risen substantially over time. Wages of workers in the construction industry have risen too. Other costs, such as costs of building materials have also risen. Rises in costs will have shifted the supply curve for new housing to the left.

Government regulation House building companies often argue that they would build more houses if only government regulations were relaxed. All new houses need planning permission. The vast majority of the land in the UK which is not already built on is not available for building. A whole variety of restrictions such as Green Belt regulations and limited access to National Parks prevent any sort of development outside urban areas. Even within built up areas, there is a very limited amount of land available for new house building. Getting planning permission for this land takes years. Initial applications are usually refused because planners feel that the development is inappropriate. The planning regime therefore ensures that house builders cannot respond quickly to large changes in house prices. If the planning regime were relaxed, this would push the supply curve for new housing to the right, allowing more houses to be built at the same price.

Technology Some argue that the supply of housing could increase if UK house builders adopted new technology in their construction techniques. In the UK, the typical dwelling is still built using bricks and mortar. On the Continent and in the USA, many houses are built using pre-fabricated techniques where much of the dwelling is built off site and then assembled on site. These techniques, it is argued, would produce lower cost

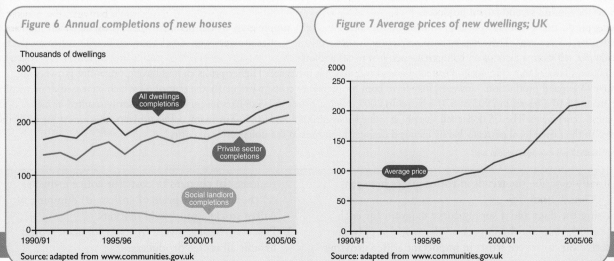

Figure 6 Annual completions of new houses

Thousands of dwellings

All dwellings completions
Private sector completions
Social landlord completions

Source: adapted from www.communities.gov.uk

Figure 7 Average prices of new dwellings; UK

£000

Average price

Source: adapted from www.communities.gov.uk

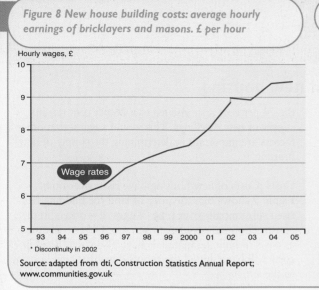

Figure 8 New house building costs: average hourly earnings of bricklayers and masons. £ per hour

Source: adapted from dti, Construction Statistics Annual Report; www.communities.gov.uk

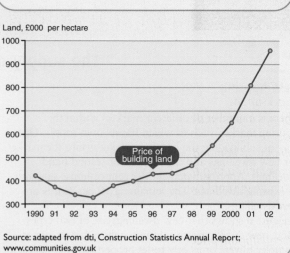

Figure 9 Average price of building land, £000 per hectare

Source: adapted from dti, Construction Statistics Annual Report; www.communities.gov.uk

houses, pushing the supply curve to the right.

The supply of new housing is a major political issue in the UK. The environmental and rural lobbies argue that almost all new housing must be built within existing urban areas to prevent the 'concreting over' of Britain. Planning regulations effectively ensure that this is what actually occurs. The result is that the lack of supply

forces building land prices up and increases the cost of new homes. The only way to increase supply substantially would be to ease planning restrictions, building in what is now countryside. This is unlikely to occur in the immediate future given the strength of the environmental and rural lobbies.

DataQuestion — Coffee

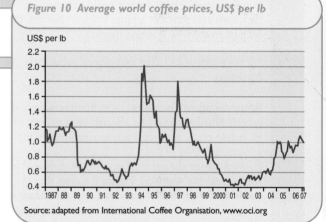

Figure 10 Average world coffee prices, US$ per lb

Source: adapted from International Coffee Organisation, www.oci.org

Commodity prices have soared over the past few years but coffee has not shared in this bonanza for producers. In fact, coffee prices have never recovered from the collapse of the coffee cartel in 1989.

Before 1989, a number of countries agreed to limit sales and production of coffee on world markets. In 1989, this arrangement collapsed. To make the cartel work, individual countries had withheld stocks of unsold coffee. Over the next few years, these stocks were sold off in addition to normal annual production. This caused a glut of coffee in world markets.

Prices rebounded when Brazil, one of the world's largest coffee producers, was hit by frost in 1994. Severe frost can seriously damage coffee bushes and reduce their yield. Frost hit Brazil again in 1995. There followed a period of four or five years of good prices. This provided the incentive for many coffee producers to increase their production of coffee. For example, Vietnam went from being an insignificant grower of coffee to the world's second largest producer.

Rising production eventually outstripped demand for coffee. In 2000, supply grew by 3.5 per cent when world demand for coffee only increased by 1.5 per cent. There was a sharp correction in coffee prices. Coffee growers were quick to react. Brazil's coffee production, for example, fell from a peak of 55 billion bags per year to 30 million.

By 2005 prices began to rise again. Production, however, has not increased. Higher prices should have given coffee growers an incentive to expand production. However, they have been hit by higher costs, particularly the cost of oil which increased dramatically from around $10 a barrel in 2002 to $70 a barrel in 2007. Higher prices in US dollars has also not necessarily resulted in higher prices in domestic currencies. The US dollar fell sharply in value between 2005 and 2007. For many coffee growers, this meant the price they received in their own local currency barely changed despite sharp rises in the dollar price of coffee.

Source: adapted from www.ico.org/news.asp.

1. Briefly describe the trends in coffee prices between 1987 and 2006.
2. Using the data and a supply curve diagram for each example, explain the impact on the world supply of coffee of: (a) severe frosts in important coffee growing regions; (b) changes in costs for coffee growers; (c) changes in the price of coffee; (d) dumping of coffee stocks onto world markets.
3. Discuss whether severe frosts in Vietnam would benefit all coffee producers.

Summary

1. The equilibrium or market clearing price is set where demand equals supply.
2. Changes in demand and supply will lead to new equilibrium prices being set.
3. A change in demand will lead to a shift in the demand curve, a movement along the supply curve and a new equilibrium price.
4. A change in supply will lead to a shift in the supply curve, a movement along the demand curve and a new equilibrium price.
5. Markets do not necessarily tend towards the equilibrium price.
6. The equilibrium price is not necessarily the price which will lead to the greatest economic efficiency or the greatest equity.

Equilibrium price

Buyers and sellers come together in a market. A price (sometimes called the **market price**) is struck and goods or services are exchanged. Consider Table 1. It shows the demand and supply schedule for a good at prices between £2 and £10.

Table 1

Price (£)	Quantity demanded (million units per month)	Quantity supplied (million units per month)
2	12	2
4	9	4
6	6	6
8	3	8
10	0	10

Figure 1 Equilibrium
At £6, the quantity demanded is equal to the quantity supplied. The market is said to be in equilibrium at this price.

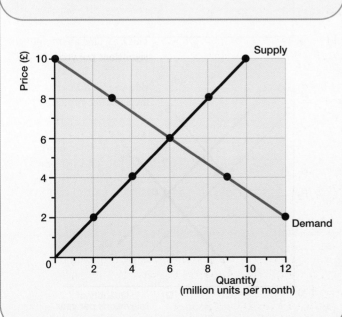

- If the price is £2, demand will be 12 million units but only 2 million units will be supplied. Demand is greater than supply and there is therefore EXCESS DEMAND (i.e. too much demand in relation to supply) in the market. There will be a **shortage** of products on the market. Some buyers will be lucky and they will snap up the 2 million units being sold. But there will be a 10 million unit shortfall in supply for the rest of the unlucky buyers in the market. For instance, it is not possible to buy some luxury cars without being on a waiting list for several years because current demand is too great.
- If the price is £10, buyers will not buy any goods. Sellers on the other hand will wish to supply 10 million units. Supply is greater than demand and therefore there will be EXCESS SUPPLY. There will be a glut or surplus of products on the market. 10 million units will remain unsold. A sale in a shop is often evidence of excess supply in the past. Firms tried to sell the goods at a higher price and failed.
- There is only one price where demand equals supply. This is at a price of £6 where demand and supply are both 6 million units. This price is known as the EQUILIBRIUM PRICE. This is the only price where the planned demand of buyers equals the planned supply of sellers in the market. It is also known as the MARKET-CLEARING price because all the products supplied to the market are bought or cleared from the market, but no buyer is left frustrated in his or her wishes to buy goods.

An alternative way of expressing the data in Table 1 is shown in Figure 1. The equilibrium price is where demand equals supply. This happens where the two curves cross, at a price of £6 and a quantity of 6 million units. If the price is above £6, supply will be greater than demand and therefore excess supply will exist. If the price is below £6, demand is greater than supply and therefore there will be excess demand.

Changes in demand and supply

It was explained in the previous two units that a change in price would lead to a change in quantity demanded or supplied, shown by a movement along the demand or supply curve. A change in any other variable, such as income or the costs of production, would lead to:

Question 1

Table 2

Price (£)	Quantity demanded (million units)	Quantity supplied (million units)
30	20	70
20	50	50
10	80	30

(a) Plot the demand and supply curves shown in Table 2 on a diagram.
(b) What is the equilibrium price?
(c) In what price range is there (i) excess demand and (ii) excess supply?
(d) Will there be a glut or a shortage in the market if the price is: (i) £10; (ii) £40; (iii) £22; (iv) £18; (v) £20?

● an **increase** or **decrease** in demand or supply and therefore
● a **shift** in the demand or supply curve.

Demand and supply diagrams provide a powerful and simple tool for analysing the effects of changes in demand and supply on equilibrium price and quantity.

Consider the effect of a rise in consumer incomes. This will lead to an increase in the demand for a normal good. In Figure 2(a) this will push the demand curve from D_1 to D_2. As can be seen from the diagram, the equilibrium price rises from P_1 to P_2. The quantity bought and sold in equilibrium rises from Q_1 to Q_2. The model of demand and supply predicts that an increase in incomes, all other things being equal (the **ceteris paribus** condition) will lead to an increase both in the price of the product and in the quantity sold. Note that the increase in income **shifts** the demand curve and this then leads to a **movement along** the supply curve.

Figure 2(b) shows the market for televisions in the early 2000s. In the early 2000s, many manufacturers introduced flat screen, slimline televisions. As a result, there was a boom in sales of these televisions and a slump in sales of older, more bulky sets. In economic terms the demand for older, bulky sets

Figure 2 Shifts in the demand and supply curves
Shifts in the demand or supply curves for a product will change the equilibrium price and the equilibrium quantity bought and sold.

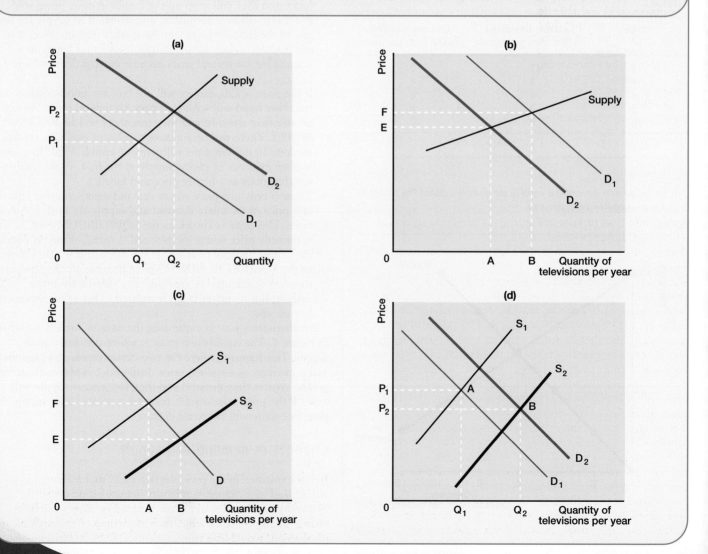

Question 2

During the 1970s the price of metals such as nickel was historically high. This prompted nickel producers to invest in new production facilities which came on stream during the late 1970s and early 1980s. But the world economy went into deep recession during the early 1980s, prompting a collapse in the world price of nickel. Producers reacted by closing facilities. Between 1980 and 1986, the industry lost about 32 500 tonnes of annual capacity compared with an annual demand of between 400 000 and 500 000 tonnes.

The world economy started to recover from 1982 but it wasn't until 1987 that a sharp increase in demand from Japanese stainless steel producers, one of the major buyers in the industry, made prices rise. In the last quarter of 1987, nickel could be bought for $1.87 per lb. By March 1988, it had soared to over $9 per lb. This price proved unsustainable. Both the US and UK economies began to go into recession in 1989 and nickel prices fell to below $3 per lb by the end of 1989.

The invasion of Kuwait by Iraq in 1990 and the subsequent large military involvement of the USA and other countries in defeating Iraq led to a rise in most metal prices. The markets feared a long drawn out war with a possible increase in demand from armaments manufacturers and a possible fall in supply if any nickel producing countries decided to side with Iraq and suspend nickel sales onto the world market. However, the swift defeat of Iraq led to a sharp fall back in price. Recession in Europe and Japan produced further falls in price between 1991 and 1993 despite the beginning of recovery in the US economy, with the price falling below $2 per lb in the last quarter of 1993. The price would have been even lower but for cutbacks in output by major nickel producers over the period.

1994 saw a sharp rise in demand as all the major industrialised countries showed economic growth. By the start of 1995, nickel prices had risen to over $3 per lb. The next major price movement occurred in 1997. An increase in productive capacity led to oversupply and falling prices. However, at the end of the year, this was compounded by the start of the Asian crisis. Several countries in East Asia, including South Korea and Thailand, experienced a financial

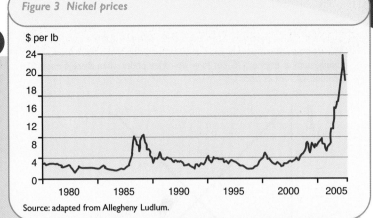

Figure 3 *Nickel prices*

Source: adapted from Allegheny Ludlum.

crisis which led to a sharp fall in domestic production. Demand for nickel from the Far East fell sharply, going below $2 per lb at the end of 1998 before recovering in price as East Asian economies bounced back in 1999 and 2000, reaching a high of nearly $5 per lb.

Fears of a recession in the world economy in 2000 and 2001 then led to a fall in the price of nickel back down to nearly $2 per lb at the end of 2002. However, growing demand from the Far East, particularly China, led to a surge in commodity prices from 2003, returning prices to levels not seen since the late 1980s.

Using demand and supply diagrams, explain why the price of nickel changed when:
(a) new production facilities came on stream in the late 1970s;
(b) there was a world recession in the early 1980s;
(c) the industry closed capacity during the early 1980s;
(d) Japanese stainless steel producers increased purchases in 1987;
(e) Iraq invaded Kuwait in 1990;
(f) all the major industrialised countries showed economic growth in 1994;
(g) the 1998 Asian crisis occurred;
(h) China, a country with the world's largest population, experienced fast economic growth between 2003 and 2007.

---

fell. This is shown by a shift to the left in the demand curve. The equilibrium level of sales in Figure 2(b) falls from 0B to 0A whilst equilibrium price falls from 0F to 0E. Note again that a shift in the demand curve leads to a movement along the supply curve.

Prices of many models of television set tended to fall in the 1970s and 1980s. The main reason for this was an increase in productive efficiency due to the introduction of new technology, enabling costs of production to fall. A fall in costs of production is shown by the shift to the right in the supply curve in Figure 2(c). At any given quantity of output, firms will be prepared to supply more television sets to the market. The result is an increase in quantity bought and sold from 0A to 0B and a fall in price from 0F to 0E. Note that there is a shift in the supply curve which leads to a movement along the demand curve.

So far we have assumed that only one variable changes and that all other variables remain constant. However, in the real world, it is likely that several factors affecting demand and supply will change at the same time. Demand and supply diagrams can be used to some extent to analyse several changes. For instance, in the 2000s the demand for flat screen and high definition television sets increased due to rising real incomes. At the same time, supply increased too because of an increase in

productive efficiency. Overall, the price of television sets fell slightly. This is shown in Figure 2(d). Both the demand and supply curves shift to the right. This will lead to an increase in quantity bought and sold. In theory, depending upon the extent of the shifts in the two curves, there could be an increase in price, a fall in price or no change in the price. Figure 2(d) shows the middle of these three possibilities.

Do markets clear?

It is very easy to assume that the equilibrium price is either the current market price or the price towards which the market moves. Neither is correct. The market price could be at any level. There could be excess demand or excess supply at any point in time.

Nor will market prices necessarily tend to change to equilibrium prices over time. One of the most important controversies in economics today is the extent to which markets tend towards market-clearing prices.

The argument put forward by neo-classical free market economists is that markets do tend to clear. Let us take the example of the coffee market. In this market, there are many producers (farmers, manufacturers, wholesalers and

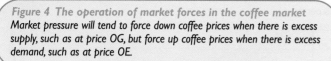

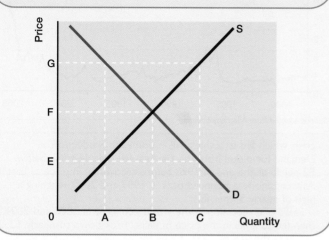

Figure 4 *The operation of market forces in the coffee market*
Market pressure will tend to force down coffee prices when there is excess supply, such as at price OG, but force up coffee prices when there is excess demand, such as at price OE.

retailers) that are motivated by the desire to make as large a profit as possible. When there is excess demand for coffee (demand is greater than supply), coffee producers will be able to increase their prices and therefore their profits and still sell all they produce. If there is excess supply (supply is greater than demand), some coffee will remain unsold. Producers then have a choice. Either they can offer coffee for sale at the existing price and risk not selling it or they can lower their price to the level where they will sell everything offered. If all producers choose not to lower their prices, there is likely to be even greater pressure to reduce prices in the future because there will be unsold stocks of coffee overhanging the market. Therefore when there is excess demand, prices will be driven upwards whilst prices will fall if there is excess supply.

This can be shown diagrammatically. In Figure 4, there is excess demand at a price of 0E. Buyers want to purchase AC more of coffee than is being supplied. Shops, manufacturers and coffee growers will be able to increase their prices and their production and still sell everything they produce. If they wish to sell all their output, they can increase their prices to a maximum

of 0F and their output to a maximum 0B, the market-clearing prices and production levels. This they will do because at higher prices and production levels they will be able to make more profit. If there is excess supply, coffee producers will be left with unsold stocks. At a price of 0G, output left unsold will be AC. Producers in a free market cannot afford to build up stocks forever. Some producers will lower prices and the rest will be forced to follow. Production and prices will go on falling until equilibrium output and price is reached. This is usually referred to as a **stable equilibrium** position.

These pressures which force the market towards an equilibrium point are often called FREE MARKET FORCES. However, critics of the market mechanism argue that free market forces can lead away from the equilibrium point in many cases. In other markets, it is argued that market forces are too weak to restore equilibrium. Many Keynesian economists cite the labour market as an example of this. In other markets, there are many forces such as government legislation, trade unions and multi-national monopolies which more than negate the power of the market.

Consumer and producer surplus

Consumer and producer surplus can be shown on a demand and supply diagram. In Figure 5, the equilibrium price is 0J. Consumer surplus, the difference between how much buyers are prepared to pay for a good and what they actually pay, is the area JHG. Producer surplus, the difference between the market price which firms receive and the price at which they are prepared to supply, is shown by the area JGF.

The amounts of consumer and producer surplus will change if either demand or supply change. For example, in Figure 6, demand increases, shown by a shift to the right in the demand curve. For suppliers, an increase in demand results in higher equilibrium output and higher prices. Suppliers will experience an increase in producer surplus. For consumers, the increase in demand shows that they are prepared to pay a higher price for the same quantity bought. They place a greater value on the good. So their consumer surplus also increases. This can be seen by the increase in the shaded areas in Figure 6.

Points to note

Equilibrium is a very powerful concept in economics but it is essential to remember that the equilibrium price is unlikely to be the most desirable price or 'right' price in the market. The most desirable price in the market will depend upon how one defines 'desirable'. It may be, for instance, the one which leads to the greatest economic efficiency, or it may be the one which leads to greatest equity. Alternatively it may be the one which best supports the defence of the country.

Demand can also equal supply without there being equilibrium. At any point in time, what is actually bought must equal what is actually sold. There can be no sellers without buyers. So actual demand (more often referred to as **realised** or **ex post** demand in economics) must always equal actual (or realised or ex post) supply. Equilibrium occurs at a price where there is no tendency to change. Price will not change if, at the current price, the quantity that consumers wish to buy (called **planned** or **desired** or **ex ante** demand) is equal to the quantity that suppliers wish to sell (called planned or desired or ex ante supply).

Therefore only in equilibrium will planned demand equal planned supply.

Figure 5 *Consumer and producer surplus*

Consumer surplus is the shaded area JGH, showing how much more consumers are prepared to pay for buying a total of 0A goods. Producer surplus is FGJ, showing how less they would have been prepared to accept in revenue for supplying 0B than they actually received.

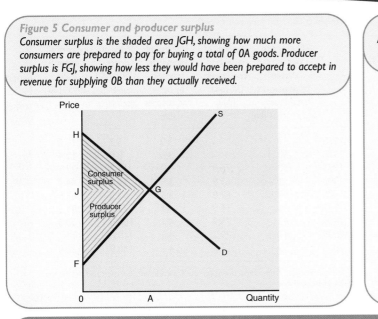

Figure 6 *Changing consumer and producer surplus*

A rise in demand from D_1 to D_2 increases consumer surplus from JGH to MKL and producer surplus from FGJ to FKM.

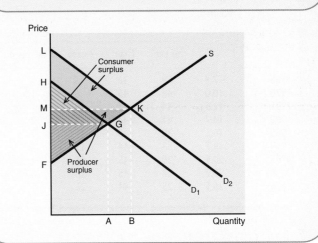

Key terms

Equilibrium price - the price at which there is no tendency to change because planned (or desired or ex ante) purchases (i.e. demand) are equal to planned sales (i.e. supply).

Excess demand - where demand is greater than supply.

Excess supply - where supply is greater than demand.

Free market forces - forces in free markets which act to reduce prices when there is excess supply and raise prices when there is excess demand.

Market clearing price - the price at which there is neither excess demand nor excess supply but where everything offered for sale is purchased.

Applied economics

Demand and supply in the passenger transport market

The quantity demanded and supplied of passenger transport in the UK over the past 50 years has almost quadrupled, as Figure 7 shows. Almost all of this growth is accounted for by a rise in the demand for car

Figure 7 *Passenger transport use*

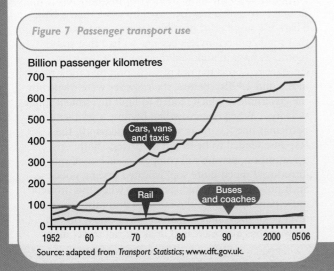

Source: adapted from *Transport Statistics*; www.dft.gov.uk.

Table 3 *Disposable income and household expenditure on passenger transport*

	Personal households' disposable income per head, £, at 2001 prices	Household expenditure on transport, £, average per week at 2001 prices	Household expenditure on transport as a percentage of total household expenditure %	Motoring expenditure as a percentage of all household expenditure on transport %
1965	4 640	30.90	9.7	74.5
1970	5 084	36.29	10.2	77.2
1975	5 873	37.78	13.8	80.2
1980	6 611	40.55	14.6	81.2
1985	7 147	44.25	15.2	84.4
1990	9 015	54.99	16.2	84.5
1995	9 978	50.16	15.1	85.7
2000	11 120	62.79	19.9	85.2
2004	12 094	65.52	16.9	85.2

1. Figures for expenditure for 1995 are 1994/5, for 2000 are 1999/2000 and for 2006 are 2005/6.
Source: adapted from *Economic Trends Annual Supplement*, Office for National Statistics; Department for the Environment, Transport and the Regions, *Transport Statistics*.

Table 4 Car ownership

	Number of private cars licensed, millions	Households with regular use of car(s) %			
		no car	I car	2 cars	3 or more
1965	7.7	59	36	5	-
1970	10.0	48	45	6	I
1975	12.5	44	45	10	I
1980	14.7	41	44	13	2
1985	16.5	38	45	15	3
1990	19.7	33	44	19	4
1995	20.5	30	45	21	4
2000	23.2	27	45	23	5
2005	26.5	25	44	26	5

Source: Department for the Environment, Transport and the Regions, *Transport Statistics.*

Table 5 National rail statistics

	National rail, passenger journeys (million)	National rail passenger kilometres (billion)
1946	I 266	47.0
1960	I 037	34.7
1985/86	686	30.4
1990/91	809	33.2
1995/96	761	30.0
2000/01	957	38.2
2006/07	I 164	46.5

Source: Department for the Environment, Transport and the Regions, *Transport Statistics.*

Table 6 Bus and coach travel

	Number of kilometres travelled by passengers on buses and coaches (bn)	Number of buses and coaches on UK roads (000)	Number of kilometres travelled by buses and coaches (bn)	Index of prices (1995=100) bus and coach fares	Index of all prices (RPI) 1995=100
1965	67	-	3.9	5.7	10.0
1970	60	-	3.6	8.0	12.4
1975	60	76.9	3.2	15.3	22.9
1980	52	69.9	3.5	36.5	44.9
1985	49	67.9	3.3	52.8	63.5
1990	46	71.9	4.1	73.8	84.6
1995	43	75.7	4.1	100.0	100.0
2000	47	79.2	4.2	119.6	114.2
2006	50	51.6	4.1	140.9	132.8

Source: adapted from Department for the Environment, *Transport and the Regions, Transport Statistics.*

Table 7 Passenger transport: consumer price indices (1995=100)

	Motor vehicles Total	of which net purchase	Rail	Bus and coach	All transport	All consumer expenditure (RPI)
1965	9.4	11.6	6.7	5.7	9.1	10.0
1970	12.0	13.6	8.5	8.0	11.7	12.4
1975	22.6	23.8	17.4	15.3	22.0	22.9
1980	47.1	55.4	39.6	36.5	45.8	44.9
1985	65.1	70.8	50.7	52.8	62.7	63.5
1990	79.4	87.8	72.3	73.8	84.6	84.6
1995	100.0	100.0	100.0	100.0	100.0	100.0
2000	119.0	94.7	116.5	119.6	114.2	114.2
2006	122.6	79.5	141.4	140.9	142.2	132.8

Source: adapted from *Economic Trends Annual Supplement*, Office for National Statistics; Department for the Environment, Transport and the Regions, *Transport Statistics.*

travel. Rail travel (national rail plus the London Underground plus light rail systems) has grown by around 60 per cent since the mid-1990s, having been broadly constant over the previous 40 years. Bus and coach travel declined until the early 1980s when it broadly stabilised. Air travel has grown significantly from 0.2 billion passenger kilometres in 1952 to 9.9 billion passenger kilometres in 2006, but today only accounts for approximately 1 per cent of the total passenger miles travelled in the UK.

Demand and income

The main reason for the growth in demand for passenger transport has been rising incomes. As Table 3 shows, real personal households' disposable income (the average income per household after income tax and inflation has been accounted for) has grown more than 2.5 times between 1965 and 2006. Consumers have tended to spend a relatively high proportion of increases in income on transport. As a result, spending on transport as a proportion of household expenditure has risen from 9.7 per cent in 1965 to 16.9 per cent in 2006. Spending on car transport has risen faster than spending on other types of passenger transport. In 1965, there were 7.7 million cars on the road as Table 4 shows. 41 per cent of households had the use of at least one car whilst spending on cars and their running costs accounted for three quarters of total household spending on transport. By 2006, there were 26.5 million cars on

the roads. 75 per cent of households had use of at least one car and spending on motor transport accounted for 85.2 per cent of total transport spending.

Rising income seems to have had little effect on overall rail travel. Between 1945 and 1985, the number of passenger journeys fell on the national rail network as shown in Table 5. Between the mid-1980s and mid-1990s, the number of journeys made was roughly constant. Since then, the number of journeys and distances travelled has increased by more than a half. There is a number of possible reasons for this. One is that road congestion has become so bad that some motorists have abandoned their cars for the train. Another reason is the rail privatisation that took place in the mid-1990s. Before, the railways were owned by the government which tended to limit investment in the railways. When overcrowding became a problem on a particular line (i.e. there was excess demand), the response tended to be to put up prices. With privatisation, private rail companies such as Virgin have introduced much more sophisticated pricing policies. Such policies include reducing fares when this attracts more passengers onto the railways and raises the total revenue of the train companies. Investment on the railways has also increased, making rail travel more attractive. In the long term, privatisation has led to an increase in the supply of rail services.

As for bus and coach travel, Table 6 shows that the long term trend has been for bus and coach travel to fall. In 1952, 92 billion passenger kilometres were travelled. By 2004, this had fallen by approximately 50 per cent. With rising incomes over the period, it could be argued that passengers have deserted buses and coaches for cars.

Bus and coach travel would then be an inferior good. However, Table 6 shows that there has been a slight upturn in bus and coach travel since the late 1990s. This perhaps reflects improved services offered by bus and coach services, or increased congestion on the roads which have led to some motorists abandoning their cars for public transport. However, the increase, at 9 per cent, over the period 1995 to 2006 is relatively small.

Demand and prices

The average price of transport has risen broadly in line with the average increase in all prices in the economy, as can be seen from Table 7. However, Table 7 shows that the price of travelling by rail, bus and coach rose substantially faster than that of travelling by car in the 1980s and 1990s. The price of bus travel continued to increase above the rate of general inflation in the early 2000s. This broad trend can be explained mainly by a reduction in subsidies to bus and rail travel and the need for bus and rail companies to adopt a more commercial, profit-orientated approach to their operations. Bus and rail also suffered greater price competition from the car. In 2006, it was relatively cheaper to travel by car than by bus or train compared to 1965 or 1995. It is not surprising that demand for car travel has outstripped demand for bus or rail travel over the period.

For the past 15 years, the government's response to growing congestion on Britain's roads has been to talk about increasing the cost of motoring. Between 1993 and 2000, the government increased the tax on petrol above the rate of inflation in an attempt to discourage car use on both congestion and environmental grounds. The government was forced to abandon this policy when an alliance of farmers and truck drivers brought the country almost to a halt for a few days in protest against rising fuel prices. The congestion charge in London is another example of government using the price mechanism to reduce demand.

However, pricing motorists off the roads is a highly unpopular policy. Partly this is because the demand for motor transport is fairly unresponsive to increases in price (i.e. demand is fairly **inelastic**. It needs very substantial increases in price to discourage potential motorists from either owning a car or making fewer journeys. For many journeys, there is no suitable alternative to car transport. For many other journeys, public transport takes longer, is far less convenient and is more expensive. Table 7 shows that the cost of motoring actually went down compared to the increase in all prices in the economy over the period 1995 to 2004 despite increases in tax. Market forces are positively

encouraging consumers to own cars and run them.

Other factors affecting the demand for transport

Demand for transport has grown for a number of other reasons apart from rising income. The population of the UK has increased. In 1951, it was 52.7 million; in 1971 it had increased to 55.9 million and in 2005 it was 60.1 million. Population-led increases in demand are set to continue with an estimated UK figure of 71.1 million by 2031.

Planning policies have led to a greater separation of housing and places of work. In Victorian England, workers tended to live within walking distance of their work. Planning regulations over the past 50 years, though, have created distinct zones within urban areas and, as a result, most people are no longer within walking distance of their place of work.

Improvements in infrastructure and advances in technology have created their own demands. Building a new motorway or bypass reduces journey times and encourages people to live further away from their place of work. Faster roads or rail links also encourage greater leisure travel. Equally, improvements in car design have made motoring more reliable and comfortable. One reason why railways failed to attract more passengers in the second half of the twentieth century was that there was not a similar increase in quality of service. For instance, the shortest journey time from London to Birmingham was longer in 1999 than it was in 1979 and rolling stock had barely improved. Privatisation of the UK's railways in the mid-1990s, however, has led to increased investment in new rolling stock and shorter journey times. Since 2000, this has led to some increase in passenger numbers.

The supply of transport

There is no 'supply curve' for transport in general or for parts of the transport industry. For instance, there is no supply curve for motor vehicle transport because no single firm or industry provides this service. There are, though, supply curves for some of the components of the service such as petrol or servicing of cars. Nor is there a supply curve for rail travel. Until 1995, the rail industry was operated by a single company, British Rail, which was a monopoly (i.e. only) supplier and there is no supply curve under monopoly. Since 1995, the industry has been privatised but the key companies in the industry, such as Railtrack or Virgin, are still monopolies in their areas of service.

However, it could been argued that there has been a supply curve for bus and coach travel since 1980 (for coaches) and 1985 (for buses) when the industry was **deregulated**. Before deregulation, the government issued licences, and in general only one licence was offered on a route, establishing monopolies. After deregulation, any firm could set up and offer regular bus services in the UK. Table 6 shows that there was an increase in the number of buses on the roads during the 1980s and 1990s, travelling more kilometres. This was despite a fall in the number of kilometres travelled by passengers. The demand curve for bus transport has therefore probably been shifting to the left as more people switch to cars. The supply curve, however, has shifted to the right with new companies coming into the market and existing companies expanding their services. Opposing this rightward shift has been a fall in government subsidies to bus companies, which, all other things being equal, would have shifted the supply curve to the left.

Price determination

The supply and demand model cannot be used in industries where there is no supply curve in the market. In the rail industry, for instance, prices are fixed by the rail companies influenced by the actions of the rail regulator. In the bus industry, where arguably there is a supply curve, fares have risen by more than the general rate of inflation since the 1980s. As Table 7 shows, fares between 1980 and 2006 rose nearly four fold whilst prices in general only increased nearly three fold. Falls in demand for bus travel due to increased demand for car travel, and an increase in supply as evidenced by the increased number of bus companies and buses, should have led to a relative fall in bus fares. Instead they rose, almost certainly due to the cuts in government subsidies during the period.

DataQuestion

Copper

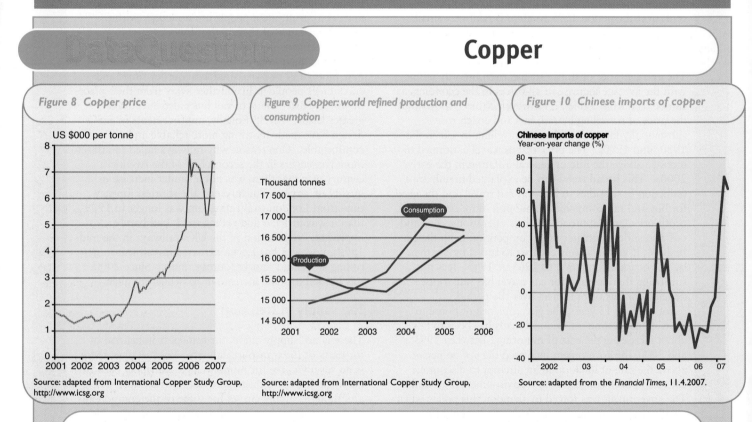

Figure 8 Copper price

US $000 per tonne

Source: adapted from International Copper Study Group, http://www.icsg.org

Figure 9 Copper: world refined production and consumption

Thousand tonnes

Consumption

Production

Source: adapted from International Copper Study Group, http://www.icsg.org

Figure 10 Chinese imports of copper

Chinese imports of copper
Year-on-year change (%)

Source: adapted from the *Financial Times*, 11.4.2007.

Mine executives and industry analysts, meeting for a copper conference in Santiago recently, expressed confidence that copper prices would remain high. In particular, China's demand is likely to continue to rise due to intensive demand for copper in construction. With stocks of copper low, any significant increase in world demand will put upward pressure on prices.

High prices are making marginally profitable mining projects more feasible. New mines, or extensions to existing mines are more likely to get the go-ahead if prices remain at their current levels. However, recent expansion of world production has led to severe cost inflation in the industry. A shortage of speciality engineering services and a scarcity of mining professionals and technicians have helped push up investment costs by 40 per cent. Labour costs in the industry over the past couple of years have risen by 20 or 30 per cent it is estimated.

Source: adapted from the *Financial Times*, 11.4.2007.

1. Using Figure 9, state how much refined copper was (a) demanded and (b) supplied by world users in 2001.
2. Using Figure 8 and Figure 9, suggest why the price of copper rose between 2002 and 2006.
3. Using Figure 10 and the data in the passage, explain how demand and supply trends in 2007 and 2008 for copper are likely to affect its price. Use demand and supply diagrams to illustrate your answer.

8 Interrelationships between markets

Summary

1. Some goods are complements, in joint demand.
2. Other goods are substitutes for each other, in competitive demand.
3. Derived demand occurs when one good is demanded because it is needed for the production of other goods or services.
4. Composite demand and joint supply are two other ways in which markets are linked.

Partial and general models

A model of price determination was outlined in the previous unit. It was explained that the price of a good was determined by the forces of demand and supply. This is an example of a **partial model**. A partial model is an explanation of reality which has relatively few variables. However, a more **general model** or wider model of the market system can be constructed which shows how events in one market can lead to changes in other markets. In this unit we will consider how some markets are interrelated.

Complements

Some goods, known as COMPLEMENTS, are in JOINT DEMAND. This means that, in demanding one good, a consumer will also be likely to demand another good. Examples of complements are:

● tennis rackets and tennis balls;
● washing machines and soap powder;
● strawberries and cream;
● DVD disks and DVD recorders.

  Economic theory suggests that a rise in the quantity demanded of one complement will lead to an increase in the demand for another, resulting in an increase in the price and quantity bought of the other complement. For instance, an increase in the quantity demanded of strawberries will lead to an increase in

demand for cream, pushing up the price of cream.

This can be shown on a demand and supply diagram. Assume that new technology reduces the cost of production of washing machines. This leads to an increase in supply of washing machines shown by a shift to the right of the supply curve in Figure 1 (a). As a result there is a fall in price and a rise in the quantity demanded of washing machines, shown by a movement along the demand curve. This in turn will increase the demand for automatic soap powder, shown by a shift to the right in the demand curve in Figure 1 (b). This leads to a rise in the quantity purchased of automatic soap powder and also an increase in its price.

Substitutes

A SUBSTITUTE is a good which can be replaced by another good. If two goods are substitutes for each other, they are said to be in COMPETITIVE DEMAND. Examples of substitutes are:

● beef and pork;
● Coca-cola and Pepsi-cola;
● fountain pens and biros;
● gas and oil (in the long term but not particularly in the short term).

Economic theory predicts that a rise in the price of one good will lead to an increase in demand and a rise in price of a substitute good.

  Figure 2 shows a rise in the price of beef, due to a fall in its supply. This leads to a fall in the quantity demanded of beef as

Figure I Complements

An increase in supply and the consequent fall in price of washing machines will lead to a rise in the quantity of washing machines and a rise in demand (shown by a shift in the demand curve) for a complementary good such as automatic washing powder.

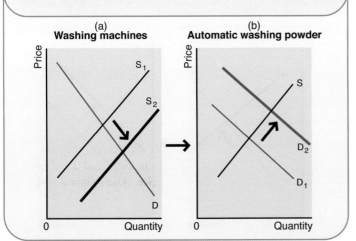

Figure 2 Substitutes

A fall in the supply of beef leading to a rise in its price will lead to a fall in the quantity demanded of beef and an increase in the demand for a substitute product such as pork.

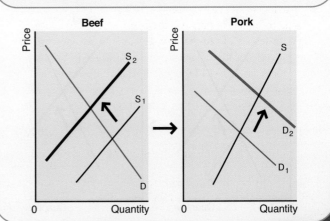

the price of beef rises. In turn, there will be an increase in the demand for pork as consumers substitute pork for beef. The demand for pork will increase, shown by a shift to the right in the demand curve for pork. This leads to a rise in the price of pork and a rise in quantity purchased.

Many substitute goods are not clearly linked. For instance, a rise in the price of foreign holidays will lead some consumers to abandon taking a foreign holiday. They may substitute a UK holiday for it, but they may also decide to buy new curtains or a new carpet for their house, or buy a larger car than they had originally planned.

Question 1

(a) It could be argued that the following pairs of products are both complements **and** substitutes. Explain why.
   (i)   Electricity and gas.
   (ii) Tea and milk.
   (iii) Bus journeys and train journeys.
   (iv) Chocolate bars and crisps.
(b) (i) For each pair of products, explain whether you think they are more likely to be complements or substitutes.
   (ii) Show on a demand and supply diagram the effect on the price of the first product of a rise in price of the second product.

Derived demand

Many goods are demanded only because they are needed for the production of other goods. The demand for these goods is said to be a DERIVED DEMAND.

For instance, the demand for steel is derived in part from the demand for cars and ships. The demand for flour is derived in part from the demand for cakes and bread. The demand for sugar is in part derived from demand for some beverages, confectionery and chocolate.

Figure 3 shows an increase in the demand for cars. This leads to an increase in quantity bought and sold. Car manufacturers will increase their demand for steel, shown by a rightward shift of the demand curve for steel. The price of steel will then increase as will the quantity bought and sold. Economic theory therefore predicts that an increase in demand for a good will

lead to an increase in price and quantity purchased of goods which are in derived demand from it.

Question 2

Milk sales have been in decline for 30 years, but one of the latest food fads has helped reverse the trend. About 35 million more litres of liquid milk were sold to consumers last year than the year before. This is not a big increase on 4.45 billion litres sold in the year to April 2004, but it represents welcome news for Britain's dairy farmers.

Liz Broadbent, director of market development at the Milk Development Council (MDC), said: 'The rise is down to an increase in the frequency of buying milk rather than people buying more during each shopping trip. The indications are that the extra milk is being used mainly in porridge, tea and coffee.'

Porridge consumption rose by 25 per cent last winter, according to TNS, which carried out market research for the MDC. Consumption of tea and coffee also improved by 17 per cent and 8 per cent respectively. According to Tesco, which saw its sales of porridge increased markedly over the year, an important factor in increased sales of porridge was the fashionability of the Glycemic or GI diet. This diet encouraged dieters to maintain their blood sugar at a steady level by having a healthy breakfast.

Gwyn Jones, chairman of the National Farmers' Union dairy board, said that the increase in milk consumption 'is certainly a welcome development, even if it's only by a small amount. Eventually it ought to mean more money for farmers but there are lots of ifs and buts.'

Source: adapted from the *Financial Times* 20.5.2005.

(a) 'Milk is in derived demand from porridge.' Explain this statement.
(b) Analyse, with the help of diagrams, the effect of the change in demand for porridge on the demand for milk.
(c) Why might there be 'lots of ifs and buts' about whether the price of milk will go up due to the increase in demand for porridge?

Composite demand

A good is said to be in COMPOSITE DEMAND when it is demanded for two or more distinct uses. For instance, milk may be used for yoghurt, for cheese making, for butter or for

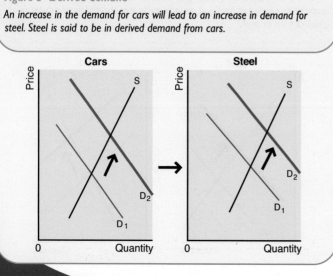

Figure 3 Derived demand

An increase in the demand for cars will lead to an increase in demand for steel. Steel is said to be in derived demand from cars.

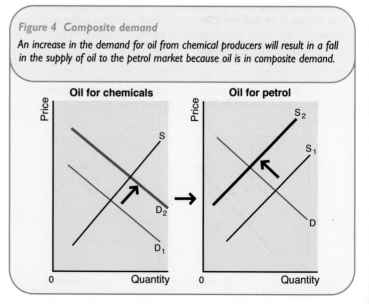

Figure 4 Composite demand

An increase in the demand for oil from chemical producers will result in a fall in the supply of oil to the petrol market because oil is in composite demand.

drinking. Land may be demanded for residential, industrial or commercial use. Steel is demanded for car manufacturing and for shipbuilding.

Economic theory predicts that an increase in demand for one composite good will lead to a fall in supply for another. Figure 4 shows that an increase in the demand by the chemical industry for oil will push the demand curve to the right, increasing both the quantity sold and the price of oil. With an upward sloping supply for oil as a whole, an increase in supply of oil to the chemical industry will reduce the supply of oil for petrol. This is shown by a shift upwards in the supply curve in Figure 4. The price of oil for petrol will rise and the quantity demanded will fall.

Economic theory therefore predicts that an increase in demand for a good will lead to a rise in price and a fall in quantity demanded for a good with which it is in composite demand.

Joint supply

A good is in JOINT SUPPLY with another good when one good is supplied for two different purposes. For instance, cows are supplied for both beef and leather. An oil well may give both oil and gas.

Economic theory suggests that an increase in demand for one good in joint supply will lead to an increase in its price. This leads to an increase in the quantity supplied. The supply of the other good therefore increases, leading to a fall in its price. Figure 5 shows that an increase in demand for beef leads to an increase in both price and quantity bought and sold of beef. More beef production will lead, as a by-product, to greater

Question 3

At the start of 2000, most customers could withdraw cash from a cash machine free of charge. Since then there has been a dramatic expansion of new cash machines which charge customers a fee for withdrawing cash, typically £1.50 for any withdrawal. Fee-charging cash machines only handle an estimated 3 per cent of all transactions with most customers getting their money from cash machines inside or outside banks where there is no charge. However, fee-charging machines tend to be situated away from banks in locations like convenience stores, pubs, petrol stations and shopping centres and are becoming increasingly popular with customers.

Many fee-charging cash machines also have a facility for playing advertisements. So a cash machine can generate revenues and profits for its owners not just by charging customers for cash withdrawals but also by selling advertising space to companies.

Source: adapted from the *Financial Times*, 15.11.2004.

A cash machine can give two products: cash for bank customers and advertising. With the help of diagrams and the concept of joint supply, explain what impact an increase in demand by bank customers for withdrawals from fee-charging cash machines might have on the price of advertising space.

supply of leather. This is shown by a shift to the right in the supply curve for leather. The price of leather will then fall and quantity demanded, bought and sold will increase.

Key terms

Competitive demand - when two or more goods are substitutes for each other.
Complement - a good which is purchased with other goods to satisfy a want.
Composite demand - when a good is demanded for two or more distinct uses.
Derived demand - when the demand for one good is the result of or derived from the demand for another good.

Joint demand - when two or more complements are bought together.
Joint supply - when two or more goods are produced together, so that a change in supply of one good will necessarily change the supply of the other goods with which it is in joint supply.
Substitute - a good which can be replaced by another to satisfy a want.

Figure 5 *Joint supply*
An increase in the demand for beef, which leads to more beef being produced, results in an increase in the supply of leather. Beef and leather are said to be in joint supply.

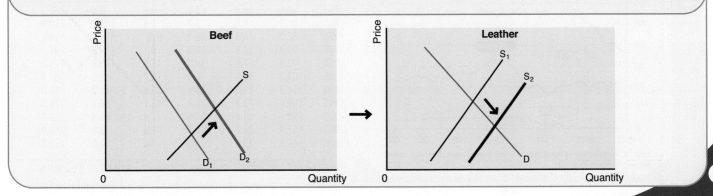

Applied economics

Commercial transport

Derived demand

Commercial transport, the transporting of goods in the UK from factory to shop for instance, is a derived demand. It is ultimately derived from the purchase of consumer goods and services. The movement of coal from a coal pit to an electricity power station is part of the long chain of production in the eventual consumption of, say, a packet of cornflakes.

Demand for commercial transport

Demand for commercial transport has grown over time as consumer incomes have risen and more goods and services have been consumed. Table 1 shows, however, that the growth in tonnage of goods moved has been relatively small since the 1960s. Much of this is due to the fact that goods have got lighter and less bulky. Far more plastic and far less metal are used today, for instance. So whilst more consumer goods are purchased, the total weight and volume have only increased a little. In contrast, Table 2 shows that there has been a significant growth over the same period in the number of tonne kilometres travelled. Each tonne is travelling a longer distance today than 40 years ago. This is the result of greater specialisation between regions and firms. In turn, this has been encouraged by the growth of the motorway network in the UK, which has allowed much faster journey times.

Substitutes

Different modes of transport are substitutes for each other. Both Tables 1 and 2 and Figure 6 indicate that there has been a switch away from rail transport to other modes, particularly road transport. In the early 1950s, railways carried slightly more freight than the

roads. By the 1960s, rail had already lost much of its market share to road haulage. However, since rail privatisation in 1995, there has been a significant increase in rail freight. Pipeline traffic has increased, mainly due to growth of gas consumption and North Sea oil production. The sudden increase in the share of water transport between 1976 and 1985 was entirely due to the growth of the North Sea oil industry.

Complements

The privatisation of British Rail led to an increase in the amount of rail freight carried. The private freight companies have proved more flexible than British Rail and have been able to drive down costs and win orders. However, the future of rail transport lies mainly as a complement to road transport. Lorries and vans will take goods to railway collection depots. The goods will then be transported by rail before being taken away again by lorry. Loading and unloading from one mode of transport to another is relatively expensive.

Table 1 Goods: total transported in millions of tonnes, Great Britain

	Road	Rail	Water: coastwise oil	Water: other	Pipelines	Total
1961	1 295	249	57		6	1 607
1965	1 634	239	64		27	1 964
1970	1 610	209	58		39	1 916
1975	1 602	176	48		52	1 878
1980	1 383	154	54	83	83	1 757
1985	1 452	122	50	92	89	1 805
1990	1 749	152	44	108	121	2 163
1995	1 701	101	47	98	168	2 115
2000	1 693	96	40	97	151	2 077
2005	1 868	108	42	91	168	2 277
2006	1 936	108	na	na	159	2 336

Source: adapted from Department for the Environment, Transport and the Regions, *Transport Statistics.*

Table 2 Goods: distance transported, total tonne kilometres (billions), Great Britain

	Road	Rail	Water: coastwise oil	Water: other	Pipelines	Total
1961	85.6	16.4	3.2	0.6	0.4	106.2
1965	108.0	15.8	3.7	0.6	1.8	129.8
1970	85.0	26.8	23.2	0.01	3.0	138.1
1975	95.3	23.5	18.3	0.1	5.9	143.1
1980	92.4	17.6	38.2	15.9	10.1	174.2
1985	103.2	15.3	38.9	18.7	11.2	187.3
1990	136.3	15.8	32.1	23.6	11.0	218.8
1995	149.6	13.3	31.4	11.1	11.1	226.6
2000	159.4	18.1	26	41.4	11.4	256.3
2005	163.4	21.7	30.3	30.6	10.8	256.8
2006	166.9	22.1	na	na	10.8	259.8

Source: adapted from Department for the Environment, Transport and the Regions, *Transport Statistics.*

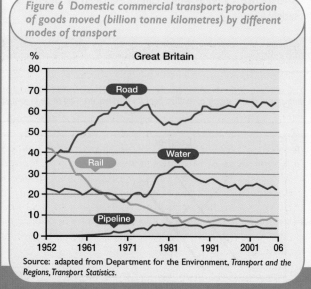

Figure 6 Domestic commercial transport: proportion of goods moved (billion tonne kilometres) by different modes of transport

Source: adapted from Department for the Environment, *Transport and the Regions, Transport Statistics.*

Therefore rail transport has proved to be economic mainly when journeys of over 300-400 miles are made by rail or when a dedicated rail link can take goods door to door, for instance from a pit head to a power station. The number of dedicated rail links could decrease in the immediate future if the electricity industry burns more gas and imported coal and less domestic coal. The Channel Tunnel should have given a significant boost to rail freight. It is ideally suited, for example, for the transport of goods such as new cars being taken from manufacturing plants to dealers in other countries. However, inefficiencies in the rail system in the UK and even more so in Europe have meant that services using the Tunnel have been too unreliable and too slow to attract much extra traffic. Rail freight in general can only grow in future if journey times become faster and services are more reliable.

Composite demand

Roads are in composite demand with commercial transport and passenger transport. At present, there is no systematic pricing mechanism for the road system. Most roads are free from congestion at all times of day. A minority of roads suffer from congestion at certain times of the day. This is a problem of scarce resources. Some potential road users react by either not travelling or travelling by an alternative mode of transport. Commuters in the London area, for instance, may choose to travel by rail, underground or bus because the opportunity cost of travelling by car is too high. Some commuters arrive earlier or later to their place of work to avoid the rush hour. Other road users accept that their road journey times will be longer in the rush hour than at other times of the day.

The more cars on the road, the greater the potential for congestion and longer journey times for freight transport. Road pricing could help the freight industry if car users were discouraged from travelling. Road pricing is when cars and lorries are charged for the use of a road, as for instance with the London congestion charge or the toll on the M6 toll motorway. However, any road pricing system is likely to place charges on lorries as well as cars. Journey times for lorries might be reduced, lowering costs, but road tolls will increase freight costs. The experience of the M6 toll motorway shows the trade off between cost and time. Lorries have avoided using the toll motorway, opened in 2004, because of what they say are too high charges. Instead, most hauliers prefer to use the M6 through Birmingham, which is free, but they risk getting held up by congestion. For these hauliers, the cost of the toll motorway is greater than that of the possible loss of time through congestion of using the free motorway. Overall, British hauliers are estimated to lose up to £20 billion a year through congestion in increased journey times. Reducing journey times through applying tolls on all congested roads would reduce these costs but hauliers would inevitably have to pay tolls too, meaning that their gain would be far less than the £20 billion.

Imposing tolls on road freight transport could act as an incentive for firms to switch some freight from road to rail. Indeed, some environmentalists have argued that revenues from road tolls should be used to subsidise rail freight to create a large shift from road to rail.

DataQuestion

Land usage

The cost of planning restrictions

Planning restrictions have increased the price of housing land. The price of farming land, for instance, is often one-thirtieth or one-fortieth of what it is when housebuilding is allowed. Hence, there are plenty of farmers willing to sell their land for residential use. A 1994 study commissioned by the Department for the Environment, however, pointed out that this is a misleading comparison because the cost of preparing farming land for housing or industrial purposes is high. Instead, it estimated the opportunity cost of housing land by looking at prices of housing land in Barnsley, where at the time there was no shortage of housing land available for sale. The cost of planning restrictions could then be calculated. For instance, in Reigate, prime commuter country in Surrey in the South of England, land prices were 3.6 times their opportunity cost. In Beverley in Yorkshire, the ratio was 2.2.

Nimbyism

A 'Nimby' is someone who says 'not in my backyard'. The word came into fashion in the 1980s to describe people who were all in favour of better facilities, better roads, more housing and more places of work to reduce unemployment so long as none of this happened in their local area.

It has often been justified by high-sounding references to preserving rural England, maintaining local amenities and protecting areas of natural beauty. Every new bypass or road upgrade seems to run through a patch of land which is the habitat of some rare species of plant or animal. However, in practice, the vast majority of Nimbys are motivated solely by the losses that they might incur if development went ahead. For instance, building a new housing estate next door is unlikely to help the property prices of existing houses in the area.

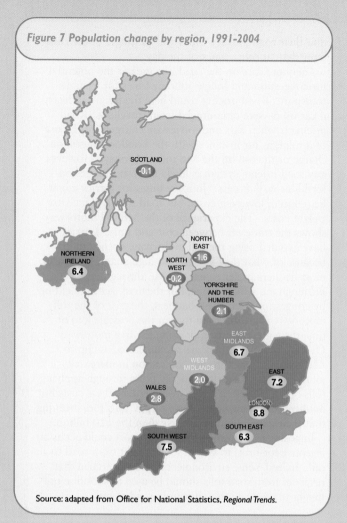

Figure 7 Population change by region, 1991-2004

Source: adapted from Office for National Statistics, *Regional Trends*.

Table 3 *Changing population and number of households, Great Britain*

	1971	1981	1991	2001	2006	2021 projected
Population	55.4	54.9	55.8	57.4	60.5	64.7
Number of households	18.6	20.2	22.4	23.8	24.2	28.0

Source: adapted from *Social Trends*, Office for National Statistics; *Regional Trends*, Office for National Statistics.

Greenbelt policies

Britain's greenbelts were established after the Second World War. They were intended to throw a cordon around urban areas to prevent their spread into the countryside. Within the greenbelt, planning restrictions are very strict about development. No new housing or industrial development is permitted. Greenbelt policies have severely restricted the supply of new land for housing and industry in the UK and contributed to the relatively high price of land in urban areas. This increases the costs of living for urban dwellers, the vast majority of people in the UK. Not only are house prices and rents much higher than they would otherwise be but the cost of services from supermarkets to cinemas is much higher. This is because high land prices paid by industry have to be paid for in the form of higher prices by consumers.

Households

The number of households in the UK is growing at a much faster rate than the slow growth in the overall population. The growth is coming partly from changes in society. The increase in divorce has created many one-person households and rising incomes mean that more young single people now have the choice between living at home with their parents or getting their own accommodation. Growth is also coming from demographic changes. There is an increasing number of elderly people who are living longer and living alone. The number of households with two parents and several children is declining.

New land for housing

New land for building houses comes from a variety of sources. 'Windfall sites' are those which come from homeowners selling part of their garden for development, or housebuilders buying a large old house, knocking it down and replacing it with a small estate of smaller houses. Another source is 'brownfield sites'. These are sites which have already been used for commercial or other urban purposes but now have a higher value as housing land. Third, and most controversially, new land can be found by small scale easing of greenbelt and other restrictions, usually amounting to just a few tens of acres in a specific locality.

1. Explain the following.
   (a) The demand for land is a derived demand.
   (b) Land is in composite demand.
   (c) Land is sometimes in joint supply.
   (d) Land is sometimes in joint demand with buildings.
2. Explain the economic relationships in the UK between land use and:
   (a) a growing population;
   (b) a shifting population geographically;
   (c) increasing affluence.
3. Do you think greenbelt regulations should be loosened to allow more house building in the UK? In your answer, consider the costs and benefits of such a change in policy. This will include an analysis of the effects on the price of houses, industrial property and agricultural land.

Summary

1. *Elasticity is a measure of the extent to which quantity responds to a change in a variable which affects it, such as price or income.*
2. *Price elasticity of demand measures the proportionate response of quantity demanded to a proportionate change in price.*
3. *Price elasticity of demand varies from zero, or infinitely inelastic, to infinitely elastic.*
4. *The value of price elasticity of demand is mainly determined by the availability of substitutes and by time.*

The meaning of demand elasticity

The quantity demanded of a good is affected by changes in the price of the good, changes in price of other goods, changes in income and changes in other relevant factors. Elasticity is a measure of just how much the quantity demanded will be affected by a change in price or income etc.

Assume that the price of gas increases by 1 per cent. If quantity demanded consequently falls by 20 per cent, then there is a very large drop in quantity demanded in comparison to the change in price. The price elasticity of gas would be said to be very high. If quantity demanded falls by 0.01 per cent, then the change in quantity demanded is relatively insignificant compared to the large change in price and the price elasticity of gas would be said to be low.

Different elasticities of demand measure the proportionate response of quantity demanded to a proportionate change in the variables which affect demand. So price elasticity of demand measures the responsiveness of quantity demanded to changes in the price of the good. Income elasticity measures the responsiveness of quantity demanded to changes in consumer incomes. Cross elasticity measures the responsiveness of quantity demanded to changes in the price of another good. Economists could also measure population elasticity, tastes elasticity or elasticity for any other variable which might affect quantity demanded, although these measures are rarely calculated.

Price elasticity of demand

Economists choose to measure responsiveness in terms of proportionate or percentage changes. So PRICE ELASTICITY OF DEMAND - the responsiveness of changes in quantity demanded to changes in price - is calculated by using the formula:

$$\frac{\text{percentage change in quantity demanded}}{\text{percentage change in price}}$$

Sometimes, price elasticity of demand is called OWN PRICE ELASTICITY OF DEMAND to distinguish it from cross price elasticity of demand.

Table 1 shows a number of calculations of price elasticity. For instance, if an increase in price of 10 per cent leads to a fall in quantity demanded of 20 per cent, then the price elasticity of demand is 2. If an increase in price of 50 per cent leads to a fall

in quantity demanded of 25 per cent then price elasticity of demand is ½.

Elasticity is sometimes difficult to understand at first. It is essential to memorise the formulae for elasticity. Only then can they be used with ease and an appreciation gained of their significance.

Table 1

Percentage change in quantity demanded	Percentage change in price	Elasticity
20	10	2
25	50	0.5
28	7	4
3	9	0.333

Question 1

Table 2

	Percentage change in quantity demanded	Percentage change in price
(a)	10	5
(b)	60	20
(c)	4	8
(d)	1	9
(e)	5	7
(f)	8	11

Calculate the price elasticity of demand from the data in Table 2.

Alternative formulae

Data to calculate price elasticities are often not presented in the form of percentage changes. These have to be worked out. Calculating the percentage change is relatively easy. For instance, if a consumer has 10 apples and buys another 5, the percentage change in the total number of apples is of course 50 per cent. This answer is worked out by dividing the change in the number of apples she has (i.e. 5) by the original number of apples she possessed (i.e. 10) and multiplying by 100 to get a percentage figure. So the formula is:

$$\text{percentage change} = \frac{\text{absolute change}}{\text{original value}} \times 100\%$$

Price elasticity of demand is measured by dividing the percentage change in quantity demanded by the percentage change in price. Therefore an alternative way of expressing this is $\Delta Q/Q \times 100$ (the percentage change in quantity demanded Q) divided by $\Delta P/P \times 100$ (the percentage change in price P). The 100s cancel each other out, leaving a formula of:

$$\frac{\Delta Q}{Q} \div \frac{\Delta P}{P} \quad \text{or} \quad \frac{\Delta Q}{Q} \times \frac{P}{\Delta P}$$

This is mathematically equivalent to:

$$\frac{P}{Q} \times \frac{\Delta Q}{\Delta P}$$

Examples of calculations of elasticity using the above two formulae are given in Figure 1.

Question 2

Table 3

	Original values		New values	
	Quantity demanded	Price (£)	Quantity demanded	Price (£)
(a)	100	5	120	3
(b)	20	8	25	7
(c)	12	3	16	0
(d)	150	12	200	10
(e)	45	6	45	8
(f)	32	24	40	2

Calculate the price elasticity of demand for the data in Table 3.

Elastic and inelastic demand

Different values of price elasticity of demand are given special names.

- Demand is price ELASTIC if the value of elasticity is greater than one. If demand for a good is price elastic then a percentage change in price will bring about an even larger percentage change in quantity demanded. For instance, if a 10 per cent rise in the price of tomatoes leads to a 20 per cent fall in the quantity demanded of tomatoes, then price elasticity is 20 ÷ 10 or 2. Therefore the demand for tomatoes is elastic. Demand is said to be **infinitely elastic** if the value of elasticity is infinity (i.e. a fall in price would lead to an infinite increase in quantity demanded whilst a rise in price would lead to the quantity demanded becoming zero).

Figure 1 *Calculations of elasticity of demand*

Example 1
Quantity demanded originally is 100 at a price of £2. There is a rise in price to £3 resulting in a fall in demand to 75. Therefore the change in quantity demanded is 25 and the change in price is £1.
The price elasticity of demand is:

$$\frac{\Delta Q}{Q} \div \frac{\Delta P}{P} = \frac{25}{100} \div \frac{1}{2} = \tfrac{1}{2}$$

Example 2
Quantity demanded originally is 20 units at a price of £5 000. There is a fall in price to £4 000 resulting in a rise in demand to 32 units.
Therefore the change in quantity demanded is 12 units resulting from the change in price of £1 000.
The price elasticity of demand is:

$$\frac{P}{Q} \times \frac{\Delta Q}{\Delta P} = \frac{5\ 000}{20} \times \frac{12}{1\ 000} = 3$$

- Demand is price INELASTIC if the value of elasticity is less than one. If demand for a good is price inelastic then a percentage change in price will bring about a smaller percentage change in quantity demanded. For instance, if a 10 per cent rise in the price of tube fares on London Underground resulted in a 1 per cent fall in journeys made, then price elasticity is 1 ÷ 10 or 0.1. Therefore the demand for tube travel is inelastic. Demand is said to be **infinitely inelastic** if the value of elasticity is zero (i.e. a change in price would have no effect on quantity demanded).
- Demand is of UNITARY ELASTICITY if the value of elasticity is exactly 1. This means that a percentage change in price will lead to an exact and opposite change in quantity demanded. For instance, a good would have unitary elasticity if a 10 per cent rise in price led to a 10 per cent fall in quantity demanded. (It will be shown in unit 10 that total revenue will remain constant at all quantities demanded if elasticity of demand is unity.)

This terminology is summarised in Table 4.

Question 3

Explain whether you think that the following goods would be elastic or inelastic in demand if their price increased by 10 per cent whilst all other factors remained constant: (a) petrol; (b) fresh tomatoes; (c) holidays offered by a major tour operator; (d) a Ford car; (e) a Mars Bar; (f) *GQ* magazine.

Graphical representations

Figure 2 shows a straight line graph. It is a common mistake to conclude that elasticity of a straight line demand curve is constant all along its length. In fact nearly all straight line demand curves vary in elasticity along the line.

- At the point A, price elasticity of demand is infinity. Here

Table 4 *Elasticity: summary of key terms*

	Verbal description of response to a change in price	Numerical measure of elasticity	Change in total outlay as price rises[1]
Perfectly inelastic	Quantity demanded does not change at all as price changes	Zero	Increases
Inelastic	Quantity demanded changes by a smaller percentage than does price	Between 0 and 1	Increases
Unitary elasticity	Quantity demanded changes by exactly the same percentage as does price	1	Constant
Elastic	Quantity demanded changes by a larger percentage than does price	Between 1 and infinity	Decreases
Perfectly elastic	Buyers are prepared to purchase all they can obtain at some given price but none at all at a higher price	Infinity	Decreases to zero

1. This is explained in unit 10.

quantity demanded is zero. Putting Q = 0 into the formula for elasticity:

$$\frac{\Delta Q}{Q} \div \frac{\Delta P}{P}$$

we see that zero is divided into ΔQ. Mathematically there is an infinite number of zeros in any number.

● At the point C, price elasticity of demand is zero. Here price is zero. Putting P = 0 into the formula for elasticity, we see that P is divided into ΔP giving an answer of infinity. Infinity is then divided into the fraction $\Delta Q \div Q$. Infinity is so large that the answer will approximate to zero.

Figure 2 *Price elasticity along a straight demand curve*
Price elasticity varies along the length of a straight demand curve, moving from infinity, where it cuts the price axis, to half way along the line, to zero where it cuts the quantity axis.

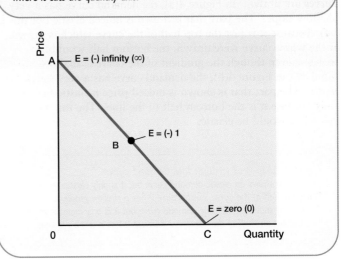

● At the point B exactly half way along the line, price elasticity of demand is 1.

It is worth noting that the elasticity of demand at a point can be measured by dividing the distance from the point to the quantity axis by the distance from the point to the price axis, BC ÷ AB. In Figure 2, B is half way along the line AC and so BC = AB and the elasticity at the point B is 1.

Two straight line demand curves discussed earlier do not have the same elasticity all along their length.

Figure 3(a) shows a demand curve which is perfectly inelastic. Whatever the price, the same quantity will be demanded.

Figure 3(b) shows a perfectly elastic demand curve. Any amount can be demanded at one price or below it whilst nothing will be demanded at a higher price.

Figure 3(c) shows a demand curve with unitary elasticity. Mathematically it is a rectangular hyperbola. This means that any percentage change in price is offset by an equal and opposite

Figure 3 *Perfectly elastic and inelastic demand curves and unitary elasticity*
A vertical demand curve (a) is perfectly inelastic, whilst a horizontal demand curve (b) is perfectly elastic. A curve with unitary elasticity (c) is a rectangular hyperbola with the formula PQ = k where P is price, Q is quantity demanded and k is a constant value.

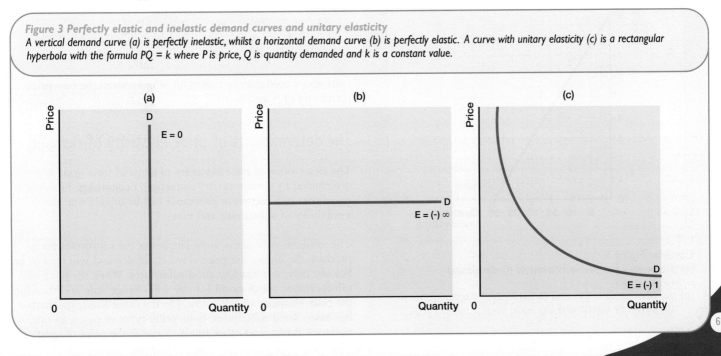

change in quantity demanded.

Another common mistake is to assume that steep demand curves are always inelastic and demand curves which have a shallow slope are always elastic. In Figure 4, two demand curves are drawn. In Figure 4(a), the demand curve has a very shallow slope. The part that is drawn is indeed elastic but this is only because it is just the top half of the curve which is drawn. If the whole curve were drawn, the bottom half would be inelastic even though the gradient of the curve is shallow. Similarly, in Figure 4(b), the demand curve has a very steep slope. The part that is shown is indeed price inelastic but this is only because it is the bottom half of the line. The top half of the steep line would be elastic.

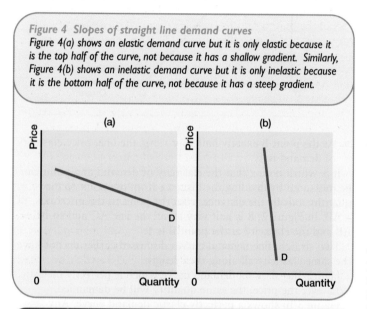

Figure 4 Slopes of straight line demand curves
Figure 4(a) shows an elastic demand curve but it is only elastic because it is the top half of the curve, not because it has a shallow gradient. Similarly, Figure 4(b) shows an inelastic demand curve but it is only inelastic because it is the bottom half of the curve, not because it has a steep gradient.

Question 4

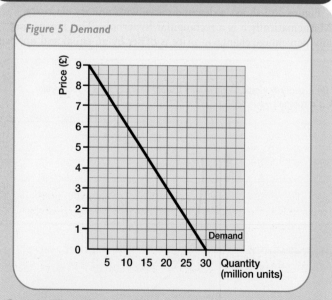

Figure 5 Demand

Consider Figure 5.
(a) Between what prices is demand (i) elastic and (ii) inelastic?
(b) At what price is demand (i) perfectly inelastic, (ii) perfectly elastic and (iii) equal to 1?

Two technical points

So far we have written of price elasticity of demand as always being a positive number. In fact any downward sloping demand curve always has a negative elasticity. This is because a rise in one variable (price or quantity) is always matched by a fall in the other variable. A rise is positive but a fall is negative and a positive number divided by a negative one (or vice versa) is always negative. However, economists find it convenient to omit the minus sign in price elasticity of demand because it is easier to deal in positive numbers whilst accepting that the value is really negative.

A second point relates to the fact that elasticities over the same price range can differ. For example, at a price of £2, demand for a good is 20 units. At a price of £3, demand is 18 units. Price elasticity of demand for a rise in price from £2 to £3 is:

$$\frac{P}{Q} \times \frac{\Delta Q}{\Delta P} = \frac{2}{20} \times \frac{2}{1} = \frac{1}{5}$$

However, price elasticity of demand for a fall in price from £3 to £2 is:

$$\frac{P}{Q} \times \frac{\Delta Q}{\Delta P} = \frac{3}{18} \times \frac{2}{1} = \frac{1}{3}$$

The price elasticity for a rise in price is therefore less than for a fall in price over the same range. This is not necessarily a problem so long as one is aware of it. One way of resolving this is to average out price and quantity. In the formulae, P becomes not the original price but the average price (i.e. the original price plus the new price divided by 2) and Q becomes the average quantity demanded (i.e. the original quantity demanded plus the new quantity demanded divided by 2). In the above example, the average price is £(2 + 3) ÷ 2 or £2.50. The average quantity demanded is (20 + 18) ÷ 2 or 19. Price elasticity of demand is then:

$$\frac{P}{Q} \times \frac{\Delta Q}{\Delta P} = \frac{2.5}{19} \times \frac{2}{1} = \frac{5}{19}$$

As you would expect, this value is in between the two price elasticities of ⅕ and ⅓.

The determinants of price elasticity of demand

The exact value of price elasticity of demand for a good is determined by a wide variety of factors. Economists, however, argue that two factors in particular can be singled out: the availability of substitutes and time.

The availability of substitutes The better the substitutes for a product, the higher the price elasticity of demand will tend to be. For instance, salt has few good substitutes. When the price of salt increases, the demand for salt will change little and therefore the price elasticity of salt is low. On the other hand, spaghetti has many good substitutes, from other types of pasta, to rice, potatoes, bread, and other foods. A rise in the price of spaghetti, all other food prices remaining constant, is likely to have a significant effect on the demand for spaghetti. Hence the elasticity of demand for spaghetti is likely to be higher than that for salt.

Width of market definition The more widely the product is defined, the fewer substitutes it is likely to have. Spaghetti has many substitutes, but food in general has none. Therefore the elasticity of demand for spaghetti is likely to be higher than that for food. Similarly the elasticity of demand for boiled sweets is likely to be higher than for confectionery in general. A 5 per cent increase in the price of boiled sweets, all other prices remaining constant, is likely to lead to a much larger fall in demand for boiled sweets than a 5 per cent increase in the price of all confectionery.

Time The longer the period of time, the more price elastic is the demand for a product. For instance, in 1973/74 when the price of oil quadrupled the demand for oil was initially little affected. In the short term the demand for oil was price inelastic. This is hardly surprising. People still needed to travel to work in cars and heat their houses whilst industry still needed to operate. Oil had few good substitutes. Motorists couldn't put gas into their petrol tanks whilst businesses could not change oil-fired systems to run on gas, electricity or coal. However, in the longer term motorists were able to, and did, buy cars which were more fuel efficient. Oil-fired central heating systems were replaced by gas and electric systems. Businesses converted or did not replace oil-fired equipment. The demand for oil fell from what it would otherwise have been. Taking the ten year period to 1985, and given the changes in other variables which affected demand for oil, estimates suggest that the demand for oil was slightly elastic. It is argued that in the short term, buyers are often locked into

spending patterns through habit, lack of information or because of durable goods that have already been purchased. In the longer term, they have the time and opportunity to change those patterns.

It is sometimes argued that **necessities** have lower price elasticities than **luxuries**. Necessities by definition have to be bought whatever their price in order to stay alive. So an increase in the price of necessities will barely reduce the quantity demanded. Luxuries on the other hand are by definition goods which are not essential to existence. A rise in the price of luxuries should therefore produce a proportionately large fall in demand. There is no evidence, however, to suggest that this is true. Food, arguably a necessity, does not seem to have a lower elasticity than holidays or large cars, both arguably luxuries. Part of the reason for this is that it is very difficult to define necessities and luxuries empirically. Some food is a necessity but a significant proportion of what we eat is unnecessary for survival. It is not possible to distinguish between what food is consumed out of necessity and what is a luxury.

It is also sometimes argued that goods which form a relatively low proportion of total expenditure have lower elasticities than those which form a more significant proportion. A large car manufacturer, for instance, would continue to buy the same number of paper clips even if the price of paper clips doubled because it is not worth its while to bother changing to an alternative. On the other hand, its demand for steel would be far more price elastic. There is no evidence to suggest that this is true. Examples given in textbooks, such as salt and matches, have low price elasticities because they have few good substitutes. In the case of paper clips, manufacturers of paper clips would long ago have raised prices substantially if they believed that price had little impact on the demand for their product.

Key terms

Elastic demand - where the price elasticity of demand is greater than 1. The responsiveness of demand is proportionally greater than the change in price. Demand is infinitely elastic if price elasticity of demand is infinity.
Inelastic demand - where the price elasticity of demand is less than 1. The responsiveness of demand is proportionally less than the change in price. Demand is infinitely inelastic if price elasticity of demand is zero.

Price elasticity of demand or own elasticity of demand - the proportionate response of changes in quantity demanded to a proportionate change in price, measured by the formula:

$$\frac{P}{Q} \times \frac{\Delta Q}{\Delta P}$$

Unitary elasticity - where the value of price elasticity of demand is 1. The responsiveness of demand is proportionally equal to the change in price.

Applied economics

Price elasticity of demand for oil

The price of oil

Oil is a key world commodity. In the 1950s and 1960s, the price of oil was relatively stable at around $2 a barrel. Since 1970, however, the price of oil has proved volatile and the actual or nominal price has increased dramatically as can be seen in Figure 6. There have been four major oil price spikes in that period.

- Between 1972 and 1975, the price of oil increased from $2 a barrel to $11 a barrel. High world growth during that period increased demand for all commodities and led to a boom in commodity prices. In the case of oil, the Yom Kippur War in 1973 between Israel and Egypt led Arab countries to threaten to cut off oil supplies to the West for selling arms to Israel. OPEC, the Organisation of the Petroleum Exporting Countries, played a key role during the crisis. Set up in 1960, it had had little impact on world oil markets up to that point. However, its response to the war was to enforce a set of limits or quotas on production of member states. By restricting supply at a time of growing demand, it led to a large rise in the price of oil. Once the political crisis was over, OPEC members continued to impose quotas to maintain high prices which were to their economic advantage.

- Another political crisis, the 1978 revolution in Iran which led to an Islamic fundamentalist government coming to power, led to the next oil price rise. The revolution severely disrupted oil production in Iran and Iran was a major supplier of oil to world markets. Between 1978 and 1980, oil prices rose from $13 a barrel to $36 a barrel.

- In the 1980s, oil prices fell from their 1980 peak. In 1990, however, this fall was reversed when the USA and its allies fought the first Gulf War against Iraq. Again it was the threat of interruption of supplies of oil which led to the price increase.

- The rise in the price of oil from the early 2000s was caused by rising world demand, particularly from the fast growing Chinese economy. By 2004-2005, OPEC countries were producing at full capacity. An inability to increase supply substantially further pushed up the price of oil.

Price elasticity of demand for oil

Economic theory would suggest that a rise in the price of oil would lead to a fall in quantity demanded. Looking at Figure 7, it can be seen that the sharp rise in the price of oil from $2 a barrel to $36 a barrel between 1972 and 1980 was associated with a sharp decline in the UK consumption of oil from 106 million tonnes in 1973 to a low of 68.6 million tonnes in 1983. An 850

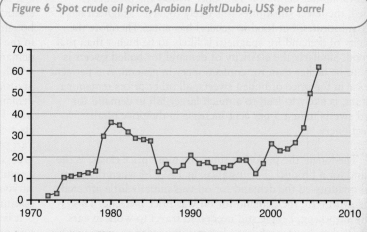

Figure 6 *Spot crude oil price, Arabian Light/Dubai, US$ per barrel*

Source: adapted from *BP Statistical Review of World Energy.*

per cent rise in the price of oil was associated with a 55 per cent fall in demand. Other factors affecting the UK demand for oil were changing over this ten year period. Incomes rose, for example, and more fuel efficient technology was developed. However, these figures would suggest that the demand for oil at the time was price inelastic.

Figure 7 shows that the UK demand for oil since 1990 has remained fairly stable at between 75 and 79 million tonnes per year. Other factors that affected demand over the period including rising incomes. However, the large rises in oil prices since 2000 seem to have had little impact on quantity demanded, again suggesting a very low price elasticity of demand for oil.

Figure 8 shows estimates of the price elasticity of demand for oil between different regions of the world. Demand is price inelastic in every instance. The UK is part of OECD Europe. This estimate puts price elasticity of demand for oil at -0.3.

Short term and long term price elasticities

In the short term, demand for oil is likely to be highly price inelastic. Consumers of oil have little choice but to buy oil to run their cars, trains or heating systems. In the longer term, demand for oil is likely to be less inelastic. This is partly because consumers can substitute oil for other forms of energy such as gas and coal. It is also because of energy saving measures which make it economical, for example, to install insulation in lofts or develop more fuel-efficient cars.

OPEC and some of its member countries like Saudi Arabia are aware that too high a price for oil could result in a long term decline in demand for oil despite rising world incomes. A large scale switch from petrol driven vehicles to ones powered by hydrogen, for example, could bring the price of oil down to below $10 a barrel. This would have a significant impact on economies such as Saudi Arabia which are highly dependent on oil revenues for their prosperity. It is in the interests of these countries to have an oil price which is as high as possible but is not so high that in encourages the long term development of technologies which considerably reduce the demand for oil.

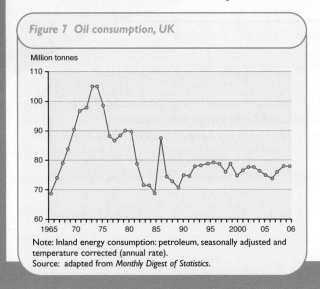

Figure 7 Oil consumption, UK

Note: Inland energy consumption: petroleum, seasonally adjusted and temperature corrected (annual rate).
Source: adapted from *Monthly Digest of Statistics*.

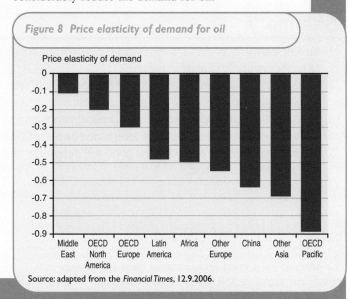

Figure 8 Price elasticity of demand for oil

Source: adapted from the *Financial Times*, 12.9.2006.

DataQuestion

Food prices

Sharply higher wheat prices will mean another increase in bread prices in the next few weeks, Premier Food, owner of the Hovis brand, said yesterday. Given price increases by other bread manufacturers, this could mean a 10 per cent increase in the price of a standard loaf.

Source: adapted from the *Financial Times*, 10.7.2007.

Consumer groups in Italy have asked consumers to boycott eating pasta for a day. They are protesting about recent rises in the price of pasta of around 20 per cent. Pasta manufacturers have been forced to increase prices by soaring wheat prices. Durum flour, the main ingredient for Italian pasta, has risen from €0.26 per kg to €0.45 per kg just in the last two months.

Source: adapted from newsvote.bbc.co.uk, 13.9.2007.

Consumers are likely to be hit by price rises for meat and dairy products as the Far East competes with the West for stocks. The Chinese, for example, have developed a taste for yoghurt, cheese and milk. Wholesale milk prices have risen from about 17p a litre to almost 25p a litre in recent months. This could push the price of a pint of milk in the shops up 10 per cent.

Source: adapted from *The Times*, 29.8.2007.

Table 5 Estimates of price elasticities of demand for selected foods

	Price elasticity
Bread	-0.40
Milk and cream	-0.36
Cereal and cereal products other than bread e.g. pasta	-0.94

Source: adapted from National Food Survey 2000, Defra.

1 Assume that the price elasticities for Hovis bread, a pint of milk and Italian pasta are those given in Table 5. Calculate the effect on demand for those products given the price rises mentioned in the data.
2 Define inelastic demand and suggest why milk and bread have such low price elasticities of demand.
3 Table 5 shows that the price elasticity of demand for all cereal and cereal products other than bread is -0.94. Discuss whether the price elasticity of demand for pasta is likely to be higher or lower than this.

Summary

1. *Income elasticity of demand measures the proportionate response of quantity demanded to a proportionate change in income.*
2. *Cross elasticity of demand measures the proportionate response of quantity demanded of one good to a proportionate change in price of another good.*
3. *Price elasticity of supply measures the proportionate response of quantity supplied to a proportionate change in price.*
4. *The value of elasticity of supply is determined by the availability of substitutes and by time factors.*
5. *The price elasticity of demand for a good will determine whether a change in the price of a good results in a change in expenditure on the good.*

Income elasticity of demand

The demand for a good will change if there is a change in consumers' incomes. INCOME ELASTICITY OF DEMAND is a measure of that change. If the demand for housing increased by 20 per cent when incomes increased by 5 per cent, then the income elasticity of demand would be said to be positive and relatively high. If the demand for food were unchanged when income rose, then income elasticity would be zero. A fall in demand for a good when income rises gives a negative value to income elasticity of demand.

The formula for measuring income elasticity of demand is:

$$\frac{\text{percentage change in quantity demanded}}{\text{percentage change in income}}$$

So the numerical value of income elasticity of a 20 per cent rise in demand for housing when incomes rise by 5 per cent is +20/+5 or +4. The number is positive because both the 20 per cent and the 5 per cent are positive. On the other hand, a rise in income of 10 per cent which led to a fall in quantity demanded of a product of 5 per cent would have an income elasticity of -5/+10 or -½. The minus sign in -5 shows the fall in quantity demanded of the product. Examples of items with a high income elasticity of demand are holidays and recreational activities, whereas washing up liquid tends to have a low income elasticity of demand.

Just as with price elasticity, it is sometimes easier to use alternative formulae to calculate income elasticity of demand. The above formula is equivalent to:

$$\frac{\Delta Q}{Q} \div \frac{\Delta Y}{Y}$$

where is change, Q is quantity demanded and Y is income. Rearranging the formula gives another two alternatives:

$$\frac{Y}{Q} \times \frac{\Delta Q}{\Delta Y} \quad \text{or} \quad \frac{\Delta Q}{Q} \times \frac{Y}{\Delta Y}$$

Examples of the calculation of income elasticity of

Table 1 Calculation of income elasticity of demand

Original quantity demanded	New quantity demanded	Original income (£)	New income (£)	$\frac{\Delta Q}{Q} \div \frac{\Delta Y}{Y}$	Numerical value
				Income elasticity of demand	
20	25	16	18	5/20 ÷ 2/16	+2
100	200	20	25	100/100 ÷ 5/20	+4
50	40	25	30	-10/50 ÷ 5/25	-1
60	60	80	75	0/60 ÷ -5/80	0
60	40	27	30	-20/60 ÷ 3/27	-3

demand are given in Table 1. Some economists use the terms 'elastic' and 'inelastic' with reference to income elasticity. Demand is income inelastic if it lies between +1 and -1. If income elasticity of demand is greater than +1 or less than -1, then it is elastic.

Question 1

Table 2

£

	Original		New	
	Quantity demanded	Income	Quantity demanded	Income
(a)	100	10	120	14
(b)	15	6	20	7
(c)	50	25	40	35
(d)	12	100	15	125
(e)	200	10	250	11
(f)	25	20	30	18

Calculate the income elasticity of demand from the data in Table 2.

Cross elasticity of demand

The quantity demanded of a particular good varies according to the price of other goods. In unit 9 it was argued that a rise in price of a good such as beef would increase the quantity demanded of a substitute such as pork. On the other hand, a rise in price of a good such as cheese would lead to a fall in the quantity demanded of a complement such as macaroni. CROSS ELASTICITY or CROSS PRICE ELASTICITY OF DEMAND measures the proportionate response of the quantity demanded of one good to the proportionate change in the price of another. For instance, it is a measure of the extent to which demand for pork increases when the price of beef goes up; or the extent to which the demand for macaroni falls when the price of cheese increases.

The formula for measuring cross elasticity of demand for good X is:

$$\frac{\text{percentage change in quantity demanded of good X}}{\text{percentage change in price of another good Y}}$$

Two goods which are substitutes will have a positive cross elasticity. An increase (positive) in the price of one good, such as gas, leads to an increase (positive) in the quantity demanded of a substitute such as electricity. Two goods which are complements will have a negative cross elasticity. An increase (positive) in the price of one good such as sand leads to a fall (negative) in demand of a complement such as cement. The cross elasticity of two goods which have little relationship to each other would be zero. For instance, a rise in the price of cars of 10 per cent is likely to have no effect (i.e. 0 per cent change) on the demand for Tipp-Ex.

As with price and income elasticity, it is sometimes more convenient to use alternative formulae for cross elasticity of demand. These are:

$$\text{Cross elasticity of good X} = \frac{\Delta Q_X}{Q_X} \div \frac{\Delta P_Y}{P_Y}$$

or

$$\frac{P_Y}{Q_X} \times \frac{\Delta Q_X}{\Delta P_Y}$$

Some economists use the terms 'elastic' and 'inelastic' with reference to cross elasticity. Demand is cross elastic if it lies between +1 and -1. If cross elasticity of demand is greater than +1 or less than -1, then it is elastic.

Question 2

Explain what estimated value you would put on the cross elasticity of demand of: (a) gas for electricity; (b) tennis shorts for tennis rackets; (c) luxury cars for petrol; (d) paper for socks; (e) CDs for MP3 downloads; (f) Sainsbury's own brand baked beans for Tesco's own brand baked beans; (g) Virgin Cola for Coca-Cola.

Price elasticity of supply

Price elasticity of demand measures the responsiveness of changes in quantity demanded to changes in price. Equally, the responsiveness of quantity supplied to changes in price can also be measured - this is called PRICE ELASTICITY OF SUPPLY. The formula for measuring the price elasticity of supply is:

$$\frac{\text{percentage change in quantity supplied}}{\text{percentage change in price}}$$

This is equivalent to:

$$\frac{\Delta Q}{Q} \div \frac{\Delta P}{P}$$

or

$$\frac{P}{Q} \times \frac{\Delta Q}{\Delta P}$$

where Q is quantity supplied and P is price.

The supply curve is upward sloping (i.e. an increase in price leads to an increase in quantity supplied and vice versa). Therefore price elasticity of supply will be positive because the top and bottom of the formula will be either both positive or both negative.

As with price elasticity of demand, different ranges of elasticity are given different names. Price elasticity of supply is:
- **perfectly inelastic** (zero) if there is no response in supply to a change in price;
- **inelastic** (between zero and one) if there is a less than proportionate response in supply to a change in price;
- **unitary** (one) if the percentage change in quantity supplied equals the percentage change in price;
- **elastic** (between one and infinity) if there is a more than proportionate response in supply to a change in price;
- **perfectly elastic** (infinite) if producers are prepared to supply any amount at a given price.

These various elasticities are shown in Figure 1.

It should be noted that any straight line supply curve passing through the origin has an elasticity of supply equal to 1. This is best understood if we take the formula:

$$\frac{P}{Q} \times \frac{\Delta Q}{\Delta P}$$

$\Delta Q/\Delta P$ is the inverse of (i.e. 1 divided by) the slope of the line, whilst P/Q, assuming that the line passes through the origin, is the slope of the line. The two multiplied together must always equal 1.

Determinants of elasticity of supply

As with price elasticity of demand, there are two factors which

Figure 1 Elasticity of supply
The elasticity of supply of a straight line supply curve varies depending upon the gradient of the line and whether it passes through the origin.

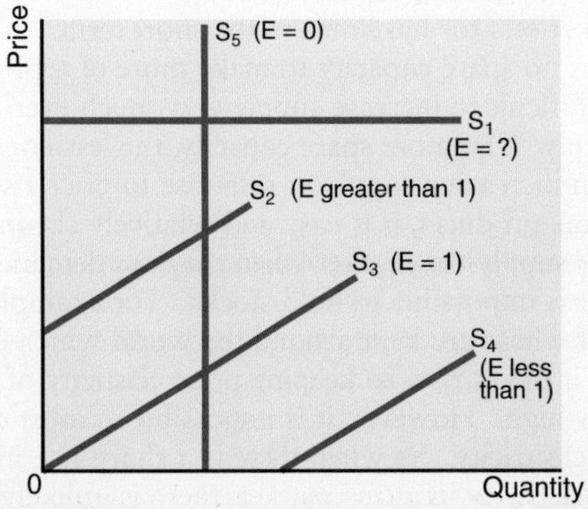

Question 3

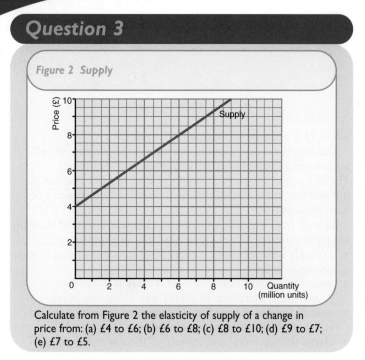

Figure 2 Supply

Calculate from Figure 2 the elasticity of supply of a change in price from: (a) £4 to £6; (b) £6 to £8; (c) £8 to £10; (d) £9 to £7; (e) £7 to £5.

determine supply elasticity across a wide range of products.

Availability of substitutes Substitutes here are not consumer substitutes but producer substitutes. These are goods which a producer can easily produce as alternatives. For instance, one model of a car is a good producer substitute for another model in the same range because the car manufacturer can easily switch resources on its production line. On the other hand, carrots are not substitutes for cars. The farmer cannot easily switch from the production of carrots to the production of cars. If a product has many substitutes then producers can quickly and easily alter the pattern of production if its price rises or falls. Hence its elasticity will be relatively high. However, if a product has few or no substitutes, then producers will find it difficult to respond flexibly to variations in price. If there is a fall in price, a producer may have no alternative but either to carry on producing much the same quantity as before or withdrawing from the market. Price elasticity of supply is therefore low.

Time The shorter the time period, the more difficult producers find it to switch from making one product to another. So in the short term, supply is likely to be more price inelastic than in the long term. There is a number of reasons why this is the case.
- Some items take a long time to make. For example, if there is a crop failure of a product like hazelnuts, it will take until the next growing season to increase supply again whatever price the market sets for hazelnuts in the short term.
- If there is no spare capacity to make more of a product, it will be difficult to increase supply very much even if prices rise sharply. The more spare capacity, the less constraint this places on increasing supply in response to price rises.
- With some products, it is easy and relatively cheap to hold stocks to supply the market when they are demanded. With others, it is impossible to hold stocks. For example, large stocks of wheat are kept around the world which can be released if prices rise, so keeping price elasticity of supply relatively high. However, it is impossible in most cases to store electricity. So when there is a sharp rise in price of electricity in a free market, there is unlikely to be

much response in terms of extra supply in the short term if the system is working at full capacity. The longer the time period, the easier it is for the market to build up appropriate stocks or to build excess capacity if stocks are not possible. So price elasticity of supply is higher in the longer term.
- Price elasticity of supply will be higher the easier it is for a firm to switch production from one product to another or for firms to enter the market to make the product.

Price elasticity of demand and total expenditure

Price elasticity of demand and changes in total expenditure on a product are linked. Total expenditure can be calculated by multiplying price and quantity:

Total expenditure = quantity purchased x price

For instance, if you bought 5 apples at 10 pence each, your total expenditure would be 50 pence. If the price of apples went up, you might spend more, less, or the same on apples depending upon your price elasticity of demand for apples. Assume that the price of apples went up 40 per cent to 14p each. You might react by buying fewer apples. If you now buy 4 apples (i.e. a fall in demand of 20 per cent), the price elasticity of demand is 20 ÷ 40 or 0.5. Your expenditure on apples will also rise (from 50 pence to 56 pence). If you buy two apples (i.e. a fall in quantity demanded of 60 per cent), your elasticity of demand is 60 ÷ 40 or 1.5 and your expenditure on apples will fall (from 50 pence to 28 pence).

These relationships are what should be expected. If the percentage change in price is larger than the percentage change in quantity demanded (i.e. elasticity is less than 1, or inelastic), then expenditure will rise when prices rise. If the percentage change in price is smaller than the percentage change in quantity demanded (i.e. elasticity is greater than 1 or elastic), then spending will fall as prices rise. If the percentage change in price is the same as the change in quantity demanded (i.e. elasticity is unity), expenditure will remain unchanged because the percentage rise in price will be equal and opposite to the percentage fall in demand.

Key terms

Cross or cross-price elasticity of demand - a measure of the responsiveness of quantity demanded of one good to a change in price of another good. It is measured by dividing the percentage change in quantity demanded of one good by the percentage change in price of the other good.
Income elasticity of demand - a measure of the responsiveness of quantity demanded to a change in income. It is measured by dividing the percentage change in quantity demanded by the percentage change in income.
Price elasticity of supply - a measure of the responsiveness of quantity supplied to a change in price. It is measured by dividing the percentage change in quantity supplied by the percentage change in price.

Question 4

(a) Suggest reasons why the demand for some foods in Table 3 is more price elastic than the demand for others.

(b) An increase in the price of which foods would be most likely to lead to
  (i) the greatest and
  (ii) the least change in household expenditure? Explain your answer.

Table 3 *Estimates of price elasticities of demand for selected household foods*

	Price elasticity
Milk and cream	-0.36
of which	
Liquid wholemilk and skimmed milks	-0.17
Cheese	-0.35
Carcass meat	-0.69
Other meat and meat products	-0.52
Fresh fish	-0.80
Processed and shellfish	-0.17
Prepared fish	0.00
Frozen fish	-0.32
Eggs	-0.28
Fats	-0.75
Sugar and preserves	-0.79
Fresh potatoes	-0.12
Fresh green vegetables	-0.66
Other fresh vegetables	-0.33
Processed vegetables	-0.60
of which	
Frozen peas	-0.68
Frozen convenience potato products	-0.58
Fresh fruit	-0.29
of which	
Bananas	-0.32
Other fruit and fruit products	-0.81
of which	
Fruit juices	-0.55
Bread	-0.40
Other cereal and cereal products	-0.94
of which	
Cakes and pastries	-0.56
Frozen convenience cereal foods	-0.69
Beverages	-0.37

Source: adapted from *National Food Survey 2000*, Defra.

Applied economics

Cross elasticities of demand for food

Many foods are substitutes for each other. Eggs are a substitute for fish; fish is a substitute for meat. Economic theory would suggest that these goods would therefore have a positive cross elasticity of demand. An increase in the price of one good would lead to an increase in demand of the substitute good, whilst a fall in price of one good would lead to a fall in demand of another.

The National Food Survey 2000 gives some evidence for this. Table 4 shows estimates of the cross elasticity of demand for three foods: carcass meat, fresh fish and eggs. In orange, going across diagonally, are the own-price elasticities of demand for each good. For example, the price elasticity of demand for carcass meat is - 0.69 (i.e. it is price inelastic). In black, reading across the rows, are the figures for cross elasticity of demand for a product with respect to the price of another. For example, the cross elasticity of demand of carcass meat with respect to the price of

fresh fish is + 0.15. The cross elasticity of demand of eggs with respect to the price of fresh fish is + 0.16.

These cross elasticities are relatively low suggesting, for example, that eggs are only a weak substitute for fresh fish or carcass meat. So a 10 per cent rise in the price of fresh fish, leading to a 8 per cent fall in demand for fresh fish (because the price elasticity of demand for fresh fish is - 0.8), is associated with only a 1.6 per cent rise in demand for eggs (because the cross price elasticity of eggs with respect to the price of fresh fish is + 0.16). Equally, a 10 per cent rise in the price of fresh fish is associated with only a 1.5 per cent rise in demand for carcass meat.

When cross elasticities are negative, it shows that goods might be complements to each other. Table 5 would suggest that milk and cream, eggs and fats are all complements. For example, the ingredients for pancakes, and some cakes include milk, eggs and fats. The National Food Survey estimates suggest that a

Table 4 *Estimates of price and cross elasticity of demand for carcass meat, fresh fish and eggs, 1988-2000*

	Elasticity with respect to the price of		
	Carcass meat	Fresh fish	Eggs
Carcass meat	-0.69	+0.15	+0.15
Fresh fish	+0.02	-0.8	+0.14
Eggs	+0.02	+0.16	-0.28

Source: adapted from HMSO, *Household Food Consumption and Expenditure.*

Table 5 *Estimates of price and cross elasticity of demand for milk and cream, eggs and fats, 1988-2000*

	Elasticity with respect to the price of		
	Milk and cream	Eggs	Fats
Milk and cream	-0.36	-0.40	-0.20
Eggs	-0.05	-0.28	-0.10
Fats	-0.04	-0.19	-0.75

Source: adapted from HMSO, *Household Food Consumption and Expenditure.*

Table 6 *Estimates of price and cross elasticity of demand for eggs, non-fresh fruit and fruit products, and meat and meat products other than carcass meat, 1988-2000*

	Elasticity with respect to the price of		
	Eggs	Non-fresh fruit and fruit products	Meat and meat products other than carcass meat
Eggs	-0.28	0.00	0.00
Non-fresh fruit and fruit products	0.00	-0.81	-0.01
Meat and meat products other than carcass meat	+0.03	-0.04	-0.52

Source: adapted from HMSO, *Household Food Consumption and Expenditure.*

10 per cent rise in the price of eggs leads to a 4 per cent fall in the quantity demanded of milk and cream. Interestingly, a 10 per cent rise in the price of milk and cream only leads to a fall of 0.4 per cent in the quantity demanded of eggs. As with the data on substitutes, the National Food Survey estimates suggest that where foods are compliments, they tend to be fairly weak compliments with numbers fairly near zero.

Where changes in the price of one good have no effect on the quantity demanded of another good, the cross elasticity of demand is zero. Table 6, which shows data from the National Food Survey, would suggest that changes in the price of eggs, non-fresh fruit and fruit products, and meat and meat products other than carcass meat have little impact on demand for each other.

DataQuestion

Clothing, footwear and transport

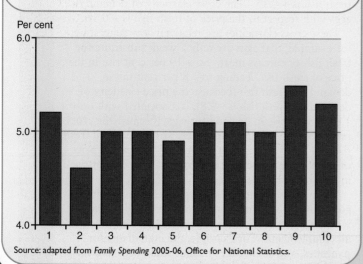

Figure 3 *Expenditure on clothing and footwear as a percentage of total expenditure by gross income decile group, 2005-2006*

Source: adapted from *Family Spending* 2005-06, Office for National Statistics.

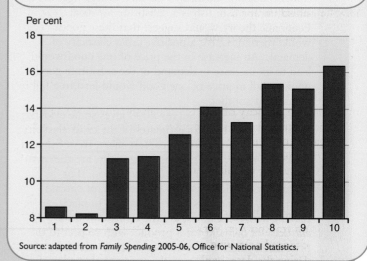

Figure 4 *Expenditure on transport as a percentage of total expenditure by gross income decile group, 2005-2006*

Source: adapted from *Family Spending* 2005-06, Office for National Statistics.

Decile groups

A population can be split into ten equal groups. These are called decile groups. In Table 8 the groups are households, which are split according to their gross income. So the first decile group is the tenth of households which have the lowest income. The fifth decile group is the tenth of households between 40 and 50 per cent of the total, whilst the tenth decile group is made up of the highest 10 per cent of households by gross income. In Table 8 data for the other 7 decile groups is available but is not printed here in order to simplify the data.

Table 7 Clothing and footwear and transport as a percentage of total household expenditure, real household disposable income 1980 to 2005-2006

	Clothing and footwear %	Transport %	Real household disposable income 1980=100
1980	8.1	14.6	100.0
1992	6.0	15.8	141.2
2005-06	5.1	13.9	200.0

Source: adapted from *Family Spending 2005-06*, Office for National Statistics.

Table 8 Weekly household expenditure, £, on clothing and footwear and transport by gross income decile group 2005-2006

	Average weekly expenditure, £		
	First decile	Fifth decile	Tenth decile
Men's outer garments	1.10	3.00	10.70
Men's under garments	0.10	0.20	0.80
Women's outer garments	3.20	6.00	21.50
Women's under garments	0.50	1.10	2.20
Boys' outer garments (5-15)	0.40	0.40	1.30
Girls' outer garments (5-15)	0.30	0.80	1.60
Infants' outer garments (under 5)	0.30	0.60	1.00
Children's under garments (under 16)	0.10	0.30	0.50
Accessories	0.30	0.50	2.00
Haberdashery and clothing hire	0.00	0.20	0.60
Dry cleaners, laundry and dyeing	0.10	0.10	1.10
Footwear	1.70	4.10	9.00
Total clothing and footwear	**8.00**	**17.30**	**52.00**
Purchase of vehicles	4.10	14.80	71.80
Petrol, diesel and other motor oils	3.70	15.00	38.20
Other motoring costs	1.90	9.00	23.80
Rail and tube fares	0.40	1.00	8.20
Bus and coach fares	0.90	1.40	1.70
Combined fares	0.50	0.30	3.60
Other travel and transport	1.70	3.40	14.80
Total transport	**13.20**	**44.80**	**161.90**
Total household expenditure on all goods and services	**153.60**	**356.70**	**989.70**
Total household income £	**0-134**	**364-472**	**1 224+**

Source: adapted from *Family Spending 2005-06*, Office for National Statistics.

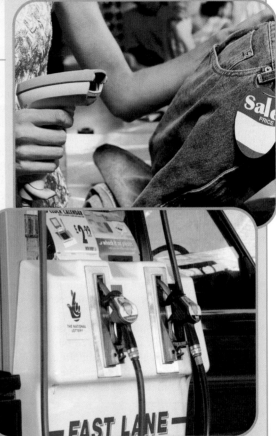

Measuring income elasticity of demand

Income elasticity of demand is measured by dividing the percentage change in quantity demanded of a good or a basket of goods by the percentage change in income of consumers. Quantity demanded is a physical number, like 100 washing machines or 1 000 shirts. However, when data for quantity is not available, a good proxy variable is expenditure. This is quantity times price. If prices remain the same as expenditure changes, then the percentage change in quantity will be the same as the percentage change in expenditure.

1. Describe how spending on clothing and footwear and on transport (a) varies with income and (b) has changed over time.
2. Using the data, explain whether 'clothing and footwear' is likely to have a higher income elasticity of demand than transport.
3. Using Table 8, explain which components of clothing and footwear and transport are likely to have the highest income elasticities.
4. Using the data in Table 8 and the concept of income elasticity of demand, discuss whether bus and coach transport has a future in the UK.

Summary

1. An increase in income will lead to an increase in demand for normal goods but a fall in demand for inferior goods.
2. Normal goods have a positive income elasticity whilst inferior goods have a negative elasticity.
3. A Giffen good is one where a rise in price leads to a rise in quantity demanded. This occurs because the positive substitution effect of the price change is outweighed by the negative income effect.
4. Upward sloping demand curves may occur if the good is a Giffen good, if it has snob or speculative appeal or if consumers judge quality by the price of a product.

Normal and inferior goods

The pattern of demand is likely to change when income changes. It would be reasonable to assume that consumers will increase their demand for most goods when their income increases. Goods for which this is the case are called NORMAL GOODS.

However, an increase in income will result in a fall in demand for other goods. These goods are called INFERIOR GOODS. There will be a fall in demand because consumers will react to an increase in their income by purchasing products which are perceived to be of better quality. Commonly quoted examples of inferior goods are:

- bread - consumers switch from this cheap, filling food to more expensive meat or convenience foods as their incomes increase;
- margarine - consumers switch from margarine to butter, although this has become less true recently with greater health awareness;
- bus transport - consumers switch from buses to their own cars when they can afford to buy their own car.

A good can be both a normal and an inferior good depending upon the level of income. Bread may be a normal good for people on low incomes (i.e. they buy more bread when their

income increases). But it may be an inferior good for higher income earners.

Normal and inferior goods are shown on Figure 1. D_1 is the demand curve for a normal good. It is upward sloping because demand increases as income increases. D_2 is the demand curve for an inferior good. It is downward sloping, showing that demand falls as income increases. D_3 is the demand curve for a good which is normal at low levels of income, but is inferior at higher levels of income.

Question 1

Table 1 Estimated household food consumption in Great Britain

	Grammes per person per week				
	1985	1990	1995	2000	2005/6
Sugar	238	171	136	105	94
Chicken	196	226	237	253	224
Bananas	80	125	176	206	225
Bread	878	797	756	720	701
Pickles and sauces	61	67	80	107	125
Butter	80	46	36	39	38

Source: adapted from *Annual Abstract of Statistics*, Office for National Statistics.

Household incomes rose between each of the years 1985, 1990, 1995, 2000 and 2005/6. Assuming that all other factors remained constant, which of the goods shown in Table 1 are normal goods and which are inferior goods?

Inferior goods and income elasticity

Inferior goods can be distinguished from normal goods by their income elasticity of demand. The formula for measuring income elasticity is:

$$\frac{\text{percentage change in quantity demanded}}{\text{percentage change in income}}$$

A normal good will always have a positive income elasticity because quantity demanded and income either both increase

Figure 1 *Normal and inferior goods*
On the quantity-income diagram, a normal good such as D_1 has an upward sloping curve, whilst an inferior good such as D_2 has a downward sloping curve. D_3 shows a good which is normal at low levels of income but is inferior at higher levels of income.

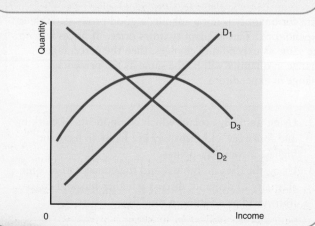

(giving a plus divided by a plus) or both decrease (giving a minus divided by a minus). An inferior good, however, will always have a negative elasticity because the signs on the top and bottom of the formula will always be opposite (a plus divided by a minus or a minus divided by a plus giving a minus answer in both cases).

For instance, if the demand for bread falls by 2 per cent when incomes rise by 10 per cent then it is an inferior good. Its income elasticity is -2/+10 or -0.2.

Giffen goods

A GIFFEN GOOD is a special sort of inferior good. Alfred Marshall (1842-1924), an eminent economist and author of a best selling textbook of his day, claimed that another eminent economist, Sir Robert Giffen (1837-1910), had observed that the consumption of bread increased as its price increased. The argument was that bread was a staple food for low income consumers. A rise in its price would not deter people from buying as much as before. But 'poor' people would now have so little extra money to spend on meat or other luxury foods that they would abandon their demand for these and instead buy more bread to fill up their stomachs. The result was that a rise in the price of bread led to a rise in the demand for bread. Another way of explaining this phenomenon is to use the concepts of INCOME and SUBSTITUTION effects. When a good changes in price, the quantity demanded will be changed by the sum of the substitution effect and the income effect.

● **Substitution effect**. If the price of a good rises, consumers will buy less of that good and more of others because it is now relatively more expensive than other goods. If the price of a good falls, consumers will buy more of that good and less of others. These changes in quantity demanded solely due to the relative change in prices are known as the substitution effect of a price change.

● **Income effect**. If the price of a good rises, the real income of consumers will fall. They will not be able to buy the same basket of goods and services as before. Consumers can react to this fall in real income in one of two ways. If the good is a normal good, they will buy less of the good. If the good is an inferior good, they will buy more of the good. These changes in quantity demanded caused by a change in real income are known as the income effect of the price change.

For a normal good the substitution effect and the income effect both work in the same direction. A rise in price leads to a fall in quantity demanded because the relative price of the good has risen. It also leads to a fall in quantity demanded because consumers' real incomes have now fallen. So a rise in price will always lead to a fall in quantity demanded, and vice versa.

For an inferior good, the substitution effect and income effect work in opposite directions. A rise in price leads to a fall in quantity demanded because the relative price of the good has risen. But it leads to a rise in quantity demanded because consumers' real incomes have fallen. However, the substitution effect outweighs the income effect because overall it is still true for an inferior good that a rise in price leads to an overall fall in quantity demanded.

A Giffen good is a special type of inferior good. A rise in price leads to a fall in quantity demanded because of the substitution effect but a rise in quantity demanded because of the income effect. However, the income effect outweighs the substitution effect, leading to rises in quantity demanded. For instance, if a 10p rise in the price of a standard loaf leads to a 4 per cent fall in

the demand for bread because of the substitution effect, but a 10 per cent rise in demand because of the income effect, then the net effect will be a 6 per cent rise in the demand for bread.

The relationship between normal, inferior and Giffen goods and their income and substitution effects is summarised in Table 2.

Giffen goods are an economic curiosity. In theory they could exist, but no economist has ever found an example of such a good in practice. There is no evidence even that Sir Robert Giffen ever claimed that bread had an upward sloping demand curve - it crept into textbooks via Alfred Marshall and has remained there ever since!

Table 2 Substitution and income effects on quantity demanded of a rise in price for normal, inferior and Giffen goods

Type of good	Effect on quantity demanded of a rise in price		
	Substitution effect	Income effect	Total effect
Normal good	Fall	Fall	Fall
Inferior good	Fall	Rise	Fall because substitution effect > income effect
Giffen good	Fall	Rise	Rise because substitution effect < income effect

Question 2

Table 3

Good	Change in price (pence per unit)	Change in quantity demanded as a result of	
		income effect	substitution effect
Bacon	+10	+5%	-8%
Bus rides	+15	+7%	-5%
Jeans	-100	+1%	+5%
Baked beans	-2	-1%	+4%
Compact discs	-150	+4%	+3%

An economist claims that she has observed the effects detailed in Table 3 resulting solely from a change in price of a product. Which of these products are normal goods, which are inferior and which are Giffen goods?

Necessities and luxuries

Some economists distinguish between **necessities** (or **basic goods**) and **luxuries** (or **superior goods**). They state that necessities have an income elasticity of less than +1 whilst luxury goods have an income elasticity of greater than +1. The problem with this distinction is that many products which have an income elasticity of less than +1 would hardly be classified as 'necessities' by most consumers. In

Table 4, for example, all the foods have an income elasticity of less than +1 and would therefore all be classified as necessities. Yet should a fruit juice be just as much a necessity as tea, milk or meat? Whilst it can be useful to discuss necessities and luxuries in theory, putting a precise value on these in terms of income elasticity of demand may not be particularly helpful.

Upward sloping demand curves

Demand curves are usually downward sloping. However, there are possible reasons why the demand curve for some goods may be upward sloping.

Giffen goods Giffen goods, a type of inferior good, have been discussed above.

Goods with snob appeal Some goods, sometimes called **Veblen goods**, are bought mainly because they confer status on the buyer. Examples might be diamonds, fur coats or large cars. The argument is that these goods are demanded because few people can afford to buy them because their price is high. If large numbers of people could afford to buy them, then the demand (the quantity buyers would buy) would be low. This might be true for some individual consumers, but economists have not found any proof that it is true for markets as a whole. Whilst some might buy diamonds only because they are expensive, the majority of consumers would buy more diamonds if their price fell because they like diamonds. So there must be some doubt as to whether snob appeal does give rise to upward sloping demand curves.

Speculative goods Throughout most of 1987, stock markets worldwide boomed. Share prices were at an all time high and the demand for shares was high too. But in October 1987 share prices slumped on average between 20 and 30 per cent. Overnight the demand for shares fell. This could be taken as evidence of an upward sloping demand curve. The higher the price of shares, the higher the demand because buyers associate high share prices with large speculative gains in the future. However, most economists would argue that what is being seen is a shift in the demand curve. The demand curve is drawn on the assumption that expectations of future gain are constant. When share prices or the price of any speculative good fall, buyers revise their expectations downwards. At any given share price they are willing to buy fewer shares, which pushes the demand curve backwards to the left.

Quality goods Some consumers judge quality by price. They automatically assume that a higher priced good must be of better quality than a similar lower priced good. Hence, the higher the price the greater the quantity demanded. As with snob appeal goods, this may be true for some individuals but there is no evidence to suggest that this is true for consumers as a whole. There have been examples where goods that have been re-packaged, heavily advertised and increased in price have increased their sales. But this is an example of a shift to the right in the demand curve caused by advertising and repackaging rather than of an upward sloping demand curve.

In conclusion, it can be seen that there are various reasons why in theory demand curves might be upward sloping. But few, if any, such goods have been found in reality. The downward sloping demand curve seems to be true of nearly all goods.

Question 3

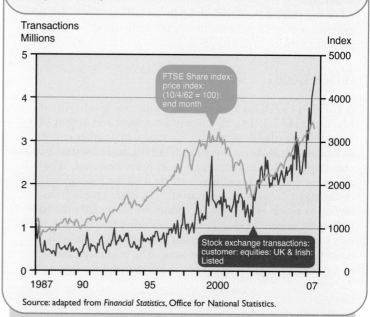

Figure 2 Number of Stock market transactions, FTSE all share price index (1962 = 100)

FTSE Share index: price index: (10/4/62 = 100): end month

Stock exchange transactions: customer: equities: UK & Irish: Listed

Source: adapted from *Financial Statistics*, Office for National Statistics.

In October 1987, prices on the London Stock Market crashed by around 25 per cent. The result was a sharp fall in the number of shares bought and sold. Similarly, in 2000, prices of 'dotcom' shares (shares in companies related to the Internet), having created a boom in share prices, fell sharply. By September 2002, the FTSE All Share Price Index stood at 1802 compared to 3242 in December 1999 at the height of the dotcom bubble. Equally, the number of shares traded per month fell from a high of 2.6 million in March 2000 to a low of 1.1 million in December 2002.

To what extent does the data support the existence of an upward sloping demand curve for shares?

Key terms

Giffen good - a special type of inferior good where demand increases when price increases.
Income effect - the impact on quantity demanded of a change in price due to a change in consumers' real income which results from this change in price.
Inferior good - a good where demand falls when income increases (i.e. it has a negative income elasticity of demand).
Normal good - a good where demand increases when income increases (i.e. it has a positive income elasticity of demand).
Substitution effect - the impact on quantity demanded due to a change in price, assuming that consumers' real incomes stay the same (i.e. the impact of a change in price excluding the income effect).

Applied economics

Income elasticities and inferior goods

Table 4 gives estimates of the income elasticity of demand for certain foods in the UK. The estimates have been calculated using data from the National Food Survey (which from 2001 was amalgamated with the Family Expenditure Survey to become the Expenditure and Food Survey) conducted by Defra (Department for the Environment, Food and Rural Affairs) and ONS (Office for National Statistics, the UK government statistical service).

The calculations pool data for the three year period 1998-2000. Sophisticated statistical techniques were used to take account of factors such as regional spending patterns and household size. The estimates are based on how food expenditure varies between households on different incomes.

Food itself, according to the data, has an income elasticity of demand of + 0.20. Hence, a 10 per cent increase in incomes leads to a 2 per cent increase in the quantity demanded of all foods. Incomes in the UK are growing at around 2.5 per cent per year on average. Growth in demand for food is increasing, therefore, at just one fifth of that amount, at around 0.5 per cent per year on average. An income elasticity of +0.20 also means that spending on food is declining as a proportion of total household expenditure over time.

Most categories of food have a positive income elasticity of demand and are therefore normal goods. For example, cheese has an income elasticity of +0.23, fish +0.27 and fresh fruit +0.30. Some foods, however, are inferior goods with negative income elasticities. In Table 4, these are liquid wholemilk, eggs, margarine, apples and tea. There is a variety of reasons why these particular foods have negative income elasticities.

- Some reflect growing awareness of what constitutes a healthy diet. So liquid wholemilk and margarine with their typically high fat content show a fall in demand as incomes increase. Higher income households tend to be more aware of health issues related to diet. They also have higher incomes to be able to afford to buy acceptable substitutes if these are more expensive.
- Some reflect changing tastes. Tea drinking is declining in the UK as consumers drink more coffee. Because coffee is more expensive than tea, this shift is arguably happening at a faster rate amongst higher income groups. Hence tea has a negative income elasticity of demand. Equally, -0.02 is so small that, according to the National Food Survey report, it is 'not statistically different from zero', i.e. the evidence would suggest that tea is on the borderline between

being a normal and an inferior good.
- Others are more difficult to explain. Healthy eating campaigns should be encouraging consumers to eat apples and yet, according to the data, apples are an inferior good with an income elasticity of -0.07. Perhaps as incomes increase, households are switching from apples to other fruit such as oranges and bananas, both of which have positive income elasticities.

The item with the highest income elasticity of demand in Table 4 is fruit juices with an income elasticity of +0.45. Fruit juices tend to be purchased more by high income households than low income households. The high cost of fruit juices and their perceived health benefits might account for this.

Table 4 Estimated income elasticities of food products

	Income elasticity
Milk and cream	0.05
of which	
Liquid wholemilk	-0.17
Cheese	0.23
Carcass meat	0.20
Fish	0.27
Eggs	-0.01
Fats	0.08
of which	
Butter	0.20
Margarine	-0.37
Sugar and preserves	0.00
Fresh potatoes	0.09
Fresh green vegetables	0.27
Fresh fruit	0.30
of which	
Apples	-0.07
Oranges	0.23
Bananas	0.12
Fruit juices	0.45
Bread	0.12
Cakes and biscuits	0.13
Beverages	0.10
of which	
Tea	-0.02
Coffee	0.16
All foods	0.20

Source: *National Food Survey 2000*, Defra.

DataQuestion

Tourism

Figure 3 Real household disposable income per head at 2003 prices, £

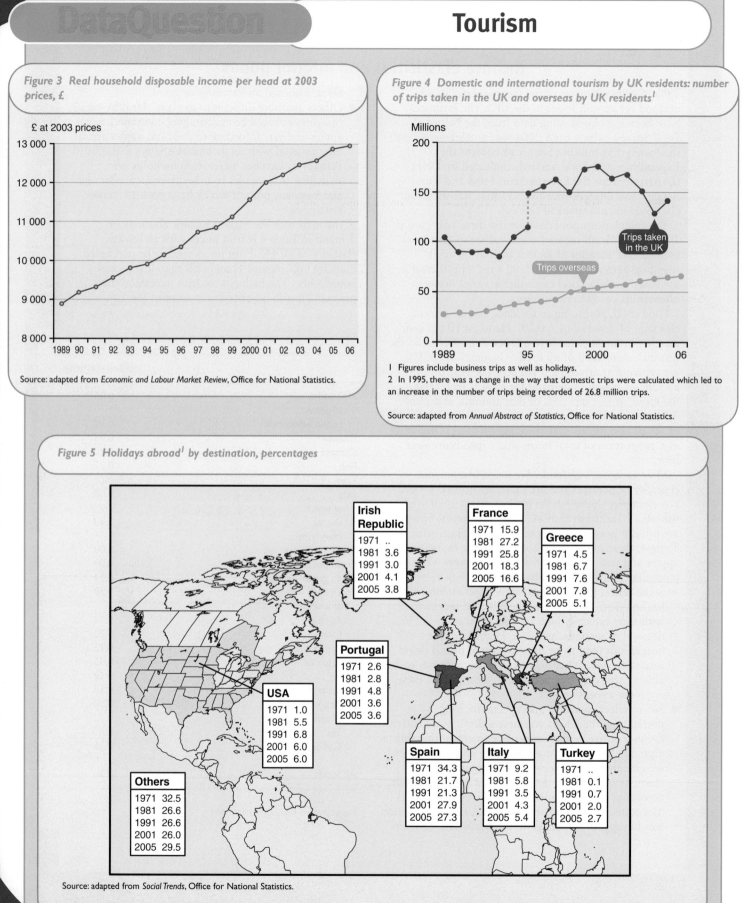

£ at 2003 prices

Source: adapted from *Economic and Labour Market Review*, Office for National Statistics.

Figure 4 Domestic and international tourism by UK residents: number of trips taken in the UK and overseas by UK residents[1]

Millions

Trips taken in the UK

Trips overseas

1 Figures include business trips as well as holidays.
2 In 1995, there was a change in the way that domestic trips were calculated which led to an increase in the number of trips being recorded of 26.8 million trips.

Source: adapted from *Annual Abstract of Statistics*, Office for National Statistics.

Figure 5 Holidays abroad[1] by destination, percentages

Irish Republic

1971	..
1981	3.6
1991	3.0
2001	4.1
2005	3.8

France

1971	15.9
1981	27.2
1991	25.8
2001	18.3
2005	16.6

Greece

1971	4.5
1981	6.7
1991	7.6
2001	7.8
2005	5.1

Portugal

1971	2.6
1981	2.8
1991	4.8
2001	3.6
2005	3.6

USA

1971	1.0
1981	5.5
1991	6.8
2001	6.0
2005	6.0

Spain

1971	34.3
1981	21.7
1991	21.3
2001	27.9
2005	27.3

Italy

1971	9.2
1981	5.8
1991	3.5
2001	4.3
2005	5.4

Turkey

1971	..
1981	0.1
1991	0.7
2001	2.0
2005	2.7

Others

1971	32.5
1981	26.6
1991	26.6
2001	26.0
2005	29.5

Source: adapted from *Social Trends*, Office for National Statistics.

1. Holidays of four nights or more taken by British residents; percentages

Table 5 Visits to the most popular tourist attractions

Great Britain				Historic houses			Millions
	1981	1991	2006		1981	1991	2006
Museums and galleries				**Historic houses and monuments**			
British Museum	2.6	5.1	4.8				
National Gallery	2.7	4.3	4.6	Edinburgh Castle	0.8	1.0	1.2
Natural History Museum	3.7	1.6	3.8	Tower of London	2.1	1.9	2.1
Tate Gallery	0.9	1.8	4.6	Stonehenge	0.5	0.6	0.9
Theme parks				**Wildlife parks and zoos**			
Blackpool Pleasure Beach	7.5	6.5	5.7	London Zoo	1.1	1.1	0.9
Pleasure Beach, Great Yarmouth	..	2.5	1.4	Chester Zoo	..	0.9	1.2
				Knowsley Safari Park	..	0.3	0.5

Source: adapted from *Social Trends*, Office for National Statistics; *Visitor Attraction Trends England 2006*, VisitBritain.

Table 6 Holiday taking: by social grade

Great Britain			Percentages[1]
	Holidays in Britain	Holidays abroad	No holiday
AB	44	59	18
C1	37	47	31
C2	38	32	38
DE	28	20	57

1. Percentage of people in each social grade taking holidays in each location. Percentages do not sum to 100 because some people take holidays in Britain and abroad.

AB = higher/middle management, administration and professional; C1 = junior management, supervisory or clerical; C2 = skilled manual; DE = semi and unskilled, lowest paid or unemployed.

Source: adapted from *Social Trends*, Office for National Statistics.

Figure 6 Domestic holidays[1] taken by United Kingdom residents: by destination, 2005

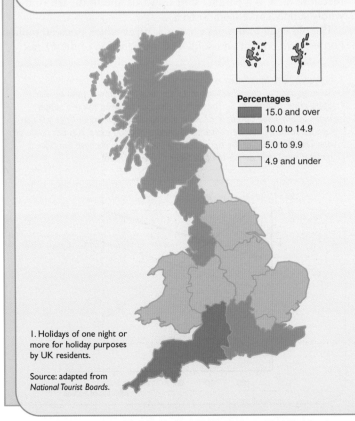

Percentages
- 15.0 and over
- 10.0 to 14.9
- 5.0 to 9.9
- 4.9 and under

1. Holidays of one night or more for holiday purposes by UK residents.

Source: adapted from *National Tourist Boards*.

1. Describe the main trends in tourism shown in the data.
2. 'A visit to Stonehenge could be classified as a normal good.' Explain what this means.
3. What evidence is there in the data that some tourist destinations and attractions are inferior goods?
4. Firms associated with tourism in the Great Yarmouth area are concerned that they are losing out in the expansion of tourism in the UK and abroad. (a) Suggest THREE reasons why a tourist might prefer to go to places such as Scotland, Cornwall, Spain or Florida rather than Great Yarmouth. (b) Discuss THREE strategies which stakeholders in the tourist industry in the Great Yarmouth area could adopt to make the income elasticity of demand more favourable to themselves.

Summary

1. Indirect taxes can be either ad valorem taxes or specific taxes.
2. The imposition of an indirect tax is likely to lead to a rise in the unit price of a good which is less than the unit value of the tax.
3. The incidence of indirect taxation is likely to fall on both consumer and producer.
4. The incidence of tax will fall wholly on the consumer if demand is perfectly inelastic or supply is perfectly elastic.
5. The incidence of tax will fall wholly on the producer if demand is perfectly elastic or supply is perfectly inelastic.

Indirect taxes and subsidies

An indirect tax is a tax on expenditure. The two major indirect taxes in the UK are VAT and excise duties.

VAT is an example of an AD VALOREM tax. The tax levied increases in proportion to the value of the tax base. In the case of VAT, the tax base is the price of the good. Most goods in the UK carry a 17.5 per cent VAT charge. Excise duties on the other hand are an example of a SPECIFIC or UNIT tax. The amount of tax levied does not change with the value of the goods but with the amount or volume of the goods purchased. So the excise duty on a bottle of wine is the same whether the bottle costs £5 or £500, but the VAT is 100 times more on the latter compared to the former. The main excise duties in the UK are on alcohol, tobacco and petrol. They should not be confused with customs duties which are levied on imports.

A SUBSIDY is a grant given by government to encourage the production or consumption of a particular good or service.

Subsidies, for instance, may be given on essential items such as housing or bread. Alternatively they may be given to firms that employ disadvantaged workers such as the long term unemployed or people with disabilities. Thay may also be given to firms manufacturing domestically produced goods to help them be more competitive than imported goods.

The incidence of tax

Price theory can be used to analyse the impact of the imposition of an indirect tax on a good. Assume that a specific tax of £1 per bottle is imposed upon wine. This has the effect of reducing supply. Sellers of wine will now want to charge £1 extra per bottle sold. In Figure 1, this is shown by a vertical shift of £1 in the supply curve at every level of output. However many bottles are produced, sellers will want to charge £1 more per bottle and therefore there is a parallel shift upwards and to the left of the whole supply curve from S_1 to S_2.

The old equilibrium price was £3.30, at which price 60 million bottles were bought and sold. The introduction of the £1 tax

Question 1

The price of a litre of unleaded petrol at the pumps is made up as follows:

	pence
Petrol cost before tax	28.6
Excise duty	53.7
	82.3
VAT @ 17.5%	14.4
Price at the pumps	96.7

Calculate the new price of petrol if:
(a) an increase in the cost of crude oil pushed up the cost of petrol before tax from 28.6p to 32.3p;
(b) the government increased excise duty from 53.7 to 58.2p;
(c) VAT was reduced from 17.5 per cent to 15 per cent;
(d) the government removed both excise duties and VAT on petrol and instead introduced a subsidy of 2p a litre.
(For each part, assume that the price at the pumps is initially 96.7p.)

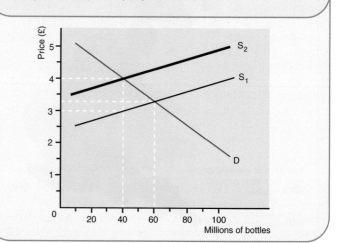

will raise price and reduce quantity demanded. The new equilibrium price is £4, at which price quantity demanded falls to 40 million bottles.

This result might seem surprising. The imposition of a £1 per bottle tax has only raised the price of a bottle by 70p and not the full £1 of the tax. This is because the INCIDENCE OF TAX is unlikely to fall totally on consumers. The incidence of tax measures the burden of tax upon the taxpayer. In this case the consumer has paid 70p of the tax. Therefore the other 30p which the government receives must have been paid by producers.

Question 2

Table 1

Price (£)	Quantity demanded	Quantity supplied
4	16	4
6	12	6
8	8	8
10	4	10
12	0	12

(a) Draw the demand and supply curves from the data in Table 1.
(b) What is the equilibrium quantity demanded and supplied?

The government now imposes a specific tax of £3 per unit.
(c) Show the effect of this on the diagram.
(d) What is the new equilibrium quantity demanded and supplied?
(e) What is the new equilibrium price?
(f) What is the incidence of tax per unit on (i) the consumer and (ii) the producer?
(g) What is (i) the tax per unit and (ii) total government revenue from the tax?
(h) By how much will the before tax revenue of producers change?

Tax revenues

Using Figure 1 we can also show the change in total expenditure before and after imposition of the tax as well as the amount of tax revenue gained by the government. The government will receive total tax revenue of £1 x 40 million (the tax per unit x the quantity sold); hence tax revenues will be £40 million. Consumers will pay 70p x 40 million of this, whilst producers will pay 30p x 40 million. Consumers will therefore pay £28 million of tax whilst producers will pay £12 million. Total spending on wine will fall from £198 million (£3.30 x 60 million) to £160 million (£4 x 40 million). Revenues received by producers will fall from £198 million (£3.30 x 60 million) to £120 million (£3 x 40 million).

Ad valorem taxes

The above analysis can be extended to deal with ad valorem taxes. The imposition of an ad valorem tax will lead to an upwards shift in the supply curve. However, the higher the price, the greater will be the amount of the tax. Hence the shift will

look as in Figure 2. Consumers will pay FG tax per unit whilst the incidence of tax on producers per unit will be HG.

Figure 2 The incidence of an ad valorem tax
The imposition of an ad valorem tax will push the supply curve upwards from S_1 to S_2. The following gives the key facts about the change:
(a) original equilibrium price and quantity, OG and OB;
(b) new equilibrium price and quantity, OF and OA;
(c) incidence of tax per unit on consumers, GF;
(d) incidence of tax per unit on producers, HG;
(e) tax per unit in equilibrium, HF;
(f) total tax paid by consumers, GKEF;
(g) total tax paid by producers, GHJK;
(h) total tax revenue of government, FHJE;
(i) change in producers' revenue, OBCG - OAJH;
(j) change in consumers' expenditure, OBCG - OAEF.

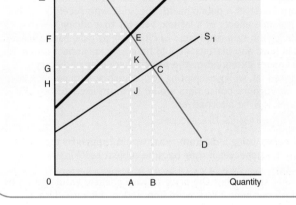

Figure 3 The effect of a subsidy on price
A subsidy of AC per unit will push the supply curve down from S_1 to S_2. The price to the consumer will fall by BC (i.e. less than the value of the subsidy per unit given).

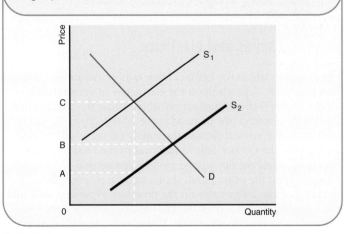

Subsidies

A subsidy on a good will lead to an increase in supply, shifting the supply curve downwards and to the right. This is shown in Figure 3. It should be noted that a subsidy of AC will not lead to a fall in price of AC. Part of the subsidy, AB, will be appropriated by producers because of the higher unit cost of production of higher levels of output (shown by the upward sloping supply curve). Prices to consumers will only fall by BC.

Question 3

The Prime Minister's Strategy Unit has suggested that taxing unhealthy foods might be part of a wider strategy to combat rising levels of obesity. In a paper, *Personal Responsibility and Changing Behaviour*, it says: 'There might even be potential to consider fiscal measures - a 'fatty food tax' - applied to food not people - or different VAT treatment for food with poor nutritional standards. This would be a signal to producers as well as consumers and serve more broadly as a signal to society that nutritional content in food is important.'

Currently, VAT is levied at the full rate of 17.5 per cent on many foods most associated with obesity, such as crisps, fizzy drinks and ice cream. But a burger bought in a supermarket, like most foods, has no VAT on it. In contrast, burgers sold in fast food restaurants carry 17.5 per cent VAT.

Tom Marshall, a public health specialist who recently studied the possible effects of a fat tax, believes that adding VAT to foods high in saturated fats - such as full-fat milk, hard cheeses, butter, buns and biscuits - could have a major impact on health. If VAT were extended to the principal sources of dietary saturated fat, while exempting goods such as orange juice and low-fat yoghurt, consumers would be more likely to buy the cheaper, low-fat alternatives.

Source: adapted from *The Times*, 19.2.2004.

(a) Explain, using a diagram, what would happen to the supply of hard cheeses if they became subject to VAT at 17.5 per cent.

(b) Analyse whether the price of hard cheeses would go up by 17.5 per cent if VAT were imposed at this rate. Use a diagram to illustrate your analysis.

(c) Why might the imposition of VAT on hard cheeses have an impact on the demand for orange juice?

(d) 'A positive impact on health of the imposition of VAT would be most likely if demand for fatty foods were price elastic.' Using a diagram, explain this statement.

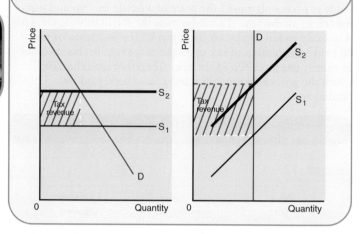

Figure 4 *Where the incidence of tax falls wholly on the consumer*
If supply is perfectly elastic or demand perfectly inelastic, then it can be seen from the graphs that the incidence of tax will fall wholly on consumers.

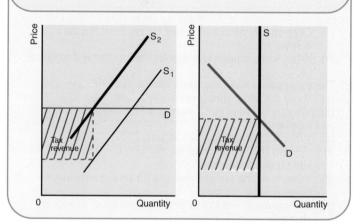

Figure 5 *Where the incidence of tax falls wholly on the producer*
If supply is perfectly inelastic or demand perfectly elastic, then it can be seen from the graphs that the incidence of tax will fall wholly on producers.

Taxes, subsidies and elasticity

The extent to which the tax incidence falls on consumers rather than producers depends upon the elasticities of demand and supply. Figure 4 shows a situation where either the supply curve is perfectly elastic or the demand curve is perfectly inelastic. In both cases, the vertical shift in the supply curve, which shows the value of the tax per unit, is identical to the final price rise. Therefore, all of the tax will be paid by consumers.

Figure 5, on the other hand, shows two cases where the incidence of tax falls totally on the producer. Producers will find it impossible to shift any of the tax onto consumers if the demand curve is perfectly elastic. Consumers are not prepared to buy at any higher price than the existing price. If the supply curve is perfectly inelastic, then the supply curve after imposition of the tax will be the same as the one before. Equilibrium price will therefore remain the same and producers will have to bear the full burden of the tax.

Generalising from these extreme situations, we can conclude that the more elastic the demand curve or the more inelastic the supply curve, the greater will be the incidence of tax on producers and the less will be the incidence of tax on consumers. So far as the government is concerned,

taxation revenue will be greater, all other things being equal, the more inelastic the demand for the product taxed. For instance, if demand were perfectly elastic, the imposition of an indirect tax would lead to quantity demanded falling to zero and tax revenue

Question 4

Table 2

	Price elasticity of demand
Food	- 0.52
Durables	- 0.89
Fuel and light	- 0.47
Services	- 1.02

Source: John Muellbauer, 'Testing the Barten Model of Household Composition Effects and the Cost of Children', *Economic Journal*.

The government wishes to raise VAT on selected goods, all these goods and services being zero-rated at present. Which categories of goods does the data suggest would yield (a) the most and (b) the least revenues? (Assume that at present the average price and the quantity demanded of goods in each category is identical.) Explain your reasoning carefully.

being zero. At the opposite extreme, if demand were perfectly inelastic, consumers would buy the same quantity after imposition of the tax as before. Hence revenue will be equal to the tax per unit times the quantity demanded before imposition. If the price elasticity of demand lies between these two extremes, the imposition of a tax will lead to a fall in quantity demanded. The higher the elasticity, the larger will be the fall in quantity demanded and hence the lower will be the tax revenue received by government. Hence, it is no coincidence that in the UK excise duties are placed on alcohol, tobacco and petrol, all of which are relatively price inelastic.

The same analysis can be applied to subsidies. In general, subsidies tend to be given where the policy objective is to reduce the price of the good. The largest fall in price will occur when either demand is highly inelastic or supply is highly elastic. If demand is very elastic or supply very inelastic, there will be very little, if any change, in price following the granting of a subsidy.

This is because producers will not pass on the subsidy to consumers. They will absorb the subsidy, which will allow them to increase their profits.

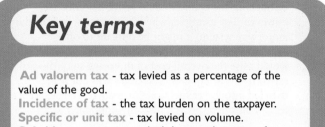

Key terms

Ad valorem tax - tax levied as a percentage of the value of the good.
Incidence of tax - the tax burden on the taxpayer.
Specific or unit tax - tax levied on volume.
Subsidy - a grant given which lowers the price of a good, usually designed to encourage production or consumption of a good.

Applied economics

Taxes, subsidies, congestion and the environment

The demand for transport keeps growing as Figure 6 shows. However, this growing demand is concentrated on motor transport. Other modes of transport, such as bus and rail, are today relatively insignificant. The increase in demand for motor transport poses two problems. One is that it is causing ever increasing congestion on the roads. The other is that it is causing a variety of environmental problems. The government, through taxes and subsidies, can tackle both problems but, as with so many complex economic issues, there are no easy and painless solutions.

Road congestion

Britain's roads are becoming ever more congested. In 1950, there were fewer than 2 million cars. Today, there are over 27 million. The Department for Transport projects that this will rise to 30 million by 2015 and 40 million by 2025. The demand for road space is therefore growing over time. The supply of road space in terms of the number of kilometres of road or the number of lanes on roads is hardly changing. Hence, key roads regularly become congested at certain times of day or certain days of the week. Figure 7 shows how average traffic speeds in London have declined over time as a result of this increasing congestion.

The overall cost of motoring is one factor which limits the demand for road space. The fixed costs of owning a car, in terms of purchase, insurance, licensing and servicing, deter those on lower incomes from owning a car. However, the decision for a car owner about whether to use a particular road is determined by the cost of fuel, the variable cost of motoring.

Raising taxes on motoring, such as raising taxes on petrol and diesel prices, is one way in which the government can price motorists off the road. However,

this is a very crude way of doing this because it gives no incentive for motorists to switch their journey times to when roads are less congested. It also hits motorists, particularly in rural areas, who rarely face any congestion.

Reducing congestion through raising taxes on fuel is also likely to be politically impossible. In 2000, the country was brought to a halt by a relatively small group of protesters from the farming and road haulage lobby who wanted the government to reduce the price of petrol through cutting taxes. Because the demand for motoring is relatively inelastic, there would have to be very large rises in tax on fuel to have an impact on congestion. Petrol would have to be, say, £5 a litre compared to £1 today, to force enough cars off the road at peak times to reduce congestion. Such prices would hit all motorists, not just those whose journeys create congestion in the first place.

Economists therefore favour taxing congestion directly. A start has already been made with the London Congestion Charge, where motorists have to pay £8 a day to enter central London. This has been highly effective at reducing congestion in central London and raising journey speeds. More broadly, the government has plans to introduce congestion charging across the whole country, currently by 2014. The hope is that all vehicles can be tracked via satellite and be charged when they travel in any zone where there is congestion. It might be politically acceptable to introduce such a charge if the revenues raised were used to reduce the tax on fuel. However, the technology is still unproven. It would also have to give significant benefits to motorists in terms of shorter journey times in congested areas.

In central London, the introduction of the Congestion Charge was accompanied by higher spending on, and subsidies for, public transport. In particular, bus services were expanded to offer an alternative to those who no longer wanted to bring their cars into Central London. Using part of the revenues from congestion charging throughout the country could prove less effective, however. For example, where cars were priced off the motorway system, it might be difficult to offer satisfactory public transport alternatives. Equally, it would raise the overall cost of motoring since the cash raised from the congestion charges was not being recycled into lower fuel taxes or reduced vehicle licence fees. This might prove politically unpopular.

The environment

Motor vehicles are environmentally damaging. Roads eat into the countryside. Scarce natural resources are used up in the making and running of vehicles. There is noise pollution in the vicinity of roads. Engines run on carbon fuels and emit greenhouse gasses which contribute to global warming. Diesel engines emit particulates which can cause cancer.

One solution to reducing the damage done to the environment is simply to reduce the number and length of journeys made. Raising taxes on fuel would therefore be a good way of achieving this. In its April 1993 Budget, the government committed itself to such a rise in taxes on petrol by 3 per cent per year in real terms for the foreseeable future, a figure which it increased to 5 per cent in its December 1993 Budget. It justified this by pointing out that petrol was cheaper in real terms in 1993 than it had been in the early 1980s. It was this policy which fuel protesters succeeded in getting the government to abandon in 2000. The vast majority of motorists put lower taxes on fuel ahead of any environmental concerns.

Another solution to at least some of the environmental problems associated with motoring is to modify vehicles themselves. Vehicles are slowly becoming more fuel efficient. Diesel engines emit fewer greenhouse gases than petrol cars. If everyone drove around in diesel powered minis, there would be considerable environmental gains. Figure 8 shows that over the period 1976 to 2006, there were some modest gains in efficiency. Distance travelled by all types of road vehicle increased 108 per cent whilst fuel consumption only increased by 70 per cent. The data also suggest that efficiency gains are increasing over time. Between 1997 and 2003, for example, distance travelled increased by 12 per cent but fuel consumption only increased by 3 per cent.

However, making incremental improvements in the efficiency of oil driven engines is unlikely to prevent the motor car from causing more damage to the environment in the future. This is because the number of motor cars worldwide will increase 5, 10 or 20 fold over the next few decades as developing economies such as China and India develop to the point where most households can afford at least one car. The only solution to this is to change the engine which powers the motor car. Electric cars driven by batteries or engines fuelled by hydrogen

have been developed but both have so many drawbacks today that they are not being widely adopted. However, in 10 or 20 years' time, circumstances may have changed and the petrol driven car with its damaging effects on the environment may have largely disappeared. It could be that the market mechanism will bring about this change. More likely, governments will intervene and through a combination of policies such as government regulations, taxes and subsidies, we will see fewer environmentally damaging vehicles on the roads.

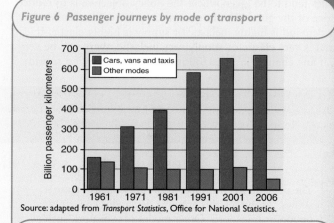

Figure 6 Passenger journeys by mode of transport

Source: adapted from *Transport Statistics*, Office for National Statistics.

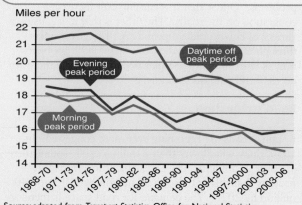

Figure 7 Average traffic speeds in London, 1968-2006

Source: adapted from *Transport Statistics*, Office for National Statistics.

Figure 8 Distance travelled and fuel consumption: all transport UK

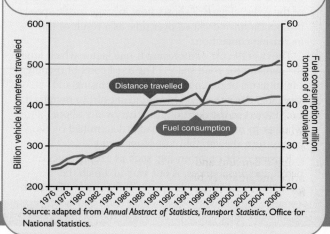

Source: adapted from *Annual Abstract of Statistics, Transport Statistics*, Office for National Statistics.

DataQuestion

SUVs

SUVs

SUVs, sports utility vehicles, are sometimes also called 'off-roaders'. They differ from ordinary cars in that they are taller, placing the driver in a higher position than other car drivers. They have 4x4 transmissions, meaning that power is directly taken to all four wheels rather than just two wheels on an ordinary car. This gives them much better grip for travelling across rough terrain such as fields or dirt tracks - hence the name 'off-roader'. They are designed to give the handling of a traditional work vehicle or utility vehicle like a farm Land Rover with the comfort of a modern car. According to a survey by YouGov, almost two thirds of the population want special taxes on sports utility vehicles. Londoners were even more strongly in favour of restrictions on 4x4s. Ken Livingstone, mayor of London, has described SUV drivers as 'complete idiots'.

Source: adapted from the *Financial Times*, 2.9.2004.

Demand for and supply of SUVs

Demand for SUVs has seen strong growth. In the past 10 years, sales have doubled with 76 000 sold in 2006 alone. They now account for 7.5 per cent of all new cars sold in the UK. Motor manufacturers have responded by developing new SUV models and all the major sellers in the UK market now have an SUV on offer. There is an added incentive for motor manufacturers in that the profit margins on SUVs are higher than on the average car. Customers seem to be less price sensitive, viewing their SUVs as luxuries for which they are prepared to pay extra.

Table 3 SUV price ranges, new, September 2007

Nissan X-trail	£17 637 - £22 999
Toyota Rav 4	£16 995 - £24 881
Mitsubishi Shogun	£21 716 - £33 269
Land Rover Discovery	£24 566 - £40 374
Suzuki Grand Vitara	£10 394 - £14 381

Source: adapted from www.smmt.co.uk, January 2007, www.broadspeed.com.

The Chelsea tractor

SUVs are sometimes known as 'Chelsea tractors'. They are used by the well heeled of one of the richest boroughs in London to do such exciting things as go to the local supermarket or pick up the children from school. They certainly would never be let out into the open countryside - that is just the fantasy which helps sell the car.

So what is the attraction for buyers? Women say they feel safer driving an SUV because they are higher up and so get better vision. They are also a tremendous status symbol. They are a very large and prominent display of wealth and social standing. Not merely can you afford to buy it, but you can also afford the high running costs of the vehicle. A YouGov Survey found that a fifth of SUV owners bought them for 'pose value'. However, in the same survey, half of the respondents who didn't own an SUV believed that 'pose value' was the main reason for owners buying them.

Source: adapted from the *Financial Times*, 2.9.2004.

Vehicle Excise Duty

The Prime Minister has been re-examining the case for penalising drivers of gas-guzzling cars. He is investigating whether to raise the highest rate of Vehicle Excise Duty on the most polluting vehicles, which would include many SUVs. Vehicle Excise Duty is a specific, flat rate, tax on the purchase of every new car.

Source: adapted from the *Financial Times*, 17.3.2007.

Fuel consumption

SUVs tend to have very poor fuel consumption. Some petrol versions do as little as 13.4 miles to the gallon in a city and 25mpg on a motorway. The environmental lobby argues that few drivers of off-roaders ever need the 4x4 capability, but the extra weight of the complex system makes the vehicles less fuel-efficient. 'It is bound to be less efficient because it has the aerodynamics of a brick and the extra weight of a four-wheel-drive drivetrain' said John Wormaid, partner at Autopolis, the consultants.

Source: adapted from the *Financial Times*, 2.9.2004.

1. Outline TWO reasons why the government might want to raise the level of Vehicle Excise Duty on SUVs. (Vehicle Excise Duty is a specific tax on the purchase of new cars.)

2. Using a demand and supply diagram, explain how the price and quantity bought of SUVs might be affected by an increase in Vehicle Excise Duty.

3. Discuss just how high the tax would need to be to bring about a significant reduction in purchases of SUVs by those who would never use their vehicles off-road.

Summary

1. The market is a mechanism for the allocation of resources.
2. In a free market, consumers, producers and owners of the factors of production interact, each seeking to maximise their returns.
3. Prices have three main functions in allocating resources. These are the rationing, signalling and incentive functions.
4. If firms cannot make enough profit from the production of a good, the resources they use will be reallocated to more profitable uses.

The role of the market

Adam Smith, in his book *An Enquiry into the Nature and Causes of the Wealth of Nations*, attacked the economic system of his day. It was a system founded upon protectionism, economic restrictions and numerous legal barriers. He presented a powerful case for a free market system in which the 'invisible hand' of the market would allocate resources to everyone's advantage. There are three main types of actor or agent in the market system. Consumers and producers interact in the **goods markets** of the economy. Producers and the owners of the factors of production (land, labour and capital) interact in the **factor markets** of the economy.

The main actors in the market

The consumer In a pure free market system it is the consumer who is all powerful. Consumers are free to spend their money however they want and the market offers a wide choice of products. It is assumed that consumers will allocate their scarce resources so as to maximise their welfare, satisfaction or utility.

The firm In a pure free market, firms are servants of the consumer. They are motivated by making as high a profit as possible. This means maximising the difference between revenues and costs.

- **Revenues**. If they fail to produce goods which consumers wish to buy, they won't be able to sell them. Consumers will buy from companies which produce the goods they want. Successful companies will have high revenues; unsuccessful ones will have low or zero revenues.
- **Costs**. If firms fail to minimise costs, then they will fail to make a profit. Other more efficient firms will be able to take their market away from them by selling at a lower price.

The price of failure - making insufficient profit to retain resources and prevent factor owners from allocating their resources in more profitable ways - will be the exit of the firm from its industry. On the other hand, in the long run firms cannot make higher than average levels of profit. If they did, new competitors would enter the industry attracted by the high profits, driving down prices and profits and increasing output.

Owners of the factors of production Owners of land, labour and capital - rentiers, workers and capitalists - are motivated by the desire to maximise their returns. Landowners wish to rent their land at the highest possible price.

Workers wish to hire themselves out at the highest possible wage, all other things being equal. Capitalists wish to receive the highest rate of return on capital. These owners will search in the market place for the highest possible reward and only when they have found it will they offer their factor for employment. Firms, on the other hand, will be seeking to minimise cost. They will only be prepared to pay the owner the value of the factor in the production process.

Question 1

'In a free market, consumers have no choice about what they can buy. Firms simply impose their wishes on the consumer.' Use the photograph to explain why this is incorrect.

The function of prices in the market

In a market, there are buyers who demand goods and sellers who supply goods. The interactions of demand and supply fix the price at which exchange takes place. Price has three important functions in a market.

Rationing Consumer wants are infinite, but we live in a world of scarce resources. Somehow, those scarce resources need to be allocated between competing uses. One function of price in a market is to allocate and ration those resources. If many consumers demand a good, but its supply is relatively scarce, then prices will be high. Limited supply will be rationed to those buyers prepared to pay a high enough price. If demand is relatively low, but supply is very high, then prices will be low. The low price ensures that high numbers of goods will be bought, reflecting the lack of scarcity of the good.

Signalling The price of a good is a key piece of information to both buyers and sellers in the market. Prices come about because of the transactions of buyers and sellers. They reflect market conditions and therefore act as a signal to those in the market. Decisions about buying and selling are based on those signals.

Incentive Prices act as an incentive for buyers and sellers. Low prices encourage buyers to purchase more goods. For consumers, this is because the amount of satisfaction or utility gained per pound spent increases relative to other goods. Higher prices discourage buying because consumers get fewer goods per pound spent. On the supply side, higher prices encourage suppliers to sell more to the market. Firms may have to take on more workers and invest in new capital equipment to achieve this. Low prices discourage production. A prolonged fall in prices may drive some firms out of the market because it is no longer profitable for them to supply.

To illustrate how these functions help allocate resources, consider two examples.

Example 1 Assume that lobbying from animal welfare groups changes consumers' tastes. In the market for fur coats, fewer fur coats will be purchased. In the short run, companies are likely to cut prices to boost demand. The fall in price is a signal that market conditions have changed. It also acts as a disincentive to production. At the new low prices, profits fall. So in the long term, some firms will leave the industry, reducing supply. When the price is in long run equilibrium, it will ration supply amongst those customers prepared to pay the new price. Factors markets too will be affected. The demand by firms in the fur industry for workers, equipment and animals will fall. So wages of fur workers may fall. This fall in wages, the price of labour, acts as a signal to workers. The incentive to work in the industry will have fallen so fewer workers will want jobs in the fur trade. Some workers will now leave the industry and get jobs elsewhere in the economy. This is the operation of the rationing function. Meanwhile, consumers will have increased their spending on other goods, for instance on imitation furs. In the short term, the price of imitation furs may rise. This acts as a signal and an incentive for existing firms to expand output and new firms to enter the market. With increased supply, there will be an increase in resources used in the production of imitation furs, an example of the rationing function of prices.

Question 2

Pioneer, the Japanese electronics manufacturer, is to close about one-quarter of its global manufacturing facilities. It will consolidate its 40 manufacturing facilities into 30 and reduce its workforce by 5 per cent, or 2 000 jobs, mostly outside Japan.

The move is in response to sharp falls in price in its main markets for plasma display panels (one type of flat screen television) and DVD recorders. Pioneer forecasts demand for plasma display panels to grow from 2.4 million in the year to the end of March 2005 to 11 million by March 2009. However, prices have recently fallen by 40 per cent. This has been due to an aggressive expansion of supply by manufacturers worldwide who have acted on predictions that flat screen televisions will replace traditional television sets. But the falls in price have led most flat screen television manufacturers to make losses on every set they now produce. Like Pioneer, they have a choice: they either have to cut their costs of manufacturing to be able to make a profit on each set sold, or they must leave the market.

Source: adapted from the *Financial Times*, 24.3.2005.

Explain how prices for flat screen televisions have:
(a) acted as signals to the market;
(b) provided incentives to consumers and firms to allocate their resources.

Example 2 There is a large increase in the number of young workers in the population. This increased supply of young workers will force their wages, the price of labour, down. The wage fall acts as a signal to firms that labour is now cheaper. It also acts as an incentive to employ more young workers because they are cheaper. Thus, the allocation of resources changes. Lower wage costs should reduce the costs of firms, which in turn may be passed on to the consumer in the form of lower prices. These lower prices will act as a signal to consumers and provide an incentive for them to increase purchases of goods, again altering the allocation of resources.

Question 3

Samsung Electronics, the South Korean manufacturer, has come from nowhere to become a global force in products such as memory chips, flat panel displays and mobile phones. Last week, the company held an unusual news conference dedicated to its new MP3 players, declaring it would increase its share of the mini hard disk-drive music player market from just 7.7 per cent now to become the world's top producer, unseating Apple which controls 70 per cent, by 2007.

Apple's iPod has proved an unexpected and spectacular success. Easy to use and with a 'cool', 'must have' image amongst its young buyers, it has transformed the fortunes of Apple. The company quadrupled its first quarter profits this year compared to last year's figures on the back of sales of the iPod.

Samsung hopes young people will be lured to its multi-functional MP3 players with a built-in voice recorder, camera and radio tuners, which will allow users to play electronic games, watch music videos and movies and take digital photographs. Technologically, the company has a strong advantage over Apple because it is the world's largest producer of flash memory chips, a key component of MP3 players. Samsung's global brand power and sales network are also expected to help it increase market share in the US. This year, the company plans to spend $40 million on marketing for its MP3 players.

Analysts warn, though, that Samsung's strategy may not work, as many consumers still prefer simple products with user-friendly interfaces, which is the strength of iPod. 'Cool' is also very difficult to capture in a copycat product. Yet it is the 'cool' factor which allows products such as Nike shoes and BMW cars to be sold at higher prices than competing products and generates large profits for their owners.

Source: adapted from the *Financial Times*, 30.3.2005.

Explain, using Samsung as an example, the role of profit in allocating resources.

Maximising behaviour

In the market mechanism, everyone is assumed to be motivated by self interest. Consumers are motivated by the desire to maximise their welfare or utility. Producers wish to maximise profits. Workers, rentiers and capitalists seek to maximise the returns from the factor that they own. This maximising behaviour determines the way in which resources are allocated.

Consumers, for instance, will spend to maximise their satisfaction or utility. They cast spending 'votes' between different products and different firms. If consumer tastes change so that they want more ice cream and fewer hot dogs, then they will spend more on ice cream and less on hot dogs. Ice cream manufacturers will collect more money from the sale of ice cream which they will use to expand production. Manufacturers of hot dogs will be forced to lay off staff, buy fewer raw materials and in the long term shut factories.

Profit and not revenue is the signal to firms to change levels of production. When consumers demand more ice cream, firms will expand production only if it is profitable to do so. Hot dog manufacturers will shut down manufacturing plant only if these resources could be used at higher profit levels elsewhere. In a free market, changes in consumer demand are met by changes in patterns of production by firms because of their desire to maximise profit.

Judging the market

Markets are one way of allocating resources. There are alternatives. For instance, the government could allocate resources as it does with defence, education or the police. Economists are interested in knowing how to judge whether markets are the best way of allocating resources. There are two main ways in which they do this.

First, they consider whether markets are **efficient** ways of allocating resources. By this, we mean whether firms produce at lowest cost and are responsive to the needs of consumers as in the ice cream and hot dog example above. Second, they consider issues of **equity**. Efficiency takes income distribution for granted. However, is income and wealth in society distributed in an acceptable way?

If resources are allocated inefficiently and inequitably, then there may be a case for governments to intervene, either by altering conditions in the market or by removing production from the market mechanism altogether. The next few units consider these complex issues.

Applied economics

Motor cars

The history of the UK motor car industry in recent decades is a good example of how markets allocate resources. In the 1950s and 1960s, the British market was insulated to a great extent from foreign competition. The British motorist bought cars made in British factories, even if some of these factories were owned by foreign companies such as Ford. It was largely a sellers' market, with demand constrained by the ability of consumers to obtain credit for the purchase of cars.

However, the car industry suffered two major weaknesses at the time. First, it failed to address problems of quality. In a sellers' market, firms had little incentive to manufacture world beating cars. Second, there was underinvestment by the industry. This was perhaps not surprising given the poor profitability of some companies. For instance, the original Mini car, first produced in 1959, failed to make a profit in its first five years of production because its price was set too low. Poor profitability led to resources being reallocated in the market. There was widespread rationalisation. Companies were taken over and car plants closed. However, the necessary investment in new production processes and facilities lagged behind the UK's main overseas competitors.

These weaknesses hit the British motor industry hard

in the 1970s and 1980s. As Figure 2 shows, imports soared, whilst exports declined. Domestic production fell from a peak of 1.9 million cars per year in 1972 to 0.9 million by 1984. What happened was that UK consumers increasingly wanted to buy foreign cars because they were better built, more reliable and, in the case of Japanese cars, more keenly priced. Lower prices for Japanese cars signalled to the market that resources should be reallocated. Foreign customers turned away from British cars too, reducing exports to a third of their 1960s levels. As British car manufacturers made losses, they responded to this market signal by closing factories, laying off workers and reducing orders for components. The reduction in demand for British made cars resulted in a fall in demand for the factors of production used to manufacture those cars.

The mid-1980s was a turning point for British motor manufacturing. Arguably the most important factor in forcing change was the arrival of Japanese manufacturers in the UK. Honda established a working partnership with the then UK owned Rover and also built an engine plant in Swindon. Nissan built a new car plant in the North East of England, followed by Toyota which set up in Derby.

This extra competition in the market forced US and

European car manufacturers in the UK market to change the way in which they designed and built cars. They adopted Japanese production methods such as just-in-time deliveries of components to factories. Workers were given far greater skills. New investment and new models were given to car plants which could show that they had high levels of productivity. British factories in particular were given a choice. Either they adopted new ways of working or they would be starved of investment and eventually closed. If British factories could not be profitable and supply the right goods, the market would force them to shut down.

Market forces also played a part in the decision by the Japanese to come to the UK. In the first half of the 1980s, the government of Margaret Thatcher pursued **supply side policies** which attracted foreign investment. Trade union power was curbed. Taxes on company profits were cut. Higher rates of tax paid by company executives were slashed. Finally, taxes paid by employers on their workers fell. The poor performance of the UK economy in the 1960s and 1970s relative to other European countries also meant that wages in the UK were now often lower than in Germany or France. Low taxes and low wages acted as powerful incentives for the Japanese and other foreign countries to set up in the UK.

In the 1990s, as Figures 1 and 2 show, the UK car industry made a substantial recovery. Domestic production increased from 1.3 million cars in 1990 to 1.8 million cars in 1999, an increase of nearly 40 per cent. Over the same period, exports rose 73 per cent whilst imports only rose 49 per cent. The market was signalling that UK car plants could be as competitive as, if not more competitive than, foreign car plants. The market was also providing an incentive for car manufacturing firms to invest in their UK car plants because they could be as profitable as, if not more profitable than, car plants abroad.

The highly competitive nature of the car industry if anything intensified in the 2000s. For example, countries in Eastern Europe which joined the EU in 2004, with their low wage labour force and low taxes, saw significant investment by multinationals. As a result, a boom in car sales in the UK, rising from 2.3 million cars a year in 2000 to 2.6 million cars a year in 2004, was supplied entirely by imports rather than an increase in domestic production. Another example of the fierce nature of competition in the market was the collapse in 2004 of Rover, the UK's only remaining UK-owned mass car manufacturer.

Despite this competition, the long term future of the UK car industry looks secure. UK car plants, for the most part, are competitive. Nissan's car plant in Sunderland has the highest labour productivity in Europe and is also Nissan's most productive plant worldwide. This shows that British car plants can be world class units if managed effectively and if their owners continue to invest in them.

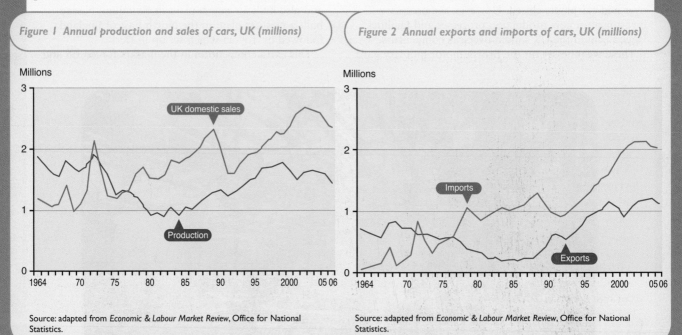

Figure 1 *Annual production and sales of cars, UK (millions)*

Millions

UK domestic sales

Production

Source: adapted from *Economic & Labour Market Review*, Office for National Statistics.

Figure 2 *Annual exports and imports of cars, UK (millions)*

Millions

Imports

Exports

Source: adapted from *Economic & Labour Market Review*, Office for National Statistics.

DataQuestion

Biofuels

Figure 3 Index of oil and biofuel prices (January 2006 = 100)

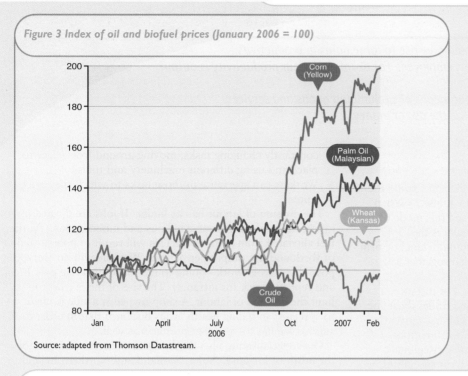

Source: adapted from Thomson Datastream.

European Union energy ministers this week agreed to set a legal requirement that, by 2020, 10 per cent of petrol and diesel used in vehicles will have to come from biofuels. Biofuels are fuels made from renewable biological materials such as corn, sugar cane, wheat and palm oil. Already, most petrol sold in the UK contains around 2 per cent ethanol made from Brazilian sugar cane. The UK government has itself said that petrol and diesel sold at the pump must contain 5 per cent biofuel by 2010.

Source: adapted from the *Financial Times*, 23.2.2007.

High prices are being felt around the world.

- Growing US demand for crop-based ethanol has pushed prices of yellow corn to a 10-year high. This in turn has lifted prices of white corn used to make tortilla flat bread, a staple food in Mexico. There have been protests on the street in Mexico about rising corn and tortilla prices.
- Farmland from Iowa to Argentina is rising faster in price than apartments in Manhattan and London for the first time in 30 years. Demand for corn used in ethanol increased the value of farm land 16 per cent in Indiana and 35 per cent in Idaho in 2006.
- US farmers plan to plant 8.4 million or 11 per cent less acres of soyabeans in 2007 compared to 2006 whilst the acreage devoted to corn will rise by 12.1 million acres or 7 per cent compared to 2006. The amount of land given over to cotton production will also fall as farmers switch to corn production. The US Department of Agriculture estimates that US demand for ethanol made from corn in 2007 will be 15 per cent more than in 2006.
- The Spanish engineering company Abengoa has

threatened to half production at its biggest bioethanol plant. The facility uses wheat, and wheat prices have risen 50 per cent this year, making production unprofitable.

Source: adapted from the *Financial Times*, 23.2.2007, 4.4.2007 and 29.6.2007.

1. Compare the changes in the price of the commodities shown in Figure 3.
2. Explain how the rationing, signalling and incentive functions are acting to allocate resources in the markets for different biofuels and related markets.
3. 'Governments forcing oil companies to include biofuels in their products will lead to much higher food prices for all and starvation for some.' Discuss whether the EU should have a 10 per cent biofuels target by 2020.

Summary

1. Specialisation and the division of labour give rise to large gains in productivity.
2. Productivity is output per unit of input employed. For example, labour productivity is output per worker.
3. Specialisation necessitates an efficient means of exchanging goods and services.
4. The most efficient means of exchange is the use of money.

Specialisation

When he was alone on his desert island, Robinson Crusoe found that he had to perform all economic tasks by himself. When Man Friday came along he quickly abandoned this mode of production and specialised. SPECIALISATION is the production of a limited range of goods by an individual or firm or country in co-operation with others so that together a complete range of goods is produced.

Specialisation can occur between nations. For instance, a country like Honduras produces bananas and trades those for cars produced in the United States. **Globalisation** is currently intensifying this process of specialisation between nations. Specialisation can also occur within economies. Regional economies specialise. In the UK, Stoke-on-Trent specialises in pottery whilst London specialises in financial services.

Specialisation by individuals is called THE DIVISION OF LABOUR. Adam Smith, in a passage in his famous book *An Enquiry into the Nature and Causes of the Wealth of Nations* (1776), described the division of labour amongst pin workers. He wrote:

A workman not educated to this business ... could scarce ... make one pin in a day, and certainly could not make twenty. But in the way in which this business is now carried on, ... it is divided into a number of branches ... One man draws out the wire, another straightens it, a third cuts it, a fourth points, a fifth grinds it at the top for receiving the head; to make the head requires two or three distinct operations; to put it on is a peculiar business, to whiten the pins is another; it is even a trade by itself to put them into the paper.

He pointed out that one worker might be able to make 20 pins a day if he were to complete all the processes himself. But ten workers together specialising in a variety of tasks could, he estimated, make 48 000 pins.

This enormous increase in PRODUCTIVITY (output per unit of input employed) arises from both increases in LABOUR PRODUCTIVITY (output per worker) and CAPITAL PRODUCTIVITY (output per unit of capital employed).

- Specialisation enables workers to gain skills in a narrow range of tasks. These skills enable individual workers to be far more productive than if they were jacks-of-all-trades. In a modern economy a person could not possibly hope to be able to take on every job which society requires.
- The division of labour makes it cost-effective to provide workers with specialist tools. For instance, it would not be profitable to provide every farm worker with a tractor. But it is possible to provide a group of workers with a tractor which they can then share.
  - Time is saved because a worker is not

constantly changing tasks, moving around from place to place and using different machinery and tools.
- Workers can specialise in those tasks to which they are best suited.

The division of labour has its limits. If jobs are divided up too much, the work can become tedious and monotonous. Workers feel alienated from their work. This will result in poorer quality of work and less output per person. Workers will do everything possible to avoid work - going to the toilet, lingering over breaks and reporting sick for instance. The size of the market too will limit the division of labour. A shop owner in a village might want to specialise in selling health foods but finds that in order to survive she has to sell other products as well.

Over-specialisation also has its disadvantages. For example, the north of England, Wales, Scotland and Northern Ireland suffered high unemployment in the 1960s, 1970s and 1980s as their traditional heavy industry, such as coal mining and shipbuilding, declined and was not replaced by enough new service sector jobs. Another problem with specialisation is that a breakdown in part of the chain of production can cause chaos within the system. Eighteen Toyota production plants in Japan were brought to a halt for two weeks in 1997 when the factory of the sole supplier of brake parts to Toyota in Japan was destroyed in a fire. Toyota had to work round the clock with new suppliers to get production going again. Equally, London businesses can be crippled by an Underground strike or a bus strike.

Money and exchange

Specialisation has enabled people to enjoy a standard of living

Question I

(a) Explain, with the help of the photograph, what is meant by 'specialisation'.
(b) What might be some of the (i) advantages to firms and (ii) disadvantages to workers of the division of labour shown in the photograph?

which would be impossible to achieve through self-sufficiency. Specialisation, however, necessitates exchange. Workers can only specialise in refuse collecting, for instance, if they know that they will be able to exchange their services for other goods and services such as food, housing and transport.

Exchange for most of history has meant **barter** - swapping one good for another. However, barter has many disadvantages and it would be impossible to run a modern sophisticated economy using barter as a means or **medium of exchange**. It was the development of **money** that enabled trade and specialisation to transform economies into what we know today. Money is anything which is widely accepted as payment for goods received, services performed, or repayment of past debt. In a modern economy, it ranges from notes and coins to money in bank accounts and deposits in building society accounts.

Key terms

Capital productivity - output per unit of capital employed.
Division of labour - specialisation by workers.
Labour productivity - output per worker.
Productivity - output per unit of input employed.
Specialisation - a system of organisation where economic units such as households or nations are not self-sufficient but concentrate on producing certain goods and services and trading the surplus with others.

Applied economics

The Boeing 787

The new Boeing 787 fuel-saving medium sized passenger jet was launched today. For Boeing, it represents a new way of working. Its previous aircraft have been mainly made in-house. The 787 is being mainly manufactured by 40 partner companies round the world. For example, the wings are being build in Japan, the composite fuselage in Italy and the US, and the landing gear in France. Only the tail fin and final assembly, accounting by about 10 per cent by value of the plane, are being done by Boeing itself.

The company is doing what Adam Smith admired in *The Wealth of Nations*, profiting from specialisation and the division of labour. It is tapping into the expertise of companies round the world. They can provide better products at cheaper prices than if Boeing had developed

and manufactured the aircraft in the traditional way. Because of specialisation, the time taken to design the aircraft has been reduced, an important competitive advantage against Boeing's rival, Airbus.

Not everyone has been a winner. The number of workers employed in Boeing's US factories would have been greater if the 787 had been produced in-house. Like so many US manufacturing jobs, the forces of globalisation have relocated those jobs elsewhere round the world. But it has helped create other jobs at Boeing particularly in the service area. With £50 billion of orders for the new plane, it has helped secure the future of Boeing.

Source: adapted from the *Financial Times*, 9.7.2007.

DataQuestion — JVC

JVC is a major Japanese electronics company. It has plants across the world including Japan and the UK, which manufacture a wide range of electronics goods such as televisions and digital camera .

1. Explain, using JVC televisions as an example, what is meant by (a) specialisation; (b) the division of labour; (c) exchange.
2. Evaluate why a company like JVC can specialise only because money exists as an efficient medium of exchange. In your answer, compare money with a less efficient medium of exchange like barter.

15 Economic efficiency and market failure

Summary

1. Static efficiency refers to efficiency at a point in time. Dynamic efficiency concerns how resources are allocated over time so as to promote technical progress and economic growth.
2. Productive efficiency exists when production is achieved at lowest cost.
3. All points on an economy's production possibility frontier are productively efficient.
4. Free markets tend to lead to efficiency.
5. Market failure occurs when markets do not function efficiently. Sources of market failure include lack of competition in a market, externalities, missing markets, information failure, factor immobility and inequality.

Efficiency

The market mechanism allocates resources, but how well does it do this? One way of judging this is to consider how **efficiently** it resolves the three fundamental questions in economics of how, what and for whom production should take place. Efficiency is concerned with how well resources, such as time, talents or materials, are used to produce an end result. In economic terms, it is concerned with the relationship between scarce inputs and outputs. There are a number of different forms of efficiency which need to be considered.

Static vs dynamic efficiency

STATIC EFFICIENCY exists at a point in time. An example of static efficiency would be whether a firm could produce 1 million cars a year more cheaply by using more labour and less capital. Another example would be whether a country could produce more if it cut its unemployment rate. Productive efficiency and other types of efficiency (discussed below) are static concepts of efficiency. Economists use them to discuss whether more could be produced now if resources were allocated in a different way. These concepts can be used, for instance, to discuss whether industries dominated by a monopoly producer might produce at lower cost if competition were introduced into the industry or whether a firm should be allowed to pollute the environment.

DYNAMIC EFFICIENCY is concerned with how resources are allocated **over a period of time**. For instance, would there be greater efficiency if a firm distributed less profit over time to its shareholders and used the money to finance more investment? Would there be greater efficiency in the economy if more resources were devoted to investment rather than consumption over time? Would an industry invest more and create more new products over time if it were a monopoly than if there were perfect competition?

Productive efficiency

PRODUCTIVE EFFICIENCY exists when production is achieved at lowest cost. There is productive inefficiency when the cost of production is above the minimum possible given the state of knowledge. For instance, a firm which produces 1 million units at a cost of £10 000 would be productively inefficient if it could have produced that output at a cost of £8 000.

Productive efficiency will only exist if there is TECHNICAL EFFICIENCY. Technical efficiency exists if a given quantity of output is produced with the minimum number of inputs (or alternatively, if the maximum output is produced with a given number of units). For instance, if a firm produces 1 000 units of output using 10 workers when it could have used 9 workers, then it would be technically inefficient. However, not all technically efficient outputs are productively efficient. For instance, it might be possible to produce 1 000 units of output using 9 workers. But it might be cheaper to buy a machine and employ only 2 workers.

Question 1

Table 1

Output	Minimum input levels	Units
	Labour	Capital
10	4	1
20	8	2
30	11	3
40	14	4
50	16	5

(a) Firm A uses 21 units of labour and 6 units of capital to produce 60 units of output. A competing firm uses 19 units of labour and 6 units of capital to produce the same output. Explain whether Firm A is more technically efficient than the competing firm.

(b) Firm B uses 24 units of labour and 7 units of capital to produce 70 units of output. Firm B pays £10 000 to employ these factors. A competing firm employs the same number of factors to produce the same level of output but only pays £8 000 for them. Explain whether Firm B is more productively efficient.

(c) Now look at Table 1. From the table, which of the following combinations are: (i) technically efficient and (ii) productively efficient if the minimum cost of a unit of labour is £100 and of a unit of capital is £500?
(1) 8 units of labour and 2 units of capital to produce 20 units of output at a cost of £1 800. (2) 15 units of labour and 4 units of capital to produce an output of 40 units at a cost of £3 500. (3) 4 units of labour and 1 unit of capital to produce 10 units of output at a cost of £1 000.

Equally, Firm A might be using a machine and two workers to produce a given output. However, if it is paying £100 000 a year for this, whilst a competing business is paying only £80 000 a year for the same factor inputs, then Firm A is productively inefficient.

Efficiency and the production possibility frontier

Productive efficiency can be illustrated using a **production possibility frontier** or **PPF**. A production possibility frontier shows combinations of goods which could be produced if all resources were fully used (i.e. the economy were at full employment).

There is productive efficiency in an economy only if it is operating on the PPF. To understand why, consider an economy where all industries except the shoe industry are productively efficient. This means that the shoe industry is not operating at lowest cost and is using more resources than is necessary for its current level of output (i.e. it is technically inefficient). If the shoe industry became technically efficient, it could produce more shoes without reducing the output of the rest of the economy. Once the shoe industry is productively efficient, all industries are productively efficient and output cannot be increased in one industry without reducing it in another industry. However, this is true about any point on the PPF. In Figure 1, the economy is initially at B, within the PPF. The shoe industry is productively inefficient because YZ more shoes could be produced without affecting the output, 0X, of the rest of the economy. At A, the shoe industry cannot produce any more shoes without taking away resources from other industries and causing their output to fall. Hence the shoe industry must be productively efficient at A.

Efficiency and economies of scale

Productive efficiency is also linked to ECONOMIES and DISECONOMIES OF SCALE. When firms increase the scale of their production, their average costs change. For example, it might cost a specialist car manufacturer producing 2 000 cars a year on average £50 000 to make each car. But if production were scaled up to, say, 2 million cars a year, the average cost of production might fall to £15 000. When average costs fall as the scale of production increases, economies of scale exist. But if average costs rise when the scale of production rises, then there are said to be diseconomies of scale.

There is a number of different reasons for, or types of, economy of scale.

● **Purchasing economies.** The greater the quantities bought of raw materials and other supplies, the lower is likely to be the average cost. Large buyers are able to negotiate larger discounts because they have more market power. It is also usually cheaper to sell large quantities. For instance, transport costs might be lower if a given quantity is delivered to one customer rather than ten as bulk orders might save on packaging.
● **Marketing economies.** Marketing costs, such as advertising or the cost of promotional leaflets, are often lower per unit sold the greater the volume of sales. The cost of an advertisement, for instance, is the same however many sales it generates. If a catalogue is sent out to customers, again the cost remains the same whatever the response.
● **Technical economies.** Larger scale machinery or plant can often be more efficient than smaller scale plant. For instance, a boat which is twice the length, breadth and depth of another boat can carry 8 times as much cargo. But it likely to cost less than four times as much to build. A large supermarket costs much less to build per square metre than a

Question 2

Privatisation (the transfer of ownerships of assets from the government to the private sector) in the UK in the 1980s and 1990s led to a considerable reduction in the number of workers employed in the industries that were privatised. In electricity, gas, the railways and water, fewer workers were employed after privatisation to produce the same amount of goods and services. In the case of coal, the output of coal and the number of miners employed declined substantially after privatisation as coal mines found that demand for UK coal fell. The main customer for coal, the electricity industry, switched to gas fired power stations and also increased its imports of cheaper foreign coal.

(a) Using a production possibility diagram, explain the effect of privatisation on productive efficiency in the UK.

Figure 1 Efficiency and the production possibility frontier
At B, the economy is productively inefficient because more shoes could be produced without affecting the amount of all other goods available. All points on the PPF are productively efficient and allocatively efficient.

Shoes (vertical axis)

Z ---- A
Y ---- ● B

0   X   All other goods

small supermarket. What's more, the larger the scale of production, the more likely it is that resources will be fully utilised. A small building firm, for instance, might own a truck which it uses only for a few hours a week to transport materials. A large firm might be able to use the truck far more intensively because it has more jobs on at any one time.

● Managerial economies. **Specialisation** is an important source of greater efficiency. In a small firm, the owner might be part time salesperson, accountant, receptionist and manager. Employing specialist staff is likely to lead to greater efficiency and therefore lower costs.

● Financial economies. Small firms often find it difficult and expensive to raise finance for new investment. When loans are given, small firms are charged at relatively high rates of interest because banks know that small firms are far more at risk from liquidation than large firms. Large firms have a much greater choice of finance and it is likely to be much cheaper to raise than for small firms.

Diseconomies of scale arise mainly due to management problems. As a firm grows in size it becomes more and more difficult for management to keep control of the activities of the organisation. There is a variety of ways of dealing with this problem. Some companies choose to centralise operations with a small, tightly-knit team controlling all activities. Sometimes a single charismatic figure, often the founder of the company, will keep tight control of all major decisions. In other companies, management is decentralised with many small subsidiary companies making decisions about their part of the business and head office only making those decisions which affect the whole group. However, controlling an organisation which might employ hundreds of thousands of workers is not easy and there may come a point where no management team could prevent average costs from rising.

Geography too may lead to higher average costs. If a firm has

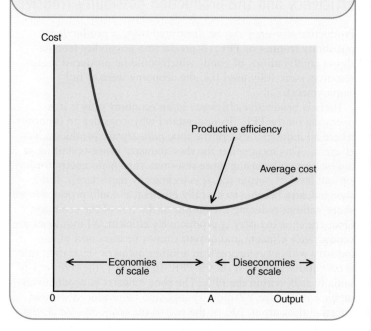

Figure 2 Economies and diseconomies of scale
The average cost is U-shaped because average costs:
• *at first fall over the output range OA showing economies of scale;*
• *rise when output exceeds OA showing diseconomies of scale.*
Productive efficiency is at output level OA where average costs of production are lowest.

to transport goods (whether finished goods or raw materials) over long distances because it is so large, then average costs may rise. Head office may also find it far more difficult to control costs in an organisation 1 000 miles away than in one on its door step.

Economies of scale can be shown on an average cost diagram. Figure 2 shows that average costs at first fall when the scale of production is increased from zero to 0A. So economies of scale exist between zero and 0A. Diseconomies of scale exist when production is higher than 0A. Here average costs are rising. The average cost curve is therefore U-shaped. Productive efficiency exists when average costs of production are at their lowest. So productive efficiency occurs at the output level 0A.

The size of economies of scale differs between industries. Economies of scale are very large in the car industry for example. In the furniture manufacturing industry, they tend to be small. Where there are large economies of scale, there tends to be relatively large firms. Few economies of scale means that small firms can compete successfully with larger firms which might be experiencing diseconomies of scale because of their size. In these industries, there is a positive disincentive for firms to grow in size.

The market and economic efficiency

Markets often lead to an efficient allocation of resources. In a market where there are many buyers and sellers, competition forces producers to produce at lowest cost. If they fail to do so, buyers will purchase their goods from lower cost firms. So competitive markets tend to lead to productive efficiency. Markets also tend towards efficiency in other ways. Customers are able to cast their spending 'votes' in the market. This determines what is produced. If consumers want to buy more

Question 3

In 2007, the Nationwide Building Society merged with its much smaller competitor, the Portman Building Society. The two building societies said that the new enlarged body would be better able to compete in the market place. 'Joining together gives us a lot of synergies, such as being to borrow at a cheaper rate and some cost savings', Nationwide Chief Executive Philip Williamson said.

The merged building society planned to close one branch in each of the 108 locations in the UK where there would now be two branches. A spokesperson said that the society would be looking to operate from a single site in all these locations. The Portman's mortgage and administration centre in Wolverhampton would also close with the loss of 250 jobs as the work was moved to existing Nationwide facilities.

The merged building society is also likely to have lower marketing costs, saving on costs such as advertising.

Source: adapted from news.bbc.co.uk, 12.9.2006 and 9.3.2007.

(a) The merger of the two building societies is likely to give rise to financial economies, technical economies and marketing economies of scale. Explain why this is likely to occur.
(b) Explain, using a cost diagram, the impact of the merger on productive efficiency.

shoes and fewer garden chairs, then shoe firms will expand production, whilst manufacturers of garden chairs will cut back on their production. Free markets allow this transfer of productive resources from one use to another.

Market failure

Markets, though, do not necessarily lead to economic efficiency. MARKET FAILURE occurs when markets lead to an inefficient allocation of resources. In some markets, there is partial market failure where the market exists but there is over production or underproduction of goods. In other cases, there is complete market failure where markets fail to lead to any production of good or services. A missing market is then said to exist.

Lack of competition in a market Economic efficiency is likely to be present in a market where there are many buyers and sellers. However, in many markets, there are either only a few buyers or a fewer sellers. In the rail transport industry, for instance, most travellers have no choice about which company to use on a particular journey. In the water industry, households are forced to buy their water from one company. In the UK soap powder market, two firms dominate sales. In the defence industry, the UK government is the only UK buyer of goods. Trade unions would like to be in a position where only union members work in a place of work. Where there is **imperfect competition**, there is likely to be market failure. Firms which dominate their markets, for instance, will attempt to charge high prices in order to make greater profit. However, they can only do this by restricting supply to the market, denying customers the ability to buy as much as they would have done if the market had been competitive. This leads to allocative inefficiency. Trade unions can push up costs to firms if they are successful in getting higher wages for their members than the market rate. This leads to productive inefficiency.

Externalities Prices and profits should be accurate signals, allowing markets to allocate resources efficiently. In reality, market prices and profits can be misleading because they may not reflect the true prices and profits to society of economic activities. These differences are known as the externalities of an economic activity. For instance, in Brazil it makes commercial sense to cut down the rain forest to create grazing land for cattle sold to the West as meat for hamburgers. However, this could lead to economic catastrophe in the long term because of global warming. The market is putting out the wrong signals, leading to a misallocation of resources.

Missing markets The market, for a variety of reasons, may fail to provide certain goods and services. Some goods such as defence (called **public goods**) will not be provided by the market. Other goods, called **merit goods**, will be underprovided. Health care and education are two examples of merit goods. Part of the reason for underprovision is that the market mechanism can be poor at dealing with risk and providing information to agents in the market.

Information failure In an efficient market, both buyers and sellers have good knowledge of the product. Sometimes, though, information is imperfect. For example, a consumer buying a soft drink is likely to have tried out a variety of drinks before. The drink being bought is likely to be something the consumer likes and so the consumer has good information about the product. However, what about the purchase of a washing machine which the consumer might only make every 8 years? In this case, the consumer might have imperfect information and make the wrong choice. Other examples relate to the problem of ASYMMETRIC INFORMATION. This is when either the buyer or seller has more information than the other party. One example is private dentists. If a dentist recommends a treatment when the patient is not in any pain, how does the patient know that the treatment is really in his best interest? Could it be that the dentist is recommending far more work than is necessary and is more interested in gaining a fee than treating the patient properly? Another common example given is second hand cars.

Externalities and missing markets are examples of market failure.

Some cars are 'lemons', constantly breaking down and requiring large repair bills. Other cars of the same make and model are very reliable. The owner of the car for sale knows whether the car is a 'lemon' or not. However, the buyer does not have this information. Should the buyer offer a high price for the car on the assumption it isn't a 'lemon' or should he offer a low price assuming it will have problems?

Factor immobility Factors of production (land, labour and capital) may be immobile. This means that they are difficult to transfer from one use to another. For instance, a train once built is only useful as a train. It cannot be changed into a car or a plane. As for labour, workers can be immobile. A coal miner made redundant might have few skills to offer in other types of work. So he or she may find it difficult to get a job. An unemployed worker in a high unemployment area might be unable or not be willing to move to a job in a low unemployment area. For instance, it may be impossible to find housing at an affordable rent or price in the low unemployment area, or the worker might not want to leave family and friends in the local area. The greater the immobility of factors, the more time it will take for markets to clear when there is a shock to the economic system. Factor immobility was one of the reasons why the North of England, Wales, Scotland and Northern Ireland suffered above average unemployment rates during the 1960s, 1970s and 1980s. Traditional heavy primary and manufacturing industries were concentrated in these areas. As they declined, workers were made redundant. However, new industry with new capital was not created in sufficient volume to compensate for the decline of old industries. Unemployed workers found it hard, if not impossible, to get jobs. Neither were sufficient workers prepared to leave these regions to find employment in low unemployment areas of the UK.

Inequality Market failure is not just caused by economic inefficiency. It can also be caused by **inequality** in the economy. In a market economy, the ability of individuals to consume goods depends upon the income of the household in which they live. Household income comes from a variety of sources.
- Wages are paid to those who work outside the household. In the labour market, different wages are paid to different workers depending on factors such as education, training, skill and location.
- Interest, rent and dividends are earned from the wealth of the

household. Wealth may include money in bank and building society accounts, stocks and shares, and property.
- Private pensions are another type of unearned income. Private pensions represent income from a pension fund which can be valued and is a form of wealth.
- Other income includes state benefits such as unemployment benefit, child benefit and state pensions.

The market mechanism may lead to a distribution of income which is undesirable or unacceptable. For instance, income levels may be so low that a household is unable to afford basic **necessities** such as food, shelter or clothing. If healthcare is only provided by the private sector, a household may not be able to afford medical care. The state may then need to intervene, either to provide income in the form of benefits, or goods and services such as healthcare to increase consumption levels.

Key terms

Asymmetric information - when either a buyer or seller has more information than the other party.
Diseconomies of scale - a rise in the average costs of production as output rises.
Dynamic efficiency - occurs when resources are allocated efficiently over time.
Economies of scale - a fall in the average costs of production as output rises.
Market failure - where resources are inefficiently allocated due to imperfections in the working of the market mechanism.
Productive efficiency - is achieved when production is achieved at lowest cost.
Static efficiency - occurs when resources are allocated efficiently at a point in time.
Technical efficiency - is achieved when a given quantity of output is produced with the minimum number of inputs.

Applied economics

The Common Agricultural Policy (CAP)

When the European Union (EU), formerly the European Community, was first formed there was a commitment to free trade between member countries. This found its first major expression in 1962 in the Common Agricultural Policy, a Community-wide policy which aimed to harmonise the agricultural policies of the original six member countries. One of the implicit aims of the CAP was to increase efficiency in the market for agricultural products. To what extent has this been achieved?

Productive efficiency has certainly increased. Table 2 shows that the number of small, relatively inefficient, farms has declined over time whilst the number of large farms over 50 hectares with lower overall costs has increased. There has been a substantial fall in employment in the agricultural sector as Table 3 shows. At the same time, due to more intensive farming methods, more use of fertilisers and machinery and higher yielding crop and animal strains, output has risen.

However, European agriculture is not fully productively efficient. There are still far too many small farmers producing on marginal land, such as in Wales or the French Alps. In 2005, considering the 27 EU member countries that had joined by 2006, the average size of a farm ranged from 1.2 hectares in Malta, to 21.1 hectares in Bulgaria, 27.9 hectares in Belgium, 52.1 hectares in France and 81.3 hectares in the UK. Small farms are unable to exploit the economies of scale enjoyed by large farms and consequently their costs of production are much higher.

However, it could be argued that the difference in productivity between farms in Europe is not as important an issue as the difference in the cost of

Table 2 *Number of holdings by size, millions*

	Total	0-5ha	5-20ha	20-50ha	50+ha
EUR-10					
1970	7.67	4.26	2.36	0.85	0.20
1987	5.00	2.32	1.53	0.78	0.37
EUR-12					
1987	6.92	3.40	2.10	0.95	0.47
1993	7.23	4.23	1.68	0.78	0.53
2000	5.18	2.65	1.33	0.64	0.56
EU-27					
2005	7.82	3.92	2.41	0.81	0.68

Note: ha is the abbreviation for hectares
Source: adapted from European Commission, *European Economy, EC Agricultural Policy for the 21st Century*, Number 4, 1994; European Commission, *The Agricultural Situation in the European Union 1997*; European Commission, *Agricultural Statistics Pocketbook*.

Table 3 *Employment in agriculture, hunting, forestry and fishing*

					Millions
	1970	1980	1990	2000	2003
Greece	1.3	1.0	0.9	0.7	0.6
Spain	3.7	2.2	1.5	1.0	0.9
France	2.8	1.8	1.4	1.0	1.0
Germany	2.3	1.4	1.1	1.0	0.9
UK	-	0.6	0.6	0.4	0.3
EU12	-	11.9	8.9	6.4	6.1
EU15	-	12.7	9.5	7.2	6.8
EU25	-	-	-	11.2	10.4

Source: European Commission, *The Agricultural Situation in the European Union 1997*; European Commission, *Agricultural Statistics Pocketbook*.

production between the EU and the rest of the world. World prices for many agricultural commodities, such as wheat or butter, have been considerably below those maintained by the complex system of tariffs, quotas and intervention prices in the EU.

Consumers lose out because of these high domestic prices. Their loss can be calculated by multiplying the amount they purchase by the difference between domestic and world farm gate prices.

However, farmers worldwide also tend to be supported by the taxpayer. Figure 2 shows the extent of the subsidies paid to farmers throughout the world. In the EU, for instance, farmers in 2005 received in subsidies an average 32 per cent of the market value of what they produced.

The agricultural market is not just productively inefficient. It is also inefficient in other ways. The fact that taxpayers throughout the developed world are having to subsidise farmers means that the marginal cost of production far exceeds the price consumers are prepared to pay. Efficiency could therefore be increased by shifting resources out of agriculture into other industries.

Over the past 20 years, there has been an increasing awareness of the costs of the CAP and other agricultural support systems. In the latest Doha round of trade talks, many Third World countries along with agricultural exporting countries such as Australia and New Zealand were fighting to get trade in agricultural products liberalised. In practice, this means both the EU and the USA dismantling their support regimes for agriculture. In the EU, there is strong resistance to a reduction in subsidies to farmers from certain countries, particularly those which benefit the most from the CAP, such as France.

The abolition of the CAP would produce losers as well as gainers. Land prices would plummet because prices for produce would fall substantially. Marginal farmers too would lose because their land would not be productive enough to support them in business. The experience of New Zealand, which almost abolished farm subsidies in the 1980s, suggests, however, that farm profits would remain roughly constant. There would be lower prices and fewer state handouts.

However, equally, the costs of production, particularly rents on farms, would fall too leaving most farmers on good farming land with broadly similar incomes.

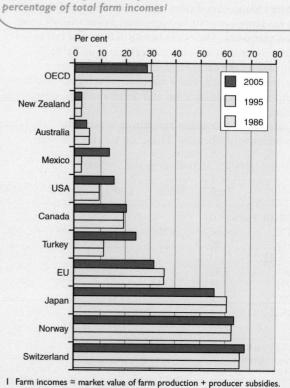

Figure 2 *Farming subsidies: producer subsidies as a percentage of total farm incomes¹*

Per cent

1 Farm incomes = market value of farm production + producer subsidies.
Source: adapted from www.oecd.org.

DataQuestion

Market failure

Tesco, the UKs largest supermarket chain, has been accused of trying to sabotage the opening of a new small store in the market town of Ludlow in Shropshire. Harry Tuffins is a small chain of four stores in the Welsh borders and Wales. Days before the opening of the new store, Tesco leafleted every house within a ten mile radius with two vouchers worth £10 off on £30 of shopping at the local Tesco. One voucher was valid for the the two weeks before Harry Tuffin's opening dates and the other covered the two weeks immediately after. The Association of Convenience Stores, the body representing small stores, has reported the matter to the Competition Commission, the government body which deals with unfair competition.

Source: adapted from *The Sunday Times*, 21.1.2007.

Yixing in China is a prosperous city of one million people. Incomes are high as the population works in more than 1 000 factories producing textiles and chemicals. However, there is a price to pay. Most of the factories are located on the local river where it is easy to transport raw materials but also untreated waste is dumped into the river. The river feeds Lake Tai, China's third-largest freshwater lake. On the lake is sited the industrial city of Wuxi. This summer, pollution in the lake became so bad that the water authorities in Wuxi were forced to cut off supplies to households in Wuxi. They were without tap drinking water for weeks. Local campaigners have claimed that the pollution is damaging both people's health and the environment.

Source: adapted from news.bbc.co.uk 18.9.2007.

The 5 million people who live in former coalmining communities have poorer standards of health, education and employment than the rest of the population, according to a report published yesterday. Average household incomes are £50 a week lower than regional averages and more than 250 000 people in coalfields are claiming incapacity benefit. 22 per cent of coalfield residents have some form of long-term illness. The proportion of 16 year olds getting five or more A-C grades at GCSE is 7 to 10 percentage points below the national average and more than half of adults have no or low-level qualifications. Unemployment is well above the national average. These communities were devastated by the closure of most of the UK's coal mining industry following the miners' strike in 1984-85. Around 250 000 jobs were lost directly and many more indirectly from the closures.

Source: adapted from the *Financial Times*, 23.3.2007.

More and more older people are working beyond the retirement age. Since 1992, the number of people above pensionable age in work has risen by 400 000 to 1.2 million, two thirds of them women. They are doing this because they realise they can't afford to live off their retirement income. The government has warned workers that they must save more for their old age, especially since life expectancy continues to rise. However, many are choosing to ignore the government warnings. Young workers in particular are failing to save, choosing instead to either take on large mortgages or spend their money to support their lifestyle.

Source: adapted from the *Financial Times*, 19.7.2007.

Burkina Faso is a land-locked country in Western Africa. With an income per head of just $516, it is one of world's poorer nations. Despite a decade of relatively high economic growth, malnutrition is still common in the countryside. Poverty sits alongside new Grecian-style villas in the capital, Ouagadougou. The increasingly wealthy political and trading classes are able to afford flashy cars and a Western life style.

Source: adapted from the *Financial Times*, 18.9.2007.

1. 'Efficiency is concerned with how well resources, such as time, talents or materials, are used to produce an end result. Market failure occurs where resources are inefficiently allocated due to imperfections in the working of the market mechanism.' Explain how market failure occurs in each of the examples given in the data.

16 Public and merit goods

Summary

1. There will inevitably be market failure in a pure free market economy because it will fail to provide public goods.
2. Public goods must be provided by the state because of the free rider problem.
3. Merit goods are goods which are underprovided by the market mechanism, for instance because there are significant positive externalities in consumption.
4. Governments can intervene to ensure provision of public and merit goods through direct provision, subsidies or regulation.

Markets and market failure

Markets may lead to an efficient allocation of resources. However, there are some goods and services which economists recognise are unlikely to be best produced in free markets. These may include defence, the judiciary and the criminal justice system, the police service, roads, the fire service and education. More controversially, some believe that the free market is poor at producing health care and housing for the less well off. There are different reasons why there might be market failure in the production of these goods.

Public goods

Nearly all goods are PRIVATE GOODS (not to be confused with goods produced in the private sector of the economy). A private good is one where consumption by one person results in the good not being available for consumption by another. For instance, if you eat a bowl of muesli, then your friend can't eat it; if a firm builds a plant on a piece of land, that land is not available for use by local farmers.

A few goods, however, are PUBLIC GOODS or PURE PUBLIC GOODS. These are goods which possess two characteristics:
- **non-rivalry** - consumption of the good by one person does not reduce the amount available for consumption by another person; sometimes this is also known as **non-diminishability** or **non-exhaustibility**;
- **non-excludability** - once provided, no person can be excluded from benefiting (or indeed suffering in the case of a public good like pollution).

There are relatively few examples of pure public goods, although many goods contain a public good element. Clean air is a public good. If you breathe clean air, it does not diminish the ability of others to breathe clean air. Moreover, others cannot prevent you from breathing clean air. Defence is another example. An increase in the population of the UK does not lead to a reduction in the defence protection accorded to the existing population. A person in Manchester cannot be excluded from benefiting even if she were to object to current defence policy, prefer to see all defence abolished, and refuse to pay to finance defence.

Goods which can be argued to be public goods are:
- defence;
- the judiciary and prison service;
- the police service;
- street lighting.

Many other goods, such as education and health, contain a small public good element.

The free rider problem

If the provision of public goods were left to the market mechanism, there would be market failure. This is because of the FREE RIDER problem. A public good is one where it is impossible to prevent people from receiving the benefits of the good once it has been provided. So there is very little incentive for people to pay for consumption of the good. A free rider is someone who receives the benefit but allows others to pay for it. For instance, citizens receive benefits from defence expenditure. But individual citizens could increase their economic welfare by not paying for it.

In a free market, national defence is unlikely to be provided. A firm attempting to provide defence services would have difficulty charging for the product since it could not be sold to benefit individual citizens. The result would be that no one would pay for defence and therefore the market would not provide it. The only way around this problem is for the state to provide defence and force everyone to contribute to its cost through taxation.

In practice, there are often ways in which providers of public

Question 1

Explain why lamp posts might be classed as a public good.

goods can exclude consumers from benefiting from the public good. The problem of free riding can to some extent be solved for these NON-PURE or QUASI-PUBLIC GOODS. For example, motorists can be made to pay a toll for using a road. Television viewers can be forced to buy subscriptions because reception is encoded. Ships entering a port can be forced to pay taxes for the upkeep of local lighthouses. However, quasi-public goods possess the second characteristic of pure public goods. They are non-rival. So for most roads, for example, one motorist travelling along the road does not exclude another motorist from travelling along the same road. When goods are non-rival, it is unlikely that the free market mechanism will provide enough of the good. How many country roads would private firms provide if they were tolled? The answer is very few because the tolls collected would not cover the building and maintenance of the road. Hence, there is a very strong case for government providing this quasi-public good.

Merit and demerit goods

Even the most fervent advocates of free market economics agree that public goods are an example of market failure and that the government should provide these public goods. However, more controversial are merit and demerit goods.

A MERIT GOOD is one which is underprovided by the market mechanism (i.e. one which some people think should be provided in greater quantities). One reason for underprovision is that individuals lack perfect **information** and find it difficult to make rational decisions when costs occur today but the benefits received only come in, say, thirty years time. Another reason is because there are significant **positive externalities** present.

Health, education and insurance are the main merit goods provided today by government in the UK. Health and insurance are two examples where consumers find it difficult to make rational choices because of time. If left totally to market forces, the evidence suggests that individuals would not give themselves sufficient health cover or cover against sickness, unemployment and old age. Young people tend to be healthy and in work. Many find it difficult to appreciate that one day they will be ill and out of work. However, the cost of health care and pensions is so great that young people can only afford them if they save for the future. If they don't, they find when they are older that they do not have sufficient resources to pay for medical services, or the insurance needed to cover them against loss of earnings due to illness or retirement. Therefore it makes sense for the state to intervene and to force young people in particular to make provision against sickness, unemployment and old age.

In the case of education, the main beneficiary (the child or student) is unlikely to be the person paying for the education. Therefore there could be a conflict of interest. It could be in the interest of the parents to pay as little as possible for the child's education but in the interest of the child to receive as high quality an education as possible. Others in society also have an interest. Children who, for instance, cannot read or write are an economic liability in the UK today. They are more likely than not to have to receive support from others rather than contribute to the nation's welfare. This is an example of a **principal agent problem** where those benefiting or losing from a decision are not the same as those making the decision and where the objectives of, and outcomes for, the two groups are different. There are many other examples of goods with a merit good element. Lack of industrial training, for instance, is seen as a major problem in the UK. Individual firms have an incentive not to train workers,

not only because it is so costly but also because their trained workers can then be poached by competitors. Rather, they go into the market place and recruit workers who have been trained at other firms' expense. This is an example again of the free rider problem. It is partly countered by the government providing funding for organisations which provide training in local areas.

A DEMERIT GOOD is one which is overprovided by the market mechanism. The clearest examples of demerit goods are drugs - everything from hard drugs such as heroin to alcohol and tobacco. Consumption of these goods produces large negative **externalities**. Crime increases, health costs rise, valuable human economic resources are destroyed, and friends and relatives suffer distress. Moreover, individuals themselves suffer and are unable to stop consuming because drugs are addictive. Therefore it can be argued that consumers of drugs are not the best judges of their own interests.

Governments intervene to correct this market failure. They have three main weapons at their disposal: they can ban consumption as with hard drugs; they can use the price system to reduce demand by placing taxes on drugs; or they can try to persuade consumers to stop using drugs, for instance through advertising campaigns.

Equity

It would be extremely improbable that a free market system would lead to a distribution of resources which every individual would see as equitable. It is therefore argued by some economists that the state has a duty to reallocate resources.

Question 2

Suggest reasons why education might be considered a merit good.

Cost of school places to rise

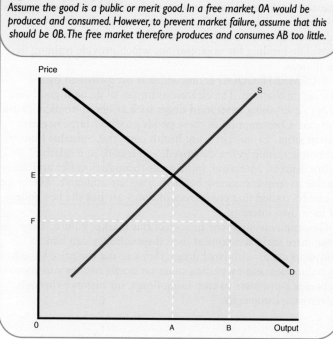

Figure 1 Market failure.
Assume the good is a public or merit good. In a free market, 0A would be produced and consumed. However, to prevent market failure, assume that this should be 0B. The free market therefore produces and consumes AB too little.

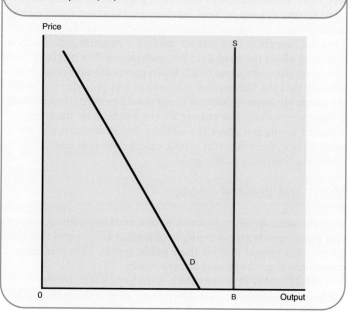

Figure 2 Direct provision.
Assume this is the market for defence. To prevent market failure, 0B should be produced. However, there is no price on the demand curve at which 0B would be demanded. The government must therefore step in and provide 0B, whatever the price of defence.

In the UK today, for instance, there is some consensus that British citizens should not die for lack of food, or be refused urgent medical treatment for lack of money.

In the UK, over 30 per cent of all public spending is devoted to social security payments. Some of these payments come from the National Insurance fund and therefore could be seen as merit goods. However, benefits such as family credit are an explicit attempt to redistribute income to those in need. It could also be argued that the free provision of services such as health and education leads to a more equitable distribution of resources.

Government intervention

Markets are likely to underprovide public and merit goods. This leads to **inefficiency** because consumers are not able to spend their money in a way which will maximise their utility (their welfare or satisfaction). For instance, households in a city would be prepared to pay a few pounds a year to have street lighting throughout the city. However, because of the free rider problem, they are reluctant to make any contribution either because they hope everyone else will pay or because they don't want to make large payments because few others are paying. It then makes sense for government to force everyone to pay through a system of taxes.

Merit goods are more controversial, partly because they contain a private good element. The main beneficiaries of health care and education, for instance, are patients and students. Governments can attempt to increase the provision of merit goods in a variety of ways.

Direct provision Governments can supply public and merit goods directly to consumers free of charge. In the UK, primary school education, visits to the doctor and roads are provided in this way. The government may choose to produce the good or service itself, as with primary school education, or it may buy in the services of firms in the private sector. General practitioners, for instance, work for themselves and

the government buys their services.

Subsidised provision The government may pay for part of the good or service (a **subsidy**) but expect consumers to pay the rest. Prescriptions or dental care are subsidised in this way in the UK.

Regulation The government may leave provision to the private sector but force consumers to purchase a merit good or producers to provide a merit good. For instance, motorists are forced to buy car insurance by law. There is an ongoing debate in industrialised countries about whether workers should be forced to pay into private pensions. Motorway service stations are forced to provide toilet facilities free of charge to motorists whether or not they purchase anything.

These different types of intervention can be seen using demand and supply curves. In Figure 1, the demand and supply curve for a public or merit good is shown. The market equilibrium output is 0A. However, assume that this level of output is too low to

Question 3

There is a variety of ways in which the government could ensure that all households have access to dental services.
(a) It could provide the service directly, making it free to all users, and raise the required finance through taxes.
(b) It could subsidise some dental treatment considered to be essential, but not subsidise other treatment. This is the present system in the UK.
(c) It could make it a legal obligation that all households take out dental insurance to cover the cost of essential dental treatment.

Discuss the relative merits of each of these options.

Figure 3 Subsidies
Assume this shows the market for a merit good. A subsidy which shifts the free market supply curve from S₁ to S₂ can lead to market failure being eliminated with output rising to 0B.

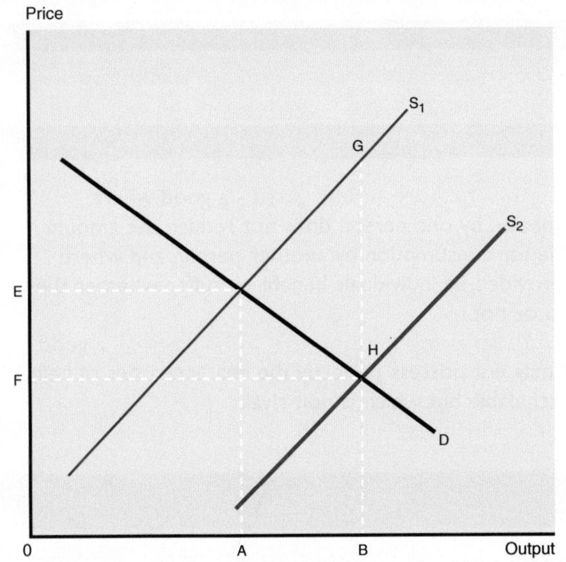

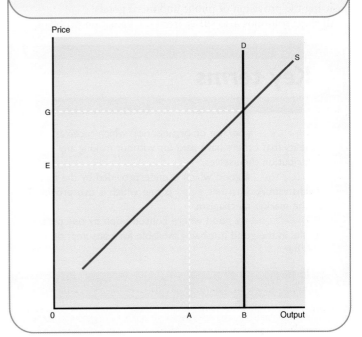

Figure 4 Regulation
Forcing motorists to buy car insurance means that the demand curve for motor insurance becomes vertical at the socially optimal output level of 0B.

ensure that welfare is maximised. Market failure would only be eliminated if output were higher at 0B.

- Direct provision of the good by government simply sees the government supplying 0B. This could be illustrated by drawing a vertical supply curve at 0B. Whatever the price of the good, the government will supply 0B. In Figure 2, a good like defence is shown. The government supplied 0B free of charge. The position of the demand curve shows that there is no price at which citizens would buy 0B of defence in a free market.

- Subsidising provision shifts the supply curve downwards so that it cuts the demand curve at output 0B. This is shown in Figure 3. The subsidy shifts the supply curve downwards from S₁ to S₂. The fall in price from 0E to 0F increases quantity demanded from 0A, where there was market failure, to the socially optimal level 0B. The level of subsidy per unit is GH.

- Regulation can work in a number of different ways but regulations serve to increase output from 0A to 0B in Figure 1. Take the example of car insurance. Whatever the price of car insurance, motorists have to buy it to drive their cars legally. So the demand curve for car insurance is perfectly inelastic, shown by the vertical demand curve in Figure 4. Equilibrium output is therefore at 0B where there is market failure. The price of motor insurance is, however, higher than it would have been if there had been no regulation at output 0A.

Advantages and disadvantages of different methods

There is a number of advantages and disadvantages to each of these solutions. The advantage of direct provision is that the government directly controls the supply of goods and services. It determines the number of hospital beds in the system because it provides them. It decides how many soldiers there are because it pays them directly. However, direct provision has disadvantages.

It may be inefficient, particularly if the government produces the good itself. Employees of the state, whether providing the good or buying it in, may have no incentive to cut costs to a minimum. It may also be inefficient because the wrong mix of goods is produced, especially if the goods are provided free of charge to taxpayers. The government may provide too many soldiers and too few hospital beds, for instance. Markets, in contrast, give consumers the opportunity to buy those goods which give the greatest satisfaction. In a market, if producers supplied too many soldiers, they would be left unsold. Firms would then move resources out of the production of defence and into the production of a good which consumers were prepared to buy.

Subsidies are a way of working through the market mechanism to increase the consumption of a good. So subsidising dental care, for instance, increases the amount of dental care provided, hopefully to a level which maximises economic welfare. Subsidies can also help those on low incomes to afford to buy goods. One problem with subsidies is that decisions about the level of subsidies can become 'captured' by producers. Subsidies then become too large to maximise welfare. For instance, it can be argued that farmers in Europe have to some extent 'captured' the Common Agricultural Policy. Instead of government ministers deciding what level of farm subsidy will maximise economic welfare, they bow to the pressure of the farming lobby. Farming subsidies then become far too large. The resultant welfare gains to farmers are far less than the welfare loss to consumers and taxpayers.

Regulation has the advantage that it requires little or no taxpayers' money to provide the good. Consumers are also likely to be able to shop around in the free market for a product which gives them good value, ensuring productive and allocative efficiency. However, regulations can impose heavy costs on the poor in society. How many poor families, for instance, could afford to pay for private health care insurance if it was a requirement for them to do so? Regulations can also be ignored. Not all motorists have insurance, for instance. If parents had a legal obligation to pay for their children to go to school, some parents would defy the law and not give their children an education. The more likely citizens are to evade regulations, the less efficient they are as a way of ensuring the provision of public and merit goods.

All these solutions also suffer from the valuation problem.

With public and merit goods, it is difficult, if not impossible, in practice to say what exactly is the socially optimal level of output for a good. If an exact value cannot be put on production and consumption of public and merit goods, then it becomes difficult to know exactly what level of output is required.

Key terms

Free rider - a person or organisation which receives benefits that others have paid for without making any contribution themselves.

Merit good - a good which is underprovided by the market mechanism. A **demerit good** is one which is overprovided by the market mechanism.

Private good - a good where consumption by one person results in the good not being available for consumption by another.

Public good or pure public good - a good where consumption by one person does not reduce the amount available for consumption by another person and where once provided, all individuals benefit or suffer whether they wish to or not.

Quasi-public good or non-pure public good - a good which may not possess perfectly the characteristics of being non-excludable but which is non-rival.

Applied economics

Lighthouses

Public goods are goods which possess the two properties of non-excludability (once provided, it is impossible to prevent others from benefiting) and non-rivalry (benefit by one does not diminish the amount by which others can benefit). Lighthouses possess both these characteristics. Once the lighthouse is working, it is impossible to prevent any ship in the area benefiting. The fact that one ship sees the lighthouse doesn't prevent other ships from seeing it as well.

Economists from Adam Smith onwards have argued that public goods need to be provided by the public sector because there is no economic incentive for the private sector to provide them. Non-excludability would mean that there would be large numbers of free-riders - individuals or firms which benefited but did not pay. For instance, how could ships be made to pay for lighthouses?

In the UK, government doesn't provide lighthouses. They are provided by Trinity House, a private corporation. However, the government has given it the right to build lighthouses. In return, the government allows it to charge each ship which visits a British port a 'light charge'. This is collected by Revenue and Customs, part of the government. Trinity House has to submit its budget to both the government and representatives of the shipping industry each year, where it has to justify the scale of its charges. So in this case, whilst the government doesn't provide the

public good, it is involved at every stage and crucially in forcing ships to pay charges for the upkeep of lighthouses.

It is in fact difficult to think of any public good for which the government doesn't provide or regulate its private provision. However, the example of lighthouses shows that a public good is not necessarily one directly provided by the government.

DataQuestion

Television

Watching television is one of the nation's favourite occupations. Almost all households have a television and on average we watch 3.8 hours per day. When television first became widely available in the UK in the 1950s, television watchers needed three things: a television set and an aerial both of which could be bought from shops, and a television licence. The licence was a tax on households owning a television, the proceeds of which were used to run the British Broadcasting Corporation, the BBC. When terrestrial commercial television in the form of ITV came on the market in 1955, television viewers didn't pay for the service. It was funded through the sale of advertisements on the channel.

Source: adapted from www.which.co.uk.

Sending out unscrambled television signals means that anyone with an aerial and a television set can receive television broadcasts, whether they have paid their licence fee or not. However, there are two other models of broadcasting in the UK where consumers are forced to pay. One is cable television. In 2007, 3.4 million households subscribed to cable. If the customer doesn't pay the subscription, their cable signal can be cut off. The other is Sky satellite television. Sky, a broadcasting company, sells equipment and cards to receive a signal. Cards are issued annually and are only sent to subscribers who pay a fee. In 2007, over 8 million households had Sky subscriptions.

Source: adapted from www.ofcom.org.uk.

Many regard the BBC as the world's best broadcaster. Partly this is because of the quality of much of its output. In commercial television, there is an incentive to produce the cheapest programmes which will appeal to a mass audience. Games shows, soaps and sitcoms are ideal formats for this. High quality programming which does not appeal to a mass audience is marginalised. Because the BBC does not have to chase ratings all the time, and because its funding does not come from advertising, it can afford to produce a wide range of material to appeal to a variety of tastes. The BBC is also world renowned for its impartiality in news and current affairs. It is independent of government and so it is not forced to churn out political propaganda. Equally, because it is not dependent on advertisers, it can tackle issues which might either offend commercial interests or lower ratings for programmes. Lastly, the BBC offers a broad range of channels from those on television to radio to the Internet.

The BBC, however, is constantly under attack from commercial broadcasters who would like to see the BBC liquidated. Commercial broadcasters would then be able to take the BBC's current audience and either charge them to view and listen, or use them as targets for advertising. Almost inevitably, the quality of broadcasting in the UK would slump to the levels seen in countries such as France, Italy and the USA.

Source: adapted from *The Guardian*, 1.4.2004.

In the 1990s and 2000s, Sky Television aggressively bid for the exclusive rights to broadcast major sporting events. One of the main reasons why it became so successful was its purchase of the broadcasting rights to Premier League football in 1992. This gave it a core subscriber base of young males who could no longer watch live Premier League matches on free-to-air BBC or ITV channels. There was concern that Sky would buy up the rights to sporting events from the football FIFA World Cup to the Olympics to the Rugby World Cup final. In 1996, the government acted by passing the Broadcasting Act. This created a list of 'Category A' sporting events which had to be broadcast on free-to-air channels. To the disappointment of many, the list did not include English test cricket matches, the golf Ryder Cup, and non-finals matches in Wimbledon tennis and the Rugby World Cup.

Source: with information from www.ofcom.org.uk.

Does quality matter in broadcasting? Does it matter whether someone is watching a critically acclaimed adaptation of a Jane Austen novel like *Pride and Prejudice* or a badly made American sitcom? Does it matter whether viewers are watching half an hour of in-depth quality news reporting or whether they only have access to three minute roundups of news sandwiched in between adverts and games shows? Some say that it doesn't matter. If you want to watch a game show rather than a wild life documentary, then it is your choice. Others argue that broadcasting has a vital role in informing and challenging viewers. Do we want to be a nation of ignorant couch potatoes or do we want to be aware, living, informed and cultured individuals?

1. Explain what is meant by a 'public good' using television broadcasting as an example.
2. It could also be argued that (a) television broadcasting is a quasi-public good and that (b) quality broadcasting is a merit good. Suggest why this might be the case.
3. Discuss whether 'liquidating the BBC', closing it down and distributing its rights to air waves to commercial broadcasters would result in market failure.

17 Externalities

3.1.4, 3.1.5

Summary

1. Externalities are created when social costs and benefits differ from private costs and benefits.
2. The greater the externality, the greater the likelihood of market failure.
3. Market failure occurs when marginal social cost and marginal social benefit are not equal at the actual level of output. There will be a welfare loss at this level of output shown by the 'welfare triangle' on a marginal social and private cost and benefit diagram.
4. Governments can use regulation, the extension of property rights, taxation and permits to reduce the market failure caused by externalities.

Private and social costs and benefits

A chemical plant may dump waste into a river in order to minimise its costs. Further down the river, a water company has to treat the water to remove dangerous chemicals before supplying drinking water to its customers. Its customers have to pay higher prices because of the pollution.

This is a classic example of EXTERNALITIES or SPILLOVER EFFECTS. Externalities arise when private costs and benefits are different from social costs and benefits. A PRIVATE COST is the cost of an activity to an individual economic unit, such as a consumer or a firm. For instance, a chemical company will have to pay for workers, raw materials and plant and machinery when it produces chemicals. A SOCIAL COST is the cost of an activity not just to the individual economic unit which creates the cost, but to the rest of society as well. It therefore includes all private costs, but may also include other costs. The chemical manufacturer may make little or no payment for the pollution it generates. The difference between private cost and social cost is the externality or spillover effect. If social cost is greater than private cost, then a NEGATIVE EXTERNALITY or EXTERNAL COST is said to exist.

However, not all externalities are negative. A company may put up a building which is not just functional but also beautiful.

The value of the pleasure which the building gives to society over its lifetime (the SOCIAL BENEFIT) may well far exceed the benefit of the building received by the company (the PRIVATE BENEFIT). Hence, if social benefit is greater than private benefit, a POSITIVE EXTERNALITY or EXTERNAL BENEFIT is said to exist.

This is often the case with health care provision (an example of a merit good). Although one individual will benefit from inoculation against illness, the social benefit resulting from the reduced risk of other members of society contracting the illness will be even greater. Positive externalities could also result from education and training. An individual may benefit in the form of a better job and a higher salary but society may gain even more from the benefits of a better trained workforce.

Activities where social benefit exceeds private benefit are often inadequately provided by a market system. In many cases this results in either state provision or a government subsidy to encourage private provision.

Market failure

The price mechanism allocates resources. Prices and profits are the signals which determine this allocation. However, a misallocation of resources will occur if market prices and profits

Question 1

(a) Why might each of the examples in the photographs give rise to positive and negative externalities?

do not accurately reflect the costs and benefits to society of economic activities.

For instance, in the case of the chemical plant, the price of chemicals does not accurately reflect their true cost to society. The private cost of production to the manufacturer is lower than the social cost to society as a whole. Because the price of chemicals is lower than that which reflects social cost, the quantity demanded of chemicals and therefore consumption of chemicals will be greater than if the full social cost were charged. On the other hand, if the water company is pricing water to consumers, it will have to charge higher prices to consumers than would have been the case without the chemical pollution. Demand for water and consumption of water will therefore be less than it would otherwise have been without the externality.

The greater the externality, the greater the market failure and the less market prices and profits provide accurate signals for the optimal allocation of resources.

Marginal costs and benefits

The difference between social costs and social benefits changes as the level of output changes. This can be shown using **marginal analysis**. The margin is a possible point of change. So the marginal cost of production is the extra cost of producing an extra unit of output. The marginal benefit is the benefit received from consuming an extra unit of output.

The marginal cost of production is likely to change as output increases. In Figure 1, it is shown as at first falling and then rising. Marginal costs fall at first because producing more can lead to greater efficiencies. However, then they start to rise.This could be because a firm is having to pay higher prices to obtain more factors of production: to employ more workers it might have to pay higher wages, for example. Or production might be less efficient if a firm is operating beyond its optimum capacity of production.

In contrast, the marginal benefit of consumption of a product falls as consumption increases. Each extra unit of consumption brings less benefit to the consumer. The marginal benefit curve is the same as the demand curve. This is because the demand curve

too shows that the value of the benefit put on the consumption of the product by a buyer.

Assume that the marginal cost curve and marginal benefit curves in Figure 1 are the costs and benefits to society. Then welfare would be maximised at a quantity level of 0A and a price of 0B. What if production and consumption are not at 0A?

● If quantity produced and consumed were greater than 0A, the extra cost of production would be greater than the extra benefit from consumption. Welfare would be improved by reducing production and consumption. So this would lead to an inefficient allocation of resources.

● If quantity produced and consumed were less than 0A, then the marginal benefit of production would be greater than the marginal cost of production. Welfare could be increased if production and consumption were increased.

Note that when this diagram is usually drawn, only the upward sloping part of the marginal cost curve is shown as in Figure 2. This is because it is assumed that the marginal benefit curve will cut the marginal cost curve when marginal cost is increasing.

Welfare losses

In many markets, social costs and private costs differ. So too do social benefits and private benefits. Figure 2 shows a situation where there are PRODUCTION EXTERNALITIES or EXTERNALITIES IN PRODUCTION. Production externalities occur when the social cost of production is greater than the private cost of production.

Figure 2 shows that at every level of output, the MARGINAL SOCIAL COST of production is higher than the MARGINAL PRIVATE COST. So the marginal social cost curve, the MSC curve, is higher and to the left of the marginal private cost curve, the MPC curve. It is assumed here that the marginal social benefit (MSB) and marginal private benefit (MPB) are the same. So the demand curve is also the MSB and MSC curves.

The market equilibrium is where the marginal private cost equals the marginal private benefit. This is at an output level of 0B and a price of 0E. If the price were higher than 0E,

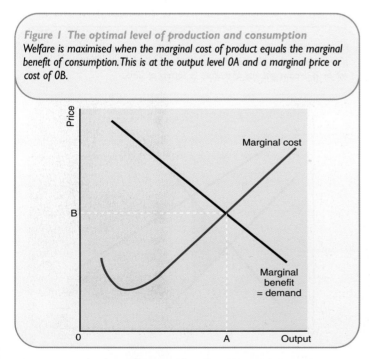

Figure 1 The optimal level of production and consumption
Welfare is maximised when the marginal cost of product equals the marginal benefit of consumption.This is at the output level 0A and a marginal price or cost of 0B.

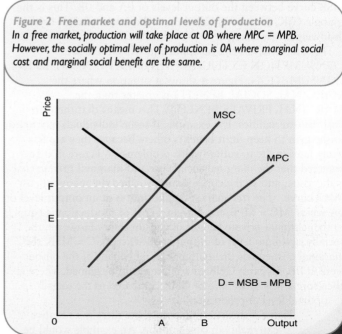

Figure 2 Free market and optimal levels of production
In a free market, production will take place at 0B where MPC = MPB. However, the socially optimal level of production is 0A where marginal social cost and marginal social benefit are the same.

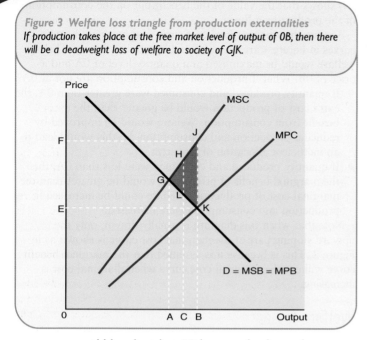

Figure 3 Welfare loss triangle from production externalities
If production takes place at the free market level of output of 0B, then there will be a deadweight loss of welfare to society of GJK.

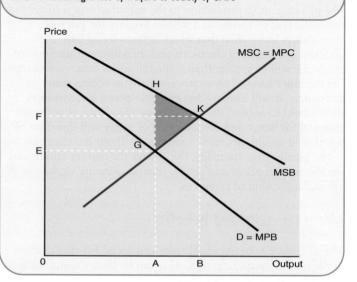

Figure 4 Welfare loss triangle from positive consumption externalities
If production takes place at the free market level of output of 0B, then there will be a deadweight loss of welfare to society of GHK.

consumers would buy less than 0B because the demand curve shows the value or utility placed by consumers on the product. If the price were lower than 0E, producers would not be prepared to supply 0B because they would make a loss on the last or marginal units produced.

However, the socially optimum level of production is lower than 0B. It is 0A where marginal social cost equals marginal social benefit (MSC = MSB). The price of 0F is higher than the free market price of 0E. This reflects the fact that the free market price does not include the production externality generated by the good.

If production and consumption takes place at 0B, then there is a welfare loss to society. The loss is the difference between the marginal social cost and the marginal private benefit shown in Figure 3. On the last unit produced, the 0Bth unit, this is JK. On the 0Cth unit, the welfare loss is HL. So the total welfare loss is the sum of the vertical distances between the MSC curve and MSB curve between the output levels of 0A and 0B. This is the triangle GJK, sometimes called the **welfare loss triangle** or the **deadweight loss triangle**.

The same analysis can be applied to when there are CONSUMPTION EXTERNALITIES or EXTERNALITIES IN CONSUMPTION. Figure 4 shows a situation where the MARGINAL SOCIAL BENEFIT is greater than the MARGINAL PRIVATE BENEFIT. This means that there are positive externalities. For example, if some individuals pay to go to the gym to keep fit, it benefits others because they are less likely later in life to suffer health problems. In Figure 4, it is assumed that the marginal social cost and marginal private cost is the same, and so the curve is simply called the marginal cost (MC) curve. The free market equilibrium is at an output level of 0A where MC = MPB, the marginal cost of production is equal to the marginal private benefit of consumption. However, the socially optimum level of output is 0B where MC = MSB, the marginal cost equals the marginal social benefit. If the output were at 0B, an extra GHK of welfare could be gained. There is therefore a loss of welfare of GHK compared to the socially optimal level of production.

Figure 5 shows a situation where there is a negative externality in consumption. An example would be

parents smoking at home and forcing children to smoke through passive smoking. The free market equilibrium is at 0A where MC = MPB. The socially optimal level of production and consumption is 0B. The welfare loss due to passive smoking is GHK.

Government policy

The government has a wide range of policies that it could use to bring about an efficient allocation of resources where externalities exist.

Regulation Regulation is a method which is widely used in the UK and throughout the world to control externalities. The government could lay down maximum pollution levels or might even ban pollution creating activities altogether. For instance, in the UK, the Environmental Protection Act 1989 laid down minimum environmental standards for emissions from over 3 500

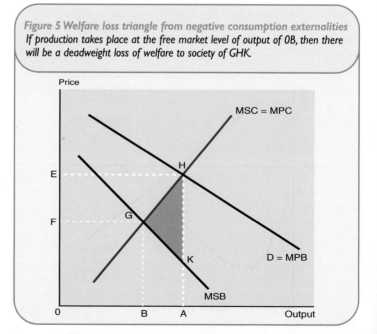

Figure 5 Welfare loss triangle from negative consumption externalities
If production takes place at the free market level of output of 0B, then there will be a deadweight loss of welfare to society of GHK.

Question 2

Small to medium sized businesses are responsible for 80 per cent of environmental crimes. Yet, according to a report by the House of Commons environmental audit committee, almost all offences fail to be detected or prosecuted by the relevant legal authorities. For example, since 2001 when businesses have had to pay to use waste tips, fly-tipping has increased by 40 per cent. This is the illegal dumping of waste by the roadside, or on waste land. The cost of dealing with fly-tipping is estimated at between £100 million and £150 million per year.

Fly-posting is another major problem, but local authorities will soon be able to recover the cost of removing fly-posting and graffiti from offending companies under the provisions of the Clean Neighbourhoods and Environment Bill. Fly-posting has been regularly used by clubs and concert promoters wishing to advertise particular events. The local area is deluged with posters strapped to lamp posts but not taken down afterwards. Local authorities then have to pay their workers to remove the posters.

The House of Commons Report said that 'unless there is a real threat of being detected, the offender will continue to offend'. The Department for Environment, Food and Rural Affairs believes that, even when prosecutions do reach the court, many companies receive unreasonably small fines for polluting.

Source: adapted from the *Financial Times*, 9.2.2005.

(a) Explain how fly-tipping creates an externality.
(b) From an economic viewpoint, why do lack of detection and small fines for environmental crimes limit the effectiveness of regulation as a way of dealing with environmental problems?
(c) Explain why matching fines to the environmental damage caused might be a better way of dealing with environmental crimes than simply levying fixed penalties.

factories involved in chemical processes, waste incineration and oil refining. There are limits on harmful emissions from car exhausts. Cars that do not meet these standards fail their MOT tests. Forty years before these MOT regulations came into force, the government banned the burning of ordinary coal in urban areas.

Regulation is easy to understand and relatively cheap to enforce. However, it is a rather crude policy. First, it is often difficult for government to fix the right level of regulation to ensure efficiency. Regulations might be too lax or too tight. The correct level would be where the economic benefit arising from a reduction in externality equalled the economic cost imposed by the regulation. For instance, if firms had to spend £30 million fitting anti-pollution devices to plant and machinery, but the fall in pollution was only worth £20 million, then the regulation would have been too tight. If the fall in pollution was worth £40 million, it implies that it would be worth industry spending even more on anti-pollution measures to further reduce pollution and thus further increase the £40 million worth of benefits.

Moreover, regulations tend not to discriminate between different costs of reducing externalities. For instance, two firms might have to reduce pollution emissions by the same amount. Firm A could reduce its emissions at a cost of £3 million whilst it might cost Firm B £10 million to do the same. However, Firm A could double the reduction in its pollution levels at a cost of £7 million. Regulations which set equal limits for all firms will mean that the cost to society of reducing pollution in this case is £13 million (£3 million for Firm A and £10 million for Firm B). However, it would be cheaper for society if the reduction could be achieved by Firm A alone at a cost of £7 million.

Extending property rights If a chemical company lorry destroyed your home, you would expect the chemical company to pay compensation. If the chemical company polluted the atmosphere so that the trees in your garden died, it would be unlikely that you would gain compensation, particularly if the chemical plant were in the UK and the dead trees were in Germany.

Externalities often arise because property rights are not fully allocated. Nobody owns the atmosphere or the oceans, for instance. An alternative to regulation is for government to extend property rights. It can give water companies the right to charge companies which dump waste into rivers or the sea. It can give workers the right to sue for compensation if they have suffered injury as a result of working for a company. It can give local residents the right to claim compensation if pollution levels are more than a certain amount.

Extending property rights is a way of **internalising the externality** - eliminating the externality by bringing it back into the framework of the market mechanism. Fifty years ago, asbestos was not seen as a dangerous material. Today, asbestos companies around the world are having to pay compensation to workers suffering from asbestosis. They have also had to tighten up considerably on safety in the workplace where asbestos is used. Workers have been given property rights which enable them to sue asbestos companies for compensation.

One advantage of extending property rights is that the government does not have to assess the cost of pollution. It is generally assumed that property owners will have a far better knowledge of the value of property than the government. There should also be a direct transfer of resources from those who create pollution to those who suffer. With regulation, in contrast, the losers are not compensated whilst polluters are free to pollute up to the limit despite the fact that the pollution is imposing costs on society.

Question 3

The death of the drinks can is now a distinct possibility in environmentally conscious Germany. Since January, a new refundable deposit of between 25 and 50 cents has been levied on most recyclable cans and bottles. The deposit in effect doubles the retail price of the drinks. Consumers can get their deposit back by returning the empty can to the retailer who sold them the can. However, this is so much trouble for most consumers (and impossible if bought from most vending machines) that sales of drinks in cans have slumped. Can manufacturers estimate that sales of cans in Germany fell by about 50 per cent in the first half of this year.

The new measures have been introduced not just to encourage recycling of cans but also to encourage consumers to move more towards using refillable bottles. Refillable bottles are used in the UK by door step milk delivery companies where empty milk bottles are returned to the dairy to be reused. The deposit, though, was too successful this year. In June, both Coca-Cola and the German Brewers' League ran out of refillable bottles and launched advertising campaigns to stop buyers hoarding them or throwing them away.

Source: adapted from the *Financial Times*, 9.7.2003.

(a) Why might cans and bottles create an externality?
(b) The German scheme is an example of extending property rights. Explain why.
(c) How will the scheme reduce externalities?

There are problems though. One is that a government may not have the ability to extend property rights. This occurs, for instance, when the cause of the externality arises in another country. How do Western governments prevent countries like Brazil from logging huge areas of forest, leading to global warming, which imposes costs on them? One way around this is to pay the agents causing the externality to stop their economic activity. So Western countries could pay countries like Brazil not to log their forests.

Another problem is that extending property rights can be very difficult in many cases. Asbestos companies, for instance, will not pay claims to asbestos workers unless it can definitely be proved that their medical condition was caused by working with asbestos. The compensation process can take years, and many ex-workers die before their cases are settled. They receive no compensation and the asbestos company has not had to include payment in its costs. This would tend to lead to a continuing overproduction of asbestos.

A final problem is that it is often very difficult even for the owners of property rights to assess the value of those rights. For instance, one homeowner might put a far higher value on trees in his or her garden than another homeowner. If a cable company lays cable in the road, cutting the roots of trees in front gardens, should the homeowner who places a high value on trees be compensated more than the homeowner who is fairly indifferent when trees die? What happens if the homeowner wanted to get rid of the trees anyway?

Taxes Another solution, much favoured by economists, is the use of taxes. The government needs to assess the cost to society of a particular negative externality. It then sets tax rates on those externalities equal to the value of the externality. This increases costs to customers by shifting the supply curve to the left. The result is a fall in demand and output and thus fewer externalities are created.

For example, the government might put a tax on petrol for cars because emissions from cars contribute to global warming. The tax should be set at the level where the tax revenues equal the cost to society of the emissions. This **internalises** the externality, as explained above, making the polluter pay the cost of pollution.

Taxes, like extending property rights, have the advantage that they allow the market mechanism to decide how resources should best be allocated. Those creating the highest levels of negative externalities have a greater incentive to reduce those externalities than those creating fewer externalities.

However, it is often very difficult for government to place a monetary value on negative externalities and therefore decide what should be the optimal tax rate. With global warming, for instance, there is considerable disagreement about its likely economic impact. Some environmentalists would argue that the potential economic costs are so large that cars should be virtually priced off the roads. At the opposite extreme, some argue that global warming, if it occurs at all, will bring net economic benefits. For instance, slightly higher temperatures will increase the amount of food that can be produced and make it easier to feed the world's growing population. There is therefore no need for taxes on petrol designed to reduce emissions.

Where positive externalities occur, governments should offer subsidies. It can be argued, for instance, that parks, libraries, art galleries, concert halls and opera houses create positive externalities. Therefore they should be subsidised. As with taxes and negative externalities, the level of

Question 4

Smoking is widely accepted to be a killer. But so too is passive smoking, the taking in of smoke fumes in a room when another person is smoking. A leaked Report from the Scientific Committee on Tobacco and Health indicated that second-hand smoke increased the risk of heart disease by an estimated 25 per cent.

The UK is about to implement the 2003 European Union Tobacco Advertising and Sponsorship Directive which orders member states to outlaw advertising in the press and other forms of media by 2005. The UK has chosen to allow tobacco companies to advertise at the point of sale so long as posters are no larger than a single A5 sheet.

The tobacco industry has long argued that advertising doesn't attract new users or increase the quantity of cigarette smoking. Instead, it shifts customer preferences between brands. It is arguing the implementation of the new ban on advertising will not hurt them. However, there is evidence that overall sales do decline with increases in taxes on tobacco. In Germany, the government over the past 18 months has increased taxes on tobacco, raising the price of a packet of cigarettes from €3.00 to €3.80 (£2.00 to £2.63). Volumes of cigarettes sold have decreased 13 per cent over the period, and are expected to fall further.

Source: adapted from the *Financial Times*, 19.10.2004.

(a) Explain why cigarette smoking causes externalities.
(b) Discuss whether the market failure caused by the sale of cigarettes is best tackled by bans on advertising **or** rising taxes. Use demand and supply diagrams and the concept of price elasticity of demand in the analysis to your answer.

subsidy should equal the positive externality created.

Permits A variation on regulating negative externalities through direct controls is the idea of issuing permits. Assume that the government wishes to control emissions of sulphur into the atmosphere. It issues permits to pollute, the total of which equals the maximum amount of sulphur it wishes to see emitted over a period of time like a year. The government then allocates permits to individual firms or other polluters. This could be done, for instance, on the basis of current levels of emissions by firms or on output of goods giving rise to sulphur emissions in production. The permits are then tradable for money between polluters. Firms which succeed in reducing their sulphur levels below their permit levels can sell their permits to other producers who are exceeding their limits.

The main advantage of permits over simple regulation is that costs in the industry and therefore to society should be lower than with regulation. Each firm in the industry will consider whether it is possible to reduce emissions and at what cost. Assume that Firm A, with just enough permits to meet its emissions, can reduce emissions by 500 tonnes at a cost of £10 million. Firm B is a high polluter and needs 500 tonnes worth of permits to meet regulations. It calculates that it would need to spend £25 million to cut emissions by this amount.

If there was simple regulation, the anti-pollution costs to the industry, and therefore to society, would be £25 million. Firm B would have to conform to its pollution limit whilst there would be no incentive for Firm A to cut pollution.

With permits, Firm A could sell 500 tonnes of permits to Firm B. The cost to society of then reducing pollution would only be £10 million, the cost that Firm A would incur, and not

Question 5

Industry reacted with fury yesterday when the government announced plans to further reduce emissions of greenhouse gases. Under the Kyoto Protocol, signed in 1997, the UK agreed to reduce emissions by 12.5 per cent from their 1990 levels. But government ministers yesterday announced a two-stage plan to cut emissions by 20 per cent from 1990 levels by 2010.

The burden will fall disproportionately on a few heavy industries, such as electricity generation, oil refining, and steel, cement, glass and paper production, which currently account for half of the UK's CO_2 emissions. These industries will have to cut their emissions quite dramatically under a new EU-wide emissions trading scheme starting in 2005. Transport and domestic emissions will not be covered. Individual industrial sites will be allocated a set number of 'emission permits'. For each tonne of CO_2 they produce over their allocation, they will have to buy extra permits from those sites which have produced less CO_2 than they are allowed to.

Business organisations warned that the effect of the scheme would be to increase electricity prices and force production offshore to countries that did not recognise the Kyoto Protocol.

Source: adapted from *The Independent*, 20.1.2004.

(a) Explain what is meant by an 'emission permit'.
(b) How can a system of tradable permits lead to a more efficient way of reducing pollution than simple regulation?
(c) Discuss whether UK producers are being put under an unfair competitive disadvantage because of the Kyoto Protocol.

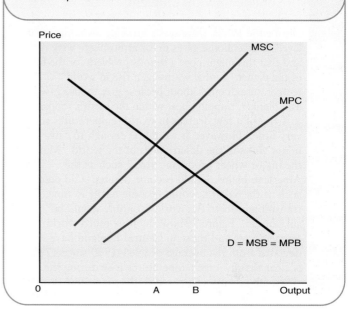

Figure 6 *Effects of different policies*

Regulation and pollution permits attempt to fix output levels at 0A, the socially optimal point of production and consumption. Extending property rights and taxes attempt to do the same thing by shifting the MPC curve upwards so that it becomes equal to to the MSC curve.

£25 million as with regulation. It might cost Firm B more than £10 million to buy the permits. It would be prepared to spend anything up to £25 million to acquire them. Say Firm A drove a hard bargain and sold the permits to Firm B for £22 million. Society would save £15 million (£25 million - £10 million), distributed between a paper profit of £12 million for Firm A and a fall in costs from what otherwise would have been the case for Firm B of £3 million.

Using diagrams to illustrate government policy

These different policies can be illustrated on a marginal social cost and benefit diagram. In Figure 6, it is assumed that externalities arise in production and so the marginal social cost is higher than the marginal private cost. The socially optimal level of production is 0A but the free market level of production is 0B.

- **Regulation** attempts to fix output at 0A. In the case of emissions, this is typically done by controlling the level of emissions. With a given state of technology, this then determines the socially optimal output level.
- **Extending property rights** attempts to make the marginal social cost curve and marginal private cost identical by shifting the MPC curve upwards. This is done by changing the externality into a private cost of production.
- **Taxation** again attempts to make the marginal social cost curve and marginal private cost the same. The tax should be levied in such a way that the marginal tax plus the MPC equals the MSC at output 0A.
- **Pollution permits** act like regulations. In theory, permits to pollute should be given so that production is limited to 0A.

Key terms

Consumption externalities or external benefits in consumption - when the social costs of consumption are different from the private costs of consumption.

Externality or spillover effect - the difference between social costs and benefits and private costs and benefits. If net social cost (social cost minus social benefit) is greater than net private cost (private cost minus private benefit), then a **negative externality** or **external cost** exists. If net social benefit is greater than net private benefit, a **positive externality** or **external benefit** exists.

Marginal social and private costs and benefits - the social and private costs and benefits of the last unit either produced or consumed.

Private cost and benefit - the cost or benefit of an activity to an individual economic unit such as a consumer or a firm.

Production externalities or externalities in production - when the social costs of production differ from the private costs of production.

Social cost and benefit - the cost or benefit of an activity to society as a whole.

Applied economics

Global warming

The environmental problem

During the 1980s, there was a growing awareness that levels of greenhouse gases in the atmosphere were rising and that this might pose a serious problem for the future of the planet. Global warming, a rise in world temperatures, comes about because greenhouse gases act as a blanket, trapping heat within the earth's atmosphere.

A rise of a few degrees in world temperatures sounds very little. However, it would be enough to cause major shifts in the desert zones of the world. Many of the major wheat producing areas, such as the American plains, would become deserts. Old deserts, such as the Sahara, would become fertile in time. The transition costs to the world economy would be substantial. Figure 7 shows by how much world temperatures and those in Central England have deviated from the average of 1961-1990 since 1772. It is clear that average temperatures rose during the twentieth century compared to the nineteenth century. It is also clear that average temperatures since 1990 have been rising compared to the historical average. Four of the five warmest years since 1772 in Central England have been since 1990.

A second problem associated with global warming is rising sea levels. Higher world temperatures would lead to some melting of the polar icecaps, releasing large volumes of water in the oceans. With a 3 degree centigrade rise in world temperatures, there could be an increase in sea levels of 30cm. This would be enough to flood areas such as the east coast of England, the Bangladesh delta and the Maldive Islands. Sea defences and dykes could and probably would be built, but the cost to the world economy would be considerable. Figure 8 shows sea level rises that have already taken place at selected sites around the UK between 1850 and 2006.

Sources of greenhouse gas emissions

Figure 9 shows that around 80 per cent of greenhouse gas emissions come from carbon dioxide. Almost all the rest is split roughly equally between methane and nitrous oxide.

In terms of who creates these emissions, roughly 90 per cent of carbon dioxide emissions are split equally between the

transport, industry and domestic sectors. Petrol and diesel fuels account for almost all transport CO_2 emissions. Industry uses power generated by burning gas, coal and oil, as well as a variety of industrial processes which in themselves release CO_2 into the atmosphere. Equally, homes use gas, electricity and oil for heating and other uses. Agriculture creates roughly half the methane and nitrous oxide emissions. Nitrous oxide comes from fertilisers that farmers put onto the

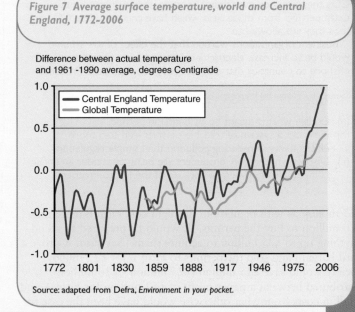

Figure 7 Average surface temperature, world and Central England, 1772-2006

Difference between actual temperature and 1961 -1990 average, degrees Centigrade

Source: adapted from Defra, *Environment in your pocket.*

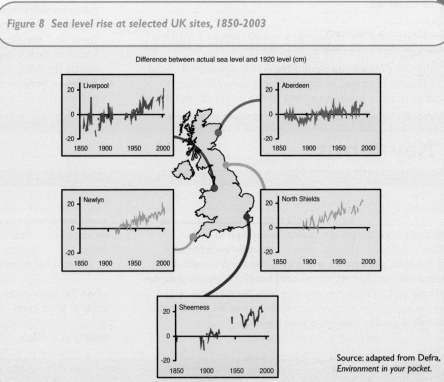

Figure 8 Sea level rise at selected UK sites, 1850-2003

Difference between actual sea level and 1920 level (cm)

Source: adapted from Defra, *Environment in your pocket.*

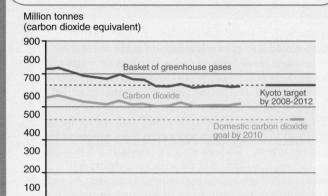

Figure 9 *UK emissions of greenhouse gases, 1990-2006*

Million tonnes
(carbon dioxide equivalent)

Source: adapted from Defra, *Environment in your pocket.*

Figure 10 *Road transport emissions and Gross Domestic Product, 1990-2005*

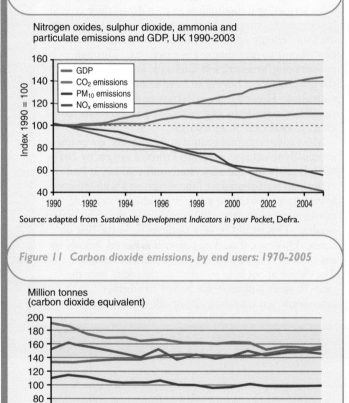

Nitrogen oxides, sulphur dioxide, ammonia and particulate emissions and GDP, UK 1990-2003

Source: adapted from *Sustainable Development Indicators in your Pocket*, Defra.

Figure 11 *Carbon dioxide emissions, by end users: 1970-2005*

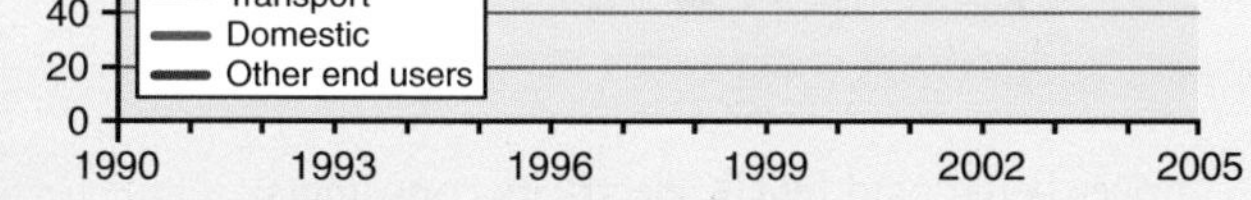

Million tonnes
(carbon dioxide equivalent)

Source: adapted from Defra, *Environment in your pocket.*

land, whilst methane comes from sheep and cattle.

Reducing greenhouse gas emissions

It is easy to assume that there is a direct link between growth in the economy and pollution: the higher the income of a country, for example, the higher its

pollution levels. However, the evidence does not bear this out. Figure 10 shows how road transport CO_2 emissions have risen far less than the increase in real income (GDP) over the period. Whilst the number of miles travelled by passenger cars increased 18 per cent, CO_2 emissions only went up 6 per cent and nitrous oxides and particulate emissions fell. There are two main reasons why higher growth may lead to less rather than more pollutions. First, as in the case of road vehicles, the technology becomes less polluting. Advances in technology mean that emissions per mile travelled has fallen. Also, most of the growth in spending has been on low pollution services anyway. Manufacturing and primary sector industries, which are big polluters, have shrunk in size.

Second, government has been implementing policies to reduce the amount of pollution. Some of these policies have come about because of agreed action on an international scale. For example, the Montreal Protocol signed in 1987 committed 93 countries, including the major industrialised nations of the world, to phasing out the use of CFCs which were destroying the earth's ozone layer. The Rio Summit of 1992, which was followed by the Kyoto Protocol of 1997, led to industrialised nations, excluding the USA, agreeing to reducing greenhouse gas emissions to 12.5 per cent less than their 1990 levels.

Figure 11 shows how greenhouse gas emissions by end user have changed since 1970. Carbon emissions of the electricity generation industry have been divided up according to who consumes the electricity. Figure 11 shows that industry has been the most successful end user in reducing carbon emissions. Reduction in domestic emissions have come almost entirely from less carbon polluting forms of electricity generation. Transport in the 1990s and early 2000s saw a small increase in carbon emissions. 'Other users' is mainly agriculture, which has made a small but not particularly significant contribution to reductions in carbon emissions.

UK policies

In signing the 1997 Kyoto Protocol, the UK government agreed to reduce its greenhouse gas emissions to 12.5 per cent less than their 1990 levels by 2010. In 2004, it went further, announcing that it would reduce emissions to 20 per cent less than their 1990 levels by 2010. The government has adopted a piecemeal approach to ensuring that it meets its greenhouse gas emission targets.

One major source of greenhouse gas emissions is industry, including the power generation industry. In 2005 the government, in conjunction with other EU countries, introduced an emissions trading scheme. Existing industrial users were given carbon permits for each site they operated. If the company created more carbon than its total permits allowed, it would have to buy permits on the open market from other companies which created less carbon than their total permits allowed. Over time, companies will be given fewer permits, giving them an incentive to reduce their carbon emissions.

Industrial users include electricity generation companies. In the 1980s and 1990s, major reductions in carbon emissions were achieved by the shrinkage of the coal industry and a shift towards more carbon efficient electricity power stations powered by gas. However, the government now faces a dilemma because of nuclear power. In 2005, around 20 per cent of UK electricity was generated by nuclear power stations. These, however, are nearing the end of their operational life. They could be replaced by building new nuclear power stations, but this would be vigourously opposed by the environmental lobby on safety grounds. Equally, they could be replaced by 'renewable' energy sources such as wind power. However, renewable energy sources are still relatively expensive. There are environmental concerns about building large numbers of 'wind farms' which 'spoil' the landscape where they are situated. Finally, there are doubts about whether renewables can provide energy security at all times of the year given that there are times when the wind doesn't blow or the sun doesn't shine and so no electricity is generated. The third alternative is to build more gas or coal fired stations, but this would lead to a significant increase in greenhouse gas emissions which would make achieving the Kyoto targets impossible.

Transport, too, poses problems for government policy. Increasing numbers of road journeys have led carbon emissions from transport to increase over time. In 1993, the Chancellor announced that the duty on fuel would be increased by 3 per cent per year above the rate of inflation to curb growth in journeys. In 1998, this was increased to 6 per cent. However, this policy was effectively abandoned in 2000 when a blockade of oil refineries by a mix of farmers and road hauliers angry at high fuel prices brought the country almost to a standstill. It is also doubtful whether higher petrol prices would lead to much reduction in the number of car journeys made because fuel is highly price inelastic. Government policy with regard to road transport is now mainly targeted at reducing congestion rather than fuel emissions. Road transport is likely to add to carbon emissions over the next decade rather than reduce them.

Growth in air transport poses even more problems for the government. With air traffic growing at 3-5 per cent per annum, it is likely that the aviation industry will contribute to higher carbon emissions in future. As with road transport, the main focus of government policy is concentrated on how to accommodate the growth of air transport rather than curbing it to achieve lower carbon emissions over time.

The government has a large number of small scale initiatives to curb carbon emissions by households. These range from encouraging householders to lag their lofts, to getting householders to turn down their central heating and getting builders to build new houses which are more energy efficient. Agriculture is also a major contributor to greenhouse gas emissions. Through encouraging 'greener', less intensive, farming methods, the government is hoping to have some impact on emissions. However, the government does not expect significant reductions in greenhouse gas emissions from either households or agriculture.

Most environmental groups argue that the government is unlikely to achieve its Kyoto Protocol targets by 2010. With households and agriculture only making at best very small contributions to the target, and with emissions from transport likely to grow, it is industry including power generation that will have to make the reduction needed. This would be very challenging at the best of times. However, if nuclear power is replaced, mainly by gas or coal fired power stations, it will be impossible. The choice about how to generate electricity over the next 20 years will probably be key to whether greenhouse gas emissions rise or fall in the UK.

DataQuestion — Nuclear power generation

In recent decades, around one fifth of electricity in the UK has been generated from nuclear power stations. However, the last nuclear power station to be built was completed in 1995. Over the next 30 years, all the UK's existing nuclear power stations will close because of age. In its 2007 Energy White Paper, the government stated that it was in favour of building new nuclear power stations for two reasons.

- Nuclear power was a relatively cheap form of generating electricity given that it produced very little greenhouse gases. Using other forms of energy generation would lead to higher prices being paid by UK electricity consumers.
- The UK needed to have a range of energy resources to ensure security of supplies. For example, the amount of electricity generated from many renewables like wind power depended on the weather. Gas supplies might be imported from abroad and those supplies could be cut off if there were an international dispute.

However, many, including environmental groups, oppose any resumption of building of nuclear stations.

Source: adapted from dti, 'The role of nuclear power in a low carbon UK economy', May 2007.

In the 2007 Energy White Paper the government published estimates of how much carbon in grams different forms of electricity generation emitted per kilowatt of energy produced. The range of estimate is shown by the horizontal distance on each block in Figure 12. The estimate is over the lifecyle of the plant. Coal and natural gas produce most of their carbon emissions when burning fuel. Wind and nuclear energy create carbon emissions when windmills and nuclear plants are manufactured, built and then taken down or decommissioned.

Figure 12 Relative carbon emissions of generating technologies

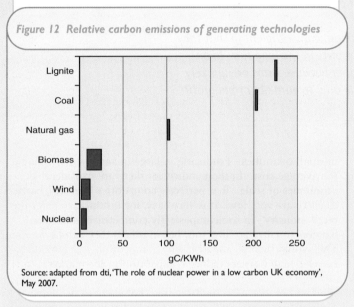

Source: adapted from dti, 'The role of nuclear power in a low carbon UK economy', May 2007.

In its 2007 Energy White Paper, the government estimated the relative cost of generating 1 megawatt of electricity at the prices of energy in November 2006. For coal and gas, it added a carbon tax of €25 per tonne of CO_2 emitted. The bars in Figure 13 show the range of prices from different plants, with a central estimate given in red for nuclear and renewable energy. For coal and gas, the red bar shows the cost of generation and the green bar the cost of the carbon tax.

Figure 13 Cost of electricity generation based on November 2006 fuel prices and a carbon price of €25 per tonne of carbon emissions

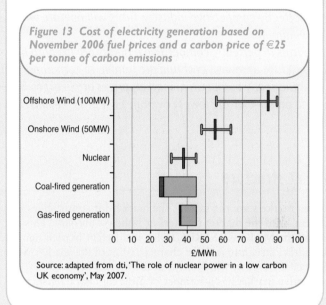

Source: adapted from dti, 'The role of nuclear power in a low carbon UK economy', May 2007.

Environmental pressure groups attacked the 2007 Energy White Paper as misguided. They were particularly critical of the government's proposals to build new nuclear power stations.

- They pointed out that whilst nuclear power provided 20 per cent of the UK's electricity, it only provided around 4 per cent of the nation's total energy.
- Nuclear power stations have a history of being more costly to build than predicted.
- The technology is inherently unsafe. If a nuclear power plant went into meltdown, as in Chernobyl in Russia in 1986, it would have devastating consequences for the local and international environment.
- The full cost of decommissioning nuclear plants is unclear but it is large. At the moment, there is no strategy for what to do with the UK's most radioactive waste which will still be dangerous in 1000 years time.

The government has totally underestimated the cost of clean up.
- There is a danger that radioactive material from nuclear power plants will fall into the hands of terrorists.
- The proposed sites for new nuclear power stations in the UK are all on the coast and could be flooded if sea levels rise significantly due to global warming.
- Although the cost of renewable energies is higher now than for gas and coal, further development will bring the cost down substantially. The true cost of gas, coal and nuclear energies are considerably underestimated. The real cost of CO_2 emissions from coal and gas plants, for example, is much higher than the current carbon levy or tax.

Source: with information from Greenpeace, the 2007 Energy White Paper - Media briefing; Friends of the Earth, Press release: Energy White Paper reaction.

1. Using examples from the data, what might be included in (a) the private cost and (b) the social cost of generating electricity from nuclear power stations?
2. Using a diagram, explain why environmental groups like Greenpeace might suggest that the current taxes on carbon emissions from coal and gas fired electricity power stations are too low.
3. An environmental pressure group suggests that motorists should be forced to cut the number of miles

they travel by 20 per cent. This would be achieved by considerably increasing the tax on petrol, trebling its price. At the same time, the number of air flights into and out of the UK should be frozen. Discuss whether these measures would be a better solution to solve the UK's energy problems than building nuclear power stations. In your answer, compare the social and private costs and benefits of the proposals.

Summary

1. Competitive markets tend to be characterised by a number of different firms, none of which is able to control the market, producing homogeneous or weakly branded goods, in a market where there are low barriers to entry and there is perfect knowledge.
2. Firms in competitive markets are likely only to earn normal profit in the long run. In a perfectly competitive industry, firms will operate where their average costs are at a minimum.
3. Firms in perfectly competitive markets are likely to be economically efficient in that they produce at lowest cost and are unable to earn abnormal profits in the long run. In an imperfectly competitive market, prices are likely to be higher because firms are unlikely to produce at the lowest average cost possible and may be able to earn abnormal profits.

Market structure

No two markets are the same. The market for sports shoes is different from the market for steel or holidays abroad. This is because the MARKET STRUCTURE is different in each market. The market structure is those characteristics of the market which influence the way in which firms in the market behave. A **competitive market** has a number of different characteristics.

A number of different firms in the industry In a competitive industry there are at least two firms in the industry. In the most competitive industries, where there is PERFECT COMPETITION, there is a large number of firms, none of which is large enough to have any economic power over the industry. In farming, for instance, there are large numbers of farms. Even the largest farm in the UK still produces only a very small fraction of total farming output. In other industries, there is IMPERFECT COMPETITION, i.e. there is not full competition in the market. In some imperfectly competitive industries, there are large numbers of small firms. In most, though, a few firms tend to dominate the industry. In the grocery retailing industry in the UK, for instance, the largest four supermarket chains sell over 50 per cent of all goods (i.e. their MARKET SHARE is more than 50 per cent). In the soap powder industry, two firms have over 80 per cent of the market.

Entry to the industry New firms are constantly being set up. Existing firms may expand their product range and enter new markets. In some markets, it is easier to set up and enter than in others. The obstacles to setting up are called BARRIERS TO ENTRY. There are many types of barrier to entry. For instance, it may be so costly to set up that only very large firms could consider entering the industry. Car manufacturing is an example. On the other hand, it is relatively cheap to set up in business as a grocery store. The law may be another barrier to entry. For instance, to set up a pharmacy in the UK, you have to have a licence. When setting up as a book publisher, you cannot print any books where the copyright is owned by another publisher. No firm in the UK is legally allowed to enter the drugs trade. Costs of production might be another barrier to entry. In industries like car manufacturing or bulk chemical production it is very expensive to produce

in small quantities. Producing in large quantities drives down the average cost. In these industries there are considerable **economies of scale**. In a perfectly competitive industry, barriers to entry are very low. It is very easy, for instance, to enter the retail industry. In some imperfectly competitive industries, barriers to entry are low too, but in others they can be very high. This would then be a reason why competition was imperfect, because high barriers reduce competition in the market.

Product homogeneity and branding For there to be perfect competition, customers must be able to have a wide choice of supplier, all of whom are selling the same product. This means the goods being sold must be HOMOGENEOUS. In farming, for instance, carrots are a standard product. No farmer can claim that his or her carrots are different from those of another farmer. The same is true for products such as steel, oil, basic chemicals and copper.

In an imperfectly competitive market, however, the product of one firm is different from that of another. Persil washing powder is different from Ariel. A Vauxhall Vectra is different from a Ford Escort. Firms are then said to BRAND their products.

Knowledge In a perfectly competitive industry, there is PERFECT KNOWLEDGE. This means that all firms have access to the same information. They can all find out what is the current market price. There are no trade secrets. All firms have access to the same information about production techniques. In an imperfectly competitive industry, there might be perfect knowledge or knowledge may be imperfect when firms have secret formulations which make their products unique. The formula for Coca-Cola, for instance, is known only to a few at Coca-Cola itself. Firms may keep knowledge about methods of production to themselves, not allowing rivals to see how a good is manufactured.

Prices, profits and costs in competitive markets

In perfectly competitive markets, like farming or copper mining:
- there are large numbers of small firms in the industry;
- there is freedom of entry to the market;
- firms produce identical or homogeneous goods;

Question 1

The dry cleaning market is shrinking. According to estimates by Mintel, the market research company, revenues have fallen by 10 per cent since 1999. It estimates that there are now about 4 500 dry cleaning outlets in the UK, compared to almost 5 300 in 2000.

Some factors behind the trend are positive. The number of high income, AB socio-economic group, adults is rising as is the number of households where both adults are out at work and thus have less time for domestic chores. Other factors, though, outweigh these positive trends. People are dressing more casually. Fewer men wear suits to the office for example. Equally, the price of formal wear, such as suits, is coming down. A growing number of people don't bother to dry clean a cheap £80 suit when the cost of cleaning is £20. Instead, they prefer to go out and buy another cheap suit.

The dry cleaning businesses which have the best chance of survival are those which provide a high quality service and whose customers buy up market, expensive, designer label clothes. New legislation will also add to dry cleaners' costs. The European Directive on solvent emissions means that dry cleaners will have to use less chemicals per item to reduce workers' exposure to dangerous fumes. Dry cleaners could face a bill of about £200 a year from their local authority just to cover the administration costs of the relevant licences. In some cases, a company will need to upgrade its cleaning machines, costing about £25 000 each. Some estimates suggest that about one quarter of the industry will disappear as a result of the new legislation.

The industry is highly fragmented. An estimated 64 per cent of the market is supplied by small independent firms. The largest player in the market is Johnson Service Group with 638 outlets nationwide but it still only has 24 per cent of the market. Supermarket groups such as Asda and Tesco are also expanding their share of the market. However, convenience, being able to pop into a shop near where you live, is still a key competitive advantage for the small independent dry cleaner.

Source: adapted from the *Financial Times*, 5.7.2005.

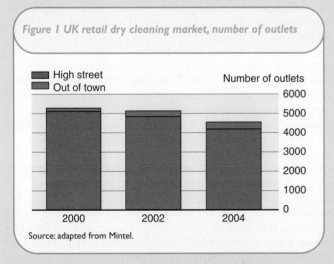

Figure 1 *UK retail dry cleaning market, number of outlets*

High street
Out of town

Number of outlets

Source: adapted from Mintel.

(a) Describe the market structure of the UK dry cleaning industry.
(b) To what extent is the UK dry cleaning industry competitive?
(c) Discuss whether the dry cleaning industry might become more competitive in future if supermarket groups such as Tesco expand further in the dry cleaning market.

● perfect knowledge exists throughout the industry.

This market structure affects the way in which firms behave. Because there is freedom of entry to a market where firms produce identical goods, all firms will charge the same price in equilibrium. To understand why, consider what would happen if a firm charged a higher price than other firms. Customers would then switch their demand to other firms because other firms are offering identical products. The firm charging the higher price will lose all its sales and go out of business. If a firm charged a lower price than all other firms, then buyers would switch away from other firms and they would all lose their customers. So they would have to cut their prices to stay in the industry.

Competition will not drive prices down to zero. In the long term, firms will only supply a good if they can make a profit. The minimum profit that a firm must make to prevent it from moving its economic resources to production of another good is called NORMAL PROFIT. If firms in a perfectly competitive industry are able to make ABNORMAL PROFITS, profit which is greater than normal profit, then new firms will be attracted into the industry. They will want to take advantage of being able to earn higher than normal profit. However, their entry will increase supply and drive prices down. The long run equilibrium price will be the one where prices are just high enough for firms to make normal profits, so no firms are being forced out of the industry, but equally no firms are being attracted into the industry.

Firms in a perfectly competitive industry will also produce at lowest average cost. Assume that one firm was a higher cost producer than other firms in the industry. It would have to charge the same price as other firms or risk losing all its customers. But then its profits would be lower than those of other firms because its costs were higher. Since all other firms are only earning normal profit, it would be making less than normal profit, the minimum profit needed to persuade the owners of the firm to keep their resources in that industry. So this firm would leave the industry because it was not sufficiently profitable.

On the other hand, assume that a firm could produce at lower cost than other firms and was making abnormal profit. Then other firms would be able to find out why this firm had lower costs because there is perfect knowledge in the industry. If it is because the firm has adopted new production methods, then these production methods will be taken up by other firms. If it is because the firm has a particularly productive factor of production, other firms will attempt to buy it, raising its price and hence its cost. For instance, if success is due to a very successful managing director, then other firms will attempt to employ him or her by offering a higher salary. In the long term, costs will become the same across the industry. They will be the minimum cost possible.

In imperfectly competitive industries:
● there may be many small firms in the industry or it could be dominated by just a few firms;
● there might be relatively free entry to the industry or there might be barriers to entry;
● firms produce branded goods;
● there may or may not be perfect knowledge.

This market structure limits competition. Because each firm is producing a slightly different branded product, it

Question 2

The great British sandwich is alive and well, even if 30 per cent of the market is made up of 'innovative' or 'exotic' products. These are products such as chicken ciabatta, or Italian chicken with sun dried tomato in focaccia, which are increasing favourites with customers tired of cheese and tomato or egg mayonnaise.

The sandwich market is highly competitive. According to the British Sandwich Association, the industry trade body, there are about 5 000 independently owned sandwich shops compared with 700 chain outlets. The chain outlets include highly successful companies such as Subway and Pret A Manger. The chain outlets bring high quality standardised products. The independent outlets offer everything from convenience on the local parade of shops to unique product offerings and a flexibility to change their offerings from week to week to satisfy local demand and tastes in Glasgow, Birmingham or London.

Since the 1990s, sales of sandwiches have steadily soared as high-income, time-pressed consumers identify the sandwich as a health alternative to fast food. Last year 1.8 billion sandwiches were sold for £3.5 billion, an increase of 5 per cent on the year before. New businesses continue to come into the market, including McDonald's, which recently added a range of toasted deli sandwiches to its menu, while Burger King now offers fresh backed baguettes. Equally, there has been no shortage of new local independent shops opening up to exploit the growing market.

Source: adapted from the *Financial Times*, 20.6.2005.

(a) Why are new entrants to the UK sandwich market unlikely to earn abnormal profit despite a growing market?

is able to some extent to decide on what price it will charge. If other firms charge lower prices, it is likely to still keep some of its customers who will remain loyal to buying its branded good.

Market power will increase the fewer the number of competitors and the higher the barriers to entry. If entry barriers are very high, firms will be able to charge higher prices without worrying that new entrants will come in and take away market share. So in imperfect competition it could be that competitive pressures are strong enough to force profits down to a normal level in the long run. However, it is more likely that firms will be charging high enough prices to earn abnormal profit.

Competition and efficiency

Perfect competition is likely to lead to economic efficiency. First, firms in a perfectly competitive industry will, in the long run, be productively efficient. As explained above, competitive pressures will ensure that firms produce at lowest average cost. If they fail to do so, they will be driven out of the industry. Second, firms will be efficient in other ways. Customers will be able to buy at the lowest price that is possible because firms are only able to make normal profit.

In contrast, firms in imperfectly competitive industries are likely to be inefficient. There is no pressure to produce at lowest average cost because firms produce branded goods. This gives them some control over how much they wish to sell, i.e. it gives them some control over where on the demand curve they sell. Firms will choose to sell where profit is maximised and this is unlikely to be the minimum average cost point. Hence, imperfectly competitive firms are unlikely to be productively efficient.

They are unlikely to be efficient in other ways. Production would be greater and prices lower if the industry were perfectly competitive. Firms in imperfect competition are likely to earn abnormal profits. If they earned only normal profit, they would have to cut prices and expand their production. Hence, in imperfect competition, firms restrict supply in order to exploit the customer for abnormal profit. Even where firms earn only normal profit, output is still likely to be lower and prices higher than if the industry were perfectly competitive. This is because firms will choose to produce where profit is maximised, in this case where they are earning just normal profit, and not where average costs are lowest.

So far, aspects of static efficiency have been explained. Perfect competition is likely to lead to productive efficiency, whilst imperfect competition is not. Therefore perfect competition is likely to lead to static efficiency, whilst imperfect competition is not. However, perfect competition may not lead to greater **dynamic efficiency**. There is no incentive to innovate over time in a perfectly competitive industry. Because there is perfect knowledge in the industry, discoveries and inventions by one firm will become quickly available for use by all other firms. There is therefore no point in spending large amounts on research and development. In imperfect competition where firms can protect innovation, for instance through patents and copyrights, they have an incentive to be innovative. If they can develop a new product which customers like, they can sell it at a high price and earn abnormal profit on it.

Question 3

Sending freight across France by rail should be straightforward. But the freight division of SNCF, France's national railway company, is dominated by powerful local divisions and poor co-ordination between them often disrupts long-distance trains. The result is high prices, long journey times and unreliable service. France is not unique. European railways have long suffered from a lack of competition leading to disorganisation and inefficiency.

This is all about to change. Since March 15, 2003, any company has the right to compete with traditional operators on cross-border rail freight on the main trans-European routes. All they need are an operating certificate and safety clearances. The law is the first stage of a drive to introduce competition on Europe's railways. In the long term, the vision is that any company will be able to offer freight services across Europe's rail tracks, however long or short the journey.

Competition has already been introduced within national railways in some countries like the UK and Germany. In the Netherlands, Ewout Sandker, policy manager for the European Shippers' Council, an industry group, says the service of Railion Nederland, the Dutch traditional rail freight operation, was transformed after it lost some contracts to private operators. 'Users saw an immediate change in the traditional railway company's behaviour, its service orientation', Mr Sandker says.

In France, SNCF is due to restructure its operations. It is also planning to invest €500 million in new locomotives to speed up journey times and increase reliability.

Matthias Raith, managing director of Rail4Chem, a new freight operator, says traditional railways have long overcharged certain customers. His company, he says, offers a cheaper, more responsive alternative. That should force traditional railways to charge more realistic prices.

Source: adapted from the *Financial Times*, 22.9.2004.

(a) How might increased competition in the European rail freight market lead to greater efficiencies in the market?

Key terms

Abnormal profit - the profit over and above normal profit.
Barriers to entry - factors which make it difficult or impossible for firms to enter an industry and compete with existing producers.
Branded good - a named good which in the perception of its buyers is different from other similar goods on the market.
Homogeneous goods - goods which are identical.
Imperfect competition - a market structure where there are several firms in the industry, each of which has the ability to control the price that it sets for its products.
Market share - the proportion of sales in a market taken by a firm or a group of firms.

Market structure - the characteristics of a market which determine the behaviour of firms within the market.
Normal profit - the profit that the firm could make by using its resources in their next best use. Normal profit is an economic cost.
Perfect competition - a market structure where there are many buyers and sellers, where there is freedom of entry and exist to the market, where there is perfect knowledge and where all firms produce a homogeneous good.
Perfect knowledge or information - exists if all buyers in a market are fully informed of prices and quantities for sale, whilst producers have equal access to information about production techniques.

Applied economics

Low-cost airlines move into the long-haul market

Low-cost carriers have transformed short-haul airline routes both in Europe and the USA. In Europe, companies like Ryanair and easyJet have entered the market and decimated the market share of most established airline companies. They have done this by cutting prices and opening up new airline routes. Prices have fallen because low-cost carriers have cut costs - everything from salaries and numbers of staff, to landing fees at airports to onboard catering to turnaround time of planes. Competition has cut prices, increased passenger numbers and reduced inefficiency in the industry.

The race is now on to take this model into the long-haul market. Traditional airline companies still have nearly 100 per cent market share on long-haul routes but this could be about to change. A number of low-cost carriers have entered the market, initially in the business-class segment. On most long-haul routes, airlines carry economy-class passengers almost at cost or even at a loss. The profit on each flight comes from charging high fares to business-class passengers. So the easiest segment to attack is the business-class segment. The transatlantic route from Europe to the America's Eastern seaboard is also the best place to start. The London-New York route is the world's busiest long-haul route with more than 4 million passengers a year. In 2005, Eos Airlines and Maxjet, two new start-up airlines, began offering all business-class services from the UK to New York. In 2007, Silverjet, another start-up, followed and L'Avion, a French start-up, began flying from Paris to New York. Two established low-cost carriers, Air Asia and Ryanair, have plans to enter the market.

Some analysts, however, question whether the low-cost business business can work on long-haul routes. They point that passengers need costly in-flight services for journeys that take many hours. Also some of the key operating factors in the short-haul model, such as quick airport turnarounds, are much tougher to achieve in long long-haul. What's more, at the bottom end of the market, established carriers offer cheap flights. The average budget ticket costs £18 per hour of flight, which is lower than the Ryanair's average on short-haul routes in Europe. To reduce fares further, airline companies like Ryanair will have to find significant economy savings. If they can't find these, they are unlikely to enter the market. Existing competition and the threat of competition from new airlines will keep the traditional airline companies lean and efficient. There may be room in the market for a few small specialist business-class airlines offering budget prices. But business-class travel is more price inelastic than economy-class travel. So traditional airlines are likely to carry on charging high prices to business-class travellers and making most of their profit from them.

DataQuestion   Outdoor equipment suppliers

The outdoor equipment market, worth £1.2 billion a year, is a tough market. In recent years, a number of high-street outdoor retailers have disappeared whilst Blacks Leisure Group has issued profit warnings and is due to close more than 40 of its stores, mainly those operating under the Milletts brand. At the same time, demand is growing, fuelled by the expansion of activity holidays for people on a 'middle-aged gap year' and concern for carbon emissions leading people to choose holidays at home. Consciousness about health and fitness is growing, although the family camping market is shrinking. About one quarter of British adults are regular walkers, climbers or participants in other outdoor activities.

Traditionally, the market has had a large proportion of small outlets. These, disproportionately located in popular walking areas such as the Lake District, provided specialist equipment to serious enthusiasts at premium prices. However, there are a significant number of customers who only walk or climb occasionally. Mass market retailers such as Halfords, Woolworths and Argos have moved into the market providing cheap tents and walking equipment. They offer value and convenience to customers who are more price sensitive and less brand aware than serious enthusiasts. The internet has also expanded the number of retailers accessible to customers. Specialist retailers based in one location now have the opportunity to sell equipment to customers across the UK.

Selling on-line is one way in which specialist retailers can fight back against competition from the likes of Argos and Halfords. Their specialist knowledge and advice is another. Each year, walkers die because they didn't have the right equipment with them. Advice can make the difference between life and death. Emphasising quality, brands and specialist knowledge attract customers to smaller retailers. Some better-known specialists, such as Cotswolds Outdoor and Graham Tiso, are trying to lure customers with new shop

formats. Bigger outlets and in-store attractions such as rock climbing walls and wet areas to test goods are becoming more common. The aim is to make stores leisure destinations in themselves in the same way that garden centres have become.

Source: adapted from the *Financial Times*, 10.4.2007.

1. Describe TWO of the trends in the outdoor equipment retailing industry outlined in the data.
2. Explain the market structure of the UK outdoor equipment retailing industry.

3. To what extent has increased competition in the UK outdoor equipment retailing industry led to economic efficiency?

19 Monopoly and efficiency

Summary

1. A monopoly exists where there is only firm in an industry.
2. Monopolies are protected from competition by barriers to entry to the industry.
3. Monopolies tend to earn abnormal profit by choosing a price higher than would be the case if the industry were competitive.
4. Monopolies are productively efficient if they are natural monopolies exploiting economies of scale and dynamically efficient if their existence leads to technological innovation.
5. Monopolies are also inefficient if they exploit customers by charging higher prices than would be the case under competition.
6. Governments can intervene to correct market failure caused by monopoly activity through taxes and subsidies, prices controls, nationalisation and privatisation, deregulation, breaking up the monopolist or reducing entry barriers.

Monopoly

A MONOPOLY exists where there is only one firm or supplier in an industry. For instance, Transco has a monopoly on UK gas pipelines whilst Railtrack has a monopoly on UK rail infrastructure. In practice, firms which have a dominant share of the market tend to be referred to as monopolists as well. For instance, Microsoft, with 90 per cent of the world's PC operating systems market, could be seen as a monopolist.

Barriers to entry

Firms gain monopoly powers in the long run because of barriers to entry to the industry. There are various barriers to entry which can create monopolies.

Legal barriers The government can create monopolies through the legal system. It can make competition illegal in an industry. For instance, in the UK only pharmacies can sell prescription drugs by law. The government has granted Virgin Trains a monopoly to run train services on the West Coast Main Line railway between Manchester and London.

Resource barriers In some industries, a monopolist may be able to buy or otherwise acquire the key resources needed to produce a good. For instance, an airline may be able to buy up the sole rights to fly from one airport to another. A supermarket chain may be able to buy the only plot of land available for development for a large supermarket in a small town. An electricity company may buy out all the other competing electricity companies in a country. Customers would then be faced with a sole supplier for the product.

Unfair competition Once created, a monopolist may defend itself through unfair competitive practices. For instance, an airline with a monopoly on a route may slash prices below cost if a new entrant comes into the market. When the new entrant is forced out, the monopolist then puts back up its fares. Or the monopolist may refuse to supply customers with other goods if it buys one good from a new entrant into the market.

Natural cost advantages Some firms are natural monopolies. They become monopolies because not even a single firm in the industry is large enough to reduce average costs to their minimum. Size can reduce average costs because of the existence of **economies of scale**.

Economies of scale Economies of scale, such as marketing economies, technical economies or financial economies, vary from industry to industry. In some industries, economies of scale are low. It is easy for small firms to be productively efficient, producing at the lowest point on the average cost curve. When this occurs, the market is likely to be competitive. In Figure 1, a firm with a market share of 1 per cent, is able fully to exploit economies of scale and produces at the lowest point on the average cost curve at output 0A. This is the **productively**

Question 1

Intel has a stranglehold on the world market for personal computer chips. It supplies 80 per cent of all chips put into personal computers (PCs). Last year it made a net profit of $7.5 billion and it makes an average 41 per cent profit over costs on every microprocessor sold. It would argue that its dominance in the market is due to superior products, backed by patents, sold at a competitive price. It would also point out that it has a strong record of bringing new products to market based on considerable research and development spending.

AMD (Advance Micro Devices) would disagree. It has around 10 per cent of the market for PC chips and has just launched a legal claim in US courts against Intel of running an illegal conspiracy to restrict AMD's share of the market. AMD claims that Intel is doing this through a system of rebates and other financial incentives. For example, AMD alleges that: 'In return for payments, (Dixons, the UK high street retailer) has agreed to keep AMD's share of its business below 10%'. Toshiba, once an important AMD customer, has also stopped buying its processors. Four times a year, Toshiba allegedly receives 'market development funds' worth $25-$30 million from Intel. This money is allegedly given on the understanding that Toshiba will not use any AMD microprocessors in its PCs.

Source: adapted from *The Sunday Times*, 3.7.2005.

(a) Explain why Intel, in practice, has a monopoly on production of microprocessors for personal computers.
(b) How might Intel have maintained its monopoly powers over the market?

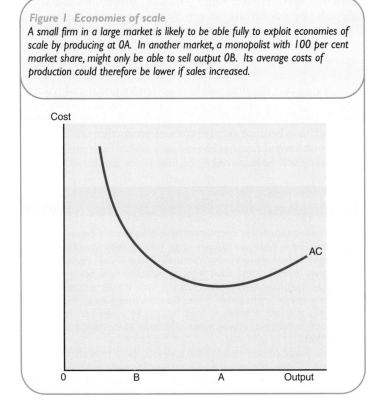

Figure 1 Economies of scale
A small firm in a large market is likely to be able fully to exploit economies of scale by producing at 0A. In another market, a monopolist with 100 per cent market share, might only be able to sell output 0B. Its average costs of production could therefore be lower if sales increased.

sets a price of 0E for its product, it can sell quantity 0A. It can choose to raise its price to 0F but it has to accept that quantity sold will fall to 0B.

The highest price is not necessarily the profit maximising price. If the price is set too high, they could lose profit. This is because the profit gained from sales at a high price could be less than the profit lost from even more sales at a lower price. For instance, a firm might charge £20 for an item costing £12 for which sales are 1 million units. It then makes a profit of £8 per item or a total of £8 million (£8 x 1 million). But it might be able to sell 2 million units if it reduced its price to £17. Its profit per unit would then only be £5, but its total profit would be £10 million (£5 x 2 million).

The profit earned is likely to be **abnormal profit**. It is higher than the minimum amount needed to keep resources employed in that industry, i.e. it is higher than normal profit. The profit is therefore higher than would be earned by the industry if it were **perfectly competitive**. In a perfectly competitive industry, fierce competition between many small firms drives the price down to the point where firms are making just enough profit to stay in

efficient point of production. In contrast, in some industries, there are such large economies of scale that only a few or just one firm can achieve the lowest average costs of production. When just one firm can produce all the output of an industry and still not fully exploit economies of scale, a NATURAL MONOPOLY is said to exist. In Figure 1, assume that there is only one firm in the industry and it produces and sells output 0B. It could reduce its average costs further but the market is not big enough for it to do this. Examples of natural monopolies include transport systems, such as pipeline networks, rail tracks and electricity power grids. If these are underutilised, which they usually are, then it is possible to lower average costs by increasing throughput in the system. This would be an example of a technical economy of scale.

Marketing barriers Monopolies can create marketing barriers, for example through advertising. High levels of advertising can create strong brands which make it difficult, if not impossible, for a new entrant to gain any significant share of the market.

Capital costs The cost of setting up in an industry may be so high that very few, if any, new entrants can enter the market. For example, setting up a new car company costs tens of millions of pounds just to create a specialist car manufacturer. To create a mass car manufacturer would cost hundreds of millions, if not billions, of pounds.

Prices and profits under monopoly

Monopolists, in the absence of government regulations, can set whatever price they choose to customers. They can choose, for instance, whether to charge £10 per item or £2. It should be remembered, though, that the higher the price they set, the lower will be the demand for the product. This is shown in Figure 2. The monopolist faces the demand curve D for its product. If it

Question 2

Tesco is the largest supermarket chain in the UK. In 2005, it announced record profits of £2 billion. In 2005, it had a market share within the grocery market of approximately 33 per cent and sold an astonishing 12.5 per cent by value of everything that is sold in Britain's shops.

Tesco, along with other supermarkets, has however come in for fierce criticism for 'ripping off the consumer' and 'ripping off suppliers'. The supermarkets counter these criticisms by pointing out that supermarkets are in intense competition with each other. But this is not always the case because in many areas, particularly rural areas, a supermarket chain may enjoy a local monopoly. The UK Competition Commission, the government monopoly watchdog, published a report in 2000 which found that Safeway, Sainsbury and Tesco had policies of 'varying prices in different geographical areas in the light of local competition'. Where a supermarket chain enjoyed a local monopoly, prices tended to be higher than in areas where customers had a range of stores within easy travelling distance.

Source: adapted from www.gnn.gov.uk, http://news.bbc.co.uk.

(a) Suggest what might be meant by a supermarket having a 'local monopoly'.
(b) Why might supermarkets increase their prices in areas where they have a local monopoly compared to areas where they are in competition from other supermarkets?
(c) Tesco claims that it charges very low prices to its customers compared to its competitors. Explain why it doesn't raise prices to earn even more profit than the £2 billion it earned in 2004-2005.

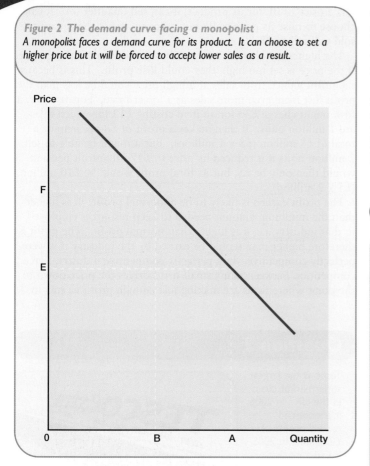

Figure 2 *The demand curve facing a monopolist*
A monopolist faces a demand curve for its product. It can choose to set a higher price but it will be forced to accept lower sales as a result.

the industry, i.e. to the point where firms only make normal profit. If there is **imperfect competition**, firms may be able to charge higher prices than under perfect competition and earn abnormal profit. Whether the price will be as high as under monopoly, or whether the total industry profits will be as high, depends degree of **monopoly power** of individual firms. A number of factors affect the degree of monopoly power.

● The higher the barriers to entry to a market or part of a market (a market segment), the greater the ability of firms in the market to charge higher prices.
● The fewer the firms in the industry, and therefore the higher the degree of concentration, the less competition there will be. So the monopoly power of individual firms is likely to be higher.
● The greater the product different ion (the difference between the product of one firm and another), the less consumers are likely to be able to substitute one product for another. So the greater the product differentiation, the greater the monopoly power of a firm.

Monopoly, efficiency and market failure

A natural monopoly will be producing at the lowest average cost possible for the level of total demand in the industry. Breaking a natural monopoly up into several smaller firms would only result in increased average costs. Hence, natural monopolies are productively efficient, i.e. production is at lowest cost compared to a more competitive industry.

However, if the monopoly is not a natural monopoly, then the effect of a break up is more complex. If the industry becomes perfectly competitive, costs will be driven

down to a minimum and hence productive efficiency will be achieved. By comparison, monopoly is productively inefficient. If the industry became imperfectly competitive, it is not possible to say whether prices or total profits would fall. Hence, it is impossible to make a comparison about productive efficiency.

As for other aspects of efficiency, a natural monopoly is inefficient in that the firm will have driven up prices and reduced output to earn abnormal profit. But splitting up the industry is unlikely to result in efficiency because prices are likely to be even higher. This is because average costs of production will be higher with several firms in the industry rather than just one.

Efficiency will be achieved if the firm is not a natural

Question 3

Land based telephone companies have traditionally been monopolies in Europe. Usually state owned, they have had a stranglehold on voice communication. Today, those monopolies face two threats. First, their legal monopolies have been taken away as they have been privatised and their markets opened up to competition from other firms. Second, they face at the extreme the loss of most of their market to a new technology: the mobile telephone, which has only been in existence since the 1980s.

Land based phone networks are, in fact, most unlikely to disappear. They possess cost advantages for large volumes of traffic over mobile phone networks. There is no limit to the

number of lines that can be laid, whereas there is a limit to the number of calls that can be made on frequencies allocated to mobile phone networks. Established land line networks also represent a 'sunk' cost - a cost that has already been paid for - and so today's cost of using the system is much lower than if the whole system had to be replaced.

Privatisation and competition have led to falling land line telephone charges in real terms. This has benefited customers as has mobile phone technology which allows customers to call from anywhere.

(a) Why might mobile phone technology represent an example of creative destruction in the telephone industry?
(b) Explain how customers have benefited from the breakdown of the monopoly of land line telephone companies.

monopolist and it is split up into a number of perfectly competitive firms. Perfect competition will ensure that prices to customers are as low as possible and that firms are only able to earn normal profit. The reduction in price from competition will expand demand and output in the industry, again benefiting customers.

However, if a monopolist is split up but only imperfect competition results, then there may be no improvement in efficiency. Prices may not fall because the new firms may still earn just as much abnormal profit, and hence output may not increase.

So far, aspects of **static efficiency** have been analysed. However, there is also **dynamic efficiency** to consider. This looks at whether efficiency occurs over a period of time rather than at a point in time. It can be argued that monopoly is dynamically efficient, whilst perfect competition is not. In perfect competition, there is no incentive for individual firms to spend on research and development. This is because there is perfect knowledge in a perfectly competitive industry. Any innovation will quickly become known throughout the industry and if it gives the firm a competitive advantage it will be copied.

With a monopoly, the benefits of any research and development can be exploited by the monopolist. If it develops a new drug, or a new machine, it can exploit that invention and earn abnormal profits. Hence, the ability to keep abnormal profits acts as an incentive for innovation.

What's more, it can be argued that the existence of monopolies and abnormal profits encourages those outside the industry to destroy monopolies by leapfrogging the technology used in the industry. This is called the **process of creative destruction**. For instance, the monopoly of the canals was destroyed by the invention of railways. Telephone and postal monopolies are being destroyed by e-mails and the Internet.

However, it can equally be argued that a monopolist could easily become complacent and lazy, sheltering behind high barriers to entry. Lack of competition reduces the incentive to innovate. Spending on research and development is always risky and the monopolist may choose to become extremely risk adverse, preferring profits now to the possibility of higher profits in the future. What's more, the monopolist may not even attempt to profit maximise. Its management may aim to make enough profit to satisfy the shareholders (profit satisficing), and then run the firm for its own benefit. This is unlikely to involve aggressive attempts to innovate.

Government intervention

Governments are able to use a number of different policies to attempt to correct the market failure caused by monopolies.

Taxes Monopolies are likely to earn abnormal profits. Governments could tax away these abnormal profits, but this is unlikely to increase efficiency. There would be no incentive for the monopolist to reduce its prices as a result. Productive inefficiency could even increase because the monopolist would have no incentive to reduce costs. After all, any reduction in costs which led to higher profit would simply be taxed away. It would also reduce any incentive to innovate since any abnormal profits earned from innovation would be taxed. In practice, there would also be the problem of how to set the tax. It is very difficult to estimate the level of abnormal profit made by a firm in a real life situation. If the government set the tax too high, it would discourage the monopolist from even making essential

Question 4

Royal Mail currently has a monopoly on the collection and delivery of letters, although it faces fierce competition in the parcels market. But from 1 January 2006, any licensed company will be able to deliver mail to business and residential customers. For a number of years, the postal market has been regulated by Postcomm. It has set prices that Royal Mail can charge for its letter service. It will continue to regulate Royal Mail prices for the foreseeable future and will be responsible for licensing companies that want to enter the market. Royal Mail will continue to have to provide a universal service, collecting mail from post boxes throughout the UK and delivering to every address. Rival companies will not have this universal obligation and will be free to set their own charges.

The reason why Postcomm will continue to regulate the market is that Royal Mail's monopoly is unlikely to be broken very fast. In the two countries in the world that have introduced competition into their postal markets - New Zealand five years ago and Sweden 12 years ago - the original monopoly supplier still has at least 90 per cent of the market.

Source: adapted from http://news.bbc.co.uk, 18 February 2005.

(a) What might be the advantages to customers of Postcomm's regulation of Royal Mail?
(b) Why might introducing competition into a market, when Royal Mail had a monopoly, benefit customers?

routine investment and the quality and quantity of the good or service produced could deteriorate increasing rather than reducing market failure. The most important advantage of a tax on monopoly profits is that it redistributes income away from the owners of monopoly firms to the rest of the society, arguably improving **equity** in the economy.

Subsidies Monopolists are likely to be allocatively inefficient because they increase prices and reduce output compared to the situation which would occur if the industry were perfectly competitive. A way of reducing prices and increasing supply is to give subsidies to the monopolist to cut its prices and produce more. Whilst this might seem a possible solution, in practice it would be difficult to implement. It would be difficult for the government to know what would be the price and level of output which would lead to efficiency. Hence, it is almost impossible to know what level of subsidy would maximise efficiency. Moreover, subsidising monopolists already earning abnormal profits would be politically unacceptable. Citizens would question why taxpayers' money was being used to increase the profits of already highly profitable firms.

Price controls If a monopolist sets its prices too high to be efficient, then the government could impose price controls, limiting the prices that the monopolist can set. This is the policy currently adopted to control UK monopoly utilities such as water, telephones and railways. It has the added advantage that there is an incentive for monopolists to increase productive efficiency. If the monopolist faces a fixed price set by the government, it can still earn higher profit if it can drive down its costs. The major drawback of price controls is that it is difficult for the government to know what price to set to maximise efficiency. The monopolist will always argue that it needs higher prices to justify investment which will lead to dynamic efficiency. For instance, the UK water industry always argues that if prices are set too low, it will have to cut back on investment to improve water quality and preserve the environment.

Nationalisation If the monopoly is a private sector company, a solution to lack of efficiency would be to NATIONALISE the firm, i.e. turn it into a state owned company. The government could then force it to set its prices to ensure efficiency. Nationalisation was a very common policy throughout the world from the 1940s onwards. However, nationalised industries came to face two major problems. First, there was no incentive for these firms to reduce costs and hence, over time, they became increasingly productively inefficient. PRIVATISATION (i.e. the transfer of ownership from the public sector back to the private sector) of industries in the 1980s and 1990s has led to considerable reductions in costs and improvements in productive efficiency. Second, governments tended to starve nationalised industries of funds for investment. This damaged dynamic efficiency. Again, privatisation has usually led to considerable increases in investment, to the benefit of customers.

Privatisation and deregulation Many monopolies in the past have been nationalised industries. As already argued, the prices they set might be nearer those needed to ensure efficiency than a private sector monopolist would have set. However, they tended to be productively and dynamically inefficient. So privatising them might increase overall efficiency. To prevent them exploiting the consumer by raising prices, the government could combine privatisation with price controls. Alternatively, it could attempt to bring competition into the industry. Either it could split the monopolist up at privatisation into a number of competing companies. Or it could DEREGULATE the industry by allowing competitors to set up in an industry previously protected by legal barriers to entry. Competition would then hopefully drive prices down towards the level at which efficiency would be achieved.

Breaking up the monopolist The government could order the break up of a monopoly. This won't necessarily lead to any increase in efficiency if the monopoly is a natural monopoly, or if the new firms are in imperfect competition with each other. It is most likely to lead to an increase in efficiency if the new firms are in perfect competition with each other. This could be very difficult to achieve. For instance, it would be impossible if the monopolist produced branded goods.

Reducing entry barriers The government could try to reduce barriers to entry to the industry. This policy would be most easy to implement if the entry barriers were legal. For instance, a way of introducing competition in the UK gas delivery service would be to abolish Centrica's legal monopoly on ownership of the UK's gas pipeline network. However, there is no guarantee that competition would develop, especially if the monopoly is also a natural monopoly. Even if there were competition, the industry might become imperfectly competitive and there might be few efficiency gains as a result.

Key terms

Deregulation - the process of removing government controls from markets.
Monopoly - a market structure where one firm supplies all output in the industry without facing competition because of high barriers to entry to the industry.
Nationalisation - the transfer of firms or assets from private sector ownership to state ownership.

Natural monopoly - where economies of scale are so large relative to market demand that the dominant producer in the industry will always enjoy lower costs of production than any other potential competitor.
Privatisation - the opposite of nationalisation, the transfer of organisations or assets from state ownership to private sector ownership.

Applied economics

DVD Technology formats

In the 1970s, the audio cassette, developed by Philips, revolutionised home recording. In the 1980s, the audio CD was launched onto the market delivering high quality sound. In the same decade, the video recorder proved a smash hit. In the early 2000s, DVDs took off. All these technologies were only successful because a variety of manufacturers supported the new technology and were prepared to share out the profits to be made from the sale of equipment and from the sale of films and music. Over the same period, there was a large number of formats which failed. Digital Audio Tape, for example, provided CD quality listening but was a tape in a cassette rather than a round CD shaped disk. Despite the fact customers could buy blank tapes on which to record, the format never took off. Customers were happy to use audio cassettes to do their recordings and listen to pre-recorded music on their CD players.

In the mid-2000s, a new format battle geared up between Sony and Toshiba. It was over high-definition DVDs. The new product would enable viewers to buy films on DVD but view them in high definition format. Relatively few televisions in people's homes today have high definition. But the assumption is that over the next ten years, more and more televisions sold will be high definition, giving better viewing quality. Part of the incentive for customers to buy the new televisions would be that they had widely available high definition DVDs to play on them. High definition DVDs, because they carry much more information than existing DVDs, would also be ideal to use in games consoles where there is ever increasing demand for more sophisticated games which need more and more memory space.

Sony and Toshiba have each produced a new high-definition DVD format, but they are incompatible with one another. Sony's Blue Ray disk technology cannot be used on Toshiba's HD-DVD machines and vice versa. Sony claims that its product is technologically superior because its disk can hold almost twice the amount of information as its rival. Toshiba points out that its disks are cheaper to make and can be made in factories making today's DVDs. Blue Ray disks would need totally new equipment to manufacture them.

For Sony and Toshiba, what is at stake is the ability to create a monopoly protected by patents. Both companies would license their technology to other manufacturers. Equally, both companies would license the format to the film studios for them to issue their films in the format. However, whoever owns the licence would get a royalty fee. Equally, they would be in charge of the technology which would give them a competitive advantage as they made small incremental improvements to the technology. In the short term, whoever owns the technology could probably get their products out into the market first and be able to charge high prices to customers wanting to have the technology immediately. The abnormal profits that the first mover could make would eventually be competed away by other manufacturers. But overall, their profits would have been higher over the life cycle of the product than their rivals.

For Sony, the stakes are high because it also owns one of the major US film companies with a vast back list of films. If it loses the battle, it will have to pay Toshiba to put its films onto Toshiba's HD-DVD format. If it wins, it will save this cost and gain licence fees from other film studios.

Format wars are a mixed blessing for consumers. On the one hand, new formats are an example of dynamic efficiency in action. Over the past 50 years, the world of audio and visual communication has been revolutionised by the audio cassette, the CD, the video recorder and the DVD. On the other hand, there is no guarantee that the best format wins out. Many argue, for example, that the video recorder format, VHS, which eventually came to dominate the market was inferior technologically to its main rival, Sony's

Betamax format.

In the short term, the existence of patents and copyright over the format may lead to higher prices than would be the case if there were no barriers to entry to the market. However, the productive and allocative inefficiency that result from this are unlikely to be great in the case of the new generation of DVDs. One reason why Sony lost its video recorder war with VHS was that it was reluctant to license the technology to other manufacturers. It learnt its lesson from this and Sony today positively wants to license its Blue Ray technology to gain its quick adoption.

The worst scenario for both manufacturers and customers is that both formats are launched and a winner only emerges after a few years. Companies will experience either higher costs or lost sales, whilst those customers who have bought into the losing format will eventually have to write off their equipment and disks to move over to the new format. Equally, if there is no agreement, there is a danger that a new technology will make the format redundant. The very fast progress in computer technology could result in consumers by-passing the new generation of DVD players in favour of something superior. This example of creative destruction would leave Sony and Toshiba unable to recoup the development costs of the high definition DVD technologies and prevent them from earning profits from sales of hardware and software.

DataQuestion

Artificial sweeteners

Tate&Lyle

In its 2005 *Annual Report and Accounts*, Tate&Lyle described itself in the following way.

'Tate&Lyle is a world leading manufacturer of renewable food and industrial ingredients. Through the use of innovative technology, we transform corn, wheat and sugar into value added ingredients for customers in the food, beverage, pharmaceutical, cosmetic, paper, packaging and building industries. We work hard to understand our customers' needs and help meet the demands of consumers for tasty, nutritious, healthy and innovative products. We are a leader in cereal sweeteners and starches, sugar refining, value added food and industrial ingredients and citric acid. We are the world number one in industrial starches and the sole manufacturers of SPLENDA ® Sucralose.'

Nutrasweet

Until the 1990s, the US company Nutrasweet held a monopoly over the world's most widely-used sweetener: aspartame. Before Nutrasweet's patents expired, it could sell a pound of aspartame for $100, and $75 of that was profit. When its patents expired at the end of the 1990s, the price of aspartame collapsed to around $9 a pound as competitors entered the market with identical generic products. In spite of strong competition, Nutrasweet has maintained a large share of the $566m aspartame market, which is still twice the size of the market for sucralose. What is more, the amount of profit made from $100 worth of sales is still a healthy $15. Nutrasweet, after a period of closing down and mothballing factories after its patents expired, is now increasing output again because of growing demand.

Splenda

Tate&Lyle owns the monopoly patent rights to sucralose, better known in the UK by its brand name Splenda. 20 per cent of the profits of the company are now derived from the product. What is more, global sales are expanding faster than the industry average. Last year, sales grew 63 per cent compared to 8 per cent growth in the broader artificial sweetener market. Tate&Lyle can't keep up with demand and is currently rationing supplies to customers whilst it builds new plant to triple production by 2007.

So profitable is sucralose that competitors are constantly trying to find ways around the patents rights to produce it legally themselves. One competitor, the US company Nutrasweet, announced this week that it is talking to potential partners in China and India about possible techniques to produce sucralose without violating patents. Tate&Lyle believes that its patents are strong enough to prevent competition until patents expire in 2020. But with several Chinese companies already producing small quantities of the sweetener, many analysts doubt that Tate&Lyle will hold out that long.

Innovation

Artificial sweeteners have traditionally been used by food manufacturers to create 'low calorie' products which appeal to customers who don't want the high calorie content of a product made with natural sugar.

Sucralose currently leads the artificial sweeteners market on taste. It the most 'natural' sweetener being made from sugar and many consumers find that it tastes the most like sugar.

However, taste is not everything in this market. Nutrasweet, the US sweetener company, has recently launched Neotame. This is so sweet and cheap to produce that $1 of Neotame can be used to replace $10 of refined sugar in a product. Some soft drink manufacturers are now mixing Neotame with natural sugar in their drinks to cut costs of production. Sales of Neotame quadrupled last year.

The holy grail of the industry, however, is to produce a truly organic, plant-based sugar substitute that would taste exactly like sugar but have minimal calories. The company which comes up with this product is set to make a fortune if it can ring fence the product with patents.

Source: adapted from the *Financial Times*, 28.9.2005, Tate&Lyle, *Annual Report and Accounts*, 2005.

1. Explain the link between a 'patent' and a 'monopoly'.
2. Using examples from the data, explain why firms take out patents.
3. Discuss whether patents in the artificial sweeteners market lead to market efficiency or market failure.

20 Market stabilisation

Summary

1. The price of a good may be too high, too low or fluctuate too greatly to bring about an efficient allocation of resources.
2. Governments may impose maximum or minimum prices to regulate a market.
3. Maximum prices can create shortages and black markets.
4. Minimum prices can lead to excess supply and tend to be maintained only at the expense of the taxpayer.
5. Prices of commodities and agricultural products tend to fluctuate more widely than the prices of manufactured goods and services.
6. Buffer stock schemes attempt to even out fluctuations in price by buying produce when prices are low and selling when prices are high.

Prices and market failure

The market mechanism establishes equilibrium prices for each good or service in the economy. However, this price or the way in which it has been set may not lead to an efficient allocation of resources. The price may fluctuate too greatly in the short term, or it may be too high or too low.

Large fluctuations in price In some markets, particularly agricultural and commodity markets, there can be large fluctuations in price over a short space of time. Prices act as signals and incentives to producers. Large fluctuations in price mean that these signals can give a very confusing picture to producers and result in over or under production in the short term, and over or under investment in the longer term. This in turn can lead to a less than optimal allocation of resources.

Too high a price The price of a good may be too high. It may be an essential item, such as bread, rice or housing, which poor households are unable to afford to buy in sufficient amounts. The government may judge these items as **merit goods**, or it may want to reduce inequalities in society and hence want to reduce their prices. Alternatively, there could be significant positive **externalities** in consumption. Too high a market price would lead to a less than optimal level of demand for the good.

Too low a price The free market price of goods like cigarettes may be too low because their consumption gives rise to significant negative externalities. Alternatively, the government may judge that too low a price is having a negative economic impact on producers. For instance, it may judge that farmers' incomes need to be raised because otherwise they would leave the land and there would be rural depopulation.

Governments can intervene in markets and change prices. For instance, they can impose indirect taxes or give subsidies. They can set maximum or minimum prices or they can establish buffer stock schemes to stabilise prices.

Prices and revenues

Governments can have other motives for market intervention other than to correct market failure. Sometimes, they intervene in markets in order to change prices for their own benefit or the benefit of their own citizens. For example, OPEC, the Organisation of the Petroleum Exporting Countries, is a group of countries which attempts to maximise its long term revenues from the sale of oil. In doing so, it switches income from oil consumers, particularly in rich industrialised countries, to the countries of its own members. In theory, this should raise the living standards of their citizens at the expense of citizens living in countries which purchase the oil. It also tends to enrich ruling elites in member OPEC countries.

Maximum prices

The government can fix a maximum price for a good in a market. In Figure 1, the free market price is P_1 and Q_1 is bought and sold. Assume that this is the market for rented accommodation. At a price of P_1 the poorest in society are unable to afford to rent houses and there is therefore a problem of homelessness. The government intervenes by fixing a maximum price for accommodation of P_2. In the very short term, this may well seem to alleviate the problem. Landlords will continue to offer Q_1 of housing whilst the poorest in society will be more able to afford the new lower cost housing. However, in the longer term, economic theory predicts that new problems will arise. At a price of P_2, demand will be higher than at P_1, whilst supply will be lower. There will in fact be an excess demand of Q_2Q_3. At the lower price, consumers will demand more housing. On the other hand, landlords will reduce their supply, for instance by selling off their properties for owner occupation, not buying new properties to rent out, or living in their own properties instead of renting them out.

Permanent rent controls will thus reduce the supply of privately rented accommodation to the market whilst increasing its demand. The market may react in a number of ways. In a law abiding society, queues or waiting lists may develop. It may be a matter of luck rather than money whether one is able to get

Figure 1 Maximum prices

OP₁ is the free market price. If the government sets a maximum price of OP₂ in the market, demand will increase to OQ₃ whilst supply will fall to OQ₂. The result will be excess demand in the market of Q₂Q₃.

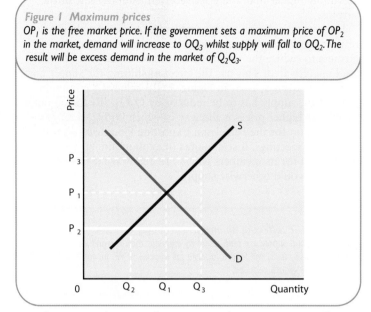

rented accommodation. The state may devise systems to allocate rented accommodation on the basis of greatest need. Landlords may develop a variety of ways in which they can get round the price controls. A black market may develop, illegal and uncontrolled, where rents are fixed at, or greater than, the free market price of P_1. Economic theory therefore predicts that

Question 1

In the 1960s, the government introduced a system of maximum rents for privately rented properties in the UK. Typically, these 'registered' rents were below the free market rent. In the late 1980s, the government reversed its policy by introducing a new type of private tenancy agreement, assured tenancies, which allowed private landlords to set whatever rent they wished. By 2006, there were very few rented properties left with registered rent contracts.

Table 1 Number of privately rented properties, UK

	Number of properties rented privately or with a job or busines
	millions
1961	5.0
1971	3.7
1981	2.4
1991	2.2
2001	2.5
2006	3.0

Source: adapted from *Housing Statistics*, Office for National Statistics.

(a) What happened to the stock of privately rented properties between 1961 and 1991?

(b) Using a demand and supply diagram, explain why the introduction of registered rents in the 1960s might have caused (i) a fall in the supply of rented property and (ii) excess demand for private rented property.

(c) Using a demand and supply diagram, explain why the introduction of assured tenancies led to a change in the quantity demanded for and supply of privately rented housing.

maximum prices may benefit some consumers - those able to obtain the goods which are controlled in price - but will disadvantage those who are prepared to pay a higher price for the good but are unable to obtain it because of a shortage of supply.

If the maximum price were set at P_3, there would be no effect on the market. P_1, the free market price, is below the maximum price and therefore nothing will happen following the introduction of maximum price controls.

Minimum prices

Minimum prices are usually set to help producers increase their incomes. Consider Figure 2, which shows the market for wheat. The free market price is P_1. The government decides that this is too low a price for farmers to receive and sets a minimum price of P_2. As a result, farmers will now grow Q_1Q_3 more wheat. Consumers will react to the new higher prices by reducing their demand by Q_1Q_2. Total excess supply of Q_2Q_3 will result.

This poses a problem for the government. With maximum prices, the government did not need to intervene when excess demand appeared. The excess demand could remain in the market forever if need be. However, this is not true of excess supply. If consumers only buy Q_2 of wheat then farmers can only sell Q_2 of wheat. Q_2Q_3 will remain unbought. Unless the government takes action, there will be strong pressure for farmers to sell this at below the minimum price. Average prices will fall until the market is cleared. The resulting price structure is likely to be very complex, some wheat being sold at the official minimum price of P_2 whilst the rest is sold at a variety of prices, the lowest of which is likely to be below the free market clearing price of P_1. Government action will have been frustrated.

So an effective minimum price structure must be accompanied by other measures. There are two main ways of dealing with this problem. The first is for the government to buy up the wheat that consumers refuse to buy (i.e. buy up the excess supply Q_2Q_3). This in turn creates problems because the government has to do something with the wheat it buys. This has been the classic problem with the Common Agricultural Policy in the European Union. A variety of solutions, such as selling wheat

Figure 2 Minimum prices

OP₁ is the free market price. If the government sets a minimum price of OP₃ in the market, supply will increase to OQ₃ whilst demand will fall to OQ₂. The result will be excess supply in the market of Q₂Q₃.

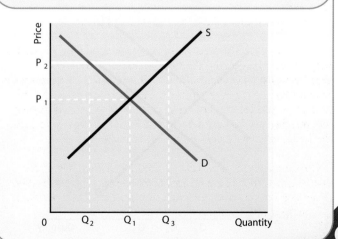

Question 2

A bumper cereals harvest across Eastern Europe has forced the European Commission to intervene, buying up and moving large amounts of surplus stocks to prevent a European-wide fall in prices. EU cereal stocks are now at their highest for a decade after EU countries produced 290 million tons in 2004, an increase of one quarter compared to 2003. The main problem has been an increase of 40 per cent in production from the ten new member states in Eastern Europe. For example, Hungarian farmers increased their production by 89 per cent whilst farmers in the Czech Republic increased their harvest by 54 per cent.

Storage is now a major problem with the EU already committed to buying up 13.5 million tons as intervention stocks. There simply isn't enough storage capacity in the new Eastern European member states to store all this grain. The Hungarian Ministry of Agriculture has requested the use of storage facilities in Belgium and Germany to help solve its storage crisis.

To reduce intervention stocks, the EU has begun offering export subsidies for the first time since 2003. Last week, it increased the payment to farmers for each ton of grain they sold for export to €10. In addition, it has offered to subsidise the transport of some grain from landlocked Eastern European countries to the nearest ports for export.

Source: adapted from www.nutraingredients.com and www.farmersjournal.

(a) Using demand and supply diagrams, explain (i) why 'EU cereal stocks are now at their highest for a decade';
(ii) how giving subsidies for grain exports can reduce EU cereal stocks.
(b) How did EU grain farmers benefit and EU taxpayers lose out from the bumper grain harvest of 2004?

mountains to Third World countries at rock bottom prices, selling it back to farmers to feed to animals, or offering it at reduced prices to those in need in the EU, or simply destroying the produce, has been adopted. All have one drawback - they cost the taxpayer money because the price paid to farmers is

inevitably higher than the price received from the sale of the surplus.

The second solution to the problem of excess supply is to restrict production. Governments can either force, or pay, farmers to reduce the size of their herds or leave part of their land uncultivated. This has the effect of shifting the supply curve to the left, from S_1 to S_2 in Figure 3. To achieve a minimum price of P_2, supply has to be reduced by Q_2Q_3. Reducing output to achieve higher prices is the way in which OPEC, the Organisation for the Petroleum Exporting Countries, operates. At regular meetings, it sets quotas (maximum limits) on production for its members which are below what these countries would otherwise supply.

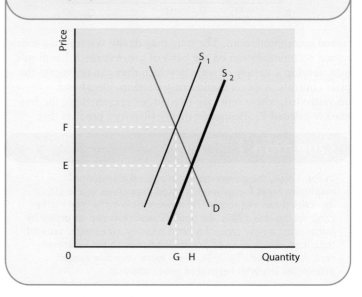

Figure 4 The effect of an increase in supply on price
If demand and supply are both relatively inelastic, then a small increase in supply from S_1 to S_2 will lead to a large fall in price of FE. Incomes will therefore be greatly reduced.

Buffer stock schemes

The free market price of **primary products** (commodities such as gold and tin, and agricultural products such as wheat and beef) tends to fluctuate much more than the price of either manufactured goods or services. This is mainly due to supply side influences. The demand for canned tomatoes or fresh tomatoes is likely to remain broadly constant over a twelve month period. However, the supply of these two products will differ. Canned tomatoes can be stored. Therefore the supply too will remain broadly the same over a twelve month period. However, the supply of fresh tomatoes varies greatly. In the summer months, supply is plentiful and the price of tomatoes is therefore low. In winter, supply is low and prices are high.

On a year to year basis, the supply of raw agricultural commodities can vary greatly according to crop yields. A bumper crop will depress prices whilst crop failure will lead to high prices. Bumper crops can be disastrous for farmers. In Figure 4, if the demand for a product is price inelastic, a large fall in price is needed to sell a little extra produce. This will greatly reduce farmers' revenues.

Equally, a poor crop can be disastrous for individual farmers. Although farm income overall will be higher than average, only

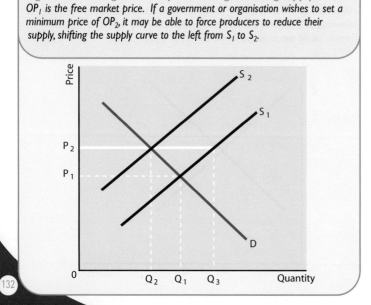

Figure 3 Achieving minimum prices through reducing supply
OP_1 is the free market price. If a government or organisation wishes to set a minimum price of OP_2, it may be able to force producers to reduce their supply, shifting the supply curve to the left from S_1 to S_2.

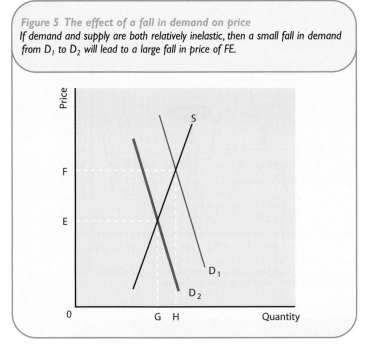

Figure 5 *The effect of a fall in demand on price*
If demand and supply are both relatively inelastic, then a small fall in demand from D₁ to D₂ will lead to a large fall in price of FE.

farmers who have crops to sell will benefit. Farmers whose crops have been mostly or completely destroyed will receive little or no income.

Manufactured goods and services also contain greater value added than primary products. The cost of a can of tomatoes is made up not only of the cost of tomatoes themselves but also of the canning process and the can. If fresh tomatoes only account for 20 per cent of the cost of a can of tomatoes, then a doubling in the price of fresh tomatoes will only increase the price of a can by just over 7 per cent.

Demand side influences can, however, also be a source of price fluctuations for commodities. In manufacturing and services,

producers devote much effort and money to stabilising demand through branding, advertising and other marketing techniques. However, Zambian copper is little different from Chilean copper. Buyers are free to buy from the cheapest source so demand fluctuates more greatly. In the short term, supply is relatively inelastic. Countries have invested in mines, oil wells and other commodity producing plant and need, often for foreign exchange purposes, to maximise output and sales. Small changes in demand, as shown in Figure 5, can produce large changes in price. Any slowdown in the world economy is likely to have a larger impact on commodities than on manufactured goods. Manufacturers may react to a small fall in their sales by cutting their stock levels and perhaps delaying the buying of stock by a few months. This results in a large, if temporary, fall in the price of raw materials. Whilst the slowdown persists, prices are likely to remain low. The converse is also true - in a boom, commodity prices go up far faster than those of manufactured goods or services.

Demand and supply influences combine to bring about large fluctuations in the price of commodities. Governments and other bodies have often reacted to this situation by intervening in the market place. One way to do this is to set up a BUFFER STOCK SCHEME which combines elements of both minimum and maximum pricing. In theory it is designed to even out price fluctuations for producers. An intervention price is set, shown as P_1 in Figure 6. If the free market price is the same as the intervention price, as in Figure 6(a), then the scheme doesn't need to intervene in the market. If the free market price is below the intervention price, as in Figure 6(b), then the buffer stock agency buys up enough supply to restore prices to the minimum price. In Figure 6(b), it increases demand by buying up Q_2Q_3. In contrast, if the free market price is above the intervention price, as in Figure 6(c), it can sell stocks it has accumulated. In Figure 6(c) it increases supply by selling Q_2Q_3, forcing the price down to the intervention level. In effect, the buffer stock shifts the demand curve for the product to the right when free market prices are below the intervention price, and shifts the supply

Figure 6 Buffer stock interventions
In (a), the free market price of P_1 is the same as the intervention price set by the buffer stock scheme and so it does not need to intervene in the market. In (b), the free market price, P_2, is below the intervention price and so it has to buy up Q_2Q_3 to bring prices back up to P_1. In (c), the free market price, P_3, is above the intervention price. So the buffer stock scheme can sell up to Q_2Q_3 from its stocks without bringing prices down below the intervention level.

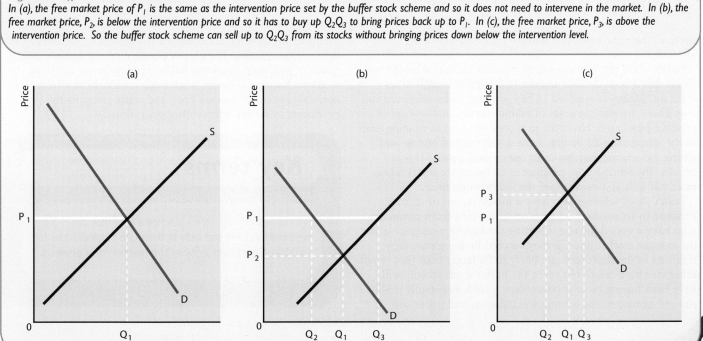

Question 3

The world tin industry has commodity agreements going back to 1921. The International Tin Council (ITC) came into being in 1956. It was able to support the price of tin during periods of low prices by buying tin for its buffer stockpile and selling tin when prices were high. During the 1970s, its stockpile of tin was not sufficiently large to prevent serious price rises in the commodity. However, the world recession of 1981-82 hit world tin consumption. The ITC was able to avoid sharp declines in tin prices by buying in the open market. However, it was only able to afford the cost of its increasing stockpile by extensive borrowing from banks and metal trading firms. In late 1985, it reached its credit limits and its supporters, such as the UK, refused to extend further credit. The International Tin Council was disbanded and its stocks sold off over a four year period. Prices did not recover their early 1980 levels until 2004 when sharp increases in demand from the booming countries of East Asia, particularly China, fuelled a commodity price boom.

Source: adapted from http://minerals.er.usgs.gov/minerals/pubs/commodity/tin/.

(a) Explain, using a demand and supply diagram, how the International Tin Council (ITC) affected the price of tin in the market.
(b) According to the data, how well did the ITC succeed in fixing prices in the 1970s and 1980s?
(c) Explain why the price of tin was low in the 1990s compared to the late 1970s and early 1980s.

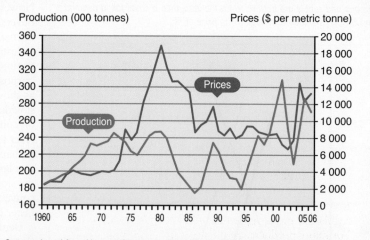

Figure 7 *Prices and world production of tin*

Source: adapted from *Historical Statistics for Mineral Commodities in the United States, Metal prices in the United States through 1998*, United States Geological Survey

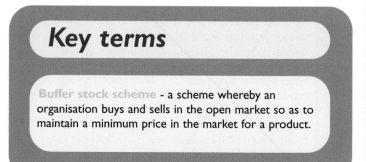

curve to the right when free market prices are above the intervention price.

Buffer stock schemes are not common. One major reason for this is that a considerable amount of capital is needed to set them up. Money is required to buy produce when prices are too low. There are also the costs of administration and storage of produce purchased. However, in theory, the overall running costs of the scheme should be low. Indeed, with skilful buying and selling the scheme may make an operational profit. This is because the scheme buys produce at or below the intervention price but sells at a price above the intervention price.

Buffer stock schemes also have a mixed record of success. Pressure to set up these schemes tends to come from producers who have a vested interest in setting the intervention price above the average market price. If they succeed in doing this, their revenues in the short term are likely to be larger than they would otherwise have been. However, the buffer stock scheme will have been buying more produce than it sold. Eventually it will run out of money, the scheme will collapse, and prices will plummet because the accumulated stocks will be sold to pay the debts of the scheme. The glut of produce on the market will result in producers receiving below average prices for some time to come. Successful buffer stock schemes are those which correctly guess the average price and resist attempts by producers to set the intervention price above it.

Key terms

Buffer stock scheme - a scheme whereby an organisation buys and sells in the open market so as to maintain a minimum price in the market for a product.

Applied economics

The Common Agricultural Policy (CAP)

One of the most important steps taken by the European Union (formerly the European Community) in its early years was to create the Common Agricultural Policy in 1958. Article 39 of the Treaty of Rome cites five objectives of agricultural policy:

● to increase agricultural productivity;
● to ensure a fair standard of living for farmers;
● to stabilise markets;
● to guarantee availability of supplies;
● to ensure fair prices for consumers.

It was hoped that the CAP would achieve this through regulation of the agricultural industry in the Union. For many products, an intervention price was established. Farmers could then choose to sell their produce on the open market or to the EU at this minimum fixed price. The EU guaranteed to buy up any amount at the intervention price. Farmers were protected from overseas competition through a complex system of tariffs (taxes on imported goods) and quotas (physical limits on the amount that could be imported). Tariffs and quotas effectively raised the price of imported agricultural produce to EU consumers. With high enough tariffs and quotas, agricultural produce from outside the EU could be kept out, allowing EU farmers to sell their own produce into their domestic markets at much higher prices than they would otherwise have been able to do.

CAP proved to be far more favourable to farmers than to consumers. The farming community in the EU became very good at lobbying their individual governments to vote for high intervention prices at the annual price fixing negotiations in Brussels. Consumers lost out in two ways. First, they had to pay directly for food which was much higher in price than it would otherwise have been if it had been bought on world markets. Second, as taxpayers, they had to pay for the heavy costs of running the CAP.

In theory, the CAP should have been fairly inexpensive to run. If there was a glut of produce on the market in one season, the EU would buy some of it at the intervention price and store it. The next season, when there was perhaps a shortage, the EU could take the produce out of storage and sell it. Prices would not fluctuate by as much as under a market system and the sale of produce would ensure that the major cost of the system would be administration and storage.

In practice, the cost of the CAP rose year after year. High intervention prices led to increased production, as economic theory would predict. Supply then began to outstrip demand. Instead of selling produce taken into storage to European consumers at a later date, mountains and lakes of produce developed, as shown in Figure 8. This produce then had to be sold, often at a fraction of the cost of production, to the former USSR, Third World countries, and to EU farmers for

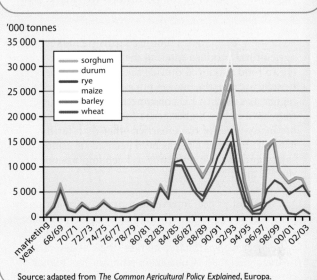

Figure 8 EU intervention stocks, cereal crops

'000 tonnes

Legend: sorghum, durum, rye, maize, barley, wheat

Source: adapted from *The Common Agricultural Policy Explained*, Europa.

use as animal feed. Some was even destroyed.

EU reform

Reform of CAP has been a long standing issue. As early as 1968, the Mansholt Plan recommended that farm size should increase to enable farmers to enjoy economies of scale and thus be better able to provide food at world market prices. By the early 1980s, political pressure was building to limit the growth of the CAP budget. In 1984, a quota system (see below) was introduced for milk production to limit production and therefore subsidies to dairy farmers. In 1988, a ceiling was introduced on the CAP budget.

However, the first fundamental changes to CAP were the MacSharry reforms of 1992. Ray MacSharry was the European Commissioner for Agriculture at the time. There were two major ways in which agriculture was affected. One was through a set-aside scheme (see below) where farmers received payments for leaving ground uncultivated rather than growing crops on it. The second was limiting the amount of financial support to selected crops and animals and replacing them by direct grants to farmers for a variety of schemes not linked to production. Giving grants to farmers which are not linked to their production levels is known as **decoupling**.

In 2003, EU farm ministers agreed on a more radical scheme to decouple farm subsidies. Between 2005 and 2012, it was agreed that EU member states would change their farm subsidy regime to eliminate most production subsidies and replace them with direct grants to farmers. The total EU agricultural budget was fixed up to 2012 and included changes needed to accommodate new Eastern European entrants to the European Union.

Economic effects of different schemes

Agricultural policy in the EU distorts free markets in a variety of ways.

External trade barriers Putting tariffs (i.e. taxes) on agricultural produce entering the EU keeps out cheap food produced outside the EU. EU farmers benefit because the market price inside the EU is higher as a result. EU consumers lose out because they have to pay higher prices for their food. There are many types of trade barrier other than tariffs. The EU, for example, has been accused of using safety and welfare standards to keep imports out of the EU area.

Intervention prices Intervention prices were minimum prices set for some (but not all) agriculture products in the EU. They were effectively minimum prices which were often above the free market price. They raised farmers' incomes. Consumers paid not just higher prices for those agricultural products but also taxes to buy up surplus produce which would then have to be disposed of in some way at less than the buying price.

Quotas Quotas on milk production were introduced in 1984. Each member country of the EU was given a milk quota, a maximum amount of milk that could be produced. This was then divided up between farmers, originally depending on how much milk they produced before quotas were introduced. Quotas were transferable. A farmer owning a quota could sell all or part it to another farmer. Quotas were set at levels

Table 2 EU farm support		
	Yearly average	
	1986-88	2005
	EU15	EU25
Transfers from consumers (€ millions)	82 142	47 159
Transfers from taxpayers (€ millions)	25 747	74 467
Budget revenues (€ millions)	1 517	533
Total support estimate (€ millions)	106 372	121 093
EU population (million)	363	456
Total support cost per head (€)	293	266
Total support estimate as percentage of GDP	2.82	1.10

Source: adapted from *Agricultural policies in OECD countries: monitoring and evaluation 2005*, OECD.

which would reduce the production of milk. In terms of demand and supply, quotas shifted the supply curve of milk to the left, reducing the equilibrium level of production but raising the equilibrium price compared to the free market price. This benefited farmers but consumers had to pay higher prices for their milk and milk-based products. The quota system was cheap to run for the EU taxpayer because dairy farmers did not receive subsidies for production of milk.

Set-aside Set-aside was introduced in 1992 for cereal farmers. They were paid for setting aside (i.e. not using) a certain proportion of their land. The land set aside had to be rotated from year to year to prevent farmers simply setting aside their least productive land. By reducing the amount of land available for production, the supply of cereals is reduced, thus raising their price. Farmers received a payment from the EU for each acre set-aside. Hence, not only did EU consumers pay higher prices for cereals than they would otherwise, but EU taxpayers had to pay a direct subsidy to farmers.

Decoupling Decoupling subsidies from production in theory should reduce, if not eliminate, production distortions. Farmers will receive a grant according to the number of acres they own, not how much they produce. Prices for agricultural products will be set by the forces of demand and supply in a free market. Consumers will therefore not pay higher prices for agricultural products as they would, say, with a system of intervention prices, set aside or quotas. In a rational world, marginal farmers who find it difficult to make a reasonable profit from agricultural activities will simply not produce. Instead, they will do nothing and collect their subsidy on their acreage. In practice, farmers are likely to be less rational. With a basic income given by the subsidy, they will be prepared to work for lower returns than they would otherwise. Hence, production is likely to be higher than if there were no subsidies at all.

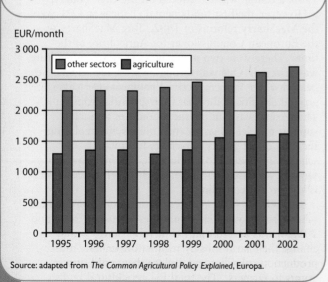

Figure 9 Farm incomes - development of average gross monthly wages in the economy and gross monthly agricultural income

EUR/month

Source: adapted from *The Common Agricultural Policy Explained*, Europa.

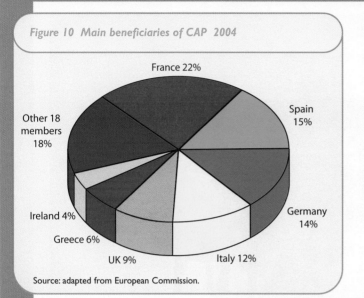

Figure 10 Main beneficiaries of CAP 2004

France 22%

Spain 15%

Germany 14%

Italy 12%

UK 9%

Greece 6%

Ireland 4%

Other 18 members 18%

Source: adapted from European Commission.

Advantages and disadvantages of the Common Agricultural Policy

The Common Agricultural Policy is highly controversial. It can be judged in a variety of ways.

Maintaining farmers' incomes One key argument for the CAP is that it transfers income from the richer non-farming community to the poorer farming community. Figure 9 shows that farm incomes on average are below those in the non-farm sector. However, there are no other industries in the EU where income transfers are made on an industrial basis. Average wages in the EU tourist industry, for example, are below those in all other industries but there is no call to subsidise the whole of the tourist industry as a result. Critics would argue that application of the general system of taxes and welfare benefits to the poorer workers in farming would be a fairer way of dealing with rural poverty than the CAP. They also point out that 80 per cent of total spending on the CAP goes to 20 per cent of the EU's largest farmers and agricultural corporations. In the UK, the largest beneficiary of the CAP was the sugar company Tate and Lyle which received £127 million in subsidies.

Cost The cost of the CAP to EU citizens has been substantial. In the past, they have not only had to pay for subsidies to the farming community through their taxes, but they have also had to pay higher prices for the food they buy because it was available at lower prices on world markets. Table 2 gives a breakdown of the cost of that support, comparing the yearly average for 1986-88 and 2005 for the EU 15 and then EU 25 countries. What it shows is that the balance of support has shifted. In 1986-88, by far the largest cost of farm support was from consumers having to pay higher prices for the food they purchased. By 2005, the reverse was true with the taxpayer picking

up most of the bill. In 2005, the cost of the CAP per head in the EU was €265, roughly equivalent to £175. A family of four people living in the UK was therefore subsidising EU farming by roughly £700 per year.

The EU budget In the 1970s, expenditure on the CAP was over 70 per cent of the EU budget. By 2005, this was approximately 50 per cent. Supporters of the CAP argue that agriculture is a key industry within the EU. Critics would point out that agriculture now accounts for only 2 per cent of EU GDP. Agriculture is of little importance to the EU economy. The opportunity cost of spending so much of the EU budget on agriculture is considerable. It would be better spent on areas such as regional assistance.

Government failure Support for reform of the CAP varies between countries across the EU. The countries which are most resistant to change tend to be those countries which most benefit from the CAP. Figure 10 shows that France is the single largest beneficiary from the CAP. For both Ireland and Greece, although they receive relatively small percentages of the total, the CAP is especially important. On average, countries receive CAP support of around 0.5 per cent of GDP. For Ireland and Greece, this is three times as large at 1.5 per cent of GDP. Critics of the CAP argue that the support of countries like France for the CAP has little to do with economic efficiency or the economic welfare of the EU. They support the CAP and resist change simply because they are the major beneficiaries of the policy.

Self sufficiency Supporters of the CAP point out that it has created a Europe which is broadly self sufficient in food. In times when a country was at war, food self sufficiency was a strategic objective. However, critics point out that in no other commodity does the EU attempt to be self sufficient. There are no objectives, for example, for the EU to be self sufficient in the production of television sets, microchips, clothes or foreign holidays. In an era of globalisation, self sufficiency in food could be argued to be an outdated goal.

Food quality and animal welfare Supporters of the CAP argue that EU farmers provide high quality food with minimum guaranteed levels of animal welfare. By implication, some food that is imported to the EU is below acceptable standards and comes from unacceptable farming practices. Critics would argue that the quality of food produced in the EU is on average no better than that produced elsewhere in the world. To be sold in the EU, imported food has to conform to certain standards anyway. Some animal rearing practices outside the EU do not conform to EU standards. However, the EU can and does impose a wide variety of conditions upon meat imported to the EU and has the power to prohibit imports if there are good reasons to do so under its trading obligations with the World Trade Organisation (WTO).

The environment

Supporters of the CAP argue that it is a key factor in supporting the rural environment. Farmers look after the countryside, ensuring that it is protected for future generations. Critics of the CAP point out that the agricultural sector is a major polluter of the environment. Animals are the major source of methane gas, a key contributor to global warming. Farmers, through the use of fertilisers and pesticides, pollute

the environment. In southern European countries, their overuse of scarce water resources for irrigation is causing major problems to the environment. Little of the rural environment, anyway, is 'natural' in any sense. It has been created over thousands of years by farmers to suit the needs of production.

Supporting the rural economy

Supporters of the CAP argue that it is needed to maintain an appropriate economic environment in rural areas. Without the CAP, some rural areas would become completely depopulated because there would be no jobs or income in the area. Other areas would suffer considerable depopulation as residents left to find jobs in towns and cities. There would be pressure on the urban environment which would have to expand to accommodate these migrants. Critics of the CAP argue that urban dwellers have no duty to support financially those living in the countryside: the countryside should not be seen as a charity. There is no benefit overall to having a thriving rural economy in a locality as opposed to seeing it completely depopulated. Urban areas have been expanding to take in people from rural areas for centuries. If towns and cities created large costs for their inhabitants, people would not have migrated to them from rural areas in the first place.

Impact on poorer countries in the world

Supporters of the CAP argue that the EU is a major importer of food from countries round the world, including poorer developing countries. The EU has helped millions of poor farmers establish markets for their products. Critics accuse the EU of damaging farming markets round the globe. First, through its system of protection for its farmers, the EU has denied access to farmers outside the EU to EU markets. Second, the EU has dumped large amounts of food onto world markets at low prices to get rid of the surpluses that its farming regime has created. This has hurt non-EU farmers because it has denied them the opportunity to sell into those markets. Critics of the EU argue that the CAP has increased world poverty over the past fifty years.

CAP is already being radically reformed

Supporters of CAP point to the radical reforms which have already been implemented and will be implemented over the next ten years. They argue that any further quickening of pace of reform will have serious consequences for the farming sector and the rural economy. Critics argue that the pace of reform is too slow and that the reforms are too timid. They point out that there are some areas of the CAP, such as the dairy sector, wine, fruit and vegetables, where there are no current plans for reform. Export subsidies and tariffs on imported food remain too high. Agriculture remains a major source of inefficiency within the EU even with the current reform programme.

DataQuestion

Rubber

The International Natural Rubber Organisation (INRO) is to break up following the withdrawal of two of the world's largest rubber producers, Thailand and Malaysia. The buffer stock scheme, set up in 1980, buys up rubber when prices fall and sells when prices rise. Members include the six leading rubber producing countries as well as the biggest consuming countries such as the US, Japan and China.

Thailand and Malaysia have become dissatisfied with the low price of rubber in world markets in recent years. They have accused INRO of failing to intervene to stop the price of rubber falling. For instance, at the start of 1998, rubber was 230 Malaysian cents a kilo. By 1999, this had fallen to 150 cents. They also accuse INRO of pursuing policies which favour member countries with low volumes of production and failing to pay sufficient attention to the interests of the three countries which account for nearly three-quarters of world production. Thailand, for instance, paid around 40 per cent of the total yearly contributions which financed INRO, but was only responsible for 30 per cent of output.

Source: adapted from the *Financial Times*, 6.10.1999

In August 2002, Malaysia, Indonesia and Thailand, the world's three largest producers of natural rubber, controlling around two thirds of world production, set up the International Rubber Consortium (IRCo). The Consortium was established to co-ordinate production and exports of the three countries. In April 2004, IRCo was officially registered with a capital of US$225 million. Its objectives are to achieve a long term price trend that is stabilised, sustainable and remunerative to farmers, and to maintain a supply-demand balance to ensure adequate supply of natural rubber in the market at fair prices.

Source: adapted from International Rubber Consortium, www.irco.biz

The collapse of the International Natural Rubber Organisation could have spelt disaster for rubber prices as stocks built up were offloaded onto the market. As it was, growing demand allowed prices to remain relatively stable, although prices fell to an all time low at the end of 2001. Since then, growing demand, especially from the booming economies of East Asia and particularly China, has driven up prices. Without this increased demand, rubber prices could easily have collapsed.

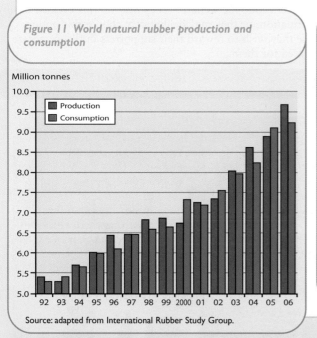

Figure 11 *World natural rubber production and consumption*

Source: adapted from International Rubber Study Group.

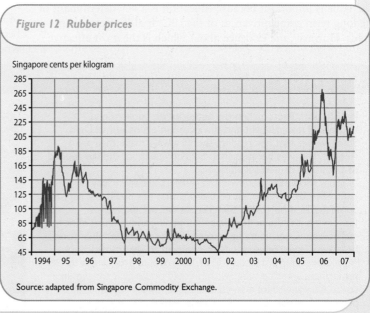

Figure 12 *Rubber prices*

Source: adapted from Singapore Commodity Exchange.

1. Explain, using INRO as an example, what is meant by a buffer stock scheme.
2. Why had INRO built up stocks of rubber by 1999?

3. To what extent could IRCo be seen as having been responsible for substantially increasing the price of rubber from 2001?

21 Government failure

Summary

1. Government failure can be caused by inadequate information, conflicting objectives, administrative costs and creation of market distortions.
2. Public choice theory suggests that governments may not always act to maximise the welfare of society because politicians may act to maximise their own welfare.

Reasons for government failure

Markets can fail. They may underprovide public and merit goods. They may lead to externalities in production and consumption. There may be wild fluctuations in price which harm both producers and consumers. One response is for governments to intervene to correct these market failures. However, if markets can fail, so too can government. GOVERNMENT FAILURE occurs when it intervenes in the market but this intervention leads to a loss of economic welfare rather than a gain. There is a number of reasons why government failure may occur.

Inadequate information Governments, like any economic agents, rarely possess complete information on which to base a decision. In some cases, the information available is positively misleading. It is not surprising, then, that governments may make the wrong policy response to a problem. For instance, governments have to make decisions about whether to fund a selective school system or a comprehensive school system. In Germany, the school system is selective. In the USA, it is comprehensive. In the UK, it is mainly comprehensive, but a significant minority of local authorities fund selective schools. The issue is important because education is a key determinant of the long term competitiveness of the UK. It also affects every child. However, the evidence about which is the most effective form of education is conflicting. In the 1960s and 1970s, the UK government supported the change from a mainly selective system to a mainly comprehensive system. In the 1980s and 1990s, the Conservative government favoured selective schools. In the 2000s the Labour government was pushing for a variety of provision and specialist schools.

Conflicting objectives Governments often face conflicting objectives. For instance, they may want to cut taxes but increase spending on defence. Every decision made by the government has an opportunity cost. Sometimes, a decision is made where the welfare gain from the alternative foregone would have been even higher. In the case of education, assume that those receiving a selective education in grammar schools receive a better education than if they were in a comprehensive school. In contrast, assume that those who fail to get into a selective school achieve less than if they were in a comprehensive school. There is now a conflict of objectives about which system to implement. Are the needs of those who would be selected for grammar schools more important than those of the rest of the school population, or vice versa? Governments may make the wrong policy decision when there are such conflicts of objective, choosing the option which gives lower economic welfare rather than higher economic welfare. They may do this because of lack of information, or they may deliberately choose this option because they wish to reward their supporters in the electorate who voted for them.

Question 1

In 1861, Mrs Beeton, then the authority on cookery and household management and the Victorian equivalent of Delia Smith, wrote that her readers should always make their own vinegar. This was because shop bought vinegar of the day tended to consist of diluted sulphuric acid.

Today, food manufacturers and retailers are so strictly controlled by government regulations that this could not happen. Some argue, though, that such regulations are excessive. Government red tape restricts the opening and running of new businesses. Consumers have to pay higher prices for their food because it costs firms money to conform to government regulations. For instance, in 1999, the costs of production to UK pig farmers went up because they could no longer rear pigs in stalls. Animal welfare activists would like to see battery hen production stopped and all chickens reared in free range conditions, but why shouldn't consumers have the choice about whether or not they buy cheaper battery produced eggs and chickens?

(a) Explain why markets fail according to the data.
(b) Discuss whether, in the examples given in the data, government intervention leads to market failure.

Administrative costs Sometimes, the administrative cost of correcting market failure is so large that it outweighs the welfare benefit from the correction of market failure. For instance, the government may put into place a scheme to help the unemployed back into work. During a year, 100 000 pass through the scheme. Of those, 50 000 would have found jobs anyway but simply use the scheme because it is advantageous for them or their employer to do so. 10 000 find a job who would otherwise not have done so. 40 000 remain unemployed. It may cost £3 000 per person per year on the scheme, giving a total cost of £300 million. This means that the cost per worker who would otherwise not have got a job is
£300 million ÷ 10 000 or £30 000 per worker. This is an enormous cost for the benefit likely to be gained by the 10 000 workers. Indeed, they almost certainly would have preferred to have been given the £30 000 rather than gain a job. Another example would be the payment of welfare benefits. If it costs £1 to pay out a £3 benefit, is this likely to improve economic welfare?

Market distortions In some cases, government intervention to correct one market failure leads to the creation of far more serious market failures. One example is government intervention in agricultural markets such as the Common Agricultural Policy. Here, governments offer farmers financial support, partly to raise farm incomes which can be low and second to even out fluctuations in income from year to year arising from changes in the size of crops. However, financial support typically leads to increases in the supply of food which may not be matched by increases in demand. The result is an over-supply of farm produce. Countries may choose to dump this over-supply on world markets at low prices. This leads to lower farm incomes for world farmers outside the European Union, destroying the markets for their produce. Higher farm incomes in Europe may be gained at the expense of lower farm incomes in Egypt or New Zealand. Agricultural markets within the EU may also be distorted. For instance, the price of beef is artificially high in the EU because of CAP support but pig prices receive no subsidy. The result is that EU consumers buy less beef and more pork than they would otherwise do if there were no government intervention. Another market distortion may occur with respect to the environment. The CAP encourages over-production of food. Marginal land is brought into production when it might otherwise be left wild. Too much pesticide and fertiliser may be used to raise yields because CAP offers too high prices to farmers. Lower prices might lead to less intensive modes of production and less destruction to wildlife.

There are many examples of market distortions in the labour market. For instance, the government may want to raise income levels for the poor by setting a high minimum wage. However, this may be so high that employers shed low paid workers, putting out of work large numbers of people whom the government wanted to protect. Similarly, the government may raise unemployment benefit to help the unemployed. However, this may discourage them from looking for work since more are now better off on the dole than working. This increases the numbers of unemployed.

Public choice theory

It is generally assumed that governments act in a way which they believe will maximise economic welfare. They may not succeed in this because of lack of information, conflicting objectives, etc.

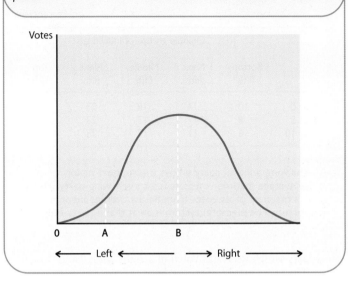

Figure 1 Voting behaviour of electors.
Politicians will tend to maximise their votes by moving to the centre ground in politics.

However, PUBLIC CHOICE THEORY suggests that governments may not attempt to maximise economic welfare at all.

Public choice theory analyses how and why public spending and taxation decisions are made. 'Consumers' or 'customers' are voters in the system. They vote for politicians and political parties who are the 'producers' in the system. Producers make decisions about how public money should be spent, about taxes and about laws. The decisions have to be 'sold' by politicians to voters.

The voters want to maximise the net benefits they get from the state. For instance, all other things being equal, voters would like the state to provide large quantities of goods and services but with minimal levels of taxation.

Politicians want to maximise their welfare too. In the simplest models, politicians are assumed to want to maximise their votes, so that they can get into power and remain in power. In more complicated models, more sophisticated assumptions can be made, such as that politicians want to get posts in government, or use their political connections to maximise their own earnings.

If politicians want to maximise their votes, then the most obvious thing to do is to appeal to the centre ground. Consider Figure 1 which shows a normal distribution of votes. A right wing politician is facing a left wing politician who has pitched his policies so that they will attract votes to the left of 0A. The obvious stance to take is for the right wing politician to pitch his policies just to the right of B, as near as possible to the middle ground whilst remaining to the right of the political spectrum. On the other hand, if the left wing politician were rational, he too would move to the centre ground to try and maximise his vote.

In practice, democracies tend to throw up governments which do veer towards the centre. It is for this reason that governments like those of Margaret Thatcher's in the 1980s were so unusual. Due to Britain's first past the post voting system, a UK party can get a majority in Parliament with as little as 40 per cent of the votes cast. With a 75 per cent turnout on polling day (i.e. 25 per cent of eligible voters don't vote), this means that a British government only has to gain the vote of 30 per cent of all voters. Not surprisingly, this sometimes allows a right

Question 2

Table 1 Shares of disposable income					
					Percentages
	Quintile groups of individuals				
	Bottom fifth	Next fifth	Middle fifth	Next fifth	Top fifth
Year 0	10	14	18	23	35
Year 5	8	12	17	23	36
Year 10	6	11	17	23	43

A right wing political party enjoys the support mainly of above average income voters. It faces a left wing party which gains a majority of its votes from below average income supporters. The electoral system is such that a party only needs 40 per cent of the vote to secure a majority in Parliament, whilst a 45 per cent vote would give it a massive majority. On average, 75 per cent of the electorate vote, but the higher the income of the individual, the more likely they are to turn out to vote. The top 20 per cent of income earners have a turnout rate of 90 per cent.

The right wing party wins an election in year 0 committed to 'increasing incentives for individuals to earn money and create wealth for the nation'. It wins two further elections in year 5 and year 10.

(a) (i) Would Table 1 suggest that the nation's welfare has been maximised?
(ii) What additional information would you need to support your conclusion?
(b) Explain why the party can win elections when the relative income position of most individuals is worsening over time.

wing party which itself has voted in a right wing leader to gain office. The same would of course be true for a left wing party in the UK which had a left wing leader.

In much of economic theory, there is a hidden assumption that governments act so as to maximise the welfare of society as a whole. Public choice theory can help explain why governments often fail to do this.

Local interests Assume that an MP has a large textile mill in her constituency which employs 1 000 workers. The company owning the mill lobbies the MP to support the imposition of higher tariffs (taxes on imports) on textiles, arguing that the mill will have to close unless foreign competition is reduced. Economic theory would probably suggest that the mill should be allowed to close and the resources released be used to produce something which the UK is better at producing. However, the MP may be frightened that losing 1 000 jobs could mean losing 1 000 votes. Therefore, she could well put pressure on the government to impose higher tariffs even if she knows that the nation's welfare would be lessened as a result.

Favouring minorities Assume that a political party can get elected with considerably less than 50 per cent of the votes, because of the nature of the voting system and because not all voters turn out on polling day. In UK national elections, as argued above, a party could get a majority with the support of just 30 per cent of voters. In a local election, where the turnout is often only 30-50 per cent, a party can get a majority with far less. Assume that those who do vote tend to possess similar characteristics. For instance, in the UK, middle class voters are more likely to vote than working class voters. In a local election, voters from one ethnic group may be far more likely to vote than voters from another ethnic group. In these situations, it is clear that politicians wishing to maximise their share of the vote will want to appeal to a minority, not the majority, because it is the minority who cast votes. A government might, for instance, introduce government spending and tax changes which leave 30 per cent of the population better off and 70 per cent worse off. This would be rational behaviour if the 30 per cent of the population better off tended to vote for that party in a first past the post system with a 75 per cent turnout.

However, it is arguable as to whether the nation's welfare would be maximised as a result.

Conflicting personal interests Politicians, parties and governments may be prone to corruption. Assume that politicians are not just interested in winning votes and retaining power, but also in gaining personal economic wealth. There may then be a conflict of interest between maximising the nation's welfare and maximising the welfare of the individual politician. Assume, for instance, that a Third World political leader can remain in power by giving massive bribes to electors at election time. Between elections, he accepts bribes from electors for granting political favours. In the process, the country fails to develop because decisions are made on the basis of maximising the wealth of the individual politician rather than that of the country. The individual politician is far better off as a rich head of a poor country than as a leader who has lost power in a fast growing country.

Short-termism In the UK, there has to be a general election at least every five years. Assume that a government wants a high growth, low inflation economy. Unfortunately, the current state of the economy at the time is one of high inflation and low growth. If the government pursues anti-inflationary policies, these will need to be long term policies if they are to be successful. However, they are also likely to push up unemployment and lead to a tough tax and low government spending regime. A government coming up to re-election has two choices. It can cut taxes, increase public spending, and cut interest rates to stimulate spending and make voters 'feel good', or it can pursue austere policies which might keep the economy on course but leave voters feeling they are not particularly well off. Assume that the austere policies are the ones which will maximise welfare in the long term, but would mean the government losing the election. It is obvious that the government will go for the reflationary policies if that means it can win the election, even though it knows this will damage welfare.

Regulatory capture Governments are responsible for regulating many areas, such as monopolies or the environment. 'Regulatory capture' means that groups such as monopolists earning abnormal profit or polluters damaging the environment can strongly influence the way they are being regulated to their own advantage. Take, for instance, a utility which is about to be privatised. The board of the utility will want to make sure that it is as easy as possible after privatisation for it to make high profits to satisfy its shareholders and maximise the pay of members of the board. It will lobby hard to have as weak powers as possible given to the regulatory body which will supervise it after privatisation. National welfare would probably be maximised if the regulatory body were given strong powers to keep consumer prices as low as possible.

However, in the short term, the government is far more likely to be wanting to maximise its own short term electoral advantage from having a successful sale of the shares and by allowing small investors (probably its own voters) to make quick gains on the share price. This requires weak regulation. Once the company has been privatised, it will want to dominate the regulator. It will do this by supplying only the information which is favourable to its case. For instance, it will tend to underestimate revenues and overestimate costs in order to make it seem that future profits will be low. The regulator, with little evidence apart from that supplied by the utility, will constantly make decisions which are in the utility's interest.

Evidence from the UK since 1984, when the first regulator was appointed, suggests that the individual appointed to head the regulatory team can be crucial in determining whether or not the regulatory body is captured. A regulator who wants to minimise confrontation with a utility (i.e. have a quiet life) will allow him- or herself to be captured.

In economic theory, it is often assumed that market failure should be corrected by government. If a monopolist is exploiting the consumer, then the government should regulate or abolish the monopoly. If a polluter is damaging the environment, then the government should act to limit the actions of those responsible. Public choice theory suggests that government may fail to act in these cases because politicians are more interested in maximising their own rewards (such as votes to stay in power) than in maximising the nation's welfare. Indeed, in some cases, politicians maximising their own rewards may lead to an even greater loss of economic welfare than if market failure had been left unregulated. At one extreme, some economists argue that governments should intervene as little as possible in the economy because their interventions are likely to be more damaging than the problems they are trying to solve. On the other hand, it is argued that politicians are not all out to maximise their own self-interest. Some politicians do act in the public interest even when this does not accord with their own self-interest. A left wing MP, for instance, who votes for higher income tax rates on higher income earners is likely to pay more in tax as a result. This doesn't mean to say that he or she won't vote in favour. The more a political system can encourage its politicians to act in the public interest, the more it will accord with the traditional view that government acts as an impartial actor in the economic system, intervening to maximise national welfare.

Key terms

Government failure - occurs when government intervention leads to a net welfare loss compared to the free market solution.

Public choice theory - theories about how and why public spending and taxation decisions are made.

Applied economics

Government failure and environmental policy

Governments round the world are facing increasing pressure to implement measures which will help solve environmental problems. A wide variety of policies is in use. However, in many circumstances, it could be argued that they create more problems than they solve. The result is government failure rather than a solution to market failure.

Landfill taxes

The UK Landfill Tax was first introduced in 1996. It was designed to solve a market failure. Households

and firms were disposing of rubbish to landfill sites but were not paying the full social cost of the disposal. For example, taking material to landfill creates CO_2 emissions from lorries. Local residents next to landfill sites suffer noise and other types of pollution. New landfill sites destroy the environment on which they are situated. Leakages from landfill sites can also cause environmental problems. Materials which could have been recycled at low cost were simply being thrown away. In theory, a landfill tax extends property rights and internalises the externality. Because households and firms now have to pay the full social cost of

is no difference made between landfill targets in London where land is scarce and Northumbria where population densities are much lower. Second, there are conflicting objectives. 'Green taxes' have political impact and help governments get elected into office. It could be that higher green taxes are a way of winning votes.

Carbon offsetting

Carbon offsetting occurs when an economic agent creates carbon emissions in one activity and then reduces them, or offsets them, in another. One example is air flights. It is now standard practice for airlines to ask passengers booking a flight whether they would like to pay extra to offset the carbon emissions they will create. The money is used to fund schemes such as planting trees which reduce CO_2 or developing renewable energy which saves on emissions from coal and gas fired power stations.

At the moment, governments have played little part in carbon offsetting schemes. These are private contracts between individual economic agents. However, there are reservations about how effective carbon offsetting is. It is difficult, for a start, to get exact offsets. The same trees planted in different locations, for example, will have different growth rates and will react differently to the soil in which they are planted. This affects the amount of CO_2 which they will store. More problematic is that not all the money given for carbon offsets is being spent efficiently. Some projects are started but are not completed for a variety of reasons. High administration costs and even fraud were found by the *Financial Times* when it reported on such schemes in 2007.

It is likely that at some point in the future the government will step in to regulate carbon offsetting schemes to correct the market failure currently being generated. However, this could in turn lead to government failure. For example, the cost of regulating schemes might be larger than the benefits gained from greater efficiency and transparency of existing schemes. Regulation might deter some carbon offsetting schemes from going ahead.

Carbon emissions trading

Carbon emissions trading schemes are a form of tradeable pollution permits. Currently, the most developed scheme is the European Union Emission Trading Scheme. The scheme began in 2005 when the EU issued firms with allowances for the amount of carbon they can emit. The total amount of allowances

disposal, they reduce the amount of waste being sent to landfill tips. Either they find ways of cutting down the amount of waste they create, or they recycle their waste.

For the purposes of the UK Landfill Tax, waste is classified into two types. Inactive waste is mainly materials used in building which cannot be recycled. Examples are concrete and soil excavated from foundations. Active waste is all other waste which includes household waste and building waste such as wood, piping and plastics. Active waste is waste which is capable of being recycled or disposed of in another way such as incineration. When first introduced in 1996, the tax on disposal of active waste at landfill sites was £7 a tonne. For inactive waste, this was £2 per tonne. By 2007/8, this had risen to £24 per tonne for active waste but inactive waste was still £2 per tonne. By 2010/11, the government have announced it will be £48 per tonne for active waste and £2.50 per tonne for inactive waste.

It can be argued that the Landfill Tax has been a great success. It has altered behaviour. In 1997-1998, the quantity of waste deposited at landfill sites was 96 million tonnes. By 2005/06, this had fallen to 72 million tonnes, a fall of 25 per cent. It is also clear that households and firms were not paying the full social cost of landfill before 1996.

However, it is also likely that the Landfill Tax has created government failure. First, the UK government has little precise information about the social costs and benefits of landfill disposal and its alternatives. It is unclear as to what is the socially optimal level of landfill use. For example, recent evidence suggests that local communities protest much more vigorously about the opening of an incineration plant for waste than a new landfill site. Their perception is that the pollution created by an incineration plant is much greater than that created by a landfill site. UK government targets for waste disposal are in practice set by the EU. There

represents the maximum amount of carbon emissions that can be emitted throughout the EU. This maximum amount is related to the EU's commitments under treaties such as the Kyoto agreement. Firms which do not use up all their allowances can then trade them for cash with other firms. In theory, this is a cheaper way to reduce carbon emissions than through regulation because it provides incentives for firms to reduce their carbon emissions in the most cost-effective way.

However, the scheme has been criticised. The scheme only covers half of the EU carbon emissions, targeting large carbon emitters such as power stations and heavy industry. These industries feel that they have been unfairly penalised and put under a competitive disadvantage. Economic theory suggests that if only some firms are taxed, there is sometimes a misallocation of resources which outweighs the misallocation present in the first place. Another criticism was that the 2005-2007 scheme was too lax and did little to curb emissions. Too lax a scheme could mean that the costs of compliance and administration outweigh any benefits. The scheme also distributed carbon allowances to existing polluters according to how much carbon they were emitting at the start of the scheme - so called 'grandfathering'. Arguably, this was done mainly for political reasons because of lobbying from firms that would be affected. However, greater economic efficiency could probably have been achieved if the carbon permits had been auctioned to the highest bidder. This is an example of government failure.

Renewable energy certificates

Renewable energy certificates can be seen as a negative carbon emission trading scheme. Instead of firms having to acquire carbon certificates to emit carbon, firms which generate renewable energy are given renewable energy certificates. They can then sell these to firms generating carbon and which need carbon certificates. In the UK, the government has created the Renewable Obligations Scheme where renewable energy certificates can legally offset the need for UK firms to buy carbon permits from the European Union Emission Trading Scheme. However, critics argue that the scheme has been relatively ineffective at encouraging anything other than wind power and even then incentives within the scheme have been weak.

Renewable energy itself is highly controversial. Critics argue that renewable energies can create as many if not more negative externalities as they create positive externalities. Few local communities want any wind turbines

located in their area because of their visual impact on the landscape and alleged problems with noise. Bio-fuels, where fuel is manufactured from corn for example, perpetuates ecologically damaging intensive farming methods. It can also send the price of basic foodstuffs rocketing as the experience of 2007 has shown. At worst, this could cause starvation in Third World countries amongst the poor who can no longer afford to pay the high prices. The proposed barrage across the estuary of the river Severn, which could generate 5-7 per cent of the UK's electricity, has been opposed by environmentalists because it will destroy rare wildlife habitats. Excessive use of renewable energy resulting from government incentives could itself lead to government failure.

DataQuestion

Bio-fuels and US pork-barrel politics

The world is rushing towards its end. Global warming, according to the gloomiest predictions, will raise temperatures so much that most life on this planet will disappear within the next 100 years. However, there is a solution and it comes from a farm near you. Farmers will grow crops such as corn or sugar cane. This will absorb CO_2 from the atmosphere. The crop can then be converted into bio-fuel and, mixed with conventional petrol or diesel, can be used to power vehicles. Bio-fuels will then be carbon neutral rather than emitting CO_2 as with the burning of oil.

In the United States, bio-fuels are already big business. In 2007, one quarter of the country's corn crop is set to be converted into ethanol which will then be mixed with conventional petrol and diesel products. There are already 116 ethanol plants with 79 under construction and 200 more planned. The major oil company ConocoPhillips in partnership with Tyson Foods wants to expand the industry by processing animal fats from the food group's herds and flocks and blending it with conventional fuel.

However, all this is only coming about because of subsidies. The US government is already paying $8.4 billion per year in subsidies for corn and ethanol production, which equates to 79 cents per litre. Petrol blended with ethanol has reduced tax of 5.3 cents per gallon. Then the oil industry gets a subsidy of 51 cents per gallon for blending the ethanol with petrol. This makes US ethanol a very expensive source of renewable energy. This is especially so when you take into account the fact that Brazilian ethanol, made from much more efficient sugar cane, is being kept out of US markets by a 51 cents a gallon tax on imports.

Devoting so much land to growing bio-fuels is not supported even by environmentalists. They point out that growing bio-fuel crops leads to soil acidification, high use of fertilisers and pesticides and bio-diversity loss. The rapid expansion of bio-fuels has also led to sharp increases in the prices of many agricultural products. Corn, for example, is used as a major feedstock for animals. So meat prices are likely to rise.

Ethanol plant.

Devoting extra land to corn means less wheat is produced, pushing up the price of bread. It is the poor, particularly in the Third World, who will suffer most from rising prices.

To understand why all this is happening, you need to consider traditional American pork-barrel politics. The farming lobby and the oil lobby have always had enormous influence in Washington. Farm subsidies, which go mainly to large agri-businesses rather than small farmers, remain substantial. Bio-fuels are just the latest, very profitable, way for these lobbies to milk the US taxpayer. Then there is the location of the states most involved in growing bio-fuel crops. One leading state is Iowa. This just happens to be one of the key states which votes early on to select the presidential candidates for each party. No presidential candidate who wants to get his party's nomination for president can afford to upset the voters of Iowa. The state gets a disproportionate amount of its income from agriculture. So no presidential candidate can afford to be less than enthusiastic about bio-fuels.

Source: adapted from the *Financial Times*, 20.7.2007; OECD, *Biofuels: is the cure worse than the Disease?*, 2007; EA2020, *Peak Soil: why biofuels are not sustainable and a threat to America's national security*.

1. Explain how increasing the output of bio-fuels could (a) help solve the problem of market failure in the market for fuels or (b) create an example of government failure.

2. Using public choice theory, explain why there might be an overproduction of bio-fuels in the USA.

Summary

1. Macroeconomics is concerned with the economy as a whole whilst microeconomics is the study of individual markets within the economy.
2. National economic performance can be measured in a number of different ways. Four key macroeconomic variables are the economic growth rate, unemployment, inflation and the current account balance.

Microeconomics and macroeconomics

MICROECONOMICS is the study of individual markets within an economy. For instance, microeconomics is concerned with individual markets for goods or the market for labour. Housing, transport, sport and leisure are all mainly microeconomic topics because they concern the study of individual markets.

In contrast, MACROECONOMICS is concerned with the study of the economy as a whole. For instance, macroeconomics considers the total quantity produced of goods and services in an economy. The price level of the whole economy is studied. Total levels of employment and unemployment are examined. Housing becomes a macroeconomic issue when, for instance, rises in house prices significantly affect the average level of all prices in the economy.

National economic performance

One of the reasons why macroeconomics is useful is because it tells us something about the performance of an economy. In particular, it allows economists to compare the economy today with the past. Is the economy doing better or worse than it was, say, ten years ago? It also allows economists to compare different economies. Is the Japanese economy doing better than the US economy? How does the UK compare with the average in Europe?

An economy is a system which attempts to resolve the basic economic problem of scarce resources in a world of infinite wants. An economic system is a mechanism for deciding what is to be produced, how production is to take place and who is to receive the benefit of that production. When judging the performance of an economy, one of the criteria is to consider how much is being produced. The more that is produced, the better is usually considered the economic performance. Another criterion is whether resources are being fully utilised. If there are high levels of unemployment, for instance, the economy cannot be producing at its potential level of output. Unemployment also brings poverty to those out of work and therefore affects the living standards of individuals. The rate at which prices rise is important too. High rates of price rises disrupt the workings of an economy. A national economy must also live within its means. So over a long period of time, the value of what it buys from other economies must roughly equal what it sells. In this, it is no different from a household which cannot forever overspend and accumulate debts.

Economic growth

One of the key measures of national economic performance is the rate of change of output. This is known as economic growth. If an economy grows by 2.5 per cent per annum,

output will double roughly every 30 years. If it grows by 7 per cent per annum, output will approximately double every 10 years. At growth rates of 10 per cent per annum, output will double every 7 years.

There is a standard definition of output based on a United Nations measure which is used by countries around the world to calculate their output. Using a standard definition allows output to be compared between countries and over time. This measure of output is called **gross domestic product** or **GDP**. So growth of 3 per cent in GDP in one year means that the output of the economy has increased by 3 per cent over a 12 month period.

Economic growth is generally considered to be desirable because individuals prefer to consume more rather than fewer goods and services. This is based on the assumption that wants are infinite. Higher economic growth is therefore better than lower economic growth. Periods when the economy fails to grow at all, or output shrinks as in a RECESSION or DEPRESSION, are periods when the economy is performing poorly. The depression years of the 1930s in Europe and the

Question 1

Table 1 Economic growth rates

				Average yearly changes, %	
	1961-73	1974-1979	1980-1989	1990-1999	2000-2007
United States	3.9	2.5	2.5	3.0	2.6
Japan	9.6	3.6	4.0	1.7	1.8
Germany	4.3	2.4	2.0	2.2	1.6
France	5.4	2.8	2.3	1.7	2.0
Italy	5.3	3.7	2.4	1.5	1.4
Mexico	6.6	6.1	2.0	3.0	3.0
United Kingdom	3.1	1.5	2.4	2.1	2.7

Source: adapted from OECD, Historical Statistics, Economic Outlook.

(a) Which country had the highest average yearly growth rate between (i) 1961 and 1973; (ii) 1974 and 1979; (iii) 1980 and 1989; (iv) 1990 and 1999; (v) 2000 and 2007?
(b) 'Mexico enjoyed a better economic performance than Germany over the period 1961 to 2007'. Does the evidence support this statement?
(c) In 1961, the UK enjoyed one of the highest living standards in Europe. By the mid-1990s, as measured by GDP, it lagged behind countries such as France and Germany. By 2007, the UK had caught up again with its main European competitors. Explain how the data show this story of the UK's poor relative economic performance over the period 1961 to the mid-1990s and its subsequent improvement.

Question 2

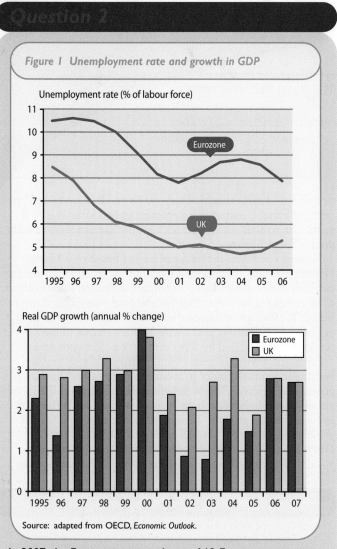

Figure 1 Unemployment rate and growth in GDP

Unemployment rate (% of labour force)

Real GDP growth (annual % change)

Source: adapted from OECD, *Economic Outlook*.

In 2007, the Eurozone was made up of 13 European countries, including France and Germany. 12 of these countries were the founder members of the 1999 European Monetary Union which led to the creation of a single European currency. The UK decided not to join and in 2007 was still not a member.

(a) Compare the economic performance of the UK with countries in the Eurozone.

(b) Suggest why the UK's unemployment record between 1995 and 2007 was better than that for the Eurozone.

Americas, for instance, were years when poverty increased and unemployment brought misery to millions of households.

Unemployment

Unemployment is a major problem in society because it represents a waste of scarce resources. Output could be higher if the unemployed were in work. It also leads to poverty for those who are out of work. So high unemployment is an indicator of poor national economic performance. Conversely, low unemployment is an indicator of good national economic performance.

Economic growth and unemployment tend to be linked. Fast growing economies tend to have low unemployment. This is because more workers are needed to produce more goods and services. Low levels of economic growth tend to be associated with rising levels of unemployment.

Over time, technological change allows an economy to produce more with fewer workers. If there is little or no economic growth, workers are made redundant through technological progress but fail to find new jobs in expanding industries. If growth is negative and the economy goes into recession, firms will lay off workers and unemployment will rise.

Fast economic growth, then, will tend to lead to net job creation. More jobs will be created than are lost through the changing structure of the economy. So another way of judging the performance of an economy is to consider its rate of job creation.

Inflation

Inflation is the rate of change of average prices in an economy. Low inflation is generally considered to be better than high inflation. This is because inflation has a number of adverse effects. For instance, rising prices mean that the value of what savings can buy falls. If a person had £50 in savings and the price of DVDs went up from £10 to £25, then they would be worse off because their savings could only now buy 2 DVDs compared to 5 before. Another problem with inflation is that it disrupts knowledge of prices in a market. If there is very high inflation, with prices changing by the month, consumers often don't know what is a reasonable price for an item when they come to buy it.

Today, inflation of a few per cent is considered to be acceptable. When inflation starts to climb through the 5 per cent barrier, economists begin to worry that inflation is too high. Inflation was a major problem for many countries including the UK in the 1970s and 1980s. In the UK, inflation reached 24.1 per cent in 1975, for instance. However, these levels of inflation are nothing compared to the **hyperinflation** experienced by countries such as Argentina and Brazil in the 1980s. Prices were increasing by up to 1 000 per cent per year.

The current balance

A household must pay its way in the world. If it spends more than it earns and takes on debt, then at some point in the future it must repay that debt. Failure to repay debt can lead to seizure of assets by bailiffs and the household being barred from future borrowing. The same is true of a national economy. A nation's spending on foreign goods and services is called **imports**. It earns money to pay for those imports by selling goods and services, known as **exports**, to foreigners. If imports are greater than exports then this must be financed, either through borrowing or running down savings held abroad. The economic performance of a country is sound if, over a period of time, its exports are either greater than or approximately equal to its imports. However, if its imports are significantly greater than exports, then it could face difficulties.

Where exports of goods and services are greater than imports, there is said to be a **current account surplus**. Where imports exceed exports, there is a current account deficit. Deficits become a problem when foreign banks and other lenders refuse to lend any more money. A 'credit crunch' like this occurred, for instance, in Mexico in 1982 and Thailand in 1998. Countries have to respond to restore confidence. This is likely to involve cutting domestic spending, which leads to less demand for imports. Cutting domestic spending, though, also leads to reduced economic growth and rising unemployment. So the current account position of a country is an important indicator of performance.

In July 2005, four terrorists planted bombs on London's underground and buses, killing 52 people and injuring many more. London is a major tourist destination and inevitably there was a wave of cancellations for London hotels in the aftermath of the bomb.

The World Travel and Tourism Council (WTTC) made an immediate impact assessment of the likely effects of the bombings on UK tourism. It predicted that in 2005 there would be nearly 600 000 fewer visitors to the UK, down from 31 million visitors. The contribution of travel and tourism to UK GDP would fall by £927 million, a 2 per cent fall in this contribution. UK Tourism contributes £185 billion to GDP and represents 4 per cent of the total. It directly and indirectly creates 2.8 million jobs.

The WTTC's conclusion was that the effects of the bombings on UK tourism would continue to be felt through to 2007. Jean-Claude Baumgarten, President of the WTTC, said the day after the bombings: 'This assumes that UK authorities undertake at least similarly strong measures of reassurance and encouragement to regain and rebuild visitor confidence and that no further events take place in the meantime.'

Source: adapted from www.wttc.org.

What impact might the 2005 London bombings have had on the performance of the UK economy (a) in the short term; (b) in the long term?

Government objectives

Governments attempt to manipulate the economy so as to improve its economic performance. Different economies perform in different ways. So what is possible for the UK economy might be very different from what is possible for the Chinese economy or the Russian economy. However, typically, governments have four main macroeconomic objectives.

- Economic growth should be as high as possible. The UK economy has grown at approximately 2.5 per cent per annum over the past 50 years. This has been fairly typical of western European economies and the USA too. So the UK government currently has an unofficial objective of seeing the economy grow at 2.5 per cent and would like to be able to increase this to 3.0 per cent. In China, with growth rates averaging 10 per cent per annum over the past thirty years, the Chinese government aims to achieve yearly growth rates of up to 10 per cent.
- Unemployment should be as low as possible. It is impossible to have zero unemployment in a market economy because there are always workers moving between jobs. They might have a new job to go to but it hasn't yet started, or they might be looking for a new job. The UK government has no official target for UK unemployment. However, it would like to see unemployment continue to fall from its present levels. In the 1950s and 1960s, UK unemployment was between 250 000 and 500 000 and the typical unemployment rate was 1.5 per cent. In 2007, the workforce was much larger but unemployment rates were higher at around 3 per cent. What's more, this does not include

several million people of working age who were long term sick. So the UK government would like to see further falls in unemployment.

- Inflation should be low but not necessarily zero. Inflation is the only indicator of macroeconomic performance for which there is an official target in the UK. The central target in 2007 was 2 per cent.
- The balance of payments on current balance should broadly balance over time. Exports and imports for an economy like the UK are very large. So annual deficits or surpluses of even tens of billions of pounds can be relatively unimportant. However, history shows that large sustained deficits on the current account can lead to economic crises. So governments might have to intervene if the current account is threatening the rest of the economy.

Governments also have other major objectives apart from those to do with economic growth, unemployment, inflation and the balance of payments on current account. One objective relates to the **distribution of income**. Some governments attempt to make the distribution of income more equal. So the Labour government elected in 1997 had this commitment. Other governments, such as the Conservative government of Margaret Thatcher in the 1980s, are committed to making the distribution of income less equal.

Another objective of most governments today is to reduce damage to the **environment**. There is no simple measure of the impact of economy activity on the environment. So a wide variety of measures have to be used from tonnes of waste sent to landfill sites to CO_2 emissions into the atmosphere. Governments do not aim to eliminate pollution and environmental damage since this would be impossible. However, they set targets and impose limits on different environmental outcomes of economic activity.

In this, my 11th budget, my report to the country is of rising employment and rising investment; continued low inflation and low interest and mortgage rates; and this is a Budget to expand prosperity and fairness for Britain's families - and it is built on the foundation of the longest period of economic stability and sustained growth in our country's history. I can report the British economy is today growing faster than all the other G7 economies - growth stronger this year than the euro area, stronger than Japan and stronger even than America. Our forecast and the consensus of independent forecasts agree that looking ahead to 2008 and 2009 inflation will also be on target. Mr Deputy Speaker, six months ago when we published the Stern report on climate change, we set a framework for environmental action combining a call to personal and social responsibility, with European and international co-operation. Since then we have secured support for a strengthened European carbon trade scheme on the road to a global scheme.

Source: excerpts from *The Budget Speech*, March 2007.

(a) Name **four** economic objectives mentioned in the 2007 Budget Speech.
(b) What evidence was there in the speech that the UK was succeeding in meeting its growth and inflation objectives but failing in its environmental objectives?

Trade-offs

Governments cannot necessarily achieve all their objectives at any single point in time. There are frequently trade-offs that have to be made. For example, in the short term, lower unemployment might only be achievable if there is higher inflation. This is known as the Phillips curve relationship. The reason why is that lower unemployment is typically associated with fast economic growth. Fast economic growth tends to put upward pressure on prices. Equally, fast economic growth for the UK economy is often associated with a worsening balance of payments on current account. This is because UK consumers buy more imported goods with their high incomes. However, in countries like China or Japan, faster economic growth is often caused by booms in export sales which in turn lead to current account surpluses. Trade-offs will be explored in much more detail in many of the macroeconomic units of this book.

Key terms

Depression - a period when there is a particularly deep and long fall in output.
Macroeconomics - the study of the economy as a whole, including inflation, growth and unemployment.
Microeconomics - the study of the behaviour of individuals or groups within an economy, typically within a market context.
Recession - a period when growth in output falls or becomes negative. The technical definition now used by governments is that a recession occurs when growth in output is negative for two successive quarters (i.e. two periods of three months).

Applied economics

A tale of four economies

The USA, Germany, Japan and the UK are four of the largest economies in the world. They form part of the G7 group (the other three being France, Italy and Canada) which meets regularly to discuss common economic problems. For much of the post-war period, Japan and Germany were seen as highly successful. They had high economic growth, low inflation, low unemployment and a persistent current account surplus. The USA was less successful mainly because its growth rate seemed low in comparison with Japan and much of continental Europe. As for the UK, it seemed to have a disappointing economic performance with slow growth and persistent inflation and balance of payment problems.

The 1990s, though, saw a reversal of fortunes as Figures 2 to 5 show. Japan's growth rate at the start of the decade was not untypical of what it had achieved during the previous four decades. However, it became bogged down in a series of recessions interspersed with short periods of positive economic growth. Over the period 1991-2006, it only averaged economic growth of 1.3 per cent per annum, compared to the 4-10 per cent range of its 'economic miracle' years of the 1950s to 1980s. Inflation reflected depressed demand. In 1995, prices fell and this was followed by six years of price stability or falls between 1999 and 2006. In the 1990s, unemployment remained low, but by the end of the decade was beginning to rise as years of low economic growth resulted in a shake out of jobs from Japanese industry. By 2006, unemployment was double what it

had been in 1991.

The period 1991-2006 was difficult for Germany too. Part of its problems arose from the cost of reunification of East Germany with West Germany in 1990. East Germany had been a **command economy** within the Soviet sphere of influence since 1945. By 1990, East Germany was a relatively inefficient economy where output per head was far below that of its highly successful western neighbour. Reunification resulted in a transfer of resources from West Germany to East Germany. Despite this, the East German economy remained a drag on the performance of the German economy as a whole. Growth for the reunited German economy was relatively slow after 1991. By the late 1990s, the failure of the German economy to pick up after reunification began to be blamed on its 'social' economic model which it shared with low growth countries, such as France and Italy. 'Social Europe' was growing slowly because it lacked flexibility

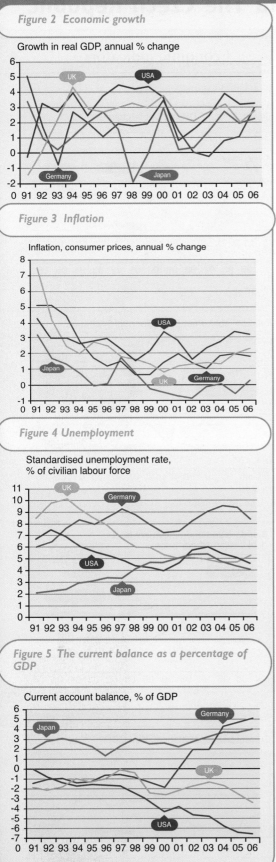

Figure 2 Economic growth

Growth in real GDP, annual % change

Figure 3 Inflation

Inflation, consumer prices, annual % change

Figure 4 Unemployment

Standardised unemployment rate, % of civilian labour force

Figure 5 The current balance as a percentage of GDP

Current account balance, % of GDP

Source: adapted from OECD, *Economic Outlook*.

in its markets. Government red tape, high taxes on labour, difficulties in sacking workers and other **supply side** constraints were discouraging firms from investing and taking on workers. The result was low growth and high unemployment. By 2006, German unemployment was still 40 per cent higher than its 1991 level. Inflation, which rose at the start of the 1990s following reunification, fell back quickly to below 2 per cent, partly a reflection of low economic growth and lack of demand.

The story for the USA and the UK was the reverse for that of Germany and Japan. Both the USA and the UK, after decades of relatively low economic growth, saw their position transformed into relatively high economic growth countries. Between 1960 and 1990, the US's long term growth rate had been around 2.5 per cent per year. However, from 1992, economic growth averaged over 3 per cent. Strong economic growth was also combined with subdued inflation.

In the UK, after a deep recession in the early 1990s, the economy bounced back and enjoyed average growth of 2.9 per cent between 1993 and 2006. This compared to a 2.6 per cent average for the period 1950-1990 and 2.3 per cent for 1970-1990. Unemployment nearly halved between its peak in 1993 and 2006 whilst inflation also fell.

The performance of the four economies on the current account of the balance of payments can be interpreted in two ways. One is to argue that the persistent current account deficits of the UK and the USA will drag down future growth of these economies. If the deficits have been financed through borrowing to pay for current spending, the money will one day have to be repaid with interest. Just as heavy borrowing now by a household means lower consumption in the future when the debt has to be repaid, so it could be with both the UK and the USA. On this argument, Japan, which has run a persistent surplus, will benefit in the future. On the other hand, if the current account deficits have been caused by inflows of investment capital, where foreigners are investing in UK and US businesses, then the economies of the UK and the USA have been strengthened, not weakened over the period. If, for example, Japan is using part of its current account surplus to invest in new car plants in the UK, the British economy is likely to benefit in the long term. Economists are divided about whether the current account deficits and surpluses the UK, USA, Germany and Japan have had, and will have, an effect on economic performance.

It could be argued that the performance of the UK and the US economies has barely changed since the 1970s and 1980s. An increase in the average economic growth rate of around half a percent looks fairly insignificant. However, it should be taken in the context of the fall in the long term growth rate of countries like Germany and Japan. In the 1970s and 1980s, Japan and Germany were growing at up to twice the rate of the UK and the USA. Since 1991, the growth rates of Japan and Germany have been half that of the UK and the USA. This turnaround has been used to argue that the 'Anglo-Saxon economic model' associated with free markets and globalisation is superior to the 'social economic model' of countries like Germany associated with more controlled markets and protectionism. By 2006, the UK's economic performance looked extremely good compared to that of Germany. The USA was outperforming its long term economic rival, Japan. The only worrying feature of the performance of the UK and the USA was their persistent current account deficits.

DataQuestion — Ireland and The Czech Republic

Ireland

Ireland joined the European Union at the same time as the UK in 1973. When it joined, it was one of the poorer EU members and consequently attracted a considerable amount of EU regional aid as well as benefiting from agricultural subsidies from the EU Common Agricultural Policy (CAP).

Successive Irish governments pursued two sets of policies which were, arguably, to prove crucial in its economic success. One was to spend generously on education so that by the 1990s, the workforce of Ireland was as richly endowed with human capital as its economic rivals. The other was, for example through grants and tax breaks, to attract foreign companies to set up in Ireland. Not only did these directly and indirectly create jobs, but they encouraged Irish companies to come up to world class standards.

With many low wage countries in Central and Eastern Europe having joined the EU in 2004, and possibly more to come over the next ten years, Ireland faced the same problem as other Western European EU members: can they compete successfully or will they see jobs drain away to the East? For Ireland, is this the end of its economic boom time and will its growth rate fall to the Western European average of little more than 2 per cent per annum?

The Czech Republic

Until 1990, the Czech Republic was a command economy and part of the Eastern Bloc. Relatively poor by Western standards, its trade was orientated towards other Eastern Bloc countries such as Poland, East Germany and the Soviet Union.

From 1990, it began a transition to democracy and a free market economy. Much of the industry owned by the state was privatised (i.e. sold off to the private sector). Trade was re-orientated towards Western Europe. However, the transition was painful. Inefficient firms closed down. Other enterprises had to scale back their production. Increases in GDP in some sectors of the economy were offset by decreases in other sectors. Czech consumers and producers showed a preference for imported goods over Czech-made products. In 2004, the Czech Republic joined the European Union. It looked to the success of economies such as Ireland and Portugal following their accession to the European Union as a model for its own future development.

1. Compare the economic performance of the Czech Republic and Ireland over the period 1994 to 2006.
2. What problems may the Czech Republic and Ireland face in the future and how might these problems impact on the future economic performance of these two countries?

Economic indicators

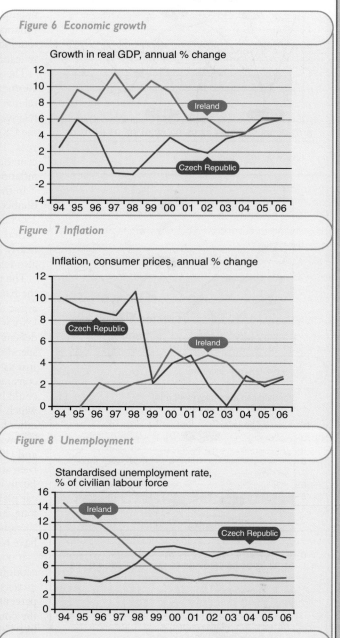

Figure 6 Economic growth

Growth in real GDP, annual % change

Figure 7 Inflation

Inflation, consumer prices, annual % change

Figure 8 Unemployment

Standardised unemployment rate, % of civilian labour force

Figure 9 The current balance as a percentage of GDP

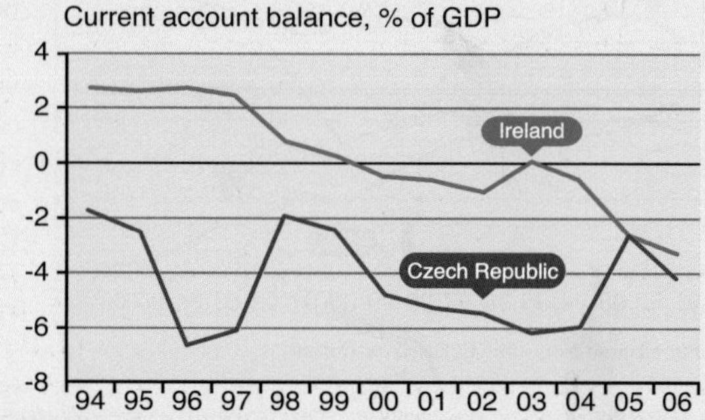

Current account balance, % of GDP

Source: adapted from OECD, *Economic Outlook*.

Summary

1. There are four phases to the economic cycle including boom, recession, slump and recovery.
2. Positive and negative output gaps exist when actual GDP is above and below the trend rate of growth of the economy.

The economic cycle

Over time, real output in the UK economy has risen. For the period 1950-2007, the average annual rate of real economic growth was 2.5 per cent. However, in the short term, the rate of growth of output fluctuates above and below this long term average or trend rate rate of growth. These fluctuations are known as the BUSINESS CYCLE or TRADE CYCLE or ECONOMIC CYCLE. All business cycles are slightly different. However, they tend to have four main phases. These are illustrated in Figure 1.

Peak or boom When the economy is in boom, GDP is growing particularly fast. Unemployment is likely to be low and spending high. The rate of growth of GDP is likely to be above its long term trend rate. There will be inflationary pressures due to expanding aggregate demand. Firms will increasing their investment to cope with demand.

Downturn In a downturn, the economy is slowing down. The rate of growth of GDP will be falling and unemployment will be rising. Consumer and investment spending will be slowing and inflationary pressures will be falling.

Recession or trough or slump or depression At the bottom of the economic cycle, the rate of growth of GDP may be close to zero or may be negative. The deeper the recession, the larger will be the fall in the GDP and the longer the recession will last. In a recession, unemployment will be high and possibly still rising. Consumers and firms will be reluctant to take on debt because they fear they will not be able to repay it. Firms will be reluctant to invest in case they cannot sell the goods produced by the new investment. Inflation will be low and could even be negative.

Recovery or expansion In a recovery, the rate of growth of GDP begins to pick up again. Consumers and firms begin to regain confidence and spend more. Unemployment begins to fall.

In the UK, the government defines recession as where GDP falls in at least two successive quarters. On this definition, the last recession in the UK occurred in 1990-1991. Since then, the pattern of the trade cycle has followed the pattern set in the 1950s and 1960s. Recessions have been very mild. GDP has not fallen. Rather the rate of growth of GDP has dipped below its long term trend rate of growth. In a boom, the rate of growth of GDP has been slightly above the average long term rate of growth. When the economic cycle is very mild, the terms 'depression' and 'recovery' tend not be used. Economists and media commentators tend to talk about the economy going from recession to boom and back again to recession.

There are many different reasons why the short run rate of

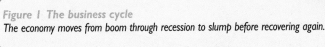

Figure 1 The business cycle
The economy moves from boom through recession to slump before recovering again.

growth of GDP may fluctuate around its long term trend. But they can be classified into two main types.

- **Demand-side shocks** are shocks which affect aggregate demand. For example, there may be a sudden collapse in stock market prices which sends consumer confidence plummeting, or the central bank may raise interest rates sharply because inflation is getting too high, or the world economy may go into recession, hitting UK exports sharply and so sending the UK economy into recession.
- **Supply-side shocks** are shocks which affect aggregate supply. For example, a large rise in world commodity prices could raise the price level substantially in the UK, leading to lower spending and a recession. An outbreak of trade union militancy which saw large wage increases in the economy could again raise the price level substantially and send the economy into recession.

The output gap

The difference between the actual level of GDP and its estimated long term value at a point in time is known as the OUTPUT GAP. In Figure 2, the straight line is the trend rate of growth in GDP over a long period of time. It is assumed that this shows the level of GDP associated with the productive potential of the economy. The actual level of GDP varies around the trend growth line. This fluctuation is the business cycle. When the economy is in recession and there is high unemployment and deflation, the actual level of

153

GDP will be below the trend line. A NEGATIVE OUTPUT GAP is then said to exist. In an inflationary boom, the actual level of GDP is likely to be above the trend line. A POSITIVE OUTPUT GAP then exists.

Figure 2 The output gap

The trend rate of growth of GDP approximates the growth in productive potential of the economy. When actual GDP falls below this or rises above it, there is said to be an output gap. When actual GDP growth falls below this, there is a negative output gap. When actual GDP growth rises above it, there is a positive output gap.

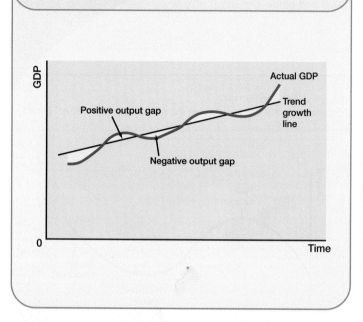

Key terms

Business or economic or trade cycle - regular fluctuations in the level of economic activity around the productive potential of the economy. In business cycles, the economy veers from recession, when it is operating well below its productive potential, to booms when it is likely to be at or even above its productive potential.

Output gap - the difference between the actual level of GDP and the productive potential of the economy. There is a **positive output gap** when actual GDP is above the productive potential of the economy and it is in boom. There is a **negative output gap** when actual GDP is below the productive potential of the economy.

Applied economics

The end of the economic cycle?

The UK government defines a recession as being where GDP falls in two successive quarters. The GDP data expressed in £bn in Figure 3 shows that between 1988 and 2007, there was only one period when this occurred, between the 2nd quarter of 1991 and the 2nd quarter of 1992. So has the economic cycle disappeared in recent years?

Figure 4 also shows quarterly changes in GDP expressed as annual percentages. This shows clearly that there are fluctuations in the rate of growth of GDP. These fluctuations are not random but follow a pattern which looks very much like an economic cycle. So peaks and troughs can be seen from the GDP growth line in Figure 4 centred round a trend rate of growth of 2.9 per cent between

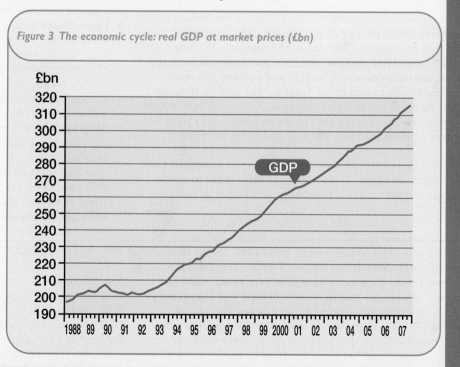

Figure 3 The economic cycle: real GDP at market prices (£bn)

1995 and 2007. When the rate of growth has dipped below the trend rate of growth, newspapers and economic commentators have talked about the UK going 'into recession' and there being a 'downturn' in the economy. Equally, when the rate of growth has been above the trend rate of growth, the talk has been of 'boom times' in the economy.

So recent economic experience would suggest that the economy is no longer lurching from negative to positive economic growth rates. Instead, the economy is experiencing very mild fluctuations in the level of economic activity, but these fluctuations are still occurring on a regular basis. The economic cycle looks alive and well even if, fortunately, it is very mild.

Figure 4 *Annual percentage change in real GDP*

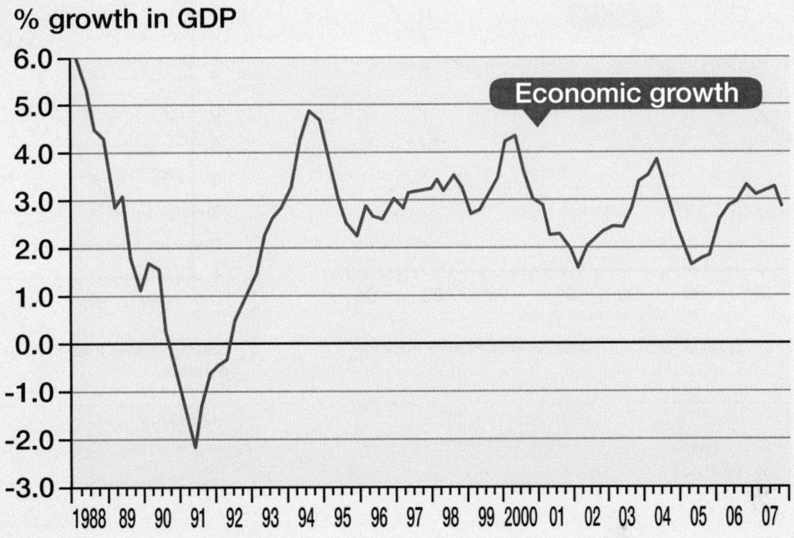

DataQuestion   Boom and bust 1987-1994

The Lawson boom

The last major recession in the UK occurred in the early 1990s. It followed was is now called the 'Lawson boom'. Nigel Lawson was Chancellor of the Exchequer between 1983 and 1989. Between 1983 and 1987, the economy grew at an average rate of 3.6 per cent compared to the post-war average of 2.5 per cent. The economy seemed to be performing extremely well. A number of factors helped fuel the boom.

The government cut taxes. House prices rose fast. Interest rates fell. Then in 1988, inflation began to rise. The government responded by raising interest rates. The economy began to slow down and by 1991 had entered into an official recession as GDP fell in two successive quarters.

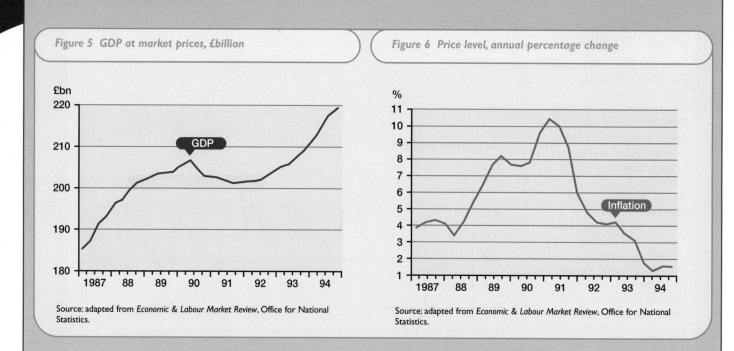

Figure 5 GDP at market prices, £billion

Source: adapted from *Economic & Labour Market Review*, Office for National Statistics.

Figure 6 Price level, annual percentage change

Source: adapted from *Economic & Labour Market Review*, Office for National Statistics.

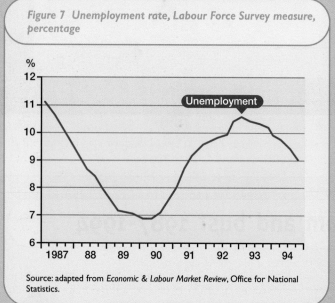

Figure 7 Unemployment rate, Labour Force Survey measure, percentage

Source: adapted from *Economic & Labour Market Review*, Office for National Statistics.

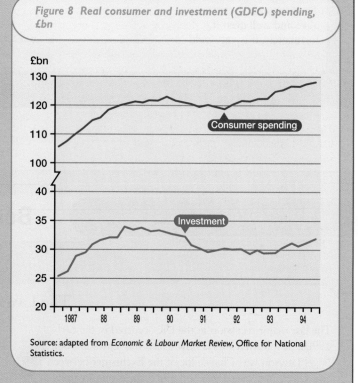

Figure 8 Real consumer and investment (GDFC) spending, £bn

Source: adapted from *Economic & Labour Market Review*, Office for National Statistics.

1. Explain the phases of the economic cycle, illustrating your answer from the data.

2. 'The end of the Lawson boom was caused by a demand side shock.' Explain what this might mean.

Summary

1. National income can be measured in three ways: as national output, national expenditure or national income.
2. The most commonly used measure of national income is Gross Domestic Product (GDP). Other measures include Gross National Product (GNP) and Net National Product (NNP). All these measures can be at market prices or factor cost.
3. National income statistics are used by academics to formulate and test hypotheses. They are used by policy makers to formulate economic policy both on a microeconomic and macroeconomic level. They are often used as a proxy measure for the standards of living and to compare living standards between countries and within a country over time.
4. National income statistics can be inaccurate because of statistical errors, the existence of the black economy, of non-traded sectors, and difficulties with valuing public sector output.
5. Problems occur when comparing national income over time because of inflation, the accuracy and presentation of statistics, changes in population, the quality of goods and services and changes in income distribution.
6. Further problems occur when comparing national income between countries. In particular, an exchange rate has to be constructed which accurately reflects different purchasing power parities.

Income, output and expenditure

Macroeconomics is concerned with the economy as a whole. A key macroeconomic variable is the level of total output in an economy, often called NATIONAL INCOME. There are three ways in which national income can be calculated. To understand why, consider a very simple model of the economy where there is no foreign trade (a CLOSED ECONOMY as opposed to an OPEN ECONOMY where there is foreign trade) and no government. In this economy, there are only households and firms which spend all their income and revenues.

- Households own the WEALTH of the nation. They own the stock of land, labour and capital used to produce goods and services. They supply these factors to firms in return for rents, wages, interest and profits - the rewards to the factor of production. They then use this money to buy goods and services.
- Firms produce goods and services. They hire factors of production from households and use these to produce goods and services for sale back to households.

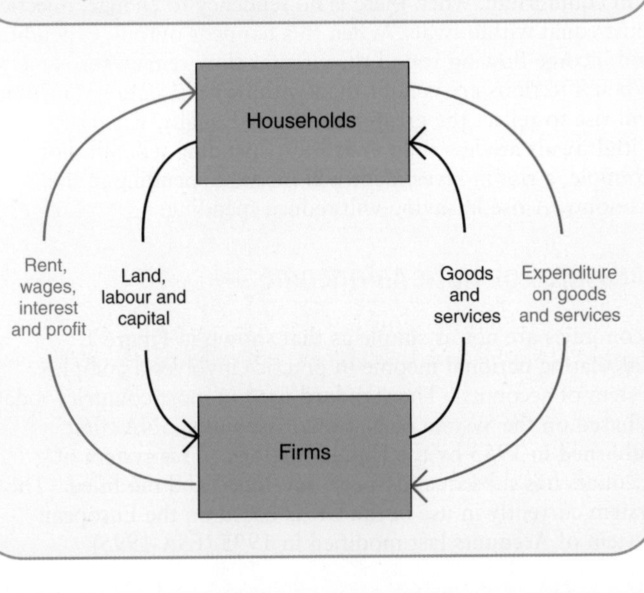

The flow from households to firms is shown in Figure 1. The flow of money around the economy is shown in colour. Households receive payments for hiring their land, labour and capital. They spend all that money on the goods and services produced by firms (consumption). An alternative way of putting this is to express these money payments in real terms, taking into account changes in prices. The real flow of products and factor services is shown in black. Households supply land, labour and capital in return for goods and services. The CIRCULAR FLOW OF INCOME MODEL can be used to show that there are three ways of measuring the level of economic activity.

National output (O) This is the value of the flow of goods and services from firms to households. It is the black line on the right of the diagram.

National expenditure (E) This is the value of spending by households on goods and services. It is the red line on the right of the diagram.

National income (Y) This is the value of income paid by firms to households in return for land, labour and capital. It is the blue line on the left of the diagram.

So income, expenditure and output are three ways of measuring the same flow. To show that they must be identical and not just equal, we use the '$\equiv$' sign.

$$O \equiv E \equiv Y$$

Injections and withdrawals

The simple circular flow of income model in Figure 1 can be made more realistic by adding injections and withdrawals. An INJECTION into the circular flow is spending

Figure I The circular flow of income in a simple economy
Households supply factors of production to firms in return for rent, wages, interest and profit. Households spend their money on goods and services supplied by firms.

Households

Rent, wages, interest and profit

Land, labour and capital

Goods and services

Expenditure on goods and services

Firms

Table 1

	£bn
Rent	5
Wages	75
Interest and profit	20

The figures in Table 1 represent the only income payments received by households. There are no savings, investment, government expenditure and taxes or foreign trade in the economy.

(a) Draw a circular flow of income diagram. Label it at the appropriate place with the value of: (i) income, (ii) output and (iii) expenditure.
(b) How would your answer be different if wages were £100 billion?

which does not come from households. There are three injections.

● Investment is spending by firms on new capital equipment like factories, offices and machinery. It is also spending on stocks (or inventories) of goods which are used in the production process.
● Government spending is spending by central and local government as well as other government agencies.
● Exports is spending by foreigners on goods and services made in the UK.

A WITHDRAWAL or LEAKAGE from the circular flow is spending which does not flow back from households to firms. There are three withdrawals which correspond to the three injections.

● Saving by households is money which is not spent by households. Equally, firms do not spend all of their money

Figure 2 *Injections and withdrawals and the circular flow*
Investment, government spending and exports are injections into the circular flow. They raise spending. Saving, taxes and imports are withdrawals and reduce spending.

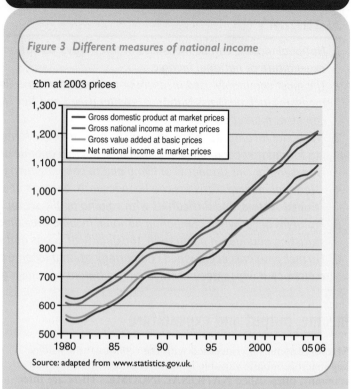

Figure 3 *Different measures of national income*

£bn at 2003 prices

- Gross domestic product at market prices
- Gross national income at market prices
- Gross value added at basic prices
- Net national income at market prices

Source: adapted from www.statistics.gov.uk.

(a) Briefly explain the difference between each measure of national income shown on the graph.
(b) 'Changes in GDP at market prices broadly reflect changes in other measures of national income over time.' To what extent do the data support this?

on wages and profits but may save some of it.
● Taxes paid to the government take money from both households and firms.
● Imports from abroad are bought both by households and firms. The money paid in taxes then does not flow back round the circular flow.

A circular flow diagram which includes injections and withdrawals is shown in Figure 2.

In equilibrium, when there is no tendency to change, injections must equal withdrawals. When this happens output, expenditure and income flowing round the circular flow remain the same. When injections are greater than withdrawals, national income will rise to reflect the greater spending. Equally, when withdrawals are less than injections, spending will fall. For example, a rise in investment will increase spending in the economy. A rise in saving will reduce spending.

Measures of national income

Economies are not as simple as that shown in Figure 1. Calculating national income in practice involves a complex system of accounts. The standard used in most countries today is based on the System of National Accounts (SNA) first published in 1953 by the United Nations. This system of accounts has subsequently been developed and modified. The system currently in use in the UK is based on the European System of Accounts last modified in 1995 (ESA 1995).

The key measure of national income used in the UK is GROSS DOMESTIC PRODUCT (GDP). This is at market prices, which means it is a measure of national income that includes the value of **indirect taxes** (taxes on expenditure) like VAT. Indirect taxes are not part of the output of the economy, so this measure inflates the actual value of national income. GDP also includes the value of exports and imports and is therefore a more complex measure of national income than in the simple circular flow model described earlier. There are other measures of national income.

Gross value added (GVA) at basic cost This is GDP minus indirect taxes plus subsidies on goods. Indirect taxes minus subsidies is called the basic price adjustment.

Gross national income (GNP) at market prices GROSS NATIONAL INCOME (GNP) is GDP plus income earned abroad on investments and other assets owned overseas minus income paid to foreigners on their investments in the UK.

Net national income at market prices Each year, the existing capital stock or physical wealth of the country depreciates in value because of use. This is like depreciation on a car as it gets older. If individuals run down their savings to finance spending, their actual income must be their spending minus how much they have used from their savings. Similarly with a country, its true value of income is gross (i.e. before depreciation has been taken into account) national income minus depreciation. This is net national income.

GDP at market prices is the main headline figure used for national income because the data to calculate it is most quickly available. When comparing over time and between countries, movements in GDP at market prices are broadly similar to movements in other measures of national income. So it is a good guide to what is happening in the economy and can be used to judge the performance of the economy.

Transfer payments

Not all types of income are included in the final calculation of national income. Some incomes are received without there being any corresponding output in the economy. For instance:
- the government pays National Insurance and social security benefits to individuals, but the recipients produce nothing in return;
- students receive student grants from government, but again produce nothing which can be sold;
- children receive pocket money and allowances from their parents;
- an individual selling a second hand car receives money, but no new car is created.

These incomes, called TRANSFER PAYMENTS, are excluded from final calculations of national income. For instance, government spending in national income is **public expenditure** minus spending on benefits and grants.

Why is national income measured?

National income is a measure of the output, expenditure and income of an economy. National income statistics provide not only figures for these totals but also a breakdown of the totals. They are used in a number of different ways.
- Academic economists use them to test hypotheses and build models of the economy. This increases our understanding of how an economy works.
- Government, firms and economists use the figures to forecast changes in the economy. These forecasts are then used to plan for the future. Government may attempt to direct the economy, making changes in its spending or its taxes at budget time. Groups such as trade unions or the CBI will make their own recommendations about what policies they think the government should pursue.
- They are used to make comparisons over time and between countries. For instance, national income statistics can be used to compare the income of the UK in 1950 and 2007, or they can be used to compare France's income with UK income. Of particular importance when making comparisons over time is the rate of change of national income (i.e. the rate of economic growth).
- They are used to make judgements about economic welfare. Growth in national income, for instance, is usually equated with a rise in living standards.

The accuracy of national income statistics

National income statistics are inaccurate for a number of reasons.

Statistical inaccuracies National income statistics are calculated from millions of different returns to the government. Inevitably mistakes are made: returns

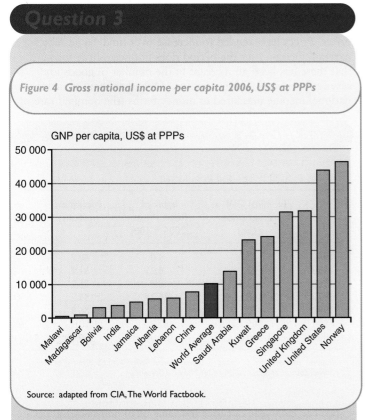

Question 3

Figure 4 Gross national income per capita 2006, US$ at PPPs

GNP per capita, US$ at PPPs

Source: adapted from CIA, The World Factbook.

(a) What statistics do governments need to collect in order to be able to calculate GNP per capita?
(b) How might (i) an economist and (ii) a government use these statistics?

Question 4

Researchers from the University of Cyprus have estimated the size of the hidden economy in the UK to be at least 10.6 per cent of GDP. They looked at the incomes of the self-employed and compared them to their expenditure using the Family Expenditure Survey compiled by the Office for National Statistics (FES). They compared this with the incomes and expenditure of employed workers such as civil servants who were unlikely to have any hidden income. They estimated that households where the head of the household was a blue collar worker and self-employed reported only 46 per cent of their income to the tax authorities. Households whose self-employed head was in a white-collar occupation on average reported only 61 per cent of their income. Given that reported self-employment income is around 12.3 per cent of GDP, this means that self-employment related black economy activities in the UK amount to 10.6 per cent of GDP.

Workers who are employed may also have undeclared part-time jobs which would increase the size of the black economy. Their ability to avoid tax, however, is limited because their employers deduct their tax from their pay packet through the PAYE (Pay As You Earn) scheme. In 2004, there were 3.6 million self-employed workers and 24.6 million employees.

Source: adapted from 'Estimates of the black economy based on consumer demand approaches', P.Lyssiotou, P.Pashardes and T.Stengos, *Economic Journal*, July 2004 and *Monthly Digest of Statistics*, Office for National Statistics.

(a) Explain why there is an incentive for workers to work in the 'hidden economy'.
(b) UK tax authorities estimate that painters and decorators, cleaners, taxi drivers and gardeners tend to evade tax. Suggest why these workers, rather than teachers or civil servants, are more likely to work in the 'hidden economy'.
(c) The UK government is currently aiming to create a more flexible workforce, with a greater proportion of part-time, casual and self-employed workers. What are the implications of this for the size of the hidden economy?

are inaccurate or simply not completed. The statistics are constantly being revised in the light of fresh evidence. Although revisions tend to become smaller over time, national income statistics are still being revised decades after first publication.

The hidden economy Taxes such as VAT, income tax and National Insurance contributions, and government regulations such as health and safety laws, impose a burden on workers and businesses. Some are tempted to evade taxes and they are then said to work in the BLACK, HIDDEN OR INFORMAL ECONOMY. In the building industry, for instance, it is common for workers to be self-employed and to under-declare or not declare their income at all to the tax authorities. Transactions in the black economy are in the form of cash. Cheques, credit cards, etc. could all be traced by the tax authorities. Tax evasion is the dominant motive for working in the hidden economy but a few also claim welfare benefits to which they are not entitled. The size of the hidden economy is difficult to estimate, but in the UK estimates have varied from 7 to 15 per cent of GDP (i.e. national income statistics underestimate the true size of national income by at least 7 per cent).

Home produced services In the poorest developing countries in the world, GNP per person is valued at less than £100 per year. It would be impossible to survive on this

amount if this were the true value of output in the economy. However, a large part of the production of the agricultural sector is not traded and therefore does not appear in national income statistics. People are engaged in subsistence agriculture, consuming what they produce. Hence the value of national output is in reality much higher. In the UK, the output of the services of housewives and househusbands is equally not recorded. Nor is the large number of DIY jobs completed each year. The more DIY activity, the greater will be the under-recording of national output by national income statistics.

The public sector Valuing the output of much of the public sector is difficult because it is not bought and sold. This problem is circumvented by valuing non-marketed output at its cost of production. For instance, the value of the output of a state school is the cost of running the school. This method of valuation can yield some surprising results. Assume that through more efficient staffing the number of nurses on a hospital ward is reduced from 10 to 8 and the service is improved. National income accounts will still show a fall in output (measured by a drop in the two nurses' incomes). In general, increased productivity in the public sector is shown by a fall in the value of output. It looks as though less is being produced when in fact output remains unchanged.

Comparing national income over time

Comparing the national income of the UK today with national income in the past presents problems.

Prices Prices have tended to increase over time. So an increase in national income over the period does not necessarily indicate that there has been an increase in the number of goods and services produced in the economy. Only if the rate of increase of national income measured in money terms (the nominal rate of

Question 5

Table 2 *GDP, prices and population*

	Nominal GDP at market prices (£bn)	Index of Retail Prices (2006 = 100)	Population (millions)
1948	12.0	4.0	48.7
1958	23.1	6.2	51.7
1968	43.5	8.4	55.2
1978	168.1	25.2	56.2
1988	470.7	54.0	56.9
1998	865.7	82.2	58.5
2006	1 300.0	100.0	60.6

Source: adapted from *Economic & Labour Market Review, Monthly Digest of Statistics, Annual Abstract of Statistics*, Office for National Statistics.

(a) For each year, calculate the value of: (i) nominal GDP per head of the population; (ii) real GDP per head of the population at 2006 prices.
(b) To what extent is it possible to judge from the data whether living standards increased over the period 1948-2006?

economic growth) has been greater than the increase in prices (the inflation rate) can there be said to have been an increase in output. So when comparing over time, it is essential to consider real and not **nominal** changes in income.

The accuracy and presentation of statistics National income statistics are inaccurate and therefore it is impossible to give a precise figure for the change in income over time. Moreover, the change in real income over time will also be affected by the inflation rate. The inevitable errors made in the calculation of the inflation rate compound the problems of inaccuracy. The method of calculating national income and the rate of inflation can also change over time. It is important to attempt to eliminate the effect of changes in definitions.

Changes in population National income statistics are often used to compare living standards over time. If they are to be used in this way, it is essential to compare national income per capita (i.e. per person). For instance, if the population doubles whilst national income quadruples, people are likely to be nearer twice as well off than four times.

Quality of goods and services The quality of goods may improve over time due to advances in technology but they may also fall in price. For instance, cars today are far better than cars 80 years ago and yet are far cheaper. National income would show this fall in price by a fall in national income, wrongly implying that living standards had fallen. On the other hand, pay in the public sector tends to increase at about 2 per cent per annum faster than the increase in inflation. This is because pay across the economy tends to increase in line with the rate of economic growth rather than the rate of inflation. Increased pay would be reflected in both higher nominal and real national income but there may well be no extra goods or services being produced.

Defence and related expenditures The GDP of the UK was higher during the Second World War than in the 1930s, but much of GDP between 1940 and 1945 was devoted to defence expenditure. It would be difficult to argue that people enjoyed a higher standard of living during the war years than in the pre-war years. So the proportion of national income devoted to defence, or for instance to the police, must be taken into account when considering the standard of living of the population.

Consumption and investment It is possible to increase standards of living today by reducing investment and increasing consumption. However, reducing investment is likely to reduce standards of living from what they might otherwise have been in the future. As with defence, the proportion of national income being devoted to investment will affect the standard of living of the population both now and in the future.

Externalities National income statistics take no account of **externalities** produced by the economy. National income statistics may show that national income has doubled roughly every 25 years since 1945. However, if the value of externalities has more than doubled over that time period, then the rate of

growth of the standard of living has less than doubled.

Income distribution When comparing national income over time, it is important to remember that an increased national income for the economy as a whole may not mean that individuals have seen their income increase. Income distribution is likely to change over time, which may or may not lead to a more desirable state of affairs.

Comparing national income between countries

Comparing national income between economies is fraught with difficulties too. Income distributions may be different. Populations will be different and therefore it is important to compare per capita income figures. National income accounts will have varying degrees of inaccuracy, caused, for instance, by different sizes of the informal economy in each country. National income accounting conventions will differ.

There is also the problem of what rate of exchange to use when comparing one country's national income with anothers'. The day to day market exchange rate can bear little relation to relative prices in different countries. So prices in some countries, like Switzerland or West Germany, can be much higher at official exchange rates than in France or Italy. Therefore if national income statistics are to be used to compare living standards between countries it is important to use an exchange rate which compares the cost of living in each country. These exchange rates are known as PURCHASING POWER PARITIES. For instance, if a typical basket of goods costs 2 Euros in France and £1 in the UK, then national income should be converted at an exchange rate of 2 Euros to the £1, even if the market exchange rate gives a very different figure.

Even this is not accurate enough. In some countries, consumers have to purchase goods which in others are free. For instance, Sweden spends a greater proportion of its national income than Italy on fuel for heating because of its colder climate. However, this extra expenditure does not give the Swedes a higher standard of living. Again, countries are different geographically and one country might have higher transport costs per unit of output than another because of congestion or having to transport goods long distances. In practice, it is almost impossible to adjust national income figures for these sorts of differences.

Income and wealth

National income tends to be correlated with national wealth. Wealth is a **stock** of assets which produce a **flow** of income over time. Countries with high levels of wealth, which includes both human wealth and non-human wealth, tend to produce higher levels of income than countries with low levels of wealth. The wealthiest nation in the world, the USA, also has the highest national income. A poor country like Tanzania with relatively little wealth also has a low national income. Wealth can be mismanaged and used poorly. So there is not a perfect correlation between wealth and income.

Key terms

Circular flow of income - a model of the economy which shows the flow of goods, services and factors and their payments around the economy.

Closed economy - an economy where there is no foreign trade.

Gross domestic product (GDP) and gross national product (GNP) - measures of national income which exclude and include respectively net income from investments abroad, but do not include an allowance for depreciation of the nation's capital stock.

Hidden, black or informal economy - economic activity where trade and exchange take place, but which goes unreported to the tax authorities and those collecting national income statistics. Workers in the hidden economy are usually motivated by the desire to evade paying taxes.

Injections - in the circular flow of income, spending which is not generated by households including investment, government spending and exports.

National income - the value of the output, expenditure or income of an economy over a period of time.

Open economy - an economy where there is trade with other countries.

Purchasing power parities - an exchange rate of one currency for another which compares how much a typical basket of goods in one country costs compared to that of another country.

Transfer payments - income for which there is no corresponding output, such as unemployment benefits or pension payments.

Wealth - a stock of assets which can be used to generate a flow of production or income. For example, physical wealth such as factories and machines is used to make goods and services.

Withdrawals or leakages - in the circular flow of income, spending by households which does not flow back to domestic firms. It includes savings, taxes and imports.

Applied economics

The UK and the USA

The UK has a lower GDP than the USA. In 2006, US GDP was $13 060 billion compared to £1300 billion for the UK. At a market exchange rate of $1.8429 to the pound, this meant that the US economy produced 5.5 times as much output as that of the UK.

Crude national income statistics like these have a story to tell when making inter-country comparisons but they are only a small part of the story. For a start, populations may be vastly different. The population of the USA at 301.2 million is five times the size of that of the UK. A better comparison might therefore be GDP per capita. US GDP per capita in 2006 was $43 800 (or £23 800 at market exchange rates) compared to $39 400 (or £21 380 at market exchange rates) for the UK. So the USA produces more than the UK per person. The USA also has a lower cost of living. So the gap between the two countries is larger when compared using purchasing power parity exchange rates. At PPP rates expressed in US dollars, US GDP per capita is $43 800 but UK GDP per capita is only $31 800. Measured at purchasing power rates, the average US citizen has an income which is 38 per cent higher than that of the average UK citizen.

In making comparisons about living standards, national income is only one among many factors to be taken into account. One other factor is the distribution of income. Table 3 shows that income in the UK is slightly more evenly distributed than in the USA. In the UK, the poorest 20 per cent enjoyed 6.1 per cent of the

national cake compared to 5.4 per cent in the USA. At the other end of the income scale, the top 20 per cent in the UK received 44 per cent of the national cake compared to 45.8 per cent in the USA.

Another group of factors which are important relates to how national income is distributed between different types of expenditure. In 2006, spending by the state accounted for 45.1 per cent of GDP compared to 36.4 per cent in the USA. One reason for this is spending on healthcare. In the UK, healthcare is mostly provided by the state. In the USA, healthcare is mostly provided by the private sector. In the UK, there is universal access to free health care. In the USA, only the retired and those on low incomes have access to free health care, accounting for around 27 per cent of the population. Approximately 57 per cent of the population are covered by health insurance schemes through their employer. 16 per cent of the population, or 47 million people, are uninsured and have to fund all medical bills themselves. Despite the fact that 16 per cent of the population are not covered, the USA has the world's highest spending on health care as a proportion of GDP. In 2006, it was 15.2 per cent compared to 8.0 per cent for the UK. Despite spending almost twice as much on healthcare as the UK, the USA performs worse on a variety of medical statistics than the UK. For example, life expectancy is 77.5 years in the USA but 79.5 years in the UK. Infant mortality rates are 6 per thousand in the USA but only 5 per thousand in the UK.

Healthcare is one reason why public spending differs between the UK and the USA. In general, welfare spending is lower in the USA as a proportion of GDP. Individuals are expected to be less dependent on the state. One area where government spending is higher in the USA than the UK is defence. In 2005, defence expenditure was 4.1 per cent of GDP in the USA compared to 2.6 per cent in the UK. In terms of quality of life, there are differences of opinion about whether higher defence spending in the USA is increasing quality of life compared to the UK or reducing it.

There is a wide range of other quality of life measures that could be taken into consideration, as Table 4 shows. The UK has a high population density with most of its population crammed into urban centres with limited space. The USA has a low population density. Houses and housing plots tend to be much larger in the USA. Equally the cost of housing tends to be lower. Crime rates are higher in the USA. The homicide rate is nearly three times as high in the USA as in the UK.

Overall, the USA is a good place to live for those who have a good job and a good income. The safety net for the poor is weaker than in the UK. So low income workers, the unemployed and the retired may be better off in the UK.

Table 3 Income distribution

| | | Percentage share of income | | | |
	Lowest 20%	Next 20%	Middle 20%	Next 20%	Highest 20%
USA (2000)	5.4	10.7	15.7	22.4	45.8
UK (1999)	6.1	11.4	16.0	22.5	44.0

Source: adapted from World Bank, *World Development Indicators*.

Table 4 Standard of living measures, 2006

	Average life expectancy	Infant mortality rates	Defence spending	Population density	Homicide rate	Carbon dioxide emissions per capita
	years	per thousand	% of GDP	People per sq km 2005	Per 100 000 inhabitants	metric tonnes
USA	77.5	6	4.1	32	5.9	20.2
UK	79.5	5	2.3	249	2.0	9.2

Source: adapted from World Bank, *World Development Report*; en.wikipedia.org

DataQuestion

Living standards

Table 5 National income and population indicators 2005

	PPP estimates of gross national income per capita ($)	Population millions	Gross national income ($million)	Gross national income per capita ($)	Population, % of population aged 0-14
Tanzania	730	38	12.7	340	43
Kenya	1 170	34	18.0	530	43
Pakistan	2 350	156	107.3	690	38
Indonesia	3 720	221	282.2	1 280	28
China	6 600	1 305	2 263.8	1 740	21
Colombia	7 420	46	104.5	2 290	31
Russian Federation	10 640	143	639.1	4 460	15
Czech Republic	20 140	10	109.2	10 710	15
New Zealand	23 030	4	106.7	25 960	21
UK	32 690	60	2 263.7	37 600	18
USA	41 950	296	12 969.6	43 740	21

Table 6 Health indicators

	Life expectancy at birth, years, 2005	Under-five mortality rate, per thousand of the population 2005	Prevalence of child malnutrition, % of children under 5 underweight 2005	Access to safe water, % of population 2000	Access to sanitation facilities, % of urban population 2000
Tanzania	46.3	122.0	21.8	58	53
Kenya	49.0	120.0	21.2	57	47
Pakistan	64.9	99.0	-	89	89
Indonesia	67.8	28.0	24.6	76	71
China	70.3	27.0	10.0	76	66
Colombia	72.8	21.4	7.0	92	96
Russian Federation	65.5	17.5	-	96	93
Czech Republic	75.0	5.0	0.0	100	99
New Zealand	79.6	6.0	0.0	100	100
UK	78.9	6.0	0.0	100	100
USA	77.0	7.0	0.0	100	100

Table 7 Education

	Adult illiteracy, % of people aged 15 and older, 2000-04	School enrolment, % gross, 2005		Primary completion rate, total (% of relevant age group)	Ratio of girls to boys in primary and secondary education, %
		Primary	Secondary		
Tanzania	31	110.5	-	71.6	-
Kenya	26	112.2	48.8	95.0	95.8
Pakistan	50	87.3	26.9	63.2	75.4
Indonesia	10	117.3	63.1	101.1	97.2
China	9	112.8	74.3	-	99.4
Columbia	7	112.0	78.1	96.9	103.6
Russian Federation	1	128.7	91.9	-	98.9
Czech Republic	-	101.2	95.8	102.3	100.5
New Zealand	-	102.2	122.7	-	104.1
UK	-	106.7	105.1	100.0	101.5
USA	-	99.0	94.7	100.0	100.3

Table 8 Selected indicators

	Paved roads, % of total, 2000	Fixed line and mobile phone subscribers (per 1 000 people), 2005	Internet users (per 1 000 people), 2005	Electric power consumption (kwh per capita), 2000	High-technology exports (% of manufactured 2005	Military expenditure (% of GDP), 2005 exports),
Tanzania	-	8.4	1.2	58.5	1.2	1.0
Kenya	12.1	142.9	32.4	111.9	3.9	1.4
Pakistan	56.0	115.9	67.4	373.5	1.6	3.3
Indonesia	57.1	270.6	72.5	400.4	16.3	0.9
China	82.5	570.2	85.1	992.7	30.6	2.0
Colombia	-	657.0	105.4	803.7	4.9	3.7
Russian Federation	-	1 118.7	152.3	5 208.8	8.1	3.7
Czech Republic	100.0	1 465.0	269.5	5 693.7	8.1	1.8
New Zealand	62.8	1 283.0	671.9	8 911.8	14.2	1.0
UK	100.0	1 615.5	473.5	6 031.0	28.0	2.6
USA	-	1 070.0	439.4	13 667.4	31.8	4.1

Source: adapted from World Bank, *World Development Report*; World Bank, *Country Profiles*.

1. You have been asked to write an article for a magazine of no more than 1 000 words. The editor wants you to compare the standard of living of 11 countries using national income statistics. Using the data provided, in your article: (a) make such a comparison; (b) discuss the limitations of using national income statistics to compare living standards between countries, giving examples of how different economic indicators might provide an additional or perhaps even better basis for making a comparison.

Summary

1. Consumption can be divided into spending on durable goods and non-durable goods.
2. The consumption function shows the relationship between consumption and its determinants, the main one being income.
3. Increases in wealth will lead to an increase in consumption.
4. Expected inflation tends to lead to a rise in saving and a fall in consumption. The effect of households attempting to restore the real value of their stock of savings more than outweighs the effect of households bringing forward their purchases of goods.
5. The rate of interest and the availability of credit particularly affect the consumption of durable goods.
6. A change in the structure of the population will affect both consumption and saving. The greater the proportion of adults aged 35-60 in the population, the higher is likely to be the level of saving.
7. Keynesians hypothesise that consumption is a stable function of current disposable income in the short run.
8. The life cycle hypothesis and the permanent income hypothesis both emphasise that consumption is a stable function of income only in the very long run. In the short run, other factors such as the rate of interest and wealth can have a significant impact upon consumption and savings.

Defining consumption and saving

CONSUMPTION in economics is spending on consumer goods and services over a period of time. Examples are spending on chocolate, hire of videos or buying a car. Consumption can be broken down into a number of different categories. One way of classifying consumption is to distinguish between spending on **goods** and spending on **services**. Another way is to distinguish between spending on DURABLE GOODS and NON-DURABLE GOODS. Durable goods are goods which, although bought at a point in time, continue to provide a stream of services over a period of time. A car, for instance, should last at least 6 years. A television set might last 10 years. Non-durable goods are goods and services which are used up immediately or over a short period of time, like an ice-cream or a packet of soap powder.

SAVING is what is not spent out of income. For instance, if a worker takes home £1 000 in her wage packet at the end of the month, but only spends £900, then £100 must have been saved. The saving might take the form of increasing the stock of cash, or an increase in money in a bank or building society account, or it might take the form of stocks or shares. Income in this case is DISPOSABLE INCOME, income including state benefits such as child benefit and interest on, say, building society shares, but after deductions of income tax and National Insurance contributions.

Consumption and income

There is a number of factors which determine how much a household consumes. The relationship between consumption and these factors is called the CONSUMPTION FUNCTION. The most important determinant of consumption is disposable income. Other factors, discussed in sections below, are far less important but can bring about small but significant changes in the relationship between consumption and income.

Assume that one year a household has an income of £1 000 per month. The next year, due to salary increases, this rises to £1 200 per month. Economic theory predicts that the consumption of the household will rise.

How much it will rise can be measured by the MARGINAL PROPENSITY TO CONSUME (MPC), the proportion of a change in income that is spent:

$$MPC = \frac{\text{Change in consumption}}{\text{Change in income}} = \frac{\Delta C}{\Delta Y}$$

where Y is income, C is consumption and Δ is 'change in'. If the £200 rise in income leads to a £150 rise in consumption, then the marginal propensity to consume would be 0.75 (£150 ÷ £200).

For the economy as a whole, the marginal propensity to consume is likely to be positive (i.e. greater than zero) but less than 1. Any rise in income will lead to more spending but also some saving too. For individuals, the marginal propensity to consume could be more than 1 if money was borrowed to finance spending higher than income.

The AVERAGE PROPENSITY TO CONSUME (or APC) measures the average amount spent on consumption out of total income. For instance, if total disposable income in an economy were £100 billion and consumption were £90 billion, then the average propensity to consume would be 0.9. The formula for the APC is:

$$APC = \frac{\text{Consumption}}{\text{Income}} = \frac{C}{Y}$$

Table 1 Real consumption and household disposable income

		£bn at 2003 prices
	Consumption	Disposable income
1965	260.6	268.8
1966	265.2	275.0
1975	328.8	347.6
1976	330.2	346.3
1985	402.2	425.5
1986	427.8	443.1
1995	541.1	588.5
1996	561.8	602.4
2005	760.2	775.1
2006	776.0	783.6

Source: adapted from *Economic & Labour Market Trends*, Office for National Statistics.

(a) Using the data, explain the relationship between consumption and disposable income.

(b) (i) Calculate the MPC and the APC for 1966, 1976, 1986, 1996 and 2006.

(ii) What happened to saving during these years?

The number of mortgages being approved fell to its lowest level for more than nine years in November, sending out a strong signal that house prices are set for further falls. The number of loans is an important indicator for consumer spending. Most economists regard a slowdown in consumer spending as a risk to the UK economy over the next year.

Higher house prices lead directly to more consumer spending because people feel wealthier. But Ben Broadbent at Goldman Sachs, the investment bank, argues that consumer spending is more likely to be affected by a slowdown in house turnover than a decline in house prices. He said: 'When you move house, you have to buy a lot of stuff, such as carpets, curtains and fridges. There is already a trend towards slower retail sales and we expect data over the next weeks that will include the Christmas period to reflect this more strongly.'

Consumer spending is also linked to mortgage equity release, when housebuyers take out a larger mortgage than they need to buy a house and then spend the difference. Equally, existing homeowners may remortgage their house, taking on a bigger mortgage and spending the balance. Mortgage equity withdrawal totalled £12.4bn between July and September, down from £13.0bn in the previous quarter.

Source: adapted from the *Financial Times*, 5.1.2005.

Explain three ways in which the housing market can affect consumption levels.

In a rich industrialised economy, the APC is likely to be less than 1 because consumers will also save part of their earnings.

Wealth

The wealth of a household is made up of two parts. **Physical wealth** is made up of items such as houses, cars and furniture. **Monetary wealth** is comprised of items such as cash, money in the bank and building societies, stocks and shares, assurance policies and pension rights.

If the wealth of a household increases, consumption will increase. This is known as the WEALTH EFFECT. There are two important ways in which the wealth of households can change over a short time period.

- A change in the price of houses. If the real price of houses increases considerably over a period of time, as happened in the UK from the mid-1990s to 2007, then households feel able to increase their spending. They do this mainly by borrowing more money secured against the value of their house.
- A change in the value of stocks and shares. Households react to an increase in the real value of a household's portfolio of securities by selling part of the portfolio and spending the proceeds. The value of stocks and shares is determined by many factors. One of these is the rate of interest. If the rate of interest falls, then the value of stocks will rise. So consumption should be stimulated through the wealth effect by a fall in the rate of interest.

Inflation

Inflation, a rise in the general level of prices, has two effects on consumption. First, if households expect prices to be higher in the future they will be tempted to bring forward their purchases. For instance, if households know that the price of cars will go up by 10 per cent the next month, they will attempt to buy their cars now. So expectations of inflation increase consumption and reduce saving.

However, this can be outweighed by the effect of inflation on wealth. Rising inflation tends to erode the real value of money wealth. Households react to this by attempting to restore the real value of their wealth (i.e. they save more). This reduces consumption.

Overall, rising inflation in the UK tends to reduce consumption. The negative effect on consumption caused by the erosion of real wealth more than offsets the positive effect on consumption caused by the bringing forward of purchases.

The rate of interest

Households rarely finance expenditure on **non-durables** such as food or entertainment by borrowing money. However, much of the money to buy **durables** such as cars, furniture, kitchen equipment and hi-fi equipment comes from credit finance. An increase in the rate of interest increases the monthly repayments on these goods. This means that, effectively, the price of the goods has increased. Households react to this by reducing their demand for durables and thus cutting their consumption.

Many households also have borrowed money to buy their houses. Increased interest rates lead to increased mortgage repayments. Again, this will directly cut spending on other items and perhaps, more importantly, discourage households from borrowing more money to finance purchases of consumer durables.

It has already been explained above that a rise in the rate of interest reduces the value of stocks on stock markets and thus reduces the value of household wealth. This in turn leads to a fall in consumption.

Question 3

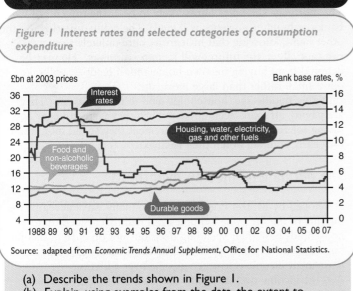

Figure 1 Interest rates and selected categories of consumption expenditure

£bn at 2003 prices

Bank base rates, %

Interest rates

Housing, water, electricity, gas and other fuels

Food and non-alcoholic beverages

Durable goods

1988 89 90 91 92 93 94 95 96 97 98 99 00 01 02 03 04 05 06 07

Source: adapted from *Economic Trends Annual Supplement*, Office for National Statistics.

(a) Describe the trends shown in Figure 1.
(b) Explain, using examples from the data, the extent to which interest rates affect consumption.

The availability of credit

The rate of interest determines the price of credit. However, the price of credit is not the only determinant of how much households borrow. Governments in the past have often imposed restrictions on the availability of credit. For instance, they have imposed maximum repayment periods and minimum deposits. Before the deregulation of the mortgage market in the early 1980s in the UK, building societies rationed mortgages. They often operated queueing systems and imposed restrictive limits on the sums that could be borrowed. When these restrictions are abolished, households increase their level of debt and spend the proceeds. Making credit more widely available will increase consumption.

Expectations

Expectations of increases in prices tend to make households bring forward their purchases and thus increase consumption. Expectations of large increases in real incomes will also tend to encourage households to increase spending now by borrowing more. So when the economy is booming, autonomous consumption tends to increase. On the other hand, if households expect economic conditions to become harsher, they will reduce their consumption now. For instance, they might expect an increase in unemployment rates, a rise in taxes or a fall in real wages.

The composition of households

Young people and old people tend to spend a higher proportion of their income than those in middle age. Young people tend to spend all their income and move into debt to finance the setting up of their homes and the bringing up of children. In middle age, the cost of homemaking declines as a proportion of income. With more income available, households often choose to build up their stock of savings in preparation for retirement. When they retire, they will run down their stock of savings to

supplement their pensions. So if there is a change in the age composition of households in the economy, there could well be a change in consumption and savings. The more young and old the households, the greater will tend to be the level of consumption.

The determinants of saving

Factors which affect consumption also by definition must affect saving (remember, saving is defined as that part of disposable income which is not consumed). The SAVINGS FUNCTION therefore links income, wealth, inflation, the rate of interest, expectations and the age profile of the population with the level of saving. However, because a typical AVERAGE PROPENSITY TO SAVE (the APS - the ratio of total saving to total income calculated by Saving ÷ Income) is 0.05 to 0.2 in Western European countries, income is far less important in determining saving than it is in determining consumption. Factors other than income are therefore relatively more important. This explains why, in the UK, for instance, the APS has varied from 0.12 to 0.04 between the 1980s and mid-2000s. The MARGINAL PROPENSITY TO SAVE (the proportion that is saved out of a change in income calculated by Change in saving ÷ Change in income) is equally unstable for these reasons.

Question 4

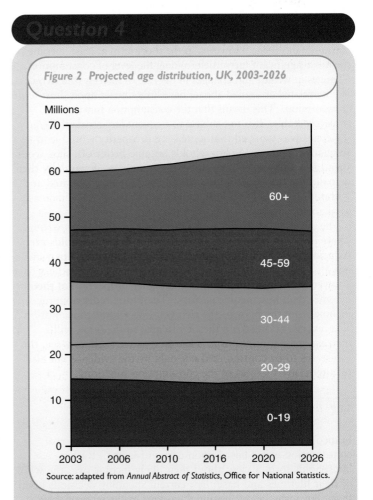

Figure 2 Projected age distribution, UK, 2003-2026

Millions

60+

45-59

30-44

20-29

0-19

2003 2006 2010 2016 2020 2026

Source: adapted from *Annual Abstract of Statistics*, Office for National Statistics.

What effects do you think that the changing structure of the population to 2026 is likely to have on consumption and saving?

Confusion **sometimes** arises between 'saving' and 'savings'. Saving is a **flow** concept which takes place over a period of time. Saving is added to a **stock** of savings fixed at a point in time. A household's stock of savings is the accumulation of past savings. For instance, you might have £100 in the bank. This is your stock of savings. You might then get a job over Christmas and save £20 from that. Your saving over Christmas is £20. Your stock of savings before Christmas was £100 but afterwards it was £120. The savings function explains the relationship between the flow of savings and its determinants. It attempts to explain why you saved £20 over Christmas. It does not explain why you have £100 in the bank already.

The Keynesian consumption function

John Maynard Keynes was one of the greatest economists working in the first half of the twentieth century. He was the founder of modern macroeconomics, the subject of much of the rest of this book. It was he who first popularised the idea that consumption was linked to income. 'Keynesian' means that an idea is linked to an idea first put forward by Keynes. Keynesian economists are economists who work within the framework first established by Keynes.

The Keynesian consumption function lays stress upon the relationship between planned current consumption and current disposable income. Other factors, particularly the availability of credit, can have an important impact upon expenditure on consumer durables. However, in the short term at least, income is the most significant factor determining the level of consumption. Changes in wealth and changes in the rate of interest (the two can be interrelated as argued above) have little impact upon short term consumption. This means that the consumption function is relatively stable. It is not subject to frequent large scale shifts.

Keynes was worried that increasing prosperity would lead to a stagnant economy. As households became better off, they would spend less and less of their increases in income. Eventually their demand for consumer goods would be completely satiated and without increases in spending, there could be no more increases in income.

The evidence of the past 70 years has proved Keynes wrong. There does not seem to be any indication that households are reducing their MPCs as income increases. However, this view has also led Keynesians to argue that higher income earners have a lower MPC (and therefore save a higher proportion of their income) than low income earners. Therefore, redistributing income from the poor to the rich will lower total consumption. The reverse, taking from the rich to give to the poor, will increase total consumption. However, as we shall now see, this too seems to be contradicted not only by the evidence but also by alternative theories of the consumption function.

The life cycle hypothesis

Franco Modigliani and Albert Ando suggested that current consumption is not based upon current income. Rather, households form a view about their likely income over the whole of their lifetimes and base their current spending decisions upon that. For instance, professional workers at the start of their careers in their early 20s may earn as much as manual workers of the same age. But the APC of professional workers is likely to be higher. This is because professional workers expect to earn more in the future and are prepared to

borrow more now to finance consumption. A professional worker will expect, for instance, to buy rather than rent a house. The mortgage she takes out is likely to be at the top end of what banks or building societies will lend. The manual worker, on the other hand, knowing that his earnings are unlikely to increase substantially in the future, will be more cautious. He may be deterred from buying his own home and, if he does, will take out a small rather than large mortgage.

During middle age, households tend to be net savers. They are paying off loans accumulated when they were younger and saving for retirement. During retirement they spend more than they earn, running down their savings.

The permanent income hypothesis

Developed by Milton Friedman, this in many ways develops the insights of the life cycle hypothesis. Friedman argued that households base their spending decisions not on current income but on their PERMANENT INCOME. Broadly speaking, permanent income is average income over a lifetime. Average income over a lifetime can be influenced by a number of factors.
- An increase in wealth will increase the ability of households to spend money (i.e. it will increase their permanent income). Hence a rise in wealth will increase actual consumption over a lifetime.
- An increase in interest rates tends to lower both stock and share prices. This leads to a fall in wealth, a fall in permanent income and a fall in current consumption.
- An increase in interest rates also leads to future incomes being less valuable. One way of explaining this is to remember that a sum of money available in the future is worth less than the same sum available today. Another way is to consider borrowing. If interest rates rise, households will need either to earn more money or cut back on their spending in the future to pay back their loans. Therefore, the real value of their future income (i.e. their permanent income) falls if interest rates rise.
- Unexpected rises in wages will lead to an increase in permanent income.

Friedman argued that the long run APC from permanent income was 1. Households spend all their income over their lifetimes (indeed, Friedman defined permanent income as the income a household could spend without changing its wealth over a lifetime). Hence, the long run APC and the MPC are stable.

In the short run, however, wealth and interest rates change. Measured income also changes and much of this change is unexpected. Income which households receive but did not expect to earn is called transitory income. Initially, transitory income will be saved, as households decide what to do with the money. Then it is incorporated into permanent income. The MPC of the household will depend upon the nature of the extra income. If the extra income is, for instance, a permanent pay rise, the household is likely to spend most of the money. If, however, it is a temporary rise in income, like a £10 000 win on the lottery, most of it will be saved and then gradually spent over a much longer period of time. Because the proportion of transitory income to current income changes from month to month, the propensity to consume from current income will vary too. So in the short run, the APC and the MPC are not constant. This contradicts the Keynesian hypothesis that current consumption is a stable function of current income.

Key terms

Average propensity to consume - the proportion of total income spent. It is calculated by C ÷ Y.

Average propensity to save - the proportion of a total income which is saved. It is calculated by S ÷ Y.

Consumption - total expenditure by households on goods and services over a period of time.

Consumption function - the relationship between the consumption of households and the factors which determine it.

Disposable income - household income over a period of time including state benefits, less direct taxes.

Durable goods - goods which are consumed over a long period of time, such as a television set or a car.

Marginal propensity to consume - the proportion of a change in income which is spent. It is calculated by Δ C ÷ Δ Y.

Marginal propensity to save - the proportion of a change in income which is saved. It is calculated by Δ S ÷ Δ Y.

Non-durable goods - goods which are consumed almost immediately like an ice-cream or a packet of washing powder.

Permanent income - the income a household could spend over its lifetime without reducing the value of its assets. This approximates to the average income of a household over its lifetime.

Savings function - the relationship between the saving of households and the factors which determine it.

Saving (personal) - the portion of households' disposable income which is not spent over a period of time.

Wealth effect - the change in consumption following a

Applied economics

Consumption in the UK

The composition of consumption expenditure

Total real consumption roughly trebled between 1964 and 2007. However, as Figure 3 shows, there were significant differences in the rate of growth of the components of expenditure. Real spending on food and non-alcoholic drinks, for instance, only increased by approximately 60 per cent whilst spending on communication, which includes mobile phones, increased 12 fold. Real expenditure on alcoholic drink and tobacco remained constant whilst spending on restaurants and hotels increased 150 per cent. These changes partly reflect a number of different factors. As incomes increase, how consumers choose to spend the extra they earn differs from how they spend their existing income. So they choose not to spend very much extra on food, but quite a lot more on recreation and culture, which is reflected in the different income elasticities of demand for products. Some products, such as mobile phones, were not available in 1965. Increased spending reflects a desire to buy into these new technologies. Some changes also reflect changes prices. The price of clothing and footwear has fallen considerably over the past 30 years with globalisation of production. This has arguably led to a significant rise in total spending on clothing and footwear.

Consumption and income

Keynesian theory suggests that income is a major determinant of consumption. The evidence in Figure 4 would tend to support this theory. Over the period 1955 to 2006, real households' disposable income rose 4.1

times whilst real consumers' expenditure increased by 3.8 times. Keynesian theory would also suggest that the average propensity to consume declines as incomes rise over time. Figure 5 would tend not to support this. The average APC in the 1960s was 0.94. It fell slightly in the 1970s and 1980s, stabilised in the 1990s but then rose again between 2000-2006. Note that in Figure 6 income used to calculate the APC is defined as households' disposable income **plus** an adjustment for the net equity of households in pension funds. It is the accounting convention used by the Office for National Statistics (ONS). This produces a slightly lower value of the APC than if only households' disposable income were included. There is considerable fluctuation of the APC, however, around these long term averages. For instance, there was a sharp rise in the APC between 1986 and 1988 during the Lawson boom, and between 1997 and 2004 in the prolonged upswing experienced at the time, whilst the APC fell to less than 0.9 in the two major recessions of 1980-82 and 1990-92. This would suggest that other factors can be important in determining consumption apart from income.

Other determinants of consumption

Economists in the 1960s and early 1970s were fairly confident that the relationship between consumption and income was highly stable. However, from the mid-1970s a number of key variables which can affect consumption were subject to large changes and this had a small but significant effect on the average propensity to consume.

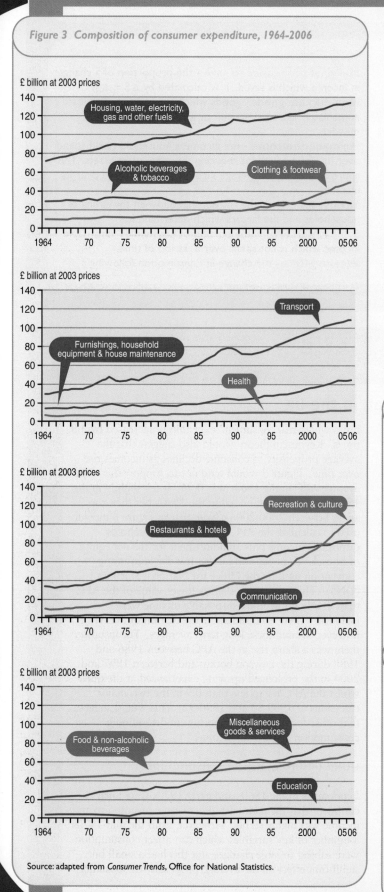

Figure 3 *Composition of consumer expenditure, 1964-2006*

£ billion at 2003 prices

Housing, water, electricity, gas and other fuels

Alcoholic beverages & tobacco

Clothing & footwear

£ billion at 2003 prices

Transport

Furnishings, household equipment & house maintenance

Health

£ billion at 2003 prices

Recreation & culture

Restaurants & hotels

Communication

£ billion at 2003 prices

Food & non-alcoholic beverages

Miscellaneous goods & services

Education

Source: adapted from *Consumer Trends*, Office for National Statistics.

Wealth A sharp appreciation in household wealth was a key feature of most of the 1980s. Figure 6 shows that share prices rose considerably between 1980 and 1987. This increase in stock market values was a key element in persuading households to increase their spending in 1986 and 1987. In October 1987, on 'Black Monday', world stock markets crashed and 25 per cent of the value of shares on the London Stock Exchange was wiped out. This helped knock consumer confidence and the subsequent poor performance of share prices was one factor which reduced the average propensity to consume in the late 1980s and early 1990s. Equally, UK stock markets put in a strong performance in the second half of the 1990s, fuelled towards the end by sharp rises in shares of companies related to the Internet. This contributed to strong growth in consumer spending whilst the fall in share prices following the bursting of the 'dot-com' bubble helped subdue consumer spending. The revival in share prices from 2003 also helped buoy up consumer demand.

Many households do not own shares but the majority own their home. Again, in the mid-1980s the boom in house prices shown in Figure 7 was a major determinant of increased consumer spending during the Lawson boom. Equally, the fall in house prices in the early 1990s

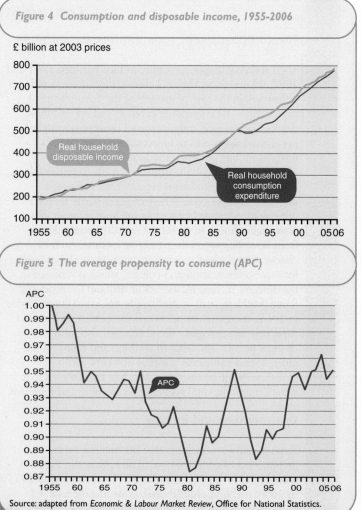

Figure 4 *Consumption and disposable income, 1955-2006*

£ billion at 2003 prices

Real household disposable income

Real household consumption expenditure

Figure 5 *The average propensity to consume (APC)*

APC

APC

Source: adapted from *Economic & Labour Market Review*, Office for National Statistics.

Figure 6 London Stock Market prices (FT Ordinary Share Index, 1962=100) and the average propensity to consume

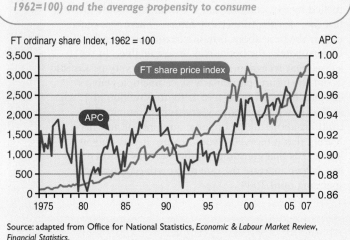

Source: adapted from Office for National Statistics, *Economic & Labour Market Review, Financial Statistics.*

Figure 7 Average house prices, £ at 2006 prices, and the average propensity to consume

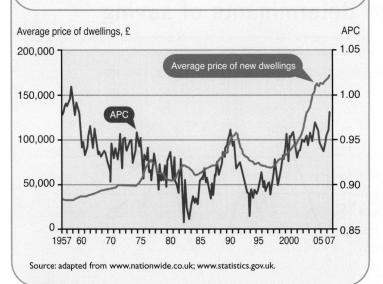

Source: adapted from www.nationwide.co.uk; www.statistics.gov.uk.

played an important role in dampening consumption. The stagnation in house prices which followed until 1996 helped break growth in consumer spending. Then, with the subsequent boom in house prices there was strong growth in consumer spending.

Inflation Periods of high inflation tend to be marked by a falling APC and vice versa. Following the rise in inflation during the late 1980s, consumers reacted by increasing their savings and reducing the average propensity to consume. They wanted to rebuild the real value of their wealth. Equally, the low inflation of the mid-1990s to 2007 contributed to a rise in spending out of income. The relationship between inflation and consumption is shown in Figure 8.

The rate of interest The rate of interest has a significant impact on spending, particularly on items typically bought on credit such as consumer durables. Figure 9 shows that during the Lawson boom of 1986-88,

Figure 8 Inflation (RPI, % change year on year) and the average propensity to consume

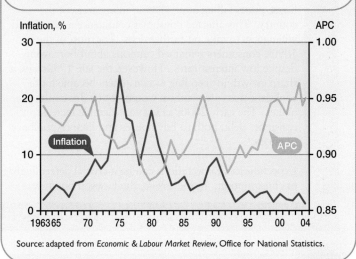

Source: adapted from *Economic & Labour Market Review*, Office for National Statistics.

relatively low interest rates helped fuel a consumer spending boom. The raising of bank base rates to 15 per cent in 1988 and the period of high interest rates which followed was the key factor which helped reduce growth in consumer spending and pushed the economy into recession. The reduction of interest rates from 1992 onwards then helped the recovery during the rest of the 1990s. The changes in the rate of interest between 1995 and 2004 were relatively small compared to the changes in the 1980s. A rise in interest rates of 2 per cent does not have the same impact as a rise in interest rates of, say, 8 per cent seen during the 1980s. Therefore, the rises and falls in interest rates from 1995 onwards had an impact on consumer spending but these were relatively small. Certainly, they were not large enough to bring about reductions in total consumer spending.

Interest rates affect consumption in a number of ways. Higher interest rates makes borrowing more expensive and in particular hits spending on consumer durables. It also makes it more expensive to buy a house using a mortgage. The rise in interest rates in the late 1980s

Figure 9 Interest rates and the change in real consumer expenditure

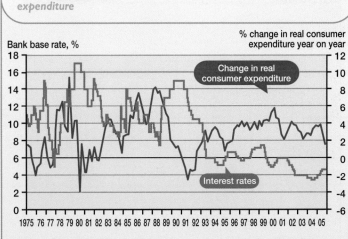

Source: adapted from Office for National Statistics, *Economic & Labour Market Review*.

helped bring about a crash in the housing market, with house prices falling after 1989 in many areas of the country. This affected consumer confidence and reduced willingness to take on further debt. For most of the 1990s, consumers remained cautious about borrowing despite low interest rates. However, the late 1990s saw a sharp growth in spending as consumers became more confident that interest rates would not be driven sharply higher. The early 2000s saw a considerable increase in consumer debt, both to buy houses and finance purchase of goods.

Expectations Expectations can be a crucial determinant of consumption. In the 1980s, the Lawson boom was

fuelled by expectations that the economy would grow at fast rates for the foreseeable future. There was much talk at the time about Britain's 'economic miracle'. Unfortunately, the boom was unsustainable. In the subsequent recession, consumers became very pessimistic about the future, particularly since unemployment climbed from 1.5 million in 1989 to 3 million in 1993. In the subsequent recovery, consumers remained cautious about taking on large amounts of new debt, fearing that a recession would recur. It was only in the late 1990s that consumer confidence was restored and this helped increase the rate of growth of consumer spending until 2004.

DataQuestion   The determinants of saving

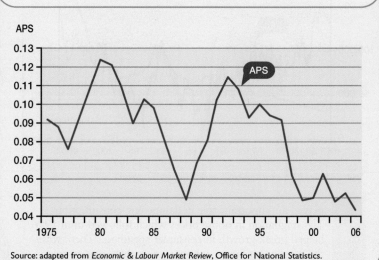

Figure 10 The average propensity to save (APS), 1975-2006

Source: adapted from *Economic & Labour Market Review*, Office for National Statistics.

You have been asked to write a report for a bank on the determinants of saving in the economy. Use the data here and in the Applied Economics section to construct your report.

- Briefly outline trends in saving and the APS since 1975.
- Briefly outline the main factors which affect saving in the economy.
- Produce a case study of the period 1975 to 2006 to illustrate your discussion.

Summary

1. Investment is the purchase of capital goods which are then used to create other goods and services. This differs from saving, which is the creation of financial obligations.
2. Marginal efficiency of capital theory suggests that investment is inversely related to the price of capital - the rate of interest.
3. Factors which shift the MEC or investment demand schedule include changes in the cost of capital goods, technological change, and changes in expectations or animal spirits.
4. The accelerator theory suggests that investment varies with the rate of change in income.
5. The past and current profitability of industry too may be more important than future rates of return on capital in determining current investment.

A definition of investment

Economists use the word INVESTMENT in a very precise way. Investment is the addition to the **capital stock** of the economy - factories, machines, offices and stocks of materials, used to produce other goods and services.

In everyday language, 'investment' and 'saving' are often used to mean the same thing. For instance, we talk about 'investing in the building society' or 'investing in shares'. For an economist, these two would be examples of saving. For an economist, investment only takes place if real products are created. To give two more examples:

- putting money into a bank account would be saving; the bank buying a computer to handle your account would be investment;
- buying shares in a new company would be saving; buying new machinery to set up a company would be investment.

A distinction can be made between **gross** and **net** investment. The value of the capital stock depreciates over time as it wears out and is used up. This is called **depreciation** or **capital consumption**. Gross investment measures investment before depreciation, whilst net investment is gross investment less the value of depreciation. Depreciation in recent years in the UK has accounted for about three-quarters of gross investment. So only about one-quarter of gross investment represents an addition to the capital stock of the economy.

Another distinction made is between investment in **physical capital** and in **human capital**. Investment in human capital is investment in the education and training of workers. Investment in physical capital is investment in factories etc.

Investment is made both by the public sector and the private sector. Public sector investment is constrained by complex political considerations. In the rest of this unit, we will consider the determinants of private sector investment in physical capital.

Marginal efficiency of capital theory

Firms invest in order to make a profit. The profitability of investment projects varies. Some will make a high **rate of return**, some will yield a low rate of return and others will result in losses for the company. The rate of return on an investment project is also known as the MARGINAL EFFICIENCY OF CAPITAL (MEC).

At any point in time in the economy as whole, there exists a large number of possible individual investment projects. Table 1 shows an economy where there are £4bn of investment projects with an MEC of 20 per cent and above, £8bn with an MEC of 15 per cent and above and so on.

How much of this investment takes place will depend upon the rate of interest in the economy. If the rate of interest is 20 per cent, then firms having to borrow money will make a loss if they undertake any project with an MEC of less than 20 per cent. Hence, planned investment will be £4bn. If, on the other hand,

Question 1

Using the photograph, showing the interior of a UK bank, give examples of: (a) past investment in physical capital; (b) past investment in human capital; (c) saving; (d) capital consumption.

Table 1 Planned investment and the marginal efficiency of capital

Marginal efficiency of capital (% per year)	Planned investment (£bn per year)
20	4
15	8
10	12
5	16

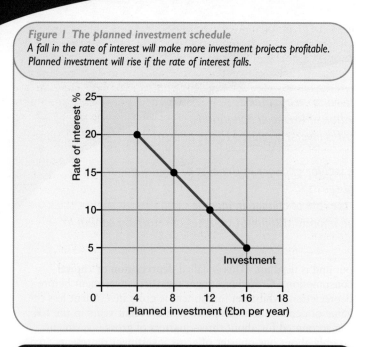

Figure 1 The planned investment schedule
A fall in the rate of interest will make more investment projects profitable. Planned investment will rise if the rate of interest falls.

In our explanation above, the rate of interest was assumed to be the rate of interest at which firms have to borrow money. However, most investment by firms in the UK is financed from RETAINED PROFIT. This is profit which is not used to pay dividends to shareholders or taxes to the government, but is kept back by the firm for its own use. This does not alter the relationship between the rate of interest and investment. Firms which keep back profits have a choice about what to do with the money. They can either invest it or save it. The higher the rate of interest on savings, such as placing the money on loan with banks or other financial institutions, the more attractive saving the money becomes and the less attractive becomes investment. Put another way, the higher the rate of interest, the higher the **opportunity cost** of investment and hence the lower will be the amount of planned investment in the economy.

Factors which shift the planned investment schedule

Cost of capital goods If the price of capital goods rises, then the expected rate of return on investment projects will fall if firms cannot pass on the increase in higher prices. So increases in the price of capital goods, all other things being equal, will reduce planned investment. This is shown by a shift to the left in the planned investment schedule in Figure 2.

Technological change Technological change will make new capital equipment more productive than previous equipment. This will raise the rate of return on investment projects, all other things being equal. Hence, technological change such as the introduction of computer aided machinery will raise the level of planned investment at any given rate of interest. This is shown by a shift to the right in the planned investment schedule.

Expectations Businesses have to form views about the future. When calculating the possible rate of return on future

Question 2

Table 2 Average cost of funds (as % of sales) of top spending companies on research and development

	Chemicals	Pharmaceuticals	Engineering	Electronics and electrical equipment
Japan	2.1%	2.8%	2.2%	1.5%
Germany	3.8%	5.1%	2.1%	2.9%
France	5.0%	n.a.	2.5%	2.8%
US	5.9%	9.5%	3.0%	4.2%
UK	5.6%	12.5%	3.1%	5.8%

Source: adapted from DTI, R&D Scoreboard.

The UK's high interest rates in the 1980s and 1990s put British industry at a severe disadvantage. It meant that fewer projects were worth taking on because the thresholds for returns were higher. Table 2 shows the cost of investment funds measured as a percentage of sales revenues for firms in different industries. In all these industries, the UK had the highest or nearly the highest cost of funds.

Source: adapted from the *Financial Times*.

(a) Explain, using a diagram, why high interest rates may have put British industry at a disadvantage in investment.
(b) During the 1990s and 2000s, UK interest rates have been above those in the rest of the EU. What are the possible implications for UK investment if Britain were to join the euro?

Figure 2 Shifts in planned investment
An increase in the cost of planned capital will reduce the rate of return on investment projects. Therefore at any given rate of interest, planned investment will fall. This is shown by a shift to the left in the planned investment schedule. Changes in technology which make capital more productive raise the level of planned investment, shown by a shift to the right of the schedule.

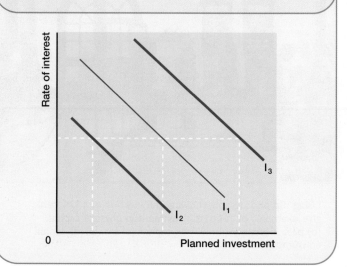

the rate of interest is 5 per cent, then all investment projects with an MEC of 5 per cent or more will be profitable. Hence, planned investment will be £16bn. So the conclusion of marginal efficiency of capital theory is that planned investment in the economy will rise if the rate of interest falls. This relationship, using the figures from Table 1, is shown in Figure 1.

Assume that I_1 in Figure 2 shows the planned investment schedule for the UK. Is it more likely to shift to I_2 or I_3 if: (a) there is a rise in the real prices of commercial property; (b) the government announces a billion pound programme to encourage the use of computers in industry; (c) the economy grew much faster than expected last year and forecasts show this set to continue; (d) the price of computers and computer aided tools falls; (e) prices on the New York Stock Exchange crash?

investment, they have to make assumptions about future costs and future revenues. If managers become more pessimistic about the future, they will expect the rate of return on investment projects to fall and hence planned investment will be reduced. If, on the other hand, they become more optimistic their expectations of the rates of return on investment projects will tend to rise. Hence planned investment will rise and this will be shown by a shift to the right in the investment schedule. Keynes called the expectations of businessmen their 'animal spirits'. He believed that expectations were crucial in determining changes in investment, and that these expectations could change suddenly.

Government policy Government can play a crucial role in stimulating private sector investment. This will be discussed in more detail in the unit on supply-side policies.

The accelerator theory

The ACCELERATOR THEORY of investment suggests that the level of planned investment varies with the rate of change of income or output rather than with the rate of interest. To see why this might be the case, consider Table 3.

Table 3

Year	Annual output £m	Number of machines required	Investment in machines
1	10	10	0
2	10	10	0
3	12	12	2
4	15	15	3
5	15	15	0
6	14	14	0

A firm producing toys needs one machine to produce £1m of output per year. The machines last 20 years and for the purpose of this example we will assume that none of the firm's machines need replacing over the time period being considered (so we are considering net and not gross investment). Initially in year 1 the firm has £10m worth of orders. It already has 10 machines and therefore no investment takes place. In year 2, orders remain unchanged and so again the firm has no need to invest. However, in year 3 orders increase to £12m. The firm now

needs to invest in another two machines if it is to fulfil orders. Orders increase to £15m in year 4. The firm needs to purchase another 3 machines to increase its capital stock to 15 machines. In year 5, orders remain unchanged at £15m and so investment returns to zero. In year 6, orders decline to £14m. The firm has too much capital stock and therefore does not invest.

In this example investment takes place when there is a change in real spending in the economy. If there is no change in spending, then there is no investment. What is more, the changes in spending lead to much bigger changes in investment. For instance, the increase in spending of 25 per cent in year 4 (from £12m to £15m) resulted in an increase in investment of 50 per cent (from 2 machines to 3 machines). In reality, it should be remembered that about 75 per cent of gross investment is replacement investment which is far less likely than net investment to be affected by changes in income. Even so, the accelerator theory predicts that investment spending in the economy is likely to be more volatile than spending as a whole.

The simplest form of the accelerator theory can be expressed as:

$$I_t = a (Y_t - Y_{t-1})$$

where I_t is investment in time period t, $Y_t - Y_{t-1}$ is the change in real income during year t and a is the accelerator coefficient or CAPITAL-OUTPUT RATIO. The capital-output ratio is the amount of capital needed in the economy to produce a given quantity of goods. So if £10 of capital is needed to produce £2 of goods, then the capital-output ratio is 5. The theory therefore predicts that changes in the level of investment are related to past changes in income.

This accelerator model is very simplistic. There is a number of factors which limit the predictive power of the model.

- The model assumes that the capital-output ratio is constant over time. However, it can change. In the long term, new technology can make capital more productive. In the shorter term, the capital-output ratio is likely to be higher in a recession when there is excess capacity than in a boom.
- Expectations may vary. Businesses may choose not to satisfy extra demand if they believe that the demand will be short lived. There is little point in undertaking new investment if the extra orders will have disappeared within six months. On the other hand, businesses may anticipate higher output. Despite constant income, they may believe that a boom is imminent and invest to be ahead of their rivals.
- Time lags involved are likely to be extremely complicated. Changes in investment are likely to respond to changes in income over several time periods and not just one.
- Firms may have excess capacity (i.e. they can produce more with current levels of capital than they are at present doing). If there is an increase in income, firms will respond not by investing but by bringing back into use capital which has been mothballed or by utilising fully equipment which had been underutilised.
- The capital goods industry will be unable to satisfy a surge in demand. Some investment will therefore either be cancelled or delayed.

Despite these qualifications, evidence suggests that net investment is to some extent linked to past changes in income. However, the link is relatively weak and therefore other influences must be at work to determine investment.

Profits

About 70 per cent of industrial and commercial investment in the UK is financed from retained profit. Some economists argue that many firms do not consider the opportunity cost of investment. They retain profit but rarely consider that it might be better used saved in financial assets. They automatically assume that the money will be spent on investment related to the activities of the firm. The rate of interest is then much less important in determining investment. Investment becomes crucially dependent upon two factors.

- The amount of retained profit available. So the poor investment record of companies in the UK compared to many competitors overseas over the past 50 years may be due to the fact that UK companies pay out a larger

percentage of their profits in dividends to their owners. This leaves less for investment.

- The availability of suitable investment projects. If firms do not have suitable investment projects to hand, they will bank the cash or pay it out to shareholders in dividends. New technology or new products can act as a spur to investment on this view.

Question 4

$$I_t = 2 (Y_t - Y_{t-1})$$

(a) In year 0 income was £100m. In subsequent years, it grew by 5 per cent per annum. Calculate the level of investment in years 1 to 5.

(b) Compare what would happen to investment in each year if income grew instead by (i) 10 per cent and (ii) 2.5 per cent.

Key terms

Accelerator theory - the theory that the level of planned investment is related to past changes in income.
Capital-output ratio - the ratio between the amount of capital needed to produce a given quantity of goods and the level of output.
Investment - the addition to the capital stock of the economy.
Marginal efficiency of capital - the rate of return on the last unit of capital employed.
Retained profit - profit kept back by a firm for its own use which is not distributed to shareholders or used to pay taxation.

Applied economics

Investment in the UK

The composition of investment

Gross investment is called **gross fixed capital formation** (GFCF) in UK official statistics. Figure 3 shows the composition of investment in 1979 and 2006. Significant changes in this composition are apparent from the data.

- In real terms, investment in housing has risen from £33.0 bn to £45.7 bn. However, as a percentage of total investment, it has fallen one third, from 34 per cent to 21 per cent. Within these totals, there has been a significant fall in public sector housing (mainly council housing), but a rise in private sector housing investment.
- Investment in 'other machinery and equipment' has more than trebled compared to an approximate doubling in real GDP. This investment ranges from milking machines to machine lathes to computers and desks.
- Investment in 'other new buildings and structures', has more than doubled, outpacing the percentage growth in real GDP. This includes new factories and offices.
- Investment in transport equipment has barely changed in real terms, but as a proportion of total investment has nearly halved. This is investment in ships

and aircraft.

Table 4 shows how the composition of investment has changed by industry. 1989 was an exceptional year for investment. The Lawson boom of 1986-88 had left many firms short of capacity. They had therefore sharply increased their spending on investment. Many firms came to regret this because the economy then went into a deep recession, between 1989 and 1992, leaving them with excess capacity. Even by 1996, four years into the recovery, investment was 15 per cent below its 1989 peak. Firms were reluctant to invest either because they had continued spare capacity or they feared that the economy would fail to recover. The prolonged period of economic growth of the late 1990s and early 2000s, however, saw investment increase and by 2004 was 11 per cent above its 1989 level.

The pattern of investment spending to some extent reflects trends in output between sectors of the economy. Primary industries, including agriculture and mining, have seen their share of output decline between 1989 and 2004. As a consequence, investment in these industries has been relatively static or fallen. Manufacturing output has increased only by a few per cent but real investment in manufacturing has halved. Investment by the

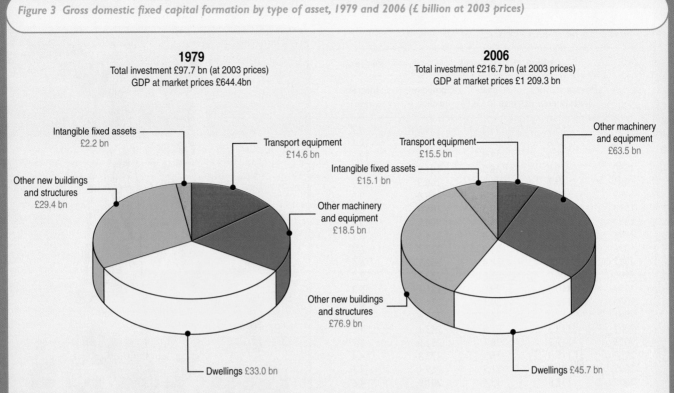

Figure 3 *Gross domestic fixed capital formation by type of asset, 1979 and 2006 (£ billion at 2003 prices)*

1979
Total investment £97.7 bn (at 2003 prices)
GDP at market prices £644.4bn

2006
Total investment £216.7 bn (at 2003 prices)
GDP at market prices £1 209.3 bn

Intangible fixed assets £2.2 bn
Transport equipment £14.6 bn
Other new buildings and structures £29.4 bn
Other machinery and equipment £18.5 bn
Dwellings £33.0 bn

Transport equipment £15.5 bn
Other machinery and equipment £63.5 bn
Intangible fixed assets £15.1 bn
Other new buildings and structures £76.9 bn
Dwellings £45.7 bn

Source: adapted from *Economic Trends Annual Supplement, Monthly Digest of Statistics,* Office for National Statistics.

construction industry has increased by 76 per cent, reflecting particularly an increase in construction of retail and office space. The 63 per cent increase in education, health and social work, investment mainly in new buildings and equipment reflects growing spending in public services, particularly after the election of the Labour government in 1997.

The determinants of investment

Economic theory suggests that there may be several determinants of private sector investment. The accelerator theory suggests that investment is a function of changes in income. The growth of the economy, measured for example by past changes in income, might be the crucial factor. Neo-classical theory argues that the rate of interest is the most important determinant, whilst other theories point to the current level of profits as significant.

The evidence tends to support the ideas that the level of investment is determined by a number of variables. In Table 5 there is some weak correlation between investment and changes in income, profits and the rate of interest. However, these variables tend to move together throughout the business or trade cycle and so changes in investment may in themselves affect the three variables in the data.

Table 4 *GDP and gross capital formation by industry*

	£ billion, at 2003 prices			% change
	1989	1996	2004	1989-2004
GDP at market prices	813.0	914.3	1 154.3	42.0
Total gross fixed capital formation	182.6	156.0	201.8	10.5
of which				
Construction	2.7	1.1	4.7	76.0
Education, health & social work	6.2	6.7	10.1	62.9
Transport, storage & communication	16.0	16.5	22.6	41.1
Investment in dwellings etc.	43.0	32.2	49.7	15.5
Other services	8.9	7.9	10.6	18.9
Public administration & defence	10.5	10.0	13.0	24.3
Distribution, hotels & catering	17.8	15.7	17.8	0.5
Business services & finance	33.5	24.5	31.6	-5.8
Electricity, gas & water supply	5.9	5.4	5.2	-12.6
Agriculture, hunting, forestry and fishing	3.0	3.3	2.6	-15.5
Mining & quarrying	7.7	4.9	4.2	-44.6
Manufacturing	23.6	21.8	11.1	-52.9

Source: adapted from *United Kingdom National Accounts* (Blue Book), Office for National Statistics.

Table 5 *Determinants of investment*

	£ billion, at 2003 prices			Per cent
	Private sector investment	Annual change in GDP	Company profits	Interest rate[1]
1987	55.5	33.2	179.9	9.7
1988	67.6	37.9	187.9	10.1
1989	75.8	17.4	191.4	13.8
1990	75.8	6.3	181.0	14.8
1991	69.7	-11.2	166.3	11.7
1992	67.1	1.7	169.8	9.6
1993	64.6	18.3	185.8	6.0
1994	67.8	35.7	208.3	5.5
1995	73.1	25.4	214.5	6.7
1996	80.7	24.8	227.3	6.0
1997	88.8	28.4	232.2	6.6
1998	106.0	31.6	232.7	7.2
1999	110.3	29.6	231.1	5.3
2000	115.2	38.1	231.1	6.0
2001	117.0	24.7	225.6	5.1
2002	118.3	21.9	243.1	4.0
2003	117.2	30.1	257.6	3.7
2004	119.9	36.4	273.3	4.4
2005	123.5	21.2	269.1	4.7
2006	132.8	33.4	281.0	4.6

1. London clearing banks, base rate: annual average.

Source: adapted from *Economic & Labour Market Review; Monthly Digest of Statistics*, Office for National Statistics.

DataQuestion

Investment

Figure 4 *Investment by and output of manufacturing industry, and GDP, quarterly (£ billion at 2003 prices)*

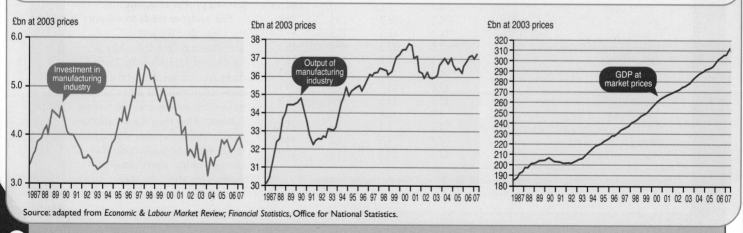

Source: adapted from *Economic & Labour Market Review; Financial Statistics*, Office for National Statistics.

Figure 5 *Short term interest rates[1] and investment by manufacturing industry, quarterly*

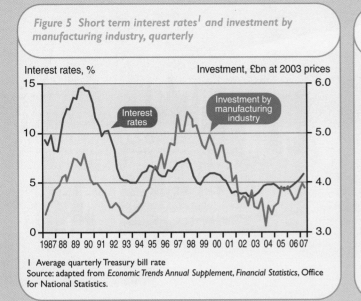

Interest rates, %   Investment, £bn at 2003 prices

Interest rates

Investment by manufacturing industry

1 Average quarterly Treasury bill rate
Source: adapted from *Economic Trends Annual Supplement*, *Financial Statistics*, Office for National Statistics.

Figure 6 *Profits of and investment by manufacturing industry, yearly, (£ billion at 2003 prices)*

£bn at 2003 prices

Company profits

Investment by manufacturing industry

Source: adapted from *National Income Blue Book, Monthly Digest of Statistics*, Office for National Statistics.

Figure 7 *The UK output gap[1] and investment by manufacturing industry*

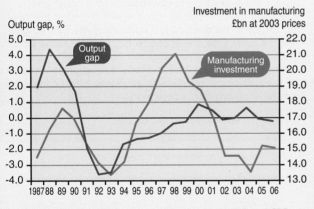

Output gap, %   Investment in manufacturing £bn at 2003 prices

Output gap

Manufacturing investment

1 Deviation of actual GDP from trend GDP as a percentage of trend GDP.
Source: adapted from *Monthly Digest of Statistics*, Office for National Statistics; *Economic Outlook*, OECD.

1. Briefly outline the trends in manufacturing investment between 1987 and 2007.
2. Taking each possible determinant of investment (a) explain why economic theory suggests there is a link between the two variables and (b) evaluate whether the evidence from 1987 to 2007 supports the theory.

3. A manufacturing company is reviewing its investment policies. Evaluate which macroeconomic variable is the most important variable that it should take into consideration when making an investment decision.

Summary

1. Government spending, exports and imports are an important part of total demand in the economy.
2. Government spending is influenced by factors such as the need to provide public and merit goods as well as a desire to control total spending in the economy.
3. Demand for exports and imports is influenced by factors such as their price, exchange rates, changes in the state of the world economy, and non-price factors including quality of goods.

Reasons for government spending

Government plays a crucial role in modern economies. One way in which they intervene is by spending money on a wide variety of goods and services. For example, they provide public goods such as defence and the judiciary. They also provide merit goods such as education and healthcare.

The size of government spending varies from country to country. In a modern economy, the government will fund defence, the police and judiciary, roads and education. There are then wide divergencies between economies. In a free market economy like the United States, the private sector is expected to provide goods such as health care, housing and social care. In a mixed economy, the state will provide many of these goods. Some mixed economies, like Sweden, have much higher state involvement than countries like the UK.

Much of government spending is fixed from year to year. Schools must be funded. Warships must be fuelled. Pensions must be paid. However, governments vary what they spend their money on and how much they spend from year to year. Government announcements about changes in spending are made in **budgets**.

Typically, changes in government spending reflect changing priorities about how to spend money. A government might choose to spend more on education and less on defence next year, for example. However, changes in government spending can also be made deliberately to affect total spending in the economy. Higher government spending can boost total spending and so affect variables such as unemployment and inflation.

The impact of changes in government spending on total spending in the economy depends on levels of taxation. If the government raises taxes by the same amount as a rise in its spending, then there might be little impact on total spending in the economy. On the other hand, a rise in total spending with no change in taxation will have more impact.

Government spending can be greater than government receipts such as taxation. When this happens there will be a **budget deficit**. When government spending is less than government receipts such as taxation, there will be a **budget surplus**. A rise in government spending with no change in taxation will either reduce a budget surplus or increase a budget deficit.

Question 1

Since 2001, public finances have been worsening. Government spending has grown faster than taxes. The result is that the budget has moved from a healthy surplus to a substantial deficit. The Chancellor has increased government spending to pay for much needed improvements in the health and education systems. But he hasn't raised taxes fast enough to pay for the extra doctors and nurses and the new hospitals.

At the same time, the economy has been receiving a boost. The extra spending over taxes has been adding to demand and helping to create jobs and reduce unemployment. Cutting off the spending could dampen economic activity and even put the economy into a recession.

Source: adapted from the *Financial Times*, 22.3.2007.

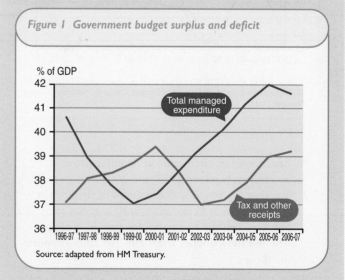

Figure 1 Government budget surplus and deficit

Source: adapted from HM Treasury.

(a) Using examples from the data, explain two reasons why a government increases its spending.
(b) Using the circular flow of income model, analyse the impact of an increase in the budget deficit on income.

Exports and imports

Exports are goods and services sold to foreigners. **Imports** are goods and services bought from foreigners. Exports are an important part of total demand in an economy like the UK. The demand for exports and imports is influenced by a number of factors.

Price Buyers make decisions partly on the price of a good. The higher the price, the lower the quantity demanded. The price itself depends upon a variety of supply factors including costs. Over the past 15 years, production of low and medium technology manufactured goods has gone from high wage economies like the UK to low wage economies like China. So imports into the UK from China have increased because UK domestic producers can no longer compete.

The exchange rate The exchange rate is the price at which one currency is sold for another. A rise in the value of the pound means that it costs foreigners more to buy pounds with their local currency. This makes exports from the UK less price competitive and hence UK exports are likely to fall. Equally, a rise in the value of the pound means that UK buyers can buy foreign currency more cheaply with pounds. So imports become more price competitive to UK buyers. A fall in the value of the pound leads to the opposite result. UK exports become more price competitive to foreign buyers. In contrast, UK buyers find that imports become less price competitive.

World and UK income When the world economy is booming, foreign income is rising fast. This provides UK exporters with an opportunity to sell more exports. When foreign markets slump, UK exports will fall because foreigners can no longer afford to buy as many goods from the UK. Sometimes there are world wide booms and recessions. At other times, individual economies go into boom or slump. In the first half of the 2000s, for example, economic growth was slow in the EU and so UK exporters found it hard to increase their exports to the rest of the EU. When the UK goes into a recession, foreign companies selling imports to the UK will find trading conditions difficult and imports may fall. In contrast, a boom in the UK economy will suck in imports from abroad as UK buyers spend their extra income.

Non-price factors Exports and imports may be bought solely on price. This is particularly true where goods are of standard quality. Copper, steel or wheat, for example, are standard commodities which tend to be traded on price. However, many products are unique in quality. They may have a unique design protected by patents. It may be a unique service, such as next day delivery. So a whole range of non-price factors affects the competitiveness of exports and imports.

Applied economics

EEF

EEF, the organisation which represents UK manufacturing companies, said that British firms were coping well with the export challenge. In a report published in 2007, *Export support: How UK firms compete abroad*, it said that most British manufacturers had increased their dependence on exports since the late 1990s. As Figure 2 shows, 90 per cent of UK manufacturing companies sell to other western European EU countries whilst 45 per cent sell goods to China.

One key reason for the success of British exporting companies has been the strong economic growth in many overseas countries. Whilst the UK enjoyed a period of above average growth from 1995 of between 2.5 and 3 per cent per annum, the USA has grown even faster. China, a key market, has been growing at nearly 10 per cent per annum.

Another reason for export success has been that UK companies have exploited niche markets. These markets have allowed them to exploit new technologies or make small numbers of products to order. Foreign owned firms with subsidiary companies in the UK have been better at exporting from the UK than UK owned firms. Foreign

owned firms tend to be larger which in export markets can give a variety of competitive advantages such as economies of scale or greater product knowledge. Foreign owned firms also tend to more attuned to globalisation and more aware of which markets they can exploit.

However, UK manufacturers have tended to pull out of markets where they have to compete on price on mass produced or low technology items. They cannot compete with low wage cost countries such as China. Some UK companies have exploited this trend by moving such production to low cost countries and then exporting the goods worldwide. Production might be done in China but the profits are earned by the UK company.

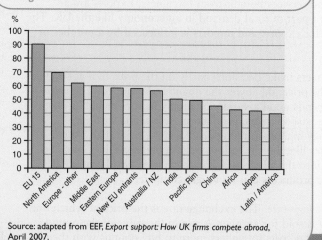

Figure 2 Overseas markets: percentage of UK companies selling to those markets

Source: adapted from EEF, *Export support: How UK firms compete abroad*, April 2007.

DataQuestion

DEK

DEK is the world's largest maker of specialist printing machines for the production of circuit boards used in the electronics industry. It has two factories, one in Weymouth in the UK and the other in China. Total production in 2006 was £100 million, with about 60 per cent of that coming from the Weymouth plant. Around 95 per cent of output from Weymouth is exported.

Part of the success of the company comes from its technology. Customers place their orders for specialist machines which come in about 150 basic variants. High levels of automation at the Weymouth plant mean that costs are only slightly higher than at its Chinese plant where wages are much lower. Automation means that wages account for only a very small part of total cost. Highly efficient production methods mean that a customer ordering a machine today can expect to receive it two weeks later from Britain via air freight.

Source: adapted from the *Financial Times*, 23.4.2007.

1. Explain two reasons why DEK is a successful exporter.

2. To what extent can UK exporters like DEK be successful against Chinese manufacturers in future?

Summary

1. The aggregate demand curve is downward sloping. It shows the relationship between the price level and equilibrium output in the economy.
2. A movement along the aggregate demand curve shows how equilibrium income will change if there is a change in the price level.
3. A shift in the aggregate demand curve is caused by a change in variables such as consumption and exports at any given price level.
4. The multiplier increases any impact on aggregate demand and national income of changes in an injection to the circular flow.

Aggregate demand

Demand for an individual good is defined as the quantity that is bought at any given price. In this unit, we will consider what determines AGGREGATE demand. 'Aggregate' in economics means a 'total' or 'added up' amount. AGGREGATE DEMAND is the total of all demands or expenditures in the economy at any given price.

National expenditure is one of the three ways of calculating national income, usually measured as GDP. National expenditure is made up of four components.

- **Consumption (C).** This is spending by households on goods and services.
- **Investment (I).** This is spending by firms on investment goods.
- **Government spending (G).** This includes current spending, for instance on wages and salaries. It also includes spending by government on investment goods like new roads or new schools.
- **Exports minus imports (X - M).** Foreigners spend money on goods produced in the DOMESTIC ECONOMY. Hence it is part of national expenditure. However, households, firms and governments also spend money on goods produced abroad. For instance, a UK household might buy a car produced in France, or a British firm might use components imported from the Far East in a computer which is sold to Germany. These imported goods do not form part of national output and do not contribute to national income. So, because C, I, G and X all include spending on imported goods, imports (M) must be taken away from C + I + G + X to arrive at a figure for national expenditure.

National expenditure or aggregate demand (AD) can therefore be calculated using the formula:

$$AD = C + I + G + X - M$$

The aggregate demand curve

The AGGREGATE DEMAND CURVE shows the relationship between the price level and the level of real expenditure in the economy. Figure 1 shows an aggregate demand (AD) curve. The price level is put on the vertical axis whilst real output is put on the horizontal axis.

The **price level** is the average level of prices in the economy. Governments calculate a number of different measures of the

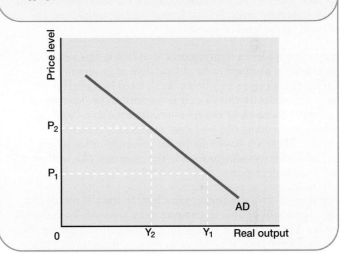

Figure 1 The aggregate demand curve
A rise in the price level will lead, via a rise in interest rates, to a fall in the equilibrium level of national income and therefore of national output. Hence the aggregate demand curve is downward sloping.

price level. In the UK, for instance, the most widely quoted measure is the **Consumer Prices Index**, figures for which are published every month and are widely reported in the news. A change in the price level is **inflation**.

Real output on the horizontal axis must equal real expenditure and real income. This is because, in the circular flow model of the economy, these are three different ways of measuring the same flow. The aggregate demand curve plots the level of expenditure where the economy would be in an equilibrium position at each price level, all other things being equal.

Demand curves are nearly always downward sloping. Why is the aggregate demand curve the same shape? One simple answer is to consider what happens to a household budget if prices rise. If a household is on a fixed income, then a rise in average prices will mean that they can buy fewer goods and services than before. The higher the price level in the economy, the less they can afford to buy. So it is with the national economy. The higher the price, the fewer goods and services will be demanded in the whole economy.

A more sophisticated explanation considers what happens to the different components of expenditure when prices rise.

Consumption Consumption expenditure is influenced by the **rate of interest** in the economy. When prices increase, consumers (and firms) need more money to buy the same number of goods and services as before. One way of getting more money is to borrow it and so the demand for borrowed funds will rise. However, if there is a fixed supply of money available for borrowing from banks and building societies, the price of borrowed funds will rise. This price is the rate of interest. A rise in interest rates leads to a fall in consumption, particularly of durable goods such as cars which are commonly bought on credit.

Another way a rise in the price level affects consumption is through the **wealth effect**. A rise in the price level leads to the real value of an individual consumer's wealth being lower. For instance, £100 000 at today's prices will be worth less in real terms in a year's time if average prices have increased 20 per cent over the 12 months. A fall in real wealth will result in a fall in consumer spending.

Investment As has just been explained, a rise in prices, all other things being equal, leads to a rise in interest rates in the economy. Investment is affected by changes in the rate of interest. The higher the rate of interest, the less profitable new investment projects become and therefore the fewer projects will be undertaken by firms. So, the higher the rate of interest, the lower will be the level of investment.

Government spending Government spending in this model of the economy is assumed to be independent of economic variables. It is exogenously determined, fixed by variables outside the model. In this case, it is assumed to be determined by the political decisions of the government of the day. Note that government spending (G) here does not include transfer payments. These are payments by the government for which there is no corresponding output in the economy, like welfare benefits or student grants.

Exports and imports A higher price level in the UK means that foreign firms will be able to compete more successfully in the UK economy. For instance, if British shoe manufacturers put up their prices by 20 per cent, whilst foreign shoe manufacturers keep their prices the same, then British shoe manufacturers will become less competitive and more foreign shoes will be imported. Equally, British shoe manufacturers will find it more difficult to export charging higher prices. So a higher UK price level, with price levels in other economies staying the same, will lead to a fall in UK exports.

Hence, aggregate demand falls as prices rise, first, because increases in interest rates reduce consumption and investment and, second, because a loss of international competitiveness at the new higher prices will reduce exports and increase imports.

Question 1

In 1975, inflation rose to a peak of 24.1 per cent. Real GDP fell in both 1974 and 1975. In 1980, inflation rose to a peak of 18.0 per cent and real GDP fell in 1980 and 1981. In 1990, inflation rose to a peak of 9.5 per cent. GDP fell in 1991 and 1992.

How might economic theory account for this?

Shifts in the AD curve

The aggregate demand (AD) curve shows the relationship between the price level and the equilibrium level of real income and output. A change in the price level results in a **movement along** the AD curve. Higher prices lead to falls in aggregate demand.

Shifts in the aggregate demand curve will occur if there is a change in any other relevant variable apart from the price level. When the AD curve shifts, it shows that there is a change in real output at any given price level. In Figure 2, the shift in the AD curve from AD_1 to AD_2 shows that at a price level of P, real output increases from Y_1 to Y_2. There is a number of variables which can lead to a shift of the AD curve. Some of these variables are real variables, such as changes in the willingness of consumers to spend. Others are changes in **monetary variables** such as the rate of interest.

Consumption A number of factors might increase consumption spending at any given level of prices, shifting the AD curve from AD_1 to AD_2 in Figure 2. For instance, unemployment may fall, making consumers less afraid that they will lose their jobs and more willing to borrow money to spend on consumer durables. The government might reduce interest rates, again encouraging borrowing for durables. A substantial rise in stock market prices will increase consumer wealth which in turn may lead to an increase in spending. A reduction in the relative numbers of high saving 45-60 year olds in the population will increase the **average propensity to consume** of the whole economy. New technology which creates new consumer products can lead to an increase in consumer spending as households want to buy these new products. A fall in income tax would increase consumers' disposable income, leading to a rise in consumption.

Investment One factor which would increase investment spending at any given level of prices, pushing the AD curve from AD_1 to AD_2 in Figure 2, would be an increase in business

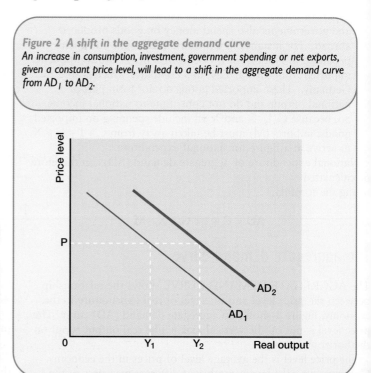

Figure 2 A shift in the aggregate demand curve
An increase in consumption, investment, government spending or net exports, given a constant price level, will lead to a shift in the aggregate demand curve from AD_1 to AD_2.

Explain, using a diagram, the likely effect of the following on the aggregate demand curve for the UK.

(a) The increase in real investment expenditure between 2000 and 2005.
(b) The pushing up of interest rates by the government from 7.5 per cent in May 1987 to 15 per cent in October 1989.
(c) The large cuts in taxes in the Lawson Budget of 1987.
(d) The 50 per cent per cent fall in London Stock Market prices (FTSE 100) between December 1999 and January 2003.
(e) The fall in the savings ratio from a peak of 11.7 per cent in 1992 to a low of 3.7 per cent in 2004.
(f) The increase in planned government spending on education and health care by the Labour government 2000-2007.
(g) The more than 25 per cent rise in the average value of the pound against other currencies between 1996 and 2000.

confidence - an increase in 'animal spirits' as John Maynard Keynes put it. This increase in business confidence could have come about, for instance, because the economy was going into boom. A fall in interest rates ordered by the government would lead to a rise in investment. An increase in company profitability would give firms more retained profit to use for investment. A fall in taxes on profits (corporation tax in the UK) would lead to the rate of return on investment projects rising, leading to a rise in investment.

Government spending Government spending can change automatically because of previous government spending commitments, or the government can announce changes to its spending. A rise in government spending with no change in taxation will lead to a fall in its budget surplus or a rise in its deficit. This will increase aggregate demand, pushing the AD curve to the right from AD_1 to AD_2 in Figure 2. A fall in government spending with no change in taxation will lead to a shift to the left in the aggregate demand curve.

Exports and imports A number of factors can affect the balance between exports and imports. For example, a rise in the exchange rate is likely to lead to lower exports but higher imports. Exports minus imports will therefore fall, reducing aggregate demand. This is shown by a shift in the aggregate demand curve to the left. In contrast, an improvement in innovation and quality of UK manufactured goods is likely to lead to a rise in exports. This will increase aggregate demand and shift the aggregate demand curve to the right from AD_1 to AD_2 in Figure 2.

The multiplier

If there is an increase in, say, investment of £1, what will be the final increase in national income? John Maynard Keynes argued in his most famous book, *The General Theory of Employment, Interest and Money*, published in 1936, that national income would increase by more than £1 because of the MULTIPLIER EFFECT.

To understand why there might be a multiplier effect, consider what would happen if firms increased spending on new factories by £100m. Firms would pay contractors to build the factories. This £100m would be an increase in aggregate demand. The contractor would use the money in part to pay its workers on the project. The workers would spend the money, on everything from food to holidays. This spending would be an addition to national income. Assume that £10m is spent on food. Food manufacturers would in turn pay their workers who would spend their incomes on a variety of products, increasing national income further. John Maynard Keynes argued that this multiplier

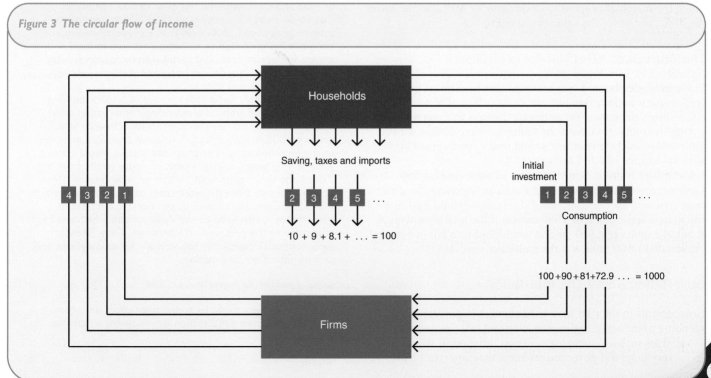

Figure 3 *The circular flow of income*

effect would increase jobs in the economy. Every job directly created by firms through extra spending would indirectly create other jobs in the economy.

This process can be shown using the **circular flow of income model**. Assume that households spend 9/10ths of their gross income. The other 1/10th is either saved or paid to the government in the form of taxes. Firms increase their spending by £100m, money which is used to build new factories. In Figure 3, this initial £100m is shown in stage 1 flowing into firms. The money then flows out again as it is distributed in the form of wages and profits back to households. Households spend the money, but remember that there are **withdrawals** of 0.1 of income because of savings and taxes. So only £90m flows back round the economy in stage 2 to firms. Then firms pay £90m back to households in wages and profits. In the third stage, £81m is spent by households with £19 million leaking out of the circular flow. This process carries on with smaller and smaller amounts being added to national income as the money flows round the economy. Eventually, the initial £100m extra government spending leads to a final increase in national income of £1 000m. In this case, the value of the MULTIPLIER is 10.

If leakages from the circular flow in Figure 3 had been larger, less of the increase in investment would have continued to flow round the economy. For instance, if leakages had been 0.8 of income, then only £20m (0.2 x £100m) would have flowed round the economy in the second stage. In the third stage, it would have been £4m (0.2 x £20m). The final increase in national income following the initial £100m increase in investment spending would have been £125m.

The multiplier model states that the higher the leakages from the circular flow, the smaller will be the increase in income which continues to flow round the economy at each stage following an initial increase in spending. Hence, the higher the leakages, the smaller the value of the multiplier. Leakages are what is not spent. So, another way of saying this is that the multiplier is smaller when the ratio of consumption to income is lower. The ratio of consumption to income at the margin is called the **marginal propensity to consume** or **MPC**. So the lower the MPC, the lower the value of the multiplier.

The multiplier effect and injections

In the example above, it was assumed that investment increased. Investment is an **injection** into the circular flow. The multiplier effect shows the impact on aggregate demand and income of a change in an injection. So if the multiplier were 2, then a £100 million increase in investment would lead to an increase in national income of £200 million.

Investment is not the only injection into the circular flow. Government spending and exports are also injections. So a rise in government spending of, say, £200 million would lead to a rise in national income of £800 million if the multiplier were 4. A fall in exports of £500 million would lead to a fall in national income of £1 500 million if the multiplier were 3.

Governments and the multiplier

Governments in the past have used changes in government spending to influence national income and macroeconomic variables such as unemployment and inflation. It would be very helpful if governments knew that an extra £1 in

government spending would produce an extra, say, £2 in national income. However, in practice, it is not so simple.

- It is difficult to measure the exact size of the multiplier. Sophisticated econometric models have to be used which describe the workings of the economy. They are not completely accurate. Equally, changes can happen in an economy which can alter the size of the multiplier from one period to the next.
- The multiplier effect is not instantaneous. A £100 increase in government spending today does not increase national income by £200 today. It takes time for the money to flow round the circular flow. So there are time lags between the increase in the government spending and the final increase in national income.
- Economists disagree about the exact size of the multiplier. However, in general it is considered to be relatively low, between 1 and 2. Increases in investment or government spending do not give very large increases in national income.

Important notes

Changes and shifts in AD Aggregate demand analysis and aggregate supply analysis are more complex than demand and supply analysis in an individual market. You may already have noticed, for instance, that a change in interest rates could lead to a movement along the aggregate demand curve or lead to a shift in the curve. Similarly, an increase in consumption could lead to a movement along or a shift in the curve. To distinguish between

Question 3

The small town of Bo'ness was once the centre of a booming economy. A port, situated on the Forth estuary on the east coast of Scotland, it was once only second in importance to Edinburgh's port of Leith. Today, it has fallen on hard times. Its port was closed to commercial shipping in 1958 and the town now has only 15 000 inhabitants. All that could change if a proposed £150 million development scheme goes ahead. ING Real East, a property development company, has proposed an ambitious scheme to build a marina for leisure craft, 700 harbour-front apartments and townhouses, a 100-bedroom hotel and waterside shops, restaurants, cafes and bars.

The town centre has a rich heritage of historic buildings and this year was granted outstanding conservation area status. It already houses the Scottish Rail Museum, which draws 60 000 visitors a year. Tourism is therefore important to the local economy. The proposed marina would act as a good staging post for leisure craft en route to the Falkirk Wheel, the spectacular boat lift that provides vessels cross-country passage from the west coast to the east coast via the Union Canal with the Firth and Forth Canal. The government is also keen to see development which would take some of the pressure off Edinburgh. Only 20 miles away, Scotland's capital city has virtually full employment and an overheated housing market.

Source: adapted from the *Financial Times*, 1.12.2004.

Explain how there might be a multiplier effect on income from the proposed £150 million development scheme in Bo'ness.

movements along and shifts in the curve it is important to consider what has caused the change in aggregate demand.

If the change has come about because the price level has changed, then there is a movement **along** the AD curve. For instance, a rise in the price level causes a rise in interest rates. This leads to a fall in consumption. This is shown by a movement up the curve.

If, however, interest rates or consumer spending have changed for a different reason than because prices have changed, then there will be a **shift** in the AD curve. A government putting up interest rates at a given price level would lead to a shift in the curve.

Levels and changes As with any economic analysis, it is important to distinguish between absolute changes and rates of change. For example, a fall in the level of investment will lead to a fall in aggregate demand, all other things being equal. However, a fall in the rate of change of investment, when this rate of change is positive, means that investment is still rising. If growth in investment has fallen from 5 per cent to 3 per cent, investment is still increasing. So a fall in the rate of growth of investment will lead to an increase in aggregate demand and a shift of the AD curve to the right.

Key terms

Aggregate - the sum or total.
Aggregate demand - the total of all demands or expenditures in the economy at any given price.
Aggregate demand curve - shows the relationship between the price level and equilibrium national income. As the price level rises the equilibrium level of national income falls.
Domestic economy - the economy of a single country.

Multiplier - the figure used to multiply a change in autonomous expenditure, such as investment, to find the final change in income. It is the ratio of the final change in income to the initial change in autonomous expenditure.
Multiplier effect - an increase in investment or any other autonomous expenditure will lead to an even greater increase in income.

Applied economics

Aggregate demand 1979-2007

In 1979, a new Conservative government under Margaret Thatcher was elected into office. The economy had been through very difficult times in the 1970s. Imported inflation had been a major problem and trade unions had militantly pushed up wages in an attempt to maintain the real value of their members' earnings. On coming into office, she faced rapidly rising inflation. Partly this was because of a world oil crisis where OPEC was ultimately able to increase the price of oil threefold between 1978 and 1982. Partly it was because wage inflation had taken off again.

Margaret Thatcher was strongly influenced by the relatively new and fashionable monetarist idea that inflation was solely caused by excessive increases in the money supply. If the money supply increased, this pushed up aggregate demand. Too much money, and so excess demand, chasing too few goods could only lead to increases in prices. To reduce the rate of growth of the money supply, she raised interest rates from 12 per cent in May 1979 to 17 per cent in November 1979 as Figure 4 shows. High interest rates of over 10 per cent, which were maintained for four years, depressed both

consumption and investment, reducing aggregate demand. The economy went into a major recession, with unemployment climbing from 1.3 million in 1979 to 3.1 million in 1983. As Figure 5 shows, a negative output gap of 7 per cent of GDP opened up in 1981. Aggregate demand was far below its trend level.

As interest rates fell, the economy began to recover and aggregate demand began to rise again. Part of the monetarist philosophy was that excessive growth of the money supply was usually caused by excessive government borrowing. So the government attempted to reduce government spending and even raised taxes in 1981. This limited the growth in aggregate demand from 1981 onwards.

Nevertheless, the economy was in the recovery phase of the trade cycle. Between 1983 and 1988, it grew at above its trend rate of growth of 2.5 per cent. Interest rates were still at historically high levels, averaging 10-12 per cent, but consumption and investment grew despite this. A housing boom began to develop, which further encouraged consumption.

By 1987, the government had convinced itself that

Britain was experiencing an 'economic miracle' due to its economic policies and that a 4 per cent per annum growth rate was sustainable in the long term. There was a substantial tax cutting budget in March 1987 which saw the top rate of income tax fall from 60 per cent to 40 per cent. Lower taxes led to higher disposable income and hence higher consumption. Inflation remained low, so households did not have to increase their savings levels to rebuild the real value of their wealth. The stock market also saw share prices increasing, adding to households' wealth. Unemployment fell sharply, halving from 3 million to 1.8 million between 1986 and 1989. All these factors led to increasing levels of consumer confidence. Households were more willing than before to take out loans and were less willing to save.

By 1988, the economy was operating at 5.5 per cent above its productive potential. Firms sharply increased their investment spending and planned to take advantage of the many profitable opportunities that were now available. In the meantime, importers took advantage of the UK's inability to satisfy domestic demand and a dangerously high current account deficit was recorded.

In 1988, the government realised that the economy had overheated and that inflation would increase sharply if it did not take action. So it raised interest rates and by late 1989, as Figure 4 shows, they stood at 15 per cent, double their lowest 1988 value. This led to a slowdown in consumer spending. The housing market collapsed as borrowers were less willing to take out mortgages to finance new purchases. Existing mortgage borrowers found their mortgage payments increasing sharply, reducing their ability to spend. Lower house prices lowered household wealth and severely dented consumer confidence. So too did rising unemployment, which doubled between 1989 and 1993. Firms cut back their investment spending as they found themselves with too much productive capacity, as Figure 5 shows. Government spending remained tight although there was

some increase in it after John Major became Prime Minister in 1989. As for exports, their growth remained subdued because high interest rates kept the value of the pound high. The government also made the policy mistake of taking the pound into the Exchange Rate Mechanism (ERM) of the European Monetary Union (the precursor to the euro and monetary union) at too high a level. This forced it to keep interest rates high to defend the value of the pound. Britain was forced to leave the ERM by currency speculation in September 1992. By that time, falling levels of aggregate demand meant that GDP was lower than it was in the last quarter of 1988, nearly four years earlier.

Leaving the ERM allowed the government to reduce interest rates rapidly at a time when inflation had fallen to around 2 per cent per annum. The period 1993-2007 was then characterised by above average rates of growth. 1993-1997 can be seen as the recovery from the deep recession of 1990-1992. The period 1997-2007 can be seen as a prolonged period when the economy was growing at roughly its trend rate of growth, as Figure 5 would suggest.

The drivers of aggregate demand have fluctuated over the period 1993-2007.

- Consumer spending has tended to increase at a faster rate than growth in aggregate demand overall. This has been fuelled by low interest rates and easy credit. Low interest rates have kept the cost of borrowing low to purchase consumer durables such as cars and electronic equipment. Rising house prices have also produced rising wealth which has encouraged consumer spending boom.
- Government spending growth was low between 1995 and 2000 because of political commitments to keep both government spending and taxes low. However, after 2001, the government raised its spending substantially to pay for improvement to health care and education. Taxes failed to keep pace with the growth in spending. As a result, there was a substantial boost to

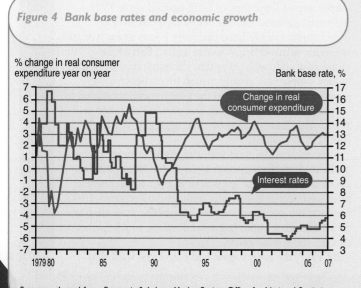

Figure 4 Bank base rates and economic growth

Source: adapted from *Economic & Labour Market Review*, Office for National Statistics.

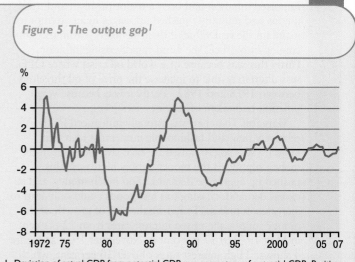

Figure 5 The output gap[1]

1 Deviation of actual GDP from potential GDP as a percentage of potential GDP. Positive numbers show actual GDP is above potential GDP, whilst negative numbers show actual GDP is below potential GDP.

Source: adapted from HM Treasury, *Economic Cycles*, 2005; *Budget 2007 - the economy*.

aggregate demand from government spending from 2001.
- Exports were hit by a financial crisis in Asia in 1997 and by a downturn in the US economy in 2001 made worse by the attacks on the World Trade Centre of 9/11. It could be argued that these two events were the major cause of the faltering of the UK economy in 1998

and again in 2002-2003. However, exports bounced back after 2003 as the world economy grew strongly. Imports equally grew strongly as UK consumers and firms bought goods and services from overseas. The net impact of exports minus imports after 2003 was to depress aggregate demand because imports grew more strongly than exports.

DataQuestion

Aggregate demand 2000-2007

Figure 6 Real growth in GDP and its components, % change year on year

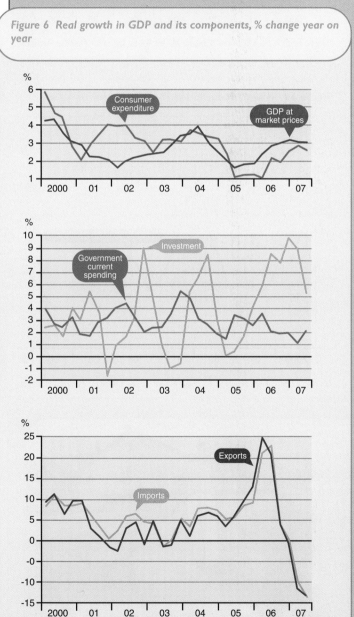

Source: adapted from *Economic & Labour Market Review*, Office for National Statistics.

Figure 7 GDP and its components, 2nd quarter 2007

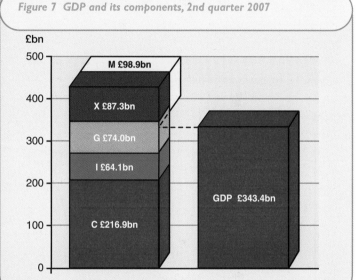

Source: adapted from *Economic Trends*, Office for National Statistics.

Figure 8 Short term interest rates

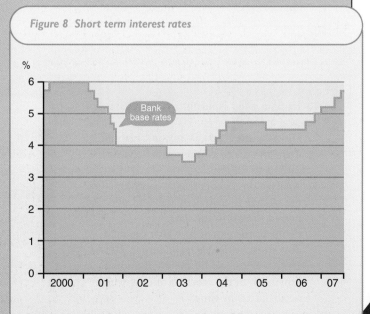

Source: adapted from *Economic & Labour Market Review*, Office for National Statistics.

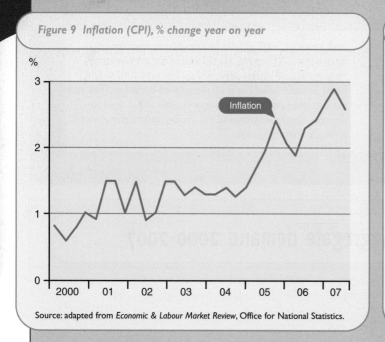

Figure 9 Inflation (CPI), % change year on year

%

Inflation

Source: adapted from *Economic & Labour Market Review*, Office for National Statistics.

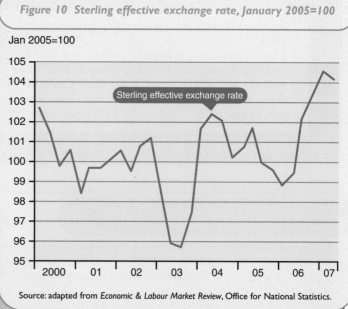

Figure 10 Sterling effective exchange rate, January 2005=100

Jan 2005=100

Sterling effective exchange rate

Source: adapted from *Economic & Labour Market Review*, Office for National Statistics.

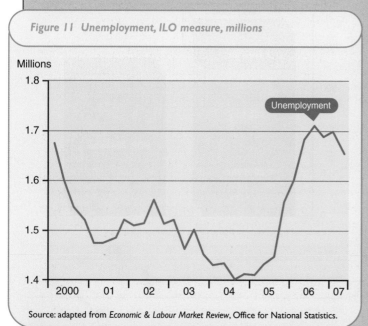

Figure 11 Unemployment, ILO measure, millions

Millions

Unemployment

Source: adapted from *Economic & Labour Market Review*, Office for National Statistics.

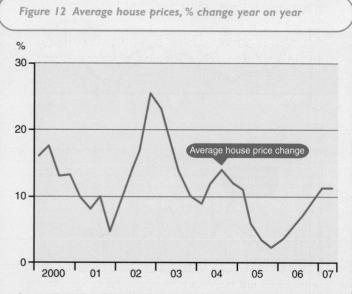

Figure 12 Average house prices, % change year on year

%

Average house price change

Source: adapted from *Economic & Labour Market Review*, Office for National Statistics.

1. Explain what is meant by 'aggregate demand'.
2. Describe the trend, if any, in aggregate demand and its components between 2000 and 2007.
3. Analyse the factors which contributed to the change in aggregate demand over the period shown in the data.
4. Evaluate the extent to which the mild downturn in the UK economy in 2001-2002 was caused by the international downturn in the world economy which occurred at the time.

Summary

1. The aggregate supply curve shows the level of output in the whole economy at any given level of average prices.
2. In the short run, it is assumed that the prices of factors of production, such as money wage rates, are constant. Firms will supply extra output if the prices they receive increase. Hence in the short run, the aggregate supply curve is upward sloping.
3. An increase in firms' costs of production will shift the short run aggregate supply curve upwards, whilst a fall in costs will shift it downwards.
4. In the long run, it is assumed that the prices of factors of production are variable but that the productive capacity of the economy is fixed. The long run aggregate supply curve shows the productive capacity of the economy at any given price level.
5. The long run aggregate supply curve shows the productive capacity of the economy in the same way that a production possibility frontier or the trend rate of growth shows this productive capacity.
6. Shifts in the long run aggregate supply curve are caused by changes in the quantity or quality of factors of production or the efficiency of their use.
7. In the long run, it is assumed that the prices of factors of production are variable but that the productive capacity of the economy is fixed. The long run aggregate supply curve shows the productive capacity of the economy at any given price level.
8. The long run aggregate supply curve shows the productive capacity of the economy in the way that a production possibility frontier or the trend rate of growth shows this productive capacity.

The short run aggregate supply curve

In unit 6, it was argued that the supply curve for an industry was upward sloping. If the price of a product increases, firms in the industry are likely to increase their profits by producing and selling more. So the higher the price, the higher the level of output. The supply curve being talked about here is a **microeconomic** supply curve. Is the **macroeconomic** supply curve (i.e. the supply curve for the whole economy) the same?

The macroeconomic supply curve is called the AGGREGATE SUPPLY CURVE, because it is the sum of all the industry supply curves in the economy. It shows how much output firms wish to supply at each level of prices.

In the short run, the aggregate supply curve is upward sloping. The short run is defined here as the period when money wage rates and the prices of all other factor inputs in the economy are fixed. Assume that firms wish to increase their level of output. In the short run, they are unlikely to take on extra workers. Taking on extra staff is an expensive process. Sacking them if they are no longer needed is likely to be even more costly, not just in direct monetary terms but also in terms of industrial relations within the company. So firms tend to respond to increases in demand in the short run by working their existing labour force more intensively, for instance through overtime.

Firms will need to provide incentives for workers to work harder or longer hours. Overtime, for instance, may be paid at one and a half times the basic rate of pay. Whilst basic pay rates remain constant, earnings will rise and this will tend to put up both the average and marginal costs per unit of output. In many sectors of the economy, where competition is imperfect and where firms have the power to increase their prices, the rise in labour costs will lead to a rise in prices. It only needs prices to rise in some sectors of the economy for the average price level in

the economy to rise. So in the short term, an increase in output by firms is likely to lead to an increase in their costs which in turn will result in some firms raising prices. However, the increase in prices is likely to be small because, given constant prices (e.g. wage **rates**) for factor inputs, the increases in costs (e.g. wage **earnings**) are likely to be fairly small too. Therefore the short run aggregate supply curve is relatively price elastic. This is shown in Figure 1. An increase in output from Q_1 to Q_2 leads to a moderate rise in the average price level of $P_1 P_2$.

If demand falls in the short run, some firms in the economy will react by cutting their prices to try and stimulate extra orders. However, the opportunities to cut prices will be limited. Firms will be reluctant to sack workers and their overheads will remain the same, so their average cost and marginal cost will barely be altered. Again, the aggregate supply curve is relatively price elastic.

Shifts in the short run aggregate supply curve

The SHORT RUN AGGREGATE SUPPLY CURVE shows the

Question 1

Using a short run aggregate supply curve, explain the likely effect on the price level of the following, assuming that the prices of all factor inputs are fixed.
(a) In 1988, output in the UK economy boomed. Real GDP rose by 5 per cent, an increase which has yet to be repeated.
(b) In 1991, there was a recession in the UK economy and output fell. Real GDP declined by 1.5 per cent, the last time in recent economic history a fall occurred.

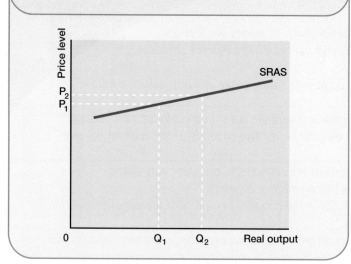

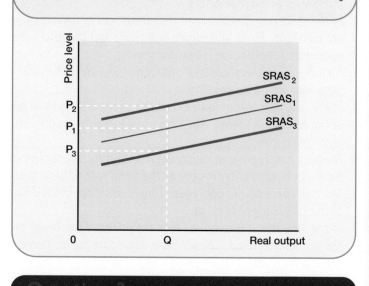

relationship between aggregate output and the average price level, assuming that money wage rates in the economy are constant. But what if wage rates do change, or some other variable which affects aggregate supply changes? Then, just as in the microeconomic theory of the supply curve, the aggregate supply curve will shift.

Wage rates An increase in wage rates will result in firms facing increased costs of production. Some firms will respond by increasing prices. So at any given level of output, a rise in wage rates will lead to a rise in the average price level. This is shown in Figure 2 by a shift in the short run aggregate supply curve from $SRAS_1$ to $SRAS_2$.

Raw material prices A general fall in the prices of raw materials may occur. Perhaps world demand for commodities falls, or perhaps the value of the pound rises, making the price of imports cheaper. A fall in the price of raw materials will lower industrial costs and will lead to some firms reducing the prices of their products. Hence there will be a shift in the short run aggregate supply curve downwards. This is shown in Figure 2 by the shift from $SRAS_1$ to $SRAS_3$.

Taxation An increase in the tax burden on industry will increase costs. Hence the short run aggregate supply schedule will be pushed upwards, for instance from $SRAS_1$ to $SRAS_2$ in Figure 2.
 When there is a large change in wage rates, raw material prices or taxation, a SUPPLY SIDE SHOCK is said to occur. A supply side shock, like a doubling of the price of oil, can have a significant impact on aggregate supply, pushing the short run aggregate supply curve upwards.

The long run aggregate supply curve

In the short run, changes in wage rates or the price of raw materials have an effect on the aggregate supply curve, shifting the SRAS curve up or down. Equally, a rise in real output will lead to a movement along the SRAS curve.
 In the long run, however, there is a limit to how

Using diagrams, show the likely effect of the following on the long run aggregate supply curve.
(a) Real national output in the 2nd quarter of 1992 was the same as in the fourth quarter of 1988 but average prices had increased 27 per cent over the period.
(b) In 2004-2005, the price of crude oil approximately doubled.
(c) Between 2000 and 2004, average money earnings in the UK economy rose by 16.7 per cent.

much firms can increase their supply. They run into capacity constraints. There is a limit to the amount of labour that can be hired in an economy. Capital equipment is fixed in supply. Labour productivity has been maximised. So it can be argued that in the long run, the aggregate supply curve is fixed at a given level of real output, whatever the price level. What this means is that the long run aggregate supply curve is vertical on a diagram showing the price level and real output.
 Figure 3 shows such a vertical LONG RUN AGGREGATE SUPPLY CURVE or LRAS CURVE. The long run aggregate supply curve shows the productive potential of the economy. It shows how much real output can be produced over a period of time with a given level of factor inputs, such as labour and capital equipment, and a given level of efficiency in combining these factor inputs. It can be linked to three other economic concepts.
● The LRAS curve is the level of output associated with production on the production possibility frontier of an economy. In Figure 4, any point on the boundary AB is one which shows the level of real output shown by the LRAS curve.
● The LRAS curve is the level of output shown by the trend or long term average rate of growth in an economy. When output is above or below this long term trend level, an output

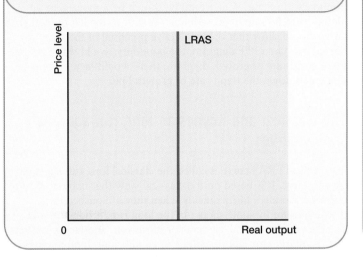

Figure 3 *The classical long run aggregate supply curve*
Classical economics assumes that in the long run wages and prices are flexible and therefore the LRAS curve is vertical. In the long run, there cannot be any unemployment because the wage rate will be in equilibrium where all workers who want a job (the supply of labour) will be offered a job (the demand for labour). So, whatever the level of prices, output will always be constant at the full employment level of income.

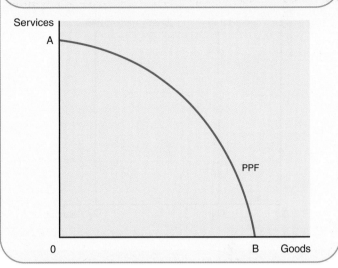

Figure 4 *A production possibility frontier*
Any point on the production possibility frontier AB shows the potential output of the economy when all resources are fully utilised. The long run aggregate supply curve also shows the potential output of the economy. At any point in time, if the economy is operating on its long run aggregate supply curve, then it will be operating at one of the points along the production possibility frontier.

gap is said to exist. In Figure 5, the economy is growing along the trend rate of growth of AB. There are short term fluctuations in actual output above and below the trend rate. This shows that actual output can be above or below that given by the long run aggregate supply curve. When actual output is above the trend rate on Figure 5 in the short run, and so to the right of the LRAS curve in Figure 3, economic forces will act to bring GDP back towards its trend rate of growth. Equally, when it is below its trend rate of growth, and so to the left of the LRAS curve in Figure 3, the same but opposite forces will bring it back to that long run position.

● The LRAS curve shows the level of FULL CAPACITY output of the economy. At full capacity, there are no underutilised resources in the economy. Production is at its long run maximum. In the short run, an economy might operate beyond full capacity, creating a positive output gap. However, this is unsustainable and the output in the economy must fall back to its full capacity levels.

Shifts in the long run aggregate supply curve

The long run aggregate supply curve is likely to shift over time. This is because the quantity and quality of economic resources changes over time, as does the way in which they are combined. These changes bring about changes in the productive potential of an economy.

Causes of shifts in the LRAS curve include:
● education and training which raises the skills of the workforce and levels of productivity (output per worker);
● investment in capital equipment which raises the stock of physical capital and hence pushes out the production possibility boundary;
● technological advances which allow new products to be made or existing products to be produced with fewer resources;
● increased world specialisation through international trade which allows production to be located in the cheapest and most efficient place in the world economy;

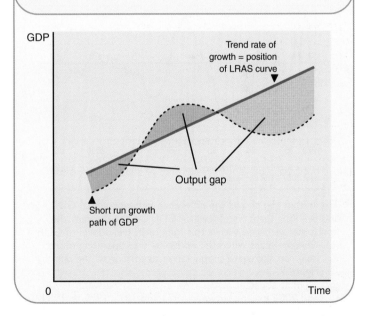

Figure 5 *The trend rate of growth for an economy*
At any point in time, the level of output shown by the long run aggregate supply is on the line of the trend rate of growth of output.

● improved work practices, such as just-in-time production which increase the productivity of both labour and capital;
● changes in government policy, such as the removal of unnecessary business regulation, which increases the efficiency of firms.

Figure 6 shows how a growth in potential output is drawn on an aggregate supply diagram. Assume that the education and skills of the workforce increase. This should lead to labour becoming more productive, in turn leading to an increase in the productive potential of the economy at full employment. The long run aggregate supply curve

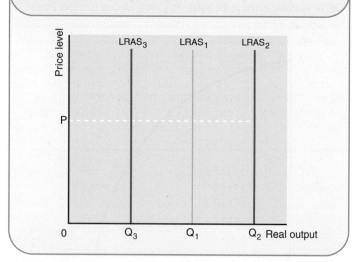

will then shift from $LRAS_1$ to $LRAS_2$, showing that at a given level of prices, the economy can produce more output. A fall in potential output, caused for instance by a fall in the size of the labour force, would be shown by a leftward shift in the curve, from $LRAS_1$ to $LRAS_3$.

A shift to the right in the LRAS curve shows that there has been economic growth. On a production possibility frontier (PPF) diagram, it would be represented by a movement outwards on the boundary. In Figure 5, it would be shown by a movement up along the trend rate of growth line. A shift to the left in the LRAS curve would show that the productive potential of the economy has fallen. On a PPF diagram, the boundary would shift inwards. On a trend rate of growth diagram, there would be a movement along and down the trend rate of growth line.

The classical and Keynesian long run aggregate supply curves

The vertical LRAS curve is called the **classical long run aggregate supply curve**. It is based on the classical view that markets tend to correct themselves fairly quickly when they are pushed into disequilibrium by some shock. In the long run, product markets like the markets for oil, cameras or meals out, and factor markets like the market for labour, will be in equilibrium. If all markets are in equilibrium, there can be no unemployed resources. Hence, the economy must be operating at full capacity on its production possibility boundary.

Keynesian economists, however, point out that there have been times when markets have failed to clear for long periods of time. Keynesian economics was developed out of the experience of the Great Depression of the 1930s when large scale unemployment lasted for a decade. If it had not been for the Second World War, it could be that high unemployment would have lasted for twenty or thirty years. John Maynard Keynes famously said that 'in the long run we are all dead'. There is little point in studying and drawing

Figure 7 *Output gap estimates*

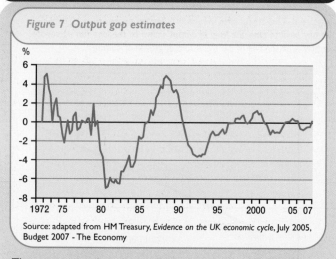

Source: adapted from HM Treasury, *Evidence on the UK economic cycle*, July 2005, Budget 2007 - The Economy

The output gap shows the difference between actual GDP and the long term trend level of GDP. On the diagram, the horizontal zero line shows this long term trend level of GDP.
(a) Give six years when the economy was operating on its long run aggregate supply curve, according to the data in Figure 7.
(b) GDP at constant prices rose every year between 1972 and 2004 except between 1973 and 1975, 1979 to 1983 and 1990 to 1992. Using a diagram, explain what happened to the long run aggregate supply curve between the six years given in your answer to (a).
(c) The economy experienced deep recessions between 1973 and 1975, 1979 and 1983, and 1990 to 1992. In these recessions, manufacturing suffered particularly badly, with many factories closing, never to reopen again, and some workers became deskilled, resulting in their inability ever to find another job in their working lifetime. Using a diagram, explain what might have happened to the long run aggregate supply curve for the UK economy in these years.

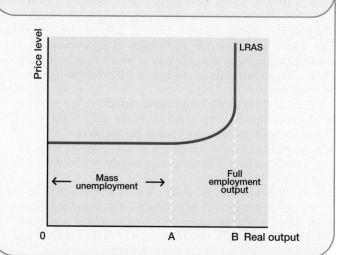

vertical long run aggregate supply curves if it takes 20-30 years to get back to the curve when the economy suffers a demand side or supply side shock.

Keynesian economists therefore suggest that the long run aggregate supply curve is the shape shown in Figure 8.

- At an output level of OB, the LRAS curve is vertical as with the classical LRAS curve. OB is the full capacity level of output of the economy. It is when the economy is on its production possibility boundary.
- At an output level below OA, the economy is in a deep and prolonged depression. There is mass unemployment. In theory, unemployment should lead to wages falling. If there is too

much supply of labour, the price of labour will fall. However, in a modern economy, there are many reasons why wages are **sticky downwards**. There might be a national minimum wage which sets a floor for wages. Trade unions might fight to maintain wage levels. High unemployment might persist in one area of the country when there is full employment in another area because of labour immobility. Firms may not want to lower wages because this could demotivate their staff and lead to lower productivity. So at output levels below OA, markets, and in particular the labour market, fail to clear. Firms can hire and fire extra workers without affecting the wage rate. Wages are stuck and there is persistent disequilibrium in the long run. Hence, there is no pressure on prices when output expands.

- At an output level between OA and OB, labour is becoming scarce enough for an increase in demand for labour to push up wages. This then leads to a higher price level. The nearer output gets to OB, the full employment level of output, the greater the effect of an increase in demand for labour on wages and therefore the price level.

Question 4

A survey by analyst IDS claims that an increasing number of companies now have their lowest pay rate set at the level of the minimum wage. The report states that increases in the National Minimum Wage (NMW) have 'had a widespread impact on a broad range of lower paying organisations', with 55 per cent of retail chains now setting their lowest rate of pay at £5.05 an hour, the NMW. This is an increase on last year when the figure was 45 per cent of retail chains.

The National Minimum Wage is also affecting pay structures, with wages rises being given to workers on above the minimum wage when the government raises the actual minimum wage. The IDS survey found that two-thirds of employers in the hotels sector had been directly affected by the latest rise in the NMW.

However, the report said that 'Estimates by economists in the mid-1990s that up to 1.7 million jobs would be lost if a minimum wage were to be introduced now look very wide of the mark.' In fact 'despite NMW increases running ahead of both inflation and average earnings over the past three years, there has been no negative employment effect. Employment in lower paying sectors such as retail, restaurants, hospitality and leisure has been growing.'

In contrast, earlier this month the British Retail Consortium called for a 'fundamental review' of the aims of the NMW, claiming that the proposed increase in October 2006 could lead to around 35 000 jobs losses in the retail sector. It claims that retailers 'simply cannot go on absorbing further increases in their fixed costs - of which labour is one of the biggest.'

Source: adapted from http://news.viewlondon.co.uk.

(a) Explain why a national minimum wage might (i) prevent the labour market from clearing and (ii) lead to a long run aggregate supply curve (LRAS) which is not vertical.
(b) Explain whether the data support the view that in the UK the national minimum wage prevents the LRAS curve from being vertical.

Key terms

Aggregate supply curve - the relationship between the average level of prices in the economy and the level of total output.
Full capacity - the level of output where no extra production can take in the long run with existing resources. The full capacity level of output for an economy is shown by the classical long run aggregate supply curve.
Long run aggregate supply curve - the aggregate supply curve which assumes that wage rates are variable, both upward and downwards. Classical or supply side economists assume that wage rates are flexible. Keynesian economists assume that wage rates may be 'sticky downwards' and hence the economy may operate at less than full employment even in the long run.
Short run aggregate supply curve - the upward sloping aggregate supply curve which assumes that money wage rates are fixed.
Supply side shocks - factors such as changes in wage rates or commodity prices which cause the short run aggregate supply curve to shift.

Applied economics

The case of oil

As Figure 9 shows, in 1973 a barrel of oil cost $2.83. A year later the price had risen to $10.41. This price rise was possibly the most important world economic event of the 1970s. The trigger for the rise came from a war - the Yom Kippur war - when Egypt attacked Israel and was subsequently defeated. The Arab nations, to show support for Egypt, decreed that they would cut off oil supplies from any country which openly supported Israel. Because the demand for oil in the short run is highly price inelastic, any small fall in the supply of oil is enough to bring large increases in prices. After the war finished, the oil producing nations through their organisation OPEC (the Organisation for Petroleum Exporting Countries) realised that it was possible to maintain a high price for oil by limiting its supply (i.e. by operating a cartel). Since then OPEC has operated a policy of restricting the supply of oil to the market.

Oil prices rose rather more slowly between 1974 and 1978. However, between 1978 and 1982 the average price of a barrel of oil rose from $13.03 to $31.80.

Again, a political event was a major factor in triggering the price rise. The Shah of Iran, ruler of an important oil producing country, was deposed by Muslim fundamentalists led by the Ayatollah Khomeini. The revolution plunged Iran into economic chaos and the new rulers, fiercely anti-Western, showed little interest in resuming large scale exports of oil. A small disruption in oil supplies, a situation exploited by OPEC, was again enough to send oil prices spiralling.

In 1990, Iraq invaded Kuwait but was expelled in the Gulf War of 1991. This produced a short lived spike in oil prices but oil prices subsequently fell and by 1998, averaged only $12.21 a barrel. Cutting production quotas enabled OPEC to raise prices again to over $20 a barrel. However, from 2003 to 2005, another boom in oil prices occurred with oil prices at times reaching over $100 a barrel. The main cause of this boom was the relentless increase in demand for oil by fast growing Asian countries, particularly China. Underinvestment by OPEC countries in their oil production facilities over a twenty year period meant that, by 2005, the world oil industry was operating at maximum capacity. Increases in demand could only push prices up.

These three periods of sharp oil price rises all had an important effect on the short run aggregate supply curve of the UK economy. Oil price rises increase the costs of firms. So at any given level of output, firms need to charge higher prices to cover their costs. As a result, the short run aggregate supply curve shifts upwards. The oil price rises of 1973-75 and 1979-81 were a major contributor to the rises in inflation at the time shown in Figure 10. Significantly, though, the oil price increase from 2003 had very little impact on inflation. One reason was that the average amount of

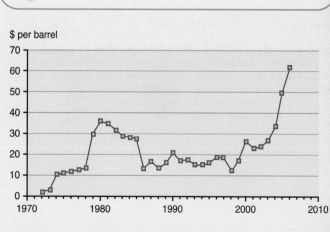

Figure 9 Price of oil

$ per barrel

Source: adapted from *BP Statistical Review of World Energy*.

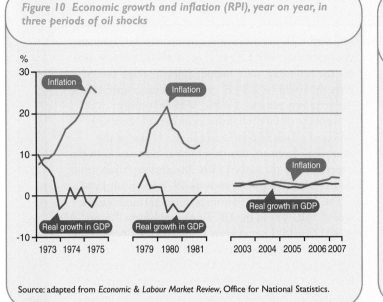

Figure 10 *Economic growth and inflation (RPI), year on year, in three periods of oil shocks*

Source: adapted from *Economic & Labour Market Review*, Office for National Statistics.

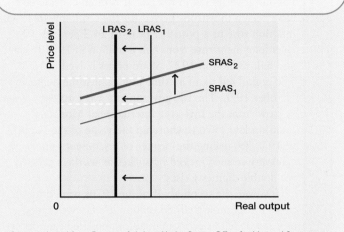

Figure 11 *The effect of steep rises in oil prices on aggregate supply*
A large rise in the price of oil will push the short run aggregate supply curve upwards and possibly shift the long run aggregate supply curve to the left.

Source: adapted from *Economic & Labour Market Review*, Office for National Statistics.

oil used to generate £1 of GDP was far less during this period than in 1975 or 1981. Greater energy efficiency and the decline of manufacturing industry were the main reasons for this. Another reason for the small impact of the oil price rise was that UK firms found it much more difficult to pass on price rises to their customers than in 1975 or 1981. The economic climate was more competitive and firms tended to absorb oil prices rather than pass them on.

Many economists argue that the oil price rises of 1973-75 and 1979-1981 also reduced the productive potential of the UK economy, shifting the long run aggregate supply curve to the left, as shown in Figure 11. The rise in oil prices meant that some capital equipment which was oil intensive became uneconomic to run. This equipment was mothballed and then scrapped, leading to a once-and-for-all fall in the amount of capital in the economy. Because the economy was far less oil dependent in 2003-2007, this scrapping of equipment was negligible. Firms had become reluctant to invest in equipment using oil when there were good substitutes because they were afraid of a large rise in oil prices.

DataQuestion

Aggregate supply, 1974-79

Between February 1974 and May 1979, there was a Labour government in the UK. It is often considered to have been a disastrous period for the economy. In 1975, inflation rose to a post-war peak of 24.2 per cent. Unemployment rose from half a million in 1974 to one and half million in 1977. Share prices halved in 1974. The pound fell to an all time low against the dollar in October 1976. The UK government was forced to borrow from the IMF (the International Monetary Fund) in late 1976 to shore up the value of the pound. In 1978-79, during the 'winter of discontent', the economy seemed racked by strikes as workers pressed for double digit pay rises.

However, the second half of the 1970s were difficult times for all industrialised economies. Growth rates worldwide fell as economies accommodated the supply-side shock of the first oil crisis in 1973-4. Table 1 shows that the growth in real GDP in the UK economy was above its long run trend rate of growth of 2.5 per cent per annum in three of the six years during the period;

and although the average yearly growth rate over the six years was only 1.5 per cent, if 1973, a boom year for the economy, were included, the average rate of growth would be 2.3 per cent. Investment spending in the economy remained static, with investment as a percentage of GDP slightly declining. This perhaps reflected a lack of confidence in the future of the economy. Even so, this should be contrasted with the experience of the early 1980s. Investment fell in 1980 and 1981 and did not reach its 1979 levels till 1984.

The 1970s were inflationary times throughout the world. Inflation in the UK accelerated from 7.5 per cent in 1972 to 15.9 per cent in 1974 and 24.1 per cent in 1975. However, the government adopted firm anti-inflationary policies in 1975 and inflation subsequently fell to 8.3 per cent in 1978, before rising again to 13.4 per cent in 1979 as pressure from wages and import prices, including the second round of oil price rises, worsened.

Table 1   Selected economic indicators, UK 1974-79

	Real growth in GDP	Gross investment	Inflation (RPI)	Change in import prices	Change in average earnings
	%	% of GDP	%	%	%
1974	-1.5	14.8	15.9	46.2	18.5
1975	-0.6	14.6	24.1	14.1	26.6
1976	2.8	14.4	16.6	22.3	15.9
1977	2.4	13.9	15.9	15.8	8.8
1978	3.2	13.8	8.3	3.8	13.2
1979	2.8	13.8	13.4	6.4	15.2

Source: adapted from *Economic Trends Annual Supplement*, Office for National Statistics.

1. Consider both the passage and the table carefully. Discuss, using diagrams, what happened to aggregate supply in the second half of the 1970s: (a) in the short run and (b) in the long run.

Summary

1. The economy is in equilibrium when aggregate demand equals aggregate supply.
2. In the short run, equilibrium occurs when aggregate demand equals short run aggregate supply.
3. In the classical model, where wages are completely flexible, the economy will be in long run equilibrium at full employment. In the Keynesian model, where wages are sticky downwards, the economy can be in long run equilibrium at less than full employment.
4. In the classical model, a rise in aggregate demand will in the short run lead to an increase in both output and prices, but in the long run the rise will generate only an increase in prices. In the Keynesian model, a rise in aggregate demand will be purely inflationary if the economy is at full employment, but will lead to an increase in output if the economy is below full employment.
5. A rise in long run aggregate supply in the classical model will both increase output and reduce prices. Keynesians would agree with this in general, but would argue that an increase in aggregate supply will have no effect on output or prices if the economy is in a slump.
6. Factors which affect aggregate demand may well affect aggregate supply and vice versa, although this may occur over different time periods. For instance, an increase in investment is likely to increase both aggregate demand and aggregate supply.

Equilibrium output in the short run

The previous two units outlined theories of aggregate demand and aggregate supply. Both Keynesian and classical economists agree that in the short run the aggregate demand curve is downward sloping whilst the aggregate supply curve is upward sloping. The equilibrium level of output in the short run occurs at the intersection of the aggregate demand and aggregate supply curves. In Figure 1, the equilibrium level of income and output is 0Q. The equilibrium price level is 0P.

An increase in aggregate demand will shift the aggregate demand curve to the right. Aggregate demand is made up of consumption, investment, government spending and export minus imports. So an increase in aggregate demand will result from an increase in one of these components. For example:
- a fall in interest rates will raise both consumption and investment;

- a fall in the exchange rate will boost exports and reduce imports;
- a lowering of income tax will raise consumption because households will now have higher disposable income.

Figure 2 shows the impact of a rise in aggregate demand on equilibrium output and the price level. The aggregate demand curve shifts from AD_1 to AD_2. Equilibrium output then rises from $0Q_1$ to $0Q_2$ whilst the price level rises from $0P_1$ to $0P_2$. A rise in aggregate demand therefore increases both real output and the price level in the short run. The opposite is also true. A fall in aggregate demand will lead both to a fall in real output and a fall in the price level.

A fall in short run aggregate supply will shift the SRAS curve upwards and to the left. A variety of factors could bring about a fall in short run aggregate supply. For example:
- wages of workers might rise;

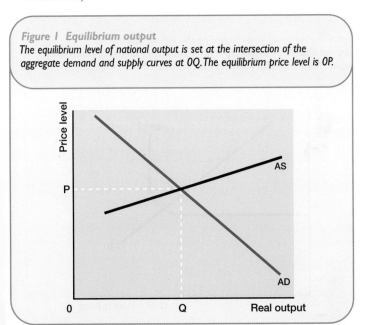

Figure 1 Equilibrium output
The equilibrium level of national output is set at the intersection of the aggregate demand and supply curves at 0Q. The equilibrium price level is 0P.

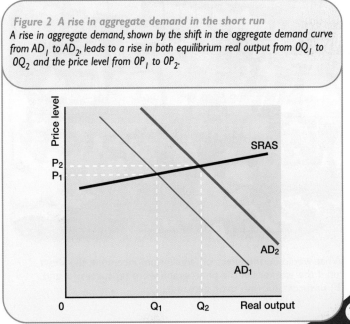

Figure 2 A rise in aggregate demand in the short run
A rise in aggregate demand, shown by the shift in the aggregate demand curve from AD_1 to AD_2, leads to a rise in both equilibrium real output from $0Q_1$ to $0Q_2$ and the price level from $0P_1$ to $0P_2$.

Figure 3 A fall in aggregate supply in the short run

A fall in short run aggregate supply, shown by the shift in the SRAS curve from $SRAS_1$ to $SRAS_2$, leads to a fall in equilibrium real output from $0Q_1$ to $0Q_2$ and a rise in the price level from $0P_1$ to $0P_2$.

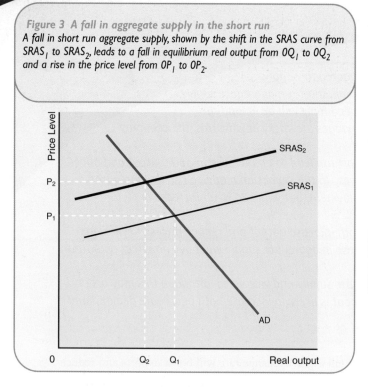

Figure 4 Long run equilibrium in the classical model

Long run equilibrium output is $0Q$, the full employment level of output, since wages are flexible both downwards as well as upwards.

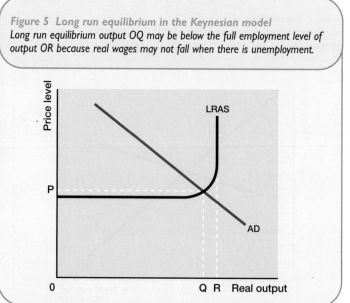

is also true. A rise in aggregate supply, shown by a downward shift to the right of the SRAS curve, will lead to a rise in equilibrium output and a fall in the price level.

Equilibrium output in the long run

In the long run, the impact of changes in aggregate demand and supply are affected by the shape of the long run aggregate supply curve. Classical economists argue that in the long run the aggregate supply curve is vertical, as shown in Figure 4. Long run equilibrium occurs where the long run aggregate supply curve (LRAS) intersects with the aggregate demand curve. Hence equilibrium output is $0Q$ and the equilibrium price level is $0P$. Associated with the long run equilibrium price level is a short run aggregate supply curve (SRAS) which passes through the point where LRAS = AD. The long run aggregate supply curve shows the supply curve for the economy at full employment. Hence there can be no unemployment in the long run according to classical economists.

- raw material prices might go up;
- taxes on goods and services might be raised by the government.

Figure 3 shows the impact of a fall in aggregate supply on equilibrium output and the price level. The SRAS curve shifts from $SRAS_1$ to $SRAS_2$. Equilibrium output then falls from $0Q_1$ to $0Q_2$. At the same time, the price level rises from $0P_1$ to $0P_2$. A fall in short run aggregate supply therefore leads to a fall in output but a rise in the price level in the short run. The opposite

Question 1

What would be the effect on equilibrium income in the short run if the workers in the photograph were (a) successful and (b) unsuccessful with their demands?

Figure 5 Long run equilibrium in the Keynesian model

Long run equilibrium output OQ may be below the full employment level of output OR because real wages may not fall when there is unemployment.

Keynesian economists argue that the long run aggregate supply curve is as shown in Figure 5. The economy is at full employment where the LRAS curve is vertical at output OR - a point of agreement with classical economists. However, the economy can be in equilibrium at less than full employment. In Figure 5 the equilibrium level of output is OQ where the AD curve cuts the LRAS curve. The key point of disagreement between classical and Keynesian economists is the extent to which workers react to unemployment by accepting real wage cuts.

Classical economists argue that a rise in unemployment will lead rapidly to cuts in real wages. These cuts will increase the demand for labour and reduce its supply, returning the economy to full employment quickly and automatically. Keynesian economists, on the other hand, argue that money wages are sticky downwards. Workers will refuse to take money wage cuts and will fiercely resist cuts in their real wage. The labour market will therefore not clear except perhaps over a very long period of time, so long that it is possibly even not worth considering.

Having outlined a theory of equilibrium output, it is now possible to see what happens if either aggregate demand or aggregate supply changes.

A rise in aggregate demand

Assume that there is a rise in aggregate demand in the economy with long run aggregate supply initially remaining unchanged. For instance, there may be an increase in the wages of public sector employees paid for by an increase in the money supply, or there may be a fall in the marginal propensity to save and a rise in the marginal propensity to consume. A rise in aggregate demand will push the AD curve to the right. The classical and Keynesian models give different conclusions about the effect of this.

The classical model A rise in aggregate demand, in the classical model, will lead to a rise in the price level but no change in real output in the long run. In Figure 6, the aggregate demand curve shifts to the right from AD_1 to AD_2. This could have been

Question 2

In his Budget of 1981, with unemployment at 3 million and still rising, the Chancellor of the Exchequer, Geoffrey Howe, raised the level of taxes and significantly reduced the budget deficit in order to squeeze inflationary pressures. In a letter to *The Times*, 364 economists protested at what they saw as the perversity of this decision.

(a) Geoffrey Howe was influenced by classical economic thinking. Using a diagram, explain why he believed that his policy (i) would help reduce inflation and (ii) not lead to any increase in unemployment.
(b) The economists who wrote the letter to The Times could broadly be described as Keynesian. Using a diagram, explain why they believed that it was folly to increase taxes at a time when the economy was in the grip of the worst recession since the 1930s.

caused by a fall in interest rates, for example. The equilibrium price level rises from $0P_1$ to $0P_2$ but equilibrium real output remains the same at $0Q$. In the classical model, no amount of extra demand will raise long run equilibrium output. This is because the long run aggregate supply curve shows the maximum productive capacity of the economy at that point in time.

The movement from one equilibrium point to the next can also be shown on an AD/AS diagram. Assume there is a rise in aggregate demand, which shifts the aggregate demand curve from AD_1 to AD_2. In the short run, this will result in a movement up the SRAS curve. In Figure 7, output will rise from 0L to 0M and this will be accompanied by a small rise in the price level from 0N to 0P. This will move the economy from A to B.

However, the economy is now in long run disequilibrium. The full employment level of output is 0L, shown by the position of the long run aggregate supply curve. The economy is therefore

---

Figure 6 *A rise in aggregate demand in the classical model*
A rise in aggregate demand in the long run will shift the aggregate demand curve from AD_1 to AD_2. The equilibrium price level will rise from $0P_1$ to $0P_2$ but there will be no change in equilibrium real output..

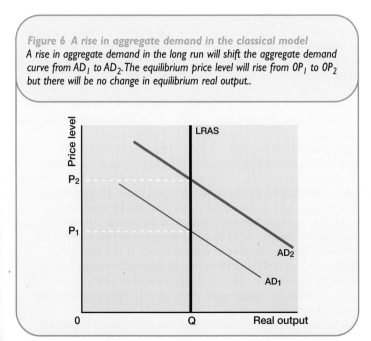

Figure 7 *The classical model in the short and long run*
A rise in aggregate demand shown by a shift to the right in the AD curve will result in a movement along the SRAS curve. Both output and prices will increase. In the long run, the SRAS curve will shift upwards with long run equilibrium being re-established at C. The rise in demand has led only to a rise in the price level.

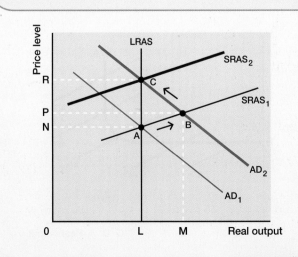

operating at over-full employment. Firms will find it difficult to recruit labour, buy raw materials and find new offices or factory space. They will respond by bidding up wages and other costs. The short run aggregate supply curve is drawn on the assumption that wage rates and other costs remain constant. So a rise in wage rates will shift the short run aggregate supply curve upwards. Short run equilibrium output will now fall and prices will keep rising. The economy will only return to long run equilibrium when the short run aggregate supply curve has shifted upwards from $SRAS_1$ to $SRAS_2$ so that aggregate demand once again equals long run aggregate supply at C.

The conclusion of the classical model is that increases in aggregate demand will initially increase both prices and output (the movement from A to B in Figure 7). Over time prices will continue to rise but output will fall as the economy moves back towards long run equilibrium (the movement from B to C). In the long term an increase in aggregate demand will only lead to an increase in the price level (from A to C). There will be no effect on equilibrium output. So increases in aggregate demand without any change in long run aggregate supply are purely inflationary.

The Keynesian model In the Keynesian model, the long run aggregate supply curve is shaped as in Figure 8. Keynesians would agree with classical economists that an increase in aggregate demand from, say, AD_4 to AD_5 will be purely inflationary if the economy is already at full employment at 0D.

But if the economy is in deep depression, as was the case in the UK during the early 1930s, an increase in aggregate demand will lead to a rise in output without an increase in prices. The shift in aggregate demand from AD_1 to AD_2 will increase equilibrium output from 0A to 0B without raising the price level from 0P as there are unused resources available.

The third possibility is that the economy is a little below full employment, for instance at 0C in Figure 8. Then a rise in aggregate demand from AD_3 to AD_4 will increase both equilibrium output and equilibrium prices.

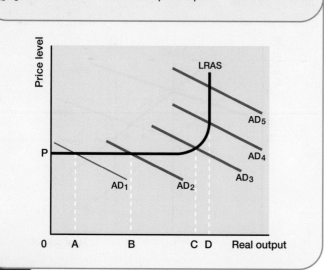

Figure 8 The Keynesian model
If the economy is already at full employment, an increase in aggregate demand in the Keynesian model creates an inflationary gap without increasing output. In a depression, an increase in aggregate demand will increase output but not prices. If the economy is slightly below full employment, an increase in aggregate demand will increase both output and prices.

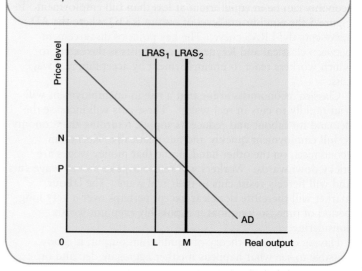

Figure 9 An increase in aggregate supply in the classical model
A shift to the right of the LRAS curve will both increase equilibrium output and reduce the price level.

In the Keynesian model, increases in aggregate demand may or may not be effective in raising equilibrium output. It depends upon whether the economy is below full employment or at full employment.

A rise in long run aggregate supply

A rise in long run aggregate supply means that the potential output of the economy has increased (i.e. there has been genuine economic growth). Rises in long run aggregate supply which are unlikely to shift the aggregate demand curve might occur if, for instance, incentives to work increased or there was a change in technology.

The classical model In the classical model, an increase in long run aggregate supply will lead to both higher output and lower prices. In Figure 9 a shift in the aggregate supply curve from $LRAS_1$ to $LRAS_2$ will increase equilibrium output from OL to OM. Equilibrium prices will also fall from ON to OP. Contrast this conclusion with what happens when aggregate demand is increased in the classical model - a rise in prices with no increase in output. It is not surprising that classical economists are so strongly in favour of **supply side policies** (this is why they are often referred to as 'supply side' economists).

The Keynesian model In the Keynesian model, shown in Figure 10, an increase in aggregate supply will both increase output and reduce prices if the economy is at full employment. With aggregate demand at AD_1, a shift in the aggregate supply curve from $LRAS_1$ to $LRAS_2$ increases full employment equilibrium output from Y_E to Y_F. If the economy is at slightly less than full employment, with an aggregate demand curve of AD_2, then the shift to the right in the LRAS curve will still be beneficial to the economy, increasing output and reducing prices. However, Keynesians disagree with classical economists that supply side measures can be effective in a depression. If the aggregate demand curve is AD_3, an increase in aggregate supply has no effect on equilibrium output. It remains obstinately stuck at Y_D. Only an increase in aggregate demand will move the economy out of depression.

It is now possible to understand one of the most important

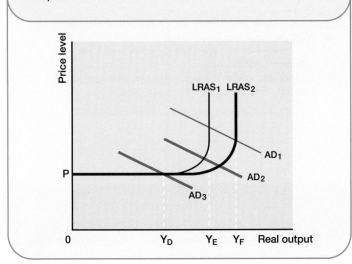

Figure 10 An increase in aggregate supply in the Keynesian model
The effect of an increase in long run aggregate supply depends upon the position of the aggregate demand curve. If the economy is at or near full employment, an increase will raise output and lower prices. However, if the economy is in depression at Y_D*, an increase in LRAS will have no impact on the economy.*

controversies in the history of economics. During the 1930s, classical economists argued that the only way to put the millions of unemployed during the Great Depression back to work was to adopt supply side measures - such as cutting unemployment benefits, reducing trade union power and cutting marginal tax rates and government spending. John Maynard Keynes attacked this orthodoxy by suggesting that the depression was caused by a lack of demand and suggesting that it was the government's responsibility to increase the level of aggregate demand. The same debate was replayed in the UK in the early 1980s. This time it was Keynesians who represented orthodoxy. They suggested that the only quick way to get the millions officially unemployed back to work was to expand aggregate demand. In the Budget of 1981, the government did precisely the opposite - it cut its projected budget deficit, reducing aggregate demand and argued that the only way to cure unemployment was to improve the supply side of the economy.

Question 3

In June 1995, a new French government unveiled a stiff budget designed to reduce high unemployment levels by 700 000 and bring down a high budget deficit from 5.7 per cent of GDP to 5.1 per cent of GDP within the fiscal year. The measures included:

- a substantial FF19bn cut in government spending affecting all ministries apart from justice and culture, with defence bearing nearly 50 per cent of the cuts;
- a rise in corporation tax from 33.3 per cent to 36.6 per cent;
- a rise in the standard rate of VAT from 18.6 per cent to 20.6 per cent;
- a 10 per cent rise in wealth tax;
- a 40 per cent cut in employment taxes paid by firms on employment of workers at or near the minimum wage level;
- new programmes targeted particularly at youth in difficulties, offering training, apprenticeship and other policies to bring people into the workforce;
- a rise in the minimum wage by 4 per cent;
- a rise in state pensions by 0.5 per cent;
- measures to stimulate the housing market, particularly focused on lodgings for people on lower incomes.

Using diagrams, explain what effect these measures would have on aggregate supply according to:
(a) classical or supply side economists,
(b) Keynesian economists.

Increasing aggregate demand and supply

In microeconomics, factors which shift the demand curve do **not** shift the supply curve as well and vice versa. For instance, an increase in the costs of production shifts the supply curve but does **not** shift the demand curve for a good (although there will of course be a **movement along** the demand curve as a result). However, in macroeconomic aggregate demand and aggregate supply analysis, factors which shift one curve may well shift the other curve as well. For instance, assume that firms increase their planned investment. This will increase the level of aggregate demand. However, in the long run it will also increase the level of aggregate supply. An increase in investment will increase the capital stock of the economy. The productive potential of the economy will therefore rise. We can use aggregate demand and supply analysis to show the effects of an increase in investment.

An increase in investment in the classical model will initially shift the aggregate demand curve in Figure 11 to the right from AD_1 to AD_2. There will then be a movement along the short run aggregate supply curve from A to B. There is now long run disequilibrium. How this will be resolved depends upon the speed with which the investment is brought on stream and starts to produce goods and services. Assume that this happens fairly quickly. The long run aggregate supply curve will then shift to the right, say, from $LRAS_1$ to $LRAS_2$. Long run equilibrium will

Figure 11 An increase in investment expenditure
An increase in investment will increase aggregate demand from AD_1 *to* AD_2*, and is likely to shift the long run aggregate supply curve from* $LRAS_1$ *to* $LRAS_2$*. The result is an increase in output and a small fall in prices.*

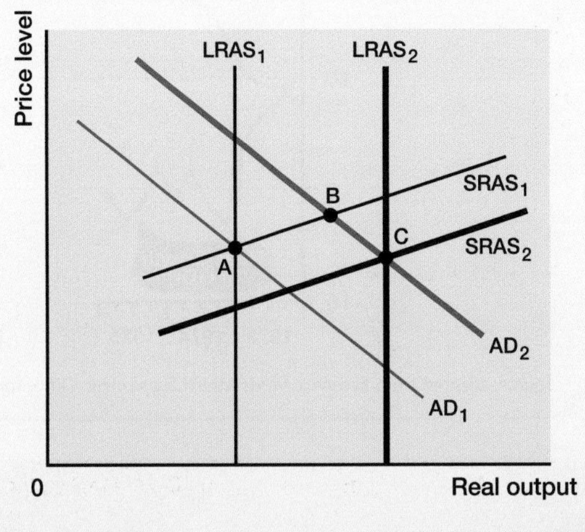

be restored at C. Output has increased and the price level fallen slightly. There will also be a new short run aggregate supply curve, SRAS$_2$. It is below the original short run aggregate supply curve because it is assumed that investment has reduced costs of production.

Not all investment results in increased production. For instance, fitting out a new shop which goes into receivership within a few months will increase aggregate demand but not long run aggregate supply. The long run aggregate supply curve will therefore not shift and the increased investment will only be inflationary. Equally, investment might be poorly directed. The increase in aggregate demand might be greater than the increase in long run aggregate supply. Here there will be an increase in equilibrium output but there will also be an increase in prices. The extent to which investment increases output and contributes to a lessening of inflationary pressure depends upon the extent to which it gives a high rate of return in the long run.

Question 4

Using a classical model of the economy, explain the effect of the following on: (i) aggregate demand; (ii) short run aggregate supply; (iii) output and prices in the long run.
(a) A 10 per cent rise in earnings.
(b) An increase in real spending by government on education and training.
(c) An increase in the average long term real rate of interest from 3 per cent to 5 per cent.

Applied economics

Stagflation, 1974-76, 1979-1981 and 1988-1990

In a simple Keynesian model, rising inflation is associated with falling unemployment and vice versa. The experience of the 1950s and 1960s tended to support the hypothesis that there was this trade off between the two variables. However, in 1973-75, 1979-1981 and 1988-91 there were both rising inflation and rising unemployment, as shown in Figure 12. This combination of stagnation and inflation came to be called **stagflation**.

The stagflation of the first two of these periods was caused by a large rise in oil prices, an example of an external supply side shock to the economy. The rise had the effect of raising the short run aggregate supply curve from SRAS$_1$ to SRAS$_2$ in Figure 13. The economy shifted from A to B. As can be seen from the diagram, prices rose and output fell.

In the first oil crisis, inflation rose from 9.1 per cent in 1973 to 15.9 per cent in 1974 and 24.1 per cent in 1975, before falling back to 16.5 per cent in 1976. Real GDP on the other hand fell by 1.5 per cent in 1974 and 0.8 per cent in 1975, before resuming an upward path in 1976.

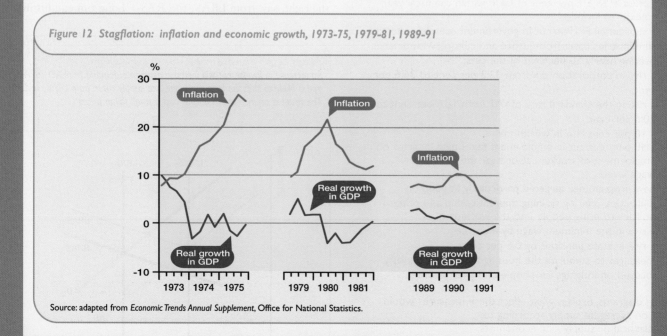

Figure 12 *Stagflation: inflation and economic growth, 1973-75, 1979-81, 1989-91*

Source: adapted from *Economic Trends Annual Supplement*, Office for National Statistics.

In the second oil crisis, inflation rose from 8.3 per cent in 1978 to 13.4 per cent in 1979 and 18.0 per cent in 1980, before falling back again in 1981. Real GDP fell by 2 per cent in 1980 and 1.2 per cent in 1981.

The classical model would suggest that, all other things being equal, the economy would fall back to A from B. Full employment would be restored at the old price level. The above figures indicate that this did not happen. This was because the aggregate demand curve shifted to the right at the same time as the short run aggregate supply curve was shifting to the left. This led to continued inflation as output rose from 1976 and again from 1982. The rise in aggregate demand in the first period was partly due to the then Labour government increasing the budget deficit, as well as increases in the money supply (the inflation was **accommodated**). Treasury estimates of the output gap suggest that the economy returned to its long run productive potential, at C in Figure 35.10, in 1978. In the second period, 1979-1981, taxation rose and government spending fell during the downturn in the economy, although the money supply increased again. This difference in fiscal stance is a partial explanation of why the rise in unemployment was lower and the rise in inflation higher in the first period than in the second period. It can be argued that the shift to the right in the aggregate demand curve was greater in the mid-1970s than in the early 1980s.

The result was that the economy took much longer to return to the point C on its LRAS curve in this second period. Treasury estimates of the output gap suggest this did not occur until 1986.

The period of stagflation between 1988 and 1990 was different from the two previous periods. This was caused, not by a supply side shock but by a demand side shock. The Conservative government was partly responsible for stoking up an unsustainable boom in 1986-88, called the 'Lawson boom' after Nigel Lawson, the Chancellor of the Exchequer at the time. When inflation began to rise, it reacted by raising interest rates from 7.5 per cent in May 1988 to 15 per cent in October 1989 and keeping them at those levels for nearly a year. This, together with a high value of the pound, produced a prolonged recession lasting through to the end of 1992 despite the fact that inflation peaked in the 3rd quarter of 1990. The economy did not return to production on the LRAS curve until 1997.

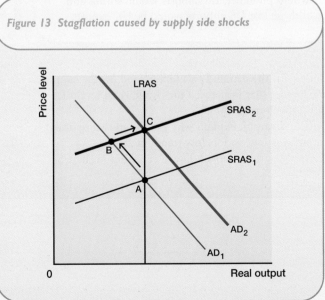
Oil crises have led to inflation.

In all three periods of stagflation, the long run aggregate supply curve was probably still shifting to the right. The productive potential of the economy was increasing despite the actual fall in GDP being recorded. However, some economists argue that these periods of stagflation destroyed some of that productive potential. Capital equipment became redundant through lack of demand and was scrapped. Workers became long term unemployed, deskilled and demotivated, some never to work again. On this argument, stagflation is responsible for slowing down the growth of the productive potential of the economy. So the long run aggregate supply curve shifts less quickly to the right, leading to permanently lower equilibrium output and a higher price level.

Figure 13 *Stagflation caused by supply side shocks*

DataQuestion

The UK economy, 2005-06

Disappointing year for the economy

2005 has not been a boom year for the economy. Economic growth has been below trend whilst unemployment has very slightly risen. The housing market has been subdued, with average house price rises of a 'mere' 5 per cent, even if 5 per cent is arguably the right long term rate of growth of house prices. Consumers have not been increasing their spending as much as in previous years, hit by a variety of factors including higher interest rates, higher petrol prices and higher gas and electricity bills.

2005 could have been worse

At the same time, 2005 could have been much worse. Oil prices rising at times to over $60 a barrel, nearly twice the price of 12 months earlier, could have sparked off much higher inflation, as indeed it did in the 1970s. The same rising oil prices and the general steep rise in world commodity prices could have sparked a recession in the world wide economy, causing Britain's exports to slump and sending it too into a recession. Consumers could have taken real fright at deteriorating economic conditions and decided to cut back on their borrowing and increase their saving by considerably reducing their spending. The US economy, with its huge imbalances, could have suddenly gone into recession. It remains extremely vulnerable to overseas lenders which are financing the US current account deficit of over 5 per cent of GDP. If that finance dried up, the value of the dollar would plummet, US imports would shrink and some of those lost US imports would be UK exports.

Dangers for 2006

Dangers remain for 2006. The greatest danger is probably external, from a world recession. However, British consumers could cut back on their spending. The government is fortunately in the middle of a large expansion of public spending and has proved reluctant to increase its taxes too much to pay for it. So the government sector should provide a positive boost to GDP. With luck, it will be enough to keep the output gap close to zero and the economy on course.

1. Outline (a) the demand side factors and (b) the supply side factors that influenced the equilibrium level of national output in 2005.
2. Using a diagram, explain why the rise in real national output was low and 'below trend' in 2005.
3. Using a diagram, explain how a recession in the US economy could affect the equilibrium level of real output and the price level of the UK economy.
4. To what extent is it important that the output gap should be 'close to zero' and the economy is kept 'on course'?

Summary

1. Economic growth is the change in potential output of the economy shown by a shift to the right of the production possibility frontier. Economic growth is usually measured by the change in real national income.
2. Economic growth is caused by increases in the quantity or quality of land, labour and capital and by technological progress.

Economic growth

Economies change over time. Part of this change involves changes in productive capacity - the ability to produce goods and services. Increases in productive capacity are known as ECONOMIC GROWTH. Most economies today experience positive economic growth over time. For example, the UK economy is growing at around 2.5 per cent per annum. This means that its productive potential is doubling roughly every 25 years. The Chinese economy is growing at around 10 per cent per annum. This means its productive potential is doubling roughly every 7 years.

The productive potential of an economy can fall as well as rise. Recent wars in Africa, for example, have lead to negative economic growth for some countries. Equally, the collapse of communism in the early 1990s and the move to a market economy for countries like Russia or Poland led initially to a fall in productive potential because of the economic disruption caused.

The production possibility frontier

Production possibility frontiers (PPFs) can be used to discuss economic growth. The PPF shows the maximum or **potential** output of an economy. When the economy grows, the PPF will move outward as in Figure 1. A movement from A to C would be classified as economic growth. However, there may be unemployment in the economy. With a PPF passing through C, a movement from B (where there is unemployment) to C (full employment) would be classified as ECONOMIC RECOVERY rather than economic growth. Hence, an increase in national income does not necessarily mean that there has been economic growth. In practice it is difficult to know exactly the location of an economy's PPF and therefore economists tend to treat all increases in GNP as economic growth.

Figure 1 can also be used to show the conflict between investment and consumption. One major source of economic growth is investment. All other things being equal, the greater the level of investment the higher will be the rate of growth in the future. However, increased production of investment goods can only be achieved by a reduction in the production of consumption goods if the economy is at full employment. So there is a trade off to be made between consumption now and consumption in the future. The lower the level of consumption today relative to the level of investment, the higher will be the level of consumption in the future.

The causes of economic growth

Fluctuations in the level of GDP around the trend rate of growth

are caused by demand and supply side shocks. However, what explains why the productive potential of the economy increases over time?

National output can be increased if there is an increase in the quantity or quality of the inputs to the production process. Output can also be increased if existing inputs are used more efficiently. This can be expressed in terms of a **production function**:

$$\text{Output} = f \text{ (land, labour, capital, technical progress, efficiency)}$$

The remainder of this unit will concentrate on the ways in which the quantity and quality of the factors of production can be increased and on what determines technical progress.

Land

Different countries possess different endowments of land. Land in economics is defined as all natural resources, not just land itself. Some countries, such as Saudi Arabia, have experienced large growth rates almost solely because they are so richly endowed. Without oil, Saudi Arabia today would almost certainly be a poor Third World country. Other countries have received windfalls. The UK, for instance, only started to exploit its oil and gas resources in the mid 1970s. However, most economists argue that the exploitation of raw materials is unlikely to be a significant source of growth in developed economies, although it can be vital in developing economies.

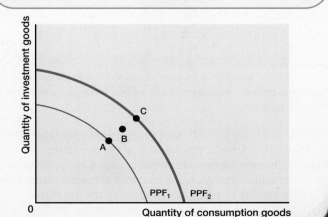

Figure 1 Production possibility frontiers
A movement from A to C would represent economic growth if there were a shift in the production possibility frontier from PPF_1 to PPF_2. A movement from B to C would represent economic recovery if the production possibility frontier was PPF_2.

Question 1

'Garbage jobs' are holding back the Spanish economy. These are jobs which are short term, offer little security and give few benefits. Of the 900 000 jobs created in the Spanish economy last year, two thirds of them carried contracts of six months or less. Temporary contracts now cover more than 35 per cent of all jobs in Spain compared to an EU average of 12 per cent.

On the plus side, the widespread use of temporary contracts has helped Spain more than halve its official unemployment rate since the 1993 recession. There are now officially 60 per cent more people in work compared to 1993.

However, temporary contracts offer little, if any, training. The goal of young people with university degrees is to get a job with a permanent contract, such as a civil service post. This, economists fear, is discouraging young people from being entrepreneurial. Those with a permanent contract don't want to leave their jobs unless it is to take another one offering a permanent contract. This discourages labour mobility and labour flexibility. 'Garbage jobs' have ultimately led to Spain failing to improve its poor labour productivity record compared to the rest of Europe.

Source: adapted from the *Financial Times*, 21.10.2005.

(a) Explain why Spain has an unemployment problem compared to the rest of the Euro area and the USA.
(b) Explain three factors which might have caused Spain to grow less fast than it might otherwise have done in the 1990s and 2000s.

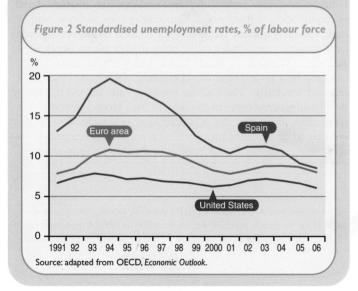

Figure 2 *Standardised unemployment rates, % of labour force*

Source: adapted from OECD, *Economic Outlook*.

Labour

Increasing the **number** of workers in an economy should lead to economic growth. Increases in the labour force can result from three factors.

Changes in demography If more young people enter the workforce than leave it, then the size of the workforce will increase. In most western developed countries the population is relatively stable. Indeed, many countries are experiencing falls in the number of young people entering the workforce because of falls in the birth rate from the late 1960s onwards.

Increases in participation rates Nearly all men who wish to work are in the labour force. However, in most Western countries there exists a considerable pool of women who could be brought into the labour force if employment opportunities were present. In the UK, for instance, almost all of the increase in the labour force in the foreseeable future will result from women returning to or starting work.

Immigration A relatively easy way of increasing the labour force is to employ migrant labour. In the UK, for example, there have been large inward flows of migrant labour from Eastern Europe in recent years. It should be noted that increasing the size of the labour force may increase output but will not necessarily increase economic welfare. One reason is that increased income may have to be shared out amongst more people, causing little or no change in income per person. If women come back to work, they have to give up leisure time to do so. This lessens the increase in economic welfare which they experience.

Increasing the size of the labour force can increase output but increasing the quality of labour input is likely to be far more important in the long run. Labour is not **homogeneous** (i.e. it is not all the same). Workers can be made more productive by education and training. Increases in **human capital** are essential for a number of reasons.

- Workers need to be sufficiently educated to cope with the demands of the existing stock of capital. For instance, it is important for lorry drivers to be able to read, typists to spell and shop assistants to operate tills. These might seem very low grade skills but it requires a considerable educational input to get most of the population up to these elementary levels.
- Workers need to be flexible. On average in the UK, workers are likely to have to change job three times during their lifetime. Increasingly workers are being asked to change roles within existing jobs. Flexibility requires broad general education as well as in-depth knowledge of a particular task.
- Workers need to be able to contribute to change. It is easy to see that scientists and technologists are essential if inventions and new products are to be brought to the market. What is less obvious, but as important, is that every worker can contribute ideas to the improvement of techniques of production. An ability of all workers to take responsibility and solve problems will be increasingly important in the future.

Capital

The stock of capital in the economy needs to increase over time if economic growth is to be sustained. This means that there must be sustained investment in the economy. However, there is not necessarily a correlation between high investment and high growth. Some investment is not growth-related. For instance, investment in new housing or new hospitals is unlikely to create much wealth in the future. Investment can also be wasted if it takes place in industries which fail to sell products. For instance, investment in UK shipbuilding plants during the late 1970s and early 1980s provided a poor rate of return because the shipbuilding industry was in decline. Investment must therefore be targeted at growth industries.

Technological progress

Technological progress increases economic growth in two ways.

- It cuts the average cost of production of a product. For instance, a machine which performed the tasks of a simple scientific calculator was unavailable 100 years ago. 50 years ago, it needed a large room full of expensive equipment to do this. Today calculators are portable and available for a few pounds.
- It creates new products for the market. Without new products, consumers would be less likely to spend increases in their income. Without extra spending, there would be less or no economic growth.

Efficiency

The way in which the factors of production are used together is vital for economic growth. Increased efficiency in the use of resources in itself will bring about rises in output.

In a market economy, competition should lead to greater efficiency. Firms which use more efficient production techniques will drive less efficient firms out of the market. Firms which develop new, better products will drive old products out of the market. So economic growth can come about because of government policies which promote competition and protect innovation. For example, policies such as privatisation, deregulation and control of monopolies should increase competition. Laws which protect patents and copyright will encourage innovation.

Markets promote efficiency but they can also fail. So government may have to step in to redress market failure. In the past, some have argued that market failure is so widespread that the government should own most, if not all, of industry. This socialist or communist view is mostly rejected today. The problem was that in communist countries like Russia, government failure became so great that it outweighed any benefits from the correction of market failure. However, in countries like France, Germany and Italy today, many still argue that the government should be highly interventionist. They argue that by owning key industries like electricity, gas and the postal service and providing subsidies to other key industries, the state can promote economic growth.

In Third World countries, many of the features of a functioning market economy may be missing. Resources are then combined inefficiently. For example, laws may not exist which protect property rights, or laws may exist but the state may take assets away from private citizens and businesses through corruption, bribery and a judiciary which doesn't uphold the law. If property rights are not protected, citizens and

firms have little incentive to save and invest in the long term. Widescale bribery leads to resources being appropriated by a few individuals rather than being used in the most efficient manner across the economy. Another problem is that there may be no properly functioning capital markets. Farmers in rural areas, for example, may have no access to banks. They are then cut off from access to relatively cheap loans to expand their businesses. At worst, there may be civil war and a complete breakdown of government. Civil wars lead to negative growth as assets, both physical and human, are destroyed.

Four distinctions

Economic growth is typically measured by the rate of change of output or GDP. When measuring GDP, four important distinctions should be made.

- Economic growth is typically measured by the rise in the output of goods and services over time. Economic growth is changes in **real** GDP and not changes in **nominal** GDP which also includes increases in prices. Real GDP over time has to be measured using one year's prices. So for example, economic growth for 1988-2008 might be measured with all prices adjusted to 2006 prices.
- Real GDP is a proxy measure of the **volume** of goods and services produced. It is equal to the quantity produced in an economy. The **value** of goods and services produced is

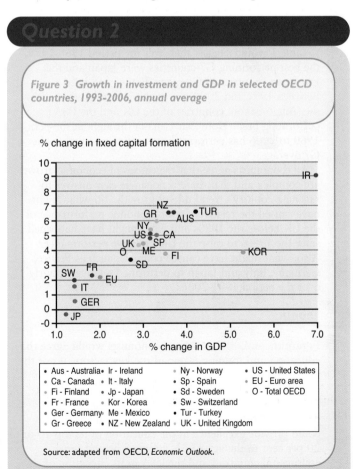

Question 2

Figure 3 Growth in investment and GDP in selected OECD countries, 1993-2006, annual average

% change in fixed capital formation

Aus - Australia	Ir - Ireland
Ca - Canada	It - Italy
Fi - Finland	Jp - Japan
Fr - France	Kor - Korea
Ger - Germany	Me - Mexico
Gr - Greece	NZ - New Zealand
Ny - Norway	US - United States
Sp - Spain	EU - Euro area
Sd - Sweden	O - Total OECD
Sw - Switzerland	
Tur - Turkey	
UK - United Kingdom	

Source: adapted from OECD, *Economic Outlook.*

(a) What relationship would economic theory suggest exists between investment and economic growth?
(b) To what extent is this relationship shown by the data?

Key terms

Economic growth - growth in the productive potential of the economy. It is typically measured by growth in real GDP although this is only a proxy measure because actual GDP can be above or below the productive potential of the economy at a point in time.
Economic recovery - the movement back from where the economy is operating below its productive potential to a point where it is at its productive potential.

volume times the average price. So a proxy measure of the volume of goods produced can be calculated by taking the nominal value of GDP and dividing it by the price level.

● **Total GDP** is the total amount of GDP produced in an economy. However, when comparing living standards, it is often more important to compare **GDP per capita** or total GDP divided by the size of the population. Similarly, growth in GDP per capita, which takes into account both change in GDP and the change in population, is often more useful when comparing

living standards than simply using growth in total GDP.

● Falling economic growth does not mean that the level of GDP itself is falling. China is currently growing at 10 per cent per annum. If its growth rate fell to 2 per cent per annum, its GDP would still be rising by 2 per cent each year. A falling rate of growth simply means that GDP is not rising as fast as before. So it is very important to distinguish between the **level** of GDP and the **rate of growth** of GDP. Only if the rate of growth of GDP became negative would GDP be falling.

Applied economics

Britain's growth rate

Worries about Britain's growth rate date back over a century. In Edwardian times, for example, it was not difficult to see the economic advance of Germany and France and compare it with the poor economic performance of the UK economy. Britain's poor growth performance persisted in the 1950s, 1960s and 1970s. As Table 1 shows, the UK had the lowest average annual rate of growth between 1960 and 1979 of the seven largest industrial economies of the world (the **Group of Seven** or **G7**). By the 1980s and 1990s, however, the UK had ceased to be at the bottom of the growth league. In the 1990s, for the first time, the UK's average rate of growth was almost equal to the G7 average. In the 2000s, it was higher than the G7 average.

Table 1 would suggest that over the period 1960-1979, the best performing G7 countries were Japan and the European countries of Germany, France and Italy. Between 1991 and 2006, the position was reversed with the 'Anglo-Saxon' countries of the UK and the USA performing best. Note that Canada throughout the period 1960 to 2006 has performed better than or equal to the G7 average.

All economists agree that the causes of economic growth are complex and that there is no single easy answer to raising a country's trend rate of growth. So what might have caused the relatively poor economic performance of the UK before the 1980s and what might have happened since the 1980s to raise the UK's relative performance? Also, what might have caused countries such as France, Germany, Italy and Japan to performed relatively poorly over the period 1991-2006?

Labour

Education and training Most economists would agree that education and training is one of the key factors, if not the most important factor, in determining long run growth rates. For much of the 20th century, countries such as France and Germany were perceived by some to have better education systems than the UK. Whilst the UK could provide excellence in the education of its top 10 or 20 per cent to the age of 21, it lagged behind some continental countries and the USA in its education of the bottom 80 per cent. In the USA, where standards for children to the age of 18 tend to be fairly low, there is a widespread acceptance that the majority of post-18 year

olds will stay on and do some form of college course. The USA still has the highest proportion of 18-24 year olds in full time education of any country in the world. Germany's system of technical and craft education has been seen as a major contributor to its economic success over the past 50 years. Japan has an education system which delivers high standards across the ability range.

In the UK, academic children going through to A levels and university degrees received an education which was as, good as, if not better than, their French, German or US peers. However, education for the rest was arguably poor. In the 1960s and 1970s, governments put opportunity and equality at the top of their list of priorities. Comprehensive schools were introduced to give all children a better chance of success whilst the number of university places was considerably increased to give young people more access to higher education. It wasn't till the 1980s that much emphasis was put on the quality of education and lifting standards. The 1980s saw the introduction of the National Curriculum in schools, Ofsted inspections of schools and school league tables. In the 1990s, new national vocational qualifications (NVQs) were introduced, designed to provide qualifications for training in work. Their school or college based equivalent, GNVQs, were introduced to help those for whom academic A level and GCSE examinations were not suitable. The 1990s also saw the introduction of targets into education, for instance for achievement in National Curriculum tests. Targets were intended to raise standards in schools which performed poorly, and to give good schools an incentive to achieve even better results. In 1997, the Labour government under Tony Blair was elected which, for the first time, put education as a top priority in its manifesto. Since 1997, education has been specifically linked by government to the long term performance of the economy. Education spending has been raised as a proportion of GDP and a target of getting 50 per cent of the 18-21 year olds into some form of higher education has been set. It could be argued that the relative improvement of the British educational system compared to other G7 countries has played a part in helping the UK achieve relatively higher growth.

Catching up Why can China grow by 10 per cent per annum whilst the UK barely manages a quarter of that?

Table 1 *Average annual growth in GDP, G7 countries, 1960-2004*

(%)

	1960-67	1968-73	1974-79	1980-90	1991-2000	2001-06
Canada	5.5	5.4	4.2	2.8	2.8	2.6
United States	4.5	3.2	2.4	3.3	3.3	2.5
United Kingdom	3.0	3.4	1.5	2.6	2.6	2.5
France	5.4	5.5	2.8	2.4	2.4	1.6
Japan	10.2	8.7	3.6	3.9	3.9	1.4
Germany	4.1	4.9	2.3	2.3	2.3	1.0
Italy	5.7	4.5	3.7	2.3	2.3	0.9
Average G7	5.0	4.4	2.7	2.8	2.8	1.8

Source: adapted from OECD, *Historical Statistics, Economic Outlook.*

One suggestion is that the high economic growth rate represents the gains from transferring workers from low productivity agriculture to higher productivity manufacturing and service industries. If a worker can produce £500 per year in output as an agricultural worker but £1 000 working in a factory, then the act of transferring that worker from agriculture to industry will raise the growth rate of the economy. This theory was popular in explaining why the UK performed badly relative to the rest of the EU in the 1950s and 1960s. In 1960-67, for instance, the average proportion of agricultural workers in the total civilian working population of the then Common Market was 18.1 per cent, but was only 4.2 per cent in the UK. By the 1990s, the proportion of workers in agriculture was less than 5 per cent in France and Germany and there was little scope for major transfers of labour out of the primary sector in northern Europe. Hence, this competitive advantage viz a viz the UK has disappeared. However, this theory can still explain why countries like China or Poland, with large amounts of labour in agriculture, can grow at rates several times that of EU countries.

Flexible labour markets In the 1990s, the UK government saw flexible labour markets as key to its **supply side reforms**. Labour markets are flexible when it is relatively easy for firms to hire and fire labour, and for workers to move between jobs. Inflexible labour markets create market failure, partly because they tend to lead to unemployment. There are many different aspects to creating flexible labour markets. One is education and training, discussed above. An educated workforce is more attractive to firms and helps workers to change jobs when the need arises. Another aspect is government rules and regulations about employment. Health and safety laws, maximum working hours, minimum wages, minimum holiday entitlements, redundancy regulations and maternity and paternity leave are all examples of government imposed rules which increase the cost of employment to firms and reduce the ability of firms to manage their workforces to suit their production needs.

It is argued that, in EU countries, firms have to comply with too many rules and regulations. They then become reluctant to take on workers, leading to high unemployment and lower growth. In contrast, the UK and the US have fewer regulations and this partly explains their higher growth rates in the 1990s and 2000s. Other aspects of flexible labour markets include pensions and housing. If workers are to move between jobs easily, they must carry with them pension rights. If they lose their pension rights every time they change job, they will be reluctant to move. Difficulty in obtaining housing discourages workers from moving between geographical areas. Part time working is important too. In flexible labour markets, workers should be able to choose how many hours they wish to work and how many jobs they have at any time. If work structures are such that part time working is discouraged, then the skills of many workers at home bringing up children are likely to go unutilised. Equally, there may not be enough full time work in the economy, but flexible labour markets should mean that workers could choose to build up **portfolios** of jobs, making several part time jobs equal to one full time one.

Taxes Another argument put forward is that taxes can have an important impact on growth levels. Before 1979, it could be argued that Britain's tax regime discouraged work, enterprise and investment. For example, the Labour government during 1974-1979 introduced a top marginal tax rate on earned income of 83 per cent. Average tax rates had also been rising since the 1950s as the size of the state expanded and government spending rose. The Conservative government elected in 1979 was committed to lowering the tax burden by lowering levels of government spending. By 1997, when it was defeated at the polls, it had succeeded in limiting government spending to around 40 per cent of GDP, up to 10 per cent less than many of its continental EU rivals. Since then, both the level of government spending as a proportion of GDP and taxation have risen. Increased public spending has been necessary to fund increases in expenditure on health and education. Nevertheless, by 2007, the UK still had relatively low taxes compared to its main EU partners. These relatively low taxes since the 1990s can be argued to be a cause of the UK's higher economic growth.

Lower taxes help in a number of ways. Some economists argue that low taxes encourage workers with no job to enter the labour force, and those with jobs to work harder. This can lead to higher economic growth. Also, low taxes paid by firms on employing labour encourage firms to employ labour. In France and Germany, social security taxes paid by firms on the labour they employ are relatively high. This discourages them from employing labour, leading to high unemployment. This means that there are large unemployed resources which could act as a drag on long term growth. Equally, high taxes on labour and profits can discourage inward investment by foreign companies wanting to set up plants in a country. Inward investment doesn't just create jobs and wealth directly. It often acts as a competitive spur to domestic firms which have to compete with the new entrants. Improving efficiency and developing new products in response can raise growth rates.

Immigration In recent years, net migration, the difference between immigration and emigration, has been positive, averaging 200 000 per annum. Around 500 000 migrants per annum have been arriving in the UK, many of them young males and, since the EU was expanded in 2004, from Eastern Europe. This boost to the population has almost certainly increased the UK's rate of growth of GDP simply because there are now more workers in the population.

Countries which attract and accept migrants, such as the USA and Canada, tend to grow faster simply because of the impact of migrants on output in the economy.

Capital

Table 2 shows that the UK has consistently devoted less of its GDP to investment than other G7 countries. Economic theory would suggest that investment - the addition to the physical capital stock of the country - is essential for economic growth. How can an economy increase its growth rate if it does not increase the amount it is setting aside to increase the productive potential of the economy? There is a number of possible explanations for why investment and growth rates may or may not be linked.

Quality, not quantity Some economists have argued that it is not the quantity of investment that is important but its direction. The two classic examples used for the UK are Concorde (the supersonic plane) and the nuclear power programme. Large sums of public money were poured into the development of Concorde and the nuclear power programme in the 1960s. Both proved uncommercial. In this view, increasing investment rates without there being the investment opportunities present in the economy would have little or no effect on growth rates. The money would simply be wasted. Moreover, how could investment be increased in an economy? The simplest way would be for government to spend more on investment, either through its own programmes, by investing directly in industry, or through subsidies. Free market economists would then argue that the government is a very poor judge of industries and projects which need further investment. The money would probably be squandered on today's equivalents of Concorde. Only if firms increase investment of their own accord in free markets can growth increase. Even this is no guarantee of success. In the late 1980s and early 1990s, Japanese industry increased its investment because of very low interest rates on borrowed money. In 1986, Japan spent 27.3 per cent of its GDP on investment. In 1990, this peaked at 32.2 per cent. Despite this, the Japanese economy spent much of the 1990s in recession, with an average growth rate of just 1.5 per cent. In retrospect, Japanese companies had clearly overinvested. There was far too much capacity for the levels of production required.

Short-termism In the USA and the UK, banks do not invest in companies. They lend to companies over fairly short time periods, typically up to five years, but many loans (e.g. overdrafts) are repayable on demand. Shares in companies are owned by shareholders, and these shares are traded on stock markets. Stock markets are driven by speculators who are not interested in where a company might be in five or ten years time. They are only interested in the size of the next dividend payment or the price of the share today. In contrast, in Germany and Japan banks own large proportions of industry through shareholdings. The banks are interested in the long term development of companies. Losses this year are less important if the long term future of a company is bright and secure. It is therefore argued that US and UK stock markets lead to short-termism. Firms will only invest if

they can make a quick profit to satisfy shareholders who are only interested in the financial performance of the company over, say, 12 months. In Germany and Japan, firms can afford to make long term investment decisions even if these involve poorer short term performance, secure in the knowledge that their shareholders are interested in the long term future of the business.

Supporters of US style capitalism argue that long termism can mask poor investment decisions. When the Japanese economy went into a prolonged period of low or negative growth following the economic bubble of the late 1980s, Japanese companies often failed to take the necessary steps to restructure despite making substantial losses over a lengthy period of time. Without the pressures of shareholders wanting a fast return, they preferred to safeguard the interests of management and workers. This has contributed to the problems of Japanese industry. In France, Germany and Italy, long termism has not prevented them suffering lower economic growth rates than the USA. Indeed, the pressures of globalisation and the single market within the EU are making their firms more short termist. They are finding that their companies are facing the threat of takeover by US or UK companies. One way of fighting this is to increase short term profitability.

Lack of savings The USA and the UK have relatively low savings ratios. Given that over the long term exports roughly equal imports for a country, and the government budget deficit tends to fluctuate around a fixed proportion of GDP, then savings must roughly equal a constant proportion of investment. Higher savings will thus allow higher investment. In the UK, firms have large tax incentives to save through not distributing all their profits to shareholders. This retained profit could be increased through even lower taxation, or the government could increase its savings by moving to a budget surplus. Individuals could be persuaded to save more again through tax incentives.

Innovation The UK spends a relatively low proportion of its GDP on research and development (R&D). For most of the post-war period, an above average share of that R&D has been devoted to defence research. Hence, some economists argue that R&D spending in total needs to be increased for higher growth, and a larger proportion needs to be spent on civilian projects. The UK's poor R&D record is shown in Figure 4. Others argue that it is not so much the quantity that is important as the use to which R&D is put.

Table 2 Gross fixed capital formation as a percentage of GDP
Per cent

	1960-67	1968-73	1974-79	1980-90	1991-2000	2001-06
Canada	22.6	22.1	23.5	22.0	18.9	20.2
United States	18.1	18.4	18.8	19.1	17.9	18.6
United Kingdom	17.7	19.1	19.4	18.7	16.7	16.6
France	23.2	24.6	23.6	21.0	18.8	19.4
Japan	31.0	34.6	31.8	29.7	28.2	23.5
Germany	25.2	24.4	20.8	22.2	22.0	18.1
Italy	24.9	24.0	24.0	22.4	19.8	20.8

Source: adapted from OECD, *Historical Statistics*, United Nations Statistics Division.

It is often pointed out that the UK has a good international record in making discoveries and in inventions. However, too many of those have not been taken up by UK businesses. Instead, the ideas have gone overseas and been used by foreign firms as the bases for world-beating products. In this argument, UK firms have been very poor in the past at making a commercial success of R&D.

Catching up Catching up can apply to capital as well as to labour. For instance, a new DVD factory in China is likely to increase labour productivity (output per worker) far more than a new DVD factory in the UK. This is because the workers in China are more likely to have been employed in very low productivity jobs before than in Britain. So, countries like China can import foreign technologies and take huge leaps in productivity, which is then reflected in high economic growth rates. Some economists argue that, in the long run, all countries will arrive at roughly the same output per worker and grow at the same rate. This is because technology is internationally available. Countries can bring their capital stock up to the level of the most productive country in the world. Countries like the USA, however, which has grown at around 2.5 per cent per annum since the Second World War, can't take huge technological leaps like this. It has to create new technologies and new products to sustain its growth.

One argument put forward to explain the US economy's superior performance compared to European countries like France and Germany during the 1990s and 2000s is that its companies have invested much more heavily in IT (information technology). Not only has IT spending as a proportion of GDP been higher, but US companies have integrated IT into their operations much more deeply. The USA has therefore gained a technological advantage over other developed countries which has allowed it to sustain its growth rate whilst many other developed countries have fallen behind.

Privatisation and deregulation Capital may be tied up in relatively unproductive firms or industries. Releasing this capital can increase growth rates. The experience of the 1980s and 1990s in the UK has been that privatisation and deregulation are powerful ways of improving capital productivity. Nationalised industries, such as water, electricity, coal, gas and the railways were inefficient in the 1960s and 1970s. They employed too much capital and too much labour. Privatisation saw output per unit of capital and labour increase substantially as workforces were cut and assets sold off or closed down. The process was painful. In the coal industry, for instance, nearly 200 000 workers lost their jobs between 1980 and 2000. However, in a fast changing economy, failure to move resources between industries leads to inefficiency and slower growth.

Openness to imports One way of protecting domestic jobs is to erect protectionist barriers against imports. For instance, foreign goods can be kept out by imposing high taxes on imports (called **tariffs** or **customs duties**). It can be argued, though, that protectionism is likely to lead to lower long term economic growth. This is because domestic firms can become insulated from world best

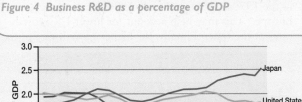

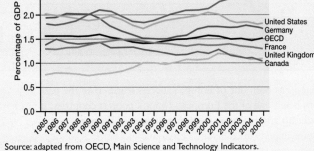

Figure 4 Business R&D as a percentage of GDP

Source: adapted from OECD, Main Science and Technology Indicators.

practice. There is reduced incentive to invest and innovate if more competitive goods from abroad are kept out of the domestic market.

France and Germany in the 1990s and 2000s have perhaps been more protectionist in their policies than the UK and the USA. Because France and Germany are part of the EU, there is a limit to the amount of protectionism that they can implement compared to other EU countries such as the UK. However, one example of protectionism was the failure of most EU countries to open up their service industries such as banking to foreign competition for much of the 1990s and early 2000s. Equally, countries like France and Germany failed to open up utility markets such as electricity, gas and telecommunications over the same period. Part of the superior performance of the UK and US economies over the period might be due to increased foreign competition in markets other than those traditionally exposed to trade.

Export-led growth Some Third World countries have grown particularly fast over the past 40 years. Their growth has tended to be fuelled by exports. Countries like South Korea, Taiwan and China have been highly successful in selling their goods into Western markets. As with low protectionist barriers to imports, successful exporting requires domestic firms to be competitive with the best firms around the world. This encourages efficiency and investment, both important in promoting economic growth. The UK has some world class industries such as financial services. However, for much of the past 40 years, its balance of payments on current account has been in deficit. This would suggest that growth in the UK has not particularly been export led.

Macroeconomic management

Some economists argue that recessions do not affect long term growth rates. Growth lost in a recession is made up in the boom which follows. Others argue that the fall in GDP in deep recessions may never be recouped in the subsequent upturn. This is because in a deep recession, labour can become de-skilled, leading to permanently higher unemployment. Capital can also be destroyed as firms cut costs, pulling down factories and throwing away equipment. The UK suffered deeper and longer recessions in the 1970s, 1980s and early 1990s than countries in Europe. This may help account for lower UK growth rates at the time. Equally, the higher growth rate in the UK in the 1990s and 2000s may be because the UK avoided a recession in the middle 1990s and early 2000s, which afflicted European countries.

DataQuestion — Ireland's economic miracle

Ireland has been one of Europe's success stories over the past 30 years. From being one of the European Union's poorest countries, it has now caught up and is among the richer nations of Europe.

Some experts trace Ireland's economic success back to the introduction of free secondary education in the 1960s. Cuts in taxes on businesses in the 1980s and cuts in top rates of income tax on earners provided a boost for business and enterprise. The 1980s also saw an increase in the labour force with the traditional net outflow of labour from Ireland reversing to become a net inflow. Today, an annual 30 000 more workers arrive in Ireland than leave to seek jobs abroad, attracted by a booming job market. Multinational companies were attracted to Ireland from the 1970s onwards by its educated, English speaking workforce and low business taxes. Jobs have been created in manufacturing and service industries, whilst jobs in low productivity agriculture have been in decline. The enormous productivity gains from these trends have allowed Irish workers to see large pay rises over time without unit labour costs rising too much. Centralised wage agreements have allowed the government to introduce flexible working practices. In exchange for wage moderation, income tax was cut.

Typical of Ireland's success story is Galway. Digital Computers set up a mainframe computer factory in the city in 1971 and became an important employer in the area. Changing patterns of demand saw the factory close in 1994. Since then, Galway has reinvented itself and hosts one of the world's largest clusters of medical device manufacturing companies. Today there are 28 companies in the city employing 5 000 people. 15 of these are locally owned, many headed by former Digital Computers employees.

Source: adapted from the *Financial Times*, 27.5.2005.

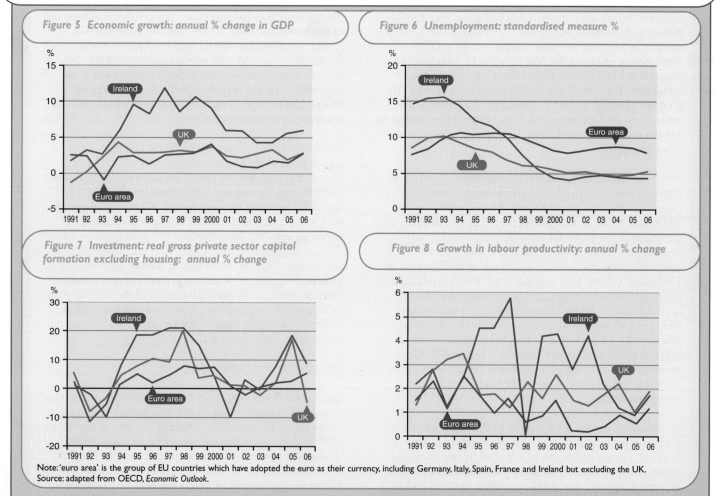

Figure 5 Economic growth: annual % change in GDP

Figure 6 Unemployment: standardised measure %

Figure 7 Investment: real gross private sector capital formation excluding housing: annual % change

Figure 8 Growth in labour productivity: annual % change

Note: 'euro area' is the group of EU countries which have adopted the euro as their currency, including Germany, Italy, Spain, France and Ireland but excluding the UK.
Source: adapted from OECD, *Economic Outlook*.

1. (a) Explain what is meant by economic growth.
    (b) Compare the recent growth performance in Ireland with the UK and the whole euro area.

2. Discuss whether higher levels of capital investment can solely account for Ireland's superior economic performance since 1991.

Summary

1. Unemployment is a stock concept, measuring the number of people out of work at a point in time. Unemployment will increase if the number of workers losing jobs is greater than the number of people gaining jobs.
2. Four types of unemployment can be distinguished: frictional unemployment caused by workers taking time to move jobs; seasonal unemployment caused by some jobs only being available at certain times of the year structural unemployment caused by a failure of labour markets to respond to long term changes in the economy; and cyclical unemployment caused by a lack of aggregate demand in recessions.

The measurement of unemployment

Unemployment, the number of people out of work, is measured at a point in time. It is a **stock concept**. However, the level of unemployment will change over time.

Millions of people seek jobs each year in the UK. Young people leave school, college or university seeking work. Former workers who have taken time out of the workforce, for instance to bring up children, seek to return to work. Workers who have lost their jobs, either because they have resigned or because they have been made redundant, search for new jobs.

Equally, millions of workers lose their jobs. They may retire, or leave work to look after children or they may resign or be made redundant from existing jobs.

Unemployment in an economy with a given labour force will rise if the number of workers gaining jobs is less than the number of people losing their jobs. In the first half of 2007, for instance, 1.2 million workers lost their jobs. However, the numbers gaining jobs were slightly higher per month than the numbers losing jobs. The result was a net fall in unemployment over the period. This flow of workers into or out of the stock of unemployed workers is summarised in Figure 1.

Unemployment will also increase if there is a rise in the number of people seeking work but the number of jobs in the economy remains static. During most years in the 1970s and 1980s, there was a rise in the number of school leavers entering the job market as well as more women wanting a job in the UK. It can be argued that at least some of the increase in unemployment in these two decades was a reflection of the inability of the UK economy to provided sufficient new jobs for those extra workers in the labour force.

Types of unemployment

Unemployment occurs for a variety of reasons. A number of different types of or reasons for unemployment can be distinguished.

Frictional unemployment Most workers who lose their jobs move quickly into new ones. This short-term unemployment is called FRICTIONAL UNEMPLOYMENT. There will always be frictional unemployment in a free market economy and it is not regarded by most economists as a serious problem. The amount of time spent unemployed varies. The higher the level of

Question I

Table I Unemployment flows, 2005-2007

	Thousands	
	Inflow	Outflow
2005 Q3	603.2	591.1
2005 Q4	624.7	591.2
2006 Q1	622.3	594.0
2006 Q2	617.3	603.3
2006 Q3	627.8	627.0
2006 Q4	624.3	644.7
2007 Q1	630.4	663.2
2007 Q2	611.7	649.9

Source: adapted from *Economic & Labour Market Review*, Office for National Statistics.

(a) In which quarters did unemployment: (i) increase; and (ii) decrease? Explain your answer.
(b) Explain whether unemployment was higher or lower in the 2005 3rd quarter than in 2007 2nd quarter.

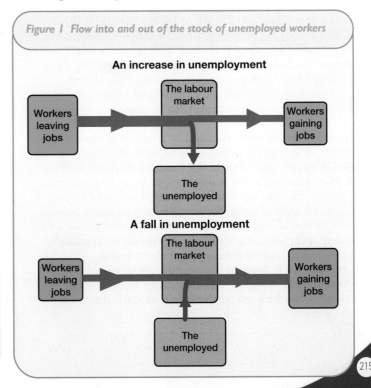

Figure I Flow into and out of the stock of unemployed workers

215

unemployment benefits or redundancy pay, the longer workers will be able to afford to search for a good job without being forced into total poverty. Equally, the better the job information available to unemployed workers through newspapers, jobcentres, etc. the shorter the time workers should need to spend searching for jobs.

Seasonal unemployment Some workers, such as construction workers or workers in the tourist industry, tend to work on a seasonal basis. SEASONAL UNEMPLOYMENT tends to rise in winter when some of these workers will be laid off, whilst unemployment falls in summer when they are taken on again. There is little that can be done to prevent this pattern occurring in a market economy where the demand for labour varies through the year.

Structural unemployment Far more serious is the problem of STRUCTURAL UNEMPLOYMENT. This occurs when the demand for labour is less than its supply in an individual labour market in the economy. One example of structural unemployment is **regional unemployment**. Throughout the post-war period, the South of England has tended to be at full employment while regions such as Northern Ireland have consistently suffered unemployment. This has occurred because of a lack of mobility of factors of production between the regions. Another example is **sectoral unemployment**. The steel and shipbuilding industries in the UK declined sharply in the late 1970s and early 1980s leaving a considerable number of skilled workers unemployed. Unfortunately their skills were no longer needed in the economy and without retraining and possible relocation, they were unable to adapt to the changing demand. **Technological unemployment** is another example of structural unemployment. Groups of workers across industries may be put out of work by new technology. Again, without retraining and geographical mobility these workers may remain unemployed.

Cyclical or demand-deficient unemployment Economies tend to experience business cycles. These are movements from boom to recession over time. CYCLICAL or DEMAND-DEFICIENT UNEMPLOYMENT is unemployment which occurs when the economy is not in boom. It is when there is insufficient aggregate demand in the economy for all workers to get a job. In a recession, it is not just workers who are unemployed. Capital too is underutilised. So factories and offices can remain empty. Machinery and equipment can lie unused.

Cyclical unemployment is caused by a lack of demand in the economy. Frictional, seasonal and structural unemployment are caused by supply side factors. For example, if labour markets were more efficient, workers would move from job to job more quickly. So the time taken to get a new job would be shorter. In the case of frictional unemployment, an increase in the amount of information of jobs available to jobseekers would reduce the time they spent searching for a job. In the case of structural unemployment, making it easier to get cheap rented accommodation in areas of low unemployment would help workers in areas of higher unemployment to move. Better retraining of workers would also help reduce structural unemployment.

Question 2

The economy is currently in recession and the following workers are unemployed. Explain under which type of unemployment their circumstances might be classified.

(a) Katie Morris is a 30 year old in Devon with a husband and two children. She works in the local hotel trade in the summer months on a casual basis but would like to work all the year round.
(b) John Penny, aged 22 and living in London, was made redundant a couple of weeks ago from a furniture store which closed down. He is currently seeking work in the retail sector.
(c) Manus O'Brien lives in Belfast in Northern Ireland. Aged 56, he last had a job 12 years ago working in a local factory.
(d) Clare Livingstone, aged 31, lost her job 6 months ago working as a surveyor for an estate agent in Guildford in the South East of England. She is currently looking for another surveyor's job but the local housing market is very depressed.
(e) Gavin Links, aged 40, has been out of work for 18 months. A former manager of a factory in the West Midlands, he is seeking a similar job within travelling distance of where he currently lives.

Using diagrams to illustrate unemployment

Unemployment can be illustrated using a variety of diagrams. Figure 2 shows a production possibility diagram. The economy is operating at its productive potential when it is somewhere on the production possibility frontier such as at point A. There are unemployed resources when the economy is operating within the frontier such as at point B.

Aggregate demand and supply analysis can be used to distinguish between demand side and supply side causes of unemployment. In Figure 3, the economy is in short run equilibrium at an output level of 0A. However, what if the LRAS curve is to the right of this point? Then there must be cyclical or demand-deficient unemployment. The economy is in

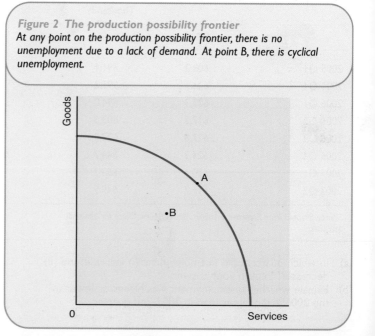

Figure 2 The production possibility frontier
At any point on the production possibility frontier, there is no unemployment due to a lack of demand. At point B, there is cyclical unemployment.

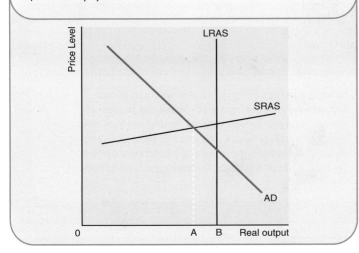

Figure 3 *Cyclical unemployment* The economy is in equilibrium in the short run at an output level of 0A. This is below the level of 0B, shown by the long run aggregate supply curve, where there would be no demand-deficient unemployment.

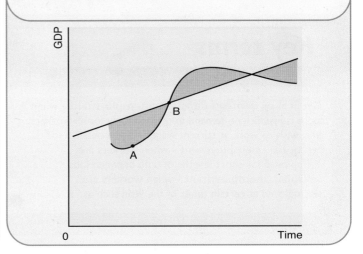

Figure 5 *Unemployment and the output gap* Cyclical unemployment occurs if the actual level of income is below its long run trend level, for example at A.

recession. Output at 0A does not represent the productive potential of the economy which is higher at 0B. However, if there is an increase in aggregate demand, shown in Figure 4 by the shift in the aggregate demand curve from AD₁ to AD₂, full employment can be restored.

The same point can be illustrated using the concept of the output gap. The trend growth of the economy is shown by the upward sloping straight line in Figure 5. At point A, there is a negative output gap and the economy is in recession. So there is cyclical unemployment. An increase in demand will move the economy to B and eliminate demand-deficient unemployment.

Supply side causes of unemployment include frictional, seasonal and structural unemployment. In Figure 4, there is likely to be some frictional, seasonal and structural unemployment at an output level of 0B. This is because the long run aggregate supply curve is drawn on the assumption that there are limited resources and markets may work imperfectly. For example, some workers may be structurally unemployed because they do not have the right skills for the jobs on offer in

the market. This lack of skills is taken into account when drawing the long run aggregate supply curve. If through training they acquire new skills and then get jobs, this leads to a rightward shift of the long run aggregate supply curve. A fall in frictional, seasonal and structural unemployment is shown by a rightward shift of the long run aggregate supply curve.

In Figure 5, the long run trend line of growth is drawn assuming the gradual shift to the right in the long run aggregate supply curve shown in Figure 4. If the long run trend rate of growth is 2.5 per cent, then in Figure 4, the LRAS curve is shifting to the right by 2.5 per cent per year on average. So the trend rate of growth assumes there will be supply side improvements to the economy over time. This may or may not include supply side improvements which reduce frictional, seasonal or structural unemployment. However, past evidence would suggest that existing structural unemployment tends to

Question 3

In a study of 6000 employed and unemployed workers, a team of academics found that the unemployed had poor psychological health. They were more likely to be depressed, less likely to mix with people in work and had little access to social support networks or to information about jobs. One of the team, Richard Lampard of Warwick University, concluded that unemployment directly increases the risk of marriage break-up, finding that the chances of the marriage of an unemployed person ending in the following year are 70 per cent higher than those of a person who has never been out of work.

The study also found that men in low-paid insecure jobs suffered almost the same level of psychological distress as those who were out of work altogether. It was found that there was a close correlation between perceived job security and psychological well-being. Women were found to be just as distressed by lack of paid work, but less affected by the prospect of an insecure low-paid job.

(a) What problems face the unemployed, according to the article?
(b) Why might these problems give rise to costs not just for the unemployed but also for society as a whole?

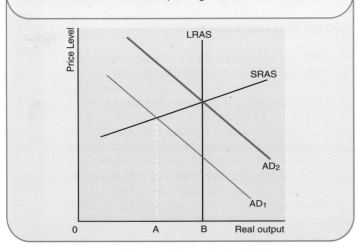

Figure 4 *Eliminating cyclical unemployment* The cyclical unemployment in the economy at the short run equilibrium of 0A can be eliminated by raising aggregate demand, shown by the shift in the aggregate demand curve from AD₁ to AD₂.

fall over time. Of course, there may be new supply side shocks which lead to new structural unemployment. If the long run trend rate of growth could be raised, say from 2.5 per cent to 3.0 per cent, there is a greater likelihood that structural unemployment will fall. A rise in the long run trend rate of growth would be shown by a shift upwards in the trend growth line in Figure 5.

Key terms

Cyclical or demand-deficient unemployment - when there is insufficient demand in the economy for all workers who wish to work at current wage rates to obtain a job.
Frictional unemployment - when workers are unemployed for short lengths of time between jobs.
Seasonal unemployment - when workers are unemployed at certain times of the year, such as building workers or agricultural workers in winter.
Structural unemployment - when the pattern of demand and production changes leaving workers unemployed in labour markets where demand has shrunk. Examples of structural unemployment are regional unemployment, sectoral unemployment or technological unemployment.

Applied economics

Measures of unemployment

In economic theory, the unemployed are defined as those without a job but who are seeking work at current wage rates. Measuring the number of unemployed in an economy, however, is more difficult than economic theory might suggest. There are two basic ways in which unemployment can be calculated.

- Government can undertake a survey of the population to identify the employed and the unemployed. The international standard for this method has been produced by the International Labour Organisation (ILO) and is the basis for the **Labour Force Survey** (LFS) conducted by the government in the UK. The Labour Force Survey generates monthly **LFS unemployment** statistics, sometimes called **ILO unemployment** statistics.
- The government can count all those who register as unemployed. In the UK, **claimant count** unemployment statistics are produced based on the numbers claiming benefit for being unemployed.

Unemployment is expressed in two ways. It can be stated as an absolute figure, as millions of workers, or it can be stated as a relative measure, as a percentage of the workforce, the **unemployment rate**. Expressing it in millions gives a clear indication of the numbers affected by unemployment. Expressing it as percentage is better when the number of workers in the economy is changing. For instance, using absolute figures to compare US unemployment with UK unemployment may not be helpful because there are about five times as many workers in the US as in the UK. Comparing it as a percentage allows a more meaningful comparison to be made. Equally, the size of the workforce is likely to change over time. In 1950 in the UK, there were 23.7 million in the labour force of which 0.4 million

were unemployed on a claimant count basis. In 2007, there were 30.8 million in the labour force of which 1.7 million were unemployed on the ILO measure. Unemployment was much higher in 2007, but so too was the size of the workforce.

The claimant count

Until 1997, the main measure of UK unemployment was the claimant count. However, the claimant count figure had come under increasing criticism because it was felt to be open to government manipulation. In the 1980s and 1990s, the UK government introduced over 30 different changes to the way in which the claimant count was calculated, most of which served to reduce the numbers officially unemployed. Not only was the claimant count open to manipulation but it was also not an internationally recognised way of measuring unemployment. Hence, it could not be used to compare UK unemployment levels with those in other countries.

ILO (or LFS) unemployment

In 1998, the newly elected Labour government decided to make the ILO count the main measure of unemployment in the UK. ILO unemployment figures had been collected first on a biannual (once every two years) basis in 1973, and then annually from 1984. In 1993, it became a quarterly count and since 1997 has been monthly. The ILO count is taken from a wider survey of employment called the Labour Force Survey (LFS). 60 000 households, with over 100 000 adults, are surveyed. The questionnaire used covers household size and structure, accommodation details, basic demographic characteristics, such as age, sex, marital status and ethnic origin, and economic activity. To be counted as unemployed, an individual has to be without a paid job, be available to start a job within a fortnight and has either looked for work at some time in the previous four weeks or been waiting to start a job already obtained.

ILO unemployment compared to the claimant count

Figure 6 shows that ILO unemployment figures differ significantly from claimant count figures. ILO unemployment tends to be above claimant count unemployment in a recovery and boom situation, but roughly equal to it in a recession.

ILO unemployment is likely to be above the claimant count figure because the claimant count excludes a number of key groups of unemployed workers.

● Many female unemployed workers are actively looking for work (and are therefore included in ILO unemployment) but are not entitled to benefits for being unemployed. For instance, they might not have built up sufficient National Insurance contributions to qualify for unemployment benefit, a National Insurance benefit. They may also be living in a household where the husband or partner is earning too high a wage for them to qualify for means tested benefit.

● Older, particularly male, workers in their 50s and 60s may be collecting a pension from their previous employer or be supported financially by their spouse. They are therefore not entitled to benefits but may be actively seeking work.

● Workers are not entitled to register as unemployed with the DSS until they have been out of work for a number of weeks. However, anyone interviewed for the ILO count who is unemployed and is looking for work is counted as unemployed regardless of how long they have been unemployed.

The claimant count, however, may include some

unemployed who would not be included in the ILO count. For instance, those working in the **hidden economy** may claim benefits for being unemployed but actually be in work, usually as a self employed worker.

Both the ILO and claimant counts could be argued to underestimate overall unemployment.

● They do not include part time workers who are actively seeking full time work, for instance.

● Those on government training and work schemes who would prefer to be in proper employment are not included. This particularly affects young workers.

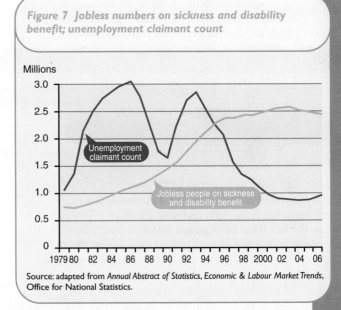

Figure 7 *Jobless numbers on sickness and disability benefit; unemployment claimant count*

Source: adapted from *Annual Abstract of Statistics, Economic & Labour Market Trends*, Office for National Statistics.

Table 2 *Employment and unemployment, UK, spring each year, seasonally adjusted, millions*

	Total in employment Millions	ILO unemployed Spring each year (millions)
1989	26.7	2.1
1990	26.9	2.0
1991	26.4	2.4
1992	25.6	2.8
1993	25.3	3.0
1994	25.4	2.8
1995	25.7	2.5
1996	26.0	2.3
1997	26.4	2.0
1998	26.7	1.8
1999	27.1	1.8
2000	27.4	1.6
2001	27.7	1.4
2002	27.9	1.5
2003	28.2	1.5
2004	28.4	1.4
2005	28.7	1.4
2006	28.9	1.7
2007	29.0	1.7

Source: adapted from *Economic & Labour Market Review*, Office for National Statistics.

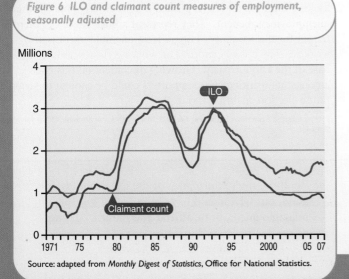

Figure 6 *ILO and claimant count measures of employment, seasonally adjusted*

Source: adapted from *Monthly Digest of Statistics*, Office for National Statistics.

- There are some out of work who are not actively seeking work or receiving benefits for being unemployed but who would take a job if offered. This mainly applies to women bringing up families. Table 2 illustrates this point. Between its peak in 1993 and 2007, ILO unemployment fell by 1.3 million whilst the total in employment increased by 3.8 million.
- Some unemployed workers have been taken off the unemployment registers by moving them onto sickness and disability benefits. As Figure 7 shows, numbers claiming sickness and disability benefits have risen from 0.7 million in 1979 to 2.4 million in 2006. Areas of the country with relatively high unemployment also have relatively high levels of sickness and disability benefit

claimants. Some economists argue that all those on sickness and disability benefits should be included amongst the unemployed since all could work given the right working conditions.

However, both measures of unemployment could be argued to overestimate unemployment. Some of those out of work find it almost impossible to get a job. Those with physical and mental disabilities, some ex-criminals or some with no qualifications find the job market very difficult. Some economists would argue that these workers are unemployable and therefore should not be counted as unemployed. A minority of those working in the hidden economy may claim benefits and may declare on surveys that they are out of work and seeking work.

DataQuestion

UK unemployment

When Mr Blair came to power in 1997, just over 2 million people were out of work. Having fallen to 1.4 million in 2001, unemployment has risen again and now stands at 1.7 million according to the Office for National Statistics, which uses the widely-recognised International Labour Organisation (ILO) counting system. Although the way unemployment is measured has changed over the years, both the ILO measure, which counts the number of people seeking work, and the claimant count, are roughly the same as they were in 1979. In percentage terms it is slightly higher at 5.5 per cent compared with 4.7 per cent in 1979. In 1979, the Labour government lost power to the Conservatives partly because of a highly successful Conservative Party advertising campaign with the slogan 'Labour isn't working'. Today, unemployment doesn't seem to be an electoral issue. What has changed?

Part of the answer lies with how unemployment is distributed. In 1979, although it was a boom year for the economy, unemployment was much higher than it had been ten years earlier. Manufacturing industry was declining across the UK creating pools of long term unemployed workers in every region and area of the UK. Today, although there are pockets of high unemployment, it is not a problem for the country as a whole. For instance, 9.4 per cent of workers are unemployed in the Poplar and Canning Town East End of London constituency of Employment Relations Minister Jim Fitzpatrick. But next door in Canary Wharf and then further on into the City of London, there are shortages of

workers.

Employment growth has also changed. Since 1997, an extra 2.7 million people have got work. The service sector is booming and there has been a big increase in women in employment, although many of these have taken low paid part-time jobs. In 1979, although the number in work had increased by 600 000 compared with 1971, the outlook for jobs was gloomy. In fact, employment didn't reach its 1980 levels again until 1988.

There is also record prosperity in the UK. Most people feel better off with growing incomes and access to cheap credit. The unemployed have shared in this growing prosperity with higher benefits and access to improving public services.

Not all agree that unemployment is no longer an economic or electoral issue. The number receiving incapacity benefit has climbed from 1.4 million in 1979 to 2.4 million today. Many of these are simply the long term unemployed who have given up looking for a job and been pushed onto a different benefit than unemployment benefit. They represent a huge waste of potential output for the economy. Longer term unemployment is also a working class phenomenon. The working classes are the electoral base of the Labour party. Growing discontent on this issue amongst its working class supporters could be enough to swing a future election against Labour.

Source: adapted from news.bbc.co.uk, 7.6.2007; *Monthly Digest of Statistics*, Office for National Statistics.

1. Explain the difference between the claimant count and the ILO measure of unemployment used in the UK.
2. 'Unemployment in the UK was structural rather than cyclical both in 1979 and 2007.' Explain what this means and give evidence from the passage to support the truth of the statement.
3. 'In 2007, the performance of the UK economy was good, but GDP could have been higher but for unemployment, both official and hidden.' Using diagrams, evaluate this statement.

33 Inflation

Summary

1. Inflation is a general sustained rise in the price level.
2. Inflation is measured by calculating the change in a weighted price index over time. In the UK, the two main measures are the Retail Price Index and the Consumer Price Index.
3. Inflation may be demand-pull or cost-push depending on whether it is caused by excessive demand or rising costs.

The meaning of inflation

INFLATION is defined as a sustained general rise in prices. The opposite of inflation - DEFLATION - is a term which can have two meanings. Strictly speaking it is defined as a fall in the PRICE LEVEL. However, it can also be used to describe a slowdown in the rate of growth of output of the economy. This slowdown or recession is often associated with a fall in the **rate of inflation**. Before the Second World War, recessions were also associated with falls in prices and this is the reason why deflation has come to have these two meanings.

A general rise in prices may be quite moderate. CREEPING INFLATION would describe a situation where prices rose a few per cent on average each year. HYPER-INFLATION, on the other hand, describes a situation where inflation levels are very high. There is no exact figure at which inflation becomes hyper-inflation, but inflation of 100 or 200 per cent per annum would be deemed to be hyper-inflation by most economists.

Question I

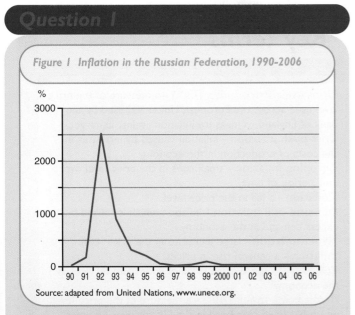

Figure I Inflation in the Russian Federation, 1990-2006

Source: adapted from United Nations, www.unece.org.

(a) Describe the changes in prices in the Russian Federation shown in the data.
(b) To what extent could the Russian Federation be said to have experienced hyper-inflation during the period shown?

Measuring inflation

Inflation is the change in average prices in an economy over a given period of time. The price level is measured in form of an index. So if the price index were 100 today and 110 in one year's time, then the rate of inflation would be 10 per cent.

There are many ways of calculating averages. In the UK, there are two main measures of inflation. The RETAIL PRICE INDEX (RPI) has been calculated for the past 50 years. The CONSUMER PRICE INDEX (CPI) is a more recent measure. The CPI is based on a common measure used by all EU countries. So CPI statistics have the advantage that they can be used to compare inflation in, say, France and Germany with the UK.

The causes of inflation

Inflation can be caused by two main factors: too much demand in the economy or rising costs.

Demand-pull inflation In the market for oil, a significant rise in demand for oil with no increase in supply will lead to a rise in the price of oil. The same occurs at a macroeconomic level. If aggregate or total demand rises and there is no increase in aggregate supply, then DEMAND-PULL INFLATION is likely to occur. Demand-pull inflation is caused by excessive demand in the economy. When there is too much demand, the price level, (or average level of prices in the economy) will rise. Excessive increases in aggregate demand in the UK can come about for a variety of reasons.
- Consumer spending may rise excessively. Interest rates could be low and consumers are spending large amounts on their credit cards, or consumer confidence could be rising because house prices are rising.
- Firms may substantially increase their spending. Perhaps they are responding to large increases in demand from consumers and need extra capacity to satisfy that demand.
- The government might be increasing its spending substantially, or it could be cutting taxes.
- World demand for UK exports may be rising because of a boom in the world economy.

Cost-push inflation Inflation may also occur because of changes in the supply side of the economy. COST-PUSH INFLATION occurs because of rising costs. There are four major sources of increased costs.

Question 2

Pay settlements have risen sharply to a six year high. This has triggered concerns that wage demands will fuel inflation. In turn this could lead to workers stepping up their wage demands to offset the higher cost of living. Some analysts are pointing out that strong consumer demand could add to inflationary pressures. They point out that firms are now more willing to raise prices and widen their profit margins in response to growth in sales. On the other hand, labour productivity is also growing, offsetting the impact of wage increases on costs. There is also the likelihood that the Bank of England will raise interest rates if inflation threatens to go too high.

Source: adapted from the *Financial Times*, 2.2.2007.

(a) Explain two factors mentioned in the article which might be causing cost-push inflation.
(b) Explain one factor mentioned in the article which might be causing demand-pull inflation.
(c) Explain two factors mentioned in the article which might limit inflationary pressures.

- Wages and salaries account for about 70 per cent of national income and hence increases in wages are normally the single most important cause of increases in costs of production.
- Imports can rise in price. An increase in the price of finished manufactured imports, such as television sets or cars, will lead directly to an increase in the price level. An increase in the price of imported semi-manufactured goods and raw materials, used as component parts of domestically produced manufactured goods, will feed through indirectly via an increase in the price of domestically produced goods.
- Profits can be increased by firms when they raise price to improve profit margins. The more price inelastic the demand for their goods, the less will such behaviour result in a fall in demand for their products.
- Government can raise indirect tax rates or reduce subsidies, thus increasing prices.

Firms will try to pass on increases in their costs to customers. For example, if a firm gives a 5 per cent pay rise to its workers, and wages account for 80 per cent of its costs, then it will need to increase prices by 4 per cent (80 per cent of 5 per cent) to maintain its profit margins. Competition in the market may mean that it finds it difficult to pass on these price rises and maintain sales. However, if costs are rising over time, firms will have to increase their prices and this leads to inflation.

Sometimes, inflation may be primarily demand-pull in nature. In other time periods, it may be mainly cost-push. In a stable but growing economy with no demand-side or supply-side shocks, inflation is likely to be caused by a mix of the two factors.

Key terms

Consumer Price Index (CPI) - a measure of the price level used across the European Union and used by the Bank of England to measure inflation against its target.
Cost-push inflation - inflation caused by increases in the costs of production in the economy.
Creeping inflation - small rises in the price level over a long period of time.
Deflation - a fall in the price level.
Demand-pull inflation - inflation which is caused by excess demand in the economy.
Hyper-inflation - large increases in the price level.
Inflation - a general rise in prices.
Price level - the average price of goods and services in the economy.
Retail Price Index (RPI) - a measure of the price level which has been calculated in the UK for over 60 years and is used in a variety of contexts such as by the government to index welfare benefits.

Applied economics

Inflation in the Lawson boom, 1986-1989

In the first half of the 1980s, the inflation rate fell from 18.0 per cent in 1980 to 4.6 per cent in 1983. Inflation then hovered in the 5 per cent range for the next five years but in mid-1988 it began to increase again. By the end of 1990, the annual growth of the Retail Price Index was over 10 per cent. Why was there this doubling of the inflation rate?

One cause was too much demand in the economy. As can be seen from Table 1, the rate of growth of real GDP increased from a rate of 3-4 per cent between 1983 and 1986 to 4-6 per cent between the last quarter of 1986 and 1988. In the first quarter of 1988, it peaked at the unsustainable level of 5.9 per cent. This very fast growth quickly reduced unemployment from over 3 million in the first half of the 1980s to 1.6 million by the last quarter of 1989, with areas such as the South East of England suffering severe shortages of many types of labour.

Another way of viewing excess demand is to consider the output gap at the time. Figure 2 shows that the economy was in deep recession at the start of the 1980s with actual output nearly 5 per cent below its trend rate of output. By 1986, this negative output gap had been eliminated and the economy was operating slightly above its potential level. At the height of the Lawson boom in 1988 and 1989, the economy was operating at over 5 per cent above its trend rate. This was unsustainable and inevitably led to rising inflation.

Table 1 also shows cost-push inflationary pressures. Wages are the most significant cost for employers on average. From 1984, there was a gradual increase in the rate of growth of earnings. In the first quarter of 1984, it was 6.1 per cent per annum, but by 1989 it was nearly 10 per cent. This could provide evidence for a cost-push explanation of the rise in inflation.

In fact, it is likely that the increased inflation from 1988 onwards was due to a combination of the above factors.

Most economists would accept that aggregate demand increased from 1986 relative to aggregate supply. Spending was fuelled partly by lower interest rates, but also because of deregulation in the financial markets. In particular, the second half of the 1980s saw the aggressive selling of mortgages as building societies, freed from many of their previous constraints, encouraged customers to borrow money. Banks too entered the mortgage market in an aggressive manner. People moving houses tended to

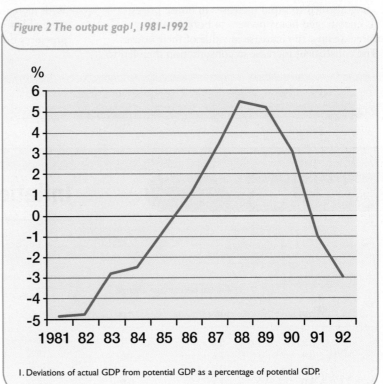

Figure 2 The output gap[1], 1981-1992

%

1. Deviations of actual GDP from potential GDP as a percentage of potential GDP.

Table 1 Inflation and its possible determinants

		%	% change over previous 12 months		Millions
		Inflation	Real GDP	Average earnings	Unemployment (claimant count)
1983	Q1	4.9	3.0	8.8	3.2
1984	Q1	5.2	4.0	6.1	3.2
1985	Q1	5.4	2.2	7.5	3.3
1986	Q1	5.0	3.8	8.4	3.4
	Q2	2.8	3.3	8.1	3.3
	Q3	2.7	3.8	7.4	3.3
	Q4	3.5	4.9	8.0	3.2
1987	Q1	3.9	3.9	7.2	3.2
	Q2	4.2	3.9	7.5	3.1
	Q3	4.3	5.6	7.9	2.9
	Q4	4.1	4.8	8.4	2.8
1988	Q1	3.3	5.9	8.8	2.7
	Q2	4.3	5.3	8.3	2.5
	Q3	5.5	4.5	8.4	2.3
	Q4	6.5	4.2	9.6	2.1
1989	Q1	7.8	2.8	9.3	2.1
	Q2	8.2	3.0	9.3	1.9
	Q3	7.7	1.7	9.9	1.8
	Q4	7.6	1.1	8.7	1.6

Source: adapted from *Economic Trends Annual Supplement, Monthly Digest of Statistics,* Office for National Statistics.

borrow more than they needed to cover the cost of the house purchase and used the cash to buy everything from carpets and curtains to new cars. Increased lending also led to rapid increases in house prices. This encouraged home owners to borrow money secured against the increase in value of their houses.

The consequent increase in consumption then led to increased investment by industry at a time when export sales were growing fast too. Extra spending which led to increased output meant that unemployment fell. With increased tightness in the labour market, workers were able to secure higher wage increases, which led to pressures on costs and prices.

DataQuestion — Inflation, 1997-2006

Table 2 Prices

| | Annual percentage change | | |
	RPI	RPIX	CPI
1997	3.2	2.8	1.8
1998	3.4	2.6	1.6
1999	1.5	2.3	1.3
2000	3.0	2.1	0.8
2001	1.8	2.1	1.2
2002	1.7	2.2	1.3
2003	2.9	2.8	1.4
2004	1.3	2.2	1.3
2005	2.8	2.3	2.1
2006	2.8	2.3	2.1

Source: adapted from *Economic & Labour Market Review*, Office for National Statistics.

Table 3 Demand: the output gap and changes in real GDP

	Real GDP annual % change	Output gap actual GDP % deviation from trend GDP
1997	3.2	-1.0
1998	3.3	-0.4
1999	3.0	-0.3
2000	3.8	0.8
2001	2.4	0.5
2002	2.1	-0.1
2003	2.8	0.0
2004	3.3	0.6
2005	1.8	-0.1
2006	2.9	-0.2

Source: adapted from *Economic & Labour Market Review*, Office for National Statistics; *Economic Outlook*, OECD.

Table 4 Supply side factors

	Output per worker whole economy, annual % change	Net migration (immigration - emigration) 000s	Unemployment rate, ILO %
1997	1.3	47	7.2
1998	2.5	139	6.3
1999	1.7	163	6.1
2000	2.6	163	5.6
2001	1.3	172	4.9
2002	1.0	153	5.2
2003	1.9	151	5.0
2004	2.2	223	4.8
2005	0.9	185	4.7
2006	2.1	200	5.4

Source: adapted from *Economic & Labour Market Review*, *International Migration*, Office for National Statistics.

Table 5 *Cost changes: average earnings, import prices and profits*

	Annual percentage change		
	Average earnings	Import prices	Profits[1]
1997	4.2	-6.7	9.4
1998	5.2	-5.1	3.0
1999	4.8	-6.1	2.6
2000	4.5	3.4	-0.4
2001	4.5	-0.9	-0.6
2002	3.5	-2.5	5.0
2003	3.4	-0.7	8.5
2004	4.4	-0.5	9.9
2005	4.0	4.2	1.7
2006	4.1	3.7	4.0

1. Profit at current prices: gross trading profit or private non-financial corporations excluding UK continental shelf companies.

Source: adapted from *Economic & Labour Market Review*, Office for National Statistics.

The Bank of England has asked you, as one of their economists, to prepare a report on the main causes of inflation during the period 1997-2006.

1. Briefly describe the main trends in the economy during the period.
2. 'Inflation during the period was entirely caused by excess demand in the economy'. Evaluate whether this is a correct analysis of the evidence presented in the data.

Summary

1. The balance of payments accounts are split into two parts. The current account records payments for the exports and imports of goods and services. The capital account records saving, investment and speculative flows of money.
2. The current account is split into two parts: trade in visibles and trade in invisibles.
3. The balance of payments accounts must always balance. However, component parts of the accounts may be positive or negative. If there is a surplus on the current account, then outflows on the capital account must be greater than inflows.
4. A current account surplus is often seen as a sign of a healthy economy, whilst a current account deficit is seen as a cause for worry. But current account deficits are not necessarily bad as they may be a sign of borrowing which could finance expansion.
5. A current account deficit is most unlikely to be financed by government. The balance of payments deficit and the government deficit are two completely different entities.

The balance of payments

The BALANCE OF PAYMENTS ACCOUNT is a record of all financial dealings over a period of time between economic agents of one country and all other countries. Balance of payments accounts can be split into two components:

- the CURRENT ACCOUNT where payments for the purchase and sale of goods and services are recorded;
- the CAPITAL and FINANCIAL ACCOUNTS where flows of money associated with saving, investment, speculation and currency stabilisation are recorded.

Flows of money into the country are given a positive (+) sign on the accounts. Flows of money out of the country are given a negative (-) sign.

The current account

The current account on the balance of payments is itself split into **several** components.

Trade in goods Trade in goods is often called trade in VISIBLES. This is trade in raw materials such as copper and oil, semi-manufactured goods such as car components and finished manufactured goods such as cars and DVD players. Visible exports are goods which are sold to foreigners. Goods leave the country, whilst payment for these goods goes in the opposite direction. Hence visible exports of, say, cars result in an **inward** flow of money and are recorded with a positive sign on the balance of payments account. Visible imports are goods which are bought by domestic residents from foreigners. Goods come into the country whilst money **flows out**. Hence visible imports of, say, wheat are given a minus sign on the balance of payments. The difference between visible exports and visible imports is known as the BALANCE OF TRADE.

Trade in services A wide variety of services is traded internationally, including financial services such as banking and insurance, transport services such as shipping and air travel, and tourism. Trade in services is an example of trade in INVISIBLES. These are intangible services. Exports of invisibles are bought by foreigners. So an American tourist paying for a stay in a London hotel is an invisible export. So too is a Chinese company buying insurance in the City of London or a Taiwanese company hiring a UK owned ship. With invisibles, money flows into the UK, as it would if a French company bought a machine manufactured in the UK, a visible export for the UK. Hence, on the official UK balance of payments accounts, invisible service exports are called export credits in services. Imports of services for the UK are services which are bought from foreigners. A holiday taken by a UK national in Spain would be an invisible import for the UK. So too would be a UK firm hiring a private jet from a German company. With invisible imports, money flows abroad. Hence they are called debits on the official UK balance of payments accounts.

Income and current transfers Not all flows of money result from trade in goods and services. **Income** results from the loan of factors of production abroad. For the UK, most of this income is generated from interest, profits and dividends on assets owned abroad. Equally, interest, profits and dividends on UK assets owned by foreigners have to be paid out. For some countries, their main income comes from the repatriation of earnings from national workers in foreign countries. For example, a Pakistani national may work in Kuwait and send back income to support his family in Pakistan. Current transfers are a range mainly of

A country has the following international transactions on current account: exports of manufactured goods £20bn; imports of food £10bn; earnings from foreign tourists £5bn; interest, profits and dividends paid to foreigners £4bn; purchase of oil from abroad £8bn; earnings of nationals working overseas which are repatriated £7bn; sale of coal to foreign countries £2bn; payments by foreigners to domestic financial institutions for services rendered £1bn.

(a) Which of these items are: (i) visible exports; (ii) exports of services; (iii) income and current transfer credits; (iv) visible imports; (v) imports of services; (vi) income and current transfer debits.?
(b) Calculate: (i) the balance of trade; (ii) the balance on all invisibles; (iii) the current balance.
(c) How would your answers to (b) be different if it cost the country £3bn to transport its exports (i) in its own ships and (ii) in the ships of other countries?

government transfers to and from overseas organisations such as the European Union. Income and current transfers are examples of invisibles along with trade in services.

The CURRENT BALANCE is the difference between exports and total imports. It can also be calculated by adding the balance of trade in goods with that of services, income and current transfers.

Current account deficits and surpluses

The balance of payments account shows all the inflows of money to and the outflows of money from a country. Inflows must equal outflows overall and therefore the balance of payments must always balance. This is no different from a household. All the money going out from a household in spending or saving over a period of time must equal money coming in from earnings, borrowings or running down of savings. If a household spends £60 going out for a meal, the money must have come from somewhere.

However, there can be surpluses or deficits on particular parts of the account. Using the example of the household again, it can spend more than it earns if it borrows money. The same is true of a national economy. It can spend more on goods and services than it earns if it borrows money from overseas. So it can have a CURRENT ACCOUNT DEFICIT, where exports are less than imports, by running a surplus on its capital account. Equally, it can run a CURRENT ACCOUNT SURPLUS, exporting more than it imports, by running a deficit on its capital and financial account. A deficit on the capital account for the UK means that it invests more abroad than foreigners invest in the UK.

Often, the media talk about a 'balance of payments deficit'. Strictly speaking, there can never be a balance of payments deficit because the balance of payments must always balance, i.e. it must always be zero. What the media are, in fact, referring to is either a balance of trade deficit or a current account deficit. Similarly, the term '**trade gap**' is a term used in the media, usually to mean a deficit on the balance of trade in goods.

Causes of changes in the current account balance

The current account balance will change over time. It may move from surplus to deficit, for example, or a deficit may get larger. To explain why this occurs, we need to distinguish between the factors which affect trade in goods and services and those which affect income and current transfers.

Trade in goods and services Goods and services sold to foreigners are exports. Goods and services bought by domestic consumers, firms and government from overseas are imports. Exports and imports change over time for a variety of reasons.

- The exchange rate may change. A rise in the exchange rate will tend to increase imports and reduce exports. A fall in the exchange rate will tend to reduce imports and increase exports.
- The price in national currencies of goods and services may change. For example, an increase in labour productivity (output per worker) will reduce costs of production and so should lead to a fall in the price of the product, all other things being equal. An increase in domestic inflation will push up a variety of costs to firms. For example, workers are likely to demand higher wages to compensate them for the

impact of higher inflation. So firm's prices are likely to rise, making them less competitive against foreign suppliers, all other things being equal.

- Many goods and services are non-homogenous. This means the product of one firm is different from that of another firm. It may be the quality of the product, its design, its functions and features, its aesthetic appearance or after-sales service that differ. For example, a Mars Bar is different from a Twix although both are chocolate bars. A beach holiday in Benidorm in Spain is different from a walking holiday in the Alps even though both are holidays. Exporters can gain a competitive advantage by improving their product and making it better than products from other firms.
- Aggregate demand may change in the domestic economy or in the world economy. A world recession, for example, will hit UK exports. A UK recession will lead to lower imports as consumers and firms buy fewer goods and services. In contrast, a world boom should raise UK exports. A boom in the UK is likely to see a rise in imports.

Income and current transfers The relative importance of income and current transfers differs from country to country. For some Third World countries, the repatriation of earnings of people working abroad is very important. Curbs on migrant workers in host countries can then hit those earnings hard. The UK records a large surplus on the profit and interest on assets owned abroad. A world recession which hits the profits made by foreign firms partly or wholly owned by UK investors will reduce this surplus. An improvement in the investment strategies of foreigners investing in UK assets could lead to a deterioration in the surplus.

When is a current account deficit or surplus a problem?

Current account deficits are generally seen as undesirable and a sign of economic weakness. Conversely, current account surpluses are usually seen as signs of the economic strength of a country. This, though, is a very crude way of analysing the balance of payments. One reason why this is crude is because the size of the current account surplus or deficit is important in deciding its significance. Using the analogy of the household again, if the income of a household is £100 000 per year and its spending over the year is £100 010, it has overspent. However, overspending by £10 on an income of £100 000 in one year is of almost no significance. On the other hand, take a household living solely from state benefits. If income is £100 per week, and spending is £110, then this household is likely to be in serious trouble. Unless it has substantial savings to draw on, overspending £10 each week on an income of £100 will soon become unsustainable. Where will the £10 per week come from? If it is from borrowing, then the money must eventually be repaid, eating into a very low income.

This is also the case for a national economy. If the country runs a current account deficit year after year, but this current account deficit is very small in relation to national income over time, then it is of little significance economically. Equally, if a country runs a large deficit over a short period of time, but then follows this with a large surplus over the next period, then it is relatively unimportant. Only if the current account deficit or surplus is large in relation to income and is sustained over a period of time does it really matter.

Question 2

The Czech Republic, since 1990, has been relatively successful in making the transition from being a command economy, where the state dominated every economic decision, to a market economy, where markets are used to allocate a significant proportion of an economy's resources. Over the period 1994-2008, average economic growth in the Euro area (the EU countries which have adopted the euro including France, Germany and Italy) was an estimated 2.2 per cent, two thirds that of the Czech Republic.

Inevitably, in opening itself up to other markets, it has sucked in significant levels of imports. Czech consumers have bought cheaper and better quality goods from other countries, whilst Czech businesses have imported raw materials and capital goods from abroad.

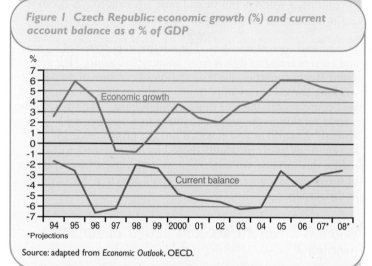

Figure 1   Czech Republic: economic growth (%) and current account balance as a % of GDP

*Projections

Source: adapted from *Economic Outlook*, OECD.

(a) Use the data to explain why the Czech Republic has been a success story in the 1990s and 2000s.
(b) Discuss whether its large current account deficits. throughout the period are a problem for the Czech Republic.

Large sustained current account deficits

Large sustained current account deficits are usually considered undesirable because they become unsustainable. Deficits on the current account may occur because the government of a country spends excessively on foreign goods and services. Or it could be private firms and individuals which are spending too much, importing far more than they are exporting. Whether it is government or the private sector, the current account deficit has to be financed. Either the level of borrowings abroad is increased, or there is a net run down in savings and investments held abroad. Governments and firms can borrow abroad so long as foreign lenders think that they can repay the loans with interest in the future. But if the current account deficit is large and sustained, there usually comes a point when lenders think that the borrowers may **default** on their loans (i.e. not pay them). Lenders then stop lending. At this point, the country is in serious difficulties.

Countries like Poland, Brazil and Uganda in the 1980s, and Thailand and South Korea in the 1990s, have all faced this **credit crunch**, the point at which foreign lenders refuse to lend any more. They are then forced to return their current account to equilibrium. This means cutting down on imports, or exporting more goods which previously might have been sold on the domestic market. Citizens therefore have fewer goods available to them and their consumption and standard of living falls.

If the economy is fundamentally strong, the adjustment will be painful but relatively short, lasting just a few years perhaps. For countries which have very weak economies, the credit crunch can have a negative impact for decades. In sub-Saharan Africa, the credit crunch which occurred in the early 1980s led to Western banks and other agencies refusing to lend significant sums for the next 20 years. This crippled the economies of certain countries and deprived them of foreign funds which could have helped them to grow.

However, large sustained current account deficits may be beneficial to an economy. It depends on its rate of **economic growth**. If an economy is growing at 3 per cent per annum, but is running a large current account deficit of 5 per cent of GDP per annum, then it will run into problems. Its foreign debt as a percentage of GDP is likely to grow over time. However, if the economy is growing at 10 per cent per annum, and there is a current account deficit of 5 per cent of GDP, accumulated foreign debt as a percentage of GDP is likely to fall. Although foreign debt in absolute terms will be growing, the income of the country available to repay it will be growing even faster. Countries like the USA in the nineteenth century, and South Korea and Malaysia in the late part of the twentieth century, have all run significant current account deficits over a period of time, but they have tended to benefit from this because the money has been used to strengthen their growth potential. Even so, both South Korea and Malaysia were caught up in a credit crunch in the late 1990s when foreign lenders judged that too much had been lent to East Asian economies. High levels of foreign borrowing carry risks for countries even when their economies are highly successful on measures of national economic performance such as economic growth, unemployment and inflation.

Large sustained current account surpluses

Some countries run large sustained current account surpluses. One reason for this is that the government of the country keeps its exchange rate artificially low. China, for example, currently adopts such a policy. The advantage is that a low exchange rate encourages exports but makes imports less competitive. Strong exports help create jobs and boost economic growth. Another possible advantage of exporting more than importing is that a country can increase its net foreign wealth. This is a strategy being pursued by some Middle Eastern oil exporting countries such as Saudi Arabia and Kuwait. It has the benefit that the economy then should receive ever increasing amounts of income from that wealth, which can be used to buy more foreign goods and services than would otherwise be the case. This is like a household which consistently saves money. In the long term, it can use the interest on that saving to buy more goods than it would otherwise have been able to afford.

A sustained current account surplus may also make sense if there are long term structural changes occurring. Japan ran large current account surpluses during the last quarter of the twentieth century, consequently building up its net wealth

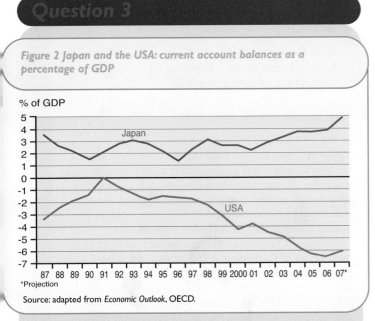

Question 3

Figure 2 Japan and the USA: current account balances as a percentage of GDP

% of GDP

*Projection

Source: adapted from *Economic Outlook*, OECD.

(a) Compare the current account balance of the USA with that of Japan during the late 1980s, 1990s and 2000s.

(b) Discuss the possible benefits and costs to Japan of running a persistent current account surplus.

overseas. However, in the first half of the twenty first century, the structure of the Japanese population will change dramatically. From having very few pensioners in proportion to workers, the population will age significantly and there will be a high proportion of pensioners to workers. It could well be that Japan will run down its wealth overseas to pay for the goods and services consumed by non-productive pensioners. Japan could therefore move from having sustained current account surpluses to current account deficits.

Large sustained current account surpluses have their disadvantages though. First, they reduce what is available for consumption now. If the surplus were eliminated, resources used for exports could be diverted to produce goods for domestic consumption. Or the country could increase imports, again increasing the amount available for consumption.

Second, sustained current account surpluses cause friction between countries. If China has a current account surplus, the rest of the world must have a deficit. If China is a net lender, building up wealth overseas, the rest of the world must be a net borrower, building up debts overseas. Countries which attempt to reduce their current account deficits can only be successful if other countries reduce their current account surpluses. On a microeconomic level, trade unions and firms in deficit countries often accuse firms in surplus countries of 'poaching' jobs. If China reduced its trade surplus by reducing exports to the United States, then firms in the United States might be able to fill the gap created by expanding their output.

In practice, the benefits to one country of another country reducing its surplus are likely to be small. If China's exports fall, US producers are just as likely to find that other countries like South Korea or the UK fill the market gap. When the USA has a large current account deficit and China a large surplus, a reduction in the Chinese surplus will improve the current account positions of many countries around the world, not just

that of the USA. The benefit of a large reduction in the Chinese surplus to any single country, even to the USA, the largest economy in the world, will be relatively small.

Government deficits and balance of payments deficits

One common mistake is to assume that any current account deficit is paid for by the government. Another common mistake is to assume that government borrowing is the same as the current account deficit. The current account is made up of billions of individual transactions. Each one is financed in a different way. So a UK firm importing machinery will use different finance from a family taking a holiday in France. A Chinese firm buying specialist car parts from a UK company will finance this in a different way from a German firm buying insurance from a broker at Lloyds of London. If a current account deficit has been caused mainly by excessive government spending, then the government is likely to have borrowed at least some of the money from abroad. However, a current account deficit may be caused mainly by private consumers and firms buying too many imports and borrowing the money from abroad to pay for them. The relationship between the current account deficit, private sector borrowing and government borrowing is therefore complex and depends upon individual circumstances.

Governments may choose to attempt to correct current account deficits or surpluses. They have a variety of ways in which they could attempt this, which have various advantages and disadvantages. These are discussed later in this book. However, governments may choose to do nothing and allow free market forces to correct any imbalances. The last time the UK government and the Bank of England attempted to influence directly the current account was in the 1970s.

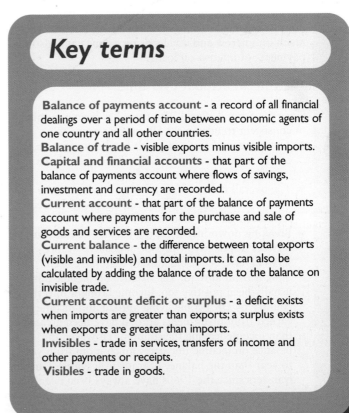

Key terms

Balance of payments account - a record of all financial dealings over a period of time between economic agents of one country and all other countries.
Balance of trade - visible exports minus visible imports.
Capital and financial accounts - that part of the balance of payments account where flows of savings, investment and currency are recorded.
Current account - that part of the balance of payments account where payments for the purchase and sale of goods and services are recorded.
Current balance - the difference between total exports (visible and invisible) and total imports. It can also be calculated by adding the balance of trade to the balance on invisible trade.
Current account deficit or surplus - a deficit exists when imports are greater than exports; a surplus exists when exports are greater than imports.
Invisibles - trade in services, transfers of income and other payments or receipts.
Visibles - trade in goods.

Applied economics

The UK current account

The parts of the current account

The Office for National Statistics divides the UK current account into four parts, shown in Table 1.

- Trade in goods. Exports of goods minus imports of goods is equal to the balance of trade in goods.
- Trade in services. The main services traded are transport (such as shipping or air transport), travel and tourism, insurance and other financial services, and royalties and licence fees.
- Income. Some countries, such as Pakistan or Egypt, earn substantial amounts from the repatriation of income from nationals working abroad. For the UK, such income is relatively unimportant. Nearly all income in the UK balance of payments accounts relates to UK investments abroad and to foreign investments in the UK (investment income).
- Current transfers. Most current transfers relate to the UK's membership of the European Union. The UK has to pay part of its tax revenues to the EU, but in return receives payments such as agricultural subsidies or regional grants.

Visibles in the account are the trade in goods. Invisibles are the trade in services, income and current transfers. In terms of relative size, invisibles outweigh visibles. The most important invisible is not trade in services but income. Current transfers are relatively insignificant. The UK's current balance is therefore crucially dependent not just on trade in goods and services, but also on income from foreign investments. Comparing this to a household, it is as if the financial soundness of the household is dependent not just on wage earnings and spending, but also very much on interest and dividends on savings and also on payments of interest on loans.

The current account over time

Since the Second World War, there has been a number of consistent trends on the UK current account.

- The balance of trade in goods has been negative, as can be seen from Figure 3. Visible exports have tended to be less than visible imports.
- The overall balance on trade in services, income and current transfers has been positive. Invisible credits have been greater than invisible debits.
- Breaking down invisibles, the balance of trade in services has nearly always been positive - more services have been sold abroad than have been bought from abroad. The balance on income has usually been positive too. Income brought into the country by UK people living abroad and income earned from investments abroad have been greater than income leaving the country. However, the balance on income fluctuates much more from year to year than the balance of trade in services. Current transfers since the 1960s have always been negative.

Since joining the EU in 1973, most of the negative balance is due to the UK paying more into EU coffers than receiving in grants.

The size of the current account balances

In the 1950s and 1960s, the current account posed a major problem for the UK. At the time, the value of the pound was fixed against other currencies. In years when the current account went into deficit, currency speculators tended to sell pounds sterling in the hope that the government would be forced to devalue the pound, i.e. make it less valuable against other currencies. Quite small current account deficits as a percentage of GDP, as in 1960 or in 1964, thus presented large problems for the government of the day.

From the 1970s, the pound was allowed to float, changing its value from minute to minute on the foreign exchange markets. Figure 4 shows that there were two periods when the UK's current account position could have become unsustainable in the long term. In 1973-75 the UK, along with most Western countries, suffered a severe economic shock from a rise in commodity prices, particularly oil prices. Following the Yom Kippur war of October 1973 between Egypt and Israel, the members of OPEC chose to restrict supply of oil to the west and as a result its price quadrupled. Import prices rose sharply and the current account approached 4 per cent of GDP in 1974. The UK government was forced to

Table 1 The current balance, 2006 (£m)

Trade in goods		
Export of goods	245 105	
Import of goods	328 736	
Balance on trade in goods		- 83 631
Trade in services		
Export of services	124 586	
Import of services	95 392	
Balance of trade in services		29 194
Balance on trade in goods and services		- 54 437
Income		
Credits	241 350	
Debits	222 795	
Balance		18 555
Current transfers		
Credits	16 165	
Debits	28 064	
Balance		- 11 899
Current balance		- 47 781

Source: adapted from *The Pink Book*, United Kingdom Balance of Payments, Office for National Statistics.

react by cutting domestic spending, which in turn reduced demand for imports. In 1986-89, there was another sharp deterioration in the current account due to the 'Lawson boom', named after the then Chancellor, Nigel Lawson. Fast increases in domestic spending led to sharp increases in imports.

Since the late 1980s, the current account has been consistently in deficit within a range of 0.2 per cent of GDP to 4 per cent of GDP. It could be argued that this should pose long term problems for the UK. If the UK is consistently spending more than it is earning abroad, this will lead to a long term build-up of debt. Just as households who consistently borrow more and more money should get into financial difficulties, so too should a country.

There are two reasons which might explain why the UK has not encountered problems relating to its persistent current account deficits in the 1990s and 2000s. One is that the deficits are manageable given the economy's average growth rate of between 2.5 and 3.0 per cent over the period. For a household, so long as income is rising faster than debt, there should be no debt problem. Certainly, the financial markets have not shown any particular concern about the UK's current account deficits. Foreign lenders have not refused to lend UK borrowers any more money as they did, for example, to countries such as Mexico, South Korea or Poland when they had debt crises over the past 30 years.

The other reason is that the current account deficit is not the main determinant of the net debt owed by UK citizens, businesses and government to foreigners. The main determinant is changing asset values, such as stock market prices in New York or bond prices in Frankfurt. Since 1997 the net debt of the UK, the difference between what UK households, businesses and government own abroad and what they owe to foreigners, has varied from plus 49 per cent of GDP to minus 150 per cent. Such huge swings are accounted for not by current account deficits but by changes in asset values.

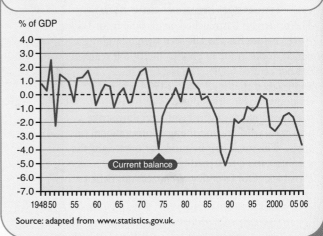

Figure 4 The current balance as a percentage of GDP

Source: adapted from www.statistics.gov.uk.

Figure 5 Balances of trade in services, total income and current transfers as a percentage of GDP

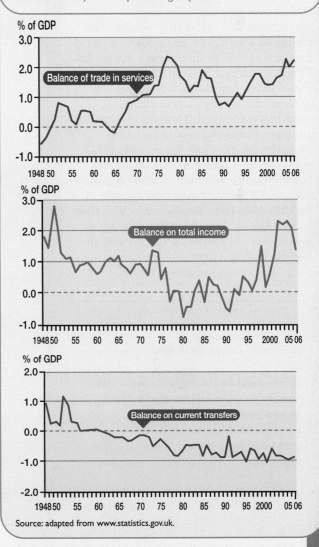

Source: adapted from www.statistics.gov.uk.

Figure 3 The balance of trade in goods, and the balance of trade in services, income and current transfers, as a percentage of GDP

DataQuestion

The trade gap

Trade gap at an all time high

The trade gap has reached an all time record. Never before has the UK seen such a large deficit in our trade in goods. In 2006 it reached 6.4 per cent of GDP. The last time it approached that level was in 1974 when the economy was in crisis due to a result of overspending by government, crippling strike action by workers and the first international oil crisis. The trade gap in goods far outweighs the surpluses the UK earned last year on its invisibles. Our overall current account deficit recorded in 2006 was 3.7 per cent of GDP.

The mystery of our investment income

Strange things are happening abroad. According to the latest statistics for 2006, the UK earned a net 1.5 per cent of GDP on its net foreign assets. What that means is that the UK earned 1.5 per cent more on the foreign assets owned by UK householders, businesses and government than foreigners earned on UK assets that they owned. However, the statistics also show that the value of foreign assets owned by the UK is less than the value of UK assets owned by foreigners. UK households, businesses and government in 2006 owed to foreigners 10 per cent more than the value of the UK's assets they owned abroad. With these sorts of figures, we ought to be paying out more than we receive. Obviously, UK investors are better at making a return on their overseas assets than foreign investors in the UK.

1. Describe the changes in the balance of trade and total investment income shown in the data.
2. What might be the implications for the current account balance of the changes shown in the data?
3. Discuss the extent to which the deterioration in the 'trade gap' in 2006 might have been of economic significance.

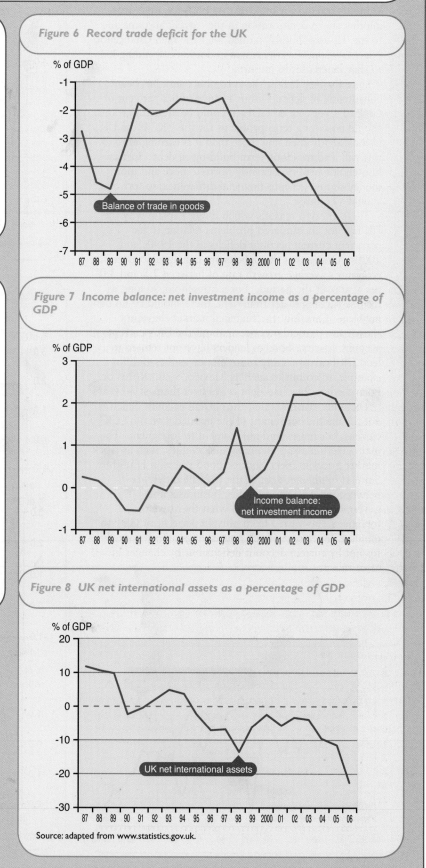

Figure 6 Record trade deficit for the UK

Balance of trade in goods

Figure 7 Income balance: net investment income as a percentage of GDP

Income balance: net investment income

Figure 8 UK net international assets as a percentage of GDP

UK net international assets

Source: adapted from www.statistics.gov.uk.

Summary

1. Fiscal policy, the manipulation of government spending, taxation and borrowing, affects aggregate demand. It can also affect the pattern of economic activity.
2. The effect on aggregate demand of a change in government spending or taxation is increased because of the multiplier effect.
3. Classical economists argue that fiscal policy cannot, in the long term, affect the level of output. Hence, it cannot influence unemployment, but can raise inflation.
4. Keynesian economists argue that fiscal policy can affect both output and prices. Hence, fiscal policy can be used to influence both inflation and unemployment.
5. Fiscal policy cannot, as a demand side policy, influence long term economic growth, but it can be used to help an economy out of a recession or reduce demand pressures in a boom.
6. Fiscal policy, through its effect on aggregate demand, can influence imports and the current balance.

Fiscal policy

The UK government has been responsible for between 40 and 50 per cent of national expenditure over the past 20 years. The main areas of public spending are the National Health Service, defence, education and roads. In addition, the government is responsible for transferring large sums of money round the economy through its spending on social security and National Insurance benefits. All of this is financed mainly through taxes, such as income tax and VAT.

In the post-war era, governments have rarely balanced their budgets (i.e. they have rarely planned to match their expenditure with their receipts). In most years, they have run BUDGET DEFICITS, spending more than they receive. As a result, in most years governments have had to borrow money. In the UK, the borrowing of the public sector (central government, local government and other state bodies such as nationalised industries) over a period of time is called the PUBLIC SECTOR NET CASH REQUIREMENT (PSNCR). In three fiscal periods, between 1969-70, 1988-91 and 1999-2001, the UK government received more revenue than it spent. The normal budget deficit was turned into a BUDGET SURPLUS. There is then a negative PSNCR. A budget surplus allows the government to pay off part of its accumulated debt. This debt, called the NATIONAL DEBT, dates back to the founding of the Bank of England in 1694.

The government has to make decisions about how much to spend, tax and borrow. It also has to decide on the composition of its spending and taxation. Should it spend more on education and less on defence? Should it cut income tax by raising excise duties? These decisions about spending, taxes and borrowing are called the FISCAL POLICY of the government.

There are two key dates in the year for fiscal policy. One is the day of the BUDGET which occurs in March. In the Budget, the Chancellor gives a forecast of government spending and taxation in the coming financial year. Changes in taxation are also announced. The other key date occurs in November or December with the Chancellor's **Pre-Budget Report** and **Comprehensive Spending Review**. In this report, the Chancellor gives another forecast of government spending and taxation and announces the government's spending plans for the year. The financial year in the UK starts on 6 April and runs until 5 April the following year.

Aggregate demand

Government spending and taxation changes have an effect on aggregate demand. A rise in government spending, with the price level constant, will increase aggregate demand, pushing the AD curve to the right as in Figure 2.

Equally, a cut in taxes will affect aggregate demand. A cut in taxes on income, such as income tax and National Insurance contributions, will lead to a rise in the disposable income of households. This in turn will lead to a rise in consumption expenditure and hence to a rise in aggregate demand. This rise,

Question 1

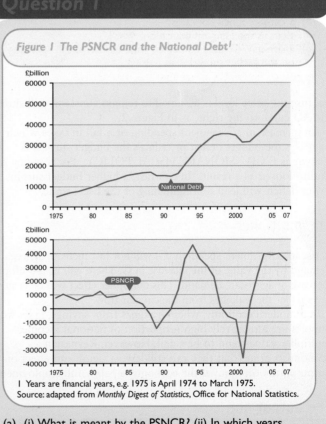

Figure 1 *The PSNCR and the National Debt*[1]

£billion

National Debt

£billion

PSNCR

1 Years are financial years, e.g. 1975 is April 1974 to March 1975.
Source: adapted from *Monthly Digest of Statistics*, Office for National Statistics.

(a) (i) What is meant by the PSNCR? (ii) In which years did the government have a budget surplus?
(b) Using examples from the data, explain the link between the PSNCR and the National Debt.
(c) If a government wanted to pay off its National Debt over a number of years, how could it achieve this?

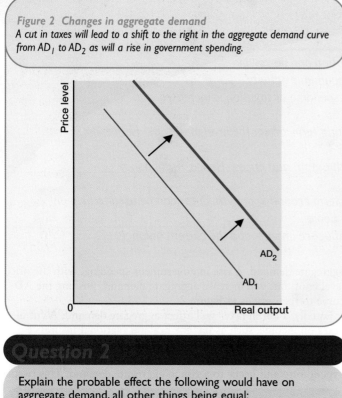

Figure 2 *Changes in aggregate demand*
A cut in taxes will lead to a shift to the right in the aggregate demand curve from AD$_1$ to AD$_2$ as will a rise in government spending.

Question 2

Explain the probable effect the following would have on aggregate demand, all other things being equal:
(a) a rise in income tax rates;
(b) a cut in council tax rates;
(c) a cut in spending on education;
(d) a rise in VAT rates combined with an increase in spending on the NHS.

because the price level is assumed to remain constant, will shift the AD curve to the right, as in Figure 2.

An increase in government spending or a fall in taxes which increases the budget deficit or reduces the budget surplus is known as EXPANSIONARY FISCAL POLICY. Fiscal policy is said to **loosen** as a result. In contrast, a higher budget surplus or lower deficit will lead to a **tightening** of the fiscal stance.

The multiplier

A rise in government spending (G) will not just increase aggregate demand by the value of the increase in G. There will be a multiple increase in aggregate demand. This **multiplier effect** will be larger the smaller the leakages from the circular flow.

In a modern economy, where leakages from savings, taxes and imports are a relatively high proportion of national income, multiplier values tend to be small. However, Keynesian economists argue that they can still have a significant effect on output in the economy if the economy is below full employment.

The output gap

Changes in government spending and taxation have an impact on the size of the output gap. In Figure 3, the actual path of GDP over time is shown by the red line. Between time period 2 and 3, the economy is going through a downturn or recession with actual GDP below its trend level. There is a negative output gap. Between time period 1 and 2, the

economy is in boom, with GDP above its trend level. There is a positive output gap. Through its fiscal policy, however, the government can reduce the impact of the cycle, shown by the blue line. By increasing spending relative to taxation and adopting an expansionary fiscal policy, it can bring the actual level of GDP up closer to the trend level between time periods 2 and 3. By cutting its spending relative to taxation and adopting a tighter fiscal stance, it can bring the actual level of GDP down closer to the trend level between time periods 1 and 2.

Figure 3 *Fiscal policy and the output gap*
Through adjusting its level of spending and taxation, governments can bring the actual level of GDP closer to its trend level. When there is a negative output gap, governments should spend more and tax less. When there is a positive output gap, governments should spend less and tax more.

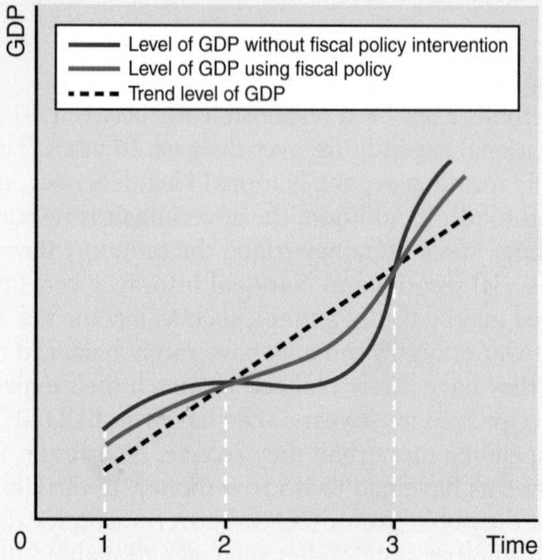

The goals of government policy

The government has four major macroeconomic policy goals. These are to achieve full employment with little or no inflation in a high growth economy with an external balance (current account) equilibrium. Fiscal policy affects each of these variables through its impact on aggregate demand.

Fiscal policy can be used to achieve a wide variety of objectives. For example, it can be used to improve standards of health care through increased spending on the health service of a country. It can be used to make incomes less unequal by taxing the wealthier and giving benefits to the less well off. However, when it is used to influence directly the level of aggregate demand it becomes an example of a DEMAND SIDE POLICY or a policy of DEMAND MANAGEMENT. Whether governments deliberately use fiscal policy to influence aggregate demand or not, changes in the balance between government spending and taxation have an effect on the four key objectives of government policy: inflation, unemployment, the rate of economic growth and the balance of payments.

Inflation An increase in government spending or a fall in taxes which leads to a higher budget deficit or lower budget surplus will have a tendency to be inflationary. A higher budget deficit or lower budget surplus leads to an increase in aggregate demand. In Figure 4, this is shown by a shift in the aggregate demand curve to the right. This in turn leads to an increase in

increase in aggregate demand will lead to increasing inflation. The nearer the level of full employment at OD, the greater will be the rise in inflation from a given rise in government spending or fall in taxes.

Unemployment A greater budget deficit or a lower budget surplus will tend to reduce the level of unemployment, at least in the short term. A greater budget deficit will lead to an increase in aggregate demand which, as shown in Figure 4, will lead to a higher equilibrium level of output. The higher the level of output the lower is likely to be the level of unemployment.

As with inflation, there is a variety of factors which determines the extent to which unemployment will fall. The smaller the change in government spending and taxation, the less impact it will have on aggregate demand and the labour market. If the long run aggregate supply schedule is vertical, then increases in aggregate demand can only lead to higher inflation and they will have no impact on the level of output and unemployment. In the

Question 3

The Labour government which took office in February 1974 barely had a majority in Parliament and therefore was unwilling to increase taxes and cut public expenditure to tackle soaring inflation and a large balance of payments deficit. In November 1974, another general election took place and this time the Labour government secured a workable majority. In the 1975 Budget, it cut planned public expenditure and increased taxes, both by over £1 000 million. Further cuts in public expenditure were announced in 1976. The budget deficit fell from £10 161 million in 1975 to £8 899 million in 1976 and to £5 419 million in 1977. However, the government relaxed its fiscal stance in 1978, and the budget deficit increased to £8 340 million.

(a) What is meant by 'the multiplier'?
(b) Explain, using the concept of the multiplier, the likely effect that the change in fiscal policy between 1974 and 1976 had on national income.
(c) Using a diagram, discuss the impact that the change in the government's fiscal stance in 1978 is likely to have had on prices and output.

the price level from P_1 to P_2. So inflation increases.

The extent to which there is an increase in inflation depends on a number of factors. One is the size of the change in government spending or taxation. If the change in the budget deficit or surplus is very small, it will have little impact on the price level. Another factor is the shape of the aggregate supply curve. The short run aggregate supply curve is likely to be relatively shallow and so an increase in aggregate demand is likely to have a relatively small impact on prices. In the long term, however, the aggregate supply curve could vary from being horizontal to vertical. Classical economists argue that the long run aggregate supply curve (LRAS) is vertical. So, in Figure 5, an increase in aggregate demand has a relatively large effect on inflation. In contrast, the Keynesian view suggests that the LRAS curve is L shaped. In Figure 6, where the LRAS curve is horizontal, the economy has high levels of unemployment. Any increase in aggregate demand to AD_2 will have no impact on prices. If the level of output rises beyond OB, however, an

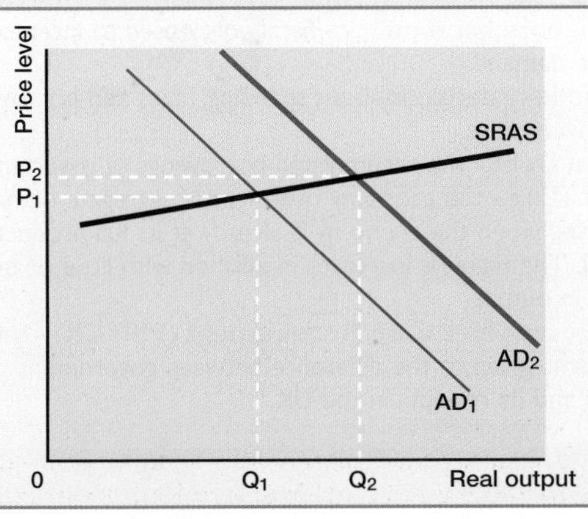

Figure 5 *The long run classical view*

In the long run, classical economists argue that expansionary fiscal policy has no effect on equilibrium output and therefore cannot reduce unemployment. However, it will lead to a higher level of prices.

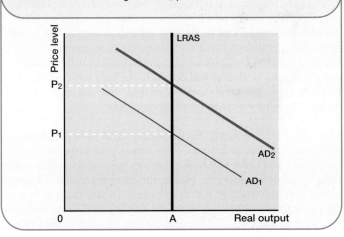

Figure 4 *Fiscal policy and aggregate demand*

A rise in government spending or a cut in taxes will shift the aggregate demand curve to the right from AD_1 to AD_2. In this short run this will be inflationary because the equilibrium price level will rise from P_1 to P_2, but equilibrium output will expand from Q_1 to Q_2.

Figure 6 *The Keynesian view*

The effectiveness of fiscal policy depends upon how close the economy is to full employment. At output levels below OB, expansionary fiscal policy can increase output and reduce unemployment without increasing inflation. Between OB and OD, expansionary fiscal policy will increase both output and inflation. At full employment, OD, expansionary fiscal policy will result only in extra inflation.

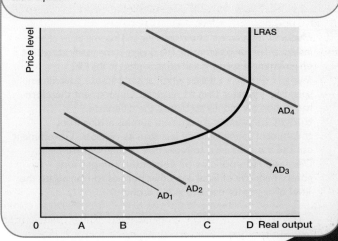

classical model, shown in Figure 5, the economy is in equilibrium at output 0A. An increase in the budget deficit might push the level of output beyond 0A in the short term because the SRAS is upward sloping, but in the long term it will revert to 0A. Hence, in the classical model, demand side fiscal policy cannot be used to alter unemployment levels in the long term. In a Keynesian model, this is also true if the economy is at full employment, at 0D in Figure 6. But at output levels below this, expansionary fiscal policy will lead to higher output and lower unemployment. If output is below 0B, expansionary fiscal policy can bring about a fall in unemployment without any increase in inflation.

Economic growth Expansionary fiscal policy is unlikely to affect the long term growth rate of an economy. This is because economic growth is caused by supply side factors such as investment, education and technology. However, expansionary fiscal policy is likely, in the short term, to increase GDP. As Figure 4 shows, in the short term an increase in aggregate demand will lead to higher output. Keynesian economists argue that expansionary fiscal policy is an appropriate policy to use if the economy is in recession below full employment. So in Figure 6, expansionary fiscal policy could be used to shift the aggregate demand curve from, say, AD_3 to AD_4. This would then return the economy to operating at full capacity on its production possibility frontier. Fiscal policy which pushes the aggregate demand curve beyond AD_4 would lead to no extra growth in output, but would be highly inflationary. In this situation, the economy would be OVER-HEATING. Classical economists argue that fiscal policy cannot be used to change real output in the long term because the long run aggregate supply curve is vertical. Shifting aggregate demand as in Figure 5 has no effect on output.

The balance of payments Expansionary fiscal policy leads to an increase in aggregate demand. This means that domestic consumers and firms will have more income and so will increase their spending on imports. Hence, the current account (exports minus imports) position will deteriorate. Tighter fiscal policy, on the other hand, will reduce domestic demand and hence demand for imports will fall. The current account position should then improve. There may be other less important influences on exports and imports. For instance, if domestic demand falls because of tighter fiscal policy, then domestic firms may increase their efforts to find markets for their goods by looking overseas.

Explain, using diagrams, the likely impact of the following on unemployment, inflation, economic growth and the current balance.
(a) The large rises in government spending on health and education between 2003 and 2007 which were not totally matched by increases in taxation.
(b) The virtual freezing of government spending in the early 1980s at a time when tax revenues were rising.

Equally, a fall in aggregate demand due to tighter fiscal policy should moderate the rate of inflation. British goods will be lower priced than they would otherwise have been. Hence, they will be more competitive against imports and foreigners will find British exports more keenly priced. This should lower imports and raise exports, improving the current account position.

Trade offs

Changing aggregate demand has different effects on key macroeconomic variables. The government may not be able to achieve improvements in one without bringing about a deterioration in the other, at least in the short term.
- Expanding the economy to bring it out of recession and reduce unemployment is likely to lead to higher inflation.
- Tightening fiscal policy to reduce inflation is likely to lead to higher unemployment and lower levels of GDP.
- Contracting the domestic economy by tightening fiscal policy to improve the current account situation will also lead to lower inflation, but will increase unemployment.

A rise in demand could lead to changes in income distribution and damage to the environment due to higher production levels. Fiscal policy therefore needs to be used in conjunction with other policies if the government is to steer the economy towards lower inflation and unemployment, higher growth and a current account equilibrium.

Affecting the pattern of economic activity

Fiscal policy can be used to influence **macroeconomic** variables

Key terms

Budget - a statement of the spending and income plans of an individual, firm or government. The Budget is the yearly statement on government spending and taxation plans in the UK.
Budget deficit - a deficit which arises because government spending is greater than its receipts. Government therefore has to borrow money to finance the difference.
Budget surplus - a government surplus arising from government spending being less than its receipts. Government can use the difference to repay part of the National Debt.
Demand side policies or demand management - government use of fiscal and other policies to manipulate the level of aggregate demand in the economy.

Expansionary fiscal policy - fiscal policy used to increase aggregate demand.
Fiscal policy - decisions about spending, taxes and borrowing of the government.
National Debt - the accumulated borrowings of government.
Over-heating - the economy over-heats if aggregate demand is increased when the economy is already at its full productive potential. The result is increases in inflation with little or no increase in output.
Public Sector Net Cash Requirement (PSNCR) - the official name given to the difference between government spending and its receipts in the UK.

such as the level of demand in the economy. However, it can also be used to influence the **distribution of income**. Through taxes and spending, income can be redistributed in general from those who are better off to those who are worse off. At a **microeconomic level**, fiscal policy is used to influence the pattern of economic activity.

- By providing goods and services directly, the government influences the level of provision of goods such as public and merit goods. If left to free market forces, these goods would either be underprovided or not provided at all.

- Through public spending and taxes, the government influences the pattern of economic activity in the private sector. For example, taxes on cigarettes discourage their consumption. Charges on waste disposal reduce the amount of waste going to land fill sites. Subsidies to firms taking on unemployed workers encourage them to employ workers who otherwise might not get a job. Building a new motorway in Scotland might attract more industry to Scotland at the expense of the South East of England.

Applied economics

A history of fiscal policy

1950-1975

During the period 1950-75, fiscal policy was probably the most important way in which governments manipulated aggregate demand. During the 1950s, governments learnt to use the 'fiscal levers' with more and more confidence. In a recession, such as in 1958, the government would cut taxes to stimulate spending in the economy. This might also be accompanied by public spending increases, although it was recognised that these would take longer to multiply through the economy than tax cuts. In a boom, when the economy was over-heating, as in 1960, the government would increase taxes and possibly cut public spending.

Borrowing in the economy was mainly controlled through direct controls on banks and building societies, specifying who was allowed to borrow money, or through controls on hire purchase, the most common way of financing the purchase of consumer durables.

In the 1960s, governments began to recognise some of the limitations of fiscal policy. The Labour government of 1964-66 experimented briefly with a National Plan, an attempt to model the economy in terms of the inputs and outputs of each industry. This plan was then to be used to help the government identify where particular industries were failing or creating 'bottlenecks' and might need further investment. This supply side experiment was abandoned as the economy faced yet another sterling crisis, which ultimately ended in the pound being devalued in 1967. Another policy used from 1966 was an incomes policy - government limits on the pay rises that could be given to workers. This supply side measure was designed to lower inflation whilst allowing the economy to grow and enjoy low rates of unemployment.

The last bout of traditional Keynesian demand management came in 1972-73 when the government cut taxes and increased public spending to put the economy into boom. This boom, called the Barber boom (after Anthony Barber, the then Chancellor of the Exchequer), ended disastrously as inflation spun out of control, fuelled by the oil price increases of 1973-74.

1975-1997

The mid-1970s saw a wholesale disillusionment with traditional Keynesian demand management techniques. A classical model of the economy became increasingly accepted as the model for governments to work with. In 1976, the Labour Prime Minister of the day, Jim Callaghan, in addressing his party conference, stated that: 'We used to think that you could just spend your way out of a recession, and increase employment by cutting taxes and boosting government spending. I tell you in all candour that that option no longer exists, and that in so far as it ever did exist, it worked by injecting inflation into the economy.'

The view was taken that cutting taxes produced only a temporary increase in aggregate demand. Unemployment would fall and growth would rise. However, as in the Barber boom, the medium term consequences would be a rise in the inflation rate. To reduce inflation, the government would have to tighten its fiscal stance by raising taxes. Aggregate demand would fall and the economy would return to its equilibrium position but at a higher level of prices and of inflation.

From 1979, when Margaret Thatcher won her first general election, fiscal policy was used for two separate purposes. First, it was used for micro-economic objectives as part of supply side policy for the government. For instance, income tax was cut to increase incentives to work. Second, it was used to ensure that monetary targets were met. In particular, it was felt that changes in the PSNCR (known as the PSBR at the time), such as might come about if taxes were cut, would have no effect on aggregate demand if the money for the tax cuts was genuinely borrowed from the non-bank sector. For instance, if the government cut taxes by £1 and financed this by borrowing from the non-bank sector, then there could be no increase in aggregate demand. The taxpayer would have £1 extra to spend but the lender to the government would have £1 less to spend. On this view, increases in the PSNCR completely **crowd-out** other expenditure in the economy resulting in no increase in aggregate demand. They could only work in a Keynesian manner if the increase in the PSNCR was financed through printing the money (the government has the unique power in the economy to print money) and thus increasing the money supply.

During the period of the Lawson boom (1986-89, named after Nigel Lawson, the then Chancellor) and the following recession (1990-92), the government allowed public spending and taxes to change in line with output and employment. Therefore, in the boom, the government allowed a large budget surplus to emerge. In the recession, the PSNCR was allowed to grow and by 1993 had reached over 5 per cent of GDP. In 1994-95, the government used active fiscal policy to cut this large deficit, increasing tax rates and introducing new taxes, whilst keeping a tight rein on public spending. On Keynesian assumptions, this put a brake on aggregate demand as it increased during the recovery. On classical assumptions, the tax increases had no effect on aggregate demand because the accompanying cuts in government borrowing released resources for the private sector to borrow and spend. One of the main reasons why the government felt it was so important to reduce the PSNCR was because of concerns that otherwise the National Debt would grow out of control.

Since 1997

In 1997, a Labour government under Tony Blair was elected. Tony Blair was succeeded as Prime Minister in 2007 by his Chancellor, Gordon Brown. Like previous governments since the mid- 1970s, the two post 1997 Labour administrations did not believe that fiscal policy should be used to manage aggregate demand. Demand management was left to the Bank of England through its operation of **monetary policy**. Instead, fiscal policy was used to achieve a number of objectives such as:

- expanding health and education: government spending was increased to finance an expansion of the provision of merit goods such as health and education;
- lessening income inequality: taxes and government spending were used to make the distribution of income less unequal;
- supply side reforms: rates of tax and government spending programmes were used to improve the performance of the supply side of the economy;
- maintaining the possibility of joining the European Monetary Union: one of the criteria for joining was that the UK should have stable public finances, with annual government borrowing at less than 3 per cent

of GDP. Note that the way in which the British government measures its annual borrowing and its National Debt is different from the measures used by the EU. The British government measure is more flattering to UK public finances than the EU measure.

There was a recognition that changes in government spending and taxation could play a positive role in the trade cycle. In a recession, when the output gap was negative, government spending would increase because of increased welfare benefits to the unemployed. Tax revenues would also fall because households and businesses would have less income and be spending less. Higher government spending and lower tax revenues would increase aggregate demand from what it would otherwise have been and help pull the economy out of recession. Equally, in a boom, when the output gap was positive, government would be raising large amounts of extra tax whilst its spending on welfare benefits would fall. This would dampen growth in aggregate demand, helping to prevent the economy from overheating.

The government was also concerned that the National Debt should not increase substantially as a proportion of national income. In 1998, the government therefore announced two new 'fiscal rules'.

- The **golden rule** stated that government would only borrow money to invest over the whole period of a trade cycle. It could increase borrowing to finance current expenditure such as welfare payments or wages in a recession, but this would have to be matched by repayments of debt in a boom. Therefore, government spending and taxation could help reduce the size of the fluctuation experienced in a trade cycle by influencing aggregate demand. However, over the whole cycle, net borrowing for this purpose would be zero. The government is allowed, however, to be a net borrower to finance its capital expenditure (i.e. investment), such as the building of new motorways or new hospitals.
- The **public debt rule** stated that the ratio of public debt to national income would be held at a 'stable and prudent' level over the trade cycle at less than 40 per cent of GDP.

Figures 10 and 11 in the data question show the extent to which the government achieved those objectives up to 2007.

DataQuestion   The pre-budget report: October 2007

In his October 2007 Pre-Budget Report, the Chancellor announced a number of changes to both government spending and taxation. For example, there would be additional spending by 2010-11 of £14.5 billion on education, £900 million on science and £3.6 billion on transport.

Overall, he predicted that total government expenditure in

2008-09 would increase by £28.2 billion compared to the estimated amounts for 2007-08. Tax and other receipts would rise by £30 billion compared to the estimated outturn for 2007-08. Public sector borrowing would therefore hardly change compared to the previous year's outturn.

Figure 7 The output gap

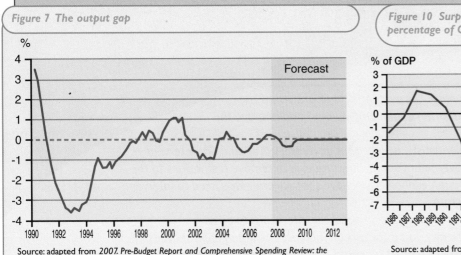

Source: adapted from *2007 Pre-Budget Report and Comprehensive Spending Review: the economy and public finances - supplementary charts and tables*, HM Treasury.

Figure 10 Surplus/deficit on government current budget as a percentage of GDP

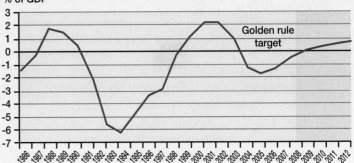

Source: adapted from *2007 Pre-Budget Report and Comprehensive Spending Review: the economy and public finances- supplementary charts and tables*, HM Treasury.

Figure 8 Growth in GDP

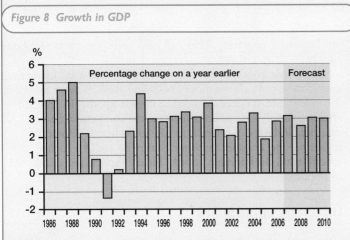

Source: adapted from *2007 Pre-Budget Report and Comprehensive Spending Review*, HM Treasury.

Figure 11 National debt as percentage of GDP

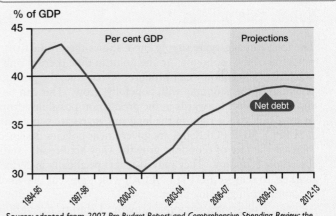

Source: adapted from *2007 Pre-Budget Report and Comprehensive Spending Review: the economy and public finances- supplementary charts and tables*, HM Treasury.

Figure 9 Inflation (annual % change in CPI)

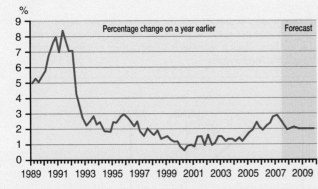

Source: adapted from *2007 Pre-Budget Report and Comprehensive Spending Review*, HM Treasury.

Figure 12 Estimated impact of changes in fiscal policy on GDP

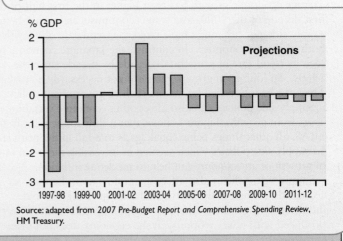

Source: adapted from *2007 Pre-Budget Report and Comprehensive Spending Review*, HM Treasury.

1. Explain how the Chancellor proposed to change government spending, taxation and government borrowing in his 2007 Pre-Budget Report.
2. Figure 12 shows how changes in government spending and taxation in one year affected GDP in that year. To what extent did the changes in fiscal policy over the period 1997-2007 help smooth out the effects of the trade cycle?
3. 'The changes in total government spending, taxation and government borrowing in the 2007 Pre-Budget Report will have no impact on GDP, unemployment and inflation.' Evaluate this statement.
4. To what extent were the Chancellor's plans announced in October 2007 in accordance with his 'fiscal rules'?

239

Summary

1. *Supply side policies are designed to increase the average rate of growth of the economy. They may also help reduce inflation and unemployment and improve the current account position.*
2. *Some economists, called supply side economists, believe that governments should not intervene in the workings of the free market. The government's role, they argue, is to remove restrictions to the operations of individual markets. Keynesian economists believe that governments need to intervene on the supply side to correct market failure.*
3. *Aggregate supply in the economy can be increased if government intervenes to ensure that labour markets operate more efficiently and if there is an increase in human capital over time.*
4. *Governments need to encourage firms to invest and take risks if aggregate supply is to increase.*
5. *Privatisation, deregulation and increased competition can increase aggregate supply.*
6. *Regional policy and inner city policy can also increase aggregate supply.*

Supply side policies

The long run aggregate supply curve shows the productive potential of the economy. At any point in time there is only so much that an economy can produce. Over time, the productive potential of the economy will, hopefully, grow. This can be shown by a shift outwards in the production possibility frontier or by a shift to the right in the long run aggregate supply curve.

SUPPLY SIDE POLICIES are government policies designed to increase the rate of economic growth. They act broadly across the whole economy. They may also act specifically in certain markets to remove BOTTLENECKS which prevent the whole economy from growing faster.

Figure 1 illustrates economic growth. A shift to the right in the LRAS curve increases output from 0A to 0B. In the UK and the USA, the trend rate of growth for most of the second half of the twentieth century has been around 2.5 per cent. However, average economic growth has been higher in the first half of the first decade of the 2000s and some economists claim that better supply side policies might have lifted the trend rate of growth for both of these economies. In contrast, the Japanese economy has seen its trend rate of growth fall decade by decade since the 1960s. So long term growth rates are not necessarily a constant. They can be influenced by factors such as government policy.

Supply side policies can also affect other economic variables apart from growth. Figure 1 shows that a shift to the right in the LRAS, all other things being equal, leads to a fall in the price level. So supply side policies which succeed in increasing the trend rate of growth of an economy can help to moderate inflation.

Supply side policies also affect unemployment. Economies are constantly changing, with new industries growing and old industries dying. Over time, new technology allows more to be produced with fewer workers. If the economy does not grow fast enough, more workers can lose their jobs in a year than new jobs are created. Unemployment therefore grows. In contrast, fast economic growth is likely to see more new jobs being created than old jobs are lost and so unemployment falls. Faster economic growth in the UK and the US in the second half of the 1990s has been associated in both countries with falling unemployment. There comes a time, as in the UK in the 1950s, when the economy is at full employment and everyone who wants a job is able to get one. Supply side policies can then play a crucial role in ensuring that inflation does

not become a problem. They can help keep growth in aggregate supply equal to growth in aggregate demand.

Supply side policies affect the current account too. Increasing aggregate supply allows more goods and services to be available for export and reduces the need to import goods. In practice, effective supply side policies increase the competitiveness of domestic industry in relation to foreign industry. Domestic goods become cheaper or better quality or are of a higher specification than foreign goods. Hence exports rise compared to imports.

Different approaches

Economists agree that government can affect the supply side of the economy. However, they disagree about how this should be done.

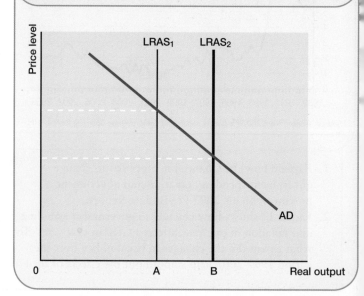

Figure 1 Supply side policies
Effective supply side policies push the long run aggregate supply curve to the right. This increases economic growth and reduces inflationary pressures. It may also bring about a reduction in unemployment and lead to higher exports and lower imports.

Supply side economists Supply side economists tend to be associated with free market economics. They believe that free markets promote economic efficiency and that government intervention in the economy is likely to impair economic efficiency. Government still has a vital role to play in the economy, according to these economists. Government is responsible for creating the environment in which free markets can work. This means eliminating the barriers which exist to the perfect working of markets. SUPPLY SIDE ECONOMICS therefore tends to be the study of how government can intervene using **market orientated** policies.

Interventionist economists Some economists believe that free markets often fail to maximise economic efficiency in the economy. Governments therefore have to correct **market failure**. This means intervening in free markets to change the outcome from that which it would otherwise have been.

In the rest of this unit, we will consider these two types of supply side policy - market orientated policies and interventionist policies.

Labour market policies

The level of aggregate supply is determined in part by the quantity of labour supplied to the market and the productivity of that labour. For instance, all other things being equal, an economy with 10 million workers will produce less than an economy with 20 million workers. Equally, an economy where workers have little **human capital** will have a lower output than one where there are high levels of human capital. Free market economists argue that there is a number of ways in which the quantity and quality of labour are restricted because markets are not allowed to work freely.

Trade unions The purpose of a trade union is to organise workers into one bargaining unit. The trade union then becomes a monopsonist, a sole seller of labour, and prevents workers from competing amongst themselves in the job market. Economic theory predicts that if trade unions raise wage rates for their members, then employment and output will be lower in otherwise competitive markets. So free market economists argue that government must intervene to curb the power of trade unions, for instance by reducing their ability to strike.

State welfare benefits Workers are unlikely to take low paid jobs if state benefits are a little below or equal to the pay being offered. Hence, state benefits reduce the level of aggregate supply because more workers remain unemployed. Free market economists argue that the solution is to cut state unemployment benefits to encourage workers to take on low paid jobs. An alternative approach is to give benefits or tax credits to those who take on low paid jobs. For there to be a positive incentive to work, the benefit plus pay must be greater than the benefits the worker would have received had he been out of work.

Minimum wages If there is a minimum wage which is set above the market clearing wage, then unemployment will be created. Minimum wages prevent some workers who would be prepared to work for lower pay from getting jobs. Hence aggregate supply is lowered. Free market economists tend to argue that minimum wages should be abolished.

Marginal tax rates High marginal rates of tax (the rate of tax on the last £1 earned or spent) discourage economic activity. A tax on cigarettes leads to fewer cigarettes being bought. A tax on work (income tax) leads to people working less. A tax on profits (corporation tax) is a disincentive to firms to make profits. Lowering certain taxes will therefore raise the level of economic activity and increase aggregate supply.

Supply side economists believe that the supply of labour is relatively elastic. A reduction in marginal tax rates on income will lead to a significant increase in 'work'. This could mean individuals working longer hours, being more willing to accept promotion, being more geographically mobile, or simply being prepared to join the workforce.

Work is, arguably, an inferior good, whilst leisure, its alternative, is a normal good. The higher an individual's income, the less willing he or she is to work. So a cut in marginal tax rates will have a negative income effect at the margin (i.e. the worker will be less willing to work). However, a cut in marginal tax rates will have a positive substitution effect because the relative price of work to leisure has changed in favour of work (i.e. the worker will be more willing to work).

Supply side economists believe that the substitution effect of a tax cut is more important than the income effect and hence tax cuts increase incentives to work. If cutting marginal income tax rates encourages people to work harder and earn more, then in theory it could be that tax revenues will increase following a tax cut. For instance, if 10 workers, each earning £10 000 a year, pay an average 25 per cent tax, then total tax revenue is £25 000 (10 x £10 000 x 0.25). If a cut in the tax rate to 20 per cent were to make each worker work harder and increase earnings to, say, £15 000, tax revenues would increase to £30 000 (10 x £3 000). This is an example of the LAFFER

Question 1

A number of studies has been completed discussing the link between income tax cuts and incentives to work. For instance, Brown and Dawson (1969) surveyed all the studies published between 1947 and 1968 making links between tax rates and hours worked. They found that high taxation acted as a disincentive to working longer hours for between 5 and 15 per cent of the population. These workers were mainly people who could choose to vary their hours of work relatively easily - the wealthy, rural workers, the middle aged and those without families. On the other hand, a smaller group of people tended to increase their hours of work when taxes were higher. These were typically part of large families, young, less well-off urban dwellers.

In a 1988 study by C V Brown, it was found that the substantial increase in tax allowances in the 1988 Budget only increased the number of hours worked in the economy by 0.5 per cent. The cut in the basic rate of tax had no effect at all on hours worked whilst the massive cut in the top rate of tax from 60 per cent to 40 per cent only had a small effect in stimulating extra hours of work by the rich.

(a) Explain why tax rates might have an effect on incentives to work.
(b) To what extent have tax cuts increased the number of hours worked?
(c) What are the implications of the two studies described in the passage for the shape of the Laffer curve?

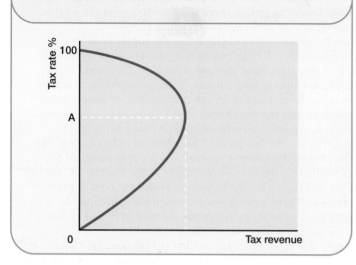

Figure 2 The Laffer curve
As tax rates increase, economic activity is discouraged and hence the rate of growth of tax revenues falls. Above 0A, an increase in tax rates so discourages economic activity that tax revenues fall.

CURVE effect, named after Professor Arthur Laffer who popularised the idea in the late 1970s. Figure 2 shows a Laffer curve, which plots tax revenues against tax rates. As tax rates increase, the rate of growth of tax revenue falls because of the disincentive effects of the tax. 0A shows the maximum revenue position of the tax. At tax rates above 0A, an increase in the tax rate so discourages economic activity that tax revenues fall.

Poverty and unemployment traps The combination of marginal rates of income tax and withdrawal of benefits can lead to poverty and unemployment traps. The POVERTY or EARNINGS TRAP occurs when a low income working individual or household earns more, for example by gaining promotion, getting a better paid job or working more hours, but the net gain is little or even negative. It occurs because as income increases, welfare benefits are withdrawn. Equally, the individual or household might start to pay tax. For example, if an individual loses 50p in benefits when earning an extra £1, and then pays income tax and National Insurance contributions at 30 per cent, then the net gain from earning the extra £1 is only 20p (£1 - 50p - 30p). The effective marginal rate of tax here is 80 per cent. If the benefit loss were 90p in the pound, the individual would be 20p worse off. The effective marginal rate of tax here would be 120 per cent. The poverty trap is a major disincentive for those working and receiving benefits to work harder or increase their skills. The UNEMPLOYMENT TRAP occurs when an individual is little better off or is even worse off getting a job than staying unemployed because of loss of benefits and taxation. The unemployment trap, where it occurs, is a major disincentive for the unemployed to find work. One solution to both kinds of trap is to lower welfare benefits but this increases poverty. The other solution is to reduce taxes on income and the rate of welfare benefit withdrawal as incomes increase. This is a more expensive solution for the government and the taxpayer.

Taxes on labour Firms will not take on workers if their total wage cost is too high. Part of the total cost is the wages of workers. However, many countries tax firms for employing labour, often by imposing employer contributions to state

social security funds. In the UK, for instance, employers have to pay National Insurance employers' contributions. The higher the tax, the fewer workers will be employed and hence the lower will be the level of aggregate supply.

Reducing the cost of changing jobs In a modern fast-changing economy, workers are likely to be changing jobs on a relatively frequent basis. Some workers will even become **portfolio workers**, having a mix of part-time jobs at any one time rather than a single full time job. If the labour market is such that workers find it difficult to get new jobs when they are made redundant, then unemployment will rise and aggregate supply will fall. So the government must ensure that **barriers to mobility** between jobs are as low as possible. One important barrier to mobility can be pensions. If pension rights are typically provided by individual employers, then a worker who is frequently moving from employer to employer will lose out. Hence, governments should give workers the opportunity to provide for their own pension which they can take with them from job to job. Another problem in the UK has been a lack of geographical mobility due to rigidities in the housing market. If house prices in the south of England are much higher than in the north, then workers will be discouraged from moving from north to south. Equally, if workers are unable to rent houses at an affordable rent in an area, then low paid workers will not be able to move into that area to take up jobs.

Education and training Increasing the level of human capital of workers is vital if economies are to develop. Increased levels of

Question 2

In a recent report on the UK economy, the OECD (Organisation for Economic Co-operation and Development) highlighted weaknesses in the UK education and training system that were hindering its growth performance. It was particularly critical of educational provision for less academic students. It said that 'much more could still be done to improve basic literacy and numeracy, thus providing a strong foundation for continued learning'. It also argued that 'continuously improving the relevance and quality of vocational programmes is as important as it is to expand their provision'.

It was worried that the tax and benefits system might discourage individuals from acquiring intermediate skills. It pointed out that, whilst gross earnings of workers with intermediate skills were significantly higher than those of low skilled workers, net income was little different if those workers had children because of tax credits that low skilled, low pay workers can claim. For 16-18 year olds, pilot schemes which have paid teenagers to stay in education appear to have boosted engagement in continued learning. But an alternative might be to increase the very light taxation faced by teenagers taking a job at 16.

Source: adapted from OECD, *Economic Survey of the United Kingdom 2005*.

(a) Using a diagram, explain why the quality of the labour force is so important for the long term growth of the UK economy.
(b) Suggest why improving 'basic literacy and numeracy' might be important for increase the long term human capital stock of the economy.
(c) Explain why taxes and benefits might be a disincentive to acquire skills in the UK.

education and training will raise the marginal revenue product of workers (i.e. will raise the value of output of workers). This in turn will shift the aggregate supply curve to the right. The value of human capital in the economy is one of the most important determinants of the level of aggregate supply.

The capital market

Increasing the capital stock of the country, such as its factories, offices and roads, will push the aggregate supply curve to the right. According to classical economists, the government has a key role to play in this.

Profitability Firms invest in order to make a profit. The higher the rate of profit, the more investment will take place. Hence, government must create an environment in which firms can make profits for their owners. One way of doing this is by reducing taxes on company profits. Another is to reduce inheritance tax which might be paid by a small business owner when passing on his or her business to a family relative. Another is to reduce taxes on employing workers. Reducing the amount of government red tape, like planning permissions, can also help reduce costs and increase profitability.

Allocating scarce capital resources The government is in a poor position to decide how to allocate resources. It should leave this as much as possible to the private sector. Hence, state owned companies should be **privatised** wherever possible. Government should offer only limited taxpayers' money to subsidise industry. The government should stay well clear of trying to 'back winning companies'.

Increasing the range of sources of capital available to firms Firms can be constrained in their growth if they are unable to gain access to financial capital like bank loans or share capital. Government should therefore encourage the private sector to provide financial capital, particularly to small businesses. They may, for instance, offer tax incentives to individuals putting up share capital for a business.

The goods market

Inefficient production will lead to a lower level of aggregate supply. For instance, if UK car workers produce 50 per cent fewer cars per worker with the same equipment as German workers, then the level of aggregate supply in the UK can obviously be increased if UK labour productivity is raised. The government has a key role to play in increasing efficiency.

Free market economists argue that the most important way of securing increased efficiency is through encouraging **competition**. If firms know that they will go out of business if they do not become efficient, then they have a powerful incentive to become efficient producers. The government can increase competition in the market in a number of ways.

Encouraging free trade Fierce foreign competition results in a domestic industry which has to be efficient in order to survive. The government should therefore liberalise trade, removing tariffs (taxes) and other barriers to imports.

Encouraging small businesses Small businesses can operate in markets where there are no large businesses. Competition here

is intense. However, small businesses can operate in markets where there are very large firms. Small businesses then force larger firms to remain cost competitive. Otherwise the larger firms will lose market share.

Privatisation Privatising firms, and in the process creating competition between newly created firms, eliminates the distortions created by the operation of public sector monopolies.

Deregulation Removing rules about who can compete in markets will encourage competition.

Interventionist approaches

Interventionist economists would tend to take a different approach to government policy and aggregate supply. They would tend to focus on issues of where free markets fail. For instance, they would agree with free market economists that a key aspect of government policy must be to increase education and training. However, whereas free market economists would argue that training should be left to individual companies or groups of companies in a local area, interventionist economists would argue that training is best organised by government. The state should, for instance, impose levies on firms to finance state organised training placements and schemes.

With regard to investment in physical capital, free market economists would argue that profit should direct the level and pattern of investment. Interventionist economists would argue that if investment is insufficient in the economy, then the government should intervene and, for instance, use taxes to set up state owned companies or subsidise investment by private industry.

In the 1950s and 1960s in the UK, the main supply side problem was that of regional inequality with the north of England, Scotland and Northern Ireland experiencing higher

Question 3

Britain's offshore industry has reacted angrily to the UK Chancellor's decision to impose an extra 10 per cent tax on profits from North Sea oil fields. It will raise an estimated £6.5 billion in revenue for the government over the next three years. The UK Offshore Operators Association said that: 'It is almost beyond comprehension that the government has failed to grasp the vulnerability of the industry's future in the UK. His move could not come at a worse time. North Sea activity has recovered remarkably since 2002 when it was last hit by a punitive tax charge.' It went on to say that: 'It will deter investment in new fields and make older fields less attractive for increased recovery. Moreover, the impact will be felt significantly by smaller oil and gas producers. The unexpected tax hit on the industry in 2002 led to a major slump in investor confidence in the North Sea. Exploration and development activity fell to record lows as investment left the North Sea for other less challenging parts of the globe with lower costs.'

Source: adapted from Press Release, United Kingdom Offshore Operators Association, December 2005.

(a) Explain the link between company taxes and North Sea oil exploration and development.
(b) What impact might the 10 per cent extra tax on North Sea oil profits have on long run aggregate supply?

unemployment rates than the south and the Midlands. The interventionist policy response was a mixture of offering incentives to firms investing in high unemployment regions and making it difficult for firms to expand in low unemployment regions.

Supply side policies and aggregate demand

Supply side policies can have an impact on aggregate demand. For example, any supply side policy which results in higher government spending or lower taxes will increase or reduce aggregate demand directly through changes in levels of spending. However, supply side policies can also have indirect effects. Supply side policies which succeed in reducing unemployment, for example, might lead to a rise in consumer confidence. In turn, this will encourage households to borrow more money and so raise aggregate demand. Hence, supply side policies can sometimes lead to both increases and decreases in an economic variable. For example, supply side policies which succeed in increasing investment will in the long term shift the aggregate supply curve to the right reducing inflationary pressures. But the increase in investment in the short term will increase aggregate demand, increasing inflationary pressures.

Question 4

Scientific innovation, knowledge transfer, skills enhancement and transport improvements are main elements of the £100 million spending plan, unveiled today, which is intended to kick-start the north of England's economy.

The Northern Way business plan is an attempt by three northern regional development agencies to tackle the north-south divide in economic performance. The Northern Way has put the output gap between north and south at £30 billion. It calculated this by comparing the Gross Value Added per capita of the three northern regions with the all-England average in the five years 1999-2003.

The £100 million will fund a variety of initiatives to improve the competitiveness of the three regions. For example, £15 million will be spent funding centres of excellence in leadership, innovation and the skills for sustainable communities. £12 million will produce some small but significant transport improvements and develop the case for a new approach to transport investment in the North. £3 million will help establish a new £6.5 million National Industrial Biotechnology Facility in the Tees Valley.

Source: adapted from the *Financial Times* 20.6.2005; Press Release, The Northern Way, 20.6.2005.

Using examples from the passage, explain how assistance from the government might increase aggregate supply.

Key terms

Bottleneck - a supply side constraint in a particular market in an economy which prevents higher growth for the whole economy.

Laffer curve - a curve which shows that at low levels of taxation, tax revenues will increase if tax rates are increased; however, if tax rates are high, then a further rise in rates will reduce total tax revenues because of the disincentive effects of the increase in tax.

Poverty or earnings trap - occurs when an individual is little better off or even worse off when gaining an increase in wages because of the combined effect of increased tax and benefit withdrawal.

Supply side economics - the study of how changes in aggregate supply will affect variables such as national income; in particular, how government microeconomic policy might change aggregate supply through individual markets.

Supply side policies - government policies designed to increase the productive potential of the economy and push the long run aggregate supply curve to the right.

Unemployment trap - occurs when an individual is little better off or even worse off when getting a job after being unemployed because of the combined effect of increased tax and benefit withdrawal.

Applied economics

Supply side policies in the UK

Since 1979, the government has been committed to implementing supply side policies aimed at improving the workings of free markets. A wide range of measures have been introduced which are described below.

The labour market

Trade union power In the 1960s and 1970s, there was a fierce debate about trade union power. It was widely recognised that trade unions, which at their membership peak in 1979 represented half of all UK workers, had considerable power in the workplace at the time. In 1979, the Conservative party under Margaret Thatcher was elected into office with a manifesto pledge to reduce trade union power and make UK industry more flexible and competitive. A number of Acts were passed which effectively made secondary picketing illegal and firms gained the power to sue trade unions involved for damages. Industrial action called by a union now had to be approved by a secret ballot of its membership. Secret ballots were also made compulsory for elections of trade union leaders. Closed shops, places of work where employers agreed that all workers should be trade union members, became more difficult to maintain and enforce. The government also took an extremely hard line with strikes in the public sector, refusing to give in to union demands. The breaking of strikes, such as the miners' strike of 1983-85, increased the confidence of private employers to resist trade union demands. By the mid-1990s, with the loss of over one quarter of their members since 1979, trade unions had become marginalised in many places of work and considerably weakened in others.

The election of a Labour government in 1997 did not reverse this position. In 1999, it passed the Employee Relations Act 1999 which forced employers to recognise the negotiating rights of trade unions if a majority of workers in the workplace voted in favour. However, whilst this might increase union membership in the long term, it is unlikely in itself to greatly increase union power.

Wage bargaining Supply side economists view collective bargaining as an inflexible way of rewarding workers. They advocate individual pay bargaining with payment systems based on bonuses and performance related pay. By reducing the power of trade unions, the government in the 1980s and early 1990s went some way to breaking collective bargaining. It encouraged employers to move away from national pay bargaining to local pay bargaining. In the public sector, it attempted to move away from national pay agreements to local ones. The Labour government elected in 1997 was more sympathetic to trade unions but made it clear it would not reverse most of the trade union reforms of the 1980s and early 1990s. However, the 1999 Employee Relations Act increased the ability of trade unions to force recognition by employers of their negotiating rights. At the same time, the signing of the Social Chapter influenced some larger firms to set up works councils which involve trade unions. The government is also supporting greater social partnerships between businesses and unions which may also encourage collective bargaining.

State welfare benefits Supply side economists tend to argue that welfare benefits can be a major disincentive to work. The benefit system needs to avoid creating **poverty traps** (where an increase in wages leads to a fall in income for a worker after tax has been paid and benefits withdrawn) and **unemployment traps** (where unemployed workers find that they can receive a higher income from remaining unemployed than by taking low paid jobs). In the 1980s, one solution to this was to cut the real value of benefits for low income households. It was made more difficult to collect unemployment benefits and the unemployed

came under much greater pressure to accept jobs that were offered or take up places on training schemes. The Labour government elected in 1997 was committed both to reducing poverty and unemployment. Its main initiative to get round both the unemployment and poverty traps was the Working Families Tax Credit, introduced in 1999, and replaced by the Child Tax Credit and the Working Tax Credit in 2003. These increased the take home pay of low income earners by giving them benefits paid through their earnings. Even so, effective marginal rates of tax for some low paid can still be far more than the 40 per cent top rate of income tax paid by high income earners. With regard to unemployment, some economists argue that much of the fall in unemployment in the 1990s and 2000s occurred simply because the long term unemployed were shifted onto disability and incapacity benefits. In the early 2000s, the government made some attempt to make it more difficult to claim these benefits and to get some of those already on these benefits onto training schemes or into work. By 2008, however, success had been very limited.

Social legislation Legislation protecting the rights of workers goes back to the nineteenth century when curbs were placed on the employment of children and of women. Over time, workers have gained more and more rights. For example, workers are protected by law from the moment they apply for a job to the time they leave. Holiday entitlements, maternity and paternity leave, sickness, disability, training, health and safety and discrimination are all covered by legislation. In 1997, the UK signed the Social Chapter of the Maastricht Treaty 1992, which gave Brussels the right to introduce regulations covering conditions of employment in the UK. Businesses tend to view regulations as 'red tape' which impairs their competitiveness. However, most other European countries, such as France and Germany, have more onerous regulations and view the UK as being relatively lightly regulated.

Training and education Education and training are recognised by the government as keystones of its supply side policies. Whilst the education of the top 20 or 30 per cent of the population by ability has traditionally been, by international standards, excellent, the education of the rest of the population has tended to be at best mediocre and at worst poor. Since the 1980s, the government has attempted to address these problems in a variety of ways. One has been to take central control of the curriculum in schools, for example through the National Curriculum established in the 1980s and more recently through numeracy and literacy initiatives. Another has been to set targets for schools and colleges for student attainment. Another has been through inspection of schools and colleges, such as the work of Ofsted. The idea of competition between schools, and a much greater variety of schools which parents may choose for their children, has been experimented with and remains a central plank of government policy. Successive governments have encouraged more students to stay on in education to 18 and 21. Today training in the UK is the responsibility of a variety of bodies including Regional Development Agencies, Learning and Skills Councils and the Small Business Service.

Much work has been done on providing vocational routes through education, although reform of the vocational framework begun in the 1980s has produced mixed results. This has arguably meant that the educational pathway for less academic students remains poorer than in many of our industrial competitors. Training in the workplace has also come in for continued criticism and lifelong training for workers in the UK, particularly those with low skills, continues to be criticised by international organisations like the OECD.

Marginal tax rates Marginal income tax rates by 1979 were very high. The standard rate of income tax was 33 per cent whilst the highest rate on earned income was 83 per cent. The incoming Conservative government made it a priority to cut these and within ten years the highest marginal income tax rate was 40 per cent, where it has remained since. Income tax cuts were designed in part to increase incentives to work. Incentives to accumulate wealth were given by cuts in both inheritance tax and capital gains tax rates. Employers too have gained with Employers National Insurance contributions falling. The UK has continued to have almost the lowest social security taxes on

employers and employees in Europe.

Help to businesses

If aggregate supply is to increase, the private sector needs to expand. Hence, according to supply side economists, the government needs to create an environment in which business can flourish.

Small businesses Small businesses are important in the economy because they provide new jobs and can become the the big businesses of tomorrow. Conservative governments between 1979 and 1997 placed particular importance on the development of an 'enterprise culture' and laid the groundwork for many of the policies which are in operation today. Existing small businesses are helped through reduced rates on taxes on profits (corporation tax) and tax allowances for investment. They may be eligible for short term loans in circumstances when a commercial bank would refuse to lend to them. Advice is available from the Small Business Service. Regulation ('red tape') is often less for small businesses than large businesses. However, the burden of regulation on small businesses is often heavier because they have fewer resources and less expertise to deal with the regulations with which they have to comply. New small businesses can get a variety of help from grants and loans for training.

Innovation and research Since 1997, the government has been keen to promote innovation and research. Tax allowances have traditionally been available to businesses spending on innovation and research. However, there is a variety of programmes which enable some businesses to gain grants for research and development (R&D), and to set up knowledge transfer networks between industry and an academic establishment.

Goods markets

It is argued that competition increases both productive and allocative efficiency. Markets should therefore be made as competitive as possible. Encouraging competition was central to government policy after 1979.

Deregulation and privatisation In the 1980s, the government introduced policies to privatise state owned companies and deregulate markets. Nearly all state owned companies were privatised by the end of the 1990s including British Telecom and the gas industry. Central government departments and local authorities were encouraged to offer such services as waste collection or cleaning to tender rather than employing staff directly to provide the service. Many controls were abolished, such as legal restrictions on pub opening hours and Sunday trading. Since 2000, the government has further increased the involvement of the private sector in providing public sector services. For example, 2004 saw the opening of the UK's first private toll motorway. In the NHS, the government is contracting out operations to private sector health companies. Many new buildings, such as schools and hospitals, are being built and operated by the private sector and the Private Finance Initiative (PFI). The private sector companies are then leasing back the facilities to the state sector for its use. In 2006, the postal letter service was opened up for the first time to serious competition.

Encouragement of international free trade Fierce foreign competition results in a domestic industry which has to be efficient in order to survive. Since 1979, governments have tended to advocate policies of free trade on most issues. For instance, they have been more willing than most other European governments to see greater free trade in agriculture. The UK has also been one of the most welcoming to foreign companies wanting to set up in the UK.

Regional and industrial policy

Before 1979, the main focus of supply side policies was regional and industrial policy. Regional policy aimed to help poorer regions of the UK to attract businesses and create jobs. Industrial policy aimed to help industries which were undergoing difficult trading conditions, such as textiles, shipbuilding, the motor manufacturing industry, coal mining and steel. Since 1999, each region of the UK had a Regional Development Agency (RDA) working to create jobs and improve the competitiveness of the region. The most high profile work of the nine RDAs has been giving grants to incoming foreign companies wanting to set up large showcase manufacturing plants. However, most of their spending is spread amongst a wide range of initiatives, from grants to small start up businesses, to promoting training of workers, to encouraging infrastructure developments such as new roads or airports.

DataQuestion

Supply side economics

France, unlike the UK or the USA, tends to be mistrustful of free market supply side economics. In the 2007 presidential elections, the different candidates put forward a range of policies which were interventionist rather than free market in nature. The Socialist candidate, for example, Ségolène Royal proposed a sharp rise in the level of the minimum wage, an extension of the law to more workers giving them a right to work a basic 35 hour week, and giving state-funding for young people to get their first job. The cap which limits taxes paid by individuals on their income and wealth to 60 per cent would be abolished, increasing taxes for very high income earners and wealthy individuals. Firms that paid large amounts of their profit to shareholders in dividends would pay higher taxes on profits than firms which retained profit to invest back in the company. Aid given to companies which set up in high unemployment areas would have to be repaid if they subsequently moved the jobs created abroad.

Nicholas Sarkozy, the right wing candidate who won the election, was slightly more free market in his approach. He proposed cutting the limit on taxes on income and wealth paid by individuals from 60 per cent to 50 per cent. Firms would not have to pay any employer taxes on overtime pay given to workers who worked more than the 35 hour week. There would be a more flexible contract of employment for employees which would give employers more rights to sack them. Unemployment benefits would be cut if an unemployed person turned down two job offers. Taxes would be cut for private investment in start up companies. Taxes on company profits would be cut to the European average. However, companies which gave increases in dividends which were much higher than the increases they gave to workers in wages would be taxed more heavily on their profits.

Source: adapted from the *Financial Times*, 30.3.2007.

1. **Explain how any four of the measures proposed by the two candidates might increase economic growth of the French economy.**

2. **Discuss whether Ségolène Royal's policies were more interventionist than those of Nicholas Sarkozy.**

Summary

1. Governments can influence the economy through the use of monetary policy – the control of monetary variables such as the rate of interest, the money supply and the volume of credit.
2. Changing interest rates can change the level of aggregate demand through its effect on consumer durables, the housing market, household wealth, saving, investment, exports and imports.
3. A rise in interest rates is likely to reduce inflationary pressures, but lead to lower growth in output and have an adverse effect on unemployment. Exports are likely to fall, but the impact on imports is uncertain and so the overall impact on the current account is likely to vary from economy to economy.
4. The use of monetary policy gives rise to a variety of trade offs such as greater inflation or greater unemployment.

Money and the rate of interest

Government can, to some extent, control the rate of interest and the amount of money circulating in the economy. They can also affect the amount of borrowing or credit available from financial institutions like banks and building societies. MONETARY POLICY is the manipulation of these monetary variables to achieve government objectives.

The RATE OF INTEREST is the price of money. This is because lenders expect to receive interest if money is supplied for loans to money markets. Equally, if money is demanded for loans from money markets, borrowers expect to have to pay interest on the loans.

At various times in the past, governments have used credit controls, such as restrictions on the amount that can be borrowed on a mortgage or on hire purchase, as the main instrument of monetary policy. Equally, some governments have attempted directly to control the supply of money, the amount of money available for spending and borrowing in the economy. In recent years, the rate of interest has been the key instrument of monetary policy. For instance, both the Bank of England and the Federal Reserve Bank, the central bank of the USA, have used interest rates to achieve their policy objectives.

Aggregate demand

The rate of interest affects the economy through its influence on aggregate demand (AD). The higher the rate of interest, the lower the level of aggregate demand. There is a variety of ways in which interest rates affect the AD curve.

Consumer durables Many consumers buy consumer durables such as furniture, kitchen equipment and cars on credit. The higher the rate of interest, the greater the monthly repayments will have to be for any given sum borrowed. Hence, high interest rates lead to lower sales of durable goods and hence lower consumption expenditure.

The housing market Houses too are typically bought using a mortgage. The lower the rate of interest, the lower the mortgage repayments on a given sum borrowed. This makes houses more affordable. It might encourage people to buy their first house or to move house, either trading up to a more expensive house or trading down to a smaller property. There are three ways in which this increases aggregate demand. First, an increase in demand for all types of housing leads to an increase in the number of new houses being built. New housing is classified as investment in national income accounts. Increased investment leads to increased aggregate demand. Second, moving house stimulates the purchase of consumer durables such as furniture, carpets and kitchens. This increases consumption. Third, moving house may release money which can be spent. A person trading down to a cheaper house will see a release of equity tied up in their home. Those trading up may borrow more than they need for the house purchase and this may be used to buy furniture or perhaps even a new car.

Wealth effects A fall in rates of interest may increase asset prices. For instance, falling interest rates may lead to an increase in demand for housing, which in turn pushes up the price of houses. If house prices rise, all homeowners are better off because their houses have increased in value. This may encourage them to increase their spending. Equally, a fall in interest rates will raise the price of government bonds. Governments issue bonds to finance their borrowing. They are sold to individuals, assurance companies, pension funds and others who receive interest on the money they have loaned to government. Like shares, bonds can go up and down in value. Rises in the price of bonds held by individuals or businesses will increase their financial wealth, which again may have a positive impact on consumer expenditure.

Saving Higher interest rates make saving more attractive compared to spending. The higher the interest rate, the greater the reward for deferring spending to the future and reducing spending now. This may lead to a fall in aggregate demand at the present time.

Investment The lower the rate of interest, the more investment projects become profitable. Hence the higher the level of investment and aggregate demand. Equally, a rise in consumption which leads to a rise in income will lead, in turn, to a rise in investment. Firms will need to invest to supply the extra goods and services being demanded by consumers.

The exchange rate A fall in the interest rate is likely to lead to a fall in the value of the domestic currency (its exchange rate). A fall in the value of the pound means that foreigners can now get more pounds for each unit of their currency. However, UK residents have to pay more pounds to get the same number of US dollars or Japanese yen. This in turn means that goods priced in pounds become cheaper for foreigners to buy, whilst foreign goods become more expensive for British firms to buy. Cheaper

Retailers are calling for a further cut in interest rates today after a survey showed another month of weak sales. According to the British Retail Consortium (BRC) survey published today, like-for-like sales, excluding the effect of new stores, were running below last year's levels for a fifth consecutive month. Kevin Hawkins, the BRCs director-general, said: 'Any growth came from heavy discounting, which is not sustainable. The underlying position is still weak and unlikely to improve unless and until there are further cuts in interest rates.' His call was echoed by Geoff Cooper, chief executive officer of Travis Perkins, the builders' merchant and owner of Wickes, which reported falling sales yesterday. 'We don't see consumer confidence or the housing market picking up for the rest of the year', he said.

Source: adapted from the *Financial Times*, 6.9.2005.

(a) Why did (i) Kevin Hawkins and (ii) Geoff Cooper want a cut in interest rates?

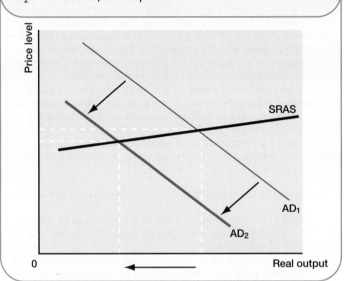

Figure 1 A rise in interest rates
A rise in interest rates shifts the aggregate demand curve left from AD_1 to AD_2. This leads to a fall in the price level.

British goods should lead to higher exports as foreigners take advantage of lower prices. In contrast, more expensive foreign goods should lead to fewer imports as British buyers find foreign goods less price competitive. Greater export levels and fewer imports will boost aggregate demand.

Policy objectives

The government has four key macroeconomic policy objectives - to control inflation and unemployment, to maintain a current account equilibrium and to secure high economic growth. Interest rate policy can affect all of these.

Inflation Interest rate policy today is used mainly to control inflation. Figure 1 shows a shift to the left in the aggregate demand curve caused by a rise in interest rates. This leads to a lower equilibrium price level.

Higher interest rates in practice rarely lead to the falling prices shown in Figure 1. This is because in modern economies aggregate demand tends to increase over time irrespective of government policy. For instance, most workers get pay rises each year, which increases aggregate demand. Profits of companies tend to increase which allows higher dividends to be paid to shareholders. A shift to the right in the aggregate demand curve from AD_1 to AD_2 caused by the annual round of pay rises is shown in Figure 2. This leads to a rise in the price level. If the government then increases interest rates, aggregate demand shifts back to the left to AD_3. Prices are then higher than at the start of the year with AD_1 but are not as high as they would otherwise have been. Interest rates have thus moderated the increase in the price level, i.e. they have moderated the inflation rate.

A loosening of monetary policy by lowering interest rates shifts the aggregate demand curve to the right and leads to a higher equilibrium level of prices. Looser monetary policy tends therefore to be inflationary.

Unemployment Tightening monetary policy by raising interest rates will tend to lead to a fall in equilibrium output, as shown in Figure 1. Lower output is likely to be associated with lower levels of employment and hence unemployment is likely to rise. Loosening monetary policy by allowing interest rates to fall, on the other hand, is likely to lead to lower unemployment.

The long run policy implications could be different, though. According to classical economists, the long run aggregate supply curve is vertical. Changing the level of interest rates will therefore have no impact on either output or unemployment in the long run. In Figure 3, a fall in interest rates pushes the aggregate demand curve to the right but real output remains at 0A. However, there is an increase in the price level. For classical economists, then, any fall in unemployment in the short term caused by a loosening of monetary policy will not be sustained in the long term. Unemployment will revert to its original level.

For Keynesian economists, the impact of loosening monetary policy depends upon how near the economy is to full

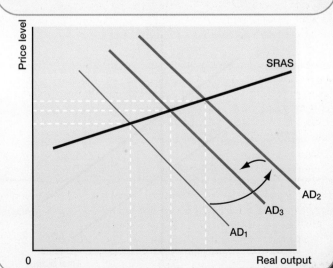

Figure 2 A rise in interest rates with increasing aggregate demand
Aggregate demand tends to increase over time. Raising interest rates moderates the increase. Instead of shifting to AD_2, the aggregate demand curve only shifts to AD_3. Inflation is thus lower than it would otherwise have been.

Question 2

In its Minutes for August 2005, the Monetary Policy Committee of the Bank of England explained why it had cut interest rates by 0.25 per cent. Part of the reason was a 'gentle labour market loosening since the turn of the year'. The total number of hours worked per week and the employment rate had fallen whilst unemployment had risen a little. Growth in average earnings of workers had 'eased a little since the start of the year'.

Inflation in prices of inputs to the service sector had 'eased'. In contrast, inflation in prices of inputs to the manufacturing sector were running at their highest level since 1986, due mainly to large increases in oil prices. Despite this bad news from manufacturing, price inflation of goods and services produced by both manufacturing and service industries (output inflation) had 'eased further'.

Source: adapted from Bank of England, Monetary Policy Committee Minutes, August 2005.

(a) Explain the links between inflation (as measured by the RPI or CPI) and (i) wage increases; (ii) costs of materials and other inputs to firms.
(b) Why does an easing of wage increases and material cost increases allow the Bank of England to change interest rates?

employment. In Figure 4, the nearer the economy is to 0A, the full employment level of output, the less impact falling interest rates will have on output and unemployment and the more they will have on inflation.

Economic growth Economic growth is a long run phenomenon. Shifting the aggregate demand curve is unlikely to have an impact on the position of the long run supply curve. The only possible link is if lower interest rates encourage investment which in turn increases the capital stock of the economy and its productive potential. Monetary policy can, however, be used to influence booms and recessions. In a boom, tighter monetary policy will reduce aggregate demand and thus lower the

increase in short run output. In a recession, looser monetary policy may increase aggregate demand and hence increase equilibrium output. Some economists argue that severe recessions depress the long run trend rate of growth. Physical and human capital are destroyed and the economy starts its recovery from a lower level than would otherwise be the case. These economists would argue that keeping the output gap low throughout the trade cycle leads to a higher long term growth rate than if the output gap is large in successive cycles. Monetary policy can play a part in keeping the economy near to its long run trend rate of growth.

The current balance In the 1950s and 1960s, the UK government used monetary policy to influence the current balance. Higher interest rates lead to lower aggregate demand. This reduces the amount of imports purchased and hence improves the current account position. On the other hand, higher interest rates should also raise the value of the currency.

Question 3

The Bank of England yesterday cut official interest rates by 0.25 per cent for the fourth time since September, citing a 'continuous slowdown' in the UK economy. Ciaràn Barr, senior UK economist at Deutsche Bank in London, said: 'We feel there is more to come. January's data are expected to be on the soft side, with the killer statistic being the first fall in gross domestic product since the second quarter of 1992.' Kate Barker, the Confederation of British Industry's chief economic adviser, said further rate cuts would be needed to ward off an outright recession. 'With continued weak global trends restraining prices in many sectors, inflation pressure is minimal', Ms Barker said.

Source: adapted from the *Financial Times*, 8.1.1999.

(a) Explain what was happening to the UK economy in late 1998.
(b) How might the 0.25 per cent cut in interest rates have affected (i) output and (ii) inflation?

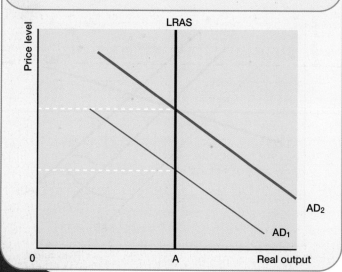

Figure 3 *Interest rates and the classical long run aggregate supply curve*
If the long run aggregate supply curve is vertical, changing interest rates will have no effect on either output or unemployment.

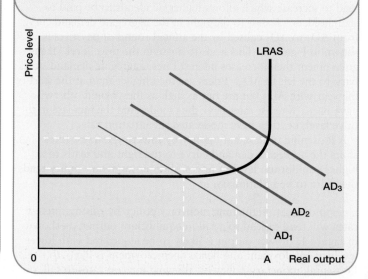

Figure 4 *Interest rates and the Keynesian long run aggregate supply curve*
The nearer to full employment at 0A, the less impact a fall in interest rates will have on output and employment and the more on inflation.

Key terms

Bank base rate - the interest rate which a bank sets to determine its borrowing and lending rates. It offers interest rates below its base rate to customers who deposit funds with it, whilst charging interest rates above base rate to borrowers.

Central bank - the financial institution in a country or group of countries typically responsible for the printing and issuing of notes and coins, setting short term interest rates, managing the country's gold and currency reserves and issuing government debt.

Instrument of policy - an economic variable, such as the rate of interest, income tax rates or government spending on education,

which is used to achieve a target of government policy.

Monetary policy - the attempt by government or a central bank to manipulate the money supply, the supply of credit, interest rates or any other monetary variables, to achieve the fulfilment of policy goals such as price stability.

Rate of interest - the price of money, determined by the demand and supply of funds in a money market where there are borrowers and lenders.

Target of policy - an economic goal which the government wishes to achieve, such as low unemployment or high growth.

A higher value of the pound will make it more difficult for UK firms to export and easier for foreign firms to sell imports to the UK. This will lead to a worsening of the current account position. Which effect is the larger varies from economy to economy and depends upon how sensitive imports are to falls in domestic income (i.e. the value of income elasticity of demand for imports). It also depends upon how sensitive exchange rates are to changes in interest rates and the sensitivity of exports and imports to changes in exchange rates (i.e. the values of price elasticity of demand for exports and imports).

Trade offs

The use of monetary policy, like other government policies such as fiscal policy, can have trade offs between objectives.

- A rise in interest rates in the short term might reduce inflation, but, because of the fall in aggregate demand, it might increase unemployment and reduce the rate of growth of GDP. The fall in aggregate demand or spending in the economy is also likely to lead to a fall in imports, spending on foreign goods. Hence a rise in interest rates might lead to an improvement in the current account position in the balance of payments.

- A fall in interest rates has the converse effect. It might reduce unemployment and stimulate growth in GDP. However, it is likely to lead to a rise in the inflation rate and a deterioration in the current account on the balance of payments.

Changes in interest rates can also impact on other government policy objectives.

- Consistently high interest rates may lead to a high value of the exchange rate and low investment. Both of these may damage the economy's international competitiveness.

- Interest rate changes can affect the distribution of income in a variety of ways. For example, higher interest rates should benefit savers at the expense of borrowers. Given that pensioners are significant savers and young workers are significant borrowers, higher interest rates will result in a redistribution of income from young workers to pensioners.

Monetary policy may also conflict with other types of policy. For example, fiscal policy may be expansionary at a time when the Bank of England is tightening monetary policy by raising interest rates. The government may be pursuing supply side policies to raise investment when interest rates are being raised to reduce inflation.

Applied economics

The functions of the central bank in the UK

Since 1997, monetary policy in the UK has been controlled by the Bank of England. This is the CENTRAL BANK of the UK. Central banks tend to have a number of functions.

- They are responsible for the issue of notes and coins. These are sold to the banking system which in turn passes them on to customers as they withdraw cash from their accounts.

- They supervise the financial system, often in conjunction with other bodies specifically set up to regulate distinct parts of the financial system.

- They manage a country's gold and currency reserves. These can be used to influence the level of the exchange rate.

- They act as bankers to the government, usually managing the National Debt of the country. They arrange for the issue of new loans to cover current borrowing by a government.

- They act as bankers to the banking system. Usually, they act as lender of last resort. If a bank gets into short term difficulties, not able to raise enough cash to meet demands from its customers, the central bank will supply cash to the banking system to relieve this liquidity shortage.

Targets and instruments

Although the Bank of England is independent of the UK government, its activities are still broadly controlled by government. With regard to monetary policy, the government sets the Bank a TARGET for inflation which it has to achieve. This target was initially set at maintaining inflation, as measured by the RPIX, within a range of 1 to 4 per cent and subsequently modified to 2.5 per cent plus or minus 1 per cent per annum. Today the target is 2.0 per cent plus or minus 1 per cent as measured by the CPI. The Bank of England, therefore, has not been given any targets concerning the other three main macroeconomic policy objectives of government - unemployment, growth and the current account. These are influenced by other policies such as fiscal policy and supply side policies.

Since the mid-1980s, the Bank of England has chosen the rate of interest as its main INSTRUMENT of monetary policy. Each month, it announces whether or not it will change bank base rates. In the 1950s and 1960s, controls on credit (the borrowing of money) were significant instruments of monetary policy as well. In the 1970s and early 1980s, the emphasis shifted to the control of the money supply, the total stock of money in the economy. However, these proved unsatisfactory in an open economy like the UK, where it was increasingly easy for borrowers to gain access to funds abroad and where there was increasing competition between financial institutions.

Bank base rates

BANK BASE RATE is the rate of interest around which the main UK banks fix their lending and borrowing rates. Customers who lend money (i.e. deposit money) with a bank will get a rate of interest less than the base rate. Customers who borrow money will be charged a rate higher than base rate. The difference or spread between borrowing and lending rates is used by the bank to pay its operating costs and provide it with a profit. Each bank can in theory fix its own base rate. However, competitive pressure means that all banks have the same base rate. If one bank had a higher base rate, it would attract more deposits from other banks but would lose customers who wanted to borrow money. It could easily end up with far too much on deposit and too little being lent out. The reverse would be true if a bank set its base rate below that of other banks.

The Bank of England controls base rates through its day to day provision of money to the banking system. In practice, banks in the UK can't decide to have a different base rate from the rate of interest set by the Bank of England, which is technically called the **repo rate.**

Bank base rates are short term rates of interest. They influence other interest rates in other money markets. For instance, building societies are likely to change their interest rates if bank base rates change. If they don't, they face customers moving their business to banks who might offer more competitive deposit or borrowing rates. However, many customers only use banks or only use building societies. Many would not switch their savings from one to the other if a small difference in interest rates appeared, so sometimes building societies will not change their interest rates if the Bank of England changes bank base rates by, say, one quarter of a per cent. There are many other money markets which are even less linked to bank base rates. Credit card rates, for instance, don't tend to change if bank base rates change by 1 or 2 per cent. Long term interest rates may also not be affected by changes in short term rates of interest. Therefore, the Bank of England only has very imperfect control of all the different money markets in the UK.

Factors affecting the decision to change interest rates

The decision whether to change interest rates in any one month is taken by the Monetary Policy Committee (MPC). This is a group of 9 people. Five are from the Bank of England, including the Governor of the Bank of England. The other four are independent outside experts, mainly professional economists. Inflation is the Bank of England's only target. Therefore, the Monetary Policy Committee considers evidence about whether inflationary pressure is increasing, decreasing or remaining stable at the time. If it believes that inflationary pressure is increasing, it is likely to raise interest rates to reduce aggregate demand. If inflationary pressure is weak, it can cut interest rates to boost aggregate demand and allow unemployment to be reduced and output to increase. In coming to any decision, it looks at a wide range of economic indicators.

For instance, it will consider the rate of increase in average earnings. If wages are rising at a faster rate than before, this could be an indication that labour is becoming scarcer in supply. The same could then also be true of goods and services. Equally, faster rising wages could feed through into higher costs for firms. They would then be forced to pass on these costs to customers and so this would be inflationary.

Another indicator is house prices. If house prices are rising fast, it is an indicator that households have money to spend which could spill over into higher demand for goods and services. Higher house prices also add to household wealth and could encourage them to borrow more, which would increase aggregate demand.

The exchange rate is important too. If the exchange rate is falling, it will make British exports more competitive and imports less competitive. This will increase aggregate demand. A rising exchange rate, on the other hand, will tend to reduce aggregate demand.

The output gap is another significant indicator. This measures the difference between the actual level of output and what economists estimate is the potential level of output of the economy. If all factors of production are fully utilised, any increase in aggregate demand will lead to higher inflation.

Problems facing the Monetary Policy Committee

One of the problems facing the Monetary Policy Committee is that economic data for one month is unreliable. If the statisticians say that average earnings increased 0.564 per cent last month, it is almost certain that this is not totally accurate. Therefore the members of the MPC have to make judgments about how plausible are the statistics presented to them.

Another problem is that economists don't agree about exactly how the economy works. Some economists might attach more importance, for instance, to an increase in wage inflation than others. All economists accept that the real world is so complicated that it is often difficult to capture it and

portray it in economic theories and models. Finally, the data is often contradictory. Some indicators will suggest an increase in inflationary pressures whilst others will show a decrease. It is less common for most of the economic data to be pointing in the same direction. This is especially a problem if the Committee is being successful at controlling inflation over a period of time. Then, the output gap is likely to be around zero, with economic resources fully utilised. It is unlikely that one month's figures will show any clear trend. This is very different from a situation where there is, say, a large negative output gap, showing the economy operating at well below its productive potential and with high unemployment. Then it is likely to be clear that interest rates could be cut without inflation moving above its target level. Equally, if there is a large positive output gap, the situation is unsustainable in the long term and increased inflation is almost inevitable. Then it is clear that interest rates must rise to choke off demand.

DataQuestion — Will the Bank of England cut interest rates today?

The Monetary Policy Committee, meeting today, will have to decide whether to change interest rates. Industry and retailers want to see interest rates cut. They are complaining of a lack of spending in the economy. On the other hand, the Monetary Policy Committee might feel that inflationary pressures are still too strong to justify a cut in interest rates.

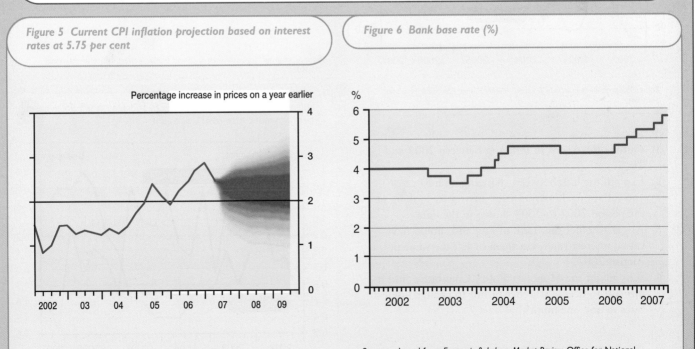

Figure 5 *Current CPI inflation projection based on interest rates at 5.75 per cent*

Percentage increase in prices on a year earlier

Source: adapted from Bank of England, *Inflation Report*, August 2007.

Figure 6 *Bank base rate (%)*

Source: adapted from *Economic & Labour Market Review*, Office for National Statistics.

Figure 7 Current projection of real GDP growth based on constant interest rates at 5.75 per cent

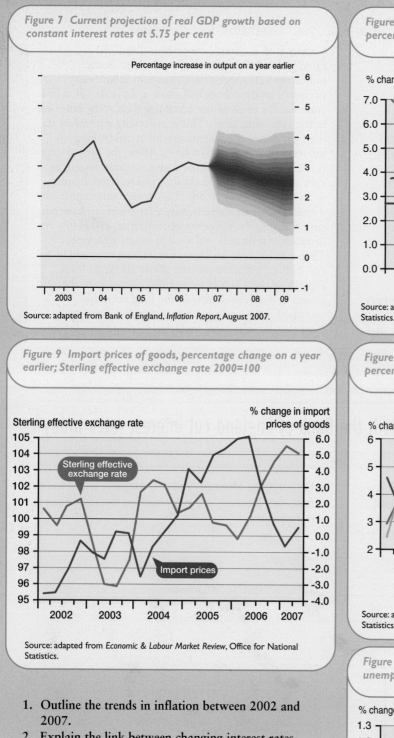

Percentage increase in output on a year earlier

Source: adapted from Bank of England, *Inflation Report*, August 2007.

Figure 8 Real household consumption, real retail sales, percentage change on a year earlier

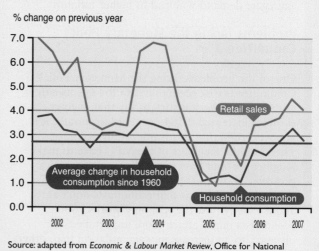

% change on previous year

Retail sales

Average change in household consumption since 1960

Household consumption

Source: adapted from *Economic & Labour Market Review*, Office for National Statistics.

Figure 9 Import prices of goods, percentage change on a year earlier; Sterling effective exchange rate 2000=100

Sterling effective exchange rate

% change in import prices of goods

Sterling effective exchange rate

Import prices

Source: adapted from *Economic & Labour Market Review*, Office for National Statistics.

Figure 10 Average earnings growth, including bonuses, percentage change on a year earlier

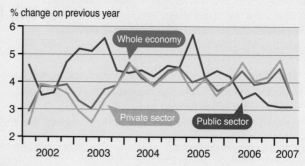

% change on previous year

Whole economy

Private sector

Public sector

Source: adapted from *Economic & Labour Market Review*, Office for National Statistics.

Figure 11 Employment, percentage change on previous year; unemployment rate (ILO), per cent

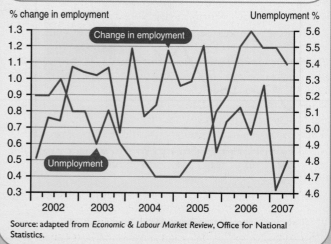

% change in employment

Unemployment %

Change in employment

Unmployment

Source: adapted from *Economic & Labour Market Review*, Office for National Statistics.

1. Outline the trends in inflation between 2002 and 2007.
2. Explain the link between changing interest rates and inflation. Illustrate your answer by looking at the period 2002 to 2007 shown in the data.
3. Assess whether the Bank of England should have raised interest rates, cut them or left the same in August 2007.
4. Why might the Monetary Policy Committee find it difficult to decide whether or not to change interest rates in any one month?

Summary

1. The value of a currency in a floating exchange rate system is determined by the forces of demand and supply.
2. Governments can influence the value of their currency by changing interest rates and by intervening directly on the foreign exchange markets using their gold and foreign currency reserves.
3. A rise in the value of a currency is likely to reduce exports but increase imports. A fall in the value of a currency is likely to increase exports but reduce imports.
4. Raising the exchange rate is likely to benefit inflation but will tend to reduce output, increase unemployment and lead to a deterioration in the current account. A fall in the exchange rate is likely to increase both inflation and output, reduce unemployment and lead to an improvement in the current account.

Exchange rate systems

The value of currencies like the US dollar, the Japanese yen and Britain's currency, the pound sterling, is determined by the foreign currency markets. At any point in time, there are buyers in the market for a currency and there are sellers. The forces of demand and supply then determine the price of the currency.

This system of determining exchange rates is known as a **free or floating exchange rate system**. There have been and still are other types of system. For instance, the value of the pound was fixed against the US dollar between 1946 and 1971. The Bank of England guaranteed to exchange pounds for US dollars at a **fixed exchange rate**. This is an example of a fixed exchange rate system. Before 1914, the world's major currencies were fixed in value in relation to gold. In Europe, before the euro became the official currency of the eurozone, each separate currency was fixed against each other at a specific rate. The value of the French franc could not change against the German deutschmark. Today, the euro itself is allowed to float against other currencies and so its value is determined within a floating exchange rate system.

This unit will consider exchange rate policy within a floating exchange rate system. This is the situation that faces the government in the UK and the European Central Bank which controls the euro today.

Influencing the exchange rate

Exchange rate policy tends to be administered by the **central bank** of a country which controls exchange rates and its gold and foreign currency reserves. It is important to understand that some governments, through their central banks, choose to allow free market forces to determine the exchange rate of their currency. For example, the UK government and Bank of England do not attempt to influence the value of the pound. Other central banks, like the Bank of Japan or the People's Bank of China, have an active policy of manipulating exchange rates. Central banks with an active exchange rate policy can influence the value of their currency in two main ways.

Interest rates Increasing domestic interest rates is likely to increase the value of the currency. This is because higher interest rates in, say, the UK makes depositing money in London more attractive. Savings are attracted into the UK from overseas, whilst UK firms and institutions are less attracted to sending their savings to New York, Tokyo or Paris. Hence the demand

for pounds is likely to increase, shown by a shift to the right in the demand curve for pounds, whilst the supply decreases, shown by a shift to the left in the supply curve. This results in a new higher equilibrium price.

Use of gold and foreign currency reserves Central banks have traditionally kept gold and foreign currency reserves. These are holdings of gold and foreign currencies which can be used to alter the value of a currency. If the Bank of England wanted to increase the value of the pound, it would sell some of its foreign currency reserves in exchange for pounds. This would increase the demand for the pound and hence raise its price. If it wanted to reduce the value of the pound, it would sell pounds for foreign currency, increasing supply and hence reducing the equilibrium price.

The ability of governments to influence the exchange rate is limited when the currency is floating. Almost all flows of money across the foreign exchanges are speculative and don't relate to the purchase of actual exports or imports. These flows of HOT MONEY are generated by individual speculators, hedge funds and banks attempting to make a profit by dealing in foreign exchange. They are so large that a country's foreign currency reserves could be used up within days trying to support a value of the exchange rate which the markets believed was too high. Equally, interest rate differentials between countries have to be substantial to have a significant impact on the value of the currency. Even so, governments can and do intervene to nudge exchange rates in directions which they believe desirable.

How exchange rate movements affect the economy

Exchange rate movements mainly affect the real economy through their effects on exports and imports. A rise or APPRECIATION in the exchange rate will tend to make exports more expensive to foreigners but imports cheaper to domestic customers. A fall or DEPRECIATION in the exchange rate will have the reverse effect, making exports cheaper and imports more expensive.

To understand why, consider a good priced at £100 which is being sold for export to the US by a UK firm. If the exchange rate is £1=$1, the US customer will have to pay $100. If the value of the pound rises to £1=$2, then the US customer will have to pay $200 for it. At the new higher

Question 1

The pound rose yesterday to its highest level against the dollar since Black Wednesday, the day in September 1992 when the pound was forced out of the Exchange Rate Mechanism. One factor was a report by the Organisation for Economic Co-operation and Development (OECD) which said that the Bank of England would need to increase its interest rates to control inflation. Another factor was reports that Asian central banks have been shifting their foreign exchange rate holdings out of dollars into other currencies such as the pound. Central banks in Japan, China and South Korea in recent years have been selling their own domestic currencies in exchange for US dollars in an attempt to weaken the value of their own currencies.

Source: adapted from the *Financial Times*, 2.12.2004.

(a) Explain why a rise in domestic interest rates by the Bank of England might affect the exchange rate value of the pound.
(b) Explain why the sale of South Korean Won or Japanese Yen by the South Korean and Japanese central banks for US dollars might affect the value of the Won or the Yen.

exchange rate, the US customer has to pay more dollars to acquire the same number of pounds as before.

Similarly, consider a good priced at $100 in the US. If the exchange rate is £1=$1, then it will cost a UK customer £100. If the exchange rate rises to £1=$2, the cost to the UK customer will fall to £50.

A rise in the value of the pound will make UK firms less price competitive internationally. British exporters will find their orders falling as foreign customers switch to other, cheaper sources. In domestic markets, British firms will find that foreign imports are undercutting their prices and gaining market share. Exactly how much EXPORT and IMPORT VOLUMES, the number of goods sold, will change depends upon their price elasticity of demand. If the price elasticity of demand for exports is elastic, with a value of, say, 2, then a 10 per cent rise in the price of exports to foreigners will result in a 20 per cent fall in export volumes.

Firms may, however, adopt a different response to an appreciation or depreciation of the currency. They may choose to keep prices to customers in their currency the same. For instance, with the good priced at £100 which is sold to the USA, the British firm could decide to keep the price at $100 when the exchange rate appreciates from £1=$1 to £1=$2. What this means is that the British exporter would then only receive £50 for the good. The British firm would not lose market share as a result, but it would see its profit margins fall. There are two reasons why an exporter might be prepared to accept a lower price for the product in domestic currency terms. First, it may think that the foreign currency movement is temporary. For marketing reasons, it does not want to be constantly changing its foreign currency price every time there is a small change in the exchange rate. Second, it may have been earning **abnormal profit** previously, a higher level of profit than the minimum needed to keep the firm supplying the good.

If firms keep their prices to customers the same in their currencies, then export and import volumes will remain unchanged. However, profitability will have changed. If a currency appreciates in value, exporters will be forced to cut their prices in their own currency to maintain prices in foreign currencies. Their profitability will decline and

it will become less attractive to export. Export values will fall too because, although volumes have remained the same, prices in domestic currency terms will have fallen. As for imports, foreign firms importing to the UK that choose to keep their sterling prices the same will see their profits rise. This will give them a greater incentive to sell into the UK. They might choose, for instance, to advertise more aggressively. Import volumes are therefore likely to rise, increasing import values as a result.

A third alternative is that firms may choose to change their export and import prices but not by as much as the change in the exchange rate. For instance, assume that the value of the pound rises 10 per cent against the US dollar. A UK exporting firm may choose to absorb 6 per cent of the rise by reducing the pound sterling price by 6 per cent and passing on the remaining 4 per cent by raising the dollar price. Profit margins fall and there could be some loss of market share because US customers now face higher prices. However, this might be better for the firm than either cutting its sterling price by 10 per cent, eating into its profit margins, or raising US dollar prices by 10 per cent and risking losing substantial market share.

Which type of strategy a firm chooses to use to some extent depends upon the industry in which it operates. For commodity products, like steel, wheat or copper, firms are likely to have little control over their market. They will be forced to pass on price rises or falls to customers as exchange rates change. Firms which can control their markets, like car manufacturers, tend to leave prices unaltered as exchange rates change.

The macroeconomic impact of changes in exchange rates

Changes in exchange rates can affect the performance of an economy.

Question 2

British cheese manufacturers, like most exporters to the USA, are suffering from the recent large rise in the value of the pound against the dollar. It has risen from $1.56 to the pound in November 2002 to $1.79 in December 2003.

Neal's Yard Dairy, a UK seller of high quality cheese, is partially protected because its US customers are less price sensitive than many. Its dollar prices have risen by an average 10 per cent over the past year. 'People go into a shop and spend the same amount on cheese. If the prices have increased, then they buy less', said Jason Hinds, sales manager of Neal's Yard. Exporters of non-niche, commodity cheeses are in for tougher times. Customers buy these purely on price. Stephen Jones, managing director of Summerdale International, a cheese export agency in Taunton, said its global sales could drop from £3m to £2m next year. UK exporters are relieved, though, that they are not in the euro area. The euro has appreciated far more against the US dollar than the pound. Jason Hinds said: 'Our products in the US look cheap compared to cheeses from France or Italy.

Source: adapted from the *Financial Times*, 6.1.2004.

(a) Explain the impact that the rise in the value of the pound against the dollar in 2003 had on UK cheese exporters.
(b) Why might the rise in the value of the euro against the dollar have given British cheese exporters a competitive advantage?

Inflation A rise in the exchange rate is likely to moderate inflation for two reasons. First, a higher exchange rate will tend to lead to a fall in import prices, which then feeds through to lower domestic prices. As explained above, some importers will choose to keep their foreign currency prices the same in order to increase their profit margins. However, other importers will cut their foreign currency prices. The extent to which a rise in the exchange rate leads to a fall in domestic prices depends upon what proportion of importers choose to cut prices.

Second, a higher exchange rate will lead to a fall in aggregate demand. Exports will fall and imports will rise as explained above. The fall in aggregate demand then leads to a fall in inflation. The extent to which aggregate demand falls depends upon the price elasticity of demand for exports and imports.

The higher the price elasticities, the greater will be the change in export and import volumes to changes in prices brought about by the exchange rate movement.

The reverse occurs when there is a depreciation of the exchange rate. Import prices will tend to rise, feeding through to higher domestic inflation. Aggregate demand will rise as exports become more price competitive and imports less price competitive. As a result, inflation will tend to increase.

Economic growth A change in the exchange rate may have an impact on long term growth rates. A higher exchange rate which discourages exports and encourages imports may lead to lower domestic investment, and vice versa for a lower exchange rate. However, the main impact of a changing exchange rate will be felt on short run output. A rise in the exchange rate will dampen output in the short term because exports fall and imports rise, leading to a fall in aggregate demand. A fall in the exchange rate will lead to rising exports and falling imports, raising aggregate demand and thus equilibrium output.

Unemployment A rise in the exchange rate will tend to increase unemployment. This is because an exchange rate rise will tend to lower aggregate demand and thus equilibrium output. A fall in the exchange rate will tend to reduce unemployment. Changes in unemployment will be felt unequally in different sectors of the economy. In those industries which export a significant proportion of output, or where imports are important, there will tend to be larger changes in employment and unemployment as a result of exchange rate changes. In industries, particularly some service industries, where little is exported or imported, changes in the exchange rate will have little effect on employment and unemployment.

The current balance A rise in the exchange rate is likely to lead to a deterioration in the current balance. A rise in the exchange rate will lead to lower exports as they become less price competitive. The volume of imports is likely to rise leading to higher import values. So the current account position (exports minus imports) is likely to deteriorate. On the other hand, a fall in the exchange rate is likely to lead to an improvement in the current balance. Exports are likely to rise, but imports fall.

Question 3

In 2003 and 2004, the Japanese central bank spent an estimated £150bn buying up US dollars with Japanese yen to depress the value of the yen against the dollar. This was part of a much longer period of intervention in foreign currency markets going back to 1991, all designed to lower the yen:US$ exchange rate. The Japanese economy in the early 2000s was in a weak state having spent much of the previous decade either in recession or experiencing low growth. The Japanese central bank wanted to support the recovery of the Japanese economy with a low exchange rate.

However, since March 2004 intervention has stopped. One possible reason is that the Japanese central bank has become concerned about the recent boom in commodity prices. Japan is a major importer of commodities such as oil, having few natural resources itself. The lower the value of the yen, the higher the cost of imported commodities for Japanese manufacturers. Imported inflation poses a threat both to the competitiveness and profitability of Japanese companies and to the economy as a whole.

Figure 1 Japan, annual percentage growth in export volumes and GDP; $ oil prices and $ index of all other primary commodities

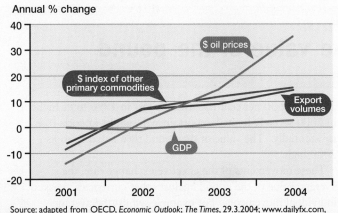

Source: adapted from OECD, *Economic Outlook; The Times,* 29.3.2004; www.dailyfx.com, May 2005.

(a) Explain how Japan's central bank used its intervention in foreign currency markets as an instrument of policy to improve the performance of the Japanese economy.
(b) Using Figure 1, discuss the extent to which this intervention was successful in achieving its aims.

Key terms

Appreciation or depreciation of a currency - a rise or fall in the value of a currency when the currency is floating and market forces determine its value.
Export and import volumes - the number of exports and imports. In statistics, they are usually expressed in index number form. They can be calculated by dividing the value of total exports or imports by their average price.
Hot money - short term, speculative flows of money across foreign exchanges, made in order to make a profit on the difference between the buying and selling price of the currency.

Applied economics

UK government policy

Since September 1992, the UK government has chosen not to use the exchange rate as an instrument of policy. Instead, it has allowed the pound to float freely on the foreign exchange markets. So it has not used either interest rates or its foreign currency reserves to affect the price of sterling.

This policy has been very much influenced by the experience during the period 1990-92. In 1990, the Conservative government with John Major as Chancellor of the Exchequer decided to join the Exchange Rate Mechanism (ERM) of the European Monetary Union (EMU). This was a mechanism designed to stabilise the value of European exchange rates prior to the creation of a single currency, the euro. Any single ERM currency was fixed in value against other currencies within the ERM within a band. For instance, the French franc was fixed against the German deutschmark within a 2.5 per cent band. So the French franc could appreciate or depreciate in value against the deutschmark but within very narrow limits.

The British government's main economic concern since 1988 had been combating inflation, which had risen from 4 per cent in 1987 to 10 per cent in 1990. It decided to enter the ERM at a high value for the pound. This put pressure on import prices and prevented a future fall in the exchange rate from reigniting inflation. Between 1990 and September 1992, it used its foreign currency reserves to keep the value of the pound within its band against other European currencies. More importantly, it was forced

to keep interest rates high. By 1991, inflation was falling rapidly but the economy was in a deep recession. The government wanted to ease monetary policy by cutting interest rates, but was prevented from cutting them as much as they wanted because high interest rates were needed to keep the value of the pound high. In September 1992, the pound came under fierce selling pressure. Despite the government using an estimated £30 billion in foreign currency reserves buying up pounds to keep its value within its band, speculation continued against the pound. On Black Wednesday, September 15, the government was forced to abandon its membership of the ERM. The pound rapidly fell 15 per cent in value.

This illustrates the problem that governments face when attempting to defend a value for the currency. Speculative flows of money are so large that it can be difficult for a government to prevent the markets from driving the currency up or down in value.

Since 1992, the UK government has chosen not to defend any particular value of the pound. However, the United Kingdom periodically reviews whether or not to join the single European currency. If it does join, it will have to peg the pound against the euro and it, together with the European Central Bank, will have to defend that value for a period of time. Under current arrangements the pound would eventually be abolished and the euro would become the UK's currency. Once the pound has disappeared, exchange rate policy will no longer be the responsibility of the UK government. It will pass to the European Central Bank.

DataQuestion

The value of the pound

In October 1990, the British government fixed the value of the pound against a basket of European currencies which would eventually become the euro. It fixed the pound at a deliberately high value because it wanted to reduce inflation within the economy. The high value of the pound meant that exports became less competitive whilst imports became more competitive. However, less than two years later, in September 1992, the government was forced to take the UK out of the Exchange Rate Mechanism (ERM). Free market forces now determined the value of the pound, pushing it quickly down by over 15 per cent.

In 1996, free market forces pushed up the average value of the pound again, and it eventually reached a high in

2000. The 30 per cent rise from its low in 1996 to its high in 2000 severely limited export growth, whilst imports rose substantially. The value of the pound then eased from its 2000 high.

These movements of the effective exchange rate, the average value of the pound against other currencies, masked individual movements. For example, whilst the average value of the pound fell between 2000 and 2003, the value of the pound against the dollar rose significantly. This meant that whilst UK exporters in general benefited from currency movements over this period, UK exporters to the US suffered.

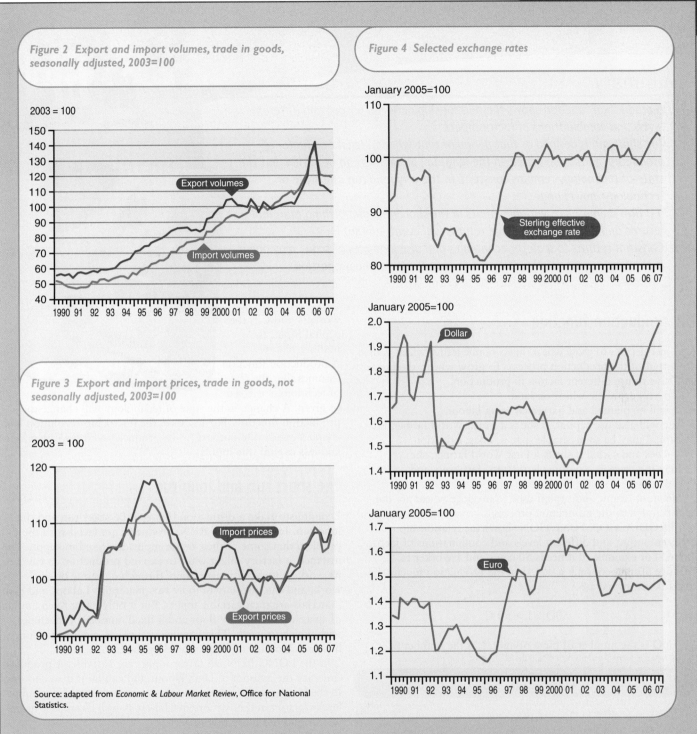

Figure 2 *Export and import volumes, trade in goods, seasonally adjusted, 2003=100*

2003 = 100

Figure 3 *Export and import prices, trade in goods, not seasonally adjusted, 2003=100*

2003 = 100

Figure 4 *Selected exchange rates*

January 2005=100

Sterling effective exchange rate

January 2005=100

Dollar

January 2005=100

Euro

Source: adapted from *Economic & Labour Market Review*, Office for National Statistics.

1. Using the data in Figure 4, describe briefly what happened to the value of the pound between 1990 and 2007. Support your description with statistics.
2. Explain how the fall in the effective exchange rate of the pound between 1992 and 1996 might have affected (a) export and import volumes; (b) average export and import prices; (c) the profitability of UK exporting firms.
3. What impact on the economic performance of the UK might the fall in the value of the pound against the euro have had between 2000 and 2007?

39 Production

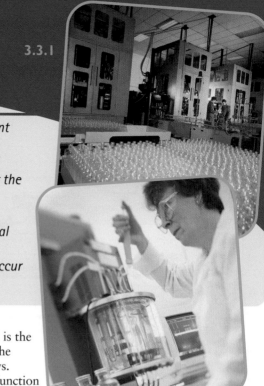

Summary

1. A production function shows the relationship between output and different levels and combinations of factor inputs.
2. The short run is defined as that period of time when at least one factor of production cannot be varied. In the long run, all factors can be varied, but the state of technology remains constant. In the very long run, the state of technology may change.
3. If a firm increases its variable inputs in the short run, diminishing marginal returns and diminishing average returns will eventually set in.
4. Constant returns to scale, or economies and diseconomies of scale, may occur in the long run when all factors are changed in the same proportion.

The production function

A farmer decides to grow wheat. In economic terms, wheat is then an output of the production process. To grow wheat, the farmer will have to use different factors of production.

● She will grow the wheat on land.
● It will be planted and harvested using labour.
● She will also use capital. If she is a Third World farmer, the capital may be some simple spades, hoes, irrigation ditches and sacks. If she is a First World farmer, she may use tractors, combine harvesters, fertilizers and pesticides.

The land, labour and capital used to produce wheat are the factor inputs to the production process.

A PRODUCTION FUNCTION shows the relationship between output and different levels and combinations of factor inputs. For example, if it needs 50 cows and 1 worker to produce 50 pints of milk a day, then the production function could be expressed as:

$$50Q = L + 50 C$$

where Q is the number of pints of milk, L is the number of workers and C is the capital input, the number of cows.

A production function assumes that the state of technology is fixed or given. A change in the state of technology will change the production function. For instance, the microchip revolution has enabled goods (the outputs) to be produced with fewer workers and less capital (the inputs).

The short run and long run

Economists make a distinction between the short run and the long run. In the SHORT RUN, producers are faced with the problem that some of their factor inputs are fixed in supply. For instance, a factory might want to expand production. It can get its workers to work longer hours through overtime or shift work, and can also buy in more raw materials. Labour and raw materials are then variable inputs. But it only has a fixed amount of space on the factory floor and a fixed number of machines with which to work. This fixed capital places a constraint on how much more can be produced by the firm.

In the LONG RUN, all factor inputs are variable. A producer can vary the amount of land, labour and capital if it so chooses. In the long run, the firm in the above example could move into a larger factory and buy more machines, as well as employ more labour and use more raw materials.

In the long run, existing technologies do not change. In the VERY LONG RUN, the state of technology can change. For instance, a bank would be able to move from a paper-based system with cheques, bank statements and paper memos to a completely electronic paperless system with cards, computer terminal statements and memos.

The way that the short run and the long run are defined in the theory of production means that there is no standard length of time for the short run. In the chemical industry, a plant may last 20 years before it needs replacing and so the short run might last 20 years. In an industry with little or no permanent physical capital, the short run may be measured in months or even weeks. The short run for a market trader, who hires everything from the stall to a van and keeps no stock, may be as short as one day, the day of the market when she is committed to hiring equipment and selling stock.

Question 1

C W Cobb and P H Douglas, two American economists, estimated, in an article published in 1938, that the production function for US manufacturing industry between 1900 and 1922 was:

$$x = 1.10 \ L^{0.75} \ C^{0.25}$$

where x is an index of total production per year, L is an index of labour input and C an index of capital input.

Using a calculator with a power function, calculate the increase in the index of production if:
(a) the quantity of labour inputs were increased by
    (i) 10% and (ii) 20%;
(b) the quantity of capital inputs were increased by
    (i) 20% and (ii) 30%;
(c) the quantity of both labour and capital inputs were increased by (i) 30% and (ii) 50%.

Question 2

General Motors (GM) is still the world's largest automobile manufacturer, just, but it is in dire difficulties. Its North American operations made a loss of $1.6 billion in the first nine months of this year. It is for this reason that the company announced today that it would cut 30 000 hourly paid production jobs in North America, about 22 per cent of its production workforce. Another 2 500 salaried jobs would also go. The company proposed closing or scaling back operations at about a dozen US and Canadian locations. Total production capacity in North America would fall 16 per cent from about 5 million cars a year to 4.2 million.

The company is to continue its research into producing alternatives to the petrol driven car, looking at battery driven cars, hybrid cars running on both petrol and batteries, and cars powered by other fuels such as hydrogen.

Source: adapted from money.cnn.com, 21.11.2005.

Explain carefully what would be the time scale (short run, long run or very long run) for GM:
(a) buying tyres from a supplier;
(b) making over 30 000 workers redundant and closing plants in North America;
(c) changing from manufacturing petrol driven cars to cars powered by hydrogen.

The short run: diminishing returns

In the short run at least one factor is fixed. Assume for example that a firm uses only two factors of production: capital, in the form of buildings and machines, which is fixed and labour which can be varied. What will happen to output as more and more labour is used?

Initially, output per worker is likely to rise. A factory designed for 500 workers, for instance, is unlikely to be very productive if only one worker is employed. But there will come a point when output per worker will start to fall. There is an optimum level of production which is most productively efficient. Eventually, if enough workers are employed, total output will fall. Imagine 10 000 workers trying to work in a factory designed for 500. The workers will get in each other's way and result in less output than with a smaller number of workers. This general pattern is known as the LAW OF DIMINISHING RETURNS or the LAW OF VARIABLE PROPORTIONS.

Total, average and marginal products

The law of diminishing returns can be explained more formally using the concepts of total, average and marginal products.

Question 3

You wish to employ cleaners to clean your house. They will use your own cleaning equipment (brooms, mops, dusters, polish etc.). Using the law of diminishing returns, explain what would happen if you employed 1 cleaner, 5 cleaners, 20 cleaners or 1 000 cleaners to clean at one time.

- TOTAL PRODUCT is the quantity of output produced by a given number of inputs over a period of time. It is expressed in physical terms and not money terms. (Indeed, economists often refer to total physical product, average physical product and marginal physical product to emphasise this point.) The total product of 1 000 workers in the car industry over a year might be 30 000 cars.
- AVERAGE PRODUCT is the quantity of output per unit of input. In the above example, output per worker would be 30 cars per year (the total product divided by the quantity of inputs).
- MARGINAL PRODUCT is the addition to output produced by an extra unit of input. If the addition of an extra car worker raised output to 30 004 cars in our example, then the marginal product would be 4 cars.

Now consider Table 1. In this example capital is fixed at 10 units whilst labour is a variable input.
- If no workers are employed, total output will be zero.
- The first worker produces 20 units of output. So the marginal product of the first worker is 20 units.
- The second worker produces an extra 34 units of output. So the marginal product of the second worker is 34 units. Total output with two workers is 54 units (20 units plus 34 units). Average output is 54 ÷ 2 or 27 units per worker.
- The third worker produces an extra 46 units of output. So total output with three workers is 100 units (20 plus 34 plus 46). Average output is 100÷3 or approximately 33 units per worker.

Table 1 *Total, average and marginal products*

Units

Capital	Labour	Physical product as labour is varied		
		Marginal	Total	Average[1]
10	0		0	0
		20		
10	1		20	20
		34		
10	2		54	27
		46		
10	3		100	33
		51		
10	4		151	38
		46		
10	5		197	39
		33		
10	6		230	38
		20		
10	7		251	36
		-17		
10	8		234	29

1. Rounded to the nearest whole number.

Initially, marginal product rises, but the fifth worker produces less than the fourth. **Diminishing marginal returns** therefore set in between the fourth and fifth worker. Average product rises too at first and then falls, but the turning point is later than for marginal product. **Diminishing average returns** set in between 5 and 6 workers.

The law of diminishing returns states that if increasing quantities of a variable input are combined with a fixed input, eventually the marginal product and then the

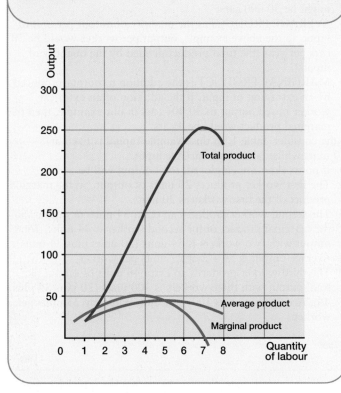

Figure 1 *Total, average and marginal product*
The curves are derived from the data in Table 46.1. Note that diminishing marginal returns set in before diminishing average returns. Note too that the marginal product curve cuts the average product curve at its highest point, whilst the total product curve falls when the marginal product curve cuts the horizontal axis.

average product of that variable input will decline.

It is possible to draw total, average and marginal product curves. The curves in Figure 1 are derived from the data in Table 1. All three curves first rise and then fall. Marginal product falls first, then average product and finally total product.

The long run: returns to scale

The law of diminishing returns assumes that firms operate in the short run. In the long run, firms can vary all their factor inputs. What would happen to the output of a firm if, for instance, it were to increase all its inputs by the same proportion? There are only three possibilities.

● INCREASING RETURNS TO SCALE occur if an equal percentage increase in inputs to production leads to a more than proportional increase in output. If a firm doubles its land, labour and capital inputs, but as a consequence trebles its output, then increasing returns to scale have occurred. For instance, if as in Table 3, 1 unit of capital and 1 unit of all other factors of production are used, then 20 units of output are produced. Doubling the inputs to 2 units of capital and 2 units of all other factors more than doubles output to 50 units. An increase in inputs by 50 per cent from 2 to 3 units of all factors increases output by more than 50 per cent from 50 units to 80 units. Therefore the firm is operating under conditions of increasing returns to scale.

    ● CONSTANT RETURNS TO SCALE occur if an equal percentage increase in inputs to production leads to the same percentage increase in output. For example,

Question 4

Table 2

		Units
Capital	Labour	Total product
10	1	8
10	2	24
10	3	42
10	4	60
10	5	70
10	6	72

Table 46.2 shows the change in total product as the quantity of labour increases and all other factor inputs remain constant.
(a) Calculate the average and marginal product at each level of labour input.
(b) Draw the total, average and marginal product curves on a graph.
(c) At what level of output do (i) diminishing marginal returns and (ii) diminishing average returns set in?

if a firm doubles its inputs and this leads to a doubling of output, then constant returns to scale occur.
● DECREASING RETURNS TO SCALE occur if an equal percentage increase in inputs to production leads to a less than proportional increase in output. So decreasing returns to scale occur if a firm trebles its inputs but only doubles its output.

Table 3 *Increasing returns to scale*

		Units of capital		
		1	2	3
Units of all	1	20	35	45
other factors	2	30	50	65
of production	3	35	63	80

Question 5

Table 4

		Units of labour				
		1	2	3	4	5
Units of all	1	1	2	4	5	6
other factors	2	2	3	6	8	10
of production	3	3	5	9	11	12
	4	5	7	10	12	13
	5	7	9	11	13	14

The table shows the output of a firm given different levels of factor inputs over the long run. Over what range does the firm experience:
(a) increasing returns.
(b) constant returns.
(c) decreasing returns to scale?

Key terms

Average product - the quantity of output per unit of factor input. It is the total product divided by the level of output.

Law of diminishing returns or variable proportions - if increasing quantities of a variable input are combined with a fixed input, eventually the marginal product and then the average product of that variable input will decline. Diminishing returns are said to exist when this decline occurs.

Long run - the period of time when all factor inputs can be varied, but the state of technology remains constant.

Marginal product - the addition to output produced by an extra unit of input. It is the change in total output divided by the change in the level of inputs.

Production function - the relationship between output and different levels and combinations of inputs.

Returns to scale - the change in percentage output resulting from a percentage change in all the factors of production. There are increasing returns to scale if the percentage increase in output is greater than the percentage increase in factors employed, constant returns to scale if it is the same and decreasing returns to scale if it is less.

Short run - the period of time when at least one factor input to the production process can be varied.

Total product - the quantity of output measured in physical units produced by a given number of inputs over a period of time.

Very long run - the period of time when the state of technology may change.

Applied economics

Increasing returns at petrol stations

The production function

Petrol stations provide a service to their customers. They buy in fuel and other merchandise in large quantities, store it and then sell it in smaller quantities to customers when they want to make their purchases. Other inputs apart from stock to this production process include the land on which the petrol station is built, capital in the form of buildings and equipment, and labour.

Changing product mix

Petrol stations tended originally to be attached to garages which repaired and perhaps also sold cars. Garages aimed to provide a complete service to the motorist. Increasingly, however, petrol stations were built without the provision of other garage services. This enabled them to benefit from specialisation.

By the 1970s, petrol stations started to undergo another change. New petrol stations began to be built by the supermarket chains. They were able to undercut existing petrol station prices by selling large volumes of petrol and by buying at lowest prices on the world oil markets. While there were few supermarket petrol stations in a region, this posed little threat to traditional suppliers. By the late 1980s, however, supermarket petrol stations could be found in most localities. Traditional petrol stations started to close under the fierce price competition.

In 1990, there were around 20 000 petrol retail sites in the UK but this had more than halved to 9 382 by 2006. The number of supermarket sites had increased over the same period from 369 to 1294. But the number of petrol retail sites owned by the major oil companies had declined from 6 500 to 2 217 whilst the number of independent retailers had gone from 13 000 to 5 280. The supermarket price discounters had won a decisive victory over more expensive oil company and independent sites.

Increasing returns

Petrol stations rarely operate at maximum capacity. Most could supply petrol to more customers without having to increase the size of their site or install new pumps. So more petrol sales could be achieved by combining existing capital with more petrol. Petrol companies have also realised for many years that other goods could be sold from petrol stations. Typically, this started off with confectionery and a few motor products like oil. However, they have increasingly turned petrol station kiosks into mini convenience stores. By combining groceries, snack foods, motor products and newspapers, they have again been able to achieve increasing returns to scale, selling more products without increasing their stock of fixed capital.

DataQuestion

Overfishing

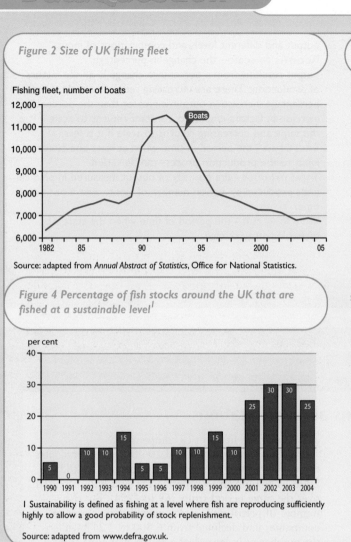

Figure 2 Size of UK fishing fleet

Fishing fleet, number of boats

Boats

Source: adapted from *Annual Abstract of Statistics*, Office for National Statistics.

Figure 4 Percentage of fish stocks around the UK that are fished at a sustainable level[1]

per cent

1 Sustainability is defined as fishing at a level where fish are reproducing sufficiently highly to allow a good probability of stock replenishment.

Source: adapted from www.defra.gov.uk.

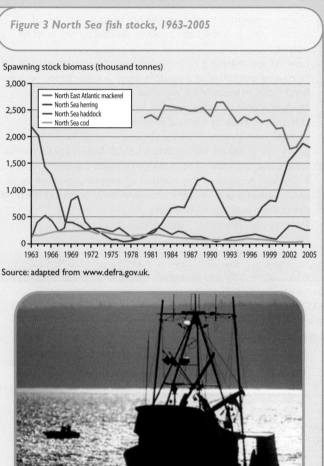

Figure 3 North Sea fish stocks, 1963-2005

Spawning stock biomass (thousand tonnes)

- North East Atlantic mackerel
- North Sea herring
- North Sea haddock
- North Sea cod

Source: adapted from www.defra.gov.uk.

In the early 1950s, the world fish catch was a little over 20 million tonnes. By 2005 it had risen to nearly 93.8 million tonnes. But there were warning signals coming from different fisheries around the world that overfishing was destroying the industry as early as the 1960s. From Newfoundland to the Mediterranean to the North Sea, fish stocks were reaching critical levels. Off Newfoundland, the fishing industry destroyed the fish stock in the 1980s. In Europe, the EU and member governments were forced to introduce a quota scheme to restrict fish catches, much to the anger of the fishing industry which had been expanding dramatically. The problem is that fish stocks are not infinite. If the fish population is not kept at a critical level, fish stocks will decline over time and eventually will completely collapse. The United Nations Food and Agriculture Organisation (FAO) in 2007 estimated for 2005 that 17 per cent of the world's fisheries were being over exploited, 7 per cent were already depleted and 1 per cent were recovering from depletion. 52 per cent were fully exploited, defined as being fished to their maximum biological productivity. Putting more boats into these areas would produce hardly any additional output. Only 23 per cent of the world's fisheries are underexploited and could sustain moderate increases in fishing.

Source: With information from *The State of World Fisheries and Aquaculture*, FAO.

1. Outline the problem of overfishing.
2. Giving examples from the data, explain why fishing was subject to diminishing returns both in the UK waters and worldwide.
3. Four possible solutions to the problem of overfishing include tightening existing quotas on fish catches, banning all fishing in a particular fishery, reducing the number of boats licensed to fish and increasing taxes on fish sales. Discuss these solutions, evaluating whether they would help solve the problem and who might benefit and lose out from their implementation.

40 Costs

Summary

1. Economists use the word 'cost' of production in a way different from its general usage. Economic cost is the opportunity cost of production.
2. There is a difference between total, average and marginal costs as well as fixed and variable costs.
3. The short run average and marginal cost curves are U-shaped because of the law of diminishing returns.
4. The long run average and marginal cost curves are U-shaped too because of economies and diseconomies of scale.
5. There is a difference between internal and external economies of scale.
6. The long run average cost curve of a firm is an envelope for the firm's short run average cost curves.

The economic definition of cost

Economists use the word 'cost' in a very specific sense. The ECONOMIC COST of production for a firm is the opportunity cost of production. It is the value that could have been generated had the resources been employed in their next best use.

For instance, a market trader has some very obvious costs, such as the cost of buying stock to sell, the rent for her pitch in the market and the petrol to get her to and from the market. Money will be paid for these and this will be an accurate reflection of opportunity cost. However, there are a number of hidden costs. Resources which have an opportunity cost but for which no payment is made must have an IMPUTED COST. There is a number of examples that can be used to illustrate imputed cost.

Labour A market trader working on her own account may calculate that she has made £50 'profit' on a day's trading. However, this may not include the value of her own time. If she could have earned £40 working in another job for the day, then her economic profit is only £10. Hence, the opportunity cost of her labour must be included as an economic cost of production.

Financial capital A small businessman may start a company with his own money investing, say, £50 000. The economic cost of production must include the opportunity cost of that start-up capital. If he could have earned 10 per cent per annum in an alternative investment, then the economic cost (the opportunity cost) is £5 000 per year.

Depreciation The **physical capital** of a company will deteriorate over time. Machines wear out, buildings need repairs, etc. Moreover, some capital will become obsolete before the end of its physical life. The economic cost of depreciation is the difference between the purchase price and the second hand value of a good. A car, for instance, which lasts for 8 years does not depreciate at 12½ per cent each year. In the first year, cars depreciate on average by 40 per cent. Therefore a company paying £10 000 for a new car which depreciates by 40 per cent over its first year only has an asset worth £6 000 at the end of the year. £6 000 is the monetary value of the opportunity cost of keeping the car rather than selling it at the end of that year.

Goodwill A firm trading over a number of years may acquire a good reputation. It may produce branded goods which become

household names. The goodwill of these brands has an opportunity cost. They could be sold to a rival company. Therefore the interest foregone on the potential sale value of these must be included as an economic cost.

Economists differ in their use of the word 'cost' from accountants, tax inspectors, businesses and others. Accountants have developed specific conventions about what is and what is not a cost and what should and should not be included on a balance sheet, and an accountant's balance sheet may be very different from that of an economist.

Fixed and variable costs

Economists distinguish between two types of cost: fixed and variable cost.

A FIXED COST (also called an INDIRECT or OVERHEAD COST) is a cost which does not vary directly with output. As production levels change, the value of a fixed cost will remain constant. For instance, a company may rent premises. The rent

Question 1

A business woman runs her own business. Over the past twelve months, she has paid £18 000 for materials and £9 000 in wages to a worker whom she employs. She runs the business from premises which her parents own. These premises could be rented out for £10 000 a year if she were not occupying them. She has £40 000 worth of her own capital tied up in the business. She is a trained teacher and at present works exactly half of her time in a school earning £15 000. She could work full time as a teacher (earning £30 000 a year) if she didn't run the business. The current rate of interest is 5 per cent. The total revenue of her business over the past 12 months was £60 000.

(a) On the basis of these figures, what were the costs she actually paid out and what were her economic costs?
(b) Did she make a profit last year?

265

on the premises will remain the same whether the company produces nothing or produces at full capacity. If a firm pays for an advertising campaign, the cost will be the same whether sales remain constant or increase. Costs commonly given as examples of fixed costs are capital goods (e.g. factories, offices, plant and machinery), rent and rates, office staff and advertising and promotion.

A VARIABLE (or DIRECT or PRIME) COST is a cost which varies directly with output. As production increases, so does variable cost. For instance, a steel maker will use iron ore. The more steel produced, the more iron ore will be needed, so the cost of iron ore is a variable cost. Raw materials for production are the clearest example of variable costs for most firms. It is not always easy to categorise a cost as either fixed or variable. Many costs are SEMI-VARIABLE COSTS. Labour is a good example. Some firms employ a permanent staff, which could be classified as a fixed cost. They might ask the permanent staff to do overtime when necessary, or employ temporary labour. These costs would be classified as variable. However, permanent staff could be seen as a variable cost if a firm were willing to hire and fire staff as its output changed. In practice, firms do adjust staff numbers with output, but the adjustment is sluggish and therefore the cost of labour is neither variable nor fixed - it is semi-variable.

In the **short run**, at least one factor input of production cannot be changed. Therefore, in the short run, some costs are fixed costs whilst others will be variable. In the long run, all factor inputs can vary, so in the long run, all costs will be variable costs.

Question 2

Rachel Hughes owns a whole food vegetarian restaurant. Explain which of the following costs would be most likely to be fixed costs, variable costs or semi-variable costs for her business: rice; rent; wages of casual staff; interest payments on a loan; electricity; cooking oil; pots and pans; her own wage; VAT.

Total, average and marginal cost

It is important to distinguish between the total, average and marginal costs of production. The TOTAL COST (TC) of production is the cost of producing a given level of output. For instance, if a manufacturer produces 100 units a week and its weekly costs come to £1 million, then £1 million is the total cost of production. Increased production will almost

Table 1 Total costs of production

(1)	(2)	(3)	(4)
Output (per week)	Total variable cost (£)	Total fixed cost (£)	Total cost (columns 2+3) (£)
0	0	200	200
1	200	200	400
2	300	200	500
3	600	200	800
4	1 200	200	1 400
5	2 000	200	2 200

Table 2 Average costs of production₁

(1)	(2)	(3)	(4)
Output (per week)	Average variable cost (£)	Average fixed cost (£)	Average total cost (columns 2+3) (£)
1	200	200	400
2	150	100	250
3	200	67	267
4	300	50	350
5	400	40	440

1. Rounded to the nearest pound.

certainly lead to a rise in total costs. If the manufacturer increased output to 200 units a week, it would need to buy more raw materials, increase the number of workers, and generally increase its factor inputs.

This is illustrated in Table 1. At an output level of 1 unit per week, the total cost of production is £400. If output were 2 units per week, total costs would rise to £500.

The total cost of production is made up of two components:
- TOTAL VARIABLE COST (TVC) which varies with output;
- TOTAL FIXED COST (TFC) which remains constant whatever the level of output.

So in Table 1, total variable cost increases from zero to £2 000 as output increases from zero to 5 units per week, whilst total fixed costs remain constant at £200 whatever the level of output. Total variable costs when added to total fixed costs are equal to total cost. Mathematically:

$$TVC + TFC = TC$$

The AVERAGE COST OF PRODUCTION is the total cost divided by the level of output. For instance, if a firm makes 100 items at a total cost of £1 000, then the average cost per item would be £10. If a firm made 15 items at a cost of £30, then the average cost of production would be £2. Mathematically:

$$AC = \frac{TC}{Q}$$

where AC is average cost, TC is total cost and Q is quantity or the level of output.

Average cost, like total cost, is made up of two components.
- AVERAGE VARIABLE COST (AVC) is total variable cost divided by the level of output.
- AVERAGE FIXED COST (AFC) is total fixed cost divided by the level of output.

The average costs of production for the example in Table 1 are given in Table 2.

MARGINAL COST is the cost of producing an extra unit of output. For instance, if it costs £100 to produce 10 items and £105 to produce 11 items, then the marginal cost of the eleventh item is £5. If it costs £4 to produce 2 items but £10 to produce 3 items, then the marginal cost of the third unit is £6. Mathematically, marginal cost (MC) is calculated by dividing the change in total cost ($\triangle$TC) by the change in total output ($\triangle$Q).

Table 3 Marginal costs of production

(1)	(2)	(3)
Output (per week)	Total cost (£)	Marginal cost per unit of output (£)
1	400	400
2	500	100
3	800	300
4	1400	600
5	2200	800

$$MC = \frac{\triangle TC}{\triangle Q}$$

The marginal costs of production for the figures in Tables 1 and 2 are given in Table 3.

Diminishing returns and short run costs

In the short run a firm will be faced with employing at least one factor input which can not be varied. For instance, it might have a given number of machines or a fixed quantity of office space. If it were to increase output by using more of the variable factor inputs, diminishing marginal returns and then diminishing average returns would set in eventually.

Diminishing returns are a technical concept. Therefore, they are expressed in terms of physical inputs and physical product (the output of the firm). However, it is possible to express physical inputs in terms of costs. For example, a firm which employed 5 workers at a wage of £200 per week, and had no other costs, would have total weekly costs of £1 000. If each worker produced 200 units of output, then the average cost per unit of output would be £1 [£1 000 ÷ (5 x 200)]. The marginal cost of the 200 units produced by the fifth worker would be her wage (£200), and so the marginal cost per unit of output would be £1 (£200 ÷ 200).

Question 3

Table 4

£

Output	Total fixed cost	Total variable cost	Total cost	Average fixed cost	Average variable cost	Average cost	Marginal cost
0	40						
1		6					
2		11					
3		15					
4			60				
5			66				

(a) Complete Table 4, calculating the missing figures.

Short run cost schedules

Having looked at inputs, it is now possible to see how the law of diminishing returns affects short run costs. Table 6 is an example of how this can be done. It is assumed that the firm can employ up to 8 workers at identical wage rates (i.e. the supply of workers over the range 1 to 8 is **perfectly elastic**). The price of capital per unit is £100 and the price of labour is £200 per unit.

Capital is the fixed factor of production. Therefore whatever the level of production, total fixed cost will be £1 000 (10 units x £100). Total variable cost will increase as more and more labour is added. Therefore, the total variable cost of producing 20 units is £200 (1 unit of labour x £200), of 54 units it is £400 (2 units of labour x £200), and so on.

Total cost is total fixed cost plus total variable cost. Once the three measures of total cost have been worked out, it is possible to calculate average and marginal costs. Alternatively, it is possible to calculate marginal cost per unit by finding the cost of the additional labour and dividing it by the marginal physical product. In our example, the cost of hiring an extra worker is a constant £200. Therefore, the marginal cost of producing, say, an extra 34 units once 20 have been made is £200 (the cost of the second worker). The marginal cost per unit is then £200 ÷ 34. Average variable cost can be calculated in a similar manner.

Question 4

Table 5

	Units
Labour	Total physical product
1	20
2	45
3	60
4	70

Table 5 shows how total physical product changes as the number of units of labour changes with a fixed quantity of capital. The cost of the capital employed is £200. The firm can employ any number of workers at a constant wage rate per unit of labour of £50. What is the value of:
(i) total fixed costs (ii) total variable costs (iii) total costs
(iv) average fixed costs (v) average variable costs
(vi) total average cost (vii) marginal cost,
if the firm employs,
(a) 1 unit of labour; (b) 2 units of labour;
(c) 3 units of labour; (d) 4 units of labour?

Short run cost curves

The cost schedules in Table 6 can be plotted on a graph (Figure 1) to produce cost curves.

Total cost curves The total fixed cost (TFC) curve is a horizontal straight line, showing that TFC is constant whatever the level of output. The total cost (TC) and total variable cost (TVC) curves are parallel because the vertical distance between the two (the difference between TC and TVC) is the constant total fixed cost. The inflections in the TC and TVC curves are

Table 6

Capital	Labour	Total physical product (output)	Total cost[1]			Average cost[2]			Marginal cost
			TVC	TFC	TC	AVC	AFC	ATC	MC
10	0	0	0	1000	1000	0	-	-	
									10.0
10	1	20	200	1000	1200	10.0	50.0	60.0	
									5.9
10	2	54	400	1000	1400	7.4	18.5	25.9	
									4.3
10	3	100	600	1000	1600	6.0	10.0	16.0	
									3.9
10	4	151	800	1000	1800	5.3	6.6	11.9	
									4.3
10	5	197	1000	1000	2000	5.1	5.1	10.2	
									6.1
10	6	230	1200	1000	2200	5.2	4.3	9.6	
									9.5
10	7	251	1400	1000	2400	5.6	4.0	9.6	
									22.2
10	8	260	1600	1000	2600	6.8	3.8	10.0	

Units   £

1. Assuming that capital costs £100 per unit and labour costs £200 per unit.
2. The three measures of average cost have been calculated to the nearest decimal from total figures. ATC therefore does not always equal AVC+AFC because of rounding.

caused by the change from increasing returns to diminishing returns.

Average cost curves The average fixed cost (AFC) curve falls as output increases because fixed costs represent an ever decreasing proportion of total cost as output increases. The average cost (AC) curve and average variable cost (AVC) curve fall at first and then rise. They rise because diminishing average returns set in. The vertical distance between the AC and AVC curves is the value of average fixed cost. This must be true because average cost minus average variable cost is equal to average fixed cost.

Marginal cost curve The marginal cost (MC) curve at first falls and then rises as diminishing marginal returns set in.

Points to note

U-shaped AC and MC curves The MC and AC curves in Figure 1 are 'U-shaped'. This is a characteristic not just of the sample figures in Table 6, but of all short run MC and AC curves. They are U-shaped because of the law of diminishing returns. The lowest point on the MC and the AVC curves shows the point where diminishing marginal returns and diminishing average returns set in respectively.

Product and cost curves The marginal and average cost curves shown in Figure 1 are mirror images of the marginal and average product curves that could be drawn from the same data in Table 6. Marginal and average physical product rise when marginal and average cost fall, and vice versa. This is what should be expected. If marginal physical product is rising, then the extra cost of producing a unit of output must fall, and similarly with average physical product and average variable cost. For instance, when the second worker produces 34 units, the third worker 46 units and the fourth

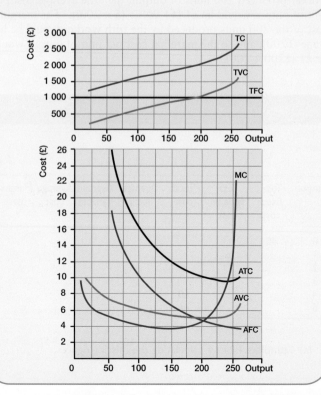

Figure 1 The shape of short run cost curves
The shape of the average and marginal cost curves is determined by the law of diminishing returns. The curves are drawn from the data in Table 6. Assuming constant factor prices, diminishing marginal returns set in at an output level of 145 when the marginal cost curve is at its lowest point. Diminishing average returns set in at the lowest point of the average variable cost curve at an output of 210 units.

worker 51 units, the marginal cost of production must be falling because the increase in output is rising faster than the increase in cost. When marginal physical product is falling, the extra cost of producing a unit of output must rise for the same reason. However, the cost and product curves will only be mirror images of each other if there are constant factor costs per unit. If, for instance, we assumed that the unit cost of labour rose as more workers were employed, so that the average wage of three workers was higher than the average wage of two, then the product and cost curves would not be mirror images.

MC curve cuts AC curve at its lowest point In Figure 1, the marginal cost curve cuts the average cost curve and average variable cost curve at their lowest points. To understand why this must be so, consider the example of a group of students whose average height is 6 feet. A new student (the marginal student) arrives in the group. If the student is above 6 feet then the average height of the group will now rise. If the student is less than 6 feet, the average height of the group will fall. If the student is exactly 6 feet tall, then the average height of the group will stay the same. Now apply this to average and marginal cost. If the average cost curve is falling, then the cost of an extra unit of output (the marginal cost) must be less than the average cost. If average cost is rising, it must be true that the cost of an extra unit of output is even higher than the average cost. When average cost is neither rising nor falling, marginal cost must be the same as average cost. Hence we know that:

- the average cost curve is above the marginal cost curve when average cost is falling;
- the average cost curve is below the marginal cost curve when average cost is rising;
- average cost and marginal cost are equal for all levels of

output when average cost is constant; if the average cost curve is U-shaped, this means that marginal cost will be equal to and will cut the average cost curve at its lowest point.

The same chain of reasoning applies to the relationship between the average variable cost curve and the marginal cost curve.

Economies of scale and long run average cost

In the long run, all factors of production are variable. This has an effect on costs as output changes. To start with, long run costs fall as output increases. **Economies of scale** are then said to exist. For instance, a firm quadruples its output from 10 million units to 40 million units. However, total costs of production only increase from £10 million to £20 million. The average cost of production consequently falls from £1 per unit (£10m ÷ 10m) to 50p per unit (£20m ÷ 40m).

Empirically (i.e. from studying real examples of the costs of firms), economists have found that firms do experience economies of scale. As firms expand in size and output, their long run average costs tend to fall. At some point, which varies from industry to industry, long run average costs become constant. However, some firms become too large and their average costs begin to rise. They are then said to experience **diseconomies of scale**. For instance, if a firm doubled its output, but as a result its costs were four times as high, then the average cost of production would double.

This pattern of falling and then rising long run average costs is shown in Figure 2. At output levels up to 0A, the firm will enjoy falling long run average costs and therefore experience economies of scale. Between output levels of 0A and 0B, long run average costs are constant. To the right of 0B, long run average costs rise and the firm faces diseconomies of scale.

LRAC in Figure 2 is drawn given a set of input prices for costs. If the cost of all raw materials in the economy rose by 20 per cent, then there would be a shift upward in the LRAC curve. Similarly, a fall in the wage rates in the industry would lead to a downward shift in the LRAC curve.

The optimum level of production

Productive efficiency is said to exist when production takes place at lowest cost. If the long run average cost curve is U-shaped, then this will occur at the bottom of the curve when constant returns to scale exist. The output range over which average costs are at a minimum is said to be the OPTIMAL LEVEL OF PRODUCTION. In Figure 2 the optimal level of production occurs over the range AB.

The output level at which lowest cost production starts is called the MINIMUM EFFICIENT SCALE (MES) of production. In Figure 2, the MES is at point A. If a firm is producing to the left of the MES, then long run average costs will be higher. To the right, they will either be the same (if there are constant returns) or will be increasing (if there are diseconomies of scale).

Sources of economies of scale

Economies of scale occur for a number of reasons.

Technical economies Economies and diseconomies of scale can exist because of **increasing** and **decreasing** returns to scale. These economies and diseconomies are known

Question 5

Table 7

		Units
Capital	Labour	Total product
10	0	0
10	1	8
10	2	24
10	3	42
10	4	60
10	5	70
10	6	72

Table 7 shows the change in total product as more labour is added to production and all other factor products remain constant. The price of capital is £1 per unit whilst labour is £2 per unit.

(a) Calculate the following over the range of output from zero to 72 units: (i) total fixed cost; (ii) total variable cost; (iii) total cost; (iv) average fixed cost; (v) average variable cost; (vi) average total cost; (vii) marginal cost.
(b) Plot each of these cost schedules on graph paper, putting the total cost curves on one graph and the average and marginal cost curves on another.
(c) Mark on the graph the point where (i) diminishing marginal returns and (ii) diminishing average returns set in.

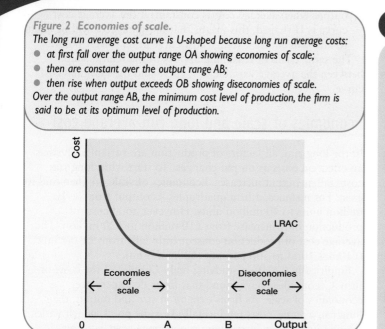

Figure 2 *Economies of scale.*
The long run average cost curve is U-shaped because long run average costs:
- *at first fall over the output range OA showing economies of scale;*
- *then are constant over the output range AB;*
- *then rise when output exceeds OB showing diseconomies of scale.*
Over the output range AB, the minimum cost level of production, the firm is said to be at its optimum level of production.

Question 6

Table 8

| Output | | Long run average cost (£) | | | |
(million units)	Firm A	Firm B	Firm C	Firm D	Firm E
1	10	20	16	19	20
2	8	18	14	18	17
3	5	16	15	17	15
4	5	11	17	16	14
5	5	10	20	15	14
6	5	10	24	14	14
7	6	11	30	13	14

For each firm, A to E, give:

(a) the range of output over which there are:
  (i) economies of scale; (ii) diseconomies of scale;
(b) the optimum level or range of output;
(c) the minimum efficient scale of production.

as **technical economies**. They arise from what happens in the production process. For instance, many firms find that they need equipment but are unable to make maximum use of it. A small builder may use a cement mixer on average only 3 days a week. If he were able to take on more work he might be able to use it 5 days a week. The total cost of the cement mixer is the same whether it is used for 3 days or 5 days a week (apart from possible depreciation) but the average cost per job done will be lower the more it is used. This is an example of an **indivisibility**. The larger the level of output, the less likely that indivisibilities will occur.

Technical economies arise too because larger plant size is often more productively efficient. For instance, because an oil tanker is essentially a cylinder, doubling the surface area of the tanker (and therefore doubling the approximate cost of construction) leads to an approximately three-fold increase in its carrying capacity. It is generally cheaper to generate electricity in large power stations than in small ones. The average cost of production of a car plant making 50 000 cars a year will be less than that of one making 5 000 cars a year.

So far, it has been assumed that unit costs are constant. However, unit costs may change as a firm changes in size. Other factors, apart from technical economies, can then lead to economies and diseconomies of scale.

Managerial economies Specialisation is an important source of greater efficiency. In a small firm, the owner might be part time salesman, accountant, receptionist and manager. Employing specialist staff is likely to lead to greater efficiency and therefore lower costs. The reason why small firms don't employ specialist staff is because staff often represent an indivisibility.

Purchasing and marketing economies The larger the firm the more likely it is to be able to buy raw materials in bulk. Bulk buying often enables these firms to secure lower prices for their factor inputs. Large firms are also able to enjoy lower average costs from their marketing operations. The cost of a sales force selling 40 different lines of merchandise is very

much the same as one selling 35 lines. A 30 second TV commercial for a product which has sales of £10 million per annum costs the same as a 30 second TV commercial for one which has sales of only £5 million per annum.

Financial economies Small firms often find it difficult and expensive to raise finance for new investment. When loans are given, small firms are charged at relatively high rates of interest because banks know that small firms are far more at risk from bankruptcy than large firms. Large firms have a much greater choice of finance and it is likely to be much cheaper than for small firms.

Question 7

Boots and Alliance UniChem, with combined sales of £13.8 billion, are to merge in a £7 billion deal. Boots has a retail chain of 1 400 health and beauty stores in the UK. It also has 13 per cent of the wholesale drug market in the UK as well as a wholesale distribution network in Europe. UniChem has a European network of around 1 300 pharmacies, 939 of which are in the UK trading under the Alliance Pharmacy name. It also has a large wholesale operation across Europe, including 27 per cent of the UK market. Following the merger, the combined group will have retail outlets in five EU countries and wholesale distribution in eleven EU countries. It hopes to generate cost savings of £100 million over four years. For example, it hopes that its greater buying power will enable it to negotiate better prices from drug manufacturers. It also hopes to sell Boots products, such as Soltan sun cream and No 7 make up, through existing UniChem outlets, starting with southern European countries.

Source: adapted from the *Financial Times*, 1.10.2005, 4.10.2005.

(a) What economies of scale might the new company enjoy as a result of the merger between Boots and Alliance UniChem?

Diseconomies of scale

Diseconomies of scale arise mainly due to management problems. As a firm grows in size it becomes more and more difficult for management to keep control of the activities of the organisation. There is a variety of ways of dealing with this problem. Some companies choose to centralise operations with a small, tightly-knit team controlling all activities. Sometimes a single charismatic figure, often the founder of the company, will keep tight control of all major decisions. In other companies, management is decentralised with many small subsidiary companies making decisions about their part of the business and head office only making those decisions which affect the whole group. However, controlling an organisation which might employ hundreds of thousands of workers is not easy and there may come a point where no management team could prevent average costs from rising.

Geography too may lead to higher average costs. If a firm has to transport goods (whether finished goods or raw materials) over long distances because it is so large, then average costs may rise. Head office may also find it far more difficult to control costs in an organisation 1 000 miles away than in one on its door step.

Movements along and shifts in the long run average cost curve

The long run average cost curve is a boundary. It represents the minimum level of average costs attainable at any given level of output. In Figure 3, points below the LRAC curve are unattainable. A firm could produce above the LRAC boundary, but if it were to do this it would not use the most efficient method to produce any given level of output. Thus a firm could, for instance, produce at the point A, but it would be less efficient than a firm producing the same quantity at the point B.

Figure 3 The LRAC as a boundary
The LRAC curve is a boundary between levels of costs which are attainable and those which are unattainable. If a firm is producing on the LRAC curve, then it is producing at long run minimum cost for any given level of output, such as at point B. If long run production is inefficient, cost will be within the LRAC boundary such as at point A.

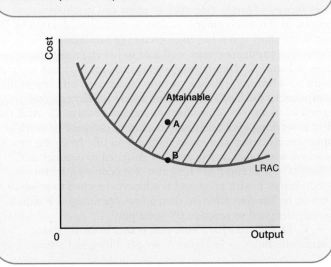

Question 8

Grimsby and its surrounding area has a concentration of about 500 food companies. Around half the companies are involved in seafood processing. Most are small and medium-sized companies, but big firms such as Young's Bluecrest Seafood and Northern Foods are also represented. Currently, around 90 per cent of inward investment to the area is from food manufacturing companies, of which 60 per cent is international.

There are excellent transport links specialising in handling food. Humberside airport, for example, handles perishable foods, whilst the local ports of Immingham and Grimsby handle over 50 million tonnes of freight a year. There is an increasing quantity of food imports, particularly fish from Iceland, The Faroes and Denmark, for local processing.

North East Lincolnshire specialises in cold perishable food products and has around 1.4 million cubic metres of public and private cold storage.

Grimsby is hoping to further strengthen its food cluster by developing a 200 acre business park which would include the existing 6 acre Europarc already housing a number of food companies such as Headland Foods, Baxters and Kwoks. If given the go ahead, it would involve building a network of shared-user waste, water recovery and energy generation facilities. According to Andrew Moore, North East Lincolnshire Council economic development officer, 'such a facility would help companies by reducing the cost of transporting and disposing of waste. It would include processing facilities and pipework for the transport of waste oil for conversion to biodiesel.'

Source: adapted from *Food Manufacture*, 1.8.2004.

(a) Explain the possible sources of external economies of scale for food companies in North East Lincolnshire, including Grimsby.

An increase in output which leads to a fall in costs would be shown by a movement along the LRAC curve. However, there is a variety of reasons why the LRAC might shift.

External economies of scale The economies of scale discussed so far in this unit have been INTERNAL ECONOMIES OF SCALE. Internal economies arise because of the growth in output of the firm. EXTERNAL ECONOMIES OF SCALE arise when there is a growth in the size of the industry in which the firm operates. For instance, the growth of a particular industry in an area might lead to the construction of a better local road network, which in turn reduces costs to individual firms. Or a firm might experience lower training costs because other firms are training workers which it can then poach. The local authority might provide training facilities free of charge geared to the needs of a particular industry. The government might assist with export contracts for a large industry but not a small industry. External economies of scale will shift the LRAC curve of an individual firm downwards. At any given level of output, its costs will be lower because the industry as a whole has grown.

Taxation If the government imposes a tax upon industry, costs will rise, shifting the LRAC curve of each firm upwards. For instance, if the government increased employers' National Insurance contributions, a tax upon the

In the long run, all factors are variable. Points A, D and G show long run cost curves at different levels of production. If the firm in the short run then expands production, average costs may fall or rise to B, E or H respectively. But they will be above the long run costs, C, F and J, for those levels of output because the cost of production with at least one fixed factor is likely to be higher than the cost if all factors were variable.

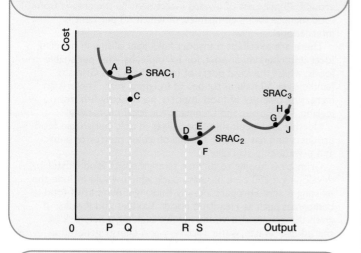

Figure 5 *The long run average cost curve envelope*
The long run average cost curve is an envelope for all the associated short run average cost curves because long run average cost is either equal to or below the relevant short run average cost.

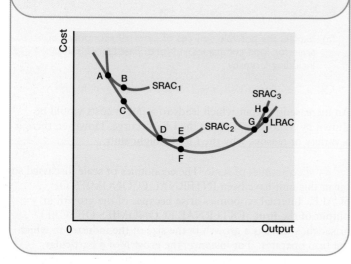

wage bill of a company, the total cost of labour would rise, pushing up average costs.

Technology The LRAC curve is drawn on the assumption that the state of technology remains constant. The introduction of new technology which is more efficient than the old will reduce average costs and push the LRAC curve downwards.

External diseconomies of scale These will shift the long run average cost curve of individual firms in the industry upwards. They occur when an industry expands quickly. Individual firms are then forced to compete with each other and bid up the prices of factor inputs like wages and raw materials.

Question 9

General Motors bought a 50 per cent stake in Saab, the Swedish car manufacturer, in 1989. However, it has been a poor investment, given that Saab has recorded losses in most years since then. Sales have been disappointing and Saab has failed to produce cars which customers have found attractive. One consequence is that Saab's Trollhättan plant has operated at far less than full capacity and Saab's production costs are high compared to other plants. In 2002, GM's patience ran out and it sent in two US executives to sort the company out. Part of their strategy was to reduce overstaffing at Trollhättan by making part of the workforce redundant. More efficient working has reduced the number of hours taken to make a car at the plant from 50 hours in 2002 to 30 hours today.

Average costs of production have also been cut by increasing production, the result of new, more attractive models being launched onto the market. However, the plant is still operating below capacity. The company hopes to increase production by 30 000 cars a year by building a new estate car at the plant, taking production up to the 160 000-170 000 level a year. It is also investigating building a small Cadillac at the plant to get it up to full working capacity.

Source: adapted from the *Financial Times*, 11.3.2004.

(a) 'In 2002, the Trollhättan plant was not operating on either its short run average cost curve boundary or its long run average cost curve boundary.' Using a diagram, explain this statement.
(b) Explain, using a diagram showing the long run average cost curve envelope and a short run average costs curve, why increasing production at Trollhättan would reduce short run average costs.

The relationship between the short run average cost curve and the long run average cost curve

In the short run, at least one factor is fixed. Short run average costs at first fall, and then begin to rise because of diminishing returns. In the long run, all factors are variable. Long run average costs change because of economies and diseconomies of scale. In the long run, a company is able to choose a scale of production which will maximise its profits. Assume in Figure 4 that it decides to produce in the long run at point A. It buys factors of production such as plant and machinery to operate at this level. Later it wishes to expand production by PQ but in the short run it has fixed factors of production. Expanding production may well lead to lower average costs as it does in Figure 4. Diminishing average returns have not set in at point A. However, production must be less cost efficient at B compared to the long run situation where the firm could have varied all its factors of production and produced at C. At B the firm is working with plant and machinery designed to work at optimum efficiency at a lower output level 0P. At C, the firm is working with plant and machinery designed to produce at C.

Similarly, if D and F are long run cost positions, a firm producing at E with plant and machinery designed to produce at D must be less cost effective than a firm operating at F with a factory designed to produce 0S of output.

A, C, D, F, G and J are least cost points in the long run. Combining these, as in Figure 5, we get a long run average cost curve. For each point on this curve there is an associated short run average cost curve, such as AB. If the firm operates in the short run at the point where the short run cost curve just touches (is tangential to) the long run cost curve, then it is operating where the company thought it would operate when it was able to vary all its factor inputs.

If short run output is different from this position, then its short run costs will be higher than if it could have varied all its factors of production. However, it could be higher or lower than the tangency point depending upon whether diminishing returns have or have not set in.

The long run average cost curve is said to be the envelope for the short run average cost curves because it contains them all.

Key terms

Average cost - the average cost of production per unit, calculated by dividing the total cost by the quantity produced. It is equal to average variable cost + average fixed cost.

Economic cost - the opportunity cost of an input to the production process.

External economies of scale - falling average costs of production, shown by a downward shift in the average cost curve, which result from a growth in the size of the industry within which a firm operates.

Fixed or indirect or overhead costs - costs which do not vary as the level of production increases or decreases.

Imputed cost - an economic cost which a firm does not pay for with money to another firm but is the opportunity cost of factors of production which the firm itself owns.

Internal economies of scale - economies of scale which arise because of the growth in the scale of production within a firm.

Marginal cost - the cost of producing an extra unit of output.

Minimum efficient scale of production - the lowest level of output at which long run average cost is minimised.

Optimal level of production - the range of output over which long run average cost is lowest.

Semi-variable cost - a cost which contains within it a fixed cost element and a variable cost element.

Total cost - the cost of producing any given level of output. It is equal to total variable cost + total fixed cost.

Variable or direct or prime costs - costs which vary directly in proportion to the level of output of a firm.

Applied economics

Economies of scale

Economic theory suggests that, in the long run, a firm will first experience economies of scale, but eventually diseconomies of scale will set in. The long run average cost curve is therefore U-shaped. However, research in this area tends to support the view that long run average cost curves in practice are not U-shaped but L-shaped. Firms experience economies of scale, but when output reaches the minimum efficient scale of production, average costs do not start to climb but remain constant. For instance, CF Pratten (1971) studied 25 industries, including newspapers, soap, oil, bread and steel and found L-shaped rather than U-shaped long run average cost curves.

Figure 6 shows an estimate of economies of scale in three areas of vehicle production: diesel engine production, commercial vehicles and cars. For instance, there was an approximate 34 per cent fall in costs if car production increased from 100 000 to 2 million. The minimum efficient scale of production for cars had not been reached by the 2 million level although the largest

falls in costs occurred at production levels between 0 and 500 000. The market for commercial vehicles and diesel engines was much smaller than for cars, and manufacturers had not reached their minimum scale of production according to the study. Larger production volumes would further reduce costs to those shown in Figure 6.

The sources of economies of scale in car manufacturing are shown in Table 9. For instance, the minimum efficient scale of production for the casting of an engine block was 1 million units a year whilst in final assembly it was 250 000 units. Economies of scale were greatest in research and development at 5 million units a year.

The car industry has steadily moved to exploit economies of scale in recent years. Many car manufacturers have merged or been taken over, including General Motors and Daimler Benz, Renault and Nissan, Peugeot and Citroen, Volkswagen and Seat and Skoda, and Ford and Mazda. Motor manufacturers have cut component costs by reducing the number of their suppliers. Each supplier then tends to supply greater volumes enabling them to exploit economies of scale. Research and development and production costs have been cut by reducing the number of platforms on which cars are built. A platform is basically the chassis. Building, say, five different models on one basic platform means that there are economies of scale in the production of the platforms, only one set of development costs is incurred in the design of the platform and expensive time between design and production is reduced.

At the same time, car manufacturers have been increasing the number of models offered for marketing reasons. Customers want greater choice. The challenge

Table 9 Economies of scale in car production

	Minimum efficient scale of production volume output per year (millions)
Technical economies	
Casting of engine block	1
Casting of various other parts	0.1-0.75
Power train (engine, transmission, etc.) machining and assembly	0.6
Pressing of various panels	1-2
Paint shop	0.25
Final assembly	0.25
Non-technical economies	
Advertising	1.0
Sales	2.0
Risks	1.8
Finance	2.5
Research and development	5.0

Source: G.Rhys, 'The motor industry: an overview, '*Developments in Economics*', edited by G.B.J. Atkinson, Causeway Press.

has therefore been how to reduce the minimum efficient scale of production for any one model. Sharing components between as many different models of car as possible has been one key way of achieving this. Another has been the ever increasing automation of the production line which allows different variants of car to be produced on the same line.

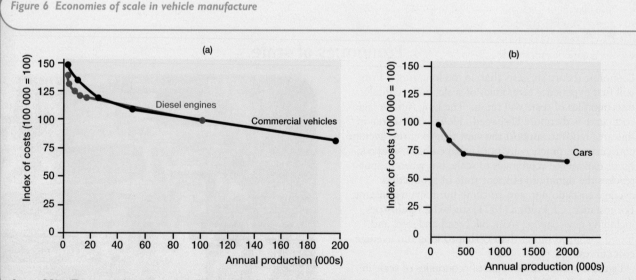

Figure 6 Economies of scale in vehicle manufacture

Source: G.Rhys, 'The motor industry: an overview, '*Developments in Economics*', edited by G.B.J. Atkinson, Causeway Press.

DataQuestion

Container shipping

Container shipping is booming as globalisation creates more and more seaborne trade. However, it isn't just trade that is growing, so too is the size of container ships. A new generation of ships is currently being built which will revolutionise trade between Asia and the USA and Europe. These are ships which can carry 8 000 twenty foot equivalent units (TEUs), a standard volume measure in shipping. Even larger ships with capacities of up to 12 000 TEUs are widely expected to follow within the new few years.

The move to ever larger ships is driven by lower costs. Larger ships enjoy greater economies of scale than smaller ships. They are cheaper to build per TEU, and fuel costs per TEU are lower as are crew costs. Ever since the first container ship sailed in 1956, vessels have been getting larger to take advantage of greater efficiencies.

Not everyone, though, is confident that the new 8 000+ TEU ships will prove profitable. One concern is port facilities. Only a very small number of container ports can accommodate the new vessels. This restricts where the ships can load and unload and leads to less flexibility if there is a bottleneck at a particular port. Equally, the new ships are too big for both the Panama Canal and the Suez Canal, which limits the routes on which they can operate. Effectively, they will be constrained to the route from Asia to the West Coast of North America and the Europe-Far East route around the tip of Africa.

Another concern is bottlenecks in onward transportation. Every day that a container ship is in port is a day of extra cost. Very large vessels will take longer to load and unload than smaller vessels but unloading can only take place if the containers are quickly moved on from the port. In Vancouver in Canada, for example, there are concerns that the already over-stretched rail lines to eastern Canada won't be able to handle the large single loads of containers from the new ships.

Handling the efficient loading and unloading of the new ships will require clockwork precision. Some are concerned that there will be too many hitches in the system between the ship operators, the clients sending containers to the ports, the port authorities and rail and road hauliers. The larger the ship, the more it will cost to have it tied up in port and not at sea.

Some analysts also predict that from 2006 the growth in shipping capacity will outstrip growth in cargo volumes. If there is too much shipping chasing too little container traffic, shipping freight rates will plummet. Ships will also be forced to sail with less than full capacity of containers on board. They then won't be operating at maximum efficiency and costs per container carried will rise.

Despite these concerns, the industry itself is, for the most part, convinced that the future lies with bigger ships. That is why nearly one third of the ships currently on order are 8 000+ TEU vessels when they account for less than 1 per cent of current container shipping.

Source: adapted from the *Financial Times*, 17.12.2004.

Table 10 *Container ship capacity*

Container capacity (TEUs*)	On order 2004-2008 ('000 TEUs)	Current fleet ('000 TEUs)
<500	0	138
500-999	86	430
1 000-1 499	80	608
1 500-1 999	98	694
2 000-2 499	69	613
2 500-2 999	309	657
3 000-3 999	142	956
4 000-4 999	475	1 133
5 000-5 999	429	776
6 000-6 999	240	537
7 000-7 999	232	206
8 000+	954	48
Total	3 175	6 796

* Twenty foot equivalent units.

1. Explain why large container ships might enjoy greater economies of scale than smaller ships.
2. An 8 500 TEUs vessel sets sail with containers whose volume is only 5 000 TEUs. Another vessel, whose size is 5 000 TEUs, sets sail from the same port to the same destination carrying a full load of 5 000 TEUs.

Using a long run average cost envelope diagram, compare the possible average costs of the two vessels for the journey.

3. Discuss whether there are likely to be any potential diseconomies of scale from operating the new larger container ships.

Summary

1. Economists distinguish between total revenue, average revenue and marginal revenue.
2. The average revenue curve is the demand curve.
3. If the price remains the same as sales increase, then marginal revenue and average revenue are the same and the demand curve is horizontal.

Total, average and marginal revenues

A firm's revenues are its receipts of money from the sale of goods and services over a time period such as a week or a year. Revenues can be either total revenue, average revenue or marginal revenue.

- TOTAL REVENUE (TR) is the total amount of money received from the sale of any given level of output. It is the total quantity sold times the average price received. For example, if a company sold 100 machines at an average price of £1 million each over a year, then its total revenue would be £100 million.
- AVERAGE REVENUE (AR) is the average receipt per unit sold. It can be calculated by dividing total revenue by the quantity sold. For example, if total revenue for a company is £50 million and it sold 50 machines over a year, then its average revenue would be £1 million. If all output is sold at the same price, then average revenue must equal the price of the product sold.
- MARGINAL REVENUE (MR) is the receipts from selling an extra unit of output. It is the difference between total revenue at different levels of output. For example, if total revenue were £70 million when 70 machines were sold but £80 million when 71 machines were sold, then the marginal revenue from the last machine sold is £10 million.

Revenue curves

Different revenue curves can be drawn given different assumptions about average revenue. One assumption is that a firm receives the same price for each good sold. This is shown in Table 1. The price is £5. As the price is the same however many are sold, this must also be equal to the average revenue. The total revenue increases as total sales increase. The marginal revenue, the additional revenue from each unit sold, is also £5 at all levels of sales.

This data can be illustrated on a diagram. Figure 1 shows the total revenue curve. Figure 2 shows the average and marginal revenue curves. Note that because the price of the good remains the same, the average and marginal curves are identical. The line is also horizontal, showing that whatever the level of output, average and marginal revenue remain the same at £5. The average revenue curve is the demand curve because it shows the relationship between average price and quantity sold. So at any quantity sold, marginal revenue equals average revenue equals demand.

Table 2 shows a situation where a firm has to lower its price to achieve higher sales. So the average revenue, or average price, is falling as sales get larger. Table 2 shows that when sales reach 6 units, total revenue begins to fall. The loss in revenue from having to accept a lower price more than

Table 1 Total average and marginal revenue

Sales	Average revenue £	Total Revenue £	Marginal Revenue £
1	5	5	
			5
2	5	10	
			5
3	5	15	
			5
4	5	20	
			5
5	5	25	
			5
6	5	30	
			5
7	5	35	
			5
8	5	40	
			5
9	5	45	
			5
10	5	50	

Figure 1 Total revenue when price is constant
The total revenue curve is upward sloping as sales increase.

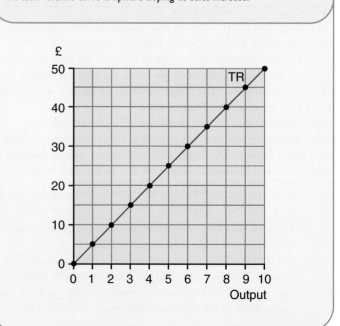

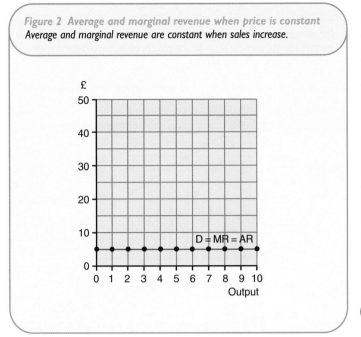

Figure 2 *Average and marginal revenue when price is constant*
Average and marginal revenue are constant when sales increase.

outweighs the increase in revenue from extra sales. As a result, marginal revenue becomes negative. Each extra unit sold brings in negative extra revenue.

Figures 3 and 4 show the total, average and marginal revenue curves derived from the data in Table 2. The total revenue curve at first rises and then falls. The average revenue curve is downward sloping. The marginal revenue curve is also downward sloping. It slopes more steeply than the average revenue curve. Mathematically, the slope is twice as steep and, measuring the distance horizontally on the graph, marginal revenue is always exactly half average revenue. The average revenue curve is also the demand curve because it shows the relationship between average price and quantity sold. So average revenue equals demand.

Table 2

Sales	Average revenue £	Total Revenue £	Marginal Revenue £
1	30	30	
			24
2	27	54	
			18
3	24	72	
			12
4	21	84	
			6
5	18	90	
			0
6	15	90	
			-6
7	12	84	
			-12
8	9	72	
			-18
9	6	54	
			-24
10	3	30	

Revenue and price elasticity

When the price received by a firm for a good is constant, the average revenue, marginal revenue and demand curves for the good are identical. They are horizontal. This means that price elasticity of demand for the good is perfectly elastic. Whatever the percentage in quantity demanded for the good, there is no change in price of the good.

However, when the price of a good declines as sales increase, there is likely to be a change in price elasticity of demand along the average revenue curve. In the unit 'Price elasticity of demand', it was explained that if demand was price inelastic, a rise in price would bring about a rise in total spending by consumers, which is the same as a rise in total revenue for a firm or firms. If the percentage fall in quantity demanded is less than the percentage rise in price, then total revenue will increase. Conversely, if demand is price elastic, then a percentage rise in price will bring about an even larger percentage fall in quantity demanded. The result will be a fall in total revenue.

Question 1

Table 3

Sales (million units)	Average revenue (£)	Total revenue (£)	Marginal revenue (£)
1	20		
2	18		
3	16		
4	14		
5	12		
6	10		
7	8		
8	6		
9	4		
10	2		

Calculate (a) total revenue and (b) marginal revenue at each level of sales from 1 million to 10 million.

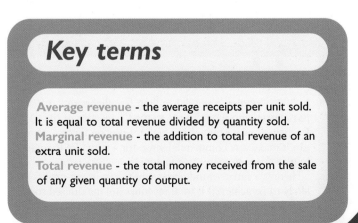

Key terms

Average revenue - the average receipts per unit sold. It is equal to total revenue divided by quantity sold.
Marginal revenue - the addition to total revenue of an extra unit sold.
Total revenue - the total money received from the sale of any given quantity of output.

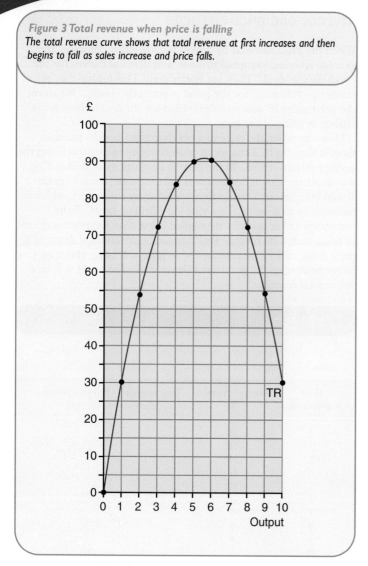

Figure 3 *Total revenue when price is falling*
The total revenue curve shows that total revenue at first increases and then begins to fall as sales increase and price falls.

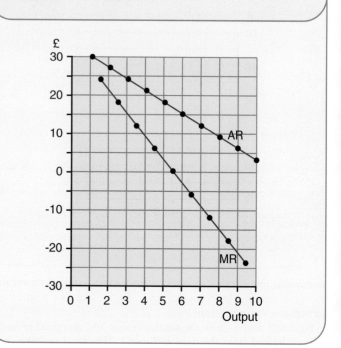

Figure 4 *Average and marginal revenue when price is falling*
The average and marginal revenue fall as sales increase. The average revenue curve is also the demand curve for the good because it shows the average price received at each level of sales.

In terms of marginal revenue, demand is price elastic so long as marginal revenue is positive i.e. total revenue is rising. When marginal revenue is negative, demand is price inelastic. In Figure 4, therefore, only that part of the marginal revenue where price is elastic is shown.

The average revenue curve is also the demand curve for the good. The top half of the curve in Figure 4 shows demand as being price elastic. The bottom half of the curve shows demand being price inelastic.

Price elasticity of demand is 1 or unitary when total revenue is maximised. This is when marginal revenue is zero.

This can be seen in Table 2 and Figure 3. At sales levels up to 6 units, demand is price elastic because falls in price are resulting in rises in total revenue. At sales levels above this, demand is price inelastic. Falls in price result in falls in total revenue.

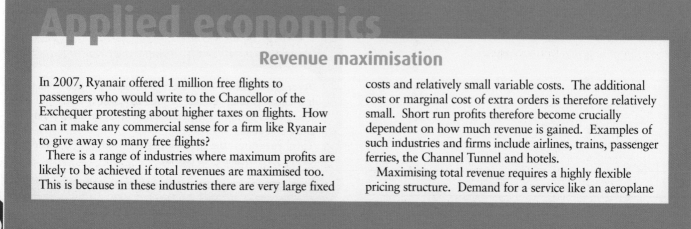

Applied economics

Revenue maximisation

In 2007, Ryanair offered 1 million free flights to passengers who would write to the Chancellor of the Exchequer protesting about higher taxes on flights. How can it make any commercial sense for a firm like Ryanair to give away so many free flights?

There is a range of industries where maximum profits are likely to be achieved if total revenues are maximised too. This is because in these industries there are very large fixed

costs and relatively small variable costs. The additional cost or marginal cost of extra orders is therefore relatively small. Short run profits therefore become crucially dependent on how much revenue is gained. Examples of such industries and firms include airlines, trains, passenger ferries, the Channel Tunnel and hotels.

Maximising total revenue requires a highly flexible pricing structure. Demand for a service like an aeroplane flight differs according to the time of the day, the day of the week, the week of the year and from year to year. Different groups of passengers are also prepared to pay different fares for fairly small differences in levels of service. For example, an airline might be able to charge double or treble the fare to a business person by allowing them to go straight to the front of the check-in queue at the airport, allowing them to sit in a special curtained off section at the front of the plane and giving them a few free sandwiches and a drink on board.

Another way of saying this is that the price elasticity of demand for the product varies considerably between customers. For a business person having to get to a meeting by 10 o'clock in the morning, the price elasticity of demand is low. For a pensioner couple who have no time commitments and are prepared to travel to an out of the way airport at any time of the day or night, price elasticity of demand is high.

Maximising total revenue means that marginal revenue will be almost zero on some sales. Taking airlines as an example, companies like Ryanair have achieved considerable publicity for offering flights at almost zero price. The number of these seats is very limited and represents only a tiny fraction of the number of seats offered over a whole year. They are also used as part of marketing to generate enquiries from passengers who go on to buy flights at higher prices. However, economic theory would suggest that for airline companies, getting a passenger onto a plane who has paid almost nothing for the flight is better than having an empty seat which generates no revenue.

DataQuestion

Finchfield Cycles

Finchfield Cycles is a UK company based in Leeds which sells bicycles. In recent years, with a growing trend towards healthier living, exercise and cycling to work, demand for its bicycles has grown considerably. Five years ago, sales were 10 000 a year. Today they are 20 000. Despite selling at £400 each, there is a long waiting list for the bicycles due to bottlenecks in production.

The company's sales director has been researching different pricing strategies. He estimates they could sell 25 000 a year and not have to drop their prices. To push sales beyond 25 000 a year would require some easing of prices. He estimates that the company could sell 30 000 a year at £360 but a move to 35 000 a year would have to see prices drop to £320. 40 000 sales a year would probably need a price of £280.

An alternative strategy would be to segment the market. Currently around half of all sales go overseas and they are sold at the same price per unit as home sales. The overseas sales, the sales director believes, are more price sensitive. He estimates that over the sales range 10 000 to 20 000, price elasticity of demand is 4. In contrast, price elasticity of demand for home sales he estimates is 2 for the equivalent sales range.

1. (a) From the data, assuming no bottlenecks in production and no differential pricing, what does the sales director believe would be total sales at a price of (i) £400; (ii) £360; (iii) £320; (iv) £280?
   (b) From this data, draw an accurate (i) total revenue curve; (ii) average revenue curve; (iii) marginal revenue curve. You would find this easier if you used graph paper.
   (c) Calculate the price elasticity of demand between the four price points, assuming that the higher price is the initial price.

2. If prices were cut by different amounts for overseas sales compared to home sales to get higher sales, which prices should be cut the most? Explain your answer.

Summary

1. Profit is the difference between revenue and costs.
2. Profit is maximised at a level of output where the difference between total revenue and total cost is greatest.
3. At this profit maximising level of output, marginal cost = marginal revenue.
4. An increase in costs will lower the profit maximising level of output.
5. An increase in revenues will raise the profit maximising level of output.
6. In the short run, profit maximising firms will operate so long as their revenue is greater than their variable cost.

Profit

Profit is the difference between **revenue** (the receipts of the firm) and costs (the monies paid out by the firm). A firm will make the most profit (or **maximum** profit) when the difference between total revenue and total cost is greatest.

This is shown in Table 1. Total revenue is shown in the second column whilst total cost is in the third column. Profit is the difference between the two. At low levels of production, the firm will make a loss. The BREAK-EVEN point, where total revenue equals total cost, is reached at an output level of 3 units. Thereafter profit increases as output increases.

Normal and abnormal profit

Cost for an economist is different from that for an accountant or business period. The economic cost of production is its opportunity cost. It is measured by the benefit that could have been gained if the resources employed in the production process had been used in their next most profitable use. If a firm could have made £1 million profit by using its resources in the next best manner, then the £1 million profit is an opportunity cost for the firm. In economics this profit, which is counted as an economic cost, is called **normal profit**.

If the firm failed to earn normal profit, it would cease to produce in the long run. The firm's resources would be put to better use producing other goods and services where a normal profit could be earned. Hence, normal profit must be earned if factors of production are to be kept in their present use.

Abnormal profit (also called PURE PROFIT, or ECONOMIC PROFIT or SUPERNORMAL PROFIT) is the profit over and above normal profit (i.e. the profit over and above the opportunity cost of the resources used in production by the firm).

Table 1

Output	Total revenue (£)	Total cost (£)	Profit (£)
1	25	35	-10
2	50	61	-11
3	75	75	0
4	100	90	10
5	125	106	19
6	150	123	27
7	175	148	27
8	200	182	18
9	225	229	-4

Table 2

Output	Marginal revenue (£)	Marginal cost (£)	Addition to total profit (£)
1	25	35	-10
2	25	26	-1
3	25	14	11
4	25	15	10
5	25	16	9
6	25	18	8
7	25	25	0
8	25	34	-9
9	25	47	-22

It is important to remember that the firm earns normal profit when total revenue equals total cost. However, total revenue must be greater than total cost if it is to earn abnormal profit.

In Table 1, there are two levels of output where profit is highest at £27. However, the profit separated out in the table is abnormal profit. Normal profit is included as part of total cost. Therefore the firm will choose to produce at the higher of the two levels of output, at 7 units. The 7th unit of output does not increase abnormal profit because this is zero on the 7th unit. But it increases the amount of normal profit. Therefore producing 7 units rather than 6 units will increase total normal profit.

Question 1

A business person leaves his £70 000 a year job to set up a company from which he draws a salary of £30 000 in its first year, £50 000 in its second year and £70 000 in its third year. He puts £50 000 of his own savings into the company as start up capital which previously had been invested and could earn a rate of return of 10 per cent per annum. Accountants declare that the costs of the firm over the first twelve months were £250 000, £280 000 in the next twelve months and £350 000 in the third year. Revenues were £270 000 in the first year, £310 000 in the second year and £450 000 in the third year.

For each year, calculate the firm's:
(a) accounting profit;
(b) economic profit;
(c) normal profit.

Question 2

Table 3

Output (million units)	Total revenue (£ million)	Total cost (£ million)
1	10	8
2	20	14
3	30	20
4	40	30
5	50	50
6	60	80

(a) Calculate the total profit at each level of output.
(b) What is the profit maximising level of output?
(c) Calculate the marginal revenue and marginal cost of production at each level of output.
(d) Explain, using the data, why MC = MR at the profit maximising level of output.

Profit maximisation: the MC = MR rule

Marginal cost and marginal revenue can also be used to find the profit maximising level of output. Marginal cost is the addition to total cost of one extra unit of output. Marginal revenue is the increase in total revenue resulting from an extra unit of sales.

Table 2 shows the marginal cost and marginal revenue figures derived from Table 1. Marginal revenue minus marginal cost gives the extra profit to be made from producing one more unit of output. The firm makes a loss of £10 on the first unit, and £1 on the second. The third unit of output yields a profit of £11, the fourth £10 and so on. So long as the firm can make additional profit by producing an extra unit of output, it will carry on expanding production. However, it will cease extra production when the extra unit yields a loss (i.e. where marginal profit moves from positive to negative). In Table 2, this happens at an output level of 7 units. The seventh unit contributes nothing to abnormal profit.

However, as explained above, cost includes an allowance for normal profit and therefore the firm will actually produce the seventh unit. The eighth unit yields a loss of profit of £9. The firm will therefore not produce the eighth unit if it wishes to maximise its profit.

Economic theory thus predicts that profits will be maximised at the output level where marginal cost equals marginal revenue.

Cost and revenue curves

These same points can be made using cost and revenue curves. The revenue curves in Figure 1 are drawn on the assumption that the firm receives the same price for its product however much it sells (i.e. demand is perfectly price elastic). So the total revenue curve increases at a constant rate. The marginal revenue curve is horizontal, showing that the price received for the last unit of output is exactly the same as the price received for all the other units sold before.

The total revenue and total cost curves show that the firm will make a loss if it produces between 0 and B. Total cost is higher than total revenue. B is the break-even point. Between B and D the firm is in profit because total revenue is greater than total cost.

Figure 1 *The profit maximising level of output*
Profit is maximised at the level of output where the difference between total revenue and total cost is at its greatest, at 0C. This is the point where marginal cost equals marginal revenue. 0B and 0D are break-even points.

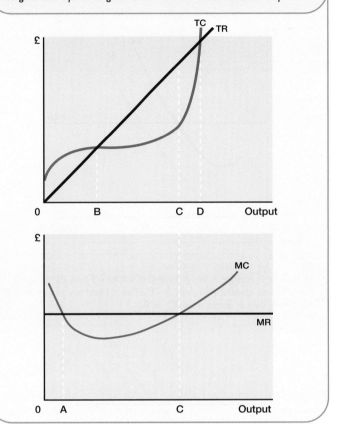

However, profit is maximised at the output level C where the difference between total revenue and total cost is at a maximum. If the firm produces more than D, it will start making a loss again. D, the second break-even point on the diagram, is the maximum level of output which a firm can produce without making a loss. So D is the sales maximisation point subject to the constraint that the firm should not make a loss.

Now consider the marginal cost and marginal revenue curves. It can be seen that the profit maximising level of output, 0C, is the point where marginal cost equals marginal revenue. If the firm produces an extra unit of output above 0C, then the marginal cost of production is above the marginal revenue received from selling the extra unit. The firm will make a loss on that extra unit and total profit will fall. On the other hand, if the firm is producing to the left of 0C the cost of an extra unit of output is less than its marginal revenue. Therefore the firm will make a profit on the extra unit if it is produced. Generalising this, we can say that the firm will expand

Question 3

(a) From the data in Table 3, draw two graphs showing (i) total revenue and total cost curves and (ii) marginal revenue and marginal cost curves. Draw the graphs one underneath the other using the same scale on the output axis.
(b) Mark on each of the graphs (i) the break-even levels of output and (ii) the profit maximising level of output.

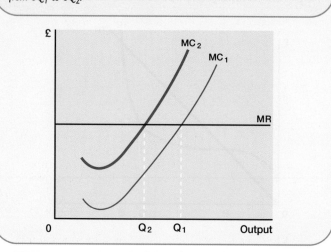

Figure 2 An increase in costs
An increase in costs of production which pushes up the marginal cost curve from MC_1 to MC_2 will lead to a fall in the profit maximising level of output from $0Q_1$ to $0Q_2$.

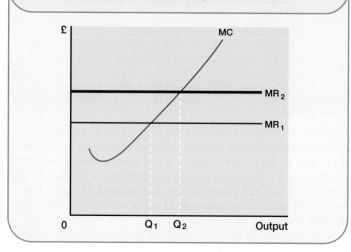

Figure 3 An increase in revenue
An increase in revenue at any given level of output will push the marginal revenue curve upwards from MR_1 to MR_2. This will lead to a rise in the profit maximising level of output from $0Q_1$ to $0Q_2$.

production if marginal revenue is above marginal cost. The firm will reduce output if marginal revenue is below marginal cost.

It should be noted that there is another point in Figure 1 where MC = MR. This is at the point A. It isn't always the case that the marginal cost curve will start above the marginal revenue curve at the lowest level of output. However, if it does, then the first intersection point of the two curves, when marginal cost is falling, is not the profit maximising point. The MC = MR rule is therefore a **necessary** but not **sufficient** condition for profit maximisation. A second condition has to be attached, namely that marginal cost must be rising as well.

Shifts in cost and revenue curves

It is now possible to analyse in greater depth the effects of changes in costs or revenues on output. Assume that costs, such as the price of raw materials, increase. This will mean that the marginal cost of production at every level of output will be higher. The marginal cost curve will shift upwards as shown in Figure 2. The profit maximising level of

output will fall from $0Q_1$ to $0Q_2$. Hence a rise in costs will lead to a fall in output.

On the other hand a rise in revenue will lead to an increase in output. Assume that revenue increases at every given level of output. Perhaps consumers are prepared to pay higher prices because their incomes have increased, or the good has become more fashionable to purchase. This will push the marginal revenue curve upwards as shown in Figure 3. The profit maximising level of output will then rise from $00Q_1$ to $00Q_2$.

Shut down point in the short run

Firms are not always able to operate at a profit. They may be faced with operating at a loss. Neo-classical economics predicts that firms will continue in production in the short run so long as they cover their variable costs.

Consider Table 4. The company would lose £20 million in any period in which it shut down its plant and produced nothing. This is because it still has to pay its fixed costs of £20 million even if output is zero. Total fixed costs represent the maximum loss per period the company need face.

The table shows that the firm is facing a steadily worsening trading situation. Its costs remain the same throughout, but each period its revenue declines. In period 1, total revenue exceeds total costs. The firm makes a profit of £10 million if production takes place. In period 2, it makes no profit by operating its plant (although it should be remembered that cost includes an allowance for normal profit).

However, this is better than the alternative of shutting down and making a £20 million loss. So too is producing in period 3. Although the company makes a loss of £10 million, it will continue to produce because the alternative to not producing is a loss of £20 million. In period 4 the company is on the dividing line between whether to produce or not. In period 5, the

Table 4

£ million

Period	Total variable cost	Total fixed cost	Total cost	Total revenue	Profit or loss — If production takes place	Profit or loss — If plant is shut down
1	30	20	50	60	+10	-20
2	30	20	50	50	0	-20
3	30	20	50	40	-10	-20
4	30	20	50	30	-20	-20
5	30	20	50	20	-30	-20

Question 4

Consider the data in Table 3. What is the new profit maximising level of output if:
(a) marginal revenue falls to £6 million at each level of output;
(b) marginal revenue increases to £20 million at each level of output;
(c) marginal cost increases by £4 million at each level of output;
(d) total cost increases by £5 million at each level of output;
(e) total revenue doubles at each level of output?

Question 5

A profit maximising company has fixed costs of £10 million. Its variable costs increase at a constant rate with output. The variable cost of production of each unit is £1 million. Explain whether it will produce:
(a) 10 units if total revenue is £30 million;
(b) 15 units if total revenue is £25 million;
(c) 20 units if total revenue is £22 million;
(d) 25 units if total revenue is £20 million.

Key terms

Break-even point - the levels of output where total revenue equals total cost.

Question 6

A firm has total fixed costs of £900 and variable costs of £1 per unit.
(a) What will be the price per unit if it sets out to manufacture 300 units a week and make a 25 per cent profit over costs?
(b) Demand is not as great as the company hoped. If it maintains its price, what is the minimum number of units that must be sold per week if the company is to break-even?
(c) Demand is 150 units per week. The company is offered an order for an extra 350 units a week if it drops its price on all units sold to £3 per unit. However, it believes that demand will slowly increase in the future to the planned 300 units a week if the original price is maintained. Should the firm accept the order?

company will clearly not produce. Its operating losses would be greater than if the plant were shut down.

So short run profit maximisation implies that a firm will continue to produce even if it is not fully covering its total costs. It will only shut down production when its total revenue fails to cover its total variable cost.

Applied economics

Book sales

It is July 16. Stores up and down the country are in the process of selling 2 million copies of *Harry Potter and the Half-Blood Prince*. Some stores opened at midnight to be the first to sell copies. In the US, an estimated 5 million copies are being sold on the same day.

The price customers paid to get a copy of Harry Potter varied enormously. The recommended retail price was £16.99. Waterstones, the book store, was selling it at £11.99. At WH Smith, it was £9.99. At Tesco it was £7.97. For the very price conscious, it was selling for just £4.99 at KwikSave.

Were these various stores profit maximising? To profit maximise, marginal cost must equal marginal revenue. The marginal cost may have differed between stores because the publisher, Bloomsbury, could have offered different retailers different prices according to how many books they ordered. WH Smith had pre-sold half a million copies, so their order could have been in excess of 500 000. Stores ordering more copies, such as Tesco which ordered 1 million copies, may have secured a better deal from Bloomsbury. Typically, publishers will offer a discount of between 40 and 60 per cent off the recommended retail price to retailers, to allow them to cover their costs and make a

profit. A retailer getting a discount of 60 per cent would pay Bloomsbury £6.79. If Tesco, for example, had secured such a deal, it would have left it with £1.18 per book to cover distribution costs and make the normal profit which is part of the economist's definition of cost. Waterstones may have sold a much lower volume and so may not have had the buying economies of scale that Tesco secured. Its marginal cost may have been higher than Tesco's and hence it had to gain a higher level of marginal revenue to profit maximise.

KwikSave's pricing strategy, though, could have been said to have yielded a loss on the purchase of the book since it was selling it at a discount of 70 per cent below the recommended retail price. Its marginal cost may have been higher than the marginal revenue of £4.99. However, marginal cost and revenue can be interpreted more widely. The majority of KwikSave's customers will not just have bought Harry Potter. They will have filled up a basket with other goods too. To profit maximise, a fairer comparison could be to look at the marginal cost to KwikSave of the whole shopping basket compared to the marginal revenue paid by the customer. A Harry Potter book could have been classified as a 'loss leader', an item sold below

cost to lure customers into the store to buy a range of goods on which the company would make a profit. Equally, the large supermarket chains such as Tesco could have considered the marginal cost and marginal revenue of the whole basket of goods a customer might buy when pricing their Harry Potter books. For Waterstones, or WH Smith, the likelihood is that most customers would not have purchased anything else when they bought their Harry Potter book. To maximise profit, they may have had to sell the volume where MC = MR of the book alone.

DataQuestion

Brick firm in lay-offs

Workers at Black Country brickmaker Baggeridge will be laid off after Christmas because of soaring gas prices which have hit company profits. Around 40 workers at the Sedgley and Kingsbury, near Tamworth, factories will be affected by the closures which are set to last until the end of January. The two factories have been chosen because they both make solid bricks which use up more energy. Chief Executive Alan Baxter said: 'From an energy viewpoint, we really can't afford to run these two factories. We are paying around £1 a therm for gas, while in France and Germany they are paying between 35p and 40p. It is not a free and fair market.'

Baggeridge has four plants in the West Midlands. Chairman Alexander Ward, said: 'Trading conditions were challenging with the cost of our main fuel, natural gas, increasing and demand for bricks reducing.'

Source: adapted from *Express & Star*, 14.12.2005.

1. Explain, using a diagram, what had happened to the marginal cost of production at Baggeridge.
2. Explain, using another diagram, what probably happened to marginal revenue at Baggeridge given that the demand for bricks was 'reducing'.
3. Combining these two diagrams, explain why Baggeridge decided to close down two of its factories temporarily.

Summary

1. Shareholders, managers, workers, government, consumers and others influence decision making in a firm.
2. Neo-classical theory assumes that firms are short run profit maximisers. In the short run, such firms will operate so long as their revenue is greater than their variable cost.
3. The neo-Keynesian theory of the firm assumes that firms are long run profit maximisers.
4. Managerial theories assume that managers maximise their own utility subject to a profit satisficing constraint.
5. Some economists argue that firms maximise their sales revenue or their sales.
6. Behavioural theories assume that decision making within a firm is not controlled by any one group, such as shareholders, but by all parties involved with the firm.

Control

The question of what motivates a firm in its actions can only be answered if there is a clear understanding of who controls the decision making process. This control is likely to lie with one or more of the firm's **stakeholders**. In a UK context these are as follows.

The owners or shareholders It might seem obvious to state that it is the owners or shareholders of a company who control it. This is perhaps true for small businesses where the owner is also the director or manager of the business. The owner of a small local corner shop, for instance, who also runs the shop will make the decisions about the business. However, it is less obvious that owners control the business they own when there is a very large number of shareholders.

Directors and managers Shareholders in a public limited company elect directors to look after their interests. Directors in turn appoint managers who are responsible for the day to day running of the business. Therefore there may be a divorce between ownership and control. The only way in which owners can influence decision making directly is by sacking directors at the Annual General Meeting (AGM) of the company. In practice the company needs to be in serious difficulties to stir sufficient shareholders for this to happen. Shareholders can also sell their shares, forcing the share price down and making the company more vulnerable to a takeover bid. If there is a takeover the directors and managers may well lose their jobs and hence there is pressure on managers to perform well.

The workers The workers, particularly through their trade unions, may be able to exert strong pressure on a company. They do not have the power to run the company in the way that shareholders or managers might be able to do. However, they can have an important influence on matters such as wages (and therefore costs), health and safety at work and location or relocation of premises.

The state The state provides an underlying framework for the operation of the company. Legislation on taxation, the environment, consumer protection, health and safety at work, employment practices, solvency and many other issues forces companies to behave in a way in which they might otherwise not do in an unregulated environment.

The consumer The consumer, through organisations such as the Consumers' Association or various trade organisations, can bring pressure to bear on companies in an attempt to make them change their policies. This form of influence is often rather weak; **consumer sovereignty** is more important. In a free market, consumers cast their spending votes amongst companies. Companies which do not provide the products that consumers wish to buy will go out of business whilst companies which are responsive to consumers' needs may make large profits. According to this argument, it is the consumer who ultimately controls the company. This assumes that consumer sovereignty exists. In practice, firms attempt to manipulate consumer preferences by marketing devices such as advertising. Firms are therefore not the powerless servants that theory implies.

Short run profit maximisation

In neo-classical economics it is assumed that the interests of owners or shareholders are the most important. Just as consumers attempt to maximise utility and workers attempt to maximise their rewards from working, so shareholders will be motivated solely by maximising their gain from the company. Therefore it is argued that the goal of firms is to maximise profits.

Neo-classical economics assumes that it is short run profits that firms maximise. They equate marginal cost and marginal revenue in the short term to decide on their level of production. In markets where there is heavy branding, such as soap powders, prices are likely to be stable. However, in commodity industries where firms are producing homogeneous goods like copper, paper or wheat, prices are likely to be unstable. Short run profit maximisation implies that firms will be prepared to supply even if they make a loss in the short run so long as price is above the average variable cost of production. In the long run, firms must cover all their costs or they will leave the market.

Long run profit maximisation

Neo-Keynesian economists believe that firms maximise their long run profit rather than their short run profit. This is based upon the belief that firms use COST PLUS PRICING techniques. The price of a product is worked out by calculating the average total cost of operating at full capacity and adding a profit mark-up. The price set and therefore the profit aimed for is based upon the long run costs of the firm.

Short run profit maximisation implies that firms will adjust both price and output in response to changes in market conditions. However, according to neo-Keynesians, rapid price adjustments may well damage the firm's position in a market. Consumers dislike frequent price changes. Price cuts may be seen as a sign of distress selling and large buyers may respond by trying to negotiate even larger price reductions. Price increases may be interpreted as a sign of profiteering, with consumers switching to other brands or makes in the belief that they will get better value for money. Price changes also involve costs to the company because price lists need to be changed, sales staff informed, advertising material changed, etc. Therefore it is argued that firms attempt to maintain stable prices whilst adjusting output to changes in market conditions.

This may mean that a firm will produce in the short run even if it fails to cover its variable cost. If it takes the view that in the long run it may make a profit on production of a particular good, it may prefer to produce at a loss rather than disrupt supplies to the market. Equally, it may cease production in the short run even if it can cover its variable costs. It may prefer to keep prices above the market price in the short run and sell nothing if it believes that price cutting in the short run would lead to a permanent effect on prices and therefore profits in the long run.

Managerial theories

Managerial theories of the firm start from the assumption that there is some divorce between ownership and control of

companies. The shareholders are assumed to be a different group of people from the managers of the company. Shareholders will wish to see profits maximised.

However, it is far from obvious that managers will share this goal. As workers they will attempt to maximise their own rewards. These may include their own pay and fringe benefits, their working conditions, their power within the organisation, their ability to appropriate resources, and the amount of effort they have to make. For instance, a manager may be more interested in which company car he or she will get, whether there is time to play golf on a Wednesday afternoon, or whether there is an extra £1 million available for the budget, than whether the company has maximised its profits at the end of the financial year.

This does not mean to say that making a profit is not important. Managers have to be seen to be efficient enough to justify their salaries. A shareholders' revolt is always a possibility. Some directors may take it upon themselves to promote actively the interests of the owners of the company. There is always the threat of takeover or bankruptcy leading to a loss of jobs, so managers have to make enough profit to satisfy the demands of their shareholders. This is known as PROFIT SATISFICING. However, once a satisfactory level of profits has been made, the managers are free to maximise their own rewards from the company.

One theory, put forward in the 1950s by William Baumol, was that firms would attempt to **maximise sales revenue** rather than profit. The size of firms can be measured in a variety of ways but, in general, they are not compared according to profit. Instead, size tends to be measured by the value of assets, stock market value or sales revenue. The larger the size of the firm, the higher is likely to be the pay and prestige of senior managers. So if management rather than owners are in charge of the day to day running, maximising sales revenue might be an objective of the firm. **Maximising sales** rather than sales revenue might be an alternative objective, particularly if sales can be increased at the same average price as previous sales. If this is the case, then sales maximisation and sales revenue maximisation are the same. Another more complicated theory put forward by O. Williamson postulates that managers have a utility function consisting of factors such as salary, size of the workforce directed by the manager, the amount of money under his or her control and the number of perks, such as company cars, that the manager receives.

Behavioural theories

Behavioural theories of the firm, pioneered by the American economist Herbert Simon, argue that decision making within a company is done not by any one group but by all groups involved in the firm. It is only by studying the relative power of each group and the power structures within the organisation that the way in which a firm behaves can be understood.

For instance, it could be argued that in the 1960s and the 1970s trade unions were very powerful in large companies. They were influential in increasing the share of revenues allocated to wages and reducing the share that went to shareholders. During the 1980s and 1990s, government legislation and mass unemployment seriously weakened the power of unions in the UK. At the same time, shareholders became more conscious of their right to make profits. The result was a large increase in the returns to shareholders, which could be seen as being financed by a reduction in the returns to the workers of the firm.

Question 1

In 2005, Malcolm Glazer, the US sports tycoon, won control of Manchester United in a £790 million takeover bid. Not known as a football fan, Malcolm Glazer owns a variety of sporting assets in the US including Tampa Bay Buccaneers American Football team. It is thought he wants to exploit the Manchester United brand name, particularly in the USA, to boost profitability.

Most of the takeover is being financed through loans at high rates of interest. This has fuelled fears among fans, who fiercely oppose the Glazer takeover, that the club will be milked for cash to repay the loans and to provide profits for Glazer. Fans fear that ticket prices will go up, merchandising will be ruthlessly exploited and there won't be any investment in new players. Comparisons have been made between the Russian millionaire Roman Abramovich who, having bought Chelsea, has spent heavily to create an unstoppable team, and Malcolm Glazer who, it is feared will be selling off star players to raise cash.

Constitutional Affairs Minister Harriet Harman said the government had urged Mr Glazer to have talks with fans, the Football Association and the club in order to ensure there was 'constructive involvement'. She said: 'Manchester United is very important to English football and the government is keeping a very close eye on the situation.'

Alex Ferguson has said he will be remaining as manager of Manchester United. His role will continue to be key in the successful running of the club. It is not known what the players think of the takeover.

Source: adapted from news.bbc.co.uk, 12.5.2005.

(a) Explain who are the stakeholders in Manchester United.
(b) Suggest what might be the objectives of the different stakeholders in the club after the takeover.

Question 2

Compass, the UK food service group, has paid its two most senior directors more than £1 million each into their pension funds. Sir Francis Mackay, chairman, and Mike Bailey, chief executive, are both leaving the company this year. Sir Francis Mackay's pension rights now stand at £16.1 million, whilst Mike Bailey's stand at just over £15 million.

The company defended the payments, saying they reflected their age and length of service. It said that Mike Bailey was paid £1.1 million last year whilst Francis Mackay was paid nearly £550 000. Bailey, along with other executive directors, had waived performance bonuses they would have been paid for meeting turnover targets, a bonus which would have been worth £300 000 to Bailey.

The pension payment has come in for criticism from a number of quarters. Compass has performed poorly in recent years, with its share price falling from a high of 500p to 229p today. Pre-tax profits for the 2005 financial year were £171 million, down 54% on the £370 million achieved in 2004. It announced in December 2005 that it would reduce the benefits of its final salary pension schemes for 30 000 current members as one way of plugging a £532 million deficit in those schemes, up one quarter from last year. The company employs 85 000 people in the UK and 420 000 around the world, mostly on low wages. The high turnover of staff means that few have joined the company pension schemes.

A senior fund manager at one institutional shareholder said: 'These are very well-paid executive directors who are continuing to do well out of Compass, thanks to their pensions. You do wonder whether it's appropriate.'

Source: adapted from www.moneyweek.com, 29.11.2005, *Accountancy Age*, 22.12.2005, *The Sunday Times*, 8.1.2006.

(a) Briefly explain what is meant by 'managerial theories of the firm'.
(b) Discuss whether or not the example of Compass would support such theories.

Question 3

During the 1960s and 1970s, it was difficult to see who controlled the Fleet Street newspaper industry. Owners of the newspapers were often rich entrepreneurial-type figures who allowed their titles to make little or no profit in return for the prestige and influence over the UK public that ownership gave them. Trade unions had a virtual veto on changes in working practices. Trade unions, not management, controlled shop floor appointments. The ability to call wildcat strikes which would lose a paper its entire production run for a day ensured that shop floor workers earned wages which bore no resemblance to the wages of workers in other comparable occupations.

Consumers rewarded with more sales those newspapers which included more page 3 pin-ups and less serious political news. Governments, meanwhile, made public noises about deteriorating press standards whilst in private attempting to get the press to toe the current party line. Management were caught in the middle, attempting to balance all the conflicting demands made of them.

New technology and soaring property prices put paid to all this. In the 1980s it became apparent that newspapers could make large profits for their owners. The key to success was to sack as many shop floor workers as possible and replace them with machines.

Those kept on would be paid reduced rates. Fleet Street offices could be sold off at vast profit on a soaring property market, the proceeds more than paying for a move to new technology premises elsewhere. The unions resisted but not even continual mass pickets and what came to be called the 'Wapping riots' in 1986 could prevent change.

Today, union power is much reduced and, in some newspaper jobs, unions are not recognised by management for negotiating purposes. Newspapers are more profit orientated although most of the British press arguably can still be relied upon to support the Conservative Party.

To what extent can behavioural theories of the firm explain the history of the Fleet Street newspaper industry?

Shareholders are more important today in company board rooms and workers less important than they were 20 years ago.

Behavioural theories assume that each group has a minimum level of demands. Shareholders demand that the firm makes a satisfactory level of profits. The government demands that laws be obeyed and taxes paid. Workers will require a minimum level of pay and work satisfaction if they are to stay with the company. Consumers demand a minimum level of quality for the price they pay for goods purchased. Local environmentalists may be able to exert enough moral pressure on the company to prevent gross over-pollution.

Other goals

Some firms have clearly distinct aims apart from those mentioned above. Consumer co-operatives aim to help consumers (although there is considerable debate in the UK as to whether they do not, in practice, serve the interests of their workers and management more). Worker co-operatives are often motivated by a desire either to maintain jobs or to produce a particular product, such as health foods. There have been examples of philanthropic owners in the past, such as Joseph Rowntree or Edward Cadbury, who have placed great priority on improving the living conditions of their workers. Nationalised industries in the UK prior to 1979

had a whole range of goals from avoiding a loss to maintaining employment to providing a high quality service.

So it is simplistic to argue that all firms aim to maximise profit. However, there is much evidence to suggest that large firms whose shares are freely traded on stock exchanges, and which are vulnerable to takeover, place the making of profit very high on their list of priorities. Therefore it is not unreasonable to make an assumption that, in general, firms are profit maximisers.

Key terms

Cost-plus pricing - the technique adopted by firms of fixing a price for their products by adding a fixed percentage profit margin to the long run average cost of production.

Profit satisficing - making sufficient profit to satisfy the demands of shareholders.

Applied economics

The role of the shareholder

Shareholder power

In both the UK and the USA, large companies tend to claim that shareholders are powerful. Company chairs make referrals to 'serving the interest of shareholders' or 'maximising shareholder value'. However, the power of the shareholders tends to be an indirect one. Annual general meetings (AGMs) of quoted companies are poorly attended, annual shareholder reports are not understood (even when read) by many shareholders, and directors rely on getting blocks of proxy votes before AGMs from key investors to push through any resolutions they recommend, including their own election to the board.

On the whole, shareholders' power lies not in being able to influence decisions directly, but in their ability to sell their shares freely. If enough shareholders are disappointed with a company's performance and sell their shares, then the share price will fall and make the company an attractive takeover target. The directors and management of a company taken over could, at worst, face immediate redundancy. So in the UK and the USA, shareholder power is vitally dependent upon free and open stock markets.

There has been some revival of direct shareholder power in the USA. Individual speculators wanting to make money have bought blocks of shares in companies which they consider are performing poorly. They have then used their voting rights to agitate for reform. Sometimes they have secured a seat on the board of directors. Once changes of policy have been implemented and monetary benefits have accrued to shareholders, perhaps in the form of higher dividends, a much higher share price or the issue of free shares in companies which have been split off from the main company, the speculator sells out and turns his or her attention to another company. Despite a trend towards more aggressive individual shareholders in the USA, most US companies and UK companies can still ride out shareholder dissatisfaction without necessarily implementing change.

In continental Europe and Japan, shareholder power is exercised in a different way. It is far more difficult for companies to be taken over for a variety of reasons. One is that, in some countries, a considerable number of publicly quoted companies have large family shareholdings and families tend to be more reluctant to sell than institutional investors. Equally in some countries, banks are major shareholders and they are reluctant to sell. In others, there are intricate networks of corporate cross-holdings where companies own shares in other companies.

In Spain, shareholdings are not even disclosed but bank, family and corporate cross shareholdings tie up control of most companies. In France, it is estimated

that more than half of the 200 largest quoted or unquoted companies are family controlled and many of the rest have key blocks of shares held either by the government or by single private shareholders. In Germany, three large banks, which for more than a century have financed German industry, have huge stakes. In Japan, companies prevent individual shareholders from becoming too powerful by buying them out or diluting their shareholding by the issue of more shares. There is also a strong tradition of corporate cross holdings.

Short-termism

For many years now, there has been a debate in the UK about whether or not the system of shareholding has a major influence on the behaviour of firms. There are those who argue that the UK system leads to 'short-termism'. Companies are forced to pursue the goal of maximising short term profit for fear that they will otherwise be taken over. This makes it difficult for them to pursue other objectives, particularly investment both in capital equipment and in their workers which have long pay-back periods.

In contrast, on the Continent and in Japan many companies can afford to take a long term view. Ultimately the company will only survive if it makes a profit. However, profit should increase if the company grows over time. Hence it is the interests of the company which are paramount. The company is not just the shareholders, but also the workers, the management, the customers and the local citizens. Because shareholders do not expect their companies to maximise short term profits, management is free to invest in a way which will maximise the long term growth of the company.

In the 1970s and 1980s, it seemed that taking the long term view produced superior results over a longer period. Companies in Europe and in Japan prospered and their economies grew at higher rates than those of the UK and the USA. However, in the 1990s and 2000s, the Anglo-Saxon short term shareholder model seemed to gain superiority. Many Japanese companies overinvested at the end of the 1980s. When the Japanese economy went into recession in the early 1990s, they were left with far too much capacity and many struggled to make a profit throughout the decade. By the turn of the millennium, many Japanese companies were sacking workers and restructuring to survive. The consensus based model was breaking down. In South Korea, where Japanese long termism had seen the growth of industrial giants, the Asian crisis of 1997-1998 revealed these companies to be debt ridden and over extended. They were forced to retrench, and some subsidiaries were sold off to US companies. In Europe, partly because of changing commercial attitudes but also because of EU regulations which forced open European capital markets, UK and US firms were taking over key firms which were available for sale. In some sectors, continental firms were found to be inefficient in comparison with their UK and US counterparts.

Short termism, then, whilst it clearly has its inadequacies, also has strengths. It prevents complacency and inertia in firms which a long term perspective can allow to gain hold.

DataQuestion

Nike

In its 2005 company Annual Report and Accounts, Nike printed a question and answer section from the new Chief Executive Officer and President of the company, William Perez. What follows is part of that section.

How will you know you are succeeding in this job? If we can sustain the growth, which obviously gets more challenging as the company gets larger. If we can keep the Nike Brand healthy, and if we can establish Starter and Converse[1] as major players in the market - that will look like success to me.

What is a great mistake you think big companies make? Complacency. If we start reading our own press, we have big problems. We have to be as hungry tomorrow as we were yesterday - as hungry as Phil Knight[2] was back when

he was selling shoes out of his car. My sense is that the people here are very hungry to achieve new success. I know I am.

How do you accomplish that when you are already number one? You redefine the market in bigger chunks so that you can aspire to double your business. A lot of companies make the mistake of narrowly defining the business segments in which they are working so they can talk to themselves about being market leaders. I worry about complacency, but then again, this company has proven time and time again that it can continue to grow.

1. *Starter and Converse are two of Nike's newer brands.*
2. *Phil Knight was the founder of the company.*
Source: adapted from Nike, *Annual Report and Accounts*, 2005

In January 2006 Perez, the CEO, resigned. His successor, Mark Parker, an existing Nike employee, in a press statement, stated the following.

'I've spent my life building the Nike brand, and I'm excited to lead one of the world's most dynamic organisations,' Parker said. 'I am committed to continue delivering profitable growth for our shareholders, creating distinctive product innovation and compelling brand connections for consumers, and building strong relationships with our retail partners. We have a strong management team in place that I will continue to develop, and I have tremendous confidence in our ability to continue growing the Nike, Inc. portfolio and delivering long-term value to shareholders.'

Source: adapted from www.nike.com.

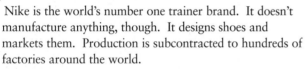

Nike is the world's number one trainer brand. It doesn't manufacture anything, though. It designs shoes and markets them. Production is subcontracted to hundreds of factories around the world.

In the 1990s, it was singled out by US campaigners concerned to highlight the poor conditions that workers in the Third World faced making goods for the rich first world. It started in 1992 when Jeff Ballinger, a US based activist working in Indonesia, published a report about conditions in the country's factories, detailing labour abuses, unsanitary conditions and forced overtime. Student groups in the US lobbied for independent monitoring of factories of companies selling goods on US campuses, threatening Nike's share of a $2.4bn business in college wear. Activist groups such as Global Exchange bombarded the media with anti-Nike stories.

Despite making a serious attempt to become more responsible as a global company, it continued to attract criticism. In 2000, for example, a BBC documentary accused Nike of using child labour in Cambodia. The company as a result reviewed all 3800 workers' records and interviewed those it suspected were under age.

However, it couldn't verify that all the workers were adult. As a result, it pulled out of production in Cambodia. Oxfam Community Aid Abroad, the Australian-based organisation that closely monitors Nike, alleges that the company has 'consistently moved production of its sneakers to wherever wages are lowest and workers' human rights are most brutally oppressed'. It says most of Nike's Indonesian workers who are parents are forced by their financial circumstances to live apart from their children. Nike's factory monitoring programme 'looks good on paper but ... in practice achieves very little'.

In 2004, Nike settled a law suit in California for $1.5 million brought by Mark Kasky, a labour rights activist. The company was charged with false advertising based upon public statements it had made defending its labour practices. Following that, in 2005, it published a corporate responsibility report. This included a list of its suppliers, the first time any company had done this. Such openness is one sign that Nike is taking this issue seriously.

Source: adapted from the *Financial Times*, 21.12.2000, 7.3.2002, 18.6.2002 and 13.4.2005.

'If you have a body, you are an athlete.' Bill Bowerman said this a couple of decades ago. The guy was right. It defines how he viewed the world, and it defines how Nike pursues its destiny. Ours is a language of sports, a universally understood lexicon of passion and competition. A lot has happened at Nike in the 33 years since we entered the industry, most of it good, some of it downright embarrassing. However, through it all, we remain totally focused on creating performance opportunities for everyone who would benefit, and offering empowering messages for everyone who would listen.

We feel lucky to have a genuine, altruistic reason to be: the service of human potential. That's the great benefit of sports, and we're glad to be in the middle of it.

... Nike employs approximately 24 300 people, and every one of them is significant to our mission of bringing inspiration and innovation to every athlete in the world. ... We operate on six continents. Our suppliers, shippers, retailers and service providers employ close to 1 million people. ... We see a bigger picture today than when we started, one that includes building sustainable business with sound labour practices. We retain the zeal of youth yet act on our responsibilities as a global corporate citizen.

Source: adapted from www.nike.com, filed under 'The company: the facts', 1.2.2006.

According to Nike, the following is the mission of Nike as a company.

The Nike Mission

To bring inspiration and innovation to every athlete* in the world.

*If you have a body, you are an athlete.

The asterisk is a quote from Bill Bowerman. Who is he? Legendary track and field coach at the University of Oregon. A teacher who showed athletes the secrets of achievement. Co-founder of Nike. Husband, father, mentor. From him we derive our mission. Through his eyes we see our future.

Source: www.nike.com.

1. Explain, using examples from the data, who might be the stakeholders in Nike.
2. According to Bill Perez, what might be the goals of the company?
3. Discuss the extent to which the interests of stakeholders in Nike (a) conflict and (b) coincide.

Summary

1. Market structures are the characteristics of a market which determine firms' behaviour within the market.
2. The number of firms within a market may vary from one (as in monopoly), to several (as in oligopoly), to a large number (as in monopolistic competition or perfect competition).
3. Barriers to entry prevent potential competitors from entering a market.
4. Industries may produce homogeneous or differentiated (branded) goods.
5. Perfect knowledge or imperfect knowledge may exist in an industry.
6. Firms may be independent or interdependent.

Market structure

MARKET STRUCTURES are the characteristics of a market which determine firms' behaviour. Economists single out a small number of key characteristics:

- the number of firms in the market and their relative size;
- the number of firms which might enter the market;
- the ease or difficulty with which these new entrants might come in;
- the extent to which goods in the market are similar;
- the extent to which all firms in the market share the same knowledge;
- the extent to which the actions of one firm will affect another firm.

The number of firms in an industry

The number of firms in an industry may vary from one to many. In the UK market for letter deliveries to household doors, the Post Office is essentially the sole supplier. In agriculture, on the other hand, there are tens of thousands of farms supplying potatoes and carrots to the market in the UK.

- A **monopoly** is said to exist where there is only one supplier in the market.
- In a market dominated by a few large producers, the market structure is **oligopolistic**. In an oligopolistic market there may be a large number of firms, but the key characteristic is that most are small and relatively unimportant, whilst a small number of large firms produces most of the output of the industry.
- In **perfect competition** or in monopolistic competition there is a large number of small suppliers, none of which is large enough to dominate the market.

The degree to which large firms dominate an industry is known as MARKET CONCENTRATION. This can be measured using **concentration ratios**, which consider the MARKET SHARE of the leading firms in an industry. These are explained in detail in the Applied Economics section of this unit.

Barriers to entry

Market structures are not only affected by the number of firms in an industry and their relative output, but also by the potential number of new entrants to the market. Firms in an industry where there are unlikely to be any new entrants may behave differently from firms in an industry where there are many strong potential competitors.

Question 1

(a) How many firms are there in each of the industries in which these particular firms operate?
(b) In which of these industries do a few large firms dominate?

There is a number of BARRIERS TO ENTRY which prevent potential competitors from entering an industry.

Capital costs Buying a local corner shop is relatively cheap and therefore the entry cost to most forms of retailing is low. Buying a car plant or an aluminium smelter, on the other hand, is extremely expensive. Entry costs to these industries are very high and only large companies on the whole can pay them. Capital costs therefore represent a very important barrier to entry and vary from industry to industry.

Sunk costs SUNK COSTS are costs which are not recoverable. For instance, a woman may set up a gardening business, buying a lawnmower, a van, garden tools and paying for advertising. If the business folds, she will be able to get some money back by selling the van, the tools and mower, but she won't be able to get any of the money back from the advertising. The cost of advertising and the difference between the purchase price and resale price of the capital equipment would be her sunk costs. High sunk costs will act as a barrier to entry because the cost of failure for firms entering the industry will be high. Low sunk costs, on the other hand, will encourage firms to enter an industry because they have little to lose from failure (the theory of contestable markets).

Scale economies In some industries, economies of scale are very large. A few firms operating at lowest average cost (the **optimum level of production**) can satisfy all the demand of buyers. This will act as a barrier to entry because any new firm entering the market is likely to produce less and therefore have much higher average costs than the few established producers. In some industries, it could be that a few firms supplying the whole industry are still unable to exploit fully the potential economies of scale. A NATURAL MONOPOLY is then likely to result, with just one firm surviving in the industry, able to beat off any new entrants because it can produce at lowest cost.

Natural cost advantages Some producers possess advantages because they own factors which are superior to others and which are unique (i.e. have no close substitutes). For instance, a petrol station site on a busy main road is likely to be superior to one in a sleepy country village. A stretch of desert in Saudi Arabia with oil underneath may be superior for oil production to the most beautiful of the Derbyshire Dales. The Victoria and Albert Museum should be able to attract more visitors because of its wide collection than a small provincial town museum. As a result, they will either be able to produce at lower cost or be able to generate higher revenues than their potential competitors.

Legal barriers The law may give firms particular privileges. Patent laws can prevent competitor firms from making a product for a given number of years after its invention. The government may give a firm exclusive rights to production. For instance, it may give broadcast licences to commercial television companies or it may make nationalised industries into monopolies by legally forbidding private firms to set up in the industry, as has been the case with the Post Office in the UK.

Marketing barriers Existing firms in an industry may be able to erect very high barriers through high spending on advertising and marketing. The purpose of these is to make consumers associate a particular type of good with the firm's product, creating a powerful brand image. One example of this from 50 years ago was the success of the Hoover company with its vacuum cleaner. Even today, many people still refer to vacuum cleaners as 'hoovers'. Similarly, a personal stereo was called a 'Walkman', the brand name of Sony which first put it on the market. In the UK detergent industry, a national launch of a new brand of soap or washing powder will cost in excess of £10 million. Soap and washing powders are low technology products whose costs of production are relatively low. Marketing barriers, however, make the industry almost impossible to enter.

Limit pricing Firms in an industry may choose to set lower prices than they would charge if they maximised their short run profits. They do this to keep out new entrants. If they only earn normal profit, new firms will not be attracted into the industry. This strategy is known as LIMIT PRICING. The strategy helps the firms to maximise long run profits. If new firms did enter the industry, this could lead to existing firms losing their abnormal profits anyway. They would also lose sales and so their normal profit would be lower. It is better to accept lower profits in the short run to preserve profit in the

Question 2

(a) Compare and contrast the barriers to entry to the UK food retailing industry, the international oil industry and the UK banking industry.

long run. Limit pricing is a barrier to entry because it keeps new entrants out of the industry.

Anti-competitive practices Firms may deliberately restrict competition through restrictive practices. For instance, a manufacturer may refuse to sell goods to a retailer which stocks the products of a competitor firm. A manufacturer may refuse to sell a good, when it has a monopoly in production, unless the buyer purchases its whole range of goods. Firms may be prepared to lower prices for long enough to drive out a new entrant to the business.

These barriers to entry may be divided into two groups. Some occur inevitably. These are known as **innocent entry barriers**. Most cost advantages fall into this category. However, other barriers are created by firms in the industry **deliberately** to keep out potential competitors. Marketing barriers limit pricing and anti-competitive practices are examples of these.

The extent to which there is freedom of entry to a market varies enormously. Manufacturing industries, with high capital costs and with extensive marketing power, tend to have higher barriers than service industries. However, many service industries have high barriers too. Banking, for instance, has a high capital cost of entry, legal permission is required, and marketing barriers are high. In the professions, like law, architecture and accountancy, new entrants are kept out by enforcement of minimum qualification levels, qualifications which are impossible to obtain except through working in the profession itself.

Barriers to exit

In most industries, BARRIERS TO EXIT are low. Barriers to exit are barriers which prevent a firm from leaving an industry quickly and at little cost. Barriers to exit include the cost and time of making employees redundant, selling premises and stock or notifying customers and suppliers. Barriers to exit increase when employment laws make it more difficult to make staff redundant. However, there may be other barriers to exit. A firm may be locked into a contract to supply another firm to which, if it breaks the contract, it will have to pay a large penalty. Or it may have leased premises where the individual owner has to continue paying the lease even if the business is closed down. In these circumstances, the firm may make a smaller loss by staying in the industry than by closing down.

Product homogeneity and branding

In some industries, products are essentially identical whichever firm produces them. Coal, steel and potatoes are examples. This does not mean to say that there are not different grades of coal or types of steel, but no producer has a monopoly on the production of any such grade or type. Goods which are identical are called HOMOGENEOUS GOODS.

Firms find it much easier to control their markets if they can produce goods which are NON-HOMOGENEOUS. Differentiating their product from those of their competitors, and creating BRANDS allows them to build up brand loyalty. This in turn leads to a reduction in the elasticity of demand for their product. A branded good may be physically no different from its competitors, or it may be slightly different, but branding has value for the firm because consumers think that the product is very different, so different that rival products are a very poor substitute for it. This perception is built up through advertising and marketing and enables firms to charge higher prices without losing very much custom (i.e. demand is relatively inelastic).

Knowledge

Buyers and sellers are said to have PERFECT INFORMATION or PERFECT KNOWLEDGE if information about prices, output and products is readily available. Therefore, if one firm were to put up its prices, it would lose all its customers because they would go and buy from elsewhere in the industry. Hence, there can only be one price in the market.

Perfect knowledge also implies that a firm has access to all information which is available to other firms in its industry. In UK agriculture, for instance, knowledge is widely available. Farmers can obtain information about different strains of seeds,

---

Question 3

Coca-Cola is the world's most valuable brand. According to the Interbrand consultancy, the brand is worth $67.5bn. In 2004, the company had sales of $21.9bn and net profits were $4.8bn. The average human on this planet consumed 75 servings annually of its products, up from 49 in 1994.

However, the company has recently been in difficulties. In the 1980s and 1990s, the company staked everything on a single product, Coca-Cola. In contrast, its rivals such as Pepsi diversified into a wide range of drinks and food. When sales of Coca-Cola stalled at the end of the 1990s, the company could not fall back on growing sales of other products. 'The magic has leaked out of the Coca-Cola brand', according to Tom Pirko, president of BevMark, a consultancy. 'How do you recreate that magnetism for a whole new generation that has much less loyalty to big monolithic brands like Coke? That's a very hard and expensive task.' When Coca-Cola appointed Neville Isdell as new chairman and chief executive in 2004 to turn the company round, one of his first acts was to commit an additional $400 million a year to marketing and innovation. This represented an acknowledgement that underinvestment in brands and product development was among the main causes of Coke's troubles. 'The company believed that all it had to do was churn out the product and people would buy it', according to Tom Pirko.

However, Coca-Cola the drink, is highly addictive for Coca-Cola the company. The problem is that Coca-Cola has high profit margins. It makes less profit per $1 of sales on most on its other products. Bottled water is a huge growth market at the moment, for instance, but profit margins on bottled water are much lower than on Coca-Cola. It is also expensive to develop and grow other brands. There are enormous economies of scale in marketing a single Coca-Cola drink compared to five or ten smaller brands with the same combined revenues.

Source: adapted from the *Financial Times*, 22.9.2005.

(a) What are the benefits and costs to Coca-Cola, the company, of owning the world's most valuable branded product?
(b) To what extent do consumers benefit from being offered branded goods, such as Coca-Cola, rather than non-branded goods, to purchase?

Question 4

Boeing, the US aircraft manufacturer, looks set to beat Airbus, the European aircraft manufacturing consortium, in numbers of orders placed for 2005. Boeing said it had clocked up 1 002 new orders whilst the total for Airbus is expected to be below 1 000. 2005 has been a year of keen competition between the two companies. In December, for example, Boeing lost out to Airbus for an order for 150 planes from Chinese Airlines. On the other hand, Airbus lost out to Boeing for a $10 billion order from Australia's Qantas Airways.

Source: adapted from uk.us.biz.yahoo.com, 6.1.2006.

(a) Explain, using the example of aircraft manufacturing, what is meant by 'interdependence' in a market.

the most effective combinations of fertilizers and pesticides and when it is best to plant and reap crops.

Perfect knowledge does not imply that all firms in an industry **will** possess all information. An inefficient farmer might not bother to gather relevant information which is readily available. In the short term, the farmer might survive, although in the longer term the farm will be driven out of business by more efficient competitors. Equally, perfect information does not imply that all firms know everything about their industry and its future. Farmers do not know if in 6 months' time a drought will destroy their crops. They have to work on the basis of probability. Perfect knowledge only means that all firms have the same access to information.

Firms have imperfect knowledge where, for instance, there are industrial secrets. Individual firms may not know the market share of their competitors or they may be unaware of new technology or new products to be launched by rival companies. Information could then act as a barrier to entry, preventing or discouraging new firms from entering the industry.

There is **asymmetric information** in a market when there is imperfect knowledge in the market and some firms have more information than others. Firms with more information are likely to be better decision makers and this will give them a competitive advantage. There may also be asymmetric information between firms and customers leading to market failure. When firms have more information than customers, there can be a misallocation of resources when firms exploit this information gap to their advantage.

Interrelationships within markets

There are two possible relationships between firms in an industry. Firms may be **independent** of each other. This means that the actions of any one firm will have no significant impact on any other single firm in the industry. In agriculture, for instance, the decision of one farmer to grow more wheat this season will have no direct impact on any other farmer. It will not affect his next door neighbour. This independence is one reason why perfect knowledge exists to some degree in agriculture. There is no point in keeping secrets if your actions will not benefit you at the expense of your competitors.

If firms are **interdependent** then the actions of one firm will have an impact on other firms. An advertising campaign for one brand of soap bar, for instance, is designed mainly to attract customers away from other brands. Firms are more likely to be interdependent if there are few firms in the industry.

Competition and market structure

The neo-classical theory of the firm recognises a number of market structures derived from the characteristics above. In later units these market structures will be considered in greater detail. Here, however, the key features are summarised. In neo-classical theory, there are three main types of market structure.
- **Perfect competition.** A large number of firms, each producing a homogeneous good, compete in the industry. None of the firms is large enough to have a direct impact on any other firm or on the market price of the good. There is freedom of exit and entry to the industry.
- **Monopoly.** There is only one firm in the industry. Barriers to entry make it impossible for new firms to enter.
- **Imperfect competition.** This exists where there are at least two firms in the industry, and the industry is not perfectly competitive. For instance, non-homogeneous goods may be produced, there may be imperfect knowledge or firms may be interdependent, or some combination of these.

Firms in imperfectly competitive industries can compete in a number of ways. For instance, they can compete on:
- **price** - offering a lower price should attract more orders;
- **quality** - consumers are likely to prefer a better quality good;
- **after-sales service**;
- **delivery date** - a buyer may look elsewhere if a firm cannot deliver quickly and on time;
- **image** - building a strong brand image through advertising and other forms of marketing is likely to be a major factor in determining demand for the product.

In perfect competition, firms are not in direct competition with each other. One firm can expand output without affecting either the price received by or the sales of another firm. Each firm is a price taker, facing a perfectly elastic demand curve. However, competition is 'perfect' because any firm which charges a higher price than its competitors, or sells an inferior product, will lose all its sales as perfectly informed consumers buy elsewhere in the market. The discipline of the market is so strong in a perfectly competitive industry that, in the long run, productive inefficiency (production at above minimum cost) cannot exist.

Key terms

Barriers to entry - factors which make it difficult or impossible for firms to enter an industry and compete with existing producers.

Barrier to exit - factors which make it difficult or impossible for firms to cease production and leave an industry.

Brand - a name, design, symbol or other feature that distinguishes a product from other similar products and which makes it non-homogeneous.

Concentration ratio - the market share of the largest firms in an industry. For instance, a five firm concentration ratio of 60 per cent shows that the five largest firms in the industry have a combined market share of 60 per cent.

Homogeneous goods - goods made by different firms but which are identical.

Imperfect competition - a market structure where there are several or a relatively large number of firms in the industry, each of which has the ability to control the price that it sets for its products.

Limit pricing - when a firm, rather than short run profit maximising, sets a low enough price to deter new entrants from coming into its market.

Market concentration - the degree to which the output of an industry is dominated by its largest producers.

Market share - the proportion of sales in a market taken by a firm or a group of firms.

Market structure - the characteristics of a market which determine the behaviour of firms within the market.

Natural monopoly - where economies of scale are so large relative to market demand that the dominant producer in the industry will always enjoy lower costs of production than any other potential competitor.

Non-homogenous goods - goods which are similar but not identical made by different firms, such as branded goods.

Perfect knowledge or information - exists if all buyers in a market are fully informed of prices and quantities for sale, whilst producers have equal access to information about production techniques.

Sunk costs - costs of production which are not recoverable if a firm leaves the industry.

Applied economics

Industry and concentration ratios

What is an industry or market?

How many firms are there in an industry or market (here we will assume that the two terms can be used interchangeably)? The answer to this question will depend on how we define the market or industry. For instance, the economy could be split up into three very broad market classifications - the market for primary goods, the market for secondary goods and the market for tertiary goods. There is a large number of firms operating in each of these markets. At the other extreme, one could ask how many UK firms produce balls for use in professional cricket. This is an extremely narrow market in which there are only two producers.

It should be obvious that the more narrowly a market is defined, the more likely it is that there will be relatively few producers. In the transport market, there are bus companies, rail companies, airlines, etc. In the air transport market, there will be fewer companies. In the market for air travel to the Isle of Skye there is only one company.

The Standard Industrial Classification

The Office for National Statistics (ONS) conducts regular censuses of production in the UK. The statistics record production levels in different industries using the Standard Industrial Classification 1992. This is a classification system which subdivides industry into broad divisions. For instance, Section C comprises mining and quarrying. Section D is manufacturing, whilst Section E is electricity, gas and water. Each section is then divided into sub-sections. Sub-section DA, for instance, is food, drink and tobacco. DB is textiles and textile products. The ONS classification is one way of grouping firms into individual industries, each sub-section representing an industry or group of industries.

Concentration ratios

Having classified firms into industries, it is possible to see how many producers there are in the industry. The number of producers is likely to be less important in studying the behaviour of the industry than the economic power of individual producers within the industry. One way of measuring this potential power is to calculate how important the top few companies in the market are . It can be done by looking at their importance in terms of market share in the industry, how many workers they employ or some other measure. This measure is then called a CONCENTRATION RATIO.

A three-firm concentration ratio would be the total share of the market (by output, employment or some other measure) held by the three largest producers in the industry; a four-firm concentration ratio would be the total share of the market held by the four largest producers.

Figure 1 shows the concentration ratios of food retailers in the UK in June 2007. One firm, Tesco, had 31.6 per cent of the food retail market by sales. The top three firms (Tesco, Asda and Sainsbury) had 64.4 per cent. The top four firms (Tesco, Asda, Sainsbury, Morrisons had 75.6 per cent of the market. This means that outside the top four supermarket chains, all other food retailers, including supermarket chains Waitrose and Somerfield, only had 24.4 per cent of the market.

Concentration in food retailing has been growing over time. There are considerable economies of scale to be achieved in food retailing, which large supermarkets pass on to their customers in the form of lower prices. Large supermarkets are also able to offer their customers one stop shopping, very important when many consumers work and have limited time to spend on activities such as shopping. Finally, they offer a much wider range of choice than small outlets. At present, the large supermarket chains are still gaining market share from small businesses.

The large supermarket chains in the UK would claim that the high concentration ratios found in the industry do not prevent the industry from being highly competitive. Critics would argue that, in practice, competition is limited. The top four supermarkets have such enormous economies of scale that they can easily be price competitive against smaller rivals. However, prices of many food items are exactly the same in local areas between rival large supermarkets. Competition at this level is imperfect and allows some of the top supermarket chains to earn abnormal profits.

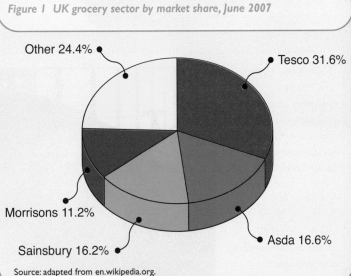

Figure 1 UK grocery sector by market share, June 2007

Other 24.4%

Tesco 31.6%

Morrisons 11.2%

Asda 16.6%

Sainsbury 16.2%

Source: adapted from en.wikipedia.org.

DataQuestion

Eurostar

November 1994 saw the first Eurostar train pass through the Channel Tunnel with fare paying passengers from London to Paris. Since then, Eurostar has gradually been gaining market share on the London to Paris route against rival airline services and coach services. By 2007, Eurostar had gained 71 per cent of the market. Airlines were struggling with the competition from Eurostar which typically gave faster journey times from central London to central Paris including check-in times. The airline with the highest market share is now Air France with just under 12 per cent. The airline bmi discontinued its service between London and Paris in early 2007 whilst there were no longer any airline services between London's second airport, Gatwick, and Paris.

Eurostar offers a fast, reliable, efficient and comfortable service between the two capital cities. The potential competition from airlines means that it has to keep its fare relatively low. In November 2007, for example, the cheapest return fare was £55 whilst the most expensive Business Premier return ticket was £225. Some would argue that its cheap fares have been massively subsidised by bond and shareholders in Eurotunnel, the group that built the Channel Tunnel and was forced to write off billions of pounds in debt. The charge made by Eurotunnel to Eurostar for allowing trains to pass through the tunnel is only a fraction of the sunk costs of the tunnel itself.

Competition doesn't just come from airlines. People can drive to Paris. For tourists, other destinations also provide competition. If tourists didn't like Eurostar's services to Paris, they might choose to fly to Rome or Prague for their holiday. Business travellers, in contrast, have no such choice. If they have to get to a meeting in Paris, they have to use some form of transport to make the meeting.

The Eurostar phenomenon is part of a wider pattern of changes in transport. High speed trains have devastated airline passenger numbers between cities where connections have opened up. For example, when the Paris to Marseille high speed train route was opened in 2002, rail only held 22 per cent of the market. By 2006 it was 69 per cent. The high speed train link between Paris and Brussels has a 52 per cent market share and there are no longer any direct airline flights between the two cities. The rest of the market is coach services. The shorter the journey time by train, the greater the market share of the train compared to airlines.

Source: adapted from www.eurostar.com, www.prnewswire.com, www.oag.com, www.businesstraveleurope.com.

1. List six key characteristics of the market structure of a market like the London to Paris travel market.
2. Analyse the market structure of the London to Paris route.

3. Discuss whether Eurostar will eventually gain 100 per cent market share on the London to Paris route.

45 Perfect competition

Summary

1. In a perfectly competitive market it is assumed that there is a large number of small firms that produce a homogeneous product. Firms are price-takers. There are no barriers to entry or exit and there is perfect knowledge.
2. The demand curve facing an individual firm is perfectly elastic because the firm is a price taker. This means that price = AR = MR.
3. The short run supply curve of the firm is its marginal cost curve above its average variable cost curve.
4. If firms in the short run are making abnormal profits, new firms will enter the industry, increasing market supply and thus reducing price. This will continue until only normal profits are being made.
5. If production is unprofitable, firms will leave the industry, reducing market supply and increasing price. This will continue until only normal profits are being made.
6. In long run equilibrium, AR = AC because no abnormal profits are made.

Assumptions

The model of **perfect competition** describes a market where there is a high degree of competition. The word 'perfect' does not mean that this form of competition produces ideal results or maximises economic welfare; in other words, the word 'perfect' should not have any **normative** overtones.

A perfectly competitive market must possess four characteristics.

- There must be many **buyers and sellers** in the market, none of whom is large enough to influence price. Buyers and sellers are said to be **price takers**. This type of market has many relatively small firms that supply goods to a large number of small buyers.
- There is **freedom of entry to and exit from** the industry. Firms must be able to establish themselves in the industry easily and quickly. Barriers to entry must therefore be low. If a firm wishes to cease production and leave the market, it must be free to do so.
- Buyers and sellers possess **perfect knowledge** of prices. If one firm charges a higher price than the market price, the demand for its product will be zero as buyers will buy elsewhere in the market. Hence the firm has to accept the market price if it wishes to sell into the market (i.e. it must be a price taker).
- All firms produce a **homogeneous** product. There is no branding of products and products are identical.

There are relatively few industries in the world which approximate to this type of market structure. One which might is agriculture. In agriculture there is a large number of farmers supplying the market, none of whom is large enough to influence price. It is easy to buy a farm and set up in business. Equally it is easy to sell a farm and leave the industry. Farmers on the whole possess perfect knowledge. They know what prices prevail in the market, for instance from the farming press. Finally, farmers produce a range of homogeneous products. King Edward potatoes from one farm are indistinguishable from King Edward potatoes from another. In Europe and in many countries around the world, farming is in certain instances not a perfectly competitive market. This is because governments may interfere in the market, buying and selling to fix a price.

Demand and revenue

It is an assumption of the model of perfect competition that there is a large number of sellers in the market. Assume that one

of these firms decides to double output. Industry supply will increase, pushing the supply curve to the right. However, the increase in supply is necessarily very small because the firm is

Question 1

US butter producers are still enjoying good times. Drought in Australia in 2002 led to significant falls in Australian milk output and it has yet to recover its 2001 peaks. Australia is a major exporter of dairy products. Strong economic growth in both the USA and the Far East led to strong growth in demand for dairy products in those countries. Lastly, the large fall of the exchange rate of the dollar particularly against the euro has given US producers a new strong competitive advantage against foreign imports. In 2005, US dairy farmers reacted by increasing the size of their herds and increasing milk output. This led to a moderation of milk and butter prices compared to their 2004 peaks.

Figure 1 US butter prices[1]

1. US support price is the minimum price guaranteed to US butter producers by the US government.
Source: adapted from United States Department of Agriculture, Foreign Agriculture Service, Dairy: World Markets and Trade, December 2005.

(a) Discuss why producers in the world butter market might be said to operate in a perfectly competitive market.

299

small. In fact it will be so small that the resulting movement along the demand curve will be impossible to distinguish and the price will not change.

This can be seen in Figure 2. The area around the existing equilibrium point has been enlarged. An increase in supply by one firm has shifted the supply curve from S_1 to S_2, reducing equilibrium price by AC and increasing equilibrium quantity demanded and supplied by CB. However, AC is so small that it has no effect on the overall equilibrium price of 0E and it is impossible to draw two supply curves thinly enough to show this shift in supply.

In agriculture, for instance, it would be surprising if the decision of one farmer to double wheat output were to have any perceptible influence on equilibrium price. His or her extra output is so insignificant that it cannot affect the market price for wheat. Of course, if all farmers were to double their wheat output, the price of wheat would collapse. However here we are interested only in the effect on price of the production decisions of a single farm.

A firm in perfect competition can therefore expand output or reduce output without influencing the price. Put another way, the firm cannot choose to raise price and expect to sell more of its product. It can lower its price but there is no advantage in this since it can sell its entire output at the higher market price. The demand curve for an individual firm is therefore horizontal i.e. **perfectly elastic** as in Figure 3. (Note that if a firm expanded output sufficiently its demand curve would become downward sloping, but then the industry would be made up of one large firm and many small firms and would no longer be perfectly competitive.)

The perfectly elastic demand curve facing a perfectly competitive firm also means that it is a PRICE TAKER. It has no choice about what price it receives for its product. Either it accepts the market price or it can choose not to sell. At a cattle auction, for example, farmers can choose either to sell at the auction price or take their cattle home

The demand curve facing a perfectly competitive firm is also

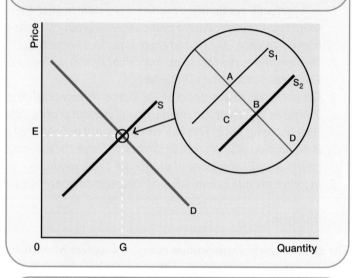

Figure 2 The effect of an increase in supply by one firm in a perfectly competitive industry
An increase in supply by one firm from S_1 to S_2 will have such a small effect on total supply that equilibrium price will remain at OE.

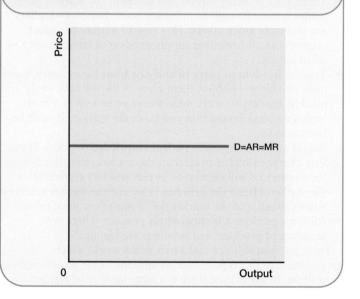

Figure 3 The demand curve facing a firm in perfect competition
A change in output by the firm will have no effect on the market price of the product. Therefore the firm faces a perfectly elastic demand curve. This is also the firm's average and marginal revenue curve.

the firm's average and marginal revenue curve. If a firm sells all its output at one price, then this price must be the average price or average revenue received. If a firm sells an extra or marginal unit, it will receive the same price as on preceding units and therefore the marginal price or revenue will be the same as the average price or revenue.

Cost and supply curves

In a perfectly competitive market, the supply curve of the firm will be its marginal cost curve.
● The marginal cost of production is the lowest price at which a firm would be prepared to supply an extra unit of output. For instance, if the marginal cost were £3 when price received was £5, then the firm would be able to make £2 **abnormal**

Question 2

Table 1 Market demand and supply

Quantity demanded (million units)	Quantity supplied (million units)	Price (£)
1 000	6 000	10
3 000	4 000	8
5 000	2 000	6

(a) Draw the market demand and supply curves on graph paper.
(b) There are 1000 firms in the industry each producing the same quantity. One firm now doubles its output.
   (i) Show the effect of this on market demand and supply.
   (ii) On a separate graph draw the demand curve facing the firm.
(c) All firms in the industry now double their output.
   (i) Show the effect of this on market demand and supply.
   (ii) What will be the effect on the demand curve for the individual firm?

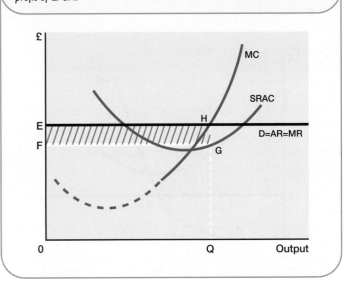

Figure 5 Short run profit maximisation
The firm produces at its profit maximising equilibrium level of output OQ where MC = MR. Because AR is greater than AC, it makes an abnormal profit of EFGH.

Figure 4 The firm's supply curve
The marginal cost of production is the lowest price at which a profit maximising firm will sell a marginal unit of production. Therefore the marginal cost curve is the supply curve for the firm. However, in the short run the firm may stay in production so long as it can cover its average variable costs. Hence the short run supply curve is the marginal cost curve above average variable cost as in Figure 4(a). In the long run a firm will leave the industry if it makes a loss. Hence, the supply curve in the long run is the marginal cost curve above the average cost curve as in Figure 4(b).

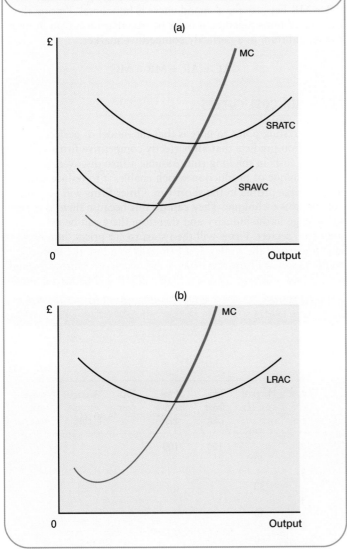

the marginal cost curve above its average variable cost curve - the thick portion of the marginal cost curve in Figure 4(a).

In the long run there are no fixed costs and the average total cost and average variable cost curves are one and the same. The firm will not produce unless it can cover all its costs. Therefore in the long run, the firm's supply curve is the marginal cost curve above its average cost curve as shown in Figure 4(b).

The supply curve for the industry can be constructed by horizontally summing the individual supply curves of each firm.

Short run equilibrium

In perfect competition it is assumed that firms are short run profit maximisers. Therefore the firm will produce at that level of output where marginal cost equals marginal revenue (the MC= MR rule). The price it charges is fixed by the market because the individual firm is a price-taker.

Figure 5 shows one possible short run equilibrium situation. The demand curve is perfectly elastic at a price of 0E. The marginal cost curve cuts the marginal revenue curve at H and hence the equilibrium, profit maximising level of output for the firm is 0Q. At this level of output, average revenue (QH) is higher than average cost (QG) and so the firm will make an abnormal profit. This is given by the shaded area EFGH and is average profit (EF) multiplied by the quantity produced (FG).

Figure 6 gives another possible situation. Here the firm is making a loss at its equilibrium, profit maximising (or in this case loss minimising) level of output 0Q where MC = MR. Price 0F is lower than average cost and hence the firm makes a total loss of EFGH. The firm will stay in production if this loss is smaller than the loss it would make if it shut down (i.e. so long as average revenue is above average variable cost).

Long run equilibrium

In the long run, a perfectly competitive firm will neither make losses nor abnormal profits.

Consider a situation where firms were making

profit (profit over and above the **normal profit** included in cost on that unit). The firm would definitely produce this marginal unit. If marginal cost were £3 when price were £3 it would still produce this marginal unit because it would earn normal profit on it. However, if marginal cost were £3 when price was £2 it would not produce the extra unit because it would make a £1 loss on it.

● In the short run, a firm will not necessarily shut down production if it makes a loss. A firm has fixed costs which it has to pay whether it closes down and produces nothing or whether it continues to operate. Any revenue over and above variable cost will make some contribution towards paying its fixed costs. Therefore it will only close down (i.e. cease to supply) if average revenue or price is below average variable cost.

The firm's short run supply curve will therefore be that part of

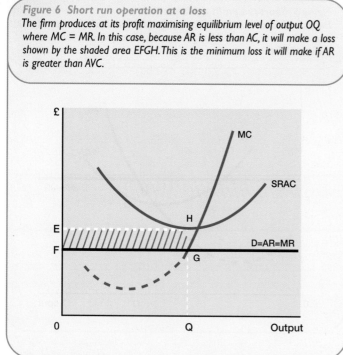

Figure 6 Short run operation at a loss
The firm produces at its profit maximising equilibrium level of output OQ where MC = MR. In this case, because AR is less than AC, it will make a loss shown by the shaded area EFGH. This is the minimum loss it will make if AR is greater than AVC.

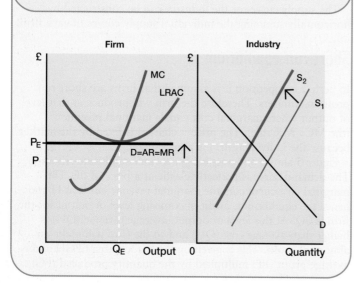

Figure 7 Long run equilibrium following short run losses
If losses are being made in the short run firms will leave the industry, pushing the supply curve from S_1 to S_2. At S_2 there will no longer be any pressure for firms to leave because they will be able to make normal profits on their operations.

losses. In the long term, some firms would leave the industry. It is pointless carrying on production in the long term at a loss. If firms leave the industry, total supply will fall. The more firms that leave the industry, the greater will be the fall in supply and the greater will be the rise in price of the product. Firms will continue to leave the industry until the industry as a whole returns to profitability. This is shown in Figure 7. When the supply curve is S_1 the firm is making a loss. Firms leave the industry, pushing the supply curve to the left. With S_2, the price is just high enough for firms to make **normal profit**. If on the other hand a firm were making abnormal profit in the short run, other firms would enter the industry

eager to gain high profits. This is shown in Figure 9. At a price of P, firms are making abnormal profit. This encourages new entrants to the industry, increasing supply from S_1 until with S_2 the price is just low enough for firms to make a normal profit.

In the long run, then, competitive pressures ensure equilibrium is established where the firm neither makes abnormal profits or losses. This means that in equilibrium, average revenue equals average cost (AR = AC). It should also be remembered that MC = MR because the firm is profit maximising and that AR = MR because the demand curve is horizontal. Putting these three conditions together, it must be true that for a firm in long run equilibrium in a perfectly competitive market:

$$AC = AR = MR = MC$$

Long run cost curves

One interesting point to note is that the model of perfect competition predicts that all perfectly competitive firms will have identical costs in the long run. Assume a firm discovers some new technique of production which enables it to reduce costs and increase profits in the short run. Other firms will respond by copying this technique. They can do this because there is perfect knowledge in the industry and therefore there can be no industrial secrets. Firms will then start to cut prices, hoping to be able to expand their sales. If a firm fails to adopt the new techniques, it will start to make a loss when other firms expand supply and undercut its price. Eventually it will be forced either

Question 3

Table 2

£

Output	Marginal cost (£)	Total fixed cost	Total variable cost	Total cost	Average variable cost	Average total cost
2		100	100			
	40					
3						
	30					
4						
	40					
5						
	60					
6						
	100					
7						

Table 2 shows the costs of production of a firm.

(a) Calculate for levels of output from 2 to 7 units: (i) total fixed cost (ii) total variable cost; (iii) total cost; (iv) average variable cost; (v) average total cost.
(b) Plot the firm's short run supply curve on a graph.
(c) Would a firm cease production (1) in the short run and (2) in the long run if the sales price per unit were: (i) £80; (ii) £70; (iii) £60; (iv) £50; (v) £40; (vi) £30?

Question 4

The price of gold has been increasing for the past five years, after decades in the doldrums. Exactly why remains a mystery. Some argue that currency instability has driven some investors to seek a safe haven in gold. Others see the booming Indian economy, with its appetite for gold jewellery, as a key factor. Others argue that the gold price has been pushed up by speculative activity betting on higher gold prices in the future. On the other hand, new gold production from the world's mines has been declining slowly in recent years. South African mines in particular are now mature and it has become more difficult to extract ore. Gold prospectors have had to move to more remote, risky and higher cost regions of the world to find new sources. The average cost of production for mined gold has risen to $362 an ounce, but with gold currently at over $500 an ounce, there are still substantial profits to be made from gold mining.

Source: adapted from the *Financial Times*, 21.12.2005.

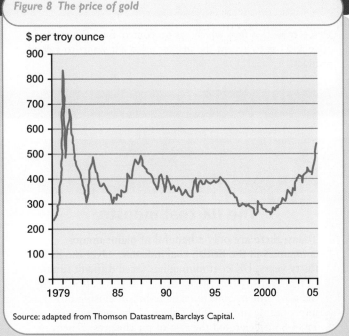

Figure 8 The price of gold

Source: adapted from Thomson Datastream, Barclays Capital.

(a) Using a perfect competition diagram alongside a demand and supply diagram, explain how both rising demand and rising costs have led to an increase in the price of gold.
(b) Explain, using a perfect competition diagram, why mining companies are actively exploring for and developing new mines.

---

to leave the industry because it is uncompetitive, or to adopt the latest production techniques.

Alternatively, a firm may possess some unique factor of production. It may have an exceptional manager, or find that it is far better sited than other firms. In a perfectly competitive world, the manager will be able to demand increases in salary which match the extra profit that she is generating for the firm. If the firm fails to pay this, she will be headhunted by another firm which realises the potential of the manager to create profits. As for the better site, the firm could sell it to another firm in the industry for a much higher price than those sites owned by competitors. Therefore the opportunity cost of the site is much higher than other sites and it is the opportunity cost, not the accounting cost, that is shown in economists' cost curves.

Figure 9 Long run equilibrium following short run abnormal profit

If abnormal profits are being made in the short run, firms will enter the industry, pushing the supply curve from S₁ to S₂. At S₂ firms will no longer be attracted into the industry because they will only be able to make normal profits on their operations.

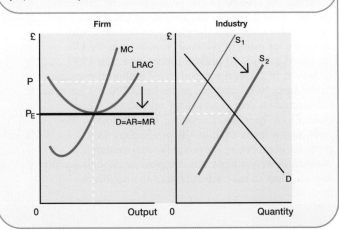

Question 5

Claire Hampton has been looking for premises to set up a flower shop. In her local market town, the main street is High Street which has on it multiples such as Boots, TopShop and Next. There is a vacant property on High Street, currently a charity shop, with a lease of £50 000 a year. Just round the corner in a side street is another vacant property, almost identical in size, with a lease of £20 000 a year.

(a) Use the theory of perfect competition to explain the difference in annual lease payments between the two properties.

Key terms

Price taker - a firm which has no control over the market price and has to accept the market price if it wants to sell its product.

Applied economics

The UK coal industry

Today, there are only a handful of major mining companies in the British coal industry. Over the past thirty years, UK coal mining has faced difficult times. In the 1980s, when the industry was still nationalised, the government continued its policy of closing down unprofitable mines. The failure of the miners' strike in 1984-85 accelerated the rate of pit closures. Then, in 1994, the industry was privatised. The preceding privatisation of the electricity and gas industries in the late 1980s and early 1990s introduced fierce competition into the energy market. For the first time, the UK electricity industry, the major customer of the British coal industry, was able to choose whether to buy British coal or foreign coal or whether to use coal or another fuel, particularly gas, to generate electricity. British coal mines were exposed to the harsh reality of a perfectly competitive market.

The market for coal is a world wide market. In 2006, total world production was 6.2 billion tonnes, of which the UK accounted for 0.3 per cent. Transport is a significant cost and so less efficient coal mines can only survive if they are near to their customers. Coal itself is a homogeneous product, although it comes in many different grades and qualities. There is perfect knowledge in the coal mining industry, with easy access for firms to coal mining technology and to information about prices. There is no buyer or seller in the market large enough to be able to influence price. In the UK market, although a few electricity generating companies are the major buyers of coal, UK mining companies can sell to overseas customers. Hence there is a large number of potential buyers in the world market for UK coal.

In the UK, the coal producers had signed a relatively generous five year contract with electricity producers in 1993. This could not prevent the decline in coal sales shown in Figure 10, but it ensured the survival of some of the industry. In December 1998, the contracts were renegotiated and this time the electricity power generating firms forced the price down to world price levels. Before, coal producers were getting around 140p a gigajoule; after it was about 120p, almost the same as the 119p cost of production at the time.

UK coal mining companies responded to the

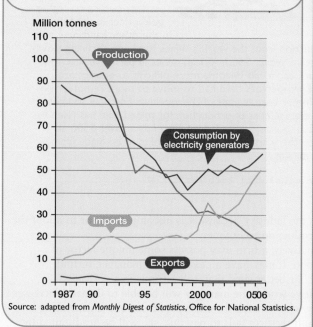

Figure 10 UK coal production, imports and exports; consumption by electricity generators, million tonnes

Source: adapted from *Monthly Digest of Statistics*, Office for National Statistics.

downward pressure on both sales and prices by closing mines and increasing productivity at those that remained. As Figure 10 shows, UK production continued to fall whilst imports of coal continued to rise. In 1987, coal imports were less than 10 per cent production. In 1997, imports were 40 per cent of domestic the volume of UK production. By 2006, imports were 2.7 times the volume of UK production. Demand for coal from the electricity industry, which accounts for most of the coal consumed in the UK, stabilised around 50 million tonnes a year in 1997. However, in 2006, it jumped to 57 million tonnes due to the surge in oil and gas prices from 2003. Coal was substituted on cost grounds for oil and gas. This should have been good news for UK producers. But 2006 saw a further fall in UK production. In a perfectly competitive market, UK coal mining companies were simply not competitive enough against foreign firms to take advantage of the upturn in demand.

Steel

Figure 11 Steel price: hot rolled coil dry

Steel price
Hot rolled coil dry ($ per tonne)

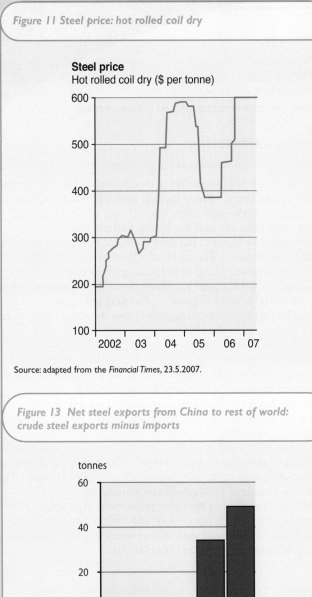

Source: adapted from the *Financial Times*, 23.5.2007.

Figure 12 World crude steel production

Million tonnes

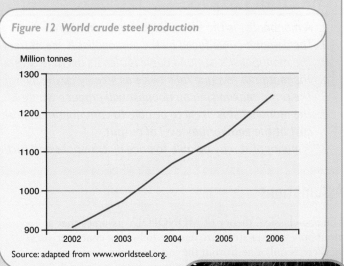

Source: adapted from www.worldsteel.org.

The world steel industry is fragmented. Although there is a number of very large firms in the market, there are thousands of smaller firms too. Today, it is relatively easy for a firm to set up a small steel plant and compete with bigger players in the market. Steel is traded internationally. UK buyers, for example, might source their steel from Russia or the Far East.

Steel prices have risen since 2002 on the back of surging demand from China. But Chinese steel producers have been expanding their production facilities. In 2006, China became a net steel exporter. Chinese imports have fallen substantially and are expected to continue falling over the next two years. That has left non-Chinese producers with less demand for their products, despite growing sales in markets other than China.

Non-Chinese producers are likely to cut back their production rather than make losses on their marginal production. This should limit the price falls they experience. Even so, it will hit their profits hard. In October 2007, EU steel firms filed a complain with the European Commission asking for duties (taxes) to placed on steel coming from China. The European Confederation of Iron and Steel Industries said the EU market had been 'inundated' by imports. As a result, EU prices had been undercut 'by up to 25%' and threatened thousands of jobs.

Source: adapted from the *Financial Times*, 23.5.2007; news.bbc.co.uk 29.10.2007.

Figure 13 Net steel exports from China to rest of world: crude steel exports minus imports

tonnes

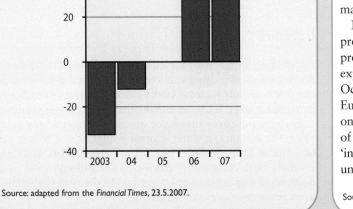

Source: adapted from the *Financial Times*, 23.5.2007.

1. Why might the world steel market be perfectly competitive?
2. Using a perfect competition diagram, explain why increased Chinese production might have led to falls in the prices, output and profits of EU steel producers in 2007.

3. Discuss whether EU (a) steel producers and (b) EU steel consumers would benefit from a tariff being placed on imports of steel from China.

Summary

1. A monopolist is the sole producer in an industry.
2. The demand curve faced by the monopolist is the market demand curve.
3. The monopolist's demand curve is also its average revenue curve.
4. The marginal revenue falls twice as steeply as the average revenue curve.
5. The profit maximising monopolist will produce where MC = MR and price on its demand curve.
6. The monopolist is likely to be able to earn abnormal profit because average revenue will be above average cost at the equilibrium level of output.
7. A monopolist may be able to price discriminate and further increase abnormal profit.

Assumptions

The neo-classical theory of MONOPOLY assumes that a monopoly market structure has the following characteristics:

- there is only one firm in the industry - the monopolist;
- barriers to entry prevent new firms from entering the market;
- the monopolist is a short run profit maximiser.

There are many industries in the world economy which possess most or all of these characteristics. In the UK, for instance, there are examples of monopolies in the gas, electricity, telecommunications, rail transport and water supply industries. All these monopolies were once state owned, but were privatised in the 1980s and 1990s without the creation of genuine competition.

Sources of monopoly power

Monopolies acquire and maintain power over their markets for a variety of reasons.

Question 1

British Gas was created by the Labour government of 1945-1951 from a network of local gas companies, some owned by local authorities. As a nationalised industry, it was the sole supplier of piped gas in the UK. In 1986, the industry was privatised as one company, retaining the legal power to be the sole supplier of gas. Then the government decided that there would be considerable efficiency gains if the gas market were to become competitive. In 1988, the company was forced to allow other gas companies to supply gas to industrial customers using British Gas pipelines. In 1996, British Gas was split into two parts. Transco owned the gas pipeline network and would earn revenues from charging other gas companies to transport gas into homes and business premises. British Gas, renamed Centrica, retained the gas supply business. However, in 1997-98, the gas market to domestic users was opened up to other companies. Now, both homes and businesses could choose which supplier to use, although all the gas was transported through Transco pipelines. Following the entry of a number of companies into the residential gas supply market, the market share of British Gas by March 2007 had fallen to 46 per cent and it was widely predicted that British Gas would continue to lose market share in the near future.

(a) To what extent was British Gas a monopoly supplier of gas in the UK in (i) 1986; (ii) 1990; (iii) 2007?
(b) To what extent was the gas industry a monopoly in 2007?

Barriers to entry Monopolists are protected from new entrants by barriers to entry. These include legal barriers, sunk costs, capital costs, scale economies, natural cost advantages, anti-competitive practices and marketing barriers including advertising. By keeping out new entrants, monopolists can then control the market. The higher the barriers to entry, the stronger the power of the monopolist over its market. For example, in the UK, legal barriers prevent firms from setting up new pharmacies in local areas. Planning permission regulations give large supermarket chains monopoly powers in some local areas in the UK.

Product differentiation and the number of near competitors Some monopolists sell products which are clearly differentiated from rival products. For example, households have to buy electricity from an electricity distributor. Gas, oil or batteries are very poor substitutes for electricity. Similarly, on the Manchester to London route, the railway has a strong monopoly because airline flights or road transport are much more inconvenient and the journey time can be much longer. The higher the degree of product differentiation, the stronger the monopoly power. The lower the degree of product differentiation, the larger the number of competitors the monopolist faces in practice. For example, Mars Foods has a monopoly on the production of Mars Bars, but the monopoly is very weak because a number of competitors produce similar chocolate bars.

Revenue curves

A monopoly firm is itself the industry. As the industry faces a downward sloping demand curve, so too must the monopolist. It can therefore only increase sales by reducing price, or increase price by reducing sales. It can set either price or output but not both.

The demand curve shows the quantity bought at any given price. For instance, a water company might sell 2 billion gallons of water at 1p per gallon. This price is the same as its average revenue; on average it will receive 1p per gallon, so the downward sloping demand curve facing the firm is also the average revenue curve of the firm.

If average revenue is falling, marginal revenue must be falling too and at a faster rate. For example, assume a firm sells 10 units at £20 each. To sell an eleventh unit, it needs to lower its price, say to £19. Not only will it have to lower its price on the eleventh unit, but it will also have to lower its price on the other 10 units. This is because it cannot charge a higher price to some consumers than others (although we will see later on in this unit that it is possible in limited cases). There is a loss of

Table 1

Quantity	Average revenue or price £	Total revenue £	Marginal revenue £
0			
			8
1	8	8	
			4
2	6	12	
			0
3	4	12	
			-4
4	2	8	
			-8
5	0	0	

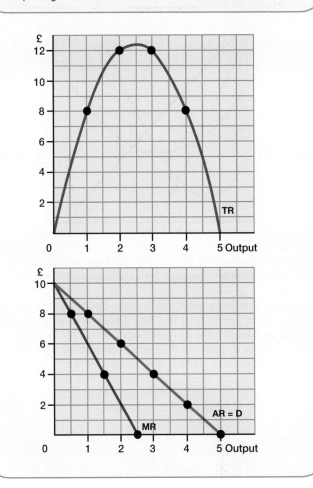

Figure 1 The revenue curves of a monopolist

A monopolist, being the sole supplier in the industry, faces a downward sloping demand or average revenue curve. Marginal revenue falls at twice the rate of average revenue and becomes zero when total revenue is maximised.

revenue not just of £1 on the sale of the eleventh unit but of a further £10 on the first 10 units. Total revenue increases from £200 (£20 x 10 units) to £209 (£19 x 11 units), so marginal revenue on the eleventh unit is £9 (£209 - £200) whilst the average revenue on selling 11 units is £19 (£209 ÷ 11 which is, of course, the price).

Table 1 gives a further example of falling marginal and average revenues. Note that the fall in marginal revenue is twice as large over any given change in quantity as the fall in average revenue. This is true of all straight line average revenue curves. Plotting these figures on a diagram, we arrive at Figure 1. The marginal revenue figures, as with all marginal figures, are plotted half way between 'whole' output figures, so the marginal revenue of the second unit is plotted half way between 1 and 2 units. It can be seen that at any given level of output, average

revenue is twice marginal revenue. Total revenue is maximised when marginal revenue is zero. If marginal revenue (the addition to total revenue) becomes negative then total revenue will automatically fall. Total revenue is zero if average revenue, the price received per unit of output, is zero too.

Equilibrium output

The neo-classical theory of the firm assumes that a monopolist will be a short run profit maximiser. This means that it will produce where MC = MR.

Figure 2 adds the traditional U-shaped average and marginal cost curves to the average and marginal revenue curves outlined above.

- **The equilibrium profit maximising level of output** is 0A where MC = MR.
- **The price** will be 0E. Buyers are prepared to pay 0E for this output. We know this because the average revenue curve is also the demand curve and the demand curve shows the maximum price buyers will pay for any given level of ouput.
- **Abnormal profit** of EFGC will be made. The abnormal profit per unit (GF) is the difference between the average revenue received (AF) and the average cost incurred (AG). 0A units are sold. Therefore total abnormal profit is

Question 2

Table 2

Output (units per week)	Marginal revenue £
0	
	10
1	
	7
2	
	4
3	
	1
4	
	-2
5	

(a) Calculate (i) total revenue and (ii) average revenue at output levels 0 to 5 units.
(b) (i) Draw the axes of a graph with revenue from £0 to £10 and output from 0 to 10. (ii) Plot the marginal and average revenue curves. (iii) Extend the average revenue curve to the output axis assuming that average revenue continues to fall at the same rate as in the table.
(c) What is the value of marginal revenue when total revenue is at a maximum?

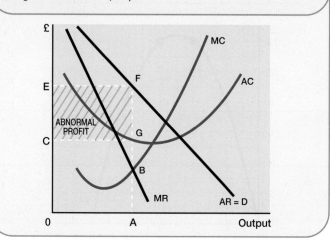

Figure 2 Profit maximising output
The monopolist will maximise profits by producing where MC = MR at OA. It will base its prices on its average revenue curve, charging OE. It will be able to earn abnormal profit of EFGC because average revenue is greater than average cost at this level of output.

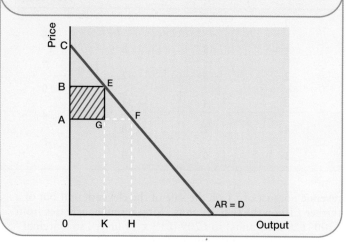

Figure 3 The appropriation of consumer surplus
A monopolist can appropriate ABEG of consumer surplus by price discriminating selling OK output to those consumers prepared to pay a minimum OB, and selling KH to other consumers only prepared to pay a minimum OA.

0A x FG, or the area EFGC. Note that this is abnormal profit because economic cost includes an allowance for normal profit.

Note also that price is not equal to the intersection of the MC and MR curves (i.e. price is not AB). This is because the firm, although deciding on the level of output by the MC = MR condition, fixes its price on the average revenue or demand curve. Also abnormal profit is not the area EF x FB (i.e. it is not the area between the average revenue curve and the marginal revenue and cost curves). Profit per unit is the difference between average revenue and average cost.

Discriminating monopoly

Some buyers in the market will almost certainly be prepared to pay a higher price for a product than other buyers. For instance, a rail commuter is likely to be prepared to pay more for a journey at 8 o'clock in the morning to take her to work than would a shopper. A millionaire faced with the need for heart surgery is likely to pay more than a person on a low income with the same complaint. This can be illustrated on a monopoly diagram. In Figure 3, the profit maximising output for a monopolist is assumed to be 0H and 0A is therefore the profit maximising price. 0A represents the maximum price that the marginal consumer is prepared to pay. Other consumers are prepared to pay a higher price. If output were only 0K, the marginal consumer would be prepared to pay 0B. The area ACF represents the area of consumer surplus when price is 0A, the difference between what consumers are prepared to pay in total for a good and what they actually pay.

A monopolist may be able to split the market and PRICE DISCRIMINATE between different buyers. In Figure 3, the monopolist may be able to charge 0B for 0K of output, and then charge a lower price of 0A for KH of output. In this way, the monopolist appropriates ABEG of consumer surplus when price is 0A in the form of higher profit (i.e. higher producer surplus).

There is a number of different ways in which a monopolist may choose to discriminate.

- Time. It may charge a different price at different times of the day or week, as do the electricity distribution companies or rail companies.
- Place. It may vary price according to the location of the buyer. The same car can be bought at different prices in different countries of the EU, for instance.
- Income. It may be able to split up consumers into income groups, charging a high price to those with high incomes, and a low price to those with lower incomes. Examples of this can be found in medical practice and amongst lawyers. Hairdressers (who may be local monopolists) offering reduced rates to pensioners are likely to be price discriminating according to income too.

Three conditions must hold if a monopolist is to be able to price discriminate effectively.

- The monopolist must face different demand curves from separate groups of buyers (i.e. the elasticity of demand of buyers must differ). If all buyers had the same demand curve, then the monopolist could not charge different prices to buyers.
- The monopolist must be able to split the market into distinct groups of buyers, otherwise it will be unable to distinguish between those consumers prepared to pay a higher price and those prepared to a pay a lower price.
- The monopolist must be able to keep the markets separate at relatively low cost. For instance, it must be able to prevent buyers in the high priced market from buying in the low price market. If a German car company sells its cars at 25 per cent less in Belgium than in the UK, then it must be able to prevent UK motorists and UK retailers from taking a day trip to Belgium to buy those cars. Equally, it must be able to prevent traders from buying in the low price market and selling into the high price market at a price which undercuts that of the monopolist.

Price discrimination can be analysed using the concepts of marginal cost and marginal revenue. Assume that the monopolist is able to divide its market into two and that the costs of production are identical for both markets.

The firm needs to allocate production between the two markets so that the marginal revenue is identical for each market if it is to maximise profit. To understand why, take a situation where marginal revenue in one market, A, is higher than in another market, B. The firm could increase its total revenue from a given output by switching goods from B to A. Marginal revenue

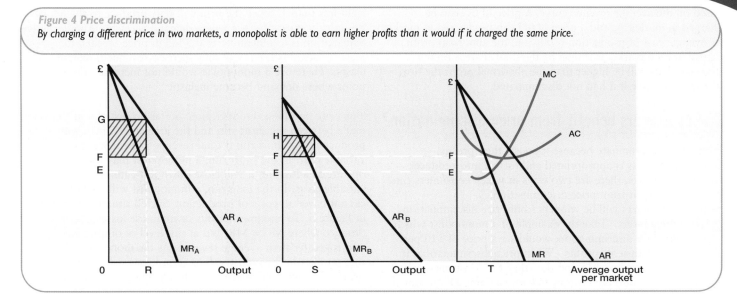

Figure 4 Price discrimination
By charging a different price in two markets, a monopolist is able to earn higher profits than it would if it charged the same price.

in market B will now rise because it can charge a higher price if it sells less. Marginal revenue in market A will fall because it has to lower price to sell more. For instance, if marginal revenue in market A were £10 when it was £6 in market B, then the firm could gain an extra £4 of revenue by switching the marginal unit of production from market B to market A. It will carry on switching from market B to A until there is no more advantage in doing so, which occurs when the marginal revenues are the same.

In Figure 4, the demand curves in markets A and B are drawn

first. From these demand or average revenue curves, the marginal revenue curves in each market can then be calculated. The average and marginal revenue curves for the total market can be calculated by summing horizontally the average and marginal revenue curves in each market. The profit maximising monopolist will produce where MC = MR across the whole market, at output level 0T. This output (0T) is then split between the two markets (0R and 0S) so that the marginal revenue is equal in both individual markets (0E). In each market, a firm's price will be

Question 3

Table 3 BT together option charges for calls to mobile phones from fixed lines, 2007

Calls from fixed lines to charge bands*	Price (pence per minute excluding VAT, rounded to 2 decimal places)		
	Daytime Mon to Fri 8am - 6pm	Evening & Night-time Mon to Fri before 8am and after 6pm	Weekend All day Sat & Sun
fm1	14.74	14.74	7.19
fm2	13.95	11.61	5.92
fm3	15.57	12.39	6.25
fm4	15.07	9.21	4.61
fm5	14.06	11.39	6.36
fm6	12.28	9.82	5.92

Source: adapted from www.bt.com.

* Bands depend on where the two phones are located, so a call to a mobile phone paying fm1 charges will be in a different area to fm4, for example.

(a) Using diagrams, explain why BT has such a complicated tariff structure for users.

based on the average revenue curve. A price of 0G can be charged in market A, and a price of 0H can be charged in market B. Average cost of production is 00F and the abnormal profit earned in each market is shown by the shaded areas on the diagram. This will be higher than the abnormal profit the firm would have made if it had not discriminated.

Can consumers benefit from price discrimination?

Firms price discriminate because it boosts their profits. Consumer surplus is appropriated and turned into producer surplus. However, there are two ways in which consumers can sometimes benefit from price discrimination.

- Some customers will be winners from price discrimination and others losers. Take the example of a monopolist which, without price discrimination, would set a price of £10 per unit to maximise its profits. When price discriminating, it sets two prices, one £15 and the other £8. Customers who pay £15 lose out, but customers who pay only £8 are gainers. Some of these customers are ones who would otherwise would have paid £10. Others are customers who would not have bought the product at all at a price of £10. Price discrimination not only results in cheaper prices for some customers but it also expands the market.
- In some cases, a monopolist would not supply at a profit maximising single price because it would make a loss. Its average revenue curve would be above its average cost curve at every level of output, but by price discriminating, it might be able to raise revenues to a point at which average cost at least equalled average revenue. At this point it would produce because it would be earning normal profit.

Four technical points

Absence of a supply curve in monopoly In perfect competition, the supply curve of the firm is its marginal cost curve above average cost in the long run. In monopoly, there is no supply curve which is determined independently of demand.
Look back at Figure 2. The firm will produce at output 0A because that is the output where MC = MR. Now assume that demand changes in such a way that the marginal revenue curve is much steeper but still passes through the point B. If the MR curve is steeper, so too will be the AR curve. The firm will now be able to charge a much higher price than 0E for its product. For each differently sloped MR curve that passes through the point B, the firm will charge a different price to the consumer. The firm is prepared to supply 0A output at a variety of different prices, depending upon demand conditions, so no supply curve for the monopolist can be drawn. (Contrast this with the firm in perfect competition. Falls in demand which reduce prices received by the firm will result in a fall in quantity supplied as the firm moves down its supply curve.)

A monopolist will produce only where demand is elastic Look back to Figure 1. It should be obvious that the firm will not produce more than 2½ units of output. If it produces 3 units, it will almost certainly have higher costs than if it produces 2½ units but total revenue will fall. Profit therefore is bound to fall. 2½ units is the output where marginal revenue is zero. It is also the point where price elasticity of demand is unity because we are now half way along the demand or average revenue curve. To the left, elasticity is greater than 1, to the

right less than 1. Since the firm will only produce to the left of 2½ units, it must produce where demand is elastic. An alternative explanation is to remember that a fall in price (needed to increase quantity sold) will only increase revenue if demand is elastic. Therefore a monopolist would not increase sales to the point where demand became inelastic.

Short run and long run operation So far no distinction has been made between the short run and the long run. A firm will produce in the short run if total revenue is greater than total variable cost. In the short run, a monopolist may therefore operate at a loss but it will close down if it cannot cover its variable costs. In the long run, a monopolist will not operate if it cannot cover all costs of production. Such a situation is shown in Figure 5. To maximise profits or minimise losses, it will produce where MC = MR, but at this level of output average cost is greater than average revenue. As the monopolist is the sole supplier in the industry, long term losses will mean that no firm will supply and hence the industry will cease to exist.

Degrees of price discrimination Sometimes, price discrimination is described in terms of three degrees of price discrimination.

- First-degree discrimination or perfect price discrimination occurs when a business charges each customer a different price, that price being the profit maximising price for the monopolist. This is the most profitable solution for a monopolist because it is able to convert all consumer surplus ACEF in Figure 3 into producer surplus. Consider Figure 3. If the profit maximising level of production is 0H, then it is able to charge a price of almost 0C to the first customer, 0E to the n'th customer and 0F to the last customer. In doing so, it appropriates all the consumer surplus ACF that there would have been if the monopolist had charged the same price of 0A to all customers. ACF becomes producer surplus. In practice, there are very few situations where a monopolist is able to discriminate to this degree.
- Second-degree discrimination occurs when the monopolist price discriminates according to the volume of purchase by a particular customer. For example, a gas company may charge a higher price for the first 100 therms used per month and a lower price for all other gas consumed on top of 100 therms.

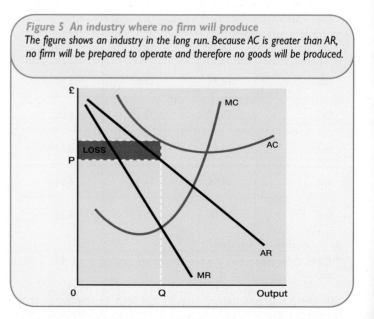

Figure 5 An industry where no firm will produce
The figure shows an industry in the long run. Because AC is greater than AR, no firm will be prepared to operate and therefore no goods will be produced.

A taxi firm may have a fixed charge of £3.50 for any journey up to 2 miles and then £1 a mile thereafter.

● Third-degree discrimination occurs when the monopolist splits customers into two or more separate groups. This is the most common type of discrimination and is described diagrammatically in Figure 4.

Question 4

Draw two diagrams showing the change in equilibrium output of a profit maximising monopolist if: (a) its marginal revenue increases; (b) its marginal cost increases.

Key terms

Price discrimination - charging a different price for the same good or service in different markets.
Monopoly - a market structure where one firm supplies all output in the industry without facing competition because of high barriers to entry to the industry.

Applied economics

Virgin Wolverhampton to London

When British Rail was broken up in 1996, Virgin won the franchise to operate trains on the West Coast line. This included taking over the Wolverhampton to London line. In one respect, this is a monopoly service. No other train operator has the legal right to run express services from Wolverhampton through Birmingham New Street Station and Milton Keynes down to London Euston. The terms of the franchise issued by the government therefore constitute a legal barrier to entry to this market.

However, travellers have alternatives. There are three train operators running from Birmingham to London: Virgin, Silverlink and Chiltern Railways. Wolverhampton passengers can therefore travel to Birmingham and change to either Silverlink or Chiltern. Silverlink only runs stopping trains to London Euston with a typical journey time one hour longer than Virgin. The rolling stock itself is suburban carriages designed for short journeys rather than the InterCity rolling stock of Virgin. The journey is therefore far less comfortable. As for Chiltern, it operates out of different stations from Virgin. At Birmingham, it runs out of Snow Hill Station. Most trains into Birmingham, including Virgin trains, go to Birmingham New Street. Making a connection between New Street and Snow Hill requires a 5 minute walk or a journey on public transport. In London, Chiltern Railways goes to Marylebone Station, not Euston Station. Both Silverlink and Chiltern Railways offer cheaper tickets from Birmingham to London than Virgin, particularly at peak times. However, their services have proved poor substitutes for those travelling from Wolverhampton to London. Virgin, therefore, has a strong monopoly on rail journeys from Wolverhampton to London.

Price discrimination

As a monopolist, Virgin is able to price discriminate. The range of prices on the Wolverhampton to London route is shown in Table 4. It splits up the market in many ways. First, it price discriminates by the time of day and weekday/weekend when the journey is taken. Those who need to get to London from Wolverhampton by 9 a.m. on a weekday tend to have a low price elasticity of demand. They tend to be business travellers, many of whom have their journey paid for them by their employer. Virgin can charge high prices without losing too many passengers amongst this group.

Second, it price discriminates on advance booking. Virgin, along with a number of other rail companies, has decided that it is in its interests to encourage as much advance booking as possible. It improves cash flow because tickets are paid for in advance. It locks passengers into travelling when, on the day, they might otherwise have chosen not to travel by Virgin or travel at all. It also spreads passenger loads. Passengers unable to book a ticket to travel at the most popular times may switch to a less popular time. Advance booking allows passengers to book a seat, which is important if there is likely to be overcrowding on the train, but also the cheapest tickets on the Wolverhampton to London route are only available by booking in advance for a specifically timed journey. They are likely to be bought by passengers with the highest price elasticity of demand: those who would otherwise not travel if the price were much higher. Only a very small proportion of seats on a train are available at the cheapest price and many trains have no value tickets allocated to them, so Virgin can advertise low prices without losing too much revenue. It can also offer the bargain hunter travel at a less crowded and popular time, allowing Virgin to spread travel numbers during the day.

Virgin has a large number of other ways in which it price discriminates. It encourages children and families to travel by offering reductions for children and Family Rail Cards. Students can get reductions by buying a Student Rail Card. Old Age Pensioners are offered a similar card.

Virgin's pricing policy over time would suggest that it has a keen understanding of price elasticity of demand.

Table 4 Virgin Trains Wolverhampton-London return fares[1]

	1995 £	2007 £	Percentage increase 1995-2007
First class open	82.00	204.00	149
Standard class open	57.00	123.00	116
Cheap day return (1995)/ Saver (2007)[2]	19.50	39.10	101
Cheapest pre-booked fare[3]	15.00	20.00	33

1. 1995 prices are British Rail fares prior to the takeover of the route by Virgin.
2. Ticket can be bought on the day of travel.
3. Ticket can only be bought by booking at least one day in advance.

Its lowest cost fares have changed by only 33 per cent between 1995 and 2007, as Table 4 shows. However, Virgin has significantly increased its standard, no restriction fares. The cost of travelling to London first class for a business traveller has increased by 149 per cent. By charging higher prices, it has been able to appropriate the consumer surplus of business customers and turn this into profit or producer surplus for itself. At the bottom end of the market, it has encouraged larger numbers of private customers to travel at less popular times of the day. Every extra passenger that would otherwise not have travelled on these services is nearly 100 per cent profit for Virgin because the marginal cost of taking them is virtually zero.

DataQuestion

Motorway service stations

The British motorway service station is an example of a local monopoly. Protected by government from competitors setting up a service station next door, they have been a feature of motorway travel since the first motorways were built in the 1960s, but the legal monopoly comes at a price for their owners. The government lays down stringent conditions about the operation of the service stations. For example, they have to be open 24 hours a day, 365 days a year. They must provide a range of services including free toilets. This is very important when surveys show that the vast majority of people who go to a motorway service station head for the toilet first. Motorway service stations cannot by law be a meeting place for more than 12 people to prevent them becoming conference centres. Alcohol cannot be sold. There are also other restrictions on what they sell, to prevent them becoming retail or leisure parks. Some of the restrictions force the motorway service stations to provide services which motorway motorists might need. Some of the restrictions are designed to prevent the service station becoming a 'destination in its own right'.

For decades, service stations have been seen as infrastructure assets, offering their owners steady but unspectacular profit growth in a regulated environment with limited competition, but over the past few years, motorway service owners have become more aggressive in their search for profit. One key development has been the signing of partnerships between established brand names and service stations. McDonald's, Burger King, Costa Coffee and Marks & Spencer are just some of the retail brands that have appeared. Well-known brands help lift sales of products. Customers are more likely to buy a McDonald's hamburger than an unbranded motorway service station hamburger. Equally, customers are unlikely to buy the evening meal they are going to eat when they get home from a motorway service branded shop, but they will do if the shop is a Marks & Spencer outlet. The goal is to leverage the selling space at motorway service stations so that when customers have a toilet or coffee stop, they spend more than they do at the moment.

Source: adapted from the *Financial Times*, 10.3.2007.

1. Explain why a motorway service station has a 'local monopoly'.
2. Motorway service stations tend to charge higher prices for products than a supermarket which might be sited just off a motorway junction. Using a monopoly diagram, explain why motorway service station prices might be higher.
3. The price of a McDonald's hamburger is higher at a motorway service station than in one of its high street outlets. Using the theory of price discrimination and a diagram, analyse why McDonald's charges different prices.
4. Discuss whether expanding sales at motorway service station outlets will benefit consumers.

Summary

1. Most markets are oligopolistic.
2. An oligopolistic market is one where a small number of interdependent firms compete with each other.
3. Non-price competition is an important feature of oligopolistic markets.
4. Oligopoly may be collusive or non-collusive. Collusion enables individual producers to share monopoly profits with other producers.
5. Cartels may collapse. Individual members have an incentive to cheat on the agreement. Non-cartel members may increase their market share at the expense of cartel members.

The importance of oligopoly

Most markets could be said to be imperfectly competitive. A few are monopolistically competitive but the majority are CONCENTRATED MARKETS, dominated by a few suppliers.

Question 1

Table 1

					% of the market	
	USA	Western Europe	UK	France	Latin America	China
Wrigley	54	43.2	89.4	37.9	5.7	54.9
Cadbury Schweppes	25.4	21.4	2.0	49.5	69.7	3.1
Other	20.6	35.4	8.6	12.6	24.6	42

In the UK, Wrigley is the dominant seller of chewing gum. Wrigley is also the world's number one manufacturer of gum, but it isn't dominant in every market. In France, or Latin America, for example, Cadbury Schweppes is the market leader.

Cadbury Schweppes increased its competitive challenge to Wrigley two years ago when it bought the US number two gum manufacturer, Adams. Cadbury Schweppes is twice the size of Wrigley and has a formidable distribution system worldwide. It can push gum through the same sales channels as its other confectionery products. Equally, Wrigley, which relies for 90 per cent of its sales on gum, is renowned for its ability to get the product to consumers. In the fast growing but undeveloped Chinese market, for example, sticks of Wrigley Doublemint gum are sold at small kiosks in rural areas.

Another way Cadbury Schweppes hopes to compete with Wrigley is on product development. Gum is a highly versatile product which can be made in a wide range of flavours and textures. Different packaging also can add value to the product for the consumer and allow the manufacturer to charge higher prices.

Source: adapted from the *Financial Times*, 19.10.2005.

(a) Why could the market for chewing gum be said to be oligopolistic?

Therefore the theory of OLIGOPOLY is arguably the most important of the theories of the firm. Yet there is no single dominant model of oligopoly within economics. Rather there is a number of competing models which make different assumptions and draw different conclusions. Some of these models will be outlined in this and the next three units, but first the characteristics of an oligopolistic market will be described.

Market structure

For an industry to be called 'oligopolistic', there must be two key aspects of its market structure.

- Supply in the industry must be concentrated in the hands of relatively few firms. For instance, an industry where the three largest firms produce 80 per cent of output would be oligopolistic. Note that alongside a few very large producers there may also be a much larger number of very small firms, so an industry with 100 firms, where the three largest firms produced 80 per cent of the output, would still be classed as oligopolistic.
- Firms must be interdependent. The actions of one large firm will directly affect another large firm. In perfect competition, firms are independent. If one farmer decides, for instance, to grow more wheat, that will have no impact on price or sales of other farmers in the industry. In oligopoly, if one large firm decides to pursue policies to increase sales, this is likely to be at the expense of other firms in the industry. One firm is likely to sell more only by taking away sales from other firms.

In addition, the neo-classical theory of oligopoly assumes that:

- there are barriers to entry to the industry. If there were no barriers, firms would enter the industry to take advantage of the abnormal profits characteristic of oligopolies and would reduce the market share of the few large producers in the industry.

Market conduct

Oligopoly can be defined by market structure. However, firms in some markets which have an oligopolistic market structure can behave as if they were in a highly competitive market, so sometimes it is better to define oligopoly in terms of market conduct, the behaviour of firms in a market. Oligopolistic market conduct has a number of features.

Non-price competition In a perfectly competitive market, firms producing homogeneous goods compete solely on price. In the short run, factors such as delivery dates might assume some importance, but in the long term price is all that matters. In an imperfectly competitive market, price is often not the most important factor in the competitive process. Firms decide upon a MARKETING MIX - a mixture of elements which form a coherent strategy designed to sell their products to their market. The marketing mix is often summarised in the '4 Ps'. Firms produce a **product** which appeals to their customers. The product may or may not be differentiated from rivals' products. A **price** needs to be set but this could be above or below the price of competing products depending upon the pricing strategy to be used. For instance, a high price will be set if the product is sold as a high quality product. A low price will be set if the firm wishes to sell large quantities of a standard product. **Promotion** (advertising and sales promotion) is essential to inform buyers in the market that the good is on sale and to change their perceptions of a product in a favourable manner. A good distribution system is essential to get the product to the right **place** at the right time for the customer.

Many markets are dominated by **brands**. A branded good is one which is produced by a particular firm and which appears to possess unique characteristics. These may be real characteristics, such as a unique formulation or a unique design. A Mars Bar or a Rolls Royce car, for instance, are unique products, but often more important than the real characteristics are the imagined characteristics of the product in the mind of the buyer. This image is likely to have been created by advertising and promotion, so it is possible for the same baked beans or the same breakfast cereal to be packaged differently and sold on the same supermarket shelves at different prices. Often the higher priced branded product will sell far better than the lower priced unbranded product despite the fact that the product itself is the same.

Question 2

The UK tinned vegetable market is not an attractive one for new entrants. The market has been in steady decline in recent years, with sales falling from £209 million in 1998 to £188 million in 2004. Seventy per cent of the market is accounted for by own label products of the major supermarket chains.

Bonduelle, the French manufacturer, has now taken on the challenge of this difficult market. It believes it can succeed by differentiating itself in two ways. First, it is selling its vegetables in square laminated paper boxes known as 'Tetra Recarts'. Although they only have a shelf life of two years compared to three or four for cans, they are simple to open and lighter than cans to carry. Being square, they can be positioned more closely together on supermarket shelves. The theory is that the more cartons the company can place on a shelf, the more retailers can sell. Second, the boxes will contain combinations of vegetables rather than the typical single vegetable found in tins.

In much of the rest of Europe, the canned vegetable market is growing. For example, in France, it increased by 20 per cent between 1998 and 2004, whilst over the same period in Spain it increased by 62 per cent. Bonduelle hopes its new UK offerings will excite British consumers to buy more in this product category.

Source: adapted from the *Financial Times*, 15.7.2005.

(a) Explain, using the example of the canned vegetable market, how firms in an oligopolistic market compete.

Price rigidity Prices in oligopolistic markets seem to change far less than in perfectly competitive markets. Despite changes in underlying costs of production, firms are often observed to maintain prices at a constant level.

L-shaped average cost curves Economic studies have established that in the real world average variable cost curves are often more L-shaped than U- shaped. Over a wide range of output, large firms face the same average variable costs whether they increase or decrease output, as shown in Figure 1.

Collusion Collusion is often a feature of the behaviour of firms in oligopolistic markets where it is not illegal. Collusive oligopoly will now be considered in more detail.

Collusive and non-collusive oligopoly

Oligopolistic firms may compete amongst themselves. When this occurs, NON-COLLUSIVE or COMPETITIVE OLIGOPOLY is said to exist. However, there is a very strong incentive for oligopolistic firms to COLLUDE. This means they make agreements amongst themselves so as to restrict competition and maximise their own benefits. COLLUSIVE OLIGOPOLY is said to exist when oligopolistic firms collude and form a CARTEL.

To understand the benefits of collusion, consider Table 2. It

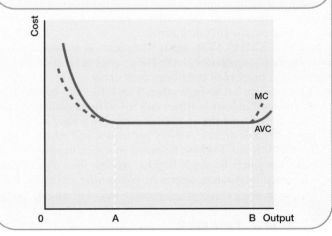

Figure 1 L-shaped average cost curve
Many firms in practice seem to face an L-shaped average cost curve. The minimum efficient scale of production extends over a wide range of output, from 0A to 0B in this diagram.

Table 2

Million units			£ millions
Output	Average revenue	Average cost (including normal profit)	Total abnormal profit
(a)	(b)	(c)	(b - c) x a
1	10	5	5
2	9	5	8
3	8	5	9
4	7	5	8
5	6	5	5
6	5	5	0

Question 3

The De Beers diamond cartel was one of the oldest cartels operating in the world. De Beers is the world's largest diamond producer, mining around 40 per cent of world production, mainly from its mines in Africa. Until 2000, through its Central Selling Organisation (CSO), it attempted to buy up all the world's diamond production. It then sold these uncut diamonds to customers at regular sales. It attempted to regulate the price by selling fewer diamonds when prices were falling and selling more when prices were rising. In 1999, it held a stockpile of unsold diamonds of $5.2 billion.

However, in 2000, it announced that it would cease to act as a cartel. There was a number of reasons for this. One was that an increasing proportion of world diamond production was being sold outside of the Central Selling Organisation. Producers in countries such as Russia were finding it more profitable to sell directly to the market rather than sell to the CSO because they could get better prices. Another problem was the rising cost to De Beers of buying diamonds from other producers. It was also attempting to mop up diamonds which were being mined illegally in war torn countries such as Angola and the Democratic Republic of Congo. These diamonds came

to be called 'blood diamonds' because their sale often passed through guerrilla and insurgent groups which used the money to buy arms. De Beers feared that the image of diamonds as a whole would become tainted in the same way that the fur trade had acquired a bad reputation. A further reason was growing worldwide demand for diamonds, particularly from India and China. In the USA, selling De Beers diamonds was illegal under anti-trust laws. Abandoning the cartel would enable De Beers to sell into the US market directly.

Source: adapted from the *Financial Times*, 15.12.1998, 28.6.2005; *The New York Times*, 13.7.2000; *The Wall Street Journal*, 13.7.2000.

(a) Explain how De Beers' Central Selling Organisation might have raised prices and profits for diamond producers in the cartel before 2000.
(b) Why was there an incentive for producers outside the cartel to cheat?
(c) Why might De Beers have considered it in its best interests to dismantle its cartel because of (i) rising demand for diamonds and (ii) the mining of diamonds in war torn areas of the world?

shows the cost and revenues for an oligopolistic industry. If barriers to entry were low, firms would find it difficult to earn abnormal profit. Long run output would then be 6 million units where abnormal profit is zero, but, if they colluded, they could force up the price by restricting output and engaging in anti-competitive practices which would keep new entrants out of the industry. The profit maximising output for the combined industry is 3 million units. If each firm in the industry agreed to halve its current output, £9 million of abnormal profit could be shared between the colluding firms.

FORMAL COLLUSION exists when firms in a cartel make agreements amongst themselves. For a cartel to function effectively, a number of conditions must apply.

- An agreement has to be reached. This is likely to be easiest in oligopolistic industries where only a few firms dominate the market; the larger the number of firms, the greater the possibility that at least one key participant will refuse to collude. It is also likely to be easiest in stable, mature industries where no single firm has recently been able to gain advantage by pursuing aggressive competitive strategies. For

instance, collusion is far more likely in a mature industry like steel manufacturing or cement making than in a rapidly changing industry like the computer industry.
- Cheating has to be prevented. Once an agreement is made and profitability in the industry is raised, it would pay an individual firm to cheat so long as no other firms do the same. For instance, it would pay a small cartel producer with 10 per cent of the market to expand production to 12 per cent by slightly undercutting the cartel price. The profit it would lose by the small cut in price on the 10 per cent is more than offset by the gain in profit on the sale of the extra 2 per cent. However, if every producer does this, the market price will quickly fall to the free market level and all firms will lose the privilege of earning abnormal profit.
- Potential competition must be restricted. Abnormal profits will encourage not only existing firms in the industry to expand output but also new firms to enter the industry. Firms already in the industry which don't join the cartel may be happy to follow the policies of the cartel in order to earn abnormal profits themselves. To prevent this,

Key terms

Cartel - an organisation of producers which exists to further the interests of its members, often by restricting output through the imposition of quotas, leading to a rise in price.

Collusion - collective agreements between producers which restrict competition.

Collusive oligopoly - when firms in an oligopolistic industry form a cartel and collude, typically to restrict output and raise prices and profits.

Concentrated market - a market where most of the output is produced by a few firms.

Formal collusion - when firms make agreements among themselves to restrict competition, typically by reducing output, raising prices and keeping potential competitors out of the market.

Marketing mix - different elements within a strategy designed to create demand for a product.

Non-collusive or competitive oligopoly - when firms in an oligopolistic industry compete amongst themselves and there is no collusion.

Tacit collusion - when firms collude without any formal agreement having been reached or even without any explicit communication between the firms having taken place.

cartel firms could agree to drive other firms which compete too aggressively out of the market. Cartel firms could also agree to increase barriers to entry to the industry.

Formal collusion is illegal in the EU, the Unied States and many other countries. The most famous cartel today is not between firms but between countries. OPEC countries, with less than half of current world output but with most of the world's oil reserves, manipulate the price of oil by restricting supply.

Countries are given production quotas which are renegotiated every six months at OPEC meetings.

However, firms may engage in TACIT COLLUSION. This is when firms in an industry understand that it is in their own best interests to restrict supply and competition. Firms monitor each other's behaviour closely. `Unwritten rules are developed which become custom and practice which define ways in which firms may or may not compete.

Applied economics

The market for salt

The UK market for the production of salt is highly concentrated. In 2005, as Figure 1 shows, the two firm concentration ratio for the sale of PDV (Pure Dried Vacuum salt) and compacted salt was 94 per cent. This was an increase from 2004 when the two firm concentration ratio was 85 per cent. This increase in concentration occurred because the UK's largest salt producer, British Salt, acquired the number three producer, NCSW (New Cheshire Salt Works Limited), in 2004.

There are significant barriers to entry to the industry. One barrier to entry is financial. Demand for salt is declining and existing salt manufacturers are faced with excess capacity at their existing plants. The firms already in the market are not making significant new investments and this would indicate that the potential rate of return on any investment is not high enough to justify the building of a new plant. Another barrier to entry is marketing. Existing customers, such as local authorities buying salt to grit roads, food companies or distributors buying in bulk and selling in smaller quantities, tend to have long established relationships with an individual salt producer. Customers put a value on quality, reliability and overall security of supply. Although price is a factor in purchase, salt is not a significant cost for any ultimate end user.

Imports are not significant for two reasons. One is that salt is a low value, high bulk product where transport costs can be a significant part of total cost. Second, imports from outside the European Union are discouraged because there is a tariff (tax) of up to €2.60 per tonne on salt imported from outside the EU.

Imports, though, ultimately have a significant impact on the UK market. Producers in the salt market are interdependent. The actions of the number one producer in the market, British Salt, has an impact on sales of the number two producer, Salt

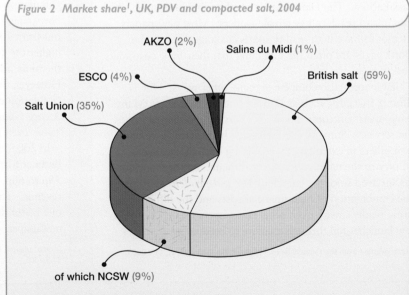

Figure 2 *Market share[1], UK, PDV and compacted salt, 2004*

AKZO (2%)
Salins du Midi (1%)
ESCO (4%)
British salt (59%)
Salt Union (35%)
of which NCSW (9%)

1. Figures add up to 101 per cent because of rounding.

Source: adapted from Competition Commission, *British Salt Ltd/New Cheshire Salt Works Ltd: A report on the acquisition by British Salt Ltd of New Cheshire Salt Works Ltd*, 2005.

Union. Economic theory would suggest that oligopolists will be able to earn abnormal profit because price competition would be limited. In the UK salt market, the ability of the two main salt producers to push up prices is limited by the price of imports. Significant rises in the price of salt by the two main UK producers would lead to loss of market share and a substantial rise in imports. The current prices charged are just low enough to keep out nearly all imports and allow British Salt and Salt Union to earn at least normal profit.

The takeover of NCSW by British Salt illustrates the problems that UK salt producers currently face. The owners of NCSW had decided to close the company down by 2006 because rising energy and other costs would have made their single plant in Cheshire unprofitable given that they would not have been able to pass on these higher costs to customers in higher prices. British Salt bought NCSW because it wanted to acquire NCSW's customers. After the acquisition, NCSW's Cheshire plant was closed as planned and production transferred to British Salt's plant at Middlewich. This had considerable spare capacity. By moving production to Middlewich, British Salt was able to move down its short run average cost curve, cutting short run average costs. This should have raised its profitability.

The UK salt production industry can therefore be seen as oligopolistic. Barriers to entry are high, but not high enough to allow existing producers to earn substantial abnormal profits. Producers have limited ability to increase prices in response, say, to increases in costs. Price rigidity is therefore a feature of this market.

DataQuestion

The national newspaper market

The national newspapers compete fiercely with one another for sales. Each newspaper attempts to appeal to a core set of readers through the stories they run, the editorial slant and how the newspaper is presented. For example, both *The Guardian* and *The Independent* appeal to well educated centre and left-leaning readers. *The Times* and *The Daily Telegraph* appeal to better educated right wing readers. *The Sun* is a working class Tory newspaper. The *Daily Mirror* is working class Labour. The *Daily Mail* is a right wing newspaper which attempts to reach out to female readers. Most newspapers attempt to have high quality sports coverage because the sports pages are often the first thing that their male customers read.

Newspapers also compete in many other ways. One is offering free gifts, such as DVDs or tickets to events. Many newspapers run competitions or offers for discounted goods and services. Some newspapers have been more successful than others in extending their offering onto the Internet.

Entry to the national market is difficult. No new entrant has survived since the launch of *The Independent* in 1986. The combination of high financial costs and the difficulty of luring readers away from other newspapers means that most new launches fail through a failure to become profitable.

Source: adapted from the *Financial Times*, 13.9.2005; *The Sunday Times*, 11.9.2005.

In the 1990s, there was a fierce price war amongst newspapers. News International, owners of *The Sun* and *The Times*, slashed the cover price of its newspapers to gain market share. With *The Times*, it was successful in significantly increasing circulation, partly at the expense of *The Independent* which did not have the financial resources to cut its price and *The Daily Telegraph*. Circulation is important because most of a newspaper's revenues come not from the cover price but from advertising. The higher the circulation, the higher the advertising prices that can be charged and the more advertising is attracted to the newspaper. However, there is a limit to how much extra circulation can be gained from cutting cover prices. A core *Guardian* reader will not transfer to *The Times* even if it is one quarter of the price.

In 2005, as *The Guardian* launched its new Berliner format, *The Times* lifted its cover price from 55p to 60p, netting itself an extra £8 million in revenue. This was a recognition that price is only one factor amongst many which attract readers to a newspaper.

Source: adapted from the *Financial Times*, 13.9.2005; *The Sunday Times*, 11.9.2005.

The Guardian is taking a big gamble. It has invested £80 million in three new printing presses at two sites in east London and Manchester. The presses are needed to produce a new look newspaper. For 184 years, the paper was printed in broadsheet format, the same size as, say, the *Financial Times*. From today, it will be printed in the 'Berliner' format, a smaller size used by the German newspaper, the *Berliner*.

The Guardian is not the first newspaper recently to change size. *The Independent* and then *The Times* moved to tabloid size in 2003 and 2004. When *The Independent* went tabloid (or 'compact'), it was a tactic to make itself more popular to readers. It gambled that some potential customers were finding the broadsheet format of quality newspapers too unwieldy to read. Arguably, it was right: today, sales are up by 40 000 compared with the last day of its appearance in broadsheet format. *The Times* is up by 60 000 since it went compact.

The Guardian is hoping to lift its sales. It needs to

because its sales have fallen 6.3 per cent over the past year, to a level not seen since 1978.

Source: adapted from the *Financial Times*, 13.9.2005; *The Sunday Times*, 11.9.2005.

Figure 3 National newspapers[1]: average circulation April 2005 compared to November 2007

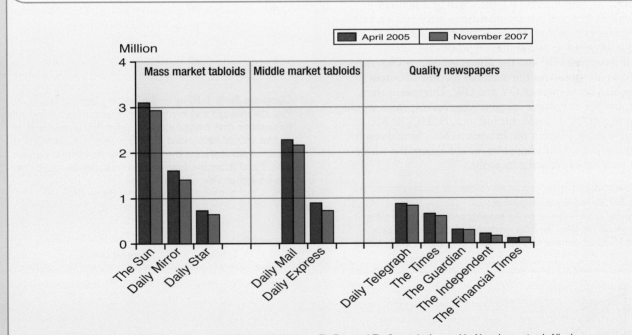

1. The *Daily Express* and the *Daily Star* are both owned by Express Newspapers. *The Times* and *The Sun* are both owned by News International. All other newspapers are owned independently.

Source: adapted from www.abc.org.uk.

1. **Explain the market characteristics of the UK national daily newspaper market.**

2. **Using the theory of oligopoly, discuss why *The Guardian* chose to launch a new design of paper in 2005.**

48 The kinked demand curve theory of oligopoly

Summary

1. The neo-classical kinked demand curve model assumes that a firm will reduce its price if a competitor starts a price war, but will leave price unchanged if a competitor raises its price.

3.3.3

The neo-classical kinked demand curve model

One model of oligopoly was developed in the late 1930s by Paul Sweezy in the USA and R Hall and C Hitch in the UK. Any theory of oligopoly must make an assumption about how one firm will react to the actions of another firm. The kinked demand curve model assumes that there will be an asymmetrical reaction to a change in price by one firm. If the firm increases its price, other firms will not react. The firm which has increased its price will then lose market share. On the other hand, if it reduces its price its competitors will reduce price too in order to prevent an erosion of their market share. The firm will gain little extra demand as a result. The demand curve therefore facing a firm is more elastic for a price rise than for a price fall.

This is shown in Figure 1. Price is initially at OP. If the firm increases price to OR it will lose far more sales than it would gain if it reduced price by an equal amount. This occurs because of the different reactions to price increases and decreases by competitors. Therefore the demand curve is kinked around the original price. If the demand curve (i.e. the average revenue curve) is kinked, then this produces a discontinuous marginal revenue curve. At output level OQ, there will be a jump in marginal revenue between a small increase in price and a small decrease in price (an example of this is given in Question 1).

The firm is assumed to be a short run profit maximiser. Therefore if the price is OP and the firm is producing OQ, the marginal cost curve must cut the marginal revenue at output OQ, somewhere between price OV and OW. This means that there are a number of possible marginal cost curves which would produce a price of OP. It could, for instance, be MC_1 or MC_2. Assume that it is MC_1 then a rise in costs to MC_2 would result in no change in price. The oligopolist would absorb the whole of the cost increase by reducing its profit.

This theory provides one explanation of why prices in oligopoly are relatively stable. Changes in costs which shift the marginal cost curve will not change either the profit maximising level of output or the profit maximising price.

Question 1

Table 1
£

Output	Average revenue	Total revenue	Marginal revenue
1	49	49	
			45
2	47		
3	45		
3	45		
			25
4	40		
5	35		
6	30		

(a) Complete Table 1, filling in the missing figures.
(b) Plot the average and marginal revenue curves on a graph. Remember that marginal revenue for the second unit of output should be plotted at output level 1½, the third at 2½, etc. Also mark on the graph a vertical line at output level 3 and draw the marginal revenue curves up to the line on either side of it as in Figure 1.
(c) Why is the marginal revenue curve discontinuous?
(d)

Table 2

Output	Marginal cost (£)
	40
2	
	32
3	
	36
4	

Draw the marginal cost curve in Table 2 onto your graph.

(e) Why is the firm in equilibrium at an output of 3 units?
(f) Explain what would happen to equilibrium output and price if marginal cost (i) rose by £4 and (ii) fell by £2 at every level of output.

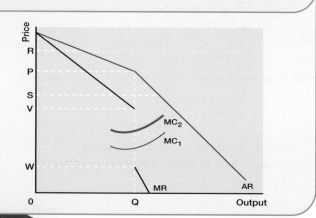

Figure 1 The kinked demand curve model
With a demand curve kinked round the prevailing price OP, a rise or fall in marginal cost will not affect the profit maximising level of output or price. Hence this model can be used to explain relative price stability in oligopolistic markets.

Game theory

The kinked demand curve theory can be seen as a simple example of game theory applied to oligopoly. One firm, Firm A, has three strategies, to keep its price the same, to raise price or to lower price. If it raises price or lowers its price, it will be worse off. This is because of how other firms will react. Only if it keeps price the same, will it be at least as well off as before.

All firms in the industry will be worse off if one firm lowers its price because their strategy will be to follow with their own price cuts. A **price war** is therefore damaging to all. However, if one firm raises prices, this represents an opportunity for other firms to gain market share. Their strategy will be to leave prices

the same in the hope of raising sales and profits.

Weaknesses in the theory

However, there is a number of weaknesses in the theory. First there is no explanation of how the original price, P, was arrived at. Second, the theory only deals with price competition and ignores the effects of non-price competition. Third, the model assumes a particular reaction by other firms to a change in price of a firm's product. It is unlikely that firms will react in exactly this way all the time. A much wider range of possible reactions needs to be explored.

Applied economics

Cardiff Bus

In 2007, the Office for Fair Trading, the government body responsible for making markets work well for consumers, issued a provisional ruling concerning Cardiff Bus. In 2004, a new bus company, 2 Travel, set up routes in Cardiff with fares lower than Cardiff Bus. Cardiff Bus responded in a way predicted by the kinked demand curve theory of oligopoly. It lowered its prices, introducing a 'no frills' service.

Both companies were interdependent. 2 Travel made a loss on its services because it failed to gained enough market share from Cardiff Bus. Cardiff Bus also made a loss because it lost market share to 2 Travel and was carrying passengers at lower prices than before. However,

Cardiff Bus was in a better position to survive these losses. 2 Travel withdrew its services in February 2005. Cardiff Bus responded by withdrawing its own 'no frills' services and increased its prices on the routes where it had been in competition with 2 Travel.

The Office for Fair Trading accused Cardiff Bus of predatory pricing. This occurs when a company deliberately lowers its prices to drive a new entrant out of the market. Cardiff Bus responded by saying that it would vigorously defend its position and it did not believe that it had infringed competition law. It had merely responded to new competition by lowering prices without the intention of forcing 2 Travel to drop its services.

DataQuestion — Low-cost flights for Eastern Europe

Established airlines flying to Romania and Bulgaria are in for a big shock this year. A number of low-cost airlines have announced plans to set up routes to the two countries which, so far, have only been served by higher cost established airlines. For example, the best British Airways return fare from London to Bucharest is €240. But on 15 January, Wizz-Air, a Hungarian based operator, will launch the first low-cost direct flight between the two capital cities for around €150. Prices could well continue to fall as more competition arrives. easyJet, for example, is expected to open up services within the next 12 months.

Why the sudden flurry of competitive activity? Although Romania and Bulgaria became members of the European Union on 1 January 2004, there was no open access to their airports. Airlines had to secure landing rights from the government and the two governments limited competition to protect their national airlines. However, as from January 1 of this year, this barrier to entry has disappeared. Under EU law, any operator with a European Union air carrier licence no longer needs government permission to secure landing rights.

Source: adapted from the *Financial Times*, 5.1.2007.

1. Explain why the airline market for flights to and from Romania and Bulgaria might be described as oligopolistic.
2. Use the kinked demand curve theory to explain why an established carrier like British Airways might reduce its fares in response to the entry of low-cost carriers to its

   Eastern European markets.
3. Discuss whether the kinked demand curve theory might explain the market for air travel between London and Romania once a number of low-cost carriers have entered the market.

49 Game theory

Summary

1. Game theory explores the reactions of one player to changes in strategy by another player.
2. Dominant strategies exist where a single strategy is best for a player irrespective of what strategy the other player adopts.
3. In Nash equilibrium, neither player is able to improve their position given the choice of the other player.
4. Oligopoly is characterised by price stability. One explanation of this is that changing price is a very risky strategy for one firm because it will provoke a reaction by other firms.
5. Non-price competition, including branding, is common in oligopolistic markets. It is a less risky strategy than price competition.
6. Collusion enables oligopolistic firms to move to their most profitable output level.
7. The large number of different market strategies available to oligopolistic firms may result in permanent disequilibrium in the market.

Game theory

Central to any understanding of oligopoly is interdependence. The actions of one large firm in the industry will directly affect all other firms in the industry. It is therefore essential, in any theory of oligopoly, to understand the nature and consequences of those reactions.

One very powerful tool for analysing oligopolistic behaviour is GAME THEORY. It has a wide variety of applications, from playing cards through to nuclear deterrence. In a game the players are interdependent. The best move for a player depends upon how the other players will react.

Dominant strategies

Consider Table 1 which shows a PAYOFF MATRIX. There are just two firms in the industry (it is a DUOPOLY). Each firm has two strategies. It can either raise the price of its product or leave it unchanged. The figures in the box represent the payoffs from the interaction of strategies by the two firms. In this case, they are the change in profits for firm A (in blue) and firm B (in red) which would result from each strategy.

Which strategy should firm A use? Firm A is better off raising price whatever strategy firm B chooses to adopt.

- If firm B chooses to raise its price, firm A will make an extra £5 million if it raises its price too, compared to just £2 million extra profit if it left prices the same.
- If firm B chooses to leave its price the same, firm A could make an extra £3 million profit by raising its price. If it leaves its price the same, and firm B does the same, it makes no extra profit at all.

Which strategy should firm B use? Firm B would equally choose to raise its price whatever strategy firm A adopted.

- It could earn either £5 million or £1 million in extra profit if it raised price.
- If it left price unchanged, the corresponding amounts would be £3 million and £0 depending on firm A's strategy.

So both firms have DOMINANT STRATEGIES. A dominant strategy is one where a single strategy is best for a player irrespective of what strategy the other player adopts. The interaction of these dominant strategies in

Figure 1 leads to an equilibrium. It is in both firms' best interests to raise price, with a payoff which is shown in the top left hand box of Table 1. It is an equilibrium because neither firm has an incentive to reconsider its decision. Both are better off than before and neither could move to another box where they would be even better off.

Table 1 Dominant strategies

		Firm B	
		Raise price	Leave price unchanged
Firm A	Raise price	+£5m/+£5m	+£3m/+£3m
	Leave price unchanged	+£2m/+£1m	£0/£0

Nash equilibrium

Dominant strategy equilibria don't occur that often. In most games, the best strategy for one firm depends on what strategy the other firm adopts. Consider Table 2. This shows two firms with two strategies: to lower price or to leave price the same.

Assume that firm B chooses to lower its price. What would be the best strategy for firm A? If it lowers its price too, it will increase its profits by £5 million. However, if it keeps its price the same, it will see a fall in profit of £2 million. Therefore, the best strategy for firm A, if firm B chooses to lower its price, is to lower its price too.

What is the best strategy for firm B if firm A chooses to lower its price? Lowering its price too would see an increase in profits of £2 million. Whilst leaving price unchanged would see a fall in profits of £1 million. Therefore, firm B's optimum strategy is to lower its price.

In Table 2, both firms lowering their prices is a NASH EQUILIBRIUM, named after John Nash, a US mathematician who formulated this proposition in 1951. In a Nash equilibrium, neither player is able to improve their position given the choice of the other player. It is an equilibrium because neither player has an incentive to change their choice strategy given the choice of strategy of the other player.

However, in a payoff matrix there may be more than one Nash equilibrium. In Table 2, both firms leaving their price unchanged is a Nash equilibrium. If firm A leaves its price unchanged, firm B would be worse off if it lowered its price. Equally, firm A would be worse off by lowering price if firm B's chosen strategy was to leave price unchanged. Equally, in a payoff matrix there may be no Nash equilibria if firms stick to a single choice (known as a **pure strategy**). However, John Nash showed that every game had a Nash equilibrium if players did not always use the same strategy (they adopted a **mixed strategy**). Therefore a firm might sometimes lower its price and sometimes keep its price the same.

Table 2 *Nash equilibrium*

		Firm B	
		Lower price	Leave price unchanged
Firm A	Lower price	+£5m/+£2m	-£1m/-£1m
	Leave price unchanged	-£2m/-£1m	£0/£0

Price stability

One commonly observed feature of oligopoly is price stability. Firms maintain stable prices over a pricing season which may last from 6 months to several years. Price stability may be a rational strategy for oligopolists.

If an oligopolistic firm raises price, it risks losing market share if its competitors do not follow suit. Lower market share could lead to lower profits and, if investment and research and development budgets are cut, a reduced ability to compete in the long run.

If it lowers its price, it risks starting a price war. It could be that the size of the market will expand as consumers buy more of the industry's products. However, the benefits in the form of larger sales could well be more than offset by losses in revenue due to lower prices. All firms in the industry could see sharp falls in profits as they battle it out. Eventually, prices will have to rise again to restore profitability and the firm which started the price war could have lost market share.

Therefore changing prices is a risky strategy. When prices do change, all firms tend to change their prices by the same percentage. For instance, a rise in the interest rate by one large building society tends to lead to a rise in all building society interest rates. A rise in petrol prices by one company is usually matched by the other petrol suppliers.

Game theory can be used to explain this. Consider Table 3. There are just two firms in the industry and each firm has two strategies. It can either raise the price of its product or leave it unchanged. The numbers in the payoff matrix show how profit will change if the two firms adopt particular strategies. Table 3 shows a particular type of game, a ZERO SUM GAME. In a zero sum game, the gains of one player are matched by equal and opposite losses for the other player. When gains and losses are added up, they always equal zero.

Firm A has no dominant strategy. If firm B raises its price, firm A would prefer to raise its price too because it can increase

profits by £10 million. However, if firm B leaves its price unchanged, firm A would prefer to leave its price unchanged too.

What strategy should firm A pursue? One rational strategy would be to minimise risk. This is called a **maximin** strategy. In this strategy, the firm aims to maximise the minimum gains it can get. If firm A raises its price, the worst case scenario is that firm B will leave its price unchanged. This will result in a loss of £2 million for firm A. If, instead, firm A chooses to leave its price unchanged, the worst that can happen is that it will see no change in profit. Therefore, minimising its risk, it will choose to leave its price unchanged.

Firm B will choose to leave its price unchanged too if it pursues a maximin strategy. If it raises price, its worst case scenario is that firm A raises its price too and it loses £10 million in profit. If it keeps its price the same, at worst it

Table 3 *A zero sum game which leads to price stability*

		Firm B	
		Raise price	Leave price unchanged
Firm A	Raise price	+£10m/-£10m	-£2m/+£2m
	Leave price unchanged	+£1m/-£1m	£0/£0

Table 4

		Firm B	
		Lower price	Leave price unchanged
Firm A	Lower price	-£10m/-£20m	+£5m/-£27m
	Leave price unchanged	-£13m/+£5m	0

Question 1

The major building societies tend to move their saving and mortgage interest rates at the same time, usually following a change in bank base rates, the rate of interest around which banks structure their saving and borrowing rates. Occasionally, building societies have responded to government concern and not raised interest rates to mortgage borrowers when banks have increased their rates. The result has been a flow of funds from building societies to banks as savers have switched their money to take advantage of higher interest rates. Equally, at such times, building societies have tended to increase their share of the mortgage market at the expense of the banks. Before too long, the building societies have been forced to raise their interest rates in order to attract back the savings to meet the demand for mortgage loans.

Use game theory to explain why building societies tend to move their interest rates in line with each other and with those of the banks.

will see no change in profit.

Both firms, therefore, pursuing a maximin strategy, will leave their price unchanged. This is an equilibrium solution because there is no incentive for either of the firms to change their strategy. It is a Nash equilibrium position because neither firm is able to improve its position given the choice of the other player.

Now consider Table 4 which shows a game where two firms competing against other have a choice between cutting their prices and leaving them the same.

It is clear from the table that it is in both firms' interests to leave prices unchanged. If one firm decides to lower its price in order to gain market share, the other firm would suffer a large drop in profits. For instance, firm A would lose £13 million in profits if it left its price unchanged when firm B lowered its price. It would prefer to lower its price too and limit the loss in profits to £10 million. The same is true for firm B. If it dropped its price and firm A did not react, it would increase its profit. However, if firm A reacted by dropping its price too, the resulting price war would have disastrous consequences for both sides.

Many economists have argued that firms avoid risk (they are said to be 'risk averse'). Competition is always risky and strategies which aim to reduce market share and profits of competitors especially so. 'The best of all monopoly profits is a quiet life', argued J R Hicks (1935).

Non-price competition

A characteristic of oligopoly is the lack of price competition. Price wars can be very damaging for firms in an oligopolistic industry. Therefore firms choose to compete in other ways apart from price. An advertising campaign, for instance, by firm A is likely to be limited in cost and may increase market share. Other firms in the industry may react by launching their own advertising campaign, but there is a reasonable chance that the advertising campaign of the competitors may not be as good, plus the fact that advertising may expand the market as a whole. The reward for firm A will be a small increase in market share and, presumably, profits. Other firms, however, will not be hit too hard and so will not take drastic measures which might affect the profitability of all firms in the industry. On the other hand, firm A's campaign may back-fire if another firm launches a more successful advertising campaign. However, the potential loss is unlikely to be very great.

This suggests that, in oligopoly, firms might not attempt to drive their main rivals out of the market. This would be an extremely risky strategy which might lead to themselves being the victim of such a move. Rather, oligopolists limit competition in order to limit the risks to their own market shares and profits.

Non-price competition is also a very powerful means of deterring potential competitors - firms which might enter the industry. This is discussed further below.

Branding

Interdependence limits the ability of oligopolistic firms to exploit markets to their own benefit. Ideally oligopolistic firms would like to turn themselves into monopolists with full control of their markets. One way of doing this is by the creation of strong brands. A strong brand has two major advantages for a producer.
- A strong brand has few good substitutes so far as the buyer is concerned. The firm is therefore able to charge a premium price (a relatively high price for the good) and earn monopoly profit on the good without seeing too great a fall in demand for it.

Table 5

		Firm B	
		Low price	High price
Firm A	Low price	£15m/£10m	£25m/£5m
	High price	£10m/£20m	£20m/£25m

Question 2

American comic books represent a small niche market in the much larger market for magazines in the UK. In 1994, three companies dominated this niche market. Marvel Comics, which publishes Spider-man, The Fantastic Four and The X-Men, held 40 per cent of the market. DC Comics, which publishes comics featuring Superman and Batman, held 30 per cent of the market. Finally, Image Comics, publishers of Spawn and Youngblood, held 24 per cent of the market.

There is no real price competition. Prices of comics are fixed in comparison with prices of rival comics. Instead, comics compete on the strength of their story lines and characters. Free gifts, special editions and graphic novels help keep existing customers loyal or attract new customers.

Until 1992, the market had been essentially a duopoly, with DC Comics and Marvel Comics carving up sales between them. Many others had tried to establish themselves, but lacked knowledge and money to create a range of comics which could compete with the two large companies. However, in 1992 a group of artists left Marvel Comics to set up the successful Image Comics. They were able to establish themselves for two reasons. The Image artists had gained considerable reputations through their work at Marvel. This 'core group' of artists attracted a large number of consumers to purchase the new Image comics and was able to create new characters which instantly appealed to consumers. Heavy promotion of the products by the company was also an important factor in generating sales.

At the turn of the 21st century the picture was much the same as in 1994. Marvel Comics and DC Comics between them held 77 per cent of the market. Image Comics had a 13 per cent market share. However, by 2005 the market had become almost totally dominated by Marvel and DC Comics.

(a) How do American comic book publishers establish a brand image?
(b) Use game theory to suggest why Marvel Comics and DC did not engage in a price war to drive Image Comics out of the market in 1992 and 1993.
(c) Why might game theory suggest that it is worthwhile to a company to pay key employees more than the going rate for the job?

- It is very difficult for competitors to challenge the supremacy of the brand. For instance, Kellogg's Corn Flakes, Mars Bars, and Jaguar cars all have stable demands at premium prices in the short run. In the long run, tastes may change or new strong brands may appear. However, even then old brands, such as Ovaltine, Horlicks or Ambrosia rice pudding may continue to be highly profitable to their owners, still commanding premium prices at lower sales volumes but with little or no development costs.

Strong brands are difficult to create, which is why many firms prefer to take over other companies and their brands at very high prices rather than attempt to establish new brands. To establish a new brand, a company usually has to produce an innovative product (innovative could mean anything from changing the colour or smell of a product to a radically new technological breakthrough) and then market it effectively. The failure rate of new brands in some markets such as food and confectionery can be as high as nearly 100 per cent. With this in mind, it is hardly surprising that a firm would be prepared to pay millions of pounds for an established brand rather than employ research workers to devise new products.

Collusion

Another way in which an oligopolist can turn itself into a monopoly is by colluding with other firms. In markets which are unregulated by government, there is a strong tendency for firms to collude (i.e. to join together and act as if they were one firm). Cartels and anti-competitive practices were the norm in British manufacturing industry before such practices were made illegal in the 1950s.

Game theory can help us understand why this is the case. Consider Table 5. The figures show the profits to be gained by two firms, A and B, depending upon whether they adopt a high or low price strategy. Firm A, whose profit figures are in blue, would like to adopt a low price strategy in opposition to a high price strategy by its rival. That would result in profits of £25 million, but it can see that firm B would not allow such a situation because its profits would only be £5 million. However, a high price strategy for firm A would be worse because it would face making the lowest possible profit, £10 million, should firm B choose to adopt a low price strategy. Therefore firm A will choose a low price strategy, hoping that firm B will adopt a high price strategy, but more realistically knowing that it too will adopt a low price strategy. Firm A will then make a profit of £15 million - the highest minimum profit it can make.

Firm B will adopt a low price strategy too. Although it stands to gain £25 million in profit by a high price strategy, if firm A too goes for a high price stategy, it risks only making £5 million if firm A were to go for a low price. Therefore it will maximise its minimum profit of £10 million and go for a low price strategy.

The result is that both firms adopt low price strategies because they fear the reactions of their competitor. They would have been considerably better off if they had both adopted high price strategies. The only way to get into the high price 'box' is for the two firms to come to some form of understanding that they will not adopt low price strategies (i.e. they must collude).

The figures shown in Table 3 are an example of what is often called the PRISONERS' DILEMMA. Substitute profits for prison sentences and prices for pleading guilty or not guilty. If both prisoners kept apart in different cells plead not guilty, then they will be released through lack of evidence. However, if one prisoner pleads guilty, then he will get a reduced sentence and the other will get a heavier sentence. If both plead guilty they will get heavy sentences. If they could get together (i.e. collude) they would choose to plead not guilty. But in isolation they cannot trust the other prisoner, so each chooses to plead guilty and they both suffer.

Cartels are usually unstable because it would normally be in the interests of one of the players to attempt to cheat on any agreement made. In Table 5, assume that both firms collude and agree to charge a high price. For Firm B, both firms charging high prices is the best outcome it could obtain with an increase in profits of £25 million. However, for firm A, it would be better if it could cut its prices so long as firm B kept its prices high. Cutting prices would increase its sales and market share. Table 5 implies that firm A could increase profits from £20 million to £25 million by selling more at a lower price. There are various ways it could 'cheat'. It could offer secret discounts to customers. It could openly cut prices but pretend that these discounts were the exception rather than the norm.

The possibility of cheating means that those players which stand to lose most from cheating must be able to enforce the rules agreed by the cartel. For example, OPEC in the 1980s and 1990s was beset by some countries cheating on their agreements. High prices were enforced by agreed production quotas. Countries negotiated a maximum level of production for their oil industry. However some countries regularly produced more than their maximum. This lowered the world price of oil, but the individual cheating country was still better off because profits were higher, selling more at a slightly lower price than less at a higher price. In 1986, Saudi Arabia, which had tended to agree to production cuts at OPEC meetings to underpin the price of oil, suddenly increased its production. Prices collapsed and all OPEC members were worse off. Saudi Arabia's strategy was to punish the cheating countries in OPEC. It subsequently cut back its production to raise oil prices, but it had shown what could happen to cheats if they refused to stick to the rules of the cartel. From 1986, other OPEC members saw that the actions of Saudi Arabia posed a CREDIBLE THREAT. This is a course of action that other players in a game believe will be taken by another player if they persist in pursuing strategies which are against that player's interests.

Multi-firm, multi-strategy options

So far, only two-firm, two-option situations have been discussed. In reality there are likely to be more than two firms in the market, each with more than two policy options. For instance, a six policy zero-sum game for two firms is shown in Table 6. There are 36 (6x6) different possible solutions to this game. If there were 3 firms in the industry, the number of possible solutions would rise to 216 (6x6x6).

Game theory predicts, then, that there is a large number of different possible outcomes in an oligopolistic setting. Given this very large number, it is perhaps not surprising that economic theory has found it difficult to provide one unified model which would explain price and output decisions in the industry.

Question 3

In 2005, fifty of Britain's top fee paying schools were astonished to receive notification from the Office of Fair Trading (OFT) that they were in breach of competition law and faced fines possibly totalling millions of pounds. Schools from Ampleforth College, Eton College, Millfield School and Westminster College to Worth School had, from 1997 on, taken part in a survey, known as the 'Sevenoaks Survey'. Between February and June each year, the schools concerned gave details of their intended fee increases and fee levels for the academic year beginning in September. Sevenoaks School then collated that information and circulated it, in the form of tables, to the schools concerned. The information in the tables was updated and circulated between four and six times each year as schools developed their fee increase proposals in the course of their annual budgetary processes. The Office for Fair Trading deemed that 'this regular and systematic exchange of confidential information as to intended fee increases was anti-competitive and resulted in parents being charged higher fees than would otherwise have been the case'.

Parents sending their children to these fee paying public schools are unlikely to make choices on the basis of a difference of a few hundred pounds in school fees when yearly fees for boarders now typically exceed £20 000. However, schools often justify fee increases by pointing out that similar schools are charging £X more this year. With demand highly price inelastic, not to increase fees by at least the average fee increase for similar schools is to lose revenue unnecessarily.

Source: adapted from www.oft.gov.uk.

Use game theory to suggest why the 50 schools found it in their interest to exchange information about their proposed level of fees for the forthcoming academic year. In your answer, compare a situation where a school increased its fees by the average for other schools and one where it increased its fees by less than the average.

Table 6, A zero sum game with six different strategies

			Firm B					
			Price			Advertising expenditure		
		Raise	Lower	Leave unchanged	Raise	Lower	Leave unchanged
Firm A	Price	Raise	£10m	-£5m	-£10m	£2m	-£1m	-£2m
		Lower	£2m	-£1m	-£4m	-£1m	£2m	£1m
		Leave unchanged	£3m	-£5m	0	£2m	-£4m	0
	Adv. exp.	Raise	-£1m	£7m	£5m	£3m	-£5m	-£1m
		Lower	£2m	-£3m	-£5m	£4m	-£2m	-£1m
		Leave unchanged	£2m	-£2m	0	£3m	-£1m	0

Key terms

Credible threat - a course of action that other players in a game believe will be taken by another player if they persist in pursuing strategies which are against that player's interests.
Dominant strategy - one where a single strategy is best for a player irrespective of what strategy the other player adopts.
Duopoly - an industry where there are only two firms.
Game theory - the analysis of situations in which players are interdependent.
Nash equilibrium - in game theory, where neither player is able to improve their position given the choice of the other player; it is an equilibrium because neither player has an incentive to change their choice of strategy given the choice of strategy of the other player.
Payoff matrix - in game theory, shows the outcomes of a game for the players given different possible strategies.
Prisoners' dilemma - a game where, given that neither player knows the strategy of the other player, the optimum strategy for each player leads to a worse situation than if they had known the strategy of the other player and been able to co-operate and co-ordinate their strategies.
Zero sum game - a game in which the gain of one player is exactly offset by the loss by other players.

Applied economics

PC operating systems

90 per cent of personal computers today use an operating system produced by Microsoft. The company's near monopoly on operating systems was the result of several games played out in the 1970s and 1980s.

In the 1970s, the world's dominant computer manufacturing company at the time, IBM, became concerned that its traditional market in large main frame computers was about to come under threat from revolutionary small machines called personal computers. It decided to manufacture its own personal computer but needed a software operating system to make it work. Rather than produce the operating system itself, IBM decided to buy MSDos, an existing operating system 'off the shelf' sold to IBM by Bill Gates, founder of Microsoft.

The contract between IBM and Microsoft allowed Microsoft to licence MSDos to any computer manufacturer. Over the next ten years, a number of computer manufacturers launched their own PCs with MSDos. These different computers could talk to each other. Software which worked on one MSDos machine worked on other MSDos machines, even if they were produced by different manufacturers. In retrospect, IBM should probably have insisted on retaining control of MSDos. As it was, MSDos became extremely profitable whilst IBM struggled to make profits from selling its PCs.

In 1984, Apple, founded by two students who created the world's first personal computer in 1976, launched a new revolutionary operating system named Macintosh. This operating system looked and worked like the operating systems we have today, with a desktop display and navigation via a mouse rather than simply a keyboard. Apple and Microsoft were now engaged in a game which would eventually control billions of pounds of revenues per year. Apple, like IBM, arguably played the game poorly. It thought it could persuade PC users to abandon other companies and buy both their hardware - the computer - and their software - the Macintosh operating system - from them. They charged a premium price for the package and initially made large profits by winning a small share of the market. However, Apple's prices were too high, and customers valued the ability to share software between different machines using MSDos. Apple crucially refused to licence its operating system to other computer manufacturers. Microsoft meanwhile worked hard on producing something which would have some of the ease of use of the Macintosh system. In 1985, it launched Windows version 1.0 which was a crude development of MSDos. It wasn't until 1990 when it launched Windows 3.0, that it came up which something which proved a hit with customers and could rival the Macintosh system. Apple in the 1980s never reached the critical mass of sales needed for Macintosh to become the standard world wide operating system. The mistake it made, just like IBM before it, was that it failed to recognise that the highest profits would be made not in manufacturing computers but in licensing an operating system which would become a universal standard.

Today, Microsoft doesn't have to worry about competition from Apple in computer operating systems. However, a new game is being played out between Microsoft and Linux. The Linux operating system is open source software, which means that it is free to the user. In contrast, Windows is expensive, retailing at around £100 for a personal user. Linux was first developed in the 1990s by Linus Torvalds, a Finnish university student. Since then, a whole variety of free software has developed around the Linux system including word processing packages. However, Linux is not totally free. There is a cost to the user in installing and getting to know how to use the system. For businesses, this involves extensive retraining of staff.

Microsoft could respond to the Linux threat by cutting its prices. However, it would probably need a substantial price cut to have much effect on market share. Say Microsoft could maintain its present prices and retain 80 per cent rather than its current 90 per cent of the market. The alternative is to cut prices in half and retain 89 per cent. For Microsoft, the strategy is clear: it is far more profitable to maintain prices and lose a little market share since the marginal cost of production is virtually zero. For Linux, it can't alter its strategy because Linux is not owned by any profit making body and users can only use it if they agree to it being free. In the PC market, Microsoft is probably fairly safe. However, Linux could prevent it from monopolising associated markets. Linux rather than Microsoft, for example, is being used by Sony in its PlayStation 3 video game console. In mobile phones, it forms the backbone for the Symbion OS software. On the net, Wikipedia, the free online encyclopaedia, uses Linux rather than Microsoft. Outside the PC market, any company developing a new product which needs an operating system is wary of using Microsoft because it has seen how Microsoft has exploited its monopoly in the PC market. Perhaps if Microsoft had not been such an aggressive player in the computer operating systems market, it might have been much more successful at entering other markets. Monopoly profits made in computers has perhaps lost Microsoft profits in related areas which will be the growth areas of the future.

London newspapers

Do you inflict pain on yourself right now to sustain your strength in the long term? Or do you continue to enjoy the good life for as long as possible, accepting that somebody else will almost certainly inflict far greater pain at some moment in the future? That is the question the *Evening Standard*, and its owner Associated Newspapers, has been facing up to as it decides how best to deal with the threat of competition to its near-monopoly position among London's newspapers.

On the face of it, the *Evening Standard* has been doing very badly for a long time. Like nearly all local evening newspapers in the UK, its circulation has been in decline. In 1960, 2.2 million copies of three rival newspapers including the *Evening Standard* were sold daily. In 1980, when the *Evening Standard* gained its monopoly, sales had fallen to 600 000. By 2004, this had fallen to around 340 000.

However, circulation is not everything. Whilst the number of copies sold has continued to fall, advertising revenue has increased. Evening paper revenues across the country have fallen by 19 per cent over the past ten years despite increases in the price of newspapers. On the other hand, revenues from advertising have increased 34 per cent in real terms over the same period. Despite falling sales, newspapers are more profitable than ever with an average three quarters of revenue coming from advertising and just one quarter from the cover price.

In London, the *Evening Standard* is fairly safe from competition from a new entrant wanting to charge readers for its product. Likely circulation and advertising revenue would be too small to cover costs. However, it is vulnerable to a free newspaper entrant. In 2000, Associated Newspapers launched *Metro*, a free newspaper distributed via London's Underground network. It did this as a pre-emptive strike against any other company wishing to launch a free London newspaper and in particular against a Swedish company which has successfully launched free newspapers in many of the world's capital cities. *Metro* costs money to produce and distribute. It doesn't raise any revenues from cover prices, but, all importantly, it does generate advertising revenues. What is more, some *Metro* readers, particularly younger readers in their 20s, wouldn't have bought an *Evening*

Standard anyway. Therefore advertisers can reach audiences which the *Evening Standard* cannot, and are prepared to pay for this.

In 2004, Associated Newspapers launched Standard Lite, renamed in 2006 as *London Lite*. This was another free newspaper, distributed at lunchtimes from the same central London newsstands that sell early editions of the *Evening Standard*. *London Lite* is produced by the staff of the *Evening Standard*, so cutting production costs. *Standard Lite* was only available at lunch times to prevent sales of the *Evening Standard* to homeward bound commuters falling. It was also there to create another barrier to entry for any other newspaper group thinking of launching a free paper into this market. However, in September 2006, News International, the newspaper group which owns the *Sun* and *The Times*, launched its own free newspaper, *thelondonpaper*. This was available in the afternoon and evening. Associated Newspapers was forced to respond by making London Lite available at the same times. *London Lite* was therefore being given away free at the same time as readers were paying to buy the *Evening Standard*.

By the end of 2007, both *London Lite* and *thelondonpaper* were making a loss. Analysts were arguing that there simply wasn't enough advertising revenue to fund two free London evening newspapers. The question was then which newspaper would survive the game. Steve Auckland, managing director of Associated's free newspapers division claimed that News International was facing the bigger losses. However, they were prepared to make the losses because their goal was to drive the *Evening Standard* and its free newspaper offshoots out of the market. 'It has been open about saying that it is attacking the Standard. It thinks *thelondonpaper* can bring it down'. News International denies this. Ian Clark, general manager of News International Free Newspapers, said 'Our criterion for success is to have a profitable newspaper. It is not about killing the Standard. Anything we do is likely to have an impact on one of the Associated titles, whether it is the Standard, Metro or Lite.'

Source: adapted from the *Financial Times*, 21.12.2004; 'End of the Standard?', *Prospect Magazine*, Issue 108 March 2005; *The Independent* 16.9.2007.

---

1. Use game theory to suggest why Associated Newspapers should be running both *Metro* and *London Lite* when it already publishes the long established *Evening Standard*.

2. Use game theory to suggest why Associated Newspapers might consider temporarily lowering the price of the *Evening Standard* if a new entrant came into the market with a newspaper for which customers had to pay.

Summary

1. In a contestable market, there are one or a number of firms which profit maximise. The key assumption is that barriers to entry to the industry are relatively low, as is the cost of exit from the industry.
2. Firms in a contestable market will only earn normal profit in the long run. If they earn abnormal profit in the short run, then new firms will enter the industry and drive prices and profits down.
3. The existence of potential entrants to the industry will tend to keep profits to their normal level even in the short run because existing firms will want to deter new entrants from coming into the market.
4. Contestable markets are both productively and allocatively efficient in the long run and are likely to be efficient in the short run as well.
5. It is not necessarily possible to predict the exact output of an individual firm in a contestable market if average cost curves are L shaped.

Contestable market theory vs neo-classical theory

Many, if not most, markets in the UK and in other industrialised economies are dominated by a few producers. The **neo-classical theory of oligopoly** assumes that oligopolistic markets feature **high barriers to entry**. However, there is also evidence to suggest that many oligopolistic markets have low barriers to entry. Therefore, firms in the industry are likely to behave in a different way from that predicted by neo-classical theory. The theory of contestable markets explores the implications of low barrier to entry markets.

Assumptions

The theory of contestable markets makes a number of assumptions.
- The number of firms in the industry may vary from one (a monopolist) having complete control of the market, to many, with no single firm having a significant share of the market.
- In a CONTESTABLE MARKET, there is both freedom of entry to and exit from the market. This is a key assumption of the model. Its implications are discussed below.
- Firms compete with each other and do not collude to fix prices.
- Firms are short run profit maximisers, producing where MC = MR.
- Firms may produce homogeneous goods or they may produce branded goods.
- There is perfect knowledge in the industry.

Normal and abnormal profit

The theory of contestable markets shows that in a contestable market:
- abnormal profits can be earned in the short run;
- only normal profit can be earned in the long run.

Assume that firms in a contestable market were making abnormal profit in the short run. Then new firms would be attracted into the industry by the abnormal profit. Supply would increase and prices would be driven down to the point where only normal profit was being made. This is the same argument that is used in the theory of perfect competition. Equally, if a

Question 1

To what extent do (a) clothing manufacturers and (b) clothing retailers operate in contestable markets?

firm is making losses, it will eventually leave the industry because in the long run it cannot operate as a loss making concern.

Entry to and exit from the industry

The ability of firms to enter and leave the industry is crucial in a contestable market and is not necessarily linked to the number of firms in the industry as in neo-classical theories of the firm. In neo-classical theory, low barriers to entry are linked with a large number of firms in an industry (perfect competition and monopolistic competition) whilst high barriers are linked with few firms in the industry (oligopoly or monopoly). Perfectly competitive and monopolistically competitive industries are contestable because an assumption of both these models is that there are low barriers toentry. But what of oligopolies and monopolies?

Some barriers to entry are natural (sometimes called **innocent entry barriers**). For instance, the industry may be a natural monopoly as in Network Rail. Alternatively, there may be very high capital entry costs to the industry, as in car manufacturing. Neo-classical theory would predict that firms in these industries would earn abnormal profits. Contestable market theory suggests that this depends to a large extent on the costs of **exit** from the industry.

For instance, assume that the natural monopolist is charging high prices and earning abnormal profit. A competitor then enters the industry and takes market share by charging lower prices. The natural monopolist reacts by cutting prices and the competitor leaves the industry, unable to compete on these new lower prices because its costs are too high. So long as the cost of leaving the industry is small, it still makes sense for the competitor to have earned profit in the short run by entering the industry. The costs of exit are the sunk costs of operating in the industry (i.e. the fixed costs of production which cannot be recovered if the firm leaves the industry). Money spent on advertising would be an example of a sunk cost. So too would capital equipment which had no alternative use. If the sunk costs are low - the firm has done little advertising and capital equipment has been leased on a short term basis, for instance - then the firm has lost little by entering and then leaving the industry. However, in the meantime, it has earned profit at the expense of the existing firm in the industry.

Some barriers to entry, however, are erected by existing firms in the industry. In the soap powder market, soap powder

producers spend large amounts of money advertising and branding their products. It may still be worth a firm entering this industry if the new entrant can charge a high enough price to cover the cost of entering and then possibly being forced to leave the industry. For instance, a firm might seek to earn £10m profit over 12 months. It is then forced to leave the industry because existing firms drive down prices or increase their advertising budget. If it earned £15m operating profit but lost £5m in leaving the industry, it would still be worthwhile for the firm to have entered and operated for a year.

Potential competition

In a contestable market, firms are able to enter and leave the industry at relatively little cost. So far, we have implied that, in the short run, existing firms in a contestable market may well be earning abnormal profit. However, contestable market theory suggests that, in practice, established firms in a contestable market earn only normal profit even in the short run (i.e. they behave as if they operated in a perfectly competitive market).

Question 3

Unilever, the multinational food and home care and personal care products group, with brands such as Dove soap, Persil washing powder, Flora margarine, Walls Ice Cream and Hellman's mayonnaise, is considering extending its range of cheaply priced 'value' brands. Traditionally Unilever has sold high priced, high profit margin, premium branded goods. However, over the past twenty years it has seen a steady erosion of market share to cheaper own label brands sold by supermarkets. The supermarkets source these products from specialist manufacturers who are typically barely able to earn normal profit given the low price paid to them by the supermarkets.

Unilever has already started introducing cheaper 'value' brands in its ice cream and bouillon ranges. It will want to ensure that increased sales and market share are not gained at the expense of an acceptable level of profit.

Source: adapted from the *Financial Times*, 10.2.2006.

(a) Why might (i) the barriers to entry and (ii) the barriers to exit to the 'value' segment of the food, home care and personal care markets be relatively low for Unilever?
(b) Explain, using the theory of contestable markets, why manufacturers producing own label products for supermarkets tend to earn low levels of profit.

Question 2

Explain whether the following would make it more likely or less likely that there would be potential entrants to an industry.
(a) The inability of firms in the industry to lease capital equipment for short periods of time.
(b) Very high second hand prices for capital equipment.
(c) Heavy advertising by existing firms in the industry.
(d) The existence of a natural monopolist which was highly inefficient and had high costs of production.
(e) Patents held by an existing firm in the industry which were crucial to the manufacture of the product.
(f) Government legislation which gave monopoly rights to a single producer in the industry.

Assume that a monopolist is the established firm in an industry. If it charges prices which would lead to it earning abnormal profit, then another firm may enter the industry charging lower prices. The new entrant will remain so long as the existing firm is earning abnormal profit, taking market share away from it and reducing its overall profits. To force the new entrant out, the monopolist would have to lower its prices. If it did this, and the new entrant left, and then the monopolist put up its prices again, all that would happen is that another firm would enter the industry. The only way to prevent potential competitors from adopting 'hit and run' tactics would be for the existing firm to price at a level where it only earned normal profit.

Hence, the ability of firms to earn abnormal profit is dependent on the barriers to entry and exit to the industry, not on the number of firms in the industry as neo-classical theory would imply. With low barriers, existing firms will price such that AR = AC (i.e. no abnormal profits are being earned) because they are afraid that otherwise hit-and-run entrants to the industry will come in and damage the market for them. They are also afraid that new entrants may stay on a permanent basis, reducing the market share of existing firms in the industry.

Efficiency

In the long run, firms (apart from those which are natural monopolies) in a contestable market will operate at the bottom of their average cost curve (i.e. at the **optimal level of output** where MC = AC). To understand why, assume that they didn't operate at this level. Then a new entrant would be able to establish itself, producing at the bottom of its average cost curve and charging at this level too, undercutting other firms' prices. Existing firms would then be forced to cut costs if they wanted to stay in the industry. Hence, firms in the long run in a contestable market must be **productively efficient**.

They must also be **allocatively efficient**. It has already been argued that firms in a contestable market can only earn normal profits in the long run (i.e. AR = AC). It has just been argued that firms will be productively efficient, producing where MC = AC. Hence, since AR = AC and MC = AC, firms must produce where AR = MC. This is the condition for allocative efficiency.

Stability of contestable markets

It is not always possible to predict the level of output of a firm in a contestable market. To understand why, assume that total market demand is 300 units at a price of £10 whilst lowest average cost for a single producer is £10 at an output of 100 units. Three firms will therefore find it profitable to produce in the industry, but each firm will only earn normal profits because AC=AR. With only normal profits being earned, the industry is in long run equilibrium because there is no incentive for other firms to enter.

However, a problem arises if market demand is, for instance, 300 units but the optimal level of production for each firm is 120 units. If there were only two firms in the industry, each firm would be producing under conditions of diseconomies of scale if each produced 150 units. There would be an incentive for a new firm to enter the industry and produce the optimum lowest cost level of output of 120 units. It would be difficult to believe that the two existing firms would not react by reducing output, moving towards the optimal level. However, if there were three firms each producing the same output of 100 units, then one firm could expand output and experience greater economies of scale. The other firms in the industry would then be likely to react by expanding their own output. Market price would fall below the minimum average cost of production and firms would make losses, sending back signals that firms should cut their production. There is in fact no level of output which would produce an equilibrium situation.

This is likely to be less of a problem if average cost curves are L-shaped rather than U-shaped. If demand is 300 units, and the minimum efficient scale of production is 120 units, then two firms could produce 150 units each at lowest cost. The theory does not, however, predict whether one firm will produce 120 units and the other 180, or both produce 150 units, or some other combination, subject to a minimum of 120 units.

Key terms

Contestable market - a market where there is freedom of entry to the industry and where costs of exit are low.

Applied economics

Transport markets

Public transport markets

The public transport market is a complex mix of different markets, some of whose services are close substitutes, whilst others have little in common with each other. In terms of traditional theories of the firm, they can relatively easily be categorised.

Rail travel The railway network in the UK consists, for the most part, of monopolies. Network Rail, which

and business travellers typically have a preference for which airline they use. Second, there is limited choice on any particular route. London to New York is quite competitive, but on many routes, there is only one operator. It may be possible to get around this by changing at another airport en route, but this is a significant deterrent to passengers who want the shortest journey time. Third, popular airports like Heathrow tend to be full during the day. In the UK, there is no tradable market in airport landing slots. Therefore, airlines setting up a new service at, say, Heathrow either have to close down another of their services or use another, less popular, airport.

Lastly, air routes have traditionally been highly regulated by governments to benefit their national carriers. For instance, airlines wishing to fly from the UK to the USA have to gain permission from both the UK and US authorities. Such permissions tend to be traded - the US authorities will only give permission for a UK airline to fly to the USA if a US airline is given new rights to fly a route to the UK. Many would like to see all governments adopt 'open skies' policies where any carrier could fly to any destination in the world. There is now an open skies policy within the EU for EU airlines, and similarly US carriers have the freedom to fly anywhere internally within the USA. Even open skies policies, though, do not necessarily make markets competitive. Some airports, such as London Heathrow, are already operating at 100 per cent capacity during the day and this limits new competition in the market.

owns the infrastructure, is a natural monopoly. The train operating companies, which run services across the infrastructure, have mostly been given monopoly rights by the government which granted them their franchises. However, they have limited ability to exploit that monopoly because they are subject to regulation and also because their franchises are limited in time. The train operating companies, not surprisingly, would like to see the regulatory price regime loosened and the length of franchises extended.

Bus travel The bus industry is more complex. Nationally, there are four main groups of bus companies which dominate local bus services: Stagecoach, Arriva, Go-Ahead and First. This could therefore be considered an oligopolistic industry. However, in many areas, only one of these bus companies offers services. It may or may not be in competition with smaller bus companies. On many routes, there is only one bus service and therefore the bus company offering it has a monopoly. The ability of bus companies to exploit this monopoly depends to some extent on agreements entered into with local authorities, which often subsidise what would otherwise be loss making routes. Where a subsidy is given, the local authority is likely to fix a price for fares in the operating contract.

Air travel There is a large number of airlines operating on routes within and out of the UK. However, the market is not perfectly competitive for a number of reasons. First, airlines offer a branded service

Shipping Freight shipping tends to be a perfectly competitive market. There is a large number of shipping companies offering services between different destinations. Passenger shipping tends to be either oligopolistic or a monopoly. For instance, there are only a few companies offering cross-Channel services, whilst there is only one company offering a service between the mainland and the Isle of Wight.

Contestability and public transport markets

Neo-classical theories of perfect competition, monopolistic competition, oligopoly and monopoly may provide poor explanations of the behaviour of transport industries if different assumptions are made about the contestability of a market.

The rail industry Network Rail is an example of a natural monopoly. Along the routes that Network Rail owns, no other competitor would want to or legally be allowed to enter the market.

The passenger transport rail market is equally uncontestable in the short term. The rail operators have bought monopoly franchises from the government. However, the market becomes contestable when the franchises come up for renewal. The existing operators have sought to make the market less contestable by applying pressure on the government to extend existing franchises in return for improvements in the service they currently offer. Typically, they try to link investment in new rolling stock with franchise extension. The government, so far, has resisted this pressure. As franchises near their end, though, it becomes increasingly difficult for a train operator to justify any long term investment. This could lead to underinvestment in the railways, leading to dynamic inefficiency. When franchises do come up for renewal, there are likely to be only a few firms interested in bidding for the renewal. These are likely to be the largest of the existing rail operators. To gain the franchise, they will have to offer to invest in the service whilst taking either the lowest subsidy or paying the government the highest price for the franchise. The bidders will also have to consider how they can exit the franchise if they fail to win the renewal bid next time around.

Bus and coach transport The bus and coach industries in the UK are deregulated. This means that any company can enter the industry and compete with existing companies. The costs of entry are relatively low. To buy a few old coaches or buses is relatively cheap. For this reason, most cities have at least one small operator on some routes competing against a much larger and more established operator. Equally, most areas of the country have a dominant company which provides most of the services.

One reason is that transport authorities, part of government, tend to subsidise many routes because otherwise bus companies would not operate them. The company which receives the subsidy tends to be the dominant operator. In the long distance coach travel market, every area has a number of firms offering coaches for hire. However, the market for scheduled long distance services is again dominated by a few firms which can market their services effectively and invest enough to provide comfortable coaches on which to travel. Overall, the bus and coach transport market is contestable and this tends to prevent existing firms in the market from making abnormal profit.

Air transport Over the past twenty years, the air transport market in Europe has become much more contestable. This is because individual governments have abandoned regulations which tended to favour their own national airlines at the expense of foreign airlines. As a result, there has been enormous growth in the number of budget no-frills airlines. In contrast, on international flights outside Europe, there has been less growth because non-European governments have tended to restrict flights from foreign airlines. The capital cost of entering the market is significant, but not so significant as to deter the new entrants which have established a presence in the market in recent years. Equally the cost of exit is relatively low. A new entrant, for example, is likely to lease planes rather than buy them. Costs then become mainly variable rather than fixed and hence sunk costs are low.

Shipping Shipping tends to be a contestable market because ship owners can move their ships around from route to route depending upon demand. In the passenger transport market, for instance, the opening of the Channel Tunnel led to a reduction in the number of ships on cross-Channel routes. These ships were put to work on other routes in Northern Europe.

The transatlantic business market

Two new services are about to be launched on the transatlantic route. Both are from US start ups in the airline industry and both will fly to and from Stansted near London in the UK. Eos will fly twice daily and Maxjet once daily from Stansted to New York's JFK airport. What is special about these launches is that the services will cater for business class passengers only.

The business class passenger market on transatlantic routes is highly lucrative. Last year, all of the profit made by British Airways came from transatlantic services.

Eos is going down the route of providing a superior product to both BA's Club World and Virgin Atlantic's Upper Class Business Suite. There will be just 48 seats on the Boeing 757s it has leased, compared to the 228 seats that would be in the aircraft if it were fitted out for economy class passengers. Each passenger will have a 'unique suite seat' including 78-inch fully flat beds, cashmere blankets, china crockery and a personal DVD player. Flat bed seats are a relatively recent innovation and mean that passengers

can convert their seats into a flat bed to sleep. The list price of a return flight will be $8 400 or £3 900.

In contrast, Maxjet is offering a 'low-fare business class product'. There will be more traditional seats with generous leg room but no flat beds. It will be using Boeing 767s with 102 seats rather than the more traditional economy class/business class configuration of these planes with more than 200 seats. Prices will be 50 to 70 per cent less than those currently in the marketplace, with the lowest cost return fare at around $1 700 or £800.

Eos has been formed by a team of US entrepreneurs which has attracted $87 million in equity (share) funding, mainly from three US private equity groups.

Whether either of these two new entrants survives is dependent on a number of factors. One problem is that both have been forced to use Stansted Airport rather than Heathrow or Gatwick. This is because the number of landing and takeoff slots at both airports to the USA is fixed by international treaty and so new entrants are effectively barred from using both airports. Stansted could prove attractive to UK business travellers who live north and east of London because Stansted itself is north of London whereas Heathrow is west of London and Gatwick south of London. However, US business travellers are unlikely to have heard of this small regional airport and may be put off by its unknown qualities and relatively poorer transport links. Another problem is lack of flights. British Airways offers ten flights a day to New York. Offering one or two flights a day may not satisfy the need for convenience from many business customers. Air miles are important too. Business class travel is typically paid by companies, but the individual flyers get free air miles which can be redeemed for free gifts, and in particular free flights or free upgrades. Taking the family on a free flight to Hawaii is a powerful incentive for individuals to insist to their employers that they fly BA or Virgin Atlantic. In a recent survey, air miles came out as the second most important factor in choosing an airline, with convenient flight schedules being the first. Eos and Maxjet will have to persuade travel departments of large companies to use their services. Large companies making frequent bookings can usually negotiate a discount. However, it could be that both Eos and Maxjet will get most of their bookings from small and medium sized companies which are less tied into relationships with established airlines.

Source: adapted from the *Financial Times*, 14.10.2005.

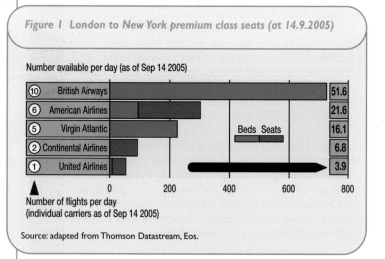

Figure 1 London to New York premium class seats (at 14.9.2005)

Number available per day (as of Sep 14 2005)

⑩ British Airways		51.6
⑥ American Airlines		21.6
⑤ Virgin Atlantic	Beds Seats	16.1
② Continental Airlines		6.8
① United Airlines		3.9

Number of flights per day
(individual carriers as of Sep 14 2005)

Source: adapted from Thomson Datastream, Eos.

Table 1 Service comparison between transatlantic carriers

	Single-class aircraft	Square feet per seat	% of seats with direct aisle access	Flat bed
Eos	Yes	21	100	Yes
Virgin Atlantic (upper)	No	16	100	Yes
British Airways (business)	No	15	50	Yes
United Airlines/American Airlines	No	14	60	No

Source: adapted from Eos.

1. Using examples from the data, explain what factors of production are used in providing airline services.
2. (a) To what extent is transatlantic business class travel price inelastic? (b) What impact might price elasticity have on the success of Eos and Maxjet?
3. Discuss whether or not the transatlantic air flight market is contestable.

Summary

1. The neo-Keynesian theory of the firm assumes that firms are long run profit maximisers which determine prices according to cost-plus pricing principles. Price stability is a feature of this model.
2. Baumol's sales maximisation model assumes that firms aim to maximise sales subject to a profit satisficing constraint.
3. Managerial theories predict that costs and output are likely to be higher than neo-classical theory would suggest.
4. Both managerial and behavioural theories predict that organisational slack is likely to be present.
5. Limit pricing occurs when firms don't attempt to maximise short run profits for fear that this will attract competitors into the market, resulting in overall smaller long run profits. Instead, they set prices which are low enough to deter new entrants from entering the market, and which result in maximum long run profits given the potential competition in the market.

The neo-Keynesian model

R Hall and C Hitch in the 1930s outlined a radically different model of the firm from existing neo-classical models. Their research indicated that firms did not equate marginal cost and marginal revenue in an attempt to maximise short run profits. Rather, firms maximised profits in the long run. Firms then determined prices by calculating costs and adding a profit mark-up (hence the term **cost-plus pricing**). Prices are stable because firms take a long term view of the market.

In the model, it is argued that firms respond to changes in demand and cost not by changing price but by changing output. A large inflow of orders will not lead to a rise in price but to an increase in production. If a manufacturer is already producing at normal full capacity, it may attempt to produce at over-full capacity by encouraging its employees to work overtime or extra shifts. In the service sector, a booming supermarket will not increase prices if it proves far more popular than expected. Rather it will allow overcrowding in the short term and in the longer term may open longer hours, open an extension or build a new supermarket close by. Alternatively, a firm may allow waiting lists to develop. (A waiting list may be helpful in some cases to the image of a product because it is a sign that there are customers who think the product is so good that they are prepared to wait to buy it.)

If demand falls or costs rise, a firm will not necessarily respond by reducing price. Rather it will reduce output. If losses threaten to become too high, it will close down production rather than reduce price which may be seen to be damaging to the longer term prospects for the product.

Prices may not change on a daily basis (as for instance for carrots or tomatoes in the agricultural market) but, equally, firms' prices are not permanently fixed. The frequency of price changes will vary from industry to industry, but a yearly review of prices is not uncommon in British manufacturing industry.

The size of the profit mark-up will vary too. However, the mark-up will tend to be higher where:
- firms in the industry are able to collude, acting as if they were a monopolist;
- there are only a few large firms in the industry, which results in less price competition;
- barriers to entry are high, limiting the possibility of new firms entering the industry;
- there is a large number of small buyers in the market, rather than a few significant buyers who are able to use their buying power to exert downward pressure on prices.

The neo-Keynesian theory of the firm is able to explain relative price stability in the market. However, it is pointed out by neo-classical economists that traditional cost curves should

Question 1

Lee Kent is a painter and decorator. He has one employee and, between them, they do all the work. Contracts come mainly from residential customers. They might want a new look to their living room, bathroom or bedroom. Or someone might have bought a new house and want it redecorating.

Lee does all his own pricing. He calculates the material costs of a job. Then he adds in wages for himself and his employee. There are also costs such as his van, the telephone and paying to have his accounts done. For these, he averages them out and charges per day worked. Finally, he adds 20 per cent as a profit margin.

Work is usually easy to come by between Easter and the end of November, but the winter can be difficult. There can be weeks when he has no work on at all, but he still has costs such as the wages of his employee or the repayments on his van.

What he finds most difficult is when a potential customer has got several quotes for a job and then keeps ringing round the contractors trying to knock the price down. Last week, for example, he had quoted a customer £2 000 for a job. This week, the customer had rung back saying that he had had a quote from another painter for £1 500 and did Lee want to revise his price? Lee knew that he had no work booked in for the following two weeks. Should he revise his quote down to £1 450?

(a) Lee is asked to quote for a job. He calculates that his total costs add up to (i) £2 000; (ii) £5 000; (iii) £8 000. In each case, calculate the price he would charge for the job.
(b) Discuss, using the concept of profit maximisation, whether Lee should revise his quote down to £1 450.

include an allowance for the cost of changing price - in other words, the insight that price changes can be costly can be incorporated within a neo-classical model.

Revenue maximisation model

Neo-classical theory assumes that firms are short run profit maximisers. In the early 1950s an American economist, W Baumol, put forward an alternative model suggesting that firms might maximise sales revenue rather than profits. He recognised that firms cannot make a loss if they are to survive in the long term, so at least some profit must be made. Managers also need to make enough profit to satisfy their shareholders.

In Figure 1, total cost and total revenue curves are drawn. The difference between the two is profit, shown by the curve at the bottom of the graph. The firm can operate anywhere between output levels 0A and 0D without making a loss. It will maximise profit at 0B. If shareholders are content to earn just normal profit and managers wish to maximise sales, then the firm will operate at 0D. On the other hand, if the minimum acceptable level of profit for shareholders is 0E, then output will be at 0C. As can be seen from the diagram, the higher the profit

satisficing level of output, the lower will be the level of output and the nearer it will be to the profit maximising level of output.

Managerial and behavioural theories of the firm

In both managerial and behavioural theories of the firm, it is argued that there is a divorce of ownership and control. In managerial theories, it is assumed that managers control the firm subject to a profit satisficing constraint.

Managerial models tend to make three clear predictions.

● Costs will be higher than neo-classical theory would predict. Higher salaries, expensive company cars and unnecessary levels of staffing have to be paid for.

● Firms will produce at higher levels of output than neo-classical theory would predict. This is because higher output and higher sales will lead to more staff being employed, which is beneficial to the utility of managers. Moreover, higher output levels may be more important in determining salary levels than increased profitability.

● In a recession, management may suffer disproportionately. In the attempt to prevent the company from sliding into loss and possible take over or bankruptcy, managers may be sacked as administration is streamlined and their salaries and perks reduced. In an economic boom, managers may benefit more than most as they are able to increase their own salaries and perks whilst increasing profits too. Shareholders find it difficult to prevent this because they are unable to gauge how much more profit the company could have made if managers had not increased costs unnecessarily.

In behavioural theories, it is argued that it is not just shareholders and managers who determine the behaviour of firms. Other interested parties, such as government, trade unions and other pressure groups like environmentalists, can have an important say too. The eventual outcome will depend upon the relative strength of the various competing parties.

Both managerial and behavioural theories predict that ORGANISATIONAL SLACK is likely to be present. Organisational slack or X-INEFFICIENCY were terms used by Professor Harvey Leibenstein to describe the tendency of firms in non-competitive markets to produce at higher than minimum cost. Therefore, when a manager receives a Jaguar when he would have been content with a Focus, or when a trade union member receives £500 a week when he would have worked for £300, or when a chargehand chooses to organise production in a traditional way when a far more efficient modern method is available, then organisational slack is present.

Organisational slack exists partly because of a lack of knowledge. Decision makers don't know the exact minimum amount for which a worker might be prepared to work, for instance. Perhaps more importantly, organisations are often very conservative. They might order components from a firm they have always dealt with even if they know that the components could be purchased more cheaply elsewhere. Or they might be reluctant to invest in new machinery because all investment is a risk, despite the fact that potentially there are considerable cost savings to be made.

Different interest groups in the firm might be able to exploit their potential power to their advantage, thus increasing organisational slack. Environmental groups, for instance, might force a firm to adopt stricter environmental standards than cost-minimisation would dictate by threatening a media campaign against the firm. Trade unions might threaten to strike, causing short term chaos, unless their demands are met.

Figure 1   Sales maximisation

A firm maximising sales will earn normal profit at an output level of OD. If shareholders demand a minimum level of profit of OE, then it will maximise sales by producing at OC. Both output levels will be above the profit maximising level of output OB.

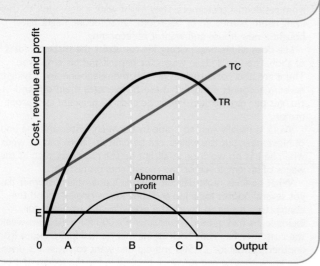

Question 2

(a) A monopolist is a revenue maximiser subject to the constraint that it needs to make normal profits to satisfy its shareholders. Draw a standard neo-classical monopoly diagram. Mark on it:
   (i) the profit maximising level of output;
   (ii) the firm's revenue maximising level of output subject to its profit constraint.

(b) Compare the effect on output and price if a monopolist moves from being a profit maximiser to being a sales maximiser.

In a recession, organisational slack tends to decline. Firms are forced to concentrate on safeguarding profits and, as a result, unnecessary costs tend to be pruned first. Everything, from the size of the company director's car to working practices on the shop floor to the provision of food in the company canteen, is likely to be affected.

Question 3

In 2006, Mittal Steel, the world's largest steelmaker, put a takeover bid in for Arcelor for £12.7 billion. Mittal Steel was founded and is run by Lakshmi Mittal. It currently has its headquarters in London and Rotterdam and has steel mills in 14 countries round the world. Arcelor was created in 2002 by the merger of three French, Luxembourg and Spanish steel companies and has its headquarters in Luxembourg.

The takeover bid was condemned both by Arcelor and by many in France and Germany. Wolfgang Munchau, writing in the *Financial Times*, said: 'If you look at the way Arcelor describes itself, it ... boasts of its size, measured in annual turnover, not profitability. It defines its goal to be "a benchmark for economic performance, labour relations and social responsibility".' Thierry Breton, France's minister of the economy, finance and industry, said: 'Arcelor .... is the world leader in its sector. The future of a business of this size is of crucial economic, industrial and social importance and has to be taken into consideration by any government whose duty is to promote national growth. ... Other stakeholders, such as employees, management, customers, suppliers and local authorities, also have the right to state their opinion. It is in the interest of the shareholders of Mittal Steel and Arcelor to listen because the success of the future company and its shareholders is also a function of stakeholders' consensus.

Source: adapted from the *Financial Times*, 30.1.2006.

Why might a behavioural model of the firm more accurately describe the behaviour of Arcelor than a short run profit maximising model?

Limit pricing

Limit pricing is when firms in an oligopolistic industry set a low enough price (the 'limit price') to deter new entrants from coming into the market. Limit pricing theories assume that firms look beyond maximising short run profits. For instance, assume that firms in an industry can earn £50 million in abnormal profit this year by charging an average price of £10 for each product sold. However, at £10, new firms would be prepared to enter the market, driving down both price and market share of existing firms in the future. It might pay existing firms to charge a lower price than £10 now and lessen the risk of new entrants coming into the market.

Consider Figure 2. Assume that existing firms in the industry all have identical cost and revenue curves. Company X, shown in the figure, produces at 0E, the level of output where its marginal cost equals its marginal revenue. 0E is therefore its profit maximising level of output. It prices at 0A on its demand curve. A new entrant comes into the market with higher costs and charges a lower price of 0B. This is the price where it just makes normal profit. How might Company X and other firms

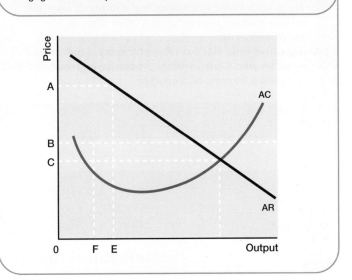

Figure 2 Limit pricing
If a new entrant proposes to come into a market charging a price of 0B, then it might be deterred from doing so if existing firms in the industry are charging less than this price.

in the industry react to the new entrant? Assuming that the new entrant could potentially take away large parts of the market, they should lower their price to below 0B. If they do this, the new entrant will be unable to make normal profit and might even make a loss. In the long term, the new entrant will leave the market. So long as the price charged by Company X is at least 0C, Company X can make at least normal profit and still undercut the price of the new entrant.

Forcing a new entrant out of the market would be easier to achieve if all existing firms in the industry colluded openly - getting together to fix prices and output to maximise profit. However, another way to achieve this would be if one firm, typically the largest, exercised PRICE LEADERSHIP. This is when one firm sets a price which other firms in the market follow. They then become PRICE FOLLOWERS. Alternatively, there may be BAROMETRIC PRICE LEADERSHIP. This is when one firm, not necessarily the largest firm and not necessarily the same firm every time, believing that a change in prices charged in the industry would benefit itself, raises or lowers its price and waits to see the reaction of other firms. If they don't change their prices, the one firm will bring its prices back into line with other firms. If they all follow, then the one firm has achieved its goal of raising or lowering price.

Firms may also fix a limit price through tacit collusion. This is when firms monitor each other's behaviour closely. Unwritten rules are developed which become custom and practice, which define ways in which firms may compete. Through tacit collusion, the limit price may be arrived at over time.

The limit price will be greater the higher the barriers to entry to the industry. This is because the higher the barriers to entry, the less likely it is that a new entrant will come into the industry. For instance, if there were large financial barriers to entry because setting up would be highly costly, then new entrants would be worried that they would lose large amounts of money if the venture proved unprofitable and they had to withdraw. A relatively small reduction from the short run profit maximising price might therefore be enough to completely deter a potential new entrant.

Key terms

Barometric price leadership - when a firm adopts the role of price leader in a market and changes its price, but will only maintain the new price if other firms equally change their price.

Organisational slack or X-inefficiency - inefficiency arising because a firm or other productive organisation fails to minimise its costs of production.

Price follower - a firm which sets its price by reference to the prices set by the price leader in a market.

Price leadership - when one firm, the price leader, sets its own prices and other firms in the market set their prices in relationship to the price leader.

Applied economics

Continental European and Japanese companies

The behaviour of large Japanese companies arguably differs from that of large US and UK companies. In the Anglo-Saxon world, shareholders are supposed to be the most important economic agents in a company. They are the owners and the company should be run for their benefit. This means maximising shareholder value. This comes in two main forms. First, companies should aim to maximise their dividend payments, which means maximising short term profits. Second, companies should aim to maximise their share price and the growth in the share price so that shareholders can make capital gains. Many companies emphasise the importance of customers or the environment. Government initiatives, such as Investors In People, stress the importance of training the workforce. However, building up a happy, loyal and productive workforce and ensuring that customers are satisfied with what they are buying are not ends in themselves. A hard working staff is only important ultimately because that staff is likely to make higher profits for the company than if it is demotivated and unhappy. Happy customers are only important because if they were unhappy they might take their custom to another company.

In continental Europe and Japan, attitudes differ. Shareholders are important, but they are only one group amongst many which influence decision making in the company. Partly this is because shareholders are unable to exert as much power. In Anglo-Saxon countries, direct shareholder involvement in the running of large companies is rare. Shareholders exert power through the buying and selling of shares on stock exchanges. A poorly performing company tends to see its share price slide as shareholders sell their stock in the face of poor dividend and share price growth. The company then becomes easy prey to a take-over bid from another company. In continental Europe and Japan, few companies are open to be taken over in this way because the majority of their voting shares are not tradeable on the stock exchange - they are owned by family members or by other large companies.

Shareholders in continental Europe and Japan are also far less likely to be short run maximisers than in Anglo-Saxon countries because of who owns shares. In the UK and the USA, banks are not allowed to hold company shares as part of their reserves. In Germany and Japan, in contrast, banks have always been encouraged to invest capital in company shares. As a consequence, bankers sit on the boards of companies in these countries. Banks are not particularly interested in short term profits. They wish to see the companies in which they own shares prosper over a long period of time. A company which produces shoddy goods might make a fast profit initially, but is unlikely to grow and prosper in the long term. Equally, shareholders in family controlled businesses are likely to be in business to secure the long term growth and prosperity of the company rather than pursuing the highest profit in the next month.

The importance of workers in a company is emphasised in the European Union through the Social Charter of the Treaty of Maastricht, 1991. Under the Charter, all large companies must have works councils, constitued from representatives of workers and management, which have some power to influence long term decision making in a company.

In Japan, workers are seen as one of the key stakeholders in a company. Large companies have traditionally had a policy of providing jobs for life whilst trade unions see it as their role to safeguard the prosperity of the company to ensure that jobs can be for life.

European and Japanese governments have a history

of being more interventionist than in the UK or the USA. In Japan, for instance, the government heavily influenced the development of individual industries in the post-war period. In France, national plans in the 1950s, 1960s and 1970s directed the growth of different sectors in the economy. Whilst direct government intervention in industry has diminished since the 1980s, no Japanese or continental Western European government has embraced the Anglo-Saxon free market model.

Anglo-Saxon firms, then, can be seen broadly as short term profit maximisers. Continental European and Japanese firms, in contrast, tend to pursue long term profit objectives. The way they work is perhaps best described by behavioural theories of the firm, where a number of competing interest groups in a

business come to a consensus about the direction the firm should pursue. However, it can be argued that the world's largest businesses are moving more to an Anglo-Saxon model. In continental Europe, increasingly firms have been bought out and become subsidiaries of Anglo-Saxon firms. This changes their corporate behaviour. Equally in Japan the very difficult economic conditions of the 1990s, when there was a prolonged recession, left many large companies in a state of financial collapse. They were forced to restructure to return to profitability and repay some of their large debts. This meant, for some companies, abandoning the policies of jobs for life, cutting staff and closing factories. Short run profit has become more important as a company goal than in the past.

DataQuestion

A traditional pub

Phil Sawyer owns and runs a traditional pub. Over the past fifteen years he has actively changed the product mix. Originally almost all the sales revenue came from drinks. Today half comes from sale of food. The menu offers traditional English dishes along with more adventurous French inspired dishes.

Phil operates a simple rule of thumb on food pricing. The cost of the food should be around one third of the price charged to customers. The remaining two thirds, the gross profit margin, pays for fixed overhead costs and the net profit earned. For instance, the food cost of a fish dish with vegetables is around £2.50, so he charges £7.49 on the menu. Part of the success of the pub is that much of the menu is changed regularly. This appeals to his regular clientele who enjoy eating out. Any new dish which fails to sell well within two weeks is withdrawn from sale. The chef sometimes

objects and tells Phil to 'give it a chance'. The chef has suggested that customers might see it as overpriced and that cutting its price could increase sales. Phil, though, is ruthless. 'If I can't sell it at a profit, then it has no place on my menu.'

Last year, the pub in the next village was bought and turned into a Mexican themed pub. It proved very popular, particularly with younger customers in their twenties. Phil was a little nervous when he saw its business take off and he noticed that fewer young customers were now visiting his pub to eat. He vaguely discussed with his chef whether changing price would have any effect on custom, but decided that price was not an issue in this situation. The key was providing value for money for his customer base. Sales the following year still grew by 6 per cent over the year, a little down on previous years but still a very satisfactory result.

1. Explain what type of pricing technique Phil Sawyer is using. Illustrate your answer from the passage.
2. Discuss how Phil Sawyer is likely to react if: (a) there are violent storms in the North Sea and the wholesale price of the fish used at Phil Sawyer's pub doubles that week; (b) there is a downturn in the local economy and unemployment rises; (c) some Saturday nights he has to turn food customers away because the eating area is full; (d) overcrowding in the restaurant becomes a regular occurrence.
3. Discuss whether there is likely to be organisational slack in the running of the pub.

52 Economic efficiency

Summary

1. Efficiency can be both static and dynamic. Productive efficiency and allocative efficiency are static measures of efficiency.
2. Productive efficiency is present if production takes place at lowest average cost. Allocative efficiency is present if the marginal cost of production equals price in all markets in an economy.
3. Dynamic efficiency exists if, for example, there is innovation in the market.
4. To judge whether there is an optimal allocation of resources in an economy, it is necessary to make value judgments about the allocation of resources. In the absence of market failure, a free market will achieve an optimal allocation of resources.
5. There are many examples of market failure, including imperfect competition and monopoly, externalities and missing markets.
6. The General Theory of the Second Best shows that in an imperfect market economy, a move towards marginal cost pricing in one industry may not lead to a Pareto improvement.

Efficiency

Efficiency is concerned with how well resources are used to resolve the three fundamental questions in economics of how, what and for whom production should take place. There are two types of **static efficiency**:

- **Productive efficiency** which occurs when production takes place at least cost;
- **Allocative efficiency** which is concerned with whether resources are used to produce the goods and services that consumers wish to buy.

Static efficiency is concerned with efficiency at a point in time. **Dynamic efficiency**, in contrast, is concerned with whether resources are used efficiently over a period of time.

Productive efficiency

Productive efficiency occurs when production takes place at least

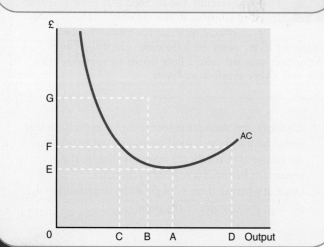

Figure 1 Productive efficiency
For a firm, productive efficiency only occurs when production takes place at lowest average cost. In this case it is at an average cost of OE and an output level of OA. There is X-inefficiency if the firm produces at a cost within the average cost boundary such as at the point G.

average cost. This can be illustrated on an average cost curve diagram. Figure 1 shows the average cost for a firm. It is productively efficient if it is producing 0A at an average cost of 0E. If it produces 0D at an average cost of of 0F, it is productively inefficient, producing too much because 0F is not the lowest average cost possible. The same argument applies if it produces at output 0C and an average cost of 0F. In this case, however, it is producing too little to be productively efficient.

There will also be productive inefficiency if the firm produces within its average cost curve boundary. If output is 0B but average cost is 0G, it is productively inefficient for two reasons. First, at output 0B, it is not achieving the lowest average cost possible as shown by the average cost curve. Second, even if it were producing on the average cost boundary, production would be too low to achieve minimum average cost. When a firm operates within rather than on its average cost boundary, there is **X-inefficiency** or **organisational slack**.

In Figure 1, 0A is the productively efficient level of output whether the average cost curve is the short run average cost curve or the long run average cost curve. A firm is productively efficient in the short run if it is operating on the bottom of its short run average cost curve. It is productively efficienct in the long run, if it is operating on the bottom of its long run average cost curve.

For an economy as a whole, there is productive efficiency if it is operating on its production possibility frontier. To understand why, consider what would be the case if one competitive firm in the economy were productively inefficient. Then it would use up too many resources to produce its output. Either by expanding or contracting output, or closing down and its production being taken over by other firms in the industry, average costs could be reduced to a minimum, so releasing resources to be used elsewhere in the economy. There is no possibility of gaining any extra production in the economy if all firms are producing at lowest cost. Hence, there must be productive efficiency only when the economy is operating on its production possibility boundary.

Allocative efficiency

ALLOCATIVE or ECONOMIC EFFICIENCY measures whether resources are allocated to those goods and services demanded by consumers. For instance, assume that consumers place equal value on the marginal consumption of shoes and jumpers. However, the last 1 million pairs of shoes produced in the economy cost 10 times as much to manufacture as an extra 1 million jumpers would have done (i.e. the economy could have produced either 1 million pairs of shoes or 10 million jumpers). It would have been more allocatively efficient if 1 million jumpers had been produced rather than the 1 million pairs of shoes because:

● consumers value the jumpers as much as the shoes;
● either an extra 9 million jumpers or 900 000 pairs of shoes or some combination of the two could have been produced **as well as** the 1 million jumpers (assuming constant costs of production).

This argument can be developed using demand and cost curves. Demand and marginal cost have a particular significance in WELFARE ECONOMICS, the study of how an economy can best allocate resources to maximise the utility or economic welfare of its citizens.

● The demand curve shows the value that consumers place on the last unit bought of a product. For instance, if a utility maximising consumer bought a pair of tights at £2, then the pair of tights must have given at least £2 worth of value (or **satisfaction** or **utility**). If total demand for a product is 100 units at a price of £10, then the value placed by consumers on the hundredth unit must have been £10. The value placed on each of the other 99 units bought is likely to be above £10 because the demand curve slopes back upwards from that point. The marginal (or extra) value of a good to the consumer (i.e. the marginal utility) is given by the price shown on the demand curve at that level of output.

● The marginal cost curve shows the cost to firms of producing an extra unit of the good. 'Cost', we will assume here, is the cost of production to society as well as to firms. In practice the **private cost** of production of the firm may differ from the **social cost** because of **externalities**, and this has important implications for allocative efficiency.

In Figure 2, two markets are shown. In the wheat market,

current output is 0B. The market price is £1 per unit, but farmers receive £3 per unit, for instance because the government subsidises production. In the gas market, output is 0E. Price is £6 but gas suppliers receive only £4, for instance because the government imposes a £2 tax per unit.

In the wheat industry, price is below marginal cost (P < MC). This means that the value that consumers place on the product is less than the cost to society of producing the product. Consumers value the last unit produced at 0B at £1 (shown on the demand curve). The cost to society of producing the last unit is £3 (shown on the marginal cost curve). Therefore consumers value the last unit of wheat purchased at £2 less than it cost to produce.

In the gas market, price is above marginal cost (P > MC). This means that the value consumers place on the last unit produced is more than the cost to society of its production. Consumers value the last unit produced at 0E at £6 whilst its cost to society is only £4. Hence consumers value the last unit of gas purchased at £2 more than it cost to produce.

This suggests that scarce resources would be more efficiently

Figure 2 *Allocative efficiency*

Transferring resources from the wheat market where price is below marginal cost to the gas market where price is above marginal cost will lead to allocative efficiency.

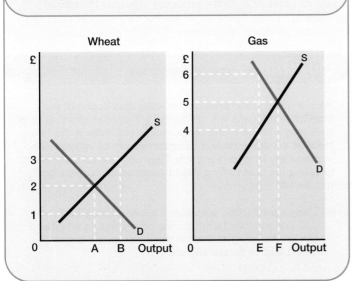

Question I

Table I

Millions	£ per unit				
	Goods			Services	
Quantity	Price	Marginal cost		Price	Marginal cost
1	10	2		10	4
2	8	4		9	5
3	6	6		8	6
4	4	8		7	7
5	2	10		6	8

The table shows the relationship between quantity demanded and price and between output and marginal cost for the only two commodities produced in an economy. Producing 1 million units of goods and 5 million units of services would not be allocatively efficient. This is because, at this level of output, the price of goods (£10 per unit) is above marginal cost (£2 per unit) whilst the price of services is below the marginal cost of production (£6 compared to £8). Consumers would be better off if resources were transferred from the production of services, where the marginal cost of production is greater than the marginal value placed on them by consumers, to the production of goods where the opposite is the case.

(a) The economy produces 3 million units of goods and 4 million units of services. Why is this an allocatively efficient level of production?

(b) Explain, using a diagram, why there would be a loss of economic efficiency if the allocation of resources changed such that: (i) only 2 million units of goods were produced and the resources released were switched to the production of services;
(ii) only 2 million units of services were produced and the resources released were switched to the production of goods.

allocated if less wheat and more gas were produced in the economy, but how much wheat and gas should be produced? If price is equal to marginal cost in both markets (P = MC), then consumers value the last unit consumed of both wheat and gas as much as it costs to produce those commodities. If the price of wheat in Figure 2 were £2 and gas £5, then it would be impossible to reallocate resources between the two industries to the advantage of consumers.

Hence allocative efficiency will exist if price is equal to marginal cost in each industry in the economy. This is a very important conclusion but we shall see below that it needs to be very heavily qualified.

If P=MC in all industries (such as wheat and gas in the above example), it is impossible to make anyone better off without making someone else worse off. The allocation of resources is then said to be PARETO EFFICIENT (after Vilfredo Pareto, an Italian economist, who first put forward this condition in 1909 in a book entitled *Manuel D'Economie Politique*). If an allocation of resources is said to be Pareto inefficient, then it must be possible to make some or all people better off without making anybody worse off.

Efficiency and the production possibility frontier

The various concepts of efficiency can be illustrated using a **production possibility frontier - PPF**. A production possibility frontier shows combinations of goods which could be produced if all resources were fully used (i.e. the economy were at full employment). Figure 3 shows the combination of goods that could be distributed between one individual, John, and all other individuals.

If there were productive inefficiency in the economy, production would take place within the boundary, for instance at points A, B or C in Figure 3. With all resources fully employed, it would be possible to move, for instance, from A to

---

Figure 3 Pareto efficient points of production

Points on the production possibility frontier, such as D, E and F, are Pareto efficient because it is not possible to produce more goods for John without reducing the production of goods for other people. Points G, H and I are unattainable whilst points A, B and C are Pareto inefficient because it is possible to increase production and produce more goods for both John and all others.

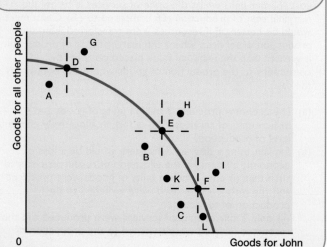

D if costs were minimised.

A, B and C are also Pareto inefficient. This is because it is possible to increase output for both John and all other people without making anyone worse off by moving to a point north east of these combinations. Production at D is therfore more efficient than at A, production at E is more efficient than at B etc.

On the other hand, D, E and F are Pareto efficient. At any of these points it is not possible to produce more for John without reducing production for all other people. This is true for all points on the production possibility frontier. Hence, all points on the PPF are Pareto efficient.

All points on the PPF also satisfy the P=MC condition, so points on the frontier are both productively and allocatively efficient.

Note that it is only possible to make Pareto efficiency statements about points which are north east and south west of each other. For instance, F is Pareto efficient whilst C is not, but K cannot be compared with F because at K all other people are better off than at F but John is worse off.

All points on the production possibility frontier are productively and allocatively (i.e. Pareto) efficient. Therefore in one sense all points on the frontier represent an OPTIMAL ALLOCATION OF RESOURCES. It is not possible to make one person better off without making another worse off. In making this judgement, we are implicitly assuming that it is not possible to say that one distribution of resources is better than another.

This gives little help to policy makers who believe that one distribution of resources is superior to another. For instance, in Figure 3, points E and F are both Pareto efficient and therefore in one sense represent an optimal allocation of resources. However, the government may believe that society would be better off if there were fewer goods for John and more goods for everybody else. It is making a value judgement about what constitutes economic welfare, so the economy would be better off at E rather than F.

Dynamic efficiency

There is dynamic efficiency in an economy when resources are allocated efficiently over time. Productive and allocative efficiency, in contrast, are examples of static efficiency, efficiency at a point in time.

One example of dynamic efficiency concerns the rate of investment. Firms invest either so that they can cut costs or to make new products. Investment can be in research and

---

Question 2

Many scientists have predicted that the destruction of the Brazilian rain forests will add to the 'greenhouse effect', in turn leading to a rise in world temperatures and a rise in sea levels. Much of the destruction is being carried out by ranchers who wish to clear land to rear cattle. They can then earn a profit by selling the beef to First World countries such as the USA and the UK.

(a) Using a production possibility frontier (putting 'beef' on one axis and 'rain forest' on the other), discuss whether a ban on the felling of trees in the Brazilian rain forests would lead to Pareto efficiency.

development, in physical non-human capital or in training workers, investment in human capital. The rate of investment by firms is determined by a number of typically short run considerations like levels of demand in the economy, interest rates and their past profitability. Dynamic inefficiency can occur if firms fail to take into account all the future costs and benefits of investment. With research and development which can have very long term pay-offs, firms may take no account of revenues to be received after, say, five years because they regard these benefits as too uncertain, but if all firms do this, there will be underinvestment in the economy as a whole in long term research and development. This will reduce the socially optimal rate of technological change over time. With the training of workers, firms may choose to 'poach' workers from firms who have good training programmes for their workers, rather than increase their costs by training them themselves. If all firms do this, there will be underinvestment in training in the economy.

Another example of dynamic efficiency concerns sustainable growth. Production uses up non-renewable resources and creates waste. Future generations face the exhaustion of some non-renewable resources like oil and natural gas. They might also be paying to clean up waste created by us today, for example from nuclear power stations. There is no exact link in economic theory between dynamic efficiency and sustainable growth. However, markets are unlikely to be dynamically efficient if their activities leave future generations considerably worse off.

The market and economic efficiency

It is possible to shows that if all markets are **perfectly competitive**, resources in the economy will be efficiently allocated.

- In long run equilibrium in a perfectly competitive market, firms will produce at the bottom of their average cost curves. Therefore there will be productive efficiency.
- For there to be allocative efficiency, the cost to society of producing an extra unit of output must equal the value placed on consumption of that good by the individual (the price = marginal cost condition). In a perfectly competitive market, firms maximise profits by producing where marginal cost = marginal revenue. Marginal revenue is equal to price because the perfectly competitive firm is a price taker. Therefore marginal cost = price. On the other hand consumers maximise their utility by equating the marginal utility of each good consumed per £1 spent. Hence price is an accurate reflection of the value of the good (the marginal utility) to the individual.

It is also true that allocative efficiency in the sense of Pareto efficiency will exist in an economy where all markets are perfectly competitive. As firms are producing at least cost, the economy must be on its production possibility frontier and therefore the allocation of resources must be Pareto efficient.

Market failure

If all markets in an economy are perfectly competitive, then two conditions must hold.

- There must be perfect competition in all goods markets. Consumers must be able to allocate their resources in a way which will maximise their utility. They must possess perfect knowledge, for instance. There must be enough consumers in

any market to prevent undue pressure being exerted on producers to their advantage. Production too must be organised under conditions of perfect competition. Each industry must comprise a large number of small producers, all of whom are price takers. There must be freedom of entry and exit to every industry and all firms must possess perfect knowledge.

- All factor markets must be perfectly competitive. There must be perfect mobility of labour, for instance. There must be no trade unions which act as monopoly suppliers of labour. Neither must there be any monopoly employers, such as the UK government with teachers and nurses. Capital must flow freely between industries and regions according to the levels of profit being made.

No real economy is like this. Imperfections exist in all sectors of modern industrialised economies, just as they do in developing economies, which **prevent** the efficient allocation of resources through the market mechanism. This is **market failure**. There is a number of different types of market failure including those arising from imperfect competition or monopoly, externalities, missing markets, information failures, malfunctioning factor markets and inequality.

Efficiency vs equity

Even if a market were efficient, it would not necessarily lead to a socially desirable distribution of resources between individuals. Both efficiency and **equity** contribute to the level of economic welfare. For instance, Pareto efficiency exists when an economy operates on its production possibility frontier, but there is an infinite number of points on the frontier. Which is the most desirable one? That question cannot be answered without some view about the distribution of resources within an economy. Most would agree that an economy where one person enjoyed

Question 3

The European Commission has fined thread producers from Germany, Belgium, The Netherlands, France, Switzerland and the UK a total of €43 million (£30 million) for operating a number of cartels. Industrial thread is used in a variety of industries to sew or embroider various products such as clothes, home furnishings, automotive seats and seat belts, leather goods, mattresses, footwear and ropes. The fines relate to three cartel agreements over the period 1990 to 2001.

The Commission raided the offices of the companies involved in November 2001. They found evidence that the thread producers had taken part in regular meetings to agree on price increases or on target increases, to exchange sensitive information on price lists or prices charged to individual customers, and to avoid undercutting suppliers' prices with a view to allocating customers between the thread producers. The Commission considered that the cartel agreements had led to a major distortion of competition, to the benefit of the producers and at the expense of customers and, ultimately, consumers.

Source: adapted from the European Commission website, europa.eu.int, 14.9.2005.

(a) Why did the thread cartel lead to inefficiency in the market?
(b) Why was it an example of market failure?

99 per cent of the resources whilst the other 100 million people were left with 1 per cent would be unlikely to provide a higher level of welfare than one where the distribution of resources was more equal. Most (but not all) would agree that it is unacceptable in today's Britain to allow people to die of hunger on our streets. The question of what distribution is desirable or is judged to maximise total welfare is a value judgement.

The theory of the second best

An economy will be economically efficient if all markets are perfectly competitive. Therefore it might seem like common sense to argue that economic efficiency will be increased in an economy where there are many instances of market failure if at least some markets can be made perfectly competitive and market distortions removed.

In the late 1950s, Richard Lipsey and Kelvin Lancaster (1956-7) published an article entitled 'On the General Theory of the Second Best'. They assumed an economy where some firms were not pricing at marginal cost. They then showed that a move towards marginal cost pricing by one firm might lead to an an increase in efficiency, but equally it could lead to a decrease in efficiency. The radical conclusion was that introducing marginal cost pricing could lead to efficiency losses rather than efficiency gains.

For instance, consider Figure 4. It shows two industries. The food industry is assumed to be monopolistic. Output is set at 0A where MC = MR (the profit maximising condition) and price is then set at 0P on the average revenue or demand curve. The entertainment industry is perfectly competitive. Output is at 0F where marginal cost equals price. Assume that resources were transferred from the entertainment industry to the food industry such that output in the food industry rose to 0B whilst output in the entertainment industry fell to 0E. The welfare gain in the food industry, shown by the difference between demand and marginal cost, is the shaded area on the graph. This is larger than the welfare loss in the entertainment industry, shown by the shaded triangle. Hence in this case there is a net welfare gain if there is a move away from perfect competition in the entertainment industry.

It can be shown that, in general, efficiency can be increased by transferring resources to industries where price is far in excess of marginal cost from industries where it is less so or where demand is less than marginal cost. Efficiency is likely to be achieved where the difference between price and marginal cost is the same throughout an economy.

This is a very important conclusion. Every economy suffers from market failure. It will never be the case that marginal cost can equal price across all sectors of the economy. Therefore simple rules or slogans such as 'competition good, monopoly bad' are unlikely to lead to good economic policy making. What the theory of the second best suggests is that distortions within an economy need to be evened out as far as possible. Eliminating them in some markets but allowing them to remain high in others could well lead to less efficiency overall than decreasing them in markets where they are high but actually increasing them in markets where distortions are low.

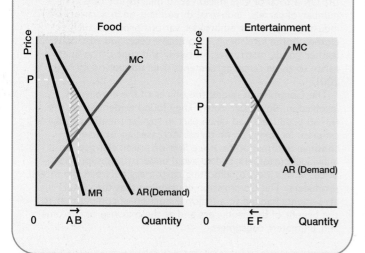

Figure 4 Resource allocation in an imperfect market
If some markets are imperfectly competitive or a monopoly, there could be efficiency gains if resources are transferred from a perfectly competitive market to the imperfectly competitive market or the monopoly. The loss of efficiency in the entertainment market, shown by the shaded area, is less than the gain in welfare in the food market in this example.

Question 4

It is difficult to imagine that many East Germans have a yearning to go back to the old days of the Communist regime before 1990. When they lived in a police state where the economy was in a terrible shape. Shortages were chronic and goods sold were shoddy. The noisy and uncomfortable Trabant car was a fitting symbol of the system. Yet today, East Germans are voting in increasing numbers for the PDS, the reformed Communist party. These voters, according to opinion polls, believe that the Communist regime was better at providing healthcare, education, industrial training, law and order, gender equality, social security and housing. These are precisely the goods which tend not to be provided by the market mechanism on which Western economies are based. As for those goods which are provided by markets, like cars or foreign holidays, these are only available to those with high enough incomes. East Germany has gone from having no unemployment under the Communist regime to an official 20 per cent today, so large sections of the East German population can't afford the goods which more efficient markets provide.

Source: adapted from the *Financial Times*, 4.11.1999.

(a) Explain why an efficient market system which provides a high average income might lead to some consumers being worse off than if they lived in an inefficient state planned economy where average incomes were much lower. Illustrate your answer with examples from the data.

Key terms

Allocative or economic efficiency - occurs when resources are distributed in such a way that no consumers could be made better off without other consumers becoming worse off. It exists in an economy if price = marginal cost in all industries.

Optimal allocation of resources - occurs when resources are efficiently used in such a way as to maximise the welfare or utility of consumers.

Pareto efficiency - occurs when no one can be made better off by transferring resources from one industry to another without making someone else worse off. Pareto efficiency is also called allocative efficiency. It exists in an economy if price = marginal cost in all industries.

Welfare economics - the study of how an economy can best allocate resources to maximise the utility or economic welfare of its citizens.

Applied economics

The misallocation of resources in transport

It is widely argued that public transport is underutilised, whilst private modes of transport, mainly the car, are overused. Partly, this view is held because cars create externalities. However, it is also true that the pricing structure of private and public transport leads directly to a misallocation of resources. When travellers consider what mode of transport to use, they will look at a number of factors.

● Feasibility. Many journeys are impossible to make using certain modes of transport. For instance, most people find it impossible to use the train to go from door to door on a journey. If they do use the train, they often have to use another mode of transport at either end of the journey. Public transport is often not available at night.

● Time. The length of the journey is important. Travellers from London to New York almost invariably today take the plane rather than the boat because of this factor. Eurostar has competed successfully with airlines on the London to Paris route because journey times door to door are often comparable.

● Comfort. Travellers often prefer cars because they are a very comfortable mode of transport. Car drivers can create their own environment within the car. Train and bus commuters, on the other hand, often dislike the journeys they make because of overcrowding and poor facilities. Another important factor, though, is cost. Decisions are made at the

margin. How much will it cost to undertake this extra journey? For the motorist, the marginal cost is the variable cost of motoring. This is petrol plus any car parking fees. The fixed costs of motoring, which include purchase, insurance and road tax, do not enter into the decision making process for a single journey. These costs have already been paid and do not change if an extra journey is made.

In contrast, the price of public transport includes both fixed and variable cost. For instance, when the train passenger buys a ticket, it includes the fixed cost of the payment to Network Rail for the use of the infrastructure and the cost of the train. On top of that is the variable cost of the train driver and the fuel. How much of the fixed cost the passenger pays depends on the pricing policy of the rail company. The tendency is for the train companies to load most of the fixed cost

onto passengers travelling at peak times.

Therefore the price that travellers pay excludes fixed costs in private motoring but, particularly for peak time travellers, includes it in public transport. Not surprisingly, this tends to make private motoring seem cheap for any single journey compared with public transport. This is particularly true if there is more than one passenger travelling in the car because the marginal cost of carrying an extra passenger is zero.

The result is that there is a misallocation of resources. In public transport, price tends to be set above the marginal cost of a single journey, whereas in private motoring, it is equal to marginal cost. The result is that too many car journeys are made and too little use is made of public transport.

It could be argued that taxes and subsidies go some way towards reducing this misallocation. Nearly all the cost of petrol today is tax, whilst public transport is not subject to VAT. Equally, many public transport services are subsidised. Even so, taxes on petrol and subsidies on public transport are probably not high enough to eliminate this misallocation. The solution favoured by economists is congestion road pricing, already introduced in Central London. The government is considering the introduction of congestion road pricing across major roads in the UK. However, it is likely to be highly unpopular and the technology is still unproven. For these reasons, the government may delay implementation and so prolong the misallocation of resources in UK transport.

DataQuestion

Grey goods

The market in grey goods expanded rapidly in the UK in the 1990s. Grey goods, or parallel import goods, are branded products bought outside normal distribution channels. The market came to a halt in 1998, however, following a judgment of the European Court. Silhouette, an upmarket Austrian sunglasses manufacturer, had sold 21 000 pairs of out of date stock to a Bulgarian company at a knock down price in 1995. The contract stipulated that they would be sold either in Bulgaria or the Soviet Union. Within months, however, they were back in Austria, being sold by the discount chain Hartlauer at cut prices. Silhouette took Hartlauer to court and eventually the European Court of Justice ruled in Silhouette's favour.

The judgment had far reaching consequences. It was standard practice for many manufacturers of branded goods to charge different prices in different markets. For instance, manufacturers' prices to US customers were on average 12 per cent lower than those for UK customers. Prices to Middle East customers, or to Eastern Europe were often much lower than European prices.

Manufacturers were, in economic terms, segmenting their market and selling at the highest price possible into each market. The growth of grey imports threatened completely to disrupt this trading pattern. Retailers like Asda and Tesco were increasingly able to bypass the manufacturer's official distribution channels and buy at knock down prices from merchants abroad. The judgment killed this trade at a stroke.

Brand owners argue that they have a right to choose their distributors. Adidas, for instance, stated that restricting the distribution network was an advantage to customers. 'We make an important commitment to our customers that our products will be consistently of high quality' it said. Many brand owners have been dismayed to find their products being sold cheaply in supermarkets. It devalues the exclusiveness of the brand and negates the image they have tried to build up through advertising and other promotion of a high class product.

Source: adapted from the Financial Times.

Sony is to launch a High Court bid to block unofficial imports of its new PlayStation Portable games console. The European launch of the console is set for 1 September but the machines have already been on sale in Japan and the USA for months.

The 'grey imports' are highly profitable for the stores selling them. Prices, at £220-£249, are typically well above the likely official price of £180 set by Sony for 1 September and profit margins can be as high as 70 per cent. Game addicts aren't simply buying the consoles because they can't wait until the official launch. They say the Japanese imports are better made than the European version. Not only is its screen, made by Sharp instead of Samsung, brighter, but the Japanese console is also 'unlocked', meaning it can play games from all over the world.

One Tottenham Court Road store selling the consoles said: 'Sony has dug its own grave. It can't realistically leave an 11 month gap between the Japanese and European release dates and not expect a grey market to develop. It's a globalised world. Gamers nowadays are completely in tune with the latest developments.'

Source: adapted from the *Financial Times*, 25.6.2005.

1. Explain why retailers, such as Tesco or electronics stores on the Tottenham Court Road, might want to sell grey imports.
2. Analyse whether the legal banning of grey imports might lead to allocative inefficiency in markets.
3. Brand owners, like Sony, Adidas, Honda or Givenchy, would argue that grey imports threaten dynamic efficiency in the EU. To what extent do you think this is likely to be the case?

53 Competition and efficiency

Summary

1. Competition is more likely to lead to productive and allocative efficiency than monopoly.
2. Competition may not necessarily lead to dynamic efficiency.
3. Firms use a wide variety of anti-competitive practices to limit competition in order to increase their profits.
4. Competition policies are used by the government to promote competition in the economy and to limit anti-competitive practices.

Competition and static efficiency

In economics, competition is generally seen as more desirable than monopoly. Competition, it is argued, drives down both costs and prices. It also increases supply and availability of goods. Consumers benefit because they can buy goods and services at the cheapest price in quantities which are not restricted by firms to make abnormal profit. Competition leads to productive and allocative efficiency.

In the unit on economic efficiency, it was shown that if all industries were perfectly competitive, then there would be both productive and allocative efficiency in the long run. This can be seen in Figure 1 which shows a diagram for a single perfectly competitive firm. In the long run, competition means that the firm cannot earn abnormal profit. Equilibrium price, P_E, is equal to the minimum price that it will accept if it is to stay in the market. At a price of P_E and an equilibrium output of Q_E, there is **productive efficiency** because production takes place at the lowest average cost possible. There is also **allocative efficiency** because price equals marginal cost.

Competition also takes place in oligopolistic markets. If the market is contestable, static efficiency will exist in the long run.

This is partly because competition will force firms to produce at lowest cost. If firms were not productively efficiency, a new firm would enter the market, produce at lowest cost, charge a lower price and thus take market share from existing inefficient producers. It is also partly because production will take place where price = marginal cost, the condition for allocative efficiency. As a result of competitive pressures, firms in a contestable market can only earn normal profits in the long run and so their average cost must equal their average revenue or price. Given that they are also productively efficient, they operate at the lowest point on their average cost curve which is cut by their marginal cost curve, so average cost equals marginal cost at the equilibrium point of production. Putting this together, price which equals average cost must also equal marginal cost.

However, there is likely to be static inefficiency in markets which are not contestable. Take an oligopolistic market which can be modelled using the kinked demand curve theory. The firm is unlikely to be productively efficient because production is unlikely to take place at lowest average cost. It is unlikely to be allocatively efficient because price is likely to be higher than marginal cost in equilibrium.

Competition and dynamic efficiency

In a competitive market, it might seem that firms will inevitably compete by producing new innovative products. If they develop a new product, they can gain a competitive advantage which, at least in the short run, will allow them to make abnormal profit. This might be true of oligopolistic or monopolistically competitive markets, but it is unlikely to be true of perfectly competitive markets.

In perfect competition, there is a large number of small firms operating in the market. No one firm will have large enough funds available for research and development. Small firms in general find it more difficult to raise finance for growth and expansion than large firms, and banks are likely to be unsympathetic if borrowed money is to be used on risky research projects. Moreover, perfect knowledge is assumed to exist in the market. The invention of one firm will quickly be adopted by other firms, so there is little or no incentive to undertake research and development.

Patent laws and copyright laws can protect the inventions of small firms, providing some encouragement to innovate. However, in markets where patent and copyright laws exist, the markets are likely to be monopolistically competitive or oligopolistic because of the assumption of perfect knowledge in perfect competition. Patent and copyright laws also create barriers to entry, so patent and copyright

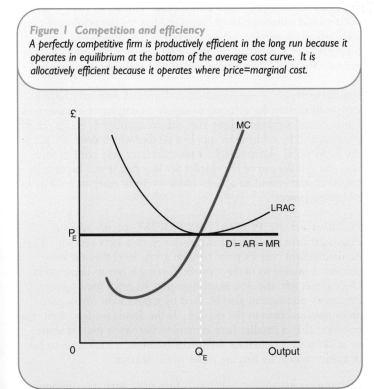

Figure 1 Competition and efficiency
A perfectly competitive firm is productively efficient in the long run because it operates in equilibrium at the bottom of the average cost curve. It is allocatively efficient because it operates where price=marginal cost.

laws create branded, non-homogenous goods.

In the few perfectly competitive industries that might be argued to exist, innovation is often provided not by individual firms but by government funded or government organised research institutions. In agriculture, for instance, major advances in crop strains in the Third World have been developed by state-funded universities and research institutes. This is an example of government correcting **market failure**. Alternatively, new crops, like GM varieties, have been developed not by farmers but by farming suppliers. These industries are oligopolistic and not perfectly competitive.

Anti-competitive practices and efficiency

Competition in a market can be reduced through the use by firms of ANTI-COMPETITIVE PRACTICES or RESTRICTIVE TRADE PRACTICES. Cartels use them to enforce their collective agreements and to deter competitors. Individual firms use them to establish or reinforce dominance in a market. They are designed to benefit the firm or group of firms which carry them out. In particular, they typically:
- raise prices from what they would otherwise be in a competitive market place;
- restrict output;
- restrict choice of product to the customer;
- raise barriers to entry, thus reducing potential competition and the incentive to produce at minimum cost;
- defend existing technologies or allow firms to earn high levels of abnormal profit on new technologies.

As such, they are designed to reduce levels of consumer surplus and raise levels of producer surplus. They lead to both productive and allocative inefficiency and are likely to lead to dynamic inefficiency. The last would not be the case if dominant firms used their abnormal profits to invest in new products and technologies.

A wide variety of anti-competitive practices is used by firms, including the following.

Resale price maintenance A firm may wish to fix a price at which its goods are sold on by a buyer. This is RESALE PRICE MAINTENANCE (RPM). This most commonly occurs with manufacturers and retailers. A manufacturer wishes to prevent competition in the market and so it will only sell to a retailer if it charges a minimum price to consumers. This RPM price is above what would otherwise be the market price for the product if there were price competition between retailers. Although the manufacturer is likely to sell less, it will be at a higher price. The manufacturer should set the price so that its profit is maximised.

Refusal to supply a competitor or customer A firm may have a variety of reasons for refusing to supply a competitor or customer. For instance, a manufacturer may enforce a policy of resale price maintenance by refusing to supply a retailer which does not sell at the RPM price. Alternatively, a manufacturer may wish to force a discount retailer out of the market for fear that it will become its largest customer and be able to erode its profit margins because of its buying power.

Predatory pricing PREDATORY PRICING occurs when a dominant firm in a market is threatened by a new entrant. The dominant firm cuts its price to such a low level that the new entrant is unable to make a profit, forcing it out of the market. Once it has left, the dominant firm puts its price back up again. Predatory pricing can also be used by a dominant firm against an established firm in the market. If the dominant firm feels, for instance, that a smaller firm is gaining too much market share, or is likely to threaten its dominant position, it may wish to take defensive action by forcing it out of the market.

Discriminatory pricing policies A firm may price discriminate.

Question 1

In 2006, the postal services market was opened to full competition. Previously, the Royal Mail had a monopoly in the collection and delivery of small letters. In October 2007, Postcomm, the independent regulator for postal services, published the results of a survey of businesses into the changes they had seen in the market.

The market research revealed that, although Royal Mail remained the dominant operator, one in five small and medium mailers and more than a third of large mailers were using more than one mail company. One in five respondents had explored alternatives to mail and had moved some of their mail to other media in the past 23 months. This confirmed the need for all postal operators to place more emphasis on customer service and innovation. More than half of respondents agreed that competition had improved choice and more than a third believed competition had improved Royal Mail's quality of service. 15 per cent of respondents believed that competition had resulted in significantly lower prices.

Source: adapted from Competitive Market Review 2007, Postcomm.

(a) Outline the benefits that increased competition in the postal market might have had in terms of (i) productive efficiency; (ii) allocative efficiency; (iii) dynamic efficiency.

For instance, a firm may offer discounts to a buyer if it also buys other products from the firm. It may charge lower prices for bulk orders. Many forms of price discrimination are anti-competitive, so firms need to be careful when using price discrimination to find out from the competition authorities whether their pricing policies are legal.

The tie in of non-related goods or services A firm may refuse to sell a good unless the buyer also purchases other goods from the firm. For instance, a firm may enjoy a dominant position in sales of one good because of genuine product superiority. It may then boost sales of another of its products which suffers much more severe competition in the market place by refusing to supply the first good unless the second is bought. This raises overall sales and is also likely to boost the price at which goods facing competition can be sold.

Refusing to allow a competitor to use essential facilities To illustrate this, consider an airport which owns its own railway station. It may refuse a train company the right to use the railway station if it threatens to compete with existing highly profitable bus or airline services. Alternatively, an ice cream manufacturer may tell its independent distributors that it will refuse to supply them if they also act as the distribution agents for a rival brand of ice cream.

Refusing to licence intellectual property rights A firm may discriminate between other firms which supply related products. For instance, a firm producing an operating system for a computer may licence use of the operating system to computer manufacturers which also install other software produced by the firm, but it may refuse to licence the operating system to other manufacturing firms which want to install software products from rival companies.

Competition policy

Governments have a variety of methods they can use to promote competition in the economy and reduce the ability of firms to engage in anti-competitive practices.

Encouraging the growth of small firms Government can encourage new entrants to some markets by encouraging the creation of new small firms. They can do this, for example, by giving training and grants to potential new entrepreneurs. They can also set lower tax rates on profits of small firms than on those of large firms.

Lowering barriers to entry In some industries, government itself is a significant barrier to entry. For example, the government might have set high taxes on imports limiting competition from abroad. Or it might limit the number of firms in a market by forcing them to have a licence to operate. Or it might impose expensive requirements in terms of employment law. Lowering these barriers to entry will increase competition. Equally, government can reduce entry barriers from within the industry. For example, if finance is a barrier to entry, government can provide schemes for low cost finance.

Making anti-competitive practices illegal In the EU and the United States, many anti-competitive practices are illegal. Firms can face large fines for engaging in anti-competitive practices. For anti-competitive legislation to be successful, the penalties

imposed on firms for breaking the law must be high enough to be a deterrent. The legislation must also be broad enough to cover all aspects of anti-competitive behaviour.

Anti-monopoly legislation Where firms enjoy considerable monopoly power, government can implement a range of policies. These are discussed in the unit on 'Monopoly and efficiency' as well as the unit on 'Mergers and the growth of firms.'

Question 2

The European Union's top anti-trust regulator yesterday slapped a record €992m fine on ThyssenKrupp and four other lift manufacturers for violating competition laws. The five companies operated a cartel in the lift industry. This was both for the installation of new lifts and for service contracts on existing lifts.

The cartel covered Germany, the Netherlands, Belgium and Luxembourg between at least 1995 and 2004. The firms co-ordinated their bids to ensure that one chosen firm would win a specific contract. When deciding whose 'turn' it was to win a contract and at what price, company employees usually met in bars and restaurants. They travelled to the countryside and even abroad to escape detection. They also used pre-paid mobile phones to avoid tracking.

Both the public sector and the private sector were hit. Contracts signed included those for the European Commission headquarters in Brussels as well as hospitals and government buildings. 'The result of this cartel is that taxpayers, public authorities and property developers have been ripped off big time', said EU spokesman Jonathan Todd. 'These companies ensured, by rigging the bids and sharing the markets, that the price paid both for the installation and the maintenance were way above what they would have been if there had been a competitive market.'

Particularly of concern was that long term maintenance contracts had been signed at inflated prices. The European Commission urged those with contracts to renegotiate them. Customers may also be able to sue their lift contractor for damages in the wake of the ruling.

Source: adapted from the *Financial Times* 22.2.2007; news.bbc.co.uk 21.2.2007.

(a) Using the term 'anti-competitive practices', explain what is meant by a 'cartel'.
(b) How did the lift manufacturers restrict competition?
(c) Discuss whether market efficiency was affected by the actions of the cartel.

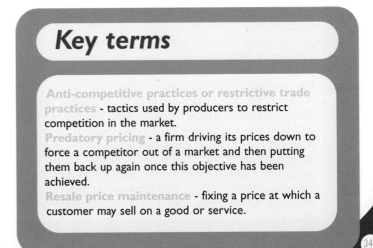

Key terms

Anti-competitive practices or restrictive trade practices - tactics used by producers to restrict competition in the market.
Predatory pricing - a firm driving its prices down to force a competitor out of a market and then putting them back up again once this objective has been achieved.
Resale price maintenance - fixing a price at which a customer may sell on a good or service.

Applied economics

Competition policy

Promoting competition

The UK government is broadly committed to promoting competition in the UK. It believes that competition benefits consumers in the short run by lowering prices and offering them a wide range of goods and services, examples of static efficiency. It also benefits citizens in the long run because increased competition improves the long run competitiveness of the economy. By remaining at least as competitive as our international rivals, the UK can continue to grow and provide jobs for its citizens, examples of dynamic efficiency.

It has a wide range of policies to promote competition.

- Trade policies tend to favour free trade, increasing the amount of competition from abroad to the UK market but also allowing UK firms to export more freely to foreign markets.
- Small firms are encouraged through a range of schemes and incentives including lower taxes on profits for small limited companies.
- The major utility industries such as gas and electricity are regulated, with the regulators given the powers to introduce more competition into the market where possible. This is discussed in the unit on '*Privatisation, Regulation and Deregulation.*'
- The public sector is being opened up to more competition, again discussed in the unit on '*Privatisation, Regulation and Deregulation.*'

Competition policy

The term 'Competition policy' in a UK context is typically used in a more restricted sense than simply government policies to promote competition. Competition policy usually refers to the legal framework to prevent firms abusing market power. It covers monopolies, discussed in the unit on *Monopoly and efficiency*, and mergers, discussed in the unit on *Mergers and the growth of firms*. In this unit, we will consider competition policy regarding anti-competitive practices.

The legal framework

UK competition law is based closely on the requirements of EU competition policy framed in the Treaty of Rome. Article 81 of the Treaty of Rome prohibits anti-competitive agreements which may affect trade between member states. Such anti-competitive agreements could prevent, restrict or distort competition and free trade in the Single Market of the European Union. Article 82 relates to monopoly situations where a firm abuses its dominant position to

restrict trade between member states. For example, a UK firm which is caught fixing prices across the EU with a French and German firm would be prosecuted by EU competition authorities.

EU law governs competition policy when it affects trade across national borders in the EU. UK law governs anti-competitive practices by firms within the UK. The Competition Act 1998 has two main parts which correspond to the two relevant articles of the Treaty of Rome. The first part prohibits anti-competitive agreements. The second part prohibits abuse of a dominant position in a market. Firms engaging in such activities can be fined up to 10 per cent of their wordwide annual sales The Enterprise Act 2002 imposed extra penalties on employees involved in cartels. Individuals caught face up to five years in prison and an unlimited fine.

Competition authorities

Responsibility for enforcing competition policy is split between a variety of bodies.

- The Office of Fair Trading (OFT) led by the Director General of Fair Trading (DGFT) is an independent body, funded by government and responsible for making markets work well for consumers. It is responsible for competition enforcement, which includes stopping and deterring abuse of dominant market positions by companies. It may investigate instances where it judges that a monopolist is abusing its dominant market position. Abuse can consist, for example, of limiting production to raise prices for customers, or limiting technical development, saving on R&D spending but at the expense of supplying higher quality goods to the customer. If it finds evidence of abuse, it can either impose sanctions directly, or refer the issue to the Competition Commission for more detailed investigation. The OFT has the power to fine firms up to 10 per cent of their turnover if found guilty of abusing their market power. In addition, competitors and customers who have lost out have the right to sue the firm for damages.
- The Competition Commission is an administrative tribunal which investigates potential monopoly situations. A firm, or group of firms acting together, is defined as having a **dominant position** if it has a market share of 40 per cent. It has a monopoly if it has a market share of at least 25 per cent. These figures could apply either to a national market or a local market. The result of an inquiry by the Commission is given in a Report. This explains the Commission's findings and lists its policy recommendations.
- Privatised monopolies, such as British Telecom or

Transco, are controlled through regulators. This is discussed in more detail in the unit Public versus private sector provision. However, if regulated firms reject the rulings of their regulator, they have the right to refer the issue to the Competition Commission for a final adjudication.

- The European Commission, through the Directorate General for Competition headed by the European Commissioner for Competition, is responsible for investigating and then punishing firms which breach EU competition law. A firm can appeal to the European Court of Justice against any fines imposed by the European Commission.

It is difficult to gauge the effectiveness of competition policy. Firms engaging in anti-competitive practices are hardly likely to be open about what is an illegal activity. The fact that competition authorities continue to find and investigate examples of anti-competitive behaviour suggest that collusion between firms and anti-competitive practices is not uncommon. The increased penalties that firms face encouraged them to conceal such practices more effectively and makes it more difficult for competition authorities to prove their existence.

DataQuestion

Airline cartel

European and US antitrust officials have raided the offices of British Airways, Lufthansa, Air France-KLM, Cargolux and other air-cargo companies as part of a transatlantic cartel probe. The raids followed allegations that the airlines had violated Article 81 of the EC treaty which outlaws cartels, price fixing and market sharing.

The rise in fuel prices over the previous 18 months has pushed up passenger and freight charges across the airline industry, leading cargo operators to impose surcharges on customers. Surcharges have also been imposed for new security measures. Groups representing customers said that these surcharges could sometimes exceed the actual transport cost. They also said that the surcharges had been very similar across different airlines.

If found guilty, the airlines face a maximum fine of 10 per cent of global annual turnover from the European Commission. In addition they could be fined by US anti-trust authorities. All the airlines whose offices were raided denied operating any form of anti-competitive practices and have promised to co-operate fully with the competition authorities. The European Commission stressed that 'the fact that the European Commission carries out such inspections does not mean that the companies are guilty of anti-competitive behaviour'.

Source: adapted from the *Financial Times* 15.2.2006; www.theAustralian.news.com.au 16.2.2006; www.ogisticsmanager.com 15.2.2006.

British Airways was today fined £270m after admitting price fixing on fuel surcharges on its long-haul flights. The Office of Fair Trading imposed a fine of £121.5 million after British Airways admitted that between August 2004 and January 2006 it colluded with Virgin Atlantic over the surcharges, added to ticket prices in response to rising oil prices, which increased from £5 to £60. The OFT said that on at least six occasions Virgin and BA discussed or informed each other about proposed changes to the surcharges, rather than setting levels independently as required by competition law.

Within hours of the OFT announcement, British Airways was hit by a $300m fine from the US Department of Justice. It was fined not just for fixing fuel surcharges for passengers but also for colluding with other airlines over cargo fuel surcharges. Korean Air was also fined $300m as part of the conspiracy. US Attorney General William W Mercer said: 'When British Airways, Korean Air and their co-conspirators got together and agreed to raise prices for passenger and air cargo fares, American consumers and businesses ended up picking up the tab for their illegal conduct. Today's enforcement actions demonstrate that the anti-trust division will investigate and prosecute illegal cartel activity - here and abroad - in order to ensure that American consumers and businesses are not harmed by illegal cartel activities.'

Source: adapted from *Guardian Unlimited*, 1.8.2007

1. Using examples from the data, explain what is meant by 'anti-competitive practices'.
2. Explain why such anti-competitive practices could have raised revenue and profit for the airlines involved.
3. Discuss whether the cartels led to inefficiency in the cargo and passenger airline markets.

Summary

1. Neo-classical theory suggests that monopoly has higher prices and lower output than perfect competition.
2. This is only likely to be true for a multi-plant monopolist. A natural monopolist may have far lower costs than if the industry were split up into competing units.
3. A monopolist might have higher costs because it needs to maintain barriers to entry. It may also suffer from X-inefficiency.
4. On the other hand, monopolies may be far more innovative than perfectly competitive firms.
5. Government may attempt to correct market failure caused by monopoly. It could tax abnormal profit away, subsidise production, set maximum prices, nationalise the industry, break it up or reduce entry barriers.

Monopoly and static efficiency

Monopoly is generally argued to be inefficient. To understand why, it is necessary to compare a perfectly competitive industry with one which becomes a multi-plant monopoly.

In a perfectly competitive industry there is a large number of small producers each operating at the bottom of the average cost curve. Each firm has therefore exploited all potential economies of scale. If new firms enter the industry because of price increases, their cost curves will be identical to the cost curves of existing firms. Equally, firms leaving the industry will have the same cost curves as those firms remaining.

If the industry became a monopoly, the new firm would be made up of a large number of small factories or plants. The monopolist would not attempt to merge these plants because they were already at their most efficient size under perfect competition. Hence the monopolist will become a MULTI-PLANT MONOPOLIST.

If, in the long run, the multi-plant monopolist wished to expand output, it would do so not by expanding an existing plant but by building a new one. It would operate the plant at its most efficient scale, at the bottom of the plant's average cost curve. If it wanted to contract output in the long run it would close down a plant rather than maintain the same number of plants each producing at less than the most efficient scale of production. Hence, the long run average cost curve for a multi-plant monopolist is horizontal. It can increase or reduce output in the long run at the same minimum average cost.

The demand curve for the monopolist is downward sloping. The marginal cost curve will be the same as the average cost curve if the AC curve is horizontal (for the same reasons that AR = MR if average revenue is constant). Hence, the cost and revenue curves facing the multi-plant monopolist are as shown in Figure 1.

If the industry were perfectly competitive, it would produce where demand equals supply (i.e. where price is equal to marginal cost). If it is a monopoly, the firm will produce at its profit maximising position where MC = MR, and price on its demand or average revenue curve. Hence, under perfect competition output will be at 0B whilst price will be at 0E. If the industry were a monopoly, long run output

would fall to 0A and price would rise to 0F. This leads to the conclusion that output will be lower and price will be higher in monopoly than under perfect competition. The multi-plant monopolist is **allocatively inefficient**.

The net social cost (or welfare cost) can be shown on the diagram. It is assumed that there are no externalities. The demand curve shows the marginal social benefit received by consumers of the product. The marginal cost curve is the marginal social cost curve, the cost to society of producing an extra unit of output. Consumers were prepared to pay 0F for the extra unit at 0A whilst it would only have cost 0E to produce. Therefore the net social cost (the difference between social benefit and social cost) on the last unit of output is EF. Similarly

---

Figure 1 Net social cost if a perfectly competitive industry becomes a monopoly

If the industry were producing under conditions of perfect competition, price and output would occur where price = MC, at output 0B and price 0E. If the industry were a monopoly, output would be where MC = MR at 0A whilst price would be on the demand curve at 0F. Price is higher and output lower in the monopoly industry. The welfare loss is the shaded triangle.

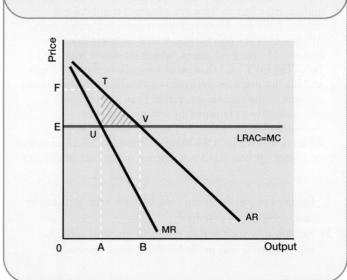

the vertical distance between the demand curve and the average cost curve shows the net social cost of each unit not produced between 0A, the monopoly output, and 0B, the output under perfect competition. Hence the net social cost to society of multi-plant monopoly production compared to production under conditions of perfect competition is the shaded triangle TUV.

The net social cost might be even greater than this triangle for two reasons.

● The monopolist might have to create and maintain barriers to entry to keep potential competitors out of the industry. For instance, it might have to spend large sums of money on advertising or other promotions. This will increase its average and marginal cost in the long run. Output will then be even lower and price even higher than if it operated under the same cost conditions as perfect competition.

● The firm may be able to shelter behind barriers to entry and as a consequence inefficiency may result. **X-inefficiency** is the term used to describe inefficiencies which occur in large organisations which are not under pressure to minimise cost. Average costs will therefore be higher than under perfect competition, resulting in even lower output and even higher prices.

Natural monopoly

So far it has been assumed that the monopolist is a multi-plant monopolist. However, many monopolies are **natural monopolies**. Natural monopolies occur in industries where not even a single producer is able to exploit fully the potential economies of scale. Hence, the dominant firm in the industry, the firm with the largest output and the lowest cost, is always able to undercut competitors in price and force them out of the industry if it so chooses.

This is shown in Figure 2. The monopolist will produce where MC = MR at output 0B and earn abnormal profit by pricing at 0F. However, it would be a nonsense to talk about making the industry more competitive. Splitting the industry into two, for instance, with each firm producing 0A (half of 0B), would increase the average cost of production from 0E to 0G. More competition in the industry would result in a loss of welfare, not a gain. It should also be noted that producing at the Pareto-efficient level of output where price = MC would result in a loss for the firm. At output 0C, average revenue is less than average cost.

Natural monopolies tend to occur in industries where fixed costs are very large. For instance, it would be inefficient to have

In 1991, the government privatised the electricity generation industry. When the industry had been owned by the government, it had operated as a single corporation. When the government sold it off, it was split into a considerable number of different companies including area companies selling electricity to local consumers and a single company which owned the national grid. Electricity generation - making electricity from fuels such as coal or nuclear power - was a multi-plant monopoly when it was a state owned business. It was split at privatisation. Nuclear power remained in government control as did the Scottish generating company. However, the mainly coal fired electricity power stations in England and Wales were split between two new companies, PowerGen and National Power.

After privatisation, the profits of the two generating companies soared as shown in Table 1.

Table 1 Profits of PowerGen and National Power

			£m
	PowerGen		National Power
1991	267		427
1992	326		525
1993	449		599
1994	477		734

(a) Assume that, before privatisation, the electricity industry priced its product as if it were a perfectly competitive industry, earning only normal profits. Assume too that it was X-efficient (producing at the lowest cost possible). Using a diagram, explain (i) where the industry would have produced and (ii) whether this would have resulted in an efficient allocation of resources.

(b) Assume that after privatisation, costs in the industry remain constant. (i) What do the figures in Table 1 indicate about normal and abnormal profit? (ii) Are resources now efficiently allocated?

(c) Assume that PowerGen and National Power were making abnormal profits in 1994 but that the industry had been X-inefficient when it was government owned before 1991. Assume also that PowerGen and National Power had succeeded in reducing costs considerably between 1991 and 1994. Would the industry have been more or less efficient in 1991 compared to 1994?

(d) In the long run, any company can become an electricity producer in the UK and sell into the market. If abnormal profits were being earned in 1994, (i) what would economic theory predict would happen in the next few years and (ii) would this be likely to lead to a more or less efficient allocation of resources?

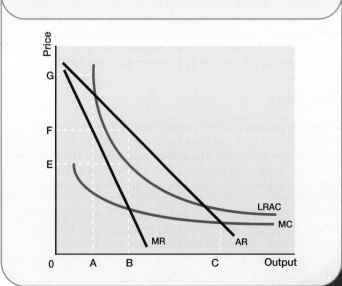

Figure 2 Natural monopoly
In a natural monopoly, economies of scale are so large that not even a single producer could fully exploit them. Competition would be highly inefficient, raising the average cost of production. The profit maximising level of output for the monopolist is 0B, but output would be greater at 0C where price = MC.

Question 2

British Telecom (BT) owns much of the fixed line network in the UK. Crucially, it owns almost all of the 'last mile' from the local telephone exchange to the telephone point in homes and businesses. Since the 1980s, BT has slowly been opening up telephone services to competition. Like Transco, which owns the UK's network of gas pipelines, or Network Rail, which owns the UK's rail infrastructure, other firms are able to hire the use of the fixed infrastructure to deliver services. What differs between BT and both Transco and Network Rail is that BT offers services directly to the customer. In comparison, Network Rail doesn't offer any train services and Transco doesn't own the gas which is pumped through its pipes.

In 2005, Cable & Wireless (C&W) filed a complaint with the independent telecommunications adjudicator concerning full telephony services. Since May 2002, it had offered a rival telephone service to home customers. Home customers choosing the service would pay all their telephone bills to C&W. Meanwhile, C&W would hire the telephone line to the home from BT to provide the service. However, C&W claimed that 40 per cent of BT customers attempting to transfer to C&W were being rejected. This was because BT was insisting that any customer transferring had to provide BT with the exact details of their address. If the details provided did not match those on BT's database, the application was rejected. A spokesperson for C&W said: 'It is like trying to crack a secret code and customers understandably think we and BT are mad when we explain why we can't transfer their account. This is in effect a barrier to competition.'

Source: adapted from the *Financial Times*, 3.3.2005.

(a) Explain why Transco, Network Rail and part of BT are natural monopolies.
(b) What part of BT is not a natural monopoly?
(c) How, according to C&W, might BT be engaging in anti-competitive practices?
(d) Suggest why it might be in BT's interests to insist on exact matching of addresses.

two railway companies with two sets of tracks in the same area running between two towns. In gas, electricity, water and telephones, it would be inefficient to have two or more sets of lines or pipes to every household so that they had the choice of which company to buy from. The Channel Tunnel is a natural monopoly too. It would make no economic sense to build a second tunnel until the first is being used to full capacity.

Innovation

So far, the analysis has been **static**. Perfect competition and monopoly have been compared at a point in time. However, there are also important **dynamic** considerations. The Austrian economist Joseph Schumpeter (1883-1950) argued that monopoly might be far more efficient over time than perfect competition.

In the unit on competition and efficiency, it was argued that perfect competition was unlikely to be dynamically efficient because there was no incentive to innovate. Low entry barriers and perfect knowledge mean that competitors can quickly copy any innovation made.

Innovation could also be lacking in a monopoly market. A monopolist, safe behind high entry barriers, may choose to take the easy life. Sleepy and inefficient, it exploits the market and earns enough profits to satisfy shareholders. Research and development, which imply potential change, are unlikely to be a high priority for this type of firm.

Schumpeter, however, argued that the reverse was likely. The monopolist would have the resources from its abnormal profits to spend on research and development. In the UK, for instance, about 70 per cent of all investment is funded from retained profit. The monopolist would also have the incentive so to spend. It would be able to exploit any new products or new techniques of production to its own advantage, safe from competitors behind its high entry barriers. Productive efficiency would increase because costs would fall. Allocative efficiency would increase because the monopolist would bring new products to the market.

Moreover, a monopolist is never safe from competition. In the 18th century, the canal seemed unassailable as a form of industrial transport. Yet during the 19th century, the monopoly of canals and the monopoly profits of canal owners were destroyed by the coming of railways. In the 20th century, the same process turned railways into loss making concerns as railway monopolists saw their markets taken away by the motor car and lorry. Schumpeter called this 'the process of creative destruction'. High barriers mean that potential competitors have to produce a substitute product which is radically better than the old. It is not good enough to add some fancy packaging or change the colour of the product or add a few gadgets. Therefore monopoly encourages fundamental rather than superficial progress, so Schumpeter argued that a system of monopoly markets was far more likely to produce efficiency over a period of time than perfect competition.

Imperfect competition

So far, monopoly has been contrasted with perfect competition. The same arguments can be used to consider the social costs or benefits of imperfect competition. In imperfect competition output is likely to be lower and price higher than in perfect competition and hence there is a net social cost. Abnormal profits are likely to be made, again imposing net social costs.

In perfect competition and in many cases of monopoly, the consumer is offered only a homogeneous product. On the other hand, imperfect competition is characterised by the selling of a large number of different branded goods. Welfare is likely to be increased if consumers can choose between many, if fairly similar, products rather than being faced with no choice at all.

Schumpeter's arguments about innovation apply to imperfect competition too. Oligopolists, for instance, are more likely to innovate than perfectly competitive firms.

The verdict?

It can now be seen that it is not possible to come to any simple conclusions about the desirability of competition in the market. Competition is by no means always 'best'. On the one hand, multi-plant monopolists and many imperfectly competitive firms may exploit the market, earning abnormal profits at the expense of consumers, reducing output and increasing price. This leads to a welfare loss. On the other hand, natural monopolies are far more efficient than any alternative competitive market

Question 3

The world's pharmaceutical industry can be split into two parts. There are those companies which exist in a tough price competitive environment manufacturing generic drugs which are out of patent. Then there are the companies which spend considerable amounts of their turnover on researching and developing new drugs. These can be sold at high prices, secure from competition through patents. One big blockbuster drug can provide a significant share of profits for one of the big drug companies like GlaxoSmithKline or AstraZeneca for over a decade whilst it remains in patent.

The market may be changing, however. New computerised methods of researching compounds are likely to lead to an explosion of new drugs on the market. The pharmaceutical companies will be wanting to sell these at premium prices. The question is whether the National Health Service, or other health systems across the world, will be able to afford to buy a wide range of new drugs for conditions which before were untreatable or where existing cheaper drugs had poor success rates.

Source: adapted from the *Financial Times*, 4.10.2005.

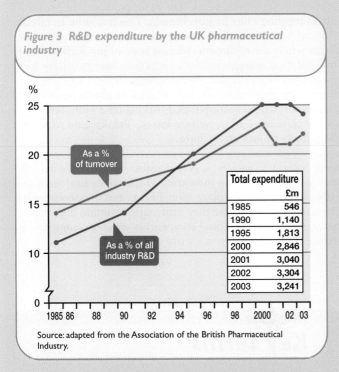

Figure 3 *R&D expenditure by the UK pharmaceutical industry*

	Total expenditure £m
1985	546
1990	1,140
1995	1,813
2000	2,846
2001	3,040
2002	3,304
2003	3,241

Source: adapted from the Association of the British Pharmaceutical Industry.

(a) What is the link between patents and monopoly in the pharmaceutical industry?
(b) Why might part of the pharmaceutical industry be described as engaged in the 'process of creative destruction'?
(c) Discuss whether patients would be better off if new drugs did not have patent protection.

structures. There may or may not be a link between monopoly and innovation.

Government policy

Governments have a range of anti-monopoly policies which they can use to improve economic efficiency.

Taxes and subsidies Abnormal profit can simply be taxed away. This may improve equity within the economic system, transferring the resources which the monopolist has expropriated from consumers back to taxpayers. Unfortunately, this will not improve allocative efficiency. A tax on profits will not affect either marginal cost or marginal revenue. Therefore the monopolist will continue to produce at less than the efficient level of output.

However, it is possible to shift the marginal cost curve downwards by providing a **subsidy**. At any given level of output, the government could subsidise production, reducing marginal cost. If the government wishes the monopolist to produce where MC = price, it will need to find out the level of output where the marginal cost curve cuts the average revenue curve before a subsidy is given. In Figure 4, this occurs at output level 0B where MC_1 = AR. The size of the subsidy required on the last unit of output is EF. This shifts the marginal cost curve to MC_2. The monopolist produces 0B because this is now the level of production where MC = MR, and society benefits because production is at a level where the true cost to society, MC_1, is equal to price. The government can recoup that subsidy by taxing away the profits made by the monopolist.

This seems an ideal solution. Unfortunately there is a number of practical problems. First, giving subsidies to private sector monopolists is likely to be politically impossible for any government. It is difficult enough for governments to subsidise nationalised industries. Second, the policy requires an accurate knowledge of cost and revenue curves. When the policy is first imposed, there is some chance that a reasonable guess can be made. However, taxes and subsidies distort the market so that in the long term it becomes very difficult to guess where hypothetical points on the curves might be. Third, it has already been discussed in detail whether allocative efficiency would increase by moving to a price = MC level of output in one

Figure 4 *Subsidising a monopolist to improve efficiency*
A profit maximising monopolist will produce at OA where MC = MR and price is OG. Output under perfect competition would be at OB, where price = MC. A subsidy of EF on the last unit of output would shift the marginal cost curve downwards from MC_1 to MC_2. The monopolist would now produce at the perfect competition level of output. The government could recoup the subsidy by a tax on profits.

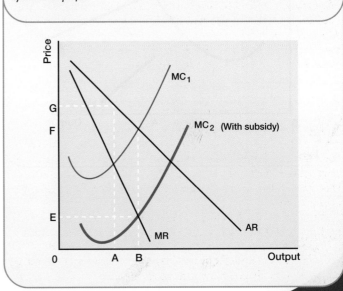

industry. Imposing taxes and subsidies assumes that there is clear understanding of what the efficiency maximising level of output and price might be.

Price controls An obvious method of controlling monopolists would be to impose price controls on their goods. The maximum price that a monopolist could charge would be set equal to the marginal social cost; in Figure 5 where MC = price. To the left of output 0A, the average revenue curve is horizontal because the government has imposed a maximum price of 0B. To the right, the free market average revenue curve reappears. If the monopolist wishes to sell more than 0A, it has to lower its price. Marginal revenue is equal to average revenue if average revenue is constant. There is then a discontinuity at 0A for the marginal revenue curve. The monopolist will produce at 0A because that is now the level of output where MC = MR. The policy works because the government has effectively turned the marginal revenue curve from being downward sloping to being horizontal up to the efficiency maximising level of output.

This type of policy is being used to control privatised industries in the UK. However, it suffers from the same defects as subsidies. It is difficult to know where the cost and revenue curves lie and what is the allocatively efficient level of output.

Nationalisation The private monopolist is assumed to maximise profit. This leads to an inefficient level of output. Another way of controlling monopoly is to change the goals of the firm. This could be achieved by nationalising the industry. The industry is then charged with maximising social welfare and not private profit.

Privatisation and deregulation Many monopolists in the past have been government owned monopolies such as gas or telephones. Their monopolies have been protected by laws preventing private firms setting up in the industry. It is difficult for state owned companies to compete on the same terms as private sector firms. Governments judge investment in a different way from a private firm. They can also always pay any debts if the firm runs up large losses. To create a 'level playing field' where all firms are competing on the same terms, it is argued that state monopolies should be privatised. At the point of privatisation, they can either be split up into competing firms or barriers to entry can be lowered so that competitors can come into the market (an example of **deregulation**), both of which are discussed below.

Breaking up the monopolist The monopolist can be broken up into competing units by government. This might be an effective solution for a multi-plant monopolist with a large number of plants where the **minimum efficient scale of production** is very low, but most monopolists or oligopolists have relatively high minimum efficient scales. The welfare gain from splitting a monopolist into a duopoly, for instance, might be negligible. In the case of natural monopolies, breaking up a monopolist would almost certainly lead to welfare losses. Breaking up cartels is more likely to increase welfare.

Reducing entry barriers It is impossible for governments to reduce entry barriers to industries which are natural monopolies. However, many multi-plant monopolists and oligopolists earn abnormal profit because they artificially maintain high entry barriers and keep potential competitors out. Governments can reduce entry barriers by a variety of means.

Figure 5 Price controls in a monopoly industry

Price controls change the shape of the average and marginal revenue curves. A maximum price of OB will produce a kinked average revenue or demand curve. To the left of OA, the average revenue curve is horizontal, showing the maximum price of OB that the firm is allowed to charge. To the right the average revenue falls because the free market price is below the maximum price. The monopolist will now produce at OA, the output level of a perfectly competitive industry where MC = price. This is because OA is now the profit maximising level of output (i.e. where MC = MR for the monopolist).

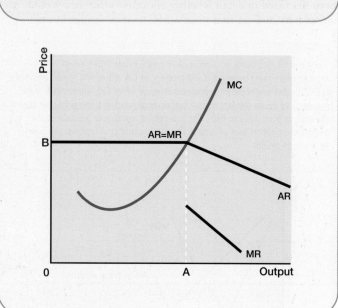

Key terms

Multi-plant monopolist - a monopoly producer working with a number of factories, offices or plants.

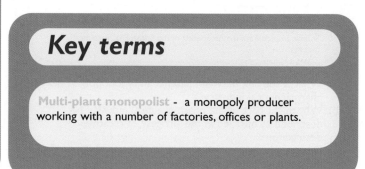

Question 4

In March 2004, Microsoft was fined a record €497 million after being found guilty of anti-competitive behaviour by the European Commission. EC competition commissioner Mario Monti said: 'The Commission has taken a decision that Microsoft has abused its virtual monopoly over the PC desktop market in Europe.' Microsoft has 90 per cent of the market for operating systems on personal computers (PCs).

Part of the original complaint was that Microsoft had 'bundled' its Media Player software in with its Windows operating system. Any new computer coming with Windows automatically had Media Player included. This meant that other software manufacturers producing products rivalling Media Player were effectively excluded from the market. Microsoft was creating a new monopoly in the market for media software, such as film or television programme downloading. The European Commission judgment meant that Microsoft had to offer a version of its Windows operating system to PC manufacturers without Windows Media Player within 90 days.

Another part of the complaint was that Microsoft did not release enough of its windows computer coding to software manufacturers wanting to develop software to run on servers using a version of Windows. Workgroup servers are the computers in a business or other organisation's network that do tasks such as allowing employees to log on, share files or route jobs to printers. Microsoft was effectively attempting to gain a monopoly on all software associated with servers.

However, in December 2005, the European Commission accused Microsoft of having failed to release enough information about its source code for competitors to develop new software. Microsoft faced the imposition of new financial penalties. Microsoft strongly disputed the European Commission's claims.

Source: adapted from the *Financial Times*, 29.3.2004, 20.1.2006.

(a) Microsoft was accused by the European Commission of either having, or attempting to develop, monopolies in two markets. What were these two markets and why were they interlinked?
(b) Why might Microsoft want to develop monopolies in these markets?
(c) How did the European Commission attempt to control Microsoft?
(d) Discuss whether other measures to control Microsoft might have been more effective in promoting competition.

Applied economics

Competition policy and monopolies

UK and EU competition policy

UK competition policy with regards to monopoly is based on European Union competition policy in Article 82 of the Treaty of Rome. This prohibits the abuse of a dominant position in a market by a firm when this affects cross border trade. In the UK, the Competition Act 1998 prohibits the abuse of a dominant position by a firm in a UK market.

A firm, or group of firms acting together, is defined as having a **dominant position** if it has a market share of 40 per cent. It has a **monopoly** if it has a market share of at least 25 per cent. These figures could apply either to a national market or a local market.

Monopolies may be investigated by the Office of Fair Trading. Where the OFT wants a more detailed investigation, it will refer the issue to the Competition Commission. The Competition Commission has the power to investigate and make recommendations. Final decisions about action are made by the OFT.

Certain industries have their own regulators. These are Ofgem in the energy markets, Ofwat in the water industry, Ofcom in the communications sector, ORR for rail services, CAA for air traffic services and Ofreg for gas and electricity in Northern Ireland. In these industries, abuses of monopoly power are investigated by the regulator rather than the OFT. If there is a dispute between the regulator and a firm in the industry, the firm can ask for the matter to be investigated by the Competition Commission.

Where the abuse affects cross border trade in the EU, the European Commission through the Director General for Competition, headed by the European Commissioner for Competition, is responsible for investigating and then punishing firms. A firm can appeal to the European Court of Justice against any fines imposed by the European Commission.

The effectiveness of policy

In the USA, monopolies are illegal because it is presumed that monopoly will always act against the public interest. The basis of UK and EU law is different. Monopoly is permissible so long as the firm or group of firms does not engage in anti-competitive practices which, for instance, raise prices to customers, restrict supply, discourage innovation or damage competitors.

The 1998 Competition Act gives greater powers to the competition authorities to curb monopolies. In the past, competition policy has often been accused of being too weak and its application inconsistent. Prior to 1998, it was often felt that governments intervened in favour of monopoly firms at the expense of customers. However, the 1998 Competition Act and the 2002 Enterprise Act have made such interventions much more difficult. The exact extent of current monopoly abuse is difficult to quantify. If it could be quantified, the OFT and the Competition Commission would be investigating those individual circumstances. However, the threat of investigation and the level of potential fines must be a deterrent to firms thinking of abusing their market position.

DataQuestion

Heathrow Airport

Heathrow misery is official. Surveys commissioned by the Office of Fair Trading say that Heathrow Airport ranks 5th out 50 big airports in terms of the charges it levies on passengers but measured on customer satisfaction it ranks 56th out of 58. The list of complaints is endless. Heathrow is notorious for losing passenger luggage coming off planes. There are long queues to check in and then to pass through security and immigration. Passengers are forced to walk miles to get to airport departure lounges. In the passenger lounges, there are broken chairs and squalid toilets. In the summer, check-in queues snake hundreds of yards into temporary marquees. Last but not least, punctuality of planes departing and arriving is appalling.

BAA, the owners of Heathrow Airport, use a variety of excuses to explain away these problems. Heathrow is a victim of its own success. The airport is just too popular and there aren't enough buildings to accommodate all the 67 million passengers who use the airport. The government imposes impossible security restrictions. It won't allow it to build new terminals or extra runways, and of course there are those school holidays which make demand very seasonal.

What BAA doesn't like to admit to is that it has an effective monopoly of air travel in southern England. By owning Heathrow, Gatwick and Stansted, it accounts for more than 80 per cent of the flights and 90 per cent of the passengers leaving the south-east and East Anglia. The three airports are money machines for BAA's shareholders. Not surprisingly, Heathrow is starved of investment, inefficient and understaffed in those areas where passengers have no choice but to put up with poor quality of service. Contrast the cramped passenger lounges with the splendour of the airport's 48 000 square metres of shopping facilities

that deliver one fifth of BAA's revenues. When BAA holds up its hands about overcrowding, it doesn't think to convert part of its gigantic shopping mall into normal passenger facilities.

The absence of competition means BAA has little if any incentive to expand capacity or to improve facilities. In fact, the current regulatory framework set by the Civil Aviation Authority (CAA) can work against the ordinary passenger. The CAA fixes maximum fees BAA can charge passengers flying to and from the airport. There is then no incentive for BAA to provide these passengers with a decent basic service. Instead, it provides an incentive for BAA to invest in anything which will bring in extra revenues, like those shopping malls. If passengers choose to stay away from Heathrow, BAA doesn't worry too much because the chances are they will fly from another BAA airport anyway.

The solution, as it would be in any other industry, is for the Competition Commission to break up the monopoly. By competing against each other, the new owners of the three main London airports would have to give a better service. That means extra investment, lower prices and greater efficiency.

Source: adapted from the *Financial Times*, 12.6.2007.

1. Why might BAA be considered to be a monopolist?
2. (a) Using a monopoly diagram, explain why BAA is likely to be both productively and allocatively inefficient.
   (b) Why is it also likely to be dynamically inefficient if it is a short run profit maximiser?
3. Discuss whether breaking up BAA's monopoly in the south of England would improve efficiency.

Summary

1. Small firms in an industry exist because economies of scale may be limited, barriers to entry low and the size of the market may be very small.

2. A healthy small firm sector in the economy may lead to increased economic efficiency if it increases competition, reduces prices and increases future efficiency.

3. Firms may grow internally or through mergers, amalgamation or takeover.

4. Mergers may be horizontal, vertical or conglomerate.

5. Firms grow in order to exploit potential economies of scale, control their markets or reduce risk through diversification.

6. Firms may choose to grow by amalgamation, for instance, because it is cheaper to buy a firm than grow internally.

7. Firms may demerge part of their business to improve performance.

8. Evidence suggests that many mergers fail to increase economic efficiency.

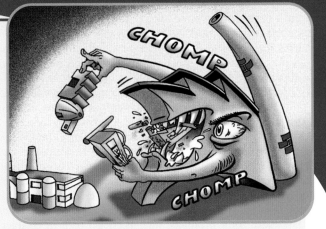

The size of firms

Although production in the UK is dominated by large firms, there are many industries where small and medium sized enterprises play a significant role.

Large firms exist for two main reasons. First, economies of scale in the industry may be significant. Only a small number of firms, producing at the minimum efficient scale of production, may be needed to satisfy total demand. The industry may be a natural monopoly where not even one firm can fully exploit potential economies of scale. Second, barriers to entry may exist which protect large firms from potential competitors. Conversely, small firms survive for the opposite reasons.

Economies of scale may be very small relative to the market size A large number of firms in an industry may be able to operate at the minimum efficient scale of production. Small firms may also be able to take advantage of the higher costs of larger firms in the industry caused by diseconomies of scale. Changing technology such as the Internet can allow small firms the same cost advantage as large firms in reaching out to customers especially in small niche markets.

The costs of production for a large scale producer may be higher than for a small company In part, this may be due to productive inefficiency - a large firm operating within its average cost curve boundary. For instance, larger firms may be poorly organised in what they see as small unimportant segments of the market (called **market niches**). Or X-inefficiency may be present. Equally, the average cost curve of a large producer may be higher in certain markets than for a small producer. For instance, a large firm may be forced to pay its workers high wages because it operates in formal labour markets. A small firm may be able to pay relatively low wages in informal labour markets. Indeed, owners of small companies can work exceptionally long hours at effective rates of pay which they would find totally unacceptable if in a normal job. Or a small producer, like a corner shop sole proprietorship, may be prepared to accept a much lower rate of return on its capital employed than would a large company.

Barriers to entry may be low The cost of setting up in an industry, such as the grocery industry or the newsagents' market, may be small. Products may be simple to produce or sell. Finance to set up in the industry may be readily available. The product

Question 1

(a) Why can small firms survive successfully in the hotel industry?
(b) What economic forces might favour hotel chains in the future?

sold may be relatively homogeneous. It may be easy for a small firm to produce a new product and establish itself in the market.

Small firms can be monopolists A monopolist offers a product for sale which is available from no other company. Many small firms survive because they offer a local, flexible and personal service. For instance, a newsagent may have a monopoly on the sale of newspapers, magazines, greetings cards, toys and stationery in a local area. Consumers may be unwilling to walk half a mile extra to buy greetings cards at a 10 per cent discount or travel 10 miles by car to a local superstore to buy a £2 toy at a 25 per cent reduction. Or the newsagent may double up as a grocery store and off-licence, opening till 10 o'clock at night and all day Sunday, again offering a service which is not offered anywhere else in the locality. A small shop could be the only place locally where informal credit is offered, or where it is possible to buy a single item instead of a pack of six. Equally in the case of some products, such as cricket balls or croquet mallets, the size of the market is so small that one or two very small firms can satisfy total demand.

Efficiency and size

There is no direct correlation between the size of a firm and economic efficiency. Some economists argue that small firms are a major source of economic efficiency in the economy.

Question 2

easyJet was founded in March 1995 to offer low cost scheduled air services within Europe. In November 1995, the company made its first flight from Luton to Edinburgh and Glasgow using two leased Boeing 737-200 aircraft. In 1996, the company bought its first aircraft and started its first international services from Amsterdam to Luton. By 2007, it had annual revenues of £1.8 billion and was carrying over 37 million passengers a year.

Source: adapted from www.easyjet.com

(a) In what sense might easyJet have contributed to greater economic efficiency in the UK economy in recent years?

- The small firms of today are the large firms of tomorrow. Historically in the UK and the USA, today's top largest 100 firms bear little relation to the list of the largest 100 firms 50 years ago. It is important to have as large a number of small firms as possible so that a few can become the large firms of tomorrow.
- Small firms provide the necessary competition to prevent large firms from exploiting their markets. Large firms would be less efficient and their prices higher if they were not aware that small firms could enter the market and take away parts of their market. In some markets, economies of scale are small relative to market size. The alternative to a large number of small firms would be multi-plant oligopolists or monopolists which would erect barriers to entry to the industry and then make abnormal profit. Prices would then be higher and output lower, leading to a loss of efficiency.

There is, however, a number of arguments which suggest that large firms can be more efficient. Large firms may be necessary to exploit economies of scale. They are more likely to be in a position to undertake research and development. Moreover, the size of firms and the number of firms in an industry is not necessarily an indication of competition or the lack of it. As the **theory of contestable markets** shows, what is important is not size or number of firms operating in the industry but the degree of potential competition. Barriers to entry are the key indicator of likely inefficiency, not the size of the firm.

The growth of firms

Firms may grow in size in two ways:
- by **internal growth**;
- by external growth through MERGER, AMALGAMATION or TAKEOVER.

Internal growth simply refers to firms increasing their output, for instance through increased investment or an increased labour force. A merger or amalgamation is the joining together of two or more firms under common ownership. The boards of directors of the two companies, with the agreement of shareholders, agree to merge their two companies together. A takeover implies that one company wishes to buy another company. The takeover may be amicable. Company X makes a bid for company Y. The board of directors considers the bid and finds that the price offered is a good price for the shareholders of the company. It then recommends the shareholders to accept the offer terms. However, the takeover may be contested. In a hostile takeover the board of directors of company Y recommends to its shareholders to reject the terms of the bid. A takeover battle is then likely to ensue. Company X needs to get promises to sell at the offer price of just over 50 per cent of the shares to win and take control.

Types of merger

Economists distinguish between three types of merger.
- A HORIZONTAL MERGER is a merger between two firms in the same industry at the same stage of production, for instance, the merger of two building societies or two car manufacturers or two bakeries.
- A VERTICAL MERGER is a merger between two firms at different production stages in the same industry. **Forward integration** involves a supplier merging with one of its buyers, such as a car manufacturer buying a car dealership, or a

Question 3

Explain whether each of the following is a horizontal, vertical or conglomerate merger.
(a) Wm Morrison (supermarket chain) with Safeway (supermarket chain) (2004).
(b) Greene King (a brewer and pub operator) with Laurel (a pub operator) (2004).
(c) Kwik-Fit with Ford (1999).
(d) British American Tobacco (a tobacco company) with Farmers Group (a US insurance group) (1988).
(e) Pete & Johnny (a manufacturer of smoothies, a crushed fruit drink) with Pepsi (the drinks and snacks group) (2005).

newspaper buying newsagents. **Backward integration** involves a purchaser buying one of its suppliers, such as a drinks manufacturer buying a bottling manufacturer, or a car manufacturer buying a tyre company.
● A CONGLOMERATE MERGER is the merging of two firms with no common interest. A tobacco company buying an insurance company, or a food company buying a clothing chain would be conglomerate mergers.

The reasons for growth

It is suggested that profit maximising companies are motivated to grow in size for three main reasons.
● A larger company may be able to exploit economies of scale more fully. The merger of two medium sized car manufacturers, for instance, is likely to result in potential economies in all fields, from production to marketing to finance. Vertical and conglomerate mergers are less likely to yield scale economies because there are unlikely to be any technical economies. There may be some marketing economies and more likely there may be some financial economies.
● A larger company may be more able to control its markets. It

may therefore reduce competition in the market place in order to be better able to exploit the market.
● A larger company may be able to reduce risk. Many conglomerate companies have grown for this reason. Some markets are fragile. They are subject to large changes in demand when economies go into boom or recession. A steel manufacturer, for instance, will do exceptionally well in a boom, but will be hard hit in a recession, so it might decide to diversify by buying a company with a product which does not have a cyclical demand pattern, like a supermarket chain. Other industries face a very uncertain future. It became fashionable in the 1970s and early 1980s for tobacco companies to buy anything which seemed to have a secure future, from grocery stores to insurance companies.

Reasons for amalgamation

Why do profit maximising companies choose to grow through amalgamation rather than through internal growth?

Cost One answer is that it is often cheaper to merge than to grow internally. For instance, a company may wish to expand and calculates that it will cost £50 million if it does so internally. It then looks to the stock markets and sees that a firm which already has the capabilities required is valued at £25 million. Even after paying the likely premium on the share price involved in takeover bids, it would be cheaper to buy the existing firm than undertake new investment. The ratio between the value of assets of a firm and its stock market price is called the **valuation ratio**. In theory, the larger the difference between asset values and stock market prices, the greater the incentive for firms to grow through takeovers rather than grow internally.

The position is often complicated because it is very difficult to place a value on the assets of a firm. In particular, it has become clear in recent years that intangible assets, particularly brands, can be more valuable than all the factories, offices, stock and other physical assets put together. A strong brand represents a guaranteed income for the foreseeable future. It is also a block on which to build. However large the company, it cannot guarantee to establish a new brand in the market place. Companies can invest money for years in the attempt to build a brand, and fail.

Asset stripping Not all companies in the merger market are necessarily interested in growing in size. Some companies specialise in asset stripping. The predator company will look for companies which have high asset values but low stock market prices. Companies being stalked may well have inefficient management who are unable to manage the company to earn the profit expected by shareholders and the stock market in general. Once a company is taken over, it will be broken up in the most profitable manner to the asset stripper. For instance, parts of the company may be sold as going concerns to other companies. Parts may be closed down. A factory site may be far more profitable sold off as building land than as a working factory. The predator company will then keep the rest to add to its portfolio of companies. A successful asset stripper will often aim to sell off some of the parts of the company for more than it paid for the whole. The part of the company which the predator might keep is then a useful addition to the profit made on the whole deal.

Rewards to management So far, it has been assumed that companies are motivated to grow because of profit, but there is much evidence to suggest that profits of merged companies are often no more and sometimes less than the combined profits of the two individual firms would have been. **Managerial and behavioural theories** of the firm can explain this by pointing out that the goal of a firm is not necessarily to maximise profit. The managers of the firm have a vested interest in seeing a firm grow because their rewards (their pay, bonuses, company cars, prestige and influence) tend to increase with the size of the firm. The managing director of a company which doubles its size overnight is likely to receive a substantial pay rise in the not-too-distant future.

Moreover, the financial markets have a strong incentive to encourage takeovers and mergers. Banks, merchant banks and other financial institutions can make very large profits from organising takeovers.

Reasons for demergers

A DEMERGER occurs when a firm splits itself into two or more separate parts to create two or more firms. The two or more new firms may be of roughly equal size. Sometimes, though, the term is used to describe the sale of a small part of a business to another business.

Demergers occur for a variety of reasons.

Lack of synergies Management may feel that there are no SYNERGIES between the parts of the firm. This means that one part of the firm is having no impact on the more efficient and profitable running of the other part of the firm. Where there are no synergies, there could even be diseconomies of scale because senior management are having to divide their time between two or more businesses which have little to do with each other.

Price The price of the demerged firms might be higher than the price of the single larger firm. For example, a firm may be valued at £300 million on a stock exchange. But if it split into two, the two new firms might be valued at £150 million and £250 million. Investors in companies base valuations on a variety of different factors but one of them is the growth prospects of a firm. If a firm has a part which is growing fast, it will be worth more than another part of equal size which is growing more slowly. The relatively poor performance of one part of a company can drag down the share price of the whole company despite the fact that other parts are performing well. Financial markets talk about 'creating value' by splitting up companies like this.

Focussed companies In the 1970s, it was fashionable to create conglomerates to diversify risk. Over the past ten years, it has become fashionable to create firms which are highly focussed on one or just a few key markets. The argument is that management can deliver higher profits and growth by concentrating their energies on getting to know and exploiting a limited range of markets. Evidence also suggests that being the market leader in terms of sales tends to be relatively more profitable than being, say, number 3 or 4 in the market, so companies therefore **divest** themselves of (i.e. sell off) parts

Key terms

Conglomerate merger - a merger between two firms producing unrelated products.
Demerger - when a firm splits into two or more independent businesses.
Horizontal merger or integration - a merger between two firms in the same industry at the same stage of production.
Merger, amalgamation, integration or takeover - the joining together of two or more firms under common ownership.
Synergy - when two or more activities or firms put together can create greater outcome than the sum of the individual parts.
Vertical merger or integration - a merger between two firms at different production stages in the same industry.

which don't fit in with their core activities. Sometimes, a firm will sell off a part cheaply which goes on to be very successful. It could be argued that the firm's management sold the part too cheaply. Equally, it can be argued that it shows that a company has only limited management resources. The part sold off would never have been successful within that particular firm because management did not have the time or expertise to make it flourish.

Mergers and efficiency

There is much controversy as to whether mergers increase economic efficiency. Productive efficiency will increase if average costs of production after the merger fall because of economies of scale. Allocative efficiency will increase if the merged company provides a wider range of goods, better quality products, etc. On the other hand, mergers tend to reduce competition in the market.

Moreover, asset stripping is very controversial. Its supporters argue that the asset stripper performs a useful economic function. The value to society of a company can be calculated by the sum of its component parts. If greater profit can be made by demolishing a factory, sacking the workforce and selling the land for shops, houses or offices than by keeping the factory operational, then the asset stripper is performing a useful social role by doing so. The asset stripper is reallocating resources according to the signals of the market. The problem is that market prices may not be an accurate reflection of true social value. Short run profit maximisation by one company may well not lead to an economically efficient outcome for society.

Question 4

Two of the world's largest consumer products groups announced their merger today. Procter & Gamble is to merge with Gillette in a deal worth $57 billion. The combined company will have annual sales of $60 billion. Although both companies sell into the same broad segment of the market, there is relatively little overlap between the two companies' brands. Around 4 per cent - 6 000 jobs - of the combined workforce will lose their jobs through rationalisation.

Analysts argue that one reason for the merger is an improved ability to deal with large supermarket chains such as Wal-Mart. Supermarkets have been driving down the prices that even giant manufacturers like Procter & Gamble can charge. With more sales, the merged company would be in a better position to negotiate higher prices. It would also be able to negotiate better marketing deals and secure prime spots for their store displays. Another argument in favour of the merger is that it will give the merged company greater

economies of scale in their supply chain. They will be able to push the products of both companies down a single supply chain rather than the two before. This will be helped by the recent introduction of radio-frequency identification (RFID) chips, the successor to bar codes. The new chips, which allow goods to be identified remotely, will make it easier to track products as they go through the supply chain, making it easier to identify when new stock needs to be delivered.

Three investment banks that worked on the merger will share between $50 million and $95 million in fees.

Source: adapted from the *Financial Times*, 31.1.2005.

(a) Suggest why Procter & Gamble chose to merge with Gillette rather than develop its own brands which would have been in competition with those of Gillette.
(b) What advantages might the combined company have because of its larger size?

Applied economics

Mergers and efficiency

Merger activity

Over the last hundred years there has been a significant growth in the importance of large firms in the UK economy. For instance, in 1949 the share of the 100 largest private enterprises in manufacturing net output was 22 per cent. By 1975, this had risen to 42 per cent. Since then it has fallen back as manufacturing industry has shrunk under competitive pressures. Most of this increase in concentration has come about through mergers, particularly horizontal mergers. There has been a similar trend in both primary and tertiary industry.

Merger activity has tended to be relatively uneven over time and tends to happen in waves. The mergers in the 1960s were often motivated by a desire to increase in size in order to gain market power or to cut costs. The abolition of restrictive trade practices by the 1956 Act in particular increased mergers. Unable to collude to rig the market in their favour, firms resorted to taking over other firms to gain sufficient control of the market to gain monopoly profits. The mergers of the 1980s were often more concerned with buying market share in what could be difficult to enter oligopolistic markets. By the late 1980s, there was also a growing realisation that only large firms would survive in many markets when a Single Market was created in the European Union in 1993.

The recession of the early 1990s led to a fall in merger activity. There were even some de-mergers,

such as the split of ICI into two companies, ICI and Zeneca. This reflected a new business awareness that two smaller companies might be more efficient than a single larger company.

Better economic conditions by the second half of the 1990s led to a resurgence of merger activity which, with a fall off in the world recession of the early 2000s, has continued to this day. The largest deals over the past ten years have tended to be international, reflecting growing globalisation. Conglomerate companies have gone out of fashion and many have been broken up. Equally, there are relatively few vertical mergers. Today, companies tend to concentrate on 'core activities', making products at one broad stage of the production process. Selling off parts of large companies which are no longer 'core' has been a major source of acquisitions for other companies. Mergers and takeovers today tend to be justified either for gaining economies of scale or increased market share. Or they are rationalised as the purchase of underperforming assets which can be transformed under new management.

The legislative background

Merger policy is governed by the Competition Act 1998 and the Enterprise Act, 2002. These two Acts lay down that mergers are initially considered by the Office of Fair Trading (OFT). The vast majority of mergers are too small to be of concern to the

regulatory authorities. Very large mergers which involve European or other foreign firms with a UK firm may be considered by the EU competition authorities, rather than the UK authorities. However, the Director General will consider it if:
- the merger involves a takeover of a firm with more than £70 million of assets worldwide;
- or the merger will create a firm with 25 per cent or more of a market;
- or it involves a firm with an existing 25 per cent or more market share;
- or the firms are in the newspaper or water industries.

The Office for Fair Trading then decides whether a merger falls into one of these categories and whether action should be taken.
- The merger may be judged to have no adverse effect on competition and be allowed to proceed.
- It may be deemed to be against the public interest but, after talks with the firms, a compromise may be reached. For instance, the firms may agree to sell off part of the new firm to reduce market dominance.
- It may be deemed against the public interest and then it will be referred to the Competition Commission.

If a referral is made to the Competition Commission, it will investigate the merger and produce a report. Based on the findings of the report, the Competition Commission will decide whether or not the merger may proceed and, if so, under what conditions. The firms involved may appeal against a decision of the Competition Commission to the Competition Appeal Tribunal whose decision is then final. In cases of 'public interest', which includes mergers of newspapers, the Secretary of State for Trade and Industry makes the final decision rather than the Competition Commission.

Mergers and economic efficiency

Evidence suggests that most mergers do not lead to any efficiency gains. Many in fact lead to losses of economic efficiency. There is a number of ways in which this could be measured.
- Profits of the combined company decline from what they might otherwise have been. This is often anticipated in the stock market where the share price of a company taking over another falls when the takeover is announced.
- Turnover falls. Mergers may well lead to 'rationalisation' of plant and other facilities. In the process the capacity of the firm falls, leading to a loss of turnover. This reduction of capacity may not be compensated for by an increase in capacity elsewhere in the economy, pushing the production possibility frontier backwards towards the origin.
- Employment falls. Rationalisation often involves reducing the workforce. These workers may then be added to a pool of long term unemployed people.

If mergers fail to improve efficiency, why do they take place? One factor is availability of finance. In booms, finance is more readily available. Stock market prices tend to be increasing, so large companies can finance acquisitions either by issuing new shares or, more likely, offering new shares in their company to the shareholders of the takeover target. Equally, interest rates tend to be lower, making it easier to borrow the money to finance acquisitions.

Another factor which fuels merger activity is the gains to be made by the economic actors in the business community. City financial institutions which help companies with takeovers and mergers have a vested self interest in promoting them. The higher the level of merger activity, the higher the fees they can collect. Equally, top managers and directors can benefit. The larger the company, the higher the total remuneration package likely to be offered to a top manager or director. Sometimes planned mergers fail to go ahead because the top executives of the two companies fail to agree on who is to get what post in the new company. This would tend to support managerial theories of the firm.

In a recession, managers and directors are often too busy fire-fighting to make long term strategic decisions such as whether to take over or merge with another company. With sales and profits falling, they are too busy trying to stabilise and reinvigorate existing business activities.

The effectiveness of merger control

Merger policy has done little to prevent the increased concentration of UK industry. Some have argued that:
- too few cases have been referred to the Competition Commission (formerly known as the Monopolies and Mergers Commission);
- there is little rationale behind the choice of which potential mergers are referred;
- this lottery is made worse by the inconsistency of the stance taken by a Competition Commission staffed by different people at different times.

It can then be argued that a much tougher line needs to be taken. In particular, companies should need to prove more than just that a merger would not be against the public interest. Merging companies should be forced to prove that the merger is likely to be in the public interest.

Free marketeers take an opposite viewpoint. They would say that governments are ill placed to decide what would be in the public interest and what would not. This is because governments cannot predict what will happen after a merger with any certainty. More government intervention would be likely to lead to a series of mistakes with beneficial mergers being stopped because of government interference. Even if it were true that most mergers lead to no increase in economic efficiency, letting the market decide is unlikely to lead to wrong decisions being made. Whatever happens, free market forces lead to better decision making than anything government could achieve.

DataQuestion

Kwik-Fit

Kwik-Fit is a car repair firm. Founded in 1971, by 1999 it had nearly 2 000 branches in the UK and in continental Europe. With profits of over £60 million, it was a successful business.

In 1999, Ford bought Kwik-Fit for £1bn ($1.6bn). Kwik-Fit wanted to expand more rapidly than its finances would allow. As part of Ford, it was hoping to gain access to finance to roll out its formula across Europe at a faster pace.

Ford was expanding outside its core motor manufacturing business. It wanted to become a leading consumer services business, controlling more of the after care market for its vehicles. Kwik-Fit, with its successful car repair business and its car insurance arm, seemed to be an ideal match. This was especially the case because Ford had for some time been attempting to enter the UK market through its own chain, called Rapid-Fit. However, sales growth and profits had proved disappointing.

Even at the time, Ford's move was contrary to industry trends. Other US manufacturers were outsourcing component supply and selling off parts and other related businesses to concentrate on their core business of vehicle development and production.

Three years later, in 2002, Ford sold Kwik-Fit for £330 million ($500 million) to a private equity firm, CVC Partners. The investment by Ford had gone wrong. Kwik-Fit was now making a loss, not helped by a downturn in the economy which made motorists more reluctant to spend money on their cars. The low price also reflected accounting problems at Kwik-Fit when PwC, investigating the company's finances, found that goods from suppliers were not being charged against profits because invoices had not been sent. The effect was to overstate profits by around £3.4 million a year. However, Ford's decision was mainly influenced by a change of strategy. By 2002, it had decided that a 'back to basics' philosophy would be more beneficial to the company in the long run. Kwik-Fit was just one of many companies that Ford sold at this time. Martin Inglis, Ford group vice president at the time and head of business strategy, said: 'Although these are good businesses, they don't align with our back-to-basics strategy. These sales further signal the progress that Ford is making on key parts of our Revitalisation Plan.'

CVC Partners is a private equity company. Its aim is to buy businesses cheaply, turn them around and then sell them at a higher price a few years later. With the

economy recovering and management more geared to expansion, Kwik-Fit rapidly turned back into a profit making company. A number of loss making sites were closed and a TV advertising campaign was launched, the first in five years. In the 2004 financial year, its turnover was £854 million and operating profits were £38.5 million.

By mid-2005, CVC Partners was in a position to sell Kwik-Fit to PAI, another private equity firm, for £800 million ($1.5 billion), over twice the price that it had paid Ford. Rob Lucus, a partner at CVC, said: 'Since our acquisition in 2002, the company has been transformed and is now delivering substantially improved financial performance. Kwik-Fit is well positioned for its next phase of growth.' Hamish McKenzie, a partner at PAI, said: 'Kwik-Fit has exceptional brand recognition in its key markets and benefits from significant growth prospects as a market leader.' He added that PAI would support Kwik-Fit's management to further strengthen Kwik-Fit's leading position in the fast-fit European market.

Source: adapted from the *Financial Times*, 18.9.1999 and 13.4.1999; www.kwik-fitinsurance.com; http://news.bbc.co.uk 28.6.2002.

1. (a) Discuss whether Ford buying Kwik-Fit was an example of a horizontal or vertical merger.
   (b) Explain what type of merger occurred when CVC or PAI bought Kwik-Fit.

2. Analyse why (a) Ford and (b) CVC and PAI decided to buy Kwik-Fit.

3. Discuss whether (a) Ford's purchase and (b) CVC's purchase of Kwik-Fit led to greater economic efficiency.

Summary

1. Technological change is associated with invention and innovation.
2. Technological change may affect a firm's production methods, its efficiency and its cost structure.
3. New technology leads to new types of products being made. This affects patterns of production and consumption.
4. Market structures can be affected by technological change. In some markets, it leads to greater competition and in other markets it leads to the creation of oligopolies and monopolies.

Technological change

Technological change and technical progress have been accelerating over time. The pace of change has been increasing as knowledge and capabilities increase. Technological change arises out of invention and innovation. Invention may be small scale. For example, the first working personal computer was developed in a garage by the founders of what would become Apple Corporation. Or it may be large scale. Putting a man on the moon required enormous research efforts in the US and elsewhere.

Invention and innovation are often linked to **research and development (R&D)** expenditures. R&D tends to be highest in industries where the reward to successful innovation is large. Typically, this means that the results of research and development can be **copyrighted** and **patented**. The firm is then able to create a **monopoly** and earn higher profits than it would if the results of the R&D process were available to all firms in the industry.

Invention and innovation are sometimes differentiated. **Invention** is the creation of a new idea. But most inventions never become commercial realities. **Innovation** is the process of transforming an invention into a process or product which will be used to produce actual goods and services. Sometimes innovation is also distinguished from improvements. An innovation is a significant change. An **improvement** is a small, incremental change to an existing process or product.

Invention and innovation may have two distinct outcomes.

- It may affect the method of production of a good or service without changing the nature of that good. For example, the use of robots on a car production line may make production more efficient but does not change the car that is being made.
- It may result in a new type of good or service. For example, technological change is currently increasing the power of computers, or expanding the range of drugs to fight diseases.

In some cases, invention and innovation result in both new methods of production and new types of products.

Methods of production

Technological change can have implications for methods of production. New technology often is **embodied** in capital equipment. For example, a new machine might contain all the latest technology. Investing in new capital equipment is likely to increase **productivity**, either capital productivity (output per unit of capital employed) or labour productivity (output per unit of labour employed).

Assume that a firm currently uses 50 units of

capital and 50 units of labour to produce 200 units of output per year. Its capital to labour ratio is therefore 1:1. It now replaces some of its machines with ones which are more technologically advanced.

- This might lead to more **capital intensive** production. For example, to produce 200 units of output, it might now need only 40 units of capital and 10 units of labour. Its capital to labour ratio has therefore risen from 1:1 to 4:1.
- Production may become more **labour intensive**. For example, to produce 200 units of output, it might now need only 20 units of capital but need 40 units of labour. The capital to output ratio has therefore fallen from 1:1 to 1:2.
- Technological change may have been **neutral** in terms of capital and labour intensities. If the introduction of new machines led to a reduction in both capital and labour to 40 units of each, the capital to output ratio would have remained the same at 1:1.

Technological change in production may have an impact on the skill levels of workers required. When Henry Ford introduced production lines to manufacture cars, he substituted machines for skilled labour. Most of the workers on the production line, instead of being skilled artisans as they were when cars were made by hand, were unskilled workers. Similarly, fast food chains like McDonald's employ production techniques which require far less skill on the part of their workers than an ordinary restaurant.

However, the trend over time is the reverse of these two examples. Technological change is demanding a more skilled workforce rather than a less skilled workforce. Unskilled workers in the UK today are at most risk from unemployment One reason for this is that the percentage of jobs in the economy which require skills is rising over time.

Costs of production

Costs of production are likely to fall due to technological change. Technological innovation is likely to be labour saving. Total, average and marginal costs of production will therefore fall at any given level of output.

In Figure 1, the long run average cost curve falls from AC_1 to AC_2. The minimum efficient scale of production (MES), the lowest point on the long run average cost curve, has increased from 0A to 0B. However, it is not always the case that the minimum efficient scale of production will rise. The change in technology may allow much smaller numbers of products to be made at lowest cost. Figure 2 shows a downward shift in the long run average cost which leads to a fall in the minimum efficient scale of production from 0A to 0B.

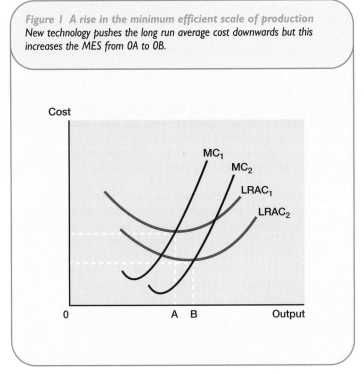

Figure 1 A rise in the minimum efficient scale of production
New technology pushes the long run average cost downwards but this increases the MES from 0A to 0B.

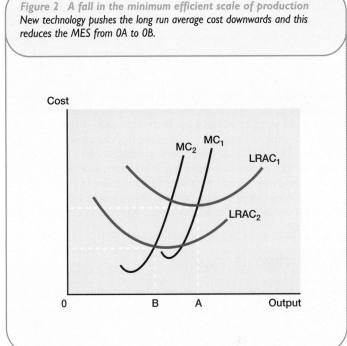

Figure 2 A fall in the minimum efficient scale of production
New technology pushes the long run average cost downwards and this reduces the MES from 0A to 0B.

In some industries, technological change has led to the minimum efficient scale of production rising. For example, in the motor manufacturing industry, Henry Ford's revolution in mass production at the start of the twentieth century increased the MES substantially. Over the past twenty years, however, manufacturers have sought technologies which will bring down the MES. In the steel industry, technological change over the past twenty years has allowed small steel mills to be as cost competitive as large mills. In the motor manufacturing industry, firms have realised that consumers wanted much more choice. **Mass customisation** means being able to produce, for example, 1 million cars in 10 000 different variants.

Technological change may have an impact on both fixed and variable costs of a business. Installing a new heating boiler which embodies the latest technology might reduce the cost of heating a firm's premises. Because heating is likely to be classified as a fixed cost, this will reduce its fixed costs. Another firm may introduce a new pattern cutting machine which reduces the amount of wastage each time a product is made. This wastage is likely to be classified as a variable cost. So variable costs fall.

Efficiency

If the introduction of new technology leads to lower costs of production, then there will be a gain in **productive efficiency**. Whether **allocative efficiency** is achieved depends on whether the firm passes on the reduction in costs to the consumer in lower prices. If price is set above marginal cost, then there will be allocative inefficiency. Productive and allocative efficiency are aspects of static efficiency. New technology results in **dynamic efficiency** when it leads to the introduction of new goods and new processes over time.

Production and consumption of goods

New technologies don't just affect how goods are produced. They also affect what is produced and what is consumed in two ways.
- New technology can significantly affect the cost and therefore the price of goods. Where technological change significantly lowers the price of goods,

Question 1

In 2008, Tata Motors, an Indian company, unveiled a new small car which will sell in India for around £1 300 before taxes. Aimed at a mass market in India where average wages are a fraction of those in the UK, it doesn't come up to the standards that are legally required in the UK or the USA. But it is part of a growing trend to make and sell cars to the growing middle classes throughout the Third World.

Tata has kept the price down to £1 300 by using lower-cost Indian engineers and out-of-the-box solutions to research and development. It won't have the specification of even the lowest specification European car. The £1 300 model is powered by a very small 600 cc engine. Labour costs will be low because the car will be manufactured in India. Tata aim to be selling 250 000 cars per year within two years of the start of production. This will give it the economies of scale necessary to keep costs down.

Source: adapted from the *Financial Times*, 4.6.2007; www.telegraph.co.uk, 12.1.2008.

(a) Explain, using a diagram, how production costs of the new Tata car will differ from those of a standard European model of car.
(b) Suggest why selling 250 000 cars a year will be necessary for Tata to be able to make a profit on the car.
(c) Discuss whether Tata is likely to use more labour intensive or more capital intensive methods of production than would a typical European manufacturer.

then demand for those goods is likely to increase. Over the last decade, China and some other Asian countries have undergone a technological transformation. It has meant that they have been able to produce a wide range of manufactured goods which previously they could not make. Combined with low wages, it has meant that the price of many goods, such as clothing and electronic goods, has fallen significantly to western customers. The result has been a much larger increase in the volume of purchases of these goods than of, say, most services which have been increasing in price over time. So the pattern of consumption has changed.

- Technological change brings new products onto the market. Goods like personal computers, DVD players, mobile phones and microwave ovens were simply not available fifty years ago. Consumer spending patterns then change to accommodate the availability of these products on the market.

The structure of markets

Technological progress influences **market structure** in many different ways.

The number of firms in an industry In some industries, new technology allows the number of firms in an industry to increase. For example, where technology reduces the minimum scale of production, there can be many more firms in the industry than before. If on the other hand technologies leads to greater economies of scale with a higher minimum scale of production, the number of firms is likely to fall. The number of firms in an industry is likely to increase if barriers to entry fall. For example, the Internet has allowed a large number of small retailers to enter the market at a time when small shops are in decline because of the economies of scale being exploited by supermarket chains. Part of these new economies of scale being exploited by supermarkets relate to increased efficiencies from the use of better computer systems, a technological advance. So in some circumstances, the number of firms in an industry may decline because a firm or a small number of firms are able to gain control of vital technologies.

Product homogeneity and non-homogeneity In some markets, particularly goods markets, new technology is backed by patents and copyright. Firms are able to create unique non-homogeneous goods for which they then typically charge a premium price. In the pharmaceuticals industry, for example, the major drug companies spend billions of pounds each year in research and development. The prize is the creation of a 'blockbuster' drug which sells into a mass market and which has no clear competitors. In other markets, particularly factor markets, new technology leads to greater product homogeneity. In the textiles industry, for example, any firm, whether in the UK or China or India, has access to the latest machines. This dissemination of technology allows a large number of textile firms to compete in the market. It then becomes very difficult for any single firm to produce a strongly branded, non-homogeneous product.

Knowledge New technologies tends to be protected by patents and copyright. Where this occurs, there is a lack of knowledge in the market. However, in other circumstances, knowledge may be perfect. For example, the container has transformed transportation, particularly sea transport, over the

past 40 years. Containers are a relatively new technology and yet no one has a patent on containerised transport. Knowledge of prices to be paid for container transport and firms willing to supply services is also widely available.

Interrelationships within markets In some markets, new technology has promoted independence of firms. In the container transport market, for example, the actions of one firm does not have an impact on other firms. In other areas, new technology has led to interdependence. In the search engine market, for example, Google and Yahoo! are interdependent because the actions of one company affects the other.

Barriers to entry New technology can break down barriers to entry. With Internet retailing, for example, start-ups no longer need physical premises on a high street. They can operate their business out of their front room. **Capital costs** and **sunk costs** can therefore be very low. On the other hand, new technology can have high capital costs and sunk costs. Building a new plant to manufacture computer chips is very costly. So too is developing a new games console or a new car filled with the latest technology. In some industries, new technology leads to increased **economies of scale** with only very large firms able to achieve the minimum efficient scale of production. Barriers to entry therefore rise. In other industries, new technology leads to a fall in barriers to entry because economies of scale are reduced. Patents and copyright attached to new technology is likely to result in greater **legal barriers** to entry. On the other hand, not all new technologies have patent protection. Also patent protection expires after a given period of time. Whilst the goal of some pharmaceutical companies is to find new drugs which can be patented, other pharmaceutical companies specialise in manufacturing drugs whose patents have expired. In the generic drug market, legal barriers are low.

Question 2

Will Apple's new iPhone transform the mobile telephone market in the same that its iPod transformed the music listening market? Customers certainly seem to like the new iPhone despite its high cost. However, the iPhone and the iPod are being sold into markets with very different characteristics. The iPod with its associated iTunes site entered a market which was weak and with no clear technological winners. The iPod and iTunes have transformed this market, expanding it far beyond what analysts might have first predicted. As a result, Apple has gained some monopoly power over the market. The iPhone is entering a very crowded market where there are already many successful products on offer at a wide variety of price points. Unlike with the iPod and iTunes, the mobile phone is likely to remain highly competitive. Companies like Nokia and Motorola are not going to roll over and let Apple gain market dominance. Through marketing and product development, they can be expected to hit back. The iPhone could then remain just one of many competing products in the market.

Source: adapted from the *Financial Times*, 26.6.2007.

(a) Explain the barriers to entry to (i) the market for mobile phone handsets such as the iPhone and (ii) the market for legal music downloads which includes iTunes.
(b) How might Apple with its iPhone affect the structure of the market for mobile phone handsets?

Competition and monopoly

New technologies can change the structure of industries. It can turn monopolies into competitive industries but can also create new monopolies. For example, in the information technology market, Microsoft with its Windows operating system, Google with its search engine, Apple with its music download site iTunes and eBay with its 'online marketplace' have effectively created monopolies in their market segments. Intel, with around 80 per cent of the PC chip market in 2007, dominates its industry. On the other hand, there is fierce competition amongst manufacturers of personal computers.

Arguably the most important factor in determining the impact of new technology on markets is to consider its effects on barriers to entry. Where new technology lowers barriers to entry to a market, it tends to create more competitive markets. Where new technology raises or creates barriers to entry, it will tend to make a market less competitive.

Applied economics

The newspaper industry

The newspaper industry has been considerably affected by new technology over the past 30 years. Part of the change has come from the introduction of new technology in the manufacturing process of newspapers. Up until the early 1980s, the production process of a UK national newspaper would have been familiar to a newspaper worker from the 1920s. Journalists would type stories onto a typewriter, or perhaps one of the new personal computers that had just been invented. The story would be handed to a compositor who would create a forme, a page image on a metal plate. The metal plate would be inked on a press and paper pages would then be produced. In the 1980s, the whole process was computerised. Journalists would type stories directly into a computer. An editor would then make up pages on screen which would be ready for the printing presses. Computerisation led to significant redundancies in newspapers as compositors and other workers at this stage of the process lost their jobs. It led to a fall in production costs for newspapers. Computerisation and improvements in technology to printing presses have continued to lower costs over time.

The information technology revolution has, however, had a downside for newspapers. Their circulation has been in decline for the past 40 years. There are many reasons for this, but one has been the development of substitute products. By the 1960s in the UK, most newspaper customers could get the news on television. Then in the 1990s, the Internet became widely available. Newspapers feared that the new technology would lead to thousands of new newspaper-type sites appearing online. 'Blogs', short pieces of writing by individuals, might become the new newspaper article. They also didn't know how to respond if other newspapers put their product online, available for free. If all newspapers went online with full editions, would anyone pay for a printed copy?

In practise, the Internet has complemented rather than competed with newspapers. Few consumers want to trawl the Internet for today's blogs. All the newspapers have put up some content online and generated revenues through selling advertising space. However, the paper edition of the newspaper remains the most read product. This is because the paper version is far more versatile when it comes to reading than any online offering. It can be read on the train or the bus, over a lunch table or whilst relaxing at home in the armchair. Online material requires a sizeable and expensive amount of hardware which is not really portable like a single newspaper.

At this stage, newspapers face more of a competitive threat from the growth of other activities. On a train, an individual might prefer to spend time texting and talking on a mobile rather than read a newspaper. At home, the substitute for a newspaper might be playing a game on the latest games console. New technologies are providing an ever wider range of attractive leisure activities. It is these trends which perhaps pose the greatest threat to newspapers in the near future.

DataQuestion

Wal-Mart

Wal-Mart was founded in 1962 by Sam Walton in Arkansas, and today is the world's largest retailer. In 2008, it was on track to sell $400 billion worth of merchandise from over 6 500 stores. Wal-Mart has a presence in the UK since it is the owner of Asda, the supermarket chain. Sam Walton started Wal-Mart as a discount retailer. He was convinced that offering lower prices than competitors was the way to success. Today, Wal-Mart remains committed to offering low prices to its customers.

Source: adapted from www.walmartstores.com.

'Truthfully, I never viewed computers as anything more than necessary overhead. A computer is not - and never will be - a substitute for getting out in your stores and learning what's going on.'

'The secret of successful retailing is to give your customers what they want. And really, if you think about it from the point of view of the customer, you want everything: a wide assortment of good quality merchandise; the lowest possible prices; guaranteed satisfaction with what you buy; friendly, knowledgeable service; convenient hours; free parking; a pleasant shopping experience.'

'You love it when you visit a store that somehow exceeds your expectations, and you hate it when a store inconveniences you, or gives you a hard time, or pretends you're invisible.'

Sam Walton writing in his memoir 'Made in America'.

Today, Wal-Mart's IT reputation is tarnished. Firstly, it has been left behind in a number of areas. For example, Wal-Mart is the world's number one retailer by sales. But on-line, it was only 13th in 2007. It didn't realise in time the importance of e-retailing. It failed to invest enough in the new channel and its web site was nowhere near as good as companies like Amazon. Second, in 2003 it embarked on a costly drive to get all suppliers to use a successor to the barcode system. This is RFID (radio frequency identification). A bar code needs to be physically read by passing it in front of a barcode scanner. An RFID tag emits a radio signal which can be read at a longer distance. For example, RFID in theory allows the possibility for a customer to pass through a checkout and all the goods in the trolley will be scanned instantly without taking them out of the trolley. By 2007, only 3 per cent of Wal-Mart's suppliers were using RFID. The technology behind the system was not properly tested and it imposed too high costs on suppliers. The push for RFID distracted Wal-Mart at a time when it needed to be focussing its efforts elsewhere.

Source: adapted from www.cio.co.uk; www.en.wikipedia.org.

Wal-Mart was once legendary in its industry for its cutting edge use of IT. It was an early adopter of bar-code scanning in the 1970s. It was the first retailer to use satellite technologies. These allowed individual stores on a daily basis to tell distribution depots what stock needed to be delivered. It accumulated a vast amount of data about sales of individual stores and purchases from individual customers. It was the first store chain to catalogue more than 100 terabytes of information. It promoted the use of electronic data interchange (EDI) with its suppliers. This meant that Wal-Mart and its suppliers were using the same standard formats for business transactions including purchasing and invoicing. In the late 1980s, it was the first company to use a continuous replenishment system with its supplier Proctor & Gamble. This was extended from 1992 to include all its suppliers. With a continuous replenishment system, the store monitors its stock levels. It knows what has been delivered. It also knows what has been sold because all goods are scanned through checkouts (the Integrated Point of Sale system or IPOS). So the store's computer system can automatically reorder stock from suppliers when stocks run low.

Source: adapted from www.cio.co.uk; www.en.wikipedia.org.

In the 1970s, 1980s and 1990s, Wal-Mart was at the forefront of using new technologies in IT. The use of barcoding and IPOS systems gave it enormous competitive advantages over its rivals. These systems allowed it to minimise the amount of stock it kept, cutting its costs. It also allowed it to replenish its stores with products that customers wanted to buy, allowing it to increase sales. What's more, its philosophy of selling goods at the lowest price proved a winning formula to grow sales.

In the 2000s, Wal-Mart has attracted criticism from industry analysts. In the USA, as in the UK, Wal-Mart customers tend to be those most attracted to low prices. These are relatively low income earners. Supermarket chains like Tesco have caught up with Wal-Mart in their use of supply-chain technology. But they also stock a much wider range of goods which appeal to more up-market customers. These goods tend to be sold at a higher profit margin. So average profit margins at Tesco are higher, for example, than at Asda. Wal-Mart has become too stuck to its goal of cutting costs and has not paid enough attention to getting products into its stores which more customers want to buy. Sam Walton, Wal-Mart's founder said that there was no 'substitute for getting out in your stores and learning what's going on'. Is this a lesson that senior management at Wal-Mart need to relearn today?

1. Explain, using examples from the data, how new technology can affect (a) methods of production; (b) costs; (c) the supply of goods and services.
2. How might the introduction of new technology have changed the structure of markets in which Wal-Mart operates?
3. To what extent can adopted new technology give a firm a competitive advantage over its rivals?

Summary

1. State ownership of key industries in the economy was the norm in western Europe for most of the post-war era. Industries were taken into state ownership for a number of reasons including the desire to achieve economies of scale, improve management and run these industries for the benefit of the whole nation.
2. Privatisation is the sale of state owned assets to the private sector.
3. A number of arguments have been used to justify privatisation including lower costs of production, increased choice, quality and innovation, wider share ownership and a reduction in state borrowing and debt.
4. Arguments used against the privatisation process include concerns about monopoly pricing, increasing inequalities in society and increasing externalities.
5. Allocative efficiency can be increased in the privatised utilities if they are either subject to greater competition or if they are regulated.
6. Deregulation can improve economic efficiency through increasing competition.
7. Competitive tendering may lead to lower costs and thus increase productive efficiency.

State ownership

As western economies developed in the late nineteenth and twentieth centuries, the role of the state grew. Governments came to intervene more actively in the management of the economy. Also, they gradually acquired ownership of many industries and became producers and providers of a wide variety of goods and services. These included:
- public goods, such as defence, police and the judiciary;
- merit goods, such as education and health;
- other goods and services, such as telephones, gas, electricity and railways - key basic industries in the economy.

By the late 1970s, state or **nationalised industries** (if organised as a separate firm, called **public corporations** in the UK) played a significant role in production in all western European countries. A number of arguments were put forward as to why the state should own and run firms.

Lower costs Nationalised industries could be more **productively efficient** than equivalent firms in the private sector. Most of the post-war nationalisation programmes involved the purchase of a number of private firms in an industry. For instance, before 1947 there were a number of private railway companies operating throughout the UK. It was argued that **economies of scale** could be achieved by merging the competing firms into one, dispensing with duplication of production resources. Moreover, competition with expenditure on advertising and promotion was seen as wasteful. The elimination of such marketing costs would result in even lower total costs of production. To a great extent, these arguments rely upon the fact that industries which were nationalised were **natural monopolies**.

Better management Supporters of nationalisation often held a very poor view of private sector management. They argued that private firms were often run in a very amateurish way by managers or owners more interested either in enjoying a quiet life or short run profit than in the welfare of the company and the economy. Nationalisation was seen as a chance to appoint efficient modern management which would run the industries to maximise net social benefit. In some of the industries, particularly coal, there was an poor record of industrial disputes. It was hoped that nationalisation would make labour relations more harmonious because workers would see the industry as 'their' industry and management would no longer see workers as enemies.

Control of monopolies Many of the nationalised firms, such as railway companies and gas suppliers, were local monopolists. Nationalisation was seen as the easiest and most effective way of controlling these monopolies and preventing them from reducing social benefit by raising prices and lowering output.

Maximisation of net social benefit and not private profit Significant **externalities** were seen to be present in the industries which were nationalised. For instance, in the coal industry it was felt that private companies had too little regard for the welfare of their workers. The safety and lives of coalminers were sacrificed for the sake of private profit. Nationalised industries were given the task of maximising net social benefit even if this meant sacrificing private profit.

Greater control of the economy State ownership of some of the most important industries in the economy (sometimes called control of the **commanding heights** of the economy) was seen as essential if the government was to manage an unstable market economy. The 1930s, for instance, were seen as an example of the inability of free market forces to bring stability and prosperity to an economy. Nationalisation was effectively a move towards a more centrally planned type of economy. In the 1970s, a number of key UK companies, such as Rolls Royce and British Leyland (which became the Rover Group), were taken into public ownership because they went bankrupt under private management. It was felt that the state had to intervene to prevent free market forces from destroying companies which played a key role in assuring the long term prosperity of the country.

A fairer distribution of resources Private firms are in business to make private profit for their owners. Before 1945 most firms were owned by the people who ran them. The family firm was the most typical business organisation. It was therefore easy for workers to see the difference in income of owners and workers. Coal miners, for instance, could compare the standard of living of their children, with barely enough to eat, badly clothed, perhaps not having a pair of shoes and sleeping several to a room, with the comparatively luxurious life-style of the mine owner's children. Capitalist profit was seen as expropriation of money which had been earned by the workers. Nationalisation was an opportunity to seize those profits and use them for the benefit of everybody in society, both workers and consumers, not just a few capitalists.

There is a number of assumptions made in these arguments which are of direct relevance to the privatisation debate.
- The public sector is seen as more efficient than the private sector. In particular, public sector management is seen as better at allocating the economy's resources than private sector management.
- The private sector is seen as exploitative of workers and consumers. State control is needed to neutralise monopoly power and the pursuit of private profit at the expense of the public interest.
- Profit is seen more as an indication of monopoly power than as a signal which allocates resources efficiently within the economy.

Overall, there was a presumption that state allocation of resources was as good as if not better than private sector allocation - or to mimic George Orwell (in '*Animal Farm*'), 'public sector good, private sector bad'.

Privatisation

Privatisation has come to be associated with the sale of large nationalised industries to the private sector. British Steel, British Gas and British Telecom are examples of public corporations which have been sold off. Such sales are just one part of a wider programme aimed at transferring resources from the public sector to the private sector. Other aspects of privatisation

include the following.
- Sales of parts of nationalised industries to the private sector. For instance, Jaguar cars was sold off from a public corporation called British Leyland, the only UK owned large car manufacturer in the 1970s and 1980s.
- Sales of individual assets of government bodies. For instance, local authorities are now forced to allow council house tenants to buy their own homes if they wish. Government departments have been encouraged to sell surplus land and buildings.
- The creation of private sector competition to state monopolies. Regulations, often created at the time of nationalisation, prevented effective competition in industries such as telecommunications, coal and gas. Abolishing these regulations has enabled competitors, such as cable companies, to enter markets previously supplied exclusively by public sector concerns.
- Compulsory competitive tendering. Many services, often local authority services, have been provided by public sector employees in the past. Dustbins have been emptied by council refuse collectors, schools cleaned by council cleaners and hospital sheets washed by health service employees. The government has now forced its own departments, local authorities, and other government bodies to put these services out to tender. Workers who previously provided the services have been sacked, although most have regained their jobs working for the private sector companies which gained the contracts.

Arguments in favour of privatisation

A number of arguments have been put forward in favour of privatisation.

Cost Publicly owned industries have no incentive to cut costs. The result is that there is likely to be X-inefficiency in the industry. There is no incentive because there is little or no mechanism by which government can bear down on costs. There is also often little comparison with what costs might be if reduced to a minimum since the state owned firm is often a monopoly. State owned industries also tend to behave like bureaucracies, where the interests of the workers are as important as the interests of the owners (the state) and consumers. **Behavioural theories of the firm** are more appropriate to understanding their decision making than traditional neo-classical profit maximising theories. A privatised profit maximising company does have an incentive to reduce cost because reduced cost is translated into higher profit. This is true whether the privatised company faces competition in the market place or whether it enjoys a monopoly. Hence privatisation leads to greater **productive efficiency**.

Choice and quality Public sector organisations have little incentive to produce goods which consumers want to buy. They tend to be 'product led' organisations, mass producing a limited range of goods and services which state employees feel is what consumers ought to be provided with. This is particularly true where the public sector organisations are monopoly or near-monopoly providers. In contrast, private sector firms have an incentive to provide both choice and quality. If they are in competitive markets, then a failure to provide choice and quality will result in consumers buying from other firms which do provide these. Even if they are monopolists, privatised firms can often raise prices and expand their market by providing quality services with choice. Higher prices and greater sales can then feed through to higher profits, the ultimate goal of private sector firms. Choice and quality are aspects of **allocative efficiency**.

Innovation As with choice and quality, state organisations have little incentive to innovate. Private sector organisations, however, can earn higher profit if they innovate and persuade consumers to buy more of their product. This increases **dynamic efficiency** in the economy.

The invisible hand of the market Market forces allocate resources so that they are used in the most efficient manner. Consumer spending decisions in a free market act like votes in a democratic election, indicating consumer preferences. Monopoly state organisations, on the other hand, lack the knowledge of consumer preferences to make efficient allocative decisions on their behalf. Moreover, governments interfere in the market place and misallocate resources for short term political objectives. Governments are the enemy of economic freedom because they have such overwhelming political power. Therefore, governments should have as little control over the economy as possible. Only the operation of free market forces will ensure the optimal allocation of resources.

Other considerations in favour of privatisation

The process of privatisation can also be used to achieve other goals.

Wider share ownership It has been argued that wider share ownership is desirable. In the past, share ownership has been too narrow. Only a few relatively rich people have chosen to invest their savings in shares. The result has been a divide between workers and capitalists, with some workers seeing share owners as parasites who skim off the profits which arise from the efforts of workers. In a wide share owning democracy, the distinction between worker and capitalist is not present because workers are also capitalists. Workers will be better able to appreciate the risks that capitalists take with their assets and will be able to see, for instance, that wage increases are not necessarily economically desirable. The wealth of the country will be more evenly spread and this too can be seen as desirable.

Reduction in public borrowing and state spending In the short term, the sale of state owned assets raises money for the government which can be used to reduce public borrowing for the year or even pay off part of the National Debt. There will also be an improvement in state finances in the long term if, as is often the case, state owned enterprises make losses and need to be subsidised. Less borrowing leads to lower interest repayments and hence less need for taxes, as do reduced subsidies to state industries.

Potential problems with privatisation

There is a number of potential problems with privatisation.

Monopoly Some state owned industries operate in a competitive market place already. Before privatisation, British Steel, for instance, although a monopoly producer in the UK, faced fierce competition from overseas steel producers. However, some were privatised as monopolies and remain monopolies. Traditional neo-classical theory would suggest that they would then exploit that position, charging high prices and restricting output, leading to a loss of allocative efficiency. Two ways around this problem are discussed below - breaking up the monopoly and regulating the monopoly.

Equity Nationalised industries do not necessarily price in the same way that a privatised company would do. The process of privatisation is likely to lead to a change in the pricing structure. This will result in there being gainers and losers amongst consumers. There will be also be a change in equity arising from ownership of shares and payouts of dividends to private shareholders.

Externalities Nationalised industries may have given greater weighting to factors such as the impact of their operations on the environment than a privatised industry. Privatisation may then lead to greater negative externalities. On the other hand, nationalised industries may not have to conform to environmental or other legislation because the state has given them exemption. In this case, privatisation will lead to fewer negative externalities.

The control of privatised companies

As explained above, some companies or industries which were privatised already operated within a competitive environment. However, others, such as electricity, gas and water in the UK, were monopolies before privatisation. If left as monopolies, they could exploit their monopoly position, leading to allocative

---

Question 2

Most privatisation was implemented by the Conservative government in the 1980s, with the government netting £110.5 billion (at 2000 prices) from sales. Over the twenty year period to 1999, consumer prices for electricity fell 24 per cent and for gas 35 per cent in real terms. For telecommunications the real price fall was 52 per cent but water prices have risen by 51 per cent and bus and coach fares by 16 per cent.

For gas and electricity, there have been no big changes in service quality despite competition in domestic supply from 1998. In telecoms, competition in the local loop has been very limited but companies have been moving in to provide residential customers a choice of provider. Subscriber waiting lists (where new customers had to wait to get a line installed) have been eliminated and there has been a reduction in call failure rates. In the water industry, there have been large amounts of investment in basic infrastructure to replace an ageing system going back to Victorian times. In the rail industry, there has been limited competition between franchisees. There has been some innovation and some improvement in service indicators. However, public perception is that service quality has deteriorated over time.

Source: adapted from the *Financial Times*, 28.9.2005.

(a) How, according to the article, has privatisation increased
(i) efficiency, (ii) choice and (iii) innovation?

inefficiency. There are two main ways in which this can be prevented.

The creation of competition There are two ways of creating competition. The first is to privatise the company or industry as a whole, but encourage other private sector companies to set up in the industry. For instance, the UK government forced British Gas to allow other gas companies to supply to both the industrial gas market and the domestic market. The second way of creating competition is to split the industry up into competing companies at the point of privatisation. For instance, electricity generation was split up into three parts at privatisation - PowerGen, National Power and Nuclear Electric.

Regulation of the industry A second route is to allow the monopoly to remain after privatisation but create a regulatory framework which prevents it from earning abnormal profit and creating allocative inefficiency. All the privatised utilities in the UK have regulators which act by limiting prices.

There are three main issues which arise from regulation. The first relates to the objective of regulation. The ultimate goal is to prevent the monopoly earning abnormal profit and to encourage it to be productively efficient (i.e. produce at lowest cost). In the USA, regulators have tended to focus on profits, limiting the amount of profit a regulated company can earn. This, it is argued, neither encourages the firm to reduce its costs nor be innovative by creating new products and new markets. In the UK, regulation has centred on prices. Privatised utilities have been set price limits but allowed to earn as much profit as they can within those limits. This, it is argued, leads to greater efficiency. If the firm cuts costs and thus becomes more productively efficient, it can retain part of or all of the gains in the form of higher profits. Equally, if the company is successful in gaining new sales and expanding its market, then it can share in this success by keeping the resulting higher profits.

A second issue arising from regulation is that of **regulatory capture**. It is argued that regulators of privatised companies can be 'captured' by the industries they are supposed to be regulating. The decisions of the regulator are often based on information which is given to them by the industry. The privatised company will obviously only want to pass on to the regulator information which supports the need to keep prices high. If the regulator assumes that the company is giving it full and impartial information, then the regulator can be said to have been 'captured' by the company because it is effectively acting in the best interests of the company, rather than the best interests of consumers. More worrying would be situations where a regulator benefited in some way from allowing weak regulation of the industry. Bribery would be one obvious way for the company to achieve this. However, an intimate association between regulator and the regulated company, where the company was paying the regulator large amounts of expenses, could well lead to the regulator failing to take an impartial approach to regulation.

The third issue concerns the quality of service and investment, issues of allocative and dynamic efficiency. This is discussed in the Applied Economics section.

Deregulation

Deregulation is the process of removing government controls from markets.

- The government may allow private firms to compete in a market which is currently being supplied by a state monopoly. An example of this would be if the government allowed private firms to compete with letter delivery against a state owned postal service.
- The government may lift regulations which prevent competition between private firms. For instance, the government may limit the number of premises in a local area which can be used for the sale of pharmaceutical drugs. Deregulation could then lead to the abolition of this licensing system, with any retailer free to sell drugs from its premises.
- The government may lift regulations when an industry is privatised. For instance, when coal was privatised in the UK, the regulation that no private coal mine could employ more than 10 workers was abolished.

Deregulation attempts to improve economic efficiency through the promotion of competition. This, it is argued, will lower costs (leading to greater productive efficiency) whilst reducing prices and increasing output (increasing allocative efficiency). A major problem with deregulation is that it encourages 'creaming' of markets (firms only providing services in the most profitable areas of the market). For instance, in the bus industry, deregulated in the 1980s, bus firms concentrated on providing bus services on profitable urban routes into town centres, arguably to the detriment of country passengers.

Contracting out and competitive tendering

The government has to provide certain goods and services because they are public or merit goods, or because state provision is more efficient or more equitable than private sector provision. However, this does not imply that the state has to be the producer of all or part of these goods and services. For instance, in the UK the state has never made the sheets that are in NHS hospitals, or the tanks that are used in the British army.

Question 3

Two electricity companies have been fined £200 000 each for stopping customers from switching to new gas or power suppliers. Ofgem, the utility industry regulator, fined Scottish Power and Npower and said it would not tolerate 'bad practices'.

Source: adapted from the *Financial Times*, 21.2.2004.

OFCOM, the new telecoms regulator, should actively encourage consumers to switch from BT, MPs on the Public Accounts Committee will say today. The call has been prompted by a complaint that BT retains an 'unacceptable' 70 per cent of fixed-line connections and a warning that the market as a whole is confusing for consumers.

Source: adapted from *The Times*, 23.3.2004.

On 2 December 2004, we set price limits for all water and sewerage companies in England and Wales for the five years from 2005 to 2010. The average price limit for 2005-06 is 13.1% (including inflation). The companies have now set their charges and in April 2005 household customers will see an average increase in their water and sewerage bills of £29 (11.8% including inflation).

Source: adapted from *Water and Sewerage Bills 2005-06*, Ofwat.

(a) Using examples from the data, explain various ways in which governments can control privatised utilities.

Question 4

The NHS is planning to spend £4.5 billion a year, nearly 6 per cent of its budget, on privately provided clinical care and facilities management. While at this week's Labour Party conference, Unison and other trade unions are calling for a halt in the use of the private sector. Chris Hamm, professor of health services management at Birmingham University and former head of strategy at the Department of Health, said there was a range of areas where private provision could grow in family doctor and community services.

Health ministers believe that the arrival of competition from private providers has helped to shake up health service hospitals and has contributed to falling waiting times and want to see the same effect in primary care. However, the extent to which the private sector has so far contributed to sharply falling waiting times is a matter of debate. It could be argued that it is extra NHS cash and waiting list targets for NHS hospitals which has helped improve NHS performance. Of the 5.5 million patients on NHS waiting lists, the private sector has only performed operations on 70 000 patients.

Source: adapted from the *Financial Times*, 26.9.2005.

(a) Why might increasing the amount of work done by the private sector for the NHS benefit patients?
(b) Why might public sector unions, such as Unison, oppose contracting out?

These are produced by private sector firms and sold to the public sector.

In theory, a government could CONTRACT OUT provision of all goods and services provided. It could employ private firms to operate everything from roads to hospitals to the army. This process is likely to be accompanied by COMPETITIVE TENDERING. The government draws up a specification for the good or service. It then invites private sector firms to bid for the contract to deliver it. The firm offering the lowest price, subject to quality guarantees, wins the contract.

The main advantage claimed for contracting out services is that the government saves money. It is argued that public sector provision is bureaucratic and inefficient. There is no incentive for public sector providers to reduce costs or be innovative. Competition, on the other hand, whether the contract goes to a private sector firm or a government body, forces down prices, leading to greater productive efficiency. The buyer of the service, the government, is also able to concentrate on deciding the exact specification of what is to be bought, rather than having to worry about how the service will be provided.

On the other hand, there is concern that private sector providers might fail to meet the specifications of the contract. Whilst this might not be too important in the area of, say, ground maintenance, it is obviously a very serious issue if a private firm is contracted to run an old people's home or if it is refitting a warship. There is also concern that only a relatively small number of firms will bid for any contract. If only two firms bid for a contract, there must be some doubt about whether either is bidding at the lowest price possible. There is also the danger of collusion, with private firms choosing to divide the market amongst themselves rather than compete.

Finally, lower costs may only be achieved because private firms pay their workers less and work them harder than if those workers were public sector employees. The apparent increase in productive efficiency arising from the lower costs of the contract may have only been achieved at the expense of redistribution in society, with taxpayers gaining and the workers involved losing.

Public Private Partnerships and the Private Finance Initiative

PUBLIC PRIVATE PARTNERSHIPS (PPPs) is a term used to describe a range of partnerships between the public sector and the private sector where the public sector and private sector companies collaborate to deliver services. There is a wide variety of forms of PPP and sometimes contracting out and competitive tendering are classified as examples of PPPs. One type of PPP is partial privatisation of a government asset. The government may sell a majority (i.e. more than 50 per cent) or minority (i.e. less than 50 per cent) stake in a state owned business to a private sector company. The business is then jointly owned and jointly run by the public sector as shareholder and private sector shareholders. Another type of PPP is when a new company is set up, jointly owned by the private sector and the public sector, to sell government services.

The most common form of PPP in the UK is the Private Finance Initiative (PFI). This is where a private sector company builds and maintains a piece of infrastructure like a school, hospital or road. The government then typically leases this facility back from the private sector on a long lease. For the private sector company or group of companies, the contract represents a guaranteed stream of income over a long period of time. Building and then maintaining or operating the piece of infrastructure gives it an opportunity to earn a profit. There is a number of possible advantages for the public sector.

- The private sector partners should have expertise in building and running a project which will deliver higher quality and lower cost than if the public sector alone were involved.
- Government is free to focus on its requirements rather than also having to worry about organising the construction and running of the facility.
- The interaction of private and public sectors should bring innovative solutions to problems. The danger with public sector only projects is that they can ignore best practice and be very conservative in their approach.
- Infrastructure projects become more affordable to the government because less government borrowing is required. The project is paid for in the lease payments made over the lifetime of the project. To the economy as a whole, there is no change in cost - a £100 million hospital costs £100 million whether it is funded by government or by a private sector company. But in effect it means that government can spend more on infrastructure projects now.

PFI projects have not always been successful.

- Sometimes, the public sector has negotiated deals which give the private sector far too large a profit. The deal has therefore not been cost effective for the taxpayer.
- The level of service provided can be inadequate. However closely performance targets are written, the PFI project can sometimes fail to meet them.
- Risk has not always been transferred from the public sector to the private sector. PFI should be risky to private sector companies participating. If they fail to deliver, they should lose out financially. However, sometimes the contract has been written in such a way that it is very difficult for the

private sector partners to lose out if there are problems. There are then reduced incentives for the private sector partners to deliver what they have promised.

- In theory, PFI projects should be more expensive than traditional government investment. The government can borrow at relatively low rates of interest because it is seen as the most secure borrower in the market. Companies have to pay higher rates of interest to borrow because they are seen as less secure. So any borrowing by the private sector to fund a PFI project will be more expensive than the equivalent government borrowing. If there are to be cost savings, the private sector partners must be more efficient in their use of resources than would have been the case if the project had been built and run by government alone.
- Trade unions argue that PFI projects seem cheaper because the private sector pays lower wages than the public sector. 'Efficiency gains' are simply a redistribution of income from often already low paid workers to the partners in a PFI project, taxpayers and the shareholders of private companies.

Internal markets

Sometimes, government decides that only it can produce a good or service. Creating a market where private sector firms compete could be wasteful, inefficient or lead to undesirable distribution of income outcomes. In this case, government can create an INTERNAL MARKET. This is where public sector providers compete amongst themselves for contracts and jobs. If a provider wins more contracts than before, money will flow into the provider and it can expand. Providers rather than see a drain of contracts, will be forced to become more efficient or face going out of business. Internal markets were implemented in the National Health Service in the 1990s. Internal markets work best when the cost of operating the market is relatively low and the efficiency gains from competition are high. If

administration costs are high, they can cancel out the gain from increased efficiency. Internal markets can also occur within private sector firms. Some manufacturing companies, for example, get individual factories which they own to compete to supply another part of the business.

Key terms

Contracted out - getting private sector firms to produce the goods and services which are then provided by the state for its citizens.

Competitive tendering - introducing competition amongst private sector firms which put in bids for work which is contracted out by the public sector.

Internal market - where parts of an organisation, such as the National Health Service or the BBC, compete against each other to provide services.

Nationalised industries and public corporations - state owned industries or companies.

Public Private Partnerships (PPPs) - a partnership between the public sector and the private sector where the public sector and private sector companies collaborate to deliver services. An example of a PPP is the Public Finance Initiative where the private sector builds and maintains infrastructure like a hospital and leases it to the government.

Applied economics

Nationalisation and privatisation in the UK

History

The state is responsible for organising the production of many goods and services. Some, such as defence and education, have traditionally been financed through taxes and have been provided free at the point of sale. However, there has also been a long tradition of the state selling goods and services in the same way that a private company might. For instance, a public postal service was established in 1840 which has grown to be today's Post Office. In 1912, the Post Office first provided a national telephone service. During the 1920s

and 1930s, successive UK governments established the British Broadcasting Corporation, the London Passenger Transport Board, the British Overseas Airways Corporation (now part of British Airways) and the Central Electricity Generating Board. Local authorities also provided many goods and services such as public baths, bus transport and gas.

Up to the Second World War, government enterprises were set up on an ad hoc basis where it was felt that state provision would be better than private provision in that particular case. However, the Labour government elected to office in 1945 believed strongly that nationalisation in general was likely to be beneficial. Clement Attlee's government nationalised coal, rail, steel, the Bank of England and road transport. It created the gas boards and electricity boards that existed for the next 40 years. The Labour Party after 1951 remained committed to further nationalisation but it was not a high priority. The two remaining firms which passed into public ownership were both firms which went bankrupt and were taken over in the national interest - Rolls Royce in 1971 by the Conservative government of Edward Heath and British Leyland cars in 1975 by Harold Wilson's Labour government.

Privatisation was not even specifically mentioned in the 1979 Conservative Party manifesto. Yet within 10 years, many public sector companies had been sold off to the private sector. Table 1 shows the timetable for the sale of state owned assets to the private sector from 1979.

Initially, relatively small companies with healthy profits were put up for sale. These were in markets where there was already competition. The first public monopoly to be privatised was British Telecom in 1984.

In the 2000s, the UK government effectively renationalised two companies. One was Railtrack, which, in 1995 on privatisation of the rail industry, was formed to own the rail infrastructure. In 2002 it became Network Rail. The other company was British Energy, the owner of the UK's more modern nuclear power stations, renationalised in 2004. Both Railtrack and British Energy effectively became bankrupt and the government decided to take action in order to safeguard the infrastructure which the two companies owned.

The example of the railways

Before 1947, the railways were private companies. Railway companies were regionally based and owned the tracks, stations and rolling stock. In 1947, the railways were nationalised only to be privatised again in 1995. The new structure of the industry was much more complex than before 1947 because the government recognised that the track was a natural monopoly but competition could be introduced into providing services over those tracks.

- Railtrack was privatised as the monopoly owner of the existing rail infrastructure. Following widespread criticism of its performance, a number of rail crashes and a sizeable increase in the government subsidy that would have been needed to keep it profitable, it was effectively renationalised in 2002. Now called Network Rail, it is a non-profit company which is run in the interests of 'members' ranging from rail companies to passengers to the government. It is responsible for maintaining and upgrading everything from rail lines to railway stations and bridges. It earns revenues from the rail companies which run trains across its tracks.
- A number of train operating companies run services along the railway network. These include National Express which operates the east coast main line, Virgin Trains which operates the west coast main line, and GoVia which operates local services in Kent. They have won a franchise from the government to run a given level of service for a fixed number of years. They receive revenues by charging passengers and often receive subsidies from government. Most train operating companies are monopolies along their routes. Where there is competition, this is often limited because one company provides a superior service to another.
- In 2008, there were four rail freight companies: Direct Rail Services, EWS, Freightliner and FirstGBRf. These compete for business in the freight market.
- Train sets (locomotives and carriages) are leased from train leasing companies (called roscos). In 2008, there were three roscos in the UK, HSBC Rail (owned by HSBC), Porterbrook (owned by Abbey National) and Angel Trains (owned by the Royal Bank of Scotland). These are responsible for maintaining existing stock and buying new stock. They receive their revenues from the train operating companies.
- There is a number of companies which compete for work repairing and maintaining railway infrastructure, as well as upgrading the system. They earn their revenues from Network Rail, which puts such work out to tender. Since the renationalisation of the track network, Network Rail has been bringing back much of the repair work and doing it itself, in-house. It was generally felt that private contractors had proved too expensive and the work they did was not up to a sufficiently high standard.

Utilities - the regulatory regime

Each of the utilities privatised in the 1980s and 1990s - British Telecom, the gas and electricity industries, the water industry and British Rail - has a regulatory body.

- Telecommunications, which includes land line

Table 1 Sale of state owned companies to the private sector			
Date begun			
1979	*British Petroleum	1987	British Airways
	*ICL		Rolls Royce
	*Ferranti		Leyland Bus
	Fairey		Leyland Truck
1981	British Aerospace		Royal Ordnance
	*British Sugar		British Airport Authority
	Cable and Wireless	1988	British Steel
	Amersham International		British Leyland
1982	National Freight Corporation	1989	Water Boards
	Britoil	1990	Electricity Area Boards
1983	*Associated British Ports	1991	Electricity Generation
	British Rail Hotels	1994	British Coal
1984	British Gas Onshore Oil	1995	British Rail
	Enterprise Oil	1996	British Energy
	Sealink Ferries	1999	National Air Traffic Services
	Jaguar Cars	2000+	British Nuclear Fuels
	British Telecom	2002	Network Rail renationalised
	British Technology Group	2004	British Energy renationalised
1986	British Gas		

*Partly owned by government at the time of sale.

telephone services, mobile phone services, television and radio, is regulated by Ofcom (formerly Oftel which only regulated telephone services).

● Gas and electricity are regulated by Ofgem. This body replaced Ofgas and Offer in 1999.
● Water is regulated by Ofwat.
● Rail is regulated by ORR.

Their task is to ensure that no firm is able to abuse what monopoly powers it has to exploit its customers. They can achieve this in four main ways - by limiting prices, prohibiting anti-competitive practices, increasing competition and setting minimum investment levels.

Price limits In the UK, price limits have been set on privatised utilities using a formula linked to the inflation rate - an RPI plus X or RPI minus X formula. Price limits are fixed for a set of period of time. In industries where the regulator expects to see efficiency gains with no substantial change in long term investment, the regulator is likely to set an RPI minus X limit. This means that prices must fall by inflation minus a fixed percentage each year. Gas, electricity and telecommunications firms have been forced to cut their prices since privatisation because of this regulatory formula. In the water industry, firms have been forced to undertake an expensive investment programme to bring the UK's water and disposal standards up to those set by the EU. Water companies were therefore allowed to increase their prices. In the rail industry, train operators are allowed to increased some of their fares, called 'regulated fares', by the rate of inflation plus 1 per cent each year. Regulated fares include season tickets and saver tickets. Unregulated fares, including open tickets which can be used anytime, can be increased in price by any amount by train operators.

Prohibiting anti-competitive practices The privatised utilities are prone to using anti-competitive practices to protect their monopolies. For instance, the electricity generators have been repeatedly accused by industrial customers of artificially manipulating prices in the electricity 'pool' - a market for electricity which fixes prices on an hour by hour basis outside of long term contracts. By restricting supply at times of shortages, they can sharply increase electricity prices for a few hours because buyers have inelastic demand. Regulators have the power to force utilities to change their behaviour and, in some cases, to impose fines.

Increasing competition Regulators, working with the government, can increase competition in an industry by abolishing legal barriers to entry. For instance, at privatisation, British Gas was given a legal monopoly on gas supply, but gradually it has been forced by the regulator to allow competitors to supply gas to customers. The regulator can also increase competition by banning anti-competitive practices by dominant firms.

In some cases, competition is not possible because part of an industry is a natural monopoly. Examples include the rail network, gas pipelines, the electricity grid and telephone lines. In these cases, regulators and governments have split the supply of a good or service from its transmission. Supply can be competitive, but transmission remains a natural monopoly.

In the gas and rail industries, the natural monopolists, Transco and Network Rail, are independent companies from product providers like British Gas or Virgin Trains. In telecommunications, electricity and water, the natural monopolists are also product providers. So, BT for instance both owns most of the land line telephone infrastructure in the UK and offers telecommunications services. Competitors have to pay BT to use its infrastructure. This is a potential source of anti-competitive practices. Competitors to BT have persistently complained that it has charged higher prices than it should and has made it difficult to establish new services. These problems have had to be sorted out by the regulator.

Competition in many industries has taken time to develop. In the gas, electricity and telecommunications markets, the original public sector monopolists have gradually lost market share as competitors come into the market and undercut them on price. Regulators have also made it much easier for customers to switch from one supplier to another. In a market like the rail freight market, the market is relatively small. This limits the possible number of firms that could operate profitably in the market. It is difficult to see how there will be more than the current four firms in the market in the future. However, four firms may be enough to ensure that costs are kept to a minimum and that there is both product and allocative efficiency in the market.

Setting minimum investment levels In the water and rail industries, the regulator has specified minimum levels of investment. This is because it has judged that there has been underinvestment in the past. In the water industry, investment is needed to bring water standards up to EU regulation levels. In the rail industry, the government wants to see a better public transport system. Investment is an essential part of persuading more people to travel by rail.

Advantages and disadvantages of privatisation

Privatisation, although fiercely opposed by many in the 1980s, is now generally considered to have been a success. Few would argue that companies such as ICL, British Steel or British Aerospace would have performed better if they had remained in state ownership.

In the gas, electricity, telecommunications, water and rail industries, privatisation, together with the regulatory regime, has led to large falls in costs. The old nationalised industries can now be seen to have been highly X-inefficient, with overmanning a particular problem. Privatisation, with large scale falls in the number of workers in these industries and the sale of many surplus assets, has led to greater productive efficiency. In the cases of gas, electricity and telecommunications, the fall in costs has been far greater than the profits that now have to be paid to shareholders. The result is that consumers have benefited through substantial price reductions in real terms. In water and rail, increases in productive efficiency have been used to pay for investment, which increases dynamic efficiency. Quality of service has, if anything, improved. Consumers tend to have greater choice and firms are more responsive to customer needs and complaints.

However, performance is often patchy. In the case of the railways, some train operators have performed better than others on measures such as punctuality (measured by the Public Performance Measure PPM) and investment. In theory, the poorest performing companies don't win back their franchises when they come up for renewal. The rail regulator, ORR, even has the power to withdraw a franchise whilst it is still running if performance is extremely poor. However, critics argue that the rail regulator is too weak and fails to apply enough pressure on companies to perform well.

DataQuestion Bus and air travel deregulation

Bus deregulation 1986

In 1986, the government deregulated the local bus industry. Before this, bus companies, mainly owned by local authorities, were legally able to maintain local monopolies. Competitors were not allowed to run rival services without the approval of local regulators. From October 1986, any bus company could run a service over any bus route and charge whatever fare it wished, subject to safety regulations.

Approximately 80-85 per cent of bus routes today are 'commercial' bus routes where the fares paid cover the costs and profit of the bus operator. A minority of bus routes are subsidised bus routes, where fare revenues are not sufficient to cover costs. Without a government subsidy, private bus companies would not run the route. So the local Passenger Transport Authority, the government body responsible for public transport in a local area, puts the route out to a competitive tender and the bus company which offers to run the route for the lowest subsidy wins the contract.

Deregulation was accompanied by the privatisation of most bus companies. Local bus companies were sold off, often to their management. In the 1990s, there was considerable consolidation in the industry as these privatised local bus companies were bought up by what today are the main five bus companies in the UK: First Group, Stagecoach, Arriva, Go Ahead and National Express.

In London, changes to bus services took a different form. Bus routes today are allocated to private sector bus operators under a process of competitive tendering. They therefore have a monopoly along the route but cannot change their fares or timetables without permission of the regulatory body, Transport for London.

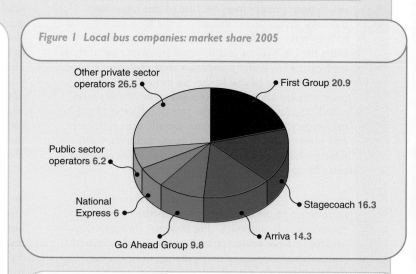

Figure 1 Local bus companies: market share 2005

Other private sector operators 26.5
First Group 20.9
Public sector operators 6.2
National Express 6
Go Ahead Group 9.8
Arriva 14.3
Stagecoach 16.3

The aims of deregulation in the bus and air travel markets

Deregulation of the bus market had a number of aims.
- Deregulation would create a competitive market. It would draw in new companies which would shake up the market. This competition would then drive down costs in the industry, creating greater productive efficiency. Firms would compete in a variety of ways such as offering lower fares, more frequent services and better quality travel with newer vehicles.
- The decline in bus passenger numbers would be stemmed because of the better service being provided by competitive firms.
- Government subsidies to bus travel would fall because of greater operating efficiencies by private bus companies.

For air travel, deregulation had similar aims.
- Competition would lead to more services and lower prices.
- Airlines would be forced to cut their costs to survive. State airlines in particular would have to become more efficient and learn to live without state subsidies.

Table 2 Passenger transport: consumer price indices (1995 = 100)

| | Motor vehicles | | Rail | Bus and | All | All consumer |
| | *of which* | | coach | transport | expenditure | |
	Total	Net purchase				(RPI)
1965	9.4	11.6	6.7	5.7	9.1	10.0
1970	12.0	13.6	8.5	8.0	11.7	12.4
1975	22.6	23.8	17.4	15.3	22.0	22.9
1980	47.1	55.4	39.6	36.5	45.8	44.9
1985	65.1	70.8	50.7	52.8	62.7	63.5
1990	79.4	87.8	72.3	73.8	84.6	84.6
1995	100.0	100.0	100.0	100.0	100.0	100.0
2000	119.0	94.7	116.5	119.6	114.2	114.2
2006	122.6	79.5	141.4	140.9	142.2	132.8

Source: adapted from *Economic Trends Annual Supplement*, Office for National Statistics; Department for the Environment, Transport and the Regions, *Transport Statistics*.

Bus deregulation is working

Bus deregulation is working. Competition has led to an expansion of bus services with more bus miles being travelled than ever before. The industry is investing in ever better buses and in innovation, such as computerised bus times at bus shelters. Bus fares are highly competitive despite increases in costs in recent years. Increased road congestion gives buses the opportunity to attract people out of their cars and back to an environmentally friendly and sustainable form of transport. Bus services are less dependent on state hand-outs. Subsidies have declined by about 30 per cent since deregulation whilst subsidies per passenger have remained roughly constant.

Bus deregulation has been a mistake

Bus deregulation has not worked. It promised competition, lower fares and a better service. Instead, on most routes, one bus company has a local monopoly and barriers to entry and exit are high enough to make the market non-contestable. Fares have gone up by more than the rate of inflation at a time when the cost of motoring has fallen. Investment has been patchy and insufficient to provide the high quality service that will prevent a continued exodus of passengers from bus to car. Most bus passengers outside of London are school children and students, pensioners with free bus passes and people on low incomes who don't have access to a car for the journey. Only in London where bus services are regulated have passenger numbers increased.

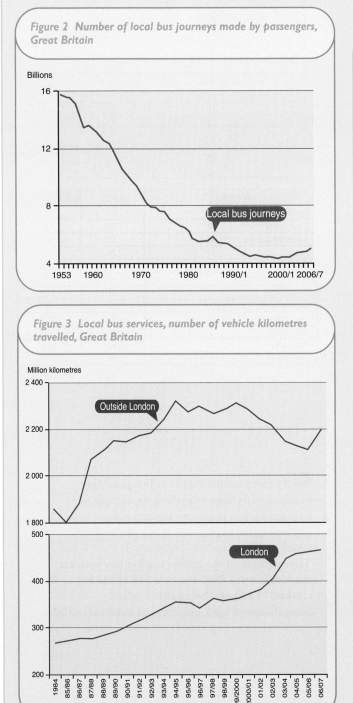

Figure 2 Number of local bus journeys made by passengers, Great Britain

Figure 3 Local bus services, number of vehicle kilometres travelled, Great Britain

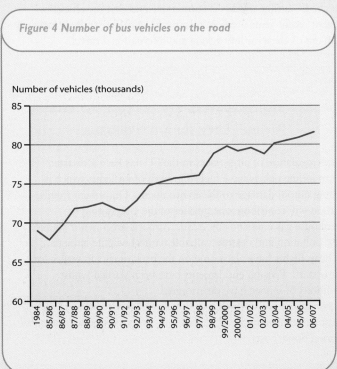

Figure 4 Number of bus vehicles on the road

Deregulation of the EU airline market

The EU airline market was deregulated in 1997. Before then, an airline from one EU country could not fly to another EU country without negotiating an agreement with the relevant authorities. Most EU countries limited competition to favour their own national airlines.

Restrictions still apply. This most significant is that airlines cannot necessarily gain landing slots at busy airports such as Heathrow Airport. This forces airlines wanting to set up new services to use less busy but often less popular airports. Some argue that the EU should force all airports to auction all their landing slots on a regular basis, such as every five years. This would lead to greater efficiency because airport slots would then be allocated to airlines most willing to pay.

Deregulation of EU airlines has been a success

Deregulation of the EU airline market has been an enormous success. It has encouraged competition, driven down prices and increased the number of routes being offered by airlines. Low cost airlines, like Ryanair and easyJet have been major winners from deregulation. They have pursued an aggressive expansion programme. The losers have tended to be the main national carriers of EU countries. In a protected environment, they could charge high fares and have high cost structures. In a deregulated environment, they have been forced to cut their costs. Many have merged or formed alliances both of which limit competition. The number of small airline companies coming into the market shows that the EU airline market is contestable and that the efficiency gains of recent years are here to stay. EU citizens can look forward to an era of cheap airline tickets and international travel.

Airline deregulation a disaster

The deregulation of air services in the EU has been a disaster. Cheap airline tickets have fuelled growth of airflights which is causing untold damage to the environment. On present trends, aviation will contribute one quarter of the UKs output of greenhouse gas emissions by 2030. Airports are a major source of noise pollution and destroy valuable natural wildlife habitats.

Cheap flights have also come on the back of cuts in wages for airline staff. Pension entitlements have been slashed whilst conditions of service have deteriorated.

Passengers have suffered too. Quality of service has declined whilst passengers are being forced to fly to out of the way airports to bring down costs.

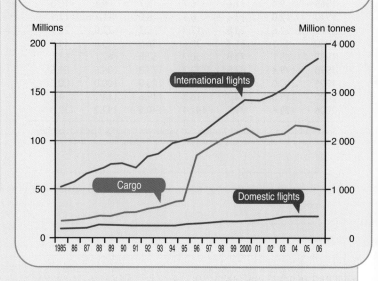

Figure 5 Number of passengers using UK airports, outward and inward (millions); cargo handled on flights to and from UK airports, (million tonnes)

Figure 6 Number of aircraft landings and take-offs, selected UK airports

Airport	1985	2006
Stansted	14	190
Newcastle	24	58
Nottingham East Midlands	27	56
Luton	28	79
Belfast	31	48
Birmingham	35	109
Edinburgh	37	116
Glasgow	51	97
Manchester	72	213
Aberdeen	79	98
Gatwick	150	254
Heathrow	288	471

Source: adapted from *Transport Statistics*, Department for Transport.

1. Briefly compare the trends in bus passenger numbers with those travelling by aeroplane.
2. Explain what is meant by deregulation, comparing the experience of the bus and air travel markets.
3. 'Deregulation of the airline market has been far more successful than deregulation of the bus market.' Evaluate the extent to which deregulation in both markets has been successful.

58 Environmental market failure

Summary

1. Externalities can lead to economic inefficiency if the marginal social cost of production is not equal to price.
2. Externalities can also redistribute real income within the economy.
3. One method for the government to control externalities is to impose regulations.
4. Another method is to internalise the externality by extending property rights.
5. A third method is to impose taxes on externalities.
6. Tradable permits are another solution to limiting the impact of externalities.

Externalities

Externalities exist when there is a difference between private costs and benefits and social costs and benefits. For instance, a factory may run at a private profit because its revenues exceed its private costs. However, it may be polluting the atmosphere as a result of its production, at no private cost to itself. It would then create an externality. If this were large enough, the social profit would be negative because social costs (private costs plus the externality) would exceed social benefits (in this case just the private benefits or revenues).

The efficient allocation of resources

Externalities imply that there is an inefficient or sub-optimal allocation of resources. Consider Figure 1. Assume that all other markets in the economy are producing at a point where marginal social cost equals marginal social benefit. Marginal cost and benefit curves are drawn on the diagram.

- Marginal cost curves are U-shaped. The cost of producing an extra unit of output is assumed to fall at first, and then to rise. This is because of diminishing marginal returns in the short run or economies and diseconomies of scale in the long run.
- Marginal benefit curves are downward sloping. This is because the benefit from consuming an extra unit of output is assumed to decline the more is consumed. The marginal benefit curve is also the demand curve for the product since the demand curve shows the value that consumers place on consuming an extra unit of the good.

Figure 1 shows that the marginal social cost of production is above the marginal private cost. Therefore, there are external costs of production in this market. The vertical distance between the two lines shows the external cost at any given level of output. The equilibrium quantity demanded and supplied in a free market would be where marginal private cost equalled marginal benefit. Market signals are such that 0R will be produced and sold at a price of 0T. However, resources could be allocated more efficiently if marginal benefit were equated with the full cost of production shown by the marginal social cost line. If all costs were taken into consideration, equilibrium quantity produced and consumed would fall to 0S whilst price would have to rise to 0V. This is what one would expect. Society needs, for instance, to consume fewer chemicals and pay a

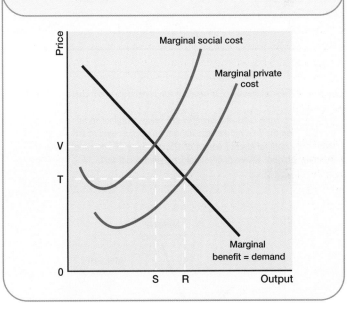

Figure 1 Allocation of resources with external costs
If marginal private cost is below marginal social cost, then the free market equilibrium production level of OR will be above the socially optimal level of output of OS, assuming all other markets in the economy produce where price equals marginal social cost.

higher price for them if their production leads to pollution of the environment.

The same analysis can be applied to external benefits. Figure 2 shows a situation where marginal private benefits are lower than marginal social benefits. The free market would lead to an underconsumption of the product. Production and consumption of 0S should lead to a more efficient allocation of resources than the free market equilibrium point of 0R.

Combining these two, Figure 3 shows a market where there are both external costs and external benefits. The free market equilibrium output point is 0R. The socially optimal point is 0S.

Welfare losses

If it is assumed that all other markets are producing where price = marginal cost (the demand or marginal benefit equalling marginal cost condition just discussed),

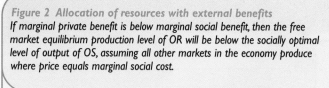

Figure 2 Allocation of resources with external benefits
If marginal private benefit is below marginal social benefit, then the free market equilibrium production level of OR will be below the socially optimal level of output of OS, assuming all other markets in the economy produce where price equals marginal social cost.

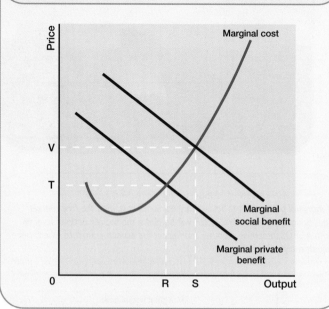

Figure 3 Allocation of resources with both external costs and benefits
If marginal private costs and benefits are below marginal social costs and benefits, then the free market equilibrium production level of OR will be above the socially optimal level of output of OS, assuming all other markets in the economy produce where price equals marginal social cost.

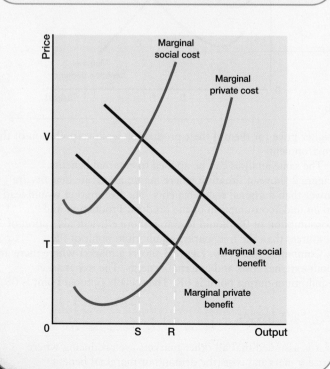

then **allocative efficiency** will exist in a market if it too produces where price = marginal cost. On the other hand, there will be allocative inefficiency if private cost or benefit differs from social cost or benefit and markets are free. The size of this allocative inefficiency can be seen in Figure 4. Production should only be at 0A if price is set equal to marginal social costs. Overproduction of AB leads to allocative inefficiency. The efficiency loss to society is given by the difference between the cost to society of production of AB (shown by the marginal social cost curve) and the value placed by society on consumption of AB (shown by the demand curve). The difference is the shaded triangle HJK. The greater the difference between marginal social cost and marginal private cost, the greater will be the net social cost shown by the area of the triangle.

It is interesting to note that the welfare loss arising from an external cost is likely to be less under conditions of imperfect competition than under perfect competition. If the market shown in Figure 4 were perfectly competitive, then the supply curve of the industry would be the marginal private cost curve and production would take place where demand equalled supply, at the point K as has already been argued above. There would be a net welfare loss of HJK.

If, on the other hand, the market were supplied by a monopolist, then production would be lower than under perfect competition. Monopolists charge a higher price than an industry with competition. Therefore, in Figure 4, the free market price under a monopolist would be higher than 0E and production would have to be lower than 0B. Hence, the welfare loss will be less than HJK. It could be the case that the monopolist will so reduce output that production is to the left of 0A. Then, there will be a welfare loss not due to overproduction but to underproduction by the monopolist. Given that there is no supply curve under monopoly, it is impossible to say whether the free market equilibrium point will result in overproduction or underproduction.

Figure 4 Social cost arising from an externality
If an industry is perfectly competitive, long run production will take place where price = marginal private cost (MPC) at output OB. This, assuming that all other markets produce where P=MC and that private and social costs and benefits are the same, is also the allocatively efficient level of production. However, if there is a negative externality leading to marginal social cost being higher than MPC in this one market, then output should be lower to maximise efficiency. The externality causes overproduction of AB.

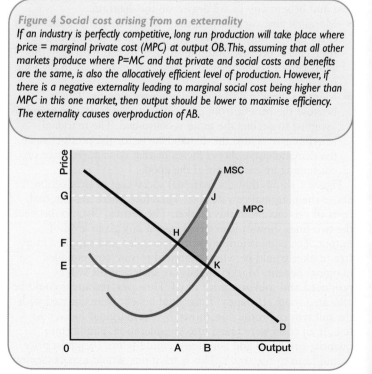

Question 1

Asbestos is a dangerous material used in a wide variety of industries including the building industry. Appreciation of its risks has grown over the past forty years. If inhaled, it can cause mesothelioma, a type of cancer, which damages the lungs and the abdomen and can lead to death. It takes 15-40 years for mesothelioma to develop. Hence, a worker today with mesothelioma is likely to have had exposure to asbestos some time between the 1960s and the 1990s. Asbestos also causes other diseases such as asbestosis, a scarring of the lung tissues. In the UK, around 1 600 people a year die from mesothelioma, a figure which will peak in 2010-2015 at about 2 000. The use of all asbestos has been banned in the UK since 1999.

Workers in the UK with asbestos-related diseases can sue the company where they were exposed to asbestos. These companies in turn have typically taken out insurance to cover the cost of claims. The Faculty and Institute of Actuaries has estimated the future cost of claims for asbestos-related diseases will be up to £20 billion. Each claim for mesothelioma currently costs insurers around £100 000 whilst asbestosis costs £50 000. However, many victims complain that the compensation process is slow and unpredictable. Some die before their cases are settled and they lose all compensation.

More worryingly, it is estimated that more asbestos is being used in Asia now than was consumed at its peak in the US 30-40 years ago, with China a big user. Many Asian workers exposed to asbestos today are unlikely to get any compensation in the future if they contract an asbestos related disease.

Source: adapted from the *Financial Times* 2.11.2004.

(a) Explain briefly the problems caused by the use of asbestos.
(b) Using a diagram, explain why, despite possible compensation, the marginal private cost of using asbestos to a company might be less than its marginal social cost.
(c) Using a diagram, explain why, in the Britain of the 1960s or China today, there was (i) allocative inefficiency and (ii) a welfare loss in the market for asbestos.

Distributional effects

Externalities don't just create potential inefficiencies. There are also distributional implications. Consider a case where a chemicals company is putting untreated waste into a river and a water supply company downstream is having to treat the water to remove the chemicals. There will then be a redistribution of income from consumers of water, the customers of the water supply company who now have to pay a higher price for their water, to consumers of chemicals who pay less than the social cost of production.

Assume that the price of chemicals is raised by a tax on output to reflect the marginal social cost of production. This should correct the market failure present in the market for chemicals. However, the water company downstream is still having to pay to clean up the pollution created by the chemical company. Only if the chemical company pays the water company will there also be efficiency in the market for water. In this case it would seem to be relatively simple for an arrangement to be made for the water company to charge the chemical company for the latter's dumping of chemical waste in the river.

Question 2

There is a growing consensus that global warming is causing an increase in natural disasters. From severe storms to flooding to drought, the climate in Europe is becoming more extreme. Global warming is caused by everyone who consumes goods and services, from gas and electricity to cars to beef. The rich tend to contribute more than the poor because they consume more products.

But the impact of global warming is uneven. Only a relatively small number of people will suffer severe economic loss from a local flood or a drought in a local area. It is also the poor who are likely to be disproportionately affected. They are least able to cope with natural disasters, often being uninsured for losses. Climate change is also affecting the poor in Third World countries where towns and villages are often built with little regard for the possibility of natural disasters and where processes such as drought and desertification are destroying the livelihoods of rural dwellers.

Source: adapted from the *Financial Times*, 29.11.2005.

(a) Use the passage to explain why using petrol to drive a car or burning gas to heat a house might cause a negative externality.
(b) What distributional impact might these activities have?
(c) Discuss whether those who suffer losses from natural disasters should be compensated by governments who would raise the cash to pay compensation through new taxes.

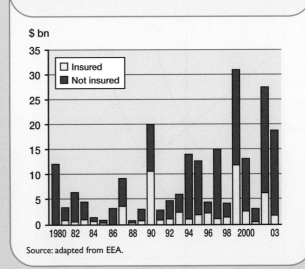

Figure 5 *Economic losses caused by weather and climate related disasters in Europe ($bn)*

Source: adapted from EEA.

But there is likely to be no such simple remedy for local residents and local anglers. Their welfare may be diminished by the polluted river. How do you decide who to compensate in the local community and how much compensation should you give? One answer which economists have suggested involves local residents and local anglers or the chemical company paying the other party an amount which is equal to the welfare loss. If citizen A is willing to pay £5 a year, and citizen B £10 a year and all other citizens £9 985, then the value of a clean river to the local community is £10 000. That is how much:

- either the chemical company should give in compensation to the local community;
- or the local community should pay to the chemical company to stop them polluting the river.

In this example, it might **seem** clear that the chemical company should pay the local community. However, to show that it is not quite as obvious as it first seems, take another example. Assume that the chemical company is making an anti-malaria drug for use in Third World countries. These drugs are cheap to produce and are widely used. If the chemical company compensates local residents for polluting the river, its costs will double and so too will the price of the drug. This will make the drug too expensive for many in the Third World and an extra 50 000 people a year will die. In this case, it might seem clear that local residents should pay the chemical company to reduce its pollution.

This shows that there is no simple answer to the question of 'who should compensate whom'. Should it be the customer of the polluting company paying through higher prices for its product, or should it be the individual, group or firm which bribes the company to stop polluting? What is more, it is often impossible to find out who exactly loses how much as a result of an externality. Therefore, taxes or other methods of reducing externalities may lead to over-compensation or under-compensation. These are issues about the distribution of income and resources more than the efficient allocation of resources.

Regulation

Regulation is a method which is widely used in the UK and throughout the world to control externalities. The government could lay down maximum pollution levels or might even ban the pollution-creating activities altogether. For instance, in the UK, the Environmental Protection Act 1989 laid down minimum environmental standards for emissions from over 3 500 factories involved in chemical processes, waste incineration and oil refining. The system is policed by HM Inspectorate of Pollution. There are limits on harmful emissions from car exhausts. Cars can be failed on their MOT test if exhausts do not meet the standard. 40 years before the MOT regulations came into force, the government banned the burning of ordinary coal in urban areas.

Regulation will only result in an efficient allocation of resources in the economy if the government equates the marginal social cost with the marginal social benefit of an activity. Consider Figure 6. The problem arising in this diagram is that marginal social cost is above marginal private cost, creating externalities. The market equilibrium production level is 0A at a price of 0E, but the optimal level of production is 0B where the price includes the private cost of 0E and the externality EF. Ideally, regulation would allow production of 0B but no more. So the supply curve would become vertical at 0B.

Figure 7 shows a situation which would justify a ban on production and consumption. If left to free market forces, 0A would be consumed where marginal private cost equals marginal private benefit. However, marginal social cost is so high that the MSC line does not cut the MPB line. At every level of output, there is a negative externality. A current example in the UK would be asbestos which has been banned from use in all new products since 1999 because of its danger to health.

If physical regulations are to be used to achieve an optimal allocation of resources, the government must be able to assess

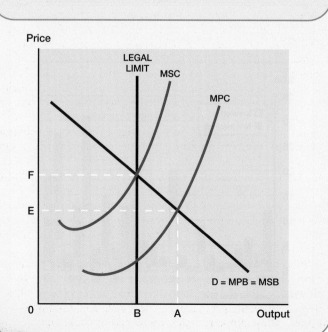

Figure 6 Regulation
Governments should impose regulations to reduce pollution to OB because this is where marginal social cost equals marginal social benefit.

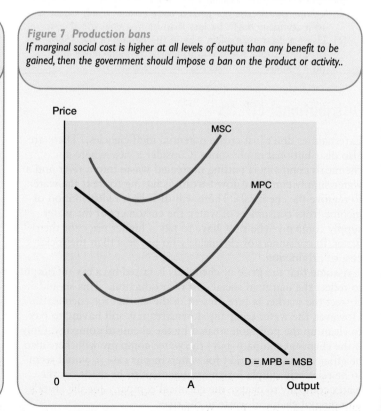

Figure 7 Production bans
If marginal social cost is higher at all levels of output than any benefit to be gained, then the government should impose a ban on the product or activity..

Question 3

Stricter controls should be placed on the spraying of pesticide on crops, as the chemicals used may be causing ill health, according to the Royal Commission on Environmental Pollution. In a report published yesterday, it said that current policy was 'inadequate' to protect the health of bystanders and those living near sprayed fields. It recommended a five-metre 'no spray zone' around fields.

Some crops, such as potatoes, receive an average of five sprayings of pesticide a year, but others more susceptible to insects, such as orchard fruits, are sprayed up to 13 times a year on average. The report found evidence of illnesses, ranging from skin rashes and respiratory irritation to immune disorders, which could be linked to pesticide use.

Peter Kendall, from the National Farmers' Union, said farmers should be spared greater regulation of their spraying practices until more research was completed. 'I think it is plainly wrong for yet more regulation to precede the science - that really is putting the cart before the horse.'

Source: adapted from the *Financial Times*, 23.9.2005.

(a) How might the current policy of pesticide spraying be tightened up?
(b) With the help of a diagram, discuss whether the proposed new measures would be too strict.

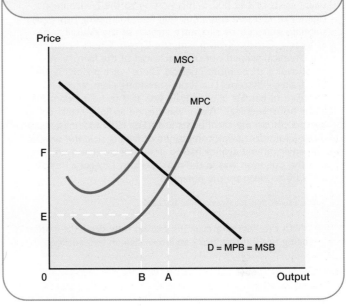

Figure 8 Extending property rights
If property rights are fully extended, a polluter would have to pay the full social cost of its activities by paying EF at the margin in compensation to those who suffer from its activities. Equally, if those who suffer paid EF at the margin to the polluter, the socially optimal level of output would be the same at OB.

accurately costs and benefits and act accordingly. If pollution controls are too lax, permitting production above 0B in Figure 6, then there will be a misallocation of resources. Firms will produce above 0B and will have no incentive to reduce pollution levels below the minimum legal requirement. On the other hand, pollution controls might be too strict. If pollution levels were fixed below 0B in Figure 6, society would make a net gain by an increase in output and the associated increase in pollution.

Extending property rights

If a chemical company lorry destroyed your home, you would expect the chemical company to pay compensation. If the chemical company polluted the atmosphere so that the trees in your garden died, it would be unlikely that you would gain compensation, particularly if the chemical plant were in the UK and the dead trees were in Germany.

Externalities often arise because property rights are not fully allocated. Nobody owns the atmosphere or the oceans, for instance. An alternative to regulation is for government to extend property rights. They can give water companies the right to charge companies which dump waste into rivers or the sea. They can give workers the right to sue for compensation if they have suffered injury or death as a result of working for a company. They can give local residents the right to claim compensation if pollution levels are more than a certain level.

Extending property rights is a way of **internalising the externality** - eliminating the externality by bringing it back into the framework of the market mechanism. This can be shown in Figure 8 where a problem arises because marginal social cost of production of a chemical is higher than marginal private cost. The equilibrium free market output is 0A whilst the socially optimal level of production is 0B. If the producers of the chemical have to pay EF to those who suffer as a result of the externality, they will only produce at 0B. This is because their marginal production costs are now 0E, their private production costs, plus EF together equally demand for the product.

However, the same result would be achieved if those suffering from the externality were to pay the chemical companies to limit production. It would be rational for property owners in a local community to offer to pay a chemical company to stop polluting the local environment if the government were failing to do anything about it. There have been suggestions, for instance, that First World countries should pay Third World countries to stop chopping down tropical rainforests, or to reduce emissions of greenhouse gases.

Who should pay whom is a question about who owns the property rights. Does a chemical company own the right to pollute? If it does, then those who suffer will have to pay the company to reduce production if they want the pollution stopped. If the property rights are owned by those who suffer the pollution, then the chemical company

Question 4

A chemicals company that polluted one of the Black Country's canals and killed thousands of fish has been hit with a huge bill. Robinson Brothers was ordered to pay £183 455 (including court costs of £62 000, compensation to the Environment Agency of £58 000 and a £60 000 fine) for letting hydrogen sulphide poison a 10 kilometre stretch of the Walsall and Ridgeacre Canals. Wolverhampton Crown Court heard that the chemical seeped out of a back wall of the factory into the canal over a three month period. There were problems with the drainage system. The drum shredding plant, which disposed of barrels of chemicals, was said to be a victim of 'poor housekeeping'. Water was turned an 'inky black' colour and people on the canal boats at Ocker Hill moorings, nearly three kilometres away, complained of feeling sick and unwell. The environment agency had to drain the canal and officers said the pollution was in the most serious category. It cost £83 000 to clean up the pollution.

Source: adapted from the *Financial Times*, 10.12.2005.

(a) With the help of a diagram, explain how the legal system is being used in this story to internalise an externality.

will have to buy the right to pollute and compensate those who suffer. An American economist, Ronald Coase, in 1960 showed that the optimal level of production of the chemical company, at 0B in Figure 8, would come about irrespective of who owned the property rights, but this would only be true if there were very low transaction costs.

In practice, transaction costs are often high. One reason is that there may be many parties which suffer from the externality. If a chemical company causes £20 million of damage each year to local households, but there are 200 000 households in the local area, it is very difficult for the 200 000 households to co-ordinate their efforts to claim compensation from the one chemical company. Equally, if 100 000 producers in the first world are emitting enough carbon to raise temperatures in Africa by 1°C, how can 100 million African farmers claim compensation from them if the yields from their harvests fall?

A second problem is that the exact cost of the externality may be difficult to assess. In theory, when a chemical company imposes costs on 20 households, each household is able to assess the cost to itself and so charge the chemical company. In practice, economic agents often find it difficult to put prices on costs or benefits. The chemical company is most likely to pay the same amount in compensation to each household, which is likely to exceed the cost to some households and be too little to compensate the losses of other households, but getting the amount right would be too difficult and costly in itself.

When there are high transaction costs, Coase showed that inefficiency would be minimised if property rights were allocated to the party which valued those property rights the most. However, governments can use a variety of other methods, such as taxes, to optimise efficiency without having to allocate property rights.

Environmental taxes

Another solution, much favoured by economists, is the use of environmental taxes. Government needs to assess the cost to society of pollution. It then sets tax rates on polluters so that the tax is equal to the value of the externality. As costs of production then increase, firms reduce their output and thus reduce their pollution emissions.

Examples of environmental taxes include road pricing taxes, such as the London Congestion Charge. In Figure 8, the marginal tax rate would be EF, set equal to the value of the externality. The optimal point of production would then become 0B.

Environmental taxes, like extending property rights, have the

Question 5

Heavy vehicles with dirty engines may have to pay a fee to drive in the area bordered by the M25 by 2008 under plans due to be put to consultation by Transport for London. The scheme - to be called the low emissions zone - would aim to reduce levels of key harmful pollutants in London's atmosphere. It would initially apply to heavy trucks, buses and coaches which emitted more pollutants than allowed under European Union legislation. Most vehicles sold after January 1 2002 meet the EU standards. Coach operators are likely to be among the worst affected because they tend to operate older vehicles than either truck or bus operators. The Confederation of Passenger Transport, which represents bus and coach operators, has objected strongly to the plans, saying that they would represent a tax on tourism. A spokesperson said the additional fee would deter tourists from elsewhere in the UK from coming on coach trips to theatrical shows or other events and might persuade some to come instead by car.

Source: adapted from the *Financial Times*, 15.9.2005.

(a) Explain, using a diagram, why the fee proposed by Transport for London might lead to greater economic efficiency.
(b) Discuss whether the objections of the Confederation of Passenger Transport should be taken into account when setting the level of the fee.

advantage that they allow the market mechanism to decide how resources should best be allocated, given that pollution is included as a cost of production. Heavy polluters have an incentive to reduce pollution emissions, whilst light polluters, who might have had to cut production under a system of government pollution regulations, can now expand production and pollution but to the benefit of society as a whole.

However, it is difficult for government to place a monetary value on pollution and therefore decide what should be the optimal tax rate. Production of some goods might still have to be banned because their environmental costs were so high that no level of taxes could adequately compensate society for their production.

Pollution permits

A variation on regulating pollution through direct controls is the idea of pollution permits. Here, the government sets a limit on the amount of pollution permitted. In Figure 8, this would be at 0B. The government then allocates permits to individual firms or other polluters. These permits can then be traded for money between polluters. For instance, one electricity generating company might have relatively modern power plants which in total let out fewer emissions than its permits allows. It could

then sell surplus permits to another electricity company which had older plants which, if allowed to run, would exceed its permits given by the government.

The main advantage of permits over simple regulation is that costs in the industry and therefore to society should be lower than with regulation. Each firm in the industry will consider whether it is possible to reduce emissions and at what cost. Assume that Firm A, with just enough permits to meet its emissions, can reduce emissions by 500 tonnes at a cost of £10m. Firm B is a high polluter and needs 500 tonnes worth of permits to meet regulations. It calculates that it would need to spend £25m to cut emissions by this amount.

- If there was simple regulation, the anti-pollution costs to the industry, and therefore to society, would be £25m. Firm B would have to conform to its pollution limit whilst there would be no incentive for Firm A to cut pollution.
- With permits, Firm A could sell 500 tonnes of permits to Firm B. The cost to society of then reducing pollution would only be £10m, the cost that Firm A would incur. It might cost Firm B more than £10m to buy the permits. It would be prepared to spend anything up to £25m to acquire them. Say Firm A drove a hard bargain and sold the permits to Firm B for £22m. Society would save £15m, distributed between a paper profit of £12m for Firm A and a fall in costs from what otherwise would have been the case for Firm B of £3m.

Question 6

Carbon prices soared yesterday, sparked by a snap of cold weather across Europe, in one of the busiest days of trading since the market was launched under the European Union's greenhouse gas emissions scheme. The scheme established a new market for carbon by setting emissions allowances for energy-intensive industries. The allowances, or pollution permits, can be bought and sold, putting a price on carbon dioxide for the first time.

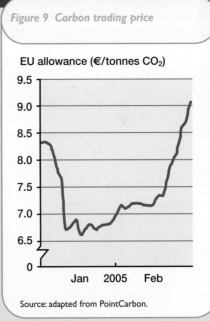

Figure 9 Carbon trading price

EU allowance (€/tonnes CO_2)

Source: adapted from PointCarbon.

Companies have received about 2.2bn allowances - each allowance equating to a tonne of carbon dioxide. Companies producing less than their limit, usually because they are more energy efficient, can sell allowances which they do not use on the open market to companies which are emitting above their allowances. Firms which do not have enough allowances to cover their emissions because they have failed to buy enough on the open market face fines of €40 a tonne.

Source: adapted from the *Financial Times*, 25.2.2005.

(a) Explain, using examples from the data, what is meant by a 'pollution permit'.
(b) Using a diagram, explain why pollution permits might be a more efficient way of limiting carbon emissions than fixing maximum emission limits on each firm and imposing fines if they breach those limits.

Applied economics

Toxic dust and externalities

In Korea, they know all about externalities. The annual April storms bring with them huge swathes of yellow dust which have come from the deserts of Mongolia. Travelling south east, the storms pass over the heavily polluted industrial areas of Northern China where they pick up high levels of dioxins and heavy metals such as copper, cadmium and lead. These pollutants are then deposited on the Korean peninsular.

The problem is getting worse. In the 1980s South Korea suffered severe yellow dust storms on about four days a year. By the 1990s, this had risen to eight and in this decade it is averaging twelve. The problem is caused by desertification. With less snow falling, grasslands are being turned into scrub. Sand is not being bound together as closely as in previous years and so is more prone to be picked up by the wind and carried thousands of miles.

The cost to South Korea is significant. The Korean Environment Institute estimates that up to 165 South Koreans, mainly elderly people and those with respiratory problems, die each year and almost 2 million more suffer from eye and breathing problems as a result of the sand. In 2006, 4 373 schools closed for at least one day, whilst 164 flights were cancelled and many more were forced to change flight paths. Carmakers are forced to change the air filters in their spray-painting factories more often. In economic terms, the Samsung Economic Research Institute estimated the economic damage from yellow dust at $5.5 billion each year.

For those suffering from respiratory problems or for Korean car makers, the yellow dust is a negative externality in two ways. First, they are forced to pay part of the cost of industrial activity in Northern China. If Northern Chinese factories had significantly better anti-pollution measures in place, they would not emit the most dangerous dioxins and heavy metals to the atmosphere. Korea is paying part of the price for the Chinese economic miracle. Second, the primary problem of desertification in Mongolia is probably being caused by global warming, which is raising temperatures in the region. With global warming, the whole of the developed world is the problem. Some countries, such as the United States, have much higher carbon emissions per capita and per unit of GDP than others. However, South Korea is also responsible in part for global warming.

How then should South Korea tackle this problem? Some possible theoretical solutions, are in practice, not possible. For example, South Korea does not have the legal jurisdiction to impose a tougher regulatory regime on Chinese producers. For the same reason, it cannot impose impose environmental taxes on Chinese polluters or introduce a pollution permit scheme for them. Taxes, regulations and pollution permits in Mongolia will also not work since the fundamental problem there is global warming.

There are two possible approaches it can use. One is to pay polluters to modify their behaviour. This is an approach already being used on a small scale. The Korean government is giving $1.2 million to Korean environmental groups to promote forestation in Mongolia. Government officials from China, Korea and Japan have met Mongolian officials to encourage the country to plant more trees and create a green belt across the Gobi desert. The South Korean government might also consider offering Korean anti-pollution technology at a subsidised price to Chinese producers. This would be far more costly than $1.2 million and might encounter political problems from a Chinese government wary of interference with national sovereignty.

The second approach is to tackle the issue of global warming. It could set itself at least some targets related to the Kyoto protocol and attempt to achieve those targets. This might mean using a wide range of measures to reduce carbon emissions from power stations, industry, transport and homes. Equally important is putting international pressure on other countries either to sign up to the Kyoto protocols or to negotiate tougher new agreements. South Korea is a country which is seeing the negative effects of global warming today. It has a much greater incentive than many other countries to be at the forefront of diplomatic efforts to sign tougher carbon emission limits.

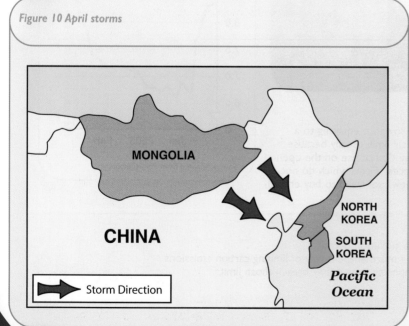

Figure 10 April storms

Source: adapted from the *Financial Times*, 10.4.2007.

DataQuestion Not in my back yard (Nimbyism)

80 per cent of the UK's population lives in towns and cities bigger than 10 000 people. These urban areas account for just 7 per cent of the UK's land mass.

11 per cent of the UK's land surface is 'concreted over' with housing, roads and other infrastructure.

Government guidance suggests building an average 30 to 50 new homes per hectare. New housing estates typically have 20-25 homes per hectare. The average density of new housing, including flats, is 40 homes per hectare.

Government guidance states that 60 per cent of new homes should be built on brownfield sites (sites which have already been built on, such as reclaimed industrial land) and 40 per cent on greenfield sites.

Source: adapted from the *Financial Times*, 20.5.2004, 16.3.2005.

Britain is a rich, modern and dynamic country, but its housing is among the oldest, pokiest and most expensive in the developed world. Continental housing is much better than housing in the UK. It is more spacious (in Germany and Switzerland, for example, new houses are on average 40 per cent larger than new houses in the UK), delivered faster, designed better and cost less.

The culprit is the UK planning system which is top down, and where local planners have little incentive to support development. In Australia, where the same system operates, there is the absurdity that, in spite of being a continent sized country with a population just 40 per cent that of the UK, land prices account for between 50 and 80 per cent of the price of a small family home in state capitals. This is due to state government policies of restricting land supply for housing, densification and imposing heavy infrastructure costs on developers.

In Switzerland, planning is bottom up, starting from the local canton. In Switzerland, building new houses means attracting new taxpayers to an area to help spread the cost of local government services. Local people can then do a simple and rational cost-benefit analysis. How much would it cost to build more homes? How much new infrastructure would have to be provided? How much damage to the local environment would there be? How much would the downsides of that development affect local inhabitants? Then how much extra tax revenue could be pumped into the local economy for the benefit of all? Would the new housing make the area a more attractive place to live? Would it help provide the sort of housing that people want to live in?

Source: adapted from the *Financial Times*, 12.9.2005.

Ministers are wrong to think that more high-density flats are needed to solve the housing problem, according to the House Builders Federation. It said the country should plan for a rise in demand for larger homes and a decline in demand for smaller ones. It pointed out that there was a basic fallacy in assuming that a big rise in one-person households must equate to a need for smaller homes. It argues that, as people become richer, they want larger homes. This does not change to any great degree as people approach retirement. Relatively few people in their mid to late 40s trade down to smaller properties when their children leave home.

Source: adapted from the *Financial Times*, 16.3.2005.

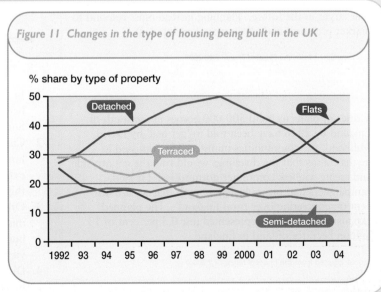

Figure 11 *Changes in the type of housing being built in the UK*

% share by type of property

In 2004, the government published the Barker Report on the supply of housing in the UK. The Report gave an estimate of the value that people put on land. Open public spaces in urban areas had a huge present value, set by the public at £10.8 million per hectare. Unspoiled forests and natural and semi-natural wetlands were valued at £1.3 million per hectare, but greenbelt land was valued at a mere £178 000 whilst intensively farmed land was valued at just £20 600 per hectare. The market too thinks that intensively farmed land has relatively little value. In South East England, the ratio of the price of residential to agricultural land is 300:1.

The planning system creates these huge distortions. By forcing people to live in crowded urban areas, it raises the price of building land and housing in our towns and cities and makes homes smaller and more cramped. The social costs of this 'imprisonment' are large now and will become ever larger in the future. Planning instead must respond to market pressures and allow more development.

Source: adapted from the *Financial Times*, 7.10.2005

Critics of plans to build 500 000 homes in the south of England by 2016 have been told to 'get real' by David Miliband, the communities minister. He dismissed as myths claims that the dwellings would ruin the countryside and create soulless commuter dormitories. He said campaigners had promulgated a 'myth that we are hell bent on concreting over rural England'. The planned expansion in housing represented just 0.3 per cent of 13 million hectares of land in England.

Source: adapted from the *Financial Times*, 17.9.2005.

Middle-class Nimbyism threatens to undermine housing growth and prospects for greater economic prosperity, Margaret Ford, the head of the government's regeneration agency, has warned. She said that Nimbyism has been 'elevated to ... an art form' in the past 30 years and was a polite, anodyne term for selfishness. 'There is nothing noble or altruistic about (Nimbyism) for its own sake. A much more adult approach would be to say we are a small attractive country and we are trying to promote the economy, therefore we have to provide decent homes and amenities for people who want to live and work here. To simply put up the shutters to development is absolutely mad', she said. While some areas were crying out for development, others were prey to a 'largely middle-class phenomenon where people want to benefit from living in a nice house and a pleasant environment but nobody else is allowed to benefit from a similarly nice environment down the road from them'.

Source: adapted from the *Financial Times*, 20.5.2004.

On its website, CPRE (Campaign to Protect Rural England) described its purpose as promoting 'the beauty, tranquillity and diversity of rural England by encouraging the sustainable use of land and other natural resources in town and country.'

It stated: 'We need strong policies for urban regeneration, so that more people will want to live in our cities (rather than quit them for smaller towns and villages), and strong policies to prevent the greater South East of England from over-heating.'

'We need to make efficient use of land by getting design and density right. We need good quality, well designed new homes - including enough family homes with gardens. We can do this at densities of around 50 homes per hectare.'

'Most people are better housed, and have more housing wealth, than ever before in history. Home ownership has been rising for decades, and so has the amount of space we enjoy per person at home. Meanwhile, household size has been falling, and so have levels of overcrowding.'

Source: adapted from www.cpre.org.uk.

1. In the UK, what might be the social costs and social benefits of building (a) more housing and (b) bigger houses?
2. Campaigners, such as the CPRE, argue that building large housing developments on greenbelt land creates negative externalities and welfare losses. Using a diagram, explain this viewpoint.
3. Others argue that planning restrictions have led to a misallocation of resources, with too few houses being built and a loss of welfare. Using a diagram, explain this viewpoint.
4. Discuss whether planning regulations on areas where new houses can be built should be abolished.

Summary

1. Cost-benefit analysis is a technique which attempts to evaluate the social costs and benefits of an economic decision.
2. Social costs and benefits may differ from private costs and benefits.
3. It is often difficult and sometimes impossible to place a price on externalities.
4. Cost-benefit analysis is often used to assess public sector investment projects.

Market failure

In a free market, decisions are based upon the calculation of **private costs and benefits**. However, there are many markets where significant **externalities** exist. This means that there are significant costs or benefits which are unlikely to be taken account of by the private economic decision maker.

COST-BENEFIT ANALYSIS is a procedure which takes into account all costs and all benefits (i.e **social costs and benefits**). Its purpose is to give guidance in economic decision making. It is used particularly by governments to evaluate important investment projects.

Costs and benefits

It is relatively easy to place a value on private costs and benefits. For instance, the government may want a toll motorway to be built round Birmingham. The company which builds and operates the motorway will be able to calculate the financial cost of constructing the road. This is the private cost to the operating company. It will also be able to calculate the revenues to be earned from tolls. These will be its private benefits. If the private benefits exceed private costs the motorway will be profitable and the operating company will be prepared to build the road.

However, there will be other costs and benefits associated with the project. These are the externalities of the road. For instance, residents near the motorway will suffer from pollution, including noise pollution. The motorway may generate more traffic on some roads joining the motorway, again increasing pollution to local residents. The motorway may go through areas of outstanding natural beauty or take away areas which have been used by local people for recreational activities such as walking. Habitats of rare species may be destroyed. Sites of historical interest may be lost. On the other hand, jobs and wealth may be created locally as industry is attracted to the area by the new motorway. Car and lorry drivers may save time using the new motorway. Traffic may be taken off some local roads, relieving congestion.

These externalities are very important costs and benefits which could be completely ignored by the operating company if it operated in a pure free market. In a cost-benefit analysis the company would attempt to place a value on these externalities in order to calculate the social cost and social benefit of the project and proceed only if social benefit exceeded social cost.

Problems with placing a value on externalities

The value of many externalities is difficult to estimate. For instance, assume that, as a result of the building of the motorway, 5 million travellers every year save on average 30 minutes each on their journey times around Birmingham. In a

Question 1

The Aberdeen Western Peripheral Route is a proposed 30 km long bypass of the city on its western side. Its building cost is currently put at between £210 million and £405 million. Local industry is supporting the building of the bypass. It claims that it will reduce congestion and journey times. It will also help attract new businesses and jobs to the area because of the improved transport links.

Opponents of the scheme, including Friends of the Earth, argue that it will have minimal impact on congestion in the centre of Aberdeen. It will encourage motorists to use their cars more and public transport less, so increasing congestion problems. The bypass will open up new development land, concreting over more of Scotland's natural land. New development will increase congestion too. Increased numbers of road journeys encouraged by the building of the new bypass will increase air pollution and reduce air quality. More car journeys will also increase greenhouse gas emissions at a time when the UK is committed to reducing them.

Source: adapted from www.foe-scotland.org.uk, March 2005.

(a) What are the main social costs and benefits of building the Aberdeen Western Peripheral Route?
(b) Which of these would be private costs and benefits to the Scottish Executive, and Aberdeen and Aberdeenshire Council, which are the two government bodies which will fund the bypass?

cost-benefit analysis, a value would need to be placed on the 2.5 million hours saved. However, it is unclear what value should be given to each hour since there is no obvious market in which a price is set for the time. A high cost estimate would assume that the time should be valued as if the travellers could have earned money during that time. This might give an estimate of £10 per hour at an average annual wage for the typical motorway user of £20 000. On the other hand, it could be assumed that the traveller places almost no value on the time saved. It could be just 50p per hour. Comparing these two estimates, we get a high estimate of £25 million and a low estimate of £1.25 million.

Even more difficult is how to place a value on a human life. Assume that the motorway takes traffic off other roads and as a result 5 fewer people are killed in road accidents each year. The value of a life today in a court case involving accidents is mainly determined by the expected earnings of the deceased. For instance, if a company director earning £500 000 per annum were killed in a road crash, together with her chauffeur earning £10 000 per year, then all other things being equal (age, family circumstances etc.) the family of the company director would receive far more compensation than the family of the chauffeur. These values, however, are open to much debate.

Other intangibles, such as pollution and illness, are very difficult to value in money terms. Even the values placed on private costs and benefits may be difficult to estimate. For instance, the operating company may charge £2 for a journey from one end of the motorway to the other. But that may not necessarily reflect the cost to the operating company of the journey. It may include a large element of monopoly profit, or it may be subsidised by the government to encourage people to use the motorway. It may therefore be necessary for the cost-benefit analysis to estimate a **shadow price** for the journey - a price which more accurately reflects the cost to the operating company of providing the service.

Question 2

Next time you eat some junk food, just remember it might cost you more than the price you paid in the supermarket or the fast food restaurant. Obesity is a growing problem worldwide, fuelled by the falling cost of food in relation to income and changing diets. In the UK today, over 20 per cent of the adult population is now obese (defined as having a body mass index over 30), up from 7 per cent in 1980. The costs of obesity are many, ranging from increased illness, to lost days at work, to premature death. The incidence of diabetes and high blood pressure is rising, with heart disease, a major killer in the western world, also up. All can be caused by being overweight.

Source: adapted from the *Financial Times*, 31.8.2004.

(a) You buy a super sized burger and fries meal in a fast food restaurant for £4.99. What might for you be (i) the private cost and (ii) the externalities of the meal?
(b) Why might an economist, calculating the costs of overeating and poor diets, put a shadow price on the lower life expectancy that results from obesity?

Costs and benefits across time

Calculations are further complicated by the fact that costs and benefits will occur at different points in time. A Channel Tunnel rail link, for instance, could still be carrying passengers in the year 2100 and beyond. Many of our major rail links today in the UK were first built over 100 years ago.

A value has to be given to future costs and benefits. Economic theory suggests that £1 of benefit in 20 years' time is worth considerably less than £1 of benefit today. This is because £1 today could be saved or invested. Each year that passes it should be worth more. For instance, if the rate of interest (or RATE OF RETURN, or RATE OF DISCOUNT) is 10 per cent per annum then £1 today is worth £1.10 in one year's time, £1.21 in two years' time, £1.33 in three years' time, £10.83 in 25 years' time and £117.39 in 50 years' time (these figures are calculated using compound interest). It must therefore be true that a benefit of £117.39 available in 50 years' time is only worth £1 today if the rate of return is 10 per cent per annum.

So in cost-benefit analysis, all future costs and benefits need to be revalued using a rate of discount. There are two ways of doing this. Either a rate of discount is assumed and all costs and benefits are calculated as if they occurred today. This is known as calculating **present values**. The NET PRESENT VALUE of an investment project is then the present value of social benefits minus the present value of social costs. Alternatively the internal rate of return on the project can be calculated. So if we knew that £1 had been invested today and the

Question 3

A rail link could be built to last either 25 years or 50 years. It has been estimated that it would cost £100 million to build it for 25 years and £200 million for 50 years. In 25 years' time the cost of upgrading it to make it last another 25 years would be £900 million.

(a) If the rate of discount (or rate of interest or rate of return) were 10 per cent, would it be cheaper to build it to last for 25 years and repair it, or build it to last for 50 years?
(b) Would your answer be different if the rate of discount was 5 per cent? Explain why.

one and only benefit were £117.39 which would be paid in 50 years' time, then we would know that the rate of return on the project would be 10 per cent per annum.

A critique of cost-benefit analysis

Cost-benefit analysis is a procedure where:
● all costs and benefits, both private and social, are identified;
● then a value is placed on those costs and benefits, wherever possible in monetary terms.

The technique is used mainly where it is assumed that market failure is present. Calculating all costs and benefits would seem to be a more rational way of evaluating an important investment project than relying upon projections of private profit or even having no facts and figures to consider.

However, cost-benefit analysis can be a very imprecise procedure. It is difficult to place a value on certain important costs and benefits and the results depend crucially upon the rate of discount of future costs and benefits used.

So the results of cost-benefit analysis should be used with caution. The assumptions made in the analysis should be explicit. Ideally a range of results should be calculated showing what would happen to costs and benefits if different assumptions were made. Social costs and benefits which cannot be valued in monetary terms should be clearly stated.

If this is done, cost-benefit analysis can be a useful tool in the evaluation of investment projects. But it should be recognised that it is only one piece of evidence amongst many and it could well be that other considerations, such as political considerations, prove ultimately to be more important.

Key terms

Cost-benefit analysis - a procedure, particularly used by governments to evaluate investment projects, which takes into account social cost and benefits.
Net present value - the present value of social benefits minus the present value of social costs.
Rate of return or rate of discount - the rate of interest or rate of profit earned on an investment project over time. The rate of discount can be used to calculate the present value of future income.

Applied economics

Cost-benefit analysis in transport

Roads

Roads in the UK are funded almost entirely by local and central government authorities. The Department for Transport has for a number of years used a computer model to conduct cost-benefit analyses of new road schemes. This computer model is called COBA (COst Benefit Analysis).

The COBA appraisal process is shown in Figure 1. On the left hand side, there are the **costs** of a project:

● Capital costs are the cost of construction, including preparation and supervision costs.
● Maintenance costs are the extra costs of maintaining the road network. For example, if without the project, the maintenance costs of the network were £100 million a year and once the project was built, the maintenance costs were £101 million a year, then the cost to be included in the cost-benefit analysis is £1 million. This calculation has to be done because most new projects are improvements to an existing road, like turning a single lane stretch of road into a dual carriageway.

On the right hand side are the **benefits** of a project. In COBA, these are called 'user costs'. As with maintenance costs, the benefits of a new scheme are the benefits minus benefits on existing roads. For example, if on an single lane existing road, there are three accidents every ten years but converting it to a dual carriageway would reduce this to one accident, then the benefit of the project is a saving of two accidents every ten years. There are three benefits included in the cost-benefit analysis.

● Changes in **time** of travel are the savings to road users. Time is valued in monetary terms. In the COBA model shown in Table 1, three different types of road user are distinguished, cars, goods vehicles and public service vehicles such as buses. For motorists and public service vehicles, three different type of use are distinguished: those working, such as taxi drivers or bus drivers, commuters, and other users such as shoppers. Time savings for drivers in the course of their work are estimated from the cost of employing those workers. Time savings for commuting and for other uses is calculated from surveys. These provide data for the price that road users put on faster journey times. The highest benefits for time saving are placed on drivers using

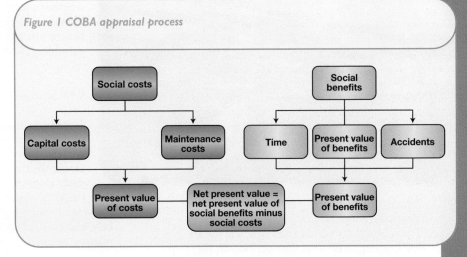

Figure 1 COBA appraisal process

their vehicle for work. The lowest is for drivers using their vehicle to do the weekly shop or fetch their children from school. The average value for all drivers placed on saving one hour of time was £9.30 in 2002.

● Changes in **operating costs** are the benefits to be gained from greater vehicle efficiency. For example, if vehicles on average spend 1 minute less at a road junction because it has been improved, then that is 1 minute less of fuel used. It also saves on other operating costs such as wear and tear on brakes.
● Changes in **accident costs** can be significant. A fatal casualty was valued at 2002 prices at £1 249 890, a serious casualty at £140 450 and a slight

Table 1 Time costs used in COBA 2002

Type of vehicle	£ per hour per occupant
Car	
Working car, driver	21.86
Non-working car, commuting	4.17
Non-working car. other	3.68
Light Goods Vehicle (LGV)	
Working vehicle, driver	8.42
Non-working LGV, commuting	4.17
Public service vehicle (PSV)	
Driver	8.42
Passenger, commuting	4.17
Passenger, other	3.68
Average vehicle	9.30

Source: adapted from *COBA Manual*, Department for Transport.

casualty at £10 830. There are also costs to property, police costs and insurance costs.

The future costs and benefits of a scheme are calculated over a 60 year time period. So the estimated benefits of a new road scheme 60 years from now are included in the calculation but benefits 70 years from now would not be included. The rate of discount used is 3.5 per cent. So a benefit worth £6.87 in 60 years time has a discounted value of £1 today. As in all cost-benefit studies, the further away in time £1 of benefit or cost, the less value is placed on it.

Inevitably, COBA has its limitations as a decision making tool. It doesn't take into account all costs and benefits. For example, the building of a new dual carriageway may have a positive impact on shop trade in a local village, or create increased noise pollution for local residents. These benefits and costs would not be included in a COBA analysis. There is also controversy about the values placed on variables such as time. Environmental groups, for example, will almost inevitably place a lower value on time saved than, say, hauliers associations.

For these reasons, since 1998, the government has stated that COBA should be only one element in the assessment of new road building and improvement schemes. The New Approach to Appraisal (NATA) assesses schemes against five criteria.

- The economy - public accounts, transport economic efficiency for business users and consumers, reliability and wider economic impacts.
- Safety - accidents and security.
- The environment - noise, local air quality, greenhouse gasses, landscape, townscape, heritage of historic resources, bio-diversity, water environment, physical fitness and journey ambience.
- Accessibility to the transport system.
- Integration - transport interchange, land-use policy and other government policies.

NATA shows clearly the problems faced by decision makers in assessing new schemes. With so many different criteria and no common measure with which to place a value on each, it becomes a matter of subjective judgement as to whether a scheme should go ahead or not. However, economists have to admit that cost-benefit analysis cannot place a value on every variable. Therefore subjective judgement is inevitable.

Rail transport

The railways are split between Network Rail, the provider of the track and other infrastructure, and the rail operating companies which run trains across the tracks. The rail operating companies make decisions about whether or not to invest based on their private costs and benefits. However, Network Rail uses cost-benefit analysis to help guide its investment decisions, including those relating to safety.

Air transport

As with the railways, ownership of infrastructure, UK airports, is split from ownership of aircraft. Airline companies operate on a commercial basis and only take into account private costs and benefits in their decision making. But UK airports are also mostly privately owned. In its 2003 White Paper, *Future of Air Transport*, the government outlined how it saw the air transport industry developing over the next few decades. However, although it recommended the expansion of a number of different airports, it did not promise to commission any cost-benefit studies of these individual proposals. The future of the UK's airports will therefore be decided by the commercial interests of their mostly private sector owners and the public sector bodies responsible for granting planning permission for developments to go ahead.

DataQuestion

Heathrow Airport

Heathrow Airport is the busiest international airport in the world with 90 airlines transporting nearly 70 million people to 180 destinations. Heathrow supports thousands of jobs, provides the vital links between the UK and the global economy, and is a crucial factor in convincing companies to locate in Britain. But today Heathrow is full. It is running at 98.5 per cent of its permitted runway capacity. It is vulnerable to foreign competitors taking away business.

There have been no major runway developments in South East England since 1946. In order to meet the demands of the UK economy, Heathrow needs to have the flexibility to grow, but accepts that growth cannot be at 'any cost' and must be within environmental limits.

Source: adapted from *Economic benefits of Heathrow Airport*, BAA Heathrow.

Note: BAA Heathrow is the owner of Heathrow Airport.

Transport Secretary Ruth Kelly has set out proposals for a third runway and a sixth terminal at Heathrow. Analysis published by the government suggests an expanded Heathrow could meet air pollution and noise limits over time. It says three runways could be operated from 2020 without breaching air quality limits thanks to developments like cleaner aircraft engines. It says take-offs and landings should be limited to 605 000 a year initially to meet noise restrictions. As old, nosier planes are phased out, this could rise to 702 000 by 2020. Currently there are 480 000 a year. A sixth terminal to serve the runway would require 700 properties to be bulldozed, including the village of Sipson.

Source: adapted from the news.bbc.co.uk, 22.11.2007.

Expanding Heathrow is crazy. Britain's airports can't expand - not if we are serious about tackling climate change. According to the government's own figures, aviation is already responsible for 13 per cent of the UK's climate impact and is one of the fastest growing sources of greenhouse gas emissions. Flying is ten times more damaging to the climate than the train yet almost a quarter of flights out of Heathrow are to destinations which are easily reachable by train like Paris and Manchester. Switching to trains for easily reachable destinations would cut out the need for Heathrow expansion. BA puts profits before the climate.

Source: adapted from www.greenpeace.org.uk

1. Explain what is meant by social costs and social benefits, using examples from the data.
2. If the government were to conduct a cost-benefit analysis of building a third runway and sixth terminal at Heathrow airport, (a) what costs and benefits might be included in the analysis and (b) what costs and benefits might be excluded because they are too difficult to quantify?
3. Assume the cost-benefit analysis of the proposed extension showed that it would generate a positive net present value. Discuss whether the scheme should go ahead.

Summary

1. In the long run, the demand curve for labour is downward sloping because capital can be substituted for labour.
2. In the short run, the downward sloping demand curve for labour can be explained by the law of diminishing returns.
3. The marginal revenue product curve of labour is the demand curve for labour. This is true whether the firm operates in a perfectly competitive or imperfectly competitive market.
4. The elasticity of demand for labour is determined by time, the availability of substitutes, the elasticity of demand for the product and the proportion of labour costs to total costs.

The downward sloping demand curve

Firms need workers to produce goods and services. The demand curve for labour shows how many workers will be hired at any given wage rate over a particular time period. A firm, for instance, might want to hire 100 workers if the wage rate were £2 per hour but only 50 workers if it were £200 per hour. Economic theory suggests that the higher the price of labour, the less labour firms will hire.

- In the long run, other things remaining equal, firms can vary all factors of production. The higher the wage rate, the more likely it is that firms will substitute machines for workers and hence the lower the demand for labour.
- In the short run, firms are likely to have an existing stock of capital. They will have to produce with a given amount of factory or office space and with a fixed amount of plant, machinery and equipment. The more workers that are added to this fixed stock of capital, the less likely it is that the last worker employed will be as productive as existing employees. Hence the wage rate would have to fall to encourage the employer to take on an extra worker.

So the demand curve for labour is likely to be downward sloping both in the long run and the short run. Why do the long run and short run demand curves slope downward and what determines the elasticity of demand for labour?

The long run demand for labour

In the long run, all factors of production are variable. A firm has complete freedom to choose its production techniques. In the Third World, where labour is cheap relative to capital, firms tend to choose labour intensive methods of production. In the First World, labour is relatively expensive and hence more capital intensive techniques of production are chosen. So in the First World, far more use is made of tractors and other machinery, whilst in the Third World, far more workers per acre are employed.

The short run demand for labour

In the short run, at least one of the factors of production is fixed. Assume that all factors are fixed except labour. The **law of diminishing returns** states that marginal output will start to decline if more and more units of one variable factor of production are combined with a given quantity of fixed factors. One common example is to imagine a plot of land with a fixed

Question 1

Table 1 Real gross capital per employee in the UK (£ at 1995 prices)

	Real gross capital per employee 1978	Real gross capital per employee 2006
Mining, quarrying, electricity, gas and water	300 000	1 690 000
Transport and communication	89 000	167 000
Manufacturing	48 000	109 000
Distribution, hotels and restaurants	17 000	42 000
Finance and business services	27 000	68 000
Construction	11 000	18 000

Source: adapted from www.statistics.gov.uk.statbase.

(a) How has real capital per employee changed over the period 1978 to 2006?
(b) Real average earnings rose 83 per cent between 1978 and 2006. Assume there was little difference in this rise between industries and that the real cost of capital did not increase over the period. Would a firm setting up in 2006 be likely to have used more or less capital intensive technique of production than in 1987? Give reasons for your answer.

number of tools where extra workers are employed to cultivate the land. Diminishing returns will quickly set in and the eleventh worker, for instance, on a one acre plot of land will contribute less to total output than the tenth worker.

This is shown in Table 2. Labour is assumed to be a variable factor of production whilst all other factors are fixed. As extra workers are employed, total output, or TOTAL PHYSICAL PRODUCT, increases. However, MARGINAL PHYSICAL PRODUCT, the number of extra units of output a worker produces, starts to decline after the employment of the second worker. So diminishing marginal returns set in with the third worker. Assume that the firm is in a perfectly competitive industry and therefore faces a horizontal, perfectly elastic demand curve. This means that the firm can sell any quantity of its product at the same price per unit. In Table 2, it is assumed that the price of the product is £10. MARGINAL REVENUE PRODUCT can then be calculated because it is the addition to revenue from the employment of an extra worker. For instance, the first worker produces 8 units and so, at a price per product unit of £10, her marginal revenue product is £80 (£10 x 8). The marginal revenue product of the second worker is £90 (£10 x the marginal physical product).

Table 2

					Per week	
1	2	3	4	5	6	7
Labour input	Total output	Marginal physical product	Price of product	Marginal revenue product (3 x 4)	Wage rate per worker	Contribution (5 - 6)
(workers)	(units)	(units)	£	£	£	£
1	8	8	10	80	70	10
2	17	9	10	90	70	20
3	25	8	10	80	70	10
4	32	7	10	70	70	0
5	38	6	10	60	70	-10
6	43	5	10	50	70	-20

It is now possible to calculate how many workers a firm will employ. The contribution to the payment of fixed costs and the earning of profit of each worker is the difference between the marginal revenue product of the firm and the cost to the firm of the worker. Assume that the firm is able to employ any number of workers at a wage rate of £70. The contribution of the first worker is £10, her marginal revenue product minus her wage (£80 - £70). The contribution of the second worker is £20 (£90 - £70). It can be seen from Table 2 that the first three workers each make a positive contribution. The fourth worker neither increases nor decreases total profit for the firm. The firm would definitely not employ a fifth worker because her employment would result in a loss of £10 to the firm. Her wage of £70 would exceed her marginal revenue product of £60. So marginal revenue product theory suggests that the firm will employ a maximum of 4 workers because this number maximises total profit (or minimises the loss) for the firm.

If the wage rate were to fall to £50, the firm would employ more workers. The fourth worker would now definitely be employed because her contribution would be £20. The fifth worker too would contribute a positive £10. The firm might also employ a sixth worker although her contribution is zero. Marginal revenue product theory therefore suggests that the lower the wage, the more workers will be employed.

The demand curve for labour

Figure 1 shows a firm's marginal revenue product curve for labour. It is downward sloping because marginal revenue product declines as output increases (as shown in Table 2). If the wage rate is 0F, the firm will employ 0B units of labour. If the wage rate rises, the firm will cut back employment to 0A. If, on the other hand, wage rates fall to 0E, then the firm will take on extra workers and increase the labour force to 0C. The marginal revenue product curve therefore shows the number of workers the firm will employ at any given wage rate, but this is the definition of the firm's demand curve for labour. Therefore the marginal revenue product curve is also the firm's demand curve for labour.

This is true for all factors of production. Figure 1

Question 2

Table 3

Number of workers employed	Total physical product per week	Total revenue product	Marginal revenue product
1	10		
2	24		
3	36		
4	44		
5	50		
6	53		

Table 3 shows the total physical product per week for a small firm as the number of workers employed varies. The price of the product sold is £10 per unit.
(a) Calculate total revenue product at each level of employment.
(b) Calculate marginal revenue product as employment increases.
(c) Explain how many workers the firm should employ if the weekly wage per worker were: (i) £60; (ii) £30; (iii) £120; (iv) £100.

shows the familiar price/quantity diagram. The price of labour is the wage rate. Quantity is the quantity of labour employed. The downward sloping marginal revenue product curve gives us the familiar downward sloping demand curve.

Shifts in the the demand curve for labour

The demand curve for labour can shift to the left or right if the marginal revenue product of a given quantity of labour changes. There are two main reasons why marginal revenue product may change given that marginal revenue product equals marginal physical product x the price of the product.

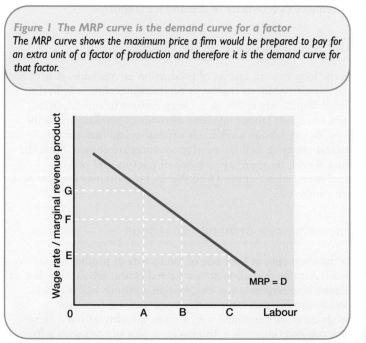

Figure 1 The MRP curve is the demand curve for a factor
The MRP curve shows the maximum price a firm would be prepared to pay for an extra unit of a factor of production and therefore it is the demand curve for that factor.

- The physical productivity (physical output per worker) of labour may change. If a group of car workers increase their output from 4 cars per day to 5 cars per day, their marginal physical product will increase and hence so too will their marginal revenue product. Employers will be prepared to pay more to workers who are more productive.
- The price of what is produced may change. If the market price of a car increases from £5 000 to £10 000, the marginal revenue product will double. Car manufacturers will then be prepared to pay more for labour.

An increase in labour productivity or an increase in the price of the product made will increase the demand for labour, shifting the demand curve to the right. Conversely, a fall in labour productivity or a fall in the price of the product will reduce the demand for labour, shifting the demand curve to the left. In Figure 2, the demand curve has shifted to the right. For any given quantity of labour, the marginal revenue product of labour has increased. So, for example, if 0A labour were employed, its MRP before the MRP increase was 0B. Now it is 0C and so the demand curve has shifted from D_1 to D_2.

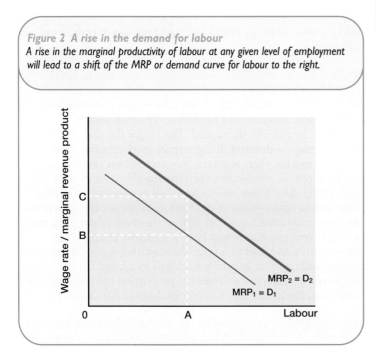

Figure 2 A rise in the demand for labour
A rise in the marginal productivity of labour at any given level of employment will lead to a shift of the MRP or demand curve for labour to the right.

Perfect and imperfect competition

So far it has been assumed that the employer is supplying goods in a perfectly competitive market. This is because it has been assumed that the firm can supply any quantity of goods to the market at the same price per unit (i.e. the firm faces a horizontal demand curve). The marginal revenue product curve falls because of diminishing returns.

However, if the employer supplies goods in an imperfectly competitive market, then it faces a downward sloping demand curve for its product. If it expands output, price per unit sold will fall. Consider Table 2 again. The fall in marginal revenue product would be even greater than that shown if the price of the product did not remain at £10 per unit, but fell as output expanded. So the marginal revenue product curve for an imperfectly competitive firm falls not only because of diminishing returns but also because the price or average revenue

Question 3

Table 4

Number of workers employed	Number of units produced and sold per week	Price per unit £
1	10	£15
2	24	£14
3	36	£12
4	44	£11
5	50	£10
6	53	£9

The firm in Table 4 produces in an imperfectly competitive market. As output increases, the price falls.
(a) Calculate (i) the total revenue product and (ii) the marginal revenue product of labour as employment increases.
(b) How many workers would the firm employ if the weekly wage were: (i) £20; (ii) £40; (iii) £60; (iv) £80; (v) £100; (vi) £120?

of the product sold falls too as output expands.

Whether the firm is perfectly or imperfectly competitive, it is still true that the demand curve for labour is the marginal revenue product curve of labour.

Determinants of the elasticity of demand for labour

The elasticity of demand for labour is a measure of the responsiveness of the quantity demanded of labour to changes in the price of labour (i.e. the wage rate. For instance, if elasticity of demand for labour were 2 and wage rates increased 10 per cent then, all other things being equal, the demand for labour would fall by 20 per cent. If demand for labour fell by 1 per cent when wage rates rose by 100 per cent, all other things being equal, then elasticity of demand for labour would be 0.01 (i.e. highly inelastic).

Time The longer the time period for adjustment, the easier it is to substitute labour for other factors of production or vice versa. In the short term, a firm may have little choice but to employ the same number of workers even if wage rates increase rapidly. Workers will have contracts of employment. There may be severe financial penalties in the form of redundancy payments if workers are sacked. Or a firm may not wish to lose skilled staff because they would be difficult to replace. In the longer term, the firm can buy new labour saving machinery and carry out changes in its methods of work which will reduce the labour employed. Hence the longer the time period, the higher will tend to be the elasticity of demand for labour.

Availability of substitutes The easier it is to substitute other factors for labour, the greater will be the response by firms to a change in real wage rates. So the better the substitutes, the higher will tend to be the elasticity of demand for labour.

Elasticity of demand for the product Labour is a

Question 4

(a) Explain whether you would expect the elasticity of demand for labour on North Sea oil rigs to be relatively high or low.

Key terms

Marginal physical product - the physical addition to output of an extra unit of a variable factor of production.

Marginal revenue product - the value of the physical addition to output of an extra unit of a variable factor of production. In a perfectly competitive product market where marginal revenue equals price, it is equal to marginal physical product times the price of the good produced.

Total physical product – the total output of a given quantity of factors of production.

Unit labour cost - cost of employing labour per unit of output or production.

derived demand. It is only demanded because the goods that it produces are demanded. For instance, if there is a collapse in demand for coal, then there will also be a collapse in the demand for coal miners. This means that the elasticity of demand for labour in an industry is directly correlated with the elasticity of demand for the product made in the industry. If the elasticity of demand for the product is low, as for instance for gas or electricity, then a sudden rise in wages which pushes up gas or electricity prices will have little effect on demand for gas or electricity. There will be little effect on employment in the industry and hence the demand for labour will be low. If, on the other hand, elasticity of demand for the product is high, elasticity of demand for labour will be high. A steel company, for instance, faces highly elastic demand for many of its products. A rise in wages not matched elsewhere in the industry

is likely to increase its prices and lead to a loss of orders and therefore jobs.

The proportion of labour cost to total cost A rise in UNIT LABOUR COSTS, the cost of employing labour per unit of production, will reduce the supply of a product, shifting the supply curve upwards and to the left. This will lead to a reduction in quantity demanded. The bigger the shift, the larger the reduction in demand. If a group of workers gains a 50 per cent pay rise but these workers only account for one per cent of the total cost of production, then the supply curve of the product will hardly shift. There will be little fall in demand and hence little loss of employment in the firm. If, however, this group of workers accounted for 50 per cent of the costs of the firm, then a 50 per cent pay rise would have a dramatic effect on the supply curve and lead to a large decrease in quantity demanded of the product. This in turn would lead to a large fall in employment. Hence, the larger the proportion of labour cost to total cost, the higher the elasticity of demand for labour.

Applied economics

Performance-related pay

Performance-related pay began to be a significant way of rewarding managers in the 1980s. Performance-related payment systems link the performance or output of an individual worker to his or her wages. It had been quite common on the shop floor for a long time. Many manual workers were on a piece-rate system. The more they produced, the higher their wages were at the end of the week. Equally, many sales people have been rewarded mainly on sales commission rather than basic pay.

Such systems can be seen as an attempt by employers to pay workers according to their revenue product. For instance, if one worker produces twice as many steel bars as another per week, it might seem logical to pay one worker more than the other. If one foreign exchange dealer generates a £1 million surplus on foreign exchange dealings over the year for his bank, whilst another only generates £100 000, then the £1 million dealer should be paid more than the other. It also enables companies to decide whether or not to retain staff. For instance, if a foreign exchange dealer is paid £200 000 a year, but only generates £20 000 a year surplus for his bank, then he should be sacked. Equally, if a company has five workers, all equally productive, but the output of one worker is sold at a loss, then one worker should be sacked.

Piece rates have become less common since the 1980s. It is felt that they encourage individualism. The emphasis in manufacturing today is on team work. Japanese production techniques, copied by many UK manufacturing companies, stress the importance of co-operation. Just-in-time manufacturing techniques, for instance, demand that workers act in the best interests of the group, not themselves.

At the same time, the 1980s saw a move away from collectivism at management level. The **entrepreneur** became a role model for many. Companies tried to identify the contribution of an individual manager or director to the business. This could then be used to set targets for future performance. It could also be used to set remuneration levels.

The 'performance' of the individual manager or director could be linked to a number of variables. At chief executive level, it could be linked to profit, share price or dividends paid. These variables are chosen because of the view that shareholders are the most important group in a company and they seek to maximise their returns on their shareholding. At a managerial level, it might be linked to factors such as costs, sales, labour productivity or customer satisfaction. All these variables ultimately affect profit, share price and dividends.

The 'pay' which is related to performance is varied. Managers and directors almost invariably are paid a basic salary. On top of this, though, they may receive cash bonuses in years when they achieve targets. Alternatively, the company may attempt to retain staff by offering rewards which can only be realised for cash in the longer term. A director may be offered shares if he or she is still with the company in three years time. Alternatively, they may be offered share options. These are opportunities given to buy shares at some point in the future at a price fixed now - usually the current share price. For instance, an executive might be given an option for 1 million shares at a price of £2, which can be exercised in three years' time if the executive is still with the company. If the share price has risen to £2.50 over that period, the executive can buy the shares in three years' time and immediately sell them on

the open market, making a profit of 50p per share or £500 000 overall. The justification for this is that a higher share price presumably indicates that the company has performed well over the period, in part because of the work of the executive.

Firms are willing to pay large salaries and bonuses to top staff because the demand for their labour is relatively inelastic. Whether a chief executive is paid £500 000 or £5 million is almost irrelevant to a company with a turnover of £1 000 million or £5 000 million. A new chief executive who increases profits from, say, £750 million per year to £1 000 million is well worth a few extra hundred thousand pounds in salary. There are also few good substitutes. A machine can replace a machine operator or a bank clerk but can't replace a chief executive.

There are two major problems with performance-related pay. First, there seems to be little overall link between the performance of companies and bonuses paid to senior executives. Whilst it is clear why some executives receive large bonuses, outsiders are often baffled as to why an executive should be given a large bonus in a year when profits have fallen. Second, it is not clear that the revenue product of a senior executive can be clearly separated from the performance of the staff under him or her. Effective leadership is important, but so too is the reaction of staff willing to make the effort to change and adapt.

Firms may be willing to pay high salaries to managers because demand for their labour is relatively inelastic.

DataQuestion

Demand for accountants

Demand for accountants has never been higher. The big four accountancy firms' most senior London-based executives have all said this year that tackling the 'skills shortage' is their number one priority. 'There have been some big, big challenges about getting and keeping the right resource,' says Mr Land, UK Chairman of Ernst & Young. 'Over the past 18 months it has been as tight as I can remember. Notwithstanding economic catastrophes, the biggest constraint on future success and growth is the availability of high quality people.'

Demand has increased because governments have introduced new reporting and regulatory requirements on businesses. This year, for example, saw the introduction of the new International Financial Reporting Standards whilst the US government implemented the Sarbanes-Oxley Act. The first of these is mind-bogglingly complex whilst the second is mind-numbingly tedious, but both take up vast amounts of accountants' time to complete. Most companies have had to hire one set of accountants to explain the rules and do the donkey work, and another set to audit the results.

However, the new work would have been even more lucrative if the big four firms had not cut their university recruitment during the post-internet downturn in the early 2000s. Graduates must train for three years to get their chartered accountancy qualification, which means that this year, when the firms need a rush of full qualified accountants, they have fewer than normal. Even trainee accountants, however, can do some of the work, which helps explain why the big four accountancy firms have

lifted their graduate recruitment to record levels this year.

The big four don't simply have a lack of trained graduates coming through their system. At the other end, they lose on average 30 per cent of trainees within a year of their becoming fully qualified. With companies, commercial banks and investment banks competing for the big four's qualified accountants, this is where the market is tightest. 'I've never seen higher demand at the newly qualified end for the ones with good degrees,' says Colin Webster, chief financial officer of Imprint, a recruitment consultancy. 'We have placed 24 and 25 year olds in the City on £55 000 to £60 000 a year, which is massive.'

The 'big four' accountancy firms dominate the world and UK accountancy markets. They are:
- PwC - PricewaterhouseCoopers;
- Deloitte;
- KPMG;
- Ernst & Young.

Table 5 Numbers of UK graduates recruited

	PwC	Deloitte	KPMG	Ernst & Young
2001	900	-	660	272
2002	950	-	519	253
2003	950	544	505	293
2004	1 000	805	636	378
2005	1 000	1 010	850	527

Source: adapted from the *Financial Times*, 26.5.2005.

1. (a) Outline briefly, using marginal revenue product theory, why demand for accountants increased in 2005. (b) Using a diagram and giving examples from the data, explain the impact of this increase on the demand curve for accountants.

2. Discuss the extent to which demand for accountants in the UK is elastic.

Summary

1. The supply curve for an individual worker is backward sloping at high levels of income.
2. Backward sloping supply curves result because the negative income effect of a wage increase outweighs the positive substitution effect.
3. The supply curve of labour to a firm, to an industry and to the economy as a whole is likely to be upward sloping.

The supply curve for an individual worker

A supply curve shows the quantity that will be supplied to the market at any given price. For an individual worker, the quantity supplied is the number of hours worked over a time period, such as a year. Neo-classical theory starts by assuming that a worker can decide how many hours to work per week and how many weeks' holiday to take per year. The price of labour is the wage per time period (i.e. the wage rate). The wage rate that determines supply is the **real wage rate** (the money or nominal wage rate divided by the price level). This is because the worker decides how many hours to work by relating it to what the wage will buy. For instance, a worker might take a job if a week's wages of £300 were to buy a television set, but she would be likely to turn it down if £300 were to only buy a newspaper.

Figure 1 shows a backward bending supply curve for labour. Between wages rates 0 and B a rise in real wage rates will lead to an increase in working hours supplied. For instance, the worker will offer to work DF extra hours if real wage rates increase from A to B. However, a rise in real wage rates above 0B, for instance from B to C, will lead to a desire for shorter working hours.

To understand why this might be the case, consider a part-time factory worker. Initially she is low paid, as are nearly all part-time workers. The firm she works for then doubles her real wage rate. She is likely to respond to this by wanting to work longer hours and perhaps become a full time worker. Further increases in real wage rates might persuade her to work overtime.

However, there are only 24 hours in a day and 365 days in a year. Eventually it is likely that increases in wage rates will make her want to reduce her working week or increase her holidays. She will value increased leisure time more than extra money to spend. Put another way, she is choosing to buy leisure time by forgoing the wages she could otherwise have earned and the goods she could otherwise have bought. This is an example of the concept of opportunity cost.

This process can be seen at work over the past 100 years in the UK. Real wage rates have risen considerably but hours worked have fallen. The typical Victorian working week was 60 to 70 hours with few or no holidays. Today, average hours worked per week for full time workers are down to about 42 hours with a typical holiday entitlement of 4 weeks per year. Workers have responded to increases in wage rates by supplying less labour.

Note that when wage rates increase, workers are likely to be able to both increase earnings **and** reduce hours worked. For instance, if real wage rates increase by 20 per cent from £10 per

Figure 1 The backward bending supply curve

The supply curve for an individual worker is assumed to be this shape because at high levels of income the worker will prefer to work shorter hours rather than receive the extra income he or she could have earned.

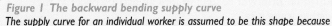
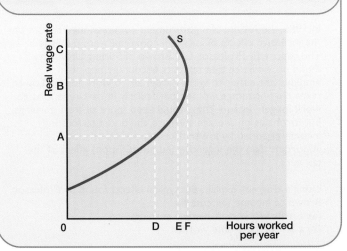

Question 1

Figure 2 Activity rates: totally economically active as % of all persons in relevant age group

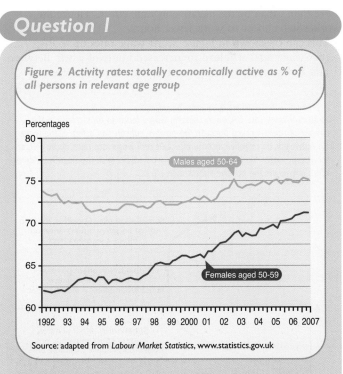

Source: adapted from *Labour Market Statistics*, www.statistics.gov.uk

(a) Real wage rates in the UK increased between 1992 and 2007. Do the data support the idea that the supply curve of labour for an individual worker is backward sloping?

hour to £12 per hour, then workers can cut their hours worked by 10 per cent from 40 hours to 36 hours per week and still see an increase in earnings from £400 per week (40 x £10) to £432 per week (36 x £12). Real wage rate increases in the neo-classical model give workers a choice between increased earnings or increased leisure time or some combination of the two.

Income and substitution effects

The backward bending supply curve occurs because of the interaction of **income and substitution** effects. An increase in real wage rates means that the reward for working, rather than not working and taking more leisure hours, increases. For instance, a worker receiving a pay rise of 10 per cent after tax and deductions can now buy 10 per cent more goods and services. The opportunity cost of not working therefore rises. Workers will therefore **substitute** work for leisure if the rate of pay increases.

However, work is arguably an **inferior good**. The higher the income, the fewer hours individuals will wish to work. For instance, it is pointless being able to buy tennis or squash equipment if you don't have the time to play. Earning more money has little use if you can't take the time off to have a holiday, go to the pub or go shopping. So the **income effect** of work tends to be negative for most individuals. The higher the income, the less work and the more leisure time is demanded.

At low levels of income, the positive substitution effect outweighs the negative income effect of a wage rise. Hence, a rise in pay for these workers leads to an increase in the number of hours worked. At higher levels of income, the positive substitution effect is likely to be equally matched by the negative income effect. Wage increases then have neither an incentive nor a disincentive effect on working hours. But at high levels of income, the positive substitution effect of a wage increase is more than offset by the negative income effect. Hence the worker will choose to work fewer hours.

This can be shown in Figure 3. At wage rates up to 0A, higher wage rates will lead to increased hours of work. Between A and B the supply curve is vertical, showing that increased

wages have no effect on hours worked. Between A and B the negative income effect cancels out the positive substitution effect as wages rise. Above 0B the supply curve slopes backward showing that the negative income effect of a wage rise more than offsets its positive substitution effect.

In the real world, many workers have little choice about how many hours they work. However, rising incomes have been associated with longer holidays and also a shorter working life. Those on higher incomes often want to retire as early as possible given that they have been able to save up enough over their working life to finance a reasonable pension. Many other workers do have the opportunity to work longer hours during the week by taking overtime. There is a limit, though, to the amount of overtime employees are prepared to work, showing the negative income effect in operation.

Monetary and non-monetary considerations

The supply of labour to a particular market is affected not just by **monetary** or **pecuniary** considerations. **Non-monetary** or **non-pecuniary** considerations can be important too. The trade-off between work and leisure has already been explained. But other non-monetary considerations include:
- job satisfaction. Workers are prepared to accept lower wages if there is greater job satisfaction. Evidence suggests, though, that higher pay is associated with greater job satisfaction because higher paid jobs tend to give workers more control over their working environment.
- location. A job may be attractive to an individual worker, for example, because it is close to relatives and friends, or it is in London with its social life.
- friends and family. Some jobs are attractive because they involve working with friends and family.
- commuting. Time taken to travel to work, the pleasantness of the journey and its cost affect people's choices of jobs.

Supply of labour to a firm

In a perfectly competitive market there are many buyers and sellers. In a perfectly competitive factor market, there are many firms hiring many individual workers. This means that an individual firm will be able to hire an extra worker at the existing wage rate.

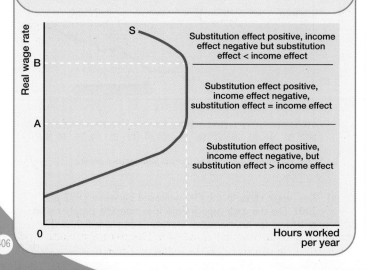

Figure 3 Substitution and income effects
Up to real wage rate 0A, an increase in wages leads to an increase in the number of hours worked because the positive substitution effect of the wage rise outweighs its negative income effect. At real wage rate rises above 0B, an increase in wages leads to a fall in hours worked, because the negative income effect outweighs the positive substitution effect.

Question 2

In 1986, the results of a government commissioned report on the incentive effects of cuts in income tax were published. The report, by Professor C V Brown of Stirling University, found no evidence that tax cuts encourage people in employment either to work harder or to work longer. Lower taxes did encourage women, particularly in part-time jobs, to work longer because they would keep more of their earnings, but for males on average earnings, the boost to existing income provided by lower taxes tended to be more important than the incentive (i.e. substitution) effect of the tax cut.

Using a diagram, explain the typical effects found by Professor Brown of income tax cuts on
(a) a male worker on average earnings and
(b) a female part-time worker.

Another way of showing increased female participation in the labour force is to calculate the female ACTIVITY RATE or PARTICIPATION RATE. This is the percentage of any given population which is in the labour force (i.e. the percentages of an age group either in work or officially counted as unemployed). There is a number of reasons why a larger proportion of females have gone out to work.

- Real wages have increased over the period. Economic theory would predict that an increase in real wages will increase the supply of labour into the market.
- Through changes in social attitudes and legislation, women now have much greater opportunities in employment than in 1971 and far more than say in 1931 or 1901. Again this means that more women are getting higher paid jobs, attracting them to make careers for themselves.
- The opportunity cost of going out to work has fallen. A hundred years ago, women created a large number of household services, from cleaning the house to baking bread to making clothes. They had to spend large amounts of time each week doing this. Today, cheap and efficient machines do much of this work. What is more, the real price of washing machines, microwaves etc. has tended to fall over time. Households have been able to afford to buy more and more of these gadgets. The result is that women have increasingly been able to combine a career with running a home. Moreover, changes in social attitudes over the past 20 years have meant that men have increasingly begun to share in domestic chores, again helping to create time for women to work in paid employment.
- Falls in the number of children in a family help explain why there was an increase in the number of women working over the period 1900 to 1970. However, the size of families with children has altered relatively little since 1970. What has changed is an increase in nursery education and in pre-school and childminding facilities. Women have found it easier to get their children looked after at an affordable cost since 1970.

Male activity rates, in contrast, have fallen. In 1971, virtually all males aged 25-65 were in the labour force. However, by the early 1990s, activity rates for men aged 50-65 had fallen to approximately 75 per cent where they have stayed since. Early retirement, ill health and disability account for why this has happened. At the other end of the age range, increased staying on rates in education account for the fall in activity rates over the past 40 years for the 16-25 year old age group.

The distribution of men and women between

different occupations is very different, as Figure 10 shows. For instance, there are almost no women in skilled trades such as plumbers or electricians. In contrast, there are very few men employed in administration and secretarial occupations, and in personal services such as care assistants. Nearly twice the proportion of male employees are managers and senior officials compared to female employees.

There is a number of possible reasons which might explain this. Traditionally, males have taken jobs which require heavy manual labour. Women, in contrast, have been associated with the caring professions such as nursing. Secretarial and clerical work is another area which has traditionally been female dominated over the past 100 years. Women are also disproportionately represented amongst occupations where there are large numbers of part-time workers. Due to child care commitments, many women prefer to work part-time rather than full time and therefore occupations which offer opportunities for part-time work are likely to attract more female workers.

Sexual equality is a relatively recent phenomenon and males are still disproportionately represented in higher paid jobs such as managers and senior officials. This could be due to discrimination against women. However, it must also reflect the fact that women are far more likely than men to take a career break to bring up children. Even a few years out of the labour force has a considerable impact on promotion prospects. Finally, the differences in Figure 10 may simply reflect occupational preferences between males and females. Males, perhaps, may prefer to mix concrete rather than act as a receptionist. This might suggest that the supply curve for any occupation is different between men and women.

Employment by age

Not only has the balance of the labour force changed between the sexes, it has also changed by age as Table 5 shows. Since 1971, there has been a significant

Figure 10 *Occupations of men and women, UK, April–June 2007*

	% of male employees	% of female employees	Male-female employees
Skilled trades	19.2	1.9	
Process, plant and machine operatives	12.1	2.1	
Managers and senior officials	18.5	11.1	
Professional occupations	13.7	12.1	
Elementary occupations	11.6	11.0	
Associate professional and technical	12.9	15.6	
Sales and customer service	4.6	11.1	
Personal service	2.3	14.5	
Administration and secretarial	4.7	20.2	
Total	100.0	100.0	

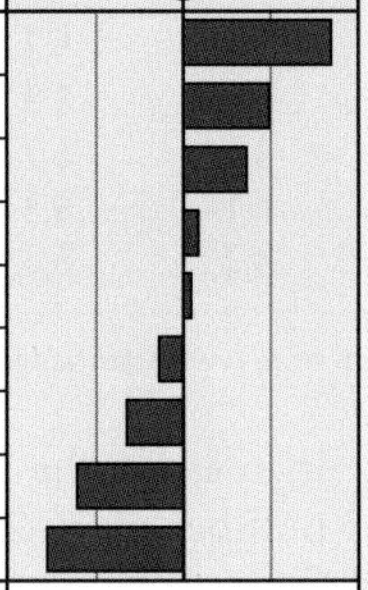

1 Figures do not add up to exactly 100 because of rounding.

Source: adapted from Labour Force Survey, Office for National Statistics.

Table 5 Employment by age, millions, UK

	16-24	25-34	35-49	50-64 (male)/ 50-59 (female)	65+ (male)/ 60+ (female)
				millions	
1971	5.1	5.3	7.9	5.0	0.6
1984	5.0	5.3	8.0	4.9	0.7
1994	3.9	6.7	9.3	4.7	0.8
2004	4.1	6.3	10.7	6.3	1.0
2007	4.2	6.3	11.0	6.5	1.3

Source: adapted from www.statistics.gov.uk.

increase in the proportion of 25-49 year workers. The number of 16-24 year old workers peaked in 1989 at 5.6 million and has since declined. The number of workers aged 50+ has jumped since the mid 1990s.

Part of the reason for these changes has been demographic. The number of births increased from the end of second world war to the mid 1960s. They then fell to 1978, rose again to 1990, fell to 2002 and are now rising again. These rises and falls create bulges of workers in the age distribution of the labour force. People born from the end of the second world war in 1945 to the mid-1960s are called 'baby boomers'. The fall in the birth rate after the mid 1960s is the key reason why the numbers in work aged 16-24 began to fall from 1989. These baby boomers have gradually pushed their way through the age range of the working population. A worker aged 50 in 2006 was born in 1956, so the numbers of workers aged 50+ can be expected to increase at least until 2015.

Another factor affecting the numbers in work aged 16-24 has been the growing proportion of particularly 16-22 year olds in full time education. At the 50+ end, there have been two factors pulling in opposite directions. One has been a trend towards early retirement, particularly seen in the 1980s and early 1990s. The other has been the willingness of the 50+

age group, particularly women, to continue working to boost their income. Those today who take early retirement frequently go on to do another job, albeit less well paid than their previous job. The combination of a retirement pension plus a lower wage can mean that they are better off financially than if they were in their previous job. The government, in response to poor pension provision in the UK, is encouraging workers to continue in employment into their 60s. This would allow a smaller number of post-baby boomer workers to support a growing number of baby-boomer pensioners.

Employment by ethnic group

Detailed statistics for the employment of different ethnic groups in the population can be found in the data question in this unit. In general, the employment patterns of those of non-white origin seem less favourable than those of the white population.

Employment by industry and region

The supply of workers to different industries and different regions has changed considerably over the past 30 years. Broadly, there has been a major shift of workers from the primary and secondary sectors of the economy to the tertiary sector. Consequently, regions heavily dependent upon coal mining and heavy manufacturing saw losses of jobs and population to regions which have traditionally specialised in light manufacturing and service industry.

Other factors affecting the labour force

There are factors other than the increased participation of women, birth rates, education and early retirement which affect the labour force.

Migration If immigration is larger than emigration, then the workforce is likely to increase. During the 1950s, the UK encouraged immigration from new Commonwealth countries to fill an acute labour shortage. In the 1960s and 1970s, following the 1961 Immigration Act, NET MIGRATION (immigration minus emigration) tended to be negative. More people left the country than entered. Since the 1980s, the trend has been reversed. Net migration currently accounts for around 50 per cent of the net population increase in the UK. It is having a significant impact on labour markets at the margin. Some argue that the low wage inflation of the late 1990s and 2000s, despite the output gap of the economy being very close to zero, can be explained by immigration of workers. The accession of a number of Eastern European states to the EU from 2004 is likely to maintain positive net migration over the next decade.

Part-time work The numbers and proportion of part-

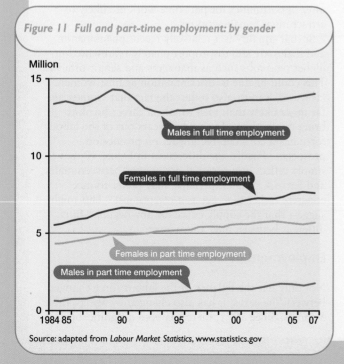

Figure 11 Full and part-time employment: by gender

Million

Males in full time employment

Females in full time employment

Females in part time employment

Males in part time employment

1984 85   90   95   00   05 07

Source: adapted from *Labour Market Statistics*, www.statistics.gov

Table 6 *Reasons why women take part-time work, UK 2004*

Reason	%
In education or training	3
Disabled	2
Caring after children or other family member	36
Found no full time job	7
Did not want full time job	19
Other	34

Source: adapted from A Manning and B Petrongolo, *The Part-Time Pay Penalty*, Centre for Economic Performance Discussion Paper no 679, March 2005.

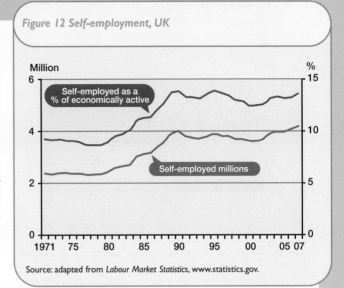

Figure 12 *Self-employment, UK*

Source: adapted from *Labour Market Statistics*, www.statistics.gov.

time workers in the workforce have been growing over the past 50 years. In 1971, for instance, 15 per cent of all employees were part-time. By 2007, this had grown to 25 per cent. Most part-time workers are female as Figure 11 shows. 43 per cent of women employees were part-timers in 2007 compared to just 11 per cent for males. Part-time working is growing amongst both males and females.

Part-time working is particularly concentrated in service industries. Workers in primary and secondary industry, such as construction and engineering, tend to be full-time male workers. The most likely explanation for this is that, historically, service industries have tended to be female dominated. They have therefore been forced to offer opportunities for part-time work because so many females prefer to work part-time rather than full-time.

The main reason why women want to work part-time is because they want or are forced to take the main responsibility for bringing up children and looking after the household as Table 6 shows. Part-time jobs enable them to fulfil these roles and hold a job. As society changes and men increasingly share in domestic responsibilities, it is likely that there will be a much greater proportion of males amongst part-time workers. Male part-time working is also likely to increase as more men take early retirement and combine their retirement with part-time employment. The increasing proportion of young people staying on in education aged 16-21 has increased part-time working too as they have been forced to seek work to supplement pocket money and grants given by parents.

Self-employment As Figure 12 shows, there was a considerable increase in self-employment during the 1980s. Since then, self-employment has remained broadly constant. The growth of self-employment in the 1980s was probably due to two main factors.

● The Conservative government of the day attempted to create an **enterprise culture**. It believed that small firms should be encouraged because they created jobs, increased competition, innovation and efficiency in markets, and increased wealth in society. Government policy was directed towards helping

small businesses and the self-employed. For instance, income tax, capital gains tax and inheritance tax were all changed to allow successful entrepreneurs to keep more of the money they earned. Various schemes lowered the cost and increased the accessibility of finance for business start ups. The unemployed were encouraged to become self-employed through grants. Training was directed at those becoming self-employed and setting up their own business.

● The economy went into a severe recession between 1980 and 1982, with unemployment rising from 1.5 million to over 3 million. Unemployment did not begin to decline until 1987, so there were six years of high unemployment. The difficulty of getting a job encouraged some workers to become self-employed and set up their own businesses. Equally, during these years there was a constant flow of workers being made redundant, some of whom were eligible for sizeable redundancy payments. This created a pool of financial capital available for these unemployed workers to set up on their own.

Since then, there has been less emphasis by government on encouraging self-employment, although small businesses continued to be a focus for government policy. Average unemployment has been lower since the early 1990s than in the 1980s and therefore there was less need for workers to become self-employed. The 1990-92 recession also led to many business failures and workers became far more aware of the risks involved in being self-employed. Since then, the period of prolonged economic growth has encouraged some workers to become self-employed. However, self-employment at 4.2 million in 2007 was approximately the same as at its peak in 1990.

Temporary work Figure 13 shows that there was a growth of temporary employment in the 1990s. As can be seen from Table 7, this was not because workers particularly seek temporary work. Only

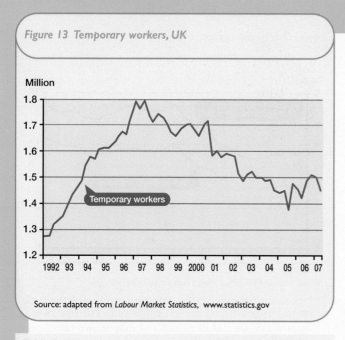

Figure 13 Temporary workers, UK

Temporary workers

Source: adapted from *Labour Market Statistics*, www.statistics.gov

Table 7 Reasons for temporary working: UK, winter 2005/06

			Per cent
Reason	All	Men	Women
Couldn't find a permanent job	25.2	28.9	22.1
Did not want a permanent job	27.5	25.0	29.4
Had a contract with period of training	7.1	8.5	6.0
Some other reason	40.2	37.5	42.3

Source: adapted from *Labour Market Trends*, Office for National Statistics.

approximately one-third of temporary workers did not want a permanent job. Rather, it reflected the wishes of firms to employ a more flexible labour force. Taking workers on permanently means that labour becomes a fixed cost. Temporary workers are a variable cost because they can be sent away at short notice. Any firm with seasonal demand for its product is therefore likely to find it attractive to employ temporary workers to cover work above that of its slackest period. Temporary workers are also used by firms which are uncertain of whether an increase in output is likely to be permanent. Sacking workers is costly and therefore to be avoided. Finally, when firms are operating efficiently, there is no slack to be taken up when workers fall ill, are away on holiday or have gone on maternity leave. Temporary workers can be used to cover these situations.

The employment of temporary workers can, however, impose costs on firms. Temporary workers can be unfamiliar with an individual's work environment and therefore not be as productive as a permanent member of staff. Motivation amongst temporary workers can also be less than with permanent staff. This is particularly true if an employee works for a long period of time for a firm but is never given a permanent contract.

Approximately 55 per cent of temporary workers

have been females. Temporary working peaked in the late 1990s and early 2000s. It can be argued that the fall in temporary working since 2001 was a reflection of the continued boom in the economy which made temporary working less attractive to workers who could find permanent jobs more easily. Temporary working is most likely to increase again if the economy goes into recession.

Hours of work and holidays Hours of work have changed little since the early 1970s. On average male full time workers have worked 41 hours per week throughout the period. However, whilst weekly hours of work have remained broadly constant, yearly hours of work have decreased because holiday entitlements have significantly increased. In 1961, workers were typically entitled to just two weeks paid holiday per year. By 2008, workers were entitled by law to four weeks paid holiday a year plus bank holidays. Many workers received even longer holiday entitlements. Long holidays and shorter working lives due to early retirement would tend to indicate that either workers prefer increases in leisure time to be in blocks of time rather than a few hours extra per week, or that employers see the 40 hour week as optimal for completing work efficiently and prefer to concede the desire for shorter hours and longer holidays or shorter working lives.

The quality of the labour force

Greater production can be achieved by using more labour. However, the size of the UK labour force is

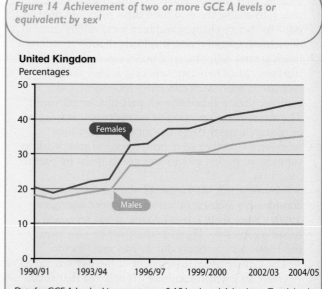

Figure 14 Achievement of two or more GCE A levels or equivalent: by sex[1]

United Kingdom
Percentages

Females

Males

Data for GCE A level achievement count 2 AS levels as 1 A level pass. Two A levels are equivalent to three or more Highers in `scotland. Pupils in Scotland generally sit Highers one year earlier than those sitting A levels in the rest of the UK. Data are for pupils in schools and further education institutions. Data prior to 1995/96, and for Wales and Northern Ireland from 2002/03, relate to schools only.

Source: adapted from www.statistics.gov.uk.

likely to change only slowly over the next 50 years. Of more significance is likely to be changes in the quality of the labour force. Rising educational standards, as shown for example by greater numbers gaining high grades at GCSE, 'A' levels, vocational qualifications and degrees, would suggest that the labour force is becoming potentially more productive over time. Figure 14 illustrates one aspect of this. A larger proportion of 17/18 year olds is gaining A levels or their equivalent. It should be noted that females have improved their performance relative to males. Male underachievement in the education system is now a target for government policy. Despite these improvements, many argue that the UK has been left behind in international terms in the quality of its labour force. This explains why governments in the 1990s and 2000s have placed such stress on education and training to improve the supply side performance of the economy.

DataQuestion

Ethnic groups in the labour force

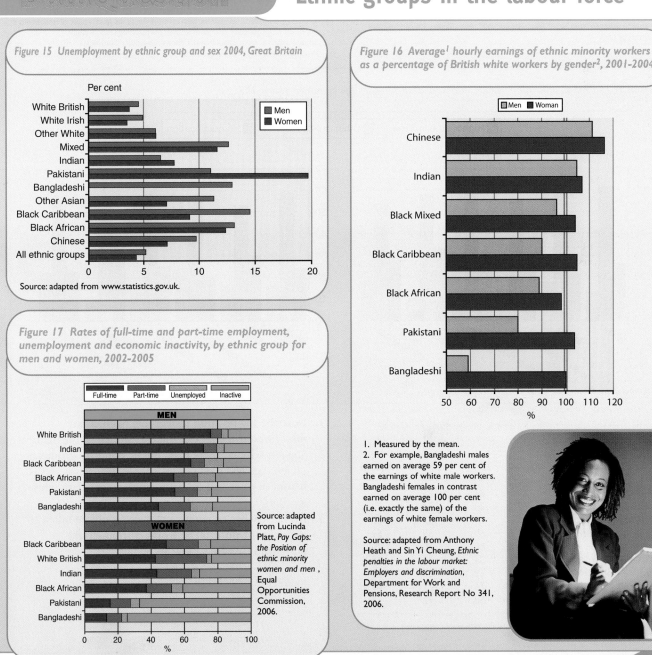

Figure 15 *Unemployment by ethnic group and sex 2004, Great Britain*

Source: adapted from www.statistics.gov.uk.

Figure 17 *Rates of full-time and part-time employment, unemployment and economic inactivity, by ethnic group for men and women, 2002-2005*

Source: adapted from Lucinda Platt, *Pay Gaps: the Position of ethnic minority women and men*, Equal Opportunities Commission, 2006.

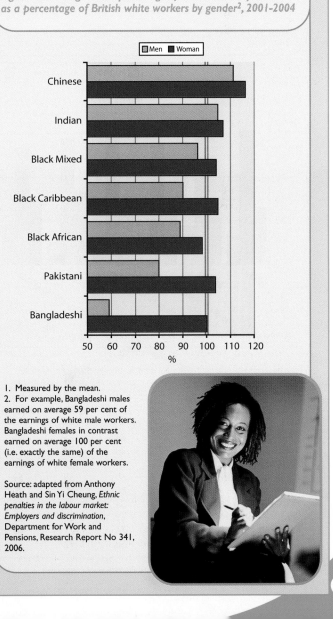

Figure 16 *Average[1] hourly earnings of ethnic minority workers as a percentage of British white workers by gender[2], 2001-2004*

1. Measured by the mean.
2. For example, Bangladeshi males earned on average 59 per cent of the earnings of white male workers. Bangladeshi females in contrast earned on average 100 per cent (i.e. exactly the same) of the earnings of white female workers.

Source: adapted from Anthony Heath and Sin Yi Cheung, *Ethnic penalties in the labour market: Employers and discrimination*, Department for Work and Pensions, Research Report No 341, 2006.

Figure 18 The acceptability of discrimination in the workplace

Question: 'Do you think that employers in Britain would be right
or wrong to refuse a job to an applicant only because of...?'
Source: Survey of British Social Attitudes, 2002

Percentage

Legend: Usually wrong / Always wrong

Categories: Religion, Black/Asian, Gay/lesbian, Age 50+, Sex, Disability

Source: adapted from *Ethnic Minorities and the Labour Market*, Prime Minister's
Strategy Unit.

Figure 19 Percentage[1] of managers, senior officials and professionals: by ethnic group[2] and sex, 2005

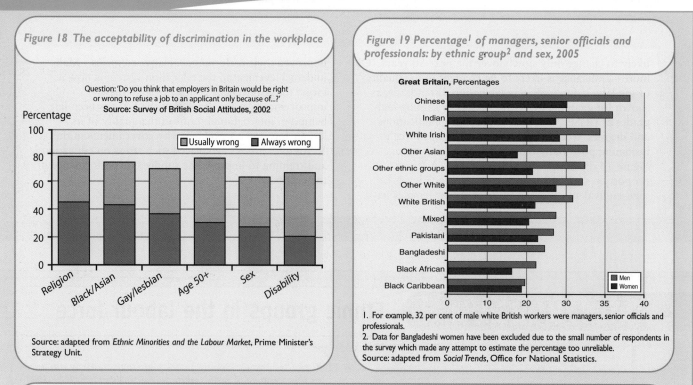

Great Britain, Percentages

Legend: Men, Women

Categories (top to bottom): Chinese, Indian, White Irish, Other Asian, Other ethnic groups, Other White, White British, Mixed, Pakistani, Bangladeshi, Black African, Black Caribbean

1. For example, 32 per cent of male white British workers were managers, senior officials and professionals.
2. Data for Bangladeshi women have been excluded due to the small number of respondents in the survey which made any attempt to estimate the percentage too unreliable.
Source: adapted from *Social Trends*, Office for National Statistics.

Figure 20 Highest qualification of men and women of working age by ethnic group, 2003

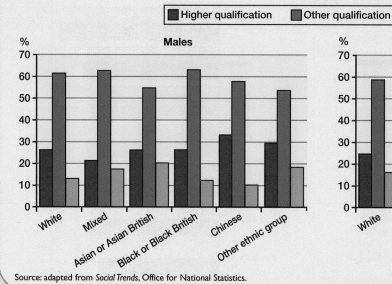

Legend: Higher qualification / Other qualification / No qualification

Males and **Females**

Categories: White, Mixed, Asian or Asian British, Black or Black British, Chinese, Other ethnic group

Source: adapted from *Social Trends*, Office for National Statistics.

Table 8 Employment rates by ethnic origin and age, Great Britain, Summer 2002 (%)

	16-24	25-44	45-59/64	All ages
All ethnic groups	64	81	73	75
White	67	83	74	77
Total mixed	49	67	57	60
Asian or Asian British	42	69	55	59
Indian	51	80	66	70
Pakistani/Bangladeshi	38	54	30	45
Black or Black British	35	69	63	60
Chinese	41	76	72	67
Other	35	58	72	57

Source: adapted from Commission for Racial Equality, www.cre.gov.uk.

1. Describe the position of workers from ethnic minorities in the labour force as shown in the data.
2. Suggest why workers from ethnic minority groups are on average less likely to (a) supply themselves to the labour market and (b) be in employment than white workers.
3. Evaluate what economic measures could be taken to improve the position of workers from ethnic minorities relative to that of whites.

Summary

1. The wage rate of labour is determined by the demand for labour and the supply of labour.
2. In an economy where labour is homogeneous and all markets are perfect, wage rates would be identical for all workers.
3. Wage differentials are caused partly by market imperfections and partly by differences in individual labour characteristics.
4. In a perfectly competitive market, individual firms face a horizontal supply curve and will hire labour up to the point where the wage rate is equal to the marginal revenue product of labour.
5. In an imperfectly competitive market, either the firm is a monopsonist or there is a monopoly supplier of labour, such as a trade union, or both. A monopsonist drives down wage rates and employment levels, whilst a monopoly supplier increases wage rates.

How wage rates are determined

Prices are determined by demand and supply. So the price of labour, the real wage rate, is determined by the demand for and the supply of labour.

The demand curve for labour in an industry is the marginal revenue product curve of labour. This is downward sloping, indicating that more labour will be demanded the lower the real wage rate. The supply curve of labour to an industry is upward sloping, indicating that more labour will be supplied if real wage rates increase. This gives an equilibrium real wage rate of 0A in Figure 1. 0B units of labour are demanded and supplied.

The demand and supply curves for labour can shift for a variety of reasons, giving new equilibrium real wage rates and levels of employment in the industry. The demand curve for labour will move to the right showing an increase in the demand for labour if the marginal revenue product of labour increases. This might occur if:

- productivity improves, perhaps due to changing technology or more flexible working practices, increasing output per worker;
- there is a rise in the selling price of the product, increasing the value of the output of each worker;
- the price of capital increases, leading to a substitution of labour for capital.

The supply curve might move to the right, showing an increase in supply, if:

- there is an increase in the number of workers in the population as a whole, perhaps because of changing demographic trends, or because government alters tax and benefit levels, increasing incentives to work;
- wages or conditions of work deteriorate in other industries, making conditions relatively more attractive in this industry.

A labour market where all workers are paid the same

Consider an economy which has the following labour market characteristics.

- Labour is homogeneous (i.e. all workers are identical, for instance in age, skill and sex).

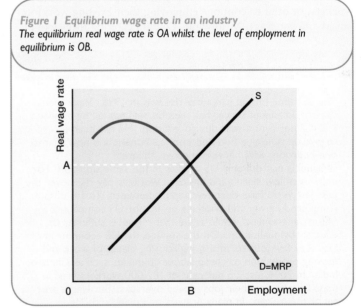

> **Figure 1 Equilibrium wage rate in an industry**
> The equilibrium real wage rate is OA whilst the level of employment in equilibrium is OB.

Question 1

(a) On a diagram, draw a demand and supply curve for labour in the DVD production industry.
(b) Mark on the diagram the equilibrium wage rate and the equilibrium level of employment.
(c) Show how the demand curve or the supply curve might shift if there is:
   (i) a fall in labour productivity;
   (ii) an increase in wage rates in all other labour markets in the economy;
   (iii) a fall in demand for DVDs;
   (iv) an introduction of new labour saving technology;
   (v) a fall in the number of 16-25 year olds in the population as a whole.

There is perfect knowledge in the labour market. For example, a worker in Scotland is as aware of job opportunities in London as a Londoner.

There is perfect mobility of labour. Workers can move at no cost between jobs in the same industry, between different industries and between geographical areas. Equally, there are no costs to firms in hiring and firing workers.

All workers and employers are price takers. There are no trade unions or monopsonist employers.

There are no barriers which prevent wages rising and falling to accommodate changes in the demand for and supply of labour.

Firms aim to maximise profit and minimise costs of production, whilst workers aim to maximise their wages.

In this perfect labour market, all workers would be paid the same wage rate. To show that this must be true, consider two markets where wage rates are different. In the Welsh steel industry, wages are higher than in the catering market in London. London catering workers would know this because there is perfect knowledge in the market. They would apply for jobs in Welsh steel firms. They would be prepared to work for less than existing Welsh steel workers so long as the wage rate was higher than their existing wage rate as caterers. Welsh steel makers, seeking to minimise cost, would then either sack their existing workers and replace them with cheaper London catering workers, or offer to continue employing their existing workforce but at a lower wage. Meanwhile, London catering firms would

Question 2

The last time Miguel had a pay rise was in 1998. Since then, the hotel banquet server has seen his real pay fall by between 1 and 2 per cent a year due to inflation. He has been forced to give up renting a two-bedroom apartment and now shares one bedroom with his wife and two children.

Miguel is not the only US worker in the same situation. For millions of low skilled and unskilled workers, pay rises over the past few years have been few and far between. This is despite rising productivity and booming profits for US companies.

Some economists would argue that Miguel is suffering the effects of globalisation. On the surface, the US economy has lost very few jobs to 'offshoring', closing places of work and moving production to cheap labour countries such as China or India. In 2004, just 2.5 per cent of 182 000 workers fired in mass lay-offs saw their jobs moved overseas. But wages are set at the margin. In many primary and manufacturing industries, workers know that they could lose their jobs overnight to Chinese or other overseas competitors if their company's costs are too high. And even if relatively few directly lose their jobs to offshoring, there are many more who fail to get a job because their company has expanded production in China and not the USA. This puts pressure on service industries like hotel banqueting. Miguel's employers can hire plenty of workers at the wage Miguel is currently paid. Perhaps Miguel should count himself lucky they haven't cut his wages.

Source: adapted from the *Financial Times*, 11.5.2005.

(a) Using diagrams, explain why the real wages of many unskilled and low skilled workers in the US are falling when the real wages of many similar Chinese workers are rising.

Question 3

Name	Petra Ellis
Age	29
Occupation	Personnel assistant
Location	Chester
Earnings	£25,000 per year

Name	Addo Tower
Age	49
Occupation	Finance director
Location	London
Earnings	£120,000 per year

Name	Mike Sellers
Age	19
Occupation	Sales assistant
Location	Tenby, West Wales
Earnings	£9,500 per year

Name	Geena Miles
Age	33
Occupation	Civil engineer
Location	Birmingham
Earnings	£48,000 per year

(a) Why do the earnings of these workers differ?

be threatened with a loss of their workers. To retain them they would need to put up their wage rates. Only when the two wage rates are equal would there be no incentive for London catering workers to become Welsh steel workers.

Why wage rates differ

In the real world, wage rates differ. One important reason is because labour is not homogeneous. Each worker is a unique factor of production, possessing a unique set of employment characteristics such as:
● age - whether young, middle aged or old;
● sex - whether male or female;
● ethnic background;
● education, training and work experience;
● ability to perform tasks - including how hard they are prepared to work, their strength and their manual or mental dexterity.

For instance, a manager of a company is likely to be paid more than a cleaner working for the same company. On the one hand, the marginal revenue product of the manager is likely to be higher. Her education, skills and work experience are likely to provide greater value to the company than the cleaner's. On the other hand, the supply of managers is lower than the supply of cleaners. Most workers in the workforce could be a cleaner, but only a few have sufficient qualities to be managers. Greater demand and less supply lead to higher wage rates for managers than cleaners.

Wage rates also differ because workers do not necessarily seek to maximise wages. Wages are only part of the net benefit workers gain from employment. Workers whose jobs are dangerous, unpleasant, tedious, where there is little chance of promotion, where earnings fluctuate and where there are few or no fringe benefits, may seek higher wages than workers whose jobs possess the opposite characteristics. Market forces will tend to lead not to equality of wage rates but to equality of net benefits to workers.

Labour is not perfectly mobile. Hence there can be unemployment and low wages in Scotland whilst employers offering much higher wages are crying out for labour in London. Part of the reason why there is a lack of mobility is the absence of perfect knowledge within the labour market. Workers in Scotland may be unaware of job opportunities in the South of England. There are also many other imperfections in the market which prevent wage rates rising or falling in response to market pressures.

Perfectly competitive labour markets

In a perfectly competitive factor market, there is a large number of small firms hiring a large number of individual workers. For the individual firm operating in such a market:
● the demand curve for labour, the marginal revenue product curve of labour, is downward sloping;
● the supply curve of labour is perfectly elastic and therefore horizontal; the firm can hire any number of workers at the existing industry wage rate.

How many workers should this type of firm employ? If a worker costs £200 per week, but increases revenue net of all other costs by only £150, then he should not be employed.

Putting this theoretically, the firm will hire workers up to the point where the marginal cost of labour is equal to the marginal

revenue product of labour. If the marginal cost were higher than marginal revenue product, for instance at 0C in Figure 2, the firm would make a loss on the output produced by the marginal worker and hence it would cut back on employment of labour. If the marginal revenue product of labour were higher than the marginal cost of labour, for instance at 0A, then it would hire more workers because these workers would generate a profit for the firm.

Hence, in Figure 2 the equilibrium level of employment by the firm is 0B. This is the point where the marginal cost of labour (the supply curve) is equal to the marginal revenue product of labour (the demand curve). The equilibrium real wage rate is 0W. This is the ruling equilibrium wage rate in the industry as a whole.

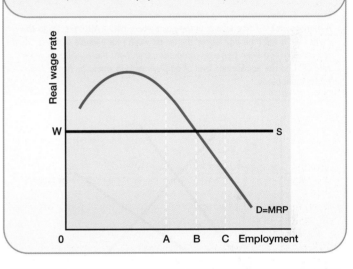

Figure 2 Equilibrium employment and wage rates for a firm in a perfectly competitive factor market
In a perfectly competitive factor market, the supply curve for labour facing the firm is horizontal. The equilibrium real wage rate, OW, is set by the industry as a whole. The firm will then employ OB workers in equilibrium.

Question 4

Table 1

Number of workers employed	Total revenue product (£ month)
1	700
2	1 300
3	1 800
4	2 200

The data show the monthly total revenue product of a profit maximising manufacturing company in a perfectly competitive industry.
(a) Plot the marginal revenue product curve on graph paper (remembering to plot the MRP half way between whole numbers on the employment axis).
(b) What would be the maximum number of workers the firm would employ if the monthly wage per worker were:
(i) £600; (ii) £400; (iii) £425; (iv) £800; (v) £525?

Imperfectly competitive labour markets

An imperfectly competitive labour market is one where:
- either the firm is a dominant or monopoly buyer of labour;
- or the firm is faced by a monopoly supplier of labour, which is most likely to be a trade union.

If the firm is the sole buyer of labour, it is called a **monopsonist**. The state, for instance, employs over 90 per cent of teachers in the UK and therefore is essentially a monopsonist. A monopsonist is able to exploit market power and therefore common sense would suggest that the monopsonist would use this power to force down wage levels.

The marginal cost of employing an extra unit of labour is higher for the monopsonist than the average cost or wage. This is because the firm has to raise wage rates to attract extra labour into the industry. So the cost of employing an extra unit of labour is not just the higher wage paid to that unit but also the extra wages that now need to be paid to all the other workers in the industry.

> *Figure 3 Monopsony in the labour market*
>
> *A monopsonist will hire labour to the point where MC = MRP (i.e. up to the point OA). It will then pay labour the lowest wage rate possible which is OE. If the industry had been perfectly competitive then both the equilibrium wage rate OF and the equilibrium level of employment OB would be higher than under monopsony.*

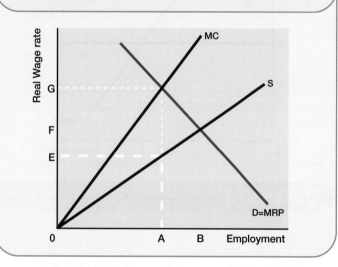

Question 5

Teachers' pay in the UK is currently determined by the findings of a School Teachers' Review Body (STRB). This takes evidence from the government, which generally wishes to keep wage increases to a minimum, and from trade unions, which want to see high increases in wages. The government can choose either to accept the recommendations of the STRB or to impose its own, invariably lower, pay deal. The government is effectively a monopsonist employer for teachers because only 9 per cent of teachers work in private sector schools.

(a) Draw a diagram to show the situation of the government facing trade unions in the market for teachers.

Assume the government decides to impose work place bargaining in teaching, with individual teachers negotiating with each school in which they are employed.

(b) Using a diagram, compare the wages and level of employment this system might create to the current system of national bargaining.

In Figure 3, the demand and supply curves for labour are drawn. The firm will employ workers up to the point where the marginal cost of an extra worker is equal to the worker's marginal revenue product. Therefore the monopsonist will employ 0A workers, the intersection of the marginal cost curve and the marginal revenue product or demand curve. The firm does not then need to pay a real wage rate of 0G to each worker. It only needs to pay a real wage rate of 0E to attract 0A workers to the industry.

If the market were perfectly competitive, employment would be 0B and the equilibrium wage rate would be 0F. So economic theory suggests that a monopsonist drives down wages and reduces employment levels compared to a perfectly competitive factor market. Note that this is similar to the perfect competition/monopoly analysis in a goods market where it is argued that a monopolist reduces output and raises prices compared to a perfectly competitive market.

The effect of a monopoly supplier of labour will be considered in the next unit on trade unions.

Applied economics

Wage determination

Wage structure by occupation

Economic theory would suggest that wage rates would be the same if all labour was homogeneous and all jobs possessed the same characteristics. In the real world workers are not identical. They differ, for instance, in where they are prepared to work, their hours of work and their levels of **human capital**. Jobs differ too. In

particular, the marginal revenue product curve for each type of job is different.

For example, Table 2 shows that in 2007 the average weekly earnings of full-time health professionals such as doctors was £1 194. This compares with full-time workers in sales occupations who earned on average £298 a week. Neo-classical economic theory suggests that such differences are due to differences in the

Table 2 Mean average gross weekly earnings and hours of work of full time workers, by occupational group, 2007

Occupation	Weekly earnings (£)	Weekly hours
Health professionals	1194	40.3
Corporate managers	863	38.5
Business and public service professionals	750	37.3
Science and technology professionals	719	38.7
Teaching and research professionals	671	33.6
Protective service occupations	665	42.4
Managers and proprietors in agriculture and services	602	40.1
Business and public service associate professionals	595	37.3
Culture, media and sports occupations	560	37.9
Science and technology associate professionals	527	39
Health and social welfare associate professionals	517	37.8
Skilled metal and electrical trades	506	42.9
Skilled construction and building trades	460	42.6
Transport and mobile machine drivers and operatives	431	47
Process, plant and machine operatives	426	42.8
Administrative occupations	379	37.6
Secretarial and related occupations	375	37
Textiles, printing and other skilled trades	366	41.8
Elementary trades, plant and storage related occupations	351	42.4
Leisure and other personal service occupations	350	38.6
Skilled agricultural trades	345	40.8
Customer service occupations	331	37.9
Caring personal service occupations	317	38.6
Elementary administration and service occupations	316	41.7
Sales occupations	298	39.1
All employees	452	39.4

Source: adapted from *Annual Survey of Hours and Earnings* (ASHE), Office for National Statistics.

Table 3 Highest and lowest paid occupations, 2007

Median gross weekly pay

Great Britain	£ per week
Highest paid	
Directors and chief executives of major organisations	1917
Senior officials in national government	1236
Medical practitioners	1188
Aircraft pilots and flight engineers	1078
Financial managers and chartered secretaries	1040
Police officers (inspectors and above)	972
Brokers	960
Air traffic controllers	935
Senior officials in local government	929
IT strategy and planning professionals	889
Managers in mining and energy	852
Solicitors and lawyers, judges and coroners	847
Lowest paid	
Kitchen and catering assistants	239
Bar staff	236
School mid-day assistants	235
Playgroup leaders/assistants	231
Floral arrangers, florists	230
Retail cashiers and check-out operators	229
Leisure and theme park attendants	226
Launderers, dry cleaners, pressers	224
Waiters, waitresses	222
Hairdressers, barbers	221
Market and street traders and assistants	202

Source: adapted from *Annual Survey of Hours and Earnings (ASHE)*, Office for National Statistics.

demand for and supply of different types of labour.

On the supply side, there are potentially far more workers with the ability and training to become manual workers than non-manual workers. In Table 3, directors and chief executives of major organisations earning £1 917 a week could become a market or street trader or assistant earning £202 a week, but the street trader could not necessarily become a successful chief executive. Occupations which are unpleasant or dangerous, or where earnings can fluctuate greatly, are likely to attract fewer workers than others where the non-pecuniary (i.e. non-monetary) advantages are much greater. Hence, earnings in construction and mining are likely to be higher than average, all other things being equal, because of the danger of the job. In general, the larger the potential supply of labour to an occupation, the lower is likely to be the level of earnings.

On the demand side, non-manual jobs are likely to carry a higher marginal revenue product than manual jobs. Without an effective manager, a company may lose thousands and perhaps millions of pounds of potential revenue or suffer high costs of production. But the company could get by without an effective office cleaner. Hence professional workers in management and administration are paid more highly than workers in catering, cleaning and hairdressing because their revenue product is greater.

So far we have assumed that labour markets are perfectly competitive and that they are in equilibrium. In practice, many of the differences in wages between occupations may be accounted for by trade unions or monopsony employers. For instance, print workers in the 1980s saw their trade union power decline as employers, such as Times Newspapers, won a number of key industrial disputes.

Alternatively, the market may be in disequilibrium. It could be argued that wage rates in low skilled jobs in parts of manufacturing are depressed today because of the continued shrinkage of manufacturing industry. On the other hand, earnings in occupations related to computers have been buoyant over the past 15 years as the industry has expanded.

Changes in wage structure by occupation

The last forty years have seen considerable changes in relative pay between different occupations. Table 3,

Directors and corporate managers earn relatively high wages.

for instance, shows that waiters and waitresses were paid £222 a week in 2007, which in real terms is little different to their pay at the start of the 1980s. In contrast, solicitors have seen their real earnings approximately double over the same period. Figure 4 shows that the top tenth of workers by earnings have increase their earnings by a larger percentage than the bottom tenth in most years over the period 1987 to 2006. Between 1987 and 2006, average earnings of the worker at the 90th decile point increased by 5.7 per cent per annum compared to 5.0 per cent for the worker at the 10th decile point. Prices rose by 3.6 per cent per annum on average.

There is a number of reasons for these trends. One has been the relative decline of primary and secondary industries in the UK and the growth of the service sector. Well paid manual jobs were concentrated in manufacturing industry and primary industries such as mining and tended to be occupied by men. The number of manual jobs in service industries has grown, but traditionally these have been low paid jobs done by women.

Another factor has been the decline of trade unionism. Union membership before 1980 was heavily concentrated amongst males in primary and secondary industries, and public sector workers. Trade unions were able to secure higher wages than the free market rate in many cases. Anti-union legislation in the 1980s weakened the power of trade unions at a time when there was considerable shrinkage in the number of jobs in primary and secondary industries. This dealt a double blow to relatively well paid male manual workers.

The government also weakened minimum wage legislation present in certain industries during the 1980s before finally abolishing minimum wages in 1993.

Globalisation has put added pressures on poorly skilled low paid workers. There has been an ever

increasing trend for work requiring high labour, low skill inputs to go to the developing world where wages are a fraction of what even low paid workers earn in the UK. In contrast, the long term trend for UK manufacturing and services in areas which are internationally traded is for the UK to specialise in producing ever more sophisticated technological products. This requires high skill labour inputs and therefore increases the demand for workers who are already better educated, better trained and better paid.

The other side of globalisation has been immigration. The UK operates a restrictive immigration policy, but workers from other EU countries are free to enter the UK labour market. In the 2000s, it can be argued that immigration has expanded the supply of workers willing to take low paid jobs and has been a factor in depressing wage rates.

The outlook for the lowest paid is better today than at the start of the 1990s. The reinstatement of the minimum wage, this time across all industries, in 1998, helped set a floor for wages. The government has set itself targets for achievement in education and training which should reduce the number of unskilled workers with no qualifications over the next 40 years. The numbers unemployed have also fallen considerably since the peaks of 3 to 3.5 million seen in the first half of the 1980s and in 1991-93. This increases the scarcity of labour and helps push up wage rates.

However, the pace of introduction of labour-saving new technology is not slowing down. It is often the least skilled jobs which are easiest to automate. There are still plenty of Third World countries with large pools of very low paid workers which can take jobs

Figure 4 Annual growth in earnings, top and bottom decile points, full-time employees[1]

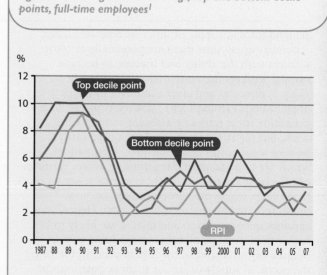

1. Data for 1987-1997 is Great Britain; 1998-2006 is UK.

Source: adapted from *Social Trends*, Annual Survey of Hours and Earnings (ASHE). Office for National Statistics.

away from the UK. Moreover, some Third World countries are also developing increasingly skilled workforces which can compete with UK workers at lower cost. This is likely to put downward pressure on many wages across the pay spectrum in the UK.

As for the highest paid, it could be argued that their wages are likely to continue to outperform the average. This is because the potential marginal revenue product of a top worker is considerable. In football, for instance, fans will pay high prices to see the best players perform on the pitch, but few want to go and see second rate footballers. The result is that the most successful clubs over the past ten years have been prepared to pay ever larger sums to their players to secure them for the club. The same is true at the top of business organisations. One person can have an enormous effect on earnings and profits for a firm, but there are only a relatively few people who can have the abilities required. The result has been an explosion in the pay of directors and top managers in firms since the 1980s.

Wage structure by gender

Females have traditionally earned less than men. Economic reasons can be put forward for this. In the past, women were denied the same educational opportunities as men and were thus unable to acquire the same level of human capital. Equally, they were denied access to all but a narrow range of jobs.

Today, possibly the most important factor causing inequality in earnings between the sexes in the UK is the unequal burden of child care. It is still more likely that women will take primary responsibility for bringing up children. Many take a career break after their first or second child or drop down to part time work. Having taken a career break, some take up low paid, part-time work which fits in to their primary role as child-carers.

Taking a career break is enormously costly in terms of human capital. Those who continue in employment will not only receive formal training, but will build up informal knowledge and understanding of new work methods, new technology, and new products. On average, earnings of both men and women rise by about 3 per cent a year when in work. The skills of the woman who left work 10 years ago in comparison will be outdated. A woman's earnings potential drops every year she is out of work. The time when women choose to leave their careers is also important. It is traditional for workers to make their most important career progressions between the ages of 20 and 30, precisely the time when many women are out of the workforce. Although illegal, because it is contrary to equal opportunities legislation, there is evidence that employers continue to respond to the less stable work patterns of women by offering less training to female employees. There is also evidence that women are passed over for promotion. At the top, many women complain of a 'glass ceiling' beyond which their male bosses refuse to promote them. To see the glass ceiling in action, it is only necessary to look at the very small numbers of women who make it onto the boards of publicly quoted companies.

Figure 5 shows the relative hourly earnings of men and women. During the first half of the 1970s, the gap between male and females earnings narrowed. This was mainly the result of the passing of the Equal Pay Act 1970 and the Sex Discrimination Act 1975. The 1970 Act made it illegal to pay women less than men if they were doing the same job. The 1975 Act guaranteed women equality of opportunity. Figure 5 would suggest that this was a once and for all gain. Relative earnings then hardly changed for a decade. Since the mid-1980s, however, there has been another narrowing of pay differentials. By 2006, the pay gap was only 13 per cent. A number of factors may have caused this.

- The upward trend which started in 1987 may have been kick-started by falling unemployment during the Lawson boom which led to labour market shortages.
- The growing proportion of well qualified women in the workforce may have exerted upward pressure.
- If the 1970s saw an upward trend in relative pay for legal reasons, perhaps from 1987 onwards there was growing social and business awareness that discrimination against women was not acceptable.
- Since the 1990s, the proportion of male workers belonging to trade unions has fallen but the proportion of female workers belonging to trade unions has remained roughly constant. If trade union membership does lead to higher wages as economic theory suggests, male wage rates should have fallen

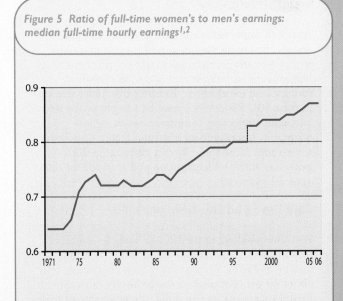

Figure 5 *Ratio of full-time women's to men's earnings: median full-time hourly earnings*[1,2]

1. The ratio of women's to men's gross hourly earnings (excluding overtime) for full-time employees at April each year. Until 1982, women aged 18 and over, men aged 21 and over. From 1983 onwards for employees on adult rates whose pay for the survey period was not affected by absence.
2. Data for 1971-1997 is for Great Britain, 1997-2006 is for UK.

Source: adapted from *Social Trends*, Office for National Statistics.

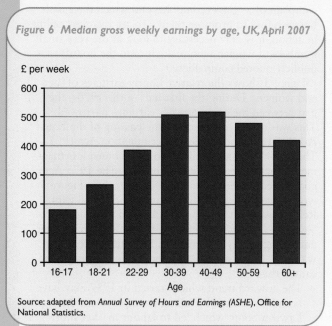

Figure 6 *Median gross weekly earnings by age, UK, April 2007*

£ per week

Source: adapted from *Annual Survey of Hours and Earnings (ASHE)*, Office for National Statistics.

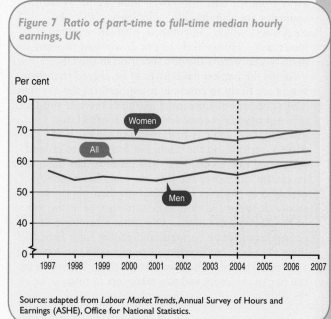

Figure 7 *Ratio of part-time to full-time median hourly earnings, UK*

Per cent

Source: adapted from *Labour Market Trends*, Annual Survey of Hours and Earnings (ASHE), Office for National Statistics.

relative to female wage rates.

However, there are still reasons why the earnings of female workers will continue to be less than for males.

- Women on average work fewer hours, and therefore even if hourly pay was the same, women would earn less per week than men.
- Many occupations, such as secretarial work, are dominated by females. It could be that the marginal revenue product of occupations traditionally filled by women is lower than that of occupations which are traditionally male dominated.

Wage structure by age

Age is an important determinant of pay as Figure 6 shows. Economic theory would suggest that older workers would receive higher rates of pay because of higher levels of human capital due to education, training and experience. To offset this, older workers in their 40s, 50s and 60s may be less physically strong and agile, important for manual work, or less adaptable, important for any job. Figure 6 provides some support for this. Weekly earnings in 2007 peaked in the 40-49 age group and then fell for those aged 50 and over.

Part-time and full-time working

Part-time workers in the UK are likely to hold less responsible jobs within an organisation. For this reason, as Figure 7 shows, they earn on average only about 60 per cent of the average hourly rates earned by full-time workers. In 2007, the wage rate of male and female part-time workers was very similar at approximately £7.25 an hour. However, because male full-time workers earn more per hour (£11.96) than female full-time workers (£10.46) on average, it

means that the ratio of hourly pay for female part-time workers to full-time workers is higher than for males, which is what Figure 7 also shows. Female workers who work part-time suffer less on average because of part-time working than males.

Wages by ethnic group

Workers from an Indian ethnic background have the highest average hourly earnings amongst males in the UK. For women, it is workers of black Caribbean origin. However, on average, workers from ethnic minorities tend to earn less than white workers. Figure 8 shows that the gap is larger for male workers than for female workers.

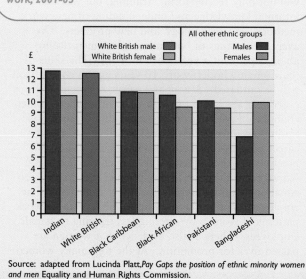

Figure 8 *Hourly earnings for those aged 25-54, full time work, 2001-05*

Source: adapted from Lucinda Platt, *Pay Gaps the position of ethnic minority women and men* Equality and Human Rights Commission.

The ratio of hourly pay for female part-time workers to full-time workers is higher than for males.

There is a number of factors which cause workers from ethnic minority groups to earn less than white workers. First, workers from ethnic minorities, on average, tend to be less qualified than white workers. This means workers from ethnic backgrounds are more likely to be in manual jobs than white workers, and also less likely to be in managerial posts. Second, workers from ethnic minorities are more likely to work in distribution (including shops), hotels, catering and in the health service than white workers. For example, according to the 2001 Census, nearly half of all Bangladeshi men, 40 per cent of Chinese men and one third of Chinese women in employment had jobs in hotels and restaurants. Nearly 40 per cent of black Caribbean women were employed in education, health and social work compared to 30 per cent for white women. Some jobs in these sectors are well paid and workers from an Indian background are disproportionately represented amongst doctors, for example. However, on average workers from ethnic minorities are more likely to be employed in industries where low pay is a prominent feature. Finally, there is evidence that pay discrimination against workers from ethnic minorities takes place, despite equal pay legislation. There is also discrimination against ethnic minority workers when it comes to recruitment, selection, promotion and training.

DataQuestion — Regional earnings and employment

Table 4 *Average (median) gross weekly earnings, April 2007*

£

	Males	Females
United Kingdom	498.30	394.00
London	643.50	518.50
South East	535.00	408.00
East	498.70	382.90
Scotland	482.20	382.00
North West	479.10	371.50
South West	476.50	363.30
West Midlands	467.40	369.70
Yorkshire and The Humber	465.10	354.70
East Midlands	463.80	354.70
Wales	441.70	356.30
North East	440.00	350.30
Northern Ireland	424.80	372.60

Source: adapted from *2007 Annual Survey of Hours and Earnings* (ASHE), First Release, November 2007, Office for National Statistics.

Table 5 *Net migration between regions*[1,2,3]

Thousands

	1981	1986	1991	1996	2001	2006
South West	20	46	22	29	32	28
South East	36	39	13	29	8	23
East	17	17	9	18	20	17
East Midlands	5	17	9	8	19	8
Wales	3	5	5	2	9	7
Scotland	-1	-12	9	-7	6	6
Northern Ireland	-3	-6	4	-1	2	2
North East	-8	-10	-1	-6	-3	1
Yorkshire and The Humber	-5	-12	0	-7	0	-1
North West	-20	-26	-9	-9	-4	-4
West Midlands	-12	-8	-5	-10	-7	-8
London	-32	-49	-53	-45	-84	-79

1. Net migration: immigration minus emigration. Positive figures in black show an increase in the population of a region whilst negative figures in red show a reduction in population of a region due to migration.
2. Only migration flows between British regions are given. International migration is not included.
3. Regions ranked by size of net migration in 2006.

Source: adapted from Population Trends, *Regional Trends*, Office for National Statistics.

Table 6 Educational qualifications, 2005-06

	Working age population with no qualifications 2007	Pupils achieving 5 or more grades A* to C at GCSE[1,2], 2005-06
		%
Northern Ireland	21	62
Wales	16	52
West Midlands	16	57
North West	14	57
Yorkshire and The Humber	14	54
Scotland	14	59
North East	13	58
East	12	60
East Midlands	12	55
London	12	59
South East	9	60
South West	9	59

1. Percentage of pupils in their last year of compulsory education.
2. Data for England is local authority maintained schools; for Scotland, Wales and Northern Ireland, it also includes all other schools including independent schools.

Source: adapted from *Economic & Labour Market Review*, Office for National Statistics; www.poverty.org.uk.

Table 7 Regional unemployment rates (claimant count)

Per cent

	1981	1986	1991	1996	2001	2007
United Kingdom	6.9	11.0	6.6	7.7	3.2	2.7
South East	na	7.2	4.1	5.5	1.6	1.6
South West	5.7	9.2	5.3	6.5	2.1	1.5
East	na	8.5	4.8	6.4	2.0	2.2
East Midlands	6.4	9.9	5.8	7.2	3.1	2.6
Yorkshire and The Humber	7.6	12.3	7.4	8.3	4.0	3.0
Wales	9.2	13.9	7.6	8.3	4.0	2.8
Scotland	8.8	13.2	8.0	7.8	4.1	2.7
Northern Ireland	11.7	16.1	12.5	11.2	4.9	2.8
West Midlands	8.3	12.7	6.6	7.6	3.8	3.7
London	4.4	9.0	6.2	9.1	3.3	3.0
North West	na	11.9	6.8	7.0	5.5	3.2
North East	na	16.7	10.2	11.1	5.7	4.0

Source: adapted from *Economic & Labour Market Review*, Office for National Statistics.

Figure 9 Cost of living comparison for housing: percentage difference in expenditure on rent compared with UK average, 2005-06

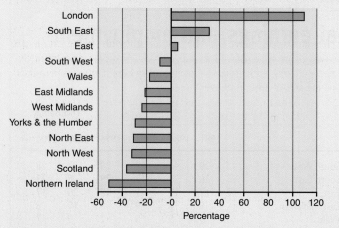

Source: adapted from *Family Spending 2005-06*, Office for National Statistics.

Figure 10 Index of output per hour worked 2005 (measured by Gross Value Added), UK = 100

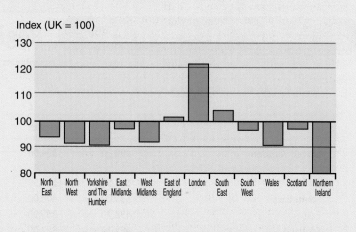

Source: adapted from *Economic & Labour Market Review*, Office for National Statistics.

1. Outline the main differences in wages and employment between the regions in the UK.
2. What economic factors might account for differences in average earnings between regions?

3. Evaluate what government policies could be pursued to reduce the earnings gap between regions.

Summary

1. Trade unions exist to further the interests of their own members.
2. Neo-classical economic theory predicts that trade unions increase wages but create unemployment in perfectly competitive industries.
3. Theory also predicts that a monopsonist buyer of labour will employ more workers and pay them a higher wage rate when bargaining with a union than in a situation where it is bargaining with a large number of individual employees.
4. Trade unions will be more powerful the larger the trade union membership, the less elastic the demand for labour and the greater the profitability of the employer.
5. Trade unions will reduce efficiency in a perfectly competitive economy, but they may increase efficiency if the economy is imperfectly competitive.
6. Trade unions may reduce costs of production for firms if they facilitate change and perform some of the tasks, such as personnel management, which management would otherwise have to undertake.

Collective bargaining

A trade union is an organisation of workers who combine together to further their own interests. Within a company organisation, an individual worker is likely to be in a relatively weak bargaining position compared to his or her employer. The employer possesses far greater knowledge about everything from safety standards to the profitability of the firm than an individual worker. Moreover, the loss of an individual worker to a firm is likely to be far less significant than the loss of his or her job to the employee.

So workers have organised themselves in unions to bargain collectively. Instead of each individual worker bargaining with the firm on a wide range of wage and employment issues, workers elect or appoint representatives to bargain on their behalf. From an economic viewpoint, trade unions act as monopoly suppliers of labour.

Trade unions play a very controversial role in the economy. Critics argue that trade unions, by forcing up wages and resisting changes in working practices, create unemployment. Neo-classical economic theory supports this view, assuming that factor markets are perfectly competitive. However, as will be argued below, it also suggests that trade unions increase employment if a trade union represents workers in a firm which is the sole buyer of labour.

Competitive industries

Trade unions act to further the interests of their members. One of the key ways in which they do this is to press for higher wages. In economic terms, they attempt to fix a minimum price for the supply of labour. This produces a kinked supply curve.

In Figure 1 the non-union demand and supply curves for labour in an industry are D and S_1 respectively. A union agreement to raise wages from the free market wage of 0A to the unionised wage rate of 0B means that employers in the industry cannot hire workers below a wage rate of 0B. The supply curve therefore is perfectly elastic (i.e. horizontal) over the employment range 0G. The union agreement does not prevent employers paying higher wages than the negotiated wage. Employers would need to pay higher wage rates if they wished to hire more workers than 0G. Above 0G the new supply curve S_2 is the same as the old supply curve S_1. The new equilibrium wage rate is 0B, the wage rate that the union negotiated. However, employment in the industry falls from 0F (the equilibrium in a non-unionised market) to 0E.

Neo-classical micro-economic theory therefore suggests that trade unions increase wages for their members, but also cause

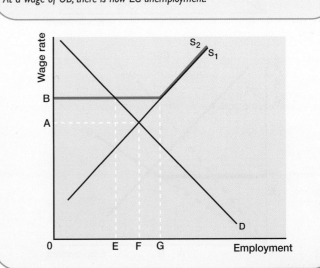

Figure 1 Trade unions in a competitive market
The entry of a trade union to a competitive factor market is likely to 'kink' the supply curve of labour. OB is the union negotiated wage rate in an industry. Employment will fall from OF to OE whilst wage rates will rise from OA to OB. At a wage of OB, there is now EG unemployment.

Question 1

Wal-Mart is the world's largest supermarket chain. It has grown in the USA by opening up stores which offer the cheapest prices on goods. It achieves this through a combination of strategies from bulk buying at low prices from manufacturers, to a computer system which tracks every item through its logistics chain, to low wages for staff. Many of its competitors have unionised staff who are paid more than Wal-Mart employees. Wal-Mart claims that its non-unionisation policy creates jobs. Critics claim that Wal-Mart destroys jobs, which it certainly does when competitors are forced out of business due to their higher costs.

Source: adapted from the *Financial Times*, 12.4.2005.

(a) 'Trade unions raise wage levels in an industry but cause a loss of jobs.' Explain, using a diagram, why Wal-Mart's claim that its non-unionisation policy creates jobs might be correct.
(b) Explain why Wal-Mart's rivals might be at a competitive disadvantage if they have unionised labour.

Figure 2 A trade union vs a monopsonist employer
A monopsonist facing a large number of employees in an industry will force wage rates down to OE and restrict employment to OA. The entry of a trade union to the industry which sets a minimum wage of OF will 'kink' the supply curve of labour and produce a discontinuity in the marginal cost curve for labour. The monopsonist has a profit incentive to hire extra workers so long as the marginal revenue product of labour, shown by the demand curve, is greater than the marginal cost of labour. Hence it will employ OB workers.

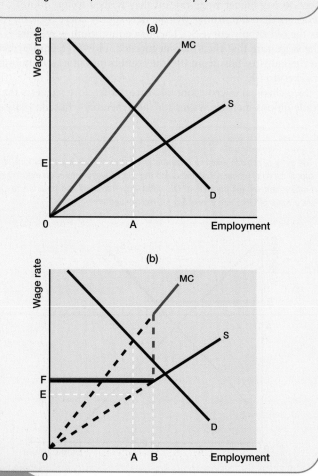

unemployment in the industry. Wages would be lower and employment higher if the industry were non-unionised.

Trade unions vs monopsony employers

Many trade unions operate in factor markets where there are monopsony employers. A sole seller of labour (the trade union) faces a sole buyer of labour (the monopsonist).

Economic theory suggests that a trade union will increase both wages and employment compared to a factor market where a monopsony employer negotiates with a large number of individual employees. Figure 2 (a) shows the wage and employment levels in an industry with a monopsonist and many individual employees. Employment is 0A and the equilibrium wage rate is 0E. Figure 2 (b) shows the entry of a trade union to the industry. Assume that the trade union forces the wage rate up to 0F. This produces a kinked supply curve. The monopsonist cannot pay a wage rate lower than 0F because of its union agreement. However, it is free to pay higher wage rates if it wishes to employ more than 0B workers. This produces a kink in the marginal cost of labour to the firm. Up to 0B, the marginal cost of labour is the same as the union negotiated wage rate. The employer can hire an extra unit of labour at that wage rate. If it employs more than 0B workers, the wage rate will rise, resulting in a jump in marginal cost at 0B. The monopsonist has a profit incentive to hire extra workers so long as the marginal revenue product of labour, shown by the demand curve, is greater than the marginal cost of labour. Hence it will employ 0B workers.

Why should a monopsonist buy more labour at a higher wage rate from a union than it would otherwise? It should be remembered that a firm bases its decision on how much labour to hire not on the wage rate (the average cost of labour) but on the marginal cost of labour. It can be seen from Figure 2 that the marginal cost of unionised labour is lower between employment levels A and B than it would have been if labour had been non-unionised. In the former case it is flat at 0F, whilst in the latter it is rising steeply above 0F.

The power of trade unions

There is a variety of factors which make trade unions more or less powerful.

Trade union membership and militancy A union which has 100 per cent membership in an industry is likely to be stronger than a union which only represents 10 per cent of potential members. It could be argued that the RMT is far more powerful in the railway industry than the Transport and General Workers Union is in the hairdressing industry. Equally, unions are more likely to call for industrial action if union members are militant. The more militant the union membership, the more costly a dispute is likely to be for an employer.

The demand curve for labour is relatively inelastic A rise in wage rates will have far less impact upon employment in the industry if the demand for labour is relatively inelastic than if it is elastic. Hence, there will be far less cost to the union of a wage rate increase in terms of lost membership and to its members in terms of lost employment.

Profitability of the employer A trade union is unlikely to be able to negotiate large wage increases with an employer on the verge of

Question 2

Table 1

Units of labour employed	Wage rate per worker, £		Marginal cost of employing 1 extra worker, £		Marginal revenue product of labour, £
	With no trade union	With a trade union	With no trade union	With a trade union	
2	4	8	4	8	16
3	5	8	6	8	14
4	6	8	8	8	12
5	7	8	10	8	10
6	8	8	12	8	8
7	9	9	14	14	6
8	10	10	16	16	4

The table shows wage rates, marginal employment costs and MRPs facing a monopsonist employer of labour.
(a) (i) What is the maximum number of workers the firm would employ if the labour force were non-unionised?
  (ii) What would be the equilibrium wage rate?
(b) What is the maximum number of workers the firm would employ if workers belonged to a trade union and it had negotiated a minimum wage rate of £8?
(c) Explain why trade unions might increase rather than decrease the level of employment in an industry.

bankruptcy. It is likely to be in a stronger position with a highly profitable firm. This implies that trade unions will be stronger in monopolistic and oligopolistic industries, where firms are able to earn abnormal profit, than in perfectly competitive industries where only normal profit can be earned in the long run.

Efficiency

Neo-classical economic theory suggests that trade unions operating in competitive industries reduce employment levels and raise wage rates. If all industries but one were perfectly competitive then a trade union in that one industry would mean that the economy as a whole was not Pareto efficient.

However, most industries in the UK are imperfectly competitive. A trade union facing a monopsonist will redress the balance of power in the industry and lead to a level of employment and a wage rate which will be nearer to the free market price of labour. It could well be that the presence of a trade union increases economic efficiency in an imperfectly competitive market. Hence the effect of trade unions on economic efficiency depends on the structure of markets in an economy.

A further important argument needs to be considered. Some economists have suggested that trade unions raise economic efficiency because they lower costs of production to the firm. The trade union performs many of the functions of a personnel department within a firm. It deals with workers' problems and obviates the need for the firm to negotiate pay with each and every worker. More importantly, it can be a good vehicle for negotiating changes in working practices. A firm may wish to

implement changes which will lead to less pleasant working conditions for its workers. Perhaps it wishes to increase the speed of the assembly line, or force workers to undertake a variety of tasks rather than just one. It may find it difficult to implement these changes on a non-unionised workforce because some workers may take unorganised industrial action or do their best to disrupt any changes being introduced. A union may help the firm to persuade workers that changes in working practices are in their own interest. The union will usually demand a price for this co-operation - higher wage rates for its members. But it still leads to an increase in economic efficiency because the firm is able to make higher profits whilst workers receive higher wage rates. According to this view, trade unions increase productivity in the economy.

Question 3

(a) How would economic theory account for the strength and weakness of union power in these industries?

Question 4

Retail union Usdaw has cooked up a unique agreement with a crack team of Chinese restaurant workers at Cathay Dim Sum in the Trafford Centre in Manchester. Restaurant director Laurence Lee approached Usdaw after discovering his 30 strong team wanted independent representation and access to union educational programmes. Usdaw General Secretary John Hannett said: 'The Yang Sing Group are very responsible employers who see the direct benefits of working with a progressive union like Usdaw and we're really looking forward to developing a strong relationship with Cathay Dim Sum that will will directly benefit both the company and our members. Our education team will be assessing the Cathay Dim Sum team to see what learning opportunities we can offer them in the future to strengthen their existing skills throughout the restaurant.'

Source: adapted from www.usdaw.org.uk 30.6.2005.

Amicus and the UK's largest printing company, Polestar, have reached an agreement for the operation of the company's new super plant at Sheffield. Commenting on the agreement, Amicus Assistant General Secretary Tony Burke said: 'This is a major investment. Although the negotiations were at times tough, Polestar recognised from the initial discussions we had that there is a major benefit to working with Amicus, not only on pay and on conditions, but also on issues such as training, health and safety, consultation with the workforce, social issues, recruitment of staff and productivity.'

Source: adapted from www.amicustheunion.org, 19.7.2005.

(a) How might the changes described in the data increase efficiency for employers?

Key terms

Closed shop - a place of work where workers must belong to a recognised trade union.

Trade union mark-up - the difference between wage rates in a unionised place of work and the wage rate which would otherwise prevail in the absence of trade unions.

Applied economics

Trade unions

Trade unions in the UK have existed for over 200 years. In the early 19th century, trade unions were outlawed for being anti-competitive. By the early 20th century there were 2 million trade union members and, as Figure 3 shows, this rose to a peak of over 13 million in 1979.

Since 1979, there has been a sharp fall in the number of trade union members. By 2006 membership had fallen to 6.6 million. There is a number of possible explanations for this radical change in union membership.

- The recessions of 1980-82 and 1990-92 both created over one and half million unemployed. The unemployed tend to allow their union membership to lapse. So it is not surprising that the drop in union membership was highest in both of these periods. The lowest fall in membership over the period 1979-1992

occurred in the boom year of 1987.

- The 1980s and 1990s saw a radical restructuring of British industry. Employment in primary industries and manufacturing, both sectors which were very highly unionised, fell significantly. The new jobs that were created tended to be in the service sector of the economy, traditionally far less unionised than manufacturing. Moreover, most of the lost jobs were full-time whilst many of the new jobs were part-time. In 2004, 31.5 per cent of all full-time workers were union members compared to only 21.1 per cent of part-time workers. Important too was that many jobs lost were traditionally male jobs and the new jobs created were traditionally female jobs. By 2006, 29.7 per cent of female workers were union members compared to just 27.2 per cent of male workers.

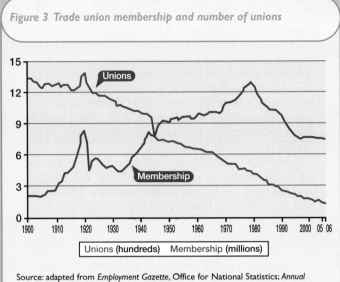

Figure 3 *Trade union membership and number of unions*

Source: adapted from *Employment Gazette*, Office for National Statistics; *Annual Abstract of Statistics*, Office for National Statistics; *Trade Union Membership*, DTI.

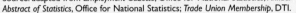

Figure 4 *Estimated mark-up of union over non-union wages*

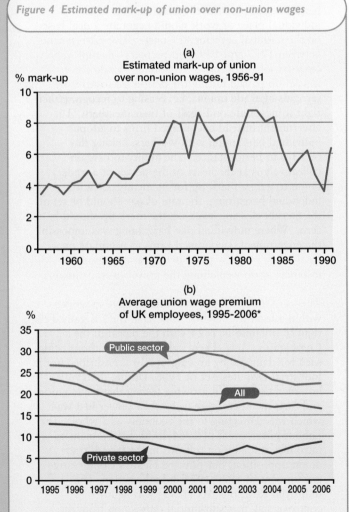

* Percentage difference in average hourly earnings of union members by sector compared with non-union employees in the same sector.

Source: adapted from *Trade Union Membership*, DTI.

● Between 1979 and 1997 government showed a marked hostility to trade unions. This has affected the willingness of workers to join unions and increased the confidence of those employers attempting to reduce or eliminate trade union activity in their workplaces.

● A perceived loss of power of trade unions has made workers less willing to join.

The trade union mark-up

Economic theory suggests that trade unions will increase wage rates for their members by shifting the supply curve of labour upwards. Studies of the UK economy tend to confirm that such a MARK-UP, the difference between actual wage rates in unionised labour markets and the wage rate which would otherwise prevail in the absence of trade unions, is indeed present. Figure 4 shows two estimates of the union mark-up covering successive periods. The methodology used to calculate the mark-up is not the same and the data in the two graphs are not strictly comparable. What both show is that a trade union-mark up exists. Workers who are unionised on average receive higher wages than workers who are non-unionised.

Sources of trade union power

A variety of factors may account for the size of the union mark-up.

Union density Union density refers to the proportion of the workforce which belongs to a trade union. Figures 3 and 4 show that over the 1950s, 1960s and 1970s trade union membership rose at the same time as the union mark-up. So the size of the mark-up may be linked to the percentage of workers belonging to a trade union. Indeed, industries which traditionally had particularly well paid manual workers, such as mining and shipbuilding, were industries which were highly unionised. Many firms within these industries were CLOSED SHOPS. In a closed shop, all workers have to belong to a recognised trade union. Closed shops are commonly assumed to increase trade union power at the expense of the employer.

The decline of union membership in the 1980s may help to account for a decline in the union mark-up in the 1980s. The power of closed shops was also weakened in the 1980s. Legislation between 1980 and 1990 limited the power of trade unions to enforce closed shop agreements. Moreover, the decline in union membership directly led to a decline in the number of informal closed shops. It is estimated that the number of manual workers covered by closed shop agreements fell from 3.7 million in 1984 to 0.5 million in 1990, for instance.

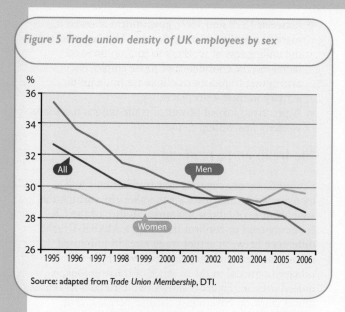

Figure 5 Trade union density of UK employees by sex

Source: adapted from *Trade Union Membership*, DTI.

Union density in the early 2000s stabilised to some extent as Figure 5 shows. It could be argued that this was due to the passing of the Employment Relations Act, 1999. This was the first piece of union legislation passed by the Labour government elected in 1997. The Act gave workers the right to union representation in a workplace if a majority of them voted in favour. However, as Figure 5 shows, union density amongst women has increased since 1999 whilst it has continued to fall for men. This is likely to reflect in part the growing participation of women in the labour force.

Union militancy The willingness of trade unions to take industrial action may be another factor influencing the size of the union mark-up. Industrial

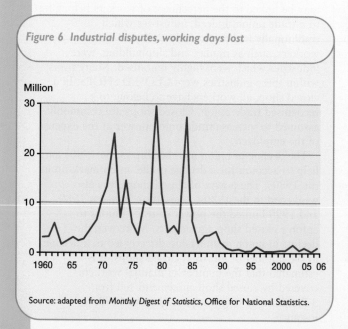

Figure 6 Industrial disputes, working days lost

Source: adapted from *Monthly Digest of Statistics*, Office for National Statistics.

action may take a variety of forms, including strikes, work-to-rules, and overtime bans. The greater the willingness of unions to strike, the more costly industrial action will be to employers and therefore the more likely it is that they will concede high pay rises. In practice, it is difficult to measure the degree of union militancy and therefore it is difficult to gauge the degree of correlation between such militancy and the change in the union mark-up.

However, Figure 6 shows that there has been a broad fall in the number of working days lost in industrial disputes since the 1970s. Workers since the 1980s have been less willing to take industrial action than in the 1970s. Again, this may help explain a fall in the union mark-up since the 1980s.

Collective bargaining Collective bargaining involves trade unions negotiating with employers. In the 1970s, large numbers of workers were covered by national agreements. Trade unions would negotiate with groups of employers representing a whole industry. In some cases, this would then be followed up by local bargaining at plant level where workers in an individual place of work would negotiate a deal based on the national agreement. Conservative governments between 1979 and 1997 put pressure on employers to cease national collective bargaining. Trade union legislation passed during the period led to firms de-recognising trade unions, i.e. ceasing to recognise their right to negotiate on behalf of their members. The government instead encouraged firms to adopt individual bargaining with workers, linking this perhaps to performance. The ability to bargain collectively is at the heart of the power of a trade union to gain a mark-up for its members. With individual bargaining, the rate of pay should be set at the market clearing level, i.e. the mark-up should be zero. Where individual pay bargaining was impossible, the government encouraged firms to negotiate on a local basis, plant by plant or region by region for instance, again weakening the power of trade unions.

The legislative background Unions have to work within a legal framework. Unions in the UK gained the right to organise in 1824 with the repeal of the Combination Acts. Their right to strike without being sued for damages by an employer was enshrined in the Industrial Disputes Act of 1906. During the 1960s, however, there was a growing feeling that trade unions and their members were using their power in a way which was damaging to the economy as a whole. The Labour government of 1964-1970 shelved plans to introduce trade union reforms in the face of trade union opposition, but Edward Heath's Conservative government of 1970-1974 did take action. The Industrial Relations Act (1971) was highly controversial, met substantial opposition from the trade union movement and failed to reduce their power effectively. It was repealed in 1974 when a new Labour government came into office and trade union rights were extended by various pieces of legislation in the following two years. The 1980s, arguably, saw a transformation in the climate of industrial relations in the UK. The Conservative government, instead of introducing large scale legislative reform, passed a number of acts each of which restricted union power at the margin. By the mid-1990s:

- secondary picketing (picketing by workers not involved in a dispute, e.g. miners picketing a school where the teachers are on strike in 'solidarity' with the teachers) had been made illegal;
- trade unions had to hold a secret ballot and gain a majority of the votes cast to call an official strike;
- social security benefits were withdrawn from the dependants of striking workers;
- union officers had to be elected by secret ballots;
- closed shop agreements were restricted and greater opportunities were given for employees to opt out of closed shops.

Power within the union movement shifted. Before 1979, small groups of workers who were willing to take unofficial strike action and certain militant trade union leaders tended to dominate at least the newspaper headlines. The reforms of the 1980s and 1990s made it more costly and more difficult for workers to take widespread unofficial action. The power of trade union leaders to call strikes was curbed because workers now had to be balloted on strike action. Moreover, the democratisation of union voting procedures made it much more difficult for militant trade union leaders to get elected to key posts within trade unions.

The government also shrewdly distanced itself from the prosecution of trade unions. Previous legislation had concentrated on criminal law, where offenders were prosecuted by the state and could be fined or imprisoned. Government always risked creating trade union 'martyrs'. Much of the union legislation of the 1980s and 1990s concentrated on civil law. Employers were given powers to sue trade unions for breaches of the law. For instance, if a trade union calls a strike without holding a secret ballot, it is the employer affected which sues the trade union for damages. The government has no power to prosecute the union.

This means that trade unions risk losing considerable sums of money if they do not comply with the law, but individual trade union members cannot gain public sympathy by being sent to prison as they could in theory under the 1971 Industrial Relations Act.

Not only has the government considerably reduced the ability of trade unions and their members to take industrial action, it also, during the 1980s and 1990s, took a strong stance with public sector trade unions. The most important trade union defeat in the public sector was the breaking of the miners' strike in 1984-5.

Furthermore, the government completely cut off the trade union movement from decision making at a national level. This contrasted with the 1960s and 1970s when governments, both Labour and Conservative, would often consult trade union leaders before making important decisions.

It is perhaps not surprising, then, that the trade union mark-up declined in the 1980s. Some groups of workers, such as miners and print workers, saw substantial cuts in their mark-up as a result of employers winning bitter strikes in the mid-1980s. In the 1990s, the government continued to implement policies designed to produce a **flexible market**. In the view of the Conservative government to 1997, trade unions would have little or no place in this market.

The Labour government elected in 1997 was more pro-union but it did not want to see a return to the industrial relations strife of the 1960s and 1970s when Labour were last in power. Instead, it wanted to see a partnership between unions and employers where unions were able to add value to the running of a firm as well as protecting their members' interests. Certainly, it had no intention of repealing most of the anti-union legislation of the 1980s.

The Employee Relations Act 1999 attempted to reverse these trends by giving workers the right to trade union recognition in the workplace where a majority voted in favour. But as Figure 7 shows, the percentage of workers (both union and non-union workers) whose pay is affected by collective agreements between trade unions and employers continued to fall. So too does the percentage of workers (both union and non-union workers) in workplaces where trade unions are present.

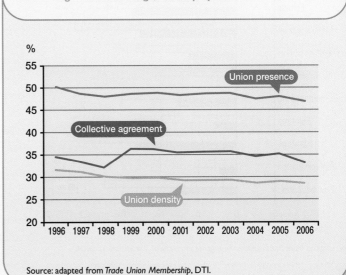

Figure 7 *Union density, presence of unions in the workplace and collective agreement coverage, UK employees*

Source: adapted from *Trade Union Membership*, DTI.

DataQuestion

The role of unions

Figure 8 Number of days lost through strikes by industry sector

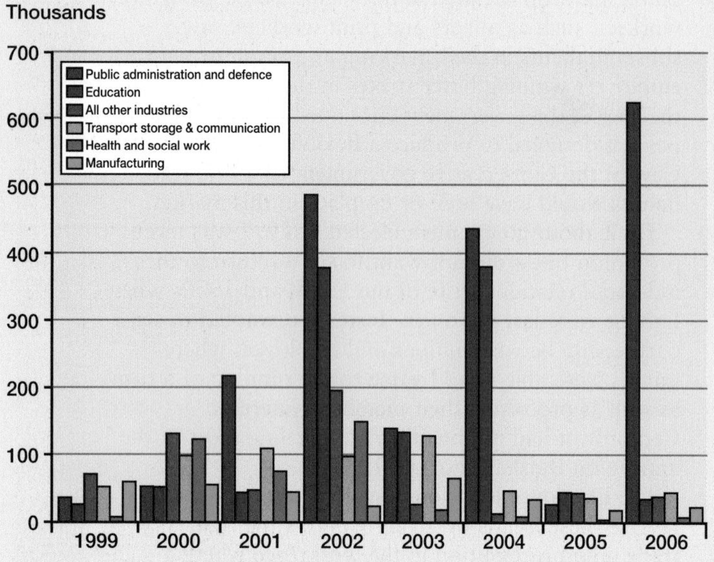
Thousands
700
600
500
400
300
200
100
0
Public administration and defence
Education
All other industries
Transport storage & communication
Health and social work
Manufacturing
1999
2000
2001
2002
2003
2004
2005
2006

Source: adapted from *Monthly Digest of Statistics*, Office for National Statistics.

The creation of large super unions will not reverse the long term decline in union membership or ease their financial problems unless they alter their strategies to suit the demands of a much-changed labour market, a study concludes today. The report, published by the Centre for Economic Performance, argues that trade union mergers have failed to address the fundamental failure to attract recruits to replace members lost through the decline of traditional industries such as manufacturing and mining.

Trade unions' ability to negotiate higher wages for their members, one of the main drivers for recruitment, has dwindled as their bargaining position has weakened. A wage premium in 1993 of about 10 per cent for private sector union members fell to just under 1 per cent by 2000. On the other hand, says the report, unions have narrowed 'the pay differential between women and men, black and white workers, manual and non-manual workers and those with health problems'.

Source: adapted from the *Financial Times*, 8.9.2005.

Figure 9 Estimated wage premium from union membership %

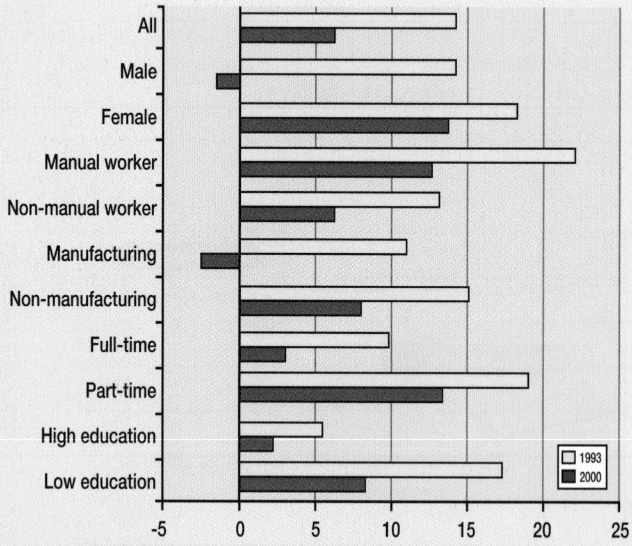
All
Male
Female
Manual worker
Non-manual worker
Manufacturing
Non-manufacturing
Full-time
Part-time
High education
Low education
1993
2000
-5
0
5
10
15
20
25

Source: adapted from *British Unions: Resurgence or Perdition?*, David Metcalf 2004.

The number of working days lost through strikes soared last year to 754 500, the highest level since 2004. More than 80 per cent of the days lost involved public sector workers. The biggest single stoppage involved more than 1 million local government workers who forced the closure of schools, libraries, local bus services, leisure centres and multi-story car parks when they walked out for 24 hours in March over proposed changes to rules allowing staff to retire early on full pensions.

Trouble for the government is not over. More than 2 million civil servants, postal workers, council staff, teachers and health workers have threatened to take industrial action in a series of disputes over below-inflation pay rises, job cuts and privatisation of services.

The number of working days lost, though, is still well below those experienced in the 1970s, when an average of 12.9 million days were lost annually and in the 1980s when 7.2 million days a year were lost through stoppages. It compares with 29.5 million days lost in 1979 during the 'winter of discontent' and a record 162 million days lost in 1926, the year of the General Strike.

Source: adapted from the *Financial Times*, 12.6.2007.

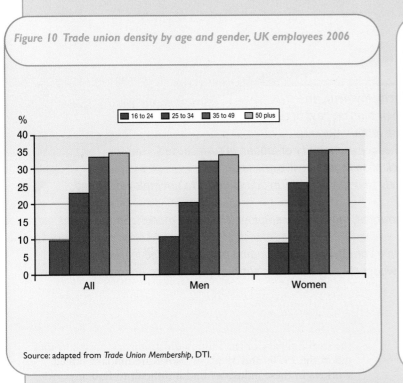

Figure 10 *Trade union density by age and gender, UK employees 2006*

Source: adapted from *Trade Union Membership*, DTI.

Members of the trade union Amicus working in the commercial printing industry have voted in favour of a new national agreement with employers. Amicus Assistant General Secretary, Tony Burke, said: 'The new Partnership at Work deal will move industrial relations in the industry into the 21st century. The new, modernised agreement takes into account the technical and economic changes that have occurred in recent years as well as reflecting the many social changes. This new agreement also looks to the future with clauses on social issues such as sick pay, the regulation of agency and temporary workers, information and consultation, and flexible working patterns. It will also mean that the industry can discuss a wide range of issues including productivity, competitiveness, new legislation, as well as social and technical issues in a different way. Discussions will take place on a regular basis between ourselves and the BPIF (the employers' federation) with the help of an independent chair to work through any issues, while recognising the interests of both sides.'

Source: adapted from www.amicustheunion.org, 28.10.2005.

Hundreds of thousands of building workers have won a 23 per cent pay increase. The deal, agreed between Ucatt, the T&G and GMB unions on one side, and the Construction Confederation on the other, covers 600 000 workers. A craftsworker's basic pay will rise from £7.30 to £9 an hour.

George Brumwell, who leads the biggest builders' union, suggested that the increase reflected a fundamental revaluing of the skills that Britain needs. Britain's construction industry has benefited from a surge in public spending aimed at repairing the country's creaking infrastructure. This has boosted the number of jobs in the construction industry by 24 000 in six months, to 1.89 million by the end of last year. But many companies are finding it hard to fill vacancies.

Source: adapted from the *Financial Times*, 17.4.2003.

1. What is the role of a trade union? Give examples from the data to illustrate your answer.
2. Analyse the effect of trade unions on wages and employment in the UK.
3. Discuss whether economic efficiency would be improved if further restrictions were placed on trade union activity.

Summary

1. In a perfectly competitive labour market, there is no unemployment, no discrimination and market forces allocate workers to their highest paid occupations.
2. In practice, there are many examples of market failure in labour markets.
3. One major cause of labour market failure in the UK is the lack of mobility of labour, in turn caused principally by failure in the housing market and by a lack of skills amongst workers.
4. In segmented labour markets, the formal sector is unlikely to make short term adjustments to unemployment and hence labour markets may be prevented from clearing.
5. Trade unions and monopsonist employers, such as government, may reduce employment in the market. So too might government policy.
6. Governments attempt to correct labour market failure in a variety of ways, including minimum wage legislation and equal pay legislation. These may lead to an increase in wages for some workers but may also lead to unemployment for others.

Efficiency, equity and market failure

An economy where all markets are perfectly competitive is Pareto efficient. All labour markets will clear. Everyone who wants a job at the going wage rate is able to obtain one and therefore there is no unemployment. There is perfect factor mobility and therefore there can be no regional or sectoral unemployment. The market mechanism will allocate workers to their highest value occupations, ensuring that total output in the economy is maximised.

In a real modern industrialised economy, few markets are perfectly competitive. There are many instances of market failure and this is true not just in the goods market but also in labour markets. Market failure can be judged against a number of criteria of efficiency including:

- full employment - the extent to which the market mechanism provides jobs for those who wish to work;
- maximum labour productivity - the extent to which the potential, the talents and the skills of workers in jobs are fully utilised in an economy.

Market failure can also be judged against different criteria of equity:

- equal opportunities - the extent to which all groups in society including women, the young, the elderly and those from ethnic minorities are not discriminated against in the labour market;
- wage differentials - the extent to which individual workers receive a 'fair' wage for the work they do.

Causes of labour market failure

There is a considerable number of ways in which labour markets are imperfect.

Mobility of labour In a perfect labour market, there is complete mobility of labour. Workers, at no cost to themselves, are free to move jobs between industries and between regions. In practice, there are major obstacles to mobility.

- Many workers have job-specific skills. For instance, a teacher could not easily become a manager. A manager could not easily become a concert pianist. A concert pianist could not easily become a chef. When industries, such as

the steel industry or the shipbuilding industry, shrink as they did in the 1970s and 1980s in the UK, redundant skilled workers in these industries find it difficult to find any employment except unskilled, low paid jobs. Industrial training by firms and by government favours young workers. So older workers find it difficult to move from industry to industry, even if they so wish.

- Knowledge is imperfect in the labour market, particularly in occupations where there is a long tradition of labour immobility. There are high SEARCH COSTS for workers and employers in finding out about employment opportunities. These search costs include time spent looking for jobs, or job applicants, and money costs such as travel, postage and advertisements. The higher the search costs, the less likely it is that a search will take place and the less labour mobility there will be.
- Workers are not just workers. They belong to families and local communities. They take a pride in their area or in the skills they have acquired over a long period of time. Many people prefer not to move around the country in pursuit of a job or a career. They prefer to remain unemployed or stay in a job which is not particularly rewarding rather than move.
- The housing market can also be a major barrier to mobility. It is difficult, if not impossible, for workers living in social accommodation, either rented from a local authority or a housing association, to get a house or flat in a different area where there might be a job. Low income or unemployed workers, particularly if they have a family, can find they cannot move from where they currently live. Equally, if there were a slump in house prices in the owner occupied sector, as happened last between 1990 and 1992, it becomes very difficult to sell a house. This limits mobility too.

Skill shortages Regions can experience skill shortages because of lack of mobility of workers. However, an economy as a whole can also experience skill shortages if education and training have not produced the right mix of workers. Appropriate education and training is therefore essential to prevent labour market failure.

Discrimination Discrimination is a major source of labour market failure. It is dealt with in more detail at the end of this unit.

Question 1

A survey published in 1993 by the CBI and Black Horse Relocation Services suggested that employee resistance to job relocation at the time was growing. Nearly 40 per cent of the 251 companies surveyed said a working spouse 'represented a key inhibitor to relocation'. Ms Sue Shortland, head of the Confederation of British Industry's relocation group, said: 'The issue of the working partner will increase with more women working and more dual-income families.' She pointed out that it was not only the temporary loss of income that caused problems but also the damage to the partner's career, promotion and income potential.

A third mentioned concern was children's education and just more than a quarter of the survey sample quoted family ties and roots as reasons for reluctance to move with the company.

The property price slump in the early 1990s was the most serious barrier to relocation. As many as 44 per cent of the sample said inability to sell their home inhibited them from being moved to another part of the country by their employer.

Source: adapted from the *Financial Times*.

(a) What barriers to labour mobility were highlighted by the 1993 survey?
(b) Explain why labour immobility can lead to inefficiency in the economy.

Trade unions and monopsony employers It is argued that trade union and monopsony employers create unemployment in the market. A full explanation of this was given in the previous unit.

Segmented labour markets Some economists have argued that labour markets are segmented so that there is little movement of labour from one market to another. One version of this argument is the DUAL LABOUR MARKET HYPOTHESIS. In the formal, primary or planning sector of the economy, workers, often unionised, are employed by large employers such as oligopolistic or monopoly firms or by government. Workers in the formal sector tend to be better qualified and better paid. In the informal, secondary or market sector, workers, mainly non-unionised, are employed by small firms or are self-employed. These workers tend to be low-skilled or unskilled workers on low pay.

In the formal sector, workers are seen as important assets by their employers. They are trained and are expected to pursue a life-long career in their occupation. They are seen as reliable, dependable and loyal. In return for these qualities, firms are prepared to give a complete remuneration package, including not just pay, but also benefits such as pension schemes, sickness benefit and paid holidays. At times, this package may be far in excess of the equilibrium wage rate (i.e. the firm could employ workers at far lower wages). However, reducing wages to take advantage of short term weaknesses in the labour market would be counter-productive in the long run. It might lead to lower morale, greater uncertainty and lower productivity amongst existing staff. If workers are brought in from outside the company, it may take time for new staff to become familiar with often complex work routines and there may be friction between these outsiders and existing company staff. Reducing wages in the short term may also deter young people, who see that wages can be volatile, from entering the industry.

In the informal sector, workers are expected to be mobile. Job security is low. Training is minimal. Workers are not expected to stay with their employers and hence little is provided in the form of extra benefits, such as sickness benefits or pension schemes.

If the economy is in fact divided into these two sectors, there are important implications for unemployment and discrimination. Market economists argue that unemployment in an industry can only be a short term phenomenon because wages will fall to clear the market. However, employers do not react to unemployment by cutting wages in the formal sector of the economy. On the contrary, workers may continue to receive pay rises in line with their career expectations. In the informal sector, there will be wage cuts which will expand employment. Overall it will take much longer for the economy to return to full employment because only the informal sector behaves in the way economic theory suggests. What is more, the process of adjustment will lead to widening income differentials. Whilst workers in the formal sector will be receiving pay rises, those in the informal sector will receive wage cuts. So the burden of adjustment falls disproportionately hard on those most likely to receive low wages.

For a variety of reasons discussed below, women and those

Question 2

Table 1 *Average earnings, inflation and unemployment, 1990-1993*

	1990	1993
Average earnings 1990 = 100		
Electricity, gas, other energy and water supply	100	122.2
Food, drink and tobacco (manufacture)	100	125.0
Education and health services	100	120.2
Motor vehicles and parts (manufacture)	100	119.5
Whole economy	100	118.5
Hotels and catering	100	118.0
Leather, footwear and clothing (manufacture)	100	117.2
Construction	100	116.5
Distribution and repairs	100	113.3
Retail price index (1990=100)	100	114.3
Unemployment (millions)	1.66	2.92

Source: adapted from Department of Employment, *Employment Gazette*.

Electricity, gas, other energy and water supply, food, drink and tobacco, education and health services and motor vehicles and parts are industries which are characterised by an above average proportion of full-time permanent jobs. Hotels and catering, leather, footwear and clothing, construction and distribution and repairs are industries which have above average proportions of part-time workers and casual workers.

The UK economy suffered a severe and prolonged recession between 1990 and 1992. How might the theory of segmented labour markets help to explain the difference in the earnings increase between the sectors at the time?

from ethnic minorities tend to form a much larger percentage of the workforce in the informal sector of the economy than in the formal sector. Hence, this dual economy reinforces discrimination against these groups.

Government policy Government policies, ranging from taxation on cigarettes to interest rate policy to health and safety legislation, affect the labour market in a variety of ways. In particular, they affect levels of employment, economic inactivity and unemployment. Each individual government policy either lessens market failure or leads to an increase in market failure. Many aspects of the debate on this issue are discussed in units on supply-side economics, but it is important to realise that government policies designed specifically to deal with labour market failure may well themselves create further labour market failure.

Correcting market failure

Governments have adopted a variety of policies in an attempt to improve both efficiency and equity in the labour market. However, some economists believe that the problems created by these policies are worse than the problems they were originally designed to counter.

Minimum wage legislation One way of tackling low pay is for the government to enforce minimum wage rates on employers.

This would seem to be an ideal solution to the problem of poverty amongst workers. However, economic theory predicts that the policy will have undesirable secondary effects. Figure 1 shows the demand and supply curves for labour in an industry. The equilibrium wage rate is 0E whilst the equilibrium level of employment is 0B. The government now imposes a minimum wage of 0F, forcing industry wage rates to rise to 0F. Firms demand AB less labour whilst BC more workers wish to gain jobs in the industry. The result is AC unemployment.

Existing workers have not necessarily benefited. 0A workers have gained higher wages. But AB workers have lost their jobs as

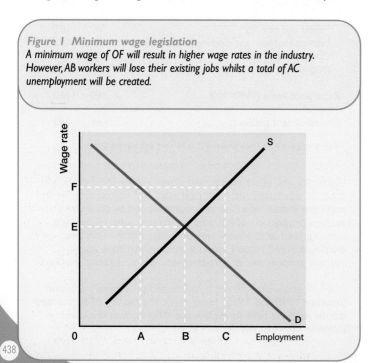

Figure 1 Minimum wage legislation
A minimum wage of OF will result in higher wage rates in the industry. However, AB workers will lose their existing jobs whilst a total of AC unemployment will be created.

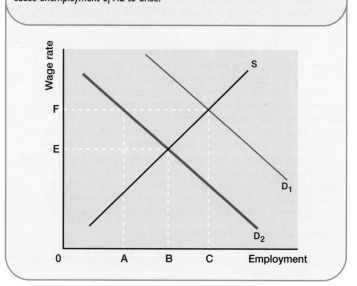

Figure 2 Minimum wages can cause unemployment
A fall in demand for labour from D₁ to D₂ should lead to a fall in wage rates from OF to OE. However, a minimum wage of OF will prevent this and will cause unemployment of AC to arise.

a result of the legislation. What is more, the workers who have lost their jobs are likely to be the least employable. Firms will have fired their least productive employees.

Minimum wage legislation can also prevent the market from clearing when there is an increase in unemployment. In Figure 2, D_1 and S are the original demand and supply curves respectively. Assume that the minimum wage is set at 0F. Then the equilibrium market wage rate is equal to the minimum wage rate and there is no unemployment. Now assume that the economy goes into recession. Demand for the industry's product falls and so the demand for labour in the industry falls (remember, labour is a derived demand). The new demand curve is D_2. If the market had been free, wage rates would have fallen to 0E and any transitional unemployment in the market would have disappeared. However, with a minimum wage of 0F, unemployment of AC is created. So it is argued that minimum wage legislation can cause unemployment.

Equal pay legislation Equal pay legislation is designed to raise the wage rates of groups of workers who perform work of equal value to other workers doing the same job who are at present paid higher wages. In the UK, equal pay legislation has been applied particularly to women and to workers from ethnic minorities.

Economic theory suggests that equal pay legislation will have the same effect as the imposition of a minimum wage. Equal pay legislation is designed to raise the wages of workers who are discriminated against. In the UK, there is evidence to suggest that it has been partially successful in achieving this. However, raising wages will reduce the demand for and increase the supply of labour. If the market was in equilibrium to start with, then the introduction of legislation would cause unemployment amongst those groups whom it is designed to benefit. There is a direct trade-off between higher pay and fewer jobs.

Health and safety legislation and other employment protection measures Government has passed many acts designed to improve the living standards of workers. For instance, health and safety legislation is designed to protect workers against accidents at work. These measures have the effect of raising the cost to firms of employing labour. Not only do firms have to pay workers a wage, but the legislation also forces a rise in labour-related costs. For instance, machines have to be made safe and minimum and maximum work temperatures have to be maintained. This shifts the supply curve upwards and to the left. At any given level of employment, workers will only work for a given wage rate plus the cost of protection measures, in turn leading to a fall in employment. Hence it is argued by free market economists that measures designed to protect the employee usually lead to a fall in employment.

The extent to which government legislation giving workers extra rights leads to a rise in unemployment depends crucially upon three factors.

● The first relates to the difference between the new rights and existing free market rights. For instance, if the market wage rate is £4 per hour and a minimum wage is set at £3 per hour, the minimum wage will have no effect. It won't raise wages in the market or create unemployment. If the minimum wage is set at £3 when market clearing rates are £2.75 per hour, there will be a small increase in average wages but equally it is unlikely that much unemployment will be created. A minimum wage of £6 with market clearing rates of £2 per hour, on the other hand, will give substantial benefits to workers employed but is likely to create substantial unemployment.

● Second, the amount of unemployment created depends on the relative elasticities of demand and supply for labour. Consider Figure 3 and compare it to Figure 1. Both diagrams relate to the introduction of a minimum wage. The market clearing wage is 0E and the minimum wage set is 0F. Unemployment of AC is created by the introduction of the minimum wage. In Figure 1, the demand and supply curves are relatively elastic between 0E and 0F. The unemployment created is large. In Figure 3, the demand and supply curves are relatively inelastic between 0E and 0F. The unemployment

created is relatively small.

Indeed if the demand for labour is perfectly inelastic, a rise in wages will have no effect on the demand for labour. One conclusion that could be drawn from the argument above is that the demand for labour is relatively less elastic in the formal sector of the economy than in the informal sector. So minimum wage legislation or equal pay legislation will have a much greater impact on jobs in the informal sector than in the formal sector. This would correspond with evidence which suggests that semi-skilled and unskilled workers have suffered disproportionately from unemployment in the 1970s and the 1980s in the UK.

● Third, what might be true for a single industry might not be true for the economy as a whole. For instance, minimum wage legislation in the hairdressing industry might result in unemployment amongst hairdressers. However, minimum wage legislation across all industries might have little or no effect on unemployment. In economics, it is not possible to conclude that the economy as a whole will behave in the same way as an individual market.

Question 3

The introduction of a 48 hour maximum working week, part of the EU working time directive, will hit some sectors of UK industry hard. Geoff Bryant, managing director of NC Engineering, which installs and services machine tools, said: 'The ending of the opt-out would outweigh every piece of red tape that we have to contend with. On a scale of 0-10, it would come in as 10 for seriousness.' He said that several of his staff of 28 often worked more than 48 hours a week, including travelling to meet customers. 'If we had to comply with this legislation, it would put us at a significant competitive disadvantage.'

Bob Fiddaman runs a 500-hectare farm in Hertfordshire. During harvesting, he hires part-time staff whose working week often exceeds 48 hours for short periods. He said: 'I can see costs in farming going up and profits going down. Farming is not a high-margin business and I can see a lot of farmers leaving the industry.'

Source: adapted from the *Financial Times*, 11.5.2005.

(a) Using a diagram, explain the possible impact of the 48 hour working week directive on employment.

Discrimination

One unfortunate feature of labour markets is discrimination. In a UK context, this is most likely to take place against women, people from ethnic minorities, people with disabilities and older workers. Discrimination comes from employers. In a market with many employers, at any given wage rate they will demand fewer workers from groups who are discriminated against. This means that the demand curve for such workers is below and to the left of where it would be if there were no discrimination. In Figure 4, this has the effect of shifting the demand curve from D_1 to D_2. Consequently, wage rates are lower and fewer workers gain jobs than would otherwise be the case.

It could also be argued that discrimination affects the supply curve of labour. If potential workers are discouraged from entering the labour market because of discrimination itself rather than lower wages, then the supply curve will

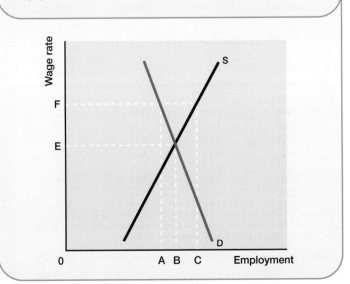

Figure 3 Inelastic demand and supply curves for labour
The more inelastic the demand and supply curves for labour, the less unemployment is created when minimum wages are introduced.

Figure 4 Discrimination

Discrimination means that employers are willing to offer fewer jobs to those workers who are being discriminated against. This has the effect of pushing their demand curve to the left. Wages are lower and fewer workers are employed.

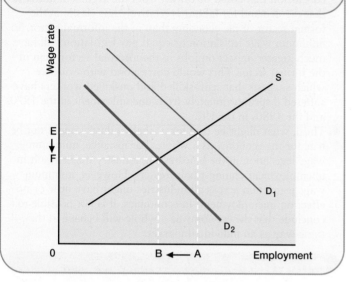

shift to the right from what it would otherwise have been. Note though that discrimination will also lead to a movement down the supply curve. Because wages are lower, fewer workers will be prepared to take jobs.

Key terms

Dual labour market hypothesis - the hypothesis that the labour market is split into two sectors: the formal sector with a relatively skilled, highly paid and stable workforce and the informal sector with a relatively unskilled, low paid and unstable workforce. **Search costs** - costs, such as money and time, spent searching for a job.

Applied economics

The minimum wage

In April 1999, the government introduced a National Minimum Wage (NMW) of £3.60 per hour for adults aged 22 and over. The rate for 18-21 year olds was set at £3, whilst employers were allowed to offer whatever they wanted for workers aged 17 and below. Table 2 shows how the minimum wage has changed since then in comparison with average earnings.

In total, it was estimated that nearly 2 million workers would see an increase in their wages when the minimum wage was first introduced in 1999, as Table 3 shows. Table 3 also shows the number of workers whose pay was raised by successive increases in the national minimum wage. For example, in April 2006 there were an estimated 1.3 million workers earning less than the new level of the minimum wage to be

introduced in October 2006, of £5.35. Most of these were earning the existing minimum wage of £5.05.

The single largest beneficiaries of the National Minimum Wage are female part-time workers. Figure 5 gives a breakdown of who was paid the minimum wage in April 2006. Nearly half of those benefiting were female part-time workers, with female and male full-time workers being the next most important

Table 3 Estimated numbers whose pay was affected by the introduction and successive increases in the National Minimum Wage

April each year	Adult minimum wage rate in April (£)	Proposed October adult minimum wage rate (£)	Number of adults earning less in April than the proposed October rate[1] (millions)
1998	-		2.0
1999	3.60	3.60	0.5
2000	3.60	3.70	0.7
2001	3.70	4.10	1.3
2002	4.10	4.20	0.9
2003	4.20	4.50	1.0
2004	4.50	4.85	1.4
2005	4.85	5.05	1.1
2006	5.05	5.35	1.3

1. The 1998 figure shows the number of workers estimated to be earning less than the minimum wage of £3.60 before it was first introduced.

Source: adapted from National Minimum Wage, Low Pay Commission Report 2007.

Table 2 National Minimum Wage hourly rates aged 22 and over and change in average earnings, UK

	National minimum wage		Average earnings
	£ per hour	Change %	Change %
1999/00	3.60		6.7
2000/01	3.70	2.8	3.8
2001/02	4.10	10.8	3.6
2002/03	4.20	2.4	3.6
2003/04	4.50	7.1	3.8
2004/05	4.85	7.8	3.1
2005/06	5.05	0.4	3.9
2006/07	5.35	5.9	3.2
2007/08	5.52	3.2	

Source: adapted from Economic and Labour Market Review, Office for National Statistics; National Minimum Wage, Low Pay Commission Report 2007.

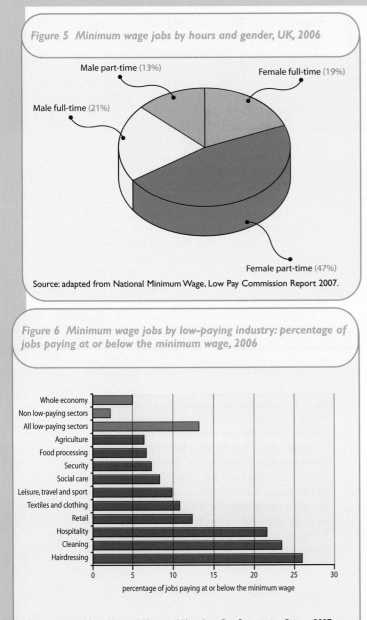

Figure 5 *Minimum wage jobs by hours and gender, UK, 2006*

Male part-time (13%)

Female full-time (19%)

Male full-time (21%)

Female part-time (47%)

Source: adapted from National Minimum Wage, Low Pay Commission Report 2007.

Figure 6 *Minimum wage jobs by low-paying industry: percentage of jobs paying at or below the minimum wage, 2006*

percentage of jobs paying at or below the minimum wage

Whole economy
Non low-paying sectors
All low-paying sectors
Agriculture
Food processing
Security
Social care
Leisure, travel and sport
Textiles and clothing
Retail
Hospitality
Cleaning
Hairdressing

Source: adapted from National Minimum Wage, Low Pay Commission Report 2007.

beneficiaries.

Low paid jobs are spread unevenly throughout the economy as Figure 6 shows. In the whole economy, 5 per cent of workers are paid at the minimum wage. In contrast, in hairdressing, 26 per cent of workers are paid at the minimum wage. The 10 lowest paying industries in the UK, ranging from agriculture to hairdressing, are shown in Figure 6. In these industries, on average 14 per cent of workers are paid at the minimum wage.

Arguments in favour of minimum wages

The main argument in favour of a national minimum wage is one of **horizontal equity**. Every worker should receive the same rate of pay for working an hour. In a market economy, this is not possible. The market produces wage differentials in order to create an efficient economy where wages act as signals, creating incentives for workers with higher skills to take on jobs with higher marginal revenue products. However, a minimum wage sets a floor below which market forces cannot drive wages. It gives a minimum reward to labour which can be seen as a 'fair' reward. It prevents workers in the UK from receiving Third World wage rates and creating a society which is highly unequal.

Minimum wages could also be argued to promote dynamic efficiency in a rich industrialised country. Firms will employ workers if their wage is equal to or less than their marginal revenue product (MRP). The MRP of labour can be raised if workers receive training and become more skilled. Equally, the MRP of labour can rise if firms invest in capital equipment. A minimum wage encourages firms to invest in both human and physical capital which can lead to higher economic growth in the long term. This will be true if low wages before the introduction of a minimum wage had led to underinvestment and an inefficient use of scarce labour.

Similarly, it can be argued that minimum wages encourage rich countries like the UK to move away from the production of low value added products to higher value added products. In the long term, if countries are to grow, they will produce ever more sophisticated products. The introduction of a minimum wage encourages this trend because it encourages investment.

In terms of world poverty, minimum wages in developed countries can help Third World countries become more competitive. Some low value, unskilled jobs will disappear in rich countries which introduce a minimum wage. Third world countries will then be able to fill the gap left by exporting those products to the rich country. This is mutually beneficial. The foreign exchange earned by the Third World country will be spent on goods and services from other countries, including exports from rich countries. They are likely to be higher value goods, those goods which rich countries have a competitive advantage in producing.

Economic theory suggests that where there is a monopsonist employer in the **market,** there will be allocative inefficiency. This is because a monopsonist will employ fewer workers at a lower rate of pay than if there is a number of employers in a market. The introduction of a minimum wage to a market where a monopsonist is paying low wages will both raise wages and raise employment. Allocative inefficiency is likely to be reduced. What's more, the taxpayer should also gain with fewer workers entitled to benefits for being on low incomes, and tax income increased as wages are higher and there are more in work.

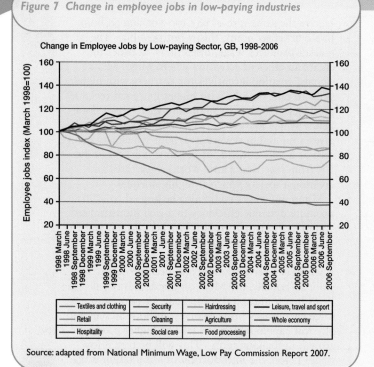

Figure 7 *Change in employee jobs in low-paying industries*

Change in Employee Jobs by Low-paying Sector, GB, 1998-2006

Source: adapted from National Minimum Wage, Low Pay Commission Report 2007.

Arguments against minimum wages

The main argument against minimum wages is that it creates unemployment. Evidence on this is contradictory. In the UK, the effect on unemployment of the introduction of the minimum wage in 1999 was probably negligible. This was because the minimum wage was set at such a low level that it had little impact on costs for employers.

The extent to which unemployment is created depends in part on whether low paid jobs are in the internationally traded goods and services sector, and the rates of the pay in our international competitors. Figure 7 shows how employment has changed in industries with a large proportion of low paid workers. The textiles industry in particular was subject to fierce international competition between 1998 and 2006 and saw job losses of over 60 per cent. Agriculture has been through difficult times over this period with both the BSE and foot and mouth crises which knocked farm incomes and therefore employment. Most low paid industries where there was no international competition saw a rise in employment, with security rising over 30 per cent. The statistics don't say what employment levels would have been if there had been no minimum wage. But the number of low paid jobs has expanded since 1998.

Evidence from abroad where national minimum wages are relatively common gives contradictory evidence. For instance, a study of the extension of the US minimum wage to Puerto Rico, a Third World economy in the Caribbean, in 1974 showed that there was a consequent fall in employment. By 1980, the Federal minimum wage was 75 per cent of the average wage in Puerto Rico's manufacturing compared to 43 per cent in mainland USA. Unemployment rose from 11.3 per cent to 23.4 per cent between 1974 and 1983, of which one-third was attributed to the rise in the minimum wage. In contrast, a 1992 study by L Katz and A Krueger of 314 fast food restaurants in Texas found that, following a 45 per cent rise in the US minimum wage in 1991, employment rose. Moreover the restaurants which had had to raise their wages the most also tended to have the largest increase in employment. The study found that for every 10 per cent rise in wages, there was a 25 per cent increase in full-time employment.

Another argument against minimum wage legislation is that it imposes compliance costs on individual firms. They have to ensure that they are meeting the requirements of the law and are able to prove to inspectors that they are so doing. This is just another example of 'red tape' which imposes particularly high costs on small firms.

Perhaps the most important argument against the minimum wage in the UK is that it does little to reduce poverty. Figure 8 shows the position of minimum wage households in household income distribution in Autumn 2002. Only 8 per cent of households in the bottom tenth of households by income distribution have someone in the household earning the minimum wage. This is because most households in the bottom decile of income are made up of households with no wage earners. Many are pensioner households but there are also single parent households and households where all the adults are unemployed. Even in the decile group with the most households with a member received the minimum wage, the third decile group, only 15 per cent of households benefit.

Figure 8 also shows the proportion of working-age households with one or more employed that have a

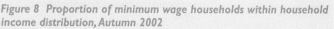

Figure 8 *Proportion of minimum wage households within household income distribution, Autumn 2002*

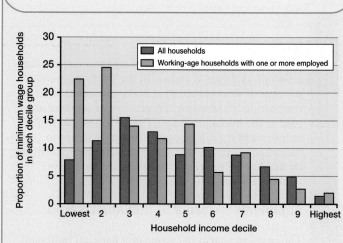

Source: adapted from *Annual Report*, Low Pay Commission.

member on the minimum wage. Nearly one-quarter of these households in the bottom two deciles have members on the minimum wage. So for households of working age with one or more employed, the minimum wage has a more significant impact compared to all households. Even so, the vast majority of households with workers do not benefit directly from the minimum wage.

DataQuestion

Social welfare models

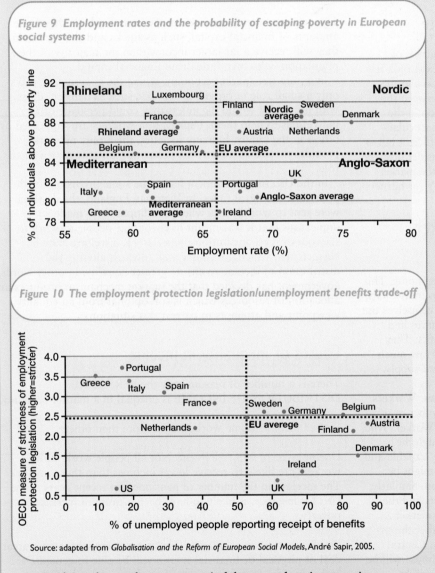

Figure 9 *Employment rates and the probability of escaping poverty in European social systems*

Figure 10 *The employment protection legislation/unemployment benefits trade-off*

Source: adapted from *Globalisation and the Reform of European Social Models*, André Sapir, 2005.

The Belgian economist André Sapir, in a recent book *Globalisation and the Reform of European Social Models,* argues that there are four distinct models of social welfare used by governments within western Europe, illustrated in Figures 9 and 10.

- The 'Nordic model' (Denmark, Finland, Sweden and the Netherlands) has the highest public spending on social protection and universal welfare provision. Labour markets are relatively unregulated but there are 'active' labour market policies whilst strong unions deliver a high degree of wage equality.
- The 'Anglo-Saxon' model (Ireland and the UK) provides quite generous social assistance of last resort, with cash transfers going mainly to people of working age. Unions are weak and the labour market relatively unregulated.
- The 'Rhineland model' (Austria, Belgium, France, Germany and Luxembourg') relies on social insurance for those out of work as well as for provision of pensions. Employment protection is stronger than in the Nordic countries. Unions are also powerful and enjoy legal support for extensions of the results of collective bargaining.
- The 'Mediterranean model' (Greece, Italy, Portugal and Spain) concentrates public spending on old-age pensions. Heavy regulation protects and lowers employment, while generous support for early retirement seeks to reduce the number of jobseekers.

Professor Sapir argues that the Anglo-Saxon and Nordic models are efficient (at least in the labour market) while the 'Rhineland' and 'Mediterranean models' are equitable.

Source: adapted from the *Financial Times*, 14.9.2005.

1. Explain why employment rates in labour markets in countries adopting the 'Rhineland model' and the 'Mediterranean model' might be low.
2. Explain why poverty is higher in countries adopting the 'Anglo-Saxon' model.
3. Discuss whether market failure is greater in countries like France and Denmark than it is in Greece or the UK.

Summary

1. In a market economy, there is a variety of reasons why the incomes of individuals and households differ, including differences in wage rates, economic activity and financial wealth.
2. A Lorenz curve and Gini coefficient can be used to show the degree of inequality in income in society.
3. There is a variety of causes of poverty but the main cause is living in a household where no one has a full time job.
4. Two types of equity or fairness can be distinguished - horizontal equity and vertical equity.
5. There can be a conflict between efficiency and equity, although redistributive government policies need not necessarily result in greater inefficiency.

Resource allocation, equality and equity

The chairperson of a large company may earn hundreds of thousands of pounds per year. A pensioner might exist on a few thousand pounds per year. This distribution of income in the economy is the result of the complex interaction between the workings of the market and government intervention in the market. Markets are impersonal. They produce a particular allocation of resources which may or may not be efficient but is almost certainly not equal. In this unit, we will consider how the market allocates resources and then consider how the market may be judged on grounds of equality and EQUITY (or fairness).

The distribution of resources in a market economy

Individuals receive different incomes in a market economy. This is because it is based on the ownership of property. Individuals, for instance, are not slaves. They are able to hire themselves out to producers and earn income. They might own shares in a company and receive dividends, a share of the profits. They might own a house from which they receive rent. How much they receive depends upon the forces of demand and supply.

Workers with scarce skills in high demand, such as chairpersons of companies, can receive large salaries. Workers with few skills and in competition with a large number of other unskilled workers are likely to receive low wages. Workers who fail to find a job will receive no wage income through the market mechanism. These workers might be highly capable and choose not to take a job. On the other hand, they might be disabled or live in a very high unemployment region. Similarly, the market decides upon the value of physical assets and the income that can be earned from them through the market mechanism. If an individual inherits a house, all other things being equal, the house will be worth more if it is in Central London than if it is in Doncaster. The rent on the house will be higher in Central London. Shares in one company will be differently priced from shares in another company, and the dividends will be different.

The owners of assets which have a high value are likely to earn a high income. The human capital of the chairperson of Barclays Bank is likely to be very high and therefore he or she will be able to command a high salary. The Duke of Westminster, the largest individual landowner in London, owns large amounts of physical capital.

This too generates large incomes. Some individuals own large amounts of financial capital, such as stocks and shares. Again, they will receive a far larger income than the majority of the population, who own little or no financial capital.

In a pure free market economy, where the government plays only a small role in providing services, such as defence, those with no wealth would die unless they could persuade other individuals to help them. Usually, non-workers are supported by others in the family. In many societies, the family network provides the social security net. Charities too may play a small role.

In the UK, the government has made some provision for the poor since medieval times. In Victorian England, the destitute were sent to workhouses where conditions were made so unpleasant that it was meant to encourage people to work to stay out of these institutions. Since 1945, a welfare state has been created which goes some way towards altering the distribution of income to ensure greater equality. In other words, government has decided that the market mechanism produces an allocation of resources which is sub-optimal from an equality viewpoint and attempts to correct this situation.

Causes of inequality in income

There is a number of reasons why the PERSONAL DISTRIBUTION OF INCOME is unequal in a market economy.

Earned income Some workers earn more than others.

Unemployment and retirement Not all people work. Non-workers are likely to receive lower incomes than those in work. The increase in the number of pensioners in recent years in the UK, for instance, is likely to have been a cause of increases in poverty.

Physical and financial wealth Those in society who own a great deal of physical or financial wealth will be able to generate a higher income from their assets than those who own little or nothing. Wealth is accumulated in two main ways. First, a significant proportion of wealthy individuals has inherited that wealth. Second, wealthy individuals may have built up their wealth over their lifetime from working or by multiplying their existing assets, for instance through playing the Stock Exchange or simply holding onto an asset which grows in value at a particularly fast rate.

Household composition How income is measured can be

important in determining inequalities. An individual may earn a high salary. However, if he or she has to support a large family, then the income per person in the household may be quite low. On the other hand, a household where there are two parent wage earners and four child wage earners may have a high income despite the fact that all six adults are individually 'low paid', so inequalities differ according to whether they are being measured per individual or per household.

Government policy The extent to which government redistributes income through taxes and benefits will affect the distribution of income.

The degree of competition in product markets Imperfectly competitive markets will result in a different distribution of income and wealth than perfectly competitive markets. Consider Figure 1. It shows the cost and revenue curves for an industry. If the industry were perfectly competitive, production would take place where price = MC at output level 0B. If the industry now became a multi-plant monopolist, output would be at 0A where MC = MR. EFG is the allocative loss to society. It is sometimes called a **deadweight loss** because the loss is not recoverable. However, there is also a transfer of income from consumers to the monopoly producer represented by the rectangle CDEF.

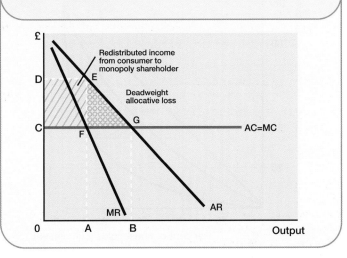

Figure 1 Allocative and distributive effects of monopoly
If the industry is perfectly competitive, it will produce at OB where price = MC. If it were a multi-plant monopolist, it would produce at OA where MC = MR. EFG is the deadweight allocative loss to society. CDEF is the total 'tax' of the monopolist on the consumer. It results in a redistribution of income from consumer to shareholder.

Question 1

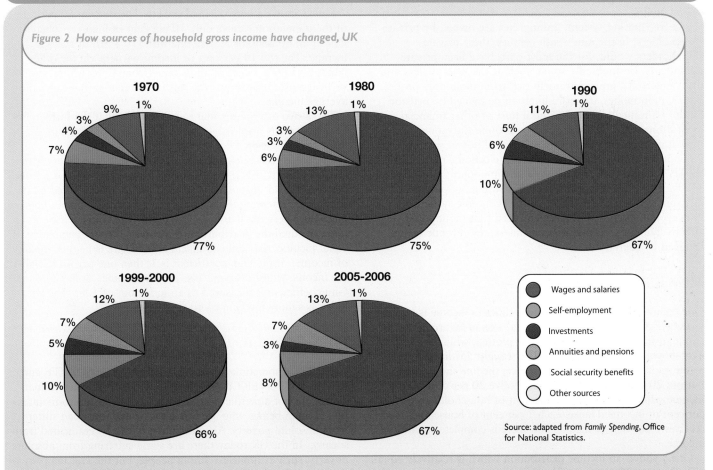

Figure 2 *How sources of household gross income have changed, UK*

Source: adapted from *Family Spending*, Office for National Statistics.

(a) How have the sources of income for UK households changed between 1970 and 2005-06?

(b) Inequalities have increased over the thirty-five year period. Using the data, suggest why this has occurred.

Figure 3 Lorenz curves
A Lorenz curve shows the degree of inequality of income in a society. The farther from the 45° line is the curve, the greater the degree of inequality.

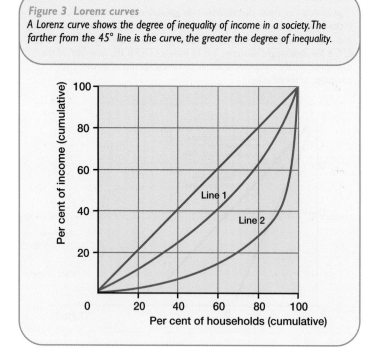

Table 1 Distribution of disposable household income¹

	Quintile groups of households				
	Bottom fifth	Next fifth	Middle fifth	Next fifth	Top fifth
1979	10	14	18	23	35
2002-03	7	12	17	24	40
2005-06	7	12	17	24	40

1. After direct taxes and benefits.
2. Figures may not add up due to rounding.

Source: adapted from *Social Trends*, Office for National Statistics.

(a) Construct three Lorenz curves from the data above.
(b) Has the distribution of income become more or less equal between 1979 and 2005-06?

Under perfect competition, the consumer would only have paid 0CFA for the output 0A. Under monopoly, consumers are forced to pay 0DEA.

In a free market system, monopolies are owned by private shareholders. In the nineteenth century, these private shareholders would, for the most part, have been private individuals. Undoubtedly some, such as the Rockefellers and the Vanderbilts, grew extremely rich from monopoly profits. Today, monopolies are more likely to be owned by pension funds, assurance companies and a host of other financial institutions which channel savings through the money and capital markets on behalf of wealthy and not so wealthy individuals. In the nineteenth century, elections, particularly in the USA, could be won or lost on this monopoly profit issue. Today, it is a less important issue because monopoly profits are distributed more widely through the economic system. However, it should still be remembered that monopolies effectively impose a 'tax' on consumers, the revenue being received by shareholders.

Measuring inequality

One common way to measure inequalities in income is to use a LORENZ CURVE. On the horizontal axis in Figure 3, the cumulative number of households is plotted, whilst the vertical axis shows cumulative income. The straight 45° line shows a position of total equality. For instance, the line shows that the bottom 20 per cent of households receive 20 per cent of total income whilst the bottom 80 per cent of households receive 80 per cent of income. Hence, each 1 per cent of households receives 1 per cent of income and there is complete equality of income.

Line 1 shows an income distribution which is relatively equal. The bottom 20 per cent of households receive 10 per cent of income. This means that they receive half the average income. The top 10 per cent of households (between 90 and 100 on the horizontal axis) receive 20 per cent of

income (from 80 to 100 on the vertical axis). So they receive twice the average income.

Line 2 shows a very unequal society. The bottom 50 per cent of the population receive only 10 per cent of income. Therefore half of all households receive one-fifth (10 ÷ 50) of average income. The top 10 per cent of income earners, on the other hand, earn 60 per cent of all income (from 40 to 100 on the vertical axis). That means the top 10 per cent earn 6 times the average income.

These two examples taken together show that the further the Lorenz curve is from the 45° line, the greater the income inequality in society.

One statistical measurement of the degree of inequality is the GINI COEFFICIENT. Mathematically, it is the ratio of the area between the 45 degree line and the Lorenz curve divided by the triangle representing the whole area under the 45 degree line. It has values between 0 and 1. The higher the Gini coefficient, the more unequal the distribution of income. If every person has equal income, the Gini coefficient is 0. There is perfect equality of income. If the Gini coefficient is 1, then one person has all the income whilst everyone else has no income. Sometimes the Gini coefficient is measured as an index out of 100. The Gini index is simply the Gini coefficient times 100.

Absolute and relative poverty

Inequality is sometimes discussed in terms of ABSOLUTE and RELATIVE POVERTY. Absolute poverty occurs when human beings are not able to consume sufficient **necessities** to maintain life. Human beings who are homeless or malnourished suffer from absolute poverty. Absolute poverty can be eradicated from society. In the UK today there are some suffering from absolute poverty, such as homeless young people, but the vast majority of the population have a sufficiently high income not to be poor in this sense. The largest concentrations of absolute poverty today are to be found in the Third World.

Relative poverty is always present in society. The poor in this

Question 3

Table 2 Gross weekly earnings, gross hourly earnings and hours worked per week, full time male and female employees[1]

	Average gross weekly earnings (£)		Hours worked per week		Average gross hourly earnings (£)		Retail Price Index (1985=100)
	Males	Females	Males	Females	Males	Females	
1971	32.9	18.3	42.9	37.4	0.74	0.47	11.5
1981	140.5	91.4	41.7	37.2	3.32	2.42	42.6
1991	318.9	222.4	41.5	37.4	7.55	5.91	76.1
2001	490.5	366.8	41.2	37.5	11.9	9.77	98.8
2007	606.1	462.8	40.7	37.4	14.90	12.38	100.0

1   Data for 1971-2001 are Great Britain from the New Earnings Survey (NES). The New Earnings Survey was replaced by the Annual Survey of Hours and Earnings (ASHE) in 2004, covering the UK. The 2005 data in Table 64 are therefore not exactly comparable to the data for 1971-2001.

Source: adapted from *New Earnings Survey, Annual Survey of Hours and Earnings*, Office for National Statistics.

(a)   To what extent has horizontal equity between males and females increased over time in the UK?

(b)   Suggest reasons why there has been this change.

sense are those at the bottom end of the income scale. There is no exact measure of this, like the poorest 10 per cent or 20 per cent of society, but Adam Smith gave one measuring rod of relative poverty when he wrote that necessities were 'whatever the custom of the country renders it indecent for creditable people, even of the lower order, to be without.'

The causes of poverty

As there is no single definition of poverty, it is impossible to give a precise analysis of the causes of poverty. However, poverty tends to be associated with a number of causal factors, many of which are interlinked.

- A disproportionate number of people without jobs are in poverty. Without a job, they don't earn income and have to fall back on other means to survive. In the UK, being without a job explains why there are higher percentages of children, the elderly and women in poverty than the average.
- Lack of human capital - education and training - tends to be associated with poverty. With little human capital, workers can only sell their services in the market for low wages. There is a positive correlation both within countries and between countries of the number of years spent in education and the level of income of an individual.
- Lack of financial capital particularly hits those who are retired. Poverty amongst old people is high because they have inadequate savings to give them a pension or other income.
- Health problems affect an individual's ability to work and earn money. There could be a physical problem like Aids or a mental health problem.

- Being dependent on others for income tends to lead to poverty. For example, the percentage of children in poverty tends to be above the percentage of adults of working age in poverty. Equally, those dependent on unemployment benefits tend to be poor.
- Inheritance is very important if sometimes difficult to quantify. Those born into poor families have a disproportionate chance of being poor themselves. This is sometimes called the 'cycle of poverty'. It is true between countries. Someone born in Tanzania today is likely to remain poor for the rest of their lives compared to someone born today in the UK. Equally, it is true within countries. A child born into a low income family is likely to receive less education and to have a lower educational achievement by the end of compulsory schooling than someone born into a middle or high income family. They are more likely to suffer health problems. Their opportunities will be more limited.
- Between countries and regions, the amount of physical capital and intellectual capital like patents is an important determinant of poverty. You are far more likely to be living off less than $100 a year if you live in a country with relatively few paved roads, hospital buildings, airports or research facilities.

The effects of poverty

As with the causes of poverty, the effects of poverty depend upon how it is defined.

- With absolute poverty, a lack of the necessities of life, then the effect will be ill health and possibly death.
- With relative poverty, ill health and death are still a hazard. Statistics show that those in relative poverty are more prone to ill health than the average and have a lower life expectancy. Partly this is because relative poverty can be associated with poorer housing, bad diets and in countries like the USA lack of access to health care. However, it is also the case that those with poor health tend to be relatively poor. Relative poverty is associated with lack of access to physical goods and services, from cars to education to holidays. Those in relative poverty within a society can have low psychological well being. Their self-esteem can be low because they know they are poor in comparison with others. They tend to have less control of their lives. They can make fewer choices about how to organise their work if they have a

Question 4

In 1976, the government replaced a scheme whereby a few per cent of handicapped people received specially adapted small cars, with Mobility Allowance, a benefit which all handicapped people with mobility problems would receive. Those who used to receive a car complained bitterly because the new Mobility Allowance was only a fraction of what a car cost to buy and run.

To what extent did the change described lead to (a) greater equity and (b) greater efficiency?

job. Outside the workplace, they often can't choose where they live or how much income they receive. These factors affect the quality of life and mental well being.

Horizontal and vertical equity

Inequalities are not necessarily unfair. For instance, assume one worker worked 60 hours per week and another, in an identical job, worked 30 hours per week. It would seem fair that the 60 hour per week worker should receive roughly twice the pay even though this would then lead to inequality in pay between the two workers. Similarly, many poor pensioners today are poor because they failed to make adequate pension provision for themselves whilst they were working. It seems only fair that a worker who has saved hard all her life through a pension scheme should enjoy a higher pension than one who has decided to spend all her money as she earned it. Nevertheless, there is an inequality in this situation. In economics, EQUITY or fairness is defined in a very precise way in order to distinguish it from inequality.

Horizontal equity HORIZONTAL EQUITY is the identical treatment of identical individuals in identical situations. Inequitable treatment can occur in a number of different situations in our society today. An Asian applicant for a job may be turned down in preference to a white applicant even though they are the same in all other respects. A woman may apply to a bank for a business loan and be refused when a male applicant for exactly the same project may have been successful. A 55 year old may be refused a job in preference to a 25 year old despite identical employment characteristics. An 18 year old may gain a place at university in preference to another solely because her father is much richer.

Vertical equity Everybody is different, from the colour of their hair to the size of their toes and from their intellectual capacities to their social background. VERTICAL EQUITY is the different treatment of people with different characteristics in order to promote greater equity. For instance, if equity were defined in terms of equality, vertical equity would imply that everybody should have the opportunity to receive the same standard of education and the same standard of health care whatever their job, race, income or social background.

Equity vs efficiency

Governments intervene in the market to redistribute income because it is widely accepted that the distribution of income thrown up by the workings of free market forces is unacceptable. In a pure free market, efficiency is maximised because all production takes place where price = MC. If a government then intervenes in the market, say by subsidising

food for the poor, imposing taxes of any kind to pay for government expenditure, subsidising housing or providing welfare benefits, it introduces a distortion in the market. Hence, government intervention leads to allocative inefficiency.

In practice there are no pure free market economies. Economies are riddled with market imperfections, such as oligopolistic and monopoly industries, monopoly unions and externalities. The theory of the second best shows that introducing another distortion, such as welfare payments to the poor, may in fact lead to greater economic efficiency. The theory suggests that efficiency will be greatest if the distortion is spread thinly across many markets rather than concentrated on a few markets. For instance, it is likely that large housing subsidies combined with no subsidies to any other goods would lead to less economic efficiency than small subsidies spread across all goods in the economy. Equally, low levels of unemployment benefit available to all unemployed workers in the economy are likely to lead to greater economic efficiency than high levels of unemployment benefit available only to male manual employees.

Key terms

Absolute poverty - absolute poverty exists when individuals do not have the resources to be able to consume sufficient necessities to survive.

Equity - fairness.

Gini coefficient - a statistical measure of inequality of income. Its value ranges from 0, where there is perfect equality of income, to 1 where income is highly unequal with 1 person having all the income and everyone else having no income. The Gini index is the Gini coefficient times 100.

Horizontal equity - the identical treatment of identical individuals or groups in society in identical situations.

Lorenz curve - shows the extent of inequality of income in society.

Personal distribution of income - the distribution of the total income of all individuals.

Relative poverty - poverty which is defined relative to existing living standards for the average individual.

Vertical equity - the different treatment of individuals or groups which are dissimilar in characteristics.

Applied economics

The distribution of income and wealth in the UK

The distribution of income

Income is distributed unevenly in the UK. Table 3 gives three measures of distribution of income between households. Original income is the gross income of households from sources such as wages and salaries, private pensions and investment income. Disposable income is gross income after income tax and National Insurance contributions have been paid but including state welfare benefits such as unemployment benefit, family credit and the state old age pension. Final income is disposable income minus indirect taxes such as VAT, but including the value of state services such as education and the National Health Service.

Table 3 *Distribution of income*[1]

	Bottom fifth	Next fifth	Middle fifth	Next fifth	Top fifth	Total
			Percentage of total			
Original income						
1976	4	10	18	26	43	100
2002/03	3	8	15	26	48	100
Disposable income						
1976	10	14	18	23	36	100
2002/03	7	12	17	24	40	100
Final income						
1976	10	14	18	23	36	100
2002/03	10	13	17	23	37	100

1. Figures may not add up to 100 due to rounding.
Source: adapted from *Social Trends*, Office for National Statistics.

The statistics give an indication of the extent of inequality in income. For instance, in 2002/03 the bottom 20 per cent of households (mostly pensioner households and those with unemployed adults) received only 3 per cent of total original income generated in the UK. That means that each household received just 0.15 (3 ÷ 20) of average income in the UK. In comparison, the top 20 per cent of households received 48 per cent of total UK original income. On average each of these households received 2.4 times (48 ÷ 20) the average income.

In a welfare state, it should be expected that the distribution of disposable income and final income would show less inequality than original income. Taxes should fall most heavily on the better off whilst benefits should be received mainly by the poorer sections of society. Table 3 shows that to some extent this is true in the UK. The share of disposable income of the bottom 20 per cent of households was

7 per cent in 2002/03 (compared to 2 per cent of original income). That means that the average household in the bottom 20 per cent received 0.35 (7 ÷ 20) of the average income. The share of the top 20 per cent of households was 40 per cent giving the average household 2 times the average income in the UK. Figures for final income (disposable income minus indirect taxes such as VAT plus the value of benefits in kind such as education and the NHS) differ little compared to disposable income although the bottom 20 per cent of households show some increase in their share of income under this measure.

It should be remembered that there will be considerable variation in income within each of the quintile groups (groups of 20 per cent). For instance, in the bottom quintile there will be some households whose final income will be markedly less than the average for the group. On the other hand in the top quintile there will be a few who will earn hundreds of times the national average income. Equally, the statistics say nothing about how many people live in a household. A one person household in the bottom quintile may have a higher income per person than a six person household in the middle quartile.

Trends in the distribution of income

For most of the 20th century, the long term trend was for income differentials to narrow. However, the period 1979 to 1990 saw a sharp increase in income inequality, as Figure 4 shows. The poorest 10 per cent of households saw only a six per cent increase in their

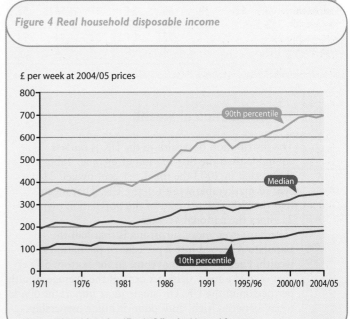

Figure 4 *Real household disposable income*

Source: adapted from *Social Trends*, Office for National Statistics.

real household disposable income. In contrast, average incomes for the top 10 per cent of households rose 46 per cent. Since 1991, however, income differentials as measured by household disposable income before deducting housing costs, have narrowed. As Figure 4 shows, over the period 1991 to 2004/05, the top 10 per cent of households saw a rise in their disposable income of approximately 20 per cent whilst the bottom 10th of households saw their disposable income rise by approximately one third.

There is a number of reasons for these trends. Wage inequalities widened considerably in the 1980s but have since remained broadly constant. The 1980s was a period of high unemployment which particularly affected low paid workers. Trade union power, too, was decreased as the government pushed through a series of 'reforms' which weakened the ability of unions to organise and strike. Low paid workers suffered disproportionately from these reforms.

Second, there was a shift in the tax burden from high income earners to low income earners in the 1980s. The top rate of income tax, for example, was cut from 83 per cent to 40 per cent. Benefits for the less well off were cut. Much of the increase in disposable income for the bottom 10 per cent of households, which contains a high proportion of pensioner households, since 1997 can be attributed to increases in benefit and cuts in tax for this group.

Table 5 Distribution of disposable income per head by region, 2005

	Gross disposable household income per head (£)
London	15 885
South East	14 941
East	14 198
South West	13 258
UK	13 279
East Midlands	12 522
Scotland	12 554
North West	12 186
West Midlands	12 133
Yorkshire and Humber	12 197
Wales	11 851
Northern Ireland	11 564
North East	11 356

Source: adapted from *Economic & Labour Market Review*, Office for National Statistics.

according to *Social Trends*, is now made up of the value of owner occupied houses.

Horizontal equity

Horizontal inequity exists in the UK in a number of different ways. One measure is the relative earnings of males and females. As Table 2 showed, there is a wide disparity between the relative earnings of males and females. Part of this can be explained by factors such as different education and training experiences, different age compositions of the male and female workforce and the loss of work experience by women during the crucial years when they might leave the

Table 4 Distribution of wealth

Percentage of marketable wealth owned by:	1911	1954	1971	1981	1991	2001	2003
Most wealthy 1%	69	43	31	21	17	22	21
Most wealthy 5%	-	-	52	40	35	42	40
Most wealthy 10%	92	79	65	54	47	54	53
Most wealthy 25%	-	-	86	77	71	72	72
Most wealthy 50%	-	-	97	94	92	94	93
Least wealthy 50%	-	-	3	6	8	6	7

Source: adapted from *Social Trends*, Office for National Statistics.

The distribution of wealth

The distribution of wealth in the UK is far less equitable than the distribution of income. Table 4 shows that in 2003 the top 1 per cent owned 21 per cent of marketable wealth in the UK. That meant that the richest 1 per cent of the population owned 21 times the national average.

Perhaps even more surprising is that half the population owned just 7 per cent of the nation's wealth. Each person on average in the bottom 50 per cent owned a mere 0.14 per cent of the average wealth per person in the UK. The single most important divide today between 'rich' and 'poor' is home ownership. Approximately one-third of marketable wealth,

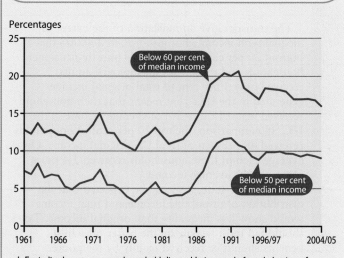

Figure 5 Proportion of people whose income is below 50 and 60 per cent of median income[1]

Percentages

Below 60 per cent of median income

Below 50 per cent of median income

1961   1966   1971   1976   1981   1986   1991   1996/97   2004/05

1. Equivalised contemporary household disposable income before deduction of housing costs.
2. Data from 1993/94 onwards are for financial years. Source of data changed in 1994/95, definition of income changed slightly and geographic coverage changed from United Kingdom to Great Britain. Geographic coverage changed from Great Britain to United Kingdom in 2002/03.

Source: adapted from *Social Trends*, Office for National Statistics.

workforce to raise children. However, despite equal pay legislation, it is unlikely that all of the difference in pay between males and females can be explained in this way and therefore horizontal inequity can be said to exist between males and females.

Another measure of horizontal inequity is the North-South divide in the UK. Table 5 shows gross disposable income per head in different regions in 2005. The South East had the highest average disposable income whilst the North East had the lowest. The difference in purchasing power is likely to be less than that implied by Table 5 because of lower prices, for instance for houses in areas outside the South.

Absolute and relative poverty

Absolute poverty is rare in the UK. One possible indicator of poverty is the number of people sleeping rough on any one night, which in England was estimated at 498 in June 2005. If there is little absolute poverty in the UK, there is, by the definition of the term, relative poverty. One common measure is to see how many people are living at or below a fraction of average income. Figure 5 shows the percentage of people whose income is below 60 per cent and 50 per cent of median income. It shows that relative poverty grew significantly in the 1980s but has since fallen.

There are those who point out that using a percentage of average income to define poverty means that, almost certainly, poverty can never be eradicated. They argue that, say, relative to our Victorian ancestors, nearly all in the UK today enjoy a very high standard of living. On the other hand, data such as in Figure 5 does show that inequality varies over time. Margaret Thatcher's government, as part of its supply side reforms, deliberately set out to increase inequalities in the 1980s and succeeded. Despite a wide range of measures aimed at tackling poverty since 1997, the Labour government under Tony Blair broadly failed to reduce relative poverty if this is measured as the proportion of people whose income is below 50 per cent of the average

DataQuestion

Equity and inequality

Figure 6 *Proportion of households of different economic type within income quintiles[1], 2005-06*

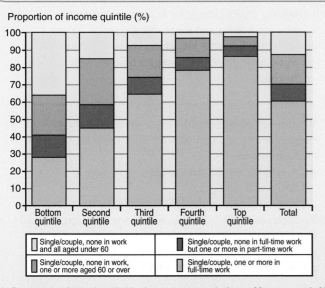

1. For example, of those households whose income is in the lowest 20 per cent, only 28 per cent of households have a member in full time work (blue bottom part of the bar) whilst 38 per cent (yellow top part of the bar from 62 per cent to 100 per cent) are households where none are in work and all are aged below 60.

Source: adapted from *Households Below Average Income, Department for Work and Pensions.*

Figure 7 *Average[1] individual income[2]: by sex and age, 2004-05*

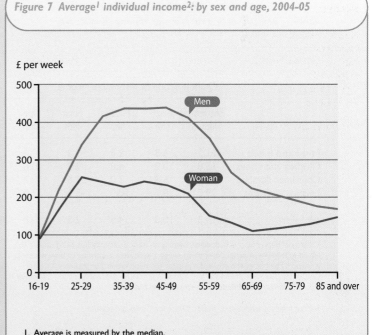

1. Average is measured by the median.
2. Income is total income which includes income from work, benefits, pensions and interest on savings.

Source: adapted from *Social Trends, Office for National Statistics.*

Table 6 The distribution of children by ethnic group by household disposable income[1], 2005-2006

Percentage of children

Ethnic group	Bottom quintile %	Second quintile %	Middle quintile %	Fourth quintile %	Top quintile %	All children %	millions
White	23	24	21	18	14	100	11.1
Mixed	29	37	20	8	6	100	0.1
Asian or Asian British	46	24	11	10	8	100	0.9
of which							
Indian	27	24	16	16	18	100	0.3
Pakistani/ Bangladeshi	60	24	8	5	2	100	0.5
Black or Black British	39	22	17	12	10	100	0.5
of which							
Black Caribbean	39	18	22	14	7	100	0.2
Black Non-Caribbean	39	24	15	11	12	100	0.3
Chinese or other ethnic group	36	18	19	10	17	100	0.2
All children	25	24	20	17	13	100	12.8

1. For example, 23 per cent of white children in 2005-06 lived in households which had disposable incomes in the bottom 20 per cent of the income distribution. 14 per cent of white children lived in the most affluent 20 per cent of households by income distribution. Adding the percentages across the table comes to 100 per cent.

Source: adapted from *Households Below Average Income*, Department for Work and Pensions.

Table 7 Relative deprivation score[1] among families with children, 2004

Great Britain   Percentages

	Quintile group of disposable income				
	Bottom fifth	Next fifth	Middle fifth	Next fifth	Top fifth
Food and meals	11.2	6.8	2.8	1.3	0.4
Clothes and shoes	15.0	10.9	4.8	2.3	0.6
Consumer durables	10.1	6.8	3.0	1.5	0.7
Leisure activities	29.0	20.7	10.0	5.3	2.0
All items	14.5	10.0	4.5	2.3	0.8

1. Material deprivation is defined as wanting an item or activity but being unable to afford it. Relative material deprivation weights each item according to how widely it is owned. The higher the score the greater the deprivation. For example 11.1 per cent of families with children in the bottom quintile by disposable income reported that they suffered deprivation in terms of food and meals.

Source: adapted from Social Trends, Office for National Statistics.

Life changes

Change can have an important effect on your income. For instance, the National Institute for Economic and Social Research (NIESR) produced evidence in the 1990s that more than half of females who separate from their partner see a significant fall in their income. They fall down the income league by at least one quintile. Splitting up is likely to be less harmful to income if you are a male. Only one quarter of males move into a lower quintile grouping after a break up. The other single most important factor which is likely to lead to a loss of income is moving away from home. Over half of children who leave the parental home fall down the income league by at least one quintile.

Equally, for women and for working couples, having a child is likely to lead to a loss of income as one parent stops working or drops down to part-time working to look after the child.

1. What types of households, experience, and what changes are most likely to lead to, (a) low incomes and (b) high incomes?
2. Analyse whether the data suggest that there is
   (a) horizontal equity and
   (b) vertical equity in the UK.
3. Since the mid-1980s, UK governments have encouraged working individuals to make private provision for their pensions. Discuss whether this is likely to reduce poverty in the UK in the next 50 years.

3.3.4, 3.3.5

Summary

1. Governments redistribute income and wealth because they believe that this will increase economic welfare.
2. They can do this through fiscal means, raising taxes from the relatively well off to spend on services and benefits for the relatively less well off.
3. Governments can also legislate to promote greater equality, for instance through passing equal pay legislation or imposing minimum wages.
4. Some economists argue that redistribution gives rise to large welfare losses. These include lower economic growth and higher unemployment. They conclude that the poor would be better off in the long term without any redistribution of income and wealth by government.
5. Other economists argue that there is little or no evidence to suggest that economies where government redistributes a considerable proportion of income and wealth perform any differently from more free market economies.
6. Critics of the market approach reply that many groups in society, such as the handicapped and the elderly, can only enjoy rising living standards if government deliberately intervenes in their favour.

The distribution of income and wealth

Free market forces give rise to a particular distribution of income and wealth in society. This distribution is unlikely to be either **efficient** or **equitable**. In previous units, we have looked at how government can correct a variety of **market failures**. This unit outlines how government might intervene to make the distribution of income and wealth in society more equitable. The current distribution of income and wealth can be seen by government as undesirable for various reasons.

- **Absolute poverty** Absolute poverty may exist in society. At the extreme, people may be dying on the streets for want of food, shelter or simple medicines.
- **Relative poverty** may be considered too great. The government may consider the gap between rich and poor in society to be too wide.
- **Horizontal equity may not exist.** For instance, men may be paid more for doing the same jobs as women. Workers from ethnic minority groups may be discriminated against in employment and housing.
- The current distribution may be seen to conflict with considerations of **economic efficiency**. For instance, it might be argued that income and wealth differentials need to be increased in order to provide incentives for people to work harder.

The first three of the above arguments suggest that income and wealth differentials should be narrowed. In recent years, however, **supply side economists** have suggested that if income differentials are too narrow, incentives will be too low for workers and risk takers and this could have a negative impact on economic growth rates.

How can governments change the distribution of income and wealth in society?

Government expenditure

Government expenditure can be used to alter the distribution of income. One obvious way is for government to provide monetary benefits to those requiring financial support. Social security and national insurance benefits now account for over 30 per cent of UK government expenditure.

However, governments may wish to target help more precisely.

Question 1

The government is proposing to move towards a system of road pricing in the UK in an attempt to solve problems of congestion on British roads. There is a variety of technologies available which might be used, one of which is a meter installed in a car which would read signals from road side beacons or gantries across the road. There is also a variety of possible metering tariffs. One is that road users will be charged for the use of roads only when roads are congested or likely to be congested. For instance, motorists might be charged to use main roads into town and city centres at peak rush hour times, or cities might charge motorists to use roads in the centre at any time of the day. Congested motorways, such as the M25, might be tolled for much of the day.

(a) To what extent is access to a road system which is free at the point of use an issue of equality of opportunity?
(b) How would the distribution of income change if the government imposed congestion metering whilst at the same time: (i) cutting the basic rate of income tax by the amount raised in the new road taxes; (ii) using the money raised from the new road taxes to subsidise public transport?

For instance, an increase in the old age pension will not necessarily relieve absolute poverty amongst some old people. They may live in houses which are damp and cold and be unable or unwilling to pay considerable sums of money to remedy the situation, so the government may choose to spend money on housing for the elderly, for instance providing low rent housing or offering renovation grants for owner-occupied property. Similarly, governments may choose to help children in need not by increasing child benefit but by offering free clothes or food coupons.

Another important area of government activity is the provision of goods and services which give citizens equality of opportunity in society. The Beveridge Report of 1942 argued that citizens should have access to a minimum standard of health care, housing and education as well as minimum incomes and employment. Some argue that education, housing and health care are no different from cars or holidays. If people have a high income, they should be able to buy better education for their children and better health care for themselves, just as they can buy better cars or more expensive holidays. Others argue that all people should have equal access to the **same** education and health care because these are basic to any standard of living in a modern industrialised economy. Private education and private health care should not be available to those who are capable of affording them.

Taxation

The taxation system plays a crucial role in determining the distribution of income in society. Taxes can be classified according to their incidence as a proportion of income.

A PROGRESSIVE TAX is a tax where the proportion of income paid in tax rises as the income of the taxpayer rises. For instance, income tax would be progressive if a worker earning £4 000 a year were to pay 5 per cent of income in tax, but 25 per cent on income of £ 40 000.

A REGRESSIVE TAX is a tax where the proportion of income paid in tax falls as the income of the taxpayer rises. An extreme example of a regressive tax was the poll tax in the UK between 1990 and 1992. The amount paid in poll tax was identical for most poll tax payers. A person earning £8 000 per year and paying £400 a year in poll tax paid exactly the same amount as a person earning £40 000, so the proportion of tax paid was different - 5 per cent of income for the person earning £8 000 a year (£400 ÷ £8 000), but only 1 per cent for the person earning £40 000 a year (£400 ÷ £40 000).

A PROPORTIONAL TAX is one where the proportion paid in tax remains the same while the income of the taxpayer changes (although the actual amount paid increases as income increases). VAT is an example of a broadly proportional tax. Whilst lower income earners spend a higher proportion of their income on zero-rated goods and services, higher income earners tend to save more of their income. Hence, the average rate of VAT paid by individuals tends to be a little less than 17.5 per cent.

The distinction between progressive, regressive and proportional taxes is made because it is important in the study of the distribution of income and wealth. The more progressive the tax, the greater the link with ability to pay the tax and the more likely it is to result in a redistribution of resources from the better off in society to the less well off.

Legislation

The government may alter the distribution of income directly through its spending and taxation decisions. However, it can also influence the behaviour of private economic agents through

---

Question 2

Between 1979 and 2008, the government introduced a number of tax changes. These included:

- in 1979, a reduction in the highest rate of income tax from 83 per cent to 60 per cent and a 2p cut in the standard rate of income tax, accompanied by an increase in the standard rate of VAT from 8 to 15 per cent;
- in 1987, a reduction in the highest rate of income tax from 60 per cent to 40 per cent and a further 2p cut in the standard rate of income tax;
- between 1990 and 1993, the replacement of the domestic rating system, a tax on property, by the council tax, another tax on property but which effectively reduced the tax on high priced properties and increased it for low priced properties. At the same time, VAT was raised by 2½ per cent to reduce average tax bills;
- between 1994 and 2000, the gradual abolition of income tax relief given to those who had taken out a mortgage to buy a home;
- in 1999, the introduction of Working Families Tax Credit, replaced by Child Credit and Working Tax Credit in 2003, a tax benefit to workers on low to median incomes with children to support.

(a) Explain the likely effect of these tax changes on the distribution of income in the UK.

Question 3

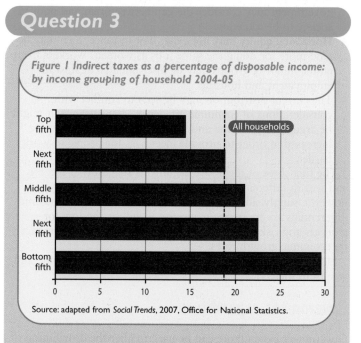

Figure 1 Indirect taxes as a percentage of disposable income: by income grouping of household 2004-05

Source: adapted from *Social Trends*, 2007, Office for National Statistics.

(a) Explain what is meant by an indirect tax.
(b) Analyse whether indirect taxes in the UK are progressive or regressive according to the data.

legislation. For instance, governments may choose to introduce minimum wage legislation, forcing employers to increase rates of pay for the lowest paid workers. They may also choose to make discrimination illegal through measures such as equal pay legislation, or they may force employers to provide benefits such as sickness benefit, pensions and medical care for their employees, or redundancy payments. They may attempt to raise the incomes of the low paid and the unemployed through effective retraining or helping workers to be more mobile geographically.

The costs of redistribution

Intervention in the economy may well lead to higher economic welfare for some, but it may also lead to lower economic welfare for others.

There is an obvious cost to those in society who lose directly from increased taxation. Some economists argue that any taxation results in a loss of freedom. The taxpayer loses the ability to choose how to allocate those scarce resources which are now being expropriated by the state. Therefore in a free society taxation should be kept to an absolute minimum. On the other hand, the LAW OF DIMINISHING MARGINAL UTILITY would suggest that taking resources away from an affluent individual to give to a poor person will lead to an increase in the combined utility of the two individuals. This law states that the higher the spending of individuals, the less utility or satisfaction they get by spending an extra pound. For instance, an extra £10 a week to a poor family would give them more utility than getting an extra £10 a week having suddenly won £1 million on the lottery. The law implies, for instance, that £1 spent on a coffee by a high income earner in the UK gives less utility than £1 spent on food by a poor individual in Bangladesh, so the implication is that redistributing income from the rich to the poor increases total utility because the loss of utility by the rich person will be less than the gain in utility by the poor person. One of the problems with this approach is that the law of marginal utility refers specifically to spending changes by a single individual. One pound is worth less to an individual earning £1 million a year than if she were only earning £5 000 a year. The law in its strictest sense cannot be used to compare income changes between individuals because it is not possible to make direct utility comparisons between individuals.

Classical or supply side economists would suggest that redistribution involves heavy costs in terms of economic growth and employment. Raising income tax rates lowers the incentives of those in employment to work, thus reducing the rate at which the aggregate supply curve shifts to the right. Classical economists would also argue that redistribution reduces the incentive of those out of work to find jobs. High unemployment benefits can make it more worthwhile to remain unemployed than to gain employment. This raises the natural rate of unemployment and depresses the level of output in the economy. Minimum wage legislation and equal pay legislation may lead to a loss of employment. Economic theory suggests that if firms are forced to pay higher wages, they will employ fewer staff. High tax rates can lead to a flight of capital and labour from an economy. Individual entrepreneurs may choose to leave the country, taking their money and skills with them. Firms may choose to locate abroad to take advantage of lower tax rates, leading to a loss of domestic jobs and income.

There is also a host of other distortions which become endemic in the system. For example, subsiding rents of council houses can lead to greater immobility of labour because those renting properties cannot afford to rent in another area. Subsidising an essential commodity like petrol can lead to greater greenhouse gas emissions and more congestion. High taxes lead to the growth of tax avoidance and evasion where a considerable amount of resources is devoted to circumventing tax legislation.

The role of government

Free market economists argue that the costs of government intervention are extremely large. They are so large in fact that any possible welfare benefits resulting from the redistribution of income from the rich to the poor are far outweighed by the welfare losses which result. They argue that economic growth will increase if taxation is low, if government regulation of the economic activities of the private sector is minimal and if state production of goods and services is kept to the barest minimum.

Question 4

Table 1 *Proportion of total income tax paid by different groups of income earners*

United Kingdom					Percentages
	1976-77	1981-82	1990-91	1997-98	2007-08
Top 1 per cent	11	11	15	20	22
Top 5 per cent	25	25	32	37	41
Top 10 per cent	35	35	42	48	52
Next 40 per cent	45	46	43	40	38
Lowest 50 per cent	20	19	15	12	10

Source: adapted from *Social Trends*, Office for National Statistics; www.hmrc.gov.uk

During the 1980s, rates of income tax were lowered. The highest rate of tax effective in 1976-77 was 83 per cent. This was lowered to 60 per cent in 1979 and then 40 per cent in 1987. The basic rate of tax fell during the same period from 33 per cent to 25 per cent. In the 1990s, the basic rate fell to 23 per cent whilst a reduced starting rate of tax of 10 per cent was introduced. However, several tax allowances, amounts of income on which no tax was paid, were abolished. In particular, the allowance given to married people was phased out, as were income tax subsidies on the purchase of homes. There were no significant changes to income tax in the first half of the first decade of the 21st century.

(a) (i) Explain why large cuts in income tax rates on the better off might lead to falls in the proportion of income tax paid by high earners.
   (ii) What actually happened to the proportion of income tax paid by high earners in the 1980s?
   (iii) Suggest TWO reasons why this might have happened and briefly discuss whether it led to an increase in economic welfare.
(b) (i) Why might the abolition of tax allowances on the purchase of homes help explain the trends in income tax paid in the 1990s?
   (ii) Discuss briefly whether this might have led to an increase in economic welfare.

The poor may lose out because there will be little in the way of state benefits, but they will be more than compensated for this through increased economic growth. The wealth generated by the better off in society will **trickle down** to the less fortunate. For instance, the poor would be better off receiving 10 per cent of a 'national cake' of £20 bn than 15 per cent of a cake of only £10 bn.

The argument that the poor would be better off if income differentials were wider rather than narrower is dependent upon a number of propositions:
- that being better off is a matter of absolute quantities rather than relative quantities;
- it must be true that high marginal income tax rates are a disincentive to work and to enterprise;
- a generous benefit system must act as a disincentive to work;
- there must be a mechanism through which increased wealth in society will benefit not just the rich but also the poor, particularly those who, for whatever, reason are unable to work.

This could be the case for many employed people but there is no mechanism apart from charity in a free market economy for groups such as the handicapped, the sick and the elderly to benefit from increased prosperity enjoyed by the rest of society.

Key terms

The law of diminishing marginal utility - for an individual, the satisfaction derived from consuming an extra unit of a good falls the greater the consumption of the good.

Progressive, regressive and proportional taxes - taxes where the proportion of income paid in tax rises, falls or remains the same respectively as income rises.

Question 5

In 1989, the Methodist Conference, the governing body of the Methodist church, attacked the government's 'divisive' social and economic policies which victimised the poor. In reply, the then Prime Minister, Margaret Thatcher, stated: 'Over the past decade living standards have increased at all points of the income distribution - that includes the poorest.'

'After allowing for inflation, a married man with two children who is in the lowest tenth of earnings has seen his take-home pay go up by 12.5 per cent'.

'Of course some have, through their own endeavours and initiative, raised their living standards further. They are also paying more in taxes, and those who earn most are contributing a higher proportion of the total that government receives from income tax'.

'You equate wealth with selfishness. But it is only through the creation of wealth that poverty can be assisted.'

'Our task is to enlarge opportunity so that more and more people may prosper.'

(a) Over the 1980s, the distribution of income became more unequal. Explain how Margaret Thatcher defended this in her reply to the Methodist Conference.

Applied economics

Redistributive policies in the UK

Taxation and spending

The Welfare State, whose foundations were laid down by Clement Attlee's Labour administration of 1945-51, should ensure that every citizen of the UK enjoys a minimum standard of living. To achieve this, higher income earners are taxed more than lower income earners and the money is used to provide a variety of

Table 2 Redistribution of income through taxes and benefits, 2002-03

£ per year and percentages

| | Quintile groups of households[1] | | | | | |
	Bottom fifth	Next fifth	Middle fifth	Next fifth	Top fifth	All households
Average per household						
Wages and salaries	2 450	7 050	14 920	26 650	45 270	19 270
Imputed income from benefits in kind	10	30	110	360	1 110	320
Self-employment income	580	660	1 330	2 390	7 150	2 420
Occupational pensions, annuities	580	1 360	2 200	2 530	3 700	2 070
Investment income	240	360	550	910	2 840	980
Other income	170	150	220	250	250	210
Total original income	4 030	9 610	19 320	33 080	60 310	25 270
plus Benefits in cash						
Contributory	2 520	3 080	2 210	1 420	930	2 030
Non-contributory	3 120	2 930	2 030	1 080	460	1 930
Gross income	9 670	15 630	23 560	35 580	61 700	29 230
less Income tax[2] and NIC[3]	470	1 370	3 320	6 440	13 690	5 060
less Council tax/Northern Ireland rates[4] (net)	440	530	670	830	960	690
Disposable income	8 760	13 730	19 570	28 310	47 050	23 480
less Indirect taxes	2 750	3 140	4 180	5 340	6 990	4 480
Post-tax income	6 010	10 590	15 390	22 970	40 060	19 000
plus Benefits in kind						
Education	2 500	1 770	1 620	1 520	850	1 650
National Health Service	2 980	3 030	2 630	2 360	2 120	2 620
Housing subsidy	80	70	40	20	-	40
Travel subsidies	70	60	60	70	100	70
School meals and welfare milk	80	30	10	-	-	20
Final income	11 710	15 550	19 750	26 940	43 130	23 410
Household type (percentages)[5]						
Retired	41	42	20	10	4	23
Non-retired without children						
1 adult no children	17	9	10	14	20	14
2 adults no children	8	10	19	28	38	21
3 adults no children	3	6	7	10	10	7
All other households without children	3	3	6	7	5	5
Non-retired with children						
1 adult with children	14	5	5	3	1	6
2 adults with children	11	18	26	23	20	20
3 adults or more with children	2	4	5	4	2	3
All other households with children	1	2	1	1	0	1
All household types	100	100	100	100	100	100

1. Equivalised disposable income has been used for ranking the households.
2. After tax relief at source on mortgage interest and life assurance premiums.
3. Employees' National Insurance contributions.
4. Council tax net of council tax benefits. Rates net of rebates in Northern Ireland.
5. Figures may not add up to 100 due to rounding.
Source: adapted from Social Trends, Office for National Statistics.

Table 3 *Taxes as a percentage of gross income by quintile group for all households, tax credits treated wholly as a benefit, 2003-04*

	Quintile groups of all households					All households
	Bottom	2nd	3rd	4th	Top	
Percentages of gross income						
Direct taxes						
Income tax[1]	3.8	7.2	10.7	13.9	18.4	13.9
Employees' NIC	1.4	2.8	4.4	5.3	4.6	4.3
Council tax & Northern Ireland rates[2]	4.9	3.6	3.0	2.5	1.7	2.5
All direct taxes	10.1	13.6	18.2	21.7	24.6	20.7
Indirect taxes						
VAT	10.6	8.0	7.3	6.3	4.9	6.3
Duty on alcohol	1.5	1.2	1.1	0.9	0.6	0.9
Duty on tobacco	3.2	1.8	1.3	0.9	0.4	1.0
Duty on hydrocarbon oils & vehicle excise	2.9	2.4	2.3	2.1	1.4	1.9
Other indirect taxes	9.6	6.6	5.6	4.8	3.6	4.9
All indirect taxes	27.9	20.0	17.6	15.0	10.0	15.1
All taxes	38.0	33.6	35.8	36.7	35.5	35.8

1. After tax relief at source on mortgage interest and life assurance premiums.
2. Council tax, domestic rates and water charges after deducting discounts, council tax benefit and rate rebates.

Source: adapted from www.statistics.gov.uk.

benefits in kind and in cash.

Table 2 is an ONS (Office for National Statistics) estimate of how this redistribution affects incomes. It is based on figures from the Family Expenditure Survey, a yearly sample of approximately 7 000 households in the UK. The households have been split into quintile groups (i.e. fifths) according to original incomes of households. For instance, the bottom fifth of households ranked by original income had an original income of just £4 030 per year. The top fifth of households had an original income of £60 310, earning on average 15 times as much.

These sharp inequalities are reduced through the effects of the tax and benefit system. Benefits in cash, contributory (i.e. National Insurance benefits) and non-contributory benefits increase the incomes of the bottom quintile of income earners from £4 030 to £9 670 a year. Whilst many benefits are targeted on low income households, some benefits are universal benefits, available to all whatever their income. The most important universal benefit is child benefit.

Benefits have to be paid for by taxes and National Insurance contributions (NICs). The tax system is often considered to be **progressive**. However, as Table 2 and 3 show, it is in practice arguably regressive. The indirect tax system is clearly regressive. For instance, the bottom fifth of households paid 27.9 per cent of their gross income in indirect taxes whilst the top fifth paid only 10.9 per cent. In contrast, direct taxes, including the council tax are progressive. The bottom

fifth of households paid 10.1 per cent of their gross income in direct taxes, whilst the top fifth paid 24.6 per cent. Overall, as Table 2 shows, whilst the top fifth of households received 15 times the amount of original income compared to the bottom fifth of households, in terms of post-tax income it was 6.7 times and as final income the ratio was only 3.7 times, so it would seem that the Welfare State is successful to some extent in reducing inequalities in society.

Government policy over time

Tables 2 and 3 illustrate the position in 2002-04. However, income inequalities change over time. As Figure 3 (in the data question) shows, during the 1960s and 1970s the percentage of individuals below half of median income fluctuated between 3 and 7 per cent. The 1980s saw a radical change, with levels of inequality rising sharply. Partly this was due to changing patterns of pay in the labour market, where higher income earners saw substantial pay increases over the decade whilst those in unskilled and semi-skilled jobs saw little if any change in their real pay. Partly, though, it was due to government policy.

- In the labour market, government policies which reduced trade union power and saw the eventual abolition of minimum wages left lower paid workers more exposed to downward pressures on pay.
- The rise in unemployment, from one and half million in 1979 to three and half million by 1986, impoverished those made unemployed and put further downward pressure on the wages of the least skilled. Throughout the 1980s, the government allowed unemployment to rise to whatever level it thought was necessary to contain inflation. Unemployment and the poverty that it brought with it were seen as a price to pay for low inflation.
- In the early 1980s, government cut the link between rises in state benefits, including pensions, and rises in wages established in the 1970s. Instead, rises in benefits were fixed to rises in prices. Given that real wages rise on average by 2.5 per cent per year, this has led to an ever widening gap between those on benefits and those in work.
- Tax changes such as the reduction of income tax paid for by an increase in VAT in 1979, the fall in the top rate of tax to 40 per cent in 1987 and the introduction of the poll tax in the late 1980s all helped to widen post tax income differentials from what they would otherwise have been.

Since 1997 and the election of the first Labour government in 18 years, there has been a commitment to reducing poverty, inequality and social exclusion. Figure 2 shows 12 objectives of government relating to poverty, inequality and social exclusion published in its Comprehensive Spending Review in October 2007. In the short term, the main thrust of government policy was to encourage those out of work to get a job. More was spent on government training schemes for the unemployed. Tax credits were introduced for the low paid to increase their after tax income. A minimum wage was introduced.

In the longer term, the government wanted to increase the employability and skills of the workforce in the future through increased spending on education and training today. Education has a long pay back period and the benefits of improved education will only begin to appear over the next 10 or 20 year period.

The government also remained committed to targeting state benefits more carefully. This meant either narrowing the number of people who were entitled to a state benefit, or means testing it (i.e. making it payable only to those below a certain level of income).

Reform of pensions proved more difficult. With an aging population, pensions have to be affordable to society in twenty or thirty years time when the bulge of 'baby boomers', born between the end of the second world war and the mid 1960s, are retired. On the other hand, pensioners have traditionally been poor. After much debate, in 2004 the Labour government announced that by 2012, there would be a significant one step increase in the state old age pension and increases would become linked to average earnings rather than average prices as at present. This would help lift many future pensioners who had no other pensions out of poverty, but it would partly be paid for by raising the state pension retirement age eventually to 68 by 2044. People would have to work longer. Decisions about state pensions took place against a backdrop of many private sector employers closing their occupational pension schemes to employers, so, the 2004 government reforms also stated that there would be compulsory savings for retirement by all workers where they were not paying into an employer's scheme. Employers would have to pay in 3 per cent of wages, employees 4 per cent and the government 1 per cent making a total saving of 8 per cent of wages.

Housing is also a major cause of poverty. In 2006, there were 100 000 households classified as homeless and in temporary accommodation provided by local authorities. Just under half of those had been in temporary accommodation for more than 6 months. In 2006, there were also 1.4 million adults living in overcrowded accommodation according to official statistics. Government policy has been to increase the numbers of houses offered for rent by social landlords whilst encouraging the growth of private rented accommodation. However, it has been frustrated in seeing sufficient growth in the overall supply of housing by its own planning restrictions and the strength of the rural and environmental lobbies. Insufficient growth of supply has driven house prices

to unaffordable levels for the relatively low paid. It could be argued that without the removal of some planning restrictions and a very large increase in the number of new dwellings built, housing will continue to be a major source of poverty and inequality in the future.

In general, the Labour government targeted certain groups in poverty: pensioners, one parent families, the out of work and children. As Figure 3 (in the data question) shows, the government had very limited success. The proportion of people today whose income is below both 50 per cent and 60 per cent of median income is substantially higher than in 1961 and 1981, although below 1991 levels.

At best, though, such policies can only eliminate absolute poverty and reduce relative poverty. In a free market economy, too little income inequality reduces incentives to work to such an extent that the economy ceases to function efficiently. In former command economies such as the Soviet Union, for instance, workers subverted the official system by getting second jobs in the illegal informal sector. Inequality is therefore desirable within limits.

Figure 2 Government objectives relating to poverty, inequality and social exclusion, October 2007

- Improve the skills of the population, on the way to ensuring a world-class skills base by 2020.
- Raise the education achievement of all children and young people.
- Narrow the gap in educational achievement between children from low-income and disadvantaged backgrounds and their peers.
- Increase the number of children and young people on the path to success.
- Maximise employment opportunity for all.
- Halve the number of children in poverty by 2010-11, on the way to eradicating child poverty by 2020.
- Address the disadvantage that individuals experience because of their gender, race, disability, age, sexual orientation, religion or belief.
- Increase the proportion of socially excluded adults in settled accommodation and employment, education or training.
- Tackle poverty and promote greater independence and well-being in later life.
- Promote better health and well-being for all.
- Increase long-term housing supply and affordability.
- Reduce the harm caused by alcohol and drugs.

Source: adapted from *Comprehensive Spending Review*, HM Treasury.

DataQuestion

Poverty in the UK

Defining poverty

The Joseph Rowntree Foundation defines a household as being in income poverty if its income is less than 60 per cent of the UK median household income. In 2005/06, this was worth £108 per week for a single adult, £186 per week for a couple with no dependent children, £223 per week for a lone parent with two dependent children and £301 per week with two dependent children. Disposable income is income after Income Tax, National Insurance contributions, Council Tax and housing costs have been deducted. The Joseph Rowntree Foundation is a social policy research and development charity.

Unemployment

Unemployment in the UK is now much lower than in many other EU countries, but those officially defined and counted as 'unemployed' do not account for all those who would like a job. A second, larger, group is those wanting work but who are not available either to start work in the next two weeks or who have not been actively seeking work in the last four weeks. Such people are termed 'the economically inactive who want work'. Whilst in 2006 there were 0.9 million adults aged 25 and over officially unemployed, there 1.5 million adults over 25 who were economically inactive but wanting work.

Almost half of all those aged 25 to retirement not in work have a disability which limits the nature of the work they can undertake.

Single adult households are far more likely than two adult ones to be workless (i.e. where no adult in the household has a job). Two fifths of lone parent households are workless, around seven times the rate for couple households. Among households without children, a quarter of single adult households are workless, around four times the rate for couple households.

Figure 3 Proportion of people whose income is below 60% and 50% of median income

Source: adapted from *Social Trends*, Office for National Statistics.

Changing poverty

The number of people living in poverty rose between 2004/05 and 2005/06 by around three-quarters of a million, to almost 13 million. This is the first time that the numbers in poverty have risen since 1996/97. At best, this indicates that progress to reduce poverty has stalled.

Over the last decade, the proportion of both children and pensioners in poverty has fallen whilst the proportion of working-age adults in poverty has remained unchanged. As a result, the pension poverty rate is now lower than the poverty rate for working-age adults - an historic shift - and more than half of the people now in poverty are working age adults.

Child poverty

3.8 million children were living in poverty in 2005/06. Half of these lived in working families and half in workless ones. Three-fifths lived in couple families while two-fifths lived with a lone parent. Of those living in households where there was a wage earner, four-fifths lived with both parents and one fifth with one parent. Of those living in households where no one worked, two thirds lived with just one parent.

Health

There are substantial inequalities in health between income levels and social classes. For example, among men aged 45-64, 45 per cent of those in the poorest fifth report a long-standing illness or disability, compared to 25 per cent for men on average incomes, and only 10 per cent of men in the richest fifth in the income range. The rate of infant death among social classes 1 to 4 is around 4 per 1 000 live births compared to 5.5 for those in social classes 5-8. Average incomes in social classes 1- 4 are higher than in 5-8.

Education

The proportion of 16-year-olds who obtained fewer than five GCSEs in 2005/06 (11 per cent) was the same as in 1999/00. 33 per cent of white 16-year-old boys in receipt of free schools meals failed to get five 'good' GCSEs (grade C or above), a far higher proportion than for any other combination of ethnic group, gender and free school meal entitlement.

People in their late 20s with no qualifications face a far higher risk than their peers of unemployment: 18 per cent compared with an average of 5 per cent. Anyone possessing at least A-levels or their nearest vocational equivalent (NVQ3) faces a below-average risk of being unemployed in their late 20s. By contrast, only graduates face a below-average risk of still being low paid by their late 20s: 10 per cent compared with an average of 25 per cent. The risk for those with no qualifications is more than 50 per cent.

Source: adapted from Joseph Rowntree Foundation , Monitoring poverty and social exclusion 2005 by Guy Palmer, Jane Carr and Peter Kenway; Monitoring poverty and social exclusion 2007 by Guy Palmer, Tom MacInnes and Peter Kenway.

Proposals to reduce poverty

Members of a private think tank have come up with a number of different ways to reduce poverty in the UK.

- Raise the minimum wage to £8.00 an hour.
- Raise the state old age pension and the limits below which pensioners can claim means tested benefits by £50 a week per pensioner on average.
- Raise child benefit by £15 per child per week.
- Raise the Job Seekers' Allowance by an average of £50 per week per worker.
- Cut the standard rate of income tax by 2p in the pound.
- Cut the higher rate of income tax from 40p in the pound to 30p in the pound.
- Provide free 24 hour nursery care and creche facilities for workers.
- Cut all benefits to workers able to work but not in work.
- Increase government spending on education and training by 10 per cent.

You have been asked to evaluate the various proposals for reducing poverty put forward by the private think tank.
1. Outline the characteristics of poverty in the UK,
2. Take each proposal and explain why it might have an impact on poverty. Assess its advantages and disadvantages as a policy measure.
3. Put forward ONE other proposal of your own for the relief of poverty and assess its costs and benefits;
4. Assess which of the proposals, or combination of proposals, is most likely to reduce poverty without imposing too great a cost on the economy.

The business cycle

Summary

1. Business cycles have been a feature of capitalist economies in the 19th and 20th centuries.
2. The business cycle has four phases - boom, recession, slump and recovery.
3. The business cycle can be explained using the AD/AS model of the economy.
4. The multiplier-accelerator theory states that cycles are caused by the interaction of the Keynesian multiplier and the accelerator theory of investment.
5. The inventory cycle theory argues that cycles are caused by regular fluctuations in the levels of stocks in the economy.
6. Long wave cycles have been explained by changes in construction levels and by changes in technology.
7. Monetarists believe that trade cycles are caused by changes in the money supply.

Characteristics of cycles

It has long been observed in economics that income and employment tend to fluctuate regularly over time. These regular fluctuations are known as **business cycles**, **trade cycles** or **economic cycles**. Figure 1 shows the various stages of a traditional cycle, such as occurred during the 19th century, during the 1930s or during the 1970s and 1980s in the UK.

- **Peak or boom**. When the economy is at a peak or is in a boom, national income is high. It is likely that the economy will be working at beyond full employment. **Overheating** is therefore present (although the economy could be at less than full employment, according to Keynesians, if there are bottlenecks in certain industries in the economy). Consumption and investment expenditure will be high. Tax revenues will be high. Wages will be rising and profits increasing. The country will be sucking in imports demanded by consumers with high incomes and businesses with full order books. There will also be inflationary pressures in the economy.

- **Downturn**. When the economy moves into a downturn, output and income fall, leading to a fall in consumption and investment. Tax revenues begin to fall and government expenditure on benefits begins to rise. Wage demands moderate as unemployment rises. Imports decline and

inflationary pressures ease.

- **Recession or depression or trough or slump**. At the bottom of the cycle, the economy is said to be in a recession or depression or trough or slump. Economic activity is at a low in comparison with surrounding years. Mass unemployment exists, so consumption, investment and imports will be low. There will be few inflationary pressures in the economy and prices may be falling (there will be **deflation** in the strict sense of the term).

- **Recovery or expansion**. As the economy moves into a recovery or expansion phase, national income and output begin to increase. Unemployment falls. Consumption, investment and imports begin to rise. Workers feel more confident about demanding wage increases and inflationary pressures begin to mount.

In the UK the government defines recession as where GDP falls in at least two successive quarters. During the 1950s and 1960s and since the mid-1990s, the UK saw much milder trade cycles, as shown in Figure 2. National income did not fall but there were regular fluctuations in the rate of economic growth. A recession occurred when the rate of economic growth fell. Recovery or expansion was present when the growth rate picked up again. The economy was in a boom when economic growth

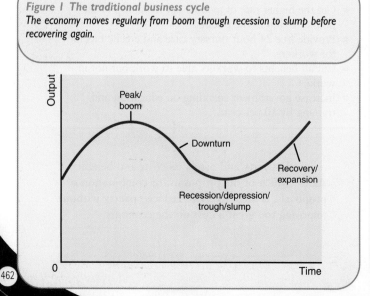

Figure 1 The traditional business cycle
The economy moves regularly from boom through recession to slump before recovering again.

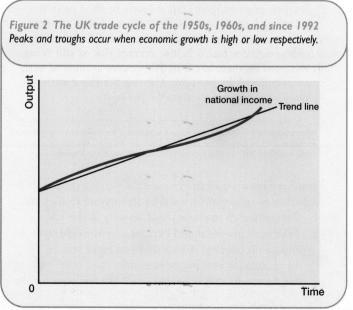

Figure 2 The UK trade cycle of the 1950s, 1960s, and since 1992
Peaks and troughs occur when economic growth is high or low respectively.

was at its highest compared to surrounding years. There were troughs too when growth was particularly low but they were not really 'slumps' in the traditional sense. In the post-war period in the UK, the business cycle has tended to last four or five years from peak to peak. This contrasts with longer seven to nine year cycles in the 19th century. Some economists have claimed that there are longer 50 year KONDRATIEV CYCLES, so named after the Russian economist who first put forward the idea.

Question 1

Table 1

	Growth of GDP %	Investment (£bn at 1985 prices)	Balance of payments current balance (£bn at 1985 prices)	Unemployment (millions)
1978	2.9	54.9	1.7	1.4
1979	2.8	56.5	- 0.9	1.3
1980	- 2.0	53.4	3.9	1.6
1981	- 1.2	48.3	8.4	2.5
1982	1.7	50.9	5.4	2.9

(a) Identify the four phases of the business cycle from the data.

Output gaps

Business cycles are movements around the long term trend rate of growth of an economy. At the height of a boom output is likely to be above what its long term growth rate would predict. In a recession it will be below it. The **output gap** measures the difference between the actual level of output and its trend level. In Figure 3 there is a negative output gap at 0A in a recession because actual output is below the trend level. There is a positive output gap at 0A, when the economy is in boom, because actual output is above its trend level.

Hysteresis

Figure 3 might suggest that there is little cost associated with fluctuations in the level of activity. Output lost in a recession is regained during a boom, leaving the economy no better or worse off in the long term. However, there are possible other costs.

● Those made unemployed during a recession, however mild, suffer a loss in their income even if the majority of workers are unaffected.
● Those on fixed incomes suffer in a boom if inflation rises. Their spending power is eroded because of higher prices.
● Some economists argue that in a deep recession, economies do not bounce back to their previous trend level of growth. This is an example of HYSTERESIS. Instead, the economy remains at a lower level of output, albeit still growing at its previous trend rate. In Figure 4, the economy starts off on a trend growth path of AA. However, a deep recession with its trough at 0R means that the economy only booms at a level consistent with a lower growth path of BB. The economy then suffers another deep recession with a trough at 0S. The trend line of growth shifts down to CC. After this, the business cycle is much shallower and actual output fluctuates around the trend line of CC. One reason why an economy may fail to recover fully from a deep recession is that there is a permanent loss of human capital. In a recession, millions can lose their jobs. Some take early retirement, with a consequent loss of output for the economy. Others suffer long periods of unemployment and become deskilled. They are therefore less productive than before. Another reason is that there can be a permanent loss of physical capital. In a recession, firms cut back on their investment. If they fail to make this up in the next boom, there is less physical capital in the economy than would otherwise have been the case. Potential output must then fall.

Business cycle models

Business cycle models can be divided into two types. **Exogenous models** argue that business cycles are started by a shock to the economic system, such as wars, revolutions, gold discoveries or large movements of population. It could be argued that the

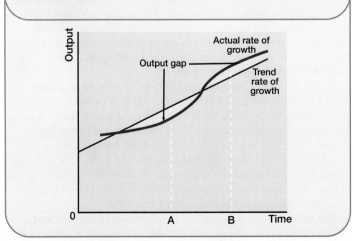

Figure 3 Output gaps
At OA there is a negative output gap because the actual level of output is below the trend level of output. At OB, it is positive because output is above its trend level.

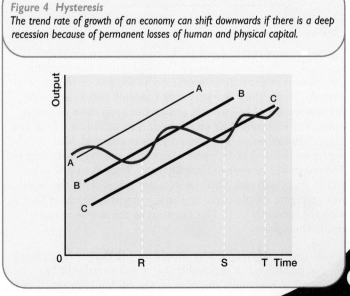

Figure 4 Hysteresis
The trend rate of growth of an economy can shift downwards if there is a deep recession because of permanent losses of human and physical capital.

four-fold increase in the price of oil in 1973-74 gave a significant supply side shock to world economies. These effects rippled through time until economies returned to equilibrium. **Endogenous theories** argue that trade cycles are caused by factors which lie within the economic system. Even if there were no supply side shocks, the economy would fluctuate regularly over time, although the fluctuations might be quite mild.

Question 2

Explain how a major world recession, an exogenous shock to the UK economy, could trigger a business cycle.

Aggregate demand and aggregate supply analysis

The business cycle can be explained using aggregate demand and aggregate supply analysis. Consider Figure 5. The economy is in both short run and long run equilibrium at A.

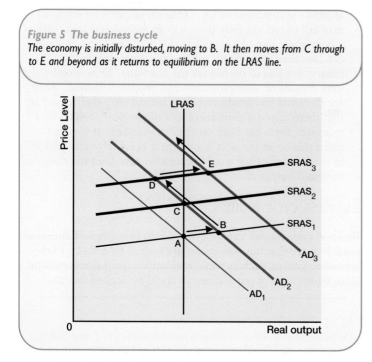

Figure 5 The business cycle
The economy is initially disturbed, moving to B. It then moves from C through to E and beyond as it returns to equilibrium on the LRAS line.

Boom An exogenous shock to the economy now shifts the aggregate demand curve from AD_1 to AD_2. For instance, the government might reduce income tax in the run up to a general election, or the stock market might suddenly boom, increasing the real wealth of households and encouraging them to spend more. The economy now moves from A to B. This is a long run disequilibrium point. The economy has overheated, with aggregate demand being greater than long run aggregate supply. The result will be over-full employment. Wage rates and other factor prices will rise. This rise in factor prices shifts the short run aggregate supply curve upwards, eventually reaching $SRAS_2$, with the economy at C. This ought to be the new long run equilibrium point.

Recession However, why should the SRAS curve stop rising at $SRAS_2$? It is possible that it will overshoot, eventually stopping at, say, $SRAS_3$ with the

economy in recession. It will be the recession which eventually brings wage inflation to a halt, not a possible long run equilibrium position. With the economy in recession, equilibrium output will have fallen, shown on the diagram by D being left of C.

Recovery Eventually, though, there will be an increase in aggregate demand at the given price level. In the move from B to D, consumers and producers have cut their real spending. Consumers will have particularly cut spending on consumer durables whilst firms will have cut investment spending. There comes a point when expenditure on these items has to start rising. Consumers, for instance, having delayed buying new cars, eventually have to replace their old cars. Firms, having deferred new investment spending, have to replace worn out machinery or stop producing. So the AD curve shifts again to the right, producing the upturn in the cycle.

Boom As consumer and business confidence returns, spending further increases to AD_3. But this produces a new short run equilibrium point where the economy is again at over-full employment, a long run disequilibrium position. Wages start to rise, pushing the SRAS curve upwards to produce the downturn in the economy.

Figure 5 shows an economy where the initial demand shock produces smaller and smaller cycles over time. Eventually, the economy will converge to a long run equilibrium position on the long run aggregate supply curve. It is likely that, before this happens, another exogenous shock will have occurred which yet again increases the amplitude of the cycle.

Different schools of economists emphasise different aspects of this basic explanation. Keynesian economists tend to emphasise the change in real variables, such as investment, which then produces fluctuations in output which characterise the business cycle. Monetarist economists tend to emphasise the role of money in the process which leads to fluctuations in prices as well as output. These individual explanations will now be discussed.

The multiplier-accelerator model

One Keynesian explanation of the business cycle is the MULTIPLIER-ACCELERATOR MODEL. The **accelerator theory** of investment says that investment is a function of past changes in income. If national income is growing, so too will investment. This increase in investment will lead to a multiple increase in national income via the **multiplier effect**. This leads to a further increase in investment. Hence the economy keeps on growing. On the other hand, if income falls, so too will investment, feeding through via the multiplier process to a further fall in income. Investment then falls again. The economy is on a downward path.

So far we have a possible explanation of why an economy might grow or contract over time but there is as yet no explanation of the trade cycle in it. There are two ways of using the multiplier-accelerator model to construct a business cycle model. The first is to construct a far more complicated accelerator model than, for instance, the $I_t = k (Y_t - Y_{t-1})$ theory. Some formulations of the accelerator model will produce regular cycles. Whether these formulations are realistic can only be gauged when they are tested against real data.

The other way is to postulate the existence of **ceilings** and **floors** in the cycle. An annual growth rate of 5 to 6 per cent has

Question 3

Table 2 Investment and national income, UK, 1994-2006

			£bn at 2003 prices
	Gross fixed capital formation	Change in gross fixed capital formation	Change in gross domestic product at market prices
1994	124.6	5.5	35.7
1995	128.3	3.7	25.4
1996	135.3	7.0	24.8
1997	144.5	9.2	28.4
1998	164.2	19.8	31.6
1999	169.1	4.9	29.6
2000	173.7	4.6	38.1
2001	178.2	4.5	24.7
2002	184.7	6.5	21.9
2003	186.7	2.0	30.1
2004	197.7	11.0	36.4
2005	200.7	3.0	21.2
2006	217.1	16.4	33.5

(a) According to Keynesian economic theory, a rise in investment will cause a rise in national income (GDP). The multiplier is the number of times that national income will rise from a given increase in income. Changes in other economic variables such as government spending and exports can also have a multiplier effect on income. Would the data support the view that there is a multiplier effect between investment and income?

(b) The accelerator theory suggests that investment is determined by changes in income over previous time periods. Would the data support this theory?

(c) Would the data support the multiplier-accelerator model?

proved unsustainable for the post-war UK economy. The economy moves to full employment and then beyond full employment. There simply isn't any more labour to be hired to sustain the boom. This puts a brake on the economy. As the rate of increase in output slows down, so the rate of growth of investment falls, producing the downturn in the economy. Similarly, national income will not keep falling to zero. At some point firms have to increase investment to replace worn-out machinery. Consumers will increasingly resist falls in their consumption and will be prepared to call on savings or borrow money to prevent their living standards falling even further. This is the turning point for the economy.

Output will begin to rise, pulling up consumption expenditure and encouraging investment expenditure.

The inventory cycle

Another Keynesian explanation of the business cycle is the INVENTORY CYCLE hypothesis. **Inventories** is another name for stocks of raw materials and finished products held by producers. For instance, a car manufacturer will hold stocks of steel, car components and finished cars.

Some economists argue that there is an inventory cycle of

business activity in the economy. Changes in inventories cause regular fluctuations in the level of national income. For instance, assume that the government increases its expenditure in real terms. Firms will initially meet part of the extra demand by supplying goods from existing stocks. So they will need to increase their production levels, firstly to replace those stocks and secondly to meet the continued extra demand from government. This leads to an increase in national income via the multiplier process. Eventually firms will have replenished their stocks to their desired levels. They will then reduce their orders from other firms to the level needed to satisfy long term demand. But this reduction in orders will produce a downturn in the economy via the multiplier process. The economy will only pick up once firms have so run down their stocks that they are forced to increase their orders again.

Question 4

Table 3 Change in stocks and GDP, 1979-1983

		£ billion at 1985 prices
	Increase in stocks and work in progress[1]	GDP[2]
1979	3.3	283.4
1980	- 3.4	277.4
1981	- 3.2	274.3
1982	- 1.3	279.2
1983	1.4	289.2

1. At market prices.
2. At basic prices.
Source: adapted from CSO, *Economic Trends Annual Supplement*.

(a) Explain how the changes in stocks and work in progress might have contributed to the change in GDP over the period 1979-1983.

Long wave cycles

A number of economists have argued that long wave cycles exist. Like the multiplier-accelerator theory and the inventory cycle theory, these theories emphasise that cycles are caused by changes in real variables.

In the inter-war period, Kuznets claimed that there was a 15-20 year building cycle. Economic fluctuations were caused by regular long cycles in building and construction.

Again in the inter-war period, a Russian economist named Kondratiev suggested that 50 year cycles existed. These were caused by lumpiness in the pace of technological change. The idea was further developed by the Austrian economist Schumpeter, who identified waves of technological progress. For instance, in the mid-nineteenth century the development of the railways was a major boost to world demand. In the early part of this century, it was the motor car and electricity that provided the stimulus to technological advance. In the post-war period up to 1970, it was the development of chemicals, plastics, nuclear power and a wide range of electrical consumer goods. Since the 1970s it has been the development of information and communication technology (ICT) and biotechnology.

These waves of innovation produce characteristic cycles. Take the micro-chip revolution. In the 1970s and early 1980s, microchips began to make an impact on products and output. Initially, some new products came onto the market (like calculators). But the biggest impact was on existing products. Costs were cut by incorporating micro-chips into existing machines. This led to a shake out of employment because the new machines could produce more output with less labour.

The world economy moved to slump both in the mid- 1970s following an oil price shock, and again in the early 1980s. On both occasions, unemployment rose substantially and remained at very high levels historically. By the mid-1990s, however, the USA economy was beginning to grow at historically high rates with falling unemployment. The 1980s and the 1990s were decades of high unemployment. The long wave cycle hypothesis would suggest that the new products appearing on the market - ranging from integrated home entertainment equipment providing digital television, internet capability with CD and games facilities, to new biotechnological drugs to cars running on non-oil based fuels - would lead to an upturn in the world economy early in the 21st century. The USA, the world's technological leader, had already begun to enjoy the benefits of the long term upswing in the second half of the 1990s, with other countries following later. By 2010 to 2020, the boom will begin to falter as exciting new products will be more difficult to invent. So economic growth rates will begin to fall. The economy will then be in its recession phase. By 2020-30, the economy will be again approaching a slump which should occur in the 2030s. Once again new technologies will emerge, but they will only help lift the world economy from recession by the 2040s.

A monetarist explanation

Milton Friedman has suggested that trade cycles are essentially monetary phenomena, caused by changes in the **money supply**. In their important book *A Monetary History of the United States, 1867-1960*, Milton Friedman and Anna Schwartz argued that US business cycles were preceded by changes in the money supply.

The argument put forward is that changes in the money supply lead to changes in real variables, such as unemployment and national income, before finally leading to an increase in prices. The path to an increased price level is not a smooth one but is cyclical. The oscillations in the cycle become more and more damped as time goes on. Of course they can become more amplified again if there is another excessive increase in the money supply.

The link between changes in the money supply and changes in income is known as the **monetary transmission mechanism**. Assume that there is a once and for all increase in the money supply when the economy is in long run equilibrium. The money supply is now greater than the **demand for money**. Economic agents, such as banks, firms and consumers, will adjust their portfolio of assets. Some of the excess supply will be used to buy physical assets - goods and services. The rest will be saved, reducing interest rates and thus encouraging the borrowing of money again to buy physical assets. The increase in consumption and investment will result in an increase in income. The economy is now in boom.

Prices will begin to rise. This, together with increased real spending, will increase the demand for money. It is most unlikely that the economy will return to equilibrium with the demand and supply for money being equal. What will happen is that the demand for money will carry on increasing so that the demand for money exceeds the supply of money. Once this happens, economic agents will start to adjust their portfolios in the opposite direction. They will cut back on purchases of physical and financial assets. Interest rates will rise. Investment and consumption will begin to fall. The economy is now in recession with falling income. This reduces the demand for money, bringing it back past the equilibrium point to the bottom of the cycle where once again supply is greater than demand for money. There will be a further bout of portfolio adjustment and aggregate demand will start to rise, bringing the economy into the recovery phase of the cycle. This will carry on, although Friedman argues that without further shocks the oscillations will become smaller and smaller over time.

Question 5

Monetarists argue that the business cycle can be explained by changes in the money supply. For instance, Friedman and Schwartz (1963) argue that the Great Depression of the 1930s in the USA was caused by a drastic fall in the supply of money. They write: 'An initial mild decline in the money stock from 1929 to 1930, accompanying a decline in Federal Reserve credit outstanding, was converted into a sharp decline by a wave of bank failures beginning in late 1930.' Those failures produced (i) widespread attempts by the public to convert deposits into currency and hence a decline in the deposit-currency ratio, and (ii) a scramble for liquidity by the banks and hence a decline in the deposit-reserve ratio.

(a) How and why, according to Friedman and Schwartz, did the US money supply contract from 1929?
(b) Suggest how this contraction in the money supply then led to depression.

Key terms

Hysteresis - the process whereby a variable does not return to its former value when changed. In terms of the business cycle, it is used to describe the phenomenon of an economy failing to return to its former long term trend rate of growth after a severe recession.
Inventory cycle - fluctuations in national income caused by changes in the level of inventories or stocks in the economy.
Kondratiev cycles - long 50 year trade cycles caused by the 'lumpiness' of technological change.
Multiplier-accelerator model - a model which describes how the workings of the multiplier theory and the accelerator theory lead to changes in national income.

Applied economics

The UK business cycle in the post-war period

Duration and amplitude

The duration of the business cycle in the UK in the post-war era has averaged 4 to 5 years from peak to peak. As Figure 6 shows, during the 1950s and 1960s booms and recessions were very mild. Recessions meant declines in the rate of growth of output rather than falls in output. However, the 1970s and 1980s saw much greater swings, and the recession of 1980-82 was the severest since the Great Depression of the 1930s, whilst the recession of 1990-92 was the longest.

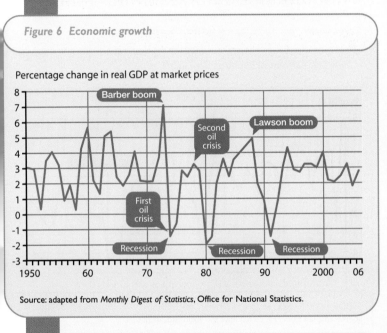

Figure 6 Economic growth

Percentage change in real GDP at market prices

Source: adapted from *Monthly Digest of Statistics*, Office for National Statistics.

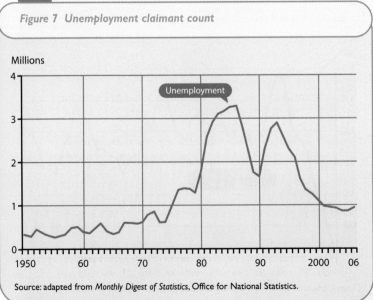

Figure 7 Unemployment claimant count

Millions

Source: adapted from *Monthly Digest of Statistics*, Office for National Statistics.

The 1950s, 1960s and early 1970s

In the 1950s, 1960s and early 1970s, booms in the economy (1954-5, 1959-60, 1964, 1968 and 1973) were associated with low unemployment, high inflation and a current account deficit on the balance of payments. It is noticeable from Figure 7 that unemployment shifted upwards in the late 1960s. The fall in unemployment that could have been expected in the boom of 1968 did not take place. This represented an upward shift in the **natural rate** of unemployment in the economy. It is an example of **hysteresis**, where an economic variable changes but does not bounce back to its original position when economic circumstances change.

1974-1979

The recession of 1974-75 was unusual in that it coincided with a severe supply side shock to the economy. The quadrupling of oil prices pushed the current account on the balance of payments into record deficit, whilst it led to an increase in the inflation rate. This produced the phenomenon of **stagflation** in 1974. There was rising inflation, a worsening balance of payments, rising unemployment and a fall in output. Within a couple of years, however, more traditional patterns reasserted themselves. The boom of 1978-79 saw faster growth, falling unemployment coupled with rising inflation and a deteriorating current account.

The recession of 1980-81

The recession of 1980-81 was even more severe than that of 1974-75 and again there was stagflation. Unemployment more than doubled and output fell by 4.2 per cent. Manufacturing industry was very badly affected, experiencing a 14.6 per cent fall in output from peak to trough. At the same time, inflation increased from 13.4 per cent in 1979 to 18.0 per cent in 1980 before falling back to 11.9 per cent in 1981. The balance of payments current account moved strongly into surplus. The recession of 1980-81 was untypical when compared to recessions of the 1950s and 1960s in many ways. The second oil crisis of 1978-79 fuelled inflation and created a downturn in the international economy which fed through to lower demand for UK exports. At the same time, North Sea oil was beginning to have a major impact on the balance of payments and led to a rise in the exchange rate, again dampening demand for UK non-oil exports. The government also, for the first time in the post-war era, reduced aggregate demand as the economy went into recession, first by increasing domestic interest rates and second by cutting public spending and raising taxes.

The 1980s and the Lawson boom

Perhaps not surprisingly, the economy took some time to recover. There was a faltering in the economy in 1984, but no major recession as the experience of the previous 30 years would have suggested. However, there was a boom in the economy in 1987-89, approximately ten years after the last major boom of 1977-79. The boom had many of the characteristics of two previous booms, in 1963-64 and 1972-74. All, in different ways, were fuelled by government policy changes. The Barber boom of 1972-74 was fuelled by a disastrous loosening of monetary policy combined with a large fiscal expansion driven by tax cuts and increases in government spending. The Lawson boom of 1987-89 too saw a failure to control growth in the money supply at an early enough point in the boom. Whilst overall fiscal policy remained broadly neutral, major income tax cuts in 1987 further boosted already strong consumer confidence which fed through into higher consumption, spending and borrowing. Increasing house prices at the time were both a symptom of inflation and a cause of rising demand and rising prices. Fast increases in house prices increase the wealth of households and encourage them to borrow and spend more. Over the three year period 1963-65, house prices rose by 20 per cent, higher than the average for the 1950s and 1960s. Over the three year period 1972-74, house prices rose 90 per cent, whilst over the four years of 1986-89 they increased 72 per cent. Certainly, the house price boom of the mid to late 1980s was encouraged by the government through generous tax concessions on mortgages and a political climate which equated home ownership with success. In all three booms, the current account on the balance of payments went into substantial deficit - 1.2 per cent of GDP in 1964, 4.2 per cent of GDP in 1974 (although this was partly caused by the oil supply side shock) and a record 5.1 per cent of GDP in 1989. This was because these booms sucked in imports as British industry failed to meet domestic demand.

The recession of 1990-92

The Lawson boom was followed by a prolonged recession. It was caused by a considerable tightening of monetary policy. Interest rates were doubled in 1988-89 from 7.5 per cent to 15 per cent in a bid by the government to stem a small rise in inflation. In 1990, the UK joined the ERM at too high a rate of the pound against other European currencies. The result was that the government was forced to maintain high interest rates to defend a weak pound throughout 1991 and 1992, long after the inflationary threat had passed. As a consequence, the recession was the longest since the 1930s. It was only when the UK was forced to leave the ERM, and the government quickly cut interest rates, so that the economy came out of recession.

Figure 8 Inflation (annual % change in RPI)

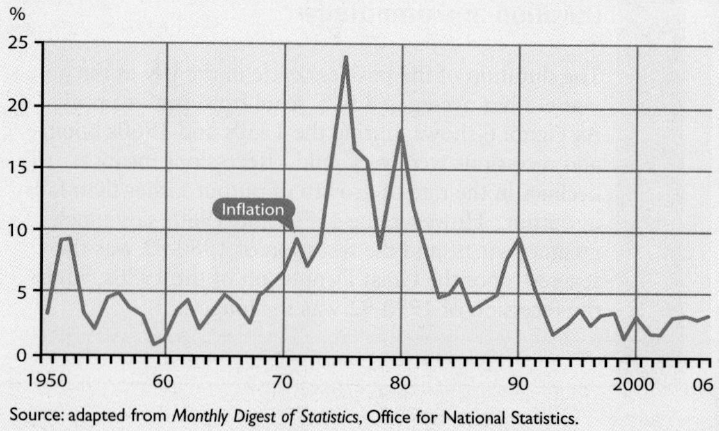

Source: adapted from *Monthly Digest of Statistics*, Office for National Statistics.

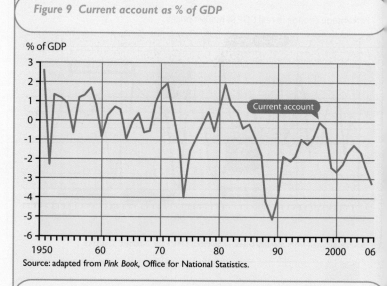

Figure 9 Current account as % of GDP

Source: adapted from *Pink Book*, Office for National Statistics.

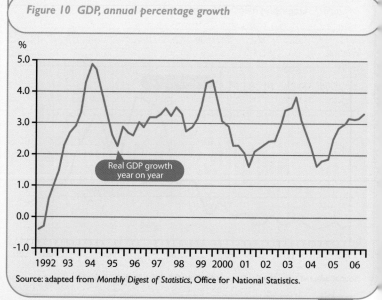

Figure 10 GDP, annual percentage growth

Source: adapted from *Monthly Digest of Statistics*, Office for National Statistics.

The period since 1992 has seen historically high economic growth combined with low inflation despite several negative supply side shocks.

Since 1992

Between 1992 and 2006, the economy reverted to the pattern of the 1950s and 1960s with a prolonged period of positive economic growth. However, within this, the sort of minor boom and recession seen in the immediate post-war period can be detected.

The post-war period would suggest that UK economic cycles last about 5 years. With a prolonged recession between 1990 and 1991, there were indeed low points in economic growth rates in 1996, 2001-2002 and 2005 as Figure 10 shows. Equally, the high points of GDP growth occurred in 1994, 2000 and 2004. However, looking at evidence from the other associated variables, it is difficult to detect this cyclical pattern. Inflation throughout the period was so low that factors other than the trade cycle were probably more important in determining the change in prices on a year by year basis. Equally, unemployment tended to fall over the whole period.

The mildness of trade cycles during this period can be attributed to two factors. First, the economic shocks experienced by the economy were relatively mild. In 1997-98, the 'Asian crisis' saw a number of countries in Asia, including South Korea, experiencing financial crises. This caused a downturn in their economies and hence a fall in demand for UK exports. In 2001, the destruction of the Twin Towers in New York by terrorists deepened a downturn in the US economy which also affected UK exports. In 2004-05, there were significant increases in oil prices which saw them returning in real terms to their late 1970s value. But all of these shocks only led to a fall in UK economic growth of at most 0.5 per cent.

The second factor which led to relative economic stability was government policy. In the 1970s and 1980s, it might be suggested that UK governments mishandled the economy at various points. Since 1992, economic policy has tended to stabilise macroeconomic variables. It can be argued that recent governments have not had to deal with the sort of economic problems that occurred in the 1970s and 1980s. Equally, though, there has been a much better understanding of how to control the economy and, arguably, mistakes have not been made.

DataQuestion

The Japanese economy

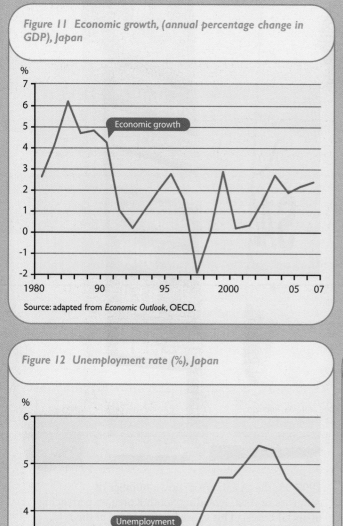

Figure 11 Economic growth, (annual percentage change in GDP), Japan

Source: adapted from *Economic Outlook*, OECD.

Japan may at last be emerging from its prolonged depression of the 1990s and early 2000s. There have been false hopes before, though. Throughout the 1990s, whenever the economy recovered, optimists predicted that Japan's boom and bust cycle might finally have ended and that the country could return to a period of prolonged positive economic growth.

One positive sign is that the Bank of Japan, the Japanese Central Bank, announced today that it would end its policy of maintaining zero interest rates in the economy. It is predicting that prices will rise rather than fall in the near future. Interest rates can therefore become positive as would be expected in a normal healthy economy. The Japanese government, however, is fearful that a rise in interest rates could kill off the present recovery and plunge the economy back into recession.

Source: adapted from new.bbc.co.uk 9.3.2006.

Figure 12 Unemployment rate (%), Japan

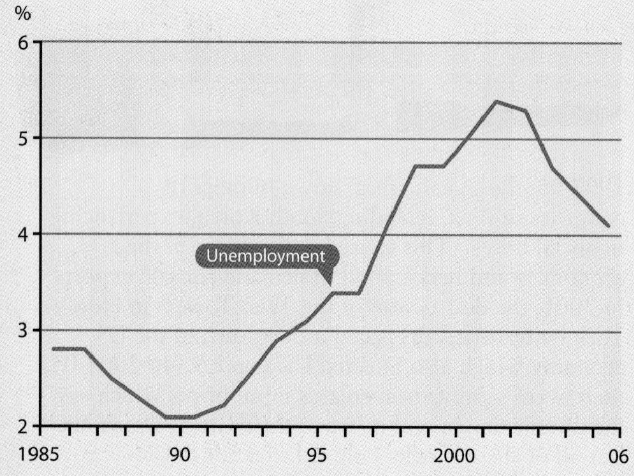

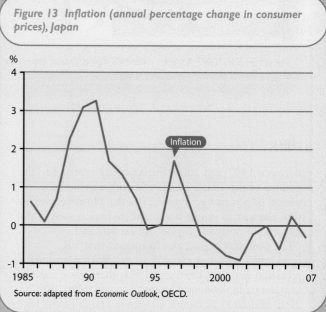

Source: adapted from *Economic Outlook*, OECD.

Figure 13 Inflation (annual percentage change in consumer prices), Japan

Source: adapted from *Economic Outlook*, OECD.

1. Identify the four phases of the business cycle from Figure 11.
2. (a) Explain the links between economic growth, unemployment and inflation in the business cycle.
   (b) To what extent do the data for Japan suggest these links exist?

3. Discuss why Bank of Japan intervention can affect the course of the Japanese business cycle.

Summary

1. National income is often used as the main indicator of the standard of living in an economy. A rise in GDP per head is used as an indication of economic growth and a rise in living standards.
2. However, there are many other important components of the standard of living, including political freedom, the social and cultural environment, freedom from fear of war and persecution, and the quality of the environment.
3. Economic growth over the past 100 years has transformed the living standards of people in the western world, enabling almost all to escape from absolute poverty.
4. Economic growth is likely to be the only way of removing people in the Third World from absolute poverty.
5. Economic growth has its costs in terms of unwelcome changes in the structure of society.
6. Some believe that future economic growth is unsustainable, partly because of growing pollution and partly because of the exploitation of non-renewable resources.

National income and economic welfare

National income is a measure of the income, output and expenditure of an economy. It is also often used as a measure of the **standard of living**. However, equating national income with living standards is very simplistic because there are many other factors which contribute to the economic welfare of individuals.

Political freedoms We tend to take civil liberties for granted in the UK. However, other governments in the world today are totalitarian regimes which rule through fear. In some countries, membership of an opposition party or membership of a trade union can mean death or imprisonment. The freedom to visit friends, to travel and to voice an opinion are likely to be more valuable than owning an extra television or being able to buy another dress.

The social and cultural environment In the UK, we take things such as education for granted. We have some of the world's finest museums and art galleries. We possess a cultural heritage which includes Shakespeare and Constable. The BBC is seen as one of the best broadcasting organisations throughout the world. However, we could all too easily live in a cultural desert where the main purpose of television programming might be to sell soap powders and make a profit. Alternatively, the arts could be used as political propaganda rather than exist in their own right.

Freedom from fear of violence If a person doesn't feel safe walking the streets or even at home, then no number of microwave ovens or videos will compensate for this loss. Equally, fears of war, arbitrary arrest, imprisonment or torture make material possessions seem relatively unimportant.

The working environment How long and hard people have to work is vital in evaluating standards of living. One reason why the average worker is far better off today than 100 years ago is because his or her working year is likely to be about half the number of hours of his or her Victorian counterpart's. Equally, the workplace is far safer today than 100 years ago. Industrial accidents were

Question 1

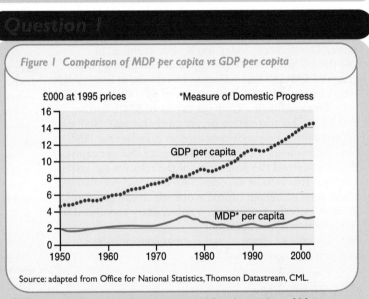

Figure 1 Comparison of MDP per capita vs GDP per capita

Source: adapted from Office for National Statistics, Thomson Datastream, CML.

It's official. 1976 was the best on record for the quality of life in Britain, according to an index of economic, social and environmental progress published by the New Economics Foundation, a think-tank. Unlike the standard GDP figure, the measure of domestic progress (MDP) takes into account social and environmental costs, including the damage done by crime, the depletion of natural resources, and pollution such as emissions of greenhouse gases. Britain in the seventies, with less crime, less income inequality, a rise in the national capital stock because of a boom in public sector investment, and lower energy consumption because there were fewer cars and centrally-heated houses, was better-off than today.

Most alternative measures of quality of life seem to show that Britain in the past was better off than today. However, those old enough to remember 1976 might be surprised that this was the best year for Britain's overall affluence. For many, the mid-1970s with record inflation, rising unemployment, strikes and no home computers, mobile phones or DVDs was a rather grey and dismal period. The MDP only captures a very small number of the variables that might go to make up a standard of living index. So perhaps GDP is a better guide after all.

Source: adapted from the *Financial Times*, 16.3.2004.

(a) Why is GDP not the only measure of the standard of living of a country?
(b) What other factors might be included in a measure of the standard of living?
(c) What are the problems identified with the MDP as a measure of the standard of living?

then commonplace and workers received little or no compensation for serious injuries or even death.

The environment Environmental issues are currently at the forefront of people's consciousness. There is an understanding that production activities can damage the environment and that in future we may well have to stop consuming certain products if we are to safeguard the environment.

The United Nations calculates a measure of the standard of living called the **Human Development Index**. This is an index based on three indicators of development:

- longevity, as measured by life expectancy at birth;
- education attainment, as measured by a combination of adult literacy and the combined first, second and third level gross enrolment ratio (numbers in education divided by population of education age);
- the standard of living as measured by real GDP per capita at purchasing power parities.

There is a good correlation between levels of GNP per capita and Human Development Index levels. For example, in 2005/06, the UK with a GDP per capita at purchasing power parity rates of $35 580 had a Human Development Index (HDI) of 0.946. China, with a GDP per capita of $7 740 had an HDI of 0.777. Tanzania, with a GDP per capita of $740, had an HDI of 0.467. This correlation occurs partly because GNP per capita is one of the three measures used to calculate the HDI. However, there is a good correlation between GNP per capita and adult literacy and the proportion of the relevant age group in education. This is to be expected. An educated population with a high level of human capital is one which can generate high levels of income. Conversely, a rich country can afford to spend large amounts on education.

Further examples of international comparisons of livings standards can be found in Unit 24.

Benefits of growth

The rate of economic growth has accelerated historically. Even five hundred years ago, most people would have seen little change in incomes over their lifetimes. In Victorian England, the economy grew at about one per cent per annum. Over the past 60 years, the UK economy has grown at an average of 2.6 per cent per annum.

Table 1 Economic growth rate of £100 over time

Year	Growth rates				
	1%	2%	3%	5%	10%
0	100	100	100	100	100
5	105	110	116	128	161
10	110	122	130	163	259
25	128	164	203	339	1 084
50	164	269	426	1 147	11 739
75	211	442	891	3 883	127 189
100	271	724	1 870	13 150	1 378 059

Growth at these rates since the end of the Second World War in 1945 has led to undreamt of prosperity for the citizens of the industrialised world. Consider Table 1. It shows by how much £100 will grow over time at different rates. At one per cent growth, income will roughly double over the lifetime of an individual. At 2 per cent, it will

The photographs show a modern kitchen and a kitchen at the start of the 20th century. To what extent do they show that economic growth has been desirable?

quadruple over a lifetime. At 3 per cent, it is doubling every twenty five years. At 5 per cent, it only takes about 14 years to double income. At 10 per cent, it only takes about 7 years to double income.

If recent growth rates are a guide to the future, average British workers in 30 years' time will earn in real terms twice what they are earning today. When they are in their seventies, they can expect workers to earn four times as much as their parents did when they were born.

These increases in income have led to the elimination of **absolute poverty** for most citizens in industrialised countries.

- Life expectancy has doubled over the past 300 years and infant mortality rates have plummeted.
- People have enough to eat and drink. What we eat and drink is nearly always fit for human consumption.
- Housing standards have improved immeasurably.
- Nearly everyone can read and write.

Future increases in income are generally desirable. Very few people would prefer to have less income rather than more income in the future (remember economics assumes that people have **infinite wants**). So economic growth has generally been considered to be highly desirable. Moreover, in 2005 only 16 per cent of the world's population lived in 'high income' countries such as the USA, the UK and Japan, with an average annual income per person of $32 500 at 2005 purchasing power parity prices. 36.5 per cent lived in 'low income' countries with an average yearly income of just $2 486, not even ten per cent of the average income of high income countries. Many who live in low and middle income countries suffer absolute poverty. It can be argued that the only way to eliminate malnutrition, disease, bad housing and illiteracy in these countries is for there to be real economic growth.

Arguments against growth

Despite the apparent benefits, the goal of economic growth is questioned by some economists and environmentalists.

The falsity of national income statistics One argument is that the increase in national income has been largely fictitious. Three hundred years ago much of the output of the economy was not traded. Women were not on the whole engaged in paid work. Much of the supposed increase in income has come from placing monetary values on what existed already. Much of the increase in income generated by the public sector of the economy comes not from increased production but from increased wages paid to public sector workers who produce the same amount of services.

Whilst there is some truth in this, it cannot be denied that material living standards have increased immeasurably over the past three hundred years. People not only consume more goods and services, they have on average far more leisure time.

Negative externalities Another argument is that modern industrialised societies have created large negative **externalities**. For instance, some put forward the view that growth has created a large pool of migrant workers, wandering from job to job in different parts of the country. They become cut off from their roots, separated from their families. The result is alienation and loneliness, particularly of the old, and the collapse of traditional family values. Crime rates soar, divorce rates increase, stress related illnesses become commonplace and more and more has to be spent on picking up the pieces of a society which is no longer content with what it has.

Supporters of this view tend to look back to some past 'golden age', often agricultural, when people lived mainly in villages as parts of large extended families. However, historical evidence suggests that such a rural paradise never existed. Life for many was short and brutish. Drunkenness was always a problem. Family life was claustrophobic and did not allow for individuality. Most people were dead by the age when people today tend to divorce and remarry.

Growth is unsustainable Perhaps the most serious anti-growth argument is that growth is unsustainable. SUSTAINABLE GROWTH can be defined as growth in the productive potential of the economy today which does not lead to a fall in the productive potential of the economy for future generations. Consider again Table 1. If a country like the UK grew at an average 3 per cent per annum then in 25 years' time national income will be twice as large as it is today; in fifty years' time, when an 18 year old student will be retired, it will be over 4 times as large; in 75 years' time, when on current life expectancy figures that student would be dead, it will be nearly 9 times as large; and in 100 years' time it will be nearly 19 times as large. If the average wage in the UK today of a full time employee was £27 000 per annum, then in 100 years' time it will have risen to £800 000 per annum in real terms.

Each extra percent increase in national income is likely to use up **non-renewable resources** such as oil, coal and copper. In the late 1970s, the Club of Rome, a forecasting institute, produced a report called 'The Limits to Growth'. The report claimed that industrialised economies as we know them would collapse. They would be caught between a growth in pollution and a decline in the availability of scarce resources such as oil, coal and timber. Oil was projected to run out in the next century and coal by the year 2400. In the 1980s and 1990s, the world was gripped by reports that people were destroying the ozone layer and raising the world's temperature through the greenhouse effect. The planet cannot support growth rates of even 1 or 2 per cent per year. Growth must stop and the sooner the better.

Economic theory suggests that the future may not be as bleak as this picture makes out. In a market economy, growing scarcity of a resource, such as oil, results in a rise in price. Three things then happen. First, demand and therefore consumption falls - the price mechanism results in conservation. Second, it becomes profitable to explore for new supplies of the resource. Third, consumers switch to substitute products whilst producers are encouraged to find new replacement products. After the massive rise in oil prices in 1973-74, the world car makers roughly halved the fuel consumption per mile of the average car

over a period of ten years through more efficient engines. Brazil developed cars which ran on fuel made from sugar. In recent years, oil companies have begun to mix biofuels with their traditional oil based fuels to sell at the pumps.

Governments too respond to pressures from scientists and the public. The activities of industry are far more regulated today in the western world than they were 30 years ago. Individual governments, for instance, have introduced strict controls on pollution emissions, regulated disposal of waste and sought to ration scarce resources like water or air through systems of tradable licences. Even more impressive has been the willingness of governments to sign international agreements designed to safeguard the environment. For instance, in 1987, 93 governments signed the Montreal Protocol to phase out production of CFC chemicals, a major contributor to the destruction of the ozone layer. Signatories to the 1997 Kyoto Protocol agreed to reduce greenhouse gas emissions by 5.2 per cent from 1990 levels between 2008-2012.

What is worrying, however, is that the market mechanism and governments are frequently slow to act. Governments and markets are not good at responding to pressures which might take decades to build up but only manifest themselves suddenly at the end of that time period. Some scientists have predicted that global warming is now already irreversible. If this is true, the problem that we now face is how to change society to cope with this. There is no clear consensus as to how we could reverse economic growth, consume less, and cope with the coming catastrophe, without creating an economic nightmare with mass starvation.

Increasing inequality Some economists have argued that economic growth is increasing inequalities in income and wealth. Karl Marx, the founder of communism in the 19th century, argued that workers would live on subsistence wages whilst all the benefits of economic growth would go to the owners of capital. It is commonly argued today that the benefits of globalisation are going mainly to the rich countries of the world and to multinational companies and very little is going to poor developing countries. The evidence is far more complex. Karl Marx has been proved wrong. Even those working on the minimum wage in the UK can consume far more goods and services than a prosperous artisan in the 19th century. As for individual economies, the picture is mixed. Average income inequalities between China and the USA are rapidly diminishing. With China growing at 10 per cent per annum and the USA at below 3 per cent, mathematically average income inequality must be falling. This doesn't mean to say that the average US citizen doesn't get more benefit in dollars than the average Chinese citizen from a growing world economy. A US citizen who gets 3 per cent of $40 000 will get more in absolute terms than a Chinese citizen who gets 10 per cent of $7 000. However, countries ranging from South Korea, Taiwan and Singapore to Ireland, Poland and Estonia have found that their high economic growth rates have either given them incomes equal to the rich nations of the world or rapidly reduced the gap between them and the rich world. In practice, whether growth leads to greater income inequality between countries and within countries is dependent partly on the chance outcomes of the market. However, it is also crucially dependent on government policy. Governments can, through provision of measures such as minimum wages, pensions, working tax credits, universal free education and health care, and tax regimes which make the rich pay a disproportionate amount of tax, ensure that the benefits of growth are widely distributed in society. As China has shown, the fastest way to relieve poverty and reduce the income differential between itself and the world's richest nation, the USA, is to grow at double digit rates per annum.

The anti-growth lobby One point to note is that supporters of the anti-growth lobby tend to be people who are relatively well off. Cutting their consumption by 25 per cent, or producing environmentally friendly alternative technologies, might not create too much hardship for them. However, leaving the mass of people in the Third World today at their present living standards would lead to great inequality. A small minority would continue to live below the absolute poverty line, facing the continual threat of malnutrition. A majority would not have access to services such as education and health care which

people in the West take for granted. Not surprisingly, the anti-growth lobby is stronger in the West than in the Third World.

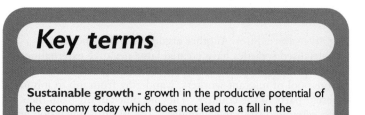

Key terms

Sustainable growth - growth in the productive potential of the economy today which does not lead to a fall in the productive potential of the economy for future generations.

Applied economics

The standard of living in the UK since 1900

GDP is often used as the major economic indicator of welfare. Table 2 shows that, on this basis, living standards in the UK rose considerably last century. Between 1900 and 1931 GDP rose 15 per cent and between 1900 and 2004 it rose 668 per cent. Population has increased too, but even when this has been taken into account, the rise in income per person is impressive.

It is possible to chart a multitude of other ways in which it can be shown that the standard of living of the British family has improved. For instance, 14.2 per cent of children in 1900 died before the age of 1. In 2007, the comparable figure was 0.5 per cent. In 1900, the vast majority of children left school at 12. Today all children stay on till the age of 16, whilst 53 per cent of 18 year olds are in full time or part time education or training. In 1900, few people were able to afford proper medical treatment when they fell ill. Today, everyone in the UK has access to the National Health Service.

Table 3 illustrates another way in which we are far better off today than a family at the turn of the century. It shows the weekly budget of a manual worker's family in a North Yorkshire iron town, estimated by Lady Bell in her book *At The Works*. The family lived off 7½ home-made loaves of 4lb (1.8kg) each thinly scraped with butter, 4lb (1.8kg) of meat and bacon, weak tea, a quart of milk and no vegetables worth mentioning. In 2005-06, whilst average consumption for five people of bread was only 3.5kg a week, tea 0.17kg and sugar 0.47kg, on the other hand meat consumption was 5.0kg, fresh potato consumption was 2.9kg, and butter, margarine, lard and other oils consumption was 0.92kg. Moreover, today's diet is far more varied and ample with fruit and vegetables apart from potatoes playing a major part. Malnutrition, not uncommon in 1900, is virtually unknown in the UK today.

The budget in Table 3 also says a great deal about

the very restricted lifestyle of the average family in 1908. Then, a family would consider itself lucky if it could take a day trip to the seaside. In comparison, individuals took an estimated 44.2 million holidays abroad in 2005.

In 1908, houses were sparsely furnished. The main form of heating was open coal fires; central heating was virtually unknown. Very few houses were wired for electricity. Table 3 shows that the typical house was lighted by oil. All the electrical household gadgets we take for granted, from washing machines to vacuum cleaners to televisions, had not been invented. The 1lb of soap in the 1908 budget would have been used to clean clothes, sinks and floors. Soap powders, liquid detergents and floor cleaners were not available. 'Gold Dust' was the popular name for an exceptionally caustic form of shredded yellow soap notorious for its ability to flay the user's hands. Compare that with the numerous brands of mild soaps available today.

Workers worked long hours, six days a week with few holidays, whilst at home the housewife faced a life of drudgery with few labour-saving devices. Accidents were frequent and old age, unemployment and sickness were dreaded and even more so the workhouse, the final destination for those with no means to support themselves.

Ecologically, the smoke-stack industries of industrial areas such as London, the Black Country and Manchester created large scale pollution. The smogs which are found in many cities such as Mexico City and Los Angeles today were common occurrences in turn-of-the-century Britain. The urban environment was certainly not clean 100 years ago.

Socially and politically, women, who formed over half the population, were not emancipated. In 1900, they did not have the vote, their place was in the home, they were often regarded as biologically inferior to men, and they were debarred from almost all public positions of influence and authority. In many ways, the standard of living of women improved more than that of men during the 20th century because of the repressive attitude held towards women 100 years ago.

Overall, it would be very difficult to look back on 1900 and see it as some golden age. For the vast majority of those in Britain today, the start of the third millennium is a paradise in comparison. However, whilst there might be little absolute poverty today, it could be argued that there is considerable relative poverty. It could also be argued that the poorest today are probably still worse off than the top 5 per cent of income earners in 1900.

Table 2 GDP, GDP per head and population, 1901-2006

	GDP (£bn at 2002 prices)	Population (millions)	GDP per head (£ at 2002 prices)
1901	152.8	38.2	4 001
1911	176.1	42.1	4 172
1921	155.8	44.0	3 540
1931	188.4	46.0	4 096
1951	294.8	50.2	5 795
1961	383.0	52.7	7 253
1971	510.7	55.9	9 130
1981	599.0	56.4	10 629
1991	777.4	57.4	13 535
2001	1 027.9	59.1	17 388
2006	1 173.1	60.6	19 358

Note: GDP is at market prices.
Source: adapted from *Social Trends, Annual Abstract of Statistics,* Office for National Statistics.

Family budget in 1908
Income 18s 6d, family of five

	s.	d.
Rent	5	6
Coals	2	4
Insurance	0	7
Clothing	1	0
Meat	1	6
14lb of flour	1	5
3½ lb of bread meal	0	4½
1lb butter		
Half lb lard	0	2½
1lb bacon	0	9
4 lb sugar	0	8
Half lb tea	0	9
Yeast	0	1
Milk	0	3
1 box Globe polish	0	1
1lb soap	0	3
1 packet Gold Dust	0	1
3 oz tobacco	0	9
7lb potatoes	0	3
Onions	0	1
Matches	0	1
Lamp oil	0	2
Debt	0	3
Total	18	6

Table 3

DataQuestion   Comparative living standards in the UK

Table 4 Income, prices and population

	1971	2006
GDP (£bn at current prices)	57.5	1 309.9
Retail Price Index (1971 = 100)	100	981
Population (millions)	55.9	60.6

Source: adapted from *Economic Trends, Annual Abstract of Statistics, Monthly Digest of Statistics,* Office for National Statistics.

Table 5 Population[1]

	Millions	
	1971	2006
Under 18	15.8	13.1
Adults not of pensionable age	31.0	36.1
Pensionable ages[1]	9.1	11.4
Total population	55.9	60.6

1 Pensionable age is 60+ for women and 65+ for men.

Source: adapted from *Annual Abstract of Statistics,* Office for National Statistics.

Table 6 Number of abortions, Great Britain

	1971-72	2005
Abortions	63 400	199 019

Source: adapted from *Social Trends,* Office for National Statistics.

Table 7 Households: by type of household and family

	1971 %	2006 %
One person		
Under state pension age	6	14
Over state pension age	12	14
One family households		
Couple no children	27	28
Couple with children	43	29
Lone parent household	7	10
Other	5	5
Total	100	100
All households (millions)	18.6	24.2

Source: adapted from *Social Trends,* Office for National Statistics.

Figure 2 Mortality: by sex and leading group of causes

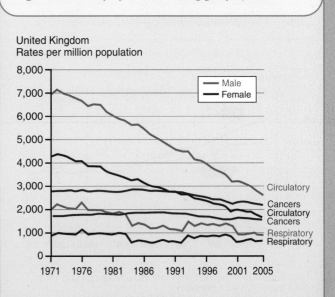

United Kingdom
Rates per million population

Source: adapted from *Social Trends,* Office for National Statistics.

Table 8 Percentage of households owning selected consumer durables

	1970-72	1981	2005-2006
Washing machine	65	78	95
Tumble dryer	0	23	58
Microwave	0	0	91
Dishwasher	0	4	35
Television	93	97	98
CD Player	0	0	88
Home computer	0	0	65
Video recorder	0	0	86
Telephone	35	75	92
Internet connection	0	0	55
Mobile phone	0	0	79

Source: adapted from *Social Trends*, *Family Spending*, Office for National Statistics.

Table 9 Education

	1970-71	2006
Ratio of pupils to teachers in state schools	22.60	17.0
Numbers in state nursery schools (millions)	0.05	0.15
Numbers in all schools (millions)	10.20	9.90
Numbers in higher education (millions)	0.62	2.49
Government spending on education as % of GDP	5.20	5.60

Source: adapted from *Social Trends*, *Annual Abstracts of Statistics*, Office for National Statistics.

Table 10 Employment and unemployment, UK, millions

	1971	2006
Employment		
Males		
full time	15.5	15.5
Females		
full time	9.0	13.3
Total unemployed[1]	0.75	0.96

1 Claimant count unemployed.

Source: adapted from *Economic and Labour Market Review*, Office for National Statistics.

Table 11 Real gross weekly earnings of selected workers, £ at 2006 prices

	1971	2005-06
Waiter/waitress	140	128
Caretaker	213	283
Bricklayer/mason	265	462
Carpenter/joiner	273	433
Nurse	140	431
Primary teacher	314	534
Solicitor	466	965
Medical practitioner	670	1 245

Source: adapted from *New Earnings Survey*, *Annual Survey of Hours and Earnings*, Office for National Statistics.

Table 12 Average daily flow of motor vehicles on motorways

		Thousands
	1971	2005
Vehicles on motorways	28.5	75.5

Source: adapted from *Transport Statistics*, Office for National Statistics.

Figure 3 Prevalence of adult cigarette smoking: by sex

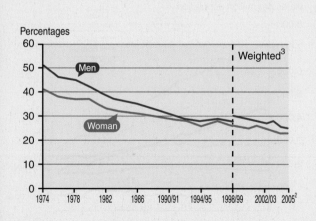

Note: weighted data after 1998/99 to compensate for non-response and to match known population distributions.
Source: adapted from *Social Trends*, Office for National Statistics.

Figure 4 Marriages and divorces

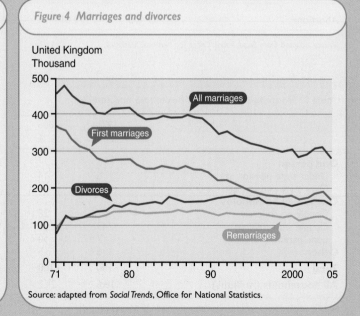

Source: adapted from *Social Trends*, Office for National Statistics.

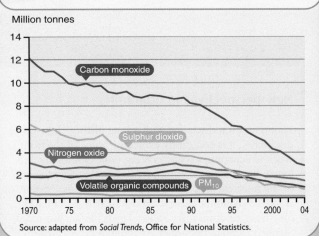

Figure 5 Proportion of adults who are obese or overweight: by sex

England
Percentages

Overweight males
Overweight females
Obese females
Obese males

Source: adapted from *Social Trends*, Office for National Statistics.

Figure 6 Emissions of selected air pollutants

Million tonnes

Carbon monoxide
Sulphur dioxide
Nitrogen oxide
Volatile organic compounds
PM_{10}

Source: adapted from *Social Trends*, Office for National Statistics.

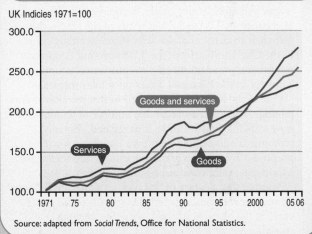

Figure 7 Environmental impact of households

United Kingdom
Index numbers (1991=100)

Waste
Water consumption
Energy consumption
Carbon dioxide emissions

Source: adapted from *Social Trends*, Office for National Statistics.

Figure 8 Volume of domestic household expenditure on goods and services

UK Indicies 1971=100

Goods and services
Services
Goods

Source: adapted from *Social Trends*, Office for National Statistics.

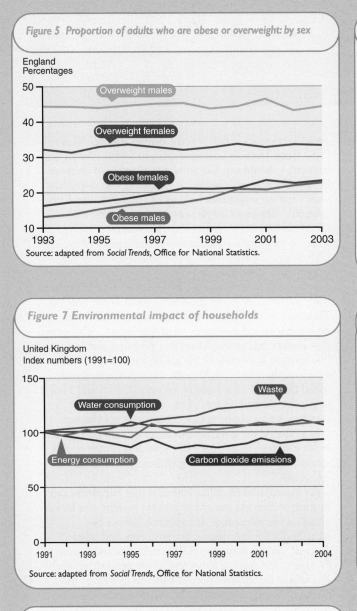

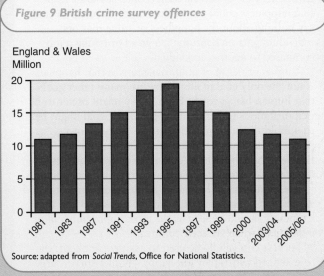

Figure 9 British crime survey offences

England & Wales
Million

Source: adapted from *Social Trends*, Office for National Statistics.

You have been asked to write a magazine article from an economic perspective comparing the early 1970s and 2006. The focus of the article is a discussion of whether living standards improved in the UK over the period. Construct the article as follows.

1. In your introduction, pick out a small number of key statistics which you feel point out the differences between the two periods.

2. In the main part of the article, compare and contrast the two periods, pointing out how living standards improved and also where it could be argued that the UK was worse off in 2006 than in the early 1970s.

3. In the conclusion, discuss whether rising GDP will be sufficient to ensure that the UK is better off in 2020 than in 2006.

Applied economics

New perspectives in economics

Economics is a discipline with a long history. Like other disciplines, it is constantly evolving. Some of the frontier work in economics today is being done developing and expanding existing theoretical models. However, some of the most exciting work today is in applying existing standard economic theory to novel situations. In 2005, an American economist, Steven Levitt, with a journalist, Stephen Dubner, published *Freakonomics: A Rogue Economist Explores the Hidden Side of Everything*, which went on to sell millions of copies worldwide. The book is made up of six chapters based on academic research done by Steven Levitt. It includes an investigation as to why almost all drug dealers earn low wages and quickly give up the occupation. It also looks at cheating by US teachers in terms of the grades they give their students and also why sumo wrestlers cheat. In the UK, Tim Harford, the 'Underground Economist', publishes a popular and easy to understand column each Saturday in the *Financial Times* on similar themes.

One of the key tools being used in this research is **data mining**. There is a considerable number of databases now available which can be interrogated. Equally, economists are creating their own databases for research purposes. By asking the right questions and formulating hypotheses, valid conclusions can be drawn.

Another key element of this new economics is linking economics with other social sciences. Over the past 50 years in the physical sciences, there has been an enormous growth for example in biochemistry and biophysics, the fusing together of biology, chemistry and physics at the borders of their disciplines. In economics, new fields of enquiry are being opened up by combining **sociology** or **psychology** with economic theory. In 2002 Daniel Kahneman, a psychologist and someone who claims to have never taken a single economics course, won the Nobel Prize in Economics for his work on **prospect theory**. Prospect theory describes decisions between alternatives that involve risk, such as buying a lottery ticket or taking out insurance. It has a base in psychology because it models how people actually behave rather than modelling how they ought to behave if they want to achieve certain outcomes. Linked to sociology and psychology is also a growing use of experiments in economics.

The economics of happiness

One branch of this new type of economics is called the ECONOMICS OF HAPPINESS or HAPPINESS ECONOMICS. One of the most often quoted comments about economics is that it is the **dismal science**. This came from Thomas Carlyle writing in 1849: 'Not a 'gay science', I should say, like some we have heard of, no a dreary, desolate and, indeed, quite abject and distressing one; what we might call, by way of eminence, the dismal science.' Thomas Carlyle was a famous writer and social commentator of the time. He was contrasting some of the negative predictions of economics of his age with a 'gay science' which at the time referred to 'life-enhancing knowledge'.

The economics of happiness has some of its theoretical roots in the work being done in England in the time of Thomas Carlyle. Jeremy Bentham was a philosopher who put forward the theory of **utilitarianism**. This stated that human beings should act in a way that would cause 'the greatest happiness of the greatest number'. This was a philosophy which could guide the individual: should I spend this £500 on a holiday for myself or should I use it to pay for the tuition fees of my child at university? It was also a philosophy which could guide government policy: should the government increase taxes on high income earners to pay for extra spending on the health service, or should taxes and spending on health care stay the same?

An assumption of utilitarianism is that happiness can be measured in the same way that the weight of a loaf of bread can be measured. If happiness cannot be measured, then individuals, governments and other decision makers cannot make the calculations necessary to ensure 'the greatest happiness of the greatest number'. The whole theory then becomes useless as a basis for decision making. Following Bentham's death, the consensus view in neo-classical economics came to be that happiness could not be measured. Economics could say nothing about the happiness or value that one individual puts on consuming a good or taking a job compared to another individual.

Another criticism of utilitarianism was that happiness is not the only goal in life There are many other goals that human beings might have. They might prefer to be rich or famous rather than happy. Their goal might be to uphold the honour of the family. Status, power, possessions, control and sex are other possibilities. People's goals differ from culture to culture and it is arguably too simplistic to reduce everything to happiness.

The economics of happiness refutes these problems and argues that happiness can indeed be measured and that happiness should be seen as the most important goal of individuals whatever their culture.

- Surveys can validly be used to ask people about the extent to which they are happy. With a survey large enough to be statistically valid, survey results produce reliable evidence about states of happiness and satisfaction. Such survey methods have been used in psychology for decades. They are backed up by neuroscience. During the 1990s, it was discovered that happiness was associated with measurable electrical activity in the brain. This could be picked up by MRI scans. So it is possible to tell physiologically whether or not someone is telling the truth when they say they are happy.

● Looking across cultures, philosophies and religions, and using evidence from sociological and psychological studies, it is clear that happiness is a goal of human beings. It is true that happiness might be given different names such as well-being, satisfaction, fulfilment or utility. But for the economics of happiness, these different names are all pointing to the same goal. Happiness can then be argued to be the most important goal. If asked, 'why do I want to be wealthy or powerful?', most people would say 'because it leads to happiness'. Wealth, power or status are not ends in themselves. They are stepping stones to happiness. Think too of the reverse question: 'Is the goal of life to be unhappy?' Or 'Does it matter that people are unhappy?' Few people would argue that they wanted to be unhappy and that it didn't matter whether their relatives and friends and other people were happy or not.

GDP and happiness

Traditional economics states that the fundamental economic problem occurs because human wants are infinite but resources are only finite. Economic growth helps solve this problem because it allows more human wants to be satisfied. Economic growth leads to rising living standards and, by implication, greater happiness.

Economists have long recognised that the quantity of goods that consumers can buy is only one part of the measurement of the standard of living. In the unit 'Economic growth and welfare', it was explained that other factors such as the social and cultural environment and political freedom contribute to the standard of living. However, there is an implicit assumption that GDP remains one of the most important components of economic welfare.

Economists using psychological surveys, though, present a more complex picture. Using surveys from across the world (cross sectional surveys), they have found that happiness and income are positively related at low levels of income but higher levels of income are not associated with increases in happiness. The idea that increases in GDP do not lead to increases in happiness is called the **Easterlin Paradox**, after Richard Easterlin, an economist, who identified this problem in a 1974 research paper. One piece of evidence for this from research conducted is illustrated in Figure 1. Using UK survey data, in Figure 2, another piece of research suggests that life satisfaction in the UK has actually declined since the 1970s despite a more than 60 per cent

rise in GDP. All the survey evidence for the USA and Japan also concludes that there has been no increase in happiness in those countries over the last 50 years.

The conclusion from research is that an increase in consumption of material goods will improve well-being when basic needs are not being met, such as adequate food and shelter. But once these needs are being met, then increasing the quantity of goods consumed makes no difference to well-being. Having a new high-definition television, or a new car when you already have a reasonable, functioning TV and car doesn't increase your well-being in the long term.

Factors affecting happiness apart from GDP

There is a number of factors which have been identified which contribute to happiness from survey evidence.

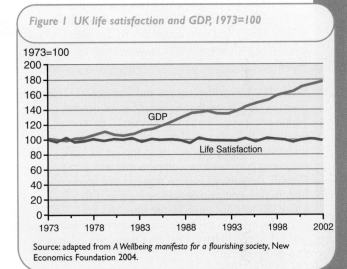

Figure 1 UK life satisfaction and GDP, 1973=100

Source: adapted from *A Wellbeing manifesto for a flourishing society*, New Economics Foundation 2004.

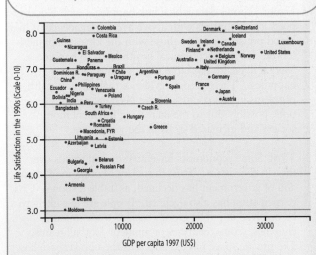

Figure 2 An international comparison of the life satisfaction and GDP of nations

Source: adapted from *A Wellbeing manifesto for a flourishing society*, New Economics Foundation 2004.

Relationships Friends and family have a very important role to play in happiness. In a 2007 research paper, the economist Nattavudh Powdthavee gave estimates of the monetary value of different types of relationships. As can be seen from Table 1, meeting friends and relatives just once or twice a month had a monetary value of £31 000 per year per capita. This should be compared with average real annual household income per capita of £9 800. Talking to neighbours on most days was worth £40 800 a year. Being married was worth £68 400. On the other hand, being divorced led to a negative monetary value of £21 600 per year. It is possible to dispute the exact size of these figures. However, the casual observer can see that individuals place a high value on relationships. Friendships are prized. Partners in a marriage give up well paid jobs for the sake of their marriage. Most divorced people seek to remarry. The high point of consumerism in today's Britain, Christmas, is one where people give gifts to each other and spend time together as families. Being alone, cut off from friends, family and even casual day to day encounters, is associated with low self-esteem, depression and mental illness.

Work Work provides income and satisfaction. However, research also shows that aspects of work depress happiness. Long commuting journeys, tight work deadlines, lack of control over how a job is done and housework have all shown up in surveys as being negatively correlated to happiness and well being. Overall, the survey evidence suggests that workers in high income countries would be happier if they had lower incomes but more leisure time. As for unemployment, in the same survey quoted in Table 1, it was calculated to have a negative happiness value of £66 400 per year.

Health Having good health has a very high monetary value in terms of happiness. In Table 1, the valuation put on excellent health is £303 000 per year. Surveys suggest that health and happiness are correlated. Figure 3 shows data which link happiness with blood pressure. Countries with above average incidence of high blood pressure are also those with the lowest happiness scores. Good psychological health leads to happiness. Mental ill health has large negative impacts on happiness. There is some evidence that mental health problems in rich countries have been increasing over time, possibly due to the increasing fragmentation of society and increased stress in the workplace.

Trust Some economists have investigated trends over time in civic issues. Trust in society of other individuals and of government has declined, as Table 2 shows. Civic participation has also declined. People are less likely to be involved in public groups such as trade unions, churches, scouts, charities or amateur football teams. The private space has expanded as the public space has diminished. Surveys suggest this is likely to have reduced

happiness. Partly this is because it limits the occasions when people meet together, form friendships, develop a positive image and give themselves a purpose in life. Civic participation also has positive externalities. When an amateur player turns up to a football practice, it benefits all the other members of the football team. Reducing civic participation reduces those positive externalities.

Relative income Although increasing absolute levels of GDP in rich countries seems to have no effect on happiness, there is a positive correlation in studies

Table 1 *Valuation of life events*

		£ per year
Meet friends and relatives		
	Once or twice a month	31 000
	Once or twice a week	47 000
	On most days	62 400
Talk to neighbours		
	Once or twice a week	22 800
	On most days	40 800
Married		68 400
Living as a couple		57 800
Separated		-5 400
Divorced		-21 600
Unemployment		-66 400
Disabled		-61 000
Health: good		237 000
Health: excellent		303 000

Source: adapted from *Putting a price tag on Friends, Relatives and Neighbours: using Surveys of Life Satisfaction to Value Social Relationships*, Nattavudh Powdthavee 2007.

Table 2 *Percentage who say 'most people can be trusted', Britain*

	%
1959	56
1981	43
1995	31

Source: adapted from *What would make a happier society?*, Richard Layard 2003.

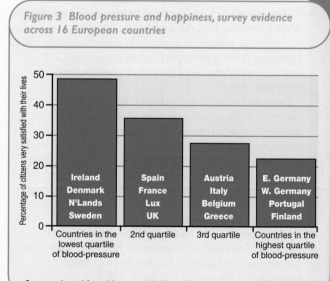

Figure 3 *Blood pressure and happiness, survey evidence across 16 European countries*

Source: adapted from *Happiness, Health and Economics*, Andrew Oswald, 2007.

Table 3 Valuation of happiness: Hungary 1995

	Rise in happiness (index)
Income	
Family income rises by 50% relative to average income	1.0
Freedom	
Quality of government improves: living in Hungary compared to Belarus 1995	2.5
Religion	
Answering yes rather than no to 'God is important in my life'	2.0
Trust	
Answering yes rather than no to 'In general people can be trusted'	1.0
Morality	
Answering yes rather than no to 'Cheating on taxes is never justifiable'	1.0

Source: adapted from *What would make a happier society?*, Richard Layard 2003.

between relative income and happiness. Surveys across countries consistently show that those with above average incomes tend to have higher levels of happiness than those with below average incomes. For example, evidence suggests that if everyone today in the UK were to see an increase in their income by 50 per cent, on average there would be no increase in happiness or well-being. On the other hand, those receiving 30 per cent more than the average income today do report being happier than those receiving 30 per cent less than the average income. There are two suggested explanations for this.

One is that income is a symbol of social status. Psychologically, we are happier if we feel we have more status. This competitive streak is 'hard-wired' into our brains and comes from our biological roots as apes. The second explanation is that above average incomes are correlated with a number of other factors which are associated with happiness. For example, those on above average income tend to enjoy better health and live longer. They have more control over their work environment and are less likely to perform short repetitive tasks. They are less likely to be unemployed.

Other factors Good government contributes to happiness. Surveys suggest, for example, that happiness under the communist regimes of the former Soviet Union and Eastern Europe was low because of the repressive nature of these regimes. Table 3 gives an estimate for the relative happiness of Hungary in 1995, a former communist state but now a democracy, compared to Belarus, which was still effectively communist. Being religious is associated with happiness. It could be that being religious is correlated with going to a church or other place of worship and being with a community. So being religious helps relationships. Or it could be that religion gives a positive purpose to life. Being moral also seems to be associated with happiness. Table 3, for example, reports survey evidence that those answering 'yes' to the question 'Cheating on

taxes is never justifiable' are happier than those who say no.

Policy implications

Increasing economic growth has traditionally been assumed to lead to an increase in economic welfare, well-being and happiness. Research from the economics of happiness suggests that this is likely to be true at current low levels of world income. Increased GDP is likely to benefit citizens of India, China or South Africa. But increasing GDP in the rich countries of the world such as the UK or the USA is unlikely to be be associated with increased well-being. The implication is that policies designed to increase GDP whatever their other consequences should be abandoned. Instead, economic policy should be directed at improving those aspects of life which most increase levels of well-being or most reduce the risk of large falls in well-being. The economics of happiness is still relatively new and there is no agreed policy agenda amongst economists who support this theory. However, examples of the sort of policy being put forward including the following.

Relationships Relationships are very important to happiness. Traditional economics suggests that labour mobility associated with flexible labour markets is a source of economic growth. However, geographic mobility breaks up family and community relationships and reduces trust by people in others. Therefore there might be net gains to society if policies were adopted to reduce geographical mobility and encourage more stable

communities. Markets might be less efficient but people might be happier.

Work Paid work leads to many examples of loss of well-being which might be addressed by government policy. For example, lengthy commuting leads to a loss of well-being. Government policies to reduce the length of time of commuter journeys would therefore increase happiness. This could come about through improving transport links. Or it could come about through planning policies which encourage workers to live nearer their place of work. Interestingly, survey evidence suggests that when workers travel together with friends or colleagues, this reduces the loss of well-being caused by commuting. This is probably because of the positive impact on happiness of relationships. Encouraging car sharing, which would have positive environmental consequences, could therefore increase happiness because people travel together and because it might reduce journey times with reduced congestion. Another example of loss of well-being is the number of hours worked by employees. Neo-classical economics suggests that taxes on income should be reduced to increase incentives to work, but it might lead to greater happiness if incentives to work longer hours were reduced through higher taxes. Unemployment and job insecurity are other examples of situations which lead to a loss of well-being. Free market economists suggest that labour laws which increase job security and make it more difficult to make workers redundant reduce economic efficiency and increase unemployment. But a combination of laws which give greater job security with job creation schemes and intensive training, seen for example in Scandinavian countries, might lead to higher levels of happiness even if they are costly to the taxpayer.

Health UK health statistics show that levels of physical health are improving in most areas. Obesity, though, is growing at an alarming rate. Obesity is linked to

increased risk of illness and also reduce quality of life. Therefore, the average level of happiness could be prevented from falling if the government made serious efforts to stem obesity. Mental health has been deteriorating over time. Yet mental health is an underfunded area of the National Health Service. Survey evidence suggests that only a quarter of people suffering from depression are being treated by the NHS. One in six of the population suffer from mental ill health such as depression, anxiety and serious phobias, 15 per cent of people will experience a major depression at some point in their lives, half of all people classified as disabled have a mental illness, and yet only 12 per cent of the NHS budget is devoted to mental health. Spending much more on mental health would increase happiness.

Economists are developing indices of happiness or well-being. These are composite indices taking a number of different variables and weighting them in order of importance similar to indices such as the UN's Human Development Index or the Index of Sustainable Economic Welfare. However, they are open to criticism about exactly what variables are included and what weightings are used. Unless a body like the United Nations produces a standardised formula, it is unlikely that a single common measure of happiness, similar to GDP for output and income, will become a target for national governments.

Key terms

The economics of happiness - investigates exactly what contributes to welfare and attempts to put values on some of these factors.

DataQuestion — Bhutan

Bhutan is one of the world's poorer countries. Situated in the Himalayas between India and China, it is a Buddhist kingdom. In 2005, average GDP measured in purchasing power parities was $5 620 and it was classified by the United Nations as a low income country.

Table 4 Selected development indicators 2005

	Bhutan	UK
GDP per capita, US$ at ppp	5 620	35 580
Life expectancy, males (2005)	62	76
Infant mortality rate (0-1 year) per 1000 live births	53	5
Tuberculosis prevalence, active 100 000 population	174	10
Percentage of population with access to improved drinking water	62	100
Percentage of the population with access to improved sanitation	70	100
Average annual rate of real GDP growth 2000-2005, percent	8	3
Energy consumption per capita oil equivalent (thousand kg), 2004	65	3 711
Internet users per 100 population	1	47

In 1972, the King of Bhutan, Jogme Singye Wangchuck, first used the term 'Gross National Happiness' to signify the direction he wanted Bhutan's economy to take. The term has never precisely been defined. However, it was an attempt to say that development was more than just increased in output as measured by the UN definition of GDP. True development was also about spiritual development, a concept which links to the country's Buddhist values.

In 1998, Bhutan's prime minister, Jigmi Thinkley identified four pillars of Gross National Happiness.
1. Sustainable and equitable socio-economic development is about improvement of physical, intellectual, social and economic health through services such as health, education, trade and commerce, road and bridge construction, employment, urban development and housing.
2. Conservation of the environment is about, for example, the law which states that the minimum tree cover in the kingdom must be 65 per cent of the land, and that hydropower projects should have minimal environmental impact.
3. Preservation and promotion of culture is about promoting Bhutanese religion, language and literature, art and architecture, performing arts, national dress, traditional etiquette, sport and recreation.
4. Good governance is moving Bhutan towards being a constitutional monarchy.

In a 2005 survey, 45 per cent of Bhutanese adults reported being very happy, 52 per cent reported being happy and only 3 per cent reported not being happy. In the USA, the comparable figures were 30 per cent very happy, 58 per cent pretty happy and 12 per cent not too happy.

A new study conducted by the University of Leicester compiled data from 178 countries and 100 global studies to map happiness across the world. Denmark came top with Switzerland 2nd, but surprisingly Bhutan was 8th. Despite having the highest average per capita GDP in the world, the USA only came 23rd whilst the UK came 41st. Most of Africa and the former Soviet republics scored worst. Burundi, Zimbabwe and the Democratic Republic of Congo were the world's least happy places. The report's author, Adrian White, said that countries with good access to healthcare and education came out on top.

Some people claim that shopping is therapeutic, but does buying things actually make people happier? In Bhutan, shopping is becoming a more regular experience especially for the urban young. There are now plenty of cheap clothes imported from a globalised marketplace available for sale. Fifty years ago, the economy was almost totally agrarian, based on subsistence agriculture where barter was the norm and money virtually unheard of. According to Kuenzang Roder, Bhutan's best known writer, people were poor but life's details had meaning. In 1998, Bhutan's king allowed in television and the Internet. This introduced a fever among the people for a different way of life and for new products. Now, at night, young people in Bhutan's capital take off their traditional dress and put on imported blue jeans to go dancing. 'The culture of fast clothes is coming in, and it's a very confusing kind of experience. Now shades of dissatisfaction with the traditional way of life are creeping in everywhere - from private living rooms to call-in radio talk shows.'

Source: adapted from en.wikipedia.org; World Bank, World Development Report; www.developments.org.uk; www.bhootan.org; news.independent.co.uk, www.le.ac.uk.

Figure 4 Subjective well-being, by country 2005-2006

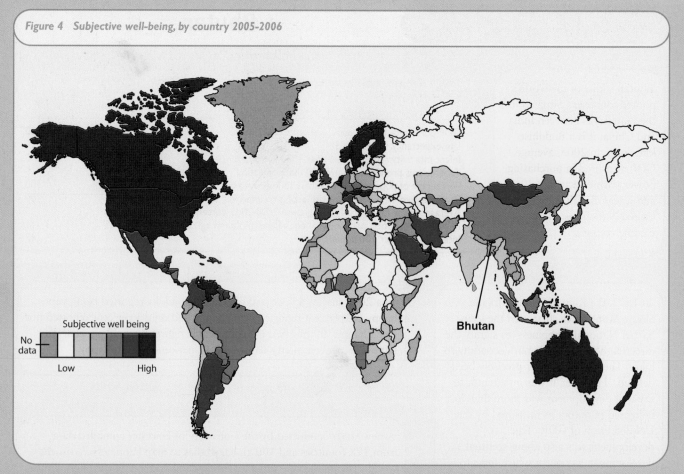

Subjective well being

No data

Low   High

Bhutan

Source: adapted from en.wikipedia.org.

1. Explain the possible distinction between GDP and happiness, using Bhutan as an example.
2. Discuss whether the main aim of Bhutan's government should be to maximise growth in GDP.

Summary

1. Cyclical unemployment and real wage unemployment occur when the labour market is in disequilibrium due to either a lack of demand for labour or because of rigidities in the labour market.
2. Frictional, seasonal and structural unemployment occur when the labour market for the whole economy is in equilibrium.
3. Cyclical unemployment is involuntary but all other types of unemployment are examples of voluntary unemployment. The rate of voluntary unemployment is called the natural rate of unemployment.
4. The short run Phillips curve suggests that there is a trade off between unemployment and inflation in the short run.
5. The long run Phillips curve suggests that when unemployment is at its natural level, there is no trade off. Higher aggregate demand simply leads to inflation.

Labour market equilibrium

Equilibrium in the labour market is achieved when the demand for labour is equal to the supply of labour. The demand for labour in an economy is determined by the marginal revenue product of labour. As more and more workers are combined with a fixed stock of land and capital, the **marginal revenue product** of labour (the addition to output of the extra worker) declines (an example of the **law of diminishing returns**). Hence the demand curve for labour is downward sloping.

The supply curve for labour in an economy is likely to be upward sloping. As real wage rates increase, more adults, particularly women, are attracted into the workforce. In the very short term, employers can also persuade existing workers to work overtime if they offer higher rates of pay.

Figure 1 shows the equilibrium level of employment in the economy. Employment is 0E whilst the equilibrium wage rate is 0W. Unemployment in the economy then occurs for two reasons. Either the labour market moves away from its equilibrium position, with actual wages being above 0W, or there is still

some measured unemployment even when the labour market is in equilibrium. These two possibilities are explored in this unit.

Unemployment when the labour market is in disequilibrium

Sometimes the labour market moves away from its equilibrium position. Figure 2 shows such a situation. The actual wage rate, 0V, is above the market clearing wage rate of 0W. Compared to the equilibrium position:
- FE fewer workers are demanded by employers because the wage rate is too high;
- EG more workers want a job because the wage rate is so high.

The result is that there is FG unemployment in the economy.

If wage rates were to fall to 0W, unemployment would fall as firms demanded more workers and some workers dropped out of the labour market, not willing to work at the lower wage rates. There is a number of reasons why the labour market can be in disequilibrium and each gives rise to a particular type of unemployment.

Cyclical or demand-deficient unemployment When an economy goes into recession, unemployment rises because there is insufficient demand within the economy. It is not just labour which becomes unemployed, factories, machines, mines, offices and farms (i.e. land and capital) become unemployed too. Figure 3 shows what happens in the labour market in a recession. The demand for labour falls, shown by a shift to the left in the demand curve. Employment used to be at 0E. Now it is at 0G with the old wage rate of 0W. This is because 0E workers want a job but only 0G workers are demanded by firms.

This unemployment of GE is cyclical or demand-deficient unemployment. It is also sometimes called **Keynesian unemployment** because it was Keynes who argued in the 1930s that the Great Depression was caused by a lack of demand within the economy. In a recession, the economy is in disequilibrium. Macroeconomic forces will work to restore the economy to its long run equilibrium position. The extra demand for goods will then generate extra demand for labour. Therefore, in the long run the demand curve for labour will shift back to the right in Figure 3. In the short run,

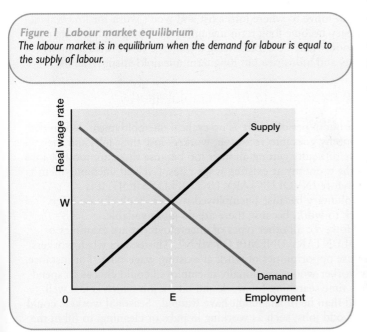

Figure 1 Labour market equilibrium
The labour market is in equilibrium when the demand for labour is equal to the supply of labour.

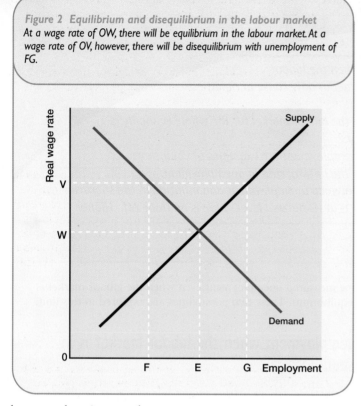

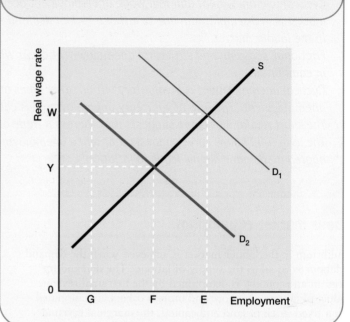

however, there is unemployment.

Classical unemployment CLASSICAL UNEMPLOYMENT or REAL WAGE UNEMPLOYMENT exists when the real wage rate is above that needed to clear the labour market even when the economy is booming. Jobs exist but workers choose not to take them because they are not prepared to accept the wages being offered, or they are unable to take them because of trade union power or government legislation. In Figure 2, the actual wage rate of 0V is too high to clear the market. What's more, wages are 'sticky downwards'. This means that there are factors preventing wages from falling to clear the market.

One reason why unemployed people refuse to take jobs is because unemployment benefit levels are too near the level of pay being offered. If benefit levels are above 0W in Figure 2, there is no point in workers accepting a job at a wage rate of 0W. The ratio between the benefit actually received and the wage a worker could receive is known as the REPLACEMENT RATIO. If the ratio were 1.0, then the unemployed would receive exactly the same from working as from being unemployed. If the ratio were 2, the unemployed would be twice as well off on the dole as working. One way of reducing the replacement ratio and giving the unemployed a greater incentive to take a job is to cut unemployment benefits.

Another reason why the labour market may fail to clear is because of minimum wage legislation. If the minimum wage is 0V in Figure 2, then there will inevitably be unemployment.

Another factor could be trade unions forcing up wages above their equilibrium level. Trade unions serve the interests of their members, nearly all of whom are in employment. Pushing up wage levels, even if this means long term job losses, is likely to be seen as advantageous by the trade union.

Unemployment when the labour market is in equilibrium

Even when the labour market is in equilibrium, there might still be unemployment for a variety of reasons explained in an earlier unit. **Frictional unemployment** will always occur in a market economy because workers take time to move between jobs. In some markets, **seasonal unemployment** will occur because of patterns of demand and supply. **Structural unemployment** will also occur because markets develop rigidities. Experience shows that it can take decades to reduce the measured unemployment caused by large scale closures of industry. Unemployed workers fail to move to where jobs exist and won't work for low wages, so they become long term unemployed. The paradox is that an economy may be experiencing a shortage of workers in many areas and industries but long term unemployment remains.

The natural rate of unemployment

In a boom period, there is no cyclical unemployment. When the economy goes into recession, workers lose their jobs and they have difficulty getting another job because there are too few jobs in the economy at existing wage rates. Cyclical unemployment is therefore INVOLUNTARY UNEMPLOYMENT. It is involuntary because unemployed workers can't choose to go back to work, because there are no jobs available.

However, all other types of unemployment are examples of VOLUNTARY UNEMPLOYMENT. This occurs when workers refuse opportunities of work at existing wage rates. For instance, a worker who is frictionally unemployed could choose to spend less time searching for work and take a job which is less well paid than he or she might have wanted. Seasonal workers could find odd jobs, such as working in pubs or cleaning, to fill in the

Question 1

The following workers in London find themselves unemployed. The level of unemployment in London has been slowly rising for the past three years. Explain how you would classify the type of unemployment faced by each of these workers.

(a) Mr Robert Quinn, 24, has been unemployed for two months after being laid off from his labouring job. 'I think the firm was short of money', he said. He could not find any jobs and his marriage had broken up.

(b) Mr David Kimber, 26, originally from Liverpool, became unemployed three weeks ago when his contract as a tower crane driver expired. 'I have been promised contracts but jobs are being put back.'

(c) Mr Kirpal Singh, 24 and single, quit two months ago after two years as a computer operator for Harrods, the department store, 10 miles away. 'It was just too far to travel every day', he said. He was optimistic about getting another job and said he was being called for second interviews.

(d) Ms Susan Morrison, 19, was pessimistic about getting another job in word processing. She left one job in January after a month when she was told she was 'not the right person' for the job. She previously resigned from British Telecom because she believed she was the lowest paid person in her office.

(e) Ms Patricia Jones, 24, a former deputy catering officer at a large London further education establishment, said: 'There was no career development being offered. I have got all the qualifications to progress in catering so I want a good job with a salary in five figures.'

(f) Mr Peter Vass, 24, a former merchandiser with Maples, the furniture group, resigned because: 'I was paid about £14 000 a year and it just was not enough.' Unemployed for 13 weeks, he was optimistic about getting a new job.

months when they are out of work from their main occupation. Those suffering from structural unemployment could get a job if they were prepared to accept a lower rate of pay or worse conditions of work. So, unemployed workers in Northern Ireland could come to the South of England to find jobs. Redundant steel workers could become bar attendants or security guards. Classical unemployment is voluntary because individual workers, trade unions or governments choose to allow unemployment to exist by maintaining too high wages. The NATURAL RATE OF UNEMPLOYMENT is the percentage of workers who are voluntarily unemployed. The economy is said to be at **full employment** when there is no involuntary unemployment in the economy. The distinction between voluntary and involuntary unemployment can be shown on diagrams. In Figure 4, the long run aggregate supply curve for the economy is drawn with an equilibrium output level of 0E. At this output level, the economy, including the labour market, is in long run equilibrium. However, some workers choose not to work at the equilibrium wage level in the economy. In Figure 4, the equilibrium wage rate is 0W. Two supply curves for labour are drawn. $S_{workers}$ shows the number of workers who are prepared to accept a job at any given wage rate. $S_{Labour\ force}$ is $S_{workers}$ plus those who claim they wish to work, but are not prepared to work at the given wage rate. Official statistics therefore show that there is EF unemployment in the economy. This unemployment is voluntary and 0E is the **natural level of employment** in the economy. EF is the **natural level of unemployment**. The **natural rate of unemployment** is the natural level of unemployment divided by the labour force, EF ÷ 0F.

What if the economy is at output level 0D in Figure 4? Here, the economy is in a recession with output below the full employment level of 0E. There will therefore be cyclical unemployment, which is involuntary unemployment. The market will return to equilibrium at 0E and in the process will reduce the level of cyclical unemployment to zero.

The extent to which unemployment is voluntary or involuntary has been a major controversy in economics. Keynesian economists have argued that most of the unemployment in the Great Depression of the 1930s and the major recessions of 1980-82 and 1990-92 was demand-deficient in nature. At the other extreme, classical economists of the rational expectations school of thought have argued that labour markets will adjust almost instantaneously to large rises in unemployment. Wage rates will fall and the labour market will clear. According to this view, there were plenty of jobs around in the 1930s and 1980s but workers refused to take them. Hence there was no involuntary unemployment.

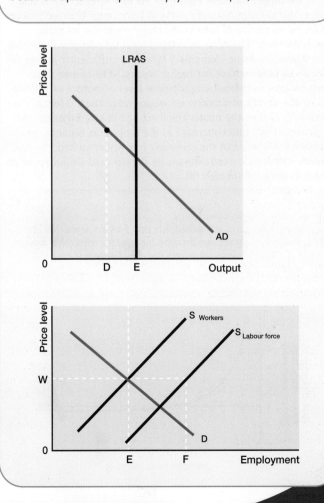

Figure 4 Voluntary unemployment

Voluntary unemployment exists when a part of the labour force refuses to work at the going wage rate. Equilibrium full employment exists at OE. At OW, the equilibrium wage rate, EF workers choose not to work. The natural rate of unemployment is therefore EF÷OF. Cyclical unemployment occurs if the economy is below the equilibrium output and employment level of OE, such as OD.

The short run Phillips curve

In 1958, Professor A W Phillips at the London School of Economics published *The Relation between Unemployment and the Rate of Change of Money Wage Rates, 1861-1957*. He showed that there was a remarkably stable relationship between the rate of change of money wages and the level of unemployment. As can be seen from Figure 5, high rates of unemployment were associated with low (and even negative) rates of change of money wage rates whilst low rates of unemployment were associated with high rates of change of money wage rates. The line of best fit came to be called the PHILLIPS CURVE.

This relationship provides a useful insight into the causes of inflation. Changes in money wage rates are a key component in changes in prices. Assume money wage rates rise by 10 per cent whilst all other factors remain constant. If 70 per cent of a firm's costs are wages, then its costs will rise by 7 per cent. It is likely to pass these costs on in the form of higher prices. These higher prices will feed through to higher costs for other firms or directly into the inflation rate (for instance, the Retail Price Index in the UK). The higher the rate of change of money wages, the higher the likely rate of inflation. Hence the Phillips curve hypothesis can be altered slightly to state that there is an inverse relationship between inflation and unemployment. When unemployment is low, inflation will be high. When unemployment is high, inflation will be low or even negative (i.e. prices will be falling).

The short run Phillips curve can be seen in the Keynesian aggregate supply curve in Figure 6. At low level levels of real output, the aggregate supply curve is horizontal because workers are prepared to accept jobs at the same wage due to high unemployment. However, at output level 0A, despite there still being unemployment, demand is labour is sufficiently strong for workers to begin to ask for higher wages. The nearer the economy gets to the full employment level of output of 0B, the greater the ability of workers to secure wage rises. Hence, inflation is higher, the nearer the level of full employment. At 0B, real output cannot increase in the long term because the productive potential of the economy has been reached. So the short run Phillips curve is shown by the upward sloping part of the curve between 0A and 0B.

In a study of 6 000 employed and unemployed workers, a team of academics found that, contrary to popular opinion, the jobless were more committed to employment than those already in work. 77 per cent were willing to take a job even if there were no financial necessity, compared with 66 per cent of those with jobs who said they would continue to work. There was no evidence that the unemployed were difficult to please in the job market. Only 12 per cent of the unemployed said they expected pay above that of the average of their employed counterparts. 45 per cent of all those out of work said they had seriously considered re-training in order to find work, with 40 per cent prepared to move area.

The study also considered whether the unemployed were intrinsically less 'employable'. Two methods were used to compare the unemployed and those in work. First, an examination of the work histories of the unemployed showed that people out of work had previously held almost exactly the same number of jobs as the employed - by far the biggest factors determining work experience were age, sex and industry. Second, the fact was that the average duration of the longest jobs of the unemployed was 74 months, and for the employed 76 months which, the study says, 'suggests employability rather than behavioural instability.'

(a) To what extent does the study outlined above suggest that unemployment is mainly voluntary?

The short run Phillips curve can also be shown using a classical aggregate demand and supply model. Assume that prices are stable and that there is an increase in aggregate demand. Perhaps planned investment has increased, or the government wishes to increase its expenditure. This will shift the aggregate demand curve to the right in Figure 7. The economy moves along its short run aggregate supply curve from

Figure 6 The Keynesian long run aggregate supply curve

Traditional Keynesian economists argue that, even in the long run, unemployment may persist because wages don't necessary fall when uneployment occurs. When there is mass unemployment output can be increased without any increases in costs and therefore prices. As the economy nears full employment, higher output leads to higher prices. At full employment the economy cannot produce any more whatever prices firms receive.

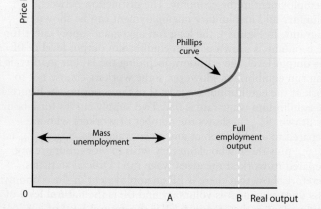

Figure 5 The Phillips curve

The original Phillips curve was derived from data from the period 1861 to 1913. Phillips then showed that the curve predicted the relationship between the rate of change of money wage rates and unemployment in the period 1913 to 1957.

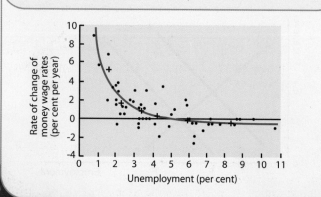

Figure 7 Aggregate demand and aggregate supply
An increase in aggregate demand from AD₁ to AD₂ will increase prices. It will also increase output and therefore reduce unemployment. This movement from A to B shows the short run Phillips curve relationship. In the long run the economy moves back to C. There is no trade-off in the long run between unemployment and inflation.

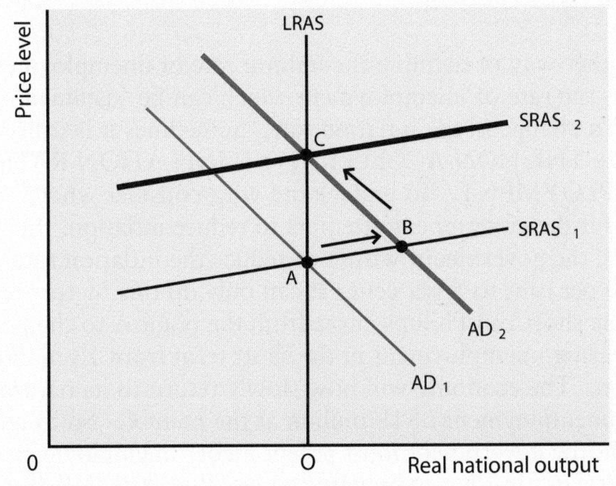

Figure 8 The long run Phillips curve
In the long run, the Phillips curve is vertical. Attempts by government to reduce unemployment below the natural rate of unemployment OA will be successful in the short run, for instance moving the economy from A to Z. But in the long run the only result will be higher inflation.

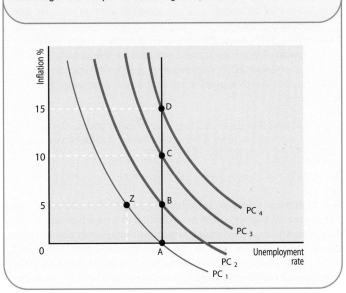

A to B. Note that the movement involves an increase in output and an increase in the price level. An increase in output is usually associated with a fall in unemployment. The increase in the price level is of course inflation. Hence the move from A to B shows the Phillips curve trade-off: higher inflation for lower unemployment. The relationship would be no different if aggregate demand fell, shifting the aggregate demand curve to the left, except that lower inflation would be traded off for higher unemployment. So the Phillips curve as originally plotted by Phillips shows what happens when the economy adjusts in the short run to a **demand-side shock**.

The long run Phillips curve with zero inflation

On classical assumptions, point B in Figure 7 is not a long run equilibrium point. Given that the economy is at full employment at the point A, the economy has moved to a position of over-full employment at B. In the labour market, workers will be able to bid up wage rates, shifting the short run aggregate supply curve upwards. The economy will only return to equilibrium at the point C where aggregate demand once again equals long run aggregate supply. The movement from B to C involves a rise in measured unemployment whilst inflation falls back to zero again when the economy reaches the point C (remember we assumed that the economy had no inflation at A and once the economy reaches C there are no forces which will increase prices any more). In the long run, therefore, there is no trade-off between inflation and unemployment.

The vertical long run Phillips curve

When inflation is zero or very low, as for instance in the UK in the 1950s or since the late 1990s, economic agents are likely to suffer from MONEY ILLUSION. This is the belief that prices are stable when in fact they might not be. For instance, if workers receive a money wage increase of 2 per cent, they may

believe they are 2 per cent better off. However, if inflation is also running at 2 per cent then they are in fact no better off at all because their real wages would be unchanged. They would then be said to be suffering from money illusion.

When economic agents become aware that inflation is eroding the value of income and wealth, they change their behaviour. Workers, for instance, may negotiate on a real terms basis. Instead of negotiating for, say, a 2 per cent wage increase, they might negotiate for 2 per cent plus the expected rate of inflation. Such behaviour affects the position of the short run Phillips curve.

In Figure 8, the original Phillips curve is PC₁. Workers and firms assume that there will be no price changes and the economy is in equilibrium at the point A. The government now increases aggregate demand, pushing the economy to the point Z on the short run Phillips curve PC₁, reducing unemployment and increasing inflation to 5 per cent. If workers suffer from money illusion, the economy will eventually return to the point A as explained above. But assume that they are more sophisticated and expect inflation to continue at 5 per cent per annum. Workers will bargain for even higher money wages which further push up prices. Hence real wages fall and workers drop out of the labour market. Unemployment will return to a level of 0A but a 5 per cent inflation rate will become permanent. The short run Phillips curve will have shifted to PC₂ and the economy will be at B. If the government attempts again to reduce unemployment, inflation will rise, say to 10 per cent on PC₂. In the long run the economy will return to unemployment 0A but on a higher Phillips curve PC₃.

The natural rate of unemployment

In Figure 8, why does the economy keep tending back towards the same level of unemployment, 0A? 0A is known as the **natural rate of unemployment**. It is the rate of unemployment which exists when the economy is

In 2005, inflation, as measured by the RPI, was 2.8 per cent. Pay deals accepted in 2005 included the following.

● In September 2005, the AUT, the union representing lecturers in Further Education colleges, accepted a 3 per cent pay deal for 2005-2006.
● In June 2005, Royal Mail managers accepted a deal worth between 3.2 per cent and 4 per cent for the coming year.
● In December 2005, workers employed by Wincanton won a pay deal worth around 4 per cent to cover a seven month period.

Explain whether these workers' decisions to accept the pay offers would have been different if inflation had been running at (a) 0 per cent and (b) 15 per cent.

in long run equilibrium (i.e. where aggregate demand equals long run aggregate supply). It was explained in an earlier unit that the economy, based on classical assumptions, tends towards its long run equilibrium level through changes in wages and prices. If the economy is below the natural rate of unemployment, then aggregate demand is above long run aggregate supply, as at the point B in Figure 7. Workers will be able to bid up wage rates, and the short run aggregate supply curve will shift upwards till long run equilibrium is once again re-established. If unemployment is above its natural rate, aggregate demand is less than long run aggregate supply. Unemployment will force workers to accept wage cuts. Firms will then take on more labour, expanding output and lowering unemployment to its natural level.

If the economy is in long run equilibrium, the labour market will also be in equilibrium. So another definition of the natural rate of unemployment is that it is the rate of unemployment which occurs when the demand for labour equals the supply of labour.

In the long run, the economy will always tend towards its natural rate of unemployment. Hence the long run Phillips curve is vertical. It is the line ABCD in Figure 8. There is no long run trade-off between unemployment and inflation. A government can reduce unemployment below its natural rate in the short run but, in the long run, unemployment will climb back up again and inflation will be higher.

Reducing inflation

Yet another way of defining the natural rate of unemployment is that it is the rate of unemployment which can be sustained without a change in the inflation rate. Sometimes it is called the NAIRU - THE NON-ACCELERATING INFLATION RATE OF UNEMPLOYMENT. To understand why, consider what happens if the government attempts to reduce inflation. In Figure 9, the government wishes to reduce the inflation rate from 10 per cent to 5 per cent. It can only do this by travelling down the short run Phillips curve from the point A to the point B, increasing unemployment in the short term from 1½ million to 3 million. The economy will now slowly return to its natural rate of unemployment of 1½ million at the point C. So to reduce inflation, the government must accept higher unemployment in the short run. If it is not prepared to pay this price, inflation will remain constant at 10 per cent with 1.5 million unemployed.

(a) Explain between what years shown in the data a normal short run Phillips curve relationship would seem to hold.
(b) (i) What is meant by the NAIRU?
    (ii) Explain between what years the NAIRU might have fallen.

Table 1 Unemployment and inflation

	Unemployment, (claimant count), millions	Inflation (RPI) %
1988	2.4	4.9
1989	1.5	7.8
1990	1.6	9.4
1991	2.3	5.9
1992	2.8	3.8
1993	2.9	1.6
1994	2.6	2.5
1995	2.3	3.4
1996	2.1	2.4
1997	1.6	3.2
1998	1.4	3.4
1999	1.3	1.5
2000	1.1	3.0
2001	1.0	1.8
2002	1.0	1.7
2003	0.9	2.9
2004	0.9	1.3
2005	0.9	2.8
2006	1.0	3.2

Source: adapted from *Economic Trends Annual Supplement*, Office for National Statistics.

Figure 9 Reducing inflation
A government can only reduce inflation by moving down the short run Phillips curve, for instance from A to B. In the long run the economy will settle at C, but a heavy price will have been paid in the form of high transitional unemployment.

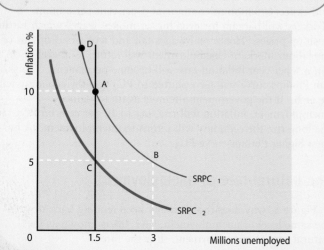

An increase in the inflation rate above 10 per cent can only come about through an increase in aggregate demand over and above what it would otherwise have been. This increase will again move the economy off the point A, this time up the short run Phillips curve to D.

So the labour market can be in equilibrium at the natural rate of unemployment (at the NAIRU) with any inflation rate. Hence, once again the long run Phillips curve is vertical. The only way to reduce the NAIRU (i.e. push the vertical long run Phillips curve to the left), according to classical economists, is to adopt supply side policies.

Keynesians, monetarists and classical economists

The theory that the Phillips curve was vertical in the long run was put forward by the founder of modern monetarism, Milton Friedman. It was he too who suggested that workers might not suffer from money illusion. Hence his theory is sometimes called the **expectations-augmented Phillips curve hypothesis or adaptive-expectations hypothesis**.

Keynesians have tended to doubt the existence of a natural rate of unemployment. This is because they believe that it takes a very long time for labour markets to clear if there is mass unemployment. In Figure 9, a government which creates unemployment of CB in order to reduce inflation may well find that the economy gets stuck with an unemployment level of 3 million. Unless it is prepared to wait perhaps a decade or more, it can only reduce unemployment by expanding demand again and accepting higher inflation.

On the other hand, New Classical economists have suggested that the short run Phillips curve does not exist. In their theory of **rational expectations** they argue that economic agents, such as workers, trade unions and employers, are able to see whether inflation and unemployment are likely to rise or fall in the future.

If the government states that it is prepared to accept a rise in unemployment in order to reduce inflation, workers will immediately moderate their wage demands in order to avoid unemployment. Inflation therefore falls immediately. So the conclusion is that the economy will always be on the vertical long run curve because economic agents perfectly adapt their expectations in the light of economic news.

Question 5

In a study of 6 000 employed and unemployed workers, a team of academics found that the unemployed had poor psychological health. They were more likely to be depressed, less likely to mix with people in work and had little access to social support networks or to information about jobs. One of the team, Richard Lampard of Warwick University, concluded that unemployment directly increases the risk of marriage break-up, finding that the chances of the marriage of an unemployed person ending in the following year are 70 per cent higher than those of a person who has never been out of work.

The study also found that men in low-paid insecure jobs suffered almost the same level of psychological distress as those who were out of work altogether. It was found that there was a close correlation between perceived job security and psychological well-being. Women were found to be just as distressed by lack of paid work, but less affected by the prospect of an insecure low-paid job.

(a) What problems face the unemployed, according to the article?
(b) Why might these problems give rise to costs not just for the unemployed but also for society as a whole?

Key terms

Classical or real-wage unemployment - when real wages are kept at such a high level that the demand for labour is greater than the supply of labour.
Involuntary unemployment - unemployment which exists when workers are unable to find jobs despite being prepared to accept work at the existing wage rate.
Money illusion - when economic agents such as workers believe that changes in money values are the same as changes in real values despite inflation (or deflation) occurring at the time.
NAIRU, the non-accelerating inflation rate of unemployment - the natural rate of unemployment, the

level of unemployment which can be sustained with a change in the inflation rate.
Replacement ratio - unemployment benefits divided by the wage an unemployed worker could receive if in work.
The natural rate of unemployment - the proportion of the workforce which chooses voluntarily to remain unemployed when the labour market is in equilibrium.
The Phillips curve - the line which shows that higher rates of unemployment are associated with lower rates of change of money wage rates and therefore inflation and vice versa.
Voluntary unemployment - workers who choose not to accept employment at the existing wage rate.

Applied economics

The causes of unemployment in the UK

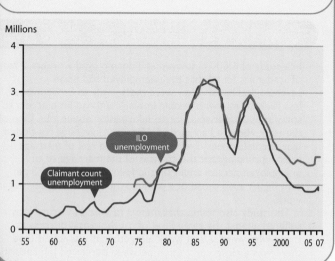

Figure 10 Unemployment, claimant count and ILO unemployed, UK millions

Unemployment in the post-war period

Figure 10 shows that unemployment since the mid-1970s was much higher than in the 1950s and 1960s on a claimant count basis. In the 1950s and 1960s, unemployment tended to be less than half a million workers. But in the 1970s, unemployment peaked at 0.9 million in 1972, 1.5 million in 1977, 3.3 million in 1986 and 2.9 million in 1993. This was not just a UK phenomenon. Unemployment rates in both Europe and the US were higher too. Unemployment in the UK and the US fell substantially in the second half of the 1990s whilst in Europe it remained stubbornly high.

The causes of unemployment since 1993

1993 saw a turning point in unemployment. Unemployment had been rising since 1989 due to a deep recession. By 1993, the claimant count level of unemployment had reached 2.9 million. Unemployment then fell during the rest of the 1990s and reached a low of 866 000 in 2004 before slightly rising again. There was a number of reasons for the fall in unemployment between 1993 and 2004.

● Cyclical unemployment fell and was arguably zero by the end of the 1990s. The successful management of the demand side of the economy both by the government through fiscal policy and the Bank of England through monetary policy, has led to the output gap being virtually zero over a

long period of time. This stability in demand growth has encouraged investment by firms and reduced the militancy of workers.

● Structural unemployment also fell. Although there continued to be a fall in manufacturing employment, this was at a much lower rate and involved fewer jobs than in the 1970s and 1980s. What's more, the service economies of the regions outside the South of England were much stronger and able to create more jobs than previously. The incoming Labour government in 1997 launched the 'New Deal' programme specifically aimed at getting young people and other groups which had difficulty finding employment into a job. Supply side reforms started in the 1980s continued to have an impact. Improved levels of education and training helped reduce structural unemployment, as did continued migration from high unemployment areas to lower unemployment areas.

● Classical unemployment fell too. Reforms of the tax and benefit system, such as the introduction of working tax credits helped increase incentives to work for those at the bottom end of the pay range.

Some economists, however, felt that the introduction of the minimum wage in 1999 and acceptance of European Union labour legislation, such as the 48 hour working week, have increased classical unemployment. They also felt that new trade union legislation, passed in 1998, which gave trade unions rights to force their negotiating rights in the workplace, have increased trade union power and thus raised unemployment.

Classical economists argue that the high unemployment seen in most of Europe since the 1990s has been the result of too high a level of union power, excessive employment taxes on firms, too generous unemployment benefits for workers and labour legislation which gave workers too many rights in the workplace. This has raised the cost of workers to employers and made them less flexible. The natural rate of unemployment has therefore been high in Europe. In contrast, they would argue that the prolonged fall in unemployment in the USA and to some extent in the UK has been the result of flexible labour markets. Trade unions are weaker, employment taxes are low and the state has a light hand in regulating the labour market. This has resulted in a falling natural rate of unemployment. On this view, both the US and UK governments have been highly successful in managing unemployment compared to their European counterparts.

However, the slight rise in unemployment between 2004-07 could signal that the UK has exhausted the benefits from its supply side reforms. The natural rate of unemployment has become stuck at around 1 million claimant count workers.

The Phillips curve

Figure 11 is a scatter diagram which shows the relationship between unemployment and inflation, the Phillips curve relationship, since 1963 in the UK. The colour coding helps to see that there is some empirical support for the idea that;

- there is an inverse relationship between unemployment and inflation over short time periods;
- the short run Phillips curve has shifted over time.

The data suggests that the short run Phillips curve shifted outwards between 1963-67 and 1980-87. This was the period when inflation rose from 2 per cent in 1963 to highs of 24 per cent in 1975 and 20 per cent in 1980. It could be argued that workers lost any money illusion that they had and bargained on the basis of 'RPI+', the rate of inflation plus whatever real increase in their wages they were seeking.

From the period 1988-94, the short run Phillips curve has arguably shifted back to the left as inflation has fallen. Inflationary expectations have fallen. By 2006, the position of the short run Phillips curve could be argued to be roughly the same as in 1963.

If the short run Phillips curve has been shifting over time, so too must the long run vertical Phillips curve and the natural rate of unemployment. Between 1963 and the mid 1980s, it was shifting outwards. From the late 1980s, it shifted inwards.

Some economists would dispute this analysis. They doubt the existence of the long run Phillips curve and the natural rate of unemployment. For example, they might point out that there was a sizeable reduction in unemployment between the period 1988-94 and 1995-98. Unemployment fell from 3 million in 1993 to 1.5 million in 1998. Such a reduction implies a very large shift backwards in the natural rate of unemployment in just a few years. This,

they would argue, is not a credible view even if the supply side reforms of the 1980s were still working their way through the economy in the 1990s.

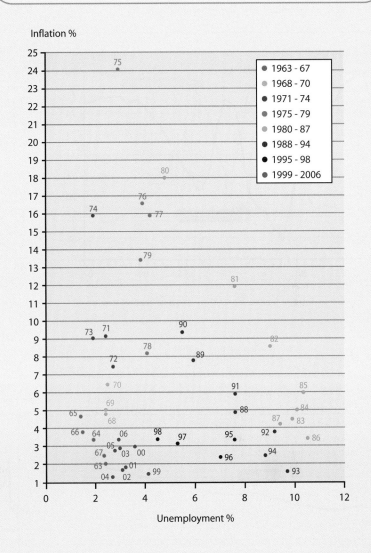

Figure 11 The Phillips curve from 1963

Source: adapted from *Economic Trends Annual Supplement*, Office for National Statistics

DataQuestion   The causes of unemployment

Figure 12 ILO employment and unemployment rates, %

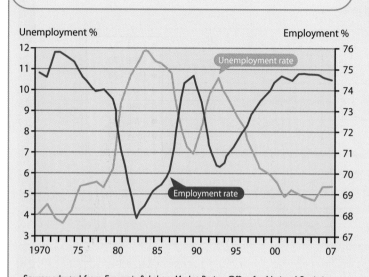

Source: adapted from *Economic & Labour Market Review*, Office for National Statistics.

Figure 14 Selected regional unemployment rates, claimant count, %

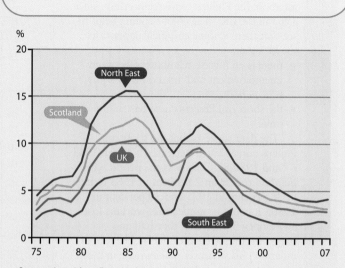

Source: adapted from *Economic & Labour Market Review*, Office for National Statistics.

Figure 13 Employee jobs in manufacturing and service industries

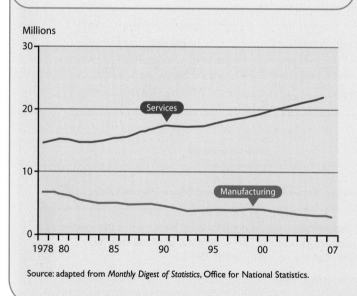
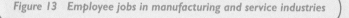

Source: adapted from *Monthly Digest of Statistics*, Office for National Statistics.

Figure 15 CBI survey of skilled labour shortages in manufacturing

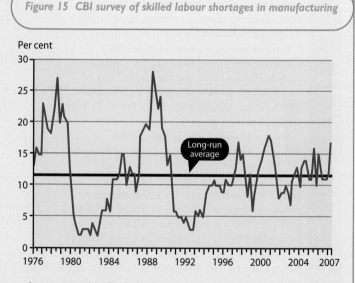

Source: adapted from *The Budget, The Economy*, Supplementary charts and tables, October 2007, HM Treasury.

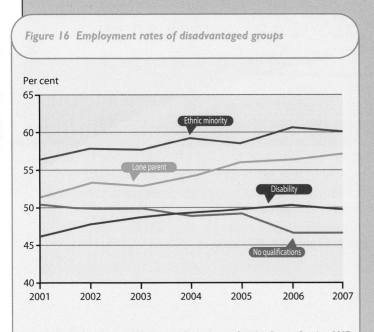

Figure 16 *Employment rates of disadvantaged groups*

Source: adapted from *Pre-budget Report and Comprehensive Spending Review*, October 2007, HM Treasury.

Figure 17 *Average employment rates by detailed ethnic groups, 1983-2003*

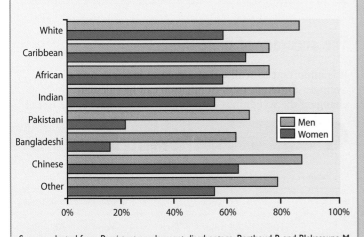

Source: adapted from Persistent employment disadvantage, Berthoud R and Blekesaune M., Department for Work and Pensions, Research Report no 416, 2007.

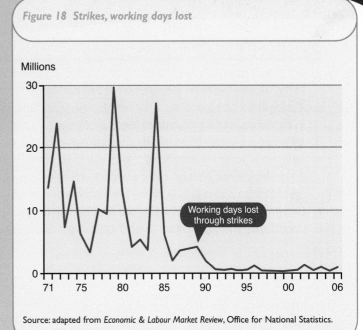

Figure 18 *Strikes, working days lost*

Source: adapted from *Economic & Labour Market Review*, Office for National Statistics.

1. A magazine has asked you to write an article on the causes of UK unemployment in recent years.
   In your article:
   (a) outline the main trends in unemployment during the period shown in the data;
   (b) explain the possible causes of unemployment, distinguishing between the main types of unemployment identified by economists;
   (c) using the data, evaluate what factors have been most important in determining unemployment levels since the early 1970s.

Summary

1. Inflation is measured by calculating the change in a weighted price index over time. In the UK, the two main measures are the Retail Price Index and the Consumer Price Index.
2. A price index only measures inflation for average households. It also cannot take into account changes in the quality and distribution of goods over time.
3. Inflation may either be caused by demand-pull or cost-push factors.
4. Inflation is generally considered to give rise to economic costs to society. These include shoe-leather and menu costs, psychological and political costs, and costs which arise from the redistribution of income in society. Some economists believe that inflation also results in higher unemployment and lower growth in the long term.
5. Deflation, falling prices, tends to lead to depressed demand in an economy.
6. Unanticipated inflation tends to give rise to higher economic costs than anticipated inflation.

Measuring inflation

The inflation rate is the change in average prices in an economy over a given period of time. The price level is measured in the form of an index. So if the price index were 100 today and 110 in one year's time, then the rate of inflation would be 10 per cent.

Calculating a price index is a complicated process. Prices of a representative range of goods and services (a **basket** of goods) need to be recorded on a regular basis. In the UK, there are two widely used measures of the price level: the Retail Price Index (RPI) and the Consumer Price Index (CPI). In theory, on the same day of the month, surveyors are sent out to record 110 000 prices for a variety of items. Prices are recorded in different areas of the country as well as in different types of retail outlets, such as corner shops and supermarkets. These results are averaged out to find the average price of goods and this figure is converted into **index number form**.

Changes in the price of food are more important than changes in the price of, say, tobacco. This is because a larger proportion of total household income is spent on food than on tobacco. Therefore the figures have to be **weighted** before the final index can be calculated. For instance, assume that there are only two goods in the economy, food and cars, as shown in Table 1. Households spend 75 per cent of their income on food and 25 per cent on cars. There is an increase in the price of food of 8 per cent and of cars of 4 per cent over one year. In a normal average calculation, the 8 per cent and the 4 per cent would be added together and the total divided by 2 to arrive at an average price increase of 6 per cent. However, this provides an inaccurate figure because spending on food is more important in the household budget than spending on cars. The figures have to be weighted. Food is given a weight of ¾ (or 0.75 or 750 out of 1 000) and cars a weight of ¼ (or 0.25 or 250 out of 1 000). The average increase in prices is 8 per cent multiplied by ¾ added to 4 per cent multiplied by ¼ (i.e. 6 per cent + 1 per cent). The weighted average is therefore 7 per cent. If the RPI were 100 at the start of the year, it would be 107 at the end of the year. In order to calculate a weighting, it is necessary to find out how money is spent. In the case of the Retail Price Index, the weighting is calculated from the results of the Expenditure and Food Survey. Each year, a few thousand households are asked to record their expenditure for one month. From these figures it is possible to calculate how the average household spends its money. (This average household, of course, does not exist except as a statistical entity.)

Table 1

Commodity	Proportion of total spending	Weight	Increase in price	Contribution to increase in RPI
Food	75%	750	8%	6%
Cars	25%	250	4%	1%
Total	100%	1 000		7%

The accuracy of price indices

It is important to realise that any price index is a weighted average. Different rates of inflation can be calculated by changing the weightings in the index. For instance, the Retail

Question 1

Table 2

Year	Weights			% annual increase in prices	
	Food	All other items	Total	Food	All other items
1	300	700	1 000	10	10
2	250	750	1 000	5	10
3	200	800	1 000	4	6
4	150	850	1 000	3	2
5	125	875	1 000	4	4
6	120	880	1 000	6	4
7	120	880	1 000	5	7
8	110	890	1 000	8	10

Table 2 shows the price index weights given to food and to all other items in each of eight years. It also shows the percentage annual increase in prices of those items.
(a) Calculate the rate of inflation (i.e. the percentage increase in prices) in each year 1 to 8.
(b) What would the price index in years 2-8 be if the price index were 100 in year 1?

Question 2

Table 3 Index of Retail Prices

	Average annual percentage change						
	1977-81	1982-86	1987-91	1992-96	1997-2000	2001-04	2005-06
General index	13.4	5.5	6.5	2.7	2.8	1.9	3.0
Pensioner index, two person household	12.8	5.3	5.3	2.8	1.6	1.6	2.9

Source: adapted from *Economic Trends Annual Supplement*, Office for National Statistics.

(a) Explain why the change in the General Index of Retail Prices may differ from the change in the Pensioner Index.

(b) A two person pensioner household where the pensioners retired in 1976 receives pensions linked to the General Index of Retail Prices. In which years would it, on average, have seen (i) an increase and (ii) a decrease in its real purchasing power? Explain why this occurs.

Price Index calculates the average price level for the average household in the UK. However, it is possible, again using data from the Expenditure and Food Survey, to calculate price indices for pensioner households or one parent households. One major difference between these households and the average household is that they spend a larger proportion of their income on food. So a 10 per cent rise in the price of food compared to a 5 per cent rise in the price of all other items will result in a higher rate of inflation for pensioners and one parent households than for the average household. In fact each individual household will have a different rate of inflation. The Retail Price Index only measures an average rate of inflation for all households across the UK.

The household spending patterns upon which the index is based also change over time. For instance, food was a far more important component of the Retail Price Index 30 years ago than it is today because spending on food was then a higher proportion of total spending. The index cannot indicate changes in the quality of goods. Cars might increase in price because their specifications improve rather than because there has been an inflationary price rise. The weights for the Retail Price Index are changed annually to take account of changes in spending patterns. However, this does not get round the fact that the average 'basket' or 'bundle' of goods purchased in 1950 and upon which the RPI for 1950 was calculated was very different from the average bundle of goods purchased in 2008.

The causes of inflation

Inflation is caused either by demand-side or supply-side factors.

Demand-pull inflation The demand-pull theory of inflation says that inflation will result if there is too much spending in relation to output. In an individual market, like the market for bananas, excess demand will lead to a rise in price. The same is true for a whole economy. If aggregate demand exceeds aggregate supply, the price level will rise and therefore there will be inflation.

Figure 1 shows an aggregate demand curve with a Keynesian aggregate supply curve. The economy is at full employment at income Y_F. Assume that there is a rise in aggregate demand from AD_1 to AD_2. This could be the result of an increase in consumer

confidence which raises autonomous consumer spending. Investment might rise because the rate of return on capital increases. The government might increase its spending. Alternatively, there might be a rise in exports because of strong economic growth in other countries. The result of these increases in real expenditure is a rise in both output and inflation. Output rises from 0A to 0B whilst the price level rises from 0E to 0F. Rising output will lead to a fall in unemployment. Falling unemployment accompanied by rising inflation is the **Phillips curve relationship**.

If the economy is already at full employment, with the aggregate demand curve at AD_3, then a rise in real expenditure which shifts the aggregate demand curve to AD_4 will lead only to a rise in inflation with no rise in output or decrease in unemployment. The Phillips curve then becomes vertical.

Policy makers today attempt to measure excess demand through output gaps. The output gap is the difference between the actual level of national income and a prediction of what it ought to be given its trend rate of growth in recent years. There is excess demand when the output gap is positive, i.e. actual national income is above its trend level. However, there can be demand-pull inflation even when the output gap is negative. As Figure 1 suggests, demand-pull inflationary pressures increase the nearer the output gap approaches zero, corresponding to the full employment level of income. For instance, the output gap may be negative overall, but certain industries or certain regions may be experiencing excess demand. So the South East of England and the service sector may be overheating when there is still excess capacity in the North East of England and in manufacturing industries.

The excess demand in the South East and in services will generate inflation throughout the economy even if other regions or industries are depressed.

Cost-push inflation The cost-push theory of inflation says that inflation is caused by changes in the supply-side of the economy which increases costs. The main types of costs in the economy

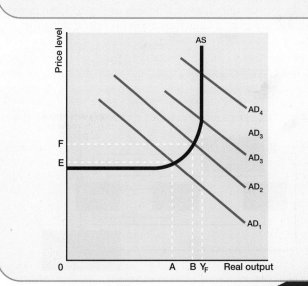

Figure 1 Demand-pull inflation
A rise in aggregate demand when the economy is at less than full employment will result in an increase in both prices and output. If the economy is at full employment, increases in aggregate demand simply lead to increases in inflation.

Table 4 Excess demand and inflation, UK

	Real GDP % change	Unemployment (claimant count) %	Inflation %
1970	2.1	2.6	6.5
1971	2.1	2.6	9.2
1972	3.7	2.9	7.5
1973	7.1	2.0	9.1
1974	-1.5	2.1	15.9
1975	-0.6	3.1	24.1
1976	2.8	4.2	16.5
1977	2.4	4.4	15.8
1978	3.2	4.4	8.3

Source: adapted from *Economic Trends Annual Supplement*, Office for National Statistics.

(a) Outline a demand-pull theory of inflation.
(b) To what extent do the data support a demand-pull theory of inflation?

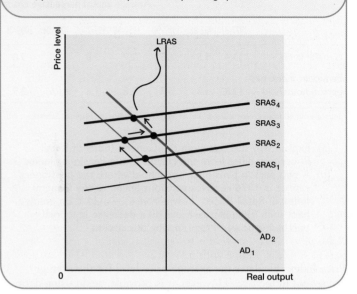

Figure 3 Cost-push inflation
An initial rise in costs leads to a chain of wage increases and increases in demand which feed back to increases in costs. Hence, the short run equilibrium level of prices in the economy is constantly moving upwards.

are wages, the price of imports, profits and indirect taxes.

The UK experience of the 1970s and early 1980s suggests that cost-push spirals can develop which lead to a long term cycle of inflation. To understand why, take the example of a country with zero inflation and few natural resources. International commodity prices of products such as oil, gas and coal increase by 50 per cent in one year. Domestic prices rise by 10 per cent as a result. Workers will now be 10 per cent worse off in real terms. So they will press for higher wages. If in the past they have become accustomed to receive a 2 per cent increase in real wages per year, they will be prepared to settle for 12 per cent. Firms pay the 12 per cent and pass on the increase in their costs in the form of higher prices. This fuels inflation. The following year, trade unions will once again fight for pay increases of 2 per cent plus the rate of inflation. In the meantime, the profits of firms will have been declining in real terms. So firms are likely to attempt to increase their profit margins in money terms, again fuelling inflation. This process, shown in Figure 2, is called a WAGE-PRICE SPIRAL or sometimes a COST-PUSH SPIRAL.

This wage-price spiral can also be seen in Figure 3. An initial price shock, say from a large increase in oil prices, shifts the

short run aggregate supply curve up from $SRAS_1$ to $SRAS_2$. With higher prices, workers demand higher wages which employers concede. This pushes the short run aggregate supply curve up even further to $SRAS_3$. The increase in wages leads to an increase in aggregate demand which shifts the aggregate demand curve to the right from AD_1 to AD_2. This further raises the price level. So workers again demand higher wage increases which employers concede. So the short run aggregate supply curve shifts up again to $SRAS_4$. And so it goes on, with wage rises fuelling both increases in costs to firms, hence shifting the SRAS curve upwards, and fuelling increases in aggregate demand.

The costs of inflation

A sustained rise in the price level is generally considered to be a problem. The higher the rate of inflation the greater the economic cost. There is a number of reasons why this is the case.

Shoe-leather costs If prices are stable, consumers and firms come to have some knowledge of what is a fair price for a product and which suppliers are likely to charge less than others. At times of rising prices, consumers and firms will be less clear about what is a reasonable price. This will lead to more 'shopping around' (wearing out your shoes), which in itself is a cost.

High rates of inflation are also likely to lead to households and firms holding less cash and more interest bearing deposits. Inflation erodes the value of cash, but since nominal interest rates tend to be higher than with stable prices, the opportunity cost of holding cash tends to be larger, the higher the rate of inflation. Households and firms are then forced to spend more time transferring money from one type of account to another or putting cash into an account to maximise the interest paid. This time is a cost.

Menu costs If there is inflation, restaurants have to change their menus to show increased prices. Similarly, shops have to change

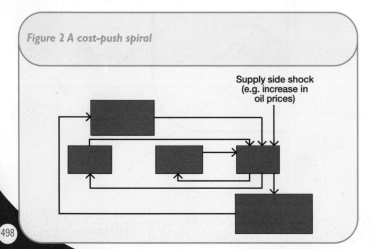

Figure 2 A cost-push spiral

Supply side shock (e.g. increase in oil prices)

their price labels and firms have to calculate and issue new price lists. Even more costly are changes to fixed capital, such as vending machines and parking meters, to take account of price increases.

Psychological and political costs Price increases are deeply unpopular. People feel that they are worse off, even if their incomes rise by more than the rate of inflation. High rates of inflation, particularly if they are unexpected, disturb the distribution of income and wealth as we shall discuss below, and therefore profoundly affect the existing social order. Change and revolution in the past have often accompanied periods of high inflation.

Redistributional costs Inflation can redistribute income and wealth between households, firms and the state. This redistribution can occur in a variety of ways. For instance, anybody on a fixed income will suffer. In the UK, many pensioners have received fixed pensions from private company pension schemes which are not adjusted for inflation. If prices double over a five year period, their real income will halve. Any group of workers which fails to be able to negotiate pay increases at least in line with inflation will suffer falls in its real income too.

If **real** interest rates fall as a result of inflation, there will be a transfer of resources from borrowers to lenders. With interest rates at 10 per cent and inflation rates at 20 per cent, a saver will lose 10 per cent of the real value of saving each year whilst a borrower will see a 10 per cent real reduction in the value of debt per annum.

Taxes and government spending may not change in line with inflation. For instance, if the Chancellor fails to increase excise duties on alcohol and tobacco each year in line with inflation, real government revenue will fall whilst drinkers and smokers will be better off in real terms assuming their incomes have risen at least by as much as inflation. Similarly, if the Chancellor fails to increase personal income tax **allowances** (the amount which a worker can earn 'tax free') in line with inflation, then the burden of tax will increase, transferring resources from the taxpayer to the government.

Unemployment and growth Some economists, mainly monetarists, have claimed that inflation creates unemployment and lowers growth. Inflation increases costs of production and creates uncertainty. This lowers the profitability of investment and makes businessmen less willing to take the risk associated with any investment project. Lower investment results in less long term employment and long term growth.

There is also a balance of payments effect. If inflation rises faster in the UK than in other countries, and the value of the pound does not change on foreign currency markets, then exports will become less competitive and imports more competitive. The result will be a loss of jobs in the domestic economy and lower growth.

The costs of deflation

Over the past fifty years, the main problem that countries have faced is high rates of inflation. However, there can also be problems associated with deflation, falling price levels. Between 1995 and 2007, Japan experienced falling prices which averaged 0.1 per cent per year and reached 0.9 per cent in 2002. This might seem insignificant but it had a serious impact on the Japanese economy. Falling prices were caused mainly by a lack of demand in the economy. However, they also caused demand to be depressed.

With falling prices, consumer confidence tends to be low. Consumers are concerned about the future and know that if they don't buy today, they might be able to buy at a cheaper price tomorrow. A lack of consumer confidence then feeds into a lack of business confidence and lower investment. Although interest rates tend to be very low with deflation, the real cost of borrowing is higher. If prices fall by, say, 1 per cent, then the real cost of borrowing is the actual or nominal interest rate plus 1 per cent.

The depressing effect on demand of deflation is the key reason why economists suggest that the ideal rate of change of the price level is a positive 1 or 2 per cent. Very low inflation means that the costs of higher inflation are avoided. At the same time, very mild inflation tends to be associated with economic growth and increasing prosperity.

Anticipated and unanticipated inflation

Some inflation is **unanticipated**; households, firms and government are uncertain what the rate of inflation will be in the future. When planning, they therefore have to estimate as best they can the expected rate of inflation. It is unlikely that they will guess correctly and hence their plans will be to some extent frustrated. On the other hand, inflation may be **anticipated**. Inflation may be a constant 5 per cent per year and therefore households, firms and government are able to build this figure into their plans.

Unanticipated inflation imposes far greater costs than anticipated inflation. If inflation is anticipated, economic agents can take steps to mitigate the effects of inflation. One way of doing this is through INDEXATION. This is where economic

Key terms

Headline rate of inflation - the increase in consumer prices including all housing costs. This is the RPI in the UK.
Indexation - adjusting the value of economic variables such as wages or the rate of interest in line with inflation.
Underlying rate of inflation - the RPIX, the increase in consumer prices excluding changes in mortgage costs, or the RPIY, which also excludes indirect taxes.
Wage-price or cost-push spiral - the process whereby increases in costs, such as wages, lead to increases in prices and this in turn leads to increases in costs to firms.

In 2005, the Index of Retail Prices rose by 2.8 per cent and in 2006 by 3.2 per cent. How might the following have been affected by the change?

(a) A pensioner on a fixed income.
(b) A bank deposit saver, given that the rate of interest on a bank deposit saving account was 2.0 per cent in 2005 and 2.5 per cent in 2006.
(c) A worker whose personal income tax allowance was £4895 between April 2005 and March 2006 and £5035 between April 2006 and March 2007.
(d) A mother with one child who received £17.00 in child benefit between April 2005 and March 2006 and £17.45 between April 2006 and March 2007.

variables like wages or taxes are increased in line with inflation. For instance, a union might negotiate a wage agreement with an employer for staged increases over a year of 2 per cent plus the change in the Retail Price Index. The annual changes in social security benefits in the UK are linked to the Retail Price Index. Economists are divided about whether indexation provides a solution to the problem of inflation. On the one hand, it reduces many of the costs of inflation although some costs such as shoe leather costs and menu costs remain. On the other hand, it reduces pressure on government to tackle the problem of inflation directly. Indexation eases the pain of inflation but is not a cure for it.

Moreover, indexation may hinder government attempts to reduce inflation because indexation builds in further cost increases, such as wage increases, which reflect past changes in prices. If a government wants to get inflation down to 2 per cent a year, and inflation has just been 10 per cent, it will not be helped in achieving its target if workers are all awarded at least 10 per cent wage increases because of indexation agreements.

Applied economics

The Retail Price Index (RPI)

Measures of inflation

In the UK, there is a wide variety of different measures of inflation. The two most commonly used are the Retail Price Index (RPI) and the Consumer Price Index (CPI).

The Retail Price Index is the traditional measure of the price level in the UK. Apart from informing economists and economics agents such as government or firms of the rate of inflation, it is also used for the indexation of pensions, state benefits and index-linked gilts (a form of long term government borrowing). Trade unions and firms may use the RPI in wage agreements and property companies may use it for calculating increases in leases (rents) on property. Utility regulators, which set prices for firms in industries such as telecommunications and water, may impose restrictions on price increases, or set price falls in terms of the RPI.

There are different measures of the RPI.

- The RPI itself measures the average price of the typical 'basket of goods' bought by the average household. It therefore measures average consumer prices.
- The RPIX excludes mortgage payments from the RPI calculation. This allows policy makers to see how prices are changed without including what can be a volatile and distorting element of the RPI, particularly when house prices are rising particularly fast or are falling.
- The RPIY excludes both mortgage payments and indirect taxes. When a government increases taxes on, say, cigarettes or petrol, these would be included in the RPI. By excluding them, policy makers are able to see how prices in the wider economy are changing. The RPIX and the RPIY are sometimes referred to as

the UNDERLYING RATE OF INFLATION, whilst the RPI is called the HEADLINE RATE OF INFLATION. The RPI is the headline rate because it is the measure which tends to be quoted in newspapers and on television and radio. The RPIX and the RPIY are underlying rates because they give a more reliable measure of trends in inflation over time.

The Consumer Price Index (CPI)

The CPI is a more recent measure of the price level and inflation. It is a measure which was developed by the European Union to be used across all countries in the EU. Before the introduction of the CPI, every country had a slightly different way of measuring the price level. The CPI in the UK before 2003 was called the Harmonised Index of Consumer Prices (HICP), 'harmonised' because it was a common measure across the EU. The CPI has only been calculated in the UK since January 1996, with estimates going back to 1988, and so this limits its use in making historical judgments about inflation. It has been used by the Bank of England to measure inflation against its target since 2003, and is therefore now the key indicator for monetary policy, replacing the RPI. However, the RPI is still widely used in other contexts. The two measures will continue to be used side by side in the future and there are no plans to phase out the calculation of the RPI.

Comparing the RPI and CPI

There is a variety of differences between the calculations of the CPI and the RPI. One important difference is that the CPI excludes a number of items relating to housing, whereas these are included in the RPI. Excluded from the CPI are council tax, mortgage interest payments, house depreciation, buildings insurance, and estate agents' and conveyancing fees. Another important difference is that the CPI uses a different way of calculating the mean value compared to the RPI. The CPI uses a geometric mean whereas the RPI uses an arithmetic mean.

Figure 4 shows how annual measures of the RPI, RPIX, RPIY and the CPI have differed since 1989. The CPI tends to be below the RPI for two reasons. One is that for most of the period 1989-2006 housing costs rose at a faster rate than other items. Since the CPI excludes many housing costs, it has tended to be lower. Second, using a geometric mean, as with the CPI, mathematically always produces a lower number than using an arithmetic mean, as with the RPI. On average, this mathematical difference has been 0.5 per cent of inflation over the period 1996-2006.

Calculating the RPI and CPI

The RPI and the CPI are calculated from the same data which is collected through monthly surveys. Two types of survey are carried out.

Prices are recorded in around 150 different areas of the UK. These locations are chosen through a random sampling method and around 30 are changed each year. 110 000 prices are collected per month of a typical 'basket of goods' bought by consumers. Around 650 items are included in the basket. Over time, what is included in the basket is changed to reflect changes in consumer spending. For example, rabbits were taken out of the index in 1955, whilst condoms were added in 1989 and credit card charges and DVD players in 2007.

In addition, a further 10 000 prices are collected centrally each month for items where local sampling would be inappropriate. Prices of goods in catalogues, utility (gas, electricity and telephone) prices, internet prices, road tolls, and mortgage interest payments are examples.

The typical basket of goods is constructed from another survey, the Expenditure and Food Survey. This survey asks around 7000 respondent households a year selected at random to keep diaries of what they spend over a fortnight. A spending pattern for the average family can then be worked out. The RPI and CPI are weighted to reflect the importance of different expenditures within the total. So the price of gas carries more weight in the index than the price of processed fruit because households spend more on gas. Figure 5 shows how weights have changed between 1962 and 2007. The proportion spent on food in the average budget has been declining over time as incomes have risen (food has a very low positive income elasticity of demand). Travel and leisure and housing and household expenditure, on the other hand, have been rising.

The CPI is based on the average basket of goods bought by all households. The RPI excludes high income households, defined as the top 4 per cent by income of households, and pensioner households which derive at least three quarters of their total income from state pensions and benefits. These two types of household are considered to have atypical spending patterns and so would distort the overall average.

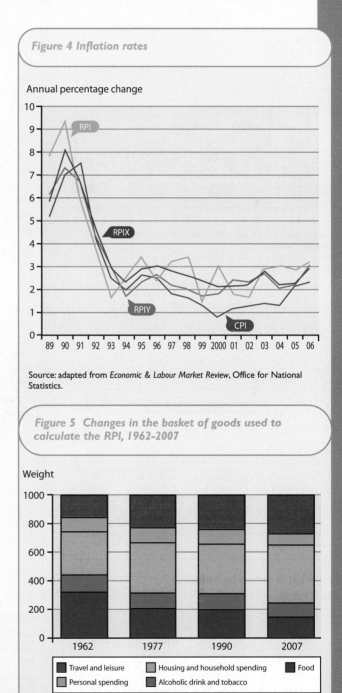

Figure 4 Inflation rates

Annual percentage change

Source: adapted from *Economic & Labour Market Review*, Office for National Statistics.

Figure 5 Changes in the basket of goods used to calculate the RPI, 1962-2007

Weight

Travel and leisure
Housing and household spending
Food
Personal spending
Alcoholic drink and tobacco

Source: adapted from *Monthly Digest of Statistics*, Office for National Statistics.

DataQuestion

Inflation

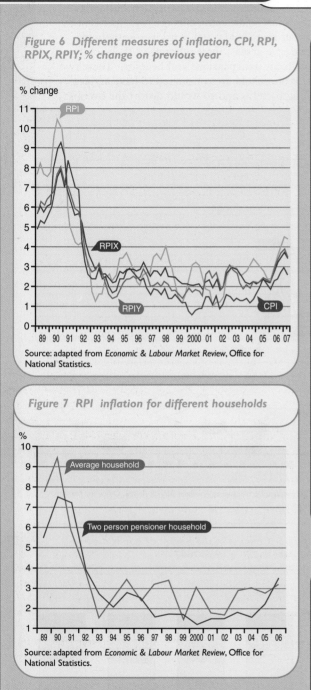

Figure 6 *Different measures of inflation, CPI, RPI, RPIX, RPIY; % change on previous year*

% change

RPI
RPIX
RPIY
CPI

Source: adapted from *Economic & Labour Market Review*, Office for National Statistics.

Figure 7 *RPI inflation for different households*

%

Average household

Two person pensioner household

Source: adapted from *Economic & Labour Market Review*, Office for National Statistics.

1. What is meant by 'inflation'?
2. Explain different ways in which inflation might be measured.
3. How might each of the following have been affected by inflation: (a) a UK pensioner, still alive today, who retired in 1989 with a company pension which remained the same and a state pension which increased in line with changes in the RPI; (b) UK 'techno-geek' who was 16 in 1989, and who loves everything from computers to mobile phones to cars; (c) a Brazilian food shopper in the early 1990s?

The RPI/CPI

What exactly does the RPI or CPI measure? Each year, items are added to the basket of goods used in the calculation of the index and each year items are removed. You won't find corsets, rabbits or men's cardigans in the RPI index any more but you will find DVDs, mobile phone handsets and frozen chicken nuggets. What's more, when the same item stays in the index, its specification may well change. This isn't true for potatoes, but it is true for, say, cameras. Forty years ago, few cameras had a built in flash. Today, even the cheapest cameras come with flash as a standard feature. Forty years ago, cars didn't come with air conditioning as standard but many do today. As for computers, whose specifications become more powerful by the year and month, how can the RPI/CPI hope to reflect such changes?

Does it matter that the basket of goods is constantly changing? The simple answer is yes. By changing the composition of the index, statisticians are not measuring the change in price of a fixed and unchanging basket of goods. Instead, they are attempting to measure changes in prices of how we spend our money. Presumably, we now buy, say, trousers rather than corsets, chicken rather than rabbits, or replica football team shirts rather than cardigans, because we prefer to do so. The amount of satisfaction to be gained from consuming some items rather than others is greater. So changes represent an increase in our living standards, the equivalent of a falling cost of living. As for increases in quality in goods, a failure to take these into account means that we overestimate the price paid for goods over time. When a software company puts additional features into a new computer game, but sells it for the same price as old computer games without these features, prices have effectively fallen but the RPI/CPI won't pick this up.

Inflation in Brazil

Before the conquest of hyper-inflation in Brazil in 1994, both Brazilian retailers and shoppers behaved in ways which seem strange today. Workers would be paid either at the end of the week or the end of the month. With prices going up every day, consumers would rush out with their pay packets and spend as much as they could afford. So retailers became used to sharp peaks in spending at the end of each week and a very large peak at the end of the month. There was little shopping around by consumers because they found it so difficult to keep up with changing prices. They had little or no idea what was a good price and what was expensive on any single shopping expedition. As for retailers, they often made their profit not from sales but from getting free credit. They would receive goods on credit, sell them immediately, but only have to pay in 30 or 60 days time. In the meantime, they could put the money in the bank and earn interest linked to the rate of inflation. In a good month, with inflation of say, 100 per cent, they could double their money.

Summary

1. The Fisher equation of exchange, states that MV≡PT. Based upon this equation, the quantity theory of money states that inflation is caused by excessive growth in the money supply.
2. Monetarists argue that in the short run, V is constant whilst T is growing slowly because T is the real rate of growth of the economy. Any increases in rate of growth of the money supply over and above the rate of growth of T will lead to inflation.
3. The monetary transmission mechanism shows the link between a rise in the money supply through to a fall in interest rates and a rise in aggregate demand, which finally leads to a rise in the price level.
4. If inflation is caused by shifts in the aggregate demand or aggregate supply curves, it can only persist if it is either validated or accommodated by an increase in the money supply.
5. Keynesian economists challenge whether there is any simple link between growth in the money supply and inflation.

The neutrality of money

In 1960 the President of France, General Charles de Gaulle, cut the value of all French money by a factor of 100. He passed a law which decreed that on 1 January 1960, 100 Francs would be called 1 Franc. So a 1 000 Franc note was reduced in value to 10 Francs. 10 000 Francs in a French bank account was only worth 100 Francs. A company which had borrowed 100 million Francs would only have to repay 1 million Francs. This change in the value of the Franc had little or no effect on the **real economy**. Because all monetary values were changed on the same day, relative values remained unchanged. Prices were only 1 per cent of their former level, but so too were wages. The company which had its loan cut by a factor of 100 still had to earn 100 times more in Francs to pay off the loan. The owner of a 1 000 Franc note saw its value reduced 100 fold, but then prices were reduced by the same factor. The note bought exactly the same quantity of goods and services as before.

This is an example of the neutrality of money. Money is said to be NEUTRAL if changes in the money supply only affect the level of prices in the economy. But economists disagree about the extent to which money is neutral. Some economists argue that changes in the money supply can have important effects on the real economy, in particular on variables such as national income and unemployment, whilst others argue that it is neutral.

The quantity theory of money

The QUANTITY THEORY OF MONEY is one of the oldest economic theories, dating back at least 500 years if not more. The theory states that increases in prices are caused solely by increases in the money supply. As Milton Friedman put it in his 1968 book *Dollars and Deficits*, 'inflation is always and everywhere a monetary phenomenon'. Advocates of the quantity theory of money are called MONETARISTS and the belief that inflation is caused solely by increases in the money supply is called MONETARISM.

Monetarism can be explained using the EQUATION OF EXCHANGE. The most famous formulation of the equation was made by Irving Fisher, an American economist who worked during the first half of this century. The FISHER EQUATION is:

$$MV \equiv PT$$

M is the total amount of money in the economy (i.e. the money supply). V is the VELOCITY OF CIRCULATION of money (sometimes also called the INCOME VELOCITY). V is the number of times the money supply changes hands over a period of time, such as a year. P is the average price of each transaction made in the economy. T is the total number of transactions made over a period of time.

The equation of exchange is an identity (i.e. it is true by definition). Assume that there is £100 of money (M) in circulation in the economy. On average, each £1 changed hands 4 times (V) during the year. So we know that £400 must have been spent during the year (M x V). If the average price of each transaction was £2 (P), there must have been 200 separate transactions (T) over the period. Similarly, if 100 transactions (T) take place over a year and each transaction was for an average of £5 (P), then the total amount spent was £500. If there was only £50 of money in circulation (M), that money must have changed hands on average 10 times during the year. So the velocity of circulation of money (V) must have been 10.

Monetarists argue that, in the short term, V and T are likely to be constant. T, the number of transactions in the economy, is equivalent to real national income or output. P times T is the same as money national income, the total value at current prices of the output of the economy. Why do monetarists argue that V and Y can be assumed to be constant?

The velocity of circulation The velocity of circulation of money is the average number of times a unit of money changes hands

Question 1

The money supply M is £200, V is 10 and T is 100.
(a) What is the value of P?
(b) The money supply now doubles. If V and T remain constant, what is the new value of P?
(c) At the new money supply level, T now increases from 100 to 150. What will happen to the price level if there is no change in the money supply and V remains constant?
(d) At the new money supply level, what is the level of
  (i) national income at constant prices and (ii) national income at current prices?
(e) If M = aP, what is the value of a at the new money supply level?

Question 2

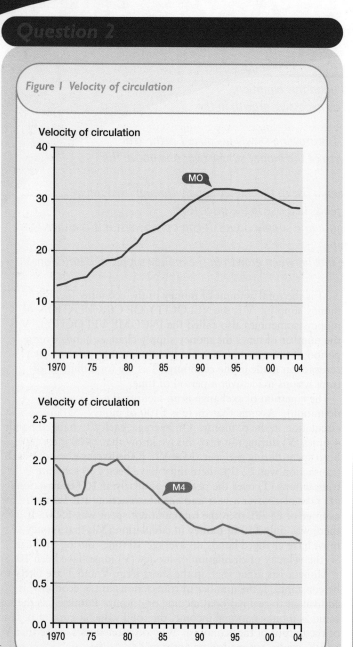

Figure I *Velocity of circulation*

Velocity of circulation [MO]

Velocity of circulation [M4]

Figure I shows two different measures of the velocity of circulation of money: that of M0, narrow money and of M4, broad money.

(a) To what extent is the velocity of circulation of money constant over time?

(b) Suggest reasons why the velocity of circulation may have changed over the period shown.

over a period of time. For instance, a £10 note may change hands 50 times a year.

One factor which determines the velocity of circulation is the way in which households receive money and make purchases.

● The velocity of circulation of broad money will tend to fall if there is a change from paying workers once a week to once a month. Households will now hold money for longer periods of time to cover expenditure later in the month.

● The increased use of **money substitutes**, such as

credit cards, will also reduce the velocity of circulation of money itself. Instead of making many separate money transactions, the card holder will make one transaction at the end of the month to the credit card company.

On the other hand, increased use of cheques and debit and credit cards will tend to lead to an increase in the velocity of circulation of notes and coins (M0). Households and firms increasingly do not keep cash as savings at home, but use it for transactions purposes. Cash card machines mean that households keep less and less cash as a proportion of income and spend it very quickly.

Another factor which is important in determining the value of V is the extent to which money is used for speculation in financial assets such as stocks and shares. If there is a large **speculative demand for money**, then V can vary as asset portfolios are switched in and out of money. Keynesians argue that when the rate of interest rises, households and firms desire to hold less money because the opportunity cost of holding money will have risen. The opportunity cost is the interest or return they could have obtained if they had placed their money in, say, a building society account or in stocks or shares. When the rate of interest rises, less money will be held to make the same number of transactions. Households and firms will make their smaller stock of money work harder (i.e. the velocity of circulation will rise).

So the debate about the value of the velocity of circulation of money is the same debate as the one about the determinants of the demand for money. Monetarists argue that the speculative

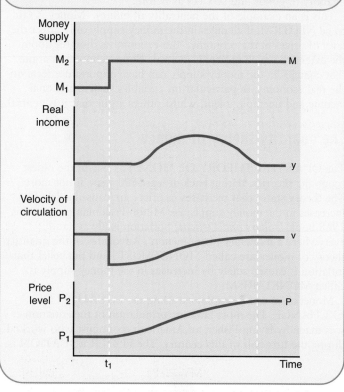

Figure 2 *The impact of a change in M on V, P and T*
An initial increase in the money supply from M_1 to M_2 leads to an immediate fall in V, the velocity of circulation of money. Then money begins to be spent, raising y and V. The rise in spending also leads to demand-pull inflation. With P rising, real income will eventually begin to fall. At the final equilibrium, V and y return to their initial levels, but P is now higher.

demand for money is relatively unimportant because money is held mainly for transactions purposes. In the long run V can change as institutional factors change, but the change will be slow. In the short run, V is broadly constant because the demand for money is a stable function of income. Keynesians, on the other hand, argue that changes in the rate of interest lead to significant changes in **liquidity preference** (i.e. the demand for money) and therefore the velocity of circulation is volatile in the short run.

National income Real national income tends to rise slowly over time. The annual growth rate of the UK economy over the past 40 years has averaged about 2.5 per cent. If $MV \equiv PT$ and V is constant, then the money supply can grow by the rate of growth of real income without generating a rise in prices. Monetarists indeed argue that the money supply should be expanded in line with real growth, otherwise prices will fall. Falling prices can be just as undesirable as inflation, but any expansion of the money supply over and above the rate of growth of real income will be inflationary, according to monetarists.

The monetary transmission mechanism

Monetarists argue that inflation is demand-pull in nature. Increases in the money supply lead to increases in aggregate demand which in turn lead to increases in the price level. The link between an increase in the money supply and inflation is known as the MONETARY TRANSMISSION MECHANISM. It can be illustrated in Figure 2.

At a point in time t_1, there is an increase in the money supply from M_1 to M_2. The immediate effect is a fall in the velocity of circulation, but as time goes on, this money begins to be spent, leading to a rise in real output and income, y. This in turn leads to demand-pull inflation and prices begin to rise. Rising prices lead to less real spending as consumers can now afford to buy less with their money. y begins to fall and equilibrium is restored when y and V are back to their original levels. In the meantime, prices have risen from P_1 to P_2.

The exact links between a rise in the money supply and a rise in prices are complex but are summarised in Figure 3. An

increase in the money supply is like an increase in the supply of bananas or apples. To restore market equilibrium, prices have to fall. The price of money is the rate of interest. So interest rates fall. Note that most central banks, including the Bank of England, now use interest rates as their main instrument of monetary policy rather than the money supply over which they have far less control. A fall in interest rates has an impact on demand in the economy in four main ways.

● A fall in money market interest rates leads to changes in a wide variety of interest rates including bank and building society borrowing and lending rates. A fall in interest rates will encourage consumers and firms to borrow. This will raise aggregate demand.

● A fall in interest rates is likely to increase many asset prices. For example, part of the increase in the money supply will feed through to higher levels of lending to house buyers. Lower interest rates will mean that house buyers can afford to borrow more money on their mortgages and offer higher prices to house vendors. Rising house prices boosts consumer confidence, and households therefore will borrow and spend more. Rising house prices also encourage households to remortgage their properties and use the proceeds to buy cars, house extensions or foreign holidays. Falling interest rates can also increase share prices. Falling interest rates are associated with higher consumer spending. So firms should be able to raise sales and increase their profits. This should raise their share price. Falling interest rates also make share

Figure 3 The monetary transmission mechanism
A rise in the money supply leads, through lower interest rates, to increased aggregate demand but also higher costs and so to higher inflation.

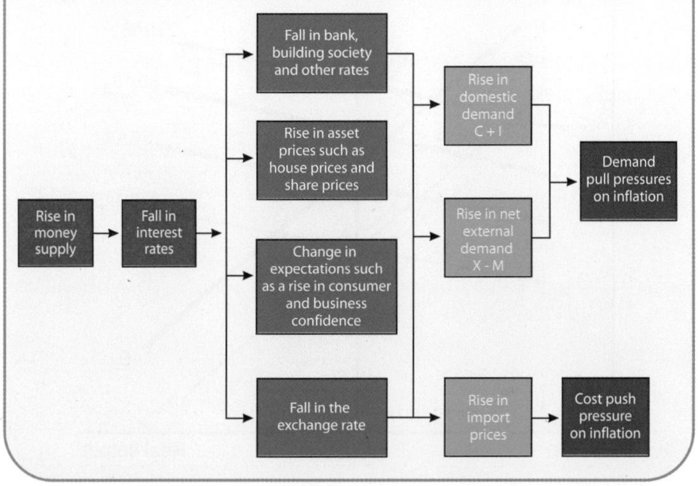

Question 3

In the long run, persistent changes in the rate of money growth are associated with changes in the rate of inflation but in the short run, monetary growth may have little impact on prices.

In recent months, growth in the quantity of notes and coin in circulation may have stabilised, having drifted lower during the past few years. The quantity of notes and coin in circulation rose by 3.9% in the year to January, having averaged almost 8% over 2002 and 2003.

By contrast annual growth in broad money (M4) was 12.6% in December 2005, the highest rate of growth since November 1990. Rapid growth in broad money has been an international phenomenon recently. M4 includes the bank deposits held by a range of non-bank financial organisations, such as pension funds and clearing houses. These organisations have been rapidly accumulating deposits over the recent past, and that has contributed to the robust growth in broad money. The implications for GDP and inflation of a build-up in their money holdings depends on why these organisations have been accumulating deposits. If they have been building up deposits to buy assets in the future, then this could lead to rising asset prices. That in turn could lead to higher spending in the economy at some point in the future. But these institutions may simply be choosing to hold more of their wealth in cash or liquid deposits. This would mean an increase in their demand for money and would have no impact on either GDP or inflation.

Source: adapted from the *Inflation Report*, February 2006, Bank of England.

(a) Using the data, explain the possible links between the money supply, the level of economic activity and inflation in 2006.

505

dividends, the share of profits given to shareholders, relatively more attractive and so share prices are bid up. Rising share prices again lead to greater consumer confidence and greater spending.

- Falling interest rates change the expectations of economic agents in the market. Falling interest rates are likely to lead to higher demand, higher pay and lower unemployment. So both consumer and business confidence are boosted which in turn leads to higher consumption and investment.
- A fall in UK interest rates, all other things being equal, should lead to a fall in the value of the pound. A fall in the value of the pound in turn should lead to higher exports and fewer imports, so boosting aggregate demand.

These four factors combined lead to a rise in aggregate demand which in turn leads to a rise in prices.

There is also a cost-push element in the transmission mechanism. The fall in the value of the pound leads to a rise in import prices. This feeds through to increased costs and so a rise in domestic prices.

The transmission mechanism can also be illustrated using aggregate demand and aggregate supply curves. An increase in the money supply will lead to an increase in aggregate demand through the transmission mechanism. Consider Figure 4. Monetarist or classical economists would argue that the long run aggregate supply curve is vertical. The equilibrium level of output is the full employment level Y_F and the initial price level is P_1. An increase in the money supply shifts the aggregate demand curve to the right from AD_1 to AD_2. Initially the economy moves up the short run aggregate supply curve $SRAS_1$ from K to L. But in the longer run, with increased prices and over-full employment, workers will demand and gain wage rate increases which will push the short run aggregate supply curve up to $SRAS_2$ and then to $SRAS_3$. N is the new long run equilibrium point where aggregate demand is once again equal to long run aggregate supply. Output, having initially risen, has returned to its long run full employment level. But prices have risen from P_1 to P_2.

Monetary accommodation and validation

Individual economies are constantly being buffeted by both demand-side and supply-side shocks. For example, in the mid to late 1980s, there was an unanticipated housing boom which led to much higher increases in aggregate demand than was expected by policy makers in government. In the mid 2000s, the price of oil increased several hundred per cent along with the price of many other raw material commodities used by industry.

Governments and central banks can react in a variety of ways to these shocks. One way is to ACCOMMODATE (for supply-side shocks) or VALIDATE (for demand-side shocks) the inflationary pressures by allowing the money supply to expand and interest rates to remain relatively low. This can be illustrated in Figure 5. The economy starts in long run equilibrium at the point A. There is then a supply-side shock, like a large rise in international commodity prices. This shifts the SRAS curve upwards to $SRAS_2$ and then $SRAS_3$. Not only is the economy suffering higher prices but at the point C there is now a negative output gap and unemployment. The economy is in recession with rising inflation. This combination of rising unemployment and rising inflation is known as STAGFLATION or SLUMPFLATION. Governments can choose to spend their way out of the recession by increasing aggregate demand. They can reduce interest rates or keep interest rates low through monetary policy. They can also increase government borrowing through effectively printing the money and increasing the money supply. This monetary accommodation in the short term in Figure 5 shifts the aggregate demand curve to the right from AD_1 to AD_2. Short run equilibrium is now at E. However, workers are likely to be demanding higher pay rises to compensate them for higher prices. A rise in wages shifts equilibrium to F. This movement from C to E to F could be the

---

Figure 4 An increase in the money supply

An increase in the money supply will shift the aggregate demand curve from AD_1 to AD_2. After an initial rise in output, shown by the movement from K to L, the economy will return to long run equilibrium at N. Prices have risen but output remains unchanged.

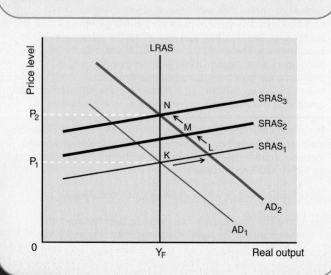

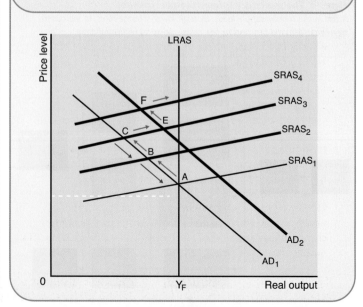

start of a **wage-price spiral**. Increases in prices lead to increases in wages lead to increases in prices. If the government constantly accommodates this by raising the money supply, then prices will carry on rising.

The reason why governments accommodate or validate economic shocks is because they want to keep unemployment low and get the economy growing again. The alternative policy response is not to increase the money supply when faced with a shock. If there is no monetary accommodation or validation, unemployment will rise as output falls. Consumer and business confidence will fall as a consequence. The fall in aggregate demand shown by the movement back up the AD curve from A to C in Figure 5. But the recession will lead to firms cutting their prices in an attempt to maintain sales. Inflation will fall. The economy will begin to recover as it moves to the point B. Eventually the economy will return to full employment at A with the original level of prices.

Monetarists argue that inflation should not be accommodated or validated. Inflation, a continuous rise in average prices, is not caused by demand or supply side shocks. It is caused by governments and central banks increasing the money supply in response to such shocks.

Today, most central banks operate monetary policy through changing interest rates. There is a general acceptance that demand and supply shocks which cause rises in inflation should be met by rises in interest rates. This effectively reduces the money supply. However, central banks like the Bank of England would also argue that the link between the money supply and inflation is unclear. So there is still debate about whether, as Milton Friedman said, 'inflation is always and everywhere a monetary phenomenon'.

Monetarist versus Keynesian views

The quantity theory of money, according to monetarists, shows that price increases are the result of increases in the money supply. This conclusion is dependent upon the assumptions that the velocity of circulation of money is constant, and that income (and therefore transactions and output) changes only slowly over time. Keynesians, on the other hand, argue that the demand for money is unstable and therefore the velocity of circulation of money is unstable too. A rise in M could be offset by a decrease in V rather than leading to a change in the price level. Keynesians also point out that monetarists assume that causality runs from M to P. But logically it could equally be true that price increases could lead to an increase in the money supply. There are two ways in which this might occur.

- Assume that the money supply is **endogenous** (i.e. it cannot be controlled by the central bank but instead is created by the banking system). A rise in wages will lead to increased demand for money from the banks. Firms will need more money to pay their workers, whilst workers will increase their demand for money because their incomes have gone up. An increased demand for money will push up interest rates and banks will find it more profitable to create money. Therefore the money supply will expand.
- If the money supply is **exogenous**, (i.e. its size is controlled by the central bank), it is not necessarily true that the central bank will choose to restrict the growth of the money supply. It may well allow the money supply to expand rather than accept the consequences of restricting its growth. This is monetary accommodation.

Economists are agreed that very large increases in the money supply will inevitably lead to high inflation. If the money supply increases by 200 per cent over a year, it would be impossible for either V or Y to change sufficiently for P to be unaffected. The monetarist-Keynesian debate centres round the effects of relatively small increases in the money supply. Are money supply increases of 5 or 10 or even 20 per cent necessarily inflationary?

Key terms

Equation of exchange (the Fisher equation) - the identity $MV \equiv PT$ where M is the money supply, V is the velocity of circulation of money over time, P is the price level and T is the number of transactions over time.
Monetarists - economists who believe that the quantity theory of money shows that inflation is always and everywhere caused by excessive increases in the money supply.
Monetary policy accommodation - a change in the nominal money supply which the government permits following a supply side shock in order to keep the real money supply constant.
Monetary policy validation - a change in the nominal money supply which the government permits following a change in aggregate demand in order to keep the real money supply constant.

Monetary transmission mechanism - the mechanism through which a change in the money supply leads to a change in national income and other real variables such as unemployment.
Neutrality of money - the theory that a change in the quantity of money in the economy will affect only the level of prices and not real variables such as unemployment.
Stagflation or slumpflation - a situation where an economy faces both rising inflation and rising unemployment.
The quantity theory of money - the theory, based on the equation of exchange, that increase in the money supply, M, will lead to increases in the price level P.
The velocity of circulation of money (or income velocity) - the number of times the stock of money in the economy changes hands over a period of time.

Applied economics

Inflation and the money supply

The quantity theory of money suggests that inflation is caused by increases in the money supply over and above the rate of real growth in the economy. If this were true, it would be possible to see a strong correlation between money supply growth and the rate of change of prices over time.

Figures 6 and 7 are scatter diagrams. They show the relationship between annual inflation, as measured by the RPI, and percentage annual changes in two measures of the money supply, narrow money M0 and broad money M4. The correlation is very weak in both cases. This could be due to the fact that changes in the money supply are compared with changes in prices on a yearly basis, rather than, say, quarterly. Or it could be that there are no time lags. So perhaps changes in the money supply in one year should be compared to changes in inflation the following year. In practice, the correlation is still weak even with quarterly data and sophisticated lags built in.

Figure 8 shows the relationship between the four variables in the Fisher equation for the UK from 1970. The 1970s and the 1990s would tend to support the view that changes in the money supply lead to a change in the rate of inflation.

- The growth in M4 between 1970 and 1972 led first to a fall in the velocity of circulation of money and then to an increase in growth in GDP. This was shortly followed by a rise in the inflation rate in 1974

and 1975. It was this experience which was particularly influential in converting many economists and politicians to monetarism.
- The fall in the rate of growth of M4 in 1973-7 led to initial rises in the velocity of circulation of money and falls in the growth of GDP, followed by

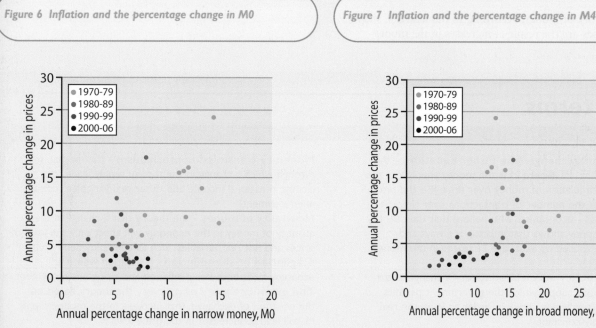

Figure 6 *Inflation and the percentage change in M0*

Legend:
- 1970-79
- 1980-89
- 1990-99
- 2000-06

Y-axis: Annual percentage change in prices (0 to 30)
X-axis: Annual percentage change in narrow money, M0 (0 to 20)

Source: adapted from Financial Statistics Freestanding, www.statistics.gov.uk

Figure 7 *Inflation and the percentage change in M4*

Legend:
- 1970-79
- 1980-89
- 1990-99
- 2000-06

Y-axis: Annual percentage change in prices (0 to 30)
X-axis: Annual percentage change in broad money, M4 (0 to 30)

Source: adapted from Financial Statistics Freestanding, www.statistics.gov.uk

falling inflation rates between 1975 and 1978.

- The fall in the rate of growth of M4 from 1989 led to falls in the rate of inflation from 1991 onwards.

However, there is little correlation between growth of M4 and inflation in the late 1970s and most of the 1980s, 1990s and 2000s. During the late 1970s and the first half of the 1980s, there was an increasing disillusionment amongst economists and politicians with what was sometimes called 'crude' monetarism (Denis Healey, Chancellor of the Exchequer from 1976 to 1979 called it 'punk' monetarism!). The targeted measures of the money supply (M1 and M3, now no longer calculated) grew at a much faster rate than inflation. In the middle 1980s, for instance, with inflation at around 5 per cent, M4 was growing in the 12-16 per cent range.

Monetarists today would argue that this arose mainly because of financial deregulation. For instance:

- exchange controls (restrictions on the ability of UK citizens to exchange pounds for other currencies) were abolished in 1979;
- controls on bank lending were removed in 1980;
- competition in the banking sector was increased, by allowing building societies to offer banking services under the Building Society Act 1986;
- the London Stock Market was deregulated in 1986.

This led to individuals and companies increasing their demand for money (i.e. controls had rationed the amount of money available to them). Increases in money holdings relative to all other variables led to falls in the velocity of circulation of money, previously thought by monetarists to be broadly constant over time. However, by the end of the 1980s, these one-off effects had fed their way throughout the economy.

There then followed a sharp fall in the growth of the money supply from 17.4 per cent for M4 in 1989 to 4.8 per cent in 1992. This was accompanied by a sharp fall in both prices and economic growth. Inflation fell from 9.4 per cent in 1990 to 1.6 per cent in 1993, whilst the economy went into a prolonged recession between 1990 and 1992. Monetarists would

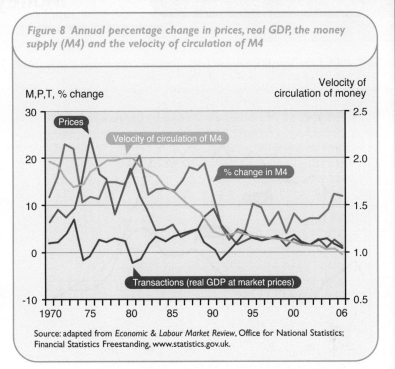

Figure 8 *Annual percentage change in prices, real GDP, the money supply (M4) and the velocity of circulation of M4*

Source: adapted from *Economic & Labour Market Review*, Office for National Statistics; Financial Statistics Freestanding, www.statistics.gov.uk.

argue that it was the sharp fall in the rate of growth of the money supply which led to first a recession and then the fall in inflation. In the second half of the 1990s and the first half of the 2000s low inflation was accompanied by economic growth above the trend rate. This, with a slow fall in the velocity of circulation of money, allowed M4 to grow between 4 and 13 per cent per annum.

For monetarists, the evidence of the past 40 years shows clearly that inflation is a monetary phenomenon. They also have an explanation for the unusual relationship between the money supply and prices in the 1980s. For Keynesians, the whole period shows that there is no predictable relationship between the money supply and prices and changes in V often absorb changes in M. Moreover, it may be that the causality is running from increases in prices to increases in the money supply, rather than the other way around as monetarists would suggest. In short, the evidence could be used to support a wide variety of conflicting opinions about the causes of inflation.

DataQuestion
Money, 1985-1992

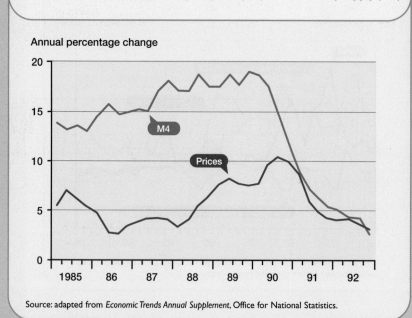

Figure 9 *Annual percentage change in prices (RPI) and the money supply (M4)*

Annual percentage change

Source: adapted from *Economic Trends Annual Supplement*, Office for National Statistics.

The Lawson boom and the subsequent recession

In the mid-1980s, the Chancellor of the Exchequer, Nigel Lawson, stoked a boom in the economy with tax cuts and low interest rates. However, when inflation began to take off in 1988, he responded by pushing up interest rates. They rose from a low of 7.5 per cent in May 1988 to a high of 15 per cent in October 1989. Interest rates were kept at 14-15 per cent until February 1991. By this time the economy was in a full blown deep recession, but at least inflation had come down, the objective of the tight monetary policy.

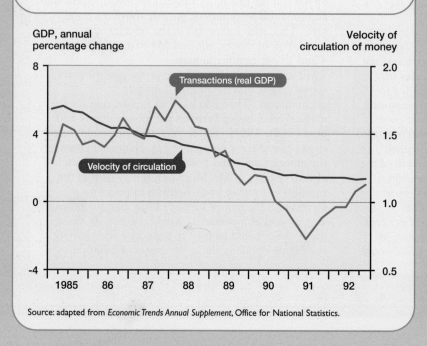

Figure 10 *Velocity of circulation of money (M4) and annual percentage change in real GDP*

GDP, annual percentage change

Velocity of circulation of money

Source: adapted from *Economic Trends Annual Supplement*, Office for National Statistics.

1. Discuss whether the period 1985-1992 would support or refute the hypothesis that changes in the money supply affect inflation through a monetary transmission mechanism.

Summary

1. Governments need to raise taxes to pay for public spending. Taxes are also used to correct market failure, to redistribute income and wealth and to manage the economy.
2. The canons of taxation are a set of principles by which taxes can be evaluated.

The reasons for taxation

Governments use taxation for a number of purposes.

To pay for government expenditure Governments need to raise finance for their expenditure programmes. They can borrow a limited amount of money for this, but most of the finance must come from taxation if inflation is to be avoided.

To correct market failure such as externalities Governments can intervene in individual markets by changing taxes and thus changing demand. For instance, tobacco consumption can be reduced by raising taxes on cigarettes, pollution can be controlled by imposing pollution taxes, or sales of books can be increased by exempting them from VAT. Used in this way, taxation becomes a way of increasing economic efficiency.

To manage the economy as a whole Taxation can have an important influence on the **macro-economic** performance of the economy. Governments may change tax rates in order to influence variables such as inflation, unemployment and the balance of payments.

To redistribute income A government may judge that the distribution of resources is inequitable. To redistribute income, it may impose taxes which reduce the income and wealth of some groups in society and use the money collected to increase the income and wealth of other groups.

Question 1

Each year in the Budget, the Chancellor of the Exchequer announces whether or not he will change the level of excise duties on tobacco. In most years, this is increased at least in line with inflation, although in some years, particularly election years, it is not increased at all. Why might the government change the level of excise duty on tobacco each year?

Direct and indirect taxes

Taxes are classified into two types. A DIRECT TAX is a tax levied directly on an individual or organisation. For instance, income tax is a direct tax because individual income earners are responsible for paying it. Corporation tax, a tax on company profits, is a direct tax too because companies have to pay it directly to the Revenue and Customs.

An INDIRECT TAX is a tax on a good or service. For instance, value added tax is an indirect tax because it is a 17.5 per cent tax on most goods and services. Council tax is an indirect tax on the notional value of a property whilst uniform business rate for businesses is an indirect tax on the notional rent of a property.

Question 2

Explain which of the following taxes are direct taxes and which are indirect:

(a) income tax; (b) National Insurance contributions; (c) inheritance tax; (d) corporation tax; (e) capital gains tax; (f) council tax; (g) VAT; (h) excise duties.

The canons of taxation

Taxation has been a source of much controversy since the first tax was introduced. Adam Smith wrote at length on the subject of taxation in his book *An Enquiry into the Nature and Causes of the Wealth of Nations*, published in 1776. He argued that a good tax was one which had four characteristics:
- the cost of collection should be low relative to the yield of the tax;
- the timing of collection and the amount to be paid should be clear and certain;
- the means of payment and the timing of the payment should be convenient to the taxpayer;
- taxes should be levied according to the ability to pay of the individual taxpayer.

These canons relate to efficiency and equity. For instance, the cost of collection is about productive efficiency. Ability to pay is about equity.

There have been examples in history where taxes did not possess these canons. For instance, at certain periods in Roman history tax collecting was privatised. The Roman government sold the right to collect taxes in a province to the highest bidder. This individual would buy the right, hoping to charge more in taxes than he paid to the Roman authorities. With luck he might make 100 per cent profit on the contract - in this case the cost of collection would hardly be low. He would terrorise the province, forcing anyone and everyone to pay as much tax as he could exact. No attempt was made to make means of payment or timing suitable to the taxpayer. It was not clear on what basis citizens were being taxed, and there was no attempt to link taxes to ability to pay, since it was the poor who were the most easily terrorised whilst better off citizens were left alone for fear that they might complain to Rome.

Economists today have argued that in addition to Adam Smith's canons, a 'good' tax should be one which:
- leads to the least loss of economic efficiency, or even increases economic efficiency;
- is compatible with foreign tax systems, and in the

case of the UK, particularly with EU tax regimes;
● automatically adjusts to changes in the price level - this is particularly important in a high inflation economy.
These three criteria relate to economic efficiency.

Sometimes it is argued that taxes should be linked to the benefits that taxpayers receive from the tax. For instance, road groups in the UK often point out that revenues from taxes on motorists far exceed government expenditure on roads. They then conclude that either taxes on motorists are too high or that spending on roads is too low. A tax whose revenue is specifically linked to an area of government spending is called a hypothecated tax. In the UK, National Insurance contributions could be argued to be a **hypothecated tax** because they are used solely to pay for spending on National Insurance benefits and make a small contribution towards the cost of the National Health Service. The benefit principle is one of equity. It is an argument which states that linking payment and benefit is 'fairer' than a tax which fails to do this.

Taxation, inefficiency and inequality

A tax is likely to lead to a fall in supply and a consequent reduction in the quantity demanded of the product or service being taxed. For instance:
● VAT and excise duties on a product push the supply curve to the left which in turn leads to a fall in the quantity demanded of the product;
● Income tax is likely to lead to a fall in the supply of labour to the market;
● Corporation tax is likely to lead to a fall in the supply of entrepreneurs to the market.

Taxes therefore distort markets. This may be beneficial in some markets, particularly if there are important negative externalities present and the tax brings private costs and benefits into line with social costs and benefits.

In other markets, taxes may lead to a loss of efficiency. For instance, if all markets were perfectly competitive, then the economy would be Pareto efficient. The introduction of a tax on one commodity, such as petrol, would then lead to a loss of efficiency in the economy because marginal cost would no longer equal price in that market. In practice, there are so many examples of market failure that it is impossible to come to any simple conclusions about whether a tax does or does not lead to efficiency losses. However, the **theory of the second best** suggests that taxes which are broadly based are less likely to lead to efficiency losses than narrow taxes. Low rates of tax spread as widely as possible are likely to be less damaging to economic welfare than high rates of tax on a small number of goods or individuals. For instance, a single rate VAT is likely to result in greater efficiency than a tax solely on petrol which raises the same revenue. Or an income tax which all earners pay is likely to lead to lower efficiency losses than an income tax paid solely by manufacturing workers.

It should be remembered that taxes are raised mainly to pay for government expenditure. Even if the imposition of taxes does lead to a loss of efficiency, this loss should be outweighed by the gain in economic efficiency resulting from the provision of **public** and **merit** goods by the government.

Taxes are also raised to ensure a redistribution of resources within the economy. There will be an increase in economic welfare if the welfare gains from a more desirable distribution of resources outweigh the welfare losses from the greater inefficiency arising from taxation.

The world's largest shipping lines may stop using UK ports because of the 'light dues' they have to pay. These are effectively a hypothecated tax on the use of harbour facilities. The revenues are used to pay the £73 million cost of providing lighthouses, buoys and beacons around Britain's shores. Ships calling at British ports have to pay up to £16 000 per visit. In other EU countries apart from Greece and the Irish Republic, lighthouses are funded out of general taxation, such as VAT and income tax.

A report commissioned by the Independent Light Dues Forum, a lobby group set up by 21 shipping lines, says that UK jobs might be lost because of light dues. Employment at ports could suffer and UK manufacturers may also shift production to the Continent to be nearer cheaper ports. This could, for example, cost some of the 800 000 jobs in the UK motor industry. The report compares port costs in Britain and on the Continent, including light dues, port dues and towage, pilotage and line handling. Although other costs are less in the UK, light dues outweigh other savings.

Source: adapted from *The Times*, 30.12.2003.

(a) Using Adam Smith's canons of taxation and the concepts of efficiency and equity, discuss whether the UK government should abolish light dues and pay for the cost of lighthouses, buoys and beacons out of general taxation.

Key terms

Direct tax - a tax levied directly on an individual or organisation, such as income tax.
Indirect tax - a tax levied on goods or services, such as value added tax or excise duties.

Applied economics

Taxation in the UK

Figure 1 Government revenues, 2007-08

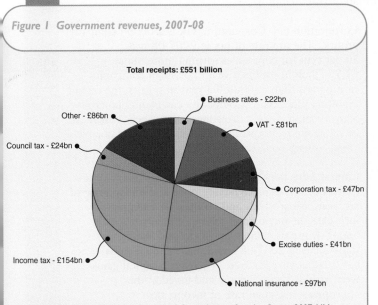

Total receipts: £551 billion

- Business rates - £22bn
- Other - £86bn
- VAT - £81bn
- Council tax - £24bn
- Corporation tax - £47bn
- Excise duties - £41bn
- Income tax - £154bn
- National insurance - £97bn

Source: adapted from *Pre-Budget Report and Comprehensive Spending Review*, 2007, HM Treasury.

Table 1 Government revenues, 2007-08

	£ billion 2007-08
HM Revenue and Customs	
Income tax (gross of tax credits)	154.1
Income tax credits	-4.5
National Insurance contributions	96.5
Value added tax	81.4
Corporation tax	46.8
Corporation tax credits	-0.5
Petroleum revenue tax	1.5
Fuel duties	24.9
Capital gains tax	4.8
Inheritance tax	3.9
Stamp duties	15.1
Tobacco duties	8.1
Spirits duties	2.3
Wine duties	2.6
Beer and cider duties	3.3
Betting and gaming duties	1.4
Air passenger duty	2.0
Insurance premium tax	2.4
Landfill tax	0.9
Climate change levy	0.7
Aggregates levy	0.3
Customer subsidies and levies	2.4
Total HMRC	**450.4**
Vehicle excise duties	5.5
Business rates	21.9
Council tax	23.7
Other taxes and royalties	15.3
Net taxes and national insurance contributions	**516.8**
Other receipts	34.4
Current receipts	**551.2**

Source: adapted from *Pre-Budget Report and Comprehensive Spending Review*, 2007, HM Treasury.

The main taxes in the UK

Figure 1 gives a broad breakdown of government revenue for 2007-2008. The largest tax by revenue is income tax, which raises a little over one quarter of all government receipts. The three largest taxes (income tax, National Insurance contributions and value added tax) raise approximately 60 per cent. If corporation tax, local authority taxes (business rates and the council tax), and excise duties (mainly on petrol, drink and tobacco) are added to these, then these taxes contribute nearly 90 per cent of government revenues. Table 1 gives a more detailed breakdown of tax and other revenues.

Income tax This is the single most important source of revenue for government. It is a tax on the income of individuals. Each person is allowed to earn a certain amount before paying income tax each year. This amount is called a **tax allowance**. One tax allowance to which everyone is entitled is the **personal allowance**. In 2007-08, this was worth £5 225, so every individual could earn £5 225 between 6th April 2007 and 5th April 2008 free of income tax. Payments into pension funds are tax free whilst additional allowances are available for the over 65s.

Income earned over the value of allowances (the tax **threshold**) is liable to tax and is called **taxable income**. In 2007-08, the first £2 230 of taxable income was taxed at the **starting rate** of 10 per cent. Income between £2 230 and £34 600 was taxed at the **basic rate** of 22 per cent. The **higher rate** of 40 per cent was paid on all taxable income over £34 600. Table 2 gives an example of how the income tax of an

Table 2 Income tax payable: an illustration

	£	£
Income before tax		60 000.00
Allowances		
Personal allowance	5 225.00	
Pension contributions	4 775.00	
Total	10 000.00	
Taxable income		50 000.00
Tax		
2 230 @10%	223.00	
32 370 @22%	7 121.40	
15 400 @40%	6 160.00	
Total tax paid	13 504.40	13 504.40
Income after tax		36 495.60

individual is calculated.

For very low income earners, such as part-time workers, the **marginal rate** of income tax is 0 per cent. This is because they can earn an extra £1 and still be within their personal tax allowance. For instance, a worker earning £4 000 a year could work an extra shift and pay no income tax on the earnings. Slightly better paid workers will have a marginal rate of 10 per cent. The majority of workers, though, earn enough to have to pay the basic rate of income tax. For high income earners, their marginal rate is 40 per cent. However, there is a difference between marginal rates of tax and average rates of tax.

Consider Table 2. This individual is earning £60 000 before tax. In 2007-08, she would have paid £13 504.40 in tax. Therefore her average rate of tax was 22.5 per cent (£13 504.40 ÷ £60 000). But her marginal rate was 40 per cent because she paid 40p in tax on the last £1 earned. **The average rate of tax is always less than the marginal rate for income tax payers.** This is because all income earners can earn a portion of their income 'tax free'. Moreover, basic and higher rate taxpayers pay lower rates of tax on part of their taxable earnings. So basic rate taxpayers in 2007-08 paid no tax on their income covered by allowances, 10 per cent on the next £2 230 and only then did their income begin to be taxed at 22 per cent.

Income tax from employed workers is collected by employers through the PAYE (pay as you earn) system. Employers are then responsible for paying the deductions to the Revenue and Customs.

National Insurance contributions (NICs) All taxes apart from NICs and local authority taxes are paid into one central fund (called the **Consolidated Fund**) and are used to pay for government spending. However, there is a separate National Insurance Fund out of which is paid National Insurance benefits, such as state pensions and Jobseekers Allowance. The National Insurance Fund also pays for a small part of the cost of the National Health Service. Strictly speaking, contributions are not taxes because they are a form of insurance premium. However, increasingly they have come to be seen, and used, by government as a form of tax. The link between payments made into the Fund and benefits taken out by individuals has been eroded over time. In 2007-2008, employed workers paid contributions of 11 per cent of earnings between £87 and £670. Unlike income tax, which is calculated on yearly income, National Insurance contributions are based on weekly income. A 17 year old student who earns £100 one week, £50 the next and nothing for the rest of the year will pay no income tax because she is within her personal allowance figure, but she will have to pay NICs in the week she earned £100 because she was above the £87 threshold. The next week, she will pay no NICs because she is below £87. In addition, employers have to pay employers' National Insurance contributions at 12.8 per cent on employees' earnings that exceed £100 per week. There are different rates of National Insurance contributions for contracted-out workers and the self-employed.

Corporation tax Corporation tax is a tax on company profits. The top rate of tax in 2007-08 was 30 per cent for companies earning more than £1.5 million in profits a year. For small companies earning less than £300 000 a year in profits, the rate of tax was 20 per cent. Companies can claim numerous allowances, including investment allowances which can be **set against** their profits. This reduces their taxable profits in any one year.

Capital gains tax This is a tax on capital gains - the difference between the buying price and selling price of an asset. Most goods and services are exempt, including the buying and selling of a person's main home. It is paid mainly on stocks and shares. Individuals in 2007-08 could make capital gains of up to £9 200 a year tax free. Thereafter, capital gains were included with income and taxed at the appropriate marginal rate of income tax.

Inheritance tax This is a tax on the value of assets left on death by an individual. In 2007-08, the first £300 000 of any inheritance was tax free. Thereafter, it was taxed at 40 per cent. There are numerous exemptions. For instance, any money left by one spouse to another is completely tax free. Also, there is no tax on gifts made during the lifetime of an individual provided that they are made 7 years before death.

Excise duties These are not to be confused with customs duties - taxes on imported goods. Excise duties are taxes levied on a narrow range of goods: fuel, alcohol, tobacco and betting. They are calculated not on value (as with VAT) but on the volume sold. For instance, excise duty is paid per litre of petrol sold. If the price of petrol rises, the amount paid in VAT rises, but the excise duty remains the same.

Value added tax This is a tax on expenditure. There are different rates of tax. Essential commodities - food, water, children's clothing, books, newspapers, magazines and public transport - are tax exempt (i.e. they are **zero rated**). Domestic fuel (gas, electricity, heating oil and coal) is taxed at a reduced rate of 5 per cent. All other goods and services are taxed at 17.5 per cent. VAT is collected by business and is imposed on the value added to a product by that business.

Petroleum revenue tax and oil royalties These are taxes on the output of North Sea oil.

Council tax Council tax is a tax imposed on domestic property by local authorities. Each dwelling has been assessed for sale value in April 1992. The property has then been put into one of 7 bands, from band A for properties up to £40 000 to band H for properties over £320 000. For instance, a £130 000 property would be put in Band F, which covers properties between £120 000 and £160 000. The local authority then fixes a charge each year to each band. The differences in charges between bands are fixed by law. For instance, properties in Band H, the highest band, pay three times the council tax of properties in Band A, the lowest band, in a local area.

Business rates Business rates are a local authority tax on business property. Each business property has been given a rateable value based on an estimate of the yearly rent at which that property might reasonably have been let. The amount paid by the business is the rateable value multiplied by a 'factor'. This factor is called the 'Uniform Business Rate'. It is fixed by the government each year and is the same for all areas of the country.

Progressive, proportional and regressive taxes

Some taxes in the UK are progressive, i.e. the higher the income, the higher the proportion of income paid in tax. Income tax is progressive because there are personal allowances and because there are three rates of tax depending upon how much is earned. For instance, in Table 2, the £60 000 income earner paid an average rate of tax of 22.5 per cent. If the same individual had a gross income of £40 000, with the same allowances and pension payments, the amount of tax paid would have been 15.8 per cent ([£6 332.40 ÷ £40 000] x 100%).

National Insurance contributions are mildly progressive up to the upper earnings limit. This is because employees can earn up to £87 a week (in 2007-08) without paying contributions. However, they become regressive for individuals earning over the upper earnings limit of £670 per week (in 2007-08). For instance, a worker earning £70 a week paid an average rate of tax of 0 per cent. A worker earning £187 a week would pay 11 per cent tax on the £100 over the £87 lower earnings limit of £87. So their average rate of tax would be 5.9 per cent ([£11 ÷ £187] x 100%). A worker earning at the top of the upper earnings limit of £670 would pay 11 per cent tax on £583 (£670 - £87) and so their average rate of tax would be 9.6 per cent ([£64.13 ÷ £670.00] x 100%). A worker earning £2 000 a week would pay 0 per cent on the first £87, 11 per cent on the next £583 and 1 per cent on the final £1 330. That makes a total tax bill of £75.26 and an average rate of tax of 3.9 per cent.

Council tax is highly regressive. The highest council tax payer only pays a maximum three times that of the lowest council tax payer, but may earn considerably more. The poorest do receive rebates on their council

tax, but this makes little difference to its regressivity.

Corporation tax could be argued to be progressive. Corporation tax leaves less profit to be distributed to shareholders. Given that shareholders tend to be higher income individuals, this means that higher income individuals tend to be more affected by corporation tax.

Capital gains tax is certainly progressive. It is paid only by those with enough assets to make capital gains over £9 000 a year (in 2007-2008). Similarly inheritance tax is in general progressive over much of the income range. Wealth and income tend to be correlated. So the larger the amount left, the larger tends to be the income of the deceased and indeed of those who inherit. Very high income earners, though, who are also very wealthy are likely to pay very little inheritance tax. This is because inheritance tax can be avoided, for instance by giving wealth away before death. The greater the wealth, the more incentive there is to avoid the tax and hence at the top of the income scale, inheritance tax might become regressive.

Indirect taxes tend to be regressive. A much larger proportion of low income households' budget is spent on alcohol, tobacco and betting than that of high income households and hence excise duties are regressive. It could be argued that VAT is progressive because items which form a disproportionate part of low income budgets, such as food and public transport, are zero rated. However, this is more than outweighed by the fact that higher income earners tend to save a larger proportion of their income than low income earners, and hence the proportion of income paid in VAT declines as income rises - a regressive effect.

In the Applied Economics section of the unit entitled 'The redistribution of income and wealth' Table 3 gives Revenue and Customs estimates of average tax rates for both direct and indirect taxes. It shows that whilst income tax and employees' National Insurance contributions tend to be progressive, other taxes tend to be regressive. Overall, the bottom fifth of households by income pay a slightly higher proportion of their gross income in tax than the top fifth. However, overall, the tax system could be seen as broadly proportional in the UK.

International comparisons

Figure 2 gives an international comparison of taxes. In the 1970s, it was argued that Britain was highly taxed and that this had contributed to low economic growth rates. In fact, Britain has tended to tax less than continental Europe whilst taxing more highly than countries such as the USA and Japan. Figure 2 shows that in 2007, the UK government collected 3.5 per cent more in revenue as a percentage of GDP than the average for the rich OECD countries but 3.3 per cent of GDP less than the euro area. The UK also tends to collect a lower proportion of taxes in direct taxes than most developed countries. Conversely, indirect taxes

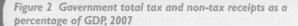

Figure 2 *Government total tax and non-tax receipts as a percentage of GDP, 2007*

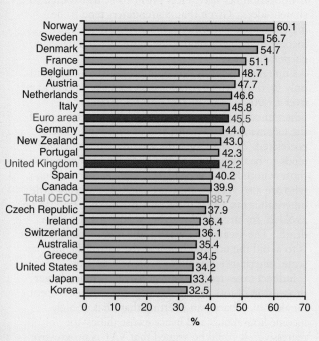

Source: adapted from *Economic Outlook*, OECD.

tend to be relatively high. Compared to continental Europe, for instance, social security taxes are far lower in the UK.

Changes in tax

Over the period 1979-2006, there were significant changes in the distribution of tax. Table 3 shows three years. 1979 and 2006 were both boom years for the economy, whilst in 1993 the UK was only just coming out of recession. This recession depressed tax receipts on income and therefore boosted the percentage of tax raised from other sources. However, the drop in the

Table 3 *Percentage contribution of different taxes to central government income[1]*

			%
	1979	1993	2006
Taxes on income			
Paid by person	32.5	27.1	32.2
Paid by corporations	7.5	8.1	10.8
Taxes on expenditure	33.1	42.6	29.6
Social security contributions	17.4	18.0	20.0
Rent, interest, dividends,			
royalties and other income	7.4	4.4	7.4
	100.0	100.0	100.0

1. Columns may not add up to 100% because of rounding.

Source: adapted from *National Income and Accounts Blue Book, Financial Statistics*, Office for National Statistics; *Pre Budget Report, 2005*, HM Treasury.

percentage of tax receipts from income tax and the rise in taxes on expenditure between 1979 and 1993 also reflected a deliberate government decision to shift the burden of tax from direct taxes to indirect taxes. Since 1993, taxes on income and other taxes have risen as a proportion of total tax receipts, reducing the relative importance of taxes on expenditure.

Income tax In the 1979 Budget, the government cut the top rate of income tax from 83 per cent on earned income and 98 per cent on unearned income to 60 per cent. Throughout the 1980s, it made it a priority to cut income tax rates. The basic rate of income tax fell from 33 per cent in 1979 to 25 per cent in 1987. The 1987 budget also saw a fall in the top rate of tax to 40 per cent. Since then, the standard rate has fallen to 22 per cent and a lower starting rate of tax has been introduced. Despite these falls in the rate of tax, the revenues from income have tended to rise for three reasons. First, although rates of income tax have been falling, governments since the late 1980s have been cutting tax allowances. In the 1990s, for instance, income tax relief on mortgage interest rate payments was gradually abolished, as was the married man's allowance and child allowances. Second, economic growth has raised the taxable income of the nation. Third, high income earners have increased their tax payments. Reductions in the top rate of tax have considerably reduced the incentive to avoid tax. For instance, there is far less incentive for millionaires to move to the Bahamas or Jersey today than there was in 1979. Moreover, widening income differentials mean that the top 10 per cent of income earners receive a larger share of total income than in 1979. More income is therefore subject to the top rate of tax. In contrast, the bottom 10 per cent receive a smaller share. The amount of untaxed income has therefore tended to fall.

VAT Value Added Tax (VAT) rates have risen and its scope has been widened. In the 1979 budget, the rate of VAT was raised from 8 per cent to 15 per cent to pay for income tax cuts. In 1991, the rate was increased to 17.5 per cent to pay for a cut in local authority poll tax. 1995 saw the introduction of VAT on domestic fuel, previously zero rated.

A reduction in the incidence of taxes on capital In the 1980s, the Conservative government considerably reduced capital gains tax and inheritance tax. These taxes bring in relatively little revenue but tended to be highly progressive. Today, with careful tax planning, taxpayers can avoid paying either tax.

Rises in excise duties In the 1990s, there was a considerable increase in excise duties on cigarettes and petrol. The former was justified on health grounds, whilst the latter was argued to be for the benefit of the environment. The increase in excise duties on cigarettes led to the UK having much higher after tax prices on cigarettes than France and Belgium. It is estimated that three quarters of all hand rolled tobacco consumed in the UK is smuggled in from the continent whilst up to a third of all cigarettes sold are contraband. As for petrol, the rises seem to have had little impact on the number of miles driven, showing that petrol is highly price inelastic in demand. The tax rises, therefore, whilst bringing in large amounts of extra revenue for the government, have not succeeded in either reducing transport congestion or limiting car exhaust emissions.

Has the tax system become more regressive?

The tax changes introduced in the 1980s served to shift the burden of taxation from the better off to those worse off. Cuts in income tax, particularly for higher rate tax payers, helped increase the post-tax incomes of the better off which was partly paid for by increases in VAT paid for by lower income households. The introduction of the poll tax in 1989-1990 hit low income earners particularly hard whilst giving substantial tax gains to the better off. In the 1990s, this trend was to some extent reversed. The poll tax was replaced by the council tax. Income tax cuts, particularly after the election of a Labour government in 1997, tended to favour the less well off. The removal of income tax allowances, such as mortgage relief, hit the better off. Overall, however, the system remains only mildly progressive.

DataQuestion

A flat tax

George Osborne, Conservative Shadow Chancellor, is planning a commission to examine the case for a flat tax. He said he wanted to see the UK move towards 'a simpler tax system which is simple to understand, where there are no loop-holes, where the very rich do not avoid tax by employing expensive accountants. I am fully conscious that we may not be able to introduce a pure flat tax, but we may be able to move towards simpler and flatter taxes ... . The rest of the world, including many countries in Europe are reducing taxes.' He denied that the system would be regressive, saying earnings up to about £10 000 to £12 000 a year would not be taxed at all.

Hong Kong adopted a flat tax in 1948. The other nine flat tax countries are all from the former Soviet bloc. They are Estonia, Latvia, Lithuania, Russia, Serbia, Slovakia, Ukraine, Georgia and Romania. The *Daily Telegraph* (19.8.2005) said that: 'The pioneer in eastern Europe is Estonia, which introduced a flat rate of 26 per cent in 1994. It has since enjoyed rapid growth and paid off its national debt. It is now cutting the rate to 20 per cent for all incomes.'

Source: adapted from newsvote.bbc.co.uk 7.9.2005; portal.telegraph.co.uk 19.8.2005.

Some economists believe that flat taxes could help revitalise the British economy. There are four main arguments in favour of a flat tax on income.
- Flat taxes are much easier to understand than the present complex income tax system where there are many allowances and four different rates of tax (0%, 10%, 22% and 40%). Simplifying the system would mean fewer loopholes for taxpayers to exploit in their drive to minimise the amount of tax they pay. Tax revenues would therefore go up because there would be less tax avoidance.
- Bringing the top rate of tax down from 40 per cent to the Adam Smith Institute's proposed rate of 22 per cent would act as a powerful incentive for higher income earners to work harder and be more entrepreneurial. At the bottom end, workers between the current personal income tax allowance level of around £5 000 and the Adam Smith Institute's proposed tax allowance level of £12 000 would now pay no tax. Again this would encourage them to work harder. Both groups would tend to earn more as a result and this would increase the amount of tax being paid.
- A flat tax would make the UK more attractive to foreign investors. Lower taxes would encourage foreign firms to set up in the UK and rich foreign individuals to take up residence in the UK.
- The combination of these three effects would boost the supply side of the economy and lead to higher economic growth. Tax revenues would actually increase as a result allowing the government to cut tax rates even further.

A flat tax is one where there is only one rate of tax. For example, in 2005, the right wing Adam Smith Institute think-tank analysed the effects of introducing a flat income tax in the UK. The rate of tax would be 22 per cent, and there would be a £12 000 personal allowance. This personal allowance would be a sum of money which could be earned but on which there would be no tax to pay. For example, a worker earning £12 000 a year would pay no income tax at all because their earnings were below the tax threshold of £12 001. A worker earning £22 000 a year would pay no tax on the first £12 000 and then 22 per cent on the remaining £10 000, making a total of £2 200. A worker earning £112 000 a year would pay no tax on the first £12 000 and 22 per cent tax on the remaining £100 000, making a total of £22 000.

Source: adapted from portal.telegraph.co.uk 19.8.2005.

The Adam Smith Institute proposals of a 22 per cent flat tax rate with a £12 000 tax free personal allowance would lead to an initial fall in income tax revenues of around one third, or about £45 billion a year. Why this is so can be seen from Table 4. The average rate of tax under this flat tax is below the average rate of tax under the present system at every point on the income range. So the average amount collected will be less under a flat tax than under the present arrangements. To bring in the same amount of revenue, either the tax free personal allowance would have to be much less or the flat rate of tax would have to be much higher.

Table 4 also shows another problem with a flat tax. On average, under the current income system, taxpayers pay 18.2 per cent of their income in income tax. Income earners in the range £4 895 to £49 999 per year pay less than this average. So too do the bottom income earners in the £50 000-£99 999 range. Looking at the number of income tax payers who fall into this category, they account for a minimum of 28.5 million taxpayers. There are only 2 million tax payers earning more than £50 000 a year. Assume that the flat tax were set at a level which brought in the same amount of income tax as at present. Such a flat tax would inevitably benefit these 2 million taxpayers. This is because at present they will almost certainly be paying a marginal 40 per cent tax rate. This might go down to say, 30 per cent, under a flat tax. They would be winners from a flat tax. If they are winners, the rest of the taxpayers would be losers. 2 million would gain and most of the other 28.5 million would lose. Very approximately, for every 1 high income earner gainer, there would be 9 lower income earner losers.

Table 4 illustrates this in another way. The top 2 million taxpayers earning over £50 000 a year pay 45 per cent of all income tax. The top 480 000 taxpayers earning over £100 000 a year pay 26 per cent of all income tax. They would be big winners from a flat tax. The bottom 28.5 million taxpayers earning less than £50 000 a year would have to pick up the tax now not being paid by the top 2 million. It would be a lot of tax and the losses to the 28.5 million taxpayers would be significant.

Source: adapted from www.hmrc.gov.uk, April 2005.

Table 4 Income tax statistics, 2005-2006[1]

Range of total income £ per year	Number of taxpayers Thousands	Total amount of tax paid per taxpayer under present income tax system £ million	Average rate of tax under present tax system %	Average rate of tax with flat tax of 22% and £12 000 personal tax allowance %
4 895-4 999	127	1	0.1	0
5 000-7 499	2 940	369	2.0	0
7 500-9 999	3 540	1 580	5.1	0
10 000-14 999	6 130	7 560	9.8	5
15 000-19 999	5 060	11 500	13.0	6.5
20 000-29 999	6 370	24 000	15.4	11.4
30 000-49 999	4 320	28 900	17.9	15.4
50 000-99 999	1 520	25 900	25.7	18.5
100 000+	480	34 200	33.4	19.4 to 22.0
All income earners above £4 895	30 500	134 000	18.2	

1 Inland Revenue estimates.

Source: adapted from www.hmrc.gov.uk, April 2005.

1. **Explain the difference between the current income tax system in the UK and the proposed flat tax.**

2. **Discuss whether a flat tax would be more efficient and more equitable than the current income tax system.**

Summary

1. The size of the state grew during the 20th century.
2. Factors which determine the optimal level of public spending include efficiency of public vs private sector provision, equity, the effects on taxation and government borrowing, and the need to intervene over the trade cycle.
3. The size of the state can be reduced through privatisation, outsourcing, internal markets, public/private sector partnerships, or the abandonment of provision.
4. Whether the state or the private sector should produce an individual good or service depends upon the criteria of productive and allocative efficiency and equity.

The size of the state

Government spending, as a proportion of national income, tended to rise worldwide during the 20th century. Two World Wars led to a significant upward shift in state spending. Then, in Europe at least, the creation of welfare states further increased spending. There is a number of factors which determine what might be the optimal level of public spending in an economy.

Efficiency Free markets can be less efficient in the production of some goods and services than the state. The free market, for instance, will produce too few **public goods** and **merit goods**. The state therefore has to organise production of services such as defence, law, order and protective services and education. Production of too few goods and services is an aspect of allocative inefficiency. Free markets, though, can also be productively inefficient. It can be argued, for instance, that health care should be provided by the state because costs, for the same level of services, are higher when it is provided by the private sector. This is to do with economies of scale and the ability of a sole buyer (a monopsonist) to drive down prices of suppliers to the market such as doctors, hospitals and drugs companies. The state should therefore produce those goods and services which it can provide more efficiently than the private sector.

Equity Free markets can produce an inequitable distribution of resources. In health care, for instance, those likely to face the largest bills are the elderly, typically in the lower income brackets of income distribution. Unless the state provides assistance, many elderly people would not be able to afford health care. Similarly, if education had to be paid for, children from poor families would suffer most. Governments therefore can be argued to have an obligation to spend in such a way as to reduce inequity.

The burden of taxation Government spending has to be paid for, typically through taxation. A country like the UK, where government spending is around 40 per cent of its GDP, has a lower tax burden than, say, Sweden, where it is nearer 60 per cent. The level of taxation can be important to both efficiency and economic growth. Taxes can act as a disincentive. For instance, high marginal rates of income tax can reduce incentives to work. High marginal rates of tax on employment reduce the willingness of employers to take on workers and can lead to higher unemployment. High tax levels can discourage overseas investors from investing in a country, whilst encouraging domestic firms to relocate abroad. This leads to a drain of capital from a country, perhaps resulting in lower economic

growth. Hence, the optimal level of government spending cannot be considered without taking into account the welfare implications of different tax levels.

Government borrowing High levels of government spending are often associated with high levels of government borrowing. This is because governments face political pressures to spend more but tax less. They can do this if they borrow more. However, ever increasing levels of government borrowing are unsustainable. Government spending levels must therefore be low enough to be financed adequately in the long run.

The trade cycle Governments may want to use their spending to smooth out the trade cycle. John Maynard Keynes advocated that governments should spend more if the economy were in a depression to increase aggregate demand. If governments finance this through increased borrowing, they must ensure that government spending falls again when the economy recovers. Otherwise, there are dangers that both government spending and levels of national debt will forever increase, which is unsustainable in the long term.

State provision of goods and services

There is a number of different models of state provision of goods

Question I

Sir Rod Eddington has been commissioned by the government to report by the middle of this year on how transport infrastructure should be improved after 2015. Business hopes his recommendations will be radical. He warned last June that the UK had 'nearly reached that point of no return' at which its transport infrastructure became so bad that it deterred foreign investment. Road congestion alone is estimated to cost companies £20 billion a year. His report is likely to assume that a national scheme of road pricing will come into force in the next 10 to 15 years.

Source: adapted from the *Financial Times*, 6.1.2006.

(a) Explain the arguments in favour of government providing improved transport infrastructure in the UK.
(b) Discuss whether revenues raised from road pricing would best be used to further improve the road network for the private motorist.

and services, shown in Figure 1.

- The public sector may both physically produce and provide (i.e. pay for out of tax revenues) goods and services. For instance, in the UK this is the case for health care, defence, education and libraries.
- The public sector may provide a good or service but not produce it. Instead it buys it in from the private sector. For instance, in the UK the government pays for the building of new roads, but it employs private sector contractors to do the work. Most places in old people's homes are paid for by local authorities, but the homes are in the private sector. The government buys in food for the army, textbooks for schools or electricity for hospitals from the private sector.
- The government may produce a good or service but sell it to the private sector. Before privatisation, government owned the gas, electricity, water and telecommunications industries, but sold these to private sector customers.
- The fourth alternative shown in Figure 1 is that the state is involved in neither the provision nor funding of services. These are goods and services produced and sold in the private sector, from cars to baked beans to package holidays.

In the 1950s, 1960s and 1970s, the state in the UK was much larger than it is today. In particular, the state owned the 'commanding heights of the economy', key industries such as coal, gas, electricity, railways and telecommunications. Since the beginning of the 1980s the size of the state has been considerably reduced in a number of ways.

Privatisation This saw the sale of state owned companies and other assets to the private sector. In Figure 1, privatisation represented a move mainly from Box B to Box C.

Outsourcing Outsourcing is the process of asking another producer to provide a good or service rather than producing it in-house. In this case, government would ask private sector firms to bid for the provision of services to the state. For instance, construction companies might be asked to tender for a road contract, or catering firms might tender for the provision of food to a school. If the good or service had previously been produced by the state, this would then be a move from Box A to Box D in Figure 1.

Figure 1 State provision 2008, UK

Paid for by

Produced by		Public sector	Private sector
	Public sector	A Libraries, hospitals	B The Post Office
	Private sector	D GP (General Practice) doctors, school buildings under PFI (Private Finance Initiative) contracts	C Motor vehicles, Ice creams

Internal markets In some cases, the government might decide that only it can both pay for and produce a good or service. However, it may decide to introduce competition by creating an internal market where different public sector providers compete amongst themselves. For instance, schools in a local area may compete for pupils. Internal markets leave a good or service in Box A in Figure 1.

Public/private sector partnerships The government can try and persuade the private sector to enter into a partnership with it. For instance, rather than pay completely for the redevelopment of a run down area, the government may invite private companies to pay part of the cost in return for a share of future revenues. The Private Finance Initiative (PFI) is another example. In this case, a private company builds and operates a building, road, bridge or other piece of infrastructure instead of government. The state then pays a 'rent' over a period of years for the use of the infrastructure before it reverts to state ownership. PFI would put provision of a good into Box D.

Abandonment of provision The government may attempt to abandon paying for a service which it also produces. For instance, new toll motorways will be paid for by the motorists that use them rather than the taxpayer (a move from Box A to Box C). The government could make patients pay for the services of their GP (a move from Box D to Box C).

Choosing between public sector and private sector provision

Whether state provision or private provision is more desirable depends on a number of factors.

Question 2

Kilmarnock Prison, Scotland's only private prison, has been in the news recently following a BBC investigation which alleged problems with the running of the jail. A representative of Premier Custodial Group accepted there had been individual failures at the prison. An undercover reporter filmed officers turning a blind eye to the use of drugs and alcohol. Three years ago, a prisoner hanged himself despite the fact that he was an 'at risk' prisoner and should have been observed every 30 minutes by warders in his cell. Two prison officers who failed to do this on the night of his suicide have since been sacked.

Scottish Nationalist member of the Scottish Parliament, Alex Neill, has called for the Scottish Prison Service to say how much it is costing taxpayers to run the prison. He is concerned that the taxpayer is not getting value for money. He said: 'This is public money which is being wasted on a private prison, which as well as being costly to run has one of the worst performing records of any prison in Scotland.'

Source: adapted from news.bbc.co.uk 10.3.2005, 22.3.2005 and 11.8.2005.

(a) Using Figure 1, explain what model of state provision is being used in the case of Kilmarnock Prison.
(b) On what economic grounds might the Scottish Prison Service have contracted out prison services to Premier Custodial Group?

Productive efficiency There can be large **economies of scale** available if a service is provided for the total population by one producer. For instance, it will almost certainly be more costly for two competing refuse collection companies to collect refuse from a housing estate than just one. Therefore, it may be more efficient for the state to organise household refuse collection rather than allow each household to employ different firms. The same might apply to the National Health Service (NHS). Costs per patient are lower than in, for example, the USA. It could be argued that this is because the NHS provides lower quality health care than in other countries. But there is evidence to suggest that there are significant economies of scale in the NHS which are not found in the private health care systems of continental Europe and the USA. For instance, bed utilisation in NHS hospitals is considerably higher than in Europe or the USA because the NHS has much greater control of when patients are to be treated. Equally, drug costs are lower because doctors in the NHS are encouraged to prescribe the minimum doses necessary of the cheapest drug available.

On the other hand, it is sometimes claimed that **diseconomies of scale** are present in organisations like the NHS. They are such large bureaucracies that management is unable to control costs and utilise resources efficiently. **X-inefficiency** raises costs as workers within the organisation manipulate the system for their own advantage. Only the break-up of the organisation and the creation of strong competition in the market place can lower costs and eliminate inefficiency. This provides a strong argument for either breaking up a public sector monopoly and then selling the competing parts to the private sector, as for instance happened to the electricity generating industry in 1991, or the creation of strong internal markets, where, say, schools or hospitals have to compete with each other for pupils or patients.

Allocative efficiency State production or tendering systems are unlikely to create much consumer choice. Households, for instance, are unlikely to have any choice about who collects their refuse or who polices their neighbourhood. Moreover, they are unable to influence the amount spent on services except perhaps indirectly through the ballot box.

Choice is much greater in the private sector. UK consumers now, for instance, have a choice about which telephone company or gas supplier to use. Since the late 1990s, households have been able to choose which company supplies them with gas. Previously they could only shop around for gas appliances or gas repair services. State provision, however, can involve an element of choice. Parents in the UK have the right to choose which school they wish to send their child to. Patients can choose their doctor. Choice may be not as great as it might seem though. Consumers of education or health care are likely to want to buy from their nearest supplier. Therefore, weak local monopolies are likely to emerge, particularly in rural areas. The 'best' schools in an area might be oversubscribed and turn applicants away. Hospitals are likely to be full and so patients are unlikely to be able to exercise much choice about when to have an operation.

Choice also implies that consumers are able to make rational choices. But there may be little **consumer sovereignty** in the market. Producers may use their market power to distort information supplied to customers. Consumers may also have extremely limited understanding of the services they are asked to buy themselves.

Distribution of resources The transfer of resources from the public sector to the private sector can have important implications for the distribution of income. For instance, when the state ceases to pay for certain activities through the tax system, individuals have to pay the full cost themselves. A student wanting to study at a drama school might before have been financed by collecting a fraction of a penny per year from local taxpayers. If the local authority ceases to pay a grant, then the student or the student's family has to pay the full cost of thousands of pounds.

Question 3

It has been suggested that local authorities should no longer provide public libraries. Instead, they could either contract out, getting a private company to run the service in return for a fee from the local authority, or the local authority could stop offering a service at all and leave the market mechanism to decide whether library services should be offered to consumers and in what form. Libraries are used by all age and income groups but are disproportionately used by females and older people.

(a) Discuss the impact of both contracting out and completely privatising the library service on efficiency and equity.

Applied economics

Public expenditure in the UK

Public expenditure totals

The public sector in the UK comprises central government, local government and government enterprises such as public corporations. Central government is responsible for approximately three-quarters of total public spending. Compared to other countries, the size of Britain's public sector is unexceptional. As shown in Table 1, it is greater as a proportion of GDP than the free market economies of the United States or Japan, at the bottom end of the range of our EU partners, but much lower than a country like Sweden which has a long tradition of high public spending.

Public expenditure totals can be divided by function, as illustrated in Figure 2.
● The largest single item of public expenditure is social protection. This covers **transfer payments** such as

child benefit and Jobseekers allowance. The most costly benefit is the state retirement pension, received by around nearly 12 million pensioners.

- Spending on **health** is the second largest category of expenditure. Most of this is accounted for by the cost of the National Health Service.
- **Education** covers local government spending on primary and secondary schools, and colleges of further education. Central government pays for higher education and research grants.
- **Personal and social services** include expenditure by local authority social services departments and children's departments on social workers, home care assistants and placements for the elderly in residential homes.
- **Transport** includes roadbuilding and maintenance as well as subsidies for train and bus services.
- **Industry, agriculture, employment and training** includes grants and subsidies to promote growth of businesses, maintenance of farms, training of workers and measures such as the New Deal to get the unemployed back to work.
- **Defence spending** is expenditure on the army, navy and airforce.
- **Public order and safety** covers spending on the police, the judiciary, prisons and the fire service.
- **Housing and the environment** covers grants to Housing Associations to build new homes and to local councils for the repairs and maintenance of their existing stock as well as expenditure on refuse collection, parks and environmental protection measures.
- **Gross debt interest** is the interest that the government has to pay on the money it has borrowed in the past - the National Debt.
- **Other expenditure** includes expenditure on overseas aid, the arts, libraries, and embassies abroad.

Trends in public expenditure

Total UK government spending in real terms has tended to rise over time as Table 2 shows. Increased income from economic growth has partly been spent on improving public services.

Trends in government spending as a percentage of GDP are more complex as Figure 3 shows.

1900-1960 The two world wars of the twentieth century caused large spikes in public spending as defence expenditure soared. The two world wars also led to new levels of public spending being established.

Table 1 Government expenditure as a percentage of GDP

	1960-67	1968-73	1974-79	1980-89	1990-99	2000-07
Sweden	34.8	44.3	54.4	62.9	64.0	56.7
France	37.4	38.9	43.3	50.2	53.4	52.9
Italy	31.9	36.0	42.9	44.9	52.8	48.0
Germany	35.7	39.8	47.5	47.8	48.1	46.7
UK	34.7	39.5	44.6	44.9	43.0	42.8
Canada	29.3	34.7	39.2	39.7	46.3	40.4
Japan	18.7	20.5	28.4	32.8	34.5	37.8
US	28.3	31.0	32.6	35.8	34.6	36.1

Source: adapted from OECD, *Historical Statistics and Economic Outlook.*

Figure 2 Government spending by function, 2007-08

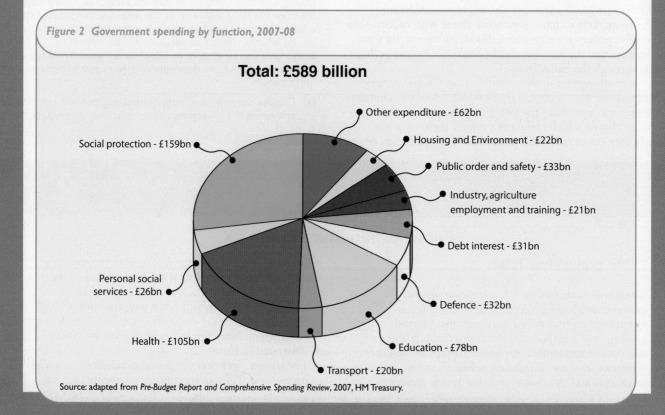

Total: £589 billion

- Other expenditure - £62bn
- Housing and Environment - £22bn
- Public order and safety - £33bn
- Industry, agriculture employment and training - £21bn
- Debt interest - £31bn
- Defence - £32bn
- Education - £78bn
- Transport - £20bn
- Health - £105bn
- Personal social services - £26bn
- Social protection - £159bn

Source: adapted from *Pre-Budget Report and Comprehensive Spending Review*, 2007, HM Treasury.

Table 2 Government total managed expenditure at 2006-07 prices

	£ billion	Index 1970-71=100
1970-71	242.7	100
1975-76	315.5	139.7
1980-81	321.2	142.2
1985-86	349.2	154.6
1990-91	353.6	156.5
1995-96	411.8	182.3
2000-01	426.1	188.6
2005-06	538.7	238.5
2006-07	550.1	243.5

Before the First World War, public expenditure was around 12 per cent of GDP. In the inter-war period, it rose to around 25 per cent, whilst after the Second World War it rose to around 35 per cent.

1960-1975 The 1960s and first half of the 1970s saw an upward trend in public spending as a percentage of GDP as the welfare state expanded. This trend came to a halt in 1975 when the then Labour government declared that the country could no longer afford to keep on spending more and more on public services. At this point, public spending was 50 per cent of GDP.

1975-1990 The move to lower public spending was reinforced by the election of a Conservative government under Margaret Thatcher in 1979. She was committed to rolling back the frontiers of the state and to reducing the tax burden. By 1988-89, public spending as a percentage of GDP had fallen to 39.4 per cent. In the decade 1980 to 1990, real public spending only rose by 10 per cent, compared to 33 per cent in the 1970s and 22 per cent in the 1990s. Between 1984 and 1989, real public spending actually fell by 3 per cent.

1990-1997 The recession of 1990-92 saw a significant increase in public spending as spending on welfare benefits tends to rise in any recession. In addition, Margaret Thatcher fell from power in 1989. Her successor, John Major, realised that it was impossible to maintain a real spending freeze in areas such as education and health and his government saw a modest growth in real spending on government services.

From 1997 In 1997, a Labour government under Tony Blair replaced John Major's Conservative government. In its election manifesto, Labour had pledged not to increase public spending, in an attempt to persuade the voters it would be fiscally responsible. Between 1996 and 1999, real public spending remained broadly unchanged. Electors, however, were growing increasingly dissatisfied with the quality of public services including the National Health Service. In 2000, the government responded by announcing a significant increase in spending on health and education to 2007-08 which would raise the proportion of government spending to approximately 43 per cent of GDP. Figure 4 shows the impact of this on health and education spending as well as on total spending. Gordon Brown, who replaced Tony Blair in 2007, was committed to maintaining public spending at high levels.

Figure 3 General government expenditure as a percentage of GDP

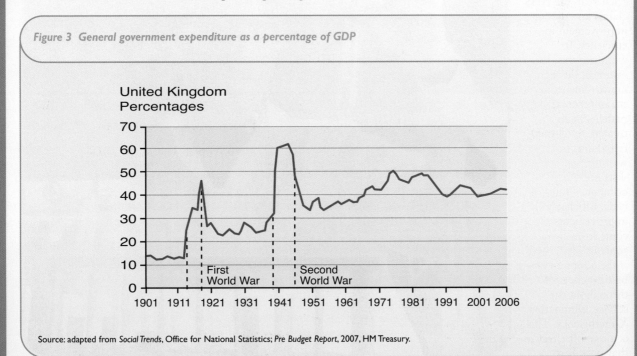

Source: adapted from *Social Trends*, Office for National Statistics; *Pre Budget Report*, 2007, HM Treasury.

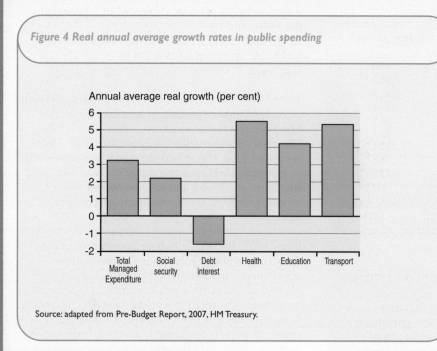

Figure 4 Real annual average growth rates in public spending

Annual average real growth (per cent)

Source: adapted from Pre-Budget Report, 2007, HM Treasury.

Are public services improving?

There are major problems in assessing whether there has been a growth in public services in recent years. Taking the National Health Service as an example, there are four key factors which need to be considered.

Efficiency gains
Each year, the NHS claims an improvement in efficiency. It measures this, for instance, through improvements in the number of patients being treated per doctor, reductions in waiting lists and occupancy rates of beds. Efficiency improvements come from two sources. First, there is the adoption of best practice throughout the service, eliminating **X-inefficiency**. This is a one-off effect in that once best

practice has been adopted, it is impossible to make further efficiency gains. Second, advances in medical knowledge, new equipment and better trained staff can increase efficiency. This, in theory, is a dynamic process and it should be possible to generate efficiency gains from this source for the foreseeable future.

The cost of the service Data are often presented 'at constant prices'. This means that figures are adjusted for the general rate of inflation in the economy (measured by the GDP deflator rather than the Retail Price Index). However, increases in real expenditure on services do not necessarily mean that the volume of services has increased. This is because inflation in the public sector is likely to be higher than inflation in the economy as a whole. The public sector is far more labour intensive than the private sector. There is also far less scope for increases in productivity. Earnings on

average increase about 2 per cent more than the increase in inflation each year. Hence the NHS has to pay more in real terms each year to buy the same number of doctors, nurses, etc.

The needs of the patients The population structure is slowly changing. In particular, there is a growth in the number of over 75 year olds. This age group is a particularly heavy user of NHS facilities. If public spending on the NHS is kept constant, the level of service to the average patient will inevitably decline.

Expectations and technology Each year, consumers expect to be able to buy better products. They expect to see more advanced cars, eat a wider range of foods and go to more exotic places for their holidays. They also expect to receive better health care. Advances in medicine mean that more and more illnesses are capable of treatment. But if these illnesses are to be treated, then extra money must be found to pay for treatment. Consumers also expect better facilities - everything from potted plants in waiting rooms, to private hospital rooms, to being able to choose the timing of medical treatment. These cost money.

Overall, there is widespread agreement that both the quality and quantity of services provided by the NHS have increased since 2000. However, critics argue that most of the extra cash pumped into the system has been wasted both on bureaucracy and on funding large pay increases for nurses and doctors. The taxpayer has not had value for money from the injection of cash. At the other extreme, some argue that the only way to improve the health service was to increase spending and that very few of the extra resources have been wasted. More information is contained in the data question.

DataQuestion The National Health Service

Growth in NHS spending

In 2000, the UK had a health service which lagged behind most other EU countries. The problem was cash. The UK was spending around one third less than other EU countries as a proportion of GDP on its health service. That gap was so huge that no amount of extra productivity in the NHS could prevent it delivering an inferior service. In the 1980s and 1990s, the Conservative government had kept down public spending on the NHS as part of its drive to keep total public spending down. It also introduced various schemes to persuade more people to use private health care. In 2000, the Labour government pledged to bring UK spending on health up to EU levels. It then embarked on a massive increase in spending which between 2001/02 and 2007/08 averaged over 7 per cent per annum. This compares with real growth in the economy of under 3 per cent. By 2007-08, spending on health in the UK was nearly 10 per cent of GDP, almost equal to the EU average.

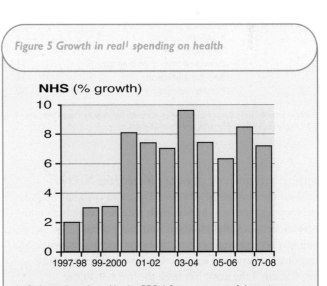

Figure 5 Growth in real[1] spending on health

NHS (% growth)

1. Cash spending adjusted by the GDP deflator, a measure of change in average prices in the economy. Because inflation in the NHS was much higher than in the economy as a whole, the increase in the volume of NHS services was much less than shown in the chart.

Source: adapted from PWC estimated based on Treasury data; Kings Fund, *Our Future Health Secured?* by Derek Wanless, John Appleby, Anthony Harrison and Darshan Patel.

Inflation in the NHS

The rate of inflation in much of the public sector is higher than the average for the whole economy. This is because the public sector produces mainly services whose main cost is wages of staff. In the NHS, two thirds of all costs are accounted by staff costs.

Inflation in the NHS was particularly affected between 2002 and 2005 by very large increases in pay for doctors and nurses. Between 2002 and 2007, pay for hospital and community health service staff rose by 30 per cent compared to just 17 per cent for average earnings in the economy as a whole. The large increases in pay were linked to new contracts. Hospital consultants received average pay increases of 25 per cent in 2002-03 and GPs 23 per cent between 2003 and 2005.

Figure 6 Rate of inflation in the NHS compared to inflation in the economy as a whole

Percentages

- NHS-specific inflation
- UK inflation (GDP deflator)

Years

Source: adapted from Kings Fund, *Our Future Health Secured?* by Derek Wanless, John Appleby, Anthony Harrison and Darshan Patel.

The quantity of services has increased

Table 4 Changes in hospital admissions 1998/9 to 2005/6

	% change
Emergency admissions	35
Non-emergency admissions	
Inpatient	-4
Day case	20
Admitted from a waiting list	-33
Booked admission	34
Planned admission	90

Source: adapted from Kings Fund, *Our Future Health Secured?* by Derek Wanless, John Appleby, Anthony Harrison and Darshan Patel.

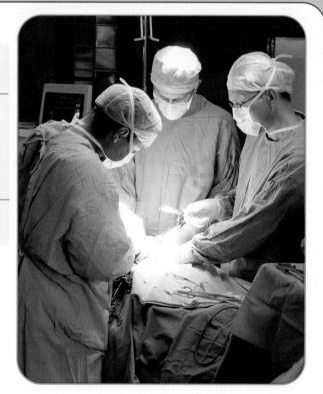

Pumping huge amounts of extra cash into the NHS has increased the number of services. The extra cash has helped fund more doctors and nurses, more intensive care beds and scanners, new hospital buildings and more drugs. The result has been shorter waiting times for operations, fewer heart deaths, improved cancer treatment and better health care. Exactly how great has been the increase in the quantity of services is often difficult to measure. For example, admissions from waiting lists have fallen and been replaced by a substantial rise in booked and planned admissions. Waiting times for operations have fallen, which is an improvement in the quality of the service. The number of operations, particularly day surgery, has increased, which is an increase in the quantity of the service. Improvements in procedures mean that operations are more successful, which is an increase in quality of service.

Is the NHS providing value for money? Certainly nurses and doctors, who over the past few years have received pay rises which make them the best paid in Europe, have done well out of rising government spending on the NHS. However, the Office for National Statistics, the government's statistical body, is not sure that taxpayers have done as well. On their figures, productivity is either stagnant or falling. Output is measured in terms of physical outcomes such as the number of operations carried out, the number of prescriptions given or the number of ambulance trips taken. Inputs are resources such as nurses and doctors. The ONS calculates that on this basis, productivity in the health service has been falling for the past decade by between 0.6 per cent and 1.3 per cent a year. Every extra £1 spent on the NHS is giving less and less output.

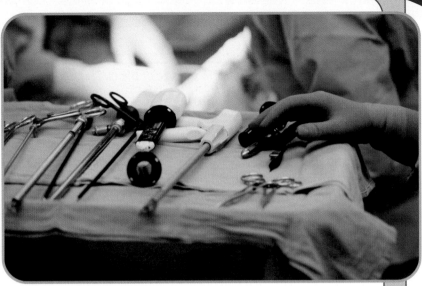

However, the ONS admits that its calculations are too crude. For example, their measures don't take into account quality of service. If waiting lists fall or a group of cancer patients survive 12 months longer on average than in the past, this isn't reflected in the ONS figures. The fact that on average we are living longer because of simple treatments to guard against heart problems and strokes isn't reflected either. The ONS wants a national debate to decide on the best approach to take.

Source: adapted from news.bbc.co.uk 28.2.2006.

Falling productivity

Huge increases in spending in recent years on the NHS have been associated with a substantial fall in NHS productivity. The increase in measured outputs have nowhere near matched the increase in cash injected into the NHS. Worse still, output per worker on some measures has fallen. Between 2000 and 2006, the number of patients admitted per consultant fell by more than 20 per cent and the number of emergency cases by 8 per cent. Unit costs have increased for all hospital services, mainly because of the very large pay increases given to health staff between 2001 and 2005.

Source: adapted from Kings Fund, *Our Future Health Secured?* by Derek Wanless, John Appleby, Anthony Harrison and Darshan Patel.

Running fast to go backwards

The NHS is faced with two crises which could lead to costs spiralling out of control. The first is that we are all living longer. Old people account for much of NHS spending. The longer we live, the greater the burden we are to the NHS. But this is a problem which has a positive side. We fund the NHS because we want to live longer.

The second crisis has no positive side. Over the past ten years, obesity levels in the population have shot up. Between 1995 and 2005, the proportion of adult males classified as obese rose by half to 23 per cent of the male population, whilst the proportion of obese women rose by 42 per cent to around 25 per cent of the female population. Nearly one in five children are now obese. Obesity causes debilitating illnesses such as diabetes and reduces average life expectancy. The NHS faces huge increases in costs over the next 20-30 years if this obesity epidemic is not reversed.

Source: adapted from Kings Fund, *Our Future Health Secured?* by Derek Wanless, John Appleby, Anthony Harrison and Darshan Patel.

1. Outline the trends in public spending on the health service since 1997.
2. Using the concepts of equity and efficiency, explain why the government might have changed its spending levels on the health service.

3. Discuss whether the government would have been better lowering taxes and allowing taxpayers to buy top up health care if they so wished rather than increasing taxes and funding extra spending in the NHS.

Summary

1. Fiscal policy, through changes in the size of the budget deficit, can have an impact on aggregate demand.
2. Government expenditure and tax revenues which change automatically as income changes are called automatic stabilisers. They break the fall of national income when the economy moves towards a depression and limit the rise of income when the economy is in boom.
3. Active fiscal policy is the deliberate manipulation of government expenditure and taxes to influence the economy.
4. Demand management through the use of fiscal policy has its limitations. There are time lags involved in the implementation of policy, economic data on which to base decisions are inadequate, economic theory itself is not sufficiently well developed for governments to be able to fine-tune the economy to meet precise targets, and continued deficits can lead to national debt problems. Countries belonging to the European Monetary Union also have restrictions placed upon their use of fiscal policy.
5. Because of these limitations, governments today tend to use monetary policy to manipulate aggregate demand.
6. Fiscal policy can be used to influence the supply side of the economy.

The objectives of fiscal policy

Fiscal policy concerns the decisions of government about its spending, taxation and borrowing. Fiscal policy is an **instrument** of policy used to achieve three main policy goals or objectives.

To improve macroeconomic performance Fiscal policy is used to achieve lower unemployment, lower inflation, higher economic growth and an improved balance of payments situation. It does this either by influencing the demand side of the economy, which is the subject of this unit; or by influencing the supply side of the economy, which is covered in the next unit.

To achieve a more desirable distribution of income and wealth Taxes and government spending are important ways in which government can affect the distribution of income and wealth. It can use fiscal policy to reduce or increase inequality. This is discussed in the unit 'The redistribution of income and wealth'.

To correct market failure at the microeconomic level Government spending and taxes are used to correct a wide range of market failures including the provision of public and merit goods, discouraging the consumption of demerit goods, improving the mobility of labour and increasing competition in product markets. These are explained in the units on various market failures.

Demand management

Fiscal policy can be used to manipulate the level of aggregate demand. This is known as DEMAND MANAGEMENT. A larger budget deficit or a smaller budget surplus will increase the government injection into the circular flow of money. There will be a multiplier impact, according to Keynesian economists, where every £1 of extra deficit or reduced surplus will lead to a more than £1 increase in final GDP. Because of this increase in GDP, policy which leads to larger budget deficits or smaller budget surpluses is known as **expansionary fiscal policy**.

In contrast, there is **deflationary fiscal policy** when the government decides to reduce a budget deficit or increase a budget surplus. This reduces the level of aggregate demand by reducing the government injection into the circular flow.

Expansionary fiscal policy should be used when there is a negative output gap and the economy is in recession. In this situation, the level of GDP is below what the long term trend growth in GDP would predict. Unemployment is likely to be above average whilst inflation is low. The rate of growth of GDP may be below average. On the other hand, the current account position may be better than would be the case if the economy were at FULL EMPLOYMENT, a level of employment where there is neither a negative or positive output gap. This is because in a recession, imports will be reduced due to a lack of spending both by consumers and firms. Conversely, deflationary fiscal policy should be used when there a positive output gap and the economy is in boom. GDP is above its long term trend rate, unemployment is below average, inflation is above average whilst the current account position is deteriorating.

Automatic stabilisers

In the 1930s, large falls in export earnings and investment spending led to the Great Depression. Today, any reduction in

---

Question 1

In March 2006, the Chancellor of the Exchequer announced a number of changes to taxes and government spending at a time when the economy was growing very slightly below its trend rate of growth. Explain whether the following are likely to be examples of automatic stabilisers or active fiscal policy.
(a) The introduction of a new higher band of Vehicle Excise Duty (the tax disk on cars) of £210 for cars which have a very high petrol consumption per mile travelled.
(b) A rise in tax revenues in 2005-2006 of 7.0 per cent, net of changes in tax rates in the 2005 Budget.
(c) A rise in average spending per pupil in state sector schools from £5 000 per annum to £8 000 over the period 2006 to 2012.
(d) Lower receipts from excise duties and VAT partly caused by moderation in household spending.

export earnings or investment would have less impact on the economy because AUTOMATIC or BUILT-IN STABILISERS are greater. Automatic stabilisers are expenditures which automatically increase when the economy is going into a recession. Conversely, they automatically fall when national income begins to rise.

Government spending and taxation are both automatic stabilisers. When the economy goes into recession and unemployment rises, the government automatically increases its social security spending, paying out more in unemployment benefits and other related benefits. The fall in aggregate demand is therefore less than it would otherwise have been. Tax revenues fall too at a faster rate than the fall in income. This is because tax rates tend to be higher on marginal income than on average income. For instance, a worker paid on commission may sell less in a recession. Her tax rate might then fall from the higher rate of 40 per cent to the basic rate of 20 per cent. If household spending has to be cut, then it is likely that consumption items such as consumer durables taxed at 17.5 per cent VAT will see falls rather than zero rated food. With the government collecting less tax, disposable incomes are higher than they would otherwise be and therefore consumption can be at a higher level than would be the case without this automatic stabiliser.

When the economy goes into boom, government spending falls as the benefit budget falls automatically. Tax revenue increases at a faster rate than the increase in income. An unemployed person will pay very little tax. Once the unemployed get jobs, they start to pay substantial amounts of direct and indirect tax. So aggregate demand is lower than it would otherwise be with these automatic stabilisers.

Active or discretionary fiscal policy

ACTIVE or DISCRETIONARY FISCAL POLICY does not rely on the economy automatically changing the amount the government spends or collects in taxes. It is the deliberate manipulation of government expenditure and taxes to influence the economy. The deliberate decision by government to cut tax rates, leading to a fall in tax revenues, would be an example of active fiscal policy. Another would be a decision to increase spending on education.

The use of fiscal policy to manipulate aggregate demand

In the 1920s and 1930s, the orthodox **classical** thinking of the day was that governments should maintain balanced budgets whatever the state of the economy. The argument was that every extra £1 of government spending would CROWD OUT £1 of private sector spending. If the government adopted expansionary fiscal policy, it would simply displace private sector spending. The net impact on national income would be zero. This was considered true whether the economy was at full employment or in a recession.

John Maynard Keynes, in his seminal book *The General Theory of Employment, Interest and Money*, argued that crowding out did not take place if the economy was in a depression. The book was published in 1936 when the world was still suffering the effects of the Great Depression of the 1930s. His views became the economic orthodoxy of the 1950s and 1960s. In the 1944 White Paper *Employment Policy* (Cmnd 6527), it was stated that: 'The government accepts as one of

---

Question 2

In a speech yesterday, Conservative leader David Cameron pledged to put Britain's economic stability above tax cuts. He said Tories would forge a low-tax economy 'over time' but 'stability and responsibility come first'. He said that high taxes and regulation were creating a 'slow furring up of the arteries of the British economy.'

Rupert Murdoch, owner of several UK newspapers including the Sun, said he believed the country was 'overtaxed', which harmed business. 'It's up to people to get on, and it's up to the government to get out of their way, tax them less, give them more incentives.'

Source: adapted from news.bbc.co.uk 23.1.2006.

(a) Explain why David Cameron might think that tax cuts might lead to instability in the UK economy.
(b) Rupert Murdoch wants government to 'get out of the way' of people by cutting both taxes and government spending. Would this be a responsible way of acting from the viewpoint of aggregate demand and the dangers of overheating the economy?

---

their primary aims and responsibilities the maintenance of a high and stable level of employment after the war'. Post war governments used fiscal policy to manage demand. In fact, in the 1950s and 1960s, unemployment was very low. So demand management was a question of FINE-TUNING the economy to a very precise level of unemployment. The term **fiscal levers** was used to illustrate the way in which Keynesian economists believed the economy could be levered into a position of full employment.

In the 1970s and 1980s, there was a monetarist counter-revolution against Keynesian orthodoxy. On a theoretical level, it was argued that the orthodox economists of the 1920s and 1930s were correct in arguing that crowding out cancelled out the impact of fiscal policy on aggregate demand. On a practical level, Western economies went through a series of crises where both high unemployment and high inflation occurred at the same time.

Today, the mainstream view is that aggregate demand should be manipulated through the use of monetary policy. Fiscal policy is best left to deal with other objectives of government such as correcting market failure or changing inequality. This is because fiscal policy has a number of limitations when it comes to the manipulation of aggregate demand.

The limitations of fiscal policy to manipulate aggregate demand

Conflicting policy objectives An instrument of policy, like fiscal policy, can only be used to manipulate one variable like unemployment or inflation. Governments in the past believed that they could achieve a variety of objectives through the use of fiscal policy. This led to STOP-GO CYCLES. When the economy was in recession, the government would use expansionary fiscal policy to reduce unemployment and stimulate growth. But the economy would overshoot and in the subsequent boom, inflation would rise and the current account would deteriorate. The government would then put on the brakes by using deflationary fiscal policy, sending the economy back into recession. The stop-go cycle was made worse by governments tending to use fiscal policy to put the economy into a boom at times of general elections. In contrast, monetary policy targets only one variable, the rate of inflation. Giving control of monetary policy to an independent central bank also prevents the manipulation of policy by government at election times.

Time lags Assume that the government announces a £500 million increase in civil servant salaries and a £500 million increase in road building. If the multiplier were 2, this would lead to a £2 000 million increase in equilibrium income in the Keynesian model. However, it may take some years for the full increase to work through the economy. The increase in civil servant salaries will work through relatively quickly. Civil servants will increase their spending within a few months of receiving the pay increase. The road building programme may take years even to start. So a government needs to be careful to take account of lags in spending when using fiscal policy to fill or remove deflationary or inflationary gaps. If a government wishes to reflate or deflate the economy quickly, it needs to change those taxes and those items of expenditure which will have an immediate impact on aggregate demand. Changing income tax rates, social security payments and public sector wages will all act quickly to change demand. Long term capital projects, such as road building or hospital building, are inappropriate for short term changes although they may be ideal in a serious longer term depression such as that which occurred during the 1930s and early 1980s.

In the past, governments have been accused of even destabilising the economy through the use of active fiscal policy. Government would reflate the economy just at a time when the economy was moving into boom of its own accord. The combination of extra private sector spending and extra public sector spending would then create a positive output gap. The more inherently stable the economy, the more potential damage there would be from wrong timing in active fiscal policy. Hence some economists argue that the inability to predict time lags accurately makes it impossible to use fiscal policy to fine-tune the economy.

Inadequacy of economic data Active fiscal policy assumes that the Chancellor knows the current state of the British economy. But statistics are notoriously unreliable. Unemployment statistics and inflation statistics are not revised after publication, but national income statistics and the balance of payments statistics are frequently revised. Moreover, there are often 'black holes' in these statistics where two or more sets of figures which should match fail to do so. In official statistics these are varyingly described as 'balancing items', 'residual errors' or 'statistical discrepancies'. If the current account on the balance of payments is in deficit, the Chancellor will not know how much of this is due to a genuine deficit and how much is due to inaccurate recording of statistics. Fine-tuning then becomes very difficult. The Chancellor could well reflate the economy even though it was at full employment because he had been misled by statistics showing a recession.

Inadequate economic knowledge Active fiscal policy assumes that we know how the economy behaves. However, there is scepticism that economics will ever be able to

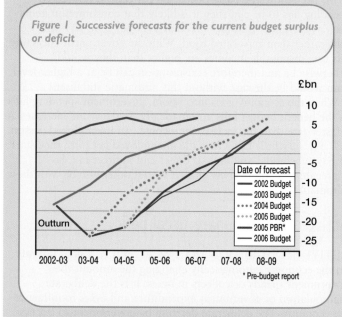
predict changes in variables to the last few per cent. This is important because so many of the variables which governments wish to control have very small values. For instance, the government may wish to reduce economic growth from 3 per cent to 1.5 per cent. But active fiscal policy is unlikely ever to be sufficiently sensitive to achieve exactly that 1.5 per cent fall.

The inadequacy of the model The computer-based macro-economic forecasting models used today by decision makers are highly complex. Even so, they provide at best an approximation of possible outcomes. Partly this is because the data that is fed into the models is not accurate, particularly the most recent data. Partly it is because models cannot capture the exact behaviour of an economy. They cannot, for instance, forecast sudden economic shocks such as the Asian crisis of 1998. Partly it also reflects the changing nature of economies. Until the 1980s, UK forecasting models failed to take into account the importance of large changes in house prices for aggregate demand, simply because large changes had not been experienced until that point. Today, there is controversy amongst model builders about the significance of the information technology revolution. Some economists argue that it has increased productivity in a way which is not being shown up by traditional models. This would enable the economy to grow at a faster rate without sparking off a rise in inflation. Other economists remain sceptical and remember the mid to late 1980s when the Conservative government of Margaret Thatcher claimed that a new 'miracle' economy had been created through its supply side reforms which would allow the economy to grow at a faster non-inflationary rate. This belief led to an overheated economy which then went into the longest recession since the 1930s.

Fiscal policy and monetary policy   Governments in Europe and the United States have, since the 1980s, tended to manage demand through **monetary policy** rather than active fiscal policy. One reason for this is that fiscal policy cannot be independent of monetary policy.

For instance, if the government increases its borrowing, this must be financed in some way. Governments, unlike households and firms, have the ability to print money to finance extra borrowing. In a modern economy, this is achieved through governments borrowing money from the banking system rather than by increasing notes and coins in circulation. Printing money, though, increases the money supply and is potentially inflationary. Printing money and increasing the money supply is a monetary policy decision. Hence fiscal policy and monetary policy are interlinked.

Governments can avoid printing money by genuinely borrowing the money for an increased budget deficit from the private sector. But this increases the demand for borrowed funds and interest rates are likely to rise. Higher interest rates will reduce the willingness of the private sector to borrow and therefore spend. So the increase in aggregate demand from a higher budget deficit will to some extent be offset by reduced aggregate demand from less private sector borrowing. This reduces the impact of fiscal policy. Allowing interest rates to rise is part of monetary policy and again this shows how monetary and fiscal policy are linked.

Higher government borrowing may not lead to higher interest rates if the economy is in a deep depression. This is called a LIQUIDITY TRAP situation. When there is a liquidity trap, borrowing can increase without changing interest rates. This occurs because interest rates are so low that they cannot fall any further. Lenders, though, are prepared to increase the supply of money without seeing a rise in interest rates. Monetary policy cannot be used to get the economy out of depression because the government cannot push interest rates down any further. So expansionary fiscal policy is the only policy option left.

The national debt   Since the Second World War, many governments have abandoned attempts to balance their budgets. They find it politically easier to spend more than they tax and borrow the difference. Demand management policies then

become a question of increasing budget deficits when the economy has high unemployment and reducing them when the economy is at full employment. In the long term, this can present a major problem for governments.

Governments are no different from individuals. If they continually borrow money, then eventually a national debt is built up which is increasingly difficult to service (i.e. pay interest on the debt). For instance, assume that a government is taking 40 per cent of national income in taxes. It has a national debt equivalent to 100 per cent of national income. Interest on the debt averages 10 per cent per annum. Then, the government has

Question 4

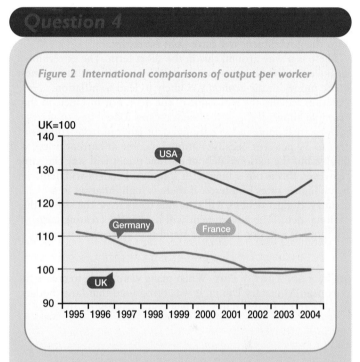

Figure 2 International comparisons of output per worker

This Budget sets out reforms in the light of the five key drivers of productivity.

● Improving *competition*, vital for the adoption of innovation and increased business efficiency;
● Promoting *enterprise*, by removing barriers to entrepreneurship and developing an enterprise culture;
● Supporting *science and innovation*, given that increasing rewards to innovation mean that the UK's economic success will depend on its ability to create new knowledge and translate it into innovative goods and services;
● Raising *skills levels*, to create a more flexible and productive workforce, which can adopt innovative technologies and enable individuals to move into new areas of work;
● Encouraging *investment*, to increase the stock of physical capital, including stronger, more efficient capital markets.

Source: adapted from *Full Budget Report*, March 2006, HM Treasury.

(a) Using the data, discuss whether the UK has improved its productivity performance compared to other countries.
(b) In his March 2006 Budget, the Chancellor announced extra cash for capital expenditure in school buildings as part of a wider initiative to increase funding for education. Discuss how this example of active fiscal policy might support the supply side of the economy in the light of the five 'key drivers of productivity'.

to pay 10 per cent of national income in interest, which amounts to one-quarter of its tax revenues (10% ÷ 40%). If it is continuing to run a budget deficit, then the proportion of taxation going on servicing the debt will increase further over time.

Eventually, lenders will begin to be scared that the government will default on its debt (i.e. it will not pay the interest and will not pay back loans as they mature). Governments in this position have to offer higher rates of interest on new loans in order to persuade lenders to take the risk of lending to them. This makes the situation worse, because the government is now having to pay even more interest on its debt. In the worst case, lenders will refuse to lend or the government will become overwhelmed by its debt and begin to default on its loans. Either way, the government will have gone bankrupt.

There is a way around this in the short term. The government, unlike an individual, can pay its debt by simply printing money. More money in the economy is likely to lead to inflation. Inflation reduces the real value of the debt. For instance, in the example above, if the government creates a doubling of prices, then the real value of the national debt will fall from 100 per cent to 50 per cent because national income at current prices will double but the national debt at current prices will stay the same. However, this is not a long term solution. Lenders will demand much higher rates of interest if there is high inflation in a country. Budget deficits will continue to increase the size of the national debt. The government will have to be creating large amounts of inflation simply to stand still in terms of national debt.

Stability and Growth Pact When plans were made to create the European Monetary Union, it was recognised that large budget deficits and a sizable national debt could destabilise the economies of individual member countries and therefore the whole monetary union. It was made a condition of membership, therefore, that fiscal deficits could not be more than 3 per cent of GDP whilst the national debt of a country could not be more than 60 per cent of GDP. Called the Stability and Growth Pact, this agreement further limits the ability of governments of member countries to use fiscal policy to steer the economy. It equally limits the policy of future applicant countries. If the UK wants to join the single currency, it must show that government finances have conformed to these criteria for a number of years before joining.

Code for Fiscal Stability In the UK, the government has had its own set of fiscal rules since 1998. Called the Code for Fiscal Stability, it has two main rules. The **golden rule** states that over the economic cycle, the government will only borrow to invest and not to fund current spending. This means that the government has pledged not to borrow to finance items of current spending such as wages and salaries, rent on buildings or heating bills for offices. It can borrow, however, to finance the construction of new hospitals and schools, or to build new roads. The **sustainable investment rule** states that the national debt will be kept at or below 40 per cent of GDP. Keeping to these rules would limit the ability of any government wishing to use fiscal policy to manipulate aggregate demand. In the eurozone, large countries like France and Germany in the first half of the 2000s breached the rules of the Growth and Stability Pact because they were in recession and were using fiscal policy to keep aggregate demand high. There is no reason why a UK government in the future could not simply set aside the Code for Fiscal Stability if it wanted to use fiscal policy as a tool of demand management. Further information about the Code for Fiscal Stability is contained in the Data Question in this unit.

Key terms

Active or discretionary fiscal policy - the deliberate manipulation of government expenditure and taxes to influence the economy.

Automatic or built-in stabilisers - mechanisms which reduce the impact of changes in the economy on national income.

Crowding out - when an extra pound of government spending leads to a reduction of one pound in private sector spending. Crowding out implies that changes in government spending or taxation will have no long term impact on the level of aggregate demand.

Demand management - government use of fiscal or other policies to manipulate the level of aggregate demand in the economy.

Fine-tuning - the attempt by government to move the economy to a very precise level of unemployment, inflation, etc. It is usually associated with fiscal policy and demand management.

Full employment - the level of output in an economy where all factors of production are fully utilised at given factor prices.

Liquidity trap - where the economy is in such a deep depression that interest rates have fallen as far as they will ever go. This means that governments cannot use monetary policy through reducing interest rates to stimulate aggregate demand. Only fiscal policy can help revive demand.

Stop/go cycle - the movement from boom to recession in the trade cycle.

Applied economics

Japan: a prolonged depression

Japan for much of the post-war period was a miracle economy. It consistently grew faster than Europe and the United States. From being a Third World country in 1945, it surpassed GDP per capita for countries such as the UK or France in the 1980s. Yet the 1990s and early 2000s were disastrous for Japan's economy.

Its problems lay in a huge asset bubble created in the second half of the 1980s. Japan had developed large trading surpluses with the rest of the world which caused trade frictions, particularly with the United States, which accused Japan of destroying its domestic industry. To make Japan less competitive, an informal agreement in 1985 (the Plazza Accord) led to countries pushing up the value of the yen on foreign currency markets. This made Japanese exports more expensive and hence less competitive. The plan worked

sufficiently for the Japanese authorities to fear that the economy would go into recession. So interest rates were pushed down. These low interest rates encouraged an investment boom in industry. The investment-GDP ratio rose from 27.3 per cent in 1986 to 32.2 per cent in 1990. Low interest rates also created an asset bubble. Share prices trebled between 1985 and 1989. Land and property prices soared.

The bubble burst in 1990. Stock market values began to fall and were soon back to their pre-bubble prices. Land prices plummeted. This led to a downturn in the economy as Figure 3 shows. Consumer spending fell as household wealth fell. Firms cut back on their investment, finding they had over invested in the second half of the 1980s and many now had spare capacity. Problems then developed

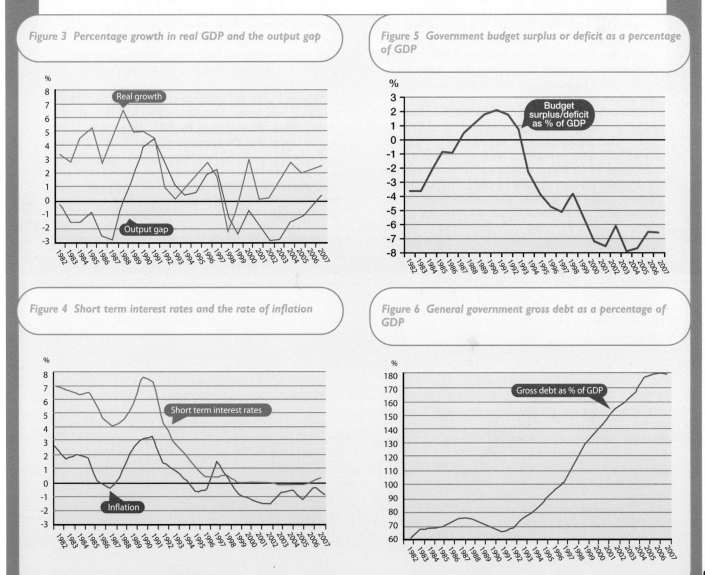

Figure 3 Percentage growth in real GDP and the output gap

Figure 5 Government budget surplus or deficit as a percentage of GDP

Figure 4 Short term interest rates and the rate of inflation

Figure 6 General government gross debt as a percentage of GDP

Source: adapted from *Economic Outlook*, OECD.

with the Japanese banking system. It had lent large sums for property purchases. With falling property prices and an economy going into recession, borrowers began to default, leaving the banks with mounting levels of bad debts. The banking system for the first half of the 1990s concealed these problems, but in the second half of the 1990s it became obvious that there would have to be a restructuring of the banking system, with banks with particularly large levels of bad debts closing.

The Bank of Japan, the Japanese central bank, found it difficult to respond. It had raised interest rates in 1989 and 1990, as Figure 4 shows, in an attempt to curb the strong economy. It then progressively cut short term interest rates down to 0.6 per cent by 1996 attempting to use monetary policy to revive the economy. It could be argued that it initially succeeded since 1996 saw an increase in economic growth to 3.4 per cent, but growth slipped back and prices in the economy actually fell as can be seen from Figure 4. From 1999, monetary policy was further relaxed until short term interest rates were 0 per cent. Low interest rates did not kick-start the economy back to long term growth in the late 1990s and early 2000s. It could be argued that Japan was suffering from a liquidity trap: a position where interest rates were very low but they failed to lead to an increase in consumption and investment.

Monetary policy, then, proved ineffective. Instead, the government increasingly used traditional Keynesian fiscal techniques to stimulate the economy. Figure 5 shows how the government's budget deficit as a percentage of GDP rose during the 1990s. It reached a peak of 8.0 per cent of GDP in 2002. To put this into context, under the Stability and Growth Pact agreement covering the euro, EU governments are not allowed normally to fix budgets where a deficit would exceed 3 per cent of GDP. Repeated deficits of 4 or 5 per cent are considered dangerous to long term prosperity. High levels of government borrowing inevitably led to increases in Japan's national debt. By 2007, this had reached nearly 180 per cent of GDP as shown in Figure 6. To put this into context, in the UK the government has a fiscal rule that its national debt must not exceed 40 per cent of GDP whilst under the Stability and Growth Pact, eurozone countries have agreed to limit their debt to 60 per cent of GDP (although most euro countries still exceed this, with the worst, Italy, having a national debt of 120 per cent of GDP in 2007).

Expansionary fiscal policy could be argued to have been a failure in the late 1990s and early 2000s. It did not prevent the Japanese economy experiencing recessions in 1998-99 and 2001-2002. On the other hand, without large injections of extra government spending, it could be argued that Japan would have suffered a prolonged slump for much of the 1990s and first half of the 2000s. In reality, both arguments are probably correct. Without expansionary fiscal policy, the economic situation would have been far worse. However, to return to long term positive economic growth, the economy had to sort out the problems that it inherited from the asset bubble of the late 1980s. In particular, banks and companies had to restructure to get rid of bad debts. Consumers also had to have more confidence to spend. By 2007, there were hopeful signs that the economy was back on a growth path. However, in the long term, the government is now going to have to deal with its enormous debt at a time when it also has to cope with a rapidly ageing population which could make the Japanese economy less dynamic.

DataQuestion   UK fiscal policy

The Government's macroeconomic framework is designed to maintain long-term stability. Stability allows businesses, individuals and the Government to plan more effectively for the long term, improving the quality and quantity of investment in physical and human capital and helping to raise productivity. Economic stability provides the essential backdrop for addressing the priorities (of government) enabling the Government to address the key social, economic and environmental challenges of the next decade.

The macroeconomic framework is based on the principles of transparency, responsibility and accountability. The monetary policy framework seeks to ensure low and stable inflation, while fiscal policy is underpinned by clear objectives and two strict rules that ensure sound public finances over the medium term whilst allowing fiscal policy to support monetary policy over the economic cycle. The fiscal rules are the foundation of the Government's public spending framework, which facilitates long-term planning and provides departments with the flexibility and incentives they need to increase the quality of public services and deliver specified outcomes. These policies work together in a coherent and integrated way, and continue to deliver unprecedented growth and stability. As the OECD recently noted, the UK economy's "strong performance is not only due to the willingness to embrace the opportunities offered by globalisation, but also to sound institutional arrangements for setting monetary and fiscal policy".

Since 1997, fiscal policy has resulted in low and stable borrowing, in contrast to previous UK experience. In the 1986-87 to 1997-98 economic cycle, net borrowing reached nearly 8 per cent of GDP, and averaged 3.1 per cent of GDP. During the current economic cycle, net borrowing has averaged 8.0 per cent of GDP and at its peak reached just 3.3 per cent of GDP. The fiscal framework has successfully supported economic stability by allowing the automatic stabilisers to operate. The fiscal framework has also protected an historically unprecedented increase in public sector net investment, whilst net debt has been maintained at a low and sustainable level.

Figure 7 UK macroeconomic stability

Figure 8 Fiscal policy supporting monetary policy

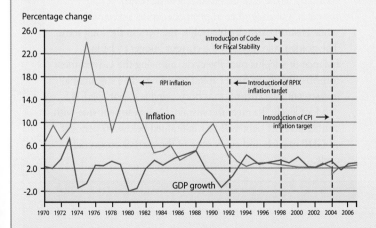

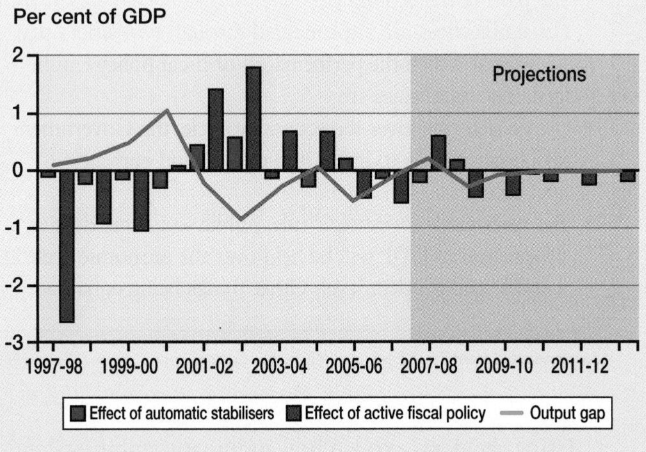

Note: The government budget deficit or surplus as a percentage of GDP is, for the purposes of this graph, equal to the effect of automatic stabilisers plus active fiscal policy.

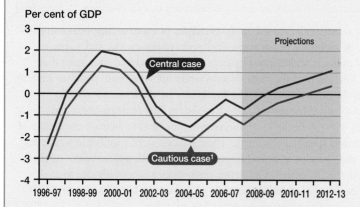

Figure 9 *The Golden Rule: cyclically-adjusted surplus/deficit on current budget*

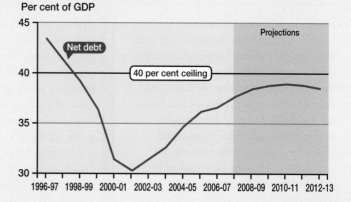

Figure 10 *Government debt as a percentage of GDP*

1. Cautious case assumes trend output 1 percentage point lower in relation to actual output than the central case.
2. The golden rule states that the government's surplus/deficit on current spending over the economic cycle will be zero.

Source: adapted from *2007 Pre-Budget Report and Comprehensive Spending Review*, HM Treasury.

The Government's fiscal policy framework is based on the five key principles set out in the Code for fiscal stability – transparency, stability, responsibility, fairness and efficiency. The Government's fiscal policy objectives are:
- over the medium term, to ensure sound public finances and that spending and taxation impact fairly within and between generations;
- over the short term, to support monetary policy and, in particular, to allow the automatic stabilisers to help smooth the path of the economy.

These objectives are implemented through two strict fiscal rules, against which the performance of fiscal policy can be judged. The fiscal rules are:
- the golden rule: over the economic cycle, the Government will borrow only to invest and not to fund current spending;
- the sustainable investment rule: public sector net debt as a proportion of GDP will be held over the economic cycle at a stable and prudent level. Other things being equal, net

debt will be maintained below 40 per cent of GDP over the economic cycle.

The fiscal rules ensure sound public finances in the medium term while allowing flexibility in two key respects:
- the rules are set over the economic cycle. This allows the fiscal balances to vary between years in line with the cyclical position of the economy; permitting the automatic stabilisers to operate freely to help smooth the path of the economy in the face of variations in demand;
- the rules work together to promote capital investment while ensuring sustainable public finances in the long term. The golden rule requires the current budget to be in balance or surplus over the cycle, allowing the Government tomorrow only to fund capital spending. The sustainable investment rule ensures that borrowing is maintained at a prudent level. To meet the sustainable investment rule with confidence, net debt will be maintained below 40 per cent of GDP in each and every year of the current economic cycle.

Source: adapted from *2007 Pre-Budget Report and Comprehensive Spending Review*, HM Treasury.

1. Using the data, explain how automatic stabilisers and active fiscal policy can help reduce cyclical fluctuations in the economy.
2. Explain why the government's golden rule and sustainable investment rule are important for the long term stability of the economy.
3. Discuss whether fiscal policy since 1997 has improved the economic performance of the economy.

Summary

1. Supply side policies are government policies designed to increase the productive potential of the economy.
2. Increasing labour productivity is key to supply side policy changes.
3. Introducing greater flexibility into labour markets is likely to increase labour productivity and long run aggregate supply.
4. Because economic decisions are made at the margin, supply side policies which target marginal decisions can be highly effective.
5. Supply side policies which affect migration will alter the quantity and skills balance of the working population.
6. Lowering taxes on business can lead to an increase in foreign direct investment into a country.
7. Aggregate demand can influence long run aggregate supply if aggregate demand is subject to large fluctuations which lead to uncertainty.

Supply side policies

Supply side policies are government policies designed to increase the productive potential of the economy and push the long run aggregate supply curve to the right. They can affect the economy in four main ways.

- They may increase the supply both of the quantity and quality of labour.
- They may raise the amount of capital employed or they may lead to the introduction of more technologically advanced capital.
- They may lead to the further exploitation of natural resources, such as oil deposits or agricultural land.
- They may increase the efficiency with which the factors of production, land labour and capital, are combined.

Labour productivity and unit labour costs

Supply side policies may affect both labour productivity and unit labour costs. Labour productivity is output per worker. Increasing labour productivity may reduce unit labour costs, the cost of labour per unit of production. For example, a firm producing one million units of output per month may introduce new technology. As a result, there is a fall in the quantity of labour needed from 100 workers to 80 workers. Output per worker will therefore increase from 10 000 units per month to 12 500 units per month. Labour productivity will have risen by 25 per cent. Assuming that average wage rates do not change from £1 000 per worker per month, the cost of labour per unit of production will fall from £0.10 per worker to £0.08. Unit labour costs have therefore fallen 20 per cent. The firm is now more competitive than before. However, if all firms in the industry also introduce new technology, relative competitiveness will remain the same.

As an economy grows, labour productivity will rise. More and more capital will be used by labour to produce goods and services. Workers will also become better trained and have more skills. Unit labour costs, however, for the whole economy will remain the same. This is because increases in productivity will be matched by increases in wages. Unit labour costs will only fall if the share of profits in GDP rises over time. Karl Marx, in the 19th century predicted that all of the benefit from the increase in labour productivity would go to the owners of capital. Workers would remain forever on subsistence wages.

History shows this not to have been the case. Whilst the shares of wages and profits in GDP do change over time, there is no overall trend across time and between countries for the owners of capital to see their share consistently rise as GDP rises.

The UK has a long-standing productivity gap with its main competitors. However, as Figure 1 shows, there has been progress in narrowing the output per worker per hour gap. The Government can use five levers to make a difference to the UK's productivity performance and effectively respond to long term challenges such as an ageing population, globalisation and climate change and technological progress. These levers are investment in workforce and skills, investment in infrastructure, tax and regulation implication, competition and market frameworks and public sector efficiency.

Source: adapted from *The 2007 Productivity and Competitiveness Indicators*, HM Treasury Department for business Enterprise & Regulatory Reform.

(a) Between 1992 and 2006, output per hour worked in the UK rose by 36 per cent. Using Figure 1, explain what happened to output per hour worked in France, Germany and the USA.
(b) Explain briefly how each of the 'five levers' could affect productivity in the UK.

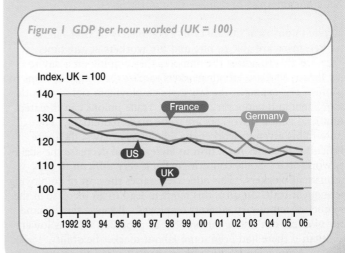

Figure 1 GDP per hour worked (UK = 100)

Index, UK = 100

Unit labour costs in individual industries and occupations, however, may change over time within an economy. Where a good or service is not traded internationally and where there is a lack of competition within a country, unit labour costs are likely to rise. For example, unit labour costs in the National Health Service or schools in the UK have risen substantially over time. Where a good or service is produced subject to a great deal of competition for example from abroad, unit labour costs tend not to rise as fast as the average and may fall. If the good or service is internationally traded, unit labour costs may be too high to allow it to be competitive and production may cease. For example, lower unit labour costs from Third World producers led to the decline of the UK textile industry in the second half of the last century.

There are a variety of supply side policies which can be used to increase labour productivity.

● Policies which lead to better education and training of workers should increase their output. Either they become more productive at the same job. Or they are able to do more complex jobs which create higher value products. Policies could include reforming the vocational education system, giving tax incentives to firms for expenditure on training, or giving workers training vouchers to spend on funding training courses.

● Policies which lead to higher levels of physical investment will increase the amount of capital per worker all other things being equal. Examples of such policies might be government grants to firms for investment, tax incentives to invest or government loans at below the commercial rate of interest for investment.

Flexible labour markets

LABOUR MARKET FLEXIBILITY is the degree to which demand and supply in a labour market respond to external changes, such as changes in demand for a product or population changes to return the market to equilibrium. If labour markets are highly flexible, there will be rapid changes in demand and supply. As a result, the natural rate of unemployment will be very low. If labour markets are highly inflexible, external shocks to the market will lead to long term disequilibrium in the market. The natural rate of unemployment will then be high.

There are many ways of classifying types of labour market flexibility. One way is to classify it according to the strategies that companies use to manage their workforces.

External numerical flexibility In a completely flexible labour market, firms are able to hire and fire workers at any time. They are able to adjust the numbers they employ on a day to day basis. Modern labour markets restrict the ability of firms to do this. For example, the law gives employment rights to both permanent and temporary workers. Trade unions can threaten industrial action if workers are to be made redundant. The more rights given to workers by employment laws, the more difficult it becomes for a firm to increase and decrease the size of its workforce. Some countries make it very difficult to sack permanent workers. This effectively raises the cost of employing permanent staff. In turn, this tends to lead to an increase in the number of temporary workers employed. Because the demand for workers has fallen, the number of people in work is lower than if there had been more labour market flexibility. Employing fewer workers may also lead to an increase in capital intensity of production. Firms buy more

capital equipment to compensate for the relatively high cost of employing labour.

Internal numerical flexibility In a completely flexible labour market, firms are able to adjust the working hours of staff to suit their needs. For example, a firm might tell its workers to work 50 hours one week and 30 hours the next. It can change workers from day shift work to night shift work. It can cancel holiday leave at a moment's notice if it needs workers to be at work to complete a contract. In practice, firms are restricted in their internal flexibility by both employment law and by workers and their trade unions. Custom and practice, as well as legally enforceable employment contracts, mean that employees work relatively fixed hours. However, firms today use a wide variety of schemes to give them greater flexibility from traditional over-time working to schemes where the firm can vary a worker's hours of work within agreed limits.

Functional flexibility Functional flexibility occurs when a firm can redeploy a worker from one job to another. To be most efficient, it requires that workers are multi-skilled. For example, a hotel may only require a receptionist for part of the day. If the receptionist can be redeployed during the rest of the day to make beds or serve in the restaurant, then costs will be lower and the hotel will be more competitive. Traditionally, trade unions have resisted functional flexibility because they argue it creates unemployment. Countries where functional flexibility is common are likely to be more competitive than countries where functional flexibility is low.

Wage flexibility In a perfectly flexible labour market, there will be complete wage flexibility. Firms will be able to adjust wages up and down according to the forces of demand and supply in the labour market. In practice, most workers are on fixed wage contracts. However, wage flexibility can be achieved for example through bonuses or individual pay bargaining. Wage flexibility is greater than, say, thirty years ago in the UK because

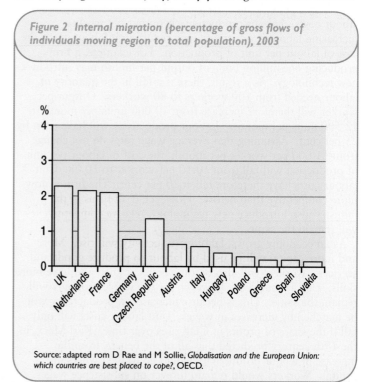

Figure 2 *Internal migration (percentage of gross flows of individuals moving region to total population), 2003*

Source: adapted rom D Rae and M Sollie, *Globalisation and the European Union: which countries are best placed to cope?*, OECD.

fewer workers are covered by collective bargaining agreement negotiated between employers and trade unions.

There are many other types of labour market flexibility. For example, **geographical flexibility** refers to the willingness of workers to move area to get a job, or the willingness of firms to relocate, for example to take advantage of the availability of labour. Figure 2 shows that within the EU, the UK has a relatively high level of mobility compared to other countries indicating its more flexible labour markets. **Industrial flexibility** refers to the willingness of workers to move from industry to industry. For example, would a factory worker made unemployed be willing to take on a job in a service sector firm?

Some argue that flexible labour markets are one of the key reasons why the US and UK economies have performed so well over the past decade. They are compared with countries in the European Union such as France, Italy and Spain which have much less flexible labour markets. In these countries, workers are given more rights by labour laws whilst trade unions tend to be stronger than in the UK. Certainly, less flexible labour markets tend to be associated with higher unemployment rates and lower participation rates in the workforce. On the other hand, stronger legislation gives workers in jobs greater employment rights. Those in jobs tend to be benefit from less labour market flexibility, at least in the short term.

Incentives at the margin

Neoclassical economists tend to argue that incentives at the margin can significantly change behaviour. Cutting marginal rates of tax on earned income, for example, leads to a significant rise in the number of hours worked by those in work and gives a significant incentive for those not working to get a job. Cutting marginal rates of tax on unearned income encourages saving. Giving income tax rebates to those who save for a pension encourages people to pay into a pension plan. Equally, cutting unemployment benefits will encourage the unemployed to get a job. The more progressive the tax and benefit system, the less incentive individuals have to work. Therefore, there is a strong economic case to make the tax and benefit system more regressive.

In the UK, there is a recognition that marginal rates of tax and benefit can influence behaviour. For example, the top rate of income tax has remained capped at 40 per cent for the past 20 years despite some arguing that a higher marginal rate would lead to a more equitable distribution of post-tax income. Equally, since 1997, the government has introduced tax credits for the low paid to give them a greater incentive to stay in employment.

However, marginal tax rates are only one influence on employment. Many who currently do not have a job face major obstacles to gaining a job. For example, for single people with young children, it might be access to good quality child care. For the over two million people receiving sickness or disability benefit, it might be getting a job which is manageable for their particular disability. Half of those on sickness or disability benefit have mental health problems rather than physical disabilities. The challenge is how to get at least some of the individuals into a workplace where they can cope and where their employer judges they are making a contribution to the output of the organisation. In countries like the Netherlands and Sweden, there are much better systems in place to help those with mental health or physical disabilities to remain in the workplace. However, these systems are expensive to run.

Migration

In recent years, there has been significant net migration into the UK of people of working age. Net inward migration of working age people increases the potential size of the labour force. With increased supply of labour, wage rates should be lower than they would otherwise have been. If the economy is at full employment, this helps reduce inflationary pressures. However, the exact impact on wages in individual occupations and on economic growth as a whole is more difficult to determine. For example, if all the immigrants were plumbers who settled in London, there would be a downward pressure on the earnings of plumbers in the London area but there would be little impact elsewhere in the economy.

Some have argued that the UK could benefit more from net immigration by targeting particular types of immigrants. This type of policy is used in countries such as the USA and Canada where those applying for visas to work in the country are more likely to be granted a visa if they have desirable skills and qualifications. This might mean skills and qualification in occupations where there is a shortage of workers; or it might mean high levels of skills, such as having a university degree. In a rich developed economy, supply side benefits are more likely to come having well educated and highly skilled workers than having low skilled workers.

Taxation and investment

The level of taxes on businesses has an impact on investment and therefore long run aggregate supply. An increase in taxes on business reduces the

Question 3

The recent rise in unemployment is due to slack in the economy rather than the recent influx of approximately 500 000 workers from Poland and other former Soviet bloc countries, according to David Blanchflower, an external member of the Bank of England's monetary policy committee. He said that there was little evidence that immigrants from eastern Europe had significantly affected the wages or employment chances of British workers since they joined the European Union in 2004. 'There is no evidence from the labour market that the natural rate of unemployment has risen in the past year' he said.

The overall impact of immigration on inflation and growth was not clear-cut. But recent immigration from east Europe was likely to have reduced the natural rate of unemployment and raised the supply potential of the economy, he said. These immigrants had helped to dampen inflationary pressures because they typically produced more than they consumed, sending a proportion of their earnings back to their homeland. There was little or no evidence that immigrants had come to the UK to claim or receive benefits. 'They have come to work' he added.

Source: adapted from the *Financial Times*, 5.1.2007.

(a) Explain, using an aggregate demand and supply diagram, how immigration could reduce inflation and increase the rate of economic growth for the UK.
(b) Discuss whether supply side policies which increased the flows of immigrants to the UK would increase labour productivity and the supply potential of the economy.

profitability of investment. With a lower rate of return, fewer investment projects will be undertaken.

Higher tax rates doesn't just affect domestic investment. They also affect investment coming in from abroad, called **foreign direct investment (FDI)**. A country can raise inward levels of FDI by lowering taxes on business. Many argue that low business taxes, for example, were a crucial part of the supply side policy mix which has led to the high economic growth of the Republic of Ireland since the 1980s.

Governments place high taxes on business for three possible reasons.

- In the long term, government spending as a proportion of GDP may be high. For example, spending by the public sector in Nordic countries, Sweden, Norway and Denmark, has exceeded 50 per cent of GDP. Taxes have to be high to finance these levels of government spending in the long term.
- Governments may choose to have relatively high taxes on business and relatively low taxes on consumers and workers. This is a political decision likely to be based on ideological grounds.
- In the short term, governments may be forced to raise tax revenues substantially because they face financial difficulties. Countries such as Italy and Japan, for example, have very high levels of public sector debt. They can reduce this by raising taxes on business.

Free market economists tend to argue that business taxes

should be low. This will encourage investment and lead to higher economic growth. This is particularly the case if a country can attract relatively large amounts of foreign direct investment as a result of a low tax policy. However, it can be argued that for large economies such as the UK, business tax levels are only one small part in business investment decision making. Levels of business tax are therefore relatively unimportant in the supply policy mix.

The contribution of demand side policies

Demand side policies can be argued to be part of the supply side policy mix for two reasons.

- Macroeconomic economic stability helps economic agents to make decisions. If the economy is lurching from boom to bust in an unpredictable way, the risk of making a bad decision increases. This is likely to lead to lower levels of investment, less labour mobility and lower consumer spending than would be the case if the economy were growing on a steady path.
- There is some evidence that steady stable GDP growth results in higher long term growth than a growth path characterised by deep recessions and unsustainable booms. This is because of the problem of **hysteresis**. In a deep recession, both physical and human capital are destroyed. Physical capital is destroyed when firms downsize or go out of business. Equipment is scrapped because there is no demand for the products it makes. There is then a permanent reduction in the capital stock of the economy from what it would otherwise have been. As for human capital, some workers made redundant in a recession will become long term unemployed. The longer the period of unemployment, the more work skills they lose making them less employable than before. There are also significant mental health issues. In the UK, over one million of those receiving sickness and disability benefits have mental health problems. Becoming long term unemployed increases possible mental health problems which in turn make it more difficult for the individual to gain or hold down a job.

Good economic management of the economy by government which minimises fluctuations in aggregate demand therefore has significant supply side benefits. It encourages investment and prevents wastage of scarce capital and labour resources.

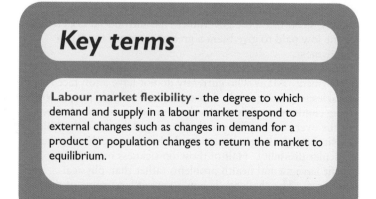

Key terms

Labour market flexibility - the degree to which demand and supply in a labour market respond to external changes such as changes in demand for a product or population changes to return the market to equilibrium.

Applied economics

Flexible labour markets in the EU

Employment protection legislation

The UK has relatively flexible labour markets compared to the rest of the EU. In the EU, there is much stricter employment protection legislation (EPL). Aspects of EPL in Europe include:

- employment contracts which make it more difficult to make workers redundant; for example, reasons for dismissal may be highly restrictive; or employers may have to undertake lengthy and costly consultations about redundancies;
- significant differences between the employment rights of permanent workers and those of temporary or casual workers; this creates a strong disincentive to employ permanent workers;
- strong legislation which protects the rights of trade unions to organise, take part in decision making in firms and take industrial action;
- restrictions on the employment of labour such as the 35 hour working week in France or the 48 hour maximum working week which covers the whole EU;
- employment contracts which make it difficult for a firm to redeploy workers from one job to another;
- increases in the cost of employing permanent labour by giving permanent labour higher benefits such as holiday entitlement rights, sickness benefits and pensions than temporary workers.

Structural unemployment (NAIRU)

The more flexible the labour market, the lower should be the level of structural unemployment, or natural rate of unemployment (NAIRU). This is because flexible labour markets imply greater mobility of workers between jobs in different industries and geographical regions. Figure 3 shows structural unemployment rates within the EU. There is evidence that flexible labour markets lead to higher natural rates of unemployment. For example, countries such as France, Italy, Spain and Germany have higher natural rates than the UK. However, other factors also affect the natural rate. For Slovakia and Poland, new accession members of the EU, their labour markets

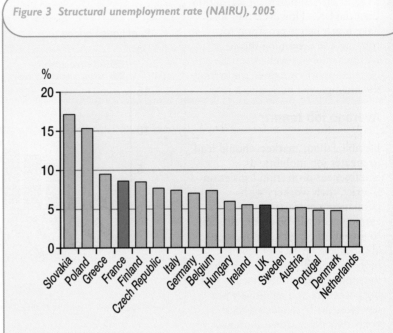

Figure 3 *Structural unemployment rate (NAIRU), 2005*

Source: adapted rom D Rae and M Sollie, *Globalisation and the European Union: which countries are best placed to cope?*, OECD.

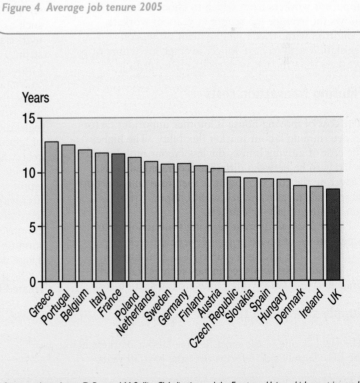

Figure 4 *Average job tenure 2005*

Source: adapted rom D Rae and M Sollie, *Globalisation and the European Union: which countries are best placed to cope?*, OECD.

have rigidities left over from the time when they were Communist countries. Countries like Sweden, Norway, Finland and Denmark have stricter employment legislation than the UK. However, they also have much better provision for training and retraining those without a job, as well as much better support structures for getting the unemployed back into a job.

Average job tenure

Flexible labour markets should lead to greater job mobility. If employment protection legislation is strict, then workers with permanent contracts of employment will be more reluctant to give up their jobs and move to another job. A lack of labour mobility is likely to lead to higher unemployment. It also means that both workers and employers are less likely to be achieving their goals. Workers are discouraged from moving jobs which might have higher pay or be more satisfying because they are afraid of leaving a secure job with strong employment rights. Firms will have a more restricted pool of applicant workers from which to choose. Figure 4 shows the average job tenure in years of workers. Countries with stricter employment protection legislation tend to have longer average job tenure of workers than the UK with relatively weak EPL.

Housing transaction costs

The cost of moving house is another important factor in determining labour market flexibility. The higher the cost of moving house, the less labour mobility there is likely to be between different geographical areas. Lowering the cost of moving is therefore an important supply side measure which would improve the functioning of labour markets.

Figure 5 shows average housing transaction costs as a percentage of house prices between different countries. The UK has relatively low housing transaction costs whilst countries such as Italy and France have relatively high housing transaction costs.

Supply side policy responses

The UK has one of the most flexible labour markets in the EU. Supply side reforms over the past 30 years

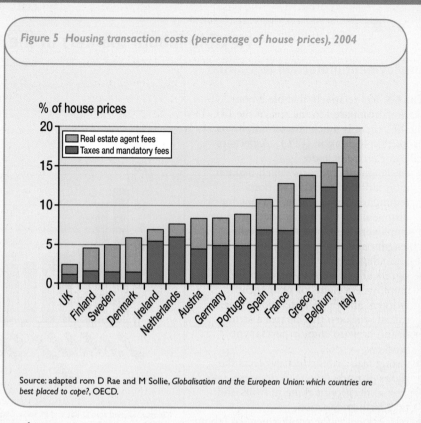

Figure 5 Housing transaction costs (percentage of house prices), 2004

Source: adapted rom D Rae and M Sollie, *Globalisation and the European Union: which countries are best placed to cope?*, OECD.

have created a labour market where labour is relatively mobile and employment protection legislation is less strong than in most other EU countries. Countries such as France and Germany have less flexible labour markets and employment protection legislation is strong. Free market economists would argue that France and Germany should adopt supply side reforms to create more flexible labour markets. They would argue this would improve economic performance. Supporters of strong employment protection legislation, however sometimes argue that the benefits of labour supply side reforms would be less than the costs. Strong employment protection legislation provide significant benefits, they would argue, to employees. They might also argue that the disadvantages of strong employment protection legislation can be reduced if, as in the Nordic countries, there are are strong policies concerning training and getting the unemployed back into work. These policies are very expensive. But they provide a necessary counterbalance to the greater unemployment created by less flexible labour markets.

DataQuestion   Northern Ireland Corporation Tax rates

Sir Anthony O'Reilly, perhaps Ireland's most successful entrepreneur, wants Northern Ireland to adopt a special low rate of corporate tax to allow it to compete with the Irish Republic. Owner and chief executive of Independent News & Media, which runs the Belfast newspaper, the Belfast Telegraph, he said: 'We have done spectacularly well as a company in the south. We believe we can do as well in the north - with just a little help from Gordon Brown and the British Treasury.'

Source: adapted from the *Financial Times*, 20.4.2007.

Figure 6 Effective average tax rates[1]

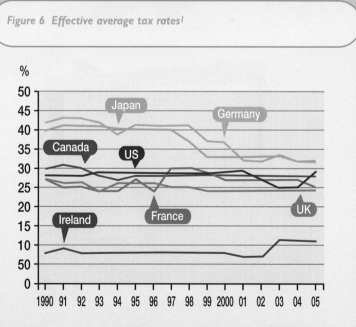

1. The effective average tax rate is the tax rate on an investment project over its lifetime, with costs and benefits discounted back to the present values. It is the most useful way of comparing tax rates for multinational firms when choosing where to locate capital.

Source: adapted from *Review of Tax Policy in Northern Ireland*, HM Treasury.

Following pressure from Northern Ireland political parties, the Chancellor of the Exchequer agreed to review tax policy in Northern Ireland. In December 2007, having been set the question 'How current and future tax policy, including the tax changes announced in the Budget 2007, can support the sustainable growth of businesses and long-term investments in Northern Ireland', the review rejected the need for tax concessions for Northern Ireland.

The Executive of Northern Ireland were disappointed with the outcome. It issued the following statement.

'The Varney Review was established in March this year to assess the extent to which the headline corporate tax rate dissuaded foreign investment from locating in Northern Ireland. Many stakeholders have argued that the low rate of tax on profits in the Republic of Ireland (12.5%) places Northern Ireland in an unfavourable location. It is the only region of the UK with a land border to a low-tax economy.

The Executive, in its July 2007 submission to the Varney team, set out a case for offering a lower rate of corporation tax in Northern Ireland. This would act as a catalyst for economic growth and transformation. A low rate of business tax is a major factor in the decision-making process of multi-national companies.

In addition to the geographical proximity to a low-tax economy, the Executive also highlighted the need to address three decades of lost investment opportunity.

'For more than three decades Northern Ireland has suffered in its ability to attract foreign investment,' Peter Robinson, the Northern Ireland Finance Minister, said. 'Resources available for economic development policy were diverted towards law and order issues and the image of the region certainly dissuaded inward investment. We will continue to argue the case for a reduction in corporation tax. The issue will not go away.'

Source: adapted from www.northernireland.gov.uk.

Figure 7 How international business executives rank the importance of different factors when making investment decisions about location[1]

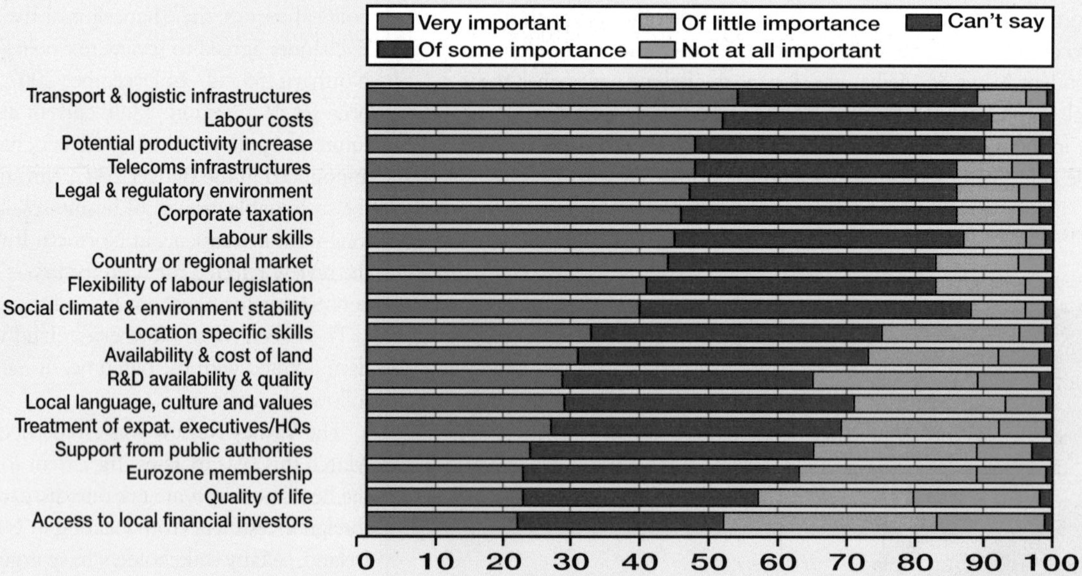
Very important
Of some importance
Of little importance
Not at all important
Can't say
Transport & logistic infrastructures
Labour costs
Potential productivity increase
Telecoms infrastructures
Legal & regulatory environment
Corporate taxation
Labour skills
Country or regional market
Flexibility of labour legislation
Social climate & environment stability
Location specific skills
Availability & cost of land
R&D availability & quality
Local language, culture and values
Treatment of expat. executives/HQs
Support from public authorities
Eurozone membership
Quality of life
Access to local financial investors
0
10
20
30
40
50
60
70
80
90
100

1. This is survey evidence from Ernst & Young's annual 'European Attractiveness Survey'. The survey gauges the opinion of international business executives across a range of industries, regions and business models about the relative importance of factors in influencing investment location.

Source: adapted from *Review of Tax Policy in Northern Ireland*, HM Treasury.

1. Using Figure 6, compare the UK's and therefore Northern Ireland's corporate tax rate with other countries.
2. Explain why lowering corporate tax rates might be an example of a supply side policy.
3. Discuss whether lowering Northern Ireland's corporate tax rate would be the most effective supply side policy change that could be made to increase the level of economic activity in the province.

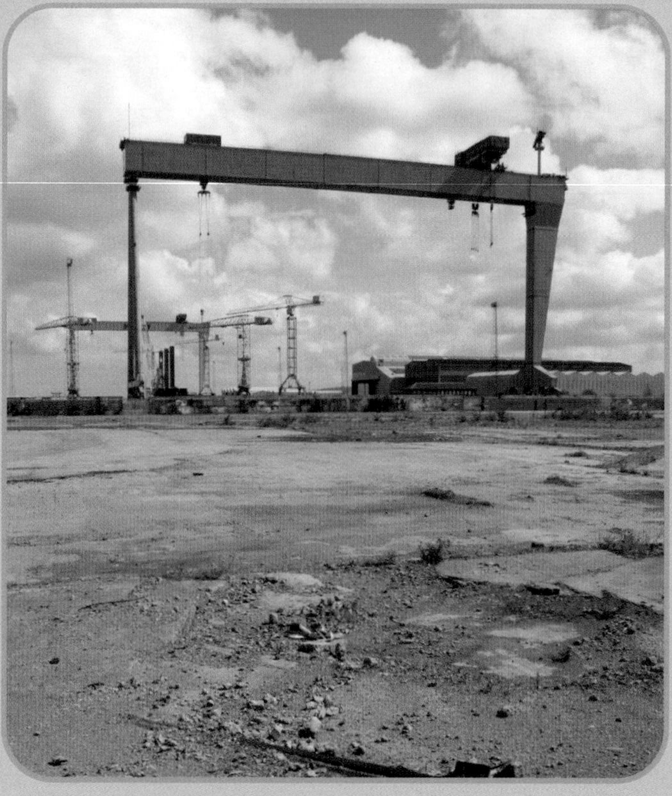

Summary

1. Money has four functions: as a medium of exchange; a unit of account; a store of value; and a standard for deferred payment.
2. Characteristics of good money include acceptability, portability, durability, divisibility and limited supply.
3. In a modern economy, cash and sight deposits are the assets which best fulfil the function of a medium of exchange. These are known as narrow monies.
4. Near monies, assets which are good units of account and stores of value and can easily be converted into assets which are a medium of exchange, include time deposits in banks and building societies. Broad money is narrow money plus near money.
5. Money substitutes, such as credit cards, are items which act as a medium of exchange but are not stores of value.
6. The money supply is the total amount of money circulating in the economy.
7. Households and firms hold their wealth in money, in non-money financial assets or in physical assets. The opportunity cost of holding money is the benefits foregone from holding other financial or physical assets.
8. The demand for money varies with income and with the rate of interest.

The functions of money

Most people today in Britain, if asked 'what is money?', would reply 'notes and coins'. What is it about notes and coins that make them money, and is there anything else which possesses these same properties? If something is to be money, it must fulfil four FUNCTIONS (i.e. it must do four things).

A medium of exchange This is the most important function of money. Money is used to buy and sell goods and services. A worker accepts payment in money because she knows that she will be able to use that money to buy products in the shops.

There is no money in a BARTER economy. Exchange is conducted directly by swapping one good with another. For instance, a farmer might pay a dozen eggs to have his horse shod or a woman might trade a carpet for a cow. This requires a **double coincidence of wants**. If the blacksmith didn't want eggs, then he might refuse to shoe the farmer's horse. If the woman with a carpet was offered a horse instead of a cow, again she might refuse to trade. Barter requires that each party to the transaction wants what the other has to trade. This is costly and difficult, if not impossible, and therefore trade is discouraged. Without trade there can be no specialisation. Without specialisation, there can be little or no increase in living standards. So barter is associated with types of economy where individuals or small groups are self-reliant, and the need for trade is small.

Money separates the two sides of a barter transaction. The farmer can sell his eggs for money. The blacksmith will accept money for shoeing the farmer's horse because he knows that he will be able buy the goods that he wants with the money.

A unit of account Money acts as a measure of value. If a dress costs £30 and a skirt costs £15, we know that the value of one dress equals the value of two skirts. At times of very high inflation, such as in Germany in 1923, money ceases to act as a unit of account. Prices may change by the hour. A dress costing £30 in the morning might only buy one skirt in the evening. High inflation therefore destroys the ability of money to perform this function. It is very difficult under a barter system to

establish an agreed unit of account as people's opinions of the value of certain items differ greatly.

A store of value A worker who receives wages is unlikely to spend the money immediately. She may defer spending because it is more convenient to spend the money later. She will do this only if what she can buy in the future is approximately equal to what she can buy today. So money links the present and the future. It acts as a store of value. High inflation destroys this link because money in the future is worth far less than money today. In the German hyperinflation of 1923, people started to refuse payment in German money because it would lose so much value by the time they had spent it.

A standard for deferred payment If a person lends money today, she will only do so if she thinks that she will be able to buy roughly the same amount of goods when it is paid back. In trade, a company which accepts an order at a fixed price today for delivery and payment in a year's time will only do so if it is confident that the money it receives will have a value which can be assessed today. So again money must link different time periods when it comes to borrowed as well as saved money. When money ceases to have this function, credit and borrowing collapse and this is very damaging to investment and economic growth in an economy.

The characteristics of money

Pigs, silver, gold, teeth, and even wives have been used as money in the past. Some cultures today still use animals as currency. However most, if not all, of these have been unsatisfactory because of their characteristics. Ideally, money should be:
- acceptable to all - it is inconvenient if a type of money is only accepted in some shops but not others for instance;
- portable - pigs, for instance, are not easy to carry around and this limits the trade which is conducted using pigs as a medium of exchange;
- durable - pigs die and teeth deteriorate; ideally money should be durable over time;
- divisible - whole live pigs can't be used to buy the

Question 1

(a) Explain which of these items might be considered 'money' and which would not.

small things in life because they are too valuable; money must be capable of being split into small denominations;
- limited - if ordinary stones are used as money, prices of goods are likely to be very high in terms of stones because they are so easy to obtain;
- difficult to forge - forgeries make money worthless and can lead to its becoming unacceptable in exchange.

Forms of money in a modern economy

In a modern economy there is a number of assets which can be classified as money.

Cash Cash means notes and coins. Cash is a **token money**. It has little or no intrinsic value (unlike gold which would be classified along with items such as pigs and

Question 2

(a) To what extent do each of the items in the previous question possess the characteristics of a good money?

cigarettes as **commodity money**). It is issued either by government or with the permission of government. Government reinforces the acceptability of cash by making it **legal tender**. This means that it must be accepted by law as a means of payment.

During much of the 19th century, bank notes were **convertible**. This meant that it was possible to go into a bank and convert the notes into something of real value: in this case, gold. However, more notes were issued than their value in gold. The value of notes and coins printed over and above the value of gold in bank vaults was called the **fiduciary issue**. Today UK bank notes are not convertible into gold and therefore all notes are **fiat** money, money made legal tender by government decree.

Cash is not perfect money. In the UK it is an almost perfect medium of exchange. But inflation affects three of the functions of money - those of a unit of account, a store of value and a standard of deferred payment. In 1975 for instance, UK inflation was nearly 25 per cent. Anyone holding £1 at the beginning of the year could only buy 75 pence worth of goods with it at the end of the year. The higher the rate of inflation, the less it can be said that cash is a 'good' money.

Money in current accounts Banks and building societies in the UK offer customers current account facilities. Current accounts (called SIGHT DEPOSIT ACCOUNTS in economic theory) have two distinguishing features. First, cash can be withdrawn on demand from the account if it is in credit. So deposits can be immediately converted into money if the account holder so wishes. Second, account holders are provided with a cheque book and debit card. Cheques and debit cards can be used to purchase goods and services. Cheque book money therefore is a medium of exchange. It is not perfect because people and firms can refuse to accept cheques and debit cards in a transaction. Moreover, little or no interest is offered on accounts and so current account deposits lose value over time with inflation, damaging their store of value function. But deposits in current accounts are nearly as good a form of money as cash.

Near monies NEAR MONIES are assets which fulfil some but not all of the functions of money. In particular, they act as units of account and stores of value but cannot be used as mediums of exchange. However, they are convertible into a medium of exchange quickly and at little cost. (The ease with which an asset can be converted into money without loss of value is termed LIQUIDITY. The more liquid an asset, the more easily it is convertible into money.) In the UK, the most obvious type of near monies is TIME DEPOSITS with banks and building societies. They pay higher rates of interest than current accounts. They are therefore used more for saving and less for making transactions than current accounts. Depositors need to give notice if they wish to withdraw from the account (hence the term 'time' deposit). Alternatively, many accounts offer instant access if an interest rate penalty is paid (i.e. the saver loses money for the privilege of instant withdrawal).

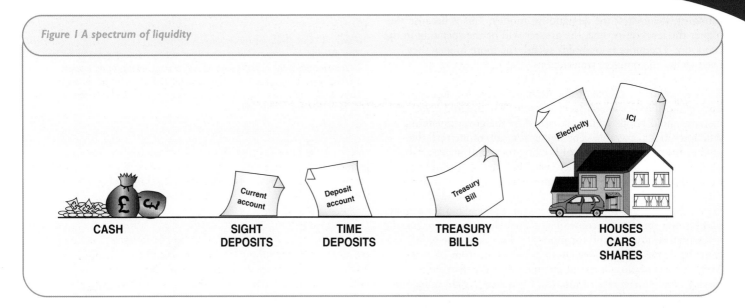

Figure I A spectrum of liquidity

CASH — SIGHT DEPOSITS — TIME DEPOSITS — TREASURY BILLS — HOUSES CARS SHARES

Non-money financial assets All financial assets can be converted into money. However, for most assets the potential penalties for doing this are great. There can be a long waiting time for withdrawal and there can be considerable loss of money from conversion. This impairs their functions as units of account and stores of value. Economists do not classify these assets as money. Shares, for instance, are easily sold, but it can take up to a month to receive the money from the sale. Shares can also change value rapidly and are therefore not a good store of value (when share prices fall) or a standard for deferred payment (when share prices rise).

Money substitutes

Money is not the only means of payment for goods and services. Charge cards and credit cards have become increasingly important over the past 30 years as a medium of exchange. But they are not stores of value. This is because possession of a card does not show that the cardholder has money in the card account. The card only represents an ability to borrow money instantly. So credit cards, for example, are not money but they are MONEY SUBSTITUTES (i.e. they are used instead of money).

The money supply

The MONEY SUPPLY is the total amount of money circulating in the economy. It has been argued above that there is no financial asset which perfectly possesses all the functions of money. So financial assets can be placed on a spectrum as in Figure 1. At the left of the spectrum is the asset which comes closest to fulfilling most of the functions of money today - cash. At the other end are assets which are extremely illiquid, such as shares in companies not traded on a stock exchange. In between there is a range of assets. As we move right, assets possess fewer and fewer of the functions of money. It is now clear that the cut off point between those assets which are money and those which are not is to some extent arbitrary.

In the UK, there is a number of official definitions of the money supply. There are two broad types of money supply definition.

● NARROW MONEY - money which can be used as a medium of exchange.

Question 3

Emma Higgins has £250 in a building society share account. She owns a £100 000 house but owes £50 000 in the form of a mortgage loan. Her current account at her bank is in credit by £200 and she has an overdraft facility of £300. In her purse she has £20 in cash. She has recently purchased £50 worth of goods using her credit card. Her credit card limit is £1 000.

(a) Explain how much money Emma Higgins possesses.

● BROAD MONEY - narrow money plus near monies. Current money supply definitions used in the UK are described below in the applied economics section.

The demand for money

Households and firms hold their wealth in a variety of different assets. Two main types of assets can be distinguished:
● **financial assets**, either monetary assets, such as cash and deposits in current accounts at banks, or non-money assets such as stocks and shares;
● **physical assets**, such as houses, buildings, cars, furniture, machinery, computers and inventories.

When economists talk about the demand for money, they do not refer to how much money people would like to have in a world where they were infinitely rich. What they mean is how much households and firms choose to hold in the form of money as opposed to holding either non-money financial assets or physical assets.

There is therefore an **opportunity cost** to a household if it holds £300 in cash. It could instead buy shares, and receive dividends and possibly capital gains. It could put money into a pension plan and increase the value of pension payments at some time in the future, or it could buy a new television and enjoy the services which it provides. Hence the price of holding money is the benefits foregone from holding another type of asset.

The demand for money is determined by two main factors.

Income The higher the level of income in the

economy, the greater the demand for money. This is because the higher the level of income, the greater will be the spending in the economy. The more households spend, the more money they need to use to complete transactions.

The rate of interest One of the alternative uses for money is to buy financial assets which yield interest. A household could, for instance, hold bonds which are issued by the government and on which interest is payable. The higher the rate of interest, the greater the opportunity cost of holding money. If interest rates on government bonds are 5 per cent, then the opportunity cost of holding £100 for one year in money is £5 in lost interest. If the rate of interest is 20 per cent, the opportunity cost is £20. Figure 2 shows this relationship between the demand for money and interest rates and income. The higher the rate of interest, the lower will be the demand for money. A rise in income would shift the demand for money curve to the right, from MD_1 to MD_2. This is because a rise in income raises the demand for money at any given rate of interest. Conversely, a fall in income would lead to a shift in the demand for money curve to the left.

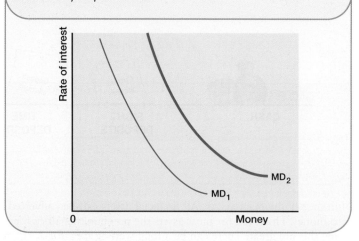

Figure 2 The demand for money
The demand for money curve is downward sloping because a rise in the rate of interest increases the attractiveness of exchanging money for an interest bearing non-money asset. A rise in income will shift the demand for money curve to the right from MD_1 to MD_2 because spending and therefore the need to have money to spend will rise.

Question 4

Kim Yip has £250 in cash, £500 in a building society account earning 5 per cent per annum interest, £400 worth of government bonds with a market rate of interest of 7 per cent, £900 worth of British Telecom shares earning a 3 per cent dividend, a house valued at £70 000 on which there is a mortgage of £40 000, furniture and personal possessions insured for £30 000, and a car worth £2 500 secondhand.
(a) What might be the opportunity cost for Kim of holding:
   (i) the £250 in cash; (ii) the £900 in British Telecom shares;
   (iii) the £70 000 house?
(b) Long term interest rates on government bonds rise by 3 per cent, all other things being equal. How might this affect Kim's holding of money?

Key terms

Barter - swapping one good for another without the use of money.
Broad money - narrow money plus near monies.
Demand for money - the total amount of money which households and firms wish to hold at a point in time.
Functions of money - money must be a medium of exchange, a store of value, a unit of account and a standard for deferred payment.
Liquidity - the degree to which an asset can be converted into money without capital loss.
Money substitutes - those which can be used as a medium of exchange but which are not stores of value. Examples are charge cards or credit cards.

Money supply - the total amount of money in circulation in the economy.
Narrow money - money which is primarily used as a medium of exchange.
Near money - an asset which cannot be used as medium of exchange in itself but is readily convertible into money and is both a unit of account and a store of value.
Sight deposit accounts - Accounts with financial institutions where deposits are repayable on demand and where a cheque book is issued. In the UK, they are more commonly called current or cheque accounts.
Time deposit accounts - accounts where interest is paid but savers are not able to withdraw without either giving notice or paying an interest rate penalty.

Applied economics

The money supply in the UK

There is no single definition of money because no financial asset possesses all the characteristics or fulfils all the functions of money perfectly. A variety of different financial assets possess some of the functions to some degree, and hence it is possible to provide a large number of definitions of the money supply. In the United Kingdom, the Bank of England monitors a variety of monetary aggregates, the main one being M4. The main measure monitored by the European Central Bank is M3. Figure 3 shows the composition of M4.

M4 is made up of three main types of asset. Notes and coins are the smallest part. The largest part is deposits by households and firms with banks and building societies. Some of the deposits are held mainly to be spent. Typically, these accounts come with a cheque book and debit card. Other deposits are held mainly as a form of saving and tend to pay higher rates of interest than cheque book accounts. Lastly, there are wholesale deposits with banks and building societies. These are very large deposits which typically are made in millions of pounds. They are made by firms and financial institutions. M4 is **broad money**, money which is used not just for spending but also for saving. The part of M4 which is used mainly for the day to day purchase of goods and services is called **narrow money**. Examples of narrow money are notes and coins and cheque book accounts with banks. Until 2005, the Bank of England published data for a definition of narrow money called M0, which was notes and coins in circulation and with banks, and banks operational balances with the Bank of England.

The Bank of England also calculates a measure called M2 (or Retail M4) which is M4 minus wholesale deposits, i.e. notes and coins plus retail deposits.

Figure 4 shows the relative size of the value of notes and coins in circulation with M2 and M4.

In the past, the Bank of England published figures for six main measures of the money supply, M0 to M5. In the 1980s, the two measures which were most closely monitored were M1 and M3. Their abandonment gives a very good example of how the definition of what constitutes money in a real economy can change very rapidly.

In the 1960s and 1970s, there was a clear division between cheque book accounts (called current accounts) operated by banks and savings accounts operated by both banks and building societies. Cheque book accounts were used for day to day spending. Savings accounts were used for longer term saving. Banks used the deposits from all types of accounts to lend out to customers. This lending helped finance everything from cars to holidays to new factories. Building societies lent out money only for mortgages on houses, an area of business which the banks traditionally did not conduct. It was judged that

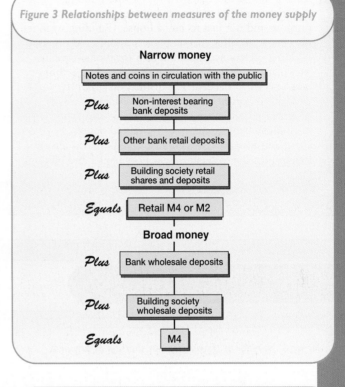

Figure 3 Relationships between measures of the money supply

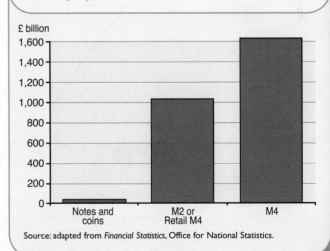
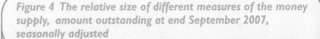

Figure 4 The relative size of different measures of the money supply, amount outstanding at end September 2007, seasonally adjusted

Source: adapted from *Financial Statistics*, Office for National Statistics.

money lent out for mortgages would not have any significant effect on spending on anything outside the housing market.

M1 measured notes and coins in circulation together with money in cheque book accounts. It was a narrow measure of the money supply. M3 was made up of

M1 plus savings accounts at banks. M4 was M3 plus savings at building societies. In the 1980s, however, the government encouraged banks and building societies to compete. Banks began to lend substantial sums in house mortgages. From 1986, building societies were allowed to lend money out for any purpose and not just to buy a house. Building societies also began to offer cheque book accounts. Many used building society accounts not as a form of saving but as a place to deposit the month's wages and withdraw it as and when needed. The distinction between deposits at banks and deposits at building societies disappeared. It was no longer possible clearly to distinguish between money that would quickly be spent and money that would be saved. It was also no longer possible to separate out how banks and building

societies would use their deposits when lent out. The distinction between M1 and M3 ceased to be very useful. Then in 1989 the Abbey National building society changed its legal status and become a bank. This created a large one-off jump in the value of M3. With further building society conversions expected, it was clear that M3 would cease to be very meaningful and that M4 should be used as the main monetary measure.

Today, the Bank of England uses its money supply data with caution precisely because what constitutes money is not entirely clear and may change very rapidly. Small changes in the rate of growth of the money supply are not considered to be significant. Only relatively large changes would be taken account of when deciding upon monetary policy.

DataQuestion

Money in the UK

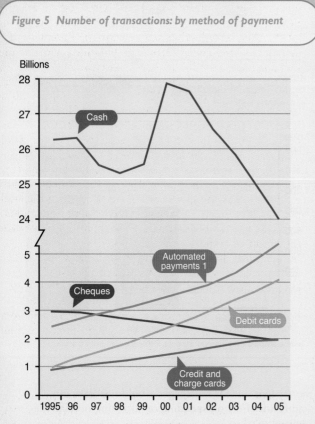

Figure 5 Number of transactions: by method of payment

Billions

Cash

Automated payments 1

Cheques

Debit cards

Credit and charge cards

1995 96 97 98 99 00 01 02 03 04 05

1. Automated payments: direct debits, standing orders, direct credits and CHAPS sterling.

Source: adapted from *Payment Trends 1995-2005: Facts and Figures*, Association for Payment Clearing Services.

Figure 6 Notes and coins in circulation

£ billion

Notes and coins

1995 96 97 98 99 00 01 02 03 04 05 06 07

Source: adapted from *Financial Statistics*, Office for National Statistics.

A manufacturer of bank notes and plastic cards has commissioned a report on prospects in the UK market for money. Write the report:
1. distinguishing between money and money substitutes;
2. explaining how the market for (a) money and (b) money substitutes has changed over the period;
3. discussing how means of payment are likely to change in the future and the implications this will have for the money supply in the UK.

Summary

1. The price of money is the rate of interest.
2. The rate of interest is determined by the demand for and supply of money.
3. An increase in the demand for money or a fall in the supply of money will increase the rate of interest. A fall in the demand for money or an increase in the supply of money will lead to a fall in the rate of interest.
4. Different interest rates exist in different money markets. Interest rates tend to move together in the same direction over long periods of time.
5. Factors which cause interest rates to differ in the same market include time, risk and administrative cost.
6. The loanable funds theory states that the rate of interest is determined by the demand for and supply of loanable funds for investment and saving.
7. The real rate of interest is the nominal rate adjusted for inflation.

Determination of the rate of interest

Economic theory suggests that, just as the price of a good is determined by the forces of demand and supply, so too is the price of money. So what is the price of money? It is how much needs to be paid if money is borrowed - it is the **rate of interest**.

Figure 1 shows the demand and supply curves of money. The demand curve for money is sometimes called the **liquidity preference schedule**. It is downward sloping because the higher the rate of interest, the more households and firms will wish to hold non-money assets such as bonds or shares. The money supply is drawn as a vertical line, showing that the supply of money remains constant whatever the rate of interest. This assumes that the central bank can and does control the supply of money in the economy independently of its price. The money supply is then said to be **exogenous** (i.e. is not linked with any variable in the economic model but is determined outside the model). It would make no difference to our conclusions here if the money supply were assumed to be upward sloping and therefore **endogenous** (i.e linked with a variable in the model, in this case the price of money, the rate of interest), with the money supply determined by the rate of interest rather than by the decisions of the central bank. The equilibrium rate of interest r_e occurs where the demand for money equals the supply of money.

Economic theory suggests that if the rate of interest is above or below this level then it will tend towards its equilibrium value.

- Assume that the rate of interest is r_1 (i.e. there is an excess demand for money). Households and firms want to hold more money than they are currently holding. They will react by selling some of their non-money assets and converting them into money. If money is defined in narrow terms such as M0, then households could increase their holdings of money by withdrawing some from building society accounts. Building societies will now have a shortfall of deposits and will react by putting up their interest rates to attract more savings. If money is defined in broad terms, households might react by selling savings such as government bonds (also known as government stock or gilts). Extra buyers for such bonds, a form of long term borrowing, will only be found if they pay out a higher financial reward through an increase in the effective interest rate paid out on them. So long term interest rates will rise. Excess demand for money will push up interest rates, leading to a movement back along the liquidity preference schedule. This will continue until households and firms are in equilibrium where the demand for money equals the supply of money.
- Now assume the converse: that there is excess supply of money such as would exist at a rate of interest of r_2. Households and firms hold more money than they wish, so they will attempt to put it into a building society, or buy bonds, shares or other types of assets. This will lead to a fall in interest rates back towards the equilibrium interest rate r_e.

Shifts in the money demand and supply curves

What happens if the demand or supply of money changes (i.e. there is a **shift** in either the money demand or supply curves)?

Assume that the liquidity preference schedule shifts to the right as in Figure 2. This means that more money is demanded at any given rate of interest. This could be caused by an increase in income, an increase in the price level (we are assuming that the LP curve shows the demand for nominal balances) or an increase in the perceived risk of holding non-monetary assets such as bonds or shares. The rate of interest

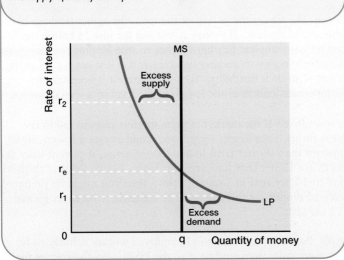

Figure 1 The equilibrium rate of interest

r_e is the equilibrium rate of interest - the rate of interest where the demand for and supply of money are equal.

551

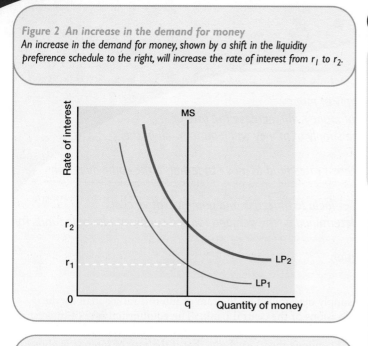

Figure 2 *An increase in the demand for money*
An increase in the demand for money, shown by a shift in the liquidity preference schedule to the right, will increase the rate of interest from r_1 to r_2.

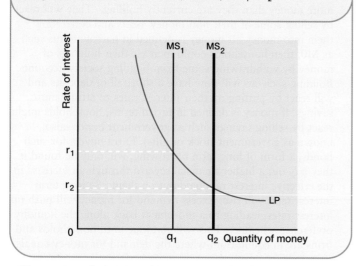

Figure 3 *An increase in the money supply*
An increase in the money supply, shown by a shift in the money supply curve to the right, will lead to a fall in the rate of interest from r_1 to r_2.

will consequently increase from r_1 to r_2. So an increase in liquidity preference shown by a shift to the right in the LP curve will increase interest rates, but not change the supply of money which is fixed by the authorities. Conversely, a fall in the demand for money will lead to a fall in interest rates.

Now assume that the government increases the supply of money. This is shown by a shift to the right in the supply curve in Figure 3. The result will be a fall in the rate of interest from r_1 to r_2. Conversely a fall in the money supply will lead to an increase in interest rates.

Different markets, different rates of interest

So far, it has been implicitly assumed that there is one market for money and one equilibrium rate of interest in the economy. This is a very useful simplification in macro-economic theory. However, in reality there are many markets for money and many rates of interest in an economy.

Draw a diagram showing the liquidity preference schedule and the money supply curve. Show the likely effect on the equilibrium rate of interest if there is:
(a) a fall in the money supply;
(b) an increase in the price level;
(c) increased use of credit cards in payment for goods and services;
(d) a fall in national income at current prices;
(e) an increase in notes and coins in circulation in the economy.

For instance, in the Treasury Bill market, the government borrows short term from banks and other large financial institutions. In the credit card market, households borrow money on credit cards from banks and other financial institutions which provide a credit card service. In the mortgage market, building societies and banks lend money to households purchasing property. If all these markets were perfect, and all loans and borrowing were identical, then the rate of interest in all markets would be the same. But there are many barriers between markets and loans which are not identical. Hence interest rates differ. For instance, when banks offer higher rates of interest on their accounts than building societies, the building societies will not suffer major drains of funds. This is partly because customers find it inconvenient to change money from one account to another. But also many customers are unaware of differences in interest rates. Equally, in some markets borrowers and lenders are locked into fixed term contracts. These are likely to be short - anything up to, say, 6 months. This means that money cannot flow into another market to take advantage of higher interest rates.

Barriers to the flow of money between markets exist but on the whole they are not high enough to insulate markets completely. When interest rates increase in the City of London, the major banks will almost certainly increase their interest rates too. The effect will ripple out into the rest of the economy. Building societies may not respond initially but they will suffer a drain of funds in the medium term if they do not increase their interest rates. So interest rates tend to move in the same direction over a period of time.

There is a number of factors which can cause interest rates to differ in the same market.

Time The longer the period of the loan, the higher tends to be the rate of interest. If money is lent out for just 24 hours, the lender has complete flexibility either to stop lending the money or to switch money to another market. If it is lent out for 25 years, there is no such flexibility. So higher interest is necessary to compensate lenders as the length of the term of a loan increases.

Expectations If the market expects interest rates to fall in the near future, then longer term loans could attract a lower rate of interest than shorter term loans. For instance, if current interest rates are 12 per cent for overnight loans, but you expect them to fall to 10 per cent in a month's time, then you might be prepared to lend money for three months at somewhere between 10 and 12 per cent.

Risk Lending money to an unemployed worker is likely to be far more risky than lending it to the HSBC. So the greater the

Question 2

Table 1 *Selected interest rates and yields, 9 November 2007*

Source	Period of loan	%
Gilt edged stock 2008	1 year	5.3
Interbank money markets	overnight	5.8-5.72
	one month	5.95-5.87
	one year	6.04-5.96
Bank base rate		5.75
Mortgage rate (Skipton Building Society capped rate)		6.49
Personal loan unsecured (Coventry Building Society)	3 years	10.0
Authorised overdraft, Nationwide Building Society		9.9
Barclaycard Platinum credit card		14.9
Miss Selfridge Account Card		29.9

Source: adapted from the *Financial Times*, 10.11.2007, www.nationwide.co.uk, www.missselfridge.co.uk.

Gilt edged stock is a form of long term loan to the UK government. Gilt edged stock 2008 was stock which was repayable in 2008 and therefore in 2007 the loan only had one year before repayment. In the interbank market in London, banks lend to each other for short periods of time from just overnight to one year. The bank base rate is the rate of interest around which banks in the UK set their interest rates. Borrowers have to pay above base rate whilst those lending to UK banks get less than base rate. Mortgages are secured loans for the purchase of houses where the lender can repossess the house if the mortgage is unpaid. Personal loans which are unsecured are loans to individuals where no security is given by the borrower. Authorised overdrafts are when customers go into the red on their bank account with the permission of their bank or building society. Store cards or account cards are issued by individual retailers and operate in a similar way to credit cards. They are typically taken out by young people on relatively low incomes.

(a) Suggest reasons why the interest rates in Table 1 differ from each other.

risk of default on the loan, the higher will be the rate of interest.

Administrative cost Lending out £100 million in lots of £100 at a time is likely to be far more administratively costly than lending out £100 million to one customer. So the higher the administration cost, the higher will tend to be the rate of interest. Equally, lenders of money may find it more costly to move their money around to gain the highest rate of interest available at a point in time than leaving their money in an existing account earning a lower rate of interest.

Imperfect knowledge Borrowers and lenders may have imperfect knowledge. For instance, credit card holders may be unaware that they could cut their interest payments by changing their credit card provider. A saver with a building society may be unaware that another building society is offering higher rates of interest on a savings account which is otherwise identical to an existing account.

Loanable funds theory

Another theory which explains how the rate of interest is determined is the LOANABLE FUNDS THEORY. Assume that the only demand for borrowed funds comes from firms or government wishing to invest. The investment schedule is downward sloping as in Figure 4. The higher the rate of interest, the lower the amount of investment. One reason for this is that the higher the rate of interest, the higher the cost to firms of borrowing money to finance investment. The higher the cost, the less profitable an investment project becomes. An investment project which might have been highly profitable if funds could be borrowed at 5 per cent might only earn normal profit at 8 per cent and be unprofitable at 15 per cent. The higher the rate of interest, the fewer investment projects are profitable and hence the lower the amount of investment.

In contrast, the savings schedule is upward sloping as shown

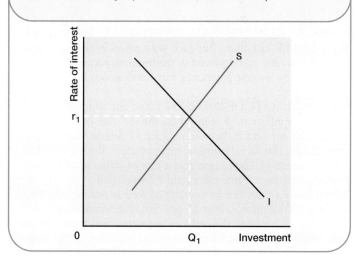

Figure 4 **Loanable funds theory**
According to the loanable funds theory, the rate of interest is determined by investment and saving in an economy. The equilibrium rate of interest is fixed where the level of savings equals the level of investment at r_1.

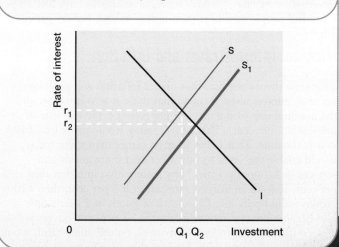

Figure 5 **An increase in the level of saving**
If at any given rate of interest households decide to save more, this will push the savings curve to the right from S to S_1. The equilibrium rate of interest in the economy will then fall from r_1 to r_2.

in Figure 4. The higher the rate of interest, the more attractive it becomes for households and firms to save. They can earn more money in interest, the higher the rate of interest.

The equilibrium rate of interest is where the investment schedule cuts the savings schedule at r_1. If, as in Figure 5, households decide to save more at any given rate of interest, perhaps because there is an increased fear of unemployment, the savings schedule shifts to the right. This will lead to a fall in the equilibrium rate of interest to r_2. A rise in investment at any given level of interest rates, would shift the investment schedule to the right and lead to a rise in the equilibrium rate of interest.

Loanable funds theory can explain how the rate of interest is determined in a simple economy where the main demand for money comes from investment and the main supply of money comes from savings. However, in a modern economy, money markets are far more complex. In an open economy like the UK, for instance, interest rates are affected by flows of money between countries. Modern economic theory, therefore, tends to use models based on the demand and supply of money to explain how interest rates are determined.

Nominal and real interest rates

When a building society offers a rate of interest of 10 per cent, it is offering a NOMINAL RATE OF INTEREST. The interest is unadjusted for inflation. But each year, prices in the economy are likely to rise. £100 placed in the building society today will, excluding any interest payments, buy fewer goods and services in a year's time.

The REAL RATE OF INTEREST is the rate of interest adjusted for inflation. For instance, the real rate of interest would be 5 per cent if the nominal rate of interest were 10 per cent and the rate of inflation were 5 per cent. With a nominal rate of interest of 12 per cent and a rate of inflation of 8 per cent, the real rate of interest would be 4 per cent.

Real interest rates can be negative as well as positive. In 1975, with the UK inflation rate at 25 per cent and nominal interest rates about 7 per cent, the real rate of interest was minus 18 per cent. Anyone saving at 7 per cent would have lost 18 per cent of the purchasing power of their money during 1975. Why do people save when real interest rates are negative? One reason is that much saving is highly illiquid. People can't liquidate assurance or pension fund contracts easily or without costs for instance. Another reason is that people need to save if only because they do not wish to spend all their income when they receive it on pay day. What's more, savers might have lost 18 per cent. But people who kept their money in cash lost 25 per cent!

Nominal interest rates and inflation

Economic theory predicts that higher inflation will push up nominal interest rates. Assume that there is zero inflation and the nominal rate of interest is 3 per cent (i.e. the real rate of interest is 3 per cent). Then, £100 today would grow into £103 in a year's time. That £100, if saved rather than spent today, would enable the saver to buy 3 per cent more goods and services in 12 months time. Now assume that inflation rises to 5 per cent. If nominal interest rates are still 3 per cent, then £100 today would only buy £98 worth of goods in a year's time because the real rate of interest is - 2 per cent. Savers would therefore save less. Borrowers, on the other hand, would borrow more because they are effectively being

paid to borrow money. The market for loanable funds would therefore fall into disequilibrium. It can only return to equilibrium when nominal rates of interest have risen to approximately the original real rate of interest of 3 per cent.

Irving Fisher, an American economist in the early part of this century, argued that a 1 per cent increase in inflation would be

Question 3

(a) Explain the possible link between nominal interest rates and inflation rates.
(b) To what extent do the data in Figure 6 support economic theory?

Figure 6 Nominal interest rates[1] and inflation[2] in OECD countries

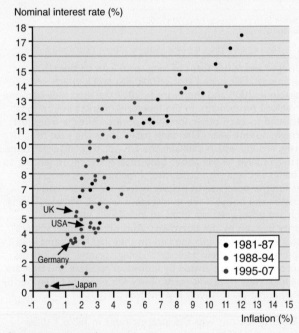

1. Short term rates, annual average.
2. Average annual percentage change in consumer prices.

Source: adapted from Historical Statistics, *Economic Outlook*, OECD.

Key terms

Loanable funds theory - the loanable funds theory of interest rate determination argues that the rate of interest is determined by the demand for and supply of loanable funds, in particular for the purchase of capital.
Nominal interest rates - interest rates unadjusted for inflation.
Real interest rates - nominal interest rates adjusted for inflation.

associated with a 1 per cent increase in nominal interest rates. Therefore, if the real rate of interest is 3 per cent, then nominal interest rates would be 13 per cent if the inflation rate were 10 per cent, 23 per cent if the inflation rate were 20 per cent and so on.

This can be seen in Figure 2. The demand for money is a demand for real balances, so when prices rise, the demand for money increases, shown by the shift to the right in the liquidity preference curve in Figure 2. But this rise in demand raises

interest rates. The analysis is more complex than this, though. Large increases in prices are associated with large increases in the money supply, so high inflation is associated with shifts to the right in the money supply curve too. What the Fisher hypothesis implies is that the shift to the right in the demand for money curve would be greater than the shift to the right in the money supply curve, and this would produce rising nominal interest rates.

Applied economics

The rate of interest in five money markets

The rate of interest in each money market in the UK is determined by the demand for and supply of money in that market. It is possible to identify the main borrowers and lenders in most money markets. For instance, in the UK domestic mortgage market, banks and building societies are the two most important suppliers of money. People wanting to borrow money to buy a house demand money. The rate of interest on a mortgage loan is low compared to, say, an ordinary overdraft or bank loan. This is mainly because a mortgage loan is secured on a property. If a borrower defaults on the loan, the bank or building society can force the borrower to sell the property and pay back the loan with the money raised, so a mortgage loan is regarded as being relatively free of risk by lenders.

Banks have traditionally been the main source of loans and overdrafts, although secondary banks and building societies entered the market in the 1970s and 1980s. The demand for money comes from individuals and companies who want to borrow to finance everything from repairing a car, to a new kitchen or a new factory. Interest rates tend to be set according to risk of default. Large companies can usually get lower rates of interest on loans than small companies, whilst individuals are charged much higher rates than on a mortgage loan. It could be argued that loans through credit cards form part of this market too. Interest rates on credit cards tend to be above overdraft and personal loan rates for individuals. Not only is the risk of default higher on a credit card than on a personal loan but there are much greater administrative costs in

handling credit card loans than in handling personal loans and overdrafts.

Figure 7 shows interest rates offered and charged by Lloyds TSB bank in November 2007. The Bank of England fixes the bank base rate. Banks, such as Lloyds TSB, borrow money from customers at rates below bank base rate. Current accounts which offer costly services such as cheques and debit cards tend to pay lower rates of interest than savings accounts. Banks then charge above base rate to customers who borrow money. Loans which carry little risk and have low administrative charges such as mortgages have relatively low interest rates. Loans where the risk of default is greater or where there is greater administrative cost, such as credit card borrowing, carry higher rates of interest.

In a City money market, such as the interbank market, discount market or local authority market, individual transactions tend to be for far greater sums of money. In the interbank market, banks borrow and lend between themselves. This can be just for 24 hours when one bank has a very short term surplus of funds, whilst another bank might need to borrow money overnight. Borrowing and lending can be for longer periods up to a year also. In the discount market, the government demands money by issuing Treasury Bills and money is supplied for their purchase mainly by financial institutions such as banks or assurance companies. In the local authority market, local authorities demand money whilst banks and other financial institutions supply funds.

Figure 7   Interest rates, Lloyds TSB Bank, 16.11.2007

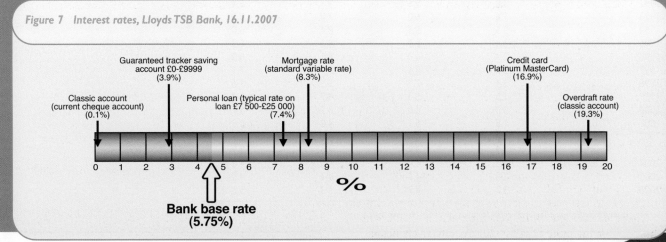

Table 2 shows interest rates in the interbank money market at a point in time. The longer the time period of the borrowing, the higher the interest rate, which is what economic theory would predict. Sometimes demand and supply conditions in some UK money markets are such that there is an 'inverted yield curve'. This means that the normal economic relationship of higher interest rates for longer borrowing is reversed. For example, the government could borrow money at a lower rate of interest if it borrowed it for ten years (through gilts) than if it borrowed for just three months (through Treasury Bills). Inverted yield curves can occur if markets believe interest rates will fall in the future.

Table 2 Interbank money market rates, 9.11.2007

Per cent

	overnight	one month	one year
Interbank money markets	5.8-5.72	5.95-5.87	6.04-5.96

Source: adapted from *Financial Times*, 10.11.2007.

DataQuestion

Interest rates and inflation

Table 3 Inflation and selected interest rates

Percentages

	Inflation rate	Banks' base rate	British government securities, long dated 20 years	Treasury Bill yield
1980	18.0	16.3	13.8	13.4
1981	11.9	13.3	14.7	15.3
1982	8.6	11.9	12.9	10.0
1983	4.5	9.9	10.8	9.0
1984	5.0	9.8	10.7	9.3
1985	6.0	12.2	10.6	11.5
1986	3.4	10.9	9.9	10.9
1987	4.2	9.7	9.5	8.4
1988	4.9	10.1	9.4	12.9
1989	7.8	13.8	9.6	15.0
1990	9.4	14.8	11.1	13.5
1991	5.9	11.7	9.9	10.4
1992	3.8	9.6	9.1	6.4
1993	1.6	6.0	7.9	5.0
1994	2.5	5.5	8.1	6.0
1995	3.4	6.7	8.3	6.3
1996	2.4	6.0	8.1	6.3
1997	3.2	6.6	7.1	7.1
1998	3.4	7.2	5.5	5.6
1999	1.5	5.3	4.7	5.7
2000	3.0	6.0	4.7	5.7
2001	1.8	5.1	4.8	3.9
2002	1.7	4.0	4.8	3.9
2003	2.9	3.7	4.6	3.9
2004	1.3	4.4	4.8	4.8
2005	2.8	4.7	4.4	4.5
2006	3.2	4.7	4.3	5.2

Source: adapted from *Economic Trends*, *Financial Statistics*, Office for National Statistics.

1. (a) What is meant by a 'real rate of interest'?
   (b) During which years shown in the data were real interest rates positive in the UK?
2. Why are some interest rates higher than others? Illustrate your answer from the data.
3. Discuss whether changes in interest rates reflect changes in the rate of inflation.

Summary

1. The main instrument of monetary policy in the UK in recent years has been the control of interest rates.
2. Interest rates are inversely related to aggregate demand, which in turn influences inflation.
3. The rate of interest is determined by the demand and supply of money.
4. Central banks can attempt to control the money supply directly rather than using interest rate policy. For instance, they can use open market operations, monetary base control or impose rules and regulations on banks.
5. Central banks may also attempt to control other monetary variables such as hire purchase credit, or lending for export contracts.
6. The higher the level of genuine government borrowing, the higher the interest rate in the market. Sometimes, though, the government chooses to finance its budget deficit by printing money and therefore increasing the money supply and not necessarily affecting interest rates.
7. Higher interest rates will lead to higher levels of the exchange rate.
8. The credit multiplier measures the number of times an increase in high powered money increases the total volume of bank deposits.
9. Monetary policy only works imperfectly, partly because the exact relationship between changes in variables is unknown, partly because the economy is constantly changing and there is therefore uncertainty, partly because data is imperfect, and partly because policy implementation can itself distort the variables that it is attempting to control.

Monetary policy

The operation of monetary policy was outlined in the earlier unit 'Monetary policy' which should be read in conjunction with this unit. Monetary policy is the attempt by the government or its agent, the central bank, to manipulate monetary variables such as the rate of interest or the money supply to achieve policy goals. The four main macro-economic policy goals are price stability, low unemployment, high economic growth and balance of payments equilibrium.

Interest rate policy

Today, the main instrument of monetary policy in Europe and the USA is the control of interest rates. Raising interest rates reduces aggregate demand because consumers spend less whilst firms reduce their investment. This occurs directly, for instance because higher interest rates increase the cost of borrowing to buy consumer durables or investment goods. It also occurs indirectly. For instance, a rise in interest rates is likely to raise the exchange rate, which in turn is likely to make exports less price competitive and imports more price competitive. Exports thus fall whilst importers can increase their sales at the expense of domestic producers. Changes in interest rates can also affect wealth, for instance changing the prices of stocks and shares, or the price of houses. These changes affect the consumption of households.

A rise in interest rates, then, reduces the level of aggregate demand. On an aggregate demand and supply curve diagram, the aggregate demand curve is shifted to the left, bringing about a lower equilibrium price level in the economy.

The money supply and the rate of interest

Central banks can only fix interest rates because they control at least part of the **money supply**. In fact, the money supply and

Question 1

There is a 'serious risk' that economic growth will fall short of the Bank of England's forecast, forcing further interest rate cuts, Stephen Nickell, a member of its monetary policy committee, has said. Consumer expenditure growth was slowing because of high oil prices, increasing slack in the labour market and high levels of household debt. There was also a possibility that household savings rates would rise, denting consumption growth. He went on to say that he saw few signs that inflationary expectations had risen, in spite of high oil prices.

Source: adapted from the *Financial Times*, 19.11.2005.

(a) Explain why the Bank of England might have cut interest rates in November 2005.

the rate of interest are completely interlinked. Consider Figure 1 which shows a downward sloping demand curve for money in a money market. The rate of interest is the price of money. The equilibrium rate of interest is determined by the demand for and supply of money. So, if the equilibrium rate of interest is r_1, then the money supply in equilibrium must be M_1. The money supply curve must therefore pass through the point A. If interest rates rise to r_2, the money supply at that equilibrium must be M_2. The money supply has therefore fallen from M_1 to M_2. The new money supply curve must have shifted backwards and passed through the point B.

In practice, when central banks announce a new rate of interest for the economy, they only fix a new rate of interest for one money market which they control. In the UK, this rate of interest is the **repo rate**. However, the repo rate then fixes the base rates of commercial banks. This in turn influences most short term interest rates, such as building society mortgage rates. It is also likely to affect longer

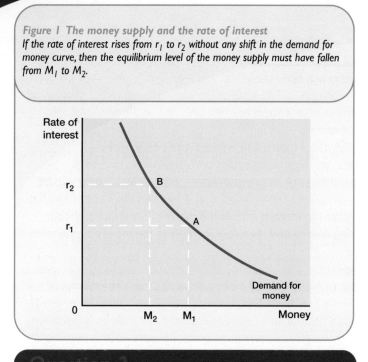

Figure 1 The money supply and the rate of interest
If the rate of interest rises from r_1 to r_2 without any shift in the demand for money curve, then the equilibrium level of the money supply must have fallen from M_1 to M_2.

Question 2

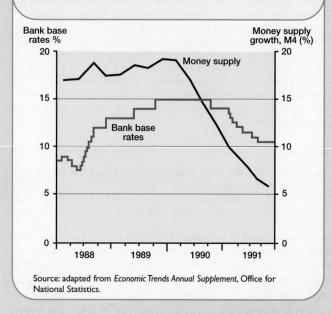

Figure 2 Money supply change (M4, percentage change on previous year) and interest rates (bank base rates, %)

Source: adapted from *Economic Trends Annual Supplement*, Office for National Statistics.

(a) Using the data to illustrate your answer, explain what is the relationship between the money supply and the rate of interest.

term interest rates, although the link is weaker, so a central bank can influence the structure of interest rates throughout the whole economy by fixing just one interest rate in one money market.

The interest rate that the central bank fixes is likely to be linked to the market in which banks borrow and lend money at very short notice. On any one day, banks may have a surplus of money which is not committed to

longer term loans to customers. They may, for instance, have received £50 million more in cheques than they paid out to other financial institutions. Some banks may be short of immediate funds, owing money, say, to other banks because their customers have paid out more in cheques than they have paid in. To cover this, banks will borrow short term, overnight (i.e. for 24 hours) typically from banks with a surplus of funds. The central bank has the unique power to print or create money. If it wants interest rates to fall, it can increase the supply of money to this market by buying back bills (short term loans it has issued) or other financial assets it owns in exchange for money. If it wants to increase interest rates, it can sell financial assets like bills to the banks for money. Hence, governments can only control interest rates if they can control at least part of the money supply.

Controlling the money supply

Controlling short term interest rates gives only indirect control over the whole money supply. In theory, there is a number of ways in which more direct control can be exercised.

Open market operations The central bank can issue government bonds and other forms of government debt. If these are bought by the non-financial sector, then money passes from the non-financial sector to the central bank. The amount of money, the money supply, is therefore reduced because, typically, money at the central bank is not counted in the money supply. This is known as OPEN MARKET OPERATIONS. The reverse is also true. The central bank can increase the supply of money by buying back part of its debt. It can do this because the central bank is the only institution with the legal power to 'print' or create money.

Monetary base control Another possible way of controlling the money supply is for the central bank to force banks to hold certain assets as a percentage of their total assets. These assets are given a variety of names, some of which are HIGH POWERED MONEY or the MONETARY BASE or RESERVE ASSETS. The central bank then attempts to control the amount of high powered money available for the banks to buy. In turn, this limits the amount of assets they can own, which limits the size of the money supply.

Rules and regulations The central bank may impose rules and regulations on banks whose deposits make up most of broad money. For instance, a central bank may impose financial penalties on banks which increase their deposits (and therefore their lending) by more than a certain percentage over a period.

Controlling other monetary variables

Today, the Bank of England closely monitors a range of other monetary variables apart from the money supply. Mortgage lending and consumer credit are two important examples. It uses information about how these are changing to decide whether or not to change interest rates, its chosen instrument of monetary policy. However, central banks can attempt to control these monetary variables directly. For instance, in the 1950s and 1960s, the Bank of England placed restrictions on hire purchase borrowing. It limited the amount that could be borrowed, stipulated the size of the deposit that had to be made and restricted the number of months within which the loan had to be paid. This made sense at the time because the commonest form of financing the purchase of consumer durables then was hire purchase. The central bank could restrict bank or building society lending for the purchase of houses if it felt that house price inflation was a serious problem. The Bank of England in the 1940s and 1950s also ordered banks to give priority for loans to firms needing the finance for exports. Central banks can force commercial banks to charge different rates of interest for different types of loan. For instance, firms wanting to invest might be given a much lower rate of interest than a personal customer wanting to buy a car.

The money supply and the budget deficit

Since the Second World War, governments have traditionally spent more money than they have raised in taxes. The result is that they have had to borrow money. In the UK, this borrowing is known as the **public sector net cash requirement**, the PSNCR. Governments have two ways of raising this money, assuming that they are not going to borrow it from foreigners. The first is to borrow the money from the general public (known as the **non-bank sector**). This has no effect on the money supply but it does affect the rate of interest. If the government wishes to increase the amount, it will have to compete for funds with consumers and firms. This extra demand for borrowed funds will increase their price (i.e. the rate of interest will rise). Conversely, a fall in the PSNCR will reduce total demand for borrowed funds and thus the rate of interest will fall. So the government cannot choose both the level of the PSNCR and the rate of interest if genuine borrowing takes place.

The government has a second option when financing the PSNCR. It could choose to print the money. In a modern economy, it does this by selling government debt to the **banking sector**. To understand why, consider a situation where the central bank sells £100 million of government debt to the banks. They pay for this and the government uses it to finance its spending. For instance, it might use it to pay the wages of civil servants. The government makes the wage payment into the bank accounts of its employees. The banks therefore receive an inflow of deposits which will roughly match the loan they have made to the government by buying its debt. But the extra deposits made by customers of the banks are an increase in the money supply. Therefore a central bank selling debt to the banking sector increases the money supply and is effectively a way of printing money. This is different from the situation where the central bank sells debt to the non-bank sector. Here the non-bank sector withdraws money from its bank accounts to pay for the purchase of the debt. When the government spends the money, the money comes back to the banks in the form of new deposits. The withdrawals and the new deposits cancel each other out, leaving no increase in the money supply.

There is a long history of governments resorting to the printing presses to finance spending. This method has the advantage that the government does not need to raise taxes. It also means that interest rates do not need to rise because increasing the money supply should lead to a fall in interest rates.

The money supply, the rate of interest and the exchange rate

The **exchange rate** is the rate at which one currency can be exchanged for another. It is a market price, and therefore the exchange rate is determined by the forces of demand and supply. Governments can intervene to try and fix the exchange rate at a particular level by either buying or selling currency. For instance, if the Bank of England wanted to make the value of the pound fall against other currencies, then it could sell pounds for currencies such as dollars and euros. But the pounds it sells must come from somewhere. If the Bank prints the money, it will raise the money supply. If it borrows the money from the public, it will raise the demand for loans and hence raise the rate of interest.

Alternatively the value of the pound can be changed by changing interest rates. A rise in interest rates in the UK will attract an inflow of funds to the country, increasing the demand for the currency and hence raising its price. The rise in interest rates can only be engineered through a fall in the money supply. So the Bank of England again faces a trade-off in its policy objectives.

The money supply, the rate of interest, the PSNCR and the exchange rate are all interlinked. If the government fixes a value for one, it cannot fix a value for others. Hence a government may choose not to control the money supply in order to control other variables such as the rate of interest.

The limitations of monetary policy

Monetary policy is used ultimately to control real variables such as inflation, economic growth and unemployment. Achieving, for instance, low inflation or low unemployment are **objectives** of monetary policy. A government may give the central bank specific **targets** to achieve, such as 2 per cent inflation. The central bank then uses **instruments** to achieve these objectives and targets. For instance, it might use interest rates or the money supply. In practice, the operation of monetary policy poses a number of difficulties for the central bank.

Question 3

In 1987 and early 1988, the value of the pound rose against other currencies. The Chancellor of the Exchequer, Nigel Lawson, believed that this would prove damaging to the economy and he attempted to limit this rise by cutting interest rates. Bank base rates fell from 11 per cent at the start of 1987 to a low of $7^1/_2$ per cent in mid-1988. However, there were worrying signs that inflation was beginning to increase. The government sharply increased interest rates to 15 per cent by the end of 1988 to brake the rise in the money supply. At the same time, the foreign exchange markets lost confidence in the pound, the value of the pound fell and the Chancellor had to raise interest rates again in 1989 to prevent the pound from falling further.

(a) Using illustrations from the passage, explain the policy conflict between control of the money supply, control of interest rates and exchange rate control.

Uncertainty Any type of policy, whether fiscal, monetary or other, is limited in its effectiveness by uncertainty. For instance, the oil price shocks of 1973-74 and 1978-79, the stock market crash of 1987, the Asian crisis of 1997-98, the 9/11 terrorist crisis of 2001 and the oil price rises of 2004-2007 all had significant effects on western economies. But these events could not have been predicted by policy makers. So an economy can be blown off course by an external event outside the control of policy makers. The policy response may then be inadequate or inappropriate if policy makers fail to assess accurately the importance of the economic shock. The economic shock may also lead to a situation where existing economic models fail to explain the new situation. In the 1970s, for instance, Keynesian and monetarist economists presented radically different views of why the oil crises had led to stagflation, the combination of high inflation with the economy being in a slump. In the 1980s, UK policy makers failed to appreciate the importance of rising house prices and rising mortgage lending on aggregate demand and inflation.

Lack of reliable data Economic data is imperfect. Data collected today are often revised as further data are accumulated. For instance, GDP figures can undergo substantial revisions over time, partly because the service sector is difficult to monitor. Policy makers have to make judgments based on the data available at the time. If GDP is growing at 2 per cent rather than 1 per cent, it can make a substantial difference to the decisions of policy makers. At 2 per cent, they might decide to raise interest rates; at 1 per cent they might decide to leave them unchanged. Yet between the two figures, there is only a 1 per cent margin of error, which is very small.

The link between monetary variables and the real economy If the money supply increases by 10 per cent, or interest rates fall by 2 per cent, policy makers do not know for certain what will be the impact on real variables such as economic growth or inflation. The Bank of England no longer attempts to control the money supply directly. The experience of the 1970s and 1980s was that there was no stable relationship between the money supply and the real economy. In contrast, there does seem to be a more stable relationship between changes in interest rates and the real economy. Even so, the exact link is not certain, and so a central bank like the Bank of England give predictions in terms of probabilities. This makes it complex for a central bank to use interest rates to steer the economy.

The money supply Economists talk about the 'money supply' as if it exists and can be quantified. In the real world, there are many different measures of the money supply depending on how 'money' is defined. What's more, there is evidence that a measure of the money supply can change its character if a central bank attempts to control it, a phenomenon known as GOODHART'S LAW. Professor Charles Goodhart argued that if policy makers attempted to manipulate one variable which had a stable relationship with another variable, then that relationship would change or break down as behaviour adapts to manipulation. He was specifically referring to the relationship between bank lending and the money supply. In the late 1970s and early 1980s, the Bank of England attempted to control the growth of the money supply because it believed that inflation was caused by increases in the money supply. The chosen measures of the money supply to be controlled were M1 and

Question 4

In November 1998, the Office for National Statistics (ONS) suspended publication of one of the most important economic series it compiles. The average earnings index was found to be giving inaccurate information. The average earnings index is a measure of how much earnings in the whole of the UK are rising. It is calculated monthly by taking data from thousands of returns from businesses. They report on whether or not they have given any pay rises during the previous month and if so, by how much.

Problems arose because of different ways of calculating the average. In October 1998, the ONS launched a new series for average earnings which used a different way of calculating the average, but as Figure 3 shows, this revised series gave very different figures from the original series. It also didn't fit in very well with what other economic indicators were showing at the time.

A government enquiry found that the revised series was based on inadequate statistical methods which gave too much importance to large changes in earnings by small businesses. In March 1999, a new series was published which followed more closely the old series.

Figure 3 Estimates in growth of average earnings

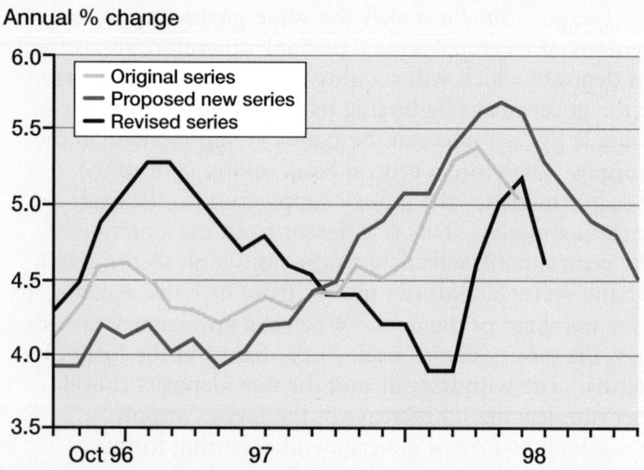

Annual % change

Original series
Proposed new series
Revised series

Source: adapted from Office for National Statistics.

(a) (i) According to the revised series, what was happening to changes in average earnings in 1997?
   (ii) Why should the Bank of England have cut interest rates on the basis of this evidence?

(b) (i) How did the evidence from the revised series conflict with that of the proposed new series?
   (ii) Why might the Bank of England's monetary policy response have been different if it had used the data from the new series?

M3. The most important components of these were deposits with commercial banks. Controls, however, led to **disintermediation**. Banks artificially reduced their recorded deposits from customers by encouraging very large customers, such as firms, to lend directly to other bank customers. The deposits and loans failed to appear on the bank's books but effectively the bank was still acting as an agent for deposits and loans. This artificially reduced the money supply. When restrictions on growth in bank deposits were abolished in 1980 by the Bank of England, there was a sudden large jump in the money supply as the money which had gone outside the official controlled system was brought back in.

Key terms

Credit multiplier - the number of times a change in reserves assets will change the assets of the banking system and thus the money supply.
Goodhart's Law - if the authorities attempt to manipulate one variable which had a stable relationship with another variable before, then the relationship will change or break down.
Open market operations - the buying and selling of financial securities in exchange for money in order to increase or decrease the size of the money supply.
Reserve assets, high powered money or the monetary base - those assets which banks have to keep either because they are needed to satisfy customers' requirements (like cash) or because the government forces banks to keep them to operate its monetary policy.

Applied economics

UK monetary policy

Controlling interest rates

As explained in the earlier unit 'Monetary Policy', UK monetary policy today centres around interest rate policy. The Bank of England controls short term interest rates in the City of London money markets. These control bank base rates, the rate of interest set by banks round which they set borrowing and lending rates. In turn, these heavily influence the rate of interest set by building societies. The link between short term interest rates and other interest rates in the economy, like the rate of interest on credit cards or longer term interest rates, is more tenuous. However, over longer periods of time all interest rates in the economy tend to move together.

The Bank of England controls short term interest rates by controlling the demand for or supply of money in the short term money markets in the City of London. Take a situation when the supply of money in these markets exceeds demand. For instance, in the late 1990s, a number of building societies and assurance companies demutualised, i.e. they ceased to be owned by their members and became public companie or part of public companies owned by shareholders. At the point of demutualisation, the members of the building society or assurance company received a payment, which might have been cash if it was being taken over, or shares in a new public limited company which would be quoted on the stock exchange. These 'windfall' gains made by society members might have ended up as new bank or building society deposits. This increases the amount of money that banks own as assets. They will initially lend this out short term on the London money markets in order to get some return on the money. This increase in supply of funds will drive down short term interest rates. The Bank of England prevents this by selling mainly Treasury Bills to the markets. Treasury Bills are 91 day loans to the government. These sales of Treasury Bills mop up the excess liquidity in the market by increasing the demand for money. The Bank of England has increased demand to match supply, and thus is able to fix the price of money, in this case the short term rate of interest.

If the supply of money in the short term markets is less than demand, the Bank of England does the opposite. This could occur, for instance, because there is a large withdrawal of funds from banks by the self employed to pay their taxes on 31 January and 31 July. The banks are then short of money and need to borrow in order to restore their liquidity. This borrowing would push up short term interest rates. Instead, the Bank of England buys 'eligible securities' from the banking system. Eligible securities are securities like repos (a form of government borrowing), Treasury Bills or Commercial Bills (91 day loans made by firms). Buying bills increases the supply of money into the markets, stabilising interest rates.

The Bank of England raises interest rates whenever it thinks that the economy is likely to be operating above its productive potential, i.e. when the output gap is positive. If actual output is above the trend rate of output, there is likely to be demand-pull inflationary pressure. If, however, the economy is operating below capacity and inflation is stable or is falling, then the Bank of England lowers interest rates to allow the economy to grow at a faster rate.

Central bank independence

Since 1997, the Bank of England has been independent of the government and in particular the Treasury, the government department led by the Chancellor of the Exchequer responsible for the overall economic management of the economy. The government sets the Bank of England a target for inflation which it has to achieve. Decision making about interest rates at the Bank of England is the responsibility of the Monetary Policy Committee (MPC), made up of four independent experts, usually professional economists, four members from the Bank of England staff and the Governor of the Bank of England. They meet every month and consider a wide range of economic statistics which help them to decide whether inflation is likely to increase, decrease or remain stable in the future. The data are often contradictory. For instance, wage rises may be increasing (a sign of possible future inflation increases), but exports might be falling (a sign of deflation and therefore falling inflationary pressures). A vote is taken and the committee is rarely unanimous.

The process has been criticised. It can be argued that the Bank of England should not be independent and the government should have retained control over such a key macro-economic weapon. It is also argued that setting interest rates should not just be about reaching an inflation target, but that other targets, such as the rate of unemployment, should be taken into consideration. Some have argued that there is an inbuilt deflationary bias to the decision making because the committee will tend to want to undershoot the inflation target (which would be seen as a 'success') rather than overshoot it (seen as 'failure'). Others argue that the Bank of England is too unaccountable and that responsibility should lie with an elected government.

However, having an independent central bank makes it far more difficult for the political party in power to manipulate the economy in its favour at election times. In the past, governments have been accused of stoking up a boom at election time in order to generate the 'feel-good' factor which will ensure them re-election only for the country to have to pay the price in terms of higher inflation and then a recession afterwards. An independent central bank is also not insensitive to other policy objectives such as growth and unemployment. The Bank of England has certainly not attempted to achieve its inflation target by having a persistent recession. Indeed, such tactics would be likely to lead to a continual undershooting of the target which in itself would be seen as a failure by the Bank of England. The US central bank, the Federal Reserve Bank, and the euro-zone central bank, the European Central Bank, are each independent, so the UK would be out of line if its central bank were not independent. Most importantly, the Bank of England has been successful in containing inflation without causing a major recession since 1997. Its track record is therefore sound.

Figure 4 shows that, compared to the 1980s and early 1990s, inflation since independence in 1997 has been low. The Bank of England has kept within its targets in almost every month. Therefore independence has guaranteed low inflation. However, it could be argued that inflation had been low since the early 1990s when monetary policy was controlled ultimately by government. If the government had operated a cautious monetary policy since 1997, the outcome could have been exactly the same. On this line of argument, Bank of England independence has not been the key reason why inflation has been low since 1997. As we don't know what would have happened to monetary policy if the Bank of England had not been independent since 1997, it is difficult to say whether independence in itself has been the key factor in securing low inflation.

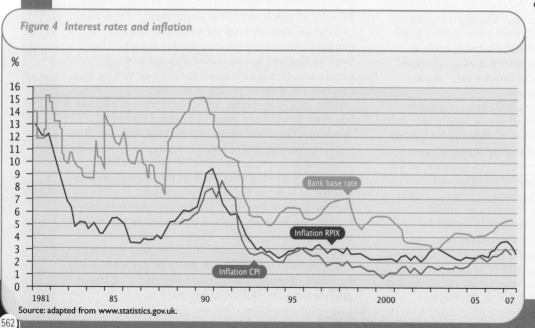

Figure 4 Interest rates and inflation

Source: adapted from www.statistics.gov.uk.

DataQuestion

The Bank of England

In 2005, the Bank of England unveiled a new macro-economic model of the UK economy. The Governor of the Bank of England, Mervyn King, introduced the model by saying: 'The new quarterly model is a valuable addition to the Bank's 'suite of models'. It does not represent a significant shift in the Committee's view of how the economy functions or of the transmission mechanism of monetary policy.' He went on: 'All economic models, however good, represent simplifications of reality and, as such, no single model can possibly address the many and varied issues that matter for economic policy. This recognition is central to the Bank's use of economic models and its approach to economic forecasting. The Bank relies on a plurality of models to help inform the Committee's projections, and these models are used as tools to help the Committee reach the economic judgements that play a critical role in shaping its projections rather than simply to generate mechanical forecasts. Economic forecasting is ultimately a matter of judgement.'

Source: adapted from *The Bank of England Quarterly Model*, Richard Harrison, Kalin Nikolov, Meghan Quinn, Gareth Ramsay, Alasdair Scott and Ryland Thomas, 2005.

The Bank of England model makes a number of predictions about how changes in interest rates affect the economy. Overall, a one per cent rise in base rates cuts gross domestic product by 0.2 to 0.35 per cent. Inflation is reduced by between 0.2 to 0.4 per cent. However, these overall effects only take place over a period of time. The path taken, the monetary transmission mechanism, is complex. There are four key links.

● Official interest rate decisions affect other interest rates in the economy, such as mortgage rates and bank deposit rates, either directly or because of expectations about future interest rate changes.
● Changes in interest rates affect the spending, saving and investment decisions of households and firms.
● Changes in interest rates also affect the value of the pound, which in turn leads to changes in demand for goods and services produced in the UK.
● Changes in the value of the pound also have a direct impact on inflation.

The effects of any interest rate change are lagged. A one per cent rise in base rates will, fairly quickly over a period of around 5 quarters, lead to the maximum fall of 0.2-0.35 per cent in GDP. After that GDP will begin to rise again back to its long run trend value. The effect on inflation is lagged behind the change in GDP. Inflation changes little in the first year after a rise in interest rates. In the second year, however, inflation falls sharply, reaching its maximum fall of between 0.2 to 0.4 per cent for every 1 per cent rise in interest rates, after 9 quarters.

Source: adapted from *The Guardian*.

Figure 5 The monetary transmission mechanism

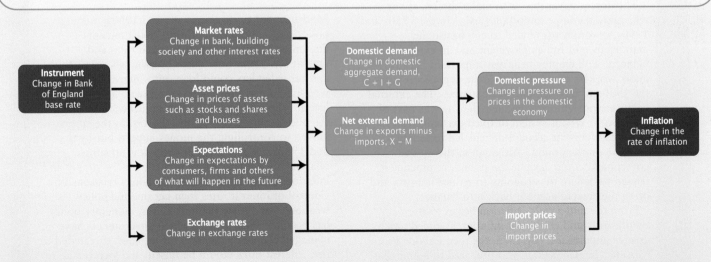

Source: adapted from www.statistics.gov.uk.

1. Explain how a rise in interest rates is likely to lead to a fall in GDP followed by a fall in inflation.
2. Analyse what might be the correct policy response for the Bank of England if inflation is rising beyond its target rate of growth but the US economy has just entered a deep recession.
3. What problems does the Bank of England face in implementing monetary policy?

Applied economics

The limits of government policy

The goals of government policy

The UK government has traditionally had four main macroeconomic goals:

● low inflation;
● low unemployment;
● high economic growth;
● equilibrium on the external balance, the current balance of the balance of payments.

In addition, it might have goals about equality and equity as well as the environment.

These are not necessarily all achievable at a point in time. For instance, in a boom, unemployment may be falling but inflation may be rising and the external balance may be going into deficit. This happened during the Lawson boom of 1986-89. Alternatively, if there is a sudden shock to the system, such as a large rise in commodity prices or a sudden recession in a major trading partner, it may not be possible to achieve any of these goals. In the mid-1970s, with the oil price shock, UK policy makers found themselves facing rising inflation and unemployment, a growing external deficit and falling economic growth. Economic growth may conflict with environmental objectives if some of the benefits of economic growth are not used to improve the environment. Economic growth achieved through some supply side policies such as cutting income tax may result in higher inequality.

This forces governments to make choices about which are the most important goals. In the 1950s and 1960s, governments tended to emphasise the maintenance of full employment and an external balance. Full employment was important because so many workers could remember the depression years of the 1930s when unemployment soared. The external balance was significant because the UK was part of the Bretton Woods system of fixed exchange rates. Significant current account deficits led to selling pressure on the pound. Although in theory the government could devalue the pound, in practice it tended to deflate the economy to reduce imports and bring the current account back into balance.

From the mid-1960s, inflation began to rise significantly and control of inflation assumed much greater importance. By 1975, the then Labour Prime Minister, Jim Callaghan, was prepared to admit that the government could not control both inflation and unemployment at the same time. Governments allowed unemployment to rise and made the control of inflation their first priority.

The external balance also became less important as a government policy objective in the 1970s. In 1971, the UK left the Bretton Woods system and the pound was allowed to float. External deficits tended to lead to falls in the value of the pound, and vice versa. However, so long as governments did not want to maintain a particular exchange rate, these were of little significance. In the mid-1980s, the then Chancellor of the Exchequer, Nigel Lawson, declared that the external balance was no longer of any policy significance. His view was that so long as deficits could be financed, it was not up to governments to decide whether households and firms wanted to borrow money to finance more imports in any one year.

By the 1990s, there was a consensus that the main short term goal of government policy should be the control of inflation. Unemployment might have to rise in the short term and GDP might have to fall to secure this objective. However, in the long term governments should be adopting supply side policies which would bring about a reduction in unemployment and a rise in the growth rate. The external balance was of no policy significance in itself. By the 2000s, government was beginning to think that full employment rather than just lower unemployment might become a realisable objective once more. Government was also committed to long term environmental targets.

Managing demand

Monetary policy In the 1950s and 1960s, monetary policy took a number of forms. Governments attempted to control credit through rules and regulations about how much building societies, banks and other lenders could loan out. Interest rates too were raised and lowered to manipulate borrowing levels. They were also used to influence the value of the pound. In the 1970s and the 1980s, the emphasis moved to controlling the money supply, but by the mid-1980s it was clear that there was no simple relationship between growth in the money supply and inflation (the quantity theory of money relationship). Control of interest rates then became the policy weapon used. Since the mid-1980s, monetary policy has been the main way in which governments have managed aggregate demand. If inflation threatened to rise, interest rates would be raised, and vice versa. In the 1980s, this was referred to as a 'one club' policy - the government only had one weapon at its disposal to steer the economy.

In 1997, the Bank of England was granted independence and given control of the operation of monetary policy. The government set it targets for inflation (e.g. to maintain it at 2.5 per cent plus or minus 1 per cent). There were fears when the Bank of England was given its independence that it would act very cautiously and tend to pursue deflationary policies to achieve its inflation target. This would have meant higher unemployment and lower growth than otherwise might be the case. In practice, the Bank of England has, according to most, attempted to set interest rates which would allow the maximum economic expansion within the constraints of its inflation target.

Fiscal policy Fiscal policy in the 1950s and 1960s was seen as being a more effective way of influencing aggregate demand than monetary policy. Governments would increase budget deficits when the economy was in recession and reduce them when the economy was overheating. In the 1970s, the traditional relationships between inflation and unemployment broke down and by the mid-1970s the economy was experiencing stagflation, high inflation and high unemployment. Traditional fiscal policy was powerless to bring down both inflation and unemployment, so governments broadly abandoned the use of active fiscal policy. However, they have allowed the automatic stabilisers within the system to manage the trade cycle. For instance, in the recession of 1990-92, the PSNCR, the Budget deficit, was allowed to rise, and peaked at £43 billion in 1993. The stated aim of the government today is that the Budget should be in balance over the trade cycle (the 'Golden Rule'). In recessions, it will be allowed to go into deficit, whilst in booms there will be a Budget surplus. This rule prevents the government from destabilising the economy by over-inflating it or inducing too severe a recession by the inappropriate use of fiscal policy.

Exchange rate policy Exchange rate policy has, for very brief periods, been used to influence inflation. In 1987-88, Nigel Lawson adopted a policy of shadowing the value of the German currency, the deutschmark. Germany had been, throughout the post-war period, a relatively low inflation economy. The argument was that by linking the pound to the deutschmark, the UK could mirror Germany's low inflation. The policy was abandoned when inflation began to rise in the UK and the Chancellor was forced to raise interest rates sharply to deflate the economy. However, the policy re-emerged in a slightly different form when the UK joined the ERM (the precursor to European Monetary Union) in 1990. The pound at the time was relatively high in value. The argument was that maintaining a high value of the pound would help keep downward pressure on inflation. It proved a costly policy mistake. By September 1990 when the UK joined the ERM, high interest rates had arguably already reduced aggregate demand sufficiently to return the economy to low inflation within 12

months. To maintain a high value of the pound, the government was forced to keep interest rates much higher than it would otherwise have wanted in 1991 and 1992 as the economy stagnated in a prolonged recession. When the UK was forced out of the ERM in September 1992 and the pound fell around 15 per cent, the government was able to cut interest rates. Both depreciation of the currency and lower interest rates soon helped the economy to come out of recession. Since then, the government has allowed the pound to float freely. However, if and when the UK joins the single currency, it will have to decide on a value for the pound on entry. Too high a value will depress aggregate demand and could lead to a prolonged recession. Too low a value will increase aggregate demand and could lead to inflation in the short term.

Prices and incomes policies In the 1960s and 1970s, governments used prices and incomes policies to suppress cost-push inflationary pressures to supress cost-push inflationary pressures. Whilst they were successful in the short term in reducing aggregate demand, they failed to address the underlying reasons why aggregate demand was rising so fast. The result was that they had little impact on long run prices.

Influencing aggregate supply

In the 1950s and 1960s, governments concentrated on industrial and regional policy to influence aggregate supply. At the time, it was felt that the UK faced two main problems: lack of competitiveness compared to other countries and regional inequalities with higher unemployment levels outside the south of England and the Midlands. In the 1970s, free market economists coined the term 'supply side economics'. They argued that efficiency could be increased if markets became free markets. In the 1980s, the Conservative government implemented a large number of supply side reforms. These included trade union reform, privatisation of state monopolies and deregulation of industries such as the bus industry. Fiscal policy, no longer used to influence aggregate demand, was used to influence aggregate supply. For instance, income tax rates were cut whilst tax and benefit incentives were given to those who started up their own businesses. Fiscal policy is still used today as one of the main ways in which governments try to influence aggregate supply. Other ways include further liberalisation of markets, such as telecommunications and air transport, and improvements in value for money in areas such as education and the health service.

Equity

Fiscal policy has been used to redistribute income and wealth in society. In the 1960s and 1970s, Labour governments favoured taxing higher income earners more heavily to gain revenue to increase benefits to those on low incomes. One of the results was a marginal income tax rate on earned income of 83 per cent for the highest earners. If these individuals also enjoyed unearned income, such as bank interest or dividends on shares, the unearned income was taxed at 98 per cent. This led to severe market distortions. High income earners avoided tax by ceasing to work, moving abroad, receiving large fringe benefits or altering their financial assets so that they earned no income but maximised untaxed capital gain.

In the 1980s, the Conservative government brought down marginal tax rates on higher income earners and also cut welfare benefits to the poor. The argument was that lowering tax rates would increase incentives to work and take risks, whilst cutting benefits would encourage the poor to take on work or work harder. The result was a significant redistribution of income from the poor to the rich.

The Labour government since 1997 has combined elements of both these strategies. It wishes to see fewer inequalities in society. It argued that the way to do this was to encourage the poor to become more self-sufficient through work and the tax and benefit system. Short term measures such as the New Deal were introduced to get people back into work quickly. Taxes and benefits were redesigned to raise disposable incomes of the low paid in work and so increase the incentive to work. In the long term, emphasis was placed on improving educational standards to make the economy as a whole more productive and more internationally competitive. This would raise incomes in general and create more jobs in the economy. A variety of other measures was introduced to reduce poverty and social exclusion, targeting pensioners, one parent families and children.

The environment

Since the 1980s, the environment has moved up the government's list of priorities. Through international agreements such as the Montreal Accords, which dealt with damage to the ozone layer, and the Kyoto Agreement, which dealt with greenhouse gas emissions, the government has committed itself to significant reductions in environmental pollution. Membership of the EU has also led to tough new limits in areas such as recycling of waste and water pollution. The government's freedom of action is very much limited by its international treaty obligations. It could be argued that the main way in which it can make policy is by persuading other countries, either at EU level or at an international level, to change policy. How international treaty obligations are met is another issue. The government faces difficult choices, for example, about greenhouse gas emissions with regard to renewable energy versus nuclear power and fossil fuels.

At a national level, the government is constantly having to make decisions about the built environment. The environmental and rural lobbies tend to argue against the building of any new roads, industrial buildings or homes outside existing built up areas. On the other hand, with the population growing and aging, more people working, and with consumers buying more goods and services, the existing infrastructure cannot cope. It can be argued that in many policy areas, government has become paralysed because it is afraid to offend individual lobby pressure groups.

Free trade and protectionism

UK governments since the Second World War have tended to favour free trade rather than protectionist policies. Since the 1950s, trade barriers have been brought down, particularly through the trade agreements negotiated through GATT, which is now the WTO (World Trade Organisation). Britain's membership of the EU in 1973 led to free trade with EU partners and further limited Britain's ability to pursue protectionist policies because such decisions were now taken at EU level. The UK, over the past ten years, has tended to be amongst those EU countries pressing for more free trade, whereas countries such as France and Italy have tended to favour a more protectionist Europe and have been less willing to liberalise trade in services within the EU.

Control of the economy

The UK government's ability to control the economy is, in many ways, severely limited and is likely to become more rather than less limited over time.

Shocks The government cannot prevent economic shocks destabilising the economy. Arguably the most important shock to hit the UK in the post-war period was the rise in oil prices between 1973 and 1981. There have many others though, including the Korean War 1950-53 and more recently the Asian crisis in 1998 and the US sub-prime mortgage crisis in 2007.

Long term shifts in consumption and trading patterns At the start of the twentieth century, one in ten workers in the UK was in the textile industry. Agriculture and coal mining were significant employers too. Today, these industries are relatively unimportant in terms of both output and employment. This is just one example of how the economy changes over time. Today, IT industries are booming and the Internet is changing the way in which the economy works. Such shifts give governments many opportunities but also leave them with many problems. In the post-war period, it could be argued that the restructuring of British industry was an important supply side constraint and limited the ability of government to influence long term economic growth. When the UK was part of the Bretton Woods system of exchange rates, Britain's lack of international competitiveness caused it recurring exchange rate problems.

International trade The UK has become a relatively more open economy over time. The greater the openness of its economy, the less a government is able to use fiscal or monetary policy to influence aggregate demand. For instance, if the government uses expansionary fiscal policy, the more open the economy, the more leaks out into greater demand for imports and the less is spent domestically. The last time a UK government used active fiscal policy to reflate the economy in 1972-73, there was a substantial increase in domestic demand but the current account deficit rose to an unsustainable level.

International treaty obligations The UK is bound by a number of international treaty obligations which limit its ability to pursue independent policies. Trade policies are influenced by both the WTO and the EU. Supply side issues, such as giving aid to individual firms, or working hours for employees, are constrained by EU law. If and when the UK joins the European Single Currency, policy will be further constrained. Monetary policy will be decided not by the Bank of England but by the European Central Bank. For fiscal policy purposes, the government will have to keep its budget deficit to a maximum of 3 per cent of GDP and the level of the National Debt will not have to exceed 60 per cent of GDP.

DataQuestion · Macroeconomic strategy

The macroeconomic policy framework

The Government's macroeconomic framework is designed to maintain long-term economic stability. Stability allows business, individuals and the Government to plan more effectively for the long term, improving the quality and quantity of investment in physical and human capital and helping to raise productivity. Economic stability provides the essential backdrop for addressing the priorities of government, enabling it to address the key social, economic and environmental challenges of the next decade.

The macroeconomic framework is based on the principles of transparency, responsibility and accountability. The monetary policy framework seeks to ensure low and stable inflation, while fiscal policy is underpinned by clear objectives and two strict rules that ensure sound public finances over the medium term while allowing fiscal policy to support monetary policy over the economic cycle. The fiscal rules are the foundation of the Government's public spending framework, which facilitates long-term planning and provides departments with the flexibility and incentives they need to increase the quality of public services and deliver specified outcomes. These policies work together in a coherent and integrated way, and continue to deliver

unprecedented growth and stability. As the OECD recently noted, the UK economy's "strong performance is not only due to the willingness to embrace the opportunities offered by globalisation, but also to sound institutional arrangements for setting monetary and fiscal policy".

The monetary policy framework has improved the credibility of policy making and continues to deliver clear benefits. Since the new framework was introduced:
- the annual increase in inflation up to December 2003, when RPIX was used as the inflation target measure, remained close to the target value of $2\frac{1}{2}$ per cent, the longest period of sustained low inflation for the past 30 years;
- inflation expectations have remained close to target following the switch to a 2 per cent CPI target. CPI inflation has averaged 2 per cent since 2003 and has moved away from its target by more than 1 percentage point on only one occasion;
- on average the UK has had the lowest inflation in the G7 so far this decade, with the exception of Japan, which has been through a protracted period of deflation. By contrast, in the 1980s and 1990s, the UK had one of the highest inflation rates among the major economies;
- long-term interest rates have averaged 5 per cent compared

with an average of just over 9 per cent in the previous economic cycle. Alongside the UK's macroeconomic stability in recent years, the effective exchange rate has also been relatively stable. The sterling effective exchange rate remains close to levels at Budget 2004.

Since 1997, fiscal policy has resulted in low and stable borrowing, in contrast to previous UK experience. In the 1986-87 to 1997-98 economic cycle, net borrowing reached nearly 8 per cent of GDP, and averaged 3.1 per cent of GDP. During the current economic cycle, net borrowing has averaged 1.0 per cent of GDP and at its peak reached just 3.3 per cent of GDP. The fiscal framework has successfully supported economic stability by allowing the automatic stabilisers to operate. The fiscal framework has also protected an historically unprecedented increase in public sector net investment, while net debt has been maintained at a low and sustainable level.

Causes of increased stability in the UK

Since the introduction of the Government's macroeconomic framework in 1997, the UK has experienced an unprecedented period of economic stability. Both relative to the rest of the post-World War II period, and relative to other G7 countries, economic volatility in the UK is low. As the IMF stated in December 2005, "macroeconomic stability in the United Kingdom remains remarkable".

There has been considerable debate on the causes of increased stability, both in the UK and across the developed world. There is strong evidence to suggest that the Government's macroeconomic framework has contributed to increased stability by creating a more certain and predictable environment for private sector decision makers:

● the credibility of monetary policy has increased since 1997. Inflation expectations have remained close to the inflation target. Short-term interest rates have been low for the longest

sustained period since the 1950s.
● the credibility of fiscal policy has increased since 1997. The Government's fiscal policy framework has restored sound public finances, and has supported monetary policy by allowing the automatic stabilisers to operate and discretionary action to be taken where appropriate.

The extent and intensity of economic shocks could also affect stability. The UK economy has maintained stability in the face of a number of shocks with economic consequences since 1997, including: a large rise and fall in equity prices, large rises in house prices and in oil prices, wars in Afghanistan and Iraq, terrorist attacks and major economic crises in Russia and East Asia. The UK has also had to adapt to an increasingly globalised economy, with growing trade and cross border investment altering the competitive environment. Structural changes and reforms have been taking place over many years which have also played an important role in increasing the UK economy's flexibility and resilience. They include, for example, reforms to competition policy legislation and reforms to encourage the economically inactive back to work.

Source: adapted from *Full Budget Report*, March 2006 and *Pre-Budget Report*, October 2007, HM Treasury.

1. In 2006, the government stated that its 'macroeconomic framework is designed to maintain long-term economic stability'. Explain what this means.

2. Analyse, using diagrams, how the monetary policy framework has increased stability.

3. To what extent could the government avoid major economic problems in the UK if stock markets in the US crashed and the US economy went into a deep and prolonged depression?

Applied economics

The characteristics of globalisation

GLOBALISATION, from an economic perspective, can be defined as the ever increasing integration of the world's local, regional and national economies into a single international market. Economic integration can be broken into four main areas:

- free trade across national boundaries of **goods and services** so that, for example, it becomes as easy for a firm in London to sell to a firm in Poland or Vietnam as it is to sell to a firm in Birmingham, Manchester or Belfast;

- free movement of **labour** between countries, in the same way that there is currently free movement of labour within the UK or within the EU;

- free movement of **capital** between countries, so that a UK pension company might invest in China, or the Chinese central bank use some of its foreign currency reserves to invest in the USA, or a US company buy a UK company;

- free interchange of **technology** and **intellectual capital** across national boundaries; so that, for example, a South African company can licence technology from the USA on exactly the same terms as a US company; or a US firm can protect its patents in China on the same terms as it can in the USA; or a UK company can use its own patented technology in a factory in Brazil in the same way that it could in one of its UK factories.

A world where there are no boundaries to trade in goods and services and there is perfect free movement of labour, capital and technology is at one end of a spectrum. Given the many boundaries that exist today, the world is nowhere near this position. At the other end of the spectrum is a world which is narrowly localised. In this world, people live in villages or small towns. Trade is the exception and people do not move from village to village. There is no exchange of capital or technology. This is a world which to some extent existed in the past in Britain and still exists in some parts of the Third World.

The term 'globalisation' is a relatively new term and only became part of everyday economic language in the 1980s. Some argue that globalisation is simply a new term for the internationalisation of economies. Internationalisation has been taking place since trade first began thousands of years ago. In Roman times, for instance, goods were traded in Europe which had originated in Africa, India and China. In the 17th and 18th centuries the East India Company, owned by British shareholders, developed strong trade links

between Britain and India. The period 1870-1913 is sometimes called the first wave of globalisation because of the significant increase in the percentage of world GDP being traded between countries. Table 1 shows that trade then fell back between 1914 and 1950 due to two world wars and the Great Depression of the 1930s when states adopted protectionist policies. Since 1950 the rate of economic integration between world economies has accelerated. An ever larger share of world GDP is exported to other countries.

For the UK, Table 2 shows that the average annual increase in exports of traded goods and services since 1950 has been 4.6 per cent. There has been a small rise in the rate of growth of exports since 1990. Figure 1 shows UK exports of traded goods and services as a percentage of GDP. There was a significant increase in the proportion of GDP exported abroad in the 1970s, possibly due to the UK joining the European Union in 1973, but there has been no trend increase since then.

The causes of globalisation

Globalisation is being caused by a complex mix of factors, none of which on their own can account for

Table 1 World exports as a percentage of world GDP, 1870-2005

	Exports as % of GDP
1870	4.6
1913	7.9
1950	5.5
1998	17.2
2005	19.4

Source: adapted from *World Trade Report 2007*, World Trade Organisation.

Table 2 Average annual percentage increase in real exports of traded goods and services, UK

	% annual growth
1950-59	3.6
1960-69	5.1
1970-79	5.2
1980-89	3.0
1990-99	5.7
2000-06	5.5
1950-06	4.6

Source: adapted from www.statistics.gov.uk/StatsBase.

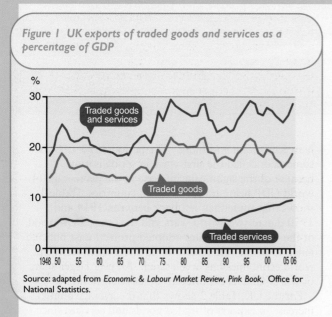

Figure 1 UK exports of traded goods and services as a percentage of GDP

Source: adapted from *Economic & Labour Market Review, Pink Book,* Office for National Statistics.

the process of globalisation. Many of the factors are interlinked. For example, trade liberalisation is causing an increase in world trade. Equally, the growth in world trade has created groups of consumers and firms which stand to benefit from further liberalisation. They then put pressure on governments to lower protectionist barriers further. Some of the causes of globalisation can be categorised in the following way.

Trade in goods For rich developed countries, goods are increasingly being manufactured abroad, many for the first time in developing countries such as China and India. This trade is occurring because developing countries are acquiring the capital equipment and the know-how to produce manufactured goods; there are efficient modes of transport to get goods to markets; and developing countries have a cost advantage in the form of very cheap labour.

Trade in services Trade in services is growing. For instance, growth in tourism is taking large numbers of visitors abroad. Call centres for customers in developed countries are being located in developing countries. India has become a world leader in writing software and then selling these skills to companies in developed countries.

Trade liberalisation Trade in goods and services is growing partly because of trade liberalisation. In the 1930s, international trade collapsed as the world went into the Great Depression and individual countries misguidedly tried to boost domestic demand by adopting fierce protectionist policies. Since 1945, protectionist barriers have gradually fallen. Lower protectionist barriers have encouraged growth in world trade.

Multinational companies Multinational (or transnational) companies have grown in number and

size. In some industries, like car manufacturing or the oil industry, this is because only large multinational companies have the economies of scale and technological knowledge to make products which are both cheap and technologically advanced. In other industries, multinational companies, particularly in food and household products, have used highly successful marketing techniques to create global brands. Coca Cola, McDonald's hamburgers, Magnum icecreams and Snickers chocolate bars are available in all five continents.

International financial flows International financial flows are becoming far greater. Countries such as China and Malaysia have financed part of their fast economic growth from inward flows of international capital.

Foreign ownership of firms Foreign ownership of firms is increasing. Many large multinational companies, for example, have invested in factories and companies in China. French firms have bought US firms. A company which started in India is now one of the world's largest steel producers after buying a number of steel companies in the developed world. Some oil rich states like Dubai, Qatar or Norway have state investment funds which buy stakes in foreign companies or purchase them outright.

Communications and IT Developments in communications and information technologies have shrunk the time needed for economic agents to communicate with each other. In industries such as software production, programmers are effectively just as near to a client's office located in, say, London if they themselves are located in India or in Kent.

The effects of globalisation

Globalisation is having a profound impact on the economies of the world. Some of these effects include the following.

Prices The relative price of goods and services is changing. Globalisation is leading to a fall in the price of some goods and services because production is being switched from high cost locations to low cost locations. For example, switching production of television sets from Wales to China will lead to a fall in labour costs because Chinese workers are prepared to work for a fraction of the wages of Welsh workers. Equally, the globalisation of technology means that a Chinese factory can employ the most advanced machines and methods of production to ensure lowest cost. However, globalisation is leading to a rise in price in some goods and services. This is because globalisation is raising average world incomes. Higher income means higher demand for individual products. Where supply is not perfectly elastic in the long run, this puts upward pressure on prices. In recent years, increased demand from China has led to a surge in commodity prices which has doubled or trebled prices of raw materials such as copper and oil.

Consumer choice The availability of goods and services has considerably increased with globalisation leading to greater consumer choice. The number of different products available in high streets, shopping centres and supermarkets is larger than it was 20 years ago. In the services market, Blackpool and Southend struggle as tourist destinations when people can go to Spain, Turkey or the Caribbean. Some argue that goods have become more homogenised. A holiday in Spain is the same as a holiday in Peru apart from the scenery. The food is 'international food', the hotels provide the same rooms and facilities, and sightseeing is packaged to suit Western tastes. Equally, the same skirt made in China may end up being bought by a girl in the UK, the USA or Japan.

Incomes Globalisation is raising world GDP. Specialisation and trade along with transfers of technology and capital are boosting production. Countries which have chosen to limit their participation in the global economy, like North Korea or Cuba, have seen their growth rates cut compared to the 1960s and 1970s.

Employment and unemployment Globalisation has seen both winners and losers in terms of employment and unemployment. For example, the transfer of much of manufacturing from Western Europe and the USA to countries such as China and Poland has led to large scale losses of jobs in these sectors in the developed world whilst there has been an increase in employment in the Third World. In Western Europe and the USA, many workers made unemployed have found new jobs, particularly in the service sector of the economy but not necessarily at the same rate of pay as before. Some have simply remained unemployed. Structural

unemployment in traditional manufacturing areas has therefore occurred. These changes, however, are not new. Throughout the Victorian era, there was a large transfer of workers from rural areas to towns and from agriculture to manufacturing and services. Globalisation might be speeding up the rate of change, but there would have been change anyway.

Income distribution Some have argued that globalisation is causing a widening of inequalities in the world. The benefits of globalisation are mainly going to the rich developed countries of the world whilst the poor in the developing world are getting poorer. The reality is far more complex because globalisation itself is a complex process. Take two examples. One is relative incomes of China compared to the USA. The Chinese economy has been growing at around 10 per cent per annum for the past 30 years whilst the US economy has only been growing at around 2.5 per cent. Inequality between China and the USA, as measured by average incomes, therefore has been falling. On the other hand, consider the wages of low skilled workers in the USA. The USA is experiencing a constant net inflow of low skill migrants particularly from Mexico and other Latin American countries. This increase in the supply of labour depresses wages at the bottom end of the US labour market and is one factor which explains why income inequalities in the USA have been rising.

Overall, the impact of globalisation on the distribution of income is dependent on two key variables: free market forces and individual government policy. They can work together for an individual country or for an individual person to lessen income inequality or widen it. For countries like South Korea or China, which have used the forces of globalisation to expand their trade, globalisation has led to rapid rises in average incomes. However, the evidence suggests that Europe and the USA are doing even better out of the trade relationship and this could

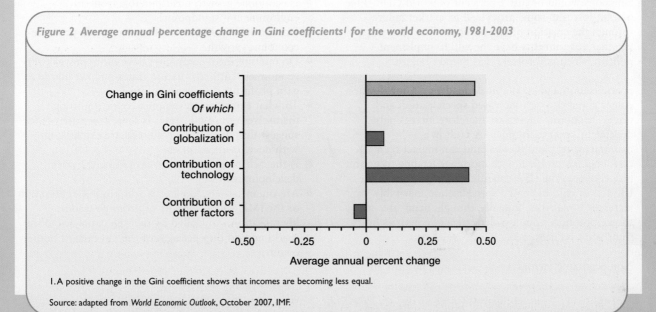

Figure 2 *Average annual percentage change in Gini coefficients¹ for the world economy, 1981-2003*

1. A positive change in the Gini coefficient shows that incomes are becoming less equal.

Source: adapted from *World Economic Outlook*, October 2007, IMF.

be leading to a widening of inequalities, particularly in comparison with countries which have not seen much expansion of their foreign trade.

It should also be remembered that globalisation is not the only factor affecting income distribution. A 2007 IMF study suggested that, using Gini coefficient data, income inequality had risen over the past twenty years, but, as Figure 2 shows, most of that was due to changes in technology. Changes in technology have disproportionately benefited skilled workers who tend to be located in developed countries. The study concluded that the contribution of trade to globalisation actually reduced income inequalities. In contrast, movements of financial capital round the globe were increasing inequalities. The study also pointed out that per capita incomes have risen across virtually all regions for even the poorest segments of the population. Absolute poverty is declining across the globe.

The environment Rising world production inevitably has an impact on the environment. If world production of wooden furniture rises, then there must be an increase in logging of trees. If world food production rises, then this must impact on the amount of land in cultivation and farming practices. If every Chinese and Indian household is to own a refrigerator, then there must be an increase in the production of iron ore and electricity. Extra demand for raw materials and increased emissions and waste have, so far, had an overall negative impact on the world environment. For example, greenhouse gas emissions continue to rise. However, environmental degradation is not inevitable and economic growth can be environmentally sustainable. Rich countries, like the UK and Sweden, have made considerable progress in many areas by using some of the proceeds of economic growth to reverse environmental degradation. The Stern Report on the environment, published in 2006, argued that the cost of stabilising greenhouse gas emissions would be just 1 per cent of world GDP. Free market forces in some areas lead to market failure through the creation of externalities. The issue is whether governments have the will to implement policies which will correct that market failure.

Specialisation and economic dependency Globalisation comes about through increased specialisation and trade. Economic agents are therefore increasingly dependent upon each other. A fault in a manufacturing plant in Thailand can impact on a UK consumer. A problem with mortgage lending to poorer households in the USA can affect interest rates in the UK and Brazil. Increased specialisation inevitably increases some risks. Equally, though, being able to source products from a wider range of countries in some ways reduces risks.

Non-economic factors Globalisation is not just an economic phenomenon. It is a political, social, technological and cultural phenomenon too. One non-economic impact is on culture. On the one hand, globalisation weakens native cultures. In particular, US culture, as seen through US films and television programmes shown throughout the world, is replacing some aspects of native culture. On the other hand, partly through migration, native cultures are spreading round the globe. Multi-cultural Britain today is very different from the Britain of the 1950s.

Politics too is affected by globalisation. Nation states have lost sovereignty, which is the ability to make choices about how their affairs are conducted. Partly this is because they have signed international treaties which limit their sovereignty. Partly it is because the forces of globalisation have become so strong that nation states cannot resist them. For example, it is difficult for a nation state to impose complete censorship on its people in the age of satellite broadcasting, the Internet or the video and DVD.

The costs and benefits of globalisation

Economists disagree about the exact costs and benefits of globalisation. For example, what are the benefits in terms of increased income; what are the environmental costs; and do the benefits of increased income outweigh these environmental costs?

Equally, there is no agreement about the extent to which it is globalisation that is bringing about these costs and benefits. For example, if the UK economy grew by 3.0 per cent last year, what proportion of this was due to globalisation? Or what proportion of the environmental degradation in Brazil is being caused by globalisation?

Arguments for and against globalisation tend to be linked to a number of other economic debates, discussed elsewhere in this book.

- Does economic growth lead to an increase in economic welfare?
- Is economic growth unsustainable from an environmental standpoint?
- Does protectionism rather than free trade promote economic growth?
- Do multinational companies have more power over economies than most nation states and act purely to gain profit for their shareholders?
- To what extent are developing countries lifting themselves out of poverty? Is there any evidence to suggest that developing countries are catching up with developed countries?
- Is the rich developed world exploiting the poor developing world?
- Are organisations, like the World Trade Organisation or the IMF, which support or promote trade liberalisation, controlled by the rich countries of the world and do they act against the interests of poorer countries?

Key terms

Globalisation - from an economic perspective, the ever increasing integration of the world's local, regional and national economies into a single international market.

DataQuestion — Globalisation

The phone in Paul Beverley's office rarely stops ringing. Last week, this producer of novelty goods took an order from a high street health chain for 105 000 odometers, another from Isle of Wight tourism bosses who wanted 50 000 island-shaped erasers, and an order from the Millennium Stadium in Cardiff for 5 000 daffodil balloons. All of them will be stamped 'Made in China'.

Source: adapted from *The Sunday Times*, 19.12.2004.

Table 3 How costs compare

	London	Hong Kong	Guangdong, China
Labour, £/hour	4.50	n/a	0.20
Office rent, £/sq ft/year	70.00	20.00	15.00
Apartment rent, £/month	3,000	2,000	500
Foreign beer, £/pint	2.50	2.50	2.00

The number of jobs created by overseas companies in the UK increased by more than half last year as the UK returned to the top of the European league table for foreign direct investment. Foreign owned businesses created 39 600 jobs in 2004-05, and foreign direct investment (FDI) was $78.5 billion. This included the £9.1 billion acquisition of Abbey National by Spain's leading bank, Santander Central Hispano.

Hans Christiansen, senior economist at the OECD, said there were several reasons for Britain's success. 'The first is simple textbook economics. The UK has been doing better on the business cycle than the continental European economies: that attracts investment. Second, the general openness of the UK economy and its proximity to the US has generated a steady stream of large mergers.'

Source: adapted from the *Financial Times*, 29.6.2005.

Figure 3 UK inward investment

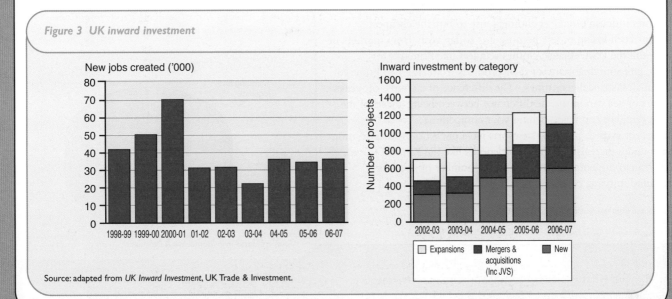

Source: adapted from *UK Inward Investment*, UK Trade & Investment.

Samsung, the Korean global conglomerate, has become the latest electronics company to quit Britain in favour of cheaper locations. It is to close its Teesside manufacturing site because of falling global prices and the lower cost of production in eastern Europe and China. The site, which employed 425 people, made flat panel PC monitors and microwave ovens. Its ordinary workers were paid £5.61 an hour compared to China and Slovakia, where the work will go, who receive respectively, 50p and £1 an hour. When the Teesside plant opened in 1995, Samsung microwaves sold for £85-£100 each, but now sell for £30. The price of flat panel screens halved last year. This year the plant is heading for a £12 million loss.

Source: adapted from the *Financial Times*, 16.1.2004.

When Beijing recently became involved in a dispute with international contractors over an infrastructure project, it turned to British barristers for advice. London-based Atkin Chambers, which was hired by the Chinese government, said the chambers' international work has increased from 30 per cent of turnover 10 years ago to about 45 per cent today.

Legal services are one of the industries that helped drive the sharp rise in services exports. But it is financial services, including banks, fund managers, insurance and securities dealers, that dominate service exports and contributed a record net £19 billion last year. No other country has enjoyed Britain's success in export earnings from its financial sector.

Source: adapted from the *Financial Times*, 12.9.2005.

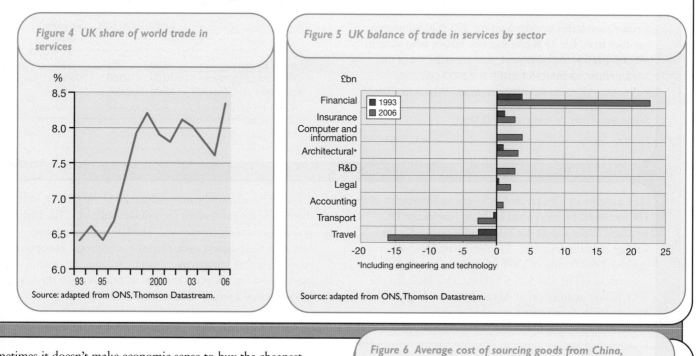

Figure 4 *UK share of world trade in services*

Source: adapted from ONS, Thomson Datastream.

Figure 5 *UK balance of trade in services by sector*

*Including engineering and technology

Source: adapted from ONS, Thomson Datastream.

Sometimes it doesn't make economic sense to buy the cheapest. China has been losing orders because it is so far away from markets in Europe and the USA. British clothes retailers like Primark, for example, are sourcing many of their products from closer to home to allow much faster delivery times. The difference of a couple of weeks transport by sea can mean the difference between being ahead of the trend in retailing and being behind your competitors.

The recent growth in China's exports have put world transportation systems under increasing stress. Bottlenecks like the Panama Canal, the US transcontinental railroads, and the number of ships have contributed to rising costs and longer delivery times.

Source: adapted from the *Financial Times*, 16.11.2004.

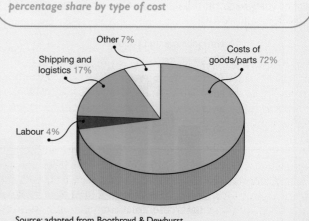

Figure 6 *Average cost of sourcing goods from China, percentage share by type of cost*

Other 7%
Costs of goods/parts 72%
Shipping and logistics 17%
Labour 4%

Source: adapted from Boothroyd & Dewhurst.

1. Explain what is meant by 'globalisation', illustrating your answer with examples from the data.
2. Analyse why globalisation is taking place, providing evidence from the data.
3. Discuss whether globalisation is having a positive impact on the UK economy today.

Summary

1. If one country has lower costs of production for a good than another country, then it is said to have an absolute advantage in the production of that good.
2. International trade will take place even if a country has no absolute advantage in the production of any good. So long as it has a comparative advantage in the production of one good, international trade will be advantageous.
3. Transport costs will limit any welfare gain from international trade. However, economies of scale in production will increase the gains from trade.
4. The terms of trade (the ratio of export prices to import prices) will determine whether trade is advantageous for a country.
5. David Ricardo thought that comparative advantage existed because of differences in labour costs between countries. In the Heckscher-Ohlin model, comparative advantage is explained by differences in factor endowments.
6. The theory of comparative advantage argues that international trade takes place because of differences in the price of products. However, much world trade is the result of non-price competition between countries. Design, reliability, availability and image are some of the factors which determine purchases of foreign goods.
7. In the theory of preference similarity, it is argued that trade takes place because consumers demand more choice than can be provided by domestic producers.

International trade

Many goods and services are traded internationally. For instance, there are international markets in oil, motor vehicles and insurance. There is a number of reasons why international trade takes place.

Differences in factor endowments Countries have different factor endowments. Saudi Arabia has large reserves of oil whilst Japan has virtually none. Costa Rica has a tropical climate suitable for growing bananas whilst the UK has a temperate climate where bananas can only be grown in artificial conditions. The USA has a large stock of skilled workers. Sudan's workforce is comparatively unskilled. The UK has a larger stock of physical capital per capita compared to Bangladesh. These differences in factor endowments lead to trade between countries. Saudi Arabia exports oil whilst Costa Rica exports bananas. The UK and the USA export high technology equipment.

Price Some countries can produce goods at a relatively cheaper cost than other countries. This may be because of the availability of natural resources, the skills of the workforce or the quality of the physical capital in the economy. There are substantial gains to be made from specialisation. Much of this unit explains this in more detail.

Product differentiation Many traded goods are similar but not identical. For instance, a small hatchback car from one motor manufacturer is very much the same as another. It will, for instance, have four wheels, four seats and an engine. However, the differences mean that some consumers in one country will want to buy a car made in another country, even if domestically produced cars are available at exactly the same price. International trade allows consumers much wider choice about the product they buy. The same basic goods or services can differ in a wide variety of ways. Specifications might be slightly different. There may be different deals on finance available. Delivery times can vary. One product may be of better quality

than another. Much of world trade is driven by a combination of these factors.

Political reasons Sometimes trade takes place or does not take place for political reasons. Countries sign trade deals with each other which lock their suppliers into doing business between each other. Or a country will place an embargo on trade with another country. For example, the USA has an embargo on most trade with Cuba and North Korea.

Economists in the 18th and 19th century developed theories centred around why differences in costs led to international trade. These theories, which will now be considered, are as relevant today as they were then.

Absolute advantage

Adam Smith, in his famous example of a pin making factory, explained how specialisation enabled an industry to increase the production of pins from a given quantity of resources. In an economy, specialisation exists at every level, from the division of labour in households to production at international level.

Consider Table 1. Assume that there are only two countries in the world, England and Portugal. They produce only two commodities, wheat and wine. Labour is the only cost, measured in terms of worker hours to produce 1 unit of output. Table 1 shows that it costs more in worker hours to produce a unit of wine in England than in Portugal. Portugal is said to have an ABSOLUTE ADVANTAGE in the production of wine. It can produce both goods but is more efficient in the production

Table 1

	Cost per unit in worker hours	
	Wheat	Wine
England	10	15
Portugal	20	10

Question 1

Table 2

	UK		France	
	Cars	Computers	Cars	Computers
(a)	10 OR	100	9 OR	108
(b)	5 OR	10	4 OR	12
(c)	20 OR	80	25 OR	75
(d)	5 OR	25	4 OR	30
(e)	6 OR	18	8 OR	16

Two countries with identical resources, UK and France, using all these resources, can produce either cars or computers or some combination of the two as shown above. Assuming constant returns to scale, state which country has an absolute advantage in the production of (i) cars and (ii) computers in each of (a) to (e) above.

of wine. On the other hand, it costs more in worker hours to produce wheat in Portugal than in England, so England has an absolute advantage in the production of wheat. It is clear that it will be mutually beneficial for England to specialise in the production of wheat and for Portugal to specialise in the production of wine and for the two countries to trade.

The same conclusion can be reached if we express relative costs in terms of absolute output. If Portugal could produce either 5 units of wheat or 10 units of wine, or some combination of the two, the relative cost of wheat to wine would be 2:1 as in Table 1. If England could produce either 9 units of wheat or 6 units of wine, the relative cost would be 3:2 as in Table 1. Hence, Portugal could produce wine more cheaply and England wheat more cheaply.

Comparative advantage

David Ricardo, working in the early part of the 19th century,

Table 3

	Cost per unit in worker hours	
	Wheat	Wine
England	15	30
Portugal	10	15

Table 4

	Production before trade		Production after trade	
	Wheat	Wine	Wheat	Wine
England (270 worker hours)	8	5	18	0
Portugal (180 worker hours)	9	6	0	12
Total	17	11	18	12

realised that absolute advantage was a limited case of a more general theory. Consider Table 3. It can be seen that Portugal can produce both wheat and wine more cheaply than England (i.e. it has an absolute advantage in both commodities). What David Ricardo saw was that it could still be mutually beneficial for both countries to specialise and trade.

In Table 3, a unit of wine in England costs the same amount to produce as 2 units of wheat. Production of an extra unit of wine means forgoing production of 2 units of wheat (i.e. the opportunity cost of a unit of wine is 2 units of wheat). In Portugal, a unit of wine costs 1½ units of wheat to produce (i.e. the **opportunity cost of** a unit of wine is 1½ units of wheat in Portugal). As relative or comparative costs differ, it will still be mutually advantageous for both countries to trade even though Portugal has an absolute advantage in both commodities. Portugal is relatively better at producing wine than wheat: so Portugal is said to have a COMPARATIVE ADVANTAGE in the production of wine. England is relatively better at producing wheat than wine: so England is said to have a comparative advantage in the production of wheat.

Table 4 shows how trade might be advantageous. Costs of production are as set out in Table 3. England is assumed to have 270 worker hours available for production. Before trade takes place it produces and consumes 8 units of wheat and 5 units of wine. Portugal has fewer labour resources with 180 worker hours of labour available for production. Before trade takes place it produces and consumes 9 units of wheat and 6 units of wine. Total production between the two economies is 17 units of wheat and 11 units of wine.

Table 5

	Output		
	Good X		Good Y
Country A	20	OR	40
Country B	50	OR	100

Question 2

Table 6

	Cost per unit in worker hours	
	Meat	Bread
UK	5	10
France	3	4

(a) Which country has comparative advantage in the production of (i) meat and (ii) bread?
(b) The UK has a total of 300 worker hours available for production whilst France has a total of 200. Before any trade took place, the UK produced and consumed 38 units of meat and 11 units of bread. France produced and consumed 20 units of meat and 35 units of bread. How much more could the two countries produce between them if each specialised and then traded?
(c) How would the answer to (a) be different, if at all, if the cost of meat and bread in France were: (i) 4 and 4; (ii) 3 and 7; (iii) 3 and 6; (iv) 6 and 12; (v) 6 and 15; (vi) 1 and 3?

If both countries now specialise, Portugal producing only wine and England producing only wheat, total production is 18 units of wheat and 12 units of wine. Specialisation has enabled the world economy to increase production by 1 unit of wheat and 1 unit of wine. The theory of comparative advantage does not say how these gains will be distributed between the two countries. This depends upon the wheat/wine exchange rate, a point discussed below.

The THEORY OF COMPARATIVE ADVANTAGE states that countries will find it mutually advantageous to trade if comparative costs of production differ. If, however, comparative costs are identical, there can be no gains from trade. Table 5 shows the maximum output of two countries, A and B, of two products, X and Y. The Table shows that country A, for instance, can either produce 20 units of good X or 40 units of good Y or some combination of both. The comparative cost or the opportunity cost of production is identical in both countries: one unit of X costs two units of Y. Hence there can be no gains from trade.

The assumptions of the theory of comparative advantage

The simple theory of comparative advantage outlined above makes a number of important assumptions.
- There are no transport costs. In reality, transport costs always exist and they will reduce and sometimes eliminate any comparative cost advantages. In general, the higher the proportion of transport costs in the final price to the consumer, the less likely it is that the good will be traded internationally.
- Costs are constant and there are no economies of scale. This assumption helps make our examples easy to understand. However, the existence of economies of scale will tend to reinforce the benefits of international specialisation. In Table 4 the gains from trade will be more than 1 unit of wheat and 1 unit of wine if England can lower the cost of production of wheat by producing more and similarly for Portugal.
- There are only two economies producing two goods. Again this assumption was made to simplify the explanation. But the theory of comparative advantage applies equally to a world with many economies producing a large number of traded goods. Table 7 shows that Chile has no absolute advantage in any product. However, it has a comparative advantage in the production of copper. Portugal has a clear comparative advantage in the production of wine whilst England has a comparative advantage in the production of apples. Exactly what and how much will be traded depends upon consumption patterns in all three countries. For instance, if neither Portugal or Chile consume apples, England will not be able to export apples to these countries.
- The theory assumes that traded goods are homogeneous (i.e. identical). Commodities such as steel, copper or wheat are

bought on price. However, a Toyota car is different from a Ford car and so it is far more difficult to conclude that, for instance, the Japanese have a comparative advantage in the production of cars.
- Factors of production are assumed to be perfectly mobile. If they were not, trade might lead to a lowering of living standards in a country. For instance, assume the UK manufactured steel but then lost its comparative advantage in steel making to Korea. UK steel making plants are closed down. If the factors of production employed in UK steel making are not redeployed, then the UK will be at less than full employment. It might have been to the UK's advantage to have kept the steel industry operating (for instance by introducing quotas) and producing something rather than producing nothing with the resources.
- There are no tariffs or other trade barriers.
- There is perfect knowledge, so that all buyers and sellers know where the cheapest goods can be found internationally.

The terms of trade

In Table 4 it was shown that England and Portugal could benefit from trade. Whether trade takes place will depend upon the TERMS OF TRADE between the two countries. From the cost data in Table 3, England could produce 2 units of wheat for every 1 unit of wine. It will only trade if it receives more than a unit of wine for every 2 units of wheat. Portugal on the other hand can produce 2 units of wheat for every 1⅓ units of wine. It will only trade if it can give England less than 1⅓ units of wine for 2 units of wheat. Hence trade will only take place if the terms of trade are between 2 units of wheat for 1 unit of wine and 2 units of wheat and 1⅓ units of wine (i.e. between 2:1 and 2:1⅓).

This is shown in Figure 1. The cost ratios of wine for two units of wheat are drawn. England will only gain from trade if the international price of wine for wheat is to the right of its existing domestic cost line. Portugal on the other hand will only gain if the international price is to the left of its domestic cost line. Hence trade will only be mutually advantageous if the terms of trade are somewhere between the two lines, the area shaded on the graph.

Question 3

Table 8

| | Cost per unit in worker hours | | | |
	DVDs	Sweaters	Beefburgers	Chocolate
England	20	10	8	20
Portugal	30	8	12	30
Chile	40	8	4	25

(a) Which country has an absolute advantage in the production of (i) DVDs; (ii) sweaters; (iii) beefburgers; (iv) chocolates?
(b) Which country has a comparative advantage in the production of (i) DVDs; (ii) sweaters; (iii) beefburgers; (iv) chocolates?

Table 7

| | Cost per unit in worker hours | | | |
	Apples	Wine	Wheat	Copper
England	10	15	20	50
Portugal	15	10	30	60
Chile	20	20	50	70

Figure 1 The terms of trade

England will find it advantageous to trade only if its terms of trade are at least 1 unit of wine for every 2 units of wheat exported. Portugal will only trade if it can receive at least 2 units of wheat for every 1⅓ units of wine exported. Therefore the terms of trade between the two countries will lie somewhere in the shaded area on the graph.

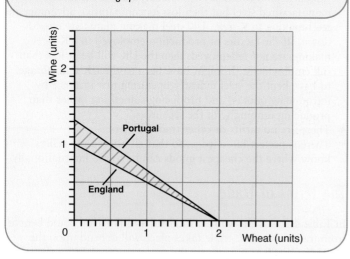

The terms of trade is defined as the ratio between export prices and import prices:

$$\text{Index of terms of trade} = \frac{\text{Index of export prices}}{\text{Index of import prices}} \times 100$$

It is an **index** because it is calculated from the weighted average of thousands of different export and import prices.

Why comparative advantage exists

David Ricardo believed that all costs ultimately could be reduced to labour costs. This belief is known as the **labour theory of value**. Hence the price of a good could accurately be measured in terms of worker hours of production. Following on from this, he argued that differences in comparative costs reflected differences in the productivity of labour.

There is an element of truth in this idea. The theory suggests that high labour productivity countries would have a comparative advantage in the production of sophisticated high technology goods whilst low labour productivity countries would have a comparative advantage in the production of low technology goods. Looking at the pattern of world trade, it is true for instance that developing countries export low technology textiles whilst developed countries export high technology computer equipment.

However, neo-classical price theory suggests that labour is not the only source of differing opportunity costs of production. For instance, the price of a piece of agricultural land can increase several times overnight if planning permission is given for residential building. This increase in value has little to do with worker hours of production. Prices and costs are, of course, linked to quantities of labour inputs, but they are also linked to forces of scarcity which can drive prices up or down.

Heckscher and Ohlin, two Swedish economists working in the inter-war period, suggested that different costs were the result not just of different labour endowments

between countries but also of different capital and land endowments. If an economy, such as India, has a large quantity of unskilled labour but little capital, then the price of capital relative to labour will be high. If, on the other hand, an economy like the USA has a large stock of capital relative to labour, then capital will be relatively cheap. Hence India will have a comparative advantage in the production of goods which can be made using unskilled labour. The USA will have a comparative advantage in the production of goods which require a relatively high capital input. Saudi Arabia is much more richly endowed with oil than France. France, on the other hand, has a rich abundance of skilled labour and capital equipment in the defence industry. Hence the theory would suggest that Saudi Arabia will specialise in producing oil, France in producing defence equipment and that the two countries will trade one product for the other.

Non-price theories of trade

The theory of comparative advantage provides a good explanation of world trade in commodities such as oil, wheat or copper. Countries with relatively rich endowments of raw materials or agricultural land specialise in the production of those commodities. It also provides a good explanation of the pattern of trade between First and Third World countries. Third World countries tend to export commodities and simple manufactured goods whilst importing more technologically sophisticated manufactures and services from the First World. However, the theory does not account for much of that half of world trade which occurs between the rich developed economies of the world.

Commodities are **homogeneous** products. There is nothing to choose between one grade of copper from Chile and the same grade from Zambia. Therefore the main determinant of demand is price. Manufactured goods and services tend to be **non-homogeneous**. Each product is slightly different. So when a consumer buys a car, price is only one amongst many factors that are considered. Reliability, availability, image, colour, shape and driving performance are just as important, if not more so. There is a wide variety of cars to choose from on the market, some produced domestically but many produced abroad. **Preference similarity theory** suggests that many manufactured goods are imported not because they are relatively cheaper than domestic goods but because some consumers want greater choice than that provided by domestic manufacturers alone. Domestic manufacturers, however, should have a competitive edge because they should be more aware of the needs of their domestic customers. This limits the extent to which foreign manufacturers can penetrate the home market.

Question 4

Look again at the data in Table 6.
(a) Show on a graph the price ratios of meat for bread in the two countries before trade.
(b) Would both countries find it mutually advantageous to trade if the international trade price ratio were 1 unit of meat for: (i) 4 units of bread; (ii) 3 units of bread; (iii) 1½ units of bread; (iv) 1 unit of bread; (v) ½ unit of bread; (vi) 2 units of bread; (vii) 1⅓ units of bread?

Question 5

For much of the first half of the 1990s, European alcoholic drinks producers saw their domestic markets as mature markets, producing little or no growth in sales. They looked to exports to grow in size. Developing a brand across international markets is a costly business. There need to be good distribution links established so that the product is available when the customer wants to buy it. Advertising, too, is essential to make customers aware of the value of the brand. Individual products are sold at premium prices. Cutting prices in times of difficulty would devalue the brand in the eyes of customers. After all, those buying Johnnie Walker whisky, Martell cognac or Pernod do so partly because they wish to show that they can afford the best drinks on the market.

In the second half of the 1990s, international drinks manufacturers were hard hit by the Asian crisis, caused by major problems in the financial systems of countries like South Korea and which led to sharp falls in GDP. For instance, Diageo saw its sales fall 40 per cent in the region. The economic rebound in 1999 and 2000 saw a sharp rise in sales, however.

Source: adapted from the *Financial Times*.

(a) Suggest why there is a market for expensive imported alcoholic drinks in countries such as Thailand, South Korea or India when there are locally produced substitutes sold at a fraction of the price.
(b) When sales fell during the Asian crisis, suggest why European drinks producers didn't respond by severely cutting prices.

Key terms

Absolute advantage - exists when a country is able to produce a good more cheaply in absolute terms than another country.
Comparative advantage - exists when a country is able to produce a good more cheaply relative to other goods produced domestically than another country.

Terms of trade - the ratio of export prices to import prices.
Theory of comparative advantage - countries will find it mutually advantageous to trade if the opportunity cost of production of goods differs.

Applied economics

UK trade flows

Table 9 UK exports and imports of traded goods and services, national income

					£ billion
	Exports		Imports		GVA[1]
	Goods	Services	Goods	Services	
1955	3.1	1.0	3.4	1.0	17.8
1965	5.0	1.6	5.2	1.7	32.8
1975	19.5	7.4	22.7	6.0	99.4
1985	78.2	23.8	81.7	17.0	321.6
1990	102.3	31.6	121.0	27.2	505.0
1995	153.6	50.6	165.6	41.6	643.7
2000	187.9	79.7	220.9	66.1	846.7
2006	244.7	124.6	322.2	95.4	1 158.9

1. Gross valued at basic prices, a measure of national income.
Source: adapted from *Economic & Labour Market Trends*, Office for National Statistics.

Total exports and imports

The UK trades in both goods and services. Table 9 shows that both exports and imports of goods have accounted for between approximately three quarters and two thirds of total exports since 1955, whilst exports and imports of services have accounted for a quarter to a third. Foreign trade has increased at a slightly faster rate than that of national income. In 1955, total exports accounted for 24 per cent of national income. By 2006, this had risen to 31.9 per cent.

Visible trade

Although the proportion of trade in goods to services has remained broadly the same in the post-war era, there

Table 10 Exports and imports by commodity (% of total value)

		1955	1975	1985	1995	2006
Food, beverages	Exports	6.0	7.1	6.3	7.3	4.5
and tobacco	Imports	36.9	18.0	10.6	9.4	7.6
Basic materials	Exports	3.9	2.7	2.7	1.9	2.0
	Imports	29.0	8.4	6.0	3.9	2.4
Fuels	Exports	4.9	4.2	21.5	6.5	10.3
	Imports	10.6	17.5	12.8	3.7	9.8
Total food and	Exports	14.8	14.0	30.5	15.7	16.8
raw materials	Imports	76.5	43.9	29.4	17.0	19.8
Semi-	Exports	36.9	31.2	25.6	28.3	26.6
manufactured	Imports	17.9	23.9	24.8	27.3	21.2
Finished	Exports	43.5	51.0	41.2	54.8	56.0
manufactured	Imports	5.3	29.9	44.0	54.7	58.4
Total	Exports	80.4	82.2	66.8	83.1	82.6
manufactures	Imports	23.2	53.8	68.8	82.0	79.6
Unclassified	Exports	4.8	3.8	2.7	1.2	0.5
	Imports	0.3	2.7	1.8	1.0	0.6

Source: adapted from *Annual Abstract of Statistics, Monthly Digest of Statistics*, Office for National Statistics.

have been some significant shifts in the composition of trade in goods. Table 10 gives a breakdown of visible trade (trade in goods) by commodity.

- Exports of fuel, nearly all of which is oil and related products, grew from less than 5 per cent in 1975 to 21.5 per cent of total visible exports by 1985. This was due to North Sea oil which first came on stream in 1976. The importance of oil exports declined from the mid-1980s. Partly this was because volumes of oil extracted from the North Sea remained relatively static whilst other export volumes have been growing at over 3 per cent per year. Partly it was because real oil prices fell. Finally, there was considerable downstream investment in new refineries which meant that more North Sea oil was bought and sold in the UK. This had the effect of reducing North Sea oil exports and also reducing imports of crude oil. However, the jump in the value of fuel exports and imports shown in Figure 10 for fuel was caused by the commodity price boom which started in 2002-2003. Oil prices shot up and caused a major shift in the relative importance of fuel to both exports and imports. High oil prices should stimulate oil exploration and development in the North Sea and may increase oil production and exports in 5 -10 years time.

- Imports of food and raw materials declined from 76.5 per cent of the total in 1955 to 19.8 per cent in 2006. In the Victorian age, Britain was known as the 'workshop of the world', importing raw materials and exporting manufactured goods. This fall would suggest that the UK has lost comparative advantage in the production of manufactured goods.

- This loss of comparative advantage in manufactured goods is clear from import figures for manufactures. In 1955, manufactures accounted for only 23.2 per

cent of imports. By 2006, this had risen to 79.6 per cent.

The decline of British manufacturing industry relative to its industrial competitors goes back 100 years. At the turn of the 20th century, many commentators were pointing out how French, German and US manufacturers were overtaking UK firms on both price and quality. In the 1960s and 1970s, industries such as the motor cycle industry and electrical goods were decimated by competition from Japan. Britain's textile industry, once one of the country's most important exporters, has shrunk due to competition, first from Europe and then from Third World countries. In contrast, there have been some success stories such as pharmaceuticals. Inward investment in the 1970s, 1980s and 1990s also transformed the competitiveness of industries such as motor manufacturing and electrical goods.

The theory of comparative advantage is often expressed in terms of relative costs of production. Whilst it is clear that the UK's loss of competitiveness in industries such as textiles has been due to higher relative costs, this is less obvious in industries such as motor manufacturing. Here, poor quality, unreliability, poor design and long delivery dates were key to the destruction of the industry in the 1970s and 1980s. Equally, high quality, reliability and good design were an essential part of the story of the revival of the British motor manufacturing industry in the 1990s and 2000s.

The loss of UK competitiveness in manufactured goods could be argued to be unimportant if manufactures can be replaced by services. However, as Table 9 shows, growth in trade in services in the post-war period has been roughly the same as growth in trade in goods. Table 9 also shows that for every 1 per cent fall in exports in goods, services exports need to grow by 2 per cent to fill the gap. This would be very difficult to achieve over a period of time, so exports of goods, particularly manufactures, are the most important way in

Table 11 Trade in services

				£ billion
	1975	1985	1995	2006
Exports				
Transport	3.4	6.1	10.2	16.7
Travel	1.2	5.4	13.0	18.3
Financial and insurance			7.9	31.9
	2.9	12.1		
Other			18.8	57.7
Total	7.5	23.6	49.9	124.6
Imports				
Transport	3.3	6.4	10.7	19.4
Travel	0.9	4.9	15.8	34.3
Financial and insurance			1.6	6.8
	1.5	4.6		
Other			13.4	34.9
Total	5.7	15.9	41.5	95.4

Source: adapted from the Blue Book, *National Income Accounts Quarterly*, Office for National Statistics; the Pink Book, *United Kingdom Balance of Payments*, Office for National Statistics.

Table 12 *Income and current transfers*

						£ billion
		1955	1975	1985	1995	2006
Income	Credits	0.5	6.5	51.4	88.1	241.1
	Debits	0.4	6.1	52.4	85.9	222.8
Current transfers	Credits	0.2	0.8	4.7	12.6	16.2
	Debits	0.1	1.1	7.6	20.1	28.1

Source: adapted from the Pink Book, *United Kingdom Balance of Payments*, Office for National Statistics.

which imports are financed and are likely to remain so.

Trade in services

Table 11 shows the composition and change in trade in services since 1975. In 2006, the UK ran a deficit on transport and tourism. For instance, UK citizens spent more on foreign holidays than foreigners taking a holiday in the UK. However, the UK has a significant comparative advantage in financial services and insurance. London is arguably the most important financial centre in the world and provides a wide range of services to foreign customers. Its comparative advantage, despite fierce competition from centres such as New York, Tokyo or Frankfurt, would seem to have grown in recent years, with financial services and insurance taking an increasing proportion of total service exports.

Income and current transfers

There is a third type of flow which forms part of the current account of the balance of payments. This is income and current transfers.

- Income is interest, profits and dividends on overseas assets. Foreigners own assets in the UK and take out income from the UK. This is a debit on the current account. Equally, UK firms and individuals own assets abroad and bring back income to the UK. This is a credit on the current account. Assets include financial assets, such as loans or shareholdings, or physical assets such as property or factories.
- Current transfers are transfers of income. This is made up of payments and receipts between the UK government and other bodies and the European Union (EU). For instance, all customs duties collected in the UK are paid to the EU. On the other hand, the EU pays large subsidies to UK farmers. The EU Social Fund gives grants to deprived regions of the UK.

Table 12 shows the UK has tended to receive more in income and current transfers than it has paid out. Income is in fact vitally important for the UK and in the 2000s has been the single most important contributor to the financing of the large deficit in the trade in goods that the UK tends to record. In 2006, income was one third of the value of all credits on the current account (i.e. the value of traded exports of goods and services, income and current transfers) and 24 per cent of all debits as Figure 3 shows. It is as if a household paid

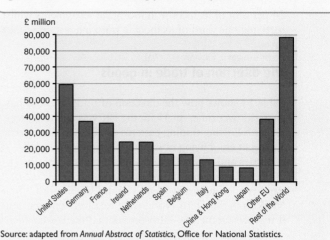

Figure 2 *The UK's main trading partners, exports 2006*

Source: adapted from *Annual Abstract of Statistics*, Office for National Statistics.

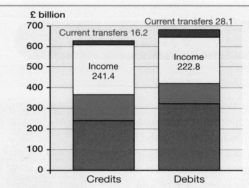

Figure 3 *Credits and debits on the current account, 2006*

Source: adapted from the Pink Book, *United Kingdom Balance of Payments*, Office for National Statistics.

Table 13 *Trade¹ by area*

				Percentage of total	
		1955	1975	1995	2006
Europe	Exports	31.9	51.3	60.5	61.8
	Imports	31.0	53.8	63.3	65.9
of which EU²	Exports	26.8	41.1	49.5	55.5
	Imports	25.9	45.1	51.0	57.3
North America	Exports	11.3	12.1	15.6	17.8
	Imports	19.8	13.5	15.3	11.4
Other developed countries³	Exports	15.3	9.6	5.8	4.8
	Imports	12.4	8.0	7.0	4.8
of which Japan	Exports	0.5	1.6	3.0	2.2
	Imports	0.6	2.8	5.0	2.5
Rest of the World	Exports	41.5	27.0	18.1	15.6
	Imports	36.8	24.7	14.4	???
of which China	Exports	-	-	0.5	1.3
	Imports	-	-	1.0	3.8

Source: adapted from *Annual Abstract of Statistics*; Office for National Statistics; *Monthly Digest of Statistics*, Office for National Statistics; the Pink Book, *United Kingdom Balance of Payments*, Office for National Statistics.

1 1955 and 1975 data are trade in goods only. 1995 and 2004 data are trade in goods and services.
2 Includes all 1995 EU countries in 1955 and 1975 percentages; 2006 data is for EU 27 members in that year.
3 Australia, New Zealand, Japan, South Africa.

24 per cent of its income in mortgage repayments whilst receiving one third of its income from interest on money saved.

The direction of trade in goods

Table 13 shows how the direction of trade in goods has changed over time. In 1955, the UK was still to a great extent following trading patterns established during the Victorian era, buying raw materials from developing countries and selling them manufactured goods. By 2006, UK trade had shifted dramatically. Over half of exports and imports were now with EU countries. Markets in the Third World were relatively unimportant. It has been argued by Eurosceptics that the UK could withdraw from the EU and rely more on its US trading connections. The UK would become the equivalent of Hong Kong or Singapore, a free trading nation benefiting from its geographical location. The problem with this idea, as Figure 2 and Table 13 show, is that the USA is a relatively unimportant trading partner with the UK. Assume that the UK left the EU and as a result the EU imposed higher tariffs and quotas on the UK. If Britain lost just 10 per cent of its exports to the EU as a result, it would have to increase exports by one third to the United States to compensate for this. It is most unlikely that UK exporters have such a comparative advantage that they could achieve this. Certainly from a trade viewpoint, Europe is vital to UK economic interests and is likely, if anything, to increase in importance over time.

DataQuestion — UK manufacturing

Mass production in Britain and other developed countries is over, according to a report published today by the EEF engineering organisation. Cheap labour costs and low cost of transport mean that countries such as China and Thailand can undercut prices for easy to produce, large volume products. However, manufacturing can still thrive in the UK. Successful manufacturing companies have turned to making specialist products for narrow market niches, where volumes are often small but design and quality are high and competition is low.

Source: adapted from the *Financial Times* 13.12.2004.

Peter Weidenbaum is moving his water filter manufacturing operation in Thailand back to his headquarters in Radcliffe, Manchester. His company, Trumeter, has been manufacturing measuring and monitoring equipment in north west England since 1937. The move back to England is the result of a £1.5 million investment in new machinery following a five year order from a German company. Automation of processes will cut the number of people required on the assembly line from 67 to 5. Peter Weidenbaum says: 'We have been able to move because there is now such a small labour component to the product. Our customer also feels comfortable with this because we don't have the quality assurance issues we sometimes experienced in south east Asia.'

Source: adapted from the *Financial Times*, 6.7.2004.

Halifax Fan makes 1 800 fans a year, most of them different, selling from between £200 to £200 000 each. 'Virtually all of them require some special engineering design to fit the product to the requirement of the customer' says Malcolm Staff, managing director. About 70 per cent of the company's fans are exported directly or indirectly.

Source: adapted from the *Financial Times*, 13.12.2004.

1. Using the concept of comparative advantage, explain why much production of mass produced manufactured goods has moved to countries such as China or Poland, whilst production of specialised low volume products has remained in countries such as the UK.
2. As countries such as China become more developed, discuss whether the UK could retain any comparative advantage in manufacturing.

Sovrin Plastics is a company in Slough which makes plastic parts for industries such as medical equipment and electronics. With annual sales of £7 million and a workforce of 135, it has found the trading environment tough in recent years. The main problem has been that many of the company's products can be made in countries such as Poland where labour costs are a quarter of those in the UK. 'In the past few years, we have lost a lot of work, both potential and actual orders, to low-cost countries' according to Mr Joiner, Sovrin's managing director. Sovrin's answer has been to move into making more customised parts that are particularly hard to produce and are manufactured in small volumes. It has also invested £600 000 in new machinery.

Source: adapted from the *Financial Times* 10.3.2005.

83 Trade policy

3.4.3

Summary

1. Although the gains from trade can be large, all countries choose to adopt protectionist policies to some extent.
2. Tariffs, quotas, voluntary export agreements and safety standards are some of the many ways in which countries limit free trade in goods and services.
3. The infant industry argument is one argument used to justify protectionism. It is claimed that young industries need protection if they are to survive the competition of larger, more established industries in other countries. When the industry has grown sufficiently, barriers can be removed.
4. It is claimed that protectionism can save jobs. However, there is a great danger that the erection of barriers for this purpose will lead to retaliation by other trading nations, resulting in an overall welfare loss.
5. Protection against dumping will only lead to a gain in long run welfare for a nation if the dumping is predatory.
6. One valid argument in favour of protectionist policies is if the importing country is a monopsonist. The imposition of tariffs will lead to a fall in the price of imports, leading to a gain in welfare for the nation at the expense of foreign suppliers and an improvement in the terms of trade.

The benefits of trade

Economists today tend to favour FREE TRADE between countries. Free trade occurs when there are no barriers to trade, such as taxes on imported goods or bans on imports. Free trade is beneficial for a number of reasons.

Specialisation The theory of **comparative advantage** shows that world output can be increased if countries specialise in what they are relatively best at producing. It makes little point, for instance, for the UK to grow bananas given its climate when they can be grown much more cheaply in Latin America. Equally, it makes little sense for Barbados to manufacture motor vehicles given the size of the island, the relatively small population, the small domestic market and its geographical location.

Economies of scale Trade allows economies of scale to be maximised and thus costs reduced. Economies of scale are a source of comparative advantage. Small countries can buy in goods and services which are produced in bulk in other countries, whilst themselves specialising in producing and exporting goods where they have developed economies of scale.

Choice Trade allows consumers the choice of what to buy from the whole world, and not just from what is produced domestically. Consumer welfare is thus increased because some consumers at least will prefer to buy foreign goods rather than domestic goods.

Innovation Free trade implies competition. A lack of free trade often leads to domestic markets being dominated by a few firms who avoid competition amongst themselves. Competition provides a powerful incentive to innovate. Not only are new goods and services being put onto the market, but firms are also competing to find production methods which cut costs and improve the quality and reliability of goods. A few firms are at the forefront of innovation in their industries. In a competitive market, however, other firms copy this innovation to remain competitive. The few countries in the world which for political reasons have chosen to isolate themselves from trade and attempt to be self-sufficient, like North Korea, have found that over time their economies have tended to stagnate. On their own, they simply do not have the resources or the incentives to keep up with the pace of innovation in the outside world.

The costs of trade

Trade between countries can be beneficial, but it can also have costs.

Overdependence Countries can become overdependent on foreign trade. Small countries in particular can become dependent on exports of one or two commodities. If the prices of those commodities fall, or demand falls, then these countries can experience large falls in GDP. Trade also opens the risk that imports will be cut for political reasons. The first oil crisis of 1973-5, for example, was caused by the threat of a refusal by Arab states to supply oil to Western countries selling arms to Israel.

Jobs Changes in demand can lead to unemployment. For example, parts of the UK suffered structural unemployment during the second half of the twentieth century as primary and manufacturing industries shrank in size due to competition from imports. The less mobile the workforce, the greater the likelihood that changes in demand due to trade will reduce output and employment over long periods of time.

Risk Trade exposes a country to many risks. Demand for a country's exports can suddenly fall or their prices can fall. Supplies can be cut by foreign countries. There can be credit crises which cut off finance for a country to pay for imports. The cost of borrowing to buy imports can suddenly rise.

Distribution of income Trade can lead to a less equal distribution of income. If the benefits of trade go mainly to other countries, then a country may find

583

itself relatively less well off. Equally, trade alters patterns of demand within a country. The benefits of trade may go mainly to rich elites within a country and the poor may even end up worse off. This widens inequality within a trading country.

The environment Trade can lead to environmental degradation and unsustainable development. Demand for timber, for example, has led to large scale deforestation in the developing world.

Loss of sovereignty Trade leads to nation states losing sovereignty. This means they lose the ability to make decisions about matters which affect them. The loss of sovereignty may be explicit because a government signs an international treaty. For example, the UK has lost sovereignty by joining the EU. Or it may be because the complex network of private trade gives power to foreign companies or foreign consumers.

Loss of culture Trade brings foreign ideas and products to an individual country. Some argue that this leads to a loss of rich traditional native culture.

Question 1

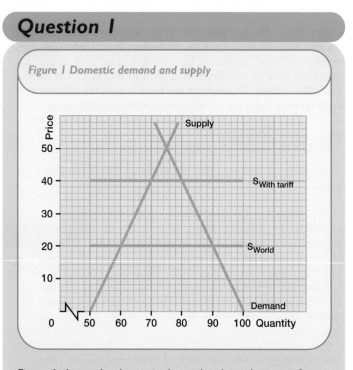

Figure 1 Domestic demand and supply

Figure 1 shows the domestic demand and supply curves for a good.
(a) What is the equilibrium price and quantity demanded and supplied domestically?
(b) The country starts to trade internationally. The international price for the product shown is 20. The country can import any amount at this price. What is:
(i) the new level of demand; (ii) the new level of domestic supply; (iii) the quantity imported?
(c) The government, alarmed at the loss of jobs in the industry, imposes a tariff of 20 per unit. By how much will: (i) domestic demand fall; (ii) domestic supply rise; (iii) imports fall?
(d) What would happen if the government imposed a tariff of 40 per unit?

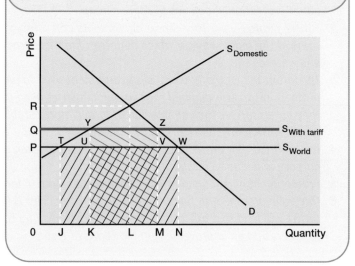

Figure 2 Tariffs
If the world price of a good is OP, a tariff of PQ will shift the supply curve upwards from S_{World} to $S_{With\ tariff}$. Domestic consumption will fall by MN whilst domestic production will rise by JK. Imports will fall from JN to KM.

Methods of protection

If a government decides that the costs of free trade outweigh the benefits, there is a large number of ways in which it can erect TRADE BARRIERS.

Tariffs A TARIFF is a tax on imported goods. It is sometimes called an IMPORT DUTY or a CUSTOMS DUTY. Tariffs can be used by governments to raise revenue to finance expenditure. However, they are most often used in a deliberate attempt to restrict imports. A tariff, by imposing a tax on a good, is likely to raise its final price to the consumer (although occasionally a foreign supplier will absorb all the tariff to prevent this from happening). A rise in the price of the good will lead to a fall in demand and the volume of imports will fall. A tariff should also help domestic producers. Some consumers will switch consumption from imported goods to domestically produced substitutes following the imposition of a tariff. For instance, if the UK imposed a tariff on sugar cane imports, British produced sugar beet would become more competitive and demand for it would rise.

This is shown in Figure 2. D is the domestic demand for a good. $S_{Domestic}$ is the domestic supply curve of the product. With no foreign trade, equilibrium output would occur where domestic demand and supply were equal at 0L. However, with foreign trade, world producers are assumed to be prepared to supply any amount of the product at a price of 0P. Consumers will now buy imported goods because the world price 0P is below the domestic price of 0R. Domestic supply will fall back along the supply curve to 0J. Demand for the good will rise to 0N. Imports must be JN if demand is 0N and domestic supply is 0J.

Now assume that the government of the country imposes a tariff of PQ per unit. The price to domestic consumers will rise to 0Q. Domestic producers will not pay the tariff. Therefore they find it profitable to expand production to 0K. Higher prices cause demand to fall to 0M. Hence imports will only be KM. Expenditure on imports will fall from JTWN (price JT

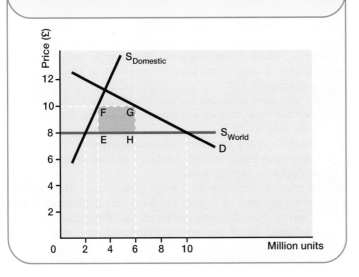

times quantity bought JN) to KYZM. Of that area KYZM, KUVM will be the revenue gained by foreign firms. The rest, UYZV, is the tax collected on the imports and will therefore go to the government.

Quotas A QUOTA is a physical limit on the quantity of a good imported. It is an example of a **physical control**. Imposing a limit on the quantity of goods imported into a country will increase the share of the market available for domestic producers. However, it will also raise the price of the protected product.

This is shown in Figure 3. The world supply price of a product is £8. Domestic demand shown by the demand curve D is 10 million units. Of that, 2 million is produced domestically. The remaining 8 million is imported. Now assume that a quota of 3 million units is imposed on imports. Because output is now 4 million units less than it would otherwise have been, price will rise to £10. Domestic production will rise to 3 million units. Domestic consumption is 6 million units. The rise in price has led to a reduction in demand of 4 million units. It should be noted that quotas, unlike tariffs, can lead to gains by importers. It is true in Figure 3 that foreign firms have lost orders for 4 million units. But those firms which have managed to retain orders have gained. They used to sell their units for £8. They can now get £10. This is a windfall gain for them, shown on the diagram by the rectangle EFGH.

Other restrictions There is a considerable number of other trade barriers which countries can erect against foreign imports. In the 1970s and 1980s, there was widespread use of **Voluntary Export Agreements**. These are a type of quota which is enforced by importers. For instance, the UK had an agreement with Japanese car manufacturers that they should not take more than 10 per cent of the UK car market. Another widespread barrier is non-competitive purchasing by governments. They are major buyers of goods and services and most governments around the world have a policy of buying only from domestic producers even if this means paying higher prices. Meeting different safety standards can lead to higher costs of production for importers. Simple tactics like lengthy delays at customs posts can also deter imports.

Arguments used to justify protection

The theory of comparative advantage states that there are major welfare gains to be made from free trade in international markets. However, protectionism has always been widespread. What arguments can be put forward to justify protectionist policies?

The infant industry argument This is one of the oldest arguments in favour of protection. Industries just starting up may well face much higher costs than foreign competitors. Partly this is because there may be large economies of scale in the industry. A new low volume producer will find it impossible to compete on price against an established foreign high volume producer. Once it is sufficiently large, tariff barriers can be removed and the industry exposed to the full heat of foreign competition. There may also be a learning curve. It takes some time for managers and workers in a new industry to establish efficient operational and working practices. Only by protecting the new industry can it compete until the

Question 2

President George Bush has decided to abandon the tariffs he put in place 20 months ago on steel imports. The import tariffs of between 8 and 30 per cent were designed to protect the US steel industry and steel jobs from fierce foreign competition. The US industry had argued that it needed protection to give it time to restructure, make investments and reduce costs in order to remain competitive against foreign imports.

The EU and Japan took the US to the World Trade Organisation (WTO) which ruled the tariffs illegal. The EU responded to the WTO judgment by threatening to impose tariffs on up to $2.2 billion worth of exports from the United States if the tariffs were not withdrawn immediately. The tariffs would have been placed on EU imports of orange juice and citrus products from Florida, motor cycles, farm machinery, textiles, shoes and other products.

US steel executives have said they feel betrayed by the repeal. Unions and the industry plan to organise a 'strong and negative response'. On the other hand, US steel customers, such as US car and car component manufacturers, were quietly relieved that tariffs were being removed since they had added to their costs.

Source: adapted from the *Washington Post*, 1.12.2003.

(a) Explain, using the example of the US steel industry, what is meant by a 'tariff'.
(b) Analyse, using a diagram, why US steel manufacturers were in favour of tariffs whilst US steel customers were against the tariffs.
(c) Who would have benefited and who would have suffered if the US government had decided to maintain tariffs on steel imports in December 2003?

Question 3

Chinese shoe manufacturers have increased their exports to the European Union by almost 700 per cent since trade restrictions were abolished in January. European shoe manufacturers have called for immediate action to stop the flood of shoes onto the market. Adolfo Urso, deputy Italian industry minister, has urged the EU Commission to 'intervene urgently' to defend Italy's shoe industry. 'It's a red alert for the import of shoes from China. The situation is dramatic for this vital component of the Made in Italy export sector' he said. 'Italy is ready to do battle in Europe to ensure commercial rules are respected' said Rossano Soldini, president of the Italian shoemaking association. He said that the industry could lose up to 40 000 of 101 000 jobs this year if China's import boom continued.

A spokesperson for Peter Mandelson, EU trade commissioner, said Brussels would look into industry complaints of dumping 'as a matter of urgency'. 'If products were exported at below the cost of production, we would not hesitate to take action', she said. This would probably mean the imposition of anti-dumping duties on imports of Chinese shoes.

Source: adapted from the *Financial Times*, 9.7.2005.

(a) What is meant by (a) 'dumping' and (b) 'duties on imports'?
(b) Discuss why European shoe manufacturers are arguing that duties should be imposed on Chinese shoes.
(c) To what extent would Europe gain from the imposition of duties on Chinese shoes?

'learning' benefits come through.

Some countries, such as Japan, have successfully developed infant industries behind high trade barriers. It is also true that many countries such as the UK have financial systems which tend to take a short view of investment. It is difficult, if not impossible, to find backers for projects which might only become profitable in 10 or even 5 years' time.

However, infant industries in general have not grown successfully behind trade barriers. One problem is that government needs to be able to identify those infant industries which will grow successfully. Governments have a poor record of picking such 'winners'. Second, industries protected by trade barriers lack the competitive pressure to become efficient. Infant industries all too often grow up to be lame duck industries. They only carry on operating because they have become skilled at lobbying government to maintain high trade barriers. Third, it is usually more efficient to use other policy weapons if a government genuinely wishes to encourage the development of a new industry. Specific subsidies, training grants, tax concessions, or even the creation of state enterprises, are likely to be better ways of creating new industries.

Job protection Another argument with a very long history is the idea that protectionism can create or at least preserve jobs. During the 1970s, the share of the UK car market taken by domestic car manufacturers shrank drastically. It would have been possible to erect trade barriers against foreign imported cars to preserve jobs in the motor car industry. However, there are two major problems with this policy. Firstly, although the policy may benefit manufacturers and their workers, consumers are likely to have less choice and pay

higher prices. Much of the gain for producers is an internal transfer of resources from domestic consumers. Moreover, foreign countries could retaliate by imposing trade restrictions on exports, leading to a loss of jobs in the domestic economy. If they do, then all countries participating in the trade war will suffer. Production will be switched from lower cost to higher cost producers, resulting in a loss of welfare for consumers. The gains from trade resulting from comparative advantage will be lost.

Dumping DUMPING can be defined in a number of ways. Broadly speaking it is the sale of goods below their cost of production, whether marginal cost, average total cost, or average variable cost. Foreign firms may sell products 'at a loss' for a variety of reasons.
- They may have produced the goods and failed to find a market for them, so they are dumped on one country in a distress sale.
- In the short run, a firm may have excess capacity. It will then sell at a price below average total cost so long as that price at least covers its variable cost.
- Low prices could represent a more serious long term threat to domestic industry. A foreign producer may deliberately price at a loss to drive domestic producers out of business. Once it has achieved this, it can increase prices and enjoy monopoly profits.

Goals of long term domination by a foreign producer might justify trade barriers, although it might be more efficient to subsidise domestic industries. It is more difficult to say whether short term distress dumping leads to a loss of domestic welfare. On the one hand, domestic producers and their workers may suffer a loss of profits and wages. The impact on employment should be limited if dumping is only a short term phenomenon. On the other hand, consumers gain by being able to buy cheap goods, even if only for a limited period.

Cheap labour Countries which have plentiful sources of cheap labour are often accused of 'unfair competition'. High labour cost countries find it difficult if not impossible to compete against products from these countries and there is pressure from threatened industries to raise trade barriers. However, cheap labour is a source of comparative advantage for an economy. There is a misallocation of resources if domestic consumers are forced to buy from high wage domestic industries rather than low wage foreign industries. Resources which are used in high cost protected industries could be used elsewhere in the economy to produce products for which the country does have a comparative advantage in production.

The terms of trade One argument in favour of tariffs for which an economic case can be made is the optimal tariff argument. In Figure 2 it was assumed that a country could import any amount at a given price because it was a relatively small buyer on the world market. However, if a country imports a significant proportion of world production, then it is likely to face an upward sloping supply curve. The more it buys, the higher the price per unit it will have to pay. At the extreme, the country may be a **monopsonist** (i.e. the sole buyer of a product).

If the country faces an upward sloping supply curve, the marginal cost of buying an extra unit will not only be the cost of the extra unit but also the extra cost of buying all other units. For instance, a country buys 10 units at £1. If it buys an eleventh unit, the price rises to £11. The cost of the eleventh

Question 4

Researchers in Thailand, India and Australia claim that excessively strict hygiene standards are increasingly being used to block food imports from developing countries. The world's leading 10 food producers are all developing countries and the main markets are the European Union, the USA and Japan. Food scares are one problem. For example, the UN Food and Agriculture Organisation reported recently that one third of global meat exports were threatened by outbreaks of bird flu and mad cow disease. 'If current bans were extended to the end of the year, trade worth up to $10 billion would be lost', it added. A World Bank study found that trade in cereals and nuts would increase by $12 billion if all 15 importing countries adopted the international Codex standards for aflatoxin contamination, which is produced by a cancer-linked mould, than if they all abided by tougher EU requirements.

Source: adapted from the *Financial Times*, 6.4.2004.

(a) According to the article, what justification is often given for blocking imports of food into the EU, the USA and Japan?
(b) Why might EU farmers benefit from such bans?
(c) Explain who are likely to be net losers from these bans.

unit is therefore £11 plus 10 x £1 - a total of £21. The decision to buy the eleventh unit will be made by individual producers and consumers. The cost to them of the eleventh unit is just £11 - the other £10 extra is borne by the producers and consumers who bought the other 10 units.

Therefore the marginal cost to the economy as a whole of buying an extra unit of imports is greater than the marginal cost to the individual. But it is the individual which makes the decision about whether to buy or not. If the marginal cost of purchase is lower for the individual than for the economy as a whole, more imports will be bought than if the individual had to pay the whole cost of purchase (i.e. the cost including the increased price of previously purchased units). This would suggest that a tariff which increased prices to the point where the cost to the individual purchaser was equal to the cost borne by society as a whole of that decision would increase economic welfare.

Imposition of a tariff will reduce demand for imported goods, and this in turn will lead to a fall in the price of imported goods (a tariff is an indirect, ad valorem or specific tax which shifts the supply curve for imported goods to the left, resulting in a fall in equilibrium price received by suppliers). Hence the terms of trade (the ratio between export prices and import prices) will rise in favour of the importing country. The importing country will be able to buy goods more cheaply. But it is important to remember that this gain will be at the expense of the exporting country. If, for instance, the UK imposed a tariff on tea, the price of tea might fall. The UK will gain but only at the expense

of, say, India and Sri Lanka. Also, if the exporting country retaliates by imposing its own tariffs, both countries could be worse off than before.

Other arguments A number of other arguments are put forward in favour of trade barriers. It is sometimes argued that a country needs a particular domestic industry for defence purposes. A country may wish to preserve a particular way of life, such as preventing depopulation of remote rural areas heavily dependent upon a particular agricultural product. It may be felt that some imports are too dangerous to be sold domestically. 'Dangerous' could range from unsafe electrical products to toxic waste to drugs. Alternatively, a country may decide that it is too dependent upon one industry. Some small Third World countries depend crucially upon one cash crop such as cocoa, bananas or sugar cane for their economic well being. These commodities are subject to large fluctuations in price on world markets. Falls in price can give rise to large falls in living standards in these economies. Diversifying, even if the newly established industries are uneconomic by world standards, could provide a valuable insurance policy against commodity price fluctuations. Trade barriers are one means of sheltering these industries from foreign competition.

In all of this, however, it is important to question whether trade barriers are the best means of achieving the desired objective. Economists tend to argue that other policies, such as subsidising industries, are likely to be more efficient than trade protection.

Key terms

Dumping - the sale of goods at less than cost price by foreign producers in the domestic market.
Free trade - international trade conducted without the existence of barriers to trade, such as tariffs or quotas.
Tariff, import duty or customs duty - a tax on imported goods which has the effect of raising the domestic price of imports and thus restricting demand for them.
Trade barriers - any measure which artificially restricts international trade.
Quota - a physical limit on the quantity of an imported group.

Applied economics

WTO and protectionism

Economic theory suggests that free trade is likely to benefit countries. By allowing each country to specialise, production will take place in locations which enjoy a comparative advantage. World trade expanded in the 19th century. As Figure 4 shows, though, the first half of the twentieth century saw a fall in trade. This was partly caused by the economic disruption of two world wars. The Great Depression of the 1930s also led countries to adopt deeply protectionist policies. Governments mistakenly believed that by keeping foreign goods out, they could save domestic jobs. In practice, all countries adopted the same mix of measures. World trade collapsed, jobs were lost in export industries and consumers were left having to pay higher prices to inefficient domestic producers when before they could buy goods from overseas at cheaper prices.

After the Second World War, there was a general recognition that these protectionist policies had been self-defeating. The Bretton Woods system of exchange rates banned competitive devaluations, whilst 23 countries in 1947 signed the General Agreement on Tariffs and Trade (GATT). Under GATT rules, member countries were not allowed to increase the degree of protection given to their domestic producers. Also, under the **most-favoured nation** clause of the agreement, a country which offered a cut in tariffs to one country had to offer the same terms to all member countries.

GATT rules prevented protection increasing, but did nothing to reduce protectionism. For this reason, GATT, and its successor organisation, the WTO (World Trade Organisation), have, over the years, organised a series of negotiations (called 'rounds') aimed at reducing tariffs and quotas. By the end of the Tokyo round of negotiations in 1979, the average tariff on industrial goods had fallen to 4.7 per cent. Between 1986 and 1994 an eighth round of negotiations, the Uruguay Round, was successfully completed. In this round, unlike previous rounds, agreements were made not just on trade of manufactures, but also agriculture and services.

● In agriculture, non-tariffs barriers, such as quotas, were dismantled and replaced by tariffs. This was intended to make the level of protectionism more transparent.
● In manufactures, the single most important agreement was dismantling protectionist barriers in textiles and garments from 2005. This has led to a substantial increase in exports, particularly from China, since then.
● In services, copyright and royalty fee agreements were tightened up, and a start made in opening up highly protected services industries such as finance and telecommunications.

The various trade rounds have been a powerful influence in expanding trade in the post-war period. Figure 5 shows that world exports of goods rose nearly four times as fast as world production of goods between 1950 and 2006. Trade in manufactured goods has risen even faster, at over seven times the rate of world production of goods.

The Doha round

The current round of talks, the Doha round, the 9th since 1945, was launched in 1999. It covers a variety of areas.
● In agriculture, Third World countries, Australia and

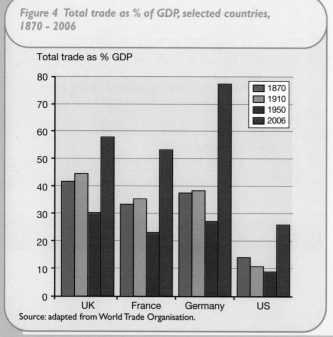

Figure 4 *Total trade as % of GDP, selected countries, 1870 - 2006*

Total trade as % GDP

Source: adapted from World Trade Organisation.

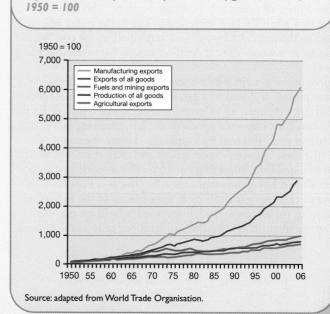

Figure 5 *World exports and production of goods, volume, 1950 = 100*

Source: adapted from World Trade Organisation.

New Zealand want substantial cuts in tariffs on imports to the highly protectionist US and EU markets. They also want an end to all export subsidies from the US and the EU. Export subsidies were used to dump unsold US and EU produce onto world markets, but were seriously damaging to agricultural producers in Third World countries.

- In manufacturing, further reductions in tariff barriers are beng negotiated.
- In services, access to markets was the key issue. In many service markets, non-tariff barriers, such as limiting the ability of foreign companies to bid for government contracts, were key to restricting trade. Forcing open markets would increase trade.
- First World countries are particularly concerned to tighten up intellectual property rights in the face of widespread piracy, whilst Third World countries want their rights over plant derived compounds and traditional knowledge and folklore protected.
- Agreements to tighten up the role of the WTO in settling trade disputes are being negotiated.

World Trade Organisation

The World Trade Organisation, set up in 1995, has two main functions.

- It encourages countries to lower protectionist barriers and thus increase trade flows between countries. It does this mainly through the various rounds of talks, the Doha round being the latest, which have occurred since the Second World War.
- It is responsible for ensuring that countries act according to the various trade agreements they have signed. Any country or group of countries can file a complaint with the WTO against the competitive practices of another country. The WTO attempts to resolve most complaints through negotiations between the two parties. Ultimately, though, the complaint can go to a panel of experts (effectively an international court), and this panel will deliver a judgment. Either side can then appeal against the judgment. However, ultimately they must accept the WTO ruling. If they reject the ruling, the country which wins the ruling has the legal right to impose trade sanctions against the exports of the losing country to impose the same damage to trade that it is suffering. When this has occurred, the losing country has quickly gone back to the negotiating table.

The WTO has come in for fierce criticism from the anti-globalisation, environmental and development lobbies. They argue that the WTO:

- allows rich countries to exploit Third World workers, paying them low wages and making them work in conditions which would be completely unacceptable in developed countries;
- is causing an environmental catastrophe in the Third World as rich countries plunder the national resources of the planet and give very little in return to poor countries;

- forces poor countries to lower their barriers to trade whilst rich countries keep their barriers in place;
- is destroying native cultures and ways of life, and is replacing it with a shallow, materialistic American lifestyle;
- is leading to the impoverishment of Third World countries whose economies are exploited by the rich countries of the world because free trade allows rich countries to force down prices of goods made in the Third World, whilst allowing their own technology-rich products to go up in price;
- gives ownership of the rules of the world trading system to a few rich countries and their multinational companies and strips power from poor countries and their citizens.

However, much of this criticism of the WTO is arguably unjustified because the WTO does not have the power to destroy cultures or force a Vietnamese worker to work for £1 a week. The WTO is there to encourage countries to negotiate rules of trade, which include mechanisms for ensuring that those rules are enforceable. It does have a pro-free trade bias but it cannot force poor countries to enter internationally binding agreements. Ultimately, the WTO is an organisation which helps develop freer trade between nations. The criticisms of the WTO are, in fact, criticisms first of free trade itself, the power of the market mechanism which does give richer countries more influence than poorer countries because they have more spending 'votes', and second the globalisation of culture.

The benefits and costs of free trade

Whether free trade is desirable is an issue which is fiercely debated. The main beneficiaries of free trade are consumers.

- They are able to buy goods and services at lower prices because they can source many of their purchases ultimately from anywhere in the world.
- They are given much greater choice of product.
- Quality and innovation is encouraged because consumers will tend to buy goods which are better quality or are more innovative at any given price.

For example, UK consumers today can buy a much greater range of clothes than they could 50 years ago. Prices of garments have fallen as trade barriers have been dismantled.

Economies, and therefore their citizens, also arguably benefit from free trade. Over the past 50 years, a large number of economic studies have found a correlation between openness to trade and economic growth. Poor countries which have become rich over the past 50 years have tended to be export orientated economies, such as South Korea, Singapore and Hong Kong. China's economic growth miracle since the mid-1970s would not have been possible without access to Western markets, finance and technology. Countries which have limited their trade for whatever reason, such as Cuba or North Korea, have performed poorly.

Third World workers employed in export industries at low rates of pay are 'exploited' in the sense that similar jobs in First World countries would carry higher rates of pay, but, they wouldn't accept these jobs if there were better alternatives. Being paid £1 a day to work in a Chinese factory is better than being paid 50p a day to work on a farm which might be the next best alternative. Equally, the job in China wouldn't exist if wages were just as high as in, say, the UK. China would not have a competitive advantage compared to the UK if wages were as high. On this argument, free trade and globalisation creates jobs in poor countries and those jobs are typically at least as well paid if not better paid than other similar jobs in the economy.

Free trade imposes costs, however. In the short term, reducing trade barriers can lead to unemployment in industries which are now exposed to foreign competition. Industries which are most likely to suffer from international competition are often those which lobby the hardest to retain protectionist barriers. In the long term, the market mechanism should lead to resources being redeployed. Workers find new jobs. But inevitably some will be losers, for instance because the new jobs are paid less well than the old ones. In the UK coal mining industry, for example, jobs were lost in the 1980s and 1990s as cheap labour, imported coal was substituted for high wage, domestically produced coal. Most UK coal miners made redundant who gained another job were forced to accept lower wages in their new job.

Greater trade which leads to greater output also implies greater use of natural resources. If the construction industry worldwide grows, for example, then more trees will be cut down to feed the industry. If more people can afford a car, then demand for oil will increase. This will lead to environmental damage in the Third World if production is uncontrolled, but free trade and protecting the environment can go together if governments round the world have the right safeguards in place. The problem is often that Third World governments do not place sufficient value on protecting their environment, whilst First World governments, firms and consumers will buy raw materials whether or not they have been produced in an environmentally friendly way.

As for damage to culture and ways of life, Coca-Cola has a mission to put its products within hands' reach of every consumer on the planet. So, unless governments ban Coca-Cola, globalisation will indeed mean that this part of American 'culture' will be exported across the world. But it is a two way process. In the UK, 'British culture' now includes Italian pizzas, Chinese acupuncture, Australian soap operas and 'ethnic' clothes. Trade has always brought with it new ideas and different ways of living which have become incorporated into local culture. Anti-globalisation protesters tend to see these changes in a negative way, but they can also be seen as positive, because they enrich different cultures.

DataQuestion

Abolition of trade restrictions in the world clothing and textiles industry

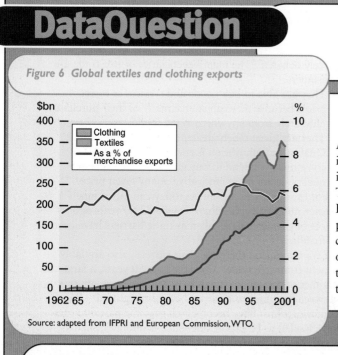

Figure 6 Global textiles and clothing exports

Source: adapted from IFPRI and European Commission, WTO.

The end of textile quotas

As part of the Uruguay world trade round, all restrictions on trade in textiles were to be abolished from 1 January 2005. The main importers are the USA and Canada and the European Union. The main exporters are Third World countries such as China and Bangladesh. An explosion of trade is expected as domestic producers in the main importing countries lose their markets to cheaper textile products from overseas. However, because China only joined the World Trade Organisation in 2004, it was forced to negotiate an agreement which allowed other countries temporarily to reimpose quotas on its exports until 2008.

The abolition of quotas worldwide will lead to a shakeout in the textile and garment industries. However, this will be an ongoing process. 'Clothing and textiles is the first manufacturing activity industrialising economies get into', says Sheila Page of Britain's Overseas Development Institute. 'It is also the first they get out of as they grow more prosperous.' Chinese workers won't stay on Third World wages forever. With very fast economic growth, their wages will rise faster than in poorer performing countries. In the process, they will lose some of their competitive advantage in textiles.

Winners and losers

The end of trade restrictions on textiles in January 2005 will create winners and losers. The winners will be the most competitive producers in the world, which will almost certainly include firms in China and Pakistan. The other winners will be consumers in Western countries who are able to buy clothes at much cheaper prices. Quotas have inflated clothing prices by creating scarcity and 'rents', price premiums that act as taxes on trade. The annual cost to US consumers has been put at $70 billion and has fallen hardest on poor families which spend a relatively large share of income on clothing. Each job saved in the US textile industry by quotas is estimated to have cost consumers an average of $170 000 a year. Once quotas are lifted, poor developing countries will be able to expand their sales by an estimated $40 billion a year, creating 27 million jobs. This is 35 times the number of jobs that will be lost in rich nations.

Losers will include firms in North America and the EU and their employees who will no longer be competitive in the world market. 770 000 jobs are likely to go. In the EU, where 2.7 million people work in clothing and textiles, it is estimated that 15 per cent of UK textile workers will lose their jobs and 13 per cent of German workers. However, some Third World countries will also suffer. Under the quota regime, many countries were able to develop export industries, selling up to their quota limits. With free trade, the least efficient of these will lose out to the most efficient countries such as China. Countries like Mauritius with higher wages compared to China could be casualties. So too could countries like Bangladesh where, although wages are low, the industry is less efficient than competitors like China. In Bangladesh, the industry employs an estimated 3 million people and generates more than three quarters of the country's exports. Losing just 20 per cent of that to China would be a national disaster.

Source: adapted from the *Financial Times* 19.7.2004.

Figure 7 *Estimated impact of pre-2005 quotas in raising the price of clothing and textiles from producing countries in US/Canada and the EU*

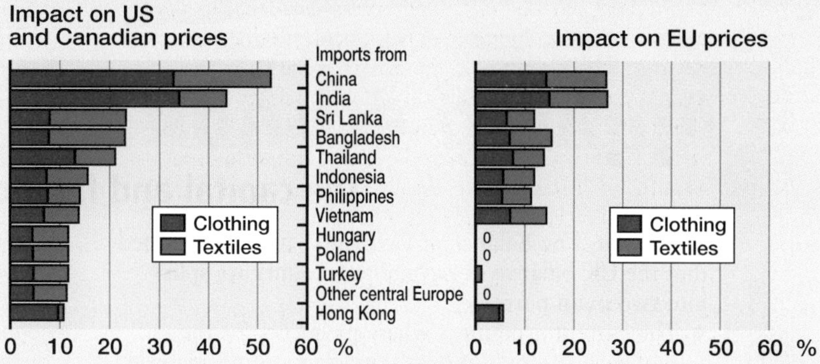

Source: adapted from IFPRI and European Commission, WTO.

Fast fashion

UK retailers are moving production from China to Eastern Europe, Turkey and India as customers' appetite for 'fast fashion' forces a fundamental rethink of supply chains.

If price were the only factor, China would win hands down. According to AT Kearney, a consultancy, a typical blouse costs £6.50 to manufacture in China against £7 in Eastern Europe, £8 in Turkey and £10 in the UK. But stores like Primark, Zara, H&M and New Look have stolen a march on their rivals by getting the latest fashion look onto their rails faster than their competitors. It takes 22 days by water to reach the UK from China, while products from Turkey can take as little as five days to arrive. Twenty years ago, more traditional retailers would buy stock 18 months in advance. Today, a retailer might pick out six key trends for the coming season. But if one or two of those really take off, it will need to be able to get extra stock of these into its stores quickly. It could equally be that the retailer hasn't spotted a key trend in advance anyway. Fast manufacture and delivery could mean the difference between a good season and a disappointing season's sales.

Source: adapted from the *Financial Times* 30.8.2005.

EU quota fiasco

Following a flood of textile imports from China, the EU forced the Chinese to agree to the short term reimposition of quotas on imports from 12 July 2005. However, on many items, Chinese exporters had already exceeded their quotas for the year by this date. The result is that an estimated 80 million trousers, pullovers and bras are now stuck in European ports. Supermarket chains like Tesco and Asda have ordered and paid for the goods but can't receive them because they are over quota. Peter Mandelson, European trade commissioner, has proposed that they are released for sale in the EU. Otherwise, he said, 'are we going to send all the unlicensed goods back to China? Who will pay for this? Who will compensate importers and retailers for the loss of contracts?'

Source: adapted from the *Financial Times*, 31.8.2005.

1. Using a diagram, explain how the textile quotas in operation before 2005 (a) created 'price premiums that act as taxes on trade'; (b) cost US consumers an estimated $70 billion annually; (c) saved jobs in high cost countries like the USA and the UK; (d) cost low price countries '$40 billion a year' in lost sales and led to 27 million fewer jobs in these economies.
2. Discuss who would gain most and lose most from the EU reimposition of textile quotas on imports from China.
3. To what extent is China (a) now and (b) in twenty years' time likely to be the most competitive country in the world producing textiles?

Applied economics

The capital and financial accounts

In the unit 'The Balance of Payments', it was explained that the UK balance of payments accounts are split into two main parts.

- The current account is where payments for the purchase and sale of goods and services are recorded.
- The capital and financial accounts is where flows of money associated with saving, investment, speculation and currency stabilisation are recorded.

The **capital account** is relatively unimportant. The largest transfers recorded are those of immigrants and emigrants bringing financial capital to the UK or taking it abroad, and of government transfers such as debt forgiveness to Third World countries or to and from the EU.

The **financial account** records almost all the flows of financial capital into and out of the UK. It is split into three main parts.

- Part of FOREIGN DIRECT INVESTMENT (FDI) is flows of money to purchase a controlling interest in a foreign firm. A controlling interest is defined as 10 per cent or more of the ordinary shares or voting power of a firm. For example, if BT were to buy 15 per cent of the shares of a telecommunications company in Brazil, with cash for the purchase transmitted from the UK to Brazil, then this would be classified as FDI. Part of FDI is reinvested earnings: profits of foreign owned companies which are reinvested in the company. If BT earned $10 million as its share of the profits made by a US subsidiary but chose to reinvest this $10 million in the company, it would be classified as FDI.
- PORTFOLIO INVESTMENT includes flows of money to purchase foreign shares where this is less than 10 per cent of the company. However, for the UK, over 90 per cent of portfolio investment is debt securities such as bonds, long term loans, issued by governments and firms.
- 'Other investments' is investment other than direct and portfolio investment. It includes trade credit, loans, purchases of currency and bank deposits.

Figure 1 shows the relative importance of the capital account and the three parts of the financial account for the UK in 2006. It also shows that there was a net inflow of funds to the UK: there was a surplus on the capital and financial accounts. This must have been true because the current account in 2006 was in deficit. The balance of payments must always add up to zero. If the current account is in deficit by £10 billion, then the financial and capital accounts must be in surplus by £10 billion.

Reasons for international capital flows

World capital flows have been growing over time at a much faster rate than growth in world GDP. This has been one aspect of **globalisation**. International capital flows occur for a number of reasons.

- Speculators are looking for quick profits. Shifting capital round the world, buying and selling debt and shares, trying to spot which currency will appreciate in value and which will fall, they are an inevitable part of the world capitalist system. International speculation is, in motivation, no different from the British old age pensioner who moves part of his savings from one bank account to another to take advantage of a higher rate of interest. Speculators perform an economic function because they help to bring adjustments in prices to reflect longer term demand, supply and price conditions.
- Capital flows are an essential part of the finance of trade. A UK resident may take out a UK loan to buy a car. A UK firm may take out a loan from abroad to finance the purchase of a machine from abroad.
- Banks in one country are finding it increasingly profitable to lend to economic agents in another country on a short term basis. A UK bank, for example, may decide to expand its operations in the French loan market.
- Individuals transfer funds abroad for a number of reasons. One is that they might have a holiday house in another country. UK residents who have holiday

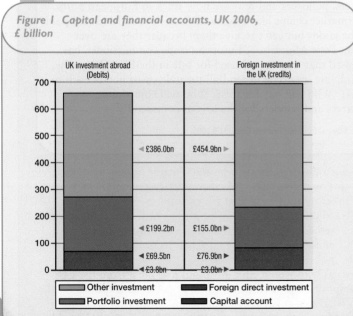

Figure 1 *Capital and financial accounts, UK 2006, £ billion*

UK investment abroad (Debits)

Foreign investment in the UK (credits)

◄ £386.0bn   £454.9bn ►

◄ £199.2bn   £155.0bn ►

◄ £69.5bn   £76.9bn ►

◄ £3.8bn   £3.0bn ►

- Other investment
- Portfolio investment
- Foreign direct investment
- Capital account

Source: adapted from the Pink Book, Office for National Statistics.

houses in Spain or France may transfer funds into a Spanish or French bank account. Tax evasion is another reason why UK residents might want to transfer funds into a foreign bank account.
● Foreign direct investment occurs because a firm in one country can see that it can make a profit by investing in the longer term in a firm in another country.
● Portfolio investment may occur for the same reasons as FDI or it may be more speculative in motivation.
● Part of portfolio investment is investment in government bonds, a form of long term loan to governments. Governments may encourage foreigners to buy their bonds to increase the amount of credit available within a national economy.

Short term and long term international capital flows

Some international capital flows are short term. A loan may be made for six months, for example. Some are long term. A government loan may be made repayable in 20 years, or a firm may buy a foreign firm.

The shorter the term of the capital flow, the more **liquid** it is likely to be. This means the shorter the capital flow, the easier it is for the owner of the investment to get back the full amount of the money. Long term capital flows therefore carry more risk.

Growth in international capital flows is important for the world economy.
● It is facilitating growth in world trade because it is helping to finance that growth.
● It is providing capital for firms that would otherwise not be able to secure finance within their own countries. This is particularly important for developing countries where there may be a lack of financial capital for investment.
● Foreign direct investment is also leading to a transfer of technology and information between countries. For developing countries, FDI is one way in which they can gain such technology from developed countries.

However, growth in international capital flows can have disadvantages.
● When one part of the world's financial system gets into difficulties, it increasingly affects the whole. In 2007, for example, US banks which had given mortgages to low income households got into difficulties. Overlending had resulted in too many households not being able to repay their loans. Fears of losses and defaults in the USA banking system led to a tightening of lending in world financial markets. One direct casualty was the UK mortgage lender, Northern Rock, which relied heavily on wholesale money markets to finance its loans. When other banks and institutions refused to lend Northern Rock enough money to carry on its day to day operations, the Bank of England was forced to intervene and act

as lender of last resort, so growth of international financial markets leads to greater risk.
● Foreign direct investment leads to national firms becoming owned by overseas firms. Some argue that this leads to exploitation of countries by multinational companies. This is discussed in more detail in the unit on multinational companies. There can also be issues of national security. When an investment vehicle for the United Arab Emirates attempted to buy six major US seaports, including New York and New Orleans owned by the UK firm P&O, there was a major outcry in the USA. It was

Figure 2 *UK share of selected international financial markets*

Source: adapted from *Key Facts*, International Financial Services London.

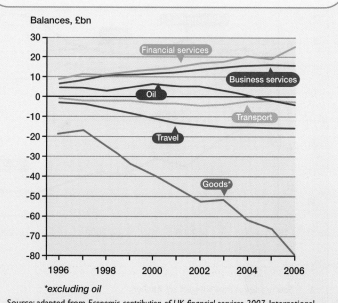

Figure 3 *UK current account trade balances*

*excluding oil

Source: adapted from *Economic contribution of UK financial services 2007*, International Financial Services London.

suggested that US national security would be at risk if an Arab country owned these ports. The sale was withdrawn.

- Availability of international credit encourages governments, firms and individuals to overborrow. As explained in the unit 'The balance of payments', there have been recurrent world financial crises due to overborrowing. For example, overborrowing by African countries in the late 1970s and early 1980s lead to two decades of poor economic performance by some of the world's poorest countries as they struggled to repay debt.

The City of London as a world financial centre

The City of London is arguably the world's top financial centre. Figure 2 shows the percentage share of a number of key financial markets enjoyed by the UK. It also shows the equivalent market share of the various US financial markets such as New York and

Chicago.

Figure 3 shows how financial services have been growing in importance for the output of the UK economy over time. Growth in financial services creates both income and jobs. In 2007, the share of financial services output in UK GDP was over 9 per cent and there were 1.1 million workers employed in the sector. Financial services are heavily concentrated in London. Nearly half the value of output of UK financial services is generated in London. This reflects the fact that over 20 per cent of the output of London's economy comes from financial services.

Financial services make a major contribution to UK exports. In 2006, 8.6 per cent of exports of goods and services were accounted for by exports of financial and insurance services. As Figure 4 shows, financial services also generate a large current account surplus. In 2006, this surplus was £25 billion, which made a significant contribution to paying for the £80 billion deficit on trade in goods.

DataQuestion — UK manufacturing

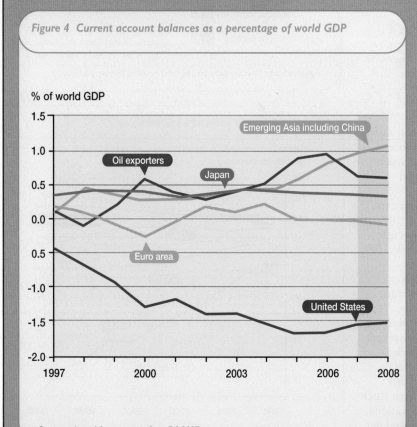

Figure 4 Current account balances as a percentage of world GDP

Source: adapted from www.imf.org 7.8.2007.

One of the main worries about the global economy over the last decade has been concern about the size of global imbalances. The US current account deficit has been running at 6 per cent of GDP for the past two years whilst the current account surplus of China has hit 12 per cent of GDP this year. Oil exporting countries have been achieving large surpluses too due to record oil prices.

The risks to the world economy are twofold. The first is that the US government attempts to solve its difficulties by imposing tariffs and other protectionist barriers. This would lead to substantially weaker global economic growth and, possibly, world recession as other countries retaliate. The second is that the rest of the world stops buying US debt as it panics about whether the US could afford to continue repayments. This would lead to a sharp fall in the dollar which, if it became a rout, could lead the US Federal Reserve Bank to raise interest rates to keep down inflation and so lead to a US recession which would spill over into a world wide recession.

Source: adapted from www.fxstreet.com, 27.11.2007.

Foreign firms are welcome to invest in China. This is despite the fact that China's exports are making the country's currency reserves balloon in size. China saw £34 billion of foreign direct investment in 2005, more than any other developing country. However, FDI flows to China were still lower per capita than to 29 out of the 30 richest countries of the world. Partly this was because mergers and acquisitions formed a relatively small part of FDI flows. The OECD argues that China could generate even faster growth and greater economic efficiency if it allowed more foreign companies to acquire Chinese companies.

Source: adapted from news.bbc.co.uk, 17.4.2007.

Oil exporters are afloat in a flood of cash. They are selling oil to the USA. Then the USA is borrowing back the money from oil exporters that it needs to pay for the oil. Oil exporters are exchanging oil in the ground for dollars in the bank. The IMF and the US government are encouraging oil-exporting economies to buy more US goods, particularly defence equipment and oil production equipment, to reduce the trade deficit. But the obvious remedy is for the USA to reduce its dependence on oil. Large subsidies to the growing bio-fuels industry in the USA is one way in which the USA is trying to reduce its oil imports. However, if the US economy collapses under the strains of record current account deficits, demand for oil worldwide could fall sharply, leading to a collapse in oil prices. Oil exporters therefore need the US economy to stay afloat if they are to continue to enjoy record growth in their incomes.

Source: adapted from www.thehindubusinessline.com, 19.3.2007.

1. Explain why (a) foreign direct investment might help the growth of the Chinese economy and (b) growth of the Chinese economy was a cause of global imbalances in 2007.

2. Explain how global imbalances could be corrected.

3. Discuss whether it should be the responsibility of the USA or of its trading partners such as China and Saudi Arabia to correct the US current account deficit.

Summary

1. The balance of payments is likely to be in disequilibrium if the value of exports and imports differs over a long period of time.
2. One policy weapon available to governments to tackle a current account deficit is to devalue the currency or allow it to depreciate. The Marshall-Lerner condition states that devaluation will be successful if the combined elasticities of demand for exports and imports exceed unity.
3. In the short term, devaluation is likely to lead to a deterioration in the current account position because of the J curve effect. In the longer term, the competitive benefits of devaluation may be eroded by cost-push inflation.
4. Deflationary policies will act to reduce imports because of the fall in total demand in the economy. Raising interest rates is one way of implementing a deflationary policy.
5. Raising interest rates is also likely to lead to a rise in the value of the currency in the short term as speculative funds are attracted into the country.
6. Protectionist measures can reduce imports but the ability of governments to implement such policies today is severely limited by international agreements.
7. Supply side policies should lead to an increase in international competitiveness over long periods of time.
8. In the short term, a country may choose to impose currency controls, restricting the supply of its currency for use in international transactions.

Balance of payments equilibrium

The balance of payments can be said to be in **equilibrium** when there is no tendency for it to change. This is most likely to occur in the short to medium term if exports are equal to imports and hence both the current and the capital account are in balance. However, equilibrium could also exist if:

- imports are greater than exports and the country is using borrowed foreign money to develop its economy as the USA did in the early part of the 19th century;
- exports are greater than imports and the country is investing the money abroad in order to finance increased imports in the future. It can be argued that Japan is in this position today given that it faces a sharp decline in its workforce and a sharp rise in the number of pensioners in the next 30 years.

In the long term, countries are unlikely to be able to continue as substantial net borrowers because other countries will refuse to lend to countries which get deeper and deeper into debt (as has happened with many Third World countries). In the long term, therefore, equilibrium will occur when exports equal imports.

If the balance of payments is in equilibrium there will be no tendency for the exchange rate to change. If, on the other hand, a country tends to export more than it imports over long periods, its exchange rate will tend to rise. The demand for the country's currency to pay for its exports will continually exceed the supply of currency offered for sale to pay for imports. Speculation may cause the exchange rate to fluctuate randomly in the short term if exchange rates are floating but the exchange rate trend is likely to be upward in the long term. If the country runs a persistent current account deficit, its exchange rate will tend to fall.

If the current account is in persistent deficit (or surplus), what measures can government take to rectify this situation? How can governments keep exchange rates up when there is persistent selling pressure from the markets?

Devaluation and revaluation

One possible way of curing a current account deficit is for the government to DEVALUE the currency. This means that it lowers the value of the currency against other currencies. Devaluation affects exports and imports because it changes their relative prices and thus their international competitiveness. The opposite of devaluation is REVALUATION, an increase in the value of the currency.

Devaluation assumes that the government pegs the value of its currency against other currencies. However, exchange rates may **float**, which means that governments allow free market forces to determine the value of the currency. A fall in the value of the currency is then called a **depreciation** of the currency. The opposite of depreciation is **appreciation** of the currency. In what follows, it will be assumed that the government does control the value of the currency and therefore the term 'devaluation' rather than 'depreciation' will be used. However, devaluation and depreciation have the same effects, as do revaluation and appreciation.

The effects of devaluation

Assume that the pound falls in value against other currencies by ten per cent. The price of imports will therefore rise in pounds sterling. With an exchange rate of $2 = £1, a US car sold to UK importers for $20 000 would have cost £10 000 in pounds sterling. With a ten per cent devaluation of the pound, the new exchange rate will be $1.8 = £1. So the cost of a $20 000 US car will be £11 111 ($20 000 ÷ 1.8). At the new price, demand is likely to fall. The effect on the total value of imports will depend upon the elasticity of demand for US cars. If demand is elastic, the percentage rise in the price of US cars will be more than offset by a percentage fall in the demand for cars. Hence the total sterling value of imported US cars will fall. (This is an application of the relationship between elasticity and revenue). If demand is price inelastic, a rise in price will lead to a rise in expenditure on US cars and hence a rise in the sterling value of US car imports.

In summary, a devaluation of the pound will:
- leave the US dollar **price** unchanged but increase the sterling price of imported goods;
- result in a fall in **import volumes**;
- lead to a fall in the **total sterling value** of imports assuming that domestic demand for imports is elastic; if demand is inelastic, there will be a rise in the sterling value of imports.

Devaluation of the pound should have no effect on the sterling price of exports. A £10 000 car exported to the USA will still be £10 000 after devaluation. But the price will have fallen in US dollars. If the value of the pound falls from $2 = £1 to $1.8 = £1, the £10 000 car will fall in price in the USA from $20 000 to $18 000. This should lead to a rise in demand for UK cars.

A devaluation will therefore:
- leave the **sterling price** of exports unchanged but reduce the price in foreign currency terms;
- lead to a rise in **export volumes**;
- increase the **total sterling value** of exports.

Devaluation and elasticity

Overall, devaluation of the pound will increase the sterling value of exports, but may or may not lead to a fall in the value of imports depending upon the elasticity of demand for imports. It is likely that, even if import values increase, export values will increase even more. Hence devaluation will result in an improved current account position. The MARSHALL-LERNER condition states that, given very stringent conditions, devaluation will result in an improvement on current account if the combined elasticities of demand for exports and imports are greater than 1. If the combined elasticities for exports and imports are less than 1, then the correct policy response to a current account deficit should be a currency **revaluation**.

Devaluation and pricing strategies

So far it has been assumed that UK exporters will choose to keep the sterling price of the products constant and change the foreign currency price, whilst importers will choose to keep the foreign currency price of their goods the same and change the sterling price. However, exporters and importers may choose a different strategy. A luxury car manufacturer, for instance, may price a model at $40 000 in the USA. If the value of the pound is $2 = £1, it will receive £20 000 per car. If the pound is now devalued to $1 = £1, the manufacturer has a choice of strategies. It could keep the sterling price constant at £20 000 and reduce the dollar price to $20 000. However, a fall in price of a luxury car may give the wrong signals to US car buyers. They may assume that the cars are no longer luxury cars. They may think that the business is not doing well in the US and is having to reduce prices in order to maintain sales. The fall in the dollar price may generate few extra sales. So the manufacturer is likely to hold constant the dollar price of $40 000 and consequently increase his profit margins. When the value of the pound rises against the dollar, the manufacturer may again choose to hold constant the dollar price. A rise in the dollar price may lead to large falls in sales if the manufacturer is in a competitive market with other luxury car manufacturers.

If both exporters and importers adopt the strategy of leaving the prices they charge to their customers unchanged, devaluation will still improve the current account position. Assume the pound is devalued.
- The sterling value of exports will rise because exporters have chosen to increase the sterling price of exported goods rather than reduce their foreign currency price. Export volumes will remain unchanged because the foreign currency price has remained unchanged. Therefore sterling export values will increase because of the sterling price increase.
- The sterling value of imports will stay the same. Foreign firms have chosen to keep the sterling price of their goods constant. Hence volumes will not change. Neither, therefore, will the sterling value of imports.

With export values increased and import values unchanged, there will be an improvement in the current account position.

Problems associated with devaluation

There are two major problems with using devaluation as a policy weapon.

The J curve The current account following devaluation is likely to get worse before it gets better. This is known as the J CURVE EFFECT and it is shown in Figure 1.

Assume the UK has a current account deficit and attempts to devalue its currency. In the short run the demand for exports and imports will tend to be inelastic. Although the foreign currency price of UK exports will fall, it takes time before other countries react to the change. Hence, the volume of exports will remain the same in the short term, before increasing in the longer term. This means that in the short term, there will be no increase in sterling export values.

Similarly, although the sterling price of imports rises, in the short term UK buyers may be stuck with import contracts they signed before devaluation. Alternatively, there may be no alternative domestic suppliers and hence firms may have to continue to buy imports. Hence, in the short term, sterling import values will rise. In the longer term, contracts can be revised and domestic producers can increase supply, thus leading to a reduction in import volumes.

Question I

The Chinese government's decision to revalue the renminbi by 2.5 per cent against the US dollar will lead to different reactions from Chinese exporters. In the textiles industry, even though profit margins are wafer thin, Chinese manufacturers are unlikely to be able to pass on the increase in the exchange rate in higher prices to their overseas customers. Even with such a small price increase, some manufacturers could lose contracts to other low cost textile producing countries such as India and Bangladesh. In the electronics industry, where there is less competition from other countries in the short term, Chinese producers are more likely to pass on the price increase to their customers.

Source: adapted from the *Financial Times*, 24.5.2005 and 22.7.2005.

Explain, using examples from the passage, what is likely to happen to (a) the price of exports, (b) the volume of exports and (c) revenues received from exports following a revaluation of a currency.

Overall, in the short term, import values will rise but export values will remain constant, thus producing a deterioration in the current account. In the longer term, export values will rise whilst import values might fall, producing an improvement in the current account position.

Cost-push inflation Devaluation generates imported inflation. This is not serious if there is a once and for all increase in prices. But if it starts up or fuels a cost-push **inflationary spiral**, then the increased competitiveness achieved by the devaluation will be quickly eroded. Keynesian economists have become increasingly sceptical of the value of devaluation as a policy weapon to cure a balance of payments deficit unless it is part of a much wider package of measures designed to increase the competitiveness and performance of a deficit economy.

Deflation

Devaluation results in EXPENDITURE SWITCHING. Foreigners buy more of our exports and less of their own and other countries' production, whilst domestic consumers buy fewer imports and more domestically produced goods. An alternative approach to curing a current account deficit is **deflation**. This is an EXPENDITURE REDUCING policy. If the government reduces aggregate demand in the economy, for instance by raising interest rates or increasing taxes, people have less money to spend so they reduce their consumption of domestically produced goods and imported goods. Imports therefore decline. Exports may also rise if domestic firms switch sales from the depressed domestic market to foreign markets.

For the UK, deflation has proved very successful in reducing imports, particularly because the UK has a very high **marginal propensity to import** in manufactured goods. The effect on exports has been less noticeable. Firms may well choose to reduce output in response to a recession in the economy rather than seek export orders.

One important policy advantage of deflation is that it is likely to reduce inflationary pressures in the economy, assuming those

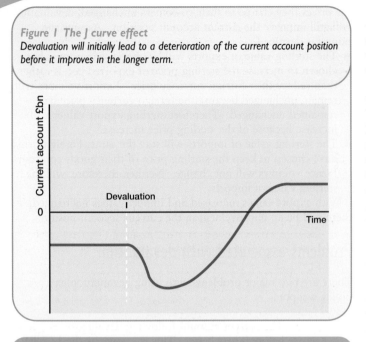

Figure 1 The J curve effect
Devaluation will initially lead to a deterioration of the current account position before it improves in the longer term.

Question 2

The British economy has benefited from the high value of the pound in recent years, but this could all come to an end if the foreign exchange rate markets become scared of Britain's growing debt problem.

Since 1995, the UK has benefited from shifts in world prices. Imports prices for the UK have fallen 16 per cent whilst export prices have only fallen 11 per cent. These trends have increased Britain's purchasing power in the world. However, the current account deficit is currently running at about 3 per cent of GDP, but would be much larger if relative prices were still at their 1995 levels. Inflation has been held down by cheap imports, allowing the Bank of England to keep interest rates at their lowest levels for four decades.

For Andrew Smithers of Smithers and Co, a City investment firm, the current account deficit has grown to a point where it will have to be narrowed. That most probably means a fall in the pound, reducing demand for imports and raising demand for exports. 'That causes a problem for the Bank of England', he says. 'The inflation rate will pick up and we will have to have higher interest rates and a bit of a recession.'

There has been a modest fall in the value of the pound already over the past 12 months, but this seems to have had little impact on import prices so far. But it is possible the impact has merely been delayed. The Bank of England in its latest Inflation Report noted that importers might be slow to put up their prices because many of their contracts are fixed for set periods, or because of the costs of changing their price lists. 'Pass-through may therefore be delayed until firms believe that the exchange rate movement is a permanent one', it said.

Source: adapted from the *Financial Times*, 10.1.2004.

(a) Explain, using the data, why the short term impact on imports of a depreciation of the pound might be different from the long term impact.
(b) Using examples from the passage, explain the problems that might occur as a result of a depreciation of the pound.

Question 3

The euro has risen in value by 30 per cent against the US dollar over the past two years. Eurozone exports to countries which buy in US dollars are feeling the heat. Heineken, for example, the world's third largest brewer by volume, announced a profit warning last month because of the impact the dollar's fall was having on revenues from exports to the USA.

Gerhard Schröder, the German Chancellor, said last month that the dollar/euro rate was 'not satisfactory' for European exports and apparently hinted that the European Central Bank might have to consider cutting interest rates to curb the euro's rise.

Source: adapted from the *Financial Times*, 11.3.2004.

(a) Explain how the European Central Bank cutting its interest rate might help companies in the eurozone which export to the USA such as Heineken.
(b) What impact might a cut in interest rates by the European Central Bank have on the current account position on the balance of payments of eurozone countries?

pressures come from the demand side of the economy. On the other hand, it also reduces growth and increases unemployment, both undesirable in themselves. In the long term, the economy must increase its international competitiveness unless the economy is to remain permanently below full employment.

Interest rates

Increased interest rates will initially bolster the value of the currency. They attract speculative inflows into the country, raising the demand for the currency. In the longer term, a rise in interest rates which, must have been generated by a fall in the supply of money, will lead to a fall in aggregate demand through the transmission mechanism. Higher interest rates deflate the economy, leading to a fall in imports and hence an improvement in the current account.

Protectionism

Increasing tariffs or quotas or other protectionist measures will reduce imports thus improving the current account position. Tariffs and quotas can both have a significant impact in the short term. However, protectionism is not much favoured by economists. First, the country is likely to find itself becoming even more internationally uncompetitive in the long run as its domestic industries have no incentive to improve their efficiency. Second, protectionism in one country invites retaliation from its trading partners. The country could find that the gains on current account from reduced imports are more than matched by losses of exports as a result of retaliation.

Increased protectionist measures are also forbidden except under certain specific circumstances by the WTO (the World Trade Organisation). Membership of a trading bloc like the European Union severely limits the ability of individual countries to limit imports through protectionist policies.

Currency controls

A government may choose to impose or tighten currency controls. These are controls on the purchase of foreign currency by domestic citizens and firms. In the late 1960s, for instance, the UK government limited the amount of currency that could be taken abroad on holiday to £50 per person. Governments could equally restrict finance for investment abroad or even for imports. The government abolished exchange controls in 1979, and today the UK government is unable to impose currency controls because of its membership of the European Union.

Supply side policies

One way of making domestically produced goods more competitive is through devaluation: altering the relative price of exports and imports. However, there are many other ways in

which domestic industry can become more competitive internationally. **Supply side policies** aimed at reducing unit labour costs, increasing investment, increasing the skills of the labour force and improving the quality and design of products, should lead to increased exports and reduced imports. Supply side policies tend to be long term policies. They cannot cure a current account deficit within, for instance, 12-24 months.

Question 4

In February 1990, the government of Bangladesh, faced with a swelling of the country's current account deficit, tightened its currency controls. Importers were required to provide a 50 per cent cash deposit when opening new letters of credit.

A letter of credit is a type of loan common in the export/import trade. Explain why the government measure outlined in the passage could lead to (a) an improvement in the current account position and (b) a rise in the value of the Bangladesh currency, the Taka.

Key terms

Devaluation and revaluation - a fall or rise in the value of the currency when the currency is pegged against other currencies.
Expenditure reducing - in a balance of payments context, government policies to reduce the level of aggregate demand in order to reduce imports and boost exports.
Expenditure switching - in a balance of payments context, government policies to switch production currently being sold domestically, to exports.
J curve effect - in the short term a devaluation is likely to lead to a deterioration in the current account position before it starts to improve.
Marshall-Lerner condition - devaluation will lead to an improvement in the current account so long as the combined price elasticities of exports and imports are greater than 1.

Applied economics

UK government policy

In the 1950s and 1960s, current account deficits were seen as a problem which demanded a policy response from government. Until 1972, the value of the pound was fixed against other currencies in the Bretton Woods System of managed exchanged rates. Current account deficits, where the demand for pounds was less than the supply of pounds, could put downward pressure on the pound, threatening to change the fixed value of the currency. Hence, the government used a range of policy measures to affect both exports and imports. In the short term, it tended to use restrictive fiscal and monetary policies (expenditure reducing policies) when the current account went into deficit. It devalued the currency twice, in 1947 and 1967, to boost the competitiveness of UK exports. Since 1972, apart from a brief period between the late 1980s and 1992, the value of the pound has been allowed to float freely against other currencies. The government has ceased to use any policies designed explicitly to affect the balance of payments in the short term.

Government does have policies designed to boost exports in the long term. It has a variety of schemes to give help and advice to exporters to win contracts and break into new markets. This is part of a wider set of supply side policies designed to boost the competitiveness of the UK economy. For example, measures to increase labour productivity should lead to a reduction in the price of exports. Measures to increase research and development should lead to more innovative products which can be sold abroad.

Global imbalances

Since the late 1990s, there have been concerns about global imbalances on the balance of payments. As Figure 2 shows, the United States has seen a gradual deterioration in its current account position since 1991, measured as a percentage of its GDP. In contrast, Japan and China have continually recorded surpluses.

In the unit on the Balance of Payments, it was explained that deficits on the current account need not be a problem for a country if they are relatively short lived and are not a large proportion of GDP. They are also not a problem if a country is growing at a fast rate and so can easily afford to repay in the future the foreign debt created today. The USA is the world's largest economy. It is growing over time but only at an average 2.5 to 3.0 per cent per annum. The size of its current account deficits from the mid 1990s onwards has meant that its foreign debt as a proportion of GDP has been increasing over time. Its deficit has not been used to accumulate capital goods for future growth. Rather, its has sucked in imports to pay for extra

consumer and government spending. There has therefore been growing concern about the US deficit.

Deficits on the current account in one country must mean that other countries have surpluses. Figure 3 shows how the composition of the US deficit has changed over time. In 2006, most of the deficit was accounted for by just three countries or groups of countries.

- The largest part of the deficit was accounted for by oil exporting countries like Saudi Arabia running surpluses with the USA. From the turn of the twenty first century, there was a large increase in world oil prices. The United States, the world's largest consumer of oil and a net importer of oil, had no choice but to pay these higher prices to secure supplies.
- As Figure 3 shows, the USA has for some time run a deficit of at least 1 per cent of its GDP with Japan. From Japan, it has bought mainly motor vehicles and other manufactured goods including electronic goods. Japanese goods have been competitively priced,

innovative and of high quality. The US deficit with Japan shows that US manufacturing is to some extent less competitive than Japanese manufacturing industry.

● Chinese exports to the USA have grown particularly fast since 2000. China has a large price competitive advantage to the USA in low to medium technology manufactured goods. This is mainly because of its low wages. Chinese workers are paid on average a small fraction of the lowest paid workers in the USA.

The US deficit poses a threat to world economic stability. The worst case scenario is that lenders decide to stop lending to the USA. They might be frightened that the USA will become a bad credit risk and that some parts of the US economic system will default on their foreign currency loans. Or the value of the dollar may fall so much that enough of those holding debt in US dollars decide to switch out of dollars into another currency. A huge sell off of US denominated debt could bring about a crisis in world financial markets. If lending to the US dries up, the USA can no longer buy more imports than it can sell exports. It must reduce its spending on imports. That would reduce world aggregate demand, at worst sending the world economy into a deep recession. World growth could become negative and millions of people would lose their jobs.

Policy solutions to global imbalances

It is difficult to see solutions to these global imbalances. One policy response would be for the US government to encourage a devaluation of the US dollar. As Figure 4 shows, the effective exchange rate (the average exchange rate against other currencies weighted according to the volume of trade with other countries) of the US dollar fell 15 per cent between 2002 and 2005 but then broadly stabilised. A US devaluation has limited impact for two reasons.

● US price elasticity of demand for imported oil is low. It is unlikely to reduce its demand for oil even if it has to pay more per barrel. Hence, its deficit with oil exporting countries is unlikely to fall in the short term whatever the value of the dollar.

● The Chinese currency, the Renminbi, is pegged to the dollar. If the value of the dollar falls, so does the Renminbi. The USA cannot devalue its way out of its deficit with China.

If a depreciation of the dollar is unlikely to have much effect, the US government has two main policy responses left. One is to reduce demand in the US. Getting US households to save more and spend less would reduce imports, so too would cutting the large US government deficit. Raising taxes and cutting government spending, however, would be politically unpopular. The second policy response is to increase the competitiveness of US industry so that the US exports more and imports less. Reducing demand would send the USA into a recession. Increasing competitiveness is a long term response which would take 5 to 10 years to have any significant effect even if it were possible to achieve.

Not surprisingly, the US government would like to see other countries implement policies to reduce its deficit.

● Oil exporting countries could increase imports of US goods. In particular, spending on extra capacity in their oil extraction industry would have two beneficial effects for the US. In the short term, the US could sell them capital equipment. In the longer term, an increase in the supply of oil would bring down its price, reducing the value of oil exports to the USA.

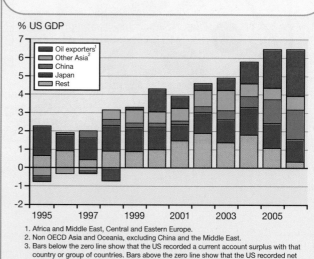

Figure 3 Geographic components of the US current account deficit

1. Africa and Middle East, Central and Eastern Europe.
2. Non OECD Asia and Oceania, excluding China and the Middle East.
3. Bars below the zero line show that the US recorded a current account surplus with that country or group of countries. Bars above the zero line show that the US recorded net deficits on current account i.e. imports were greater than exports.

Source: adapted from *Economic Outlook*, OECD.

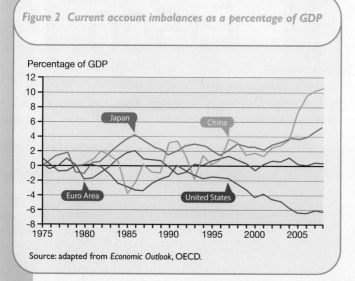

Figure 2 Current account imbalances as a percentage of GDP

Source: adapted from *Economic Outlook*, OECD.

- China could revalue the Remnimbi against the dollar. This would reduce the price competitiveness of Chinese exports to the USA. The Chinese government is unlikely to do this because it is using exports to fuel its development and economic growth. By increasing exports, it is creating wealth and jobs. Critics point out that with China running a current account surplus of nearly 10 per cent of its GDP, it could give an immediate boost to living standards by buying more imports.
- Japan could stop its depreciation of the Yen against the dollar shown in Figure 4 and buy more US imports. Japan is reluctant to do this because it spent ten years in the 1990s and early 2000s in a prolonged recession. It is using exports to boost demand and stimulate economic growth.
- Other countries, like those of the EU, could boost their aggregate demand which would stimulate growth of imports from the USA. However, countries such as those in the EU do not set their economic policies according to the needs of US exporters.

If the world continues to be willing to lend to the USA, global imbalances may reduce over time. The danger for the world economy is that global imbalances become even greater. If world lending to the USA suddenly falters, there is likely to be a global financial crisis leading to a severe world recession.

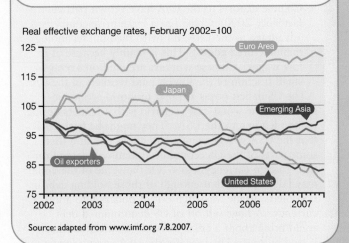

Figure 4 *Effective exchange rates, February 2002 = 100*

Real effective exchange rates, February 2002=100

Source: adapted from www.imf.org 7.8.2007.

DataQuestion Appreciation of the pound, 1996-2001

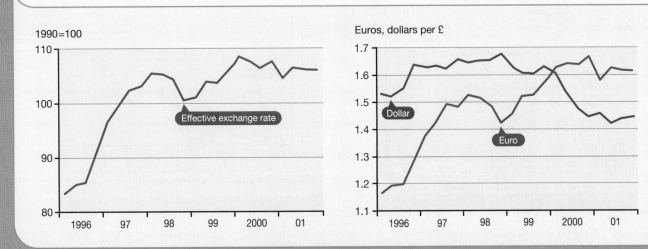

Figure 5 *Exchange rate value of the pound: effective exchange rate, euro and dollar*

1990=100 · Effective exchange rate

Euros, dollars per £ · Dollar · Euro

The value of exports and imports, measured in £s, is the volume of exports and imports times their average price. In the data here, volume and price are measured as index numbers.

Between 1996 and 2000, there was a sharp appreciation in the value of the pound which affected both exports and imports. Two other factors also affected exports and imports at the time. One was the above trend rate of growth in GDP. The other was a fall in average world prices for traded goods, the result of increasing globalisation.

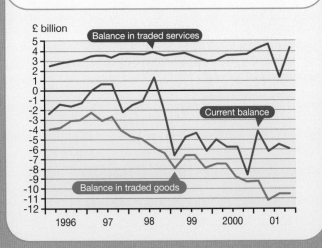

Figure 6 *Balance of payments: balance of trade in goods, balance in traded services and current balance, £ billion*

£ billion · Balance in traded services · Current balance · Balance in traded goods

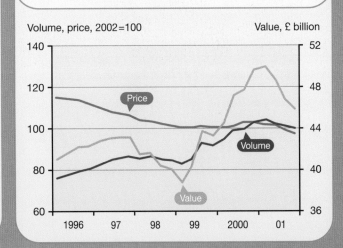

Figure 7 *Exports of traded goods by value (£ billion), volume (2002=100) and price (2002=100)*

Volume, price, 2002=100 · Value, £ billion · Price · Volume · Value

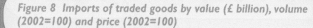

Figure 8 *Imports of traded goods by value (£ billion), volume (2002=100) and price (2002=100)*

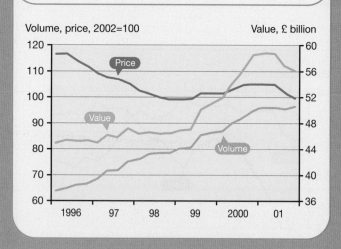

Figure 9 *Value of exports and imports of traded services (£ billion)[1]*

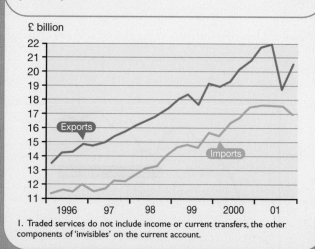

1. Traded services do not include income or current transfers, the other components of 'invisibles' on the current account.

Figure 10 *Annual percentage growth in real GDP*

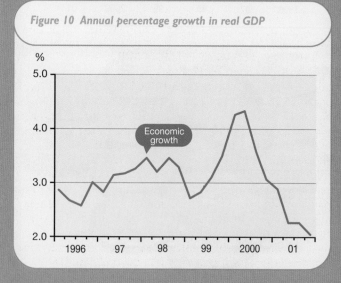

1. Outline the trends in the exchange rate of the pound sterling shown in the data.
2. Explain, using a diagram, what the J curve model suggests will happen to the current account of the balance of payments (a) in the short term and (b) in the long term.
3. To what extent can a J curve effect be seen in the data?
4. Over the period 1996 to 2001, the data show there was a sharp deterioration in the UK balance of trade and the current balance on the balance of payments. (a) Outline TWO ways in which the government or the Bank of England could have acted to check this deterioration and (b) discuss the extent to which such intervention might have been successful.

Source: adapted from *Economic & Labour Market Trends*, Office for National Statistics.

Summary

1. The exchange rate is the price at which one currency is convertible into another.
2. The equilibrium exchange rate is established where demand for a currency is equal to its supply.
3. The equilibrium exchange rate will change if there is a change in the value of exports or imports, the value of net long term foreign investment, or the volume or direction of speculative flows.
4. On a day to day basis in a free exchange market, speculation tends to be the dominant influence upon the price of a currency.
5. In the longer term, economic fundamentals relating to exports, imports and long term capital flows tend to determine the exchange rate.
6. The purchasing power parity theory of exchange rates states that exchange rates will in the long run change in line with relative inflation rates between economies.
7. Speculation tends to lead to short term exchange rate instability.

The exchange rate

Different countries use different types of **money** or **currency**. In the UK, goods and services are bought and sold with pounds sterling, in France with the euro, and in the USA with the dollar.

The rate at which one currency can be converted (i.e. bought or sold) into another currency is known as the **exchange rate**. For instance, an Indian company may wish to purchase pounds sterling. If it pays 80 million rupees to purchase £1 million, then the exchange rate is 80 rupees to the pound. A UK household may wish to buy US dollars to take on holiday to Florida. If they receive $2 000 in exchange for £1 000, then the exchange rate is $2 to the pound, or 50p to the dollar.

Question 1

Table 1

Original value of the trade weighted index	Change in exchange rate %		New value of the trade weighted index
	Country X	Country Y	
100	+10	+20	
100	+20	+10	
100	-10	+10	
100	+10	-10	
100	- 6	- 6	

Country A trades only with two countries. 60 per cent of its trade is with country X and 40 per cent with country Y.
(a) Complete the table by calculating the new value of the trade weighted index for country A following changes in its exchange rate with countries X and Y.
(b) What would be the values of the trade weighted index if country A had 90 per cent of its trade with country X and 10 per cent with country Y?
(c) Calculate the new values of the trade weighted index in (a) if the original value of the trade weighted index were not 100 but 80.

Exchange rates are normally expressed in terms of the value of one single currency against another single currency - pounds for dollars for instance, or euros for yen. However, it is possible to calculate the exchange rate of one currency in terms of a group or **basket** of currencies. The EFFECTIVE EXCHANGE RATE (a measure calculated by the International Monetary Fund) and the TRADE WEIGHTED EXCHANGE RATE INDEX (or the EXCHANGE RATE INDEX as it is often called) are two different calculations of the average movement of the exchange rate on the basis of weightings determined by the value of trade undertaken with a country's main trading partners.

To illustrate how the trade weighted index is calculated, assume that the UK trades only with the USA and France. 70 per cent of UK trade is with the USA and 30 per cent is with France. The value of the pound falls by 10 per cent against the dollar and by 20 per cent against the euro (which, incidentally, means the euro has gone up in value against the US dollar). The trade weighted index will now have changed. The fall in the dollar contributes a 7 per cent fall in the exchange rate (10 per cent x 0.7) whilst the fall in the euro contributes a 6 per cent fall (20 per cent x 0.3). The average fall is the sum of these two components (i.e. 13 per cent). If the trade weighted index started off at 100, its new value will be 87.

Equilibrium exchange rates

Currency is bought and sold on the FOREIGN EXCHANGE MARKETS. Governments may buy and sell currencies in order to influence the price of a currency. Here we will assume that governments do not intervene and that currencies are allowed to find their own price levels through the forces of **demand** and **supply**. There are then three main reasons why foreign exchange is bought and sold.
- International trade in goods and services needs to be financed. Exports create a demand for currency whilst imports create a supply of currency.
- Long term capital movements occur. Inward investment to an economy creates a demand for its currency. Outward investment from an economy creates a supply.
- There is an enormous amount of speculation in the foreign exchange markets.

The equilibrium exchange rate is established where

the demand for the currency is equal to its supply. Figure 1 shows the demand and supply of pounds priced in dollars. The market is in equilibrium at an exchange rate of $2 = £1. Buying and selling is equal to £1 000 million each day.

The demand curve is assumed to be downward sloping. If the price of the pound falls against the dollar, then the price of British goods will fall in dollar terms. For instance, if the exchange rate falls from $2 = £1 to $1 = £1, then a British good costing £1 000 will fall in price for Americans from $2 000 to $1 000. Americans should therefore buy more British goods and demand more pounds to pay for them. So a fall in the price of the pound should lead to an increase in quantity demanded of pounds, giving rise to the downward sloping demand curve. Similarly the supply curve is upward sloping because a fall in the value of the pound will increase the price of foreign imports for the British, leading them to reduce their purchases of foreign goods and therefore of foreign exchange.

All other things being equal, a fall in the value of the pound from, say, $2 to $1 is likely to make the pound look cheap and this may attract speculative buying of the pound and discourage speculative selling. This would then produce downward sloping demand curves and upward sloping supply curves for the pound sterling. However, in general on the capital side, it is unclear how buyers and sellers will react to rises and falls in the price of a currency. Given this, the justification for downward sloping demand curves and upward sloping supply curves for foreign exchange tends to rest on arguments about the buying and selling of currency for export and import payments.

Figure 2 shows that the exchange rate will change if either the demand or supply curve shifts. Equilibrium is at price 0B and output 0Q.

- If British exports to the USA increase, American firms will need to buy more pounds than before to pay for them. Hence an increase in the value of UK exports will increase the demand for pounds, shifting the demand curve from D_1 to D_2. The exchange rate will therefore rise from 0B to 0C.
- If imports from the USA increase, British firms will need to buy more dollars than before to pay for them. They will buy

these dollars with pounds. Hence an increase in the value of UK imports will increase the supply of pounds. The supply curve will shift to the right from S_1 to S_2. The equilibrium value of the pound will fall from 0B to 0A.

- If the rate of interest in the London money markets increases, US savers will switch funds into the UK. This is likely to be short term money or **hot money** which flows from financial centre to financial centre attracted by the highest rate of return. An increase in inflows on the capital account of the balance of payments will increase the demand for pounds, shifting the demand curve from D_1 to D_2, and increasing the value of the pound from 0B to 0C.
- If there is an inflow of funds for long term investment in the UK, again the demand for pounds will rise. For instance, Japanese investment in car plants in the UK will raise the demand for pounds (and increase the supply of yen) shown by the shift in the demand curve from D_1 to D_2, raising the value of the pound from 0B to 0C.
- Speculation is the single most important determinant today of the minute by minute price of the pound. If speculators believe that the value of the pound is going to fall against the dollar, they will sell pounds and buy dollars. An increase in the supply of pounds on the market, shown by the shift in the supply curve from S_1 to S_2, will lead to a fall in the price of the pound from 0B to 0A.

It is difficult to assess the level of speculative activity on the foreign exchange markets. Less than 1 per cent of daily foreign exchange transactions in London is a result of a direct buying or selling order for exports and imports or long term capital flows. However, each order tends to result in more than one transaction as foreign exchange dealers cover their exposure to the deal by buying and selling other currencies. Even if every order were to result in an extra three transactions, this would still only account for at most 4 per cent of transactions, which would suggest that speculative deals form the majority of trading on a daily basis.

Thus, in the short term, the value of a currency is dominated by speculative activity in the currency. However, there is

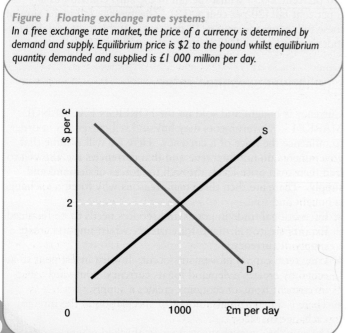

Figure 1 Floating exchange rate systems
In a free exchange rate market, the price of a currency is determined by demand and supply. Equilibrium price is $2 to the pound whilst equilibrium quantity demanded and supplied is £1 000 million per day.

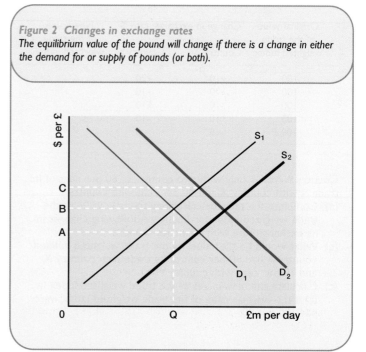

Figure 2 Changes in exchange rates
The equilibrium value of the pound will change if there is a change in either the demand for or supply of pounds (or both).

evidence to suggest that in the longer term, the value of a currency is determined by economic **fundamentals** - by exports, imports and long term capital movements.

The purchasing power parity theory of exchange rates

If purchasing power parity exists, then a given amount of currency in one country, converted into another currency at the current market exchange rate, will buy the same bundle of goods in both countries. For instance, if £1 = $2, and consumers only buy jeans, then purchasing power parity will exist if a £20 pair of jeans costs $40 in the USA. It won't exist if a pair of jeans priced at £20 in the UK is priced at $50 or $30 in the USA. If there are only two goods in the economy, food and clothing, then purchasing power parity will exist if an identical bundle of food and clothes costs £100 when it costs $200 in the USA, or £500 when it costs $1 000 in the USA.

The PURCHASING POWER PARITY (PPP) THEORY states

Question 2

Figure 3 shows the demand and supply of pounds. D and S are the original demand and supply curves respectively.

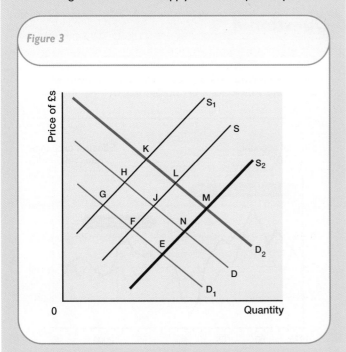

Figure 3

(a) At which point (E to N) is the market in equilibrium?
(b) To which point will the market be most likely to move in the short term if there is: (i) an increase in exports; (ii) an increase in imports; (iii) a fall in interest rates in the London money markets; (iv) a rise in takeovers of US companies by British companies; (v) a belief that the value of the euro will rise in the near future; (vi) the discovery of a huge new oil field in the North Sea; (vii) bad summer weather in the UK which sharply increases the number of foreign holidays taken; (viii) a series of prolonged strikes in the UK engineering sector of the economy?

that exchange rates in the long term change in line with different inflation rates between economies. To understand why exchange rates might change in line with inflation rates, assume that the balance of payments of the UK is in equilibrium with exports equal to imports and capital outflows equal to capital inflows, but it is suffering from a 5 per cent inflation rate (i.e. the prices of goods are rising on average by 5 per cent per year). Assume also that there is no inflation in the rest of world. At the end of one year, the average price of UK exports will be 5 per cent higher than at the beginning. On the other hand, imports will be 5 per cent cheaper than domestically produced goods. At the end of the second year, the gap will be even wider.

Starting from a PPP rate of $2 = £1, this change in relative prices between the UK and the rest of the world will affect the volume of UK exports and imports. UK exports will become steadily less price competitive on world markets. Hence sales of UK exports will fall. Imports into the UK on the other hand will become steadily more price competitive and their sales in the UK will rise. The balance of payments on current account will move into the red.

A fall in the volume of UK exports is likely to lead to a fall in the value of exports (this assumes that exports are **price elastic** and therefore the demand for pounds will fall). A rise in the value of imports will result in a rise in the supply of pounds. A fall in demand and a rise in supply of pounds will result in a fall in its value.

So the purchasing power parity theory argues that in the long run exchange rates will change in line with changes in prices between countries. For instance, if the annual UK inflation rate is 4 per cent higher than that of the USA over a period of time, then the pound will fall in value at an average annual rate of 4 per cent against the dollar over the period. In the long run, exchange rates will be in equilibrium when **purchasing power parities** are equal between countries. This means that the prices of typical bundles of traded goods and services are equal.

The causes of inflation are complex. However, one fundamental reason why economies can become less price competitive over time is **labour productivity** (i.e. output per worker). If output per worker, for instance, increases at a rate of 2 per cent per annum in the UK and 5 per cent per annum in Japan, then it is likely that the UK will become less competitive internationally than Japan over time. Wage costs are the single most important element on average in the final value of a product. In the UK, approximately 70 per cent of national income is made up of wages and salaries. Hence changes in labour productivity are an important component in changes in final costs.

Other factors affecting competitiveness

Price is an important factor in determining purchasing decisions, but it is not the only consideration. Other factors include design, quality, reliability or availability. Over long periods of time, countries can become increasingly uncompetitive internationally in one or more of these factors. Indeed it is often argued that the UK has suffered this fate over the past century. What then happens is that the economy finds it more and more difficult to export whilst imports increase. There is therefore a continual downward pressure on the exchange rate. The debate about what makes a country internationally uncompetitive is the same as the debate about why a country grows at a slower rate than other countries.

Question 3

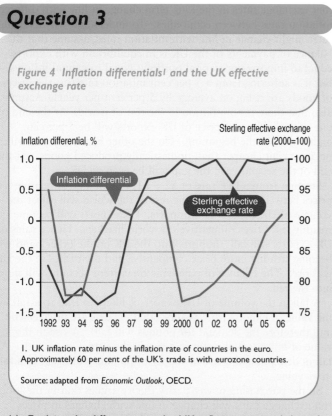

Figure 4 *Inflation differentials¹ and the UK effective exchange rate*

Inflation differential, %

Sterling effective exchange rate (2000=100)

1. UK inflation rate minus the inflation rate of countries in the euro. Approximately 60 per cent of the UK's trade is with eurozone countries.

Source: adapted from *Economic Outlook*, OECD.

(a) Explain why differences in the UK inflation rate and that of other countries might affect the value of the pound.

(b) To what extent is this relationship supported by the data?

Long term capital movements

During much of the 19th century, the USA was a net capital importer. It financed its development in part by borrowing money from Europe. Countries which are in a position to borrow money will have a higher long term exchange rate than they would otherwise have done. For instance, during the 19th century, Europeans demanded dollars to invest in the USA. This rise in demand led to a rise in the value of the dollar. Similarly, net long term lending by a country will tend to depress the exchange rate.

Speculation

Day to day exchange rate movements today are affected by speculation or short term flows of capital. Forty years ago this was different, as nearly all countries imposed a variety of EXCHANGE CONTROLS upon their currency movements. At the most extreme, currency could only be bought and sold through the central bank. In more liberal regimes, purchases could be made on the open market, but individuals and firms often had to seek permission from the central bank to trade in currency. Exchange controls have now largely been swept away in the major industrialised trading nations of the world. Vast sums of money are committed internationally and flows of just a fraction of these across exchanges can lead to large currency fluctuations.

Classical or monetarist economists in the 1960s and 1970s predicted that speculation would dampen

exchange rate fluctuations and help stabilise currencies. They argued that the exchange rate in the long term was fixed by economic fundamentals such as the balance between exports and imports. Economic fundamentals only change slowly over time and therefore market expectations of future exchange rates will only change slowly over time too. If the market believes that in two years' time the value of the pound against the dollar will be $2 = £1, and today the value of the pound is $3 = £1, then speculators will sell pounds, driving down the value of the pound towards its longer term value.

The evidence of the past 40 years suggests that this is not true. In the above example, it is just as likely that the value of the pound will go up as down even if speculators agree that in the long term the pound is overvalued at today's prices. The reason is that speculation by its very nature is short term. Speculators are not very interested in the price of sterling in 2 years' time. They are far more interested in the price of sterling in the next 30 minutes. Large sums of money can be made by buying and selling in the very short term.

It is impossible to pin-point exactly what drives short term exchange rate markets. Certainly markets tend to react in a predictable way to news about changes in economic fundamentals. A bad set of trade figures, for instance, which points to a future fall in the exchange rate, tends to lead to selling pressure today. A rise in domestic interest rates will tend to increase today's exchange rate as speculators anticipate future

Question 4

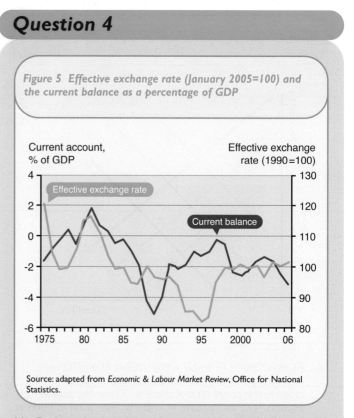

Figure 5 *Effective exchange rate (January 2005=100) and the current balance as a percentage of GDP*

Current account, % of GDP

Effective exchange rate (1990=100)

Source: adapted from *Economic & Labour Market Review*, Office for National Statistics.

(a) Explain what economic theory predicts is likely to happen to the exchange rate if the current account position deteriorates.

(b) Speculative activity should anticipate changes in economic fundamentals such as changes in the current account position. Do the data provide any evidence for suggesting that currency speculators have correctly anticipated changes in the UK current account position?

capital inflows to take advantage of the higher rates of interest. But many exchange rates are inexplicable. Speculators 'lose confidence' or 'gain confidence'. They are very influenced by the opinions of other speculators. Some individuals in the market may be extremely influential. A word spoken in a television interview or written in an article may spark off feverish buying or selling.

Some economists argue that there is no pattern at all to exchange rate movements: that they are on a **random walk** and the market is totally **chaotic**.

Even though speculation can be highly destabilising in the short term, economists tend to believe that economic fundamentals prevail in the long term.

Key terms

Effective exchange rate and trade weighted exchange rate index - measures of the exchange rate of a country's currency against a basket of currencies of a country's major trading partners.
Exchange controls - controls on the purchase and sale of foreign currency by a country, usually through its central bank.
Foreign exchange markets - the markets, organised in major financial centres such as London and New York, where currencies are bought and sold.
Purchasing power parity theory - the hypothesis that long run changes in exchange rates are caused by differences in inflation rates between countries.

Applied economics

The exchange rate, 1978-1981

Between 1978 and 1981, the effective exchange rate (EER) of the pound rose by over twenty five per cent before falling back a little, as can be seen in Table 2. There is a number of possible reasons why there should have been such a significant change in the EER.

One important factor was the change in the oil balance on the balance of payments. 1976 had seen the first production of North Sea oil and by the early 1980s production had reached its highest level. The effect was to transform a traditional deficit on trade in oil (with the UK importing all her oil requirements) to a substantial surplus. As Table 2 shows, there was a £6 000 million turnaround in the oil balance. The effect of increased production was magnified by the second oil crisis of 1978-9 which increased the price of oil from approximately $15 a barrel in 1978 to $36 a barrel in 1981. Increased exports result in greater demand for pounds and hence a higher value of the pound. So the positive change in the oil balance helped increase the EER.

Despite the positive change in the oil balance, the current balance (total exports minus imports) deteriorated in 1978-9. This was because the economy was enjoying a boom, and imports were being sucked into the country to satisfy domestic demand. However, by the early part of 1980, the economy was spiralling downwards into deep recession, which was to see a fall of 5 per cent in GDP and nearly 20 per cent in manufacturing output before the bottom in mid-1981. That led to a sharp fall in imports which, together with the effect of North Sea oil, led to a record current

Table 2 Factors affecting the exchange rate, 1979-1981

		Effective exchange rate 1985 = 100	Interest rate[1] %	Change in official reserves[2] £million	Current account balance £million	Oil balance[3] £million	Net external assets[3] £billion
1978	Q1	111.2	6.5	-46	-119		
	Q2	105.3	9.0	-2 026	458	-2 017	12.0
	Q3	106.5	10.0	54	88		
	Q4	105.7	12.0	-311	394		
1979	Q1	107.5	13.0	955	-661		
	Q2	113.0	12.0	68	-133	-686	11.0
	Q3	118.1	14.0	152	147		
	Q4	113.6	14.0	-166	-355		
1980	Q1	119.2	17.0	457	-274		
	Q2	122.1	17.0	140	-419	160	16.8
	Q3	125.1	16.0	-223	851		
	Q4	131.4	16.0	-83	1 582		
1981	Q1	135.9	14.0	319	2 752		
	Q2	131.9	12.0	-1 448	1 517	3 153	31.1
	Q3	123.1	12.0	-1 167	-68		
	Q4	120.9	15.0	-123	645		

1. Bank base rate at 15 February, 15 May, 15 August, 15 November.
2. Additions to reserves (+), falls in reserves (-).
3. Annual figures.

Source: adapted from *Economic Trends, Financial Statistics, Pink Book*, Office for National Statistics.

account surplus in 1981. This move from deficit in 1979 to record surplus in 1981, a turnaround of approximately £7 000 million on an annual basis, must have contributed to the rise in sterling between 1979 and 1981.

A further factor which is likely to have put upward pressure on the pound was the rise in interest rates. Between 1978 and 1980, bank base rates rose from 6.5 per cent to 17 per cent. This increased the interest rate differential between London and other financial centres round the world, attracting speculative flows of money into sterling. Falls in interest rates in 1980 and 1981 were followed by falls in the exchange rate in 1981.

Speculation too must have played a part in sending the EER to record levels. In 1978, there was still grave international concern about the competitiveness of the UK economy and the pound. By 1979, the pound was being seen as a petro currency. It didn't take much to look at what was happening to the oil balance to realise that the UK was likely to be in substantial surplus on current account in the early 1980s. Substantial surpluses would be likely to increase the EER, and therefore speculators bought pounds, which

had the effect of further raising the EER.

There were two factors which helped prevent the rise in the pound between 1979 and 1981 being even greater than it was. First, in November 1979, the government abolished exchange controls. These had limited the outflow of money on the capital account, reducing outflows from their free market levels. Following abolition, there was a substantial outflow of capital from the UK, reflected in the increase in net external assets of the UK shown in Table 2. Second, the Bank of England intervened in the foreign exchange markets, on the whole buying foreign currency in exchange for pounds (i.e. the supply of pounds increased). The fact that the Bank of England was intervening like this can be seen from the increase in the official foreign currency reserves of the UK during this period. When the exchange rate began to fall in 1981, the Bank of England reversed its policy. It began to buy pounds with foreign currency. This helped break the fall in the pound, but official foreign currency reserves fell.

DataQuestion — The exchange rate, 1993-2007

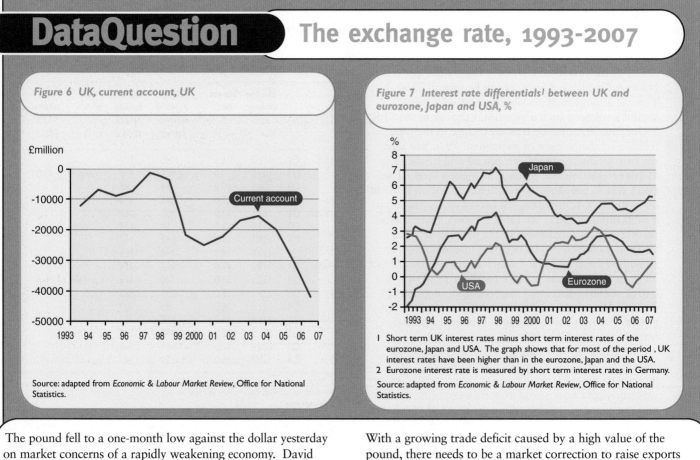

Figure 6 UK, current account, UK

Source: adapted from *Economic & Labour Market Review*, Office for National Statistics.

Figure 7 Interest rate differentials[1] between UK and eurozone, Japan and USA, %

1 Short term UK interest rates minus short term interest rates of the eurozone, Japan and USA. The graph shows that for most of the period , UK interest rates have been higher than in the eurozone, Japan and the USA.
2 Eurozone interest rate is measured by short term interest rates in Germany.

Source: adapted from *Economic & Labour Market Review*, Office for National Statistics.

The pound fell to a one-month low against the dollar yesterday on market concerns of a rapidly weakening economy. David Mann, a foreign exchange strategist at Standard Chartered Bank, said: 'Sterling is probably as strong as it will get this year. From now on, it is going to underperform the dollar and the euro.'

With a growing trade deficit caused by a high value of the pound, there needs to be a market correction to raise exports and reduce imports.

Source: adapted from the *Financial Times*, 11.5.2005.

Figure 8 Sterling exchange rates

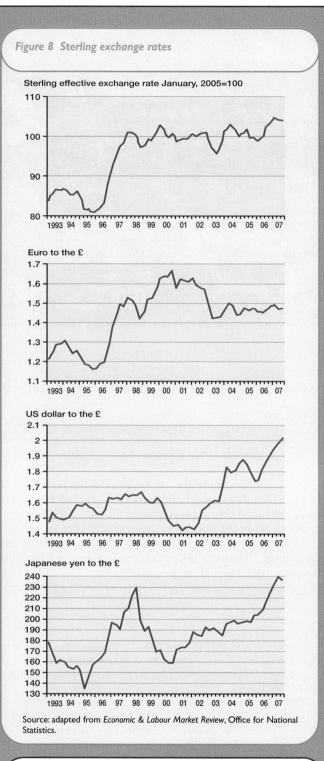

Sterling effective exchange rate January, 2005=100

Euro to the £

US dollar to the £

Japanese yen to the £

Source: adapted from *Economic & Labour Market Review*, Office for National Statistics.

Figure 9 Exports: the UK's main trading partners, 2nd quarter 2007

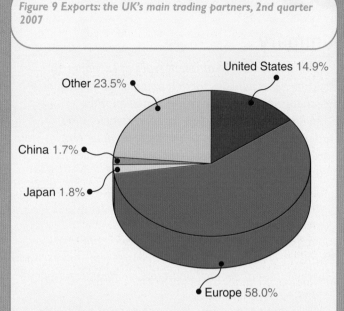

Other 23.5%

United States 14.9%

China 1.7%

Japan 1.8%

Europe 58.0%

Source: adapted from *Monthly Digest of Statistics*, Office for National Statistics.

 The pound is trading at its highest level against the US dollar for more than 26 years. High interest rates in the UK and continued bad news about the US economy have been putting upward pressure on the pound for months. Although UK interest rates are likely to have peaked, UK inflation is above the government's 2 per cent target and the Bank of England is likely to keep interest rates high for some time. However, the value of the dollar has been falling against other currencies too. The markets are worried about the continued size of the US current account deficit which, at around 5 per cent of GDP, is seen by many to be unsustainable.

Source: adapted from news.bbc.co.uk 16.4.2007 and 15.11.2007.

 The pound tumbled yesterday after it emerged that the Bank of England examined the case for a cut in interest rates this month. Minutes of a debate among the Bank's Monetary Policy Committee two weeks ago showed that some members felt that weakening inflationary pressures justified consideration of a cut in interest rates. 'Interest rates are likely to fall sooner and further than most expect,' said Jonathan Loynes of Capital Economics. The pound fell more than 1 per cent against the dollar and the euro.

Source: adapted from *The Times*, 23.12.2004.

1. Analyse whether the pound was strong or weak between (a) 1993 and 2000; (b) 2000 and 2007.
2. Discuss what might have led to the changes in the value of the pound against other currencies shown in the data.

Summary

1. There is a number of different types of exchange rate system - mechanisms for determining the conditions of exchange between one currency and another.
2. The Bretton Woods system was an example of an adjustable peg system. In the short term, currencies were fixed in value against each other. In the longer term, currencies could be devalued or revalued. Currencies were fixed in the short term by central bank intervention - the buying and selling of currency using foreign currency reserves.
3. In a floating exchange rate system, the value of a currency is determined, without central bank intervention, by the forces of demand and supply in foreign currency markets.
4. With a managed or dirty float, the price of a currency is determined by free market forces, but occasionally central banks will intervene, using their reserves to steady the price of the currency.
5. The Gold Standard was an example of a fixed exchange rate system. Currencies were pegged in value against gold and therefore they could not change in value against each other.
6. The European Monetary System was an example of a currency bloc. A group of currencies maintained fixed exchange rates against each other, but floated against other currencies.

Exchange rate systems

An EXCHANGE RATE SYSTEM is any system which determines the conditions under which one currency can be exchanged for another. It has previously been assumed that exchange rates were determined purely by the free market forces of demand and supply. This type of system is known as a free or floating exchange rate system. In contrast fixed exchange rate systems have existed in the past, where currencies have not been allowed to change in value against each other from year to year. In between, there is a variety of adjustable peg systems which combine elements of exchange rate stability in the short term with the possibility of exchange rate movements in the long term.

Adjustable peg systems

An ADJUSTABLE PEG SYSTEM is an exchange rate system where, in the short term, currencies are fixed or pegged against each other and do not change in value, whilst in the longer term the value of a currency can be changed if economic circumstances so dictate. Between the end of the Second World War and the early 1970s, exchange rates were determined by an adjustable peg system. It was known as the BRETTON WOODS SYSTEM after the town in the USA where Allied powers met in 1944 to discuss new international trade arrangements for the post-war era.

How it worked Under the system, each country fixed its exchange rate against other currencies. For instance, between 1949 and 1967, the pound was valued at US $2.80. This was known as the par value for the currency. The Bank of England guaranteed to maintain prices within a narrow 1 per cent boundary. So the price of the pound could fluctuate on a day to day basis between $2.78 and $2.82. Prices were maintained because central banks bought and sold currency. When the price of pounds threatened to go below $2.78, the Bank of England would intervene in the market and buy pounds. When the price threatened to go over $2.82, the Bank of England would sell pounds.

This is illustrated in Figure 1. The free market demand curve

---

Figure 1 Fixed exchange rate systems

The pound is pegged at $2.80 but is allowed to fluctuate within a very narrow band from $2.78 to $2.82. If market forces shift the supply curve from S_1 to S_2, the Bank of England will need to buy BD pounds to maintain the minimum price of $2.78.

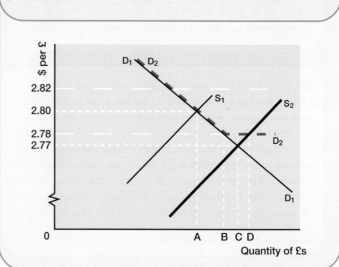

Question 1

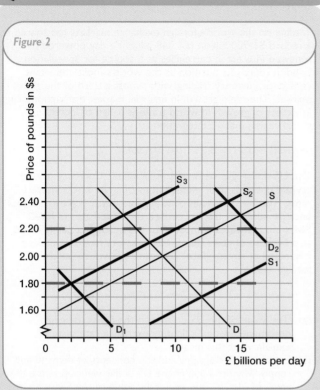

Figure 2

D and S are the free market demand and supply curves for pounds in dollars. The Bank of England is committed to keeping the dollar price of sterling between $2.20 and $1.80.

(a) What is the free market price of the pound?
(b) With a demand curve D, how much currency (in £) will the Bank of England have to buy or sell per day if the supply curve shifts from S to: (i) S_1; (ii) S_2; (iii) S_3?
(c) With a supply curve S, how much currency (in £) will the Bank of England have to buy or sell per day if the demand curve shifts from D to: (i) D_1; (ii) D_2?

If the value of the pound threatened to rise above the maximum price of $2.82, the Bank of England would sell pounds on the market, increasing the supply of pounds and thus forcing their price down. Note that in Figure 1, the supply curve of sterling under an adjustable peg system would be kinked like the demand curve, becoming horizontal (i.e. perfectly elastic) at a sterling price of $2.82. The Bank of England would be prepared to supply any amount of sterling in exchange for foreign currencies at a price of $2.82.

Adjustment mechanisms Under the Bretton Woods system, countries were committed to two major policy objectives:
● in the short term, to maintaining stable exchange rates;
● in the long term, to maintaining a balance of payments equilibrium (which they would be forced to do anyway by free market forces).

In the short term, exchange rate stability was maintained by buying and selling currencies as explained above. The system was therefore crucially dependent upon the existence of gold and foreign currency reserves held by central banks. In theory, the price of the currency was set at its long term equilibrium level. A run down in reserves caused by the need to buy the domestic currency when the currency was weak would be offset by increases in the reserves at other times when the currency was strong.

However, free market speculation could lead to very rapid depletions of a country's gold and foreign currency reserves. The UK suffered a series of **sterling crises** in the 1950s, 1960s and 1970s as speculators sold pounds believing that the UK government might devalue sterling. Governments had a limited number of options open to them if they wanted to maintain the value of their exchange rate.
● The most likely response to heavy selling pressure on the currency was to raise interest rates. This attracted speculative money from abroad, raising the demand for and therefore the price of the currency. In the medium term, a rise in interest rates would have a deflationary impact via the **transmission mechanism**.
● The government could also attempt to prevent a fall in the value of the currency by introducing **currency controls**.
● As a last resort, the central bank would turn to the **International Monetary Fund** (IMF). The founders of the system realised that there would be times when an individual country would run out of reserves. So it set up an international fund, the IMF, which would lend money to central banks when needed. Central banks would deposit part of their gold and foreign currency reserves with the IMF and in return would be able to borrow a limited amount of money when in a crisis.

Short term measures were unlikely to satisfy the market for long if speculators were selling a currency because they judged that there was a FUNDAMENTAL DISEQUILIBRIUM on the country's balance of payments. If imports were greater than exports and/or the capital account was in deficit over a long period of time, the central bank of the country would continually be buying its currency and thus running down its reserves. Eventually the reserves, including any money borrowed from the IMF, would be exhausted and the currency would have to fall in value. Governments could adopt a number of long term policies to prevent this happening.
● It was intended that governments would officially devalue their currency before markets forced this anyway.
● In practice, governments tended to deflate their

for pounds is $D_1 D_1$. In contrast, the demand curve under an adjustable peg system, $D_2 D_2$, is kinked. Above a price of $2.78, the demand curve is the same as the free market demand curve. However, at $2.78, the Bank of England is prepared to buy any amount of foreign currency to maintain the value of the pound at this minimum level. Therefore the demand curve for pounds becomes horizontal (i.e. perfectly elastic) at this price.

Assume that the supply curve is initially S_1, resulting in an equilibrium price of $2.80. 0A is bought and sold and the Bank of England does not intervene in the market.

Now assume that imports into the UK increase, shifting the supply curve for pounds to the right to, say, S_2. The new free market equilibrium price would be $2.77, below the minimum **intervention price** within the system, with 0C currency bought and sold. The Bank of England would react to this by buying pounds with gold or foreign exchange held in its reserves. To restore the exchange rate to the minimum $2.78, it has to buy BD pounds, the difference between the 0B pounds demanded by the rest of the market at $2.78 and 0D, the quantity supplied for sale.

economies, reducing imports and thus restoring a current account balance.

● Protectionist measures, such as raising tariffs and quotas, were a possibility but were illegal under WTO rule. This severely limited their use by major industrialised countries.

● Supply side policies designed to improve long term competitiveness were also a possibility.

Question 2

In 1952, the ratio of world central bank gold and foreign currency reserves to total world imports stood at 70 per cent. By 1966, this had fallen to 38 per cent.

(a) Suggest reasons why this fall is likely to have contributed to the collapse of the Bretton Woods system in the early 1970s.

Crawling peg systems

A CRAWLING PEG system is a form of adjustable peg system. A country fixes its currency value against another currency within a band. However, there is a mechanism built into the system which allows the band to rise and fall regularly over time. For instance, the band may be moved every three months. The central value could then be based on the average value of the currency in the previous three months. Crawling peg systems allow more flexibility if a country is experiencing different economic circumstances from other countries and in particular those against which its currency is pegged. It makes it much easier to adjust the value of the currency as economic circumstances change.

Floating exchange rate systems

In a pure FLOATING or FREE EXCHANGE RATE SYSTEM, the value of a currency is determined on a minute by minute basis by free market forces. Governments, through their central banks, are assumed not to intervene in the foreign exchange markets.

In theory there is no need for intervention because the balance of payments must always balance. The balance of payments will look after itself. In practice, governments find it impossible not to intervene because changes in exchange rates can lead to significant changes in domestic output, unemployment and inflation. Moreover, sharp falls in a currency are usually damaging politically and hence governments are tempted at these times to shore up the currency by buying in the market.

A system where the exchange rate is determined by free market forces but governments intervene from time to time to alter the free market price of a currency is known as a MANAGED or DIRTY FLOAT. Governments intervene by buying and selling currency as under the Bretton Woods system explained above. It is 'managed' by governments. It is 'dirty' because it is a deliberate interference with 'pure' forces of demand and supply.

Adjustment mechanisms Since the collapse of the Bretton Woods system in the early 1970s, world trade has been regulated not under a pure free exchange system but

Question 3

Trading on the world's foreign exchange markets has soared to a record $1 900 billion (£1 048 billion) a day, powered by renewed interest in currencies as a source for speculation. London retains its position as the world's most important centre for currency trading, with almost a third of the global market. The rapid growth in financial market transactions, far in excess of growth in world trade, is a sign of increasing global capital market integration.

Source: adapted from the *Financial Times*, 29.9.2004.

The US dollar this week was up in value. Currency traders revised upwards their expectations of a rise in US interest rates. The Swiss franc in contrast was down. Partly this was because currency traders revised their estimates of lower Swiss interest rates compared to the euro. But partly it was also because of news that Swiss investors have been taking advantage of strong global economic growth to purchase foreign assets.

Source: adapted from the *Financial Times* 25.3.2006.

(a) 'The value of the US dollar and the Swiss franc are determined within a floating exchange rate system.' Explain what this means.

(b) Explain, using diagrams and the concepts of demand and supply, why the value of the US dollar went up in the third week of March 2006 whilst the value of the Swiss franc went down.

under a system of managed or dirty floats. Governments have used interest rates and their gold and foreign currency reserves to manipulate the value of their currencies. Depreciation, appreciation and deflation have all been used in an attempt to alter current deficits or surpluses. Governments have found it more difficult to pursue openly protectionist policies because of international pressure for greater free trade. Currency controls too have fallen into disfavour as supply side economics has stressed the value of free markets and deregulation in promoting the international competitiveness of economies.

Fixed exchange rate systems

A fixed exchange rate system is one where a currency has a fixed value against another currency or commodity. The best known example of such a system in the past was the GOLD STANDARD, which operated in the 19th and early 20th centuries.

How it worked   Under the Gold Standard, the major trading nations made their domestic currencies **convertible** into gold at a fixed rate. For instance, in 1914 a holder of a £1 note could go to the Bank of England and exchange the note for 0.257 ounces of gold. Since French citizens could exchange French francs for a fixed amount of gold, and German citizens the same, and so on, it meant that there was a **fixed exchange rate** between the major trading currencies of the world. The domestic money supply was directly related to the amount of gold held by the central bank. For every extra 0.257 ounces of gold held by the Bank of England, it could issue £1 in paper currency (the currency was backed by gold). On the other hand, a fall in the gold reserves at the Bank of England meant an equivalent fall in the paper money in circulation.

Adjustment mechanisms A deficit on the current account of the balance of payments could not be corrected by devaluation of the currency. By the rules of the Gold Standard mechanism, the currency was fixed in value. Imbalances on the current account were corrected instead through deflation and reflation or changes in interest rates.

Assume that the UK is on the Gold Standard and that the current account is in deficit. There is therefore a net outflow of pounds to foreigners. Foreigners have no use for pounds so they will exchange those pounds for gold at the Bank of England. With less gold, the Bank of England will be forced to reduce its issue of notes (the notes handed in by foreigners for gold will effectively be destroyed). The money supply will fall and interest rates will rise. This will produce a deflation in the economy through the **transmission mechanism**. Not only will demand fall, reducing imports, but there will also be a fall in prices (predicted by the **quantity theory of money**). Exports will thus become more competitive and imports less competitive. The current account will return to equilibrium. The initial rise in unemployment caused by the fall in demand will be reversed as exports increase, returning the economy to full employment.

A small but increasing number of small countries are adopting CURRENCY BOARDS. This is a form of fixed exchange rate system where the price of one currency is fixed against another currency. Typically, currency boards fix their currencies against either the US dollar or the euro.

How it works A country fixes the value of its currency, usually against a major international currency such as the US dollar or the euro. The choice of currency is linked to foreign trade. The central bank then prints domestic currency. However, it is only able to print as much domestic currency as it has reserves of its pegged currency.

Adjustment mechanisms The adjustment mechanism is the same as with the Gold Standard. A deficit on the current account will lead to an outflow of dollars, which in turn will reduce the money supply and cause deflation. This leads to lower domestic demand and hence lower imports; and lower domestic prices and hence exports increase as they become more competitive.

Currency blocs

A country may choose to peg its currency against one other currency but allow the currency to fluctuate against all others. This would be a minimal example of a CURRENCY BLOC, a group of currencies fixed in value against each other but floating against all others.

The most important example of a currency bloc in the 1980s

and 1990s was the EUROPEAN MONETARY SYSTEM (EMS). This was a system designed to lead onto the creation of a single European currency, the euro. Participant countries agreed to keep their currencies within a band around a central reference point. If a currency threatened to break out of the band, central banks within the EMS would intervene in the market, buying or selling currency to maintain the currency in its band. The country's central bank could also change interest rates to alter its value. The whole bloc, however, floated freely against other world currencies including the dollar and the yen. If the UK is to join the euro, it will have to peg the pound against what is now the euro and show that it can maintain exchange rate stability within this system.

Like the Bretton Woods system, this is an example of a hybrid system, combining elements of fixed and floating exchange rate systems.

Question 4

In the late 1980s and early 1990s, the Argentinian economy was in deep trouble. Inflation peaked at 3 000 per cent in 1989 whilst GDP was 10 per cent lower in that year than in 1980. As part of a recovery plan, the Argentinian government introduced a currency board system in 1991. The Argentinian peso was pegged against the US dollar at an exchange rate of 1 peso to $1. Inflation fell to 3.4 per cent in 1994 but by this stage the peso was overvalued against the dollar and Argentina's main trading partners. The result was that the peg became a major source of deflation in the economy. A number of exchange rate crises in the 1990s culminated in the currency board being abandoned in 2002. The value of the peso fell by two thirds against the US dollar.

Source: adapted from en.wikipedia.org.

Estonia gained its independence from Russia in 1990. A period of rapid inflation was brought to an end when Estonia's central bank pegged its currency, the Kroon, against the German currency at the time (the mark) and created a currency board. Estonia is a relatively small country and has become dependent on trade with other countries for its prosperity. In 2004, it joined the European Union and as part of its accession treaty, committed itself to adopting the euro, which it did in January 2007. Stable prices fixed to a currency which itself was fixed against other European currencies through the Exchange Rate Mechanism (ERM), the mechanism which led to the creation of the euro, helped Estonia's rapid growth.

Source: adapted from www.bankofestonia.info, the website of the Estonian central bank.

(a) Using the examples of Argentina and Estonia, explain (i) what is meant by a 'currency board'; (ii) the advantages and disadvantages of currency boards.

Key terms

Adjustable peg system - an exchange rate system where currencies are fixed in value in the short term but can be devalued or revalued in the longer term.

Bretton Woods system - an adjustable peg exchange rate system which was used in the post-Second World War period until its collapse in the early 1970s.

Crawling peg system - an adjustable peg system of exchange rates where there is an inbuilt mechanism for regular changes in the central value of the currency.

Currency bloc - a group of currencies which are fixed in value against each other but which may float freely against other world currencies.

Currency board system - a fixed exchange rate system where a country fixes the value of its currency to another currency. Notes and coins in the domestic currency can only be printed to the value of assets in the other currency held by the central bank.

European Monetary System - a currency bloc where the participating currencies were fixed against each other within a band and where the bloc as a whole fluctuated freely against other currencies.

Exchange rate system - a system which determines the conditions under which one currency can be exchanged for another.

Free or floating exchange rate system - where the value of a currency is determined by free market forces.

Fixed exchange rate - a rate of exchange between at least two currencies which is constant over a period of time.

Fundamental disequilibrium on the balance of payments - where imports are greater than exports over a long period of time resulting in unsustainable levels of international borrowing.

Gold and foreign currency reserves - gold and foreign currency owned by the central bank of a country and used mainly to change the foreign exchange value of the domestic currency by buying and selling currency on foreign exchanges.

Managed or dirty float - where the exchange rate is determined by free market forces but governments intervene from time to time to alter the free market price of a currency.

The Gold Standard - an exchange rate system under which currencies could be converted into gold at a fixed rate, hence providing a relative price between each currency.

Applied economics

The Bretton Woods system

The Bretton Woods system, first devised in 1944, provided exchange rate stability. Hence, it can be argued that it encouraged the growth of world trade during the 1950s and 1960s.

It was intended that governments could choose how to resolve a current account deficit. They could deflate the economy, creating unemployment, reducing imports and reducing domestic inflation. This was the same adjustment mechanism as present under the Gold Standard. They could also devalue the currency. By changing the relative price of exports and imports, the economy could be made more internationally competitive without creating unemployment. However, there would be some cost in terms of imported inflation.

In practice, countries tended not to devalue except in a crisis. This was because devaluation, wrongly in the view of many economists, came to be associated with economic failure. Deficit countries tended to use deflation as the main policy weapon to deal with balance of payments problems, negating the flexibility of adjusting relative prices built into the system. The burden of adjustment also fell solely on deficit countries. There was little pressure within the system for surplus countries to reduce their surpluses, for instance by revaluing their currencies. The result was that the system became increasingly brittle. Deficit countries like the UK tended to lurch from one foreign exchange crisis to the next whilst surplus countries like West Germany resisted pressures to take any action to reduce their surpluses.

Problems were compounded by the fall in the value of gold and currency reserves as a ratio of world trade during the 1950s and 1960s. To maintain exchange rate stability, central banks bought and sold currency. So long as the central banks were the main buyers and sellers in the market, they could dictate the price of foreign exchange. However, during the 1950s and 1960s world trade expanded at a much faster rate than gold and foreign currency reserves.

In an attempt to inject greater liquidity into the international financial system, the IMF issued **Special Drawing Rights** (SDRs) to member countries in

1969. SDRs are a form of international currency which can only be used by central banks to settle debts between themselves or with the IMF. When a country needs foreign currency to defend its own currency, it can buy it with the SDRs it holds. Whilst SDRs, effectively a handout of 'free' money, increased liquidity in the system at the time, the IMF failed to allocate further SDRs to member countries. The countries which control the IMF, the industrialised nations of the world, particularly the USA, are afraid that further creation of SDRs would encourage countries, particularly in the Third World, to put off dealing with fundamental balance of payments problems by using newly distributed SDRs to finance their large current account deficits. Today, SDRs account for only about 5 per cent of world reserves.

The Vietnam war from 1965 onwards made matters worse. To finance the war the USA ran a large current account deficit and therefore was a net borrower of money on its capital account. Individuals and firms were quite happy to lend their pounds, francs, deutschmarks and other currencies to the US and in exchange receive dollars because exchange rates were fixed to the dollar and dollars were seen to be as safe as gold itself.

By the late 1960s there was a large amount of money, particularly dollars, being held outside its country of origin. Americans were holding pounds, Japanese were holding deutschmarks, Germans were holding dollars, etc. This provided the base for large speculative activity on the foreign exchanges. It had become obvious that the United States would need to devalue the dollar if it were to return to a balance of payments equilibrium. On the other hand, it was obvious that Germany and Japan, two large surplus countries, would have to revalue their currencies. There was persistent selling pressure on the dollar and buying pressure on the D-mark and yen. Central banks found it more and more difficult to match the speculative waves of buying and selling. In the early 1970s, after some traumatic devaluations and revaluations, one country after another announced that it would float its currency.

The Bretton Woods system provided a long period of exchange rate stability during which there was a significant expansion of world trade. The cost of adjustment to current account deficits was probably less than under the Gold Standard. Although deflation was widely used in response to this problem, countries also devalued their currency, trading off slightly higher imported inflation for less unemployment. However, the system was not sufficiently robust to prevent its collapse in the early 1970s.

DataQuestion — The renminbi

The Chinese central bank, the People's Bank of China, announced yesterday that it would be revaluing upwards the Chinese currency, the renminbi, by 2.1 per cent against the US dollar. Since 1994, the currency has been fixed against the US dollar.

The Chinese government has been reluctant to revalue the renminbi despite the fact that China runs a large trade surplus and the People's Bank of China has regularly intervened to keep the value of the renminbi down. In the past two years, for example, it has intervened in the foreign currency markets buying around $200 billion a year of US currency in exchange for renminbi, bringing its total foreign currency reserves to $700 billion. The rate of increase in China's foreign exchange reserves was widely seen as unsustainable.

Source: adapted from the *Financial Times*, 22.7.2005.

The new exchange rate system announced yesterday by the People's Bank of China may lead to future upward revaluations of the renminbi. The Chinese central bank described the new system as a 'peg', which would normally imply that there would be regular changes in the value of the currency. Equally, though, the Chinese government is unlikely to want to see the renminbi rise too much in value because of its impact on exports. The People's Bank of China said yesterday that it would maintain the 'renminbi exchange rate basically stable at an adaptive and equilibrium level, so as to promote the basic equilibrium of the balance of payments and safeguard macroeconomic and financial stability'.

Source: adapted from the *Financial Times*, 22.7.2005.

China has been under intense pressure in recent years from some US lobby groups to revalue the renminbi. China runs a huge surplus on its trade with the USA, reflecting its ability to undercut many US companies in price. US textile manufacturers, for example, have suffered badly at the hands of Chinese competition. In Congress, only last month, a bill was proposed to impose tariffs of 27.5 per cent on Chinese imports.

However, China points out that it runs deficits with a number of countries including Japan. It argues that US trade deficits are more to do with other factors than China's growing competitiveness.

Source: adapted from the *Financial Times*, 22.7.2005.

The Chinese government can congratulate itself that it is running a 'miracle' economy growing at 6-10 per cent per year. Much of its success is due to its outward facing policies of encouraging exports and allowing foreign companies to set up in China. Having an undervalued currency helps maintain this export momentum.

However, economic progress comes at the price of potential social instability. Millions of people are on the move from low productivity rural areas to higher productivity urban areas, particularly in the coastal provinces. Mass migration and huge changes in work have the potential to destabilise society and threaten the Communist Party's grip on power. So the last thing the Chinese government wants is an exchange rate which has large fluctuations. A stable exchange rate means that at least one uncertainty is taken out of the equation for China's exporters and importers.

Equally, building up huge foreign currency reserves is not a sensible way of operating policy in the long term. An undervalued exchange rate causes trade frictions with the risk of protectionist retaliation from other countries. It also leads in one way to lower living standards. The Chinese

are charging too low a price for their exports but are being charged too high a price for their imports. By raising their exchange rate, the Chinese could get more for their exports and pay less for their imports.

Source: adapted from the *Financial Times*, 22.7.2005

Peter Mandelson, the European Union's trade commissioner, said on Thursday that China should revalue the renminbi. He pointed out that the EU's trade deficit with China was growing $20 million every hour and would 'catch up with the US-China trade deficit in a year or so'. He went on: 'We want an end to a managed currency in China that hurts us. Even if revaluation would not, in itself, solve our trade deficits, it would help cool an

overheating (Chinese) heavy industry sector which is swollen with overcapacity and artificially cheap capital.' By revaluing the currency, the Chinese authorities had the opportunity to boost their domestic demand and encourage Chinese consumers to spend rather than save.

Source: adapted from the *Financial Times*, 9.11.2007.

1. With the help of diagrams, explain how the value of a currency is fixed in an adjustable peg system, using the renminbi as an example.
2. Analyse why the Chinese government has been under no short term economic pressure to revalue the renminbi.

3. Discuss whether the Chinese government should, over time, revalue the renminbi upwards against other currencies.

88 The advantages and disadvantages of exchange rate systems

Summary

3.4.3

1. An exchange rate system should encourage world trade, particularly through exchange rate stability. Floating exchange rate systems have proved very poor at providing exchange rate stability.
2. Economic costs of adjustment when the balance of payments of a country is in fundamental disequilibrium should be low. Adjustment mechanisms within fixed exchange rate systems, such as the Gold Standard, and to a lesser extent adjustable peg systems, such as the Bretton Woods system and the EMS, tend to create unemployment because they rely upon deflation of the economy. In contrast, floating exchange rate systems tend to give rise to inflation when currencies depreciate following current account deficits.
3. Fixed exchange rate systems, and to a lesser extent adjustable peg systems, force governments to maintain inflation rates comparable to their industrial competitors.
4. Exchange rate systems should be robust. Free exchange rate systems are the most robust because they require the least government intervention.

Judging between systems

Over the past 200 years, a variety of exchange rate systems has been in operation. This would suggest that no system is without its problems. A number of criteria can be used to judge the relative merits of different exchange rate systems.

Encouragement of world trade

World trade enables countries to specialise in the production of those goods and services in which they have a **comparative advantage**. This specialisation increases the total amount of goods available for world consumption. Hence exchange rate systems could be judged upon the extent to which they encourage or discourage world trade.

It has long been argued that exchange rate volatility, such as occurs under free floats or managed floats, discourages trade. If exchange rates fluctuate by large amounts on a day to day basis, exporters and importers will find it impossible to know what price they will receive or have to pay for deliveries in the future. For instance, a UK exporter may agree to sell goods to the US for payment in US dollars in 3 months' time. Built into the $1 million price is a 10 per cent profit margin. Over the 3 months, the pound falls in value against the dollar by 15 per cent. Not only will the exporter lose its planned profit, but it will also make a loss on the contract of about 5 per cent.

There are ways around this problem in a free or managed float regime. **Futures markets** exist, where foreign exchange can be bought at a fixed price for delivery at some point in the future. So the exporter could have bought pounds **forward**. At the time it signs the export agreement, it would have taken out a contract in the foreign exchange markets to buy $1 million worth of pounds in three months' time (which it will pay for using the $1 million gained from the export contract). It now has a guaranteed price in pounds for its contract. Of course the

forward price of pounds may be less than the price of pounds today (the spot price). But this is not important in the sense that the UK exporter will have based the export agreement price on the forward rate of the pound, and not on the current spot price. This process of buying currency forward to prevent losses is known as **hedging**.

Unfortunately, futures markets are limited in their scope. It is not possible, for instance, to buy a currency for delivery in 5 years' time. So long term contracts need other forms of insurance. This is often provided by government agencies which guarantee prices in the domestic currency for large long term export contracts. Hedging and insurance cost money and they therefore either discourage trade or raise its cost. Companies that are unable or unwilling to hedge or to insure have to decide whether or not to take the risk of proceeding with the export or import contract.

So, in general, the less volatile the currency movement, the less likely that international trade will be discouraged. Fixed exchange rate systems, such as the Gold Standard, and adjustable peg systems, such as the Bretton Woods system, are on these criteria considered to be 'better' systems than free or managed float systems.

Economic costs of adjustment

A country's balance of payments on current account can move into disequilibrium. Different exchange rate systems have different mechanisms for returning the balance of payments to equilibrium. The movement back to equilibrium may involve economic costs, such as increased unemployment or lower economic growth. The larger these transitional costs, the less attractive the exchange rate system.

The main cost of adjustment within a fixed exchange rate system or an adjustable peg system is likely to be increased unemployment. Under the Gold Standard, a current

Question 1

Britain joining the euro would lift a heavy burden from the backs of Europe's smaller businesses, most of which lack the expertise to deal with the complexities of foreign exchange markets. Smaller businesses pay a high cost for converting small amounts of foreign currencies, says Ms Jane Waters, a foreign exchange consultant. Banks typically charge 1 per cent on small deals of up to $10 000, but only 0.1 per cent on larger amounts.

Van Halteren, a Dutch meat processor with annual sales of £23m, pays about £25 000 each year to hedge the riskier currencies, such as sterling.

Many small businesses are frightened off from using the textbook exchange hedges - forward transactions or currency option arrangements - because of their perceived complexity and cost. They take evasive action. They invoice customers in their own currency; some delay making transfers of funds until currency rates are favourable; others boost prices to cover the currency risk.

All these manoeuvres carry risks. Better by far, smaller owners argue, to establish a foreign exchange framework which allows companies to get on with their business rather than having to watch currency movements.

(a) Explain, using examples from the passage, why exchange rate stability might encourage world trade.

account deficit was automatically eliminated in the long term through a fall in domestic prices. However, economists disagree about the extent to which money wage rates fall quickly in response to unemployment. Keynesian economists tend to argue that wage rate adjustment is slow. Classical or monetarist economists argue that it is a relatively quick process. The slower the adjustment, the higher the cost in terms of unemployment and lost output. Countries abandoned the Gold Standard in the early 1930s because they felt that floating exchange rates would enable their economies to reduce unemployment at a faster rate than if the exchange rate was linked to gold.

Under the Bretton Woods system, countries tended to avoid devaluing their currencies. When current accounts moved into deficit, governments tended to deflate their economies, imposing higher taxes or reducing government expenditure. Unemployment therefore rose as the rate of economic growth fell.

One of the main criticisms of floating and managed exchange rate systems is that they encourage inflationary behaviour on the part of governments. Assume that an economy has a higher inflation rate than its major trading partners and that, consequently, the current account is in deficit. Under the Bretton Woods system, governments would have been likely to tackle these two problems through deflating the economy. Under the Gold Standard, deflation would have occurred automatically. Rising unemployment and lost output are politically unpopular as well as costly economically. Under a floating exchange rate system, the exchange rate should fall automatically with a current account deficit. This leads to **imported inflation**. A government can avoid tackling domestic inflation and the current account deficit simply by allowing the exchange rate to fall continually. Hence there is no anti-inflation discipline built into the floating exchange rate system.

Moreover, tackling inflation under a floating exchange rate system can be more costly than under fixed

exchange rate systems. Assume that the government reduces the money supply and raises interest rates as part of an anti-inflation package. The rise in domestic interest rates will encourage an inflow of speculative funds on the capital account. This will increase the price of the currency. An increase in the exchange rate will make the economy less internationally competitive. Exports will fall and imports will rise, leading to a worsening of the already bad current account deficit. But falling exports and rising imports also lead to a fall in aggregate demand, pushing the economy into recession. This recession is part of the process by which inflation falls and the economy becomes more internationally competitive. The current account will only return to equilibrium when the market exchange rate is approximately equal to the **purchasing power parity rate**. It will only stay in equilibrium when the country's inflation rate is equal to that of its trading partners. Lowering inflation is a painful process and will certainly not be politically popular.

Question 2

Throughout the 1980s the UK exchange rate was determined under a floating exchange rate system, whilst the exchange rate of her main EU trading partners was determined under an adjustable peg system - the ERM. Inflation rates in all EU countries tended to fall in the first half of the 1980s and then remained low till the end of the decade. UK inflation rates tended to be 2-3 per cent higher than those of France and Germany during the period, whilst the value of the pound tended to fall. By 1987 the value of the pound was 15 per cent lower against the ECU (the basket or average of European currencies) than in 1980. However, between 1982 and 1988, average annual economic growth in the UK exceeded that of most European countries. In 1988, inflation in the UK began to accelerate again with the UK government responding by doubling interest rates to 15 per cent. The economy began to slow down. Then, in 1990, the UK joined the ERM at the very high central exchange rate of DM2.95, the same rate of exchange as prevailed on average in 1986. To maintain the value of the pound, the UK government was forced to keep interest rates at much higher levels than it probably would have wanted. The UK economy was in a very long prolonged recession between 1990 and 1992, with inflation falling rapidly to levels not seen since the 1960s. In September 1992, speculative pressure forced the pound to be suspended from the ERM. The value of the pound immediately fell over 10 per cent and the government cut interest rates from 10 per cent to 5½ per cent over the next 12 months. Growth in the economy rapidly picked up and the economy came out of recession.

(a) (i) What was true about the UK's inflation rate and rate of economic growth during the period 1982-88 compared to those of her main EU partners?

(ii) With these trends, explain what you would have expected to happen to the UK current account on the balance of payments if the value of the pound had remained constant.

(iii) Some economists and politicians argued at the time that allowing the pound to float downwards was inflationary. Explain this view.

(b) (i) Why might the fact that the UK joined the ERM in 1990 have prolonged the recession of 1990-1992?

(ii) Explain the likely impact of Britain's membership of the ERM on domestic inflation between 1990 and 1992.

Financial disciplines

Today, there are some who argue that inflation is the most important economic problem facing economies and governments. Monetarists argue that inflation is caused by excessive increases in the money supply. Under the Gold Standard, governments are unable to expand the money supply unless stocks of gold in the central bank rise first (although countries did issue a fixed amount of notes which were not backed by gold - the **fiduciary issue** - this did not affect the principle that central banks could not increase notes in circulation without corresponding increases in their stocks of gold). Changes in stocks of gold are unlikely to be very large in the short term. Hence the Gold Standard provides an important check on the ability of governments to generate inflation through the creation of money.

Equally, under an adjustable peg system, such as the Bretton Woods system, governments could not allow their inflation rates to differ greatly from those of their industrial competitors because otherwise they would lose international competitiveness, their current account would go into deficit and they would then be likely to deflate to solve this problem.

However, under a floating exchange rate system, as argued above, governments can always solve problems of international competitiveness, caused by domestic inflation, by allowing their currencies to fall in value. There is no financial discipline imposed by the system.

Robustness of the system

Some exchange rate systems are extremely robust; that is, they are unlikely to break up when economic conditions are unfavourable. The more likely it is that an exchange rate system will break up under strain, the less attractive the exchange rate system.

Fixed exchange rate systems, or adjustable peg systems, are less robust than free or managed float exchange rate systems. Countries abandoned the Gold Standard in the early 1930s during the Great Depression because they wanted to be able to devalue their currencies in order to gain competitive advantage. By devaluing, they hoped to be able to reduce imports, boost exports and thus reduce domestic unemployment. However, the rest of the 1930s, with a managed float system of exchange rates, saw a series of competitive devaluations with countries trying to export their unemployment. Competitive devaluations are ultimately self-defeating because devaluation by one country, matched by a devaluation by another country simply left exchange rates unchanged.

The unsatisfactory experience of the 1930s led to the creation of the Bretton Woods system. It broke up in the early 1970s, partly because countries failed to devalue and revalue when there was a fundamental disequilibrium on their current accounts and partly because central banks lacked reserves to counter the growing mountain of speculative money which moved so quickly from country, to country.

The managed float system of the 1970s, 1980s and 1990s has had to cope with three oil crises, and in the early 1980s, the worst world slump since the 1930s. Free and managed float systems are extremely robust because governments can allow free market forces to determine the value of the exchange rate without intervening in the market. However, the extreme volatility of exchange rates over the period has led many to advocate a return to some sort of fixed or adjustable peg system. The robustness of the system is less attractive than the exchange rate stability that can be found.

Key terms

Monetary union - when at least two countries share the same currency.

Question 3

In the early 1970s, the Bretton Woods system of exchange rates broke up. Explain why the system proved insufficiently robust.

Applied economics

Monetary unions

Monetary unions today

A MONETARY UNION occurs when at least two countries share the same currency. The most important monetary union today is the Economic and Monetary Union (EMU) of the European Union. However, there have been other monetary unions in the past. For example, the Austro-Hungarian Empire at the start of the 20th century shared a single currency. In 2008, there were four monetary unions apart from EMU.
- The Economic and Monetary Community of Central Africa, made up of a number of ex-French colonies, uses the CFA Franc.
- The West African Economic and monetary Union is another group of ex-French colonies which uses a different CFA Franc.

- The Overseas Issuing Institute issues the CFP Franc to three overseas collectivities of France in the Pacific: French Polynesia, New Caledonia and Wallis and Futuna.
- The Eastern Caribbean Currency Union is a group of Eastern Caribbean countries including Dominica, Grenada and Saint Lucia which uses the East Caribbean dollar.

There are also a number of other examples where countries use the currency of another country rather than issuing their own currency. For example, the South African rand is legal tender not just in South Africa but also in Swaziland, Lesotho and Namibia. The US dollar is used in Ecuador, El Salvador, Panama, the British Virgin Islands and the Turks and Caicos Islands.

History of the Economic and Monetary Union (EMU) of the European Union (EU)

Monetary union within the European Union has a long history going back to the late 1960s. The first agreed plant for monetary union was put forward in the Werner Report in 1970. However, difficult economic conditions in the 1970s and 1980s meant that it wasn't until 1989, with the publication of the Delors Report, that the route to today's monetary union was set out. The process was completed in 2002 when on 1 January, euro notes and coins replaced national currencies in 13 EU countries. The UK, Denmark and Sweden decided not to join and retain their national currencies. The 12 accession countries that joined the EU after 2004 have all agreed to adopt the euro as their currency within ten years of membership.

The European Central Bank (ECB)

Members of EMU have given control of monetary and exchange rate policy to the **European Central Bank (ECB)**, which was set up in 1998 and is located in Frankfurt. The ECB has a number of functions.
- It is responsible for distributing notes and coins throughout the **euro-zone**, the countries which have adopted the euro as their currency.
- As a central bank, it sets interest rates in the same way that the Bank of England sets interest rates in the UK. Like the Bank of England, decisions about interest rates are made to achieve an inflation target, which is currently to keep inflation below but close to 2 per cent. The ECB is independent of national governments in the same way that the Bank of England has independence on how to conduct policy from the UK government.
- It is responsible for maintaining a stable financial system. If banks within the euro-zone get into difficulties, it is the ECB which is responsible for dealing with any problems.
- It manages the foreign currency reserves of the Economic and Monetary Union. It can use these to intervene in the foreign exchange markets to influence the value of the euro against other currencies, although in practice it allows the euro to float freely against other currencies.

Fiscal policy rules

Interest rates are determined by the demand for and supply of money. Short term interest rates are set by the European Central Bank. However, it could find this difficult if individual member governments were borrowing large amounts and thus increasing the demand for money within the euro-zone. For this reason, governments within the euro-zone have signed the **Stability and Growth Pact**. This commits governments to:
- maintaining their annual state budgets within a maximum 3 per cent deficit;
- having a national debt of no more than 60 per cent of GDP.

Some countries when signing the Stability and Growth Pact in 1997 had national debts of nearly twice this level. The Stability and Growth Pact states that in these circumstances, states should over time bring their national debts down to the 60 per cent level. However, where governments exceed the 3 per cent deficit limit, in theory they should be fined. In practice, when a number of states in the early 2000s including France and Germany exceeded these limits, they failed to be punished by the European Commission. Nonetheless, these countries did return their state finances to within the 3 per cent limit.

The advantages of EMU

Reduced exchange rate costs A single currency means that there are no exchange rate costs in making transactions. It is as costless for a French firm based in Calais to buy from a firm in Germany as from a firm in Paris. In contrast, a French firm buying from a British firm will still have the cost of changing currency. This is not just the commission and charges imposed by banks. It is also the costs arising from the risk factor of currencies changing in value from day to day in a floating exchange rate system.

Greater price transparency With many national markets and many different currencies, customers, whether firms or households, are likely to have imperfect information about prices across the whole area. A single currency makes it easy for customers to compare prices between different countries and buy from the cheapest source. Multinational producers are far less able to price discriminate between countries by charging higher prices in some than in others to earn monopoly profits. The result has been lower prices across the euro-zone to the benefit of consumers.

More trade and greater economies of scale Reduced exchange rate costs and greater price transparency have led to more trade between member countries. There has been a wave of cross-border mergers and takeovers to create larger firms supplying across the euro-zone rather than just a single national economy. This has led to greater economies of scale, further reducing prices to customers.

Inward investment Being inside the euro-zone has given countries a competitive advantage compared to those outside the euro-zone, such as the UK. The UK itself over the past thirty years has enjoyed considerable inward investment, for instance from Japanese and US companies. One advantage to the companies is that they avoid tariffs and quotas placed on goods coming from outside the EU. They are also nearer the European market, which gives them advantages when developing new products and in marketing. However, being located in a country outside the euro-zone creates exchange rate risks and uncertainties. Companies such as Toyota have said quite explicitly that this is a negative factor in any decision about whether to expand in the UK. Conversely, one of the reasons why Eastern European countries want to join the euro is because they recognise that this will create an added incentive for multinational firms to locate in their country.

Macroeconomic management Some countries, such as Germany, were very successful in managing their economies in the post-war period. In particular, they achieved relatively low inflation. Other countries, such as Italy and the UK, were less successful. Italy's public finances, for instance, were unsustainable in the long term. Government spent too much and raised too little in taxes leading to ever higher amounts of government debt. The creation of EMU led to criteria being laid down for macroeconomic management. National governments, for instance, cannot run large budget deficits over a long period. The European Central Bank cannot be manipulated by politicians seeking re-election because it is independent of national government. However, since 2001, there has been some disillusionment with macroeconomic management by the European Central Bank. It has been criticised for holding interest rates too high, leading to a deflationary impact on countries with very low growth rates and high unemployment. Equally, the euro has not created any push for countries to implement supply side reforms.

The longer term agenda A single currency is part of a wider move towards greater European integration. The greater the economic integration, the greater the economies of scale and the lower the costs for producers. But there are potentially many other benefits that could be achieved from greater integration. For instance, having many national armies is an extremely inefficient way of providing defence for Europe. Ultimately, some would like to see political union as well as economic union. Without a single currency, this would be difficult.

The disadvantages of EMU

Transition costs The creation of a single currency inevitably created transition costs. For instance, vending machines had to be changed to take the new coins. Some bank employees lost their jobs because foreign exchange departments were cut in size. Customers had to become used to using the new money.

Loss of policy independence The UK has long suffered from structural imbalances. The South of England, for instance, might be booming with no unemployment whilst Wales or the North East of England might be seeing little economic growth and chronic unemployment. In these circumstances, it is difficult for adjust fiscal and monetary policy to accommodate the needs of all regions of the UK. For the South of England, interest rates might need to be high to deflate the economy. For Wales and the North East, interest rates might need to be low to boost aggregate demand. This sort of problem is likely to be worse the larger the area of the monetary union. In the euro-zone, for instance, interest rates between 2001 and 2006 arguably needed to be higher in the Republic of Ireland to curb strong growth whilst in France they needed to be much lower to boost low growth and reduce unemployment. Unfortunately, a single currency means there can only be one set of interest rates across the euro-zone. The European Central Bank therefore has to set interest rates to benefit the greatest number across member countries. The advantage of having national currencies is that each country is free to set its own interest rates and therefore in theory macroeconomic policies can be tailored to the national interest. In practice, governments of countries with relatively open economies (i.e. ones where exports and imports are a large proportion of GDP) have difficulty operating macroeconomic policy independently of their main trading partners. Before 1999, for instance, macroeconomic policy in the Netherlands was strongly influenced by policy in Germany. So whilst there is some loss of control of macroeconomic management for countries joining the euro-zone, it is not as great as it might at first seem.

Structural problems The 'one size fits all' nature of monetary policy in the euro-zone may lead to severe pockets of recession in some regions. This has happened in the UK over the past 50 years. A regional economy like the North East has been hard hit by the decline of mining and heavy manufacturing industry and takes decades to recover. At least in the UK, there are strong flows of money between richer and poorer regions. A region in difficulty pays less tax per head than a successful one. It also receives large transfers, for instance from the unemployment benefit system. There are no such mechanisms within the EU. Brussels only receives a small proportion of taxes paid in the EU and pays out relatively little. Much of this goes to farmers anyway. So it could be that the European Central Bank raises interest rates because of inflationary pressures in Germany, but this only makes matters worse for a region in Italy already suffering structural decline. There is then no transfer of resources from Germany to Italy which would help boost aggregate demand in the Italian region and also help deflate the German economy. The solution to this problem is for Brussels to be responsible for far more of what is currently government spending by individual nation states. This implies much more centralisation and loss of national sovereignty.

Loss of political sovereignty Some argue that monetary union presents an unacceptable loss of national sovereignty. At its simplest in the UK, some eurosceptics argue that there is a value in keeping the pound sterling as a symbol of Britishness. Others argue that foreigners should not control national economic policy. There is no doubt that the creation of a single currency has led to loss of national sovereignty since control of monetary and exchange rate policy for eurozone countries has passed to the European Central Bank.

Break up of the euro-zone A single currency can just as well be dissolved as created. In 2005, for example, some politicians in Italy were calling for their country's withdrawal from the euro to allow lower interest rates which would stimulate stagnant growth and reduce unemployment. If the euro were to fail, for whatever reason, there could be considerable transition costs in the resulting break-up. Single currencies in the past have tended to fail because of the political break up of a country or area. Examples include the Austro-Hungarian empire, which collapsed in 1918, the Soviet Union, which collapsed in 1990 and Czechoslovakia which split into two countries in 1993. Proponents of the single currency would argue that this shows the need for further economic and political integration towards some sort of indissoluble united states of Europe.

Britain and the euro

The UK has remained outside the euro and is likely to do so for the foreseeable future.
- Politically, the electorate tends to be eurosceptic and it would be difficult for a government to win a referendum on whether or not to join.
- Since 'Black Wednesday', September 1992, macroeconomic management has generally considered to have been sound. The UK's growth rate has been higher than that of the eurozone, partly because of supply-side reforms and partly because of the absence of any significant recessions. There has therefore been no push to join the eurozone.
- Neither exporters nor importers have shown that exchange rate risks and currency transaction costs have been high enough to deter growth in trade. What is more, much of the growth in trade is occurring with Far Eastern countries, such as China and India, outside of the eurozone.

Eurosceptics argue broadly that the UK economy has been doing extremely well and so why join? Pro-Europeans would reply by saying that the UK economy would have performed even better inside the euro-zone. Since a controlled experiment cannot take place, it is difficult to say which of these positions is correct.

DataQuestion — Should Britain join the euro?

The benefits of joining

The first benefit is lower transactions costs for business and consumers. We estimate these as worth about 0.1 to 0.2 per cent of GDP, £1 billion a year, the gains greater for small companies and the gains permanent.

The second is diminished exchange rate volatility, with gains for both large and small companies, especially in the manufacturing sector with again potentially the greatest gains for smaller companies.

The third benefit is greater cross-border trade and thus the potential for increased commerce and growth. Our assessment makes clear that, with Britain in the euro, British trade with the euro area could increase, perhaps by 50 per cent over 30 years.

Next, interest rates. For 30 or 40 years continental Europe has been able to combine stability with consistently lower interest rates than in Britain, to the benefit of business and of course homeowners. With Britain in the euro, business could benefit through greater access to a more integrated European capital market. And if, on the basis of sustained and durable convergence, we could lock in stability for the long term, then business could see a cut in the cost of borrowing.

Our assessment on trade and output is that inside the euro, UK national income could rise over a 30 year period by between 5 and 9 per cent, boosting, subject to convergence, potential output and national wealth by up to one quarter percentage point a year, worth up to £3 billion a year, delivering higher living standards and lower prices for consumers and households.

Source: adapted from Gordon Brown, Chancellor of the Exchequer, statement to the House of Commons, 9.6.2003.

In 1997, Gordon Brown, Chancellor of the Exchequer, laid out five tests which had to be passed if Britain was to join the euro. In 2003, in a statement to the House of Commons, he reported that, at that moment in time, only one of the five tests had been passed.

Test 1 Convergence Economic structures and the business cycle must be compatible. Changes in interest rates must have the same impact on the UK economy as they do in Europe. For example, the way that changes in interest rates feed through to spending via the housing market must be similar. Equally, the length of trade cycles must be similar and the UK trade cycle must be at the same point as the euro area business cycle. Gordon Brown said we failed on this test. 'Structural differences remain that could pose a risk to stability unless addressed.'

Test 2 Flexibility If economic problems emerge, there must be sufficient flexibility in markets to deal with them. Gordon Brown said we failed on this test. 'Considerable progress has been made to reform markets in the UK and the euro area. Yet as the persistence of volatility in inflation rates within the euro area demonstrates, we cannot be certain that there is sufficient flexibility to deal with the possible stresses. It is for these reasons that we are making structural reforms that will bring increased flexibility.'

Test 3 Investment Would joining the euro create better conditions for firms making long-term decisions to invest in the UK? For example, would euro membership make the UK a more attractive place for Japanese firms to locate? Gordon Brown said we failed this test. 'The assessment shows that inside the euro there will be new opportunities for investment.' However, there needs to be more convergence (Test 1) if this test is to be passed.

Test 4 Financial services Will the City of London, an important export earner for the UK, benefit from euro membership? This was the sole test that Gordon Brown said we passed. 'In or out of the euro, UK financial services are and will remain competitive. Future integration of financial markets inside the euro could promote the kind of diversity, flexibility and risk diversification seen in the capital markets of the USA.'

Test 5 Employment, stability and growth Will joining the euro create jobs, leading to greater economic stability and increase economic growth? Gordon Brown said we failed this test. 'The potential benefit in increased trade and competition and then higher long-term levels of output and employment is significant. Without sustainable convergence and sufficient flexibility, we would not realise the benefits for stability, jobs and investment.' He was saying that because Tests 1 and 2 had failed, it automatically meant that Test 5 failed too.

Source: adapted from Gordon Brown, Chancellor of the Exchequer, statement to the House of Commons, 9.6.2003.

Economic convergence?

Gordon Brown is widely seen as a 'eurosceptic, i.e. someone who is unsure that the current level of European integration or future plans for further integration are in Britain's best interests. Many have argued that his five tests have deliberately been formulated to make sure that they can always be failed, producing a face-saving way for him not to have to lead Britain into the euro.

Figure 1 Economic growth (change in GDP %), and output gap (% of GDP)

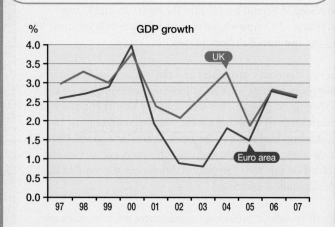

Source: adapted from *Economic Outlook*, OECD.

Figure 2 Short-term interest rates[1]

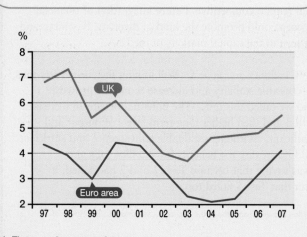

1. Three month money market rates.

Source: adapted from *Economic Outlook*, OECD.

Figure 3 Selected exchange rates against the pound, index 1st Quarter 1997 = 100

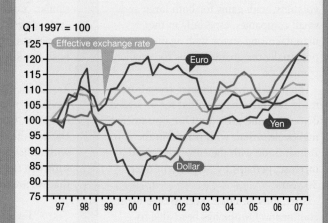

Source: adapted from *Economic & Labour Market Review*, Office for National Statistics.

Figure 4 Possible steps to joining a currency

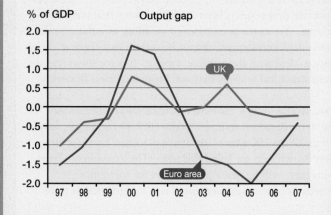

Source: adapted from the *Financial Times*.

Costs of transition

Britain's smaller businesses are facing a £6.2 billion to convert to use the euro. A survey by the Allied Irish Bank (GB) showed that conversion costs vary significantly between industries, but on average they can expect to pay £1 685. Retailers are the hardest hit, facing a bill 300 per cent higher than their colleagues in the construction industry.

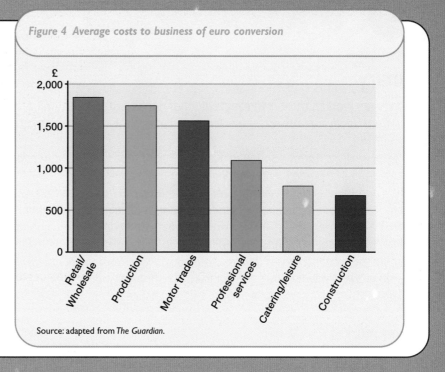

Figure 4 Average costs to business of euro conversion

Source: adapted from *The Guardian*.

Loss of sovereignty

'The surrender of British sovereignty is something I am completely opposed to. The whole idea of a single currency is untenable and would lead to instability.'
Big retailer, Midlands.

'I think things will get more expensive than at the moment. At present things can be bought cheaply off the Continent and if the single currency goes ahead things will become more expensive.'

Small construction company, North.

'Sterling is an international currency and has been for many years. Why should we move away towards an obscure bond? If we abolish the pound then we will drift into a weaker currency.'
Medium-sized manufacturer, South.

Source: adapted from the *Financial Times*.

Italy thinking of pulling out of the euro

The unthinkable is happening. Some Italian politicians are talking about Italy pulling out of the euro. They are concerned about Italy's high unemployment rate and poor growth record in recent years. Their argument is that the 'one size fits all' monetary policy of the eurozone is severely damaging the Italian economy. Pulling out would mean that Italy could devalue its currency and gain a competitive advantage over its euro partners. More Italian exports and fewer imports would boost jobs and incomes.

However, economists point out that it would be ruinous for Italy to pull out now. Italy has one of the higher national debts in the EU, which is financed at the very low interest rates which exist inside the eurozone. If it had its own currency, markets would not be willing to lend to the Italian state except at much higher interest rates. Higher Italian interest rates would more than wipe out any gains Italy could make from a lower exchange rate.

Source: adapted from the *Financial Times*, 8.6.2005.

No shortage of euro applicants

Britain might be reluctant to join the euro, but there is no shortage of applicants for euro membership from countries in Eastern Europe. All the new accession countries, as part of their treaties to join the EU, have had to sign up to joining the euro in the future. For the most part, they see euro membership as locking them into financial stability and an economic free trade zone which will boost jobs and economic growth.

1. What are the main arguments for and against the UK joining the euro?

2. Discuss whether Gordon Brown is right to keep the UK out of the euro at this point in time.

Summary

1. In a common market, there is free movement of goods and services, and factors of production. Goods and services imported from outside the common market face a common external tariff.
2. Free trade involves harmonisation in a wide range of areas, including product standards and taxation.
3. The formation of a common market will lead to trade creation and trade diversion. The greater the trade creation and the less the trade diversion, the greater will be the welfare benefits to member countries.
4. Dynamic gains from membership include economies of scale in production. Competition is likely to increase in the short run but mergers and takeovers are likely to lessen competition amongst firms in the long run.
5. Common market spending and taxation will lead to a redistribution of resources between member countries. Inevitably some countries will gain and others will lose from the common market budget.
6. Common markets may be the first step towards complete monetary and political union between member countries.

A common market

A COMMON MARKET or customs union is a group of countries between which there is free trade and which impose a COMMON EXTERNAL TARIFF on imported goods from outside the market. In theory, free trade between member countries involves goods and services as well as the factors of production.
- Land. There should be free trade in natural resources. In Europe, for instance, a British company should be free to buy land in Paris, whilst a French company should be free to own a licence to exploit North Sea oil.
- Labour. Workers should be free to work in any member country. For instance, an Italian should be able to work in London on exactly the same terms as a worker born in Birmingham.
- Capital. Capital should flow freely between countries. Of particular importance is **financial capital**. A Scottish firm should be free to borrow money in Paris to set up a factory in Italy, just as a London based firm could borrow money from a Scottish bank to invest in Wales.

Imports from outside the common market present a problem. For instance, assume that the UK imposes a tariff of 10 per cent on imports of foreign cars whilst France imposes a tariff of 20 per cent. With free trade between France and the UK, foreign importers would ship cars intended for sale in France to the UK, pay the 10 per cent tariff, and then re-export them 'tariff-free' into France. There are two ways to get round this problem.
- One way is to impose a common external tariff. All member countries agree to change their tariff structures so as to impose the same tariff on imported items. In our example, France and the UK would have to change or HARMONISE their tariffs on cars to an agreed European Union (EU) figure.
- The other way is for member countries to impose tariffs on re-exports. In our example France could impose a 10 per cent tariff on the original price of cars imported from non-member countries.

This second solution is a feature of FREE TRADE AREAS. A free trade area differs from a common market partly because of its different approach to dealing with non-member imports. It also differs because member countries are not committed to working towards closer economic integration. In a free trade area, the sole objective is free trade between member countries.

In a common market, the goal is to establish a single market in the same way that there is a single market within an individual economy. Ultimately this involves a large number of changes including:
- no customs posts between countries; just as goods and people are free to travel between Manchester and London, so they should be free to travel between London and Milan;
- identical product standards between countries; the existence of individual national safety standards on cars, for instance, is a barrier to trade just as it would be if cars sold in London had to meet different safety requirements from cars sold in Bristol;
- harmonisation of taxes; if the tax on the same car is £2 000 more in the UK than in France, then UK residents will buy their cars in France and take them back to England, distorting the pattern of trade; equally if direct taxes on income are an

Question 1

- In 1994, a group of countries, including France, Germany, Holland and Belgium, dismantled all frontier posts between their countries.
- On 1 January 2002, euro notes and coins were issued in 11 countries of the European Union, followed shortly afterwards by the withdrawal of national currencies in those countries.
- Since the 1980s, the EU has suggested that tax rates between member countries should be harmonised (i.e. made the same). This would prevent, for instance, the large scale smuggling of tobacco into the UK from France and Belgium, or the move of manufacturing plants from high labour taxed countries like Germany to low taxed countries like the UK.
- In 2004, the European Commission issued the working time directive which limited workers' hours of work per week to 48 hours throughout the EU.
- In 2006, the European Parliament approved a new services directive which would increase the ability of service sector companies to compete throughout the EU. The service sector accounts for half of the EU's GDP and two thirds of jobs.

(a) Explain why each of these illustrates how a common market works.

average 15 per cent in France and 30 per cent in the UK, some UK workers may be tempted to go and work in France;
- a common currency; having to buy foreign exchange is a barrier to trade, especially if there are exchange rate movements; hence there should be a single common market currency just as there is a single currency in the UK.

Stages of economic integration

A Hungarian economist, Bela Balassa, put forward a theory in the 1960s of stages of ever deeper economic integration. He suggested that a group of countries might go through six stages. These are summarised in Table 1.
- At the start, there would be a **preferential trading area**. This is where countries agree to reduce or abolish tariffs, quotas and other protectionist barriers on some goods being traded between them.
- This could develop into a **free trade area** where tariffs and quotas have been abolished between member countries. However, each member country may impose different tariffs and quotas on trade with countries outside the free trade area.
- In a **customs union**, there is free trade between member countries and a common external tariff.
- This might then develop into a **common market** where there is free trade not just in goods and services but also in factor markets. There is free movement of labour and capital. In the EU, the term 'single market' tends to be used to describe a common market today.
- A common market could lead onto **economic and monetary union**. In an economic union, there is a truly integrated common market together with a single currency. Having a single currency means there will be a central bank for the union which controls monetary and exchange rate policy. There will also need to be some central control of fiscal policy within the union.
- There will be **complete economic integration** when the countries in a union operate in the same way as might counties, departments, regions or areas would in a nation state. Economic integration implies some form of central government which controls a significant budget for spending and taxation across the union. Complete economic integration is therefore associated with a **political union**.

Table 1 Stages of economic integration

	Tariffs on trade between countries in the agreement	Common tariffs on imports from outside the agreement area	Free factor mobility within the area	Harmonisation of economic policies
Preferential trade agreement	Reduced	No	No	No
Free trade agreement	Eliminated	No	No	No
Customs union	Eliminated	Yes	No	Possible
Common market	Eliminated	Yes	Yes	Desirable
Economic union	Eliminated	Yes	Yes	Yes

Source: adapted from from UNCTAD secretariat.

Question 2

The accession of Eastern European countries to the EU on 1 January 2004 has led to a shake up in the agricultural industry. Polish food exports to western Europe and particularly Germany increased by 40 per cent last year. In the Czech Republic, farmers took advantage of the opening of its border with the EU to sell pork and milk to German buyers for higher prices than they could charge on the domestic market. But they themselves have faced increased competition from Poland where the agricultural sector is much larger and its costs are lower. Hungary has suffered from competition in sectors such as vegetable and fruit production as well as pork from Spain, the Netherlands and Greece.

Opening borders with the West has also meant closing borders with the East. Imports of agricultural produce into the new EU member countries from non-EU Eastern European countries such as the Ukraine, Romania and Russia have fallen as tariff barriers have gone up.

At least German farmers near the border with the Czech Republic can now console themselves with the fact that their funeral will now cost them much less if they get cremated in the Czech Republic rather than in Germany.

Source: adapted from the *Financial Times*, 15.3.2005.

(a) Using examples from the data, distinguish between trade creation and trade diversion.

In practice, unions do not necessarily evolve in the way described in this model. The European Union, for example, was never a free trade area although there were preferential trading agreements between some member countries. However, the model helps to understand the depth of economic integration which can go from fairly shallow integration with preferential trade agreements to complete economic integration with an economic union.

Trade creation and trade diversion

The **theory of comparative advantage** shows that free trade between countries is likely to increase total world production. When a small number of countries form a common market, there will be gainers and losers.

TRADE CREATION is said to take place when a country moves from buying goods from a high cost country to buying them from a lower cost country. For instance, country A might have imposed a 50 per cent tariff on imported cars. As a result, all cars sold in country A were produced domestically. It now joins a customs union. The common external tariff is 50 per cent but cars from member countries can be imported free of the tariff. Country A now buys some cars from common market countries because they are lower priced than those previously produced domestically. Consumers in country A have benefited because they are able to buy cars from a cheaper source.

TRADE DIVERSION takes place when a country moves from buying goods from a low cost producer to buying them from a higher cost producer. For instance, before entry to the European Union, the UK had low or zero tariffs on imported foodstuffs. It bought from the lowest cost producers round the world such as New Zealand and the USA. After entry, the

Question 3

Free trade in goods has been broadly achieved through the single market. But free trade in services is still a long way off. In 2006, the EU Parliament passed a much watered down directive, known as the Bolkenstein Directive after its author, liberalising some free trade in services. In goods, if a product is fit to be sold in one country under its national rules, it can be sold throughout the EU even if other countries have different rules. In services, a seller must still conform to the rules of the country in which it wishes to sell the service, so called 'country of origin' rules. So, for example, a bank, an insurance company, a hospital group or a management consultancy wanting to operate across the EU has to conform to 25 different sets of rules, one for each country in the EU.

The Bolkenstein Directive aims to sweep that away. In the version passed by the EU Parliament, some service industries will see their trade liberalised but most will not. For example, hotels and restaurants, car hire, construction, advertising services and estate agencies are covered. Excluded are postal services, legal services, social services, public transport and gambling.

The European Commission says the directive, if it covered all services, would create 600 000 jobs, boost economic growth and increase quality and choice for consumers. Opponents say that it will lead to a 'race to the bottom' with firms relocating to countries with lower wages and for the weakest consumer, environmental protection, employment and health and safety rules. A nurse in Germany said that it would lead to Eastern European workers with lower hygiene standards coming into hospitals and driving down German wages. A midwife in London was worried that the National Health Service would be able to choose the cheapest and not the best service provider.

Source: adapted from newsvote.bbc.co.uk 16.2.2006.

(a) Explain, using a demand and supply diagram for service products, why competition in services between EU providers would be likely to (i) drive down prices and (ii) create jobs.
(b) Opposition to the Bolkenstein Directive has come from trade unions. Explain, using a demand and supply for labour diagram, why trade unions in service areas such as health care and public transport might be opposed to the directive.

UK had to impose the much higher EU common external tariff. As a result it became cheaper to buy food from other EU countries such as France and Italy. France and Italy are higher cost producers than the USA and New Zealand for many food items.

In general the higher the tariffs imposed by a country before entry to a common market, the more likely it is that trade creation rather than trade diversion will take place. It is also true that the net gains will tend to be larger, the greater the volume of trade between the countries in the common market.

Free trade vs customs unions

Customs unions can be seen as a 'second best' solution in a world where there is protectionism. Economic efficiency would be maximised if there were no barriers to trade between countries. Individual economies would

also have perfectly competitive products and free labour and capital markets. In this theoretical world, comparative advantage would determine which countries produced what goods. This would be the 'first best' solution. In the real world, such conditions don't exist. Economic inefficiency arises because relatively high cost producers can shelter behind protective barriers. A customs union brings down these barriers, at least between member states. Member countries may therefore be able to switch buying from a high cost producer to a lower cost producer. However, countries will only benefit if trade creation is greater than trade diversion. Consideration must also be taken of whether there will be dynamic gains or losses from the creation of a customs union.

Economies of scale

Gains from trade creation are **static** gains. They occur once and for all following the creation of, or entry to, a common market. Membership of a common market may also result in **dynamic** gains or losses - gains or losses which occur over a period of time. One important such gain comes from **economies of scale**. In a common market, the potential size of the customer market is inevitably larger than in a national market. For instance, the European Union has 300 million inhabitants compared to 59 million for the UK. This means that important economies of scale can be achieved by national companies if they carve out a market for themselves throughout the common market. This is no easy task given that each country is likely to have different consumer preferences. However, there are some products, such as basic chemicals, which are demanded by all countries. Other products, such as cars, are relatively easily sold across national boundaries. Yet other products, such as cosmetics, may need different packaging for different countries, but the basic product is the same.

Economies of scale will be achieved over a period of time as companies expand internally or merge with other foreign companies. The size of the potential gains will be greater, the more homogeneous the tastes of consumers within the market. For instance, the gains are likely to be higher for a market comprising France and the UK than for the UK and Iran. Economies of scale bring benefits to consumers because average costs of production fall, and therefore prices are likely to fall too.

Competition

Another possible dynamic gain arises from increased competition between firms. A common market should eliminate restrictions on trade between member countries. Domestic industries will therefore face greater competition than before from firms in other member countries. Competition will encourage innovation, reduce costs of production and reduce prices. There will therefore be gains in productive and allocative efficiency.

Although there is likely to be greater competition in the short run, evidence suggests that this competition will be reduced in the long run. Competition will drive the least efficient firms out of the market, as the theory of perfect competition predicts. Other firms will seek to maintain monopoly profits by re-establishing control over their markets. They will do this by merging with or taking over foreign firms within the common market. Over time, the oligopolistic nature of competition in domestic markets will be recreated on a common market level.

This may benefit the consumer through economies of scale but it certainly will not bring the benefits that free market economists suggest.

The Austrian School of Economics argues that competition is not necessarily beneficial to the consumer. Large international monopolies, earning considerable abnormal profit, will have the resources to devote to research, development and investment. If they fail to develop products that satisfy consumer wants, their monopoly will be lost through the process of creative destruction. Competitors will break their monopoly by creating new products. This constant development of new products is far more beneficial to consumer welfare than a few per cent off the price of existing products which might result from a perfectly competitive environment.

Transfers of resources

Common markets may differ in the size and power of their institutions. The European Union has a sizeable bureaucracy, a parliament and a large budget. Money is paid into a Union budget by member countries. The money is used to pay for administration and the implementation of Union-wide policies. In the case of the European Union, the largest share of the budget has traditionally been allocated to one area of policy - the **Common Agricultural Policy**. Any budget of any size opens up the possibility that some member countries may pay more into the budget than they receive. There may therefore be a net transfer of resources from one country to another within a common market. These represent static losses and gains (i.e. once and for all losses and gains).

Perhaps more importantly, there can also be transfers of real resources from country to country. Countries in the common market which are particularly dynamic and successful are likely to attract inflows of labour and capital. Countries which have lower growth rates are likely to suffer net capital outflows and lose some of their best workers to other economies. This could heighten regional disparities, making the richer nations relatively even richer.

The process may be magnified if the successful countries are at the geographical centre of the common market whilst the less successful countries are on the fringe. Transport and communication costs tend to be lower for companies sited at the centre and higher for those at the periphery. Hence central countries tend to have a competitive advantage over fringe countries.

Neo-classical economic theory suggests that free market forces would equalise the differences between regions. An unsuccessful region will have cheap labour and cheap land. Firms will be attracted into the region to take advantage of these. In practice, this effect seems to be very weak. Cheap labour economies can easily become branch economies. Firms set up branches in these regions, employing cheap labour to perform low productivity tasks. Tasks which have high value added are completed at headquarters in higher cost areas. The result is growing economic divergence, with poorer regions losing the most skilled of their labour force to the richer regions and being left with less dynamic and less skilled workers to do less well paid jobs.

Monetary and political union

An internal common market where there are different currencies in each country imposes costs upon producers. Therefore a common market implies a move to a common currency. A common currency implies common monetary and fiscal policies. The economic implications of monetary union are discussed further in unit 96.

A common market may eventually lead to political union. Political union inevitably involves a loss of national sovereignty. Decisions which previously were made at national level will now be made at community level. This may have economic implications in that a member country will lose the ability to direct its economic affairs to its own advantage. On the other hand, it can be argued that any country which is very open (i.e. exports a high proportion of its national product) has already lost most of its ability to direct its own economic affairs because so much of its economy depends upon the spending and saving decisions of foreigners.

Question 4

Figure 1 *Estimated annual net receipts¹ from/payments to the European Union Budget 2008-13, and GNP per head 2006 (US$ at purchasing power parities)*

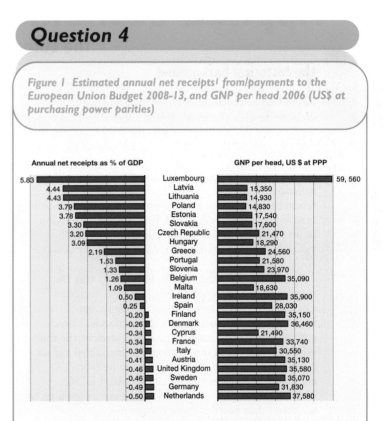

1. Net receipts for Luxembourg, Belgium and France include the spending by the EU on the European Commission, the European Court of Justice and the European Parliament located in those countries.

Source: adapted from *World Development Report*, World Bank; Bob Taylor, *Europe's World guide to the EU budget negotiations, Europe's World*, Autumn 2005.

(a) To what extent is there a correlation between low income countries and net receipts (the difference between monies paid out from the EU budget to countries and the contributions they have to make to the EU budget) in the EU?

(b) Explain how the EU budget could be used to equalise living standards between the different regions of the EU.

Key terms

Common external tariff - a common tariff set by a group of countries imposed on imported goods from non-member countries.

Common market - a group of countries between which there is free trade in products and factors of production, and which imposes a common external tariff on imported goods from outside the market.

Free trade area - a group of countries between which there is free trade in goods and services but which allows member countries to set their own level of tariffs against non-member countries.

Harmonisation - establishing common standards, rules and levels on everything from safety standards to tariffs, taxes and currencies.

Trade creation - the switch from purchasing products from a high cost producer to a lower cost producer.

Trade diversion - the switch from purchasing products from a low cost producer to a higher cost producer.

Applied economics

The European Union

The historical background

At the end of the Second World War, Europe's economies were shattered. It was realised by many western politicians that this was the direct outcome of unwise political decisions made at the end of the First World War when Germany was economically penalised for having lost the war. Huge war reparations and the isolation of Germany politically had given German fascists the chance to gain support and power, which in turn led to the Second World War. Some had a vision of co-operation and a united peaceful Europe. This vision led to the creation of today's European Union (EU).

The first step on the road to today's EU was the formation in 1952 of the European Coal and Steel Community (ECSC) by France, Germany, Italy, Luxembourg, Belgium and the Netherlands. This created a free trade area for coal and steel, at the time crucial industries in those countries. It enabled the six countries to protect their industries more from US competition. Greater output then enabled ECSC producers to reduce costs through greater economies of scale and thus become more competitive.

In 1957, the European Atomic Energy Community was formed by the same six countries to encourage the growth of the peaceful use of nuclear power. By the time the treaty had been signed, negotiations were well under way for the creation of the far more ambitious European Economic Community (EEC) or Common Market. This came into existence on 1 January 1958 after the signing of the Treaty of Rome in 1957.

The Treaty of Rome established a customs union, with provisions for the phased withdrawal of all tariffs between the six member countries and the imposition of a common external tariff on goods coming into the Community. This was finally completed in 1986. The Treaty also contained provisions which would in future allow the free flow not just of goods but also of capital and of labour between countries. Another aspect was the creation of a European policy on competition and restrictive trade practices.

The next stage of deepening the customs union occurred in 1985 with the signing of the **Single European Act (SEA)** which came into force on 1 January 1993. The 1950s and 1960s had seen the removal of tariff and quota barriers on trade in most goods between member countries. The SEA committed governments to removing the many other barriers to trade in goods which still existed. Removing the many barriers to trade in services, however, is only just starting today.

In 1991, member states signed the Treaty of Maastricht. This laid down a timetable for the creation of a monetary union. On 1 January 2002, 12 member states but not including the UK, launched a single currency and the eurozone was created.

The Treaty of Lisbon, 2007, set out a new constitution for the EU. It created the role of an EU President and removed the power of veto of member countries in key areas of decision making and extended majority voting. This will help decision making in the future.

Between 1973 and 2007, the EU was enlarged from 6 member countries to 27 countries. There are a number of countries, including Turkey, which are in negotiations with the EU to join in the future.

EU institutions

The Treaty of Rome created a number of important institutions.
- The **European Commission,** based in Brussels, is the equivalent of the civil service in the UK. At the top

are Commissioners, each with a particular responsibility for an area of community policy. The Commission is responsible for implementing agreed policies and for proposing new policies. It can be a very powerful body, partly because it is responsible for the day to day running of Community policies, but also because it is the main agent of change and progress in policy.

- The **European Council of Ministers** is a powerful body too. It is made up of a ministerial representative from each member state. When agriculture is being discussed, then countries are represented by their agriculture ministers. When broad economic issues are discussed, it will be finance ministers who are present. New policies put forward by the European Commission are either approved or rejected by the Council of Ministers. Hence, the Council of Ministers is the most important decision-making body. In most areas, there has to be a unanimous vote for a policy to be approved. However, in some areas, only a majority vote is needed.

- The **European Parliament**, based in Strasbourg, is made up of elected representatives (MEPs) from the member states. The European Parliament is a relatively weak body. Until recently, it had almost no decision-making powers at all and even since the Treaty of Maastricht (1992), when its powers were increased, it has been able to do little more than rubber stamp decisions made elsewhere. The intention is that the European Parliament will, over time, increase its powers to become more like a national parliament.

- The **European Court of Justice**, which meets in Luxembourg, is another powerful body. It is the ultimate court of law and is responsible for making judgements on EU law. It regularly passes judgements which have a significant impact on individual countries or the entire community. For instance, its judgement on equal pension rights in 1992 forced the UK government to move towards equalising the state retiring age for men and women in the UK at 65.

- The **European Central Bank** is responsible for monetary policy in the eurozone area. Its functions are described more fully in the unit 'The advantages and disadvantages of exchange rate systems'.

Common policies

The Treaty of Rome envisaged the creation of a number of common policies. The first of these to be established in 1962 was the **Common Agricultural Policy (CAP)**. To reduce inequalities between regions, there is an EU **regional policy**. The EU uses the terms **cohesion** and **convergence** to describe its objectives in this area. **Competition policy** is used to prevent firms exploiting customers when there is cross-border trade. **Social policy** is very important with the EU attempting to create a single labour market where workers have equal rights. **Transport policy** has arguably been difficult to implement because national governments have been reluctant to cede powers to the community over transport issues. **Environmental policy** linked to **energy policy** is becoming increasingly important across all aspects of community policy.

EU enlargement

Most European countries not in the EU have aspirations to join. Albania and the former states of Yugoslavia in south eastern Europe are in various stages of talks to begin membership entry. More controversially, Turkey would like to join. The advantages and problems of Turkish membership are outlined in the data question. A number of other states, such as the Ukraine, may also make applications to join.

There is a number of reasons why these countries, all of which have incomes per head well below the EU average, would like to join the EU.

- Membership of the EU would give access to much

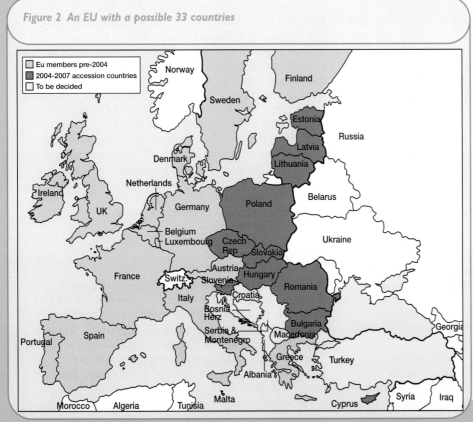

Figure 2 An EU with a possible 33 countries

Eu members pre-2004
2004-2007 accession countries
To be decided

larger markets for their goods. They are all relatively low wage economies and therefore their goods would have a price advantage within the EU.

- They would see a substantial increase in foreign direct investment into their economies. EU and other firms would buy up companies, or set up new companies, in the economies of the new member countries. They would then put considerable amounts of investment into these firms to use them as production bases either to sell back into the rest of the EU or to sell into the expanding market within the country. This investment would create jobs, output and economic growth.
- To become a member of the EU and to stay a member, new entrants would have to create legal and financial structures which were of EU standard. For example, they would have to incorporate EU law into their own legal system. This creates a framework within which firms and workers have an incentive to invest, work and create wealth. It is an essential part of creating an economy which will grow in the long term.

New entrants look at the examples of Ireland, Spain and Portugal, all of which joined the EU as relatively poor countries and quickly achieved a higher rate of economic growth. Ireland in particular has moved from one of the poorest countries in the EU on joining in 1973 to being one of the richest by the 2000s.

For the UK, expanding the size of the EU has both advantages and disadvantages.

- An expanded EU creates new markets for UK exports. It allows the UK to further specialise, exploit economies of scale and so gain from trade. These are static gains resulting from trade creation. In the short term, however, some firms will suffer loss of orders and may go out of business. Some workers will lose their jobs to foreign competition. In the long term, there is a danger that the changes could lead to structural unemployment where labour markets fail to return to equilibrium at the previous level of employment.
- New markets for UK exports and increased competition from new member countries should increase dynamic efficiency. UK firms in the traded goods and services sectors will be forced to improve their competitiveness.
- There is likely to be net migration into the UK from new member countries. This increases the size of the UK labour force and helps reduce labour shortages and bottlenecks in production. It should reduce inflation because there will be a downward pressure on wages in markets where migrants take jobs. On the other hand, wages of existing UK workers may fall in industries where there is a take-up of migrant labour. Net migration increases the pressure on housing and public services such as education and the health services.
- Financial capital will flow from the UK to new member countries. This will provide profitable investment opportunities for the UK. On the other

hand, some of that financial capital might otherwise have been invested in the UK. In time, financial capital will flow from new member countries to the UK. There could then be issues about threats to national sovereignty.

The Common Agricultural Policy

CAP remains a considerable source of friction within the EU. It takes a considerable proportion of the EU budget and yet agriculture already accounts for only a few per cent of EU GDP and employment. The EU budget for 2008-13 was agreed in 2005, fixing CAP expenditure. Reforms agreed in 2002 have, for the most part, decoupled production from subsidies preventing many problems with the growth of unsold stocks of food. However, the CAP regime was a major obstacle to agreement in world trade talks in the Doha round and encourages other world producers such as the USA to maintain their own distorting subsidy regimes at the expense of their own taxpayers and farmers in the Third World.

Furthering the single market

Despite the fact that the EU is supposed to be a common market, with free trade within its borders, there remain considerable barriers to trade particularly in service industries. This is important because services account for over 70 per cent of GDP in the EU. Barriers to trade in services are very high because, unlike trade in goods, a new entrant into a country has to conform to the laws governing production and selling of services in that country. So a UK bank, for example, has to conform to French banking laws for any operations it has in France. A bank wishing to operate in all 27 countries of the EU therefore has to conform to 27 different sets of banking regulations. In contrast, a manufacturer selling tyres can export those tyres to any country in the EU so long as they conform to the safety standards in their country of origin even if other countries have different standards.

In 2006, the European Parliament passed a directive giving a limited freeing up of trade barriers in services throughout the EU. However, countries such as France remain highly protectionist even within the EU, tending to oppose any moves to liberalise trade. Yet, in the long term, it is free trade which gives economic advantages to countries.

Political integration

Political integration is a logical outcome of greater economic integration. However, national states tend to be fiercely protective of their political rights and are reluctant to give these up to an EU superstate. In the long term, there will be greater political integration. The European Parliament, for example, will gain power at the expense of national parliaments. But progress is likely to be very slow and patchy.

DataQuestion   Turkey

On 3 October 2005, membership negotiations were symbolically opened with Turkey, which has been an associated member of the EU since 1963 and an official candidate since 1999. Negotiations are likely to be long and hard fought. Turkey will be unwilling to adopt some of the changes required by the EU, seeing them as an infringement on its sovereignty as a nation and as a threat to its culture, including the Islamic faith of most of its population. On the other hand, some European politicians, including the President of France, Jacques Chirac, and the Prime Minister of Italy, Silvio Berlusconi, have said publicly that they oppose Turkish membership because it poses a threat to European Christian civilisation.

In 1955, Turkey's per capita income was roughly double that of South Korea. In 2003, Turkey's per capita income was roughly one-third that of South Korea. What went wrong with Turkey? One way of answering this is to say that it is an unfair comparison. South Korea over the period has had one of the highest growth rates in the world. On the other hand, if South Korea, with very few natural resources, could do it, why couldn't Turkey?

One reason is that Turkey's investment and savings over the past 50 years have been too low. Today, investment in physical capital is running at around 20 to 25 per cent of GDP. Compare that to China where it is around 40 per cent. 20 to 25 per cent is simply not enough for Turkey to engage in catch up with the EU. On this level, the gap between Turkish GDP and the EU will remain fixed. Investment spending is linked to the savings ratio. Turkey doesn't save enough of its GDP to finance high investment. Given that Turkey has a very young population, and lower rates of saving are associated with aging populations, it is going to be difficult for Turkey to raise its savings ratio. As for investment in human capital, in the EU, Portugal has the worst educational performance record. Turkey's is worse than Portugal's. Education of females is particularly poor in Turkey, reflecting 'traditional' values where today only 24.3 per cent of adult women are employed in the formal economy. China's population is considerably better educated than Turkey's, yet average wages in Turkey are higher than in China.

The second reason for Turkey's relatively poor performance is linked to the first. Turkey invests too little because returns on investment are low. This is because of the poor functioning of key markets, especially the formal labour markets and financial markets, and because of ineffective economic institutions and governance at all levels.

Source: adapted from Willem H Buiter, *It's a long way to Copenhagen*, CEPS Policy Brief, March 2006.

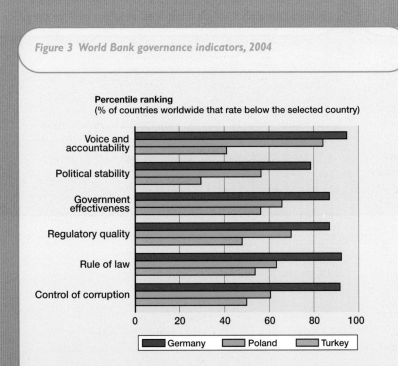

Figure 3 World Bank governance indicators, 2004

Percentile ranking
(% of countries worldwide that rate below the selected country)

- Voice and accountability
- Political stability
- Government effectiveness
- Regulatory quality
- Rule of law
- Control of corruption

0 20 40 60 80 100

■ Germany   ■ Poland   ▢ Turkey

Source: adapted from World Bank, IMF, OECD

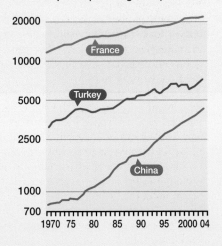

Figure 4 Real GDP per capita at purchasing power parity

$ at 1990 prices (semi-log scale)

20000
10000   France
5000   Turkey
2500
China
1000
700
1970 75   80   85   90   95   2000 04

Source: adapted from the *Financial Times*, 12.10.2005.

Turkey is a major threat to European labour markets, or so the argument goes. Once it joins, Turkish workers would be free to migrate to any EU country. This would drive down wages for existing workers and create huge unemployment. Germany already has a large Turkish population and fears that it could become much larger if Turkey joined.

Such arguments have been used before, for example to justify keeping Eastern European countries out of the EU. Even today, a number of countries including France and Germany have used their powers under the accession treaties for the 2004 wave of new entrants, to limit flows of workers from Eastern Europe until 2008. The 'Polish plumber' coming to take the Frenchman's job was a key bogeyman in the 2005 French referendum which said 'Non' to the proposed new European constitution.

In practice, the impact of immigration is complex. Immigrants create jobs because they too need hair cuts, education for their children and their plumbing fixed. Evidence suggests that first generation immigrants typically take lower paid jobs than their qualifications would suggest, and take a disproportionate number of the very lowest paid jobs in an economy. They are more likely to be in employment than the resident population. Immigrants from the 2004 accession countries are young and single, and more likely than not to return home after a year or two having earned some money and gained a knowledge of English or French or German. But some stay, and they need to be housed, their children educated and they place demands on the health service. First generation immigrants also tend to retain a strong cultural identity with their country of origin.

Table 2 Turkey and the EU 25*, some basic economic comparisons, 2003

	Turkey	EU 25
Population	70.7m	453m
GDP per head at PPP	€3 000	€21 300
Employment rate, % of working age population	45.5	62.9
Unemployment rate %	10.7	9.0
Average wage	€740	€7 505
Agricultural output, % of GDP	11.5	2.1
Industry and construction, % of GDP	27.6	27.0
Service output, % of GDP	60.9	71.0

* EU 27 in 2008.

Over the past 50 years, Turkey has not been particularly well run by western standards. Its economy has performed relatively poorly and it has had a very mixed governance record. However, since 2000, Turkey has made enormous strides in all areas of public life. Broadly, it recognises that EU membership will bring enormous benefits to Turkey. After all, looking round its borders, it can see countries which have gone different ways: countries like Iran and Syria and even Russia. The EU represents economic prosperity and political stability.

To join, it has to make further large scale reforms. These reforms will in themselves create prosperity and political stability. For the EU to rebuff Turkey would be to unleash forces in Turkey which want to take it in the direction of Iran and Syria. Not only would the EU lose economically from not having a country of 70 million people within its borders, it would also create a source of political instability which could lead to large costs for the EU.

Source: adapted from Willem H Buiter, *It's a long way to Copenhagen*, CEPS Policy Brief, March 2006; the *Financial Times*, 12.10.2005.

1. Assess the main differences between the EU 25 and Turkey.
2. Analyse the main possible advantages for
   (a) existing EU members and (b) Turkey if Turkey were to become a member of the EU.
3. Discuss whether the EU should allow Turkey to join by comparing the possible disadvantages of Turkish EU membership with the advantages.

Applied economics

Multinational companies

Multinational companies have come to play an increasingly important role in world trade. MULTINATIONAL COMPANIES (or MULTINATIONAL CORPORATIONS or TRANSNATIONAL CORPORATIONS) are companies which have significant production or service operations in at least two countries. These could be primary product companies such as Geest, Exxon Mobil or BP. They could be manufacturing companies like General Motors, Ford, Toyota or Sony. Or they could be service sector companies like Vodafone, Starbucks, the coffee shop chain, Wal-Mart, the world's largest supermarket chain which owns Asda.

Some multinationals have sales which are greater than those of some small poor countries today. However, it is important when making comparisons to understand the difference between value added and sales revenues. Wal-Mart, the world's largest retailer, had sales of approximately $370 billion in 2007. This was more than half the output of the whole of Sub-Saharan Africa with a population of 770 million. But when the GDP of a country is calculated, it is the value added of each firm which is added up, not its sales. When comparing the output of Sub-Saharan Africa with Wal-Mart, it should be Wal-Mart's value added, not its sales, that is the appropriate measure. Wal-Mart's value added is its sales minus the value of what it buys in from other firms. This includes the value of everything it buys to stock its shelves. In 2007, Wal-Mart paid approximately $275 billion to manufacturers for stock. On top of that, it also had costs such as electricity and water. Wal-Mart's value added could be estimated therefore at possibly £70 billion. This is still larger than the output of many small poor African economies. But it is less than 0.5 per cent of the output of the US economy. When comparing the size of multinationals, measures such as capital employed are more realistic indications of size than revenues.

Most multinationals operate largely in developed countries. This is where their shareholders, their headquarters, their markets and their production facilities are located. Mergers and takeovers tend to take place between companies in developed countries. A few multinationals, particularly in the primary sector, have large operations in developing countries. Examples are oil companies like Exxon Mobil and Total, and primary food companies like Geest. Many multinationals are seeing growing sales into countries like India and China.

A recent trend is for multinationals owned and controlled in developing countries to take over companies in developed countries. For example, the world's largest steel company in 2007 was Mittal Steel, an Indian company, creating by a series of takeovers of steel companies in the developed world by Mittal Steel. One of the world's largest cement manufacturers is the Mexican company Cemex, which in 2007 had operations in 50 countries across the world and owned 66 cement plants. As the developing world increases its income, more and more multinational companies will be owned by shareholders in the developing world.

Reasons for multinational companies to exist

Why do such large firms exist?

Economies of scale There are many industries where only the largest firms with world wide access to both production facilities and markets can fully exploit economies of scale. Examples of such industries include the oil and motor manufacturing industries. Typically, the amounts of capital needed are so large that small firms find it difficult to compete.

Knowledge and innovation Many multinational companies are storehouses of accumulated knowledge and powerful players in the field of innovation. For instance, it is difficult to imagine how any small enterprise could exploit oil from miles below the sea bed in the deep waters of the North Sea, or produce the technology to put a man on the moon. Genetic engineering or microchips are two examples of where multinationals are in the forefront of bringing new products to the market. Some large retailers have a more successful knowledge of what their customers want to buy than their competitors and have developed highly sophisticated logistics systems to get products from manufacturers to customers.

Branding and marketing Some multinational companies use very little technology. Instead, they rely for their world presence on branding and marketing. At some point in the past, they have produced a highly successful product in a local market. This is then rolled out into other national markets. Coca Cola or McDonald's are two examples of this. Each brand is protected from competition through patents, and heavy use of advertising and other forms of promotion.

Market and political power Some multinationals exploit market power in individual national markets to create a global business. They might have legitimate patents or copyrights or own key resources. Equally, they may build on these by **anti-competitive practices** which attempt to force existing firms out of the market and prevent new firms from entering it. Multinationals also have a long history of subverting and corrupting governments to achieve their aims. They are so large that they have considerable financial resources to be able to use either in bribing government officials and politicians, or maintaining powerful lobby organisations.

Possible advantages of multinational companies to individual countries

Multinational companies can give a variety of benefits to the individual countries in which they operate.

Home countries Individual countries gain international competitiveness if they are the national base for a multinational corporation. This is because a disproportionate amount of spending by the multinational will take place in its home country. Moreover, the resources employed are likely to be the most sophisticated within the organisation. For instance, the multinational will almost certainly have its headquarters in its home country. A disproportionate amount of research and development is likely to take place there. The home country is likely to be used as a production base, with a disproportionate number of production facilities there or with inputs being sourced from other firms in that country. One of the reasons why the developed world traditionally dominated world markets was because hardly any developing countries created successful multinationals. This is now changing with countries such as Taiwan, South Korea, China and India developing their own multinational companies which are outcompeting western companies.

Transfers of capital When Tesco sets up a new chain of supermarkets in Eastern Europe, or Toyota builds a new car plant in the UK, there is a transfer of capital from one country to another. This is called **foreign direct investment (FDI)**. FDI leads to an immediate increase in the resources available within a country. In most cases, they will in the short term lead to a multiplier effect. Construction workers for a new supermarket will spend their wages in local shops and on local produce, boosting national income. In the longer term, an increase in investment pushes the production possibility boundary of an economy outwards, which should lead to higher growth.

Transfers of knowledge With foreign direct investment comes a transfer of knowledge from one country to another. In some cases, industrial secrets are well kept. For example, despite operating in most countries in the world, no one but a few at headquarters knows the formula for Coca Cola. But Coca Cola does transfer knowledge to the local companies it works with about how to operate a bottling and distribution company. When Nissan and Toyota built plants in the UK, their production techniques were widely copied by other car

Multinationals create jobs where they set up operations. This may be in employing people directly or in employing builders, for example, to build offices and plant.

manufacturers operating in the UK. Multinationals with plants in China know that Chinese entrepreneurs and companies will constantly seek to copy and imitate what they see and then pose a real threat to their markets.

Employment Multinationals create jobs wherever they set up operations. They are sometimes criticised for only creating low level jobs for local employees whilst importing more highly skilled labour from abroad. A French hotel chain in the UK, for example, may employ local British labour for cleaning but in practice always has a French worker as the manager of each hotel. However, increasingly multinational companies recognise that creating an international employment base leads to greater productivity. Training local workers to take high level jobs within the company is an investment which strengthens the company. Training given to employees also spills over into the local economy. It raises the level of human capital. Employees leave multinationals to take jobs elsewhere in the economy and sometimes to set up their own businesses.

Taxes Multinationals pay taxes to national economies. This can then pay for government spending in areas such as health and education. Multinationals are often accused of paying as little tax as possible and seeking out locations where taxes are low. A common technique to avoid tax on profits is TRANSFER PRICING. Assume a multinational company has to make a product in country A, a country which charges high taxes on profits. The company will therefore want to make as little profit as possible in country A. The company also has operations in country B, a country which charges low taxes on profits. By selling the product made in country A at an artifically low price to its operations in country B, it can minimise its profits in country A. It then sells the product from country B at the market price, perhaps even back to customers in country A. But then it makes high profits in country B because it has bought the good at an artifically low price from country A. It still has to pay taxes on profits in country B, but its overall tax liability in countries A and B is much lower because of transfer pricing. Inevitably, because multinationals are profit seeking companies, they will seek to minimise their tax liabilities. If Slovakia offers lower taxes than the UK, this will be one factor which a US multinational will take into account when deciding where to put a new plant in the EU. Governments therefore need to weigh up the benefits of attracting investment by offering low taxes against loss of tax revenues. They also need to be robust in their dealings with multinationals to ensure that they pay their fair share of taxes.

Consumer choice Multinationals can bring greater consumer choice to a country. For example, Toyota and Nissan set up manufacturing plants in the UK to sell more cars into the UK market, Coca Cola and McDonald's set up in many countries to sell their products.

Exports Multinationals may increase a country's exports. This then increases the resources available to purchase imports. If it is an energy company like Exxon Mobil, exports of oil may be the main export for an economy.

Economic growth Multinational companies are a key component of the world trading system. By allocating resources in an efficient way, they help promote world growth. For example, multinational companies are one of the elements which explain why China and India are currently growing so fast. Without multinational companies, trade would be reduced and so too, almost certainly, would world GDP.

The possible disadvantages of multinational companies

Some argue that multinationals have a negative impact on individual economies.

Lack of accountability The size of multinationals can make them seem unaccountable to anyone. In practice, multinationals are accountable to many bodies. They are answerable, for instance, to their shareholders. Increasingly, though, they have had to account for their actions to other stakeholders. They have to obey the law of the countries in which they operate, unless government is so corrupt or weak that multinationals can evade the law. They are also subject to scrutiny by pressure groups, such as environmental groups.

Loss of national identity Multinationals are often accused of leading to lowering living standards by destroying native culture. McDonald's, for instance, has encountered opposition in some countries which see US burgers as a threat to national cuisine and eating habits. Globalisation inevitably means that there is a blurring of national identities as standards are accepted throughout the world. Standardisation can give rise to considerable benefits, though, because they allow people and firms to use common equipment, common ways of thinking and doing things, as well as helping in the purchase of products.

Footloose capitalism Multinationals have the power to move production from country to country, creating and destroying jobs and prosperity in their wake. They do this to maximise their profits. For instance, they might close a production facility in a high cost country like the UK or the USA and move it to a low cost country like India or Thailand. Globalisation is inevitably leading to a shifting of production from the developed world to the developing world. This is one key way in which the poor developing countries of the world can increase their living standards. However, multinationals are not the prime cause of this shift in production. Rather, they are responding to market forces in exactly the same way that national companies are so doing. Over the past 30 years, domestic UK companies have increasingly sourced goods from overseas to take advantage of better prices. They have closed their own manufacturing operations, or forced previous UK suppliers to close down through loss of orders. Multinationals are part of this trend which is exploiting **comparative advantage**.

Destruction of the environment A number of multinationals dominate world extraction industries such as oil or gold mining. These industries are inevitably particularly destructive of the environment. Other multinationals, such as motor manufacturers or even service companies have also been accused of destroying the environment for instance in the way in which they source their raw materials. However, any form of production could be argued to be undesirable from an environmental viewpoint. Moreover, multinational companies often have better environmental records than smaller national companies. They not only have the financial resources to be able to minimise their impact on the environment; they also have the technical knowledge and ability to innovate which can lead to minimising environmental problems.

Exploitation of poor countries The anti-globalisation movement portrays multinationals as exploiting poor countries to increase their own profits. Multinationals pay local labour the lowest wage possible. They employ child labour. Conditions of work are very poor. Natural resources are extracted and sold with hardly any compensation going to the local country. Taxes paid are minimal. Goods are sold which show no sensitivity to local culture. As little as possible is put back into the country because this would reduce the amount of profit that can be transferred back to the rich developed home country. It is correct that some individual multinational companies can be severely criticised for their historical record. It is also true that some multinational companies today are more aggressive in their pursuit of profit whatever the consequences than others. However, other multinational companies have an excellent record of dealing fairly with individual countries, local workers and local consumers. It should also be remembered that most activities of multinational companies are focussed in the developed world. So criticism of multinational companies needs to be focussed against individual companies rather than multinational companies as a group.

Corporate social responsibility

Many multinational companies have responded to criticism by implementing **corporate social responsibility (CSR)** procedures. Typically, a member of the board of the company is given responsibility for corporate social responsibility. Targets are drawn up on a wide range of issues such as the environment, employees, suppliers and customers. Policies are then put in place to achieve

those targets. Data is gathered to monitor whether targets have been achieved. Sometimes, outside auditors are used to audit results in the same way that outside auditors are used to audit company accounts.

Corporate social responsibility is a way of recognising that a company has a variety of stakeholders, each of whom have different goals. Maximising profit at the expense of the environment or workers' safety is not necessarily the goal for a company to pursue.

Critics of corporate social responsibility argue that targets set are typically arbitrary and are too low to make a substantial impact on the issue concerned. They often argue that only government regulation will force multinational companies to become socially responsible. The answer to issues about, say, illegal logging of forest in Indonesia, is for government to ban the purchase of this product. Otherwise, whilst some multinationals will not buy the timber because of their corporate social responsibility policies, other multinational companies will buy it.

The verdict

Multinationals can be easy targets for those who dislike global capitalism. Adam Smith's hidden hand of the market does make individuals relatively powerless when factories are closed and production is shifted thousands of miles away. New products, such as genetically modified food, can also raise important questions about whether such technologies should be exploited. On the other hand, without multinational companies, there would be far less trade and innovation. World output would almost certainly be considerably lower, arguably leading to lower living standards.

Free market economists would argue that the focus of any debate about multinationals is not whether they should be allowed to exist but about how government, representing all stakeholders in society, can set up regimes which can regulate the activities of multinationals for the benefit of all. For the anti-globalisation movement, multinationals are a symbol of all that is wrong with a world where profit and private greed control how resources are distributed.

Key terms

Multinational company or multinational corporation or transnational corporation - a company with significant production operations in at least two countries.
Transfer pricing - an accounting technique used by multinational companies for reducing taxes on profits by selling goods at a low price internally from a high tax country to another part of the company in a low tax country.

DataQuestion | **Multinational companies**

Corporates

Friends of the Earth is a charity which campaigns for solutions to environmental problems. In January 2008, the following was posted on their website about multinational companies.

The balance of power has shifted. Governments are losing control to huge multinational corporations. This process is putting basic human rights and vast areas of the natural world in serious danger. It's time to challenge the rise of corporate power. Each time we visit the supermarket, pay our taxes or fill up our car we fuel the growth of big companies. Behind the public face of corporations:

- Democracy is eroded. Companies often have more power than governments. They threaten to move their business to get what they want.
- Environments are destroyed. Rainforests are cleared to grow products on our supermarket shelves. Demand for palm oil has decimated forests in Borneo.
- Human rights are abused. People have no say on changes ruining their lives. Communities are thrown off their land or forced to live next to leaking oil pipes.

By law, public companies have to maximise profit and keep investors happy. This means economic growth comes before people and the planet. Did you know that 51 of the world's biggest economies are now corporations?

You shouldn't have to worry about all this when you do your weekly shop. Unfortunately some companies try to claim they are greener than they really are.

Corporates have too much power and too little incentive to care about communities and the environment. To head off such accusations, many businesses are adopting voluntary Corporate Social Responsibility (CSR) policies. CSR promises to do more than the legal minimum to protect people and the planet. But CSR is failing because it:

- Doesn't make a difference. Companies don't deliver on promises ....
- Ignore the real problems. Reports gloss over impacts of core business ....
- Is voluntary. There is no enforcement ....

Companies hide behind lobbying groups that fight on their behalf for less regulation. For example, the Confederation for British Industry (CBI) lobbies on behalf of business against laws that would benefit people and the environment.

Corporate power is out of control. The current systems are failing the planet. Governments need to regain control of big business to give rights for people and rules for big business.

Source: adapted from www.foe.co.uk.

Shell and climate change

The Shell Sustainability Report 2006 stated 'Shell was one of the first energy companies to acknowledge the threat of climate change, to call for action by governments, our industry and energy users, and to take action ourselves.

In 1998, we set ourselves voluntary targets for reducing greenhouse gas emissions from our operations. Since then Shell Renewables has built one of the broadest alternative energy portfolios of any major energy company. We have increased the supply of natural gas - the lowest carbon fossil fuel - and of the lower sulphur transport fuels needed by more fuel-efficient modern engines. The expected future costs of emitting CO_2 have been included in our investment decisions since 2000. This helps us design new projects so that they remain profitable in the carbon-constrained world that is now emerging.

Partnerships are being pursued to develop lower carbon technologies. Large scale demonstration projects to capture and store CO_2 are being given careful consideration. Our retail business runs a services of public campaigns to encourage innovation and promote energy conservation.

We stepped up our appeal to governments in 2006 to lead on this issue and introduce effective policies to combat climate change. The importance of government leadership has become clear. Without policies that reward lower CO2 technologies and create a predictable long-term cost for emitting greenhouse gas emissions, individual companies will have no incentive to make the massive investments needed.

Our appeal to government is fourfold: firstly to involve all major emitting countries and all sectors - not just industry - to avoid distorting competition; secondly, to develop stable, long term greenhouse gas targets to allow companies to plan and invest; thirdly, to use emissions trading systems more widely as a cost-effective way to manage greenhouse gas emissions from industry and to include reductions from CO_2 capture and storage in those schemes; and finally, to design better-targeted support for alternative energy sources, to help them reach the point where they can compete without further subsidies.'

Source: adapted from *The Shell Sustainability Report 2006*, Shell.

Tesco

The *TescoCorporate Responsibility Review 2006* stated:
'We sell a wide range of products, both own-brand and branded, which have palm oil as an ingredient. We do not buy palm oil directly - almost all of the palm oil used by the manufacturers of our own-brand products is bought through three of the world's largest palm oil traders. These three traders are members or affiliate members of the Roundtable on Sustainable Palm Oil (RSPO), which works to help industry identify ways of sourcing this ingredient more sustainably. In June 2006 Tesco too joined the RSPO. We hope that our participation will help the RSPO encourage other palm oil consumers to demand a sustainably sourced supply.

We want to make sure that the timber we buy is from legal, sustainable sources. We will never knowingly purchase timber from illegal sources. All sources of timber for our garden furniture are either Forest Stewardship Council (FSC) approved or members of the Tropical Forest Trust (TFT), committed to achieving the FSC standard through the certification supply programmes of ethical auditors.'

Source: adapted from *Corporate Responsibility Review 2006*, Tesco.

1. Explain what is meant by a 'multinational corporation' using examples from the data.
2. Analyse briefly (writing one paragraph on each part only) how a multinational company is likely to respond in the following situations.
   (a) An energy company finds oil in West Africa and calculates that it can make a high profit by developing the field. The government of the country has already given it the rights to develop the field.
   (b) A car manufacturer has to decide where to produce a replacement for an existing model. The existing model is produced in the UK. It calculates the cost of producing the model would be 15 per cent less if it produced the car in Slovakia in Eastern Europe.
   (c) A UK supermarket chain wants to introduce a value range of beef products. The only way it can bring the price down to its target level is to import the beef from Argentina but it has no control over how the cattle are reared and slaughtered. Should it introduce the range?
3. 'Each time we visit the supermarket, pay our taxes or fill up our car we fuel the growth of big companies.' (Greenpeace). Discuss whether economic welfare would be increased if multinational companies were broken up and limited in size.

Study skills

When you start your AS/A Level course, you should try to evaluate whether or not your study and organisational skills are effective. For instance:

- are you always present and on time for classes or lectures?
- do you always hand work in on time?
- is work done to the best of your ability?
- do you work in a suitable environment?
- do you leave time to plan and evaluate your work?
- do you participate in all learning activities in a way which helps you to learn?
- do you listen to advice and act on constructive comments about your work?

Having good study skills does not necessarily mean that work is done well in advance, or that the room where you work at home is tidy. Some students are very organised in what might at first seem chaotic situations. For instance, they might always write their essays close to the time they have to be handed in. Or their study room might look an incredible mess. However, if you work best under pressure of deadlines, and you know what is where in the mess of your room, then it could be argued that in fact you are an organised student!

In class

The core of your study is likely to take place in the classroom or lecture room. Not only will you spend a considerable proportion of your studying time in class, but what you do in the classroom and the instructions you receive there will influence what you do outside. Effective classroom skills are therefore essential. They include the following.

Attending classes regularly and on time Good organisational skills involve attending all lessons unless there are serious reasons for absence. They also involve arranging doctor's and dentist's appointments, driving lessons or holidays outside class time so that work is not missed.

Always being attentive It is important to be attentive at all times and engage in the activities being presented. Participation in class also helps other students to learn.

Making clear and concise notes during lessons Notes can act as a record of what has been said. Taking notes whilst the teacher/lecturer is talking is a form of active learning. It can help some students to focus on what is being said and identify what they don't understand. For other students, though, note taking can get in the way of understanding what the teacher or lecturer is saying. They may prefer to read handouts or notes given out by the teacher or lecturer. You have to decide what is best for you.

Asking questions of the teacher or lecturer It is unlikely that all students will understand everything that goes on in a lesson. Asking questions helps to fill in these gaps. It is also very important to keep you focussed on the lesson. If you are thinking about what you do and don't understand, you will inevitably be participating in that lesson. Formulating questions is also important for developing oral skills, which will be essential in the world outside of school or college.

Participating in classroom discussions Classroom discussions enable you to practice important key learning skills. Some students find they want to contribute more than others. Remember though that in a discussion, listening is as important as talking. All participants must respect the contributions of others. There must be a balance between communication and listening.

Preparing for the next lesson Many schools and colleges issue their students with homework diaries, or encourage them to buy one. They are a useful tool for planning and organising work. They help you to remember what you have to do and structure your out of class activities.

Planning outside the class

Planning is an essential part of good study skills. By keeping a diary, for instance, students can see at a glance what needs to be done and when. They can then mentally allocate time slots for completion of the work. For work which is not structured by the teacher or lecturer, such as coursework or revision, students need to construct a plan. Typically, this will show dates and the work to be done on or by a particular date. It may also show times during the day when work is to be done. Some students find it helpful to discipline themselves by the clock. So they plan to start, say, revision at 9.00 each morning, have a ten minute break each hour on the hour, break for lunch at 1.00, etc.

It may also be helpful to construct precise plans for day to day work outside the classroom. When you start on your AS/A level course, for instance, it might be useful to plan meticulously when you are going to complete work during the first month. This will ensure that work gets done and you have set out on your course with good work habits. Hopefully, you will then be able to relax your planning because you will have got into a sound routine for completing work.

Planning tends to increase in importance:
- the longer the task to be completed:
- the less structure is given by your school or college for its completion.

Organising time

Every student has different preferences about organising time. Some of the key issues are as follows.

Time during the week You have to decide when you want to complete your work during the week. There are likely to be conflicting claims on your time. For instance, you may have a part time job which takes priority at certain times of the week. You may have family or social commitments. You may decide that you will never work on Friday or Saturday nights (except in emergencies!). There are no right or wrong times to study. However, it is essential to build in enough time during the week to study. AS/A level examinations have been developed on the assumption that you are studying full time for 1 to 2 years.

Time during the day Some people work best in the morning, some in the afternoon and some at night. You should know whether you are a 'morning person' or otherwise. Try to work at times of day when you are most likely to learn effectively.

Breaks Breaks are essential to maintain concentration. How frequent and how long your breaks need to be varies from one individual to another. You need to find out what works best for you. Try to be as disciplined as possible in your approach to breaks. It is all too easy for the break to extend itself over the whole period when you planned to work. Get to know what is most likely to stop you from getting back to work. For instance, if you start watching television during your break, do you find that you only go back to work at the end of the programme?

Variety Some students like variety in what they do. So during an hour's work session, they may do a little on three pieces of work. Others find that they cannot cope with such short blocks of time and would rather concentrate on just one piece of work. Longer pieces of work, such as essays or coursework, may need to be broken down and completed in several different work sessions anyway.

Networking and resources

It is important that students make use of all the resources that are available to them. Here are some suggestions about how to find help when completing work.

The textbook Using a textbook effectively will help students to achieve the highest possible marks for their work. Remember that the textbook is there to help you understand a topic. The relevant section should be read before you attempt a piece of work and you are likely to want to refer to the textbook as you write. You may wish to consult a number of textbooks if, for example, you do not understand a particular area in one book.

The library Schools and colleges will have libraries, perhaps even in the classroom or lecture room, of books and other materials which can be borrowed. Reading around a topic is an essential part of preparing any work such as an essay. Libraries will also hopefully carry daily quality newspapers. Economics is about the real world. AS/A level Economics students should be aware of the major economic issues of the day and be able to discuss them.

The Internet The Internet can be very useful in the learning process. It is most perhaps useful when students are able to use the same site repeatedly. They know what is on the site and how to navigate around it. There may be more difficulties, however, when searching for general information. This requires skill in using search engines to find appropriate sites which can often take time. The Internet is likely to be very useful to students working on their own in Economics when researching coursework.

Ask the teacher/lecturer Make full use of your teacher or lecturer as a resource. If you are stuck on a piece of homework, for instance, ask the teacher or lecturer

to help you out. If you frequently need help, it is a good idea to start the homework well in advance of the date it needs to be handed in, so that you can contact the teacher or lecturer.

Network with fellow students Students may find networking with friends helpful. If they have a problem, they can call a friend or see them in school or college. Students who prefer to work in this way should be aware of which students in their teaching group are most likely to give helpful advice. Networking is a valuable tool in the learning process both to the person who receives the help and the person who gives it.

Parents, business people, etc. Parents, family members, friends or contacts in the business community may all be sources of help in different situations and for different pieces of work.

The work environment

Your work environment needs to be chosen to maximise learning. Students often work either in a library or study area, or at home in their own room. What is there about these work places which makes them effective?

Availability Your work place should be available to you when you want to study. If you like to complete as much work as possible at school or college, and work hard between time-tabled lessons, then the library might be an excellent environment for you. You may prefer to complete homework in your own home. Your bedroom may be the only place where you are guaranteed that you can work uninterrupted. Not only must a place be available but so too must the resources. If you are undertaking research, for instance, you may have to work in a library or at a computer terminal.

Music, television and noise Some students find it easy to concentrate in the midst of chaos. They like distractions and find it easier to work if they know they can also listen to music, stroke the dog or have a conversation. Many students find distractions impossible to cope with. To work effectively, they need relative peace and quiet. They might or might not like background music.

Alone or in groups Some students find that working in a group is ineffective. One person may start talking about a non-work issue and work is then never resumed. They therefore prefer to work alone. However, other students who can avoid such distractions find working in groups highly effective. It means they can instantly network with others when they have a problem.

Furniture Furniture can be very important in studying. Some students prefer to read in an armchair and write at a desk. You may find it easier to create work spaces where particular types of work can be done. Make sure that the chair you sit in is comfortable and doesn't give you back problems.

Lighting Experiment with lighting to reduce eye strain. If you find studying makes you tired very quickly, one reason might be inadequate lighting. You can also use lighting to create a mood which encourages you to study.

Movement Your work environment should allow you to move around if you wish. When trying to memorise something, for instance, some students may prefer to walk around, whereas others may prefer to sit.

Preparing for tests and examinations

Different students prepare effectively for tests or examinations in a variety of different ways. You have to find out what is most effective for you. Different methods may also be useful in different circumstances. For instance, you may want to spend most time memorising information for an essay-based examination, but for a multiple-choice examination you may want to spend most time practising past questions.

Written notes Many students use notes in their revision. Notes are useful records of what has been learned either because the student has made them and therefore hopefully can understand them, or because they have been given by the teacher or lecturer and show what material is likely to occur in the examination.

Good note taking is a skilled art. Notes are meant to be a precis, a shortening of what, for instance, might be found in a textbook. So it is important to develop a style of writing notes which does shorten material.
- Miss out common words like 'the' and 'a' which do not affect the meaning.
- Abbreviate words. For example, write 'gov' for 'government', 'C' for consumption, or 'P' for price.

Notes should be clearly laid out using headings and subheadings. Ideally, headings and subheadings should be colour coded to make them easier to skim read. The headings should provide a story in themselves which prompts you to remember the material contained underneath each heading. Highlight key terms within the notes. Star, circle or underline important points.

Some students like to work from notes written on A4 paper. Other students like to transfer notes onto small cards where there is less on each card. Whichever method you use, make sure that the notes are logically ordered and can be referred to instantly.

When memorising material from notes, some students find it helpful to think of the layout of individual pages. This then prompts memory recall of what is on the page.

The textbook Some students dislike revising from notes and prefer to use a textbook. They may find it easier, for instance, to read printed material rather than their own handwriting. They may want to use material collected together rather than a series of handouts or loose pages. Also, notes may be incomplete in places.

Some students rely on both notes and textbooks for revision. Revising from a textbook involves the same skills as revising from notes. The textbook will have chapter or unit headings, and headings and subheadings within these. These provide the skeleton on which the detail should be hung.

Pictures and visual presentations Some students find pictures particularly helpful when revising. Examples of commonly used visual presentations include mind maps, flow charts and family trees, which are illustrated in Figures 1 to 3. These illustrations summarise the main points in unit 4,

The Demand Curve, of this book. Visual presentations work through helping the student see a topic laid out. Places on the page can be visualised and connections clearly identified.

Oral methods Some students like to be 'tested' by another person on a topic to see if they have learnt the material. Repeating words or phrases can be helpful. So too can devising word associations and mnemonics. A word association is linking one word with another. For instance, you may be particularly interested in football, and decide to remember the main components of aggregate demand (consumption, investment, government spending and exports minus imports) by assigning each term to the name of a football club. Remember the football clubs and you remember the components. Alternatively, you may make up a mnemonic, a rhyme or phrase usually associated with the first letter of each word. For instance, you could have Clobber In Gap Extremely Important OR Chelsea In Goal Excitement Incident for consumption, investment, government spending, exports and imports.

Active learning Some students find it difficult just to sit and memorise material. They need to be doing something to help them remember.
- One way is to construct a set of notes, or a mind map. Once written out, the notes may be of little use, but it is in the doing that the learning has taken place.
- You may want to practice past examination questions. Multiple choice question papers, for instance, are best revised for in this way. If you practice essay questions, it is often more useful to spend scarce time writing out essay plans for a wide variety of questions than answering a few essays in detail.
- You may use published materials which give short answer questions on a topic such as 'Define economies of scale', or 'List the costs of unemployment'.
- Some students practice past homework tasks which they have been set and then compare their results with their first marked attempt.

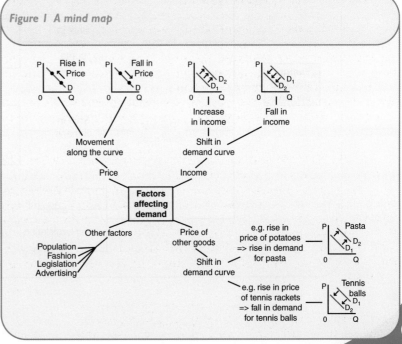

Figure 1 *A mind map*

Figure 2 Flow charts

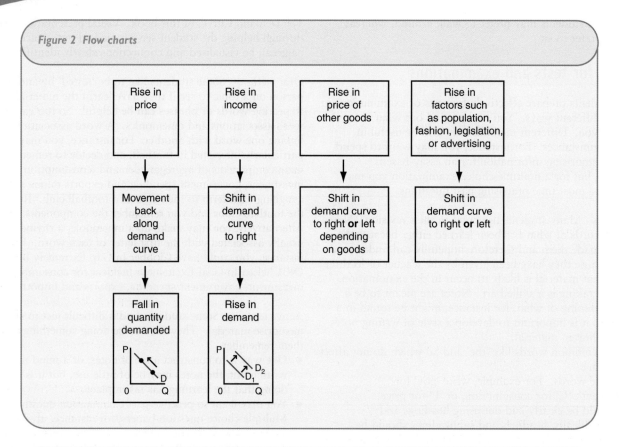

Figure 3 A family tree

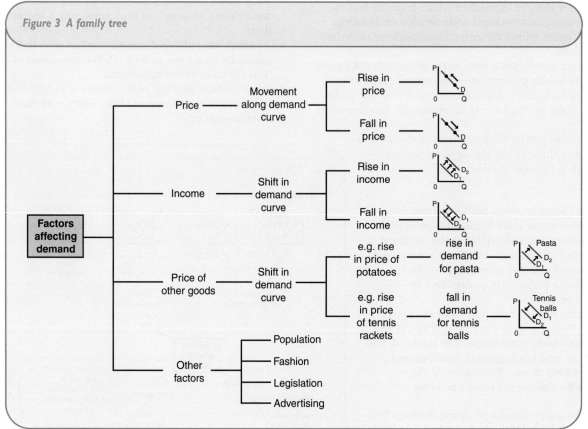

Assessment criteria

Specifications are drawn up and papers are set to test a range of assessment criteria. These are qualities and skills which a candidate must demonstrate to the examiners to gain marks in any form of assessment. In Economics at AS/A level, these assessment criteria are grouped into four areas.

Demonstration of knowledge and understanding of the specified subject content **Knowledge and understanding** requires candidates to show that they can recognise economic concepts and terms and be able to define or explain them. For instance, *Explain what is meant by economies of scale* asks for a definition of economies of scale (knowledge) and a good answer is likely to give examples to demonstrate clear understanding of the term. Knowledge and understanding are also present when economic theories are used. For instance, knowledge is required when drawing a demand and supply diagram. Has the candidate correctly identified the axes? Is the demand curve downward sloping? Is the supply curve upward sloping? Is the candidate using proper conventions by clearly labelling the axes and the demand and supply curves? Another example would be the link between interest rates and inflation. Does a candidate show knowledge of the chain of causality between a change in interest rates, a change in aggregate demand and a change in the equilibrium price level of the economy?

Application of knowledge and critical understanding to economic problems and issues arising from both familiar and unfamiliar situations Knowledge is essential for any economist, but the knowledge must be **applied** to economic problems to be of use. For instance, being able to define economies of scale is of little use if economies of scale at work in motor vehicle manufacturing cannot be recognised. Application is the skill of being able to use knowledge in a wide variety of contexts. Some of these contexts will be familiar. For instance, you might have studied leisure industries during your course and in the examination a question is set on economies of scale in leisure industries. The context may, however, be unfamiliar. For instance, you may have studied the environment as part your course. In the examination, a question on pollution permits in the USA may be set. Pollution permits is part of expected knowledge and understanding but the USA may be an unfamiliar context. Another example of application would be using mathematical formulae to work out answers to problems. Calculating a value for price elasticity of demand is application.

Analyse economic problems and issues **Analysis** is the process of breaking down information into relevant parts and then using this to understand a problem or issue. A simple piece of analysis, for instance, would be to identify a trend from a set of unemployment figures on a graph. The graph might be accompanied by a passage which contains information about why unemployment might be falling. The skill of analysis is needed to link the trend with its causes. Analysis would also be required if a candidate were asked to identify possible government policies to tackle unemployment. The candidate might have to select which policies from a list might be appropriate and justify why these policies might be effective.

Evaluate economic arguments and evidence, making informed judgements **Evaluation** requires candidates to make conclusions and argue which courses of action might be most appropriate in a situation. If a government wanted to reduce unemployment today, which would be the most effective policies for it to pursue? If global warming is to be stopped, what are the most important actions which consumers and firms must take? It is relatively easy to make a simple judgement. At this level, though, examiners expect candidates to be able to justify their answers. It is this justification which tends to carry most marks. To do this, candidates must weigh up the evidence presented to them and judge which is important and which is not. They must consider whether the information presented is reliable and whether or not it is complete enough to come to a decision. If it is not, what other information is required to come to a definitive conclusion? Candidates must also distinguish between fact and opinion.

Candidates are also assessed in Economics AS/A level on the **quality of written communication**. Candidates must:

- select and use a form and style of writing appropriate to purpose and complex subject matter. For instance, candidates must be able to write an essay, or a short answer to a question;
- organise relevant information clearly and coherently, using specialist vocabulary when appropriate. So candidates must, for instance, be able to write in paragraphs and they must be able to use terms like price elasticity or the current balance when these are required;
- ensure writing is legible, and spelling, grammar and punctuation are accurate, so that meaning is clear. Candidates must therefore write clearly, construct proper sentences and spell correctly.

Command, directive or key words

Questions typically start off with command or key words. These words indicate which skills are required when answering the question. It is important for candidates to respond in an appropriate manner. For instance, if candidates are asked to evaluate a problem, but only show knowledge and understanding, then they will lose most of the marks for that question. Command words can be grouped according to what skills will be required in an answer.

Knowledge and understanding

- Define - to give the exact meaning of a term or concept using words or mathematical symbols whose meaning is already understood by the reader, e.g. *Define what is meant by economies of scale*.
- Describe - to give an account of something, e.g. *Describe the costs of inflation*.
- Give - to state or say, e.g. *Give two examples of goods in which Saudi Arabia has a comparative advantage in production*.

- How - to present an account of something, e.g. *How does the government raise taxes?*
- Identify - to single out from other information, e.g. *Identify three factors which cause inflation.*
- Illustrate - to use examples to explain a point, e.g. *Illustrate the way in which monopolists keep out competitors from their markets.*
- List - to state in the briefest form, e.g. *List three factors which affect the demand for a product.*
- Outline - to give a short description of the main aspects or features, e.g. *Outline the arguments used by Greenpeace against genetically modified (GM) crops.*
- State - to give or say, e.g. *State three factors which affect elasticity of supply.*
- Summarise - to bring out the main points from a more complex set of data, e.g. *Summarise the main arguments in favour of government intervention.*
- What - to clarify a point, e.g. *What are the main characteristics of a perfectly competitive industry?*

Application

- Apply - use knowledge of economics to understand a situation, issue or problem, e.g. *Apply the theory of perfect competition to the market for potatoes.*
- Calculate - use mathematics to work out an answer, e.g. *Calculate the price elasticity of demand if price increases from £3 to £4.*
- Distinguish between - identify the characteristics which make two or more ideas, concepts, issues, etc. different, e.g. *Distinguish between price elasticity of demand and income elasticity of demand.*
- Explain - making clear. It is often useful to define terms and give examples in an explanation, e.g. *Explain how prices are determined in a free market.*
- Suggest - give possible reasons or ideas. These must be plausible but not necessarily correct. 'Suggest' may require candidates to analyse a problem and not just apply economic problems, e.g. *Suggest reasons why the firm did not put up its prices.*

Analysis

- Analyse - to break down into constituent parts in order to be able to understand an issue or problem. Analysis involves recognising what is important, and relating to knowledge and understanding of economics where necessary, e.g. *Analyse the reasons for the firm investing in new machinery.*
- Compare and contrast - to show the similarities and differences between two or more ideas or problems, e.g. *Compare and contrast the performance of the UK and Chinese economies over the past ten years.*
- Examine - to break down an issue or problem to understand it, e.g. *Examine the problems facing the UK economy today.*
- Investigate - to look for evidence to explain and analyse, e.g. *Investigate why the government chose to cut interest rates in May.*

Evaluation

- Assess - to analyse an economic issue or problem and then to weigh up the relative importance of different strands, e.g. *Assess the impact of high interest rates on the UK economy.*
- Comment on - invites the candidate to make their judgements based upon evidence which they have presented, e.g. *Comment on why the Bank of England thought it necessary to raise interest rates in June.*
- Critically analyse - to analyse an issue or problem and then to weigh up the relative importance of part of this analysis, e.g. *Critically analyse the problems facing the industry today.*
- Do you think - invites candidates to put forward their own opinions about an issue or problem. However, the marks will always be awarded for the quality of the arguments put forward and not for any individual opinions, e.g. *Do you think the government should have allowed the motorway to be built?*
- Discuss - to compare a number of possible views about an issue or problem and to weigh up their relative importance. A conclusion is essential, e.g. *Discuss the advantages and disadvantages of fixing rents in the housing market.*
- Evaluate - like discuss, to compare a number of possible views about an issue or problem and weigh up their relative importance. A final judgement is essential, e.g. *Evaluate the policies available to government to reduce unemployment.*
- To what extent - invites candidates to explain and analyse and then to comment upon the relative importance of arguments, e.g. *To what extent should the government rely upon interest rates to control inflation?*

Levels of response

Questions which test the higher order skills of analysis and evaluation are likely to be marked using a levels of response mark scheme. Rather than giving candidates a mark or several marks for a point made or an argument developed within an answer, the answer is marked holistically (as a whole). It is then compared to descriptions of what answers might look like in terms of the skills displayed. The answer is then put within a level. This level will have a range of marks which the examiner can award depending upon whether it is a good answer within that level or not.

For instance, a levels mark scheme might have three levels and 12 marks are awarded. The level descriptors are as follows.

Level 1

One or more reasons given, but little development of points. The answer lacks coherence and there is no valid analysis or evaluation. 1-3 marks

Level 2

Several reasons given with reasonable analysis. Arguments are expressed with some confidence and coherence. Evaluation, though, is weakly supported by evidence. 4-8 marks

Level 3

A good coverage of the main reasons. Sound analysis with clear links between the issues raised. Arguments for and against have been evaluated and a conclusion reached. 9-12 marks

Mark schemes are available from the awarding bodies. You should become familiar with the levels of response mark schemes used by examiners on the papers you will sit. To gain a mark in the highest level, candidates typically have to give evidence of all four main skills of knowledge, application, analysis and evaluation.

Multiple choice questions

Some awarding bodies use multiple choice questions as a form of assessment. They are used mainly to test lower order skills of knowledge and application. They are also a convenient way of testing breadth. A data response question or an essay is likely to cover only one topic. If there is choice, candidates may be encouraged only to revise part of the course in the hope that they will still be able to answer a full set of questions. A multiple choice test covers the whole course and therefore penalises candidates who are selective in their revision.

Success at multiple choice questions involves being thoroughly familiar with the basics of economics. It also requires skill in answering multiple choice questions, just as essays requires essay writing skills. Practice on questions is therefore very important. Using past question papers from the awarding body can also be very helpful. Not only will it help you familiarise yourself with the style of multiple choice question being used, but past questions may be reused on new papers.

There are two ways in which candidates are likely to get to a correct answer on a multiple choice question.
- Knowing the correct answer.
- Eliminating the wrong answers.

Candidates should make full use of the laws of probability. If the correct answer is not obvious, but two out of four responses can be eliminated, the chances of getting the answer right are improved from 1 in 4 for guessing to 1 in 2. Taken over a whole paper, a strategy of eliminating wrong answers can significantly improve marks.

Some multiple choice tests require candidates not just to give an answer from A to D but also to justify their answers. The written explanation should be short and to the point.

In an examination, do not spend more than the allotted time on any single question but pass over it. For instance, if there are 30 questions to be answered in 30 minutes, there is on average just 1 minute per question. Don't spend 10 minutes working out question 5. Come back at the end to the questions which you have missed out. If you have nearly run out of time, always make sure that there is an answer to every question. You will then have some chance rather than no chance to gain marks. Some candidates prefer to draw a line through incorrect responses (i.e. wrong answers) within a question and visibly isolate the correct answer.

Data response questions

Data response questions are used to test a candidate's ability to apply their knowledge and understanding to familiar or unfamiliar data. They usually also require candidates to display skills of analysis and evaluation as well.

The data presented may be verbal or in numerical form, or a mixture of both. Candidates often find data in verbal form easier to understand and interpret. However, in practice, examiners construct questions so that there is little or no difference in outcome in marks between questions which contain mainly verbal data and those which contain mainly numerical data.

Some awarding bodies only use real data, such as newspaper extracts or statistics from government sources. Others also use hypothetical or imaginary data - data which has been made up by the examiner. In some areas of Economics, it is difficult to obtain real data. Exact figures for price elasticity of demand is one example. Therefore some examiners prefer to use imaginary data for questions.

There is a number of ways in which candidates can improve their performance on data response questions in examinations.
- Read through the material thoroughly.
- Use highlighter pens to mark what you think are important words or passages.
- Highlight the key words in a question.
- Think carefully about what each question is asking of you. In particular, think about the skills you are required to display in a question.
- If there are any numerical calculations, show all your workings carefully. You may get marks for the workings even if you fail to get the final answer correct.
- Have a clear understanding of how long each answer should be. For instance, assume there are 60 marks overall, with the first two questions being awarded 5 marks each, the third question carrying 10 marks, the fourth carrying 15 marks and the last 25 marks. The first question should be roughly one fifth the length of the last question and should take only $\frac{5}{60}$ of the time to complete. Many candidates write too much on questions which carry few marks and too little on questions which carry many marks.
- Be aware of what economic concepts and theories the question is testing.
- Some candidates find it helpful to prepare plans for longer answers.
- Make sure you don't run out of time. It is usually better to abandon one part and move onto the next if you are running out of time rather than attempting to create the perfect answer on that part.
- Last parts of data response questions may expect candidates to write for around 20 minutes. These questions then become small essays and the techniques for writing essays outlined below need to be applied to them.

Sometimes, it is appropriate to use a diagram in a data response question. Some questions, in fact, specifically ask for a diagram to be drawn. There are some easy rules to remember when drawing diagrams.
- Examiners will expect to see standard diagrams which are found in any Economics textbook.
- When drawing diagrams, make sure they are large enough to be read.
- Diagrams are easier to read and look much better if they are drawn with a ruler where appropriate.
- Always label the axes and the lines or curves.
- Always refer to and explain the diagram in your written answer.

Essays

Essays are often used to test higher order skills of analysis and evaluation, although there are likely to be marks for knowledge and application in the mark scheme too. Typically, candidates are expected to write for 35 to 45 minutes on an essay title which is likely to be split into two separate but linked parts. Essay writing is a skill which needs to be practised and learnt. It requires putting together (or synthesising) a number of ideas to form one complete answer. Essays are likely to be marked using levels of response mark schemes.

Candidates can improve their essay writing skills if they can learn the following techniques.

- Before you start writing, have a clear understanding of what the question is asking. In particular, identify the skills which will be required from you to write a successful essay by looking at the command words. Identify too the areas of economics of relevance to the essay. Some candidates also find it useful to highlight the key words in an essay title to focus them on what the question is asking. For instance, take the following question: *Evaluate the policies which a government might adopt to deal with the problem of youth unemployment.* The key words here are *Evaluate*, *government policies* and *youth unemployment.* Evaluate means that you will have to compare the effectiveness of different types of government policy. You will be expected to argue that some might be more useful than others in order to gain the maximum number of marks. Government policies to deal with unemployment is the main area of economic knowledge. However, especially important is the word *youth*. Your answer must focus on *youth* unemployment if it is to get the higher marks.

- Some candidates find it useful to write out an **essay plan**. This is a brief synopsis of what you will write. It allows you to jot points down and to see how they can be organised to form a coherent whole. Often candidates start their answer and add points to their plan as they go along because writing triggers their memories. This is good practice, but always check that your new points will not unbalance the structure of your answer. Adding new material after you have written your conclusion, for instance, may gain you extra marks but it is unlikely to help you get the highest marks.

- Paragraph your essay properly. Remember that a paragraph should contain material on one idea or one group of ideas. A useful technique to use is to see a paragraph as an opening sentence which makes a point, and the rest of the paragraph as an explanation or elaboration of that point.

- Include diagrams wherever they are appropriate. Advice about the effective use of diagrams is given above.

- Write a concluding paragraph. This is especially important if you are answering an evaluation question. The conclusion gives you the opportunity to draw your points together and to weigh up the arguments put forward.

- With two part questions, ensure that you have allocated your time effectively between the two parts. Don't spend too much time on the first half of the question. It is particularly important to work out how long to spend on each part if the two parts carry very unequal mark weighting.

- Essays are continuous pieces of prose. They should not include bullet points, lists, subheadings, etc.

- Spot the story. Many essay questions are set because they cover a topical issue. Recognising what this topical issue is should help you decide what to stress in your essay. Knowledge of the issue will also give you additional material to introduce into the essay.

- Adapt your material to suit what is required. Don't write out

an answer to an essay question you have already answered in class and memorised and which is similar to the essay question set. Equally, don't write 'everything I know about' one or two key words in the essay title. For instance, answering a question about the costs of inflation by writing at length about the causes of inflation is likely to be an inappropriate answer.

- Remember there are likely to be marks for quality of language in the mark scheme. Write in a simple and clear style and pay attention to your spelling.

Report writing

Students may be required to write a report. The style of a report is different from that of an essay.

- It should begin with a section showing who the report is for, who has written it, the date it was written and the title. If the report is written under examination conditions, this may all be omitted.

- It should be broken down into a number of sections. Each section should address a particular issue. A heading should start each section to help the reader see the structure of the report. In most reports, sections are numbered in sequence.

- A section may be broken down into sub-sections, each with their own headings and their own numbers. For instance, section 3 of the report may have two sub-sections, 3.1 and 3.2.

- The report must be written in complete sentences and not in note form. However, unlike in an essay, it is acceptable to use bullet points to further structure the report.

- Use diagrams wherever appropriate. Diagrams must be part of the argument used in the report. It is important that the reader understands why they have been included.

A report will require you to draw conclusions and make judgements, i.e. show that you can evaluate an issue or problem. The evaluation can be presented at the end of the report, or it can be included in each section of the report. If it is included in each section, a conclusion or summary still needs to be written at the end to bring together what has been said earlier.

The report should also highlight missing information that would have been useful or, perhaps, was essential, to come to reasoned conclusions or recommendations. The reliability or accuracy of the information provided could also be questioned.

If the report is written in examination conditions, as with a data response question, take time at the start to read through the data given. Highlight key ideas or data. It may not be necessary to understand all the data before you start writing as this may waste important time which may be needed to write the report. However, it is important to understand what is required of you before you start writing.

Constructing a plan is essential. A report is a complex piece of writing. Identify the main headings of your report and jot down the main points which you are likely to include under each heading. You may add to your plan as you write your report if you think of new points. In an examination, you are unlikely to have the time to write a number of drafts of the report. However, outside the examination room, it would be useful to produce several drafts.